Oxford Paperback Italian Dictionary

Italian–English
English–Italian

Italiano–Inglese
Inglese–Italiano

Debora Mazza

OXFORD
UNIVERSITY PRESS

OXFORD

UNIVERSITY PRESS

Great Clarendon Street, Oxford OX2 6DP

Oxford University Press is a department of the University of Oxford.
It furthers the University's objective of excellence in research, scholarship,
and education by publishing worldwide in

Oxford New York

Auckland Bangkok Buenos Aires Cape Town Chennai
Dar es Salaam Delhi Hong Kong Istanbul Karachi Kolkata
Kuala Lumpur Madrid Melbourne Mexico City Mumbai Nairobi
São Paulo Shanghai Taipei Tokyo Toronto

Oxford is a registered trade mark of Oxford University Press
in the UK and in certain other countries

© Oxford University Press 1997, 2002

First published 1986 as *The Oxford Italian Minidictionary*
First issued (with corrections) as an Oxford University Press
paperback 1989
Reissued 1994
Second edition 1997
Reprinted with revised text 2002

British Library Cataloguing in Publication Data

Data available

Library of Congress Cataloging in Publication Data

Data available

ISBN 0-19-864522-8

9

Printed in Great Britain by
Clays Ltd, Bungay,
Suffolk

Contents/Indice

Editors/Redazione

Debora Mazza   Jane Goldie

Donatella Boi   Francesca Logi   Sonia Tinagli-Baxter

Peter Terrell   Carla Zipoli

Copy editors/Segreteria di redazione

Jacqueline Gregan   Daphne Trotter

Project management by/A cura di

LEXUS

Preface

This new edition of the Oxford Italian-English Minidictionary is an updated and expanded version of the dictionary edited by Joyce Andrews. Colloquial words and phrases figure largely, as do neologisms. Noteworthy additions include terms from special areas such as computers and business that have become a familiar feature of everyday language.

Prefazione

Questa nuova edizione del mini dizionario Oxford Italiano-Inglese è il risultato di un lavoro di ampliamento e aggiornamento della precedente edizione curata da Joyce Andrews. Un'attenzione particolare è stata rivolta a vocaboli ed espressioni colloquiali di coniazione recente e a termini relativi a settori specifici, quali l'informatica e il commercio, divenuti ricorrenti nella lingua di tutti i giorni.

Proprietary terms

This dictionary includes some words which are, or are asserted to be, proprietary names or trademarks. Their inclusion does not imply that they have acquired for legal purposes a non-proprietary or general significance, nor is any other judgment implied concerning their legal status. In cases where the editor has some evidence that a word is used as a proprietary name or trademark this is indicated by the symbol ®, but no judgment concerning the legal status of such words is made or implied thereby.

Marche depositate

Questo dizionario include alcune parole che sono o vengono considerate nomi di marche depositate. La loro presenza non implica che abbiano acquisito legalmente un significato generale, né si suggerisce alcun altro giudizio riguardo il loro stato giuridico. Qualora il redattore abbia trovato testimonianza dell'uso di una parola come marca depositata, quest'ultima è stata contrassegnata dal simbolo ®, ma nessun giudizio riguardo la stato giuridico di tale parola viene espresso o suggerito in tal modo.

Introduction

In order to give the maximum information about English and Italian in the space available, this new dictionary uses certain space-saving conventions.

A swung dash ~ is used to replace the headword within the entry.

Where the headword contains a vertical bar | the swung dash replaces only the part of the headword that comes in front of the |. For example: **efficien|te** a efficient. **~za** nf efficiency (the second bold word reads **efficienza**).

Indicators are provided to guide the user to the best translation for a specific sense of a word. Types of indicator are:

field labels (see the list on pp vii-viii), which indicate a general area of usage (commercial, computing, photography etc);

sense indicators, eg: **bore** n (of gun) calibro m; (person) seccatore, -trice mf;

typical subjects of verbs, eg: **bond** vt ⟨glue:⟩ attaccare;

typical objects of verbs, placed after the translation of the verb, eg: **boost** vt stimolare ⟨sales⟩; sollevare ⟨morale⟩;

nouns that typically go together with certain adjectives, eg: **rich** a ricco; ⟨food⟩ pesante.

A solid black circle means that the same word is being translated as a different part of speech, eg. **partition** n ... ● vt ...

English pronunciation is given for the Italian user in the International Phonetic Alphabet.

Italian stress is shown by a ' placed in front of the stressed syllable in a word.

Square brackets are used around parts of an expression which can be omitted without altering the sense.

Introduzione

Allo scopo di fornire il maggior numero possibile di informazioni in inglese e in italiano, questo nuovo dizionario ricorre ad alcune convenzioni per sfruttare al massimo lo spazio disponibile.

Un trattino ondulato ~ è utilizzato al posto del lemma all'interno della voce.

Qualora il lemma contenga una barra verticale |, il trattino ondulato sostituisce solo la parte del lemma che precede |. Ad esempio: **dark|en** vt oscurare. **~ness** n buio m (la seconda parola in neretto va letta **darkness**).

Degli indicatori vengono forniti per indirizzare l'utilizzatore verso la traduzione corrispondente al senso voluto di una parola. I tipi di indicatori sono:

etichette semantiche (vedi la lista a pp vii-viii), indicanti l'ambito specifico in cui la parola viene generalmente usata in quel senso (commercio, informatica, fotografia ecc);

indicatori di significato, es.: **redazione** nf (ufficio) editorial office; (di testi) editing;

soggetti tipici di verbi, es.: **trovarsi** vr ⟨luogo:⟩ be;

complementi oggetti tipici di verbi, collocati dopo la traduzione dello stesso verbo, es: **superare** vt overtake ⟨veicolo⟩; pass ⟨esame⟩;

sostantivi che ricorrono tipicamente con certi aggettivi, es.: **solare** a ⟨energia, raggi⟩ solar; ⟨crema⟩ sun.

Un cerchio nero pieno indica che la stessa parola viene tradotta come una diversa parte del discorso, es. **calcolatore** a ... ● nm ...

La pronuncia inglese è data usando l'Alfabetico Fonetico Internazionale.

L'accento tonico nelle parole italiane è indicato dal segno ' collocato davanti alla sillaba accentata.

Delle parentesi quadre racchiudono parti di espressioni che possono essere omesse senza alterazioni di senso.

Pronunciation of Italian

Vowels:

a is broad like *a* in *father*: **casa**.
e has two sounds: closed like *ey* in *they*: **sera**; open like *e* in *egg*: **sette**.
i is like *ee* in *feet*: **venire**.
o has two sounds: closed like *o* in *show*: **bocca**; open like *o* in *dog*: **croma**.
u is like *oo* in *moon*: **luna**.

When two or more vowels come together each vowel is pronounced separately: **buono**; **baia**.

Consonants:

b, d, f, l, m, n, p, t, v are pronounced as in English. When these are double they are sounded distinctly: **bello**.

c before **a, o** or **u** and before consonants is like *k* in *king*: **cane**.
   before **e** or **i** is like *ch* in *church*: **cena**.
ch is also like *k* in *king*: **chiesa**.
g before **a, o,** or **u** is hard like *g* in *got*: **gufo**.
   before **e** or **i** is like *j* in *jelly*: **gentile**.
gh is like *g* in *gun*: **ghiaccio**.
gl when followed by **a, e, o, u** is like *gl* in *glass*: **gloria**.
gli is like *lli* in *million*: **figlio**.
gn is like *ni* in *onion*: **bagno**.
h is silent.
ng is like *ng* in *finger* (not *singer*): **ringraziare**.
r is pronounced distinctly.
s between two vowels is like *s* in *rose*: **riso**.
   at the beginning of a word it is like *s* in *soap*: **sapone**.
sc before **e** or **i** is like *sh* in *shell*: **scienza**.
z sounds like *ts* within a word: **fazione**; like *dz* at the beginning: **zoo**.

The stress is shown by the sign ' printed before the stressed syllable.

Pronuncia inglese

SIMBOLI FONETICI

Vocali e dittonghi

æ *bad*	ʊ *put*	aʊ *now*
ɑ: *ah*	u: *too*	aʊə *flour*
e *wet*	ə *ago*	ɔɪ *coin*
ɪ *sit*	3: *work*	ɪə *here*
i: *see*	eɪ *made*	eə *hair*
ɒ *got*	əʊ *home*	ʊə *poor*
ɔ: *door*	aɪ *five*	
ʌ *cup*	aɪə *fire*	

Consonanti

b *boy*	l *leg*	t *ten*
d *day*	m *man*	tʃ *chip*
dʒ *page*	n *new*	θ *three*
f *foot*	ŋ *sing*	ð *this*
g *go*	p *pen*	v *verb*
h *he*	r *run*	w *wet*
j *yes*	s *speak*	z *his*
k *coat*	ʃ *ship*	ʒ *pleasure*

Note: ' precede la sillaba accentata.
       La vocale nasale in parole quali *nuance* è indicata nella trascrizione
       fonetica come ɒ̃: njuːɒ̃s.

Abbreviations/Abbreviazioni

adjective	*a*	aggettivo
abbreviation	*abbr*	abbreviazione
administration	*Admin*	amministrazione
adverb	*adv*	avverbio
aeronautics	*Aeron*	aeronautica
American	*Am*	americano
anatomy	*Anat*	anatomia
archaeology	*Archaeol*	archeologia
architecture	*Archit*	architettura
attributive	*attrib*	attributo
astrology	*Astr*	astrologia
automobiles	*Auto*	automobile
auxiliary	*aux*	ausiliario
biology	*Biol*	biologia
botany	*Bot*	botanica
British English	*Br*	inglese britannico
Chemistry	*Chem*	chimica
commerce	*Comm*	commercio
computers	*Comput*	informatica
conjunction	*conj*	congiunzione
cooking	*Culin*	cucina
definite article	*def art*	articolo determinativo
	ecc	eccetera
electricity	*Electr*	elettricità
et cetera	*etc*	
feminine	*f*	femminile
familiar	*fam*	familiare
figurative	*fig*	figurato
formal	*fml*	formale
geography	*Geog*	geografia
geology	*Geol*	geologia
grammar	*Gram*	grammatica
humorous	*hum*	umoristico
indefinite article	*indef art*	articolo indeterminativo
interjection	*int*	interiezione
interrogative	*inter*	interrogativo
invariable	*inv*	invariabile
(*no plural form*)		
law	*Jur*	legge/giuridico
literary	*liter*	letterario
masculine	*m*	maschile
mathematics	*Math*	matematica
mechanics	*Mech*	meccanica
medicine	*Med*	medicina
masculine or feminine	*mf*	maschile o femminile
military	*Mil*	militare
music	*Mus*	musica
noun	*n*	sostantivo

nautical	*Naut*	nautica
pejorative	*pej*	peggiorativo
personal	*pers*	personale
photography	*Phot*	fotografia
physics	*Phys*	fisica
plural	*pl*	plurale
politics	*Pol*	politica
possessive	*poss*	possessivo
past participle	*pp*	participio passato
prefix	*pref*	prefisso
preposition	*prep*	preposizione
present tense	*pres*	presente
pronoun	*pron*	pronome
psychology	*Psych*	psicologia
past tense	*pt*	tempo passato
	qcno	qualcuno
	qcsa	qualcosa
proprietary term	®	marca depositata
rail	*Rail*	ferrovia
reflexive	*refl*	riflessivo
religion	*Relig*	religione
relative pronoun	*rel pron*	pronome relativo
somebody	*sb*	
school	*Sch*	scuola
singular	*sg*	singolare
slang	*sl*	gergo
something	*sth*	
technical	*Techn*	tecnico
telephone	*Teleph*	telefono
theatrical	*Theat*	teatrale
television	*TV*	televisione
typography	*Typ*	tipografia
university	*Univ*	università
auxiliary verb	*v aux*	verbo ausiliare
intransitive verb	*vi*	verbo intransitivo
reflexive verb	*vr*	verbo riflessivo
transitive verb	*vt*	verbo transitivo
transitive and intransitive	*vt/i*	verbo transitivo e intransitivo
vulgar	*vulg*	volgare
cultural equivalent	≈	equivalenza culturale

Aa

a (**ad** *before vowel*) *prep* to; (*stato in luogo, tempo, età*) at; (*con mese, città*) in; (*mezzo, modo*) by; **dire qcsa a qcno** tell sb sth; **alle tre** at three o'clock; **a vent'anni** at the age of twenty; **a Natale** at Christmas; **a dicembre** in December; **ero al cinema** I was at the cinema; **vivo a Londra** I live in London; **a due a due** two by two; **a piedi** on *o* by foot; **maglia a maniche lunghe** long-sleeved sweater; **casa a tre piani** house with three floors; **giocare a tennis** play tennis; **50 km all'ora** 50 km an hour; **2 000 lire al chilo** 2,000 lire a kilo; **al mattino/alla sera** in the morning/evening; **a venti chilometri/due ore da qui** twenty kilometres/two hours away

a'bate *nm* abbot

abbacchi'ato *a* downhearted

ab'bacchio *nm* [young] lamb

abbagli'ante *a* dazzling ● *nm* headlight, high beam

abbagli'are *vt* dazzle. **ab'baglio** *nm* blunder; **prendere un ~** make a blunder

abbai'are *vi* bark

abba'ino *nm* dormer window

abbando'na|re *vt* abandon; leave ⟨*luogo*⟩; give up ⟨*piani ecc*⟩. **~rsi** *vr* let oneself go; **~rsi a** give oneself up to ⟨*ricordi ecc*⟩. **~to** *a* abandoned. **abban'dono** *nm* abandoning; *fig* abandon; (*stato*) neglect

abbassa'mento *nm* (*di temperatura, acqua, prezzi*) drop

abbas'sar|e *vt* lower; turn down ⟨*radio, TV*⟩; **~e i fari** dip the headlights. **~si** *vr* stoop; ⟨*sole ecc*⟩ sink; *fig* demean oneself

ab'basso *adv* below ● *int* down with

abba'stanza *adv* enough; (*alquanto*) quite

ab'batter|e *vt* demolish; shoot down ⟨*aereo*⟩; put down ⟨*animale*⟩; topple ⟨*regime*⟩; (*fig: demoralizzare*) dishearten. **~si** *vr* (*cadere*) fall; *fig* be discouraged

abbatti'mento *nm* (*morale*) despondency

abbat'tuto *a* despondent, down-in-the-mouth

abba'zia *nf* abbey

abbel'lir|e *vt* embellish. **~si** *vr* adorn oneself

abbeve'ra|re *vt* water. **~'toio** *nm* drinking trough

abbi'ente *a* well-to-do

abbiglia'mento *nm* clothes *pl*; (*industria*) clothing industry, rag trade

abbigli'ar|e *vt* dress. **~si** *vr* dress up

abbina'mento *nm* combining

abbi'nare *vt* combine; match ⟨*colori*⟩

abbindo'lare *vt* cheat

abbocca'mento *nm* interview; (*conversazione*) talk

abboc'care *vi* bite; ⟨*tubi:*⟩ join; *fig* swallow the bait

abboc'cato *a* ⟨*vino*⟩ fairly sweet

abbof'farsi *vr* stuff oneself

abbona'mento *nm* subscription; (*ferroviario ecc*) season-ticket; **fare l'~** take out a subscription

abbo'na|re *vt* make a subscriber. **~rsi** *vr* subscribe (**a** to); take out a season-ticket (**a** for) ⟨*teatro, stadio*⟩. **~to, -a** *nmf* subscriber

abbon'dan|te *a* abundant; ⟨*quantità*⟩ copious; ⟨*nevicata*⟩ heavy; ⟨*vestiario*⟩ roomy. **~te di** abounding in. **~te'mente** *adv* ⟨*mangiare*⟩ copiously. **~za** *nf* abundance

abbon'dare *vi* abound

abbor'da|bile *a* ⟨*persona*⟩ approachable; ⟨*prezzo*⟩ reasonable. **~ggio** *nm* Mil boarding. **~re** *vt* board ⟨*nave*⟩; approach ⟨*persona*⟩; (*fam: attaccar bottone a*) chat up; tackle ⟨*compito ecc*⟩

abbotto'na|re *vt* button up. **~'tura** *nf* [row of] buttons. **~to** *a fig* tight-lipped

abboz'zare *vt* sketch [out]; **~ un sorriso** give a hint of a smile. **ab'bozzo** *nm* sketch

abbracci'are *vt* embrace; hug, embrace ⟨*persona*⟩; take up ⟨*professione*⟩; *fig* include. **ab'braccio** *nm* hug

abbrevi'a|re *vt* shorten; (*ridurre*) curtail; abbreviate ⟨*parola*⟩. **~zi'one** *nf* abbreviation

abbron'zante *nm* sun-tan lotion

abbron'za|re *vt* bronze; tan ⟨*pelle*⟩. **~rsi** *vr* get a tan. **~to** *a* tanned. **~'tura** *nf* [sun-]tan

abbrusto'lire *vt* toast; roast ⟨*caffè ecc*⟩

abbruti'mento *nm* brutalization. **ab-bru'tire** *vt* brutalize. **abbru'tirsi** *vr* become brutalized

abbuf'fa|rsi *vr fam* stuff oneself. **~ta** *nf* blowout

abbuo'nare *vt* reduce

abbu'ono *nm* allowance; *Sport* handicap

abdi'ca|re *vi* abdicate. **~zi'one** *nf* abdication

aber'rante *a* aberrant

aberrazi'one *nf* aberration

a'bete *nm* fir

abi'etto *a* despicable

'abil|e *a* able; (*idoneo*) fit; (*astuto*) clever. **~ità** *nf inv* ability; (*idoneità*) fitness; (*astuzia*) cleverness. **~'mente** *adv* ably; (*con astuzia*) cleverly

abili'ta|re *vt* qualify. **~to** *a* qualified. **~zi'one** *nf* qualification; (*titolo*) diploma

abis'sale *a* abysmal. **a'bisso** *nm* abyss

abi'tabile *a* inhabitable

abi'tacolo *nm Auto* passenger compartment

abi'tante *nmf* inhabitant

abi'ta|re *vi* live. **~to** *a* inhabited ● *nm* built-up area. **~zi'one** *nf* house

'abito *nm* (*da donna*) dress; (*da uomo*) suit. **~ da cerimonia/da sera** formal/evening dress

abitu'al|e *a* usual, habitual. **~'mente** *adv* usually

abitu'ar|e *vt* accustom. **~si a** *vr* get used to

abitudi'nario, -a *a* of fixed habits ● *nmf* person of fixed habits

abi'tudine *nf* habit; **d'~** usually; **per ~** out of habit; **avere l'~ di fare qcsa** be in the habit of doing sth

abnegazi'one *nf* self-sacrifice

ab'norme *a* abnormal

abo'li|re *vt* abolish; repeal ⟨*legge*⟩. **~zi'one** *nf* abolition; repeal

abomi'nevole *a* abominable

abo'rigeno, -a *a & nmf* aboriginal

abor'rire *vt* abhor

abor'ti|re *vi* miscarry; (*volontaria-mente*) have an abortion; *fig* fail. **~vo** *a* abortive. **a'borto** *nm* miscarriage; (*volontario*) abortion. **~sta** *a* pro-choice

abras|i'one *nf* abrasion. **abra'sivo** *a & nm* abrasive

abro'ga|re *vt* repeal. **~zi'one** *nf* repeal

'abside *nf* apse

abu'lia *nf* apathy. **a'bulico** *a* apathetic

abu's|are *vi* **~ di** abuse; over-indulge in ⟨*alcol*⟩; (*approfittare di*) take advantage of; (*violentare*) rape. **~ivo** *a* illegal

a'buso *nm* abuse. **~ di confidenza** breach of confidence

a.C. *abbr* (**avanti Cristo**) BC

'acca *nf fam* **non ho capito un'~** I understood damn all

acca'demi|a *nf* academy. **A~a di Belle Arti** Academy of Fine Arts. **~co, -a** *a* academic ● *nmf* academician

acca'd|ere *vi* happen; **accada quel che accada** come what may. **~uto** *nm* event

accalappi'are *vt* catch; *fig* allure

accal'carsi *vr* crowd

accal'da|rsi *vr* get overheated; *fig* get excited. **~to** *a* overheated

accalo'rarsi *vr* get excited

accampa'mento *nm* camp. **accam-'pare** *vt fig* put forth. **accam'parsi** *vr* camp

accani'mento *nm* tenacity; (*odio*) rage

acca'ni|rsi *vr* persist; (*infierire*) rage. **~to** *a* persistent; ⟨*odio*⟩ fierce; *fig* inveterate

ac'canto *adv* near; **~ a** *prep* next to

accanto'nare *vt* set aside; *Mil* billet

accaparra'mento *nm* hoarding; *Comm* cornering

accapar'ra|re *vt* hoard. **~rsi** *vr* grab; corner ⟨*mercato*⟩. **~'tore**, **~'trice** *nmf* hoarder

accapigli'arsi *vr* scuffle; (*litigare*) squabble

accappa'toio *nm* bathrobe; (*per spiaggia*) beachrobe

accappo'nare *vt* **fare ~ la pelle a qcno** make sb's flesh creep

accarez'zare *vt* caress, stroke; *fig* cherish

accartocci'ar|e *vt* scrunch up. **~si** *vr* curl up

acca'sarsi *vr* get married

accasci'arsi *vr* flop down; *fig* lose heart

accata'stare *vt* pile up

accatti'vante *a* beguiling

accatti'varsi *vr* **~ le simpatie/la stima/l'affetto di qcno** gain sb's sympathy/respect/affection

accatto'naggio *nm* begging. **accat-'tone, -a** *nmf* beggar

accaval'lar|e *vt* cross ⟨*gambe*⟩. **~si** *vr* pile up; *fig* overlap

acce'cante *a* ⟨*luce*⟩ blinding

acce'care *vt* blind ● *vi* go blind

ac'cedere *vi* ~ **a** enter; ⟨*acconsentire*⟩ comply with

accele'ra|re *vi* accelerate ● *vt* speed up, accelerate; **~re il passo** quicken one's pace. **~to** *a* rapid. **~'tore** *nm* accelerator. **~zi'one** *nf* acceleration

ac'cender|e *vt* light; turn on ⟨*luce, TV ecc*⟩; *fig* inflame; **ha da ~e?** have you got a light?. **~si** *vr* catch fire; ⟨*illuminarsi*⟩ light up; *fig* become inflamed

accendi'gas *nm inv* gas lighter; ⟨*su cucina*⟩ automatic ignition

accen'dino *nm* lighter

accendi'sigari *nm* cigar-lighter

accen'nare *vt* indicate; hum ⟨*melodia*⟩ ● *vi* ~ **a** beckon to; *fig* hint at; ⟨*far l'atto di*⟩ make as if to; **accenna a piovere** it looks like rain. **ac'cenno** *nm* gesture; ⟨*con il capo*⟩ nod; *fig* hint

accensi'one *nf* lighting; ⟨*di motore*⟩ ignition

accen'ta|re *vt* accent; ⟨*con accento tonico*⟩ stress. **~zi'one** *nf* accentuation. **ac'cento** *nm* accent; ⟨*tonico*⟩ stress

accentra'mento *nm* centralizing

accen'trare *vt* centralize

accentu'a|re *vt* accentuate. **~rsi** *vr* become more noticeable. **~to** *a* marked

accerchia'mento *nm* surrounding

accerchi'are *vt* surround

accerta'mento *nm* check

accer'tare *vt* ascertain; ⟨*controllare*⟩ check; assess ⟨*reddito*⟩

ac'ceso *a* lighted; ⟨*radio, TV ecc*⟩ on; ⟨*colore*⟩ bright

acces'sibile *a* accessible; ⟨*persona*⟩ approachable; ⟨*spesa*⟩ reasonable

ac'cesso *nm* access; ⟨*Med: di rabbia*⟩ fit; **vietato l'~** no entry

acces'sorio *a* accessory; ⟨*secondario*⟩ of secondary importance ● *nm* accessory; **accessori** *pl* ⟨*rifiniture*⟩ fittings

ac'cetta *nf* hatchet

accet'tabile *a* acceptable

accet'tare *vt* accept; ⟨*aderire a*⟩ agree to

accettazi'one *nf* acceptance; ⟨*luogo*⟩ reception. **~ [bagagli]** check-in. **[banco] ~** check-in [desk]

ac'cetto *a* agreeable; **essere bene ~** be very welcome

accezi'one *nf* meaning

acchiap'pare *vt* catch

acchito *nm* **di primo ~** at first

acciac'ca|re *vt* crush; *fig* prostrate. **~to, -a** *a* **essere ~to** ache all over. **acci'acco** *nm* infirmity; ⟨*pl: afflizioni*⟩ aches and pains

acciaie'ria *nf* steelworks

acci'aio *nm* steel; **~ inossidabile** stainless steel

acciden'ta|le *a* accidental. **~l'mente** *adv* accidentally. **~to** *a* ⟨*terreno*⟩ uneven

acci'dente *nm* accident; *Med* stroke; **non capisce/non vede un ~** *fam* he doesn't understand/can't see a damn thing. **acci'denti!** *int* damn!

accigli'a|rsi *vr* frown. **~to** *a* frowning

ac'cingersi *vr* ~ **a** be about to

acci'picchia *int* good Lord!

acciuf'fare *vt* catch

acci'uga *nf* anchovy

accla'ma|re *vt* applaud; ⟨*eleggere*⟩ acclaim. **~zi'one** *nf* applause

acclima'tar|e *vt* acclimatize. **~si** *vr* get acclimatized

ac'clu|dere *vt* enclose. **~so** *a* enclosed

accocco'larsi *vr* squat

accogli'en|te *a* welcoming; ⟨*confortevole*⟩ cosy. **~za** *nf* welcome

ac'cogliere *vt* receive; ⟨*conpiacere*⟩ welcome; ⟨*contenere*⟩ hold

accol'larsi *vr* take on ⟨*responsabilità, debiti, doveri*⟩. **accol'lato** *a* high-necked

accoltel'lare *vt* knife

accomia'tar|e *vt* dismiss. **~si** *vr* take one's leave (**da** of)

accomo'dante *a* accommodating

accomo'dar|e *vt* ⟨*riparare*⟩ mend; ⟨*disporre*⟩ arrange. **~si** *vr* make oneself at home; **si accomodi!** come in!; ⟨*si sieda*⟩ take a seat!

accompagna'mento *nm* accompaniment; ⟨*seguito*⟩ retinue

accompa'gna|re *vt* accompany; **~re qcno a casa** see sb home; **~re qcno alla porta** show sb out. **~'tore, ~'trice** *nmf* companion; ⟨*di comitiva*⟩ escort; *Mus* accompanist

accomu'nare *vt* pool

acconci'a|re *vt* arrange. **~'tura** *nf* hair-style; ⟨*ornamento*⟩ head-dress

accondiscen'den|te *a* too obliging. **~za** *nf* excessive desire to please

accondi'scendere *vi* ~ **a** condescend; comply with ⟨*desiderio*⟩; ⟨*acconsentire*⟩ consent to

acconsen'tire *vi* consent

acconten'tar|e vt satisfy. **~si** vr be content (**di** with)

ac'conto nm deposit; **in ~** on account; **lasciare un ~** leave a deposit

accop'pare vt fam bump off

accoppia'mento nm coupling; (di animali) mating

accoppi'a|re vt couple; mate (animali). **~rsi** vr pair off; mate. **~ta** nf (scommessa) bet placed on two horses for first and second place

acco'rato a sorrowful

accorci'ar|e vt shorten. **~si** vr get shorter

accor'dar|e vt concede; match (colori ecc); Mus tune. **~si** vr agree

ac'cordo nm agreement; Mus chord; (armonia) harmony; **andare d'~** get on well; **d'~!** agreed!; **essere d'~** agree; **prendere accordi con qcno** make arrangements with sb

ac'corgersi vr **~ di** notice; (capire) realize

accorgi'mento nm shrewdness; (espediente) device

ac'correre vi hasten

accor'tezza nf (previdenza) forethought

ac'corto a shrewd; **mal ~** incautious

accosta'mento nm (di colori) combination

acco'star|e vt draw close to; approach (persona); set ajar (porta ecc). **~si** vr **~si a** come near to

accovacci'a|rsi vr crouch, squat down. **~to** a squatting

accoz'zaglia nf jumble; (di persone) mob

accoz'zare vt **~ colori** mix colours that clash

accredita'mento nm credit; **~ tramite bancogiro** Bank Giro Credit

accredi'tare vt confirm (notizia); Comm credit

ac'cresc|ere vt increase. **~ersi** vr grow larger. **~i'tivo** a augmentative

accucci'arsi vr (cane:) lie down; (persona:) crouch

accu'dire vi **~ a** attend to

accumu'la|re vt accumulate. **~rsi** vr pile up, accumulate. **~'tore** nm accumulator; Auto battery. **~zi'one** nf accumulation. **ac'cumulo** nm (di merce) build-up

accura'tezza nf care

accu'rato a careful

ac'cusa nf accusation; Jur charge; **essere in stato di ~** Jur have been charged; **la Pubblica A~** Jur the public prosecutor

accu'sa|re vt accuse; Jur charge; complain of (dolore); **~re ricevuta di** Comm acknowledge receipt of. **~to, -a** nmf accused. **~'tore** nm Jur prosecutor

a'cerbo a sharp; (immaturo) unripe

'acero nm maple

a'cerrimo a implacable

ace'tone nm nail polish remover

a'ceto nm vinegar

A.C.I. abbr (**Automobile Club d'Italia**) Italian Automobile Association

acidità nf acidity. **~ di stomaco** acid stomach

'acido a acid; (persona) sour ● nm acid

a'cidulo a slightly sour

'acino nm berry; (chicco) grape

'acne nf acne

'acqua nf water; **fare ~** Naut leak; **~ in bocca!** fig mum's the word!. **~ di Colonia** eau de Cologne. **~ corrente** running water. **~ dolce** fresh water. **~ minerale** mineral water. **~ minerale gassata** fizzy mineral water. **~ naturale** still mineral water. **~ potabile** drinking water. **~ salata** salt water. **~ tonica** tonic water

acqua'forte nf etching

ac'quaio nm sink

acquama'rina a aquamarine

acqua'rello nm = **acquerello**

ac'quario nm aquarium; Astr Aquarius

acqua'santa nf holy water

acqua'scooter nm inv water-scooter

ac'quatico a aquatic

acquat'tarsi vr crouch

acqua'vite nf brandy

acquaz'zone nm downpour

acque'dotto nm aqueduct

'acqueo a **vapore ~** water vapour

acque'rello nm water-colour

acqui'rente nmf purchaser

acqui'si|re vt acquire. **~to** a acquired. **~zi'one** nf attainment

acqui'st|are vt purchase; (ottenere) acquire. **ac'quisto** nm purchase; **uscire per ~i** go shopping; **fare ~i** shop

acqui'trino nm marsh

acquo'lina nf **far venire l'~ in bocca a qcno** make sb's mouth water

ac'quoso a watery

'acre a acrid; (al gusto) sour; fig harsh

a'crilico nm acrylic

a'croba|ta nmf acrobat. **~'zia** nf acrobatics pl

a'cronimo nm acronym

acu'ir|e *vt* sharpen. **~si** *vr* become more intense

a'culeo *nm* sting; *Bot* prickle

a'cume *nm* acumen

acumi'nato *a* pointed

a'custic|a *nf* acoustics *pl.* **~o** *a* acoustic

acu'tezza *nf* acuteness

acutiz'zarsi *vr* become worse

a'cuto *a* sharp; ⟨*suono*⟩ shrill; ⟨*freddo, odore*⟩ intense; *Gram, Math, Med* acute ● *nm Mus* high note

adagi'ar|e *vt* lay down. **~si** *vr* lie down

a'dagio *adv* slowly ● *nm Mus* adagio; ⟨*proverbio*⟩ adage

adattabilità *nf* adaptability

adatta'mento *nm* adaptation; **avere spirito di ~** be adaptable

adat'ta|re *vt* adapt; ⟨*aggiustare*⟩ fit. **~rsi** *vr* adapt. **~'tore** *nm* adaptor. **a'datto** *a* suitable (**a** for); ⟨*giusto*⟩ right

addebita'mento *nm* debit. **~ diret-to** direct debit

addebi'tare *vt* debit; *fig* ascribe ⟨*colpa*⟩

ad'debito *nm* charge

addensa'mento *nm* thickening; ⟨*di persone*⟩ gathering

adden'sar|e *vt* thicken. **~si** *vr* thicken; ⟨*affollarsi*⟩ gather

adden'tare *vt* bite

adden'trarsi *vr* penetrate

ad'dentro *adv* deeply; **essere ~ in** be in on

addestra'mento *nm* training

adde'strar|e *vt* train. **~si** *vr* train

ad'detto, -a *a* assigned ● *nmf* employee; ⟨*diplomatico*⟩ attaché; **addetti** *pl* **ai lavori** persons involved in the work. **~ stampa** information officer, press officer

addiaccio *nm* **dormire all'~** sleep in the open

addi'etro *adv* ⟨*indietro*⟩ back; ⟨*nel passato*⟩ before

ad'dio *nm & int* goodbye. **~ al celiba-to** stag night, stag party

addirit'tura *adv* ⟨*perfino*⟩ even; ⟨*assolutamente*⟩ absolutely; **~!** really!

ad'dirsi *vr* **~ a** suit

addi'tare *vt* point at; ⟨*in mezzo a un gruppo*⟩ point out; *fig* point to

addi'tivo *a & nm* additive

addizio'nal|e *a* additional. **~'mente** *adv* additionally

addizio'nare *vt* add [up]. **addizi'one** *nf* addition

addob'bare *vt* decorate. **ad'dobbo** *nm* decoration

addol'cir|e *vt* sweeten; tone down ⟨*colore*⟩; *fig* soften. **~si** *vr fig* mellow

addolo'ra|re *vt* grieve. **~rsi** *vr* be upset (**per** by). **~to** *a* pained, distressed

ad'dom|e *nm* abdomen. **~i'nale** *a* abdominal; [**muscoli**] **addominali** *pl* abdominals

addomesti'ca|re *vt* tame. **~'tore** *nm* tamer

addormen'ta|re *vt* put to sleep. **~rsi** *vr* go to sleep. **~to** *a* asleep; *fig* slow

addos'sar|e *vt* **~e a** ⟨*appoggiare*⟩ lean against; ⟨*attribuire*⟩ lay on. **~si** *vr* ⟨*ammassarsi*⟩ crowd; shoulder ⟨*responsabilità ecc*⟩

ad'dosso *adv* on; **~ a** *prep* on; ⟨*molto vicino*⟩ right next to; **mettere gli occhi ~ a qcno/qcsa** hanker after sb/sth; **non mettermi le mani ~!** keep your hands off me!; **stare ~ a qcno** *fig* be on sb's back

ad'durre *vt* produce ⟨*prova, documento*⟩; give ⟨*pretesto, esempio*⟩

adegua'mento *nm* adjustment

adegu'a|re *vt* adjust. **~rsi** *vr* conform. **~to** *a* adequate; ⟨*conforme*⟩ consistent

a'dempi|ere *vt* fulfil. **~'mento** *nm* fulfilment

ade'noidi *nfpl* adenoids

ade'ren|te *a* adhesive; ⟨*vestito*⟩ tight ● *nmf* follower. **~za** *nf* adhesion. **~ze** *npl* connections

ade'rire *vi* **~ a** stick to, adhere to; support ⟨*sciopero, petizione*⟩; agree to ⟨*richiesta*⟩

adesca'mento *nm Jur* soliciting

ade'scare *vt* bait; *fig* entice

adesi'one *nf* adhesion; *fig* agreement

ade'sivo *a* adhesive ● *nm* sticker; *Auto* bumper sticker

a'desso *adv* now; ⟨*poco fa*⟩ just now; ⟨*tra poco*⟩ any moment now; **da ~ in poi** from now on; **per ~** for the moment

adia'cente *a* adjacent; **~ a** next to

adi'bire *vt* **~ a** put to use as

'adipe *nm* adipose tissue

adi'ra|rsi *vr* get irate. **~to** *a* irate

a'dire *vt* resort to; **~ le vie legali** take legal proceedings

'adito *nm* **dare ~ a** give rise to

adocchi'are *vt* eye; ⟨*con desiderio*⟩ covet

adole'scen|te *a & nmf* adolescent. **~za** *nf* adolescence. **~zi'ale** *a* adolescent

adom'brar|e *vt* darken; *fig* veil. **~si** *vr* (*offendersi*) take offence

adope'rar|e *vt* use. **~si** *vr* take trouble

ado'rabile *a* adorable

ado'ra|re *vt* adore. **~zi'one** *nf* adoration

ador'nare *vt* adorn

adot't|are *vt* adopt. **~ivo** *a* adoptive. **adozi'one** *nf* adoption

ad *prep* = **a** (*davanti a vocale*)

adrena'lina *nf* adrenalin

adri'atico *a* Adriatic ● *nm* **l'A~** the Adriatic

adu'la|re *vt* flatter. **~'tore**, **~'trice** *nmf* flatterer. **~zi'one** *nf* flattery

adulte'ra|re *vt* adulterate. **~to** *a* adulterated

adul'terio *nm* adultery. **a'dultero**, **-a** *a* adulterous ● *nm* adulterer ● *nf* adulteress

a'dulto, **-a** *a* & *nmf* adult; (*maturo*) mature

adu'nanza *nf* assembly

adu'na|re *vt* gather. **~ta** *nf Mil* parade

a'dunco *a* hooked

ae'rare *vt* air (*stanza*)

a'ereo *a* aerial; (*dell'aviazione*) air *attrib* ● *nm* aeroplane, plane

ae'robic|a *nf* aerobics. **~o** *a* aerobic

aerodi'namic|a *nf* aerodynamics *sg*. **~o** *a* aerodynamic

aero'nautic|a *nf* aeronautics *sg*; *Mil* Air Force. **~o** *a* aeronautical

aero'plano *nm* aeroplane

aero'porto *nm* airport

aero'scalo *nm* cargo and servicing area

aero'sol *nm inv* aerosol

'afa *nf* sultriness

af'fabil|e *a* affable. **~ità** *nf* affability

affaccen'da|rsi *vr* busy oneself (**a** with). **~to** *a* busy

affacci'arsi *vr* show oneself; **~ alla finestra** appear at the window

affa'ma|re *vt* starve [out]. **~to** *a* starving

affan'na|re *vt* leave breathless. **~rsi** *vr* busy oneself; (*agitarsi*) get worked up. **~to** *a* breathless; **dal respiro ~to** wheezy. **af'fanno** *nm* breathlessness; *fig* worry

af'fare *nm* matter; *Comm* transaction, deal; (*occasione*) bargain; **affari** *pl* business; **non sono affari tuoi** *fam* it's none of your business. **affa'rista** *nmf* wheeler-dealer

affasci'nante *a* fascinating; (*persona, sorriso*) bewitching

affasci'nare *vt* bewitch; *fig* charm

affatica'mento *nm* fatigue

affati'car|e *vt* tire; (*sfinire*) exhaust. **~si** *vr* tire oneself out; (*affannarsi*) strive

af'fatto *adv* completely; **non... ~** not... at all; **niente ~!** not at all!

affer'ma|re *vt* affirm; (*sostenere*) assert. **~rsi** *vr* establish oneself

affermativa'mente *adv* in the affirmative

afferma'tivo *a* affirmative

affermazi'one *nf* assertion; (*successo*) achievement

affer'rar|e *vt* seize; catch (*oggetto*); (*capire*) grasp; **~e al volo** *fig* be quick on the uptake. **~si** *vr* **~si a** grasp at

affet'ta|re *vt* slice; (*ostentare*) affect. **~to** *a* sliced; (*sorriso, maniere*) affected ● *nm* cold meat, sliced meat. **~zi'one** *nf* affectation

affet'tivo *a* affective; **rapporto ~** emotional tie

af'fetto[1] *nm* affection; **con ~** affectionately

af'fetto[2] *a* **~ da** suffering from

affettuosità *nf inv* (*gesto*) affectionate gesture

affettu'oso *a* affectionate

affezio'na|rsi *vr* **~rsi a** grow fond of. **~to** *a* devoted (**a** to)

affian'car|e *vt* put side by side; *Mil* flank; *fig* support. **~si** *vr* come side by side; *fig* stand together; **~si a qcno** *fig* help sb out

affiata'mento *nm* harmony

affia'ta|rsi *vr* get on well together. **~to** *a* close-knit; **una coppia ~ta** a very close couple

affibbi'are *vt* **~ qcsa a qcno** saddle sb with sth; **~ un pugno a qcno** let fly at sb

affi'dabil|e *a* dependable. **~ità** *nf* dependability

affida'mento *nm* (*Jur: dei minori*) custody; **fare ~ su qcno** rely on sb; **non dare ~** not inspire confidence

affi'dar|e *vt* entrust. **~si** *vr* **~si a** rely on

affievo'lirsi *vr* grow weak

af'figgere *vt* affix

affi'lare *vt* sharpen

affili'ar|e *vt* affiliate. **~si** *vr* become affiliated

affi'nare *vt* sharpen; (*perfezionare*) refine

affinché *conj* so that, in order that

af'fin|e *a* similar. **~ità** *nf* affinity

affiora'mento *nm* emergence; *Naut* surfacing

affio'rare *vi* emerge; *fig* come to light

af'fisso *nm* bill; *Gram* affix

affitta'camere *nm inv* landlord ● *nf inv* landlady

affit'tare *vt* (*dare in affitto*) let; (*prendere in affitto*) rent; **'af'fittasi'** 'to let', 'for rent'

af'fitt|o *nm* rent; **contratto d'~o** lease; **dare in ~o** let; **prendere in ~o** rent. **~u'ario , -a** *nmf Jur* lessee

af'fligger|e *vt* torment. **~si** *vr* distress oneself

af'fli|tto *a* distressed; **~tto da** suffering from. **~zi'one** *nf* distress; *fig* affliction

afflosci'arsi *vr* become floppy; (*accasciarsi*) flop down; ⟨*morale:*⟩ decline

afflu'en|te *a & nm* tributary. **~za** *nf* flow; (*di gente*) crowd

afflu'ire *vi* flow; *fig* pour in

af'flusso *nm* influx

affo'ga|re *vt/i* drown; *Culin* poach; **~re in** *fig* be swamped with. **~to** *a* ⟨*persona*⟩ drowned; ⟨*uova*⟩ poached. **~to al caffè** *nm* ice cream with hot espresso poured over it

affol'la|re *vt*, **~rsi** *vr* crowd. **~to** *a* crowded

affonda'mento *nm* sinking

affon'dare *vt/i* sink

affossa'mento *nm* pothole

affran'ca|re *vt* redeem ⟨*bene*⟩; stamp ⟨*lettera*⟩; free ⟨*schiavo*⟩. **~rsi** *vr* free oneself. **~'tura** *nf* stamping; (*di spedizione*) postage

af'franto *a* prostrated; (*esausto*) worn out

af'fresco *nm* fresco

affret'ta|re *vt* speed up. **~rsi** *vr* hurry. **~ta'mente** *adv* hastily. **~to** *a* hasty

affron'tar|e *vt* face; confront ⟨*il nemico*⟩; meet ⟨*le spese*⟩. **~si** *vr* clash

af'fronto *nm* affront, insult; **fare un ~ a qcno** insult sb

affumi'ca|re *vt* fill with smoke; *Culin* smoke. **~to** *a* ⟨*prosciutto, formaggio*⟩ smoked

affuso'la|re *vt* taper [off]. **~to** *a* tapering

afo'risma *nm* aphorism

a'foso *a* sultry

'Africa *nf* Africa. **afri'cano, -a** *a & nmf* African

afrodi'siaco *a & nm* aphrodisiac

a'genda *nf* diary

agen'dina *nf* pocket-diary

a'gente *nm* agent; **agenti** *pl* atmosferici atmospheric agents. **~ di cambio** stockbroker. **~ di polizia** policeman

agen'zia *nf* agency; (*filiale*) branch office; (*di banca*) branch. **~ di viaggi** travel agency. **~ immobiliare** estate agency

agevo'la|re *vt* facilitate. **~zi'one** *nf* facilitation

a'gevol|e *a* easy; ⟨*strada*⟩ smooth. **~'mente** *adv* easily

aggranci'ar|e *vt* hook up; *Rail* couple. **~si** *vr* ⟨*vestito:*⟩ hook up

ag'geggio *nm* gadget

agget'tivo *nm* adjective

agghiacci'ante *a* terrifying

agghiacci'ar|e *vt fig* **~ qcno** make sb's blood run cold. **~si** *vr* freeze

agghin'da|re *vt fam* dress up. **~rsi** *vr fam* doll oneself up. **~to** *a* dressed up

aggiorna'mento *nm* up-date

aggior'na|re *vt* (*rinviare*) postpone; (*mettere a giorno*) bring up to date. **~rsi** *vr* get up to date. **~to** *a* up-to-date; ⟨*versione*⟩ updated

aggi'rar|e *vt* surround; (*fig: ingannare*) trick. **~si** *vr* hang about; **~si su** ⟨*discorso ecc:*⟩ be about; (*approssimarsi*) be around

aggiudi'car|e *vt* award; (*all'asta*) knock down. **~si** *vr* win

aggi'un|gere *vt* add. **~ta** *nf* addition. **~'tivo** *a* supplementary. **~to** *a* added ● *a & nm* (*assistente*) assistant

aggiu'star|e *vt* mend; (*sistemare*) settle; (*fam: mettere a posto*) fix. **~si** *vr* adapt; (*mettersi in ordine*) tidy oneself up; (*decidere*) sort things out; ⟨*tempo:*⟩ clear up

agglomera'mento *nm* conglomeration

agglome'rato *nm* built-up area

aggrap'par|e *vt* grasp. **~si** *vr* **~si a** cling to

aggra'vante *Jur nf* aggravation ● *a* aggravating

aggra'var|e *vt* (*peggiorare*) make worse; increase ⟨*pena*⟩; (*appesantire*) weigh down. **~si** *vr* worsen

aggrazi'ato *a* graceful

aggre'dire *vt* attack

aggre'ga|re *vt* add; (*associare a un gruppo ecc*) admit. **~rsi** *vr* **~rsi a** join. **~to** *a* associated ● *nm* aggregate; (*di case*) block

aggressi'one *nf* aggression; (*atto*) attack

aggres's|ivo *a* aggressive. **~ività** *nf* aggressiveness. **~ore** *nm* aggressor

aggrin'zare, aggrin'zire *vt* wrinkle

aggrot'tare *vt* ~ **le ciglia/la fronte** frown

aggrovigli'a|re *vt* tangle. **~rsi** *vr* get entangled; *fig* get complicated. **~to** *a* entangled; *fig* confused

agguan'tare *vt* catch

aggu'ato *nm* ambush; (*tranello*) trap; **stare in ~** lie in wait

agguer'rito *a* fierce

agia'tezza *nf* comfort

agi'ato *a* ⟨*persona*⟩ well off; ⟨*vita*⟩ comfortable

a'gibil|e *a* ⟨*palazzo*⟩ fit for human habitation. **~ità** *nf* fitness for human habitation

'agil|e *a* agile. **~ità** *nf* agility

'agio *nm* ease; **mettersi a proprio ~** make oneself at home

a'gire *vi* act; (*comportarsi*) behave; (*funzionare*) work; **~ su** affect

agi'ta|re *vt* shake; wave ⟨*mano*⟩; (*fig: turbare*) trouble. **~rsi** *vr* toss about; (*essere inquieto*) be restless; ⟨*mare:*⟩ get rough. **~to** *a* restless; ⟨*mare*⟩ rough. **~'tore, ~'trice** *nmf* (*persona*) agitator. **~zi'one** *nf* agitation; **mettere in ~zione qcno** make sb worried

'agli = **a + gli**

'aglio *nm* garlic

a'gnello *nm* lamb

agno'lotti *nmpl* ravioli *sg*

a'gnostico, -a *a & nmf* agnostic

'ago *nm* needle

ago'ni|a *nf* agony. **~z'zare** *vi* be on one's deathbed

ago'nistic|a *nf* competition. **~o** *a* competitive

agopun'tura *nf* acupuncture

a'gosto *nm* August

a'grari|a *nf* agriculture. **~o** *a* agricultural ● *nm* landowner

a'gricol|o *a* agricultural. **~'tore** *nm* farmer. **~'tura** *nf* agriculture

agri'foglio *nm* holly

agritu'rismo *nm* farm holidays, agrotourism

'agro *a* sour

agroalimen'tare *a* food *attrib*

agro'dolce *a* bitter-sweet; *Culin* sweet-and-sour; **in ~** sweet and sour

agrono'mia *nf* agronomy

a'grume *nm* citrus fruit; (*pianta*) citrus tree

aguz'zare *vt* sharpen; **~ le orecchie** prick up one's ears; **~ la vista** look hard

aguz'zino *nm* slave-driver; (*carceriere*) jailer

ahimè *int* alas

'ai = **a + i**

'Aia *nf* **L'~** The Hague

'aia *nf* threshing-floor

Aids *nmf* Aids

ai'rone *nm* heron

ai'tante *a* sturdy

aiu'ola *nf* flower-bed

aiu'tante *nmf* assistant ● *nm Mil* adjutant. **~ di campo** aide-de-camp

aiu'tare *vt* help

ai'uto *nm* help, aid; (*assistente*) assistant

aiz'zare *vt* incite; **~ contro** set on

al = **a + il**

'ala *nf* wing; **fare ~** make way

ala'bastro *nm* alabaster

'alacre *a* brisk

a'lano *nm* Great Dane

'alba *nf* dawn

Alba'n|ia *nf* Albania. **a~ese** *a & nmf* Albanian

albeggi'are *vi* dawn

albe'ra|to *a* wooded; ⟨*viale*⟩ tree-lined. **~'tura** *nf Naut* masts *pl*. **albe'rello** *nm* sapling

al'berg|o *nm* hotel. **~o diurno** *hotel where rooms are rented during the daytime*. **~a'tore, ~a'trice** *nmf* hotelkeeper. **~hi'ero** *a* hotel *attrib*

'albero *nm* tree; *Naut* mast; *Mech* shaft. **~ genealogico** family tree. **~ maestro** *Naut* mainmast. **~ di Natale** Christmas tree

albi'cocc|a *nf* apricot. **~o** *nm* apricot-tree

al'bino *nm* albino

'albo *nm* register; (*libro ecc*) album; (*per avvisi*) notice board

'album *nm* album. **~ da disegno** sketch-book

al'bume *nm* albumen

'alce *nm* elk

'alcol *nm* alcohol; *Med* spirit; (*liquori forti*) spirits *pl*; **darsi all'~** take to drink. **al'colici** *nmpl* alcoholic drinks. **al'colico** *a* alcoholic. **alco'lismo** *nm* alcoholism. **~iz'zato, -a** *a & nmf* alcoholic

alco'test® *nm inv* Breathalyser®

al'cova *nf* alcove

al'cun, al'cuno *a & pron* any; **non ha ~ amico** he hasn't any friends, he has no friends. **alcuni** *pl* some, a few; **~i suoi amici** some of his friends

alea'torio *a* unpredictable

a'letta *nf Mech* fin

alfa'betico *a* alphabetical

alfabetizzazi'one *nf ~ della popolazione* teaching people to read and write

alfa'beto *nm* alphabet

alfi'ere *nm (scacchi)* bishop

al'fine *adv* eventually, in the end

'alga *nf* seaweed

'algebra *nf* algebra

Alge'ri|a *nf* Algeria. **a~no, -a** *a & nmf* Algerian

ali'ante *nm* glider

'alibi *nm inv* alibi

alie'na|re *vt* alienate. **~rsi** *vr* become estranged; **~rsi le simpatie di qcno** lose sb's good will. **~to, -a** *a* alienated ● *nmf* lunatic

a'lieno, -a *nmf* alien ● *a* **è ~ da invidia** envy is foreign to him

alimen'ta|re *vt* feed; *fig* foment ● *a* food *attrib;* *(abitudine)* dietary. **~ri** *nmpl* food-stuffs. **~'tore** *nm* power unit. **~zi'one** *nf* feeding

ali'mento *nm* food; **alimenti** *pl* food; *Jur* alimony

a'liquota *nf* share; *(di imposta)* rate

ali'scafo *nm* hydrofoil

'alito *nm* breath

'alla = a + la

allaccia'mento *nm* connection

allacci'ar|e *vt* fasten *(cintura);* lace up *(scarpe);* do up *(vestito);* *(collegare)* connect; form *(amicizia).* **~si** *vr* do up, fasten *(vestito, cintura)*

allaga'mento *nm* flooding

alla'gar|e *vt* flood. **~si** *vr* become flooded

allampa'nato *a* lanky

allarga'mento *nm (di una strada, delle ricerche)* widening

allar'gar|e *vt* widen; open *(braccia, gambe);* let out *(vestito ecc);* *fig* extend. **~si** *vr* widen

allar'mante *a* alarming

allar'ma|re *vt* alarm. **~to** *a* panicky

al'larme *nm* alarm; **dare l'~** raise the alarm; **falso ~** *fig* false alarm. **~ aereo** air raid warning

allar'mis|mo *nm* alarmism. **~ta** *nmf* alarmist

allatta'mento *nm (di animale)* suckling; *(di neonato)* feeding

allat'tare *vt* suckle *(animale);* feed *(neonato)*

'alle = a + le

alle'a|nza *nf* alliance. **~to, -a** *a* allied ● *nmf* ally

alle'ar|e *vt* unite. **~si** *vr* form an alliance

alle'gare¹ *vt Jur* allege

alle'ga|re² *vt (accludere)* enclose; set on edge *(denti).* **~to** *a* enclosed ● *nm* enclosure; **in ~to** attached, appended. **~zi'one** *nf Jur* allegation

allegge'rir|e *vt* lighten; *fig* alleviate. **~si** *vr* become lighter; *(vestirsi leggero)* put on lighter clothes

allego'ria *nf* allegory. **alle'gorico** *a* allegorical

allegra'mente *adv* breezily

alle'gria *nf* gaiety

al'legro *a* cheerful; *(colore)* bright; *(brillo)* tipsy ● *nm Mus* allegro

alle'luia *int* hallelujah!

allena'mento *nm* training

alle'na|re *vt,* **~rsi** *vr* train. **~'tore, ~'trice** *nmf* trainer, coach

allen'tar|e *vt* loosen; *fig* relax. **~si** *vr* become loose; *Mech* work loose

aller'gia *nf* allergy. **al'lergico** *a* allergic

allerta *nf o nm inv* **stare ~** be on the alert

allesti'mento *nm* preparation. **~ scenico** *Theat* set

alle'stire *vt* prepare; stage *(spettacolo);* *Naut* fit out

allet'tante *a* alluring

allet'tare *vt* entice

alleva'mento *nm* breeding; *(processo)* bringing up; *(luogo)* farm; *(per piante)* nursery; **pollo di ~** battery hen *or* chicken

alle'vare *vt* bring up *(bambini);* breed *(animali);* grow *(piante)*

allevi'are *vt* alleviate; *fig* lighten

alli'bito *a* astounded

allibra'tore *nm* bookmaker

allie'tar|e *vt* gladden. **~si** *vr* rejoice

alli'evo, -a *nmf* pupil ● *nm Mil* cadet

alliga'tore *nm* alligator

allinea'mento *nm* alignment

alline'ar|e *vt* line up; *Typ* align; *Fin* adjust. **~si** *vr* fall into line

'allo = a + lo

al'locco *nm* tawny owl; *fig* dunce

al'lodola *nf* [sky]lark

alloggi'are *vt (persona:)* put up; *(casa:)* provide accommodation for; *Mil* billet ● *vi* put up, stay; *Mil* be billeted.

al'loggio nm (appartamento) flat; Mil billet

allontana'mento nm removal

allonta'nar|e vt move away; (licenziare) dismiss; avert ⟨pericolo⟩. ~si vr go away

al'lora adv then; (in quel tempo) at that time; (in tal caso) in that case; d'~ in poi from then on; e ~? what now?; (e con ciò?) so what?; fino ~ until then

al'loro nm laurel; Culin bay

'alluce nm big toe

alluci'na|nte a fam incredible; sostanza ~nte hallucinogen. ~to, -a nmf fam space cadet. ~zi'one nf hallucination

allucino'geno a ⟨sostanza⟩ hallucinatory

al'ludere vi ~ a allude to

allu'minio nm aluminium

allun'gar|e vt lengthen; stretch [out] ⟨gamba⟩; extend ⟨tavolo⟩; (diluire) dilute; ~e il collo crane one's neck. ~e le mani su qcno touch sb up. ~e il passo quicken one's step. ~si vr grow longer; (crescere) grow taller; (sdraiarsi) lie down

allusi'one nf allusion

allu'sivo a allusive

alluvio'nale a alluvial

alluvi'one nf flood

al'meno adv at least; [se] ~ venisse il sole! if only the sun would come out!

a'logeno nm halogen ● a lampada alogena halogen lamp

a'lone nm halo

'Alpi nfpl le ~ the Alps

alpi'nis|mo nm mountaineering. ~ta nmf mountaineer

al'pino a Alpine ● nm Mil gli alpini the Alpine troops

al'quanto a a certain amount of ● adv rather

alt int stop

alta'lena nf swing; (tavola in bilico) see-saw

altale'nare vi fig vacillate

alta'mente adv highly

al'tare nm altar

alta'rino nm scoprire gli altarini di qcno reveal sb's guilty secrets

alte'ra|re vt alter; adulterate ⟨vino⟩; (falsificare) falsify. ~rsi vr be altered; ⟨cibo:⟩ go bad; ⟨merci:⟩ deteriorate; (arrabbiarsi) get angry. ~to a ⟨vino⟩ adulterated. ~zi'one nf alteration; (di vino) adulteration

al'terco nm altercation

alter'nanza nf alternation

alter'na|re vt, ~rsi vr alternate. ~'tiva nf alternative. ~'tivo a alternate. ~to a alternating. ~'tore nm Electr alternator

al'tern|o a alternate; a giorni ~i every other day

al'tero a haughty

al'tezza nf height; (profondità) depth; (suono) pitch; (di tessuto) width; (titolo) Highness; essere all'~ di be on a level with; fig be up to

altezzos|a'mente adv haughtily. ~ità nf haughtiness

altez'zoso a haughty

al'ticcio a tipsy, merry

altipi'ano nm plateau

alti'tudine nf altitude

'alto a high; (di statura) tall; (profondo) deep; (suono) high-pitched; (tessuto) wide; Geog northern; a notte alta in the middle of the night; avere degli alti e bassi have some ups and downs; ad alta fedeltà high-fidelity; a voce alta, ad alta voce in a loud voice; ⟨leggere⟩ aloud; essere in ~ mare be on the high seas. alta finanza nf high finance. alta moda nf high fashion. alta tensione nf high voltage ● adv high; in ~ at the top; ⟨guardare⟩ up; mani in ~! hands up!

alto'forno nm blast-furnace

altolà int halt there!

altolo'cato a highly placed

altopar'lante nm loudspeaker

altopi'ano nm plateau

altret'tanto a & pron as much; (pl) as many ● adv likewise; buona fortuna! grazie, ~ good luck! thank you, the same to you

altri'menti adv otherwise

'altro a other; un ~, un'altra another; l'altr'anno last year; domani l'~ the day after tomorrow; l'ho visto l'~ giorno I saw him the other day ● pron other [one]; un ~, un'altra another [one]; ne vuoi dell'~? would you like some more?; l'un l'~ one another; nessun ~ nobody else; gli altri (la gente) other people ● nm something else; non fa ~ che lavorare he does nothing but work; desidera ~? (in negozio) anything else?; più che ~, sono stanco I'm tired more than anything; se non ~ at least; senz'~ certainly; tra l'~ what's more; ~ che! and how!

altroi'eri nm l'~ the day before yesterday

al'tronde *adv* d'~ on the other hand

al'trove *adv* elsewhere

al'trui *a* other people's ● *nm* other people's belongings *pl*

altru'is|mo *nm* altruism. ~ta *nmf* altruist

al'tura *nf* high ground; *Naut* deep sea

a'lunno, -a *nmf* pupil

alve'are *nm* hive

al'za|re *vt* lift, raise; (*costruire*) build; *Naut* hoist; ~re le spalle shrug one's shoulders; ~re i tacchi *fig* take to one's heels. ~rsi *vr* rise; (*in piedi*) stand up; (*da letto*) get up; ~rsi in piedi get to one's feet. ~ta *nf* lifting; (*aumento*) rise; (*da letto*) getting up; *Archit* elevation. ~to *a* up

a'mabile *a* lovable; (*vino*) sweet

a'maca *nf* hammock

amalga'mar|e *vt*, ~si *vr* amalgamate

a'mante *a* ~ di fond of ● *nm* lover ● *nf* mistress, lover

ama'rena *nf* sour black cherry

ama'retto *nm* macaroon

a'ma|re *vt* love; be fond of, like (*musica, sport ecc*). ~to, -a *a* loved ● *nmf* beloved

ama'rezza *nf* bitterness; (*dolore*) sorrow

a'maro *a* bitter ● *nm* bitterness; (*liquore*) bitters *pl*

ama'rognolo *a* rather bitter

ama'tore *nm* lover

ambasci'a|ta *nf* embassy; (*messaggio*) message. ~tore, ~trice *nm* ambassador ● *nf* ambassadress

ambe'due *a* & *pron* both

ambien'ta|le *a* environmental. ~'lista *a* & *nmf* environmentalist

ambien'tar|e *vt* acclimatize; set (*personaggio, film ecc*). ~si *vr* get acclimatized

ambi'ente *nm* environment; (*stanza*) room; *fig* milieu

ambiguità *nf inv* ambiguity; (*di persona*) shadiness

am'biguo *a* ambiguous; (*persona*) shady

am'bire *vi* ~ a aspire to

'ambito *nm* sphere

ambiva'len|te *a* ambivalent. ~za *nf* ambivalence

ambizi'o|ne *nf* ambition. ~so *a* ambitious

'ambra *nf* amber. am'brato *a* amber

ambu'lante *a* wandering; venditore ~ hawker

ambu'lanza *nf* ambulance

ambula'torio *nm* (*di medico*) surgery; (*di ospedale*) out-patients' [department]

a'meba *nf* amoeba

'amen *int* amen

a'meno *a* pleasant

A'merica *nf* America. ~ del Sud South America. ameri'cano, -a *a* & *nmf* American

ame'tista *nf* amethyst

ami'anto *nm* asbestos

ami'chevole *a* friendly

ami'cizia *nf* friendship; fare ~ con qcno make friends with sb; amicizie *pl* (*amici*) friends

a'mico, -a *nmf* friend; ~ del cuore bosom friend

'amido *nm* starch

ammac'ca|re *vt* dent; bruise (*frutto*). ~rsi *vr* (*metallo:*) get dented; (*frutto:*) bruise. ~to *a* dented; (*frutto*) bruised. ~'tura *nf* dent; (*livido*) bruise

ammae'stra|re *vt* (*istruire*) teach; train (*animale*). ~to *a* trained

ammai'nare *vt* lower (*bandiera*); furl (*vele*)

amma'la|rsi *vr* fall ill. ~to, -a *a* ill ● *nmf* sick person; (*paziente*) patient

ammali'are *vt* bewitch

am'manco *nm* deficit

ammanet'tare *vt* handcuff

ammani'cato *a* essere ~ have connections

amma'raggio *nm* splashdown

amma'rare *vi* put down on the sea; (*nave spaziale:*) splash down

ammas'sar|e *vt* amass. ~si *vr* crowd together. am'masso *nm* mass; (*mucchio*) pile

ammat'tire *vi* go mad

ammaz'zar|e *vt* kill. ~si *vr* (*suicidarsi*) kill oneself; (*rimanere ucciso*) be killed

am'menda *nf* amends *pl*; (*multa*) fine; fare ~ di qcsa make amends for sth

am'messo *pp di* ammettere ● *conj* ~ che supposing that

am'mettere *vt* admit; (*riconoscere*) acknowledge; (*supporre*) suppose

ammic'care *vi* wink

ammini'stra|re *vt* administer; (*gestire*) run. ~'tivo *a* administrative. ~'tore, ~'trice *nmf* administrator; (*di azienda*) manager; (*di società*) director. ~tore delegato managing director. ~zi'one *nf* administration; fatti di ordinaria ~zione *fig* routine matters

ammi'ragli|o *nm* admiral. ~'ato *nm* admiralty

ammi'ra|re *vt* admire. ~to *a* restare/

essere ~**to** be full of admiration. ~'**tore**, ~'**trice** *nmf* admirer. ~**zi'one** *nf* admiration. **ammi'revole** *a* admirable

ammis'sibile *a* admissible

ammissi'one *nf* admission; (*approvazione*) acknowledgement

ammobili'a|re *vt* furnish. ~**to** *a* furnished

am'modo *a* proper ● *adv* properly

am'mollo *nm* **in** ~ soaking

ammo'niaca *nf* ammonia

ammoni'mento *nm* warning; (*di rimprovero*) admonishment

ammo'ni|re *vt* warn; (*rimproverare*) admonish. ~'**tore** *a* admonishing. ~**zi'one** *nf Sport* warning

ammon'tare *vi* ~ **a** amount to ● *nm* amount

ammonticchi'are *vt* heap up

ammorbi'dente *nm* (*per panni*) softener

ammorbi'dir|e *vt*, ~**si** *vr* soften

ammorta'mento *nm Comm* amortization

ammor'tare *vt* pay off (*spesa*); *Comm* amortize (*debito*)

ammortiz'za|re *vt Comm* = **ammortare**; *Mech* damp. ~'**tore** *nm* shock-absorber

ammosci'ar|e *vt* make flabby. ~**si** *vi* get flabby

ammucchi'a|re *vt*, ~**rsi** *vr* pile up. ~**ta** *nf* (*sl: orgia*) orgy

ammuf'fi|re *vi* go mouldy. ~**to** *a* mouldy

ammutina'mento *nm* mutiny

ammuti'narsi *vr* mutiny

ammuto'lire *vi* be struck dumb

amne'sia *nf* amnesia

amni'stia *nf* amnesty

'**amo** *nm* hook; *fig* bait

amo'rale *a* amoral

a'more *nm* love; **fare l'**~ make love; **per l'amor di Dio/del cielo!** for heaven's sake!; **andare d'**~ **e d'accordo** get on like a house on fire; ~ **proprio** self-respect; **è un** ~ (*persona*) he/she is a darling; **per** ~ **di** for the sake of; **amori** *pl* love affairs. ~**ggi'are** *vi* flirt. **amo'revole** *a* loving

a'morfo *a* shapeless; (*persona*) colourless, grey

amo'roso *a* loving; (*sguardo ecc*) amorous; (*lettera, relazione*) love

ampi'ezza *nf* (*di esperienza*) breadth; (*di stanza*) spaciousness; (*di gonna*) fullness; (*importanza*) scale

'**ampio** *a* ample; (*esperienza*) wide; (*stanza*) spacious; (*vestito*) loose; (*gonna*) full; (*pantaloni*) baggy

am'plesso *nm* embrace

amplia'mento *nm* (*di casa, porto*) enlargement; (*di strada*) widening

ampli'are *vt* broaden (*conoscenze*)

amplifi'ca|re *vt* amplify; *fig* magnify. ~'**tore** *nm* amplifier. ~**zi'one** *nf* amplification

am'polla *nf* cruet

ampol'loso *a* pompous

ampu'ta|re *vt* amputate. ~**zi'one** *nf* amputation

amu'leto *nm* amulet

anabbagli'ante *a Auto* dipped ● *nmpl* **anabbaglianti** dipped headlights

anacro'nis|mo *nm* anachronism. ~**tico** *a* **essere** ~ be an anachronism

a'nagrafe *nf* (*ufficio*) registry office; (*registro*) register of births, marriages and deaths

ana'grafico *a* **dati** *nmpl* **anagrafici** personal data

ana'gramma *nm* anagram

anal'colico *a* non-alcoholic ● *nm* soft drink, non-alcoholic drink

a'nale *a* anal

analfa'be|ta *a* & *nmf* illiterate. ~'**tismo** *nm* illiteracy

anal'gesico *nm* painkiller

a'nalisi *nf inv* analysis; *Med* test. ~ **grammaticale/del periodo/logica** parsing. ~ **del sangue** blood test

ana'li|sta *nmf* analyst. ~**tico** *a* analytical. ~**z'zare** *vt* analyse; *Med* test

anal'lergico *a* hypoallergenic

analo'gia *nf* analogy. **a'nalogo** *a* analogous

'**ananas** *nm inv* pineapple

anar'chi|a *nf* anarchy. **a'narchico, -a** *a* anarchic ● *nmf* anarchist. ~**smo** *nm* anarchism

A.N.A.S. *nf abbr* (**Azienda Nazionale Autonoma delle Strade**) *national road maintenance authority*

anato'mia *nf* anatomy. **ana'tomico** *a* anatomical; (*sedia*) contoured, ergonomic

'**anatra** *nf* duck

ana'troccolo *nm* duckling

'**anca** *nf* hip; (*di animale*) flank

ance'strale *a* ancestral

'**anche** *conj* also, too; (*persino*) even; ~ **se** even if; ~ **domani** tomorrow also *o* too, also tomorrow

anchilo'sato *a fig* stiff

13

an'cora *adv* still, yet; (*di nuovo*) again; (*di più*) some more; **~ una volta** once more

'anco|ra *nf* anchor; **gettare l'~ra** drop anchor. **~'raggio** *nm* anchorage. **~'rare** *vt* anchor

anda'mento *nm* (*del mercato, degli affari*) trend

an'dante *a* (*corrente*) current; (*di poco valore*) cheap ● *nm Mus* andante

an'da|re *vi* go; (*funzionare*) work; **~ via** (*partire*) leave; ⟨*macchia:*⟩ come out; **~ [bene]** (*confarsi*) suit; ⟨*taglia:*⟩ fit; **ti va bene alle tre?** does three o'clock suit you?; **non mi va di mangiare** I don't feel like eating; **~ di fretta** be in a hurry; **~ fiero di** be proud of; **~ di moda** be in fashion; **va per i 20 anni** he's nearly 20; **ma va' [là]!** come on!; **come va?** how are things?; **~ a male** go off; **~ a fuoco** go up in flames; **va spedito [entro] stamattina** it must be sent this morning; **ne va del mio lavoro** my job is at stake; **come è andata a finire?** how did it turn out?; **cosa vai dicendo?** what are you talking about?. **~rsene** go away; (*morire*) pass away ● *nm* going; **a lungo ~re** eventually

'andito *nm* passage

an'drone *nm* entrance

a'neddoto *nm* anecdote

ane'lare *vt* **~ a** long for. **a'nelito** *nm* longing

a'nello *nm* ring; (*di catena*) link

ane'mia *nf* anaemia. **a'nemico** *a* anaemic

a'nemone *nm* anemone

aneste'si|a *nf* anaesthesia; (*sostanza*) anaesthetic. **~'sta** *nmf* anaesthetist. **ane'stetico** *a & nm* anaesthetic

an'fibi *nmpl* (*stivali*) army boots

an'fibio *nm* (*animale*) amphibian ● *a* amphibious

anfite'atro *nm* amphitheatre

'anfora *nf* amphora

an'fratto *nm* ravine

an'gelico *a* angelic

'angelo *nm* angel. **~ custode** guardian angel

angli'c|ano *a* Anglican. **~ismo** *nm* Anglicanism

an'glofilo, -a *a & nmf* Anglophile

an'glofono, -a *nmf* English-speaker

anglo'sassone *a & nmf* Anglo-Saxon

ango'la|re *a* angular. **~zi'one** *nf* angle shot

'angolo *nm* corner; *Math* angle. **~ [di] cottura** kitchenette

ango'loso *a* angular

an'gosci|a *nf* anguish. **~'are** *vt* torment. **~'ato** *a* agonized. **~'oso** *a* (*disperato*) anguished; (*che dà angoscia*) distressing

angu'illa *nf* eel

an'guria *nf* water-melon

an'gusti|a *nf* (*ansia*) anxiety; (*penuria*) poverty. **~'are** *vt* distress. **~'arsi** *vr* be very worried (**per** about)

an'gusto *a* narrow

'anice *nm* anise; *Culin* aniseed; (*liquore*) anisette

ani'dride *nf* **~ carbonica** carbon dioxide

'anima *nf* soul; **non c'era ~ viva** there was not a soul about; **all'~!** good grief!; **un'~ in pena** a soul in torment. **~ gemella** soul mate

ani'ma|le *a & nm* animal; **~li domestici** *pl* pets. **~'lesco** *a* animal

ani'ma|re *vt* give life to; (*ravvivare*) enliven; (*incoraggiare*) encourage. **~rsi** *vr* come to life; (*accalorarsi*) become animated. **~to** *a* animate; ⟨*discussione*⟩ animated; ⟨*strada, paese*⟩ lively. **~'tore**, **~'trice** *nmf* leading spirit; *Cinema* animator. **~zi'one** *nf* animation

'animo *nm* (*mente*) mind; (*indole*) disposition; (*cuore*) heart; **perdersi d'~** lose heart; **farsi ~** take heart. **~sità** *nf* animosity

ani'moso *a* brave; (*ostile*) hostile

'anitra *nf* = **anatra**

annac'qua|re *vt anche fig* water down. **~to** *a* watered down

annaffi'a|re *vt* water. **~'toio** *nm* watering-can

an'nali *nmpl* annals

anna'spare *vi* flounder

an'nata *nf* year; (*importo annuale*) annual amount; (*di vino*) vintage

annebbia'mento *nm* fog build-up; *fig* clouding

annebbi'ar|e *vt* cloud ⟨*vista, mente*⟩. **~si** *vr* become foggy; ⟨*vista, mente:*⟩ grow dim

annega'mento *nm* drowning

anne'ga|re *vt/i* drown

anne'rir|e *vt/i* blacken. **~si** *vr* become black

annessi'one *nf* (*di nazione*) annexation

an'nesso *pp di* **annettere** ● *a* attached; ⟨*Stato*⟩ annexed

an'nettere *vt* add; (*accludere*) enclose; annex ⟨*Stato*⟩

annichi'lire *vt* annihilate

anni'darsi *vr* nest

annienta'mento *nm* annihilation

annien'tar|e *vt* annihilate. **~si** *vr* abase oneself

anniver'sario *a & nm* anniversary. **~ di matrimonio** wedding anniversary

'anno *nm* year; **Buon A~!** Happy New Year!; **quanti anni ha?** how old are you?; **Tommaso ha dieci anni** Thomas is ten [years old]. **~ bisestile** leap year

anno'dar|e *vt* knot; do up ⟨*cintura*⟩; *fig* form. **~si** *vr* become knotted

annoi'a|re *vt* bore; (*recare fastidio*) annoy. **~rsi** *vr* get bored; (*condizione*) be bored. **~to** *a* bored

anno'ta|re *vt* note down; annotate ⟨*testo*⟩. **~zi'one** *nf* note

annove'rare *vt* number

annu'a|le *a* annual, yearly. **~rio** *nm* year-book

annu'ire *vi* nod; (*acconsentire*) agree

annulla'mento *nm* annulment; (*di appuntamento*) cancellation

annul'lar|e *vt* annul; cancel ⟨*appuntamento*⟩; (*togliere efficacia a*) undo; disallow ⟨*gol*⟩; (*distruggere*) destroy. **~si** *vr* cancel each other out

annunci'a|re *vt* announce; (*preannunciare*) foretell. **~'tore**, **~'trice** *nmf* announcer. **~zi'one** *nf* Annunciation

an'nuncio *nm* announcement; (*pubblicitario*) advertisement; (*notizia*) news. **annunci** *pl* **economici** classified advertisements

'annuo *a* annual, yearly

annu'sare *vt* sniff

annuvo'lar|e *vt* cloud. **~si** *vr* cloud over

'ano *nm* anus

anoma'lia *nf* anomaly

a'nomalo *a* anomalous

anoni'mato *nm* **mantenere l'~** remain anonymous

a'nonimo, -a *a* anonymous ● *nmf* (*pittore, scrittore*) anonymous painter/writer

anores'sia *nf Med* anorexia

ano'ressico, -a *nmf* anorexic

anor'mal|e *a* abnormal ● *nmf* deviant, abnormal person. **~ità** *nf inv* abnormality

'ansa *nf* handle; (*di fiume*) bend

an'sare *vi* pant

'ansia, ansietà *nf* anxiety; **stare/ essere in ~ per** be anxious about

ansi'oso *a* anxious

antago'nis|mo *nm* antagonism. **~ta** *nmf* antagonist

an'tartico *a & nm* Antarctic

antece'dente *a* preceding ● *nm* precedent

ante'fatto *nm* prior event

ante'guerra *a* pre-war ● *nm* pre-war period

ante'nato, -a *nmf* ancestor

an'tenna *nf Radio, TV* aerial; (*di animale*) antenna; *Naut* yard. **~ parabolica** satellite dish

ante'porre *vt* put before

ante'prima *nf* preview; **vedere qcsa in ~** have a sneak preview of sth

anteri'ore *a* front *attrib*; (*nel tempo*) previous

antiade'rente *a* ⟨*padella*⟩ nonstick

antia'ereo *a* anti-aircraft *attrib*

antial'lergico *a* hypoallergenic

antia'tomico *a* **rifugio ~** fallout shelter

antibi'otico *a & nm* antibiotic

anti'caglia *nf* (*oggetto*) piece of old junk

antica'mente *adv* in ancient times, long ago

anti'camera *nf* ante-room; **far ~** be kept waiting

antichità *nf inv* antiquity; (*oggetto*) antique

antici'clone *nm* anticyclone

antici'pa|re *vt* advance; *Comm* pay in advance; (*prevedere*) anticipate; (*prevenire*) forestall ● *vi* be early. **~ta'mente** *adv* in advance. **~zi'one** *nf* anticipation; (*notizia*) advance news

an'ticipo *nm* advance; (*caparra*) deposit; **in ~** early; (*nel lavoro*) ahead of schedule

an'tico *a* ancient; ⟨*mobile ecc*⟩ antique; (*vecchio*) old; **all'antica** old-fashioned ● *nmpl* **gli antichi** the ancients

anticoncezio'nale *a & nm* contraceptive

anticonfor'mis|mo *nm* unconventionality. **~ta** *nmf* nonconformist. **~tico** *a* unconventional, nonconformist

anticonge'lante *a & nm* anti-freeze

anti'corpo *nm* antibody

anticostituzio'nale *a* unconstitutional

anti'crimine *a inv* ⟨*squadra*⟩ crime *attrib*

antidemo'cratico *a* undemocratic

antidolo'rifico *nm* painkiller

an'tidoto *nm* antidote

anti'droga *a inv* ⟨*campagna*⟩ anti-drugs; ⟨*squadra*⟩ drug *attrib*

antie'stetico *a* ugly

antifa'scismo *nm* anti-fascism

antifa'scista *a & nmf* anti-fascist

anti'forfora *a inv* dandruff *attrib*

anti'furto *nm* anti-theft device; (*allarme*) alarm ● *a inv* ⟨*sistema*⟩ anti-theft

anti'gelo *nm* antifreeze; (*parabrezza*) defroster

antigi'enico *a* unhygienic

An'tille *nfpl* **le ~** the West Indies

an'tilope *nf* antelope

antin'cendio *a inv* **allarme ~** fire alarm; **porta ~** fire door

anti'nebbia *nm inv Auto* [**faro**] **~** foglamp, foglight

antinfiamma'torio *a & nm* anti-inflammatory

antinucle'are *a* anti-nuclear

antio'rario *a* anti-clockwise

anti'pasto *nm* hors d'oeuvre, starter

antipa'tia *nf* antipathy. **anti'patico** *a* unpleasant

an'tipodi *nmpl* antipodes; **essere agli ~** *fig* be poles apart

antiquari'ato *nm* antique trade

anti'quario, -a *nmf* antique dealer

anti'quato *a* antiquated

anti'ruggine *nm inv* rust-inhibitor

anti'rughe *a inv* anti-wrinkle *attrib*

anti'scippo *a inv* theft-proof

antise'mita *a* anti-Semitic

anti'settico *a & nm* antiseptic

antisoci'ale *a* anti-social

antista'minico *nm* antihistamine

anti'stante a *prep* in front of

anti'tarlo *nm inv* woodworm treatment

antiterro'ristico *a* antiterrorist *attrib*

an'titesi *nf inv* antithesis

antolo'gia *nf* anthology

'antro *nm* cavern

antropolo'gia *nf* anthropology. **antro'pologo, -a** *nmf* anthropologist

anu'lare *nm* ring-finger

'anzi *conj* in fact; (*o meglio*) or better still; (*al contrario*) on the contrary

anzianità *nf* old age; (*di servizio*) seniority

anzi'ano, -a *a* old, elderly; (*di grado ecc*) senior ● *nmf* elderly person

anziché *conj* rather than

anzi'tempo *adv* prematurely

anzi'tutto *adv* first of all

a'orta *nf* aorta

apar'titico *a* unaligned

apa'tia *nf* apathy. **a'patico** *a* apathetic

'ape *nf* bee; **nido** *nm* **di api** honeycomb

aperi'tivo *nm* aperitif

aperta'mente *adv* openly

a'perto *a* open; **all'aria aperta** in the open air; **all'~** open-air

aper'tura *nf* opening; (*inizio*) beginning; (*ampiezza*) spread; (*di arco*) span; *Pol* overtures *pl*; *Phot* aperture; **~ mentale** openness

'apice *nm* apex

apicol'tura *nf* beekeeping

ap'nea *nf* **immersione in ~** free diving

a'polide *a* stateless ● *nmf* stateless person

a'postolo *nm* apostle

apostro'fare *vt* (*mettere un apostrofo a*) write with an apostrophe; reprimand ⟨*persona*⟩

a'postrofo *nm* apostrophe

appaga'mento *nm* fulfilment

appa'ga|re *vt* satisfy. **~rsi** *vr* **~rsi di** be satisfied with

appai'are *vt* pair; mate ⟨*animali*⟩

appallotto'lare *vt* roll into a ball

appalta'tore *nm* contractor

ap'palto *nm* contract; **dare in ~** contract out

appan'naggio *nm* (*in denaro*) annuity; *fig* prerogative

appan'nar|e *vt* mist ⟨*vetro*⟩; dim ⟨*vista*⟩. **~si** *vr* mist over; ⟨*vista:*⟩ grow dim

appa'rato *nm* apparatus; (*pompa*) display

apparecchi'a|re *vt* prepare ● *vi* lay the table. **~'tura** *nf* (*impianti*) equipment

appa'recchio *nm* apparatus; (*congegno*) device; (*radio, TV ecc*) set; (*aeroplano*) aircraft. **~ acustico** hearing aid

appa'ren|te *a* apparent. **~te'mente** *adv* apparently. **~za** *nf* appearance; **in ~za** apparently.

appa'ri|re *vi* appear; (*sembrare*) look. **~'scente** *a* striking; *pej* gaudy. **~zi'one** *nf* apparition

apparta'mento *nm* flat, apartment *Am*

appar'ta|rsi *vr* withdraw. **~to** *a* secluded

apparte'nenza *nf* membership

apparte'nere *vi* belong

appassio'nante *a* ⟨*storia, argomento*⟩ exciting

appassio'na|re *vt* excite; (*commuovere*) move. **~rsi** *vr* **~rsi a** become excited by. ~**to** a passionate; ~**to di** (entusiastico) fond of

appas'sir|e vi wither. ~**si** vr fade

appel'larsi vr ~ **a** appeal to

ap'pello nm appeal; (chiamata per nome) rollcall; (esami) exam session; **fare l'**~ call the roll

ap'pena adv just; (a fatica) hardly ● conj [**non**] ~ as soon as, no sooner... than

ap'pendere vt hang [up]

appendi'abiti nm inv hat-stand

appen'dice nf appendix. **appendi- 'cite** nf appendicitis

Appen'nini nmpl **gli** ~ the Apennines

appesan'tir|e vt weigh down. ~**si** vr become heavy

ap'peso pp di **appendere** ● a hanging; (impiccato) hanged

appe'ti|to nm appetite; **aver** ~**to** be hungry; **buon** ~**to!** enjoy your meal!. ~**'toso** a appetizing; fig tempting

appezza'mento nm plot of land

appia'nar|e vt level; (fig) smooth over. ~**si** vr improve

appiat'tir|e vt flatten. ~**si** vr flatten oneself

appic'care vt ~ **il fuoco a** set fire to

appicci'car|e vt stick; ~**e a** (fig: appioppare) palm off on ● vi be sticky. ~**si** vr stick; (cose:) stick together; ~**si a qcno** fig stick to sb like glue

appiccica'ticcio a sticky; fig clingy

appicci'coso a sticky; fig clingy

appie'dato a **sono** ~ I don't have the car; **sono rimasto** ~ I was stranded

appi'eno adv fully

appigli'arsi vr ~ **a** get hold of; fig stick to. ~**'piglio** nm fingerhold; (per piedi) foothold; fig pretext

appiop'pare vt ~ **a** palm off on; (fam: dare) give

appiso'larsi vr doze off

applau'dire vt/i applaud. **ap'plauso** nm applause

appli'cabile a applicable

appli'ca|re vt apply; enforce ⟨legge ecc⟩. ~**rsi** vr apply oneself. ~**'tore** nm applicator. ~**zi'one** nf application; (di legge) enforcement

appoggi'ar|e vt lean (**a** against); (mettere) put; (sostenere) back. ~**si** vr ~**si a** lean against; fig rely on. **ap'poggio** nm support

appollai'arsi vr fig perch

ap'porre vt affix

appor'tare vt bring; (causare) cause. **ap'porto** nm contribution

apposita'mente adv (specialmente) especially

ap'posito a proper

ap'posta adv on purpose; (espressamente) specially

apposta'mento nm ambush; (caccia) lying in wait

appo'star|e vt post ⟨soldati⟩. ~**si** vr lie in wait

ap'prend|ere vt understand; (imparare) learn. ~**i'mento** nm learning

appren'di|sta nmf apprentice. ~**'sta- to** nm apprenticeship

apprensi'one nf apprehension; **essere in** ~ **per** be anxious about. **appren'sivo** a apprehensive

ap'presso adv & prep (vicino) near; (dietro) behind; **come** ~ as follows

appre'star|e vt prepare. ~**si** vr get ready

apprez'za|bile a appreciable. ~**'men- to** nm appreciation; (giudizio) opinion

apprez'za|re vt appreciate. ~**to** a appreciated

ap'proccio nm approach

appro'dare vi land; ~ **a** fig come to; **non** ~ **a nulla** come to nothing. **ap'pro- do** nm landing; (luogo) landing-stage

approfit'ta|re vi take advantage (**di** of), profit (**di** by). ~**'tore,** ~**'trice** nmf chancer

approfondi'mento nm deepening; **di** ~ ⟨fig: corso⟩ advanced

approfon'di|re vt deepen. ~**rsi** vr ⟨divario:⟩ widen. ~**to** a ⟨studio, ricerca⟩ in-depth

appropri'a|rsi vr take possession (**di** of); (essere adatto a) suit. ~**to** a appropriate. ~**zi'one** nf Jur appropriation. ~**zione indebita** Jur embezzlement

approssi'ma|re vt ~**re per eccesso/difetto** round up/down. ~**rsi** vr draw near. ~**tiva'mente** adv approximately. ~**'tivo** a approximate. ~**zi'one** nf approximation

appro'va|re vt approve of; approve ⟨legge⟩. ~**zi'one** nf approval

approvvigiona'mento nm supplying; **approvvigionamenti** pl provisions

approvvigio'nar|e vt supply. ~**si** vr stock up

appunta'mento nm appointment, date fam; **fissare un** ~ make an appointment; **darsi** ~ decide to meet

appun'tar|e vt (annotare) take notes; (fissare) fix; (con spillo) pin; (appuntire) sharpen. **~si** *vr* **~si su** ⟨*teoria:*⟩ be based on

appun'ti|re *vt* sharpen. **~to** *a* ⟨*mento*⟩ pointed

ap'punto¹ *nm* note; (*piccola critica*) niggle

ap'punto² *adv* exactly; **per l'~!** exactly!; **stavo ~ dicendo...** I was just saying...

appu'rare *vt* verify

a'pribile *a* that can be opened

apribot'tiglie *nm inv* bottle-opener

a'prile *nm* April; **il primo d'~** April Fools' Day

a'prir|e *vt* open; turn on ⟨*luce, acqua ecc*⟩; (*con chiave*) unlock; open up ⟨*ferita ecc*⟩. **~si** *vr* open; (*spaccarsi*) split; (*confidarsi*) confide (**con** in)

apri'scatole *nf inv* tin-opener

aqua'planing *nm* **andare in ~** aquaplane

'aquil|a *nf* eagle; **non è un'~a!** he is no genius!. **~'lino** *a* aquiline

aqui'lone *nm* (*giocattolo*) kite

ara'besco *nm* arabesque; *hum* scribble

A'rabia Sau'dita *nf* **l'~** Saudi Arabia

'arabo, -a *a* Arab; ⟨*lingua*⟩ Arabic ● *nmf* Arab ● *nm* (*lingua*) Arabic

a'rachide *nf* peanut

ara'gosta *nf* lobster

a'ranci|a *nf* orange. **~'ata** *nf* orangeade. **~o** *nm* orange-tree; (*colore*) orange. **~'one** *a* & *nm* orange

a'ra|re *vt* plough. **~tro** *nm* plough

ara'tura *nf* ploughing

a'razzo *nm* tapestry

arbi'trar|e *vt* arbitrate in; *Sport* referee. **~ietà** *nf* arbitrariness. **~io** *a* arbitrary

ar'bitrio *nm* will; **è un ~** it's very high-handed

'arbitro *nm* arbiter; *Sport* referee; (*nel baseball*) umpire

ar'busto *nm* shrub

'arca *nf* ark; (*cassa*) chest

ar'ca|ico *a* archaic. **~'ismo** *nm* archaism

ar'cangelo *nm* archangel

ar'cata *nf* arch; (*serie di archi*) arcade

arche|olo'gia *nf* archaeology. **~o'logico** *a* archaeological. **~'ologo, -a** *nmf* archaeologist

ar'chetto *nm* *Mus* bow

architet'tare *vt* *fig* devise; **cosa state architettando?** *fig* what are you plotting?

archi'tet|to *nm* architect. **~'tonico** *a* architectural. **~'tura** *nf* architecture

archivi'are *vt* file; *Jur* close

ar'chivio *nm* archives *pl*; *Comput* file

archi'vista *nmf* filing clerk

ar'cigno *a* grim

arci'pelago *nm* archipelago

arci'vescovo *nm* archbishop

'arco *nm* arch; *Math* arc; (*arma, Mus*) bow; **nell'~ di una giornata/due mesi** in the space of a day/two months

arcoba'leno *nm* rainbow

arcu'a|re *vt* bend. **~rsi** *vr* bend. **~to** *a* bent, curved; ⟨*schiena di gatto*⟩ arched

ar'dente *a* burning; *fig* ardent. **~'mente** *adv* ardently

'ardere *vt/i* burn

ar'desia *nf* slate

ar'di|re *vi* dare. **~to** *a* daring; (*coraggioso*) bold; (*sfacciato*) impudent

ar'dore *nm* (*calore*) heat; *fig* ardour

'arduo *a* arduous; (*ripido*) steep

'area *nf* area. **~ di rigore** (*in calcio*) penalty area. **~ di servizio** service area

a'rena *nf* arena

are'narsi *vr* run aground; ⟨*fig: trattative*⟩ reach deadlock; **mi sono arenato** I'm stuck

'argano *nm* winch

argen'tato *a* silver-plated

argente'ria *nf* silver[ware]

ar'gento *nm* silver

ar'gil|la *nf* clay. **~'loso** *a* ⟨*terreno*⟩ clayey

argi'nare *vt* embank; *fig* hold in check, contain

'argine *nm* embankment; (*diga*) dike

argomen'tare *vi* argue

argo'mento *nm* argument; (*motivo*) reason; (*soggetto*) subject

argu'ire *vt* deduce

ar'gu|to *a* witty. **~'zia** *nf* wit; (*battuta*) witticism

'aria *nf* air; (*aspetto*) appearance; *Mus* tune; **andare all'~** *fig* come to nothing; **avere l'~...** look...; **corrente** *nf* **d'~** draught; **mandare all'~ qcsa** *fig* ruin sth

aridità *nf* dryness

'arido *a* arid

arieggi'a|re *vt* air. **~to** *a* airy

ari'ete *nm* ram. **A~** *Astr* Aries

ari'etta *nf* (*brezza*) breeze

a'ringa *nf* herring

ari'oso *a* ⟨*locale*⟩ light and airy

aristo'cra|tico, -a *a* aristocratic ● *nmf* aristocrat. **~'zia** *nf* aristocracy

arit'metica *nf* arithmetic

arlec'chino *nm* Harlequin; *fig* buffoon

'arma *nf* weapon; **armi** *pl* arms; (*forze armate*) [armed] forces; **chiamare alle armi** call up; **sotto le armi** in the army; **alle prime armi** *fig* inexperienced, fledg[e]ling. **~ da fuoco** firearm. **~ impropria** makeshift weapon. **~ a doppio taglio** *fig* double-edged sword

armadi'etto *nm* locker, cupboard

ar'madio *nm* cupboard; (*guardaroba*) wardrobe

armamen'tario *nm* tools *pl*; *fig* paraphernalia

arma'mento *nm* armament; *Naut* fitting out

ar'ma|re *vt* arm; (*equipaggiare*) fit out; *Archit* reinforce. **~rsi** *vr* arm oneself (**di** with). **~ta** *nf* army; (*flotta*) fleet. **~'tore** *nm* shipowner. **~'tura** *nf* framework; (*impalcatura*) scaffolding; (*di guerriero*) armour

armeggi'are *vi fig* manoeuvre

armi'stizio *nm* armistice

armo'ni|a *nf* harmony. **ar'monica** *nf* **~ [a bocca]** mouth organ. **ar'monico** *a* harmonic. **~'oso** *a* harmonious

armoniz'zar|e *vt* harmonize ● *vi* match. **~si** *vr* (*colori:*) go together, match

ar'nese *nm* tool; (*oggetto*) thing; (*congegno*) gadget; **male in ~** in bad condition

'arnia *nf* beehive

a'roma *nm* aroma; **aromi** *pl* herbs. **~tera'pia** *nf* aromatherapy

aro'matico *a* aromatic

aromatiz'zare *vt* flavour

'arpa *nf* harp

ar'peggio *nm* arpeggio

ar'pia *nf* harpy

arpi'one *nm* hook; (*pesca*) harpoon

arrabat'tarsi *vr* do all one can

arrabbi'a|rsi *vr* get angry. **~to** *a* angry. **~'tura** *nf* rage; **prendersi un'~tura** fly into a rage

arraf'fare *vt* grab

arrampi'ca|rsi *vr* climb [up]. **~ta** *nf* climb. **~'tore**, **~'trice** *nmf* climber. **~'tore sociale** social climber

arran'care *vi* limp, hobble; *fig* struggle, limp along

arrangia'mento *nm* arrangement

arrangi'ar|e *vt* arrange. **~si** *vr* manage; **~si alla meglio** get by; **ar'rangiati!** get on with it!

arra'parsi *vr fam* get randy

arre'care *vt* bring; (*causare*) cause

arreda'mento *nm* interior decoration; (*l'arredare*) furnishing; (*mobili ecc*) furnishings *pl*

arre'da|re *vt* furnish. **~'tore**, **~'trice** *nmf* interior designer. **ar'redo** *nm* furnishings *pl*

ar'rendersi *vr* surrender

arren'devo|le *a* (*persona*) yielding. **~'lezza** *nf* softness

arre'star|e *vt* arrest; (*fermare*) stop. **~si** *vr* halt. **ar'resto** *nm* stop; *Med, Jur* arrest; **la dichiaro in [stato d']arresto** you are under arrest; **mandato di arresto** warrant. **arresti** *pl* **domiciliari** *Jur* house arrest

arre'tra|re *vt/i* withdraw; pull back (*giocatore*). **~to** *a* (*paese ecc*) backward; (*Mil: posizione*) rear; **numero** *nm* **~to** (*di rivista*) back number; **del lavoro ~to** a backlog of work ● *nm* (*di stipendio*) back pay

arre'trati *nmpl* arrears

arricchi'mento *nm* enrichment

arric'chi|re *vt* enrich. **~rsi** *vr* get rich. **~to**, **-a** *nmf* nouveau riche

arricci'are *vt* curl; **~ il naso** turn up one's nose

ar'ringa *nf* harangue; *Jur* closing address

arrischi'a|rsi *vr* dare. **~to** *a* risky; (*imprudente*) rash

arri'va|re *vi* arrive; **~re a** (*raggiungere*) reach; (*ridursi*) be reduced to. **~to**, **-a** *a* successful; **ben ~to!** welcome! ● *nmf* successful person

arrive'derci *int* goodbye; **~ a domani** see you tomorrow

arri'vis|mo *nm* social climbing; (*nel lavoro*) careerism. **~ta** *nmf* social climber; (*nel lavoro*) careerist

ar'rivo *nm* arrival; *Sport* finish

arro'gan|te *a* arrogant. **~za** *nf* arrogance

arro'garsi *vr* **~ il diritto di fare qcsa** take it upon oneself to do sth

arrossa'mento *nm* reddening

arros'sar|e *vt* make red, redden (*occhi*). **~si** *vr* go red

arros'sire *vi* blush, go red

arro'stire *vt* roast; toast (*pane*); (*ai ferri*) grill. **ar'rosto** *a & nm* roast

aroto'lare *vt* roll up

arroton'dar|e *vt* round; *Math ecc* round off. **~si** *vr* become round; (*persona:*) get plump

arrovel'larsi *vr* ~ **il cervello** rack one's brains

arroven'ta|re *vt* make red-hot. ~**rsi** *vr* become red-hot. ~**to** *a* red-hot

arruf'fa|re *vt* ruffle; *fig* confuse. ~**to** *a* ⟨*capelli*⟩ ruffled

arruffianarsi *vr* ~ **qcno** *fig* butter sb up

arruggi'ni|re *vt* rust. ~**rsi** *vr* go rusty; *fig* (*fisicamente*) stiffen up; ⟨*conoscenze:*⟩ go rusty. ~**to** *a* rusty

arruola'mento *nm* enlistment

arruo'lar|e *vt/i*, ~**si** *vr* enlist

arse'nale *nm* arsenal; (*cantiere*) [naval] dockyard

ar'senico *nm* arsenic

'arso *pp di* **ardere** ● *a* burnt; (*arido*) dry. **ar'sura** *nf* burning heat; (*sete*) parching thirst

'arte *nf* art; (*abilità*) craftsmanship; **le belle arti** the fine arts. **arti figurative** figurative arts

arte'fa|re *vt* adulterate ⟨*vino*⟩; disguise ⟨*voce*⟩. ~**tto** *a* fake; ⟨*vino*⟩ adulterated

ar'tefice *nmf* craftsman; craftswoman; *fig* author

ar'teria *nf* artery. ~ **[stradale]** arterial road

arterioscle'rosi *nf* arteriosclerosis, hardening of the arteries

'artico *a & nm* Arctic

artico'la|re *a* articular ● *vt* articulate; (*suddividere*) divide. ~**rsi** *vr fig* ~**rsi in** consist of. ~**to** *a* **Auto** articulated; *fig* well-constructed. ~**zi'one** *nf* **Anat** articulation

ar'ticolo *nm* article. ~ **di fondo** leader

artifici'ale *a* artificial

arti'fici|o *nm* artifice; (*affettazione*) affectation. ~**'oso** *a* artful; (*affettato*) affected

artigia'nal|e *a* made by hand; *hum* amateurish. ~**'mente** *adv* with craftsmanship; *hum* amateurishly

artigi|a'nato *nm* craftsmanship; (*ceto*) craftsmen *pl*. ~**'ano, -a** *nm* craftsman ● *nf* craftswoman

artigli|'ere *nm* artilleryman. ~**e'ria** *nf* artillery

ar'tiglio *nm* claw; *fig* clutch

ar'tist|a *nmf* artist. ~**ica'mente** *adv* artistically. ~**ico** *a* artistic

'arto *nm* limb

ar'trite *nf* arthritis

ar'trosi *nf* rheumatism

arzigogo'lato *a* fantastic, bizarre

ar'zillo *a* sprightly

a'scella *nf* armpit

ascen'den|te *a* ascending ● *nm* (*antenato*) ancestor; (*influenza*) ascendancy; *Astr* ascendant

ascensi'one *nf* ascent; **l'A~** the Ascension

ascen'sore *nm* lift, elevator *Am*

a'scesa *nf* ascent; (*al trono*) accession; (*al potere*) rise

a'scesso *nm* abscess

a'sceta *nmf* ascetic

'ascia *nf* axe

asciugabianche'ria *nm inv* (*stenditoio*) clothes horse

asciuga'ca'pelli *nm inv* hair dryer, hairdrier

asciuga'mano *nm* towel

asciu'gar|e *vt* dry. ~**si** *vr* dry oneself; (*diventare asciutto*) dry up

asci'utto *a* dry; (*magro*) wiry; ⟨*risposta*⟩ curt; **essere all'~** *fig* be hard up

ascol'ta|re *vt* listen to ● *vi* listen. ~**'tore**, ~**'trice** *nmf* listener

a'scolto *nm* listening; **dare ~ a** pay attention to; **mettersi in ~** *Radio* tune in

asfal'tare *vt* asphalt

a'sfalto *nm* asphalt

asfis'si|a *nf* asphyxia. ~**'ante** *a* ⟨*caldo*⟩ oppressive; ⟨*fig: persona*⟩ annoying. ~**'are** *vt* asphyxiate; *fig* annoy

'Asia *nf* Asia. **asi'atico, -a** *a & nmf* Asian

a'silo *nm* shelter; (*d'infanzia*) nursery school. ~ **nido** day nursery. ~ **politico** political asylum

asim'metrico *a* asymmetrical

'asino *nm* donkey; (*fig: persona stupida*) ass

'asma *nf* asthma. **a'smatico** *a* asthmatic

asoci'ale *a* asocial

'asola *nf* buttonhole

a'sparagi *nmpl* asparagus *sg*

a'sparago *nm* asparagus spear

asperità *nf inv* harshness; (*di terreno*) roughness

aspet'ta|re *vt* wait for; (*prevedere*) expect; ~**re un bambino** be expecting [a baby]; **fare ~ qcno** keep sb waiting ● *vi* wait. ~**rsi** *vr* expect. ~**'tiva** *nf* expectation

a'spetto¹ *nm* appearance; (*di problema*) aspect; **di bell'~** good-looking

a'spetto² *nm* **sala** *nf* **d'~** waiting room

aspi'rante *a* aspiring; ⟨*pompa*⟩ suction *attrib* ● *nmf* (*a un posto*) applicant;

(*al trono*) aspirant; **gli aspiranti al titolo** the contenders for the title

aspira'polvere *nm inv* vacuum cleaner

aspi'ra|re *vt* inhale; *Mech* suck in ● *vi* ~**re a** aspire to. ~'**tore** *nm* extractor fan. ~**zi'one** *nf* inhalation; *Mech* suction; (*ambizione*) ambition

aspi'rina *nf* aspirin

aspor'tare *vt* take away

aspra'mente *adv* (*duramente*) severely

a'sprezza *nf* (*al gusto*) sourness; (*di clima*) severity; (*di suono*) harshness; (*di odore*) pungency

'**aspro** *a* (*al gusto*) sour; (*clima*) severe; (*suono, parole*) harsh; (*odore*) pungent; (*litigio*) bitter

assag|gi'are *vt* taste. ~'**gini** *nmpl Culin* samples. **as'saggio** *nm* tasting; (*piccola quantità*) taste

as'sai *adv* very; (*moltissimo*) very much; (*abbastanza*) enough

assa'li|re *vt* attack. ~'**tore,** ~'**trice** *nmf* assailant

as'salto *nm* attack; **prendere d'**~ storm (*città*); *fig* mob (*persona*); hold up (*banca*)

assapo'rare *vt* savour

assassi'nare *vt* murder, assassinate; *fig* murder

assas'sin|io *nm* murder, assassination. ~**o, -a** *a* murderous ● *nm* murderer ● *nf* murderess

'**asse** *nf* board ● *nm Techn* axle; *Math* axis. ~ **da stiro** ironing board

assecon'dare *vt* satisfy; (*favorire*) support

assedi'are *vt* besiege. **as'sedio** *nm* siege

assegna'mento *nm* allotment; **fare** ~ **su** rely on

asse'gna|re *vt* allot; award (*premio*). ~'**tario** *nmf* recipient. ~**zi'one** *nf* (*di alloggio, denaro, borsa di studio*) allocation

as'segno *nm* allowance; (*bancario*) cheque; **contro** ~ cash on delivery. ~ **circolare** bank draft. **assegni** *pl* **familiari** family allowance. ~ **non trasferibile** cheque made out to 'account payee only'

assem'blea *nf* assembly; (*adunanza*) gathering

assembra'mento *nm* gathering

assen'nato *a* sensible

as'senso *nm* assent

assen'tarsi *vr* go away; (*da stanza*) leave the room

as'sen|te *a* absent; (*distratto*) absent-minded ● *nmf* absentee. ~**te'ismo** *nm* absenteeism. ~**te'ista** *nmf* frequent absentee. ~**za** *nf* absence; (*mancanza*) lack

asse'r|ire *vt* assert. ~'**tivo** *a* assertive. ~**zi'one** *nf* assertion

assesso'rato *nm* department

asses'sore *nm* councillor

assesta'mento *nm* settlement

asse'star|e *vt* arrange; ~**e un colpo** deal a blow. ~**si** *vr* settle oneself

asse'tato *a* parched

as'setto *nm* order; *Naut, Aeron* trim

assicu'ra|re *vt* assure; *Comm* insure; register (*posta*); (*fissare*) secure; (*accertare*) ensure. ~**rsi** *vr* (*con contratto*) insure oneself; (*legarsi*) fasten oneself; ~**rsi che** make sure that. ~'**tivo** *a* insurance *attrib*. ~'**tore,** ~'**trice** *nmf* insurance agent ● *a* insurance *attrib*. ~**zi'one** *nf* assurance; (*contratto*) insurance

assidera'mento *nm* exposure. **asside'rato** *a Med* suffering from exposure; *fam* frozen

assidu|a'mente *adv* assiduously. ~**ità** *nf* assiduity

as'siduo *a* assiduous; (*cliente*) regular

assil'lante *a* (*persona, pensiero*) nagging

assil'lare *vt* pester

as'sillo *nm* worry

assimi'la|re *vt* assimilate. ~**zi'one** *nf* assimilation

as'sise *nfpl* assizes; **Corte d'A~** Court of Assize[s]

assi'sten|te *nmf* assistant. ~**te sociale** social worker. ~**te di volo** flight attendant. ~**za** *nf* assistance; (*presenza*) presence. ~**za sociale** social work

assistenzi'a|le *a* welfare *attrib*. ~'**lismo** *nm* welfare

as'sistere *vt* assist; (*curare*) nurse ● *vi* ~ **a** (*essere presente*) be present at; watch (*spettacolo ecc*)

'**asso** *nm* ace; **piantare in** ~ leave in the lurch

associ'a|re *vt* join; (*collegare*) associate. ~**rsi** *vr* join forces; *Comm* enter into partnership. ~**rsi a** join; subscribe to (*giornale ecc*). ~**zi'one** *nf* association

assogget'tar|e *vt* subject. ~**si** *vr* submit

asso'lato *a* sunny

assol'dare *vt* recruit

as'solo *nm Mus* solo

as'solto *pp di* **assolvere**

assoluta'mente *adv* absolutely

assolu'tismo *nm* absolutism

asso'lu|to *a* absolute. **~zi'one** *nf* acquittal; *Relig* absolution

as'solvere *vt* perform ⟨*compito*⟩; *Jur* acquit; *Relig* absolve

assomigli'ar|e *vi* **~e a** be like, resemble. **~si** *vr* resemble each other

assom'marsi *vr* combine; **~ a qcsa** add to sth

asso'nanza *nf* assonance

asson'nato *a* drowsy

asso'pirsi *vr* doze off

assor'bente *a* & *nm* absorbent. **~ igienico** sanitary towel

assor'bire *vt* absorb

assor'da|re *vt* deafen. **~nte** *a* deafening

assorti'mento *nm* assortment

assor'ti|re *vt* match ⟨*colori*⟩. **~to a** assorted; ⟨*colori, persone*⟩ matched

as'sorto *a* engrossed

assottigli'ar|e *vt* make thin; (*aguzzare*) sharpen; (*ridurre*) reduce. **~si** *vr* grow thin; ⟨*finanze:*⟩ be whittled away

assue'fa|re *vt* accustom. **~rsi** *vr* **~rsi a** get used to. **~tto** *a* (*a caffè, aspirina*) immune to the effects; (*a droga*) addicted. **~zi'one** *nf* (*a caffè, aspirina*) immunity to the effects; (*a droga*) addiction

as'sumere *vt* assume; take on ⟨*impiegato*⟩; **~ informazioni** make inquiries

as'sunto *pp di* **assumere** ● *nm* task. **assunzi'one** *nf* (*di impiegato*) employment

assurdità *nf inv* absurdity; **~ pl** nonsense

as'surdo *a* absurd

'asta *nf* pole; *Mech* bar; *Comm* auction; **a mezz'~** at half-mast

a'stemio *a* abstemious

aste'n|ersi *vr* abstain (**da** from). **~si'one** *nf* abstention

aste'nuto, -a *nmf* abstainer

aste'risco *nm* asterisk

astig'ma|tico *a* astigmatic. **~'tismo** *nm* astigmatism

asti'nenza *nf* abstinence; **crisi di ~** cold turkey

'asti|o *nm* rancour; **avere ~o contro qcno** bear sb a grudge. **~'oso** *a* resentful

a'stratto *a* abstract

astrin'gente *a* & *nm* astringent

'astro *nm* star

astrolo'gia *nf* astrology. **a'strologo, -a** *nmf* astrologer

astro'nauta *nmf* astronaut

astro'nave *nf* spaceship

astr|ono'mia *nf* astronomy. **~o'nomico** *a* astronomical. **a'stronomo** *nm* astronomer

astrusità *nf* abstruseness

a'stuccio *nm* case

a'stu|to *a* shrewd; (*furbo*) cunning. **~zia** *nf* shrewdness; (*azione*) trick

ate'ismo *nm* atheism

A'tene *nf* Athens

'ateo, -a *a* & *nmf* atheist

a'tipico *a* atypical

at'lant|e *nm* atlas. **~ico** *a* Atlantic; **l'[Oceano] A~ico** the Atlantic [Ocean]

at'let|a *nmf* athlete. **~ica** *nf* athletics *sg*. **~ica leggera** track and field events. **~ica pesante** *weight-lifting, boxing, wrestling, etc.* **~ico** *a* athletic

atmo'sfer|a *nf* atmosphere. **~ico** *a* atmospheric

a'tomic|a *nf* atom bomb. **~o** *a* atomic

'atomo *nm* atom

'atrio *nm* entrance hall

a'troc|e *a* atrocious; (*terrible*) dreadful. **~ità** *nf inv* atrocity

atrofiz'zarsi *vr Med, fig* atrophy

attaccabot'toni *nmf inv* [crashing] bore

attacca'brighe *nmf inv* troublemaker

attacca'mento *nm* attachment

attacca'panni *nm inv* [coat-]hanger; (*a muro*) clothes hook

attac'car|e *vt* attach; (*legare*) tie; (*appendere*) hang; (*cucire*) sew on; (*contagiare*) pass on; (*assalire*) attack; (*iniziare*) start ● *vi* stick; (*diffondersi*) catch on. **~si** *vr* cling; (*affezionarsi*) become attached; (*litigare*) quarrel

attacca'ticcio *a* sticky

at'tacco *nm* attack; (*punto d'unione*) junction

attar'darsi *vr* stay late; (*indugiare*) linger

attec'chire *vi* take; ⟨*moda ecc:*⟩ catch on

atteggia'mento *nm* attitude

atteggi'ar|e *vt* assume. **~si** *vr* **~si a** pose as

attem'pato *a* elderly

at'tender|e *vt* wait for ● *vi* **~e a** attend to. **~si** *vr* expect

atten'dibil|e *a* reliable. **~ità** *nf* reliability

atte'nersi *vr* **~ a** stick to

attenta'mente *adv* attentively

atten'ta|re *vi* ~**re a** make an attempt on. ~**to** *nm* act of violence; (*contro politico ecc*) assassination attempt. ~**'tore**, ~**'trice** *nmf* (*a scopo politico*) terrorist

at'tento *a* attentive; (*accurato*) careful; ~**!** look out!; **stare** ~ pay attention

attenu'ante *nf* extenuating circumstance

attenu'a|re *vt* attenuate; (*minimizzare*) minimize; subdue ⟨*colori ecc*⟩; calm ⟨*dolore*⟩; soften ⟨*colpo*⟩. ~**rsi** *vr* diminish. ~**zi'one** *nf* lessening

attenzi'one *nf* attention; ~**!** watch out!

atter'ra|ggio *nm* landing. ~**re** *vt* knock down ● *vi* land

atter'rir|e *vt* terrorize. ~**si** *vr* be terrified

at'tes|a *nf* waiting; (*aspettativa*) expectation; **in** ~**a di** waiting for. ~**o** *pp di* **attendere**

atte'sta|re *vt* state; (*certificare*) certify. ~**to** *nm* certificate. ~**zi'one** *nf* certificate; (*dichiarazione*) declaration

'attico *nm* attic

at'tiguo *a* adjacent

attil'lato *a* ⟨*vestito*⟩ close-fitting; (*elegante*) dressed up

'attimo *nm* moment

atti'nente *a* ~ **a** pertaining to

at'tingere *vt* draw; *fig* obtain

atti'rare *vt* attract

atti'tudine *nf* (*disposizione*) aptitude; (*atteggiamento*) attitude

atti'v|are *vt* activate. ~**ismo** *nm* activism. ~**ista** *nmf* activist. **attività** *nf inv* activity; *Comm* assets *pl*. ~**o** *a* active; *Comm* productive ● *nm* assets *pl*

attiz'za|re *vt* poke; *fig* stir up. ~**'toio** *nm* poker

'atto *nm* act; (*azione*) action; *Comm, Jur* deed; (*certificato*) certificate; **atti** *pl* (*di società ecc*) proceedings; **mettere in** ~ put into effect

at'tonito *a* astonished

attorcigli'ar|e *vt* twist. ~**si** *vr* get twisted

at'tore *nm* actor

attorni'ar|e *vt* surround. ~**si** *vr* ~**si di** surround oneself with

at'torno *adv* around, about ● *prep* ~ **a** around, about

attrac'care *vt/i* dock

attra'ente *a* attractive

at'tra|rre *vt* attract. ~**rsi** *vr* be attracted to each other. ~**t'tiva** *nf* charm

attraversa'mento *nm* (*di strada*) crossing. ~ **pedonale** pedestrian crossing, crosswalk *Am*

attraver'sare *vt* cross; (*passare*) go through

attra'verso *prep* through; (*obliquamente*) across

attrazi'on|e *nf* attraction. ~**i turistiche** tourist attractions

attrez'za|re *vt* equip; *Naut* rig. ~**rsi** *vr* kit oneself out; ~**'tura** *nf* equipment; *Naut* rigging

at'trezzo *nm* tool; **attrezzi** *pl* equipment; *Sport* appliances *pl*; *Theat* props *pl*

attribu'ir|e *vt* attribute. ~**si** *vr* ascribe to oneself; ~**si il merito di** claim credit for

attri'bu|to *nm* attribute. ~**zi'one** *nf* attribution

at'trice *nf* actress

at'trito *nm* friction

attu'abile *a* feasible

attu'al|e *a* present; (*di attualità*) topical; (*effettivo*) actual. ~**ità** *nf* topicality; (*avvenimento*) news; **programma di** ~**ità** current affairs programme. ~**iz'zare** *vt* update. ~**'mente** *adv* at present

attu'a|re *vt* carry out. ~**rsi** *vr* be realized. ~**zi'one** *nf* carrying out

attu'tire *vt* deaden; ~ **il colpo** soften the blow

au'dac|e *a* daring, bold; (*insolente*) audacious;. ~**ia** *nf* daring, boldness; (*insolenza*) audacity

'audience *nf inv* (*telespettatori*) audience

'audio *nm* audio

audiovi'sivo *a* audiovisual

audi'torio *nm* auditorium

audizi'one *nf* audition; *Jur* hearing

'auge *nm* height; **essere in** ~ be popular

augu'rar|e *vt* wish. ~**si** *vr* hope. **au'gurio** *nm* wish; (*presagio*) omen; **auguri!** all the best!; (*a Natale*) Happy Christmas!; **tanti auguri** best wishes

'aula *nf* classroom; (*università*) lecture-hall; (*sala*) hall. ~ **magna** (*in università*) great hall. ~ **del tribunale** courtroom

aumen'tare *vt/i* increase. **au'mento** *nm* increase; (*di stipendio*) [pay] rise

au'reola *nf* halo

au'rora *nf* dawn

auscul'tare *vt Med* auscultate

ausili'are *a & nmf* auxiliary

23

auspicabile | avanzare

auspicabile *a* è ~ che... it is to be hoped that...

auspi'care *vt* hope for

au'spicio *nm* omen; **auspici** (*pl: protezione*) auspices

austerità *nf* austerity

au'stero *a* austere.

Au'strali|a *nf* Australia. **a~'ano, -a** *a* & *nmf* Australian

'Austria *nf* Austria. **au'striaco, -a** *a* & *nmf* Austrian

autar'chia *nf* autarchy. **au'tarchico** *a* autarchic

autenti'c|are *vt* authenticate. **~ità** *nf* authenticity

au'tentico *a* authentic; (*vero*) true

au'tista *nm* driver

'auto *nf inv* car

'auto+ *pref* self+

autoabbron'zante *nm* self-tan ● *a* self-tanning

autoambu'lanza *nf* ambulance

autoarticо'lato *nm* articulated lorry

autobio|gra'fia *nf* autobiography. **~'grafico** *a* autobiographical

auto'botte *nf* tanker

'autobus *nm inv* bus

auto'carro *nm* lorry

autocommiserazi'one *nf* self-pity

autoconcessio'nario *nm* car dealer

auto'critica *nf* self-criticism

autodi'datta *nmf* self-educated person, autodidact

autodi'fesa *nf* self-defence

auto'gol *nm inv* own goal

au'tografo *a* & *nm* autograph

autolesio'nis|mo *nm fig* selfdestruction. **~tico** *a* self-destructive

auto'linea *nf* bus line

au'toma *nm* robot

automatica'mente *adv* automatically

auto'matico *a* automatic ● *nm* (*bottone*) press-stud; (*fucile*) automatic

automatiz'za|re *vt* automate. **~zi'one** *nf* automation

auto'mezzo *nm* motor vehicle

auto'mobi|le *nf* [motor] car. **~'lismo** *nm* motoring. **~'lista** *nmf* motorist. **~'listico** *a* (*industria*) automobile *attrib*

autonoma'mente *adv* autonomously

autono'mia *nf* autonomy; *Auto* range; (*di laptop, cellulare*) battery life. **au'tonomo** *a* autonomous

auto'psia *nf* autopsy

auto'radio *nf inv* car radio; (*veicolo*) radio car

au'tore, -'trice *nmf* author; (*di pitture*) painter; (*di furto ecc*) perpetrator; **quadro d'~** genuine master

autorevo|le *a* authoritative; (*che ha influenza*) influential. **~'lezza** *nf* authority

autori'messa *nf* garage

autori'tà *nf inv* authority. **~'tario** *a* autocratic. **~ta'rismo** *nm* authoritarianism

autori'tratto *nm* self-portrait

autoriz'za|re *vt* authorize. **~zi'one** *nf* authorization

auto'scontro *nm inv* bumper car

autoscu'ola *nf* driving school

auto'stop *nm* hitch-hiking; **fare l'~** hitch-hike. **~'pista** *nmf* hitch-hiker

auto'strada *nf* motorway

autostra'dale *a* motorway *attrib*

autosuffici'en|te *a* self-sufficient. **~za** *nf* self-sufficiency

autotrasporta'|tore, ~'trice *nmf* haulier, carrier

auto'treno *nm* articulated lorry, roadtrain

autove'icolo *nm* motor vehicle

auto'velox *nm inv* speed camera

autovet'tura *nf* motor vehicle

autun'nale *a* autumn[al]

au'tunno *nm* autumn

aval'lare *vt* endorse, back ‹*cambiale*›; *fig* endorse

a'vallo *nm* endorsement

avam'braccio *nm* forearm

avangu'ardia *nf* vanguard; *fig* avant-garde; **essere all'~** be in the forefront; *Techn* be at the leading edge

a'vanti *adv* (*in avanti*) forward; (*davanti*) in front; (*prima*) before; **~!** (*entrate*) come in!; (*suvvia*) come on!; (*su semaforo*) cross now, walk *Am*; **va' ~!** go ahead!; **andare ~** (*precedere*) go ahead; ‹*orologio:*› be fast; **~ e indietro** backwards and forwards ● *a* (*precedente*) before ● *prep* **~ a** before; (*in presenza di*) in the presence of

avanti'eri *adv* the day before yesterday

avanza'mento *nm* progress; (*promozione*) promotion

avan'za|re *vi* advance; (*progredire*) progress; (*essere d'avanzo*) be left [over] ● *vt* advance; (*superare*) surpass; (*promuovere*) promote. **~rsi** *vr* advance; (*avvicinarsi*) approach. **~ta** *nf* advance. **~to** *a* advanced; (*nella notte*) late; **in**

età ~ta elderly. a'vanzo nm remainder; *Comm* surplus; avanzi pl *(rovine)* remains; *(di cibo)* left-overs

ava'ri|a nf *(di motore)* engine failure. ~'ato a *(frutta, verdura)* rotten; *(carne)* tainted

ava'rizia nf avarice. a'varo, -a a stingy ● nmf miser

a'vena nf oats pl

a'vere vt have; *(ottenere)* get; *(indossare)* wear; *(provare)* feel; ho trent'anni I'm thirty; ha avuto il posto he got the job; ~ fame/freddo be hungry/cold; ho mal di denti I've got toothache; cos'ha a che fare con lui? what has it got to do with him?; ~ da fare be busy; che hai? what's the matter with you?; nei hai per molto? will you be long?; quanti ne abbiamo oggi? what date is it today?; avercela con qcno have it in for sb ● v aux have; non l'ho visto I haven't seen him; lo hai visto? have you seen him?; l'ho visto ieri I saw him yesterday ● nm averi pl wealth sg

avia|'tore nm flyer, aviator. ~zi'one nf aviation; *Mil* Air Force

avidità nf avidness. 'avido a avid

avio'getto nm jet

'avo, -a nmf ancestor

avo'cado nm inv avocado

a'vorio nm ivory

Avv. abbr avvocato

avva'lersi vr avail oneself (of di)

avvalla'mento nm depression

avvalo'rare vt bear out *(tesi)*; endorse *(documento)*; *(accrescere)* enhance

avvam'pare vi flare up; *(arrossire)* blush

avvantaggi'ar|e vt favour. ~si vr ~si di benefit from; *(approfittare)* take advantage of

avve'd|ersi vr *(accorgersi)* notice; *(capire)* realize. ~uto a shrewd

avvelena'mento nm poisoning

avvele'na|re vt poison. ~rsi vr poison oneself. ~to a poisoned

avve'nente a attractive

avveni'mento nm event

avve'nire[1] vi happen; *(aver luogo)* take place

avve'ni|re[2] nm future. ~'ristico a futuristic

avven'ta|rsi vr fling oneself. ~to a *(decisione)* rash

av'vento nm advent; *Relig* Advent

avven'tore nm regular customer

avven'tu|ra nf adventure; *(amorosa)* affair; d'~ *(film)* adventure attrib.

~'rarsi vr venture. ~ri'ero, -a nm adventurer ● nf adventuress. ~'roso a adventurous

avve'ra|bile a *(previsione)* that may come true. ~rsi vr come true

av'verbio nm adverb

avver'sar|e vt oppose. ~io, -a a opposing ● nmf opponent

avversi|'one nf aversion. ~tà nf inv adversity

av'verso a *(sfavorevole)* adverse; *(contrario)* averse

avver'tenza nf *(cura)* care; *(avvertimento)* warning; *(avviso)* notice; *(premessa)* foreword; avvertenze pl *(istruzioni)* instructions

avverti'mento nm warning

avver'tire vt warn; *(informare)* inform; *(sentire)* feel

avvez'zar|e vt accustom. ~si vr accustom oneself. av'vezzo a avvezzo a used to

avvia'mento nm starting; *Comm* goodwill

avvi'a|re vt start. ~rsi vr set out. ~to a under way; bene ~to thriving

avvicenda'mento nm *(in agricoltura)* rotation; *(nel lavoro)* replacement

avvicen'darsi vr take turns, alternate

avvicina'mento nm approach

avvici'nar|e vt bring near; approach *(persona)*. ~si vr come nearer, approach; ~si a come nearer to, approach

avvi'lente a demoralizing; *(umiliante)* humiliating

avvili'mento nm despondency; *(degradazione)* degradation

avvi'li|re vt dishearten; *(degradare)* degrade. ~rsi vr lose heart; *(degradarsi)* degrade oneself. ~to a disheartened; *(degradato)* degraded

avvilup'par|e vt envelop. ~si vr wrap oneself up; *(aggrovigliarsi)* get entangled

avvinaz'zato a drunk

avvin'cente a *(libro ecc)* enthralling. av'vincere vt enthral

avvinghi'ar|e vt clutch. ~si vr cling

av'vio nm start-up; dare l'~ a qcsa get sth under way; prendere l'~ get under way

avvi'sare vt inform; *(mettere in guardia)* warn

av'viso nm notice; *(annuncio)* announcement; *(avvertimento)* warning; *(pubblicitario)* advertisement; a mio in my opinion. **~ di garanzia** *Jur* notification that one is to be the subject of a legal enquiry

avvi'stare *vt* catch sight of

avvi'tare *vt* screw in; screw down ‹*coperchio*›

avviz'zire *vi* wither

avvo'ca|to *nm* lawyer; *fig* advocate. **~'tura** *nf* legal profession

av'volger|e *vt* wrap [up]. **~si** *vr* wrap oneself up

avvol'gibile *nm* roller blind

avvol'toio *nm* vulture

aza'lea *nf* azalea

azi'en|da *nf* business, firm. **~ agricola** farm. **~ di soggiorno** tourist bureau. **~'dale** *a* ‹*politica, dirigente*› company *attrib*; ‹*giornale*› in-house

aziona'mento *nm* operation

azio'nare *vt* operate

azio'nario *a* share *attrib*

azi'one *nf* action; *Fin* share; **d'~** ‹*romanzo, film*› action[-packed]. **azio'nista** *nmf* shareholder

a'zoto *nm* nitrogen

azzan'nare *vt* seize with its teeth; sink its teeth into ‹*gamba*›

azzar'd|are *vt* risk. **~arsi** *vr* dare. **~ato** *a* risky; (*precipitoso*) rash. **az'zardo** *nm* hazard; **gioco d'azzardo** game of chance

azzec'care *vt* hit; (*fig: indovinare*) guess

azzuf'farsi *vr* come to blows

az'zur|ro *a* & *nm* blue; **il principe ~** Prince Charming. **~'rognolo** *a* bluish

Bb

bab'beo *a* foolish ● *nm* idiot

'babbo *nm fam* dad, daddy. **B~ Natale** Father Christmas

bab'buccia *nf* slipper

babbu'ino *nm* baboon

ba'bordo *nm Naut* port side

'babysitter *nmf inv* baby-sitter; **fare la ~** babysit

ba'cato *a* wormeaten

'bacca *nf* berry

baccalà *nm inv* dried salted cod

bac'cano *nm* din

bac'cello *nm* pod

bac'chetta *nf* rod; (*magica*) wand; (*di direttore d'orchestra*) baton; (*di tamburo*) drumstick

ba'checa *nf* showcase; (*in ufficio*) notice board. **~ elettronica** *Comput* bulletin board

bacia'mano *nm* kiss on the hand; **fare il ~ a qcno** kiss sb's hand

baci'ar|e *vt* kiss. **~si** *vr* kiss [each other]

ba'cillo *nm* bacillus

baci'nella *nf* basin

ba'cino *nm* basin; *Anat* pelvis; (*di porto*) dock; (*di minerali*) field

'bacio *nm* kiss

'baco *nm* worm. **~ da seta** silkworm

ba'cucco *a* **un vecchio ~** a senile old man

'bada *nf* **tenere qcno a ~** keep sb at bay

ba'dare *vi* take care (**a** of); (*fare attenzione*) look out; **bada ai fatti tuoi!** mind your own business!

ba'dia *nf* abbey

ba'dile *nm* shovel

'badminton *nm* badminton

'baffi *nmpl* moustache *sg*; (*di animale*) whiskers; **mi fa un baffo** I don't give a damn; **ridere sotto i ~** laugh up one's sleeve

baf'futo *a* moustached

ba'gagli *nmpl* luggage, baggage. **~'aio** *nm Rail* luggage van; *Auto* boot

ba'gaglio *nm* luggage; **un ~** a piece of luggage. **~ a mano** hand luggage, hand baggage

baggia'nata *nf* **non dire baggianate** don't talk nonsense

bagli'ore *nm* glare; (*improvviso*) flash; (*fig: di speranza*) glimmer

ba'gnante *nmf* bather

ba'gna|re *vt* wet; (*inzuppare*) soak; (*immergere*) dip; (*innaffiare*) water; ‹*mare, lago:*› wash; ‹*fiume:*› flow through. **~rsi** *vr* get wet; (*al mare ecc*) swim, bathe

bagnasci'uga *nm inv* edge of the water, waterline

ba'gnato *a* wet

ba'gnino, -a *nmf* life guard

'bagno *nm* bath; (*stanza*) bathroom; (*gabinetto*) toilet; (*in casa*) toilet, bathroom; (*al mare*) swim, bathe; **bagni** *pl* (*stabilimento*) lido; **fare il ~** have a bath; (*nel mare ecc*) [have a] swim *or* bathe; **andare in ~** go to the bathroom *or* toilet; **mettere a ~** soak. **~ turco** Turkish bath

bagnoma'ria *nm* **cuocere a ~** cook in a double saucepan

bagnoschi'uma *nm inv* bubble bath

'baia *nf* bay

baio'netta *nf* bayonet

'baita *nf* mountain chalet

bala'ustra, balaus'trata *nf* balustrade

balbet't|are *vt/i* stammer; (*bambino:*) babble. **~io** *nm* stammering; babble

bal'buzi|e *nf* stutter. **~'ente** *a* stuttering ● *nmf* stutterer

Bal'can|i *nmpl* Balkans. **b~ico** *a* Balkan

balco'nata *nf Theat* balcony, dress circle

balcon'cino *nm* **reggiseno a ~** underwired bra

bal'cone *nm* balcony

baldac'chino *nm* canopy; **letto a ~** four-poster bed

bal'dan|za *nf* boldness. **~'zoso** *a* bold

bal'doria *nf* revelry; **far ~** have a riotous time

Bale'ari *nfpl* **le [isole] ~** the Balearics, the Balearic Islands

ba'lena *nf* whale

bale'nare *vi* lighten; *fig* flash; **mi è balenata un'idea** I've just had an idea

bale'niera *nf* whaler

ba'leno *nm* **in un ~** in a flash

ba'lera *nf* dance hall

'balia *nf* wetnurse

ba'lia *nf* **in ~ di** at the mercy of

ba'listico *a* ballistic; **perito ~** ballistics expert

'balla *nf* bale; (*fam: frottola*) tall story

bal'labile *a* good for dancing to

bal'la|re *vi* dance. **~ta** *nf* ballad

balla'toio *nm* (*nelle scale*) landing

balle'rino, -a *nmf* dancer; (*classico*) ballet dancer; **ballerina** (*classica*) ballet dancer, ballerina

bal'letto *nm* ballet

bal'lista *nmf fam* bull-shitter

'ballo *nm* dance; (*il ballare*) dancing;

sala da ~ ballroom; **essere in ~** (*lavoro, vita:*) be at stake; (*persona:*) be committed; **tirare qcno in ~** involve sb

ballonzo'lare *vi* skip about

ballot'taggio *nm* second count (*of votes*)

balne'a|re *a* bathing *attrib*. **stagione ~** swimming season. **stazione ~** seaside resort. **~zi'one** *nf* **è vietata la ~zione** no swimming

ba'lordo *a* foolish; (*stordito*) stunned; **tempo ~** nasty weather

'balsamo *nm* balsam; (*per capelli*) conditioner; (*lenimento*) remedy

'baltico *a* Baltic. **il [mar] B~** the Baltic [Sea]

balu'ardo *nm* bulwark

'balza *nf* crag; (*di abito*) flounce

bal'zano *a* (*idea*) weird

bal'zare *vi* bounce; (*saltare*) jump; **~ in piedi** leap to one's feet. **'balzo** *nm* bounce; (*salto*) jump; **prendere la palla al balzo** seize an opportunity

bam'bagia *nf* cotton wool; **vivere nella ~** *fig* be in clover

bambi'nata *nf* childish thing to do/ say

bam'bi|no, -a *nmf* child; (*appena nato*) baby; **avere un ~no** have a baby. **~'none, -a** *nmf pej* overgrown child

bam'boccio *nm* chubby child; (*sciocco*) simpleton; (*fantoccio*) rag doll

'bambo|la *nf* doll. **~'lotto** *nm* male doll

bambù *nm* bamboo

ba'nal|e *a* banal; **~ità** *nf inv* banality; **~iz'zare** *vt* trivialize

ba'nan|a *nf* banana. **~o** *nm* banana-tree

'banca *nf* bank. **~ [di] dati** databank

banca'rella *nf* stall

ban'cario, -a *a* banking *attrib*; **trasferimento ~** bank transfer ● *nmf* bank employee

banca'rotta *nf* bankruptcy; **fare ~** go bankrupt

banchet'tare *vi* banquet. **ban'chetto** *nm* banquet

banchi'ere *nm* banker

ban'china *nf Naut* quay; (*in stazione*) platform; (*di strada*) path; **~ non transitabile** soft verge

ban'chisa *nf* floe

'banco *nm* (*di scuola*) desk; (*di negozio*) counter; (*di officina*) bench; (*di gioco, banca*) bank; (*di mercato*) stall; (*degli imputati*) dock; **sotto ~** under the counter; **medicinale da ~** over the counter medicines. **~ informazioni** information desk. **~ di nebbia** fog bank

'**bancomat**® *nm inv* autobank, cashpoint; (*carta*) bank card, cash card

ban'cone *nm* counter; (*in bar*) bar

banco'nota *nf* banknote, bill *Am*; **banco'note** *pl* paper currency

'**banda** *nf* band; (*di delinquenti*) gang. **~ d'atterraggio** *Aeron* landing strip. **~ rumorosa** rumble strip

banderu'ola *nf* weathercock; *Naut* pennant

bandi'e|ra *nf* flag; **cambiare ~ra** change sides, switch allegiances. **~'rina** *nf* (*nel calcio*) corner flag. **~'rine** *pl* bunting *sg*

ban'di|re *vt* banish; (*pubblicare*) publish; *fig* dispense with ⟨*formalità, complimenti*⟩. **~to** *nm* bandit. **~'tore** *nm* (*di aste*) auctioneer

'**bando** *nm* proclamation; **~ di concorso** job advertisement (*published in an official gazette for a job for which a competitive examination has to be taken*)

bar *nm inv* bar

'**bara** *nf* coffin

ba'rac|ca *nf* hut; (*catapecchia*) hovel; **mandare avanti la ~ca** keep the ship afloat. **~'cato** *nm person living in a makeshift shelter*. **~'chino** *nm* (*di gelati, giornali*) kiosk; *Radio* CB radio. **~'cone** *nm* (*roulotte*) circus caravan; (*in luna park*) booth. **~'copoli** *nf inv* shanty town

bara'onda *nf* chaos; **non fare ~** don't make a mess

ba'rare *vi* cheat

ba'ratro *nm* chasm

barat'tare *vt* barter. **ba'ratto** *nm* barter

ba'rattolo *nm* jar; (*di latta*) tin

'**barba** *nf* beard; (*fam: noia*) bore; **farsi la ~** shave; **è una ~** (*noia*) it's boring

barbabi'etola *nf* beetroot. **~ da zucchero** sugar-beet

bar'barico *a* barbaric. **bar'barie** *nf* barbarity. '**barbaro** *a* barbarous ● *nm* barbarian

'**barbecue** *nm inv* barbecue

barbi'ere *nm* barber; (*negozio*) barber's

barbi'turico *nm* barbiturate

bar'bone *nm* (*vagabondo*) vagrant; (*cane*) poodle

bar'boso *a fam* boring

barbu'gliare *vi* mumble

bar'buto *a* bearded

'**barca** *nf* boat; **una ~ di** *fig* a lot of. **~ a motore** motorboat. **~ da pesca** fishing boat. **~ a remi** rowing boat, rowboat *Am*. **~ di salvataggio** lifeboat. **~ a vela** sailing boat, sailboat *Am*. **~i'olo** *nm* boatman

barcame'narsi *vr* manage

barcol'lare *vi* stagger

bar'cone *nm* barge; (*di ponte*) pontoon

bar'dar|e *vt* harness. **~si** *vr hum* dress up

ba'rel|la *nf* stretcher. **~li'ere** *nm* stretcher-bearer

'**Barents**: **il mare di ~** the Barents Sea

bari'centro *nm* centre of gravity

ba'ri|le *nm* barrel. **~'lotto** *nm fig* tub of lard

ba'rista *nm* barman ● *nf* barmaid

ba'ritono *nm* baritone

bar'lume *nm* glimmer; **un ~ di speranza** a glimmer of hope

'**barman** *nm inv* barman

'**baro** *nm* cardsharper

ba'rocco *a & nm* baroque

ba'rometro *nm* barometer

ba'rone *nm* baron; **i baroni** *fig* the top brass. **baro'nessa** *nf* baroness

'**barra** *nf* bar; (*lineetta*) oblique; *Naut* tiller. **~ spazio** *Comput* space bar. **~ strumenti** *Comput* tool bar

bar'rare *vt* block off ⟨*strada*⟩

barri'ca|re *vt* barricade. **~ta** *nf* barricade

barri'era *nf* barrier; (*stradale*) roadblock; *Geol* reef. **~ razziale** colour bar

bar'ri|re *vi* trumpet. **~to** *nm* trumpeting

barzel'letta *nf* joke; **~ sporca** *o* **spinta** dirty joke

basa'mento *nm* base

ba'sar|e *vt* base. **~si** *vr* **~si su** be based on; **mi baso su ciò che ho visto** I'm going on [the basis of] what I saw

'**basco, -a** *nmf & a* Basque ● *nm* (*copricapo*) beret

'**base** *nf* basis; (*fondamento*) foundation; *Mil* base; *Pol* rank and file; **a ~ di** containing; **in ~ a** on the basis of. **~ dati** database

'**baseball** *nm* baseball

ba'setta *nf* sideburn

basi'lare *a* basic

ba'silica *nf* basilica

ba'silico *nm* basil

ba'sista *nm* grass roots politician; (*di un crimine*) mastermind

'**basket** *nm* basketball

bas'sezza *nf* lowness; *(di statura)* shortness; *(viltà)* vileness

bas'sista *nmf* bassist

'**basso** *a* low; *(di statura)* short; *‹acqua›* shallow; *‹televisione›* quiet; *(vile)* despicable; **parlare a bassa voce** speak quietly, speak in a low voice; **la bassa Italia** southern Italy ● *nm* lower part; *Mus* bass. **guardare in ~** look down

basso'fondo *nm* (*pl* **bassi'fondi**) shallows *pl*; **bassifondi** *pl* (*quartieri poveri*) slums

bassorili'evo *nm* bas-relief

bas'sotto *nm* dachshund

ba'stardo, -a *a* bastard; *(di animale)* mongrel ● *nmf* bastard; *(animale)* mongrel

ba'stare *vi* be enough; *(durare)* last; **basta!** that's enough!, that'll do!; **basta che** (*purchè*) provided that; **basta così** that's enough; **basta così?** is that enough?, will that do?; *(in negozio)* will there be anything else?; **basta andare alla posta** you only have to go to the post office

Basti'an con'trario *nm* contrary old so-and-so

basti'one *nm* bastion

basto'nare *vt* beat

baston'cino *nm* (*da sci*) ski pole. **~ di pesce** fish finger, fish stick *Am*

ba'stone *nm* stick; *(da golf)* club; *(da passeggio)* walking stick

ba'tosta *nf* blow

bat'tagli|a *nf* battle; *(lotta)* fight. **~'are** *vi* battle; *fig* fight

bat'taglio *nm* (*di campana*) clapper; *(di porta)* knocker

battagli'one *nm* battalion

bat'tello *nm* boat; *(motonave)* steamer

bat'tente *nm* (*di porta*) wing; *(di finestra)* shutter; *(battaglio)* knocker

'**batter|e** *vt* beat; *(percorrere)* scour; thresh *‹grano›*; break *‹record›* ● *vi* (*bussare, urtare*) knock; *‹cuore:›* beat; *‹ali ecc:›* flap; *Tennis* serve; **~e a macchina** type; **~e gli occhi** blink; **~e le mani** clap [one's hands]; **~e le ore** strike the hours. **~si** *vr* fight

bat'teri *nmpl* bacteria

batte'ria *nf* battery; *Mus* drums *pl*

bat'terio *nm* bacterium. **~'logico** *a* bacteriological

batte'rista *nmf* drummer

bat'tesimo *nm* baptism, christening

battez'zare *vt* baptize, christen

battiba'leno *nm* **in un ~** in a flash

batti'becco *nm* squabble

batticu'ore *nm* palpitation; **mi venne il ~** I was scared

bat'tigia *nf* water's edge

batti'mano *nm* applause

batti'panni *nm inv* carpetbeater

batti'stero *nm* baptistery

batti'strada *nm inv* outrider; *(di pneumatico)* tread; *S port* pacesetter

battitap'peto *nm inv* carpet sweeper

'**battito** *nm* (*del cuore*) [heart]beat; *(alle tempie)* throbbing; *(di orologio)* ticking; *(della pioggia)* beating

bat'tuta *nf* beat; *(colpo)* knock; *(spiritosaggine)* wisecrack; *(osservazione)* remark; *Mus* bar; *Tennis* service; *Theat* cue; *(dattilografia)* stroke

ba'tuffolo *nm* flock

ba'ule *nm* trunk

'**bava** *nf* dribble; *(di cane ecc)* slobber; **aver la ~ alla bocca** foam at the mouth

bava'glino *nm* bib

ba'vaglio *nm* gag

'**bavero** *nm* collar

ba'zar *nm inv* bazaar

baz'zecola *nf* trifle

bazzi'care *vt/i* haunt

be'arsi *vr* delight (**di** in)

beati'tudine *nf* bliss. **be'ato** *a* blissful; *Relig* blessed; **beato te!** lucky you!

beauty-'case *nm inv* toilet bag

bebè *nm inv* baby

bec'caccia *nf* woodcock

bec'ca|re *vt* peck; *fig* catch. **~rsi** *vr* (*litigare*) quarrel. **~ta** *nf* peck

beccheggi'are *vi* pitch

bec'chino *nm* grave-digger

'**bec|co** *nm* beak; *(di caffettiera ecc)* spout. **~'cuccio** *nm* spout

be'fana *nf* Epiphany; *(donna brutta)* old witch

'**beffa** *nf* hoax; **farsi beffe di qcno** mock sb. **bef'fardo** *a* derisory; *(persona)* mocking

bef'far|e *vt* mock. **~si** *vr* **~si di** make fun of

'**bega** *nf* quarrel; **è una bella ~** it's really annoying

be'gonia *nf* begonia

'**beige** *a & nm* beige

be'la|re *vi* bleat. **~to** *nm* bleating

'**belga** *a & nmf* Belgian

'**Belgio** *nm* Belgium

'**bella** *nf* (*in carte, Sport*) decider

bel'lezza *nf* beauty; **che ~!** how lovely!; **chiudere/finire in ~** end on a high note

'belli|co a war attrib. **~'coso** a warlike. **~ge'rante** a & nmf belligerent

'bello a nice; (di aspetto) beautiful; ⟨uomo⟩ handsome; (moralmente) good; **cosa fai di ~ stasera?** what are you up to tonight?; **oggi fa ~** it's a nice day; **una bella cifra** a lot; **un bel piatto di pasta** a big plate of pasta; **nel bel mezzo** right in the middle; **un bel niente** absolutely nothing; **bell'e fatto** over and done with; **bell'amico!** [a] fine friend he is/you are!; **questa è bella!** that's a good one!; **scamparla bella** have a narrow escape ● nm (bellezza) beauty; (innamorato) sweetheart; **sul più ~** at the crucial moment; **il ~ è che…** the funny thing is that…

'belva nf wild beast

be'molle nm Mus flat

ben vedi bene

benché conj though, although

'benda nf bandage; (per occhi) blindfold. **ben'dare** vt bandage; blindfold ⟨occhi⟩

'bene adv well; **ben ~** thoroughly; **~!** good!; **star ~** (di salute) be well; ⟨vestito, stile:⟩ suit; (finanziariamente) be well off; **non sta ~** (non è educato) it's not nice; **sta/va ~!** all right!; **ti sta ~!** [it] serves you right!; **ti auguro ~** I wish you well; **di ~ in meglio** better and better; **fare ~** (aver ragione) do the right thing; **fare ~ a** ⟨cibo:⟩ be good for; **una persona per ~** a good person; **per ~** (fare) properly; **è ben difficile** it's very difficult; **come tu ben sai** as you well know; **lo credo ~!** I can well believe it! ● nm good; **per il tuo ~** for your own good. **beni** nmpl (averi) property sg; **un ~ di famiglia** a family heirloom

bene'detto a blessed

bene'di|re vt bless. **~zi'one** nf blessing

benedu'cato a well-mannered

benefat'tore, -'trice nm benefactor ● nf benefactress

benefi'care vt help

benefi'cenza nf charity

benefici'ar|e vi **~e di** profit by. **~io, -a** a & nmf beneficiary. **bene'ficio** nm benefit. **be'nefico** a beneficial; (di beneficenza) charitable

bene'placito nm consent, approval

be'nessere nm well-being

bene'stante a well-off ● nmf well-off person

bene'stare nm consent

benevo'lenza nf benevolence. **be'nevolo** a benevolent

ben'fatto a well-made

'beni nmpl property sg; Fin assets; **~ di consumo** consumer goods

benia'mino nm favourite

be'nigno a kindly; Med benign

beninfor'mato a well-informed

benintenzio'nato, -a a well-meaning ● nmf well-meaning person

benin'teso adv needless to say, of course

benpen'sante a & nmf self-righteous

benser'vito nm **dare il ~ a qcno** give sb the sack

ben'sì conj but rather

benve'nuto a & nm welcome

ben'visto a **essere ~** go down well (da with)

benvo'lere vt **farsi ~ da qcno** win sb's affection; **prendere qcno in ~** take a liking to sb; **essere benvoluto da tutti** to be well-liked by everyone

ben'zina nf petrol, gas Am; **far ~** get petrol. **~ verde** unleaded petrol. **benzi'naio, -a** nmf petrol station attendant

'bere vt drink; (assorbire) absorb; fig swallow ● nm drinking; (bevande) drinks pl

berga'motto nm bergamot

ber'lina nf Auto saloon

Ber'lino nm Berlin

ber'muda nfpl (pantaloni) Bermuda shorts

ber'noccolo nm bump; (disposizione) flair

ber'retto nm beret, cap

bersagli'are vt fig bombard. **ber'saglio** nm target

be'stemmi|a nf swear-word; (maledizione) oath; (sproposito) blasphemy. **~'are** vi swear

'besti|a nf animal; (persona brutale) beast; (persona sciocca) fool; **andare in ~a** fam blow one's top. **~'ale** a bestial; (espressione, violenza) brutal; (fam: freddo, fame) terrible. **~alità** nf inv bestiality; fig nonsense. **~'ame** nm livestock

'bettola nf fig dive

be'tulla nf birch

be'vanda nf drink

bevi'tore, -'trice nmf drinker

be'vut|a nf drink. **~o** pp di **bere**

bi'ada nf fodder

bianche'ria nf linen. **~ intima** underwear

bi'anco a white; ⟨foglio, pagina⟩ blank

● *nm* white; **mangiare in ~** not eat fried or heavy foods; **andare in ~** *fam* not score; **in ~ e nero** ‹*film, fotografia*› black and white, monochrome; **passare una notte in ~** have a sleepless night

bian'core *nm* (*bianchezza*) whiteness

bianco'spino *nm* hawthorn

biasci'care *vt* (*mangiare*) eat noisily; (*parlare*) mumble

biasi'mare *vt* blame. **bi'asimo** *nm* blame

'Bibbia *nf* Bible

bibe'ron *nm inv* [baby's] bottle

'bibita *nf* [soft] drink

'biblico *a* biblical

bibliogra'fia *nf* bibliography

biblio'te|ca *nf* library; (*mobile*) bookcase. **~'cario, -a** *nmf* librarian

bicarbo'nato *nm* bicarbonate. **~ di sodio** bicarbonate of soda

bicchi'ere *nm* glass

bicchie'rino *nm fam* tipple

bici'cletta *nf* bicycle; **andare in ~** ride a bicycle

bico'lore *a* two-coloured

bidè *nm inv* bidet

bi'dello, -a *nmf* janitor, [school] caretaker

bido'nata *nf fam* swindle

bi'done *nm* bin; (*fam: truffa*) swindle; **fare un ~ a qcno** *fam* stand sb up

bien'nale *a* biennial

bi'ennio *nm* two-year period

bi'etola *nf* beet

bifo'cale *a* bifocal

bi'folco, -a *nmf fig* boor

bifor'c|arsi *vr* fork. **~azi'one** *nf* fork. **~uto** *a* forked

biga'mia *nf* bigamy. **'bigamo, -a** *a* bigamous ● *nmf* bigamist

bighello'nare *vi* loaf around. **bighel'lone** *nm* loafer

bigiotte'ria *nf* costume jewellery; (*negozio*) jeweller's

bigliet't|aio *nm* booking clerk; (*sui treni*) ticket-collector. **~e'ria** *nf* ticket-office; *Theat* box-office

bigli'et|to *nm* ticket; (*lettera breve*) note; (*cartoncino*) card; (*di banca*) banknote. **~to da visita** business card. **~'tone** *nm* (*fam: soldi*) big one

bignè *nm inv* cream puff

bigo'dino *nm* roller

bi'gotto *nm* bigot

bi'kini *nm inv* bikini

bi'lanci|a *nf* scales *pl*; (*di orologio, Comm*) balance. **B~a** *Astr* Libra. **~'are**

vt balance; *fig* weigh. **~o** *nm* budget; *Comm* balance sheet; **fare il ~o** balance the books; *fig* take stock

'bil|e *nf* bile; *fig* rage

bili'ardo *nm* billiards *sg*

'bilico *nm* equilibrium; **in ~** in the balance

bi'lingue *a* bilingual

bili'one *nm* billion

bilo'cale *a* two-room

'bimbo, -a *nmf* child

bimen'sile *a* fortnightly

bime'strale *a* bimonthly

bi'nario *nm* track; (*piattaforma*) platform

bi'nocolo *nm* binoculars *pl*

bio'chimica *nf* biochemistry

biodegra'dabile *a* biodegradable

bio'etica *nf* bioethics

bio'fisica *nf* biophysics

biogra'fia *nf* biography. **bio'grafico** *a* biographical. **bi'ografo, -a** *nmf* biographer

biolo'gia *nf* biology. **bio'logico** *a* biological; (*alimento, agricoltura*) organic. **bi'ologo, -a** *nmf* biologist

bi'ond|a *nf* blonde. **~o** *a* blond ● *nm* fair colour; (*uomo*) fair-haired man

bio'sfera *nf* biosphere

bi'ossido *nm* **~ di carbonio** carbon dioxide

biparti'tismo *nm* two-party system

'birba *nf*, **bir'bante** *nm* rascal, rogue. **bir'bone** *a* wicked

biri'chino, -a *a* naughty ● *nmf* little devil

bi'rillo *nm* skittle

'birr|a *nf* beer; **a tutta ~a** *fig* flat out. **~a chiara** lager. **~a scura** brown ale. **~e'ria** *nf* beer-house; (*fabbrica*) brewery

bis *nm inv* encore

bi'saccia *nf* haversack

bi'sbetic|a *nf* shrew. **~o** *a* bad-tempered

bisbigli'are *vt/i* whisper. **bi'sbiglio** *nm* whisper

'bisca *nf* gambling-house

'biscia *nf* snake

bi'scotto *nm* biscuit

bisessu'ale *a & nmf* bisexual

bise'stile *a* **anno ~** leap year

bisettima'nale *a* fortnightly

bis'nonno, -a *nmf* great-grandfather; great-grandmother

biso'gn|are *vi* **~a agire subito** we must act at once; **~a farlo** it is necessary to do it; **non ~a venire** you don't have to come. ~o *nm* need; (*povertà*) poverty; **aver ~o di** need. ~**oso** *a* needy; (*povero*) poor; ~**oso di** in need of

bi'sonte *nm* bison

bi'stecca *nf* steak

bisticci'are *vi* quarrel. **bi'sticcio** *nm* quarrel; (*gioco di parole*) pun

bistrat'tare *vt* mistreat

'bisturi *nm inv* scalpel

bi'torzolo *nm* lump

'bitter *nm inv* (*bitter*) aperitif

bi'vacco *nm* bivouac

'bivio *nm* crossroads; (*di strada*) fork

bizan'tino *a* Byzantine

'bizza *nf* tantrum; **fare le bizze** ‹*bambini:*› play up

biz'zarro *a* bizarre

biz'zeffe *adv* a ~ galore

blan'dire *vt* soothe; (*allettare*) flatter. **'blando** *a* mild

bla'sone *nm* coat of arms

blate'rare *vi* blether, blather

'blatta *nf* cockroach

blin'da|re *vt* armour-plate. ~**to** *a* armoured

blitz *nm inv* blitz

bloc'car|e *vt* block; (*isolare*) cut off; *Mil* blockade; *Comm* freeze. ~**si** *vr Mech* jam

blocca'sterzo *nm* steering lock

'blocco *nm* block; *Mil* blockade; (*dei fitti*) restriction; (*di carta*) pad; (*unione*) coalition; **in ~** *Comm* in bulk. ~ **stradale** road-block

bloc-'notes *nm inv* writing pad

blu *a & nm* blue

blue-'jeans *nmpl* jeans

'bluff *nm inv* (*carte, fig*) bluff. **bluf'fare** *vi* (*carte, fig*) bluff

'blusa *nf* blouse

'boa *nm* boa [constrictor]; (*sciarpa*) [feather] boa ● *nf Naut* buoy

bo'ato *nm* rumbling

bo'bina *nf* spool; (*di film*) reel; *Electr* coil

'bocca *nf* mouth; **a ~ aperta** *fig* dumbfounded; **in ~ al lupo!** break a leg!; **fare la respirazione ~ a ~ a** qcno give sb mouth to mouth resuscitation *or* the kiss of life

boc'caccia *nf* grimace; **far boccacce** make faces

boc'caglio *nm* nozzle

boc'cale *nm* jug; (*da birra*) tankard

bocca'porto *nm Naut* hatch

boc'cata *nf* (*di fumo*) puff; **prendere una ~ d'aria** get a breath of fresh air

boc'cetta *nf* small bottle

bocchegg'iare *vi* gasp

boc'chino *nm* cigarette holder; (*di pipa, Mus*) mouthpiece

'bocc|ia *nf* (*palla*) bowl; ~**e** *pl* (*gioco*) bowls *sg*

bocci'a|re *vt* (*agli esami*) fail; (*respingere*) reject; (*alle bocce*) hit; **essere ~to** fail; (*ripetere*) repeat a year. ~**'tura** *nf* failure

bocci'olo *nm* bud

boccon'cino *nm* morsel

boc'cone *nm* mouthful; (*piccolo pasto*) snack

boc'coni *adv* face downwards

'boia *nm* executioner

boi'ata *nf fam* rubbish

boicot'tare *vt* boycott

bo'lero *nm* bolero

'bolgia *nf* (*caos*) bedlam

'bolide *nm* meteor; **passare come un ~** shoot past [like a rocket]

Bo'livi|a *nf* Bolivia. **b~'ano, -a** *a & nmf* Bolivian

'bolla *nf* bubble; (*pustola*) blister

bol'la|re *vt* stamp; *fig* brand. ~**to** *a fig* branded; **carta ~ta** paper with stamp showing payment of duty

bol'lente *a* boiling [hot]

bol'let|ta *nf* bill; **essere in ~ta** be hard up. ~**'tino** *nm* bulletin; *Comm* list

bol'lino *nm* coupon

bol'li|re *vt/i* boil. ~**to** *nm* boiled meat. ~**'tore** *nm* boiler; (*per l'acqua*) kettle. ~**'tura** *nf* boiling

'bollo *nm* stamp

bol'lore *nm* boil; (*caldo*) intense heat; *fig* ardour

'bomba *nf* bomb; **a prova di ~** bomb-proof

bombarda'mento *nm* shelling; (*con aerei*) bombing; *fig* bombardment. ~ **aereo** air raid

bombar'd|are *vt* shell; (*con aerei*) bomb; *fig* bombard. ~**i'ere** *nm* bomber

bom'betta *nf* bowler [hat]

'bombola *nf* cylinder. ~ **di gas** gas bottle, gas cylinder

bombo'lone *nm* doughnut

bomboni'era *nf* wedding keep-sake

bo'naccia *nf Naut* calm

bonacci'one, -a *nmf* good-natured person ● *a* good-natured

bo'nario *a* kindly

bo'nifica *nf* land reclamation. **bonifi-'care** *vt* reclaim

bo'nifico *nm Comm* discount; (*bancario*) [credit] transfer

bontà *nf* goodness; (*gentilezza*) kindness

'bora *nf* bora (*cold north-east wind in the upper Adriatic*)

borbot't|are *vi* mumble; ⟨*stomaco:*⟩ rumble. **~io** *nm* mumbling; (*di stomaco*) rumbling

'borchi|a *nf* stud. **~'ato** *a* studded

bor'da|re *vt* border. **~'tura** *nf* border

bor'deaux *a inv* (*colore*) claret

bor'dello *nm* brothel; *fig* bedlam; (*disordine*) mess

'bordo *nm* border; (*estremità*) edge; **a ~** *Naut, Aeron* on board

bor'gata *nf* hamlet

bor'ghese *a* bourgeois; ⟨*abito*⟩ civilian; **in ~** in civilian dress; ⟨*poliziotto*⟩ in plain clothes

borghe'sia *nf* middle classes *pl*

'borgo *nm* village; (*quartiere*) district

'bori|a *nf* conceit. **~'oso** *a* conceited

bor'lotto *nm* borlotto bean

boro'talco *nm* talcum powder

bor'raccia *nf* flask

'bors|a *nf* bag; (*borsetta*) handbag; (*valori*) Stock Exchange. **~a dell'acqua calda** hot-water bottle. **~a frigo** coolbox. **~a della spesa** shopping bag. **~a di studio** scholarship. **~ai'olo** *nm* pickpocket. **~el'lino** *nm* purse. **bor-'sista** *nmf Fin* speculator; *Sch* scholarship holder

bor'se|llo *nm* (*portamonete*) purse; (*borsetto*) man's handbag. **~tta** *nf* handbag. **~tto** *nm* man's handbag

bo'scaglia *nf* woodlands *pl*

boscai'olo *nm* woodman; (*guardaboschi*) forester

'bosco *nm* wood. **bo'scoso** *a* wooded

'Bosnia *nf* Bosnia

'bossolo *nm* cartridge case

bo'tanic|a *nf* botany. **~o** *a* botanical ● *nm* botanist

'botola *nf* trapdoor

'botta *nf* blow; (*rumore*) bang; **fare a botte** come to blows. **~ e risposta** *fig* thrust and counter-thrust

'botte *nf* barrel

bot'te|ga *nf* shop; (*di artigiano*) workshop. **~'gaio, -a** *nmf* shopkeeper. **~'ghino** *nm Theatr* box-office; (*del lotto*) lottery-shop

bot'tigli|a *nf* bottle; **in ~a** bottled. **~e'ria** *nf* wine shop

bot'tino *nm* loot; *Mil* booty

'botto *nm* bang; **di ~** all of a sudden

bot'tone *nm* button; *Bot* bud

bo'vino *a* bovine; **bovini** *pl* cattle

box *nm inv* (*per cavalli*) loosebox; (*recinto per bambini*) play-pen

'boxe *nf* boxing

'bozza *nf* draft; *Typ* proof; (*bernoccolo*) bump. **boz'zetto** *nm* sketch

'bozzolo *nm* cocoon

brac'care *vt* hunt

brac'cetto *nm* **a ~** arm in arm

bracci'a|le *nm* bracelet; (*fascia*) armband. **~'letto** *nm* bracelet; (*di orologio*) watch-strap

bracci'ante *nm* day labourer

bracci'ata *nf* (*nel nuoto*) stroke

'bracci|o *nm* (*pl nf* **braccia**) arm; (*di fiume, pl* **bracci**) arm. **~'olo** *nm* (*di sedia*) arm[rest]; (*da nuoto*) armband

'bracco *nm* hound

bracconi'ere *nm* poacher

'brac|e *nf* embers *pl*; **alla ~e** chargrilled. **~i'ere** *nm* brazier. **~'ola** *nf* chop

'brado *a* **allo stato ~** in the wild

'brama *nf* longing. **bra'mare** *vt* long for. **bramo'sia** *nf* yearning

'branca *nf* branch

'branchia *nf* gill

'branco *nm* (*di cani*) pack; (*pej: di persone*) gang

branco'lare *vi* grope

'branda *nf* camp-bed

bran'dello *nm* scrap; **a brandelli** in tatters

bran'dire *vt* brandish

'brano *nm* piece; (*di libro*) passage

Bra'sil|e *nm* Brazil. **b~i'ano, -a** *a & nmf* Brazilian

bra'vata *nf* bragging

'bravo *a* good; (*abile*) clever; (*coraggioso*) brave; **~!** well done!. **bra'vura** *nf* skill

'breccia *nf* breach; **sulla ~** *fig* very successful, at the top

bre'saola *nf dried, salted beef sliced thinly and eaten cold*

bre'tella *nf* shoulder-strap; **bretelle** *pl* (*di calzoni*) braces

'breve *a* brief, short; **in ~** briefly; **tra ~** shortly

brevet'tare *vt* patent. **bre'vetto** *nm* patent; (*attestato*) licence

brevità *nf* shortness

'brezza *nf* breeze

'bricco *nm* jug

bric'cone *nm* blackguard; *hum* rascal

'briciol|a *nf* crumb; *fig* grain. **~o** *nm* fragment

'briga *nf* (*fastidio*) trouble; (*lite*) quarrel; **attaccar ~** pick a quarrel

prendersi la ~ di fare qcsa go to the trouble of doing sth

brigadi'ere *nm (dei carabinieri)* sergeant

bri'gante *nm* bandit; *hum* rogue

bri'gare *vi* intrigue

bri'gata *nf* brigade; *(gruppo)* group

briga'tista *nmf Pol* member of the Red Brigades

'briglia *nf* rein; **a ~ sciolta** at breakneck speed

bril'lante *a* brilliant; *(scintillante)* sparkling ● *nm* diamond

bril'lare *vi* shine; *(metallo:)* glitter; *(scintillare)* sparkle

'brillo *a* tipsy

'brina *nf* hoar-frost

brin'dare *vi* toast; **~ a qcno** drink a toast to sb

'brindisi *nm inv* toast

bri'tannico *a* British

'brivido *nm* shiver; *(di paura ecc)* shudder; *(di emozione)* thrill

brizzo'lato *a* greying

'brocca *nf* jug

broc'cato *nm* brocade

'broccoli *nmpl* broccoli *sg*

bro'daglia *nf pej* dishwater

'brodo *nm* broth; *(per cucinare)* stock. **~ ristretto** consommé

'broglio *nm* **~ elettorale** gerrymandering

bron'chite *nf* bronchitis

'broncio *nm* sulk; **fare il ~** sulk

bronto'l|are *vi* grumble; *(tuono ecc:)* rumble. **~io** *nm* grumbling; *(di tuono)* rumbling. **~one, -a** *nmf* grumbler

'bronzo *nm* bronze

bros'sura *nf* **edizione in ~** paperback

bru'care *vt (pecora:)* graze

bruciacchi'are *vt* scorch

brucia'pelo *adv* **a ~** point-blank

bruci'a|re *vt* burn; *(scottare)* scald; *(incendiare)* set fire to ● *vi* burn; *(scottare)* scald. **~rsi** *vr* burn oneself. **~to** *a* burnt; *fig* burnt-out. **~'tore** *nm* burner. **~'tura** *nf* burn. **bruci'ore** *nm* burning sensation

'bruco *nm* grub

'brufolo *nm* spot

brughi'era *nf* heath

bruli'c|are *vi* swarm. **~hio** *nm* swarming

'brullo *a* bare

'bruma *nf* mist

'bruno *a* brown; *(occhi, capelli)* dark

brusca'mente *adv (di colpo)* suddenly

bru'schetta *nf* toasted bread rubbed with garlic and sprinkled with olive oil

'brusco *a* sharp; *(persona)* brusque, abrupt; *(improvviso)* sudden

bru'sio *nm* buzzing

bru'tal|e *a* brutal. **~ità** *nf inv* brutality. **~iz'zare** *vt* brutalize. **'bruto** *a & nm* brute

brut'tezza *nf* ugliness

'brut|to *a* ugly; *(tempo, tipo, situazione, affare)* nasty; *(cattivo)* bad; **~ta copia** rough copy; **~to tiro** dirty trick. **~'tura** *nf* ugly thing

'buca *nf* hole; *(avvallamento)* hollow. **~ delle lettere** *(a casa)* letter-box

buca'neve *nm inv* snowdrop

bu'car|e *vt* make a hole in; *(pungere)* prick; punch *(biglietti)* ● *vi* have a puncture. **~si** *vr* prick oneself; *(con droga)* shoot up

bu'cato *nm* washing

'buccia *nf* peel, skin

bucherel'lare *vt* riddle

'buco *nm* hole

bu'dello *nm (pl nf* **budella**) bowel

'budget *nm inv* budget

bu'dino *nm* pudding

'bue *nm (pl* **buoi**) ox; **carne di ~** beef

'bufalo *nm* buffalo

bu'fera *nf* storm; *(di neve)* blizzard

buf'fetto *nm* cuff

'buffo *a* funny; *Theat* comic ● *nm* funny thing. **~'nata** *nf (scherzo)* joke. **buf'fone** *nm* buffoon; **fare il buffone** play the fool

bu'gi|a *nf* lie; **~a pietosa** white lie. **~'ardo, -a** *a* lying ● *nmf* liar

bugi'gattolo *nm* cubby-hole

'buio *a* dark ● *nm* darkness; **al ~** in the dark; **~ pesto** pitch dark

'bulbo *nm* bulb; *(dell'occhio)* eyeball

Bulga'ria *nf* Bulgaria. **'bulgaro, -a** *a & nmf* Bulgarian

buli'mia *nf* bulimia. **bu'limico** *a* bulimic

'bullo *nm* bully

bul'lone *nm* bolt

'bunker *nm inv* bunker

buona'fede *nf* good faith

buona'notte *int* good night

buona'sera *int* good evening

buon'giorno *int* good morning; *(di pomeriggio)* good afternoon

buon'grado: di ~ *adv* willingly

buongu'staio, -a *nmf* gourmet. **buon'gusto** *nm* good taste

bu'ono *a* good; ⟨*momento*⟩ right; **dar ~** ⟨*convalidare*⟩ accept; **alla buona** easygoing; ⟨*cena*⟩ informal; **buona notte/sera** good night/evening; **buon compleanno/Natale!** happy birthday/merry Christmas!; **~ senso** common sense; **di buon'ora** early; **una buona volta** once and for all; **buona parte di** the best part of; **tre ore buone** three good hours ● *nm* good; ⟨*in film*⟩ goody; ⟨*tagliando*⟩ voucher; ⟨*titolo*⟩ bond; **con le buone** gently; **~ sconto** money-off coupon ● *nmf* buono, **-a a nulla** dead loss

buontem'pone, -a *nmf* happy-go-lucky person

buonu'more *nm* good temper

buonu'scita *nf* retirement bonus; ⟨*di dirigente*⟩ golden handshake

burat'tino *nm* puppet

'burbero *a* surly; ⟨*nei modi*⟩ rough

bu'rocra|te *nm* bureaucrat. **buro'cra-tico** *a* bureaucratic. **~'zia** *nf* bureaucracy

bur'ra|sca *nf* storm. **~'scoso** *a* stormy

'burro *nm* butter

bur'rone *nm* ravine

bu'scar|e *vt*, **~si** *vr* catch; **~le** *fam* get a hiding

bus'sare *vt* knock

'bussola *nf* compass; **perdere la ~** lose one's bearings

'busta *nf* envelope; ⟨*astuccio*⟩ case. **~ paga** pay packet. **~'rella** *nf* bribe. **bu'stina** *nf* ⟨*di tè*⟩ tea bag; ⟨*per medicine*⟩ sachet

'busto *nm* bust; ⟨*indumento*⟩ girdle

but'tar|e *vt* throw; **~e giù** ⟨*demolire*⟩ knock down; ⟨*inghiottire*⟩ gulp down; scribble down ⟨*scritto*⟩; *fam* put on ⟨*pasta*⟩; ⟨*scoraggiare*⟩ dishearten; **~e via** throw away. **~si** *vr* throw oneself; ⟨*saltare*⟩ jump

butte'rato *a* pock-marked

buz'zurro *nm fam* yokel

Cc

caba'ret *nm inv* cabaret

ca'bina *nf* Naut, Aeron cabin; ⟨*balneare*⟩ beach hut. **~ elettorale** polling booth. **~ di pilotaggio** cockpit. **~ telefonica** telephone box. **cabi'nato** *nm* cabin cruiser

ca'cao *nm* cocoa

'cacca *nf fam* pooh

'caccia *nf* hunt; ⟨*con fucile*⟩ shooting; ⟨*inseguimento*⟩ chase; ⟨*selvaggina*⟩ game ● *nm inv* Aeron fighter; Naut destroyer

cacciabombardi'ere *nm* fighter-bomber

cacciagi'one *nf* game

cacci'a|re *vt* hunt; ⟨*mandar via*⟩ chase away; ⟨*scacciare*⟩ drive out; ⟨*ficcare*⟩ shove ● *vi* go hunting. **~rsi** *vr* ⟨*nascondersi*⟩ hide; ⟨*andare a finire*⟩ get to; **~rsi nei guai** get into trouble; **alla ~'tora** *a* Culin chasseur. **~'tore, ~'trice** *nmf* hunter. **~tore di frodo** poacher

caccia'vite *nm inv* screwdriver

ca'chet *nm inv* Med capsule; ⟨*colorante*⟩ colour rinse; ⟨*stile*⟩ cachet

'cachi *nm inv* ⟨*albero, frutta*⟩ persimmon

'cacio *nm* ⟨*formaggio*⟩ cheese

'caco *nm fam* ⟨*frutto*⟩ persimmon

'cactus *nm inv* cactus

ca'da|vere *nm* corpse. **~'verico** *a fig* deathly pale

ca'dente *a* falling; ⟨*casa*⟩ crumbling

ca'denza *nf* cadence; ⟨*ritmo*⟩ rhythm; Mus cadenza

ca'dere *vi* fall; ⟨*capelli ecc:*⟩ fall out; ⟨*capitombolare*⟩ tumble; ⟨*vestito ecc:*⟩ hang; **far ~** ⟨*di mano*⟩ drop; **~ dal sonno** feel very sleepy; **lasciar ~** drop; **~ dalle nuvole** *fig* be taken aback

ca'detto *nm* cadet

ca'duta *nf* fall; ⟨*di capelli*⟩ loss; *fig* downfall

caffè *nm inv* coffee; ⟨*locale*⟩ café. **~ corretto** espresso coffee with a dash of liqueur. **~ lungo** weak black coffee. **~ macchiato** coffee with a dash of milk.

~ ristretto extra-strong espresso coffee. **~ solubile** instant coffee. **~'ina** nf caffeine. **~'latte** nm inv white coffee.

caffetti'era nf coffee-pot

cafo'naggine nf boorishness

cafo'nata nf boorishness

ca'fone, -a nmf boor

ca'gare vi fam crap

cagio'nare vt cause

cagio'nevole a delicate

cagli'ar|e vi, **~si** vr curdle

'cagna nf bitch

ca'gnara nf fam din

ca'gnesco a **guardare qcno in ~** scowl at sb

'cala nf creek

cala'brone nm hornet

cala'maio nm inkpot

cala'mari nmpl squid

cala'mita nf magnet

calamità nf inv calamity

ca'lar|e vi come down; ⟨vento:⟩ drop; (diminuire) fall; (tramontare) set ● vt (abbassare) lower; (nei lavori a maglia) decrease ● nm (di luna) waning. **~si** vr lower oneself

'calca nf throng

cal'cagno nm heel

cal'care[1] nm limestone

cal'care[2] vt tread; (premere) press [down]; **~ la mano** exaggerate; **~ le orme di qcno** fig follow in sb's footsteps

'calce[1] nf lime

'calce[2] nm **in ~** at the foot of the page

calce'struzzo nm concrete

cal'cetto nm Sport five-a-side [football]

calci'a|re vt kick. **~'tore** nm footballer

cal'cina nf mortar

calci'naccio nm (pezzo di intonaco) flake of plaster

'calcio[1] nm kick; Sport football; (di arma da fuoco) butt; **dare un ~ a** kick. **~ d'angolo** corner [kick]

'calcio[2] nm (chimica) calcium

'calco nm (con carta) tracing; (arte) cast

calco'la|re vt calculate; (considerare) consider. **~'tore** a calculating ● nm calculator; (macchina elettronica) computer

'calcolo nm calculation; Med stone

cal'daia nf boiler

caldar'rosta nf roast chestnut

caldeggi'are vt support

'caldo a warm; (molto caldo) hot ● nm

heat; **avere ~** be warm/hot; **fa ~** it is warm/hot

calen'dario nm calendar

'calibro nm calibre; (strumento) callipers pl; **di grosso ~** ⟨persona⟩ top attrib

'calice nm goblet; Relig chalice

ca'ligine nm fog; (industriale) smog

calligra'fia nf handwriting; ⟨cinese⟩ calligraphy

cal'lista nmf chiropodist. **'callo** nm corn; **fare il callo a** become hardened to. **cal'loso** a callous

'calma nf calm. **cal'mante** a calming ● nm sedative. **cal'mare** vt calm [down]; (lenire) soothe. **cal'marsi** vr calm down; ⟨vento:⟩ drop; ⟨dolore:⟩ die down. **calmo** a calm

'calo nm Comm fall; (di volume) shrinkage; (di peso) loss

calorosa'mente adv (cordialmente) warmly

ca'lore nm heat; (moderato) warmth; **in ~** ⟨animale⟩ on heat. **calo'roso** a warm

calo'ria nf calorie

ca'lorico a calorific

calo'rifero nm radiator

calpe'stare vt trample [down]; fig trample on ⟨diritti, sentimenti⟩; **vietato ~ l'erba** keep off the grass

calpe'stio nm (passi) footsteps

ca'lunni|a nf slander. **~'are** vt slander. **~'oso** a slanderous

ca'lura nf heat

cal'vario nm Calvary; fig trial

cal'vizie nf baldness. **'calvo** a bald

'calz|a nf (da donna) stocking; (da uomo) sock. **~a'maglia** nf tights pl; (per danza) leotard

cal'zante a fig fitting

cal'za|re vt (indossare) wear; (mettersi) put on ● vi fit

calza'scarpe nm inv shoehorn

calza'tura nf footwear

calzatur'ificio nm shoe factory

cal'zetta nf **è una mezza ~** fig he's no use

calzet'tone nm knee-length woollen sock. **cal'zino** nm sock

calzo'l|aio nm shoemaker. **~e'ria** nf (negozio) shoe shop

calzon'cini nmpl shorts. **~ da bagno** swimming trunks

cal'zone nm Culin folded pizza with tomato and mozzarella or ricotta inside

cal'zoni nmpl trousers, pants Am

camale'onte nm chameleon

cambi'ale *nf* bill of exchange

cambia'mento *nm* change

cambi'ar|e *vt/i* change; move ⟨*casa*⟩; (*fare cambio di*) exchange; **~e rotta** *Naut* alter course. **~si** *vr* change. **'cambio** *nm* change; (*Comm, scambio*) exchange; *Mech* gear; **dare il ~ a** qcno relieve sb; **in ~ di** in exchange for

'camera *nf* room; (*mobili*) [bedroom] suite; *Phot* camera; **C~** *Pol, Comm* Chamber. **~ ardente** funeral parlour. **~ d'aria** inner tube. **C~ di Commercio** Chamber of Commerce. **C~ dei Deputati** *Pol* ≈ House of Commons. **~ doppia** double room. **~ da letto** bedroom. **~ matrimoniale** double room. **~ oscura** darkroom. **~ singola** single room

came'rata¹ *nf* (*dormitorio*) dormitory; *Mil* barrack room

came'ra|ta² *nmf* (*amico*) mate; *Pol* comrade. **~'tismo** *nm* comradeship

cameri'era *nf* maid; (*di ristorante*) waitress; (*in albergo*) chamber-maid; (*di bordo*) stewardess

cameri'ere *nm* manservant; (*di ristorante*) waiter; (*di bordo*) steward

came'rino *nm* dressing-room

'camice *nm* overall. **cami'cetta** *nf* blouse. **ca'micia** *nf* shirt; **uovo in ~** poached egg. **camicia da notte** nightdress

cami'netto *nm* fireplace

ca'mino *nm* chimney; (*focolare*) fireplace

'camion *nm inv* lorry *Br*, truck

camion'cino *nm* van

camio'netta *nf* jeep

camio'nista *nm* lorry driver *Br*, truck driver

cam'mello *nm* camel; (*tessuto*) camelhair ● *a inv* (*colore*) camel

cam'meo *nm* cameo

cammi'na|re *vi* walk; ⟨*auto, orologio:*⟩ go. **~ta** *nf* walk; **fare una ~ta** go for a walk. **cam'mino** *nm* way; **essere in ~** be on the way; **mettersi in ~** set out

camo'milla *nf* camomile; (*bevanda*) camomile tea

ca'morra *nf* local mafia

ca'moscio *nm* chamois; (*pelle*) suede

cam'pagna *nf* country; (*paesaggio*) countryside; *Comm, Mil* campaign; **in ~** in the country. **~ elettorale** election campaign. **~ pubblicitaria** marketing campaign. **campa'gnolo, -a** *a* rustic ● *nm* countryman ● *nf* countrywoman

cam'pale *a* field *attrib*; **giornata ~** *fig* strenuous day

cam'pa|na *nf* bell; (*di vetro*) belljar. **~'nella** (*di tenda*) curtain ring. **~'nello** *nm* door-bell; (*cicalino*) buzzer

campa'nile *nm* belfry

campani'lismo *nm* parochialism

campani'lista *nmf* person with a parochial outlook

cam'panula *nf Bot* campanula

cam'pare *vi* live; (*a stento*) get by

cam'pato *a* **~ in aria** unfounded

campeggi'a|re *vi* camp; (*spiccare*) stand out. **~'tore**, **~'trice** *nmf* camper. **cam'peggio** *nm* camping; (*terreno*) campsite

cam'pestre *a* rural

'camping *nm inv* campsite

campio'nari|o *nm* [set of] samples ● *a* samples; **fiera ~a** trade fair

campio'nato *nm* championship

campiona'tura *nf* (*di merce*) range of samples

campi'on|e *nm* champion; *Comm* sample; (*esemplare*) specimen. **~'essa** *nf* ladies' champion

'campo *nm* field; (*accampamento*) camp. **~ da calcio** football pitch. **~ di concentramento** concentration camp. **~ da golf** golf course. **~ da tennis** tennis court

campo'santo *nm* cemetery

camuf'far|e *vt* disguise. **~si** *vr* disguise oneself

'Cana|da *nm* Canada. **~'dese** *a & nmf* Canadian

ca'naglia *nf* scoundrel; (*plebaglia*) rabble

ca'nal|e *nm* channel; (*artificiale*) canal. **~iz'zare** *vt* channel ⟨*acque*⟩. **~izzazi'one** *nf* channelling; (*rete*) pipes *pl*

'canapa *nf* hemp

cana'rino *nm* canary

cancel'la|re *vt* cross out; (*con la gomma*) rub out; *fig* wipe out; (*annullare*) cancel; *Comput* delete, erase. **~'tura** *nf* erasure. **~zi'one** *nf* cancellation; *Comput* deletion

cancelle'ria *nf* chancellery; (*articoli per scrivere*) stationery

cancelli'ere *nm* chancellor; (*di tribunale*) clerk

can'cello *nm* gate

cance'ro|geno *nm* carcinogen ● *a* carcinogenic. **~'roso** *a* cancerous

can'crena *nf* gangrene

'cancro *nm* cancer. **C~** *Astr* Cancer

candeg'gi|na *nf* bleach. **~'are** *vt* bleach. **can'deggio** *nm* bleaching

can'de|la *nf* candle; *Auto* spark plug; **~'labro** *nm* candelabra. **~li'ere** *nm* candlestick

cande'lotto *nm* (*di dinamite*) stick

candida'mente *adv* candidly

candi'da|rsi *vr* stand as a candidate. **~to, -a** *nmf* candidate. **~'tura** *nf Pol* candidacy; (*per lavoro*) application

'candido *a* snow-white; (*sincero*) candid; (*puro*) pure

can'dito *a* candied

can'dore *nm* whiteness; *fig* innocence

'cane *nm* dog; (*di arma da fuoco*) cock; **un tempo da cani** foul weather. **~ da caccia** hunting dog

ca'nestro *nm* basket

cangi'ante *a* iridescent; **seta ~** shot silk

can'guro *nm* kangaroo

ca'nile *nm* kennel; (*di allevamento*) kennels *pl*. **~ municipale** dog pound

ca'nino *a & nm* canine

'canna *nf* reed; (*da zucchero*) cane; (*di fucile*) barrel; (*bastone*) stick; (*di bicicletta*) crossbar; (*asta*) rod; (*fam: hascish*) joint; **povero in ~** destitute. **~ da pesca** fishing-rod

can'nella *nf* cinnamon

can'neto *nm* bed of reeds

can'niba|le *nm* cannibal. **~'lismo** *nm* cannibalism

cannocchi'ale *nm* telescope

canno'nata *nf* cannon shot; **è una ~** *fig* it's brilliant

cannon'cino *nm* (*dolce*) cream horn

can'none *nm* cannon; *fig* ace

can'nuccia *nf* [drinking] straw; (*di pipa*) stem

ca'noa *nf* canoe

'canone *nm* canon; (*affitto*) rent; **equo ~** fair rents act

ca'noni|co *nm* canon. **~z'zare** *vt* canonize. **~zzazi'one** *nf* canonization

ca'noro *a* melodious

ca'notta *nf* (*estiva*) vest top

canot'taggio *nm* canoeing; (*voga*) rowing

canotti'era *nf* singlet

canotti'ere *nm* oarsman

ca'notto *nm* [rubber] dinghy

cano'vaccio *nm* (*trama*) plot; (*straccio*) duster

can'tante *nmf* singer

can't|are *vt/i* sing. **~au'tore, ~a-'trice** *nmf* singer-songwriter. **~icchi'are** *vt* sing softly; (*a bocca chiusa*) hum

canti'ere *nm* yard; *Naut* shipyard; (*di edificio*) construction site. **~ navale** naval dockyard

canti'lena *nf* singsong; (*ninna-nanna*) lullaby

can'tina *nf* cellar; (*osteria*) wine shop

'canto¹ *nm* singing; (*canzone*) song; *Relig* chant; (*poesia*) poem

'canto² *nm* (*angolo*) corner; (*lato*) side; **dal ~ mio** for my part; **d'altro ~** on the other hand

canto'nata *nf* **prendere una ~** *fig* be sadly mistaken

can'tone *nm* canton; (*angolo*) corner

can'tuccio *nm* nook

canzo'na|re *vt* tease. **~'torio** *a* teasing. **~'tura** *nf* teasing

can'zo|ne *nf* song. **~'netta** *nf fam* pop song. **~ni'ere** *nm* songbook

'caos *nm* chaos. **ca'otico** *a* chaotic

C.A.P. *nm abbr* (**Codice di Avviamento Postale**) post code, zip code *Am*

ca'pac|e *a* able; (*esperto*) skilled; (*stadio, contenitore*) big; **~e di** (*disposto a*) capable of. **~ità** *nf inv* ability; (*attitudine*) skill; (*capienza*) capacity

capaci'tarsi *vr* **~ di** (*rendersi conto*) understand; (*accorgersi*) realize

ca'panna *nf* hut

capan'nello *nm* **fare ~ intorno a qcno/qcsa** gather round sb/sth

capan'none *nm* shed; *Aeron* hangar

ca'parbio *a* obstinate

ca'parra *nf* deposit

capa'tina *nf* short visit; **fare una ~ in città/da qcno** pop into town/in on sb

ca'pel|lo *nm* hair; **~li** *pl* (*capigliatura*) hair *sg*. **~'lone** *nm* hippie. **~'luto** *a* hairy

capez'zale *nm* bolster; *fig* bedside

ca'pezzolo *nm* nipple

capi'en|te *a* capacious. **~za** *nf* capacity

capiglia'tura *nf* hair

ca'pire *vt* understand; **~ male** misunderstand; **si capisce!** naturally!; **sì, ho capito** yes, I see

capi'ta|le *a Jur* capital; (*principale*) main ● *nf* (*città*) capital ● *nm Comm* capital. **~'lismo** *nm* capitalism. **~'lista** *nmf* capitalist. **~'listico** *a* capitalist

capitane'ria *nf* **~ di porto** port authorities *pl*

capi'tano *nm* captain

capi'tare *vi* (*giungere per caso*) come; (*accadere*) happen

capi'tello *nm Archit* capital

capito'la|re vi capitulate. **~zi'one** nf capitulation

ca'pitolo nm chapter

capi'tombolo nm headlong fall; **fare un ~** tumble down

'capo nm head; (chi comanda) boss fam; (di vestiario) item; Geog cape; (in tribù) chief; (parte estrema) top; **a ~** (in detta-to) new paragraph; **da ~** over again; **in ~ a un mese** within a month; **gira-mento di ~** dizziness; **mal di ~** head-ache; **~ d'abbigliamento** item of clothing. **~ d'accusa** Jur charge, count. **~ di bestiame** head of cattle

capo'banda nm Mus bandmaster; (di delinquenti) ringleader

ca'poccia nm (fam: testa) nut

capocci'one, -a nmf fam brainbox

capo'danno nm New Year's Day

capofa'miglia nm head of the family

capo'fitto nm **a ~** headlong

capo'giro nm giddiness

capola'voro nm masterpiece

capo'linea nm terminus

capo'lino nm **fare ~** peep in

capolu'ogo nm main town

capo'rale nm lance-corporal

capo'squadra nmf Sport team cap-tain

capo'stipite nmf (di famiglia) pro-genitor

capo'tavola nmf head of the table

capo'treno nm guard

capouf'ficio nmf head clerk

capo'verso nm first line

capo'vol|gere vt overturn; fig re-verse. **~gersi** vr overturn; ‹barca:› capsize; fig be reversed. **~to** pp di **capovolgere ●** a upside-down

'cappa nf cloak; (di camino) cowl; (di cucina) hood

cap'pel|la nf chapel. **~'lano** nm chap-lain

cap'pello nm hat. **~ a cilindro** top hat

'cappero nm caper

'cappio nm noose

cap'pone nm capon

cap'potto nm [over]coat

cappuc'cino nm (frate) Capuchin; (bevanda) white coffee

cap'puccio nm hood; (di penna stilo-grafica) cap

'capra nf goat. **ca'pretto** nm kid

ca'pricci|o nm whim; (bizzarria) freak; **fare i capricci** have tantrums. **~'oso** a capricious; ‹bambino:› naughty

Capri'corno nm Astr Capricorn

capri'ola nf somersault

capri'olo nm roe-deer

'capro nm [billy-]goat. **~ espiatorio** scapegoat. **ca'prone** nm [billy] goat

'capsula nf capsule; (di proiettile) cap; (di dente) crown

cap'tare vt Radio, TV pick up; catch ‹attenzione›

cara'bina nf carbine

carabini'ere nm carabiniere; **carabi-ni'eri** pl Italian police force (which is a branch of the army)

ca'raffa nf carafe

Ca'raibi nmpl (zona) Caribbean sg; (isole) Caribbean Islands; **il mar dei ~** the Caribbean [Sea]

cara'mella nf sweet

cara'mello nm caramel

ca'rato nm carat

ca'ratte|re nm character; (caratteri-stica) characteristic; Typ type; **di buon ~re** good-natured. **~'ristico, -a** a char-acteristic; (pittoresco) quaint ● nf char-acteristic. **~riz'zare** vt characterize

carbon'cino nm (per disegno) char-coal

car'bone nm coal

carboniz'zare vt burn to a cinder

carbu'rante nm fuel

carbura'tore nm carburettor

car'cassa nf carcass; fig old wreck

carce'ra|rio a prison attrib. **~to, -a** nmf prisoner. **~zi'one** nf imprison-ment. **~zione preventiva** preventive detention

'carcer|e nm prison; (punizione) im-prisonment. **~i'ere, -a** nmf gaoler

carci'ofo nm artichoke

car'diaco a cardiac

cardi'nale a & nm cardinal

'cardine nm hinge

cardio'chi'rurgo nm heart surgeon. **~lo'gia** nf cardiology. **cardi'ologo** nm heart specialist. **~'tonico** nm heart stimulant

'cardo nm thistle

ca'rena nf Naut bottom

ca'ren|te a **~te di** lacking in. **~za** nf lack; (scarsità) scarcity

care'stia nf famine; (mancanza) dearth

ca'rezza nf caress; **fare una ~ a** ca-ress

cari'a|rsi vi decay. **~to** a decayed

'carica nf office; Mil, Electr charge; fig drive. **cari'care** vt load; Mil, Electr charge; wind up ‹orologio›. **~'tore** nm (per proiettile) magazine

carica'tu|ra *nf* caricature. **~'rale** *a* grotesque. **~'rista** *nmf* caricaturist

'carico *a* loaded (**di** with); ⟨*colore*⟩ strong; ⟨*orologio*⟩ wound [up]; ⟨*batteria*⟩ charged ● *nm* load; ⟨*di nave*⟩ cargo; ⟨*il caricare*⟩ loading; **a ~ di** *Comm* to be charged to; ⟨*persona*⟩ dependent on

'carie *nf* [tooth] decay

ca'rino *a* pretty; ⟨*piacevole*⟩ agreeable

ca'risma *nm* charisma. **cari'smatico** *a* charismatic

carit|à *nf* charity; **per ~à!** ⟨*come rifiuto*⟩ God forbid!. **~a'tevole** *a* charitable

carnagi'one *nf* complexion

car'naio *nm* *fig* shambles

car'nale *a* carnal; **cugino ~** first cousin

'carne *nf* flesh; ⟨*alimento*⟩ meat; **~ di manzo/maiale/vitello** beef/pork/veal

car'nefi|ce *nm* executioner. **~'cina** *nf* slaughter

carne'va|le *nm* carnival. **~'lesco** *a* carnival

car'nivoro *nm* carnivore ● *a* carnivorous

car'noso *a* fleshy

'caro, -a *a* dear; **cari saluti** kind regards ● *nmf fam* darling, dear; **i miei cari** my nearest and dearest

ca'rogna *nf* carcass; *fig* bastard

caro'sello *nm* merry-go-round

ca'rota *nf* carrot

caro'vana *nf* caravan; ⟨*di veicoli*⟩ convoy

caro'vita *nm* high cost of living

'carpa *nf* carp

carpenti'ere *nm* carpenter

car'pire *vt* seize; ⟨*con difficoltà*⟩ extort

car'pone, car'poni *adv* on all fours

car'rabile *a* suitable for vehicles; **passo ~** *vedi* **carraio**

car'raio a passo *nm* **~** entrance to driveway, garage etc where parking is forbidden

carreggi'ata *nf* roadway; **doppia ~** dual carriageway, divided highway *Am*

carrel'lata *nf* TV pan

car'rello *nm* trolley; ⟨*di macchina da scrivere*⟩ carriage; *Aeron* undercarriage; *Cinema*, *TV* dolly. **~ d'atterraggio** *Aeron* landing gear

car'retto *nm* cart

carri'e|ra *nf* career; **di gran ~ra** at full speed; **fare ~ra** get on. **~'rismo** *nm* careerism

carri'ola *nf* wheelbarrow

'carro *nm* cart. **~ armato** tank. **~ attrezzi** breakdown vehicle, wrecker *Am*. **~ funebre** hearse. **~ merci** truck

car'rozza *nf* carriage; *Rail* car, coach. **~ cuccette** sleeping car. **~ ristorante** restaurant car

carroz'zella *nf* ⟨*per bambini*⟩ pram; ⟨*per invalidi*⟩ wheelchair

carrozze'ria *nf* bodywork; ⟨*officina*⟩ bodyshop

carroz'zina *nf* pram; ⟨*pieghevole*⟩ push-chair, stroller *Am*

carroz'zone *nm* ⟨*di circo*⟩ caravan

'carta *nf* paper; ⟨*da gioco*⟩ card; ⟨*statuto*⟩ charter; *Geog* map. **~ d'argento** ≈ senior citizens' railcard. **~ assorbente** blotting-paper. **~ di credito** credit card. **~ geografica** map. **~ d'identità** identity card. **~ igienica** toilet-paper. **~ d'imbarco** boarding card. **~ da lettere** writing-paper. **~ da parati** wallpaper. **~ stagnola** silver paper; *Culin* aluminium foil. **~ straccia** waste paper. **~ stradale** road map. **~ velina** tissue-paper. **~ verde** *Auto* green card. **~ vetrata** sandpaper

cartacar'bone *nf* carbon paper

car'taccia *nf* waste paper

carta'modello *nm* pattern

cartamo'neta *nf* paper money

carta'pesta *nf* papier mâché

carta'straccia *nf* waste paper

cartave'trare *vt* sand [down]

car'tel|la *nf* ⟨*per documenti ecc*⟩ briefcase; ⟨*di cartone*⟩ folder; ⟨*di scolaro*⟩ satchel. **~la clinica** medical record. **~'lina** *nf* document wallet, folder

cartel'lino *nm* label; ⟨*dei prezzi*⟩ pricetag; ⟨*di presenza*⟩ time-card; **timbrare il ~** clock in; ⟨*all'uscita*⟩ clock out

car'tel|lo *nm* sign; ⟨*pubblicitario*⟩ poster; ⟨*stradale*⟩ road sign; ⟨*di protesta*⟩ placard: *Comm* cartel. **~'lone** *nm* poster; *Theat* bill

carti'era *nf* paper-mill

carti'lagine *nf* cartilage

car'tina *nf* map

car'toccio *nm* paper bag; **al ~** *Culin* baked in foil

carto'|laio, -a *nmf* stationer. **~le'ria** *nf* stationer's [shop]. **~libre'ria** *nf* stationer's and book shop

carto'lina *nf* postcard. **~ postale** postcard

carto'mante *nmf* fortune-teller

carton'cino *nm* ⟨*materiale*⟩ card

car'tone *nm* cardboard; ⟨*arte*⟩ cartoon. **~ animato** [animated] cartoon

car'tuccia *nf* cartridge

'**casa** *nf* house; (*abitazione propria*) home; (*ditta*) firm; **amico di ~** family friend; **andare a ~** go home; **essere di ~** be like one of the family; **fatto in ~** home-made; **padrone di ~** (*di pensione ecc*) landlord; (*proprietario*) house owner. **~ di cura** nursing home. **~ popolare** council house. **~ dello studente** hall of residence

ca'**sacca** *nf* military coat; (*giacca*) jacket

ca'**saccio** *adv* **a ~** at random

casa'**ling|a** *nf* housewife. **~o** *a* domestic; (*fatto in casa*) home-made; (*amante della casa*) home-loving; (*semplice*) homely

ca'**scante** *a* falling; (*floscio*) flabby

ca'**sca|re** *vi* fall [down]. **~ta** *nf* (*di acqua*) waterfall

ca'**schetto** *nm* [**capelli a**] **~** bob

ca'**scina** *nf* farm building

'**casco** *nm* crash-helmet; (*asciuga-capelli*) [hair-]drier; **~ di banane** bunch of bananas

caseggi'**ato** *nm* block of flats *Br*, apartment block

casei'**ficio** *nm* dairy

ca'**sella** *nf* pigeon-hole. **~ postale** post office box; *Comput* mailbox

casel'**lante** *nmf* (*per treni*) signalman

casel'**lario** *nm* **~ giudiziario** record of convictions; **avere il ~ giudiziario vergine** have no criminal record

ca'**sello** [**autostra'dale**] *nm* [motorway] toll booth

case'**reccio** *a* home-made

ca'**serma** *nf* barracks *pl*; (*dei carabinieri*) [police] station

casi'**nista** *nmf fam* muddler. ca'**sino** *nm fam* (*bordello*) brothel; (*fig: confusione*) racket; (*disordine*) mess; **un casino di** loads of

casi'**nò** *nm inv* casino

ca'**sistica** *nf* (*classificazione*) case records *pl*

'**caso** *nm* chance; (*fatto, circostanza, Med, Gram*) case; **a ~** at random; **~ mai** if need be; **far ~** pay attention to; **non far ~ a** take no account of; **per ~** by chance. **~ [giudiziario]** [legal] case

caso'**lare** *nm* farmhouse

'**caspita** *int* good gracious!

'**cassa** *nf* till; *Comm* cash; (*luogo di pagamento*) cash desk; (*mobile*) chest; (*istituto bancario*) bank. **~ automatica prelievi** cash dispenser, automatic teller. **~ da morto** coffin. **~ toracica** ribcage

cassa'**forte** *nf* safe

cassa'**panca** *nf* linen chest

casseru'**ola** *nf* saucepan

cas'**setta** *nf* case; (*per registratore*) cassette. **~ delle lettere** postbox, letterbox. **~ di sicurezza** strong-box

cas'**set|to** *nm* drawer. **~'tone** *nm* chest of drawers

cassi'**ere, -a** *nmf* cashier; (*di supermercato*) checkout assistant, checkout operator; (*di banca*) teller

'**casta** *nf* caste

ca'**stagn|a** *nf* chestnut. casta'**gneto** *nm* chestnut grove. **~o** *nm* chestnut[-tree]

ca'**stano** *a* chestnut

ca'**stello** *nm* castle; (*impalcatura*) scaffold

casti'**gare** *vt* punish

casti'**gato** *a* (*casto*) chaste

ca'**stigo** *nm* punishment

castità *nf* chastity. '**casto** *a* chaste

ca'**storo** *nm* beaver

ca'**strare** *vt* castrate

casu'**al|e** *a* chance *attrib*. **~'mente** *adv* by chance

ca'**supola** *nf* little house

cata'**clisma** *nm fig* upheaval

cata'**comba** *nf* catacomb

cata'**fascio** *nm* **andare a ~** go to rack and ruin

cata'**litico** *a* **marmitta catalitica** *Auto* catalytic converter

cataliz'**za|re** *vt fig* heighten. **~'tore** *nm Auto* catalytic converter

catalo'**gare** *vt* catalogue. ca'**talogo** *nm* catalogue

catama'**rano** *nm* (*da diporto*) catamaran

cata'**pecchia** *nf* hovel; *fam* dump

catapul'**tar|e** *vt* (*scaraventare fuori*) eject. **~si** *vr* (*precipitarsi*) dive

catarifran'**gente** *nm* reflector

ca'**tarro** *nm* catarrh

ca'**tasta** *nf* pile

ca'**tasto** *nm* land register

ca'**tastrofe** *nf* catastrophe. cata'**strofico** *a* catastrophic

cate'**chismo** *nm* catechism

cate|go'**ria** *nf* category. **~'gorico** *a* categorical

ca'**tena** *nf* chain. **~ montuosa** mountain range. **catene** *pl* **da neve** tyre-chains. **cate'naccio** *nm* bolt

cate'|**nella** *nf* (*collana*) chain. **~'nina** *nf* chain

cate'**ratta** *nf* cataract

ca'**terva** *nf* **una ~ di** heaps of

cati'nell|a *nf* basin; **piovere a ~e** bucket down

ca'tino *nm* basin

ca'torcio *nm fam* old wreck

ca'trame *nm* tar

'cattedra *nf* (*tavolo di insegnante*) desk; (*di università*) chair

catte'drale *nf* cathedral

catti'veria *nf* wickedness; (*azione*) wicked action

cattività *nf* captivity

cat'tivo *a* bad; ‹*bambino*› naughty

cattoli'cesimo *nm* Catholicism

cat'tolico, -a *a & nmf* [Roman] Catholic

cat'tu|ra *nf* capture. **~'rare** *vt* capture

caucciù *nm* rubber

'causa *nf* cause; *Jur* lawsuit; **far ~ a qcno** sue sb. **cau'sare** *vt* cause

'caustico *a* caustic

cauta'mente *adv* cautiously

cau'tela *nf* caution

caute'lar|e *vt* protect. **~si** *vr* take precautions

cauteriz'z|are *vt* cauterize. **~i'one** *nf* cauterization

'cauto *a* cautious

cauzi'one *nf* security; (*per libertà provvisoria*) bail

'cava *nf* quarry; *fig* mine

caval'ca|re *vt* ride; (*stare a cavalcioni*) sit astride. **~ta** *nf* ride; (*corteo*) cavalcade. **~'via** *nm* flyover

cavalci'oni *adv* **a ~** astride

cavali'ere *nm* rider; (*titolo*) knight; (*accompagnatore*) escort; (*al ballo*) partner

cavalle|'resco *a* chivalrous. **~'ria** *nf* chivalry; *Mil* cavalry. **~'rizzo, -a** *nm* horseman ● *nf* horsewoman

caval'letta *nf* grasshopper

caval'letto *nm* trestle; (*di macchina fotografica*) tripod; (*di pittore*) easel

caval'lina *nf* (*ginnastica*) horse

ca'vallo *nm* horse; (*misura di potenza*) horsepower; (*scacchi*) knight; (*dei pantaloni*) crotch; **a ~** on horseback; **andare a ~** go horse-riding. **~ a dondolo** rocking-horse

caval'lone *nm* (*ondata*) roller

caval'luccio ma'rino *nm* sea horse

ca'var|e *vt* take out; (*di dosso*) take off; **~sela** get away with it; **se la cava bene** he's/she's doing all right

cava'tappi *nm inv* corkscrew

ca'ver|na *nf* cave. **~'noso** *a* ‹*voce*› deep

'cavia *nf* guinea-pig

cavi'ale *nm* caviar

ca'viglia *nf* ankle

cavil'lare *vi* quibble. **ca'villo** *nm* quibble

cavità *nf inv* cavity

'cavo *a* hollow ● *nm* cavity; (*di metallo*) cable; *Naut* rope

cavo'lata *nf fam* rubbish

cavo'letto *nm* **~ di Bruxelles** Brussels sprout

cavolfi'ore *nm* cauliflower

'cavolo *nm* cabbage; **~!** *fam* sugar!

caz'zo *int vulg* fuck!

caz'zott|o *nm* punch; **prendere qcno a ~i** beat sb up

cazzu'ola *nf* trowel

c/c *abbr* (**conto corrente**) c/a

CD-Rom *nm inv* CD-Rom

ce *pron pers* (*a noi*) (to) us ● *adv* there; **~ ne sono molti** there are many

'cece *nm* chick-pea

cecità *nf* blindness

ceco, -a *a & nmf* Czech; **la Repubblica Ceca** the Czech Republic

Cecoslo'vacc|hia *nf* Czechoslovakia. **c~o, -a** *a & nmf* Czechoslovak

'cedere *vi* (*arrendersi*) surrender; (*concedere*) yield; (*sprofondare*) subside ● *vt* give up; make over ‹*proprietà ecc*›. **ce'devole** *a* ‹*terreno ecc*› soft; *fig* yielding. **cedi'mento** *nm* (*di terreno*) subsidence

'cedola *nf* coupon

'cedro *nm* (*albero*) cedar; (*frutto*) citron

C.E.E. *nf abbr* (**Communità Economica Europea**) E[E]C

'ceffo *nm* (*muso*) snout; (*pej: persona*) mug

cef'fone *nm* slap

ce'lar|e *vt* conceal. **~si** *vr* hide

cele'bra|re *vt* celebrate. **~zi'one** *nf* celebration

'celebr|e *a* famous. **~ità** *nf inv* celebrity

'celere *a* swift

ce'leste *a* (*divino*) heavenly ● *a & nm* (*colore*) sky-blue

celi'bato *nm* celibacy

'celibe *a* single ● *nm* bachelor

'cella *nf* cell

'cellofan *nm inv* cellophane; *Culin* cling film

'cellula *nf* cell. **~ fotoelettrica** electronic eye

cellu'lare *nm* (*telefono*) cellular phone ● *a* **furgone ~** police van; **telefono ~** cellular phone

cellu'lite *nf* cellulite
cellu'loide *a* celluloid
cellu'losa *nf* cellulose
'celt|a *nm* Celt. **~ico** *a* Celtic
cemen'tare *vt* cement. **ce'mento** *nm* cement. **cemento armato** reinforced concrete
'cena *nf* dinner; (*leggera*) supper
ce'nare *vi* have dinner
'cenci|o *nm* rag; (*per spolverare*) duster. **~'oso** *a* in rags
'cenere *nf* ash; (*di carbone ecc*) cinders
ce'netta *nf* (*cena semplice*) informal dinner
'cenno *nm* sign; (*col capo*) nod; (*con la mano*) wave; (*allusione*) hint; (*breve resoconto*) mention
ce'none *nm* il **~ di Capodanno/Natale** special New Year's Eve/Christmas Eve dinner
censi'mento *nm* census
cen's|ore *nm* censor. **~ura** *nf* censorship. **~u'rare** *vt* censor
'cent *nm inv* cent
centelli'nare *vt* sip
cente'n|ario, -a *a & nmf* centenarian ● *nm* (*commemorazione*) centenary. **~'nale** *a* centennial
cen'tesimo *a* hundredth ● *nm* (*di moneta*) cent; **non avere un ~** be penniless
cen'ti|grado *a* centigrade. **~metro** *nm* centimetre
centi'naio *nm* hundred
'cento *a & nm* a *or* one hundred; **per ~** per cent
centome'trista *nmf* Sport one hundred metres runner
cento'mila *nm* a *or* one hundred thousand
cen'trale *a* central ● *nf* (*di società ecc*) head office. **~ atomica** atomic power station. **~ elettrica** power station. **~ nucleare** nuclear power station. **~ telefonica** [telephone] exchange
centra'li|na *nf* Teleph switchboard. **~'nista** *nmf* operator
centra'lino *nm* Teleph exchange; (*di albergo ecc*) switchboard
centra'li|smo *nm* centralism. **~z'zare** *vt* centralize
cen'trare *vt* **~ qcsa** hit sth in the centre; (*fissare nel centro*) centre; *fig* hit on the head (*idea*)
cen'trifu|ga *nf* spin-drier. **~ [asciugaverdure]** shaker. **~'gare** *vt* Techn centrifuge; (*lavatrice:*) spin
cen'trino *nm* doily

'centro *nm* centre. **~ [città]** city centre. **~ commerciale** shopping centre, mall. **~ sociale** community centre
'ceppo *nm* (*di albero*) stump; (*da ardere*) log; (*fig: gruppo*) stock
'cera *nf* wax; (*aspetto*) look. **~ per il pavimento** floor-polish
ce'ramica *nf* (*arte*) ceramics; (*materia*) pottery; (*oggetto*) piece of pottery
ce'rato *a* (*tela*) waxed
cerbi'atto *nm* fawn
'cerca *nf* **andare in ~ di** look for
cercaper'sone *nm inv* beeper
cer'care *vt* look for ● *vi* **~ di** try to
'cerchi|a *nf* circle. **~'are** *vt* circle (*parola*). **~'ato** *a* (*occhi*) black-ringed. **~'etto** *nm* (*per capelli*) hairband
'cerchi|o *nm* circle; (*giocattolo*) hoop. **~'one** *nm* alloy wheel
cere'ale *nm* cereal
cere'brale *a* cerebral
'cereo *a* waxen
ce'retta *nf* depilatory wax
ceri'moni|a *nf* ceremony. **~'ale** *nm* ceremonial. **~'oso** *a* ceremonious
ce'rino *nm* [wax] match
cerni'era *nf* hinge; (*di borsa*) clasp. **~ lampo** zip[-fastener], zipper *Am*
'cernita *nf* selection
'cero *nm* candle
ce'rone *nm* grease-paint
ce'rotto *nm* [sticking] plaster
certa'mente *adv* certainly
cer'tezza *nf* certainty
certifi'ca|re *vt* certify. **~to** *nm* certificate
'certo *a* certain; (*notizia*) definite; (*indeterminativo*) some; **sono ~ di riuscire** I am certain to succeed; **a una certa età** at a certain age; **certi giorni** some days; **un ~ signor Giardini** a Mr Giardini; **una certa Anna** somebody called Anna; **certa gente** *pej* some people; **ho certi dolori!** I'm in such pain!. **certi** *pron pl* some; (*alcune persone*) some people ● *adv* of course; **sapere per ~** know for certain, know for sure; **di ~** surely; **~ che sì!** of course!
cer'vel|lo *nm* brain. **~'lone, -a** *nmf* hum genius. **~'lotico** *a* (*macchinoso*) over-elaborate
'cervo *nm* deer
ce'sareo *a* Med Caesarean
cesel'la|re *vt* chisel. **~to** *a* chiselled. **ce'sello** *nm* chisel
ce'soie *nfpl* shears
ce'spugli|o *nm* bush. **~'oso** *a* (*terreno*) bushy

ces'sa|re *vi* stop, cease ● *vt* stop. **~re** *nm* **il fuoco** ceasefire. **~zi'one** *nf* cessation

cessi'one *nf* handover

'**cesso** *nm sl* (*gabinetto*) bog, john *Am*; (*fig: locale, luogo*) dump

'**cesta** *nf* [large] basket. **ce'stello** *nm* (*per lavatrice*) drum

cesti'nare *vt* throw away. **ce'stino** *nm* [small] basket; (*per la carta straccia*) waste-paper basket. '**cesto** *nm* basket

'**ceto** *nm* [social] class

'**cetra** *nf* lyre

cetrio'lino *nm* gherkin. **cetri'olo** *nm* cucumber

cfr *abbr* (**confronta**) cf.

chat'tare *vi Comput* chat

che *pron rel* (*persona: soggetto*) who; (*persona: oggetto*) that, who, whom *fml*; (*cosa, animale*) that, which; **questa è la casa ~ ho comprato** this is the house [that] I've bought; **il ~ mi sorprende** which surprises me; **dal ~ deduco che…** from which I gather that…; **avere di ~ vivere** have enough to live on; **grazie! – non c'è di! ~** thank you! – don't mention it!; **il giorno ~ ti ho visto** *fam* the day I saw you ● *a inter* what; (*esclamativo: con aggettivo*) how; (*con nome*) what a; **~ macchina prendiamo, la tua o la mia?** which car are we taking, yours or mine?; **~ bello!** how nice!; **~ idea!** what an idea!; **~ bella giornata!** what a lovely day! ● *pron inter* what; **a ~ pensi?** what are you thinking about? ● *conj* that; (*con comparazioni*) than; **credo ~ abbia ragione** I think [that] he is right; **era così commosso ~ non riusciva a parlare** he was so moved [that] he couldn't speak; **aspetto ~ telefoni** I'm waiting for him to phone; **è da un po' ~ non lo vedo** it's been a while since I saw him; **mi piace più Roma ~ Milano** I like Rome better than Milan; **~ ti piaccia o no** whether you like it or not; **~ io sappia** as far as I know

checché *pron indef* whatever

chemiotera'pia *nf* chemotherapy

chero'sene *nm* paraffin

cheru'bino *nm* cherub

cheti'chella: alla ~ *adv* silently

'**cheto** *a* quiet

chi *pron rel* whoever; (*coloro che*) people who; **ho trovato ~ ti può aiutare** I found somebody who can help you; **c'è ~ dice che…** some people say that…; **senti ~ parla!** listen to who's talking!

● *pron inter* (*soggetto*) who; (*oggetto, con preposizione*) who, whom *fml*; (*possessivo*) **di ~** whose; **~ sei?** who are you?; **~ hai incontrato?** who did you meet?; **di ~ sono questi libri?** whose books are these?; **con ~ parli?** who are you talking to?; **a ~ lo dici!** tell me about it!

chi'acchie|ra *nf* chat; (*pettegolezzo*) gossip. **~'rare** *vi* chat; (*far pettegolezzi*) gossip. **~'rato** *a* essere **~rato** ⟨*persona:*⟩ be the subject of gossip; **~re** *pl* chitchat; **far quattro ~re** have a chat. **~'rone, -a** *a* talkative ● *nmf* chatterer

chia'ma|re *vt* call; (*far venire*) send for; **~re alle armi** call up. **~rsi** *vr* be called; **come ti chiami?** what's your name? **~ta** *nf* call; *Mil* call-up

chi'appa *nf fam* cheek

chiara'mente *adv* clearly

chia'rezza *nf* clarity; (*limpidezza*) clearness

chiarifi'ca|re *vt* clarify. **~'tore** *a* clarificatory. **~zi'one** *nf* clarification

chiari'mento *nm* clarification

chia'rir|e *vt* make clear; (*spiegare*) clear up. **~si** *vr* become clear

chi'aro *a* clear; (*luminoso*) bright; ⟨*colore*⟩ light. **chia'rore** *nm* glimmer

chiaroveg'gente *a* clear-sighted ● *nmf* clairvoyant

chi'as|so *nm* din. **~'soso** *a* rowdy

chi'av|e *nf* key; **chiudere a ~e** lock. **~e inglese** monkey-wrench. **~i'stello** *nm* latch

chiaz|za *nf* stain. **~'zare** *vt* stain

chic *a inv* chic

chicches'sia *pron* anybody

'**chicco** *nm* grain; (*di caffè*) bean; (*d'uva*) grape

chi'eder|e *vt* ask; (*per avere*) ask for; (*esigere*) demand. **~si** *vr* wonder

chi'esa *nf* church

chi'esto *pp di* **chiedere**

'**chiglia** *nf* keel

'**chilo** *nm* kilo

chilo'grammo *nm* kilogram[me]

chilome'traggio *nm Auto* ≈ mileage

chilo'metrico *a* in kilometres

chi'lometro *nm* kilometre

chi'mera *nf fig* illusion

'**chimic|a** *nf* chemistry. **~o, -a** *a* chemical ● *nmf* chemist

'**china** *nf* (*declivio*) slope; **inchiostro di ~** Indian ink

chi'nar|e *vt* lower. **~si** *vr* stoop

chincaglie'rie *nfpl* knick-knacks

chinesitera'pia *nf* physiotherapy

chi'nino *nm* quinine

'chino *a* bent

chi'notto *nm sparkling soft drink*

chi'occia *nf* sitting hen

chi'occiola *nf* snail; *Comput* at sign, @; **scala a ~** spiral staircase

chi'odo *nm* nail; *(idea fissa)* obsession. **~ di garofano** clove

chi'oma *nf* head of hair; *(fogliame)* foliage

chi'osco *nm* kiosk; *(per giornali)* news-stand

chi'ostro *nm* cloister

chiro'man|te *nmf* palmist. **~'zia** *nf* palmistry

chirur'gia *nf* surgery. **chi'rurgico** *a* surgical. **chi'rurgo** *nm* surgeon

chissà *adv* who knows; **~ quando arriverà** I wonder when he will arrive

chi'tar|ra *nf* guitar. **~'rista** *nmf* guitarist

chi'uder|e *vt* shut, close; *(con la chiave)* lock; turn off *(luce, acqua ecc)*; *(per sempre)* close down *(negozio, fabbrica ecc)*; *(recingere)* enclose ● *vi* shut, close. **~si** *vr* shut; *(tempo:)* cloud over; *(ferita:)* heal over; *fig* withdraw into oneself

chi'unque *pron indef* anyone, anybody ● *pron rel* whoever

chi'usa *nf* enclosure; *(di canale)* lock; *(conclusione)* close

chi'u|so *pp di* **chiudere** ● *a* shut; *(tempo)* overcast; *(persona)* reserved. **~'sura** *nf* closing; *(sistema)* lock; *(allacciatura)* fastener. **~sura lampo** zip, zipper *Am*

ci *pron (personale)* us; *(riflessivo)* ourselves; *(reciproco)* each other; *(a ciò, di ciò ecc)* about it; **non ci disturbare** don't disturb us; **aspettateci** wait for us; **ci ha detto tutto** he told us everything; **ce lo manderanno** they'll send it to us; **ci consideriamo...** we consider ourselves...; **ci laviamo le mani** we wash our hands; **ci odiamo** we hate each other; **non ci penso mai** I never think about it; **pensaci!** think about it! ● *adv (qui)* here; *(lì)* there; *(moto per luogo)* through it; **ci siamo** we are here; **ci siete?** are you there?; **ci siamo passati tutti** we all went through it; **c'è** there is; **ce ne sono molti** there are many; **ci vuole pazienza** it takes patience; **non ci vedo/sento** I can't see/hear

cia'bat|ta *nf* slipper. **~'tare** *vi* shuffle

ciabat'tino *nm* cobbler

ci'alda *nf* wafer

cial'trone *nm (mascalzone)* scoundrel

ciam'bella *nf Culin* ring-shaped cake; *(salvagente)* lifebelt; *(gonfiabile)* rubber ring

cianci'are *vi* gossip

cianfru'saglie *nfpl* knick-knacks

cia'notico *a (colorito)* puce

ci'ao *int fam (all' arrivo)* hello!, hi!; *(alla partenza)* bye-bye!, cheerio!

ciar'la|re *vi* chat. **~'tano** *nm* charlatan

cias'cuno *a* each ● *pron* everyone, everybody; *(distributivo)* each [one]; **per ~** each

ci'bar|e *vt* feed. **~ie** *nfpl* provisions. **~si** *vr* eat; **~si di** live on

ciber'netico *a* cybernetic

'cibo *nm* food

ci'cala *nf* cicada

cica'lino *nm* buzzer

cica'tri|ce *nf* scar. **~z'zante** *nm* ointment

cicatriz'zarsi *vr* heal [up]. **cicatrizzazi'one** *nf* healing

'cicca *nf* cigarette end; *(fam: sigaretta)* fag; *(fam: gomma)* [chewing] gum

cic'chetto *nm (bicchierino)* nip; *(rimprovero)* telling-off

'cicci|a *nf fam* fat, flab. **~'one, -a** *nmf fam* fatty, fatso

cice'rone *nm* guide

cicla'mino *nm* cyclamen

ci'clis|mo *nm* cycling. **~ta** *nmf* cyclist

'ciclo *nm* cycle; *(di malattia)* course

ciclomo'tore *nm* moped

ci'clone *nm* cyclone

ci'cogna *nf* stork

ci'coria *nf* chicory

ci'eco, -a *a* blind ● *nm* blind man ● *nf* blind woman

ci'elo *nm* sky; *Relig* heaven; **santo ~!** good heavens!

'cifra *nf* figure; *(somma)* sum; *(monogramma)* monogram; *(codice)* code

ci'fra|re *vt* embroider with a monogram; *(codificare)* code. **~to** *a* monogrammed; coded

'ciglio *nm (bordo)* edge; *(pl nf* **ciglia**: *delle palpebre)* eyelash

'cigno *nm* swan

cigo'l|are *vt* squeak. **~io** *nm* squeak

'Cile *nm* Chile

ci'lecca *nf* far **~** miss

ci'leno, -a *a & nmf* Chilean

cili'egi|a *nf* cherry. **~o** *nm* cherry [tree]

cilin'drata *nf* cubic capacity, c.c.; **macchina di alta ~** highpowered car

ci'lindro *nm* cylinder; (*cappello*) top hat

'cima *nf* top; (*fig: persona*) genius; **da ~ a fondo** from top to bottom

ci'melio *nm* relic

cimen'tar|e *vt* put to the test. **~si** *vr* (*provare*) try one's hand

'cimice *nf* bug; (*puntina*) drawing pin, thumbtack *Am*

cimini'era *nf* chimney; *Naut* funnel

cimi'tero *nm* cemetery

ci'murro *nm* distemper

'Cina *nf* China

cin cin! *int* cheers!

cincischi'are *vi* fiddle

'cine *nm fam* cinema

cine'asta *nmf* film maker

'cinema *nm inv* cinema. **cine'presa** *nf* cine-camera

ci'nese *a & nmf* Chinese

cine'teca *nf* (*raccolta*) film collection

ci'netico *a* kinetic

'cingere *vt* (*circondare*) surround

'cinghia *nf* strap; (*cintura*) belt

cinghi'ale *nm* wild boar; **pelle di ~** pigskin

cinguet't|are *vi* twitter. **~io** *nm* twittering

'cinico *a* cynical

ci'niglia *nf* (*tessuto*) chenille

ci'nismo *nm* cynicism

ci'nofilo *a* ⟨*unità*⟩ dog-loving

cin'quanta *a & nm* fifty. **cinquan'tenne** *a & nmf* fifty-year-old. **cinquan'tesimo** *a* fiftieth. **cinquan'tina** *nf* **una cinquantina** about fifty

'cinque *a & nm* five

cinquecen'tesco *a* sixteenth-century

cinque'cento *a* five hundred ● *nm* **il C~** the sixteenth century

cinque'mila *a & nm* five thousand

'cinta *nf* (*di pantaloni*) belt; **muro di ~** [boundary] wall. **cin'tare** *vt* enclose

'cintola *nf* (*di pantaloni*) belt

cin'tura *nf* belt. **~ di salvataggio** lifebelt. **~ di sicurezza** *Aeron, Auto* seat-belt

cintu'rino *nm* **~ dell'orologio** watchstrap

ciò *pron* this; that; **~ che** what; **~ nondimeno** nevertheless

ci'occa *nf* lock

ciocco'la|ta *nf* chocolate; (*bevanda*) [hot] chocolate. **~'tino** *nm* chocolate.

~to *nm* chocolate. **~to al latte/ fondente** milk/plain chocolate

cioè *adv* that is

ciondo'l|are *vi* dangle. **ci'ondolo** *nm* pendant. **~oni** *adv fig* hanging about

cionono'stante *adv* nonetheless

ci'otola *nf* bowl

ci'ottolo *nm* pebble

ci'polla *nf* onion; (*bulbo*) bulb

ci'presso *nm* cypress

'cipria *nf* [face] powder

'Cipro *nm* Cyprus. **cipri'ota** *a & nmf* Cypriot

'circa *adv & prep* about

'circo *nm* circus

circo'la|re *a* circular ● *nf* circular; (*di metropolitana*) circle line ● *vi* circulate. **~'torio** *a Med* circulatory. **~zi'one** *nf* circulation; (*traffico*) traffic

'circolo *nm* circle; (*società*) club

circon'ci|dere *vt* circumcise. **~si'one** *nf* circumcision

circon'dar|e *vt* surround. **~io** *nm* (*amministrativo*) administrative district. **~si di** *vr* surround oneself with

circonfe'renza *nf* circumference. **~ dei fianchi** hip measurement

circonvallazi'one *nf* ring road

circo'scritto *a* limited

circoscrizi'one *nf* area. **~ elettorale** constituency

circo'spetto *a* wary

circospezi'one *nf* **con ~** warily

circo'stante *a* surrounding

circo'stanza *nf* circumstance; (*occasione*) occasion

circu'ire *vt* (*ingannare*) trick

cir'cuito *nm* circuit

circumnavi'ga|re *vt* circumnavigate. **~zi'one** *nf* circumnavigation

'ciste *nf inv* cyst

ci'sterna *nf* cistern; (*serbatoio*) tank

'cisti *nf inv* cyst

ci'ta|re *vt* (*riportare brani ecc*) quote; (*come esempio*) cite; *Jur* summons. **~zi'one** *nf* quotation; *Jur* summons *sg*

citofo'nare *vt* buzz. **ci'tofono** *nm* entry phone; (*in ufficio, su aereo ecc*) intercom

ci'trullo *nmf fam* dimwit

città *nf inv* town; (*grande*) city

citta'della *nf* citadel

citta|di'nanza *nf* citizenship; (*popolazione*) citizens *pl*. **~'dino, -a** *nmf* citizen; (*abitante di città*) city dweller

ciucci'are *vt fam* suck. **ci'uccio** *nm fam* dummy

ci'uco *nm* ass

ci'uffo nm tuft

ci'urma nf Naut crew

ci'vet|ta nf owl; (fig: donna) flirt; [auto] **~ta** unmarked police car. **~'tare** vi flirt. **~te'ria** nf coquettishness

'civico a civic

ci'vil|e a civil. **~iz'zare** vt civilize. **~iz'zato** a ⟨paese⟩ civilized. **~izzazi'one** nf civilization. **~'mente** adv civilly

civiltà nf inv civilization; (cortesia) civility

'clacson nm inv horn. **clacso'nare** vi beep the horn, hoot

cla'mo|re nm clamour; **fare ~re** cause a sensation. **~rosa'mente** adv ⟨sbagliare⟩ sensationally. **~'roso** a noisy; ⟨sbaglio⟩ sensational

clan nm inv clan; fig clique

clandestin|a'mente adv secretly. **~ità** nf secrecy

clande'stino a clandestine; **movimento ~** underground movement; **passeggero ~** stowaway

clari'netto nm clarinet

'classe nf class. **~ turistica** tourist class

classi'cis|mo nm classicism. **~ta** nmf classicist

'classico a classical; (tipico) classic ● nm classic

clas'sifi|ca nf classification; Sport results pl. **~'care** vt classify. **~'carsi** vr be placed. **~ca'tore** nm (cartella) folder. **~cazi'one** nf classification

clas'sista nmf class-conscious person

'clausola nf clause

claustro|fo'bia nf claustrophobia. **~'fobico** a claustrophobic

clau'sura nf Relig enclosed order

clavi'cembalo nm harpsichord

cla'vicola nf collar-bone

cle'men|te a merciful; ⟨tempo⟩ mild. **~za** nf mercy

cleri'cale a clerical. **'clero** nm clergy

clic nm Comput click; **fare ~ su** click on; **fare doppio ~ su** double-click on

clic'care vi click (**su** on)

cli'en|te nmf client; (di negozio) customer. **~'tela** nf customers pl

'clima nm climate. **cli'matico** a climatic

'clinica nf clinic. **clinico** a clinical ● nm clinician

clo'na|re vt clone. **~'zione** nf cloning

'cloro nm chlorine. **~'formio** nm chloroform

clou a inv **momenti ~** highlights

coabi'ta|re vi live together. **~zi'one** nf cohabitation

coagu'la|re vt, **~rsi** vr coagulate. **~zi'one** nf coagulation

coaliz|i'one nf coalition. **~'zarsi** vr unite

co'atto a Jur compulsory

'cobra nm inv cobra

coca'ina nf cocaine. **cocai'nomane** nmf cocaine addict

cocci'nella nf ladybird

'coccio nm earthenware; (frammento) fragment

cocci|u'taggine nf stubbornness. **~'uto** a stubborn

'cocco nm coconut palm; fam love; **noce di ~** coconut

cocco'drillo nm crocodile

cocco'lare vt cuddle

co'cente a ⟨sole⟩ burning

'cocktail nm inv (ricevimento) cocktail party

co'comero nm watermelon

co'cuzzolo nm top; (di testa, cappello) crown

'coda nf tail; (di abito) train; (fila) queue; **fare la ~** queue [up], stand in line Am. **~ di cavallo** (acconciatura) ponytail. **~ dell'occhio** corner of one's eye **~ di paglia** guilty conscience

co'dardo, -a a cowardly ● nmf coward

'codice nm code. **~ di avviamento postale** postal code, zip code Am. **~ a barre** bar-code. **~ fiscale** tax code. **~ della strada** highway code.

codifi'care vt codify

coe'ren|te a consistent. **~za** nf consistency

coesi'one nf cohesion

coe'sistere vi coexist

coe'taneo, -a a & nmf contemporary

cofa'netto nm casket. **'cofano** nm (forziere) chest; Auto bonnet, hood Am

'cogliere vt pick; (sorprendere) catch; (afferrare) seize; (colpire) hit

co'gnato, -a nmf brother-in-law; sister-in-law

cognizi'one nf knowledge

co'gnome nm surname

'coi = con + i

coinci'denza nf coincidence; (di treno ecc) connection

coin'cidere vi coincide

coinqui'lino nm flatmate

coin'vol|gere vt involve. **~gi'mento** nm involvement. **~to** a involved

'coito nm coitus

col = **con** + **il**

colà *adv* there

cola'|brodo *nm inv* strainer; **ridotto a un ~brodo** *fam* full of holes. **~'pasta** *nm inv* colander

co'la|re *vt* strain; (*versare lentamente*) drip ● *vi* (*gocciolare*) drip; (*perdere*) leak; **~re a picco** *Naut* sink. **~ta** *nf* (*di metallo*) casting; (*di lava*) flow

colazi'one *nf* (*del mattino*) breakfast; (*di mezzogiorno*) lunch; **prima ~** breakfast; **far ~** have breakfast/lunch. **~ al sacco** packed lunch

co'lei *pron f* the one

co'lera *nm* cholera

coleste'rolo *nm* cholesterol

colf *nf abbr* (**collaboratrice familiare**) home help

'colica *nf* colic

co'lino *nm* [tea] strainer

'colla *nf* glue; (*di farina*) paste. **~ di pesce** gelatine

collabo'ra|re *vi* collaborate. **~'tore**, **~'trice** *nmf* collaborator. **~zi'one** *nf* collaboration

col'lana *nf* necklace; (*serie*) series

col'lant *nm* tights *pl*

col'lare *nm* collar

col'lasso *nm* collapse

collau'dare *vt* test. **col'laudo** *nm* test

'colle *nm* hill

col'lega *nmf* colleague

collega'mento *nm* connection; *Mil* liaison; *Radio ecc* link. **colle'gar|e** *vt* connect. **~si** *vr* TV, *Radio* link up

collegi'ale *nmf* boarder ● *a* (*responsabilità, decisione*) collective

col'legio *nm* (*convitto*) boarding-school. **~ elettorale** constituency

'collera *nf* anger; **andare in ~** get angry. **col'lerico** *a* irascible

col'letta *nf* collection

collet|tività *nf inv* community. **~'tivo** *a* collective; (*interesse*) general; **biglietto ~tivo** group ticket

col'letto *nm* collar

collezi|o'nare *vt* collect. **~'one** *nf* collection. **~o'nista** *nmf* collector

colli'mare *vi* coincide

col'li|na *nf* hill. **~'noso** *a* (*terreno*) hilly

col'lirio *nm* eyewash

collisi'one *nf* collision

'collo *nm* neck; (*pacco*) package; **a ~ alto** high-necked. **~ del piede** instep

colloca'mento *nm* placing; (*impiego*) employment

collo'ca|re *vt* place. **~rsi** *vr* take one's place. **~zi'one** *nf* placing

colloqui'ale *a* (*termine*) colloquial. **col'loquio** *nm* conversation; (*udienza ecc*) interview; (*esame*) oral [exam]

collusi'one *nf* collusion

colluttazi'one *nf* scuffle

col'mare *vt* fill [to the brim]; bridge (*divario*); **~ qcno di gentilezze** overwhelm sb with kindness. **'colmo** *a* full ● *nm* top; *fig* height; **al colmo della disperazione** in the depths of despair; **questo è il colmo!** (*con indignazione*) this is the last straw!; (*con stupore*) I don't believe it!

co'lomb|a *nf* dove. **~o** *nm* pigeon

co'loni|a¹ *nf* colony; **~a [estiva]** (*per bambini*) holiday camp. **~'ale** *a* colonial

co'lonia² *nf* **[acqua di] ~** [eau de] Cologne

co'lonico *a* (*terreno, casa*) farm

coloniz'za|re *vt* colonize. **~'tore**, **~'trice** *nmf* colonizer

co'lon|na *nf* column. **~ sonora** soundtrack. **~ vertebrale** spine. **~'nato** *nm* colonnade

colon'nello *nm* colonel

co'lono *nm* tenant farmer

colo'rante *nm* colouring

colo'rare *vt* colour; colour in (*disegno*)

co'lore *nm* colour; **a colori** in colour; **di ~** coloured. **colo'rito** *a* coloured; (*viso*) rosy; (*racconto*) colourful ● *nm* complexion

co'loro *pron pl* the ones

colos'sale *a* colossal. **co'losso** *nm* colossus

'colpa *nf* fault; (*biasimo*) blame; (*colpevolezza*) guilt; (*peccato*) sin; **dare la ~ a** blame; **essere in ~** be at fault; **per ~ di** because of. **col'pevole** *a* guilty ● *nmf* culprit

col'pire *vt* hit, strike; **~ nel segno** hit the nail on the head

'colpo *nm* blow; (*di arma da fuoco*) shot; (*urto*) knock; (*emozione*) shock; *Med, Sport* stroke; (*furto*) raid; **di ~** suddenly; **far ~** make a strong impression; **far venire un ~ a qcno** *fig* give sb a fright; **perdere colpi** (*motore:*) keep missing; **a ~ d'occhio** at a glance; **a ~ sicuro** for certain. **~ d'aria** chill. **~ basso** blow below the belt. **~ di scena** coup de théâtre. **~ di sole** sunstroke; **colpi** *pl* **di sole** (*su capelli*) highlights. **~ di stato** coup [d'état]. **~**

di telefono ring; **dare un ~ di telefono a qn** give sb a ring. **~ di testa** [sudden] impulse. **~ di vento** gust of wind

col'poso *a* **omicidio ~** manslaughter

coltel'lata *nf* stab. **col'tello** *nm* knife

colti'va|re *vt* cultivate. **~'tore, ~'trice** *nmf* farmer. **~zi'one** *nf* farming; *(di piante)* growing

'colto *pp di* **cogliere** ● *a* cultured

'coltre *nf* blanket

col'tura *nf* cultivation

co'lui *pron inv m* the one

'coma *nm inv* coma; **in ~** in a coma

comanda'mento *nm* commandment

coman'dante *nm* commander; *Naut, Aeron* captain

coman'dare *vt* command; *Mech* control ● *vi* be in charge. **co'mando** *nm* command; *(di macchina)* control

co'mare *nf (madrina)* godmother

combaci'are *vi* fit together; *(testimonianze:)* concur

combat'tente *a* fighting ● *nm* combatant. **ex ~** ex-serviceman

com'bat|tere *vt/i* fight. **~ti'mento** *nm* fight; *Mil* battle; **fuori ~timento** *(pugilato)* knocked out. **~'tuto** *a (gara)* hard fought

combina|re *vt/i* arrange; *(mettere insieme)* combine; *(fam: fare)* do; **cosa stai ~ndo?** what are you doing?. **~rsi** *vr* combine; *(mettersi d'accordo)* come to an agreement. **~zi'one** *nf* combination; *(caso)* coincidence; **per ~zione** by chance

com'briccola *nf* gang

combu'sti|bile *a* combustible ● *nm* fuel. **~'one** *nf* combustion

com'butta *nf* gang; **in ~** in league

'come *adv* like; *(in qualità di)* as; *(interrogativo, esclamativo)* how; **questo vestito è ~ il tuo** this dress is like yours; **~ stai?** how are you?; **~ va?** how are things?; **~ mai?** how come?; **~?** what?; **non sa ~ fare** he doesn't know what to do; **~ sta bene!** how well he looks!; **~ no!** that will be right!; **~ tu sai** as you know; **fa ~ vuoi** do as you like; **~ se** as if ● *conj (non appena)* as soon as

co'meta *nf* comet

'comico, -a *a* comic[al]; *(teatro)* comic ● *nm* funny side ● *nmf (attore)* comedian, comic actor ● *nf (a torte in faccia)* slapstick sketch

co'mignolo *nm* chimney-pot

cominci'are *vt/i* begin, start; **a ~ da oggi** from today; **per ~** to begin with

comi'tato *nm* committee

comi'tiva *nf* party, group

co'mizio *nm* meeting

com'mando *nm inv* commando

com'medi|a *nf* comedy; *(opera teatrale)* play; *fig* sham. **~a musicale** musical. **~'ante** *nmf* comedian; *fig pej* phoney. **~'ografo, -a** *nmf* playwright

commemo'ra|re *vt* commemorate. **~zi'one** *nf* commemoration

commen'sale *nmf* fellow diner

commen't|are *vt* comment on; *(annotare)* annotate. **~ario** *nm* commentary. **~a'tore, ~a'trice** *nmf* commentator. **com'mento** *nm* comment

commerci'a|le *a* commercial; *(relazioni, trattative)* trade; *(attività)* business. **centro ~le** shopping centre. **~'lista** *nmf* business consultant; *(contabile)* accountant. **~liz'zare** *vt* market. **~lizzazi'one** *nf* marketing

commerci'ante *nmf* trader, merchant; *(negoziante)* shopkeeper. **~ all'ingrosso** wholesaler

commerci'are *vi* **~ in** deal in

com'mercio *nm* commerce; *(internazionale)* trade; *(affari)* business; **in ~** *(prodotto)* on sale. **~ all'ingrosso** wholesale trade. **~ al minuto** retail trade

com'messo, -a *pp di* **commettere** ● *nmf* shop assistant. **~ viaggiatore** commercial traveller ● *nf (ordine)* order

comme'stibile *a* edible. **commestibili** *nmpl* groceries

com'mettere *vt* commit; make *(sbaglio)*

commi'ato *nm* leave; **prendere ~ da** take leave of

commise'rar|e *vt* commiserate with. **~si** *vr* feel sorry for oneself

commissari'ato *nm (di polizia)* police station

commis's|ario *nm* ≈ [police] superintendent; *(membro di commissione)* commissioner; *Sport* steward; *Comm* commission agent. **~ario d'esame** examiner. **~i'one** *nf (incarico)* errand; *(comitato ecc)* commission; *(Comm: di merce)* order; **~ioni** *pl (acquisti)* fare **~ioni** go shopping. **~ione d'esame** board of examiners. **C~ione Europea** European Commission

commit'tente *nmf* purchaser

com'mo|sso *pp di* **commuovere** ● *a* moved. **~'vente** *a* moving

commozi'one *nf* emotion. **~ cerebrale** concussion

commu'over|e *vt* touch, move. **~si** *vr* be touched

commu'tare *vt* change; *Jur* commute

comò *nm inv* chest of drawers

comoda'mente *adv* comfortably

como'dino *nm* bedside table

comodità *nf inv* comfort; (*convenienza*) convenience

'comodo *a* comfortable; (*conveniente*) convenient; (*spazioso*) roomy; (*facile*) easy; **stia ~!** don't get up!; **far ~** be useful ● *nm* comfort; **fare il proprio ~** do as one pleases

compae'sano, -a *nmf* fellow countryman

com'pagine *nf* (*squadra*) team

compa'gnia *nf* company; (*gruppo*) party; **fare ~ a qcno** keep sb company; **essere di ~** be sociable. **~ aerea** airline

com'pagno, -a *nmf* companion, mate; *Comm, Sport* partner; *Pol* comrade. **~ di scuola** schoolmate

compa'rabile *a* comparable

compa'ra|re *vt* compare. **~'tivo** *a & nm* comparative. **~zi'one** *nf* comparison

com'pare *nm* (*padrino*) godfather; (*testimone di matrimonio*) witness

compa'rire *vi* appear; (*spiccare*) stand out; **~ in giudizio** appear in court

com'parso, -a *pp di* **comparire** ● *nf* appearance; *Cinema* extra; *Theat* walk-on

compartecipazi'one *nf* sharing; (*quota*) share

comparti'mento *nm* compartment; (*amministrativo*) department

compas'sato *a* calm and collected

compassi'o|ne *nf* compassion; **aver ~ per** feel pity for; **far ~** arouse pity. **~'nevole** *a* compassionate

com'passo *nm* [pair of] compasses *pl*

compa'tibil|e *a* (*conciliabile*) compatible; (*scusabile*) excusable. **~ità** *nf* compatibility. **~'mente** *adv* **~mente con i miei impegni** if my commitments allow

compa'tire *vt* pity; (*scusare*) make allowances for

compatri'ota *nmf* compatriot

compat'tezza *nf* (*di materia*) compactness. **com'patto** *a* compact; (*denso*) dense; (*solido*) solid; *fig* united

compene'trare *vt* pervade

compen'sar|e *vt* compensate; (*supplire*) make up for. **~si** *vr* balance each other out

compen'sato *nm* (*legno*) plywood

compensazi'one *nf* compensation

com'penso *nm* compensation; (*retribuzione*) remuneration; **in ~** (*in cambio*) in return; (*d'altra parte*) on the other hand; (*invece*) instead

'comper|a *nf* purchase; **far ~e** do some shopping

compe'rare *vt* buy

compe'ten|te *a* competent. **~za** *nf* competence; (*responsabilità*) responsibility

com'petere *vi* compete; **~ a** (*compito:*) be the responsibility of

competi|tività *nf* competitiveness. **~'tivo** *a* (*prezzo, carattere*) competitive. **~'tore, ~'trice** *nmf* competitor. **~zi'one** *nf* competition

compia'cen|te *a* obliging. **~za** *nf* obligingness

compia'c|ere *vt/i* please. **~ersi** *vr* (*congratularsi*) congratulate. **~ersi di** (*degnarsi*) condescend. **~i'mento** *nm* satisfaction. **~i'uto** *a* (*aria, sorriso*) smug

compi'an|gere *vt* pity; (*per lutto ecc*) sympathize with. **~to** *a* lamented ● *nm* grief

'compier|e *vt* (*concludere*) complete; commit (*delitto*); **~e gli anni** have one's birthday. **~si** *vr* end; (*avverarsi*) come true

compi'la|re *vt* compile; fill in (*modulo*). **~zi'one** *nf* compilation

compi'mento *nm* **portare a ~ qcsa** conclude sth

com'pire *vt* = **compiere**

compi'tare *vt* spell

com'pito¹ *a* polite

'compito² *nm* task; *Sch* homework

compi'ut|o *a* **avere 30 anni ~i** be over 30

comple'anno *nm* birthday

complemen'tare *a* complementary; (*secondario*) subsidiary

comple'mento *nm* complement; *Mil* draft. **~ oggetto** direct object

comples|sità *nf* complexity. **~siva-'mente** *adv* on the whole. **~'sivo** *a* comprehensive; (*totale*) total. **com'plesso** *a* complex; (*difficile*) complicated ● *nm* complex; (*di cantanti ecc*) group; (*di circostanze, fattori*) combination; **in ~so** on the whole

completa'mente *adv* completely

comple'tare *vt* complete

com'pleto *a* complete; (*pieno*) full [up]; **essere al ~** (*teatro:*) be sold out;

la famiglia al ~ the whole family ● *nm (vestito)* suit; *(insieme di cose)* set

compli'ca|re *vt* complicate. **~rsi** *vr* become complicated. **~to** complicated. **~zi'one** *nf* complication; **salvo ~zioni** all being well

'**complic|e** *nmf* accomplice ● *a (sguardo)* knowing. **~ità** *nf* complicity

complimen'tar|e *vt* compliment. **~si** *vr* **~si con** congratulate

compli'menti *nmpl (ossequi)* regards; *(congratulazioni)* congratulations; **far ~** stand on ceremony

compli'mento *nm* compliment

complot'tare *vi* plot. **com'plotto** *nm* plot

compo'nente *a & nm* component ● *nmf* member

compo'nibile *a (cucina)* fitted; *(mobili)* modular

componi'mento *nm* composition; *(letterario)* work

com'por|re *vt* compose; *(ordinare)* put in order; *Typ* set. **~si** *vr* **~si di** be made up of

comporta'mento *nm* behaviour

compor'tar|e *vt* involve; *(consentire)* allow. **~si** *vr* behave

composi'tore, **-'trice** *nmf* composer; *Typ* compositor. **~zi'one** *nf* composition

com'posta *nf* stewed fruit; *(concime)* compost

compo'stezza *nf* composure

com'posto *pp di* **comporre** ● *a* composed; *(costituito)* comprising; **stai ~!** sit properly! ● *nm Chem* compound

com'pra|re *vt* buy. **~'tore**, **~'trice** *nmf* buyer

compra'vendita *nf* buying and selling

com'pren|dere *vt* understand; *(includere)* comprise. **~'sibile** *a* understandable. **~sibil'mente** *adv* understandably. **~si'one** *nf* understanding. **~'sivo** *a* understanding; *(che include)* inclusive. **com'preso** *pp di* **comprendere** ● *a* included; **tutto compreso** *(prezzo)* all-in

com'pressa *nf* compress; *(pastiglia)* tablet

compressi'one *nf* compression. **com'presso** *pp di* **comprimere** ● *a* compressed

com'primere *vt* press; *(reprimere)* repress

compro'me|sso *pp di* **compromet-** **tere** ● *nm* compromise. **~t'tente** *a* compromising. **~ttere** *vt* compromise

comproprietà *nf* multiple ownership

compro'vare *vt* prove

com'punto *a* contrite

compu'tare *vt* calculate

com'puter *nm* computer. **~iz'zare** *vt* computerize. **~iz'zato** *a* computerized

computiste'ria *nf* book-keeping. '**computo** *nm* calculation

comu'nale *a* municipal

co'mune *a* common; *(condiviso)* mutual; *(ordinario)* ordinary ● *nm* borough, council; *(amministrativo)* commune; **fuori del ~** out of the ordinary. **~'mente** *adv* commonly

comuni'ca|re *vt* communicate; pass on *(malattia)*; *Relig* administer Communion to. **~rsi** *vr* receive Communion. **~'tiva** *nf* communicativeness. **~'tivo** *a* communicative. **~to** *nm* communiqué. **~to stampa** press release. **~zi'one** *nf* communication; *Teleph* [phone] call; **avere la ~zione** get through; **dare la ~zione a qcno** put sb through

comuni'one *nf* communion; *Relig* [Holy] Communion

comu'nis|mo *nm* communism. **~ta** *a & nmf* communist

comunità *nf inv* community. **C~ [Economica] Europea** European [Economic] Community

co'munque *conj* however ● *adv* anyhow

con *prep* with; *(mezzo)* by; **~ facilità** easily; **~ mia grande gioia** to my great delight; **è gentile ~ tutti** he is kind to everyone; **col treno** by train; **~ questo tempo** in this weather

co'nato *nm* **~ di vomito** retching

'**conca** *nf* basin; *(valle)* dell

concate'na|re *vt* link together. **~zi'one** *nf* connection

'**concavo** *a* concave

con'ceder|e *vt* grant; award *(premio)*; *(ammettere)* admit. **~si** *vr* allow oneself *(pausa)*

concentra'mento *nm* concentration

concen'tra|re *vt*, **~rsi** *vr* concentrate. **~to** *a* concentrated ● *nm* **~to di pomodoro** tomato pureé. **~zi'one** *nf* concentration

concepi'mento *nm* conception

conce'pire *vt* conceive *(bambino)*; *(capire)* understand; *(figurarsi)* conceive of; devise *(piano ecc)*

con'cernere *vt* concern

concer'tar|e *vt Mus* harmonize; (*organizzare*) arrange. **~si** *vr* agree

concer'tista *nmf* concert performer. **con'certo** *nm* concert; (*composizione*) concerto

concessio'nario *nm* agent

concessi'one *nf* concession

con'cesso *pp di* **concedere**

con'cetto *nm* concept; (*opinione*) opinion

concezi'one *nf* conception; (*idea*) concept

con'chiglia *nf* [sea] shell

'concia *nf* tanning; (*di tabacco*) curing

conci'a|re *vt* tan; cure (*tabacco*); **~re qcno per le feste** give sb a good hiding. **~rsi** *vr* (*sporcarsi*) get dirty; (*vestirsi male*) dress badly. **~to a** (*pelle, cuoio*) tanned

concili'abile *a* compatible

concili'ante *a* conciliatory

concili'a|re *vt* reconcile; settle (*contravvenzione*); (*favorire*) induce. **~rsi** *vr* go together; (*mettersi d'accordo*) become reconciled. **~zi'one** *nf* reconciliation; *Jur* settlement

con'cilio *nm Relig* council; (*riunione*) assembly

conci'mare *vt* feed (*pianta*). **con'cime** *nm* manure; (*chimico*) fertilizer

concisi'one *nf* conciseness. **con'ciso** *a* concise

conci'tato *a* excited

concitta'dino, -a *nmf* fellow citizen

con'clu|dere *vt* conclude; (*finire con successo*) achieve. **~dersi** *vr* come to an end. **~si'one** *nf* conclusion; **in ~sione** (*insomma*) in short. **~'sivo** *a* conclusive. **~so** *pp di* **concludere**

concomi'tanza *nf* (*di circostanze, fatti*) combination

concor'da|nza *nf* agreement. **~re** *vt* agree; *Gram* make agree. **~to** *nm* agreement; *Jur, Comm* arrangement

con'cord|e *a* in agreement; (*unanime*) unanimous

concor'ren|te *a* concurrent; (*rivale*) competing ● *nmf Comm, Sport* competitor; (*candidato*) candidate. **~za** *nf* competition. **~zi'ale** *a* competitive

con'cor|rere *vi* (*contribuire*) concur; (*andare insieme*) go together; (*competere*) compete. **~so** *pp di* **concorrere** ● *nm* competition; **fuori ~so** not in the official competition. **~so di bellezza** beauty contest

concreta'mente *adv* concretely

concre|'tare *vt* (*concludere*) achieve.

~tiz'zare *vt* put into concrete form (*idea, progetto*)

con'creto *a* concrete; **in ~** in concrete terms

concussi'one *nf* extortion

con'danna *nf* sentence; **pronunziare una ~** pass a sentence. **condan'nare** *vt* condemn; *Jur* sentence. **condan'nato, -a** *nmf* convict

conden'sa|re *vt*, **~rsi** *vr* condense. **~zi'one** *nf* condensation

condi'mento *nm* seasoning; (*salsa*) dressing. **con'dire** *vt* flavour; dress (*insalata*)

condiscen'den|te *a* indulgent; *pej* condescending. **~za** *nf* indulgence; *pej* condescension

condi'videre *vt* share

condizio'na|le *a & nm* conditional ● *nf Jur* suspended sentence. **~'mento** *nm Psych* conditioning

condizio'na|re *vt* condition. **~to** *a* conditional. **~'tore** *nm* air conditioner

condizi'one *nf* condition; **a ~ che** on condition that

condogli'anze *nfpl* condolences; **fare le ~ a** offer condolences to

condomini'ale *a* (*spese*) common. **condo'minio** *nm* joint ownership; (*edificio*) condominium

condo'nare *vt* remit. **con'dono** *nm* remission

con'dotta *nf* conduct, (*circoscrizione di medico*) district; (*di gara ecc*) management; (*tubazione*) piping

con'dotto *pp di* **condurre** ● *a* **medico ~** district doctor ● *nm* pipe; *Anat* duct

condu'cente *nm* driver

con'du|rre *vt* lead; drive (*veicoli*); (*accompagnare*) take; conduct (*gas, elettricità ecc*); (*gestire*) run. **~rsi** *vr* behave. **~'tore, ~'trice** *nmf TV* presenter; (*di veicolo*) driver ● *nm Electr* conductor. **~t'tura** *nf* duct

confabu'lare *vi* have a confab

confa'cente *a* suitable. **con'farsi** *vr* **confarsi a** a suit

confederazi'one *nf* confederation

confe'renz|a *nf* (*discorso*) lecture; (*congresso*) conference. **~a stampa** news conference. **~i'ere, -a** *nmf* lecturer

confe'rire *vt* (*donare*) give ● *vi* confer

con'ferma *nf* confirmation. **confer-'mare** *vt* confirm

confes's|are *vt*, **~arsi** *vr* confess.

~io'nale *a & nm* confessional. **~i'one** *nf* confession. **~ore** *nm* confessor

con'fetto *nm* sugared almond

confet'tura *nf* jam

confezio'na|re *vt* manufacture; make ⟨*abiti*⟩; package ⟨*merci*⟩. **~to** *a* ⟨*vestiti*⟩ off-the-peg; ⟨*gelato*⟩ wrapped

confezi'one *nf* manufacture; (*di abiti*) tailoring; (*di pacchi*) packaging; **confezioni** *pl* clothes. **~ regalo** gift pack

confic'car|e *vt* thrust. **~si** *vr* run into

confi'd|are *vi* **~are in** trust ● *vt* confide. **~arsi** *vr* **~arsi con** confide in. **~ente** *a* confident ● *nmf* confidant

confi'denz|a *nf* confidence; (*familiarità*) familiarity; **prendersi delle ~e** take liberties. **~i'ale** *a* confidential; ⟨*rapporto, tono*⟩ familiar

configu'ra|re *vt Comput* configure. **~zi'one** *nf* configuration

confi'nante *a* neighbouring

confi'na|re *vi* (*relegare*) confine ● *vi* **~re con** border on. **~rsi** *vr* withdraw. **~to** *a* confined

con'fin|e *nm* border; (*tra terreni*) boundary. **~o** *nm* political exile

con'fi|sca *nf* (*di proprietà*) forfeiture. **~'scare** *vt* confiscate

con'flitt|o *nm* conflict. **~u'ale** *a* adversarial

conflu'enza *nf* confluence; (*di strade*) junction

conflu'ire *vi* ⟨*fiumi:*⟩ flow together; ⟨*strade:*⟩ meet

con'fonder|e *vt* confuse; (*turbare*) confound; (*imbarazzare*) embarrass. **~si** *vr* (*mescolarsi*) mingle; (*turbarsi*) become confused; *vr* (*sbagliarsi*) be mistaken

confor'ma|re *vt* adapt. **~rsi** *vr* conform. **~zi'one** *nf* conformity (**a** with); (*del terreno*) composition

con'forme *a* according. **~'mente** *adv* accordingly

confor'mi|smo *nm* conformity. **~sta** *nmf* conformist. **~tà** *nf* (*a norma*) conformity

confor'tante *a* comforting

confor't|are *vt* comfort. **~evole** *a* (*comodo*) comfortable. **con'forto** *nm* comfort

confron'tare *vt* compare

con'fronto *nm* comparison; **in ~** by comparison with; **nei tuoi confronti** towards you; **senza ~** far and away

confusi|o'nario *a* ⟨*persona*⟩ muddleheaded. **~'one** *nf* confusion; (*baccano*) racket; (*disordine*) mess; (*imbarazzo*)

embarrassment. **con'fuso** *pp di* **confondere** ● *a* confused; (*indistinto*) indistinct; (*imbarazzato*) embarrassed

confu'tare *vt* confute

conge'dar|e *vt* dismiss; *Mil* discharge. **~si** *vr* take one's leave

con'gedo *nm* leave; **essere in ~** be on leave. **~ malattia** sick leave. **~ maternità** maternity leave

conge'gnare *vt* devise; (*mettere insieme*) assemble. **con'gegno** *nm* device

congela'mento *nm* freezing; *Med* frost-bite

conge'la|re *vt* freeze. **~to** *a* ⟨*cibo*⟩ deep-frozen. **~'tore** *nm* freezer

congeni'ale *a* congenial

con'genito *a* congenital

congestio'na|re *vt* congest. **~to** *a* ⟨*traffico*⟩ congested; ⟨*viso*⟩ flushed. **congesti'one** *nf* congestion

conget'tura *nf* conjecture

congi'unger|e *vt* join; combine ⟨*sforzi*⟩. **~si** *vr* join

congiunti'vite *nf* conjunctivitis

congiun'tivo *nm* subjunctive

congi'unto *pp di* **congiungere** ● *a* joined ● *nm* relative

congiun'tu|ra *nf* joint; (*circostanza*) juncture; (*situazione*) situation. **~'rale** *a* economic

congiunzi'one *nf Gram* conjunction

congi'u|ra *nf* conspiracy. **~'rare** *vi* conspire

conglome'rato *nm* conglomerate; *fig* conglomeration; (*da costruzione*) concrete

congratu'la|rsi *vr* **~rsi con qcno per** congratulate sb on. **~zi'oni** *nfpl* congratulations

con'grega *nf* band

congre'ga|re *vt*, **~rsi** *vr* congregate. **~zi'one** *nf* congregation

con'gresso *nm* congress

'congruo *a* proper; (*giusto*) fair

conguagli'are *vt* balance. **congu'aglio** *nm* balance

coni'are *vt* coin

'conico *a* conical

co'nifera *nf* conifer

co'niglio *nm* rabbit

coniu'gale *a* marital; ⟨*vita*⟩ married

coniu'ga|re *vt* conjugate. **~rsi** *vr* get married. **~zi'one** *nf* conjugation

'coniuge *nmf* spouse

connazio'nale *nmf* compatriot

connessi'one *nf* connection. **con'nesso** *pp di* **connettere**

53

con'nettere *vt* connect ● *vi* think rationally

conni'vente *a* conniving

conno'ta|re *vt* connote. **~to** *nm* distinguishing feature; **~ti** *pl* description

con'nubio *nm fig* union

'cono *nm* cone

cono'scen|te *nmf* acquaintance. **~za** *nf* knowledge; (*persona*) acquaintance; (*sensi*) consciousness; **perdere ~za** lose consciousness; **riprendere ~za** regain consciousness, come to

co'nosc|ere *vt* know; (*essere a conoscenza di*) be acquainted with; (*fare la conoscenza di*) meet. **~i'tore, ~i'trice** *nmf* connoisseur. **~i'uto** *pp di* **conoscere** ● *a* well-known

con'quist|a *nf* conquest. **conqui'stare** *vt* conquer; *fig* win

consa'cra|re *vt* consecrate; ordain 〈*sacerdote*〉; (*dedicare*) dedicate. **~rsi** *vr* devote oneself. **~zi'one** *nf* consecration

consangu'ineo, -a *nmf* blood-relation

consa'pevo|le *a* conscious. **~'lezza** *nf* consciousness. **~l'mente** *adv* consciously

'conscio *a* conscious

consecu'tivo *a* consecutive; (*seguente*) next

con'segna *nf* delivery; (*merce*) consignment; (*custodia*) care; (*di prigioniero*) handover; (*Mil: ordine*) orders *pl*; (*Mil: punizione*) confinement; **pagamento alla ~** cash on delivery

conse'gnare *vt* deliver; (*affidare*) give in charge; *Mil* confine to barracks

consegu'en|te *a* consequent. **~za** *nf* consequence; **di ~za** (*perciò*) consequently

consegui'mento *nm* achievement

consegu'ire *vt* achieve ● *vi* follow

con'senso *nm* consent

consensu'ale *a* consensus-based

consen'tire *vi* consent ● *vt* allow

con'serto *a* **a braccia conserte** with one's arms folded

con'serva *nf* preserve; (*di frutta*) jam; (*di agrumi*) marmalade. **~ di pomodoro** tomato sauce

conser'var|e *vt* preserve; (*mantenere*) keep. **~si** *vr* keep; **~si in salute** keep well

conserva|'tore, -'trice *nmf Pol* conservative

conserva'torio *nm* conservatory

conservazi'one *nf* preservation; **a lunga ~** long-life

conside'ra|re *vt* consider; (*stimare*) regard. **~to a** (*stimato*) esteemed. **~zi'one** *nf* consideration; (*osservazione, riflessione*) remark

conside'revole *a* considerable

consigli'abile *a* advisable

consigli'are *vt* advise; (*raccomandare*) recommend. **~'arsi** *vr* **~arsi con qcno** ask sb's advice. **~'ere, -a** *nmf* adviser; (*membro di consiglio*) councillor

con'siglio *nm* advice; (*ente*) council. **~ d'amministrazione** board of directors. **C~ dei Ministri** Cabinet

consi'sten|te *a* substantial; (*spesso*) thick; (*fig: argomento*) valid. **~za** *nf* consistency; (*spessore*) thickness

con'sistere *vi* **~ in** consist of

consoci'ata *nf* (*azienda*) associate company

conso'lar|e[1] *vt* console; (*rallegrare*) cheer. **~si** *vr* console oneself

conso'la|re[2] *a* consular. **~to** *nm* consulate

consolazi'one *nf* consolation; (*gioia*) joy

con'sole *nf inv* (*tastiera*) console

'console *nm* consul

consoli'dar|e *vt*, **~si** *vr* consolidate

conso'nante *nf* consonant

'consono *a* consistent

con'sorte *nmf* consort

con'sorzio *nm* consortium

con'stare *vi* **~ di** consist of; (*risultare*) appear; **a quanto mi consta** as far as I know; **mi consta che** it appears that

consta'ta|re *vt* ascertain. **~zi'one** *nf* observation

consu'e|to *a & nm* usual. **~tudi'nario** *a* 〈*diritto*〉 common; 〈*persona*〉 set in one's ways. **~'tudine** *nf* habit; (*usanza*) custom

consu'len|te *nmf* consultant. **~za** *nf* consultancy

consul'ta|re *vt* consult. **~rsi con** consult with. **~zi'one** *nf* consultation

consul't|ivo *a* consultative. **~orio** *nm* clinic

consu'ma|re *vt* (*usare*) consume; wear out 〈*abito, scarpe*〉; consummate 〈*matrimonio*〉; commit 〈*delitto*〉. **~rsi** *vr* consume; 〈*abito, scarpe:*〉 wear out; (*struggersi*) pine

consu'mato *a* 〈*politico*〉 seasoned; 〈*scarpe, tappeto*〉 worn

consuma|'tore, -'trice *nmf* consumer. **~zi'one** *nf* (*bibita*) drink; (*spuntino*) snack

consu'mis|mo *nm* consumerism. **~ta** *nmf* consumerist

con'sumo *nm* consumption; (*di abito, scarpe*) wear; (*uso*) use; **generi di ~** consumer goods. **~ [di carburante]** [fuel] consumption

consun'tivo *nm* [bilancio] final statement

conta'balle *nmf fam* storyteller

con'tabil|e *a* book-keeping ● *nmf* accountant. **~ità** *nf* accounting; **tenere la ~ità** keep the accounts

contachi'lometri *nm inv* mileometer, odometer *Am*

conta'dino, -a *nmf* farm-worker; (*medievale*) peasant

contagi'are *vt* infect. **con'tagio** *nm* infection. **~'oso** *a* infectious

conta'gocce *nm inv* dropper

contami'na|re *vt* contaminate. **~zi'one** *nf* contamination

con'tante *nm* cash; **pagare in contanti** pay cash

con'tare *vt/i* count; (*tenere conto di*) take into account; (*proporsi*) intend

conta'scatti *nm inv Teleph* time-unit counter

conta'tore *nm* meter

contat'tare *vt* contact. **con'tatto** *nm* contact

'conte *nm* count

conteggi'are *vt* put on the bill ● *vi* calculate. **con'teggio** *nm* calculation. **conteggio alla rovescia** countdown

con'te|gno *nm* behaviour; (*atteggiamento*) attitude. **~'gnoso** *a* dignified

contem'pla|re *vt* contemplate; (*fissare*) gaze at. **~zi'one** *nf* contemplation

con'tempo *nm* **nel ~** in the meantime

contempo|ranea'mente *adv* at once. **~'raneo, -a** *a* & *nmf* contemporary

conten'dente *nmf* competitor. **con'tendere** *vi* compete; (*litigare*) quarrel ● *vt* contend

conte'n|ere *vt* contain; (*reprimere*) repress. **~ersi** *vr* contain oneself. **~i'tore** *nm* container

conten'tarsi *vr* **~ di** be content with

conten'tezza *nf* joy

conten'tino *nm* placebo

con'tento *a* glad; (*soddisfatto*) contented

conte'nuto *nm* contents *pl*; (*soggetto*) content

contenzi'oso *nm* legal department

con'tes|a *nf* disagreement; *Sport* contest. **~o** *pp di* **contendere** ● *a* contested

con'tessa *nf* countess

conte'sta|re *vt* contest; *Jur* notify. **~'tario** *a* anti-establishment. **~'tore, ~'trice** *nmf* protester. **~zi'one** *nf* (*disputa*) dispute

con'testo *nm* context

con'tiguo *a* adjacent

continen'tale *a* continental. **conti'nente** *nm* continent

conti'nenza *nf* continence

contin'gen|te *nm* contingent; (*quota*) quota. **~za** *nf* contingency

continua'mente *adv* (*senza interruzione*) continuously; (*frequentemente*) continually

continu|'are *vt/i* continue; (*riprendere*) resume. **~a'tivo** *a* permanent. **~azi'one** *nf* continuation. **~ità** *nf* continuity

con'tinu|o *a* continuous; (*molto frequente*) continual. **corrente ~a** direct current; **di ~o** continually

'conto *nm* calculation; (*in banca, negozio*) account; (*di ristorante ecc*) bill; (*stima*) consideration; **a conti fatti** all things considered; **far ~ di** (*supporre*) suppose; (*proporsi*) intend; **far ~ su** rely on; **in fin dei conti** when all is said and done; **per ~ di** on behalf of; **per ~ mio** (*a mio parere*) in my opinion; (*da solo*) on my own; **starsene per ~ proprio** be on one's own; **rendersi ~ di qcsa** realize sth; **sul ~ di qcno** (*voci, informazioni*) about sb; **tener ~ di qcsa** take sth into account; **tenere da ~ qcsa** look after sth; **fare i conti con qcno** *fig* sort sb out. **~ corrente** current account, checking account *Am*. **~ alla rovescia** countdown

con'torcer|e *vt* twist. **~si** *vr* twist about

contor'nare *vt* surround

con'torno *nm* contour; *Culin* vegetables *pl*

contorsi'one *nf* contortion. **con'torto** *pp di* **contorcere** ● *a* twisted

contrabban|'dare *vt* smuggle. **~di'ere, -a** *nmf* smuggler. **contrab-'bando** *nm* contraband

contrab'basso *nm* double bass

contraccambi'are *vt* return. **contrac'cambio** *nm* return

contracce|t'tivo *nm* contraceptive. **~zi'one** *nf* contraception

contrac'col|po *nm* rebound; (*di arma da fuoco*) recoil; *fig* repercussion

con'trada *nf* (*rione*) district

contrad'detto *pp di* **contraddire**

contrad'di|re *vt* contradict. **~t'torio** *a* contradictory. **~zi'one** *nf* contradiction

contraddi'stin|guere *vt* differentiate. **~to** *a* distinct

contra'ente *nmf* contracting party

contra'ereo *a* anti-aircraft

contraf'fa|re *vt* disguise; (*imitare*) imitate; (*falsificare*) forge. **~tto** *a* forged. **~zi'one** *nf* disguising; (*imitazione*) imitation; (*falsificazione*) forgery

con'tralto *nm* countertenor ● *nf* contralto

contrap'peso *nm* counterbalance

contrap'por|re *vt* counter; (*confrontare*) compare. **~si** *vr* contrast; **~si a** be opposed to

contraria'mente *adv* contrary (**a** to)

contrari|'are *vt* oppose; (*infastidire*) annoy. **~'arsi** *vr* get annoyed. **~età** *nf inv* adversity; (*ostacolo*) set-back

con'trario *a* contrary, opposite; (*direzione*) opposite; (*sfavorevole*) unfavourable ● *nm* contrary, opposite; **al ~** on the contrary

con'trarre *vt* contract

contras|se'gnare *vt* mark. **~-'segno** *nm* mark; **[in] ~segno** (*spedizione*) cash on delivery, COD

contra'stante *a* contrasting

contra'stare *vt* oppose; (*contestare*) contest ● *vi* clash. **con'trasto** *nm* contrast; (*litigio*) dispute

contrattac'care *vt* counter-attack. **contrat'tacco** *nm* counter-attack

contrat'ta|re *vt/i* negotiate; (*mercanteggiare*) bargain. **~zi'one** *nf* (*salariale*) bargaining

contrat'tempo *nm* hitch

con'tratt|o *pp di* **contrarre** ● *nm* contract. **~o a termine** fixed-term contract. **~u'ale** *a* contractual

contravve'n|ire *vi* contravene. **~zi'one** *nf* contravention; (*multa*) fine

contrazi'one *nf* contraction; (*di prezzi*) reduction

contribu'ente *nmf* contributor; (*del fisco*) taxpayer

contribu|'ire *vi* contribute. **contri-'buto** *nm* contribution

'contro *prep* against; **~ di me** against me ● *nm* **il pro e il ~** the pros and cons *pl*

contro'battere *vt* counter

controbilanci'are *vt* counterbalance

controcor'rente *a* (*idee, persona*) non-conformist ● *adv* upriver; *fig* upstream

controffen'siva *nf* counter-offensive

controfi'gura *nf* stand-in

controfir'mare *vt* countersign

controindicazi'one *nf Med* contraindication

control'la|re *vt* control; (*verificare*) check; (*collaudare*) test. **~rsi** *vr* have self-control. **~to** *a* controlled

con'trol|lo *nm* control; (*verifica*) check; *Med* check-up. **~lo delle nascite** birth control. **~'lore** *nm* controller; (*sui treni ecc*) [ticket] inspector. **~lore di volo** air-traffic controller

contro'luce *nf* **in ~** against the light

contro'mano *adv* in the wrong direction

contromi'sura *nf* countermeasure

contropi'ede *nm* **prendere in ~** catch off guard

controprodu'cente *a* self-defeating

con'trordin|e *nm* counter order; **salvo ~i** unless I/you hear to the contrary

contro'senso *nm* contradiction in terms

controspio'naggio *nm* counterespionage

contro'vento *adv* against the wind

contro'vers|ia *nf* controversy; *Jur* dispute. **~o** *a* controversial

contro'voglia *adv* unwillingly

contu'macia *nf* default; **in ~** in one's absence

contun'dente *a* (*corpo, arma*) blunt

contur'ba|nte *a* perturbing

contusi'one *nf* bruise

convale'scen|te *a* convalescent. **~za** *nf* convalescence; **essere in ~za** be convalescing

con'vali|da *nf* validation. **~'dare** *vt* confirm; validate (*atto, biglietto*)

con'vegno *nm* meeting; (*congresso*) congress

conve'nevol|e *a* suitable; **~i** *pl* pleasantries

conveni'en|te *a* convenient; (*prezzo*) attractive; (*vantaggioso*) advantageous. **~za** *nf* convenience; (*interesse*) advantage; (*di prezzo*) attractiveness

conve'nire *vi* (*riunirsi*) gather; (*concordare*) agree; (*ammettere*) admit; (*essere opportuno*) be convenient ● *vt* agree on; **ci conviene andare** it is better to go; **non mi conviene stancarmi** I'd better not tire myself out

con'vento nm (di suore) convent; (di frati) monastery

conve'nuto a fixed

convenzi|o'nale a conventional. ~'one nf convention

conver'gen|te a converging. ~za nf fig confluence

con'vergere vi converge

conver'sa|re vi converse. ~zi'one nf conversation

conversi'one nf conversion

con'verso pp di **convergere**

conver'tibile nf Auto convertible

conver'ti|re vt convert. ~rsi vr be converted. ~to, -a nmf convert

con'vesso a convex

convin'cente a convincing

con'vin|cere vt convince. ~to a convinced. ~zi'one nf conviction

con'vitto nm boarding school

convi'ven|te nm common-law husband ● nf common-law wife. ~za nf cohabitation. **con'vivere** vi live together

convivi'ale a convivial

convo'ca|re vt convene. ~zi'one nf convening

convogli'are vt convey; ⟨navi:⟩ convoy. **con'voglio** nm convoy; (ferroviario) train

convulsi'one nf convulsion. **con-'vulso** a convulsive; (febbrile) feverish

coope'ra|re vi co-operate. ~'tiva nf co-operative. ~zi'one nf co-operation

coordina'mento nm co-ordination

coordi'na|re vt co-ordinate. ~ta nf Math coordinate. ~zi'one nf co-ordination

co'perchio nm lid; (copertura) cover

co'perta nf blanket; (copertura) cover; Naut deck

coper'tina nf cover; (di libro) dust-jacket

co'perto pp di **coprire** ● a covered; ⟨cielo⟩ overcast ● nm (a tavola) place; (prezzo del coperto) cover charge; **al ~** under cover

coper'tone nm tarpaulin; (gomma) tyre

coper'tura nf covering; Comm, Fin cover

'copia nf copy; **bella/brutta ~** fair/rough copy. **~ su carta** hardcopy. **copi'are** vt copy

copi'one nm script

copi'oso a plentiful

'coppa nf (calice) goblet; (per gelato

ecc) dish; Sport cup. **~ [di] gelato** ice-cream (served in a dish)

cop'petta nf (di ceramica, vetro) bowl; (di gelato) small tub

'coppia nf couple; (in carte) pair

co'prente a (cipria, vernice) covering

copri'capo nm headgear

coprifu'oco nm curfew

copri'letto nm bedspread

copripiu'mino nm duvet cover

co'prir|e vt cover; drown ⟨suono⟩; hold ⟨carica⟩. **~si** vr (vestirsi) cover up; fig cover oneself; ⟨cielo:⟩ become overcast

coque sf **alla ~** ⟨uovo⟩ soft-boiled

co'raggi|o nm courage; (sfacciataggine) nerve; **~o!** come on. **~'oso** a courageous

co'rale a choral

co'rallo nm coral

co'rano nm Koran

co'raz|za nf armour; (di animali) shell. **~'zata** nf battleship. **~'zato** a ⟨nave⟩ armour-clad

corbelle'ria nf nonsense; (sproposito) blunder

'corda nf cord; (spago, Mus) string; (fune) rope; (cavo) cable; **essere giù di ~** be depressed; **dare ~ a qcno** encourage sb. **corde** pl **vocali** vocal cords

cordi'al|e a cordial ● nm (bevanda) cordial; **saluti ~i** best wishes. **~ità** nf cordiality

'cordless nm inv Teleph cordless

cor'doglio nm grief; (lutto) mourning

cor'done nm cord; (schieramento) cordon. **~ ombelicale** umbilical cord

core|ogra'fia nf choreography. **~'ografo, -a** nmf choreographer

cori'andoli nmpl confetti sg

cori'andolo nm (spezia) coriander

cori'car|e vt put to bed. **~si** vr go to bed

co'rista nmf choir member

cor'nacchia nf crow

corna vedi **corno**

corna'musa nf bagpipes pl

'cornea nf cornea

cor'nett|a nf Mus cornet; (del telefono) receiver. **~o** nm (brioche) croissant

cor'ni|ce nf frame. **~ci'one** nm cornice

'corno nm (pl nf **corna**) horn; **fare le corna a qcno** be unfaithful to sb; **fare le corna** (per scongiuro) touch wood. **cor'nuto** a horned ● nm (fam: marito tradito) cuckold; (insulto) bastard

'coro nm chorus; Relig choir

co'rolla nf corolla

co'rona *nf* crown; *(di fiori)* wreath; *(rosario)* rosary. **~'mento** *nm (di impresa)* crowning. **coro'nare** *vt* crown; *‹sogno›* fulfil

cor'petto *nm* bodice

'corpo *nm* body; *(Mil, diplomatico)* corps *inv*; **a ~ a ~** man to man; **andare di ~** move one's bowels. **~ di ballo** corps de ballet. **~ insegnante** teaching staff. **~ del reato** incriminating item

corpo'rale *a* corporal

corporati'vismo *nm* corporatism

corpora'tura *nf* build

corporazi'one *nf* corporation

cor'poreo *a* bodily

cor'poso *a* full-bodied

corpu'lento *a* stout

cor'puscolo *nm* corpuscle

corre'dare *vt* equip

corre'dino *nm (per neonato)* layette

cor'redo *nm (nuziale)* trousseau

cor'reggere *vt* correct; lace *‹bevanda›*

corre'lare *vt* correlate

cor'rente *a* running; *(in vigore)* current; *(frequente)* everyday; *‹inglese ecc›* fluent ● *nf* current; *(d'aria)* draught; **essere al ~** be up to date. **~'mente** *adv ‹parlare›* fluently

'correre *vi* run; *(affrettarsi)* hurry; *Sport* race; *‹notizie:›* circulate; **~ dietro a** run after ● *vt* run; **~ un pericolo** run a risk; **lascia ~!** don't bother!

corre|tta'mente *adv* correctly. **cor'retto** *pp di* **correggere** ● *a* correct; *‹caffè›* with a drop of alcohol. **~zi'one** *nf* correction. **~zione di bozze** proofreading

cor'rida *nf* bullfight

corri'doio *nm* corridor; *Aeron* aisle

corri|'dore, -'trice *nmf* racer; *(a piedi)* runner

corri'era *nf* coach, bus

corri'ere *nm* courier; *(posta)* mail; *(spedizioniere)* carrier

corri'mano *nm* bannister

corrispet'tivo *nm* amount due

corrispon'den|te *a* corresponding ● *nmf* correspondent. **~za** *nf* correspondence; **scuola/corsi per ~za** correspondence course; **vendite per ~za** mail-order [shopping]. **corri'spondere** *vi* correspond; *‹stanza:›* communicate; **corrispondere a** *(contraccambiare)* return

corri'sposto *a ‹amore›* reciprocated

corrobo'rare *vt* strengthen; *fig* corroborate

cor'roder|e *vt*, **~si** *vr* corrode

cor'rompere *vt* corrupt; *(con denaro)* bribe

corrosi'one *nf* corrosion. **corro'sivo** *a* corrosive

cor'roso *pp di* **corrodere**

cor'rotto *pp di* **corrompere** ● *a* corrupt

corrucci'a|rsi *vr* be vexed. **~to** *a* upset

corru'gare *vt* wrinkle; **~ la fronte** knit one's brows

corruzi'one *nf* corruption; *(con denaro)* bribery

'corsa *nf* running; *(rapida)* dash; *Sport* race; *(di treno ecc)* journey; **di ~** at a run; **fare una ~** run

cor'sia *nf* gangway; *(di ospedale)* ward; *Auto* lane; *(di supermercato)* aisle

cor'sivo *nm* italics *pl*

'corso *pp di* **correre** ● *nm* course; *(strada)* main street; *Comm* circulation; **lavori in ~** work in progress; **nel ~ di** during. **~ d'acqua** watercourse

'corte *nf* [court]yard; *(Jur, regale)* court; **fare la ~ a qcno** court sb. **~ d'appello** court of appeal

cor'teccia *nf* bark

corteggia'mento *nm* courtship

coreggi'a|re *vt* court. **~'tore** *nm* admirer

cor'teo *nm* procession

cor'te|se *a* courteous. **~'sia** *nf* courtesy; **per ~sia** please

cortigi'ano, -a *nmf* courtier ● *nf* courtesan

cor'tile *nm* courtyard

cor'tina *nf* curtain; *(schermo)* screen

'corto *a* short; **per farla corta** in short; **essere a ~ di** be short of. **~ circuito** *nm* short [circuit]

cortome'traggio *nm Cinema* short

cor'vino *a* jet-black

'corvo *nm* raven

'cosa *nf* thing; *(faccenda)* matter; *inter, rel* what; **[che] ~** what; **nessuna ~** nothing; **ogni ~** everything; **per prima ~** first of all; **tante cose** so many things; *(augurio)* all the best

'cosca *nf* clan

'coscia *nf* thigh; *Culin* leg

cosci'en|te *a* conscious. **~za** *nf* conscience; *(consapevolezza)* consciousness

co'scri|tto *nm* conscript. **~zi'one** *nf* conscription

così *adv* so; (*in questo modo*) like this, like that; (*perciò*) therefore; **le cose stanno ~** that's how things stand; **fermo ~!** hold it; **proprio ~!** exactly!; **basta ~!** that will do!; **ah, è ~?** it's like that, is it?; **~ ~** so-so; **e ~ via** and so on; **per ~ dire** so to speak; **più di ~** any more; **una ~ cara ragazza!** such a nice girl!; **è stato ~ generoso da aiutarti** he was kind enough to help you ● *conj* (*allora*) so ● *a inv* (*tale*) like that, such; **una ragazza ~** a girl like that, such a girl

cosicché *conj* and so

cosid'detto *a* so-called

co'smesi *nf* cosmetics

co'smetico *a & nm* cosmetic

'cosmico *a* cosmic

'cosmo *nm* cosmos

cosmopo'lita *a* cosmopolitan

co'spargere *vt* sprinkle; (*disseminare*) scatter

co'spetto *nm* **al ~ di** in the presence of

co'spicuo *a* conspicuous; ‹*somma ecc*› considerable

cospi'ra|re *vi* conspire. **~'tore, ~'trice** *nmf* conspirator. **~zi'one** *nf* conspiracy

'costa *nf* coast, coastline; *Anat* rib

costà *adv* there

co'stan|te *a & nm* constant. **~za** *nf* constancy

co'stare *vi* cost; **quanto costa?** how much is it?

co'stata *nf* chop

costeggi'are *vt* (*per mare*) coast; (*per terra*) skirt

co'stei *pron vedi* **costui**

costellazi'one *nf* constellation

coster'na|to *a* dismayed. **~zi'one** *nf* consternation

costi'er|a *nf* stretch of coast. **~o** *a* coastal

costi'pa|to *a* constipated. **~zi'one** *nf* constipation; (*raffreddore*) bad cold

costitu'ir|e *vt* constitute; (*formare*) form; (*nominare*) appoint. **~si** *vr Jur* give oneself up

costituzio'nale *a* constitutional. **costituzi'one** *nf* constitution; (*fondazione*) setting up

'costo *nm* cost; **ad ogni ~** at all costs; **a nessun ~** on no account

'costola *nf* rib; (*di libro*) spine

costo'letta *nf* cutlet

co'storo *pron vedi* **costui**

co'stoso *a* costly

co'stretto *pp di* **costringere**

co'stri|ngere *vt* compel; (*stringere*) constrict. **~t'tivo** *a* coercive. **~zi'one** *nf* constraint

costru'|ire *vt* build, construct. **~t'tivo** *a* constructive. **~zi'one** *nf* building, construction

co'stui, co'stei, *pl* **co'storo** *prons* (*soggetto*) he, she, *pl* they; (*complemento*) him, her, *pl* them

co'stume *nm* (*usanza*) custom; (*condotta*) morals *pl*; (*indumento*) costume. **~ da bagno** swim-suit; (*da uomo*) swimming trunks

co'tenna *nf* pigskin; (*della pancetta*) rind

coto'letta *nf* cutlet

co'tone *nm* cotton. **~ idrofilo** cotton wool, absorbent cotton *Am*

'cotta *nf* (*fam: innamoramento*) crush

'cottimo *nm* **lavorare a ~** do piecework

'cotto *pp di* **cuocere** ● *a* done; (*infatuato*) in love; (*sbronzo*) drunk; **ben ~** ‹*carne*› well done

cotton fi'oc® *nm inv* cotton bud

cot'tura *nf* cooking

co'vare *vt* hatch; sicken for ‹*malattia*›; harbour ‹*odio*› ● *vi* smoulder

'covo *nm* den

co'vone *nm* sheaf

'cozza *nf* mussel

coz'zare *vi* **~ contro** bump into. **'cozzo** *nm fig* clash

C.P. *abbr* (**Casella Postale**) PO Box

'crampo *nm* cramp

'cranio *nm* skull

cra'tere *nm* crater

cra'vatta *nf* tie; (*a farfalla*) bow-tie

cre'anza *nf* politeness; **mala ~** bad manners

cre'a|re *vt* create; (*causare*) cause. **~tività** *nf* creativity. **~'tivo** *a* creative. **~to** *nm* creation. **~'tore, ~'trice** *nmf* creator. **~zi'one** *nf* creation

crea'tura *nf* creature; (*bambino*) baby; **povera ~!** poor thing!

cre'den|te *nmf* believer. **~za** *nf* belief; *Comm* credit; (*mobile*) sideboard. **~zi'ali** *nfpl* credentials

'creder|e *vt* believe; (*pensare*) think ● *vi* **~e in** believe in; **credo di sì** think so; **non ti credo** I don't believe you. **~si** *vr* think oneself to be; **si crede uno scrittore** he flatters himself he is a writer. **cre'dibile** *a* credible. **credibilità** *nf* credibility

'credi|to *nm* credit; (*stima*) esteem;

comprare a ~to buy on credit. **~'tore, ~'trice** *nmf* creditor

'credo *nm inv* credo

credulità *nf* credulity

'credu|lo *a* credulous. **~'lone, -a** *nmf* simpleton

'crema *nf* cream; (*di uova e latte*) custard. **~ idratante** moisturizer. **~ pasticciera** egg custard. **~ solare** suntan lotion

cre'ma|re *vt* cremate. **~'torio** *nm* crematorium. **~zi'one** *nf* cremation

crème cara'mel *nf* crème caramel

creme'ria *nf* dairy (*also selling ice cream and cakes*)

Crem'lino *nm* Kremlin

'crepa *nf* crack

cre'paccio *nm* cleft; (*di ghiacciaio*) crevasse

crepacu'ore *nm* heart-break

crepa'pelle *adv* **a ~** fit to burst; **ridere a ~** split one's sides with laughter

cre'pare *vi* crack; (*fam: morire*) kick the bucket; **~ dal ridere** laugh fit to burst

crepa'tura *nf* crevice

crêpe *nf inv* pancake

crepi'tare *vi* crackle

cre'puscolo *nm* twilight

cre'scendo *nm* crescendo

'cresc|ere *vi* grow; (*aumentare*) increase ● *vt* (*allevare*) bring up; (*aumentare*) raise. **~ita** *nf* growth; (*aumento*) increase. **~i'uto** *pp di* **crescere**

'cresi|ma *nf* confirmation. **~'mare** *vt* confirm

'crespo *a* ⟨*capelli*⟩ frizzy ● *nm* crêpe

'cresta *nf* crest; (*cima*) peak

'creta *nf* clay

'Creta *nf* Crete

cre'tino, -a *a* stupid ● *nmf* idiot

cric *nm* jack

cri'ceto *nm* hamster

crimi'nal|e *a & nmf* criminal. **~ità** *nf* crime. **'crimine** *nm* crime

crimi'noso *a* criminal

'crin|e *nm* horsehair. **~i'era** *nf* mane

'cripta *nf* crypt

crisan'temo *nm* chrysanthemum

'crisi *nf inv* crisis; *Med* fit

cristal'lino *nm* crystalline

cristalliz'zar|e *vt,* **~si** *vr* crystallize; ⟨*fig: parola, espressione:*⟩ become part of the language

cri'stallo *nm* crystal

Cristia'nesimo *nm* Christianity

cristi'ano, -a *a & nmf* Christian

'Cristo *nm* Christ; **un povero c~** a poor beggar

cri'terio *nm* criterion; (*buon senso*) [common] sense

'criti|ca *nf* criticism; (*recensione*) review. **criti'care** *vt* criticize. **~co** *a* critical ● *nm* critic. **~cone, -a** *nmf* faultfinder

crivel'lare *vt* riddle (**di** with)

cri'vello *nm* sieve

Cro'azia *nf* Croatia

croc'cante *a* crisp ● *nm* type of crunchy nut biscuit

croc'chetta *nf* croquette

'croce *nf* cross; **a occhio e ~** roughly; **fare testa e ~** spin a coin. **C~ Rossa** Red Cross

croce'via *nm inv* crossroads *sg*

croci'ata *nf* crusade

cro'cicchio *nm* crossroads *sg*

croci'era *nf* cruise; *Archit* crossing

croci'fi|ggere *vt* crucify. **~ssi'one** *nf* crucifixion. **~sso** *pp di* **crocifiggere** ● *a* crucified ● *nm* crucifix

crogio'larsi *vr* bask

crogi[u]'olo *nm* crucible; *fig* melting pot

crol'lare *vi* collapse; ⟨*prezzi:*⟩ slump. **'crollo** *nm* collapse; (*dei prezzi*) slump

cro'mato *a* chromium-plated. **'cromo** *nm* chrome. **cromo'soma** *nm* chromosome

'cronaca *nf* chronicle; (*di giornale*) news; *TV, Radio* commentary; **fatto di ~** news item. **~ nera** crime news

'cronico *a* chronic

cro'nista *nmf* reporter

crono'logico *a* chronological

cronome'traggio *nm* timing

cronome'trare *vt* time

cro'nometro *nm* chronometer

'crosta *nf* crust; (*di formaggio*) rind; (*di ferita*) scab; (*quadro*) daub

cro'staceo *nm* shellfish

cro'stata *nf* tart

cro'stino *nm* croûton

crucci'arsi *vr* worry. **'cruccio** *nm* worry

cruci'ale *a* crucial

cruci'verba *nm inv* crossword [puzzle]

cru'del|e *a* cruel. **~tà** *nf inv* cruelty

'crudo *a* raw; (*rigido*) harsh

cru'ento *a* bloody

cru'miro *nm* blackleg, scab

'crusca *nf* bran

cru'scotto *nm* dashboard

'Cuba *nf* Cuba

cu'betto *nm* ~ **di ghiaccio** ice cube

'cubico *a* cubic

cubi'tal|e *a* **a caratteri ~i** in enormous letters

'cubo *nm* cube

cuc'cagna *nf* abundance; (*baldoria*) merry-making; **paese della ~** land of plenty

cuc'cetta *nf* (*su un treno*) couchette; *Naut* berth

cucchia'ino *nm* teaspoon

cucchi'a|io *nm* spoon; **al ~io** ⟨*dolce*⟩ creamy. **~i'ata** *nf* spoonful

'cuccia *nf* dog's bed; **fa la ~!** lie down!

cuccio'lata *nf* litter

'cucciolo *nm* puppy

cu'cina *nf* kitchen; (*il cucinare*) cooking; (*cibo*) food; (*apparecchio*) cooker; **far da ~** cook; **libro di ~** cook[ery] book. **~ a gas** gas cooker

cuci'n|are *vt* cook. **~ino** *nm* kitchenette

cu'ci|re *vt* sew; **macchina per ~re** sewing-machine. **~to** *nm* sewing. **~'tura** *nf* seam

cucù *nm inv* cuckoo

'cuculo *nm* cuculo

'cuffia *nf* bonnet; (*da bagno*) bathing-cap; (*ricevitore*) headphones *pl*

cu'gino, -a *nmf* cousin

'cui *pron rel* (*persona: con prep*) who, whom *fml*; (*cose, animali: con prep*) which; (*tra articolo e nome*) whose; **la persona con ~ ho parlato** the person [who] I spoke to; **la ditta per ~ lavoro** the company I work for, the company for which I work; **l'amico il ~ libro è stato pubblicato** the friend whose book was published; **in ~** (*dove*) where; (*quando*) that; **per ~** (*perciò*) so; **la città in ~ vivo** the city I live in, the city where I live; **il giorno in ~ l'ho visto** the day [that] I saw him

culi'nari|a *nf* cookery. **~o** *a* culinary

'culla *nf* cradle. **cul'lare** *vt* rock

culmi'na|nte *a* culminating. **~re** *vi* culminate. **'culmine** *nm* peak

'culo *nm vulg* arse; (*fortuna*) luck

'culto *nm* cult; *Relig* religion; (*adorazione*) worship

cul'tu|ra *nf* culture. **~ra generale** general knowledge. **~'rale** *a* cultural

cultu'ris|mo *nm* body-building. **~ta** *nmf* body builder

cumula'tivo *a* cumulative; **biglietto ~** group ticket

'cumulo *nm* pile; (*mucchio*) heap; (*nuvola*) cumulus

'cuneo *nm* wedge

cu'netta *nf* gutter

cu'ocere *vt/i* cook; fire ⟨*ceramica*⟩

cu'oco, -a *nmf* cook

cu'oio *nm* leather. **~ capelluto** scalp

cu'ore *nm* heart; **cuori** *pl* (*carte*) hearts; **nel profondo del ~** in one's heart of hearts; **di [buon] ~** ⟨*persona*⟩ kind-hearted; **nel ~ della notte** in the middle of the night; **stare a ~ a qcno** be very important to sb

cupi'digia *nf* greed

'cupo *a* gloomy; ⟨*suono*⟩ deep

'cupola *nf* dome

'cura *nf* care; (*amministrazione*) management; *Med* treatment; **a ~ di** edited by; **in ~** under treatment. **~ dimagrante** [slimming] diet. **cu'rante** *a* **medico curante** GP, doctor

cu'rar|e *vt* take care of; *Med* treat; (*guarire*) cure; edit ⟨*testo*⟩. **~si** *vr* take care of oneself; *Med* follow a treatment; **~si di** (*badare a*) mind

cu'rato *nm* parish priest

cura'tore, -'trice *nmf* trustee; (*di testo*) editor

'curia *nf* curia

curio's|are *vi* be curious; (*mettere il naso*) pry (**in** into); (*nei negozi*) look around. **~ità** *nf inv* curiosity. **curi'oso** *a* curious; (*strano*) odd

cur'sore *nm Comput* cursor

'curva *nf* curve; (*stradale*) bend. **~ a gomito** U-bend. **cur'vare** *vt* curve; ⟨*strada:*⟩ bend. **cur'varsi** *vr* bend. **'curvo** *a* curved; (*piegato*) bent

cusci'netto *nm* pad; *Mech* bearing

cu'scino *nm* cushion; (*guanciale*) pillow. **~ d'aria** air cushion

'cuspide *nf* spire

cu'stod|e *nm* caretaker. **~e giudiziario** official receiver. **~ia** *nf* care; *Jur* custody; (*astuccio*) case. **~ia cautelare** remand. **custo'dire** *vt* keep; (*badare*) look after

cu'taneo *a* skin *attrib*

'cute *nf* skin

cu'ticola *nf* cuticle

Dd

da *prep* from; (*con verbo passivo*) by; (*moto a luogo*) to; (*moto per luogo*) through; (*stato in luogo*) at; (*temporale*) since; (*continuativo*) for; (*causale*) with; (*in qualità di*) as; (*come*) like; **da Roma a Milano** from Rome to Milan; **staccare un quadro dalla parete** take a picture off the wall; **i bambini dai 5 ai 10 anni** children between 5 and 10; **vedere qcsa da vicino/lontano** see sth from up close/from a distance; **scritto da** written by; **andare dal panettiere** go to the baker's; **passo da te più tardi** I'll come over to your place later; **passiamo da qui** let's go this way; **un appuntamento dal dentista** an appointment at the dentist's; **il treno passa da Venezia** the train goes through Venice; **dall'anno scorso** since last year; **vivo qui da due anni** I've been living here for two years; **da domani** from tomorrow; **piangere dal dolore** cry with pain; **ho molto da fare** I have a lot to do; **occhiali da sole** sunglasses; **qualcosa da mangiare** something to eat; **un uomo dai capelli scuri** a man with dark hair; **è un oggetto da poco** it's not worth much; **l'ho fatto da solo** I did it by myself; **si è fatto da sé** he is a self-made man; **non è da lui** it's not like him

dac'capo *adv* again; (*dall'inizio*) from the beginning

dacché *conj* since

'dado *nm* dice; *Culin* stock cube; *Techn* nut

daf'fare *nm* work

'dagli = da + gli. **'dai** = da + i

'dai *int* come on!

'daino *nm* deer; (*pelle*) buckskin

dal = da + il. **'dalla** = da + la. **'dalle** = da + le. **'dallo** = da + lo

'dalia *nf* dahlia

dal'tonico *a* colour-blind

'dama *nf* lady; (*nei balli*) partner; (*gioco*) draughts *sg*

dami'gella *nf* (*di sposa*) bridesmaid

damigi'ana *nf* demijohn

dam'meno *adv* **non essere ~ (di qcno)** be no less good (than sb)

da'naro *nm* = **denaro**

dana'roso *a* (*fam: ricco*) loaded

da'nese *a* Danish ● *nmf* Dane ● *nm* (*lingua*) Danish

Dani'marca *nf* Denmark

dan'na|re *vt* damn; **far ~re qcno** drive sb mad. **~to** *a* damned. **~zi'one** *nf* damnation

danneggi|a'mento *nm* damage. **~'are** *vt* damage; (*nuocere*) harm

'danno *nm* damage; (*a persona*) harm. **dan'noso** *a* harmful

Da'nubio *nm* Danube

'danza *nf* dance; (*il danzare*) dancing. **dan'zare** *vi* dance

dapper'tutto *adv* everywhere

dap'poco *a* worthless

dap'prima *adv* at first

'dardo *nm* dart

'dar|e *vt* give; sit (*esame*); have (*festa*); **~e qcsa a qcno** give sb sth; **~e da mangiare a qcno** give sb something to eat; **~e il benvenuto a qcno** welcome sb; **~e la buonanotte a qcno** say good night to sb; **~e del tu/del lei a qcno** address sb as "tu"/"lei"; **~e del cretino a qcno** call sb an idiot; **~e qcsa per scontato** take sth for granted; **cosa danno alla TV stasera?** what's on TV tonight? ● *vi* **~e nell'occhio** be conspicuous; **~e alla testa** go to one's head; **~e su** (*finestra, casa:*) look on to; **~e sui** *o* **ai nervi a qcno** get on sb's nerves ● *nm* *Comm* debit. **~si** *vr* (*scambiarsi*) give each other; **~si da fare** get down to it; **si è dato tanto da fare!** he went to so much trouble!; **~si a** (*cominciare*) take up; **~si al bere** take to drink; **~si per** (*malato, assente*) pretend to be; **~si per vinto** give up; **può ~si** maybe

'darsena *nf* dock

'data *nf* date. **~ di emissione** date of issue. **~ di nascita** date of birth. **~ di scadenza** cut-off date

da'ta|re *vt* date; **a ~re da** as from. **~to** *a* dated

'dato *a* given; *(dedito)* addicted; **~ che** seeing that, given that ● *nm* datum. **~ di fatto** well-established fact; **dati** *pl* data. **da'tore** *nm* giver. **datore, datrice** *nmf* **di lavoro** employer

'dattero *nm* date

dattilogra'f|are *vt* type. **~ia** *nf* typing. **datti'lografo, -a** *nmf* typist

dattilo'scritto *a* *(copia)* typewritten

dat'torno *adv* **togliersi ~** clear off

da'vanti *adv* before; *(dirimpetto)* opposite; *(di fronte)* in front ● *a inv* front ● *nm* front; **~ a** *prep* before, in front of

davan'zale *nm* window sill

da'vanzo *adv* more than enough

dav'vero *adv* really; **per ~** in earnest; **dici ~?** honestly?

'dazio *nm* duty; *(ufficio)* customs *pl*

d.C. *abbr* **(dopo Cristo)** AD

'dea *nf* goddess

debel'lare *vt* defeat

debili'ta|nte *a* weakening. **~re** *vt* weaken. **~rsi** *vr* become debilitated. **~zi'one** *nf* debilitation

debita'mente *adv* duly

'debi|to *a* due; **a tempo ~** in due course ● *nm* debt. **~'tore, ~'trice** *nmf* debtor

'debo|le *a* weak; *(luce)* dim; *(suono)* faint ● *nm* weak point; *(preferenza)* weakness. **~'lezza** *nf* weakness

debor'dare *vi* overflow

debosci'ato *a* debauched

debut'ta|nte *nm* *(attore)* actor making his début ● *nf* actress making her début. **~re** *vi* make one's début. **de'butto** *nm* début

deca'den|te *a* decadent. **~'tismo** *nm* decadence. **~za** *nf* decline; *Jur* loss. **deca'dere** *vi* lapse. **decadi'mento** *nm* *(delle arti)* decline

decaffei'nato *a* decaffeinated ● *nm* decaffeinated coffee, decaf *fam*

decan'tare *vt* *(lodare)* praise

decapi'ta|re *vt* decapitate; behead *(condannato)*. **~zi'one** *nf* decapitation; beheading

decappot'tabile *a* convertible

de'ce|dere *vi* *(morire)* die. **~'duto** *a* deceased

decele'rare *vt* decelerate, slow down

decen'nale *a* ten-yearly. **de'cennio** *nm* decade

de'cen|te *a* decent. **~te'mente** *adv* decently. **~za** *nf* decency

decentra'mento *nm* decentralization

de'cesso *nm* death; **atto di ~** death certificate

de'cider|e *vt* decide; settle *(questione)*. **~si** *vr* make up one's mind

deci'frare *vt* decipher; *(documenti cifrati)* decode

deci'male *a* decimal

deci'mare *vt* decimate

'decimo *a* tenth

de'cina *nf* *Math* ten; **una ~ di** *(circa dieci)* about ten

decisa'mente *adv* definitely, decidedly

decisio'nale *a* decision-making

deci|si'one *nf* decision. **~'sivo** *a* decisive. **de'ciso** *pp di* **decidere** ● *a* decided

decla'ma|re *vt/i* declaim. **~'torio** *a* *(stile)* declamatory

declas'sare *vt* downgrade

decli'na|re *vt* decline; **~re ogni responsabilità** disclaim all responsibility ● *vi* go down; *(tramontare)* set. **~zi'one** *nf* *Gram* declension. **de'clino** *nm* decline; **in declino** *(popolarità:)* on the decline

decodificazi'one *nf* decoding

decol'lare *vi* take off

décolle'té *nm inv* décolleté, low neckline

de'collo *nm* take-off

decolo'ra|nte *nm* bleach. **~re** *vt* bleach

decolorazi'one *nf* bleaching

decom'po|rre *vt*, **~rsi** *vr* decompose. **~sizi'one** *nf* decomposition

deconcen'trarsi *vr* become distracted

deconge'lare *vt* defrost

decongestio'nare *vt* *Med, fig* relieve congestion in

deco'ra|re *vt* decorate. **~'tivo** *a* decorative. **~to** *a* *(ornato)* decorated. **~'tore, ~'trice** *nmf* decorator. **~zi'one** *nf* decoration

de'coro *nm* decorum

decorosa'mente *adv* decorously. **decoroso** *a* dignified

decor'renza *nf* **~ dal...** starting from...

de'correre *vi* pass; **a ~ da** with effect from. **de'corso** *pp di* **decorrere** ● *nm* passing; *Med* course

de'crepito *a* decrepit

decre'scente *a* decreasing. **de'crescere** *vi* decrease; *(prezzi:)* go down; *(acque:)* subside

decre'tare *vt* decree. **de'creto** *nm* decree. **decreto legge** *decree which has the force of law*

'dedalo *nm* maze

'dedica *nf* dedication

dedi'car|e *vt* dedicate. **~si** *vr* dedicate oneself

'dedi|to *a* **~ a** given to; *(assorto)* engrossed in; addicted to *(vizi)*. **~zi'one** *nf* dedication

de'dotto *pp di* dedurre

dedu'cibile *a (tassa)* allowable

de'du|rre *vt* deduce; *(sottrarre)* deduct. **~t'tivo** *a* deductive. **~zi'one** *nf* deduction

defal'care *vt* deduct

defe'rire *vt* Jur remit

defezi|o'nare *vi (abbandonare)* defect. **~'one** *nf* defection

defici'en|te *a (mancante)* deficient; *Med* mentally deficient ● *nmf* mental defective; *pej* half-wit. **~za** *nf* deficiency; *(lacuna)* gap; *Med* mental deficiency

'defici|t *nm inv* deficit. **~'tario** *a (bilancio)* deficit *attrib*

defi'larsi *vr (scomparire)* slip away

défilé *nm inv* fashion show

defi'ni|re *vt* define; *(risolvere)* settle. **~tiva'mente** *adv* for good. **~'tivo** *a* definitive. **~to** *a* definite. **~zi'one** *nf* definition; *(soluzione)* settlement

deflazi'one *nf* deflation

deflet'tore *nm* Auto quarterlight

deflu'ire *vi (liquidi:)* flow away; *(persone:)* stream out

de'flusso *nm (di marea)* ebb

defor'mar|e *vt* deform *(arto)*; *fig* distort. **~si** *vr* lose its shape. **de'form|e** *a* deformed. **~ità** *nf* deformity

defor'ma|to *a* warped. **~zi'one** *nf (di fatti)* distortion; **è una ~zione professionale** put it down to the job

defrau'dare *vt* defraud

de'funto, -a *a & nmf* deceased

degene'ra|re *vi* degenerate. **~to** *a* degenerate. **~zi'one** *nf* degeneration. **de'genere** *a* degenerate

de'gen|te *a* bedridden ● *nmf* patient. **~za** *nf* confinement

'degli = di + gli

deglu'tire *vt* swallow

de'gnar|e *vt* **~e qcno di uno sguardo** deign to look at sb. **~si** *vr* deign, condescend

'degno *a* worthy; *(meritevole)* deserving

degrada'mento *nm* degradation

degra'dante *a* demeaning

degra'da|re *vt* degrade. **~rsi** *vr* lower oneself; *(città:)* fall into a state of disrepair. **~zi'one** *nf* degradation

de'grado *nm* damage; **~ ambientale** *nm* environmental damage

degu'sta|re *vt* taste. **~zi'one** *nf* tasting

'dei = di + i. **'del** = di + il

dela'tore, -'trice *nmf* [police] informer. **~zi'one** *nf* informing

'delega *nf* proxy

dele'ga|re *vt* delegate. **~to** *nm* delegate. **~zi'one** *nf* delegation

dele'terio *a* harmful

del'fino *nm* dolphin; *(stile di nuoto)* butterfly [stroke]

de'libera *nf* bylaw

delibe'ra|re *vt/i* deliberate; **~ su/in** rule on/in. **~to** *a* deliberate

delicata'mente *adv* delicately

delica'tezza *nf* delicacy; *(fragilità)* frailty; *(tatto)* tact

deli'cato *a* delicate; *(salute)* frail; *(suono, colore)* soft

delimi'tare *vt* delimit

deline'a|re *vt* outline. **~rsi** *vr* be outlined; *fig* take shape. **~to** *a* defined

delin'quen|te *nmf* delinquent. **~za** *nf* delinquency

deli'rante *a* Med delirious; *(assurdo)* insane

deli'rare *vi* be delirious. **de'lirio** *nm* delirium; *fig* frenzy

de'litt|o *nm* crime. **~u'oso** *a* criminal

de'lizi|a *nf* delight. **~'are** *vt* delight. **~'oso** *a* delightful; *(cibo)* delicious

'della = di + la. **'delle** = di + le. **'dello** = di + lo

'delta *nm inv* delta

delta'plano *nm* hang-glider; **fare ~** go hang-gliding

delucidazi'one *nf* clarification

delu'dente *a* disappointing

de'lu|dere *vt* disappoint. **~si'one** *nf* disappointment. **de'luso** *a* disappointed

dema'gogico *a* popularity-seeking, demagogic

demar'ca|re *vt* demarcate. **~zi'one** *nf* demarcation

de'men|te *a* demented. **~za** *nf* dementia. **~zi'ale** *a (assurdo)* zany

demilitariz'za|re *vt* demilitarize. **~zi'one** *nf* demilitarization

demistificazi'one *nf* debunking

demo'cra|tico *a* democratic. **~'zia** *nf* democracy

democristi'ano, -a *a & nmf* Christian Democrat

demogra'fia *nf* demography. **demo-'grafico** *a* demographic

demo'li|re *vt* demolish. **~zi'one** *nf* demolition

'demone *nm* demon. **de'monio** *nm* demon

demoraliz'zar|e *vt* demoralize. **~si** *vr* become demoralized

de'mordere *vi* give up

demoti'vato *a* demotivated

de'nari *nmpl* (*nelle carte*) diamonds

de'naro *nm* money

deni'gra|re *vt* denigrate. **~'torio** *a* denigratory

denomi'na|re *vt* name. **~'tore** *nm* denominator. **~zi'one** *nf* denomination; **~zione di origine controllata** mark guaranteeing the quality of a wine

deno'tare *vt* denote

densità *nf inv* density. **'denso** *a* thick, dense

den'ta|le *a* dental. **~rio** *a* dental. **~ta** *nf* bite. **~'tura** *nf* teeth *pl*

'dente *nm* tooth; (*di forchetta*) prong; **al ~** *Culin* just slightly firm. **~ del giudizio** wisdom tooth. **~ di latte** milk tooth. **denti'era** *nf* dentures *pl*, false teeth *pl*

denti'fricio *nm* toothpaste

den'tista *nmf* dentist

'dentro *adv* in, inside; (*in casa*) indoors; **da ~** from within; **qui ~** in here ● *prep* in, inside; (*di tempo*) within, by ● *nm* inside

denuclearizzazi'one *nf* denuclearization

denu'dar|e *vt* bare. **~si** *vr* strip

de'nunci|a, de'nunzia *nf* denunciation; (*alla polizia*) reporting; (*dei redditi*) [income] tax return. **~'are** *vt* denounce; (*accusare*) report

denu'tri|to *a* underfed. **~zi'one** *nf* malnutrition

deodo'rante *a & nm* deodorant

dépendance *nf inv* outbuilding

depe'ri|bile *a* perishable. **~'mento** *nm* wasting away; (*di merci*) deterioration. **~re** *vi* waste away

depi'la|re *vt* depilate. **~rsi** *vr* shave (*gambe*); pluck (*sopracciglia*). **~'torio** *nm* depilatory

deplo'rabile *a* deplorable

deplo'r|are *vt* deplore; (*dolersi di*) grieve over. **~evole** *a* deplorable

de'porre *vt* put down; lay down (*armi*); lay (*uova*); (*togliere da una carica*) depose; (*testimoniare*) testify

depor'ta|re *vt* deport. **~to, -a** *nmf* deportee. **~zi'one** *nf* deportation

deposi'tar|e *vt* deposit; (*lasciare in custodia*) leave; (*in magazzino*) store. **~io, -a** *nmf* (*di segreto*) repository. **~si** *vr* settle

de'posi|to *nm* deposit; (*luogo*) warehouse; *Mil* depot. **~to bagagli** left-luggage office. **~zi'one** *nf* deposition; (*da una carica*) removal

depra'va|re *vt* deprave. **~to** *a* depraved. **~zi'one** *nf* depravity

depre'ca|bile *a* appalling. **~re** *vt* deprecate

depre'dare *vt* plunder

depressi'one *nf* depression. **de'presso** *pp di* **deprimere** ● *a* depressed

deprez'zar|e *vt* depreciate. **~si** *vr* depreciate

depri'mente *a* depressing

de'prim|ere *vt* depress. **~si** *vr* become depressed

depu'ra|re *vt* purify. **~'tore** *nm* purifier

depu'ta|re *vt* delegate. **~to, -a** *nmf* deputy, Member of Parliament

deraglia'mento *nm* derailment

deragli'are *vi* go off the lines; **far ~** derail

'derby *nm inv Sport* local Derby

deregolamentazi'one *nf* deregulation

dere'litto *a* derelict

dere'tano *nm* backside, bottom

de'ri|dere *vt* deride. **~si'one** *nf* derision. **~'sorio** *a* derisory

de'riva *nf* drift; **andare alla ~** drift

deri'va|re *vi* **~re da** (*provenire*) derive from ● *vt* derive; (*sviare*) divert. **~zi'one** *nf* derivation; (*di fiume*) diversion

dermato|lo'gia *nf* dermatology. **~'lo-gico** *a* dermatological. **derma'tologo, -a** *nmf* dermatologist

'deroga *nf* dispensation. **dero'gare** *vi* **derogare a** depart from

der'rat|a *nf* merchandise. **~e alimentari** foodstuffs

deru'bare *vt* rob

descrit'tivo *a* descriptive. **des'critto** *pp di* **descrivere**

des'cri|vere *vt* describe. **~'vibile** *a* describable. **~zi'one** *nf* description

de'serto *a* uninhabited ● *nm* desert

deside'rabile *a* desirable

deside'rare *vt* wish; (*volere*) want;

(*intensamente*) long for; (*bramare*) desire; **desidera?** what would you like?, can I help you?; **lasciare a ~** leave a lot to be desired

desi'de|rio *nm* wish; (*brama*) desire; (*intenso*) longing. **~'roso** *a* desirous; (*bramoso*) longing

desi'gnare *vt* designate; (*fissare*) fix

desi'nenza *nf* ending

de'sistere *vi* **~ da** desist from

desktop publishing *nm inv* desktop publishing

deso'lante *a* distressing

deso'la|re *vt* distress. **~to** desolate; (*spiacente*) sorry. **~zi'one** *nf* desolation

'despota *nm* despot

de'star|e *vt* waken; *fig* awaken. **~si** *vr* waken; *fig* awaken

desti'na|re *vt* destine; (*nominare*) appoint; (*assegnare*) assign; (*indirizzare*) address. **~'tario** *nm* (*di lettera, pacco*) addressee. **~zi'one** *nf* destination; *fig* purpose

de'stino *nm* destiny; (*fato*) fate

destitu'ire *vt* dismiss. **~zi'one** *nf* dismissal

'desto *a liter* awake

'destra *nf* (*parte*) right; (*mano*) right hand; **prendere a ~** turn right

destreggi'ar|e *vi*, **~si** *vr* manoeuvre

de'strezza *nf* dexterity; (*abilità*) skill

'destro *a* right; (*abile*) skilful

detei'nato *a* tannin-free

dete'n|ere *vt* hold; ⟨*polizia:*⟩ detain. **~uto, -a** *nmf* prisoner. **~zi'one** *nf* detention

deter'gente *a* cleaning; ⟨*crema*⟩ cleansing ● *nm* detergent; (*per la pelle*) cleanser

deteriora'mento *nm* deterioration

deterio'rar|e *vt* cause to deteriorate. **~si** *vr* deteriorate

determi'nante *a* decisive

determi'na|re *vt* determine. **~rsi** *vr* **~rsi a** resolve to. **~'tezza** *nf* determination. **~'tivo** *a Gram* definite. **~to** *a* (*risoluto*) determined; (*particolare*) specific. **~zi'one** *nf* determination; (*decisione*) decision

deter'rente *a & nm* deterrent

deter'sivo *nm* detergent. **~ per i piatti** washing-up liquid

dete'stare *vt* detest, hate

deto'nare *vi* detonate

de'tra|rre *vt* deduct (**da** from). **~zi'one** *nf* deduction

detri'mento *nm* detriment; **a ~ di** to the detriment of

de'trito *nm* debris

'detta *nf* **a ~ di** according to

dettagli'ante *nmf Comm* retailer

dettagli'a|re *vt* detail. **~ta'mente** *adv* in detail

det'taglio *nm* detail; **al ~** *Comm* retail

det'ta|re *vt* dictate; **~re legge** *fig* lay down the law. **~to** *nm*, **~'tura** *nf* dictation

'detto *a* said; (*chiamato*) called; (*soprannominato*) nicknamed; **~ fatto** no sooner said than done ● *nm* saying

detur'pare *vt* disfigure

deva'sta|re *vt* devastate. **~to** *a* devastated. **~zi'one** *nf* devastation; *fig* ravages *pl*

devi'a|re *vi* deviate ● *vt* divert. **~zi'one** *nf* deviation; (*stradale*) diversion

devitaliz'zare *vt* deaden ⟨*dente*⟩

devo'lu|to *pp di* **devolvere** ● *a* devolved. **~zi'one** *nf* devolution

de'volvere *vt* devolve

de'vo|to *a* devout; (*affezionato*) devoted. **~zi'one** *nf* devotion

di *prep* of; (*partitivo*) some; (*scritto da*) by; ⟨*parlare, pensare ecc*⟩ about; (*con causa, mezzo*) with; (*con provenienza*) from; (*in comparazioni*) than; (*con infinito*) to; **la casa di mio padre/dei miei genitori** my father's house/my parents' house; **compra del pane** buy some bread; **hai del pane?** do you have any bread?; **un film di guerra** a war film; **piangere di dolore** cry with pain; **coperto di neve** covered with snow; **sono di Genova** I'm from Genoa; **uscire di casa** leave one's house; **più alto di te** taller than you; **è ora di partire** it's time to go; **crede di aver ragione** he thinks he's right; **dire di sì** say yes; **di domenica** on Sundays; **di sera** in the evening; **una pausa di un'ora** an hour's break; **un corso di due mesi** a two-month course

dia'bet|e *nm* diabetes. **~ico, -a** *a & nmf* diabetic

dia'bolico *a* diabolical

dia'dema *nm* diadem; (*di donna*) tiara

di'afano *a* diaphanous

dia'framma *nm* diaphragm; (*divisione*) screen

di'agnos|i *nf* diagnosis. **~ti'care** *vt* diagnose

diago'nale *a & nf* diagonal

dia'gramma *nm* diagram

dialet'tale *a* dialect. **dia'letto** *nm* dialect

dialo'gante *a* **unità ~** *Comput* interactive terminal

di'alogo *nm* dialogue

dia'mante *nm* diamond

di'ametro *nm* diameter

di'amine *int* **che ~...** what on earth...

diaposi'tiva *nf* slide

di'ario *nm* diary

diar'rea *nf* diarrhoea

di'avolo *nm* devil; **va al ~** go to hell!; **che ~ fai?** what the hell are you doing?

di'batt|ere *vt* debate. **~ersi** *vr* struggle. **~ito** *nm* debate; (*meno formale*) discussion

dica'stero *nm* office

di'cembre *nm* December

dice'ria *nf* rumour

dichia'ra|re *vt* state; (*ufficialmente*) declare. **~rsi** *vr* **si dichiara innocente** he says he's innocent. **~zi'one** *nf* statement; (*documento, di guerra*) declaration

dician'nove *a & nm* nineteen

dicias'sette *a & nm* seventeen

dici'otto *a & nm* eighteen

dici'tura *nf* wording

didasca'lia *nf* (*di film*) subtitle; (*di illustrazione*) caption

di'dattic|a *nf* didactics *sg*. **~o** *a* didactic; (*televisione*) educational

di'dentro *adv* inside

didi'etro *adv* behind ● *nm hum* hindquarters *pl*

di'eci *a & nm* ten

die'cina = **decina**

'diesel *a & nf inv* diesel

di'esis *nm inv* sharp

di'eta *nf* diet; **essere a ~** be on a diet. **die'tetico** *a* diet. **die'tista** *nmf* dietician. **die'tologo** *nmf* dietician

di'etro *adv* behind ● *prep* behind; (*dopo*) after ● *a* back; (*di zampe*) hind ● *nm* back; **le stanze di ~** the back rooms; **le zampe di ~** the hind legs

dietro'front *nm inv* about-turn; *fig* U-turn

di'fatti *adv* in fact

di'fen|dere *vt* defend. **~dersi** *vr* defend oneself. **~'siva** *nf* **stare sulla ~siva** be on the defensive. **~'sivo** *a* defensive. **~'sore** *nm* defender; **avvocato ~sore** defence counsel

di'fes|a *nf* defence; **prendere le ~e di qcno** come to sb's defence. **~o** *pp di* **difendere**

difet't|are *vi* be defective. **~are di** lack. **~ivo** *a* defective

di'fet|to *nm* defect; (*morale*) fault, flaw; (*mancanza*) lack; (*in tessuto, abito*) flaw; **essere in ~to** be at fault; **far ~to** be

lacking. **~'toso** *a* defective; (*abto*) flawed

diffa'ma|re *vt* (*con parole*) slander; (*per iscritto*) libel. **~'torio** *a* slanderous; (*per iscritto*) libellous. **~zi'one** *nf* slander; (*scritta*) libel

diffe'ren|te *a* different. **~za** *nf* difference; **a ~za di** unlike; **non fare ~za** make no distinction (**fra** between). **~zi'ale** *a & nm* differential

differenzi'ar|e *vt* differentiate. **~si** *vr* **~si da** differ from

diffe'ri|re *vt* postpone ● *vi* be different. **~ta** *nf* **in ~ta** TV prerecorded

diffi'cil|e *a* difficult; (*duro*) hard; (*improbabile*) unlikely ● *nm* difficulty. **~'mente** *adv* with difficulty

difficoltà *nf inv* difficulty

dif'fida *nf* warning

diffi'd|are *vi* **~are di** distrust ● *vt* warn. **~ente** *a* mistrustful. **~enza** *nf* mistrust

dif'fond|ere *vt* spread; diffuse (*calore, luce ecc*). **~si** *vr* spread. **diffusi'one** *nf* diffusion; (*di giornale*) circulation

dif'fu|so *pp di* **diffondere** ● *a* common; (*malattia*) widespread; (*luce*) diffuse. **~'sore** *nm* (*per asciugacapelli*) diffuser

difi'lato *adv* straight; (*subito*) straightaway

'diga *nf* dam; (*argine*) dike

dige'ribile *a* digestible

dige|'rire *vt* digest; *fam* stomach. **~sti'one** *nf* digestion. **~'stivo** *a* digestive ● *nm* digestive; (*dopo cena*) liqueur

digi'tale *a* digital; (*delle dita*) finger *attrib* ● *nf* (*fiore*) foxglove

digi'tare *vt* key in

digiu'nare *vi* fast

digi'uno *a* **essere ~** have an empty stomach ● *nm* fast; **a ~** on an empty stomach

digni|tà *nf* dignity. **~'tario** *nm* dignitary. **~'toso** *a* dignified

digressi'one *nf* digression

digri'gnare *vi* **~ i denti** grind one's teeth

dila'gare *vi* flood; *fig* spread

dilani'are *vt* tear to pieces

dilapi'dare *vt* squander

dila'ta|re *vt*, **~rsi** *vr* dilate; (*metallo, gas:*) expand. **~zi'one** *nf* dilation

dilazio'nabile *a* postponable

dilazi|o'nare *vt* delay. **~'one** *nf* delay

dilegu'ar|e *vt* disperse. **~si** *vr* disappear

di'lemma *nm* dilemma

67

dilettante | direzione

dilet'tan|te *nmf* amateur. **~'tistico** *a* amateurish

dilet'tare *vt* delight

di'letto, -a *a* beloved ● *nm* (*piacere*) delight ● *nmf* (*persona*) beloved

dili'gen|te *a* diligent; ‹*lavoro*› accurate. **~za** *nf* diligence

dilu'ire *vt* dilute

dilun'gar|e *vt* prolong. **~si** *vr* **~si su** dwell on ‹*argomento*›

diluvi'are *vi* pour [down]. **di'luvio** *nm* downpour; *fig* flood

dima'gr|ante *a* slimming, diet. **~i-'mento** *nm* loss of weight. **~ire** *vi* slim

dime'nar|e *vt* wave; wag ‹*coda*›. **~si** *vr* be agitated

dimensi'one *nf* dimension; (*misura*) size

dimenti'canza *nf* forgetfulness; (*svista*) oversight

dimenti'car|e *vt*, **~si** *vr* **~** [*di*] forget. **dimentico** *a* **dimentico di** (*che non ricorda*) forgetful of

di'messo *pp di* **dimettere** ● *a* humble; (*trasandato*) shabby; ‹*voce*› low

dimesti'chezza *nf* familiarity

di'metter|e *vt* dismiss; (*da ospedale ecc*) discharge. **~si** *vr* resign

dimez'zare *vt* halve

diminu|'ire *vt/i* diminish; (*in maglia*) decrease. **~'tivo** *a & nm* diminutive. **~zi'one** *nf* decrease; (*riduzione*) reduction

dimissi'oni *nfpl* resignation *sg*; **dare le ~** resign

di'mo|ra *nf* residence. **~'rare** *vi* reside

dimo'strante *nmf* demonstrator

dimo'stra|re *vt* demonstrate; (*provare*) prove; (*mostrare*) show. **~rsi** *vr* prove [to be]. **~'tivo** *a* demonstrative. **~zi'one** *nf* demonstration; *Math* proof

di'namico, -a *a* dynamic ● *nf* dynamics *sg*. **dina'mismo** *nm* dynamism

dinami'tardo *a* **attentato ~** bomb attack

dina'mite *nf* dynamite

'dinamo *nf inv* dynamo

di'nanzi *adv* in front ● *prep* **~ a** in front of

dina'stia *nf* dynasty

dini'ego *nm* denial

dinocco'lato *a* lanky

dino'sauro *nm* dinosaur

din'torn|i *nmpl* outskirts; **nei ~i di** in the vicinity of. **~o** *adv* around

'dio *nm* (*pl* **'dei**) god; **D~** God

di'ocesi *nf inv* diocese

dipa'nare *vt* wind into a ball; *fig* unravel

diparti'mento *nm* department

dipen'den|te *a* depending ● *nmf* employee. **~za** *nf* dependence; (*edificio*) annexe

di'pendere *vi* **~ da** depend on; (*provenire*) derive from; **dipende** it depends

di'pinger|e *vt* paint; (*descrivere*) describe. **~si** *vr* (*truccarsi*) make up. **di'pinto** *pp di* **dispingere** ● *a* painted ● *nm* painting

di'plo|ma *nm* diploma. **~'marsi** *vr* graduate

diplo'matico *a* diplomatic ● *nm* diplomat; (*pasticcino*) millefeuille (*with alcohol*)

diplo'mato *nmf* person with school qualification ● *a* qualified

diploma'zia *nf* diplomacy

di'porto *nm* **imbarcazione da ~** pleasure craft

dira'dar|e *vt* thin out; make less frequent ‹*visite*›. **~si** *vr* thin out; ‹*nebbia:*› clear

dira'ma|re *vt* issue ● *vi*, **~rsi** *vr* branch out; (*diffondersi*) spread. **~zi'one** *nf* (*di strada*) fork

'dire *vt* say; (*raccontare, riferire*) tell; **~ quello che si pensa** speak one's mind; **voler ~** mean; **volevo ben ~!** I wondered!; **~ di sì/no** say yes/no; **si dice che...** rumour has it that...; **come si dice "casa" in inglese?** what's the English for "casa"?; **questo nome mi dice qualcosa** the name rings a bell; **che ne dici di...?** how about...?; **non c'è che ~** there's no disputing that; **e ~ che...** to think that...; **a dir poco/tanto** at least/most ● *vi* **~ bene/male di** speak highly/ill of sb; **dica pure** (*in negozio*) how can I help you?; **dici sul serio?** are you serious?; **per modo di ~** in a manner of speaking

diretta'mente *adv* directly

diret'tissima *nf* **processare per ~** *Jur* try as speedily as possible

diret'tissimo *nm* fast train

diret'tiva *nf* directive

di'retto *pp di* **dirigere** ● *a* direct. **~ a** (*inteso*) meant for. **essere ~ a** be heading for. **in diretta** ‹*trasmissione*› live ● *nm* (*treno*) through train

diret|'tore, -'trice *nmf* manager; manageress; (*di scuola*) headmaster; headmistress. **~tore d'orchestra** conductor

direzi'one *nf* direction; (*di società*)

management; *Sch* headmaster's/head-mistress's office (*primary school*)

diri'gen|te *a* ruling ● *nmf* executive; *Pol* leader. **~za** *nf* management. **~zi'ale** *a* management *attrib*, managerial

di'riger|e *vt* direct; conduct ⟨*orchestra*⟩; run ⟨*impresa*⟩. **~si** *vr* **~si verso** head for

dirim'petto *adv* opposite ● *prep* **~ a** facing

di'ritto[1], dritto *a* straight; (*destro*) right ● *adv* straight; **andare ~** go straight on ● *nm* right side; *Tennis* forehand; **fare un ~** (*a maglia*) knit one

di'ritt|o[2] *nm* right; *Jur* law. **~i d'autore** royalties

dirit'tura *nf* straight line; *fig* honesty. **~ d'arrivo** *Sport* home straight

diroc'cato *a* tumbledown

dirom'pente *a fig* explosive

dirot'ta|re *vt* reroute ⟨*treno, aereo*⟩; (*illegalmente*) hijack; divert ⟨*traffico*⟩ ● *vi* alter course. **~'tore, ~'trice** *nmf* hijacker

di'rotto *a* ⟨*pioggia*⟩ pouring; ⟨*pianto*⟩ uncontrollable; **piovere a ~** rain heavily

di'rupo *nm* precipice

dis'abile *nmf* disabled person

disabi'tato *a* uninhabited

disabitu'arsi *vr* **~ a** get out of the habit of

disac'cordo *nm* disagreement

disadat'tato, -a *a* maladjusted ● *nmf* misfit

disa'dorno *a* unadorned

disa'gevole *a* (*scomodo*) uncomfortable

disagi'ato *a* poor; ⟨*vita*⟩ hard

di'sagio *nm* discomfort; (*difficoltà*) inconvenience; (*imbarazzo*) embarrassment; **sentirsi a ~** feel uncomfortable; **disagi** *pl* (*privazioni*) hardships

disappro'va|re *vt* disapprove of. **~zi'one** *nf* disapproval

disap'punto *nm* disappointment

disar'mante *a fig* disarming

disar'mare *vt/i* disarm. **di'sarmo** *nm* disarmament

disa'strato, -a *a* devastated ● *nmf* disaster victim

di'sastro *nm* disaster; (*fam: grande confusione*) mess; (*fig: persona*) disaster area. **disa'stroso** *a* disastrous

disat'ten|to *a* inattentive. **~zi'one** *nf* inattention; (*svista*) oversight

disatti'vare *vt* de-activate

disa'vanzo *nm* deficit

disavven'tura *nf* misadventure

dis'brigo *nm* dispatch

dis'capito *nm* **a ~ di** to the detriment of

dis'carica *nf* scrap-yard

discen'den|te *a* descending ● *nmf* descendant. **~za** *nf* descent; (*discendenti*) descendants *pl*

di'scendere *vt/i* descend; (*dal treno*) get off; (*da cavallo*) dismount; (*sbarcare*) land. **~ da** (*trarre origine da*) be a descendant of

di'scepolo, -a *nmf* disciple

di'scernere *vt* discern

di'sces|a *nf* descent; (*pendio*) slope; **~a in picchiata** (*di aereo*) nosedive; **essere in ~a** (*strada:*) go downhill. **~a libera** (*in sci*) downhill race. **disce-'sista** *nmf* (*sciatore*) downhill skier. **~o** *pp di* **discendere**

dis'chetto *nm Comput* diskette

dischi'uder|e *vt* open; (*svelare*) disclose. **~si** *vr* open up

disci'oglier|e *vt*, **~si** *vr* dissolve; ⟨*neve:*⟩ thaw; (*fondersi*) melt. **disci'olto** *pp di* **disciogliere**

disci'pli|na *nf* discipline. **~'nare** *a* disciplinary ● *vt* discipline. **~'nato** *a* disciplined

'disco *nm* disc; *Comput* disk; *Sport* discus; *Mus* record; **ernia del ~** slipped disc. **~ fisso** *Comput* hard disk. **~ volante** flying saucer

discogra'fia *nf* (*insieme di incisioni*) discography. **disco'grafico** *a* ⟨*industria*⟩ record, recording; **casa disco-grafica** record company, recording company

'discolo *nmf* rascal ● *a* unruly

discol'par|e *vt* clear. **~si** *vr* clear oneself

disco'noscere *vt* disown ⟨*figlio*⟩

discontinuità *nf* (*nel lavoro*) irregularity. **discon'tinuo** *a* intermittent; ⟨*fig: impegno, rendimento*⟩ uneven

discor'dan|te *a* discordant. **~za** *nf* mismatch

discor'dare *vi* ⟨*opinioni:*⟩ conflict. **dis'corde** *a* clashing. **dis'cordia** *nf* discord; (*dissenso*) dissension

dis'cor|rere *vi* talk (**di** about). **~'sivo** *a* colloquial. **dis'corso** *pp di* **discorrere** ● *nm* speech; (*conversazione*) talk

dis'costo *a* distant ● *adv* far away; **stare ~** stand apart

disco'te|ca *nf* disco; (*raccolta*) record library. **~'caro** *nmf pej* disco freak

discre'pan|te *a* contradictory. **~za** *nf* discrepancy

dis'cre|to *a* discreet; *(moderato)* moderate; *(abbastanza buono)* fairly good. **~zi'one** *nf* discretion; *(giudizio)* judgement; **a ~zione di** at the discretion of

discrimi'nante *a* extenuating

discrimi'na|re *vt* discriminate. **~'to-rio** *a* ⟨atteggiamento⟩ discriminatory. **~zi'one** *nf* discrimination

discussi'one *nf* discussion; *(alterco)* argument. **dis'cusso** *pp di* **discutere** ● *a* controversial

dis'cutere *vt* discuss; *(formale)* debate; *(litigare)* argue; **~ sul prezzo** bargain. **discu'tibile** *a* debatable; ⟨gusto⟩ questionable

disde'gnare *vt* disdain. **dis'degno** *nm* disdain

dis'dett|a *nf* retraction; *(sfortuna)* bad luck; *Comm* cancellation. **~o** *pp di* **disdire**

disdi'cevole *a* unbecoming

dis'dire *vt* retract; *(annullare)* cancel

diseduca'tivo *a* boorish, uncouth

dise'gna|re *vt* draw; *(progettare)* design. **~'tore, ~'trice** *nmf* designer. **di'segno** *nm* drawing; *(progetto, linea)* design

diser'bante *nm* herbicide, weed-killer ● *a* herbicidal, weed-killing

disere'da|re *vt* disinherit. **~to** *a* dispossessed ● *nmf* **i ~ti** the dispossessed

diser|'tare *vt/i* desert; **~tare la scuola** stay away from school. **~'tore** *nm* deserter. **~zi'one** *nf* desertion

disfaci'mento *nm* decay

dis'fa|re *vt* undo; strip ⟨letto⟩; *(smantellare)* take down; *(annientare)* defeat; **~re le valigie** unpack [one's bags]. **~rsi** *vr* fall to pieces; *(sciogliersi)* melt; **~rsi di** *(liberarsi di)* get rid of; **~rsi in lacrime** dissolve into tears. **~tta** *nf* defeat. **~tto** *a fig* worn out

disfat'tis|mo *nm* defeatism. **~ta** *a & nmf* defeatist

disfunzi'one *nf* disorder

dis'gelo *nm* thaw

dis'grazi|a *nf* misfortune; *(incidente)* accident; *(sfavore)* disgrace. **~ata'mente** *adv* unfortunately. **~'ato, -a** *a* unfortunate ● *nmf* wretch

disgre'gar|e *vt* break up. **~si** *vr* disintegrate

disgu'ido *nm* **~ postale** mistake in delivery

disgu'st|are *vt* disgust. **~arsi** *vr* **~arsi di** be disgusted by. **dis'gusto** *nm* disgust. **~oso** *a* disgusting

disidra'ta|re *vt* dehydrate. **~to** *a* dehydrated

disil'lu|dere *vt* disenchant. **~si'one** *nf* disenchantment. **~so** *a* disillusioned

disimbal'lare *vt* unpack

disimpa'rare *vt* forget

disimpe'gnar|e *vt* release; *(compiere)* fulfil; redeem ⟨oggetto dato in pegno⟩. **~si** *vr* disengage oneself; *(cavarsela)* manage. **disim'pegno** *nm* *(locale)* vestibule

disincan'tato *a* *(disilluso)* disillusioned

disinfe'sta|re *vt* disinfest. **~zi'one** *nf* disinfestation

disinfet'tante *a & nm* disinfectant

disinfet't'are *vt* disinfect. **~zi'one** *nf* disinfection

disinfor'mato *a* uninformed

disini'bito *a* uninhibited

disinne'scare *vt* defuse ⟨mina⟩. **disin'nesco** *nm* *(di bomba)* bomb disposal

disinse'rire *vt* disconnect

disinte'gra|re *vt*, **~rsi** *vr* disintegrate. **~zi'one** *nf* disintegration

disinteres'sarsi *vr* **~ di** take no interest in. **disinte'resse** *nm* indifference; *(oggettività)* disinterestedness

disintossi'ca|re *vt* detoxify. **~rsi** *vr* come off drugs. **~zi'one** *nf* giving up alcohol/drugs

disin'volto *a* natural. **disinvol'tura** *nf* confidence

disles'sia *nf* dyslexia. **dis'lessico** *a* dyslexic

disli'vello *nm* difference in height; *fig* inequality

dislo'care *vt Mil* post

dismenor'rea *nf* dysmenorrhoea

dismi'sura *nf* excess; **a ~** excessively

disobbedi'ente *a* disobedient

disobbe'dire *vt* disobey

disoccu'pa|to, -a *a* unemployed ● *nmf* unemployed person. **~zi'one** *nf* unemployment

disonestà *nf* dishonesty. **diso'nesto** *a* dishonest

disono'rare *vt* dishonour. **diso'nore** *nm* dishonour

di'sopra *adv* above ● *a* upper ● *nm* top

disordi'na|re *vt* disarrange. **~ta'mente** *adv* untidily. **~to** *a* untidy; *(sregolato)* immoderate. **di'sordine** *nm* disorder, untidiness; *(sregolatezza)* debauchery

disorganiz'za|re *vt* disorganize. **~to** *a* disorganized. **~zi'one** *nf* disorganization

disorienta'mento *nm* disorientation

disorien'ta|re *vt* disorientate. **~rsi** *vr* lose one's bearings. **~to** *a fig* bewildered

di'sotto *adv* below ● *a* lower ● *nm* bottom

dis'paccio *nm* dispatch

dispa'rato *a* disparate

'dispari *a* odd, uneven. **~tà** *nf inv* disparity

dis'parte *adv* in **~** apart; **stare in ~** stand aside

dis'pendi|o *nm* (*spreco*) waste. **~'oso** *a* expensive

dis'pen|sa *nf* pantry; (*distribuzione*) distribution; (*mobile*) cupboard; *Jur* exemption; *Relig* dispensation; (*pubblicazione periodica*) number. **~'sare** *vt* distribute; (*esentare*) exonerate

dispe'ra|re *vi* despair (**di** of). **~rsi** *vr* despair. **~ta'mente** (*piangere*) desperately. **~to** *a* desperate. **~zi'one** *nf* despair

dis'per|dere *vt*, **~dersi** *vr* scatter, disperse. **~si'one** *nf* dispersion; (*di truppe*) dispersal. **~'sivo** *a* disorganized. **~so** *pp di* **disperdere** ● *a* scattered; (*smarrito*) lost ● *nm* missing soldier

dis'pet|to *nm* spite; **a ~to di** in spite of; **fare un ~to a qcno** spite sb. **~'toso** *a* spiteful

dispia'c|ere *nm* upset; (*rammarico*) regret; (*dolore*) sorrow; (*preoccupazione*) worry ● *vi* **mi dispiace** I'm sorry; **non mi dispiace** I don't dislike it; **se non ti dispiace** if you don't mind. **~i'uto** *a* upset; (*dolente*) sorry

dispo'nibil|e *a* available; (*gentile*) helpful. **~ità** *nf* availability; (*gentilezza*) helpfulness

dis'por|re *vt* arrange ● *vi* dispose; (*stabilire*) order; **~re di** have at one's disposal. **~si** *vr* (*in fila*) line up

disposi'tivo *nm* device

disposizi'one *nf* disposition; (*ordine*) order; (*libera disponibilità*) disposal. **dis'posto** *pp di* **disporre** ● *a* ready; (*incline*) disposed; **essere ben disposto verso** be favourably disposed towards

di'spotico *a* despotic. **dispo'tismo** *nm* despotism

dispregia'tivo *a* disparaging

disprez'zare *vt* despise. **dis'prezzo** *nm* contempt

'disputa *nf* dispute

dispu'tar|e *vi* dispute; (*gareggiare*) compete. **~si** *vr* **~si qcsa** contend for sth

dissacra'torio *a* debunking

dissangua'mento *nm* loss of blood

dissangu'a|re *vt*, **~rsi** *vr* bleed. **~rsi** *vr fig* become impoverished. **~to** *a* bloodless; *fig* impoverished

dissa'pore *nm* disagreement

dissec'car|e *vt*, **~si** *vr* dry up

dissemi'nare *vt* disseminate; (*notizie*) spread

dis'senso *nm* dissent; (*disaccordo*) disagreement

dissente'ria *nf* dysentery

dissen'tire *vi* disagree (**da** with)

dissertazi'one *nf* dissertation

disser'vizio *nm* poor service

disse'sta|re *vt* upset; *Comm* damage. **~to** *a* (*strada*) uneven. **dis'sesto** *nm* ruin

disse'tante *a* thirst-quenching

disse'ta|re *vt* **~re qcno** quench sb's thirst

dissi'dente *a & nmf* dissident

dis'sidio *nm* disagreement

dis'simile *a* unlike, dissimilar

dissimu'lare *vt* conceal; (*fingere*) dissimulate

dissi'pa|re *vt* dissipate; (*sperperare*) squander. **~rsi** *vr* (*nebbia:*) clear; (*dubbio:*) disappear. **~to** *a* dissipated. **~zi'one** *nf* squandering

dissoci'ar|e *vt*, **~si** *vr* dissociate

disso'dare *vt* till

dis'solto *pp di* **dissolvere**

disso'luto *a* dissolute

dis'solver|e *vt*, **~si** *vr* dissolve; (*disperdere*) dispel

disso'nanza *nf* dissonance

dissua'|dere *vt* dissuade. **~si'one** *nf* dissuasion. **~'sivo** *a* dissuasive

distac'car|e *vt* detach; *Sport* leave behind. **~si** *vr* be detached. **di'stacco** *nm* detachment; (*separazione*) separation; *Sport* lead

di'stan|te *a* far away; (*fig: person*) detached ● *adv* far away. **~za** *nf* distance. **~zi'are** *vt* space out; *Sport* outdistance

di'stare *vi* be distant; **quanto dista?** how far is it?

di'sten|dere *vt* stretch out (*parte del corpo*); (*spiegare*) spread; (*deporre*) lay. **~dersi** *vr* stretch; (*sdraiarsi*) lie down; (*rilassarsi*) relax. **~si'one** *nf* stretching; (*rilassamento*) relaxation; *Pol* détente. **~'sivo** *a* relaxing

di'steso, -a *pp di* **distendere** • *nf* expanse

distil'l|are *vt/i* distil. **~azi'one** *nf* distillation. **~e'ria** *nf* distillery

di'stinguer|e *vt* distinguish. **~si** *vr* distinguish oneself. **distin'guibile** *a* distinguishable

di'stinta *nf Comm* list. **~ di pagamento** receipt. **~ di versamento** paying-in slip

distinta'mente *adv* (*separatamente*) individually, separately; (*chiaramente*) clearly

distin'tivo *a* distinctive • *nm* badge

di'stin|to, -a *pp di* **distinguere** • *a* distinct; (*signorile*) distinguished; **~ti saluti** Yours faithfully. **~zi'one** *nf* distinction

di'stogliere *vt* **~ da** (*allontanare*) remove from; (*dissuadere*) dissuade from. **di'stolto** *pp di* **distogliere**

di'storcere *vt* twist

distorsi'one *nf Med* sprain; (*alterazione*) distortion

di'stra|rre *vt* distract; (*divertire*) amuse. **~rsi** *vr* get distracted; (*svagarsi*) amuse oneself; **non ti distrarre!** pay attention!. **~rsi** *vr* (*deconcentrarsi*) be distracted. **~tta'mente** *adv* absently. **~tto** *pp di* **distrarre** • *a* absent-minded; (*disattento*) inattentive. **~zi'one** *nf* absent-mindedness; (*errore*) inattention; (*svago*) amusement

di'stretto *nm* district

distribu'ire *vt* distribute; (*disporre*) arrange; deal ⟨*carte*⟩. **~'tore** *nm* distributor; (*di benzina*) petrol pump; (*automatico*) slot-machine. **~zi'one** *nf* distribution

distri'car|e *vt* disentangle; **~si** *vr fig* get out of it

di'stru|ggere *vt* destroy. **~t'tivo** *a* destructive; ⟨*critica*⟩ negative. **~tto** *pp di* **distruggere** • *a* destroyed; **un uomo ~tto** a broken man. **~zi'one** *nf* destruction

distur'bar|e *vt* disturb; (*sconvolgere*) upset. **~si** *vr* trouble oneself. **di'sturbo** *nm* bother; (*indisposizione*) trouble; *Med* problem; *Radio, TV* interference; **disturbi** *pl Radio, TV* static. **disturbi di stomaco** stomach trouble

disubbidi'en|te *a* disobedient. **~za** *nf* disobedience

disubbi'dire *vi* **~ a** disobey

disugu|agli'anza *nf* disparity. **~'ale** *a* unequal; (*irregolare*) irregular

disu'mano *a* inhuman

di'suso *nm* **cadere in ~** fall into disuse

di'tale *nm* thimble

di'tata *nf* poke; (*impronta*) finger-mark

'dito *nm* (*pl nf* **dita**) finger; (*di vino, acqua*) finger. **~ del piede** toe

'ditta *nf* firm

dit'tafono *nm* dictaphone

ditta'tor|e *nm* dictator. **~i'ale** *a* dictatorial. **ditta'tura** *nf* dictatorship

dit'tongo *nm* diphthong

di'urno *a* daytime; **spettacolo ~** matinée

'diva *nf* diva

diva'ga|re *vi* digress. **~zi'one** *nf* digression

divam'pare *vi* burst into flames; *fig* spread like wildfire

di'vano *nm* settee, sofa. **~ letto** sofa bed

divari'care *vt* open

di'vario *nm* discrepancy; **un ~ di opinioni** a difference of opinion

dive'n|ire *vi* = **diventare**. **~uto** *pp di* **divenire**

diven'tare *vi* become; (*lentamente*) grow; (*rapidamente*) turn

di'verbio *nm* squabble

diver'gen|te *a* divergent. **~za** *nf* divergence; **~za di opinioni** difference of opinion. **di'vergere** *vi* diverge

diversa'mente *adv* (*altrimenti*) otherwise; (*in modo diverso*) differently

diversifi'ca|re *vt* diversify. **~rsi** *vr* differ, be different. **~zi'one** *nf* diversification

diver|si'one *nf* diversion. **~sità** *nf inv* difference. **~'sivo** *nm* diversion. **di'verso** *a* different; **diversi** *pl* (*parecchi*) several • *pron* several [people]

diver'tente *a* amusing. **diverti'men-to** *nm* amusement

diver'tir|e *vt* amuse. **~si** *vr* enjoy oneself

divi'dendo *nm* dividend

di'vider|e *vt* divide; (*condividere*) share. **~si** *vr* (*separarsi*) separate

di'vieto *nm* prohibition; **~ di sosta** no parking

divinco'larsi *vr* wriggle

divinità *nf inv* divinity. **di'vino** *a* divine

di'visa *nf* uniform; *Comm* currency

divisi'one *nf* division

di'vismo *nm* worship; (*atteggiamento*) superstar mentality

di'vi|so *pp di* dividere. **~'sore** *nm* divisor. **~'sorio** *a* dividing; **muro ~sorio** partition wall

'divo, -a *nmf* star

divo'rar|e *vt* devour. **~si** *vr* **~si da** be consumed with

divorzi'a|re *vi* divorce. **~to, -a** *nmf* divorcee. **di'vorzio** *nm* divorce

divul'ga|re *vt* divulge; (*rendere popolare*) popularize. **~rsi** *vr* spread. **~'tivo** *a* popular. **~zi'one** *nf* popularization

dizio'nario *nm* dictionary

dizi'one *nf* diction

do *nm Mus* (*chiave, nota*) C

'doccia *nf* shower; (*grondaia*) gutter; **fare la ~** have a shower

do'cen|te *a* teaching ● *nmf* teacher; (*di università*) lecturer. **~za** *nf* university teacher's qualification

'docile *a* docile

documen'tar|e *vt* document. **~si** *vr* gather information (**su** about)

documen'tario *a & nm* documentary

documen'ta|to *a* well-documented; (*persona*) well-informed. **~zi'one** *nf* documentation

docu'mento *nm* document

dodi'cesimo *a & nm* twelfth. **'dodici** *a & nm* twelve

do'gan|a *nf* customs *pl*; (*dazio*) duty. **doga'nale** *a* customs. **~i'ere** *nm* customs officer

'doglie *nfpl* labour pains

'dogma *nm* dogma. **dog'matico** *a* dogmatic. **~'tismo** *nm* dogmatism

'dolce *a* sweet; (*clima*) mild; (*voce, consonante*) soft; (*acqua*) fresh ● *nm* (*portata*) dessert; (*torta*) cake; **non mangio dolci** I don't eat sweet things. **~'mente** *adv* sweetly. **dol'cezza** *nf* sweetness; (*di clima*) mildness

dolce'vita *a inv* (*maglione*) rollneck

dolci'ario *a* confectionery

dolci'astro *a* sweetish

dolcifi'cante *nm* sweetener ● *a* sweetening

dolci'umi *nmpl* sweets

do'lente *a* painful; (*spiacente*) sorry

do'le|re *vi* ache, hurt; (*dispiacere*) regret. **~rsi** *vr* regret; (*protestare*) complain; **~rsi di** be sorry for

'dollaro *nm* dollar

'dolo *nm Jur* malice; (*truffa*) fraud

Dolo'miti *nfpl* le **~** the Dolomites

do'lore *nm* pain; (*morale*) sorrow. **dolo'roso** *a* painful

do'loso *a* malicious

do'manda *nf* question; (*richiesta*) request; (*scritta*) application; *Comm* demand; **fare una ~ (a qcno)** ask (sb) a question. **~ di impiego** job application

doman'dar|e *vt* ask; (*esigere*) demand; **~e qcsa a qcno** ask sb for sth. **~si** *vr* wonder

do'mani *adv* tomorrow; **~ sera** tomorrow evening ● *nm* **il ~** the future; **a ~** see you tomorrow

do'ma|re *vt* tame; *fig* control (*emozioni*). **~'tore** *nm* tamer

domat'tina *adv* tomorrow morning

do'meni|ca *nf* Sunday. **~'cale** *a* Sunday *attrib*

do'mestico, -a *a* domestic ● *nm* servant ● *nf* maid

domicili'are *a* **arresti domiciliari** *Jur* house arrest

domicili'arsi *vr* settle

domi'cilio *nm* domicile; (*abitazione*) home; **recapitiamo a ~** we do home deliveries

domi'na|re *vt* dominate; (*controllare*) control ● *vi* rule over; (*prevalere*) be dominant. **~rsi** *vr* control oneself. **~'tore, ~'trice** *nmf* ruler **~zi'one** *nf* domination

do'minio *nm* control; *Pol* dominion; (*ambito*) field; **di ~ pubblico** common knowledge

don *nm inv* (*ecclesiastico*) Father

do'na|re *vt* give; donate (*sangue, organo*) ● *vi* **~re a** (*giovare esteticamente*) suit. **~'tore, ~'trice** *nmf* donor. **~zi'one** *nf* donation

dondo'l|are *vt* swing; (*cullare*) rock ● *vi* sway. **~arsi** *vr* swing. **~io** *nm* rocking. **'dondolo** *nm* swing; **cavallo/ sedia a dondolo** rocking-horse/chair

dongio'vanni *nm inv* Romeo

'donna *nf* woman. **~ di servizio** domestic help

don'naccia *nf pej* whore

donnai'olo *nm* philanderer

'donnola *nf* weasel

'dono *nm* gift

'dopo *prep* after; (*a partire da*) since ● *adv* after, afterwards; (*più tardi*) later; (*in seguito*) later on; **~ di me** after me

dopo'barba *nm inv* aftershave

dopo'cena *nm inv* evening

dopodiché *adv* after which

dopodo'mani *adv* the day after tomorrow

dopogu'erra *nm inv* post-war period

dopo'pranzo *nm inv* afternoon

dopo'sci *a & nm inv* après-ski

doposcu'ola *nm inv* after-school activities *pl*

dopo-'shampoo *nm inv* conditioner ● *a inv* conditioning

dopo'sole *nm inv* aftersun cream ● *a inv* aftersun

dopo'tutto *adv* after all

doppi'aggio *nm* dubbing

doppia'mente *adv* (*in misura doppia*) doubly

doppia|re *vt Naut* double; *Sport* lap; *Cinema* dub. ~'**tore,** ~'**trice** *nmf* dubber

'**doppio** *a & adv* double. ~ **clic** *nm Comput* double click. ~ **fallo** *nm Tennis* double fault. ~ **gioco** *nm* double-dealing. ~ **mento** *nm* double chin. ~ **senso** *nm* double entendre. **doppi vetri** *nmpl* double glazing ● *nm* double, twice the quantity; *Tennis* doubles *pl.* ~ **misto** *nm Tennis* mixed doubles ● *adv* double

doppi'one *nm* duplicate

doppio'petto *a* double-breasted

dop'pista *nmf Tennis* doubles player

do'ra|re *vt* gild; *Culin* brown. ~**to** *a* gilt; (*color oro*) golden. ~'**tura** *nf* gilding

dormicchi'are *vi* doze

dormigli'one, -a *nmf* sleepyhead; *fig* lazy-bones

dor'mi|re *vi* sleep; (*essere addormentato*) be asleep; *fig* be asleep. ~**ta** *nf* good sleep. ~'**tina** *nf* nap. ~'**torio** *nm* dormitory

dormi'veglia *nm* **essere in** ~ be half asleep

dor'sale *a* dorsal ● *nf* (*di monte*) ridge

'**dorso** *nm* back; (*di libro*) spine; (*di monte*) crest; (*nel nuoto*) backstroke

do'saggio *nm* dosage

do'sare *vt* dose; *fig* measure; ~ **le parole** weigh one's words

dosa'tore *nm* measuring jug

'**dose** *nf* dose; **in buona** ~ *fig* in good measure. ~ **eccessiva** overdose

dossi'er *nm inv* (*raccolta di dati, fascicolo*) file

'**dosso** *nm* (*dorso*) back; **levarsi di** ~ **gli abiti** take off one's clothes

do'ta|re *vt* endow; (*di accessori*) equip. ~**to** *a* ⟨*persona*⟩ gifted; (*fornito*) equipped. ~**zi'one** *nf* (*attrezzatura*) equipment; **in** ~**zione** at one's disposal

'**dote** *nf* dowry; (*qualità*) gift

'**dotto** *a* learned ● *nm* scholar; *Anat* duct

dotto'rato *nm* doctorate. **dot'tore,** ~'**ressa** *nmf* doctor

dot'trina *nf* doctrine

'**dove** *adv* where; **di** ~ **sei?** where do you come from; **fin** ~? how far?; **per** ~? which way?

do'vere *vi* (*obbligo*) have to, must; **devo andare** I have to go, I must go; **devo venire anch'io?** do I have to come too?; **avresti dovuto dirmelo** you should have told me, you ought to have told me; **devo sedermi un attimo** I must sit down for a minute, I need to sit down for a minute; **dev'essere successo qualcosa** something must have happened; **come si deve** properly ● *vt* (*essere debitore di, derivare*) owe; **essere dovuto a** be due to ● *nm* duty; **per** ~ out of duty.

dove'roso *a* only right and proper

do'vunque *adv* (*dappertutto*) everywhere; (*in qualsiasi luogo*) anywhere ● *conj* wherever

do'vuto *a* due; (*debito*) proper

doz'zi|na *nf* dozen. ~'**nale** *a* cheap

dra'gare *vt* dredge

'**drago** *nm* dragon

'**dramm|a** *nm* drama. **dram'matico** *a* dramatic. ~**atiz'zare** *vt* dramatize. ~**a'turgo** *nm* playwright. **dram'mone** *nm* (*film*) tear-jerker

drappeggi'are *vt* drape. **drap'peggio** *nm* drapery

drap'pello *nm Mil* squad; (*gruppo*) band

'**drastico** *a* drastic

dre'na|ggio *nm* drainage. ~**re** *vt* drain

drib'blare *vt* (*in calcio*) dribble. '**dribbling** *nm inv* (*in calcio*) dribble

'**dritta** *nf* (*mano destra*) right hand; *Naut* starboard; (*informazione*) pointer, tip; **a** ~ **e a manca** (*dappertutto*) left, right and centre

'**dritto** *a* = **diritto¹** ● *nmf fam* crafty so-and-so

driz'zar|e *vt* straighten; (*rizzare*) prick up. ~**si** *vr* straighten [up]; (*alzarsi*) raise

'**dro|ga** *nf* drug. ~'**gare** *vt* drug. ~'**garsi** *vr* take drugs. ~'**gato, -a** *nmf* drug addict

drogh|e'ria *nf* grocery. ~**i'ere, -a** *nmf* grocer

drome'dario *nm* dromedary

'**dubbi|o** *a* doubtful; (*ambiguo*) dubious ● *nm* doubt; (*sospetto*) suspicion; **met-**

tere in ~o doubt; **essere fuori** ~o be beyond doubt; **essere in** ~o be doubtful. ~'oso *a* doubtful

dubi'ta|re *vi* doubt; ~re di doubt; (*diffidare*) mistrust; **dubito che venga** I doubt whether he'll come. ~'tivo *a* (*ambiguo*) ambiguous

'duca, du'chessa *nmf* duke; duchess

'due *a & nm* two

due'cento *a & nm* two hundred

du'ello *nm* duel

due'mila *a & nm* two thousand

due'pezzi *nm inv* (*bikini*) bikini

du'etto *nm* duo; *Mus* duet

'duna *nf* dune

'dunque *conj* therefore; (*allora*) well [then]

'duo *nm inv* duo; *Mus* duet

du'omo *nm* cathedral

'duplex *nm Teleph* party line

dupli'ca|re *vt* duplicate. ~to *nm* duplicate. **'duplice** *a* double; **in duplice** in duplicate

dura'mente *adv* (*lavorare*) hard; (*rimproverare*) harshly

du'rante *prep* during

du'r|are *vi* last; (*cibo:*) keep; (*resistere*) hold out. ~ata *nf* duration. ~a'turo, ~evole *a* lasting, enduring

du'rezza *nf* hardness; (*di carne*) toughness; (*di voce, padre*) harshness

'duro, -a *a* hard; (*persona, carne*) tough; (*voce*) harsh; (*pane*) stale; **tieni** ~! (*resistere*) hang in there! • *nmf* (*persona*) tough person, toughie *fam*

du'rone *nm* hardened skin

'duttile *a* (*materiale*) ductile; (*carattere*) malleable

Ee

e, ed *conj* and

'ebano *nm* ebony

eb'bene *conj* well [then]

eb'brezza *nf* inebriation; (*euforia*) elation; **guida in stato di** ~ drink-driving. **'ebbro** *a* inebriated; **ebbro di gioia** delirious with joy

'ebete *a* stupid

ebollizi'one *nf* boiling

e'braico *a* Hebrew • *nm* (*lingua*) Hebrew. **e'br|eo, -a** *a* Jewish • *nmf* Jew; Jewess

'Ebridi *nfpl* **le** ~ the Hebrides

eca'tombe *nf* **fare un'**~ wreak havoc

ecc *abbr* (*eccetera*) etc

ecce'den|te *a* (*peso, bagaglio*) excess. ~za *nf* excess; (*d'avanzo*) surplus; **avere qcsa in** ~za have an excess of sth; **bagagli in** ~za excess baggage. ~za di cassa surplus. **ec'cedere** *vt* exceed • *vi* go too far; **eccedere nel mangiare** overeat; **eccedere nel bere** drink to excess

eccel'len|te *a* excellent. ~za *nf* excellence; (*titolo*) Excellency; **per** ~za par excellence. **ec'cellere** *vi* excel (**in** at)

eccentricità *nf* eccentricity. **ec'centrico, -a** *a & nmf* eccentric

eccessiva'mente *adv* excessively. **ecces'sivo** *a* excessive

ec'cesso *nm* excess; **andare agli eccessi** go to extremes; **all'**~ to excess. ~ **di velocità** speeding

ec'cetera *adv* et cetera

ec'cetto *prep* except; ~ **che** (*a meno che*) unless. **eccettu'are** *vt* except

eccezio'nal|e *a* exceptional. ~'mente *adv* exceptionally; (*contrariamente alla regola*) as an exception

eccezi'one *nf* exception; *Jur* objection; **a** ~ **di** with the exception of

ecci'ta'mento *nm* excitement. **ec'citante** *a* exciting; (*sostanza*) stimulant • *nm* stimulant

ecci'ta|re *vt* excite. ~rsi *vr* get excited. ~to *a* excited

eccitazi'one *nf* excitement

ecclesi'astico *a* ecclesiastical • *nm* priest

'ecco *adv* (*qui*) here; (*là*) there; ~! exactly!; ~ **fatto** there we are; ~ **la tua borsa** here is your bag; ~ [li] **mio figlio** there is my son; ~mi here I am; ~ **tutto** that is all

ec'come *adv & int* and how!

echeggi'are *vi* echo

e'clissi *nf inv* eclipse

'eco nmf (pl m **echi**) echo

ecogra'fia nf scan

ecolo'gia nf ecology. **eco'logico** a ecological; ⟨prodotto⟩ environmentally friendly

e commerci'ale nf ampersand

econo'm|ia nf economy; ⟨scienza⟩ economics sg; **fare ~ia** economize (**di** on). **eco'nomico** a economic; ⟨a buon prezzo⟩ cheap. **~ista** nmf economist. **~iz'zare** vt/i economize; save ⟨tempo, denaro⟩. **e'conomo, -a** a thrifty ● nmf ⟨di collegio⟩ bursar

écru a inv raw

'Ecu nm inv ECU, ecu

ec'zema nm eczema

ed conj vedi **e**

'edera nf ivy

e'dicola nf [newspaper] kiosk

edifi'cabile a ⟨area, terreno⟩ classified as suitable for development

edifi'cante a edifying

edifi'care vt build; ⟨indurre al bene⟩ edify

edi'ficio nm building; fig structure

e'dile a building attrib

edi'lizi|a nf building trade. **~o** a building attrib

edi|'tore, -'trice a publishing ● nmf publisher; ⟨curatore⟩ editor. **~to'ria** nf publishing. **~tori'ale** a publishing ● nm ⟨articolo⟩ editorial, leader

edizi'one nf edition; ⟨di manifestazione⟩ performance. **~ ridotta** abridg[e]ment. **~ della sera** ⟨del telegiornale⟩ evening news

edu'ca|re vt educate; ⟨allevare⟩ bring up. **~tivo** a educational. **~to** a polite. **~'tore, ~'trice** nmf educator. **~zi'one** nf education; ⟨di bambini⟩ upbringing. ⟨buone maniere⟩ [good] manners pl. **~zione fisica** physical education

e'felide nf freckle

effemi'nato a effeminate

efferve'scente a effervescent; ⟨frizzante⟩ fizzy; ⟨aspirina⟩ soluble

effettiva'mente adv **è troppo tardi – ~** it's too late – so it is

effet'tivo a actual; ⟨efficace⟩ effective; ⟨personale⟩ permanent; Mil regular ● nm ⟨somma totale⟩ sum total

ef'fett|o nm effect; ⟨impressione⟩ impression; **in ~i** in fact; **a tutti gli ~i** to all intents and purposes; **~i personali** personal belongings. **~u'are** vt effect; carry out ⟨controllo, sondaggio⟩. **~u'arsi** vr take place

effi'cac|e a effective. **~ia** nf effectiveness

effici'en|te a efficient. **~za** nf efficiency

ef'fimero a ephemeral

effusi'one nf effusion

E'geo nm **l'~** the Aegean [Sea]

E'gitto nm Egypt. **egizi'ano, -a** a & nmf Egyptian

'egli pron he; **~ stesso** he himself

ego'centrico, -a a egocentric ● nmf egocentric person

ego'is|mo nm selfishness. **~ta** a selfish ● nmf selfish person. **~tico** a selfish

e'gregio a distinguished; **E~ Signore** Dear Sir

eguali'tario a & nm egalitarian

eiaculazi'one nf ejaculation

elabo'ra|re vt elaborate; process ⟨dati⟩. **~to** a elaborate. **~zi'one** nf elaboration; ⟨di dati⟩ processing. **~zione [di] testi** word processing

elar'gire vt lavish

elastici|tà nf elasticity. **~z'zato** a ⟨stoffa⟩ elasticated. **e'lastico** a elastic; ⟨tessuto⟩ stretch; ⟨orario, mente⟩ flexible; ⟨persona⟩ easy-going ● nm elastic; ⟨fascia⟩ rubber band

ele'fante nm elephant

ele'gan|te a elegant. **~za** nf elegance

e'leggere vt elect. **eleg'gibile** a eligible

elemen'tare a elementary; **scuola ~** primary school

ele'mento nm element; **elementi** pl ⟨fatti⟩ data; ⟨rudimenti⟩ elements

ele'mosina nf charity; **chiedere l'~** beg. **elemosi'nare** vt/i beg

elen'care vt list

e'lenco nm list. **~ abbonati** telephone directory. **~ telefonico** telephone directory

elet'tivo a ⟨carica⟩ elective. **e'letto, -a** pp di **eleggere** ● a chosen ● nmf ⟨nominato⟩ elected member; **per pochi eletti** for the chosen few

eletto'ra|le a electoral. **~to** nm electorate

elet|'tore, -'trice nmf voter

elet'trauto nm garage for electrical repairs

elettri'cista nm electrician

elettri|cità nf electricity. **e'lettrico** a electric. **~z'zante** a ⟨notizia, gara⟩ electrifying. **~z'zare** vt fig electrify. **~z'zato** a fig electrified

elettrocardio'gramma *nm* electro-cardiogram

e'lettrodo *nm* electrode

elettrodo'mestico *nm* [electrical] household appliance

elet'trone *nm* electron

elet'tronico, -a *a* electronic ● *nf* electronics

ele'va|re *vt* raise; (*promuovere*) promote; (*erigere*) erect; (*fig: migliorare*) better; ~ **al quadrato/cubo** square/cube. ~**rsi** *vr* rise; (*edificio:*) stand. ~**to** *a* high. ~**zi'one** *nf* elevation

elezi'one *nf* election

'elica *nf* Naut screw, propeller; Aeron propeller; (*del ventilatore*) blade

eli'cottero *nm* helicopter

elimi'na|re *vt* eliminate. ~**'toria** *nf* Sport preliminary heat. ~**zi'one** *nf* elimination

éli|te *nf inv* élite. ~**'tista** *a* élitist

'ella *pron* she

el'metto *nm* helmet

elogi'are *vt* praise. **e'logio** *nm* praise; (*discorso, scritto*) eulogy

elo'quen|te *a* eloquent; *fig* tell-tale. ~**za** *nf* eloquence

e'lu|dere *vt* elude; evade (*sorveglianza, controllo*). ~**'sivo** *a* elusive

el'vetico *a* Swiss

emaci'ato *a* emaciated

e-mail *nf* e-mail; **indirizzo ~** e-mail address

ema'na|re *vt* give off; pass (*legge*) ● *vi* emanate. ~**zi'one** *nf* giving off; (*di legge*) enactment

emanci'pa|re *vt* emancipate. ~**rsi** *vr* become emancipated. ~**to** *a* emancipated. ~**zi'one** *nf* emancipation

emargi'na|to *nm* marginalized person. ~**zi'one** *nf* marginalization

ema'toma *nm* haematoma

em'bargo *nm* embargo

em'ble|ma *nm* emblem. ~**'matico** *a* emblematic

embo'lia *nf* embolism

embrio'nale *a* Biol, *fig* embryonic. **embri'one** *nm* embryo

emen|da'mento *nm* amendment. ~**'dare** *vt* amend

emer'gen|te *a* emergent. ~**za** *nf* emergency; **in caso di ~za** in an emergency

e'mergere *vi* emerge; (*sottomarino:*) surface; (*distinguersi*) stand out

e'merito *a* (*professore*) emeritus; **un ~ imbecille** a prize idiot

e'merso *pp di* **emergere**

e'messo *pp di* **emettere**

e'mettere *vt* emit; give out (*luce, suono*); let out (*grido*); (*mettere in circolazione*) issue

emi'crania *nf* migraine

emi'gra|re *vi* emigrate. ~**to, -a** *nmf* immigrant. ~**zi'one** *nf* emigration

emi'nen|te *a* eminent. ~**za** *nf* eminence

e'miro *nm* emir

emis'fero *nm* hemisphere

emis'sario *nm* emissary

emissi'one *nf* emission; (*di denaro*) issue; (*trasmissione*) broadcast

emit'tente *a* issuing; (*trasmittente*) broadcasting ● *nf* Radio transmitter

emorra'gia *nf* haemorrhage

emor'roidi *nfpl* piles

emotività *nf* emotional make-up. **emo'tivo** *a* emotional

emozio'na|nte *a* exciting; (*commovente*) moving. ~**re** *vt* excite; (*commuovere*) move. ~**rsi** *vr* become excited; (*commuoversi*) be moved. ~**to** *a* excited; (*commosso*) moved. **emozi'one** *nf* emotion; (*agitazione*) excitement

'empio *a* impious; (*spietato*) pitiless; (*malvagio*) wicked

em'pirico *a* empirical

em'porio *nm* emporium; (*negozio*) general store

emu'la|re *vt* emulate. ~**zi'one** *nf* emulation

emulsi'one *nf* emulsion

en'ciclica *nf* encyclical

enciclope'dia *nf* encyclopaedia

encomi'are *vt* commend. **en'comio** *nm* commendation

en'demico *a* endemic

endo've|na *nf* intravenous injection. ~**'noso** *a* intravenous; **per via ~nosa** intravenously

E.N.I.T. *nm abbr* (**Ente Nazionale Italiano per il Turismo**) Italian State Tourist Office

e'nergetico *a* (*risorse, crisi*) energy *attrib*; (*alimento*) energy-giving

ener'gia *nf* energy. **e'nergico** *a* energetic; (*efficace*) strong

ener'gumeno *nm* Neanderthal

'enfasi *nf* emphasis

en'fati|co *a* emphatic. ~**z'zare** *vt* emphasize

e'nigma *nm* enigma. **enig'matico** *a* enigmatic. **enig'mistica** *nf* puzzles *pl*

en'nesimo *a* Math nth; *fam* umpteenth

e'norm|e *a* enormous. ~**e'mente** *adv*

massively. **~ità** *nf inv* enormity; (*assurdità*) absurdity

eno'teca *nf* wine-tasting shop

'ente *nm* board; (*società*) company; (*filosofia*) being

entità *nf inv* (*filosofia*) entity; (*gravità*) seriousness; (*dimensione*) extent

entou'rage *nm inv* entourage

en'trambi *a & pron* both

en'tra|re *vi* go in, enter; **~re in** go into; (*stare, trovar posto*) fit into; (*arruolarsi*) join; **~rci** (*avere a che fare*) have to do with; **tu che c'entri?** what has it got to do with you? **~ta** *nf* entry, entrance; **~te** *pl Comm* takings; (*reddito*) income *sg*

'entro *prep* (*tempo*) within

entro'terra *nm inv* hinterland

entusias'mante *a* fascinating, exciting

entusias'mar|e *vt* arouse enthusiasm in. **~si** *vr* be enthusiastic (**per** about)

entusi'as|mo *nm* enthusiasm. **~ta** *a* enthusiastic ● *nmf* enthusiast. **~tico** *a* enthusiastic

enume'ra|re *vt* enumerate. **~zi'one** *nf* enumeration

enunci'a|re *vt* enunciate. **~zi'one** *nf* enunciation

epa'tite *nf* hepatitis

'epico *a* epic

epide'mia *nf* epidemic

epi'dermide *nf* epidermis

Epifa'nia *nf* Epiphany

epi'gramma *nm* epigram

epil|es'sia *nf* epilepsy. **epi'lettico, -a** *a & nmf* epileptic

e'pilogo *nm* epilogue

epi'sodi|co *a* episodic; **caso ~co** one-off case. **~o** *nm* episode

e'piteto *nm* epithet

'epoca *nf* age; (*periodo*) period; **a quell'~** in those days; **auto d'~** vintage car

ep'pure *conj* [and] yet

epu'rare *vt* purge

equa'tore *nm* equator. **equatori'ale** *a* equatorial

equazi'one *nf* equation

e'questre *a* equestrian; **circo ~** circus

equi'latero *a* equilateral

equili'bra|re *vt* balance. **~to** *a* (*persona*) well-balanced. **equi'librio** *nm* balance; (*buon senso*) common sense; (*di bilancia*) equilibrium

equili'brismo *nm* fare **~** do a balancing act

e'quino *a* horse *attrib*

equi'nozio *nm* equinox

equipaggia'mento *nm* equipment

equipaggi'are *vt* equip; (*di persone*) man

equi'paggio *nm* crew; *Aeron* cabin crew

equipa'rare *vt* make equal

équipe *nf inv* team

equità *nf* equity

equitazi'one *nf* riding

equiva'len|te *a & nm* equivalent. **~za** *nf* equivalence

equiva'lere *vi* **~ a** be equivalent to

equivo'care *vi* misunderstand

e'quivoco *a* equivocal; (*sospetto*) suspicious; **un tipo ~** a shady character ● *nm* misunderstanding

'equo *a* fair, just

'era *nf* era

'erba *nf* grass; (*aromatica, medicinale*) herb. **~ cipollina** chives *pl*. **er'baccia** *nf* weed. **er'bacee** *a* herbaceous

erbi'cida *nm* weed-killer

erbo'rist|a *nmf* herbalist. **~e'ria** *nf* herbalist's shop

er'boso *a* grassy

er'culeo *a* (*forza*) herculean

e'red|e *nmf* heir; heiress. **~ità** *nf inv* inheritance; *Biol* heredity. **~i'tare** *vt* inherit. **~itarietà** *nf* heredity. **~i'tario** *a* hereditary

ere'mita *nm* hermit

ere'sia *nf* heresy. **e'retico, -a** *a* heretical ● *nmf* heretic

e're|tto *pp di* **erigere** ● *a* erect. **~zi'one** *nf* erection; (*costruzione*) building

er'gastolo *nm* life sentence; (*luogo*) prison

'erica *nf* heather

e'rigere *vt* erect; (*fig: fondare*) found

eri'tema *nm* (*cutaneo*) inflammation; (*solare*) sunburn

ermel'lino *nm* ermine

ermetica'mente *adv* hermetically. **er'metico** *a* hermetic; (*a tenuta d'aria*) airtight

'ernia *nf* hernia

e'rodere *vi* erode

e'ro|e *nm* hero. **~ico** *a* heroic. **~'ismo** *nm* heroism

ero'ga|re *vt* distribute; (*fornire*) supply. **~zi'one** *nf* supply

ero'ina *nf* heroine; (*droga*) heroin

erosi'one *nf* erosion

e'rotico *a* erotic. **ero'tismo** *nm* eroticism

er'rante *a* wandering. **er'rare** *vi* wander; (*sbagliare*) be mistaken

er'rato *a* (*sbagliato*) mistaken

'erre *nf* ~ **moscia** burr

erronea'mente *adv* mistakenly

er'rore *nm* error, mistake; (*di stampa*) misprint; **essere in** ~ be wrong

'erta *nf* **stare all'**~ be on the alert

eru'di|rsi *vr* get educated. ~**to** *a* learned

erut'tare *vt* (*vulcano:*) erupt ● *vi* (*ruttare*) belch. **eruzi'one** *nf* eruption; *Med* rash

esacer'bare *vt* exacerbate

esage'ra|re *vt* exaggerate ● *vi* exaggerate; (*nel comportamento*) go over the top; ~**re nel mangiare** eat too much. ~**ta'mente** *adv* excessively. ~**to** *a* exaggerated; (*prezzo*) exorbitant ● *nm* person who goes to extremes. ~**zi'one** *nf* exaggeration; **è costato un'**~**zione** it cost the earth

esa'lare *vt/i* exhale

esal'ta|re *vt* exalt; (*entusiasmare*) elate. ~**to** *a* (*fanatico*) fanatical ● *nm* fanatic. ~**zi'one** *nf* exaltation; (*in discorso*) fervour

e'same *nm* examination, exam; **dare un** ~ take an exam; **prendere in** ~ examine. ~ **del sangue** blood test. **esami** *pl* **di maturità** ≈ A-levels

esami'na|re *vt* examine. ~**tore**, ~**'trice** *nmf* examiner

e'sangue *a* bloodless

e'sanime *a* lifeless

esaspe'rante *a* exasperating

esaspe'ra|re *vt* exasperate. ~**rsi** *vr* get exasperated. ~**zi'one** *nf* exasperation

esat|ta'mente *adv* exactly. ~**'tezza** *nf* exactness; (*precisione*) precision; (*di risposta, risultato*) accuracy

e'satto *pp di* **esigere** ● *a* exact; (*risposta, risultato*) correct; (*orologio*) right; **hai l'ora esatta?** do you have the right time?; **sono le due esatte** it's two o'clock exactly

esat'tore *nm* collector

esau'dire *vt* grant; fulfil (*speranze*)

esauri'ente *a* exhaustive

esauri'ri|re *vt* exhaust. ~**rsi** *vr* exhaust oneself; (*merci ecc:*) run out. ~**to** *a* exhausted; (*merci*) sold out; (*libro*) out of print; **fare il tutto** ~**to** (*spettacolo:*) play to a full house

'esca *nf* bait

escande'scenz|a *nf* outburst; **dare in** ~**e** lose one's temper

escla'ma|re *vi* exclaim. ~**'tivo** *a* exclamatory. ~**zi'one** *nf* exclamation

es'clu|dere *vt* exclude; rule out (*possibilità, ipotesi*). ~**si'one** *nf* exclusion. ~**'siva** *nf* exclusive right, sole right; **in** ~**siva** exclusive. ~**siva'mente** *adv* exclusively. ~**'sivo** *a* exclusive. ~**so** *pp di* **escludere** ● *a* **non è** ~**so che ci sia** it's not out of the question that he'll be there

escogi'tare *vt* contrive

escre'mento *nm* excrement

escursi'one *nf* excursion; (*scorreria*) raid; (*di temperatura*) range

ese'cra|bile *a* abominable. ~**re** *vt* abhor

esecu|'tivo *a* & *nm* executive. ~**'tore**, ~**'trice** *nmf* executor; *Mus* performer. ~**zi'one** *nf* execution; *Mus* performance

esegu'ire *vt* carry out; *Jur* execute; *Mus* perform

e'sempio *nm* example; **ad** *o* **per** ~ for example; **dare l'**~ **a qcno** set sb an example; **fare un** ~ give an example. **esem'plare** *a* examplary ● *nm* specimen; (*di libro*) copy. **esemplifi'care** *vt* exemplify

esen'tar|e *vt* exempt. ~**si** *vr* free oneself. **e'sente** *a* exempt. **esente da imposta** duty-free. **esente da IVA** VAT-exempt

esen'tasse *a* duty-free

e'sequie *nfpl* funeral rites

eser'cente *nmf* shopkeeper

eserci'ta|re *vt* exercise; (*addestrare*) train; (*fare uso di*) exert; (*professione*) practise. ~**rsi** *vr* practise. ~**zi'one** *nf* exercise; *Mil* drill

e'sercito *nm* army

eser'cizio *nm* exercise; (*pratica*) practice; *Comm* financial year; (*azienda*) business; **essere fuori** ~ be out of practice

esi'bi|re *vt* show off; produce (*documenti*). ~**rsi** *vr* *Theat* perform; *fig* show off. ~**zi'one** *nf* production; *Theat* performance

esibizio'nis|mo *nm* showing off. ~**ta** *nmf* exhibitionist

esi'gen|te *a* exacting; (*pignolo*) fastidious. ~**za** *nf* demand; (*bisogno*) need. **e'sigere** *vt* demand; (*riscuotere*) collect

e'siguo *a* meagre

esila'ra|nte *a* exhilarating

'esile *a* slender; (*voce*) thin

esili'a|re vt exile. **~'rsi** vr go into exile. **~to, -a** a exiled ● nmf exile. **e'silio** nm exile

e'simer|e vt release. **~si** vr **~si da** get out of

esi'sten|te a existing. **~za** nf existence. **~zi'ale** a existential. **~zia'lismo** nm existentialism

e'sistere vi exist

esi'tante a hesitating; ⟨voce⟩ faltering

esi'ta|re vi hesitate. **~zi'one** nf hesitation

'esito nm result; **avere buon ~** be a success

'esodo nm exodus

e'sofago nm oesophagus

esone'rare vt exempt. **e'sonero** nm exemption

esorbi'tante a exorbitant

esorciz'zare vt exorcize

esordi'ente nmf person making his/ her début. **e'sordio** nm opening; ⟨di attore⟩ début. **esor'dire** vi début

esor'tare vt ⟨pregare⟩ beg; ⟨incitare⟩ urge

eso'terico a esoteric

e'sotico a exotic

espa'drillas nfpl espadrilles

es'pan|dere vt expand. **~dersi** vr expand; ⟨diffondersi⟩ extend. **~si'one** nf expansion. **~'sivo** a expansive; ⟨persona⟩ friendly

espatri'are vi leave one's country. **es'patrio** nm expatriation

espedi'ent|e nm expedient; **vivere di ~i** live by one's wits

es'pellere vt expel

esperi|'enza nf experience; **parlare per ~enza** speak from experience. **~'mento** nm experiment

es'perto, -a a & nmf expert

espi'a|re vt atone for. **~'torio** a expiatory

espi'rare vt/i breathe out

espli'care vt carry on

esplicita'mente adv explicitly. **es'plicito** a explicit

es'plodere vi explode ● vt fire

esplo'ra|re vt explore. **~'tore, ~'trice** nmf explorer; **giovane ~tore** boy scout. **~zi'one** nf exploration

esplo|si'one nf explosion. **~'sivo** a & nm explosive

espo'nente nm exponent

es'por|re vt expose; display ⟨merci⟩; ⟨spiegare⟩ expound; exhibit ⟨quadri ecc⟩. **~si** vr ⟨compromettersi⟩ compromise oneself; ⟨al sole⟩ expose oneself; ⟨alle critiche⟩ lay oneself open

espor'ta|re vt export. **~'tore, ~'trice** nmf exporter. **~zi'one** nf export

esposizi'one nf ⟨mostra⟩ exhibition; ⟨in vetrina⟩ display; ⟨spiegazione ecc⟩ exposition; ⟨posizione, fotografia⟩ exposure. **es'posto** pp di **esporre** ● a exposed; **esposto a** ⟨rivolto⟩ facing ● nm Jur ecc statement

espressa'mente adv expressly; **non l'ha detto ~** he didn't put it in so many words

espres|si'one nf expression. **~'sivo** a expressive

es'presso pp di **esprimere** ● a express ● nm ⟨lettera⟩ express letter; ⟨treno⟩ express train; ⟨caffè⟩ espresso; **per ~** ⟨spedire⟩ [by] express [post]

es'primer|e vt express. **~si** vr express oneself

espropri'a|re vt dispossess. **~zi'one** nf Jur expropriation. **es'proprio** nm expropriation

espulsi'one nf expulsion. **es'pulso** pp di **espellere**

es'senz|a nf essence. **~i'ale** a essential ● nm important thing. **~ial'mente** a essentially

'essere vi be; **c'è** there is; **ci sono** there are; **che ora è? – sono le dieci** what time is it? – it's ten o'clock; **chi è? – sono io** who is it? – it's me; **ci sono!** ⟨ho capito⟩ I've got it!; **ci siamo!** ⟨siamo arrivati⟩ here we are at last!); **è stato detto che** it has been said that; **siamo in due** there are two of us; **questa camicia è da lavare** this shirt is to be washed; **non è da te** it's not like you; **~ di** ⟨provenire da⟩ be from; **~ per** ⟨favorevole⟩ be in favour of; **se fossi in te,...** if I were you,...; **sarà!** if you say so!; **come sarebbe a dire?** what are you getting at? ● v aux have; ⟨in passivi⟩ be; **siamo arrivati** we have arrived; **ci sono stato ieri** I was there yesterday; **sono nato a Torino** I was born in Turin; **è riconosciuto come...** he is recognized as... ● nm being. **~ umano** human being. **~ vivente** living creature

essic'cato a Culin desiccated

'esso, -a pron he, she; ⟨cosa, animale⟩ it

est nm east

'estasi nf ecstasy; **andare in ~ per** go into raptures over. **~'are** vt enrapture

e'state nf summer

e'sten|dere vt extend. **~dersi** vr

spread; (*allungarsi*) stretch. **~si'one** *nf* extension; (*ampiezza*) expanse; *Mus* range. **~'sivo** *a* extensive

estenu'ante *a* exhausting

estenu'a|re *vt* wear out; deplete ‹*risorse, casse*›. **~rsi** *vr* wear oneself out

esteri'or|e *a* & *nm* exterior. **~'mente** *adv* externally; (*di persone*) outwardly

esterna'mente *adv* on the outside

ester'nare *vt* express, show

e'sterno *a* external; **per uso ~** for external use only ● *nm* (*allievo*) day-boy; *Archit* exterior; (*scala*) outside; (*in film*) location shot

'estero *a* foreign ● *nm* foreign countries *pl*; **all'~** abroad

esterre'fatto *a* horrified

e'steso *pp di* **estendere** ● *a* extensive; (*diffuso*) widespread; **per ~** ‹*scrivere*› in full

e'stetic|a *nf* aesthetics *sg*. **~a'mente** *adv* aesthetically. **~o, -a** *a* aesthetic; ‹*chirurgia, chirurgo*› plastic. **este'tista** *nf* beautician

'estimo *nm* estimate

e'stin|guere *vt* extinguish. **~guersi** *vr* die out. **~to, -a** *pp di* **estinguere** ● *nmf* deceased. **~'tore** *nm* [fire] extinguisher. **~zi'one** *nf* extinction; (*di incendio*) putting out

estir'pa|re *vt* uproot; extract ‹*dente*›; *fig* eradicate ‹*crimine, malattia*›. **~zi'one** *nf* eradication; (*di dente*) extraction

e'stivo *a* summer

e'stor|cere *vt* extort. **~si'one** *nf* extortion. **~to** *pp di* **estorcere**

estradizi'one *nf* extradition

e'straneo, -a *a* extraneous; (*straniero*) foreign ● *nmf* stranger

estrani'ar|e *vt* estrange. **~si** *vr* become estranged

e'stra|rre *vt* extract; (*sorteggiare*) draw. **~tto** *pp di* **estrarre** ● *nm* extract; (*brano*) excerpt; (*documento*) abstract. **~tto conto** statement [of account], bank statement. **~zi'one** *nf* extraction; (*a sorte*) draw

estrema'mente *adv* extremely

estre'mis|mo *nm* extremism. **~ta** *nmf* extremist

estremità *nf inv* extremity; (*di una corda*) end ● *nfpl Anat* extremities

e'stremo *a* extreme; (*ultimo*) last; **misure estreme** drastic measures; **l'E~ Oriente** the Far East ● *nm* (*limite*) extreme. **estremi** *pl* (*di documento*) main points; (*di reato*) essential ele-

ments; **essere agli estremi** be at the end of one's tether

'estro *nm* (*disposizione artistica*) talent; (*ispirazione*) inspiration; (*capriccio*) whim. **e'stroso** *a* talented; (*capriccioso*) unpredictable

estro'mettere *vt* expel

estro'verso *a* extroverted ● *nm* extrovert

estu'ario *nm* estuary

esube'ran|te *a* exuberant. **~za** *nf* exuberance

'esule *nmf* exile

esul'tante *a* exultant

esul'tare *vi* rejoice

esu'mare *vt* exhume

età *nf inv* age; **raggiungere la maggiore ~** come of age; **un uomo di mezz'~** a middle-aged man

'etere *nm* ether. **e'tereo** *a* ethereal

eterna'mente *adv* eternally

eternità *nf* eternity; **è un'~ che non la vedo** I haven't seen her for ages

e'terno *a* eternal; ‹*questione, problema*› age-old; **in ~** *fam* for ever

etero'geneo *a* diverse, heterogeneous

eterosessu'ale *nmf* heterosexual

'etica *nf* ethics

eti'chetta¹ *nf* label; (*con il prezzo*) price-tag

eti'chetta² *nf* (*cerimoniale*) etiquette

etichet'tare *vt* label

'etico *a* ethical

eti'lometro *nm* Breathalyzer®

etimolo'gia *nf* etymology

Eti'opia *nf* Ethiopia

'etnico *a* ethnic. **etnolo'gia** *nf* ethnology

e'trusco *a* & *nmf* Etruscan

'ettaro *nm* hectare

'etto, etto'grammo *nm* hundred grams, ≈ quarter pound

euca'lipto *nm* eucalyptus

eucari'stia *nf* Eucharist

eufe'mismo *nm* euphemism

eufo'ria *nf* elation; *Med* euphoria. **eu'forico** *a* elated; *Med* euphoric

'euro *nm inv Fin* euro

Euro'city *nm* international Intercity

eurodepu'tato *nm* Euro MP, MEP

Eu'ropa *nf* Europe. **euro'peo, -a** *a* & *nmf* European

eutana'sia *nf* euthanasia

evacu'a|re *vt* evacuate. **~zi'one** *nf* evacuation

e'vadere *vt* evade; (*sbrigare*) deal with ● *vi* **~ da** escape from

evane'scente *a* vanishing
evan'gel|ico *a* evangelical. **evange'-lista** *nm* evangelist. **~o** *nm* = **vangelo**
evapo'ra|re *vi* evaporate. **~zi'one** *nf* evaporation
evasi'one *nf* escape; (*fiscale*) evasion; *fig* escapism. **eva'sivo** *a* evasive
e'vaso *pp di* **evadere** ● *nm* fugitive
eva'sore *nm* **~ fiscale** tax evader
eveni'enza *nf* eventuality
e'vento *nm* event
eventu'al|e *a* possible. **~ità** *nf inv* eventuality
evi'den|te *a* evident; **è ~te che** it is obvious that. **~te'mente** *adv* evidently. **~za** *nf* evidence; **mettere in ~za** emphasize; **mettersi in ~za** make oneself conspicuous

evidenzi'a|re *vt* highlight. **~'tore** *nm* (*penna*) highlighter
evi'tare *vt* avoid; (*risparmiare*) spare
evo'care *vt* evoke
evo'lu|to *pp di* **evolvere** ● *a* evolved; (*progredito*) progressive; ⟨civiltà, nazione⟩ advanced; **una donna evoluta** a modern woman. **~zi'one** *nf* evolution; (*di ginnasta, aereo*) circle
e'volver|e *vt* develop. **~si** *vr* evolve
ev'viva *int* hurray; **~ il Papa!** long live the Pope!; **gridare ~** cheer
ex+ *pref* ex+, former
'extra *a inv* extra; ⟨qualità⟩ first-class ● *nm inv* extra
extracomuni'tario *a* non-EC
extraconiu'gale *a* extramarital
extrater'restre *nmf* extra-terrestrial

Ff

fa¹ *nm inv* *Mus* (*chiave, nota*) F
fa² *adv* ago; **due mesi ~** two months ago
fabbi'sogno *nm* requirements *pl*, needs *pl*
'fabbri|ca *nf* factory
fabbri'cabile *a* ⟨area, terreno⟩ that can be built on
fabbri'cante *nm* manufacturer
fabbri'ca|re *vt* build; (*produrre*) manufacture; (*fig: inventare*) fabricate. **~to** *nm* building. **~zi'one** *nf* manufacturing; (*costruzione*) building
'fabbro *nm* blacksmith
fac'cend|a *nf* matter; **~e** *pl* (*lavori domestici*) housework *sg*. **~i'ere** *nm* wheeler-dealer
fac'chino *nm* porter
'facci|a *nf* face; (*di foglio*) side; **~ a ~a** face to face; **~a tosta** cheek; **voltar ~a** change sides; **di ~a** ⟨palazzo⟩ opposite; **alla ~a di** (*fam: a dispetto di*) in spite of. **~'ata** *nf* façade; (*di foglio*) side; (*fig: esteriorità*) outward appearance
fa'ceto *a* facetious; **tra il serio e il ~** half joking
fa'chiro *nm* fakir
'facil|e *a* easy; (*affabile*) easy-going; **essere ~e alle critiche** be quick to criticize; **essere ~e al riso** laugh a

lot; **~e a farsi** easy to do; **è ~e che piova** it's likely to rain. **~ità** *nf inv* ease; (*disposizione*) aptitude; **avere ~ità di parola** express oneself well
facili'ta|re *vt* facilitate. **~zi'one** *nf* facility; **~zioni** *pl* special terms
facil'mente *adv* (*con facilità*) easily; (*probabilmente*) probably
faci'lone *a* slapdash. **~'ria** *nf* slapdash attitude
facino'roso *a* violent
facoltà *nf inv* faculty; (*potere*) power. **~'tivo** *a* optional; **fermata ~tiva** request stop
facol'toso *a* wealthy
fac'simile *nm* facsimile
fac'totum *nmf* man/girl Friday, factotum
'faggio *nm* beech
fagi'ano *nm* pheasant
fagio'lino *nm* French bean
fagi'olo *nm* bean; **a ~** ⟨arrivare, capitare⟩ at the right time
fagoci'tare *vt* gobble up ⟨società⟩
fa'gotto *nm* bundle; *Mus* bassoon
'faida *nf* feud
fai da te *nm* do-it-yourself, DIY
fal'cata *nf* stride
'falc|e *nf* scythe. **fal'cetto** *nm* sickle.

~i'are *vt* cut; *fig* mow down. **~ia'trice** *nf* [lawn-]mower

'falco *nm* hawk

fal'cone *nm* falcon

'falda *nf* stratum; *(di neve)* flake; *(di cappello)* brim; *(pendio)* slope

fale'gname *nm* carpenter. **~'ria** *nf* carpentry

'falla *nf* leak

fal'lace *a* deceptive

'fallico *a* phallic

fallimen'tare *a* disastrous; *Jur* bankruptcy. **falli'mento** *nm* *Fin* bankruptcy; *fig* failure

fal'li|re *vi* *Fin* go bankrupt; *fig* fail • *vt* miss *(colpo)*. **~to, -a** *a* unsuccessful; *Fin* bankrupt • *nmf* failure; *Fin* bankrupt

'fallo *nm* fault; *(errore)* mistake; *Sport* foul; *(imperfezione)* flaw; **senza ~** without fail

falò *nm inv* bonfire

fal'sar|e *vt* alter; *(falsificare)* falsify. **~io, -a** *nmf* forger; *(di documenti)* counterfeiter

falsifi'ca|re *vt* fake; *(contraffare)* forge. **~zi'one** *nf* *(di documento)* falsification

falsità *nf* falseness

'falso *a* false; *(sbagliato)* wrong; *(opera d'arte ecc)* fake; *(gioielli, oro)* imitation • *nm* forgery; **giurare il ~** commit perjury

'fama *nf* fame; *(reputazione)* reputation

'fame *nf* hunger; **aver ~** be hungry; **fare la ~** barely scrape a living. **fa'melico** *a* ravenous

famige'rato *a* infamous

fa'miglia *nf* family

famili'ar|e *a* family *attrib*; *(ben noto)* familiar; *(senza cerimonie)* informal • *nmf* relative, relation **~ità** *nf* familiarity; *(informalità)* informality. **~iz'zarsi** *vr* familiarize oneself

fa'moso *a* famous

fa'nale *nm* lamp; *Auto ecc* light. **fanali** *pl* **posteriori** *Auto* rear lights

fa'natico, -a *a* fanatical; **essere ~ di calcio/cinema** be a football/cinema fanatic • *nmf* fanatic. **fana'tismo** *nm* fanaticism

fanci'ul|la *nf* young girl. **~'lezza** *nf* childhood. **~lo** *nm* young boy

fan'donia *nf* lie; **fandonie!** nonsense!

fan'fara *nf* fanfare; *(complesso)* brass band

fanfaro'nata *nf* brag. **fanfa'rone, -a** *nmf* braggart

fan'ghiglia *nf* mud. **'fango** *nm* mud. **fan'goso** *a* muddy

fannul'lone, -a *nmf* idler

fantasci'enza *nf* science fiction

fanta'si|a *nf* fantasy; *(immaginazione)* imagination; *(capriccio)* fancy; *(di tessuto)* pattern. **~'oso** *a* *(stilista, ragazzo)* imaginative; *(resoconto)* improbable

fan'tasma *nm* ghost

fantasti'c|are *vi* day-dream. **~he'ria** *nf* day-dream. **fan'tastico** *a* fantastic; *(racconto)* fantasy

'fante *nm* infantryman; *(carte)* jack. **~'ria** *nm* infantry

fan'tino *nm* jockey

fan'toccio *nm* puppet

fanto'matico *a* *(inafferrabile)* phantom *attrib*

fara'butto *nm* trickster

fara'ona *nf* *(uccello)* guinea-fowl

far'ci|re *vt* stuff; fill *(torta)*. **~to** *a* stuffed; *(dolce)* filled

far'dello *nm* bundle; *fig* burden

'fare *vt* do; make *(dolce, letto ecc)*; *(recitare la parte di)* play; *(trascorrere)* spend; **~ una pausa/un sogno** have a break/a dream; **~ colpo su** impress; **~ paura a** frighten; **~ piacere a** please; **farla finita** put an end to it; **~ l'insegnante** be a teacher; **~ lo scemo** play the idiot; **~ una settimana al mare** spend a week at the seaside; **3 più 3 fa 6** 3 and 3 makes 6; **quanto fa? – fanno 10 000 lira** how much is it? – it's 10,000 lire; **far ~ qcsa a qcno** get sb to do sth; *(costringere)* make sb do sth; **~ vedere** show; **fammi parlare** let me speak; **niente a che ~ con** nothing to do with; **non c'è niente da ~** *(per problema)* there is nothing we/you/etc. can do; **fa caldo/buio** it's warm/dark; **non fa niente** it doesn't matter; **strada facendo** on the way. **farcela** *(riuscire)* manage • *vi* **fai in modo di venire** try and come; **~ da** act as; **~ per** make as if to; **~ presto** be quick; **non fa per me** it's not for me • *nm* way; **sul far del giorno** at daybreak. **farsi** *vr* *(diventare)* get; *(sl: drogarsi)* shoot up; **farsi avanti** come forward; **farsi i fatti propri** mind one's own business; **farsi la barba** shave; **farsi la villa** *fam* buy a villa; **farsi il ragazzo** *fam* find a boyfriend; **farsi due risate** have a laugh; **farsi male** hurt oneself; **farsi strada** *(aver successo)* make one's way in the world

fa'retto *nm* spot[light]

far'falla *nf* butterfly

farfal'lino nm (cravatta) bow tie
farfugli'are vt mutter
fa'rina nf flour. **fari'nacei** nmpl starchy food sg
fa'ringe nf pharynx
fari'noso a ⟨neve⟩ powdery; ⟨mela⟩ soft; ⟨patata⟩ floury
farma|'ceutico a pharmaceutical. **~'cia** nf pharmacy; (negozio) chemist's [shop]. **~cia di turno** duty chemist. **~'cista** nmf chemist. **'farmaco** nm drug
'faro nm Auto headlight; Aeron beacon; (costruzione) lighthouse
'farsa nf farce
'fasci|a nf band; (zona) area; (ufficiale) sash; (benda) bandage. **~'are** vt bandage; cling to ⟨fianchi⟩. **~a'tura** nf dressing; (azione) bandaging
fa'scicolo nm file; (di rivista) issue; (libretto) booklet
'fascino nm fascination
'fascio nm bundle; (di fiori) bunch
fa'scis|mo nm fascism. **~ta** nmf fascist
'fase nf phase
fa'stidi|o nm nuisance; (scomodo) inconvenience; **dar ~o a qcno** bother sb; **~i** pl (preoccupazioni) worries; (disturbi) troubles. **~'oso** a tiresome
'fasto nm pomp. **fa'stoso** a sumptuous
fa'sullo a bogus
'fata nf fairy
fa'ta|le a fatal; (inevitabile) fated
fata'l|ismo nm fatalism. **~ista** nmf fatalist. **~ità** nf inv fate; (caso sfortunato) misfortune. **~'mente** adv inevitably
fa'tica nf effort; (lavoro faticoso) hard work; (stanchezza) fatigue; **a ~** with great difficulty; **è ~ sprecata** it's a waste of time; **fare ~ a fare qcsa** find it difficult to do sth; **fare ~ a finire qcsa** struggle to finish sth. **fati'caccia** nf pain
fati'ca|re vi toil; **~re a** (stentare) find it difficult to. **~ta** nf effort; (sfacchinata) grind. **fati'coso** a tiring; (difficile) difficult
'fato nm fate
fat'taccio nm hum foul deed
fat'tezze nfpl features
fat'tibile a feasible
'fatto pp di fare ● a done, made; **~ a mano/in casa** handmade/home-made ● nm fact; (azione) action; (avvenimento) event; **bada ai fatti tuoi!** mind your own business; **sa il ~ suo** he knows his business; **di ~** in fact; **in ~ di** as regards
fat'to|re nm (causa, Math) factor; (di fattoria) farm manager. **~'ria** nf farm; (casa) farmhouse
fatto'rino nm messenger [boy]
fattucchi'era nf witch
fat'tura nf (stile) cut; (lavorazione) workmanship; Comm invoice
fattu'ra|re vt invoice; (adulterare) adulterate. **~to** nm turnover, sales pl. **~zi'one** nf invoicing, billing
'fatuo a fatuous
'fauna nf fauna
fau'tore nm supporter
'fava nf broad bean
fa'vella nf speech
fa'villa nf spark
'favo|la nf fable; (fiaba) story; (oggetto di pettegolezzi) laughing-stock; (meraviglia) dream. **~'loso** a fabulous
fa'vore nm favour; **essere a ~ di** be in favour of; **per ~** please; **di ~** (condizioni, trattamento) preferential. **~ggia-'mento** nm Jur aiding and abetting. **favo'revole** a favourable. **~vol'mente** adv favourably
favo'ri|re vt favour; (promuovere) promote; **vuol ~re?** (accettare) will you have some?; (entrare) will you come in?. **~to, -a** a & nmf favourite
fax nm inv fax. **fa'xare** vt fax
fazi'one nf faction
faziosità nf bias. **fazi'oso** nm sectarian
fazzolet'tino nm ~ [di carta] [paper] tissue
fazzo'letto nm handkerchief; (da testa) headscarf
feb'braio nm February
'febbre nf fever; **avere la ~** have o run a temperature. **~ da fieno** hay fever. **febbrici'tante** a fevered. **feb'brile** a feverish
'feccia nf dregs pl
'fecola nf potato flour
fecon'da|re vt fertilize. **~'tore** nm fertilizer. **~zi'one** nf fertilization. **~zione artificiale** artificial insemination. **fe'condo** a fertile
'fede nf faith; (fiducia) trust; (anello) wedding-ring; **in buona/mala ~** in good/bad faith; **prestar ~ a** believe; **tener ~ alla parola** keep one's word. **fe'dele** a faithful ● nmf believer; (seguace) follower. **~l'mente** adv faithfully. **~ltà** nf faithfulness; **alta ~ltà** high fidelity

'**federa** nf pillowcase

fede'ra|le a federal. **~'lismo** nm federalism. **~zi'one** nf federation

fe'dina nf **avere la ~ penale sporca/pulita** have a/no criminal record

'**fegato** nm liver; fig guts pl

'**felce** nf fern

fe'lic|e a happy; (fortunato) lucky. **~ltà** nf happiness

felici'ta|rsi vr **~rsi con** congratulate. **~zi'oni** nfpl congratulations

fe'lino a feline

'**felpa** nf (indumento) sweatshirt

fel'pato a brushed; (passo) stealthy

'**feltro** nm felt; (cappello) felt hat

'**femmin|a** nf female. **femmi'nile** a feminine; (rivista, abbigliamento) women's; (sesso) female ● nm feminine. **~ilità** nf femininity. **femmi'nismo** nm feminism

'**femore** nm femur

'**fend|ere** vt split. **~i'tura** nf split; (nella roccia) crack

feni'cottero nm flamingo

fenome'nale a phenomenal. **fe'nomeno** nm phenomenon

'**feretro** nm coffin

feri'ale a weekday; **giorno ~** weekday

'**ferie** nfpl holidays; (di università, tribunale ecc) vacation sg; **andare in ~** go on holiday

feri'mento nm wounding

fe'ri|re vt wound; (in incidente) injure; fig hurt. **~rsi** vr injure oneself. **~ta** nf wound. **~to** a wounded ● nm wounded person; Mil casualty

'**ferma** nf Mil period of service

ferma'capelli nm inv hairslide

ferma'carte nm inv paperweight

fermacra'vatta nm inv tiepin

fer'maglio nm clasp; (spilla) brooch; (per capelli) hair slide

ferma'mente adv firmly

fer'ma|re vt stop; (fissare) fix; Jur detain ● vi stop. **~rsi** vr stop. **~ta** nf stop. **~ta dell'autobus** bus-stop. **~ta a richiesta** request stop

fermen'ta|re vi ferment. **~zi'one** nf fermentation. **fer'mento** nm ferment; (lievito) yeast

fer'mezza nf firmness

'**fermo** a still; (veicolo) stationary; (stabile) steady; (orologio) not working ● nm Jur detention; Mech catch; **in stato di ~** in custody

fe'roc|e a ferocious; (bestia) wild; (freddo, dolore) unbearable. **~e'mente** adv fiercely, ferociously. **~ia** nf ferocity

fer'raglia nf scrap iron

ferra'gosto nm 15 August (bank holiday in Italy); (periodo) August holidays pl

ferra'menta nfpl ironmongery sg; **negozio di ~** ironmonger's

fer'ra|re vt shoe (cavallo). **~to a ~to in** (preparato in) well up in

'**ferreo** a iron

'**ferro** nm iron; (attrezzo) tool; (di chirurgo) instrument; **bistecca ai ferri** grilled steak; **di ~** (memoria) excellent; (alibi) cast-iron; **salute di ~** iron constitution. **~ battuto** wrought iron. **~ da calza** knitting needle. **~ di cavallo** horseshoe. **~ da stiro** iron

ferro'vecchio nm scrap merchant

ferro'vi|a nf railway. **~'ario** a railway. **~'ere** nm railwayman

fertil|e a fertile. **~ità** nf fertility. **~iz'zante** nm fertilizer

fer'vente a blazing; fig fervent

fer'vere vi (preparativi:) be well under way

'**fervid|o** a fervent; **~i auguri** best wishes

fer'vore nm fervour

fesse'ria nf nonsense

'**fesso** pp di **fendere** ● a cracked; (fam: sciocco) foolish ● nm (fam: idiota) fool; **far ~ qcno** fam con sb

fes'sura nf crack; (per gettone ecc) slot

'**festa** nf feast; (giorno festivo) holiday; (compleanno) birthday; (ricevimento) party; fig joy; **fare ~ a qcno** welcome sb; **essere in ~** be on holiday; **far ~** celebrate. **~i'olo** a festive

festeggia'mento nm celebration; (manifestazione) festivity

festeggi'are vt celebrate; (accogliere festosamente) give a hearty welcome to

fe'stino nm party

festività nfpl festivities. **fe'stivo** a holiday; (lieto) festive. **festivi** nmpl public holidays

fe'stone nm (nel cucito) scallop, scollop

fe'stoso a merry

fe'tente a evil smelling; fig revolting ● nmf fam bastard

fe'ticcio nm fetish

'**feto** nm foetus

fe'tore nm stench

'**fetta** nf slice; **a fette** sliced. **~ biscottata** slices of crispy toast-like bread

fet'tuccia nf tape; (con nome) name tape

feu'dale a feudal. '**feudo** nm feud

FFSS *abbr* (**Ferrovie dello Stato**) Italian state railways

fi'aba *nf* fairy-tale. **fia'besco** *a* fairy-tale

fi'acc|a *nf* weariness; (*indolenza*) laziness; **battere la ~a** be sluggish. **fiac'care** *vt* weaken. **~o** *a* weak; (*indolente*) slack; (*stanco*) weary; (*partita*) dull

fi'acco|la *nf* torch. **~'lata** *nf* torchlight procession

fi'ala *nf* phial

fi'amma *nf* flame; *Naut* pennant; **in fiamme** aflame. **andare in fiamme** go up in flames. **~ ossidrica** blowtorch

fiam'ma|nte *a* flaming; **nuovo ~nte** brand new. **~ta** *nf* blaze

fiammeggi'are *vi* blaze

fiam'mifero *nm* match

fiam'mingo, -a *a* Flemish ● *nmf* Fleming ● *nm* (*lingua*) Flemish

fiancheggi'are *vt* border; *fig* support

fi'anco *nm* side; (*di persona*) hip; (*di animale*) flank; *Mil* wing; **al mio ~** by my side; **~ a** (*lavorare*) side by side

fi'asco *nm* flask; *fig* fiasco; **fare ~** be a fiasco

fia'tare *vi* breathe; (*parlare*) breathe a word

fi'ato *nm* breath; (*vigore*) stamina; **strumenti a ~** wind instruments; **senza ~** breathlessly; **tutto d'un ~** (*bere, leggere*) all in one go

'fibbia *nf* buckle

'fibra *nf* fibre; **fibre** *pl* (*alimentari*) roughage. **~ ottica** optical fibre

ficca'naso *nmf* nosey parker

fic'car|e *vt* thrust; drive (*chiodo ecc*); (*fam: mettere*) shove. **~si** *vr* thrust oneself; (*nascondersi*) hide; **~si nei guai** get oneself into trouble

fiche *nf* (*gettone*) chip

'fico *nm* (*albero*) fig-tree; (*frutto*) fig. **~ d'India** prickly pear

'fico, -a *fam nmf* cool sort ● *a* cool

fidanza'mento *nm* engagement

fidan'za|rsi *vr* become engaged. **~to, -a** *nmf* fiancé; fiancée

fi'da|rsi *vr* **~rsi di** trust. **~to** *a* trustworthy

'fido *nm* devoted follower; *Comm* credit

fi'duci|a *nf* confidence; **degno di ~a** trustworthy; **di ~a** (*fornitore, banca*) regular, usual; **persona di ~a** reliable person. **~'oso** *a* trusting

fi'ele *nm* bile; *fig* bitterness

fie'nile *nm* barn. **fi'eno** *nm* hay

fi'era *nf* fair

fie'rezza *nf* (*dignità*) pride. **fi'ero** *a* proud

fi'evole *a* faint; (*luce*) dim

'fifa *nf fam* jitters; **aver ~** have the jitters. **fi'fone, -a** *nmf fam* chicken

'figli|a *nf* daughter; **~a unica** only child. **~'astra** *nf* stepdaughter. **~'astro** *nm* stepson. **~o** *nm* son; (*generico*) child. **~o di papà** spoilt brat. **~o unico** only child

figli'occi|a *nf* goddaughter. **~o** *nm* godson

figli'o|la *nf* girl. **~'lanza** *nf* offspring. **~lo** *nm* boy

'figo, -a *vedi* **fico, -a**

fi'gura *nf* figure; (*aspetto esteriore*) shape; (*illustrazione*) illustration; **far bella/brutta ~** make a good/bad impression; **mi hai fatto fare una brutta ~** you made me look a fool; **che ~!** how embarrassing!. **figu'raccia** *nf* bad impression

figu'ra|re *vt* represent; (*simboleggiare*) symbolize; (*immaginare*) imagine ● *vi* (*far figura*) cut a fine figure; (*in lista*) appear, figure. **~rsi** *vr* (*immaginarsi*) imagine; **~ti!** imagine that!; **posso? – [ma] ~ti!** may I? – of course!. **~'tivo** *a* figurative

figu'rina *nf* (*da raccolta*) ≈ cigarette card

figu|ri'nista *nmf* dress designer. **~'rino** *nm* fashion sketch. **~'rone** *nm* **fare un ~rone** make an excellent impression

'fila *nf* line; (*di soldati ecc*) file; (*di oggetti*) row; (*coda*) queue; **di ~** in succession; **fare la ~** queue [up], stand in line *Am*; **in ~ indiana** single file

fila'mento *nm* filament

filantro'pia *nf* philanthropy

fi'lare *vt* spin; *Naut* pay out ● *vi* (*andarsene*) run away; (*liquido:*) trickle; **fila!** scram!; **~ con** (*fam: amoreggiare*) go out with; **~ dritto** toe the line

filar'monica *nf* (*orchestra*) orchestra

fila'strocca *nf* rigmarole; (*per bambini*) nursery rhyme

filate'lia *nf* philately

fi'la|to *a* spun; (*ininterrotto*) running; (*continuato*) uninterrupted; **di ~to** (*subito*) immediately ● *nm* yarn. **~'tura** *nf* spinning; (*filanda*) spinning mill

fil di 'ferro *nm* wire

fi'letto *nm* (*bordo*) border; (*di vite*) thread; *Culin* fillet

fili'ale *a* filial ● *nf Comm* branch

fili'grana *nf* filigree; (*su carta*) watermark

film *nm inv* film. **~ giallo** thriller. **~ a lungo metraggio** feature film

fil'ma|re *vt* film. **~to** *nm* short film. **fil'mino** *nm* cine film

'filo *nm* thread; (*tessile*) yarn; (*metallico*) wire; (*di lama*) edge; (*venatura*) grain; (*di perle*) string; (*d'erba*) blade; (*di luce*) ray; **con un ~ di voce** in a whisper; **per ~ e per segno** in detail; **fare il ~ a** qcno fancy sb; **perdere il ~** lose the thread. **~ spinato** barbed wire

'filobus *nm inv* trolleybus

filodiffusi'one *nf* rediffusion

fi'lone *nm* vein; (*di pane*) long loaf

filoso'fia *nf* philosophy. **fi'losofo, -a** *nmf* philosopher

fil'trare *vt* filter. **'filtro** *nm* filter

'filza *nf* string

fin *vedi* **fine, fino[1]**

fi'nal|e *a* final ● *nm* end ● *nf Sport* final. **fina'lista** *nmf* finalist. **~ità** *nf inv* finality; (*scopo*) aim. **~'mente** *adv* at last; (*in ultimo*) finally

fi'nanz|a *nf* finance. **~i'ario** *a* financial. **~i'ere** *nm* financier; (*guardia di finanza*) customs officer. **~ia'mento** *nm* funding

finanzi'a|re *vt* fund, finance. **~'tore, ~'trice** *nmf* backer

finché *conj* until; (*per tutto il tempo che*) as long as

'fine *a* fine; (*sottile*) thin; (*udito, vista*) keen; (*raffinato*) refined ● *nf* end; **alla ~** in the end; **alla fin ~** after all; **in fin dei conti** when all's said and done; **te lo dico a fin di bene** I'm telling you for your own good; **senza ~** endless ● *nm* aim. **~ settimana** weekend

fi'nestra *nf* window. **fine'strella** *nf* **di aiuto** *Comput* help window, help box. **fine'strino** *nm Rail, Auto* window

fi'nezza *nf* fineness; (*sottigliezza*) thinness; (*raffinatezza*) refinement

'finger|e *vt* pretend; feign ⟨*affetto ecc*⟩. **~si** *vr* pretend to be

fini'menti *nmpl* finishing touches; (*per cavallo*) harness *sg*

fini'mondo *nm* end of the world; *fig* pandemonium

fi'ni|re *vt/i* finish, end; (*smettere*) stop; (*diventare, andare a finire*) end up; **~scila!** stop it!. **~to** *a* finished; (*abile*) accomplished. **~'tura** *nf* finish

finlan'dese *a* Finnish ● *nmf* Finn ● *nm* (*lingua*) Finnish

Fin'landia *nf* Finland

'fino[1] *prep* **~ a** till, until; (*spazio*) as far as; **~ all'ultimo** to the last; **fin da** (*tempo*) since; (*spazio*) from; **fin qui** as far as here; **fin troppo** too much; **~ a che punto** how far

'fino[2] *a* fine; (*acuto*) subtle; (*puro*) pure

fi'nocchio *nm* fennel; (*fam: omosessuale*) poof

fi'nora *adv* so far, up till now

'finta *nf* pretence, sham; *Sport* feint; **far ~ di** pretend to; **far ~ di niente** act as if nothing had happened; **per ~** (*per scherzo*) for a laugh

finzi'one *nf* pretence

fi'occo *nm* bow; (*di neve*) flake; (*nappa*) tassel; **coi fiocchi** *fig* excellent. **~ di neve** snowflake

fi'ocina *nf* harpoon

fi'oco *a* weak; ⟨*luce*⟩ dim

fi'onda *nf* catapult

fio'raio, -a *nmf* florist

fiorda'liso *nm* cornflower

fi'ordo *nm* fiord

fi'ore *nm* flower; (*parte scelta*) cream; **fiori** *pl* (*nelle carte*) clubs; **a fior d'acqua** on the surface of the water; **fior di** (*abbondanza*) a lot of; **ha i nervi a fior di pelle** his nerves are on edge; **a fiori** flowery

fioren'tino *a* Florentine

fio'retto *nm* (*scherma*) foil; *Relig* act of mortification

fio'rire *vi* flower; ⟨*albero:*⟩ blossom; *fig* flourish

fio'rista *nmf* florist

fiori'tura *nf* (*di albero*) blossoming

fi'otto *nm* **scorrere a fiotti** pour out; **piove a fiotti** the rain is pouring down

Fi'renze *nf* Florence

'firma *nf* signature; (*nome*) name

fir'ma|re *vt* sign. **~'tario, -a** *nmf* signatory. **~to a** ⟨*abito, borsa*⟩ designer *attrib*

fisar'monica *nf* accordion

fi'scale *a* fiscal

fischi'are *vi* whistle ● *vt* whistle; (*in segno di disapprovazione*) boo

fischiet't|are *vt* whistle. **~io** *nm* whistling

fischi'etto *nm* whistle. **'fischio** *nm* whistle

'fisco *nm* treasury; (*tasse*) taxation; **il ~** the taxman

'fisica *nf* physics

fisica'mente *adv* physically

'fisico, -a *a* physical ● *nmf* physicist ● *nm* physique

'fisima *nf* whim

fisio|lo'gia *nf* physiology. **~'logico** *a* physiological

fisiono'mia *nf* features, face; *(di paesaggio)* appearance

fisiotera'pi|a *nf* physiotherapy. **~sta** *nmf* physiotherapist

fis'sa|re *vt* fix, fasten; *(guardare fissamente)* stare at; arrange *(appuntamento, ora)*. **~rsi** *vr (stabilirsi)* settle; *(fissare lo sguardo)* stare; **~rsi su** *(ostinarsi)* set one's mind on; **~rsi di fare qcsa** become obsessed with doing sth. **~to** *nm (persona)* person with an obsession. **~zi'one** *nf* fixation; *(osessione)* obsession

'fisso *a* fixed; **un lavoro ~** a regular job; **senza fissa dimora** of no fixed abode

'fitta *nf* sharp pain

fit'tizio *a* fictitious

'fitto[1] *a* thick; **~ di** full of ● *nm* depth

fitto[2] *nm (affitto)* rent; **dare a ~** let; **prendere a ~** rent; *(noleggiare)* hire

fiu'mana *nf* swollen river; *fig* stream

fi'ume *nm* river; *fig* stream

fiu'tare *vt* smell. **fi'uto** *nm* [sense of] smell; *fig* nose

'flaccido *a* flabby

fla'cone *nm* bottle

fla'gello *nm* scourge

fla'grante *a* flagrant; **in ~** in the act

fla'nella *nf* flannel

'flash *nm inv Journ* newsflash

'flauto *nm* flute

'flebile *a* feeble

'flemma *nf* calm; *Med* phlegm. **flem'matico** *a* phlegmatic

fles'sibil|e *a* flexible. **~ità** *nf* flexibility

flessi'one *nf (del busto in avanti)* forward bend

'flesso *pp di* **flettere**

flessu'oso *a* supple

'flettere *vt* bend

flir'tare *vi* flirt

F.lli *abbr* **(fratelli)** Bros

floppy disk *nm inv* floppy disk

'flora *nf* flora

'florido *a* flourishing

'floscio *a* limp; *(flaccido)* flabby

'flotta *nf* fleet. **flot'tiglia** *nf* flotilla

flu'ente *a* fluent

flu'ido *nm* fluid

flu'ire *vi* flow

fluore'scente *a* fluorescent

flu'oro *nm* fluorine

'flusso *nm* flow; *Med* flux; *(del mare)* flood[-tide]; **~ e riflusso** ebb and flow

fluttu'ante *a* fluctuating

fluttu'a|re *vi (prezzi, moneta:)* fluctuate. **~zi'one** *nf* fluctuation

fluvi'ale *a* river

fo'bia *nf* phobia

'foca *nf* seal

fo'caccia *nf (pane)* flat bread; *(dolce)* ≈ raisin bread

fo'cale *a (distanza, punto)* focal. **foca-liz'zare** *vt* get into focus *(fotografia)*; focus *(attenzione)*; define *(problema)*

'foce *nf* mouth

foco'laio *nm Med* focus; *fig* centre

foco'lare *nm* hearth; *(caminetto)* fireplace; *Techn* furnace

fo'coso *a* fiery

'foder|a *nf* lining; *(di libro)* dust-jacket; *(di poltrona ecc)* loose cover. **fode'rare** *vt* line; cover *(libro)*. **~o** *nm* sheath

'foga *nf* impetuosity

'foggi|a *nf* fashion; *(maniera)* manner; *(forma)* shape. **~'are** *vt* mould

'fogli|a *nf* leaf; *(di metallo)* foil. **~'ame** *nm* foliage

fogli'etto *nm (pezzetto di carta)* piece of paper

'foglio *nm* sheet; *(pagina)* leaf. **~ elet-tronico** *Comput* spreadsheet. **~ rosa** ≈ provisional driving licence

'fogna *nf* sewer. **~'tura** *nf* sewerage

fo'lata *nf* gust

fol'clo|re *nm* folklore. **~'ristico** *a* folk; *(bizzarro)* weird

folgo'ra|re *vi (splendere)* shine ● *vt (con un fulmine)* strike. **~zi'one** *nf (da fulmine, elettrica)* electrocution; *(idea)* brainwave

'folgore *nf* thunderbolt

'folla *nf* crowd

'folle *a* mad; **in ~** *Auto* in neutral; **an-dare in ~** *Auto* coast

folle'mente *adv* madly

fol'lia *nf* madness; **alla ~** *(amare)* to distraction

'folto *a* thick

fomen'tare *vt* stir up

fond'ale *nm Theat* backcloth

fonda'men|ta *nfpl* foundations. **~'tale** *a* fundamental. **~to** *nm (di principio, teoria)* foundation

fon'da|re *vt* establish; base *(ragionamento, accusa)*. **~to** *a (ragionamento)* well-founded. **~zi'one** *nf* establishment; **~zioni** *pl (di edificio)* foundations

fon'delli *nmpl* **prendere qcno per i ~** pull sb's leg

fon'dente *a* ⟨cioccolato⟩ dark

'fonder|e *vt/i* melt; ⟨colori:⟩ blend. **~si** *vr* melt; *Comm* merge. **fonde'ria** *nf* foundry

'fondi *nmpl* (denaro) funds; (di caffè) grounds

'fondo *a* deep; **è notte fonda** it's the middle of the night ● *nm* bottom; (fine) end; (sfondo) background; (indole) nature; (somma di denaro) fund; (feccia) dregs *pl*; **andare a ~** ⟨nave:⟩ sink; **da cima a ~** from beginning to end; **in ~** after all; **in ~ in ~** deep down; **fino in ~** right to the end; ⟨capire⟩ thoroughly. **~ d'investimento** investment trust

fondo'tinta *nm* foundation cream

fon'duta *nf* fondue made with cheese, milk and eggs

fo'netic|a *nf* phonetics *sg*. **~o** *a* phonetic

fon'tana *nf* fountain

'fonte *nf* spring; *fig* source ● *nm* font

fo'raggio *nm* forage

fo'rar|e *vt* pierce; punch ⟨biglietto⟩ ● *vi* puncture. **~si** *vr* ⟨gomma, pallone:⟩ go soft

'forbici *nfpl* scissors

forbi'cine *nfpl* (per le unghie) nail scissors

for'bito *a* erudite

'forca *nf* fork; (patibolo) gallows *pl*

for'cella *nf* fork; (per capelli) hairpin

for'chet|ta *nf* fork. **~'tata** *nf* (quantità) forkful

for'cina *nf* hairpin

'forcipe *nm* forceps *pl*

for'cone *nm* pitchfork

fo'resta *nf* forest. **fore'stale** *a* forest *attrib*

foresti'ero, -a *a* foreign ● *nmf* foreigner

for'fait *nm inv* fixed price; **dare ~** (abbandonare) give up

'forfora *nf* dandruff

'forgi|a *nf* forge. **~'are** *vt* forge

'forma *nf* form; (sagoma) shape; *Culin* mould; (da calzolaio) last; **essere in ~** be in good form; **a ~ di** in the shape of; **forme** *pl* (del corpo) figure *sg*; (convenzioni) appearances

formag'gino *nm* processed cheese. **for'maggio** *nm* cheese

for'mal|e *a* formal. **~ità** *nf inv* formality. **~iz'zarsi** *vr* stand on ceremony. **~'mente** *adv* formally

for'ma|re *vt* form. **~rsi** *vr* form;

(svilupparsi) develop. **~to** *nm* size; (di libro) format; **~to tessera** ⟨fotografia⟩ passport-size

format'tare *vt* format

formazi'one *nf* formation; *Sport* lineup. **~ professionale** vocational training

for'mi|ca *nf* ant. **~'caio** *nm* anthill

'formica® *nf* (laminato plastico) Formica®

formico'l|are *vi* ⟨braccio ecc:⟩ tingle; **~are di** be swarming with; **mi ~a la mano** I have pins and needles in my hand. **~io** *nm* swarming; (di braccio ecc) pins and needles *pl*

formi'dabile *a* (tremendo) formidable; (eccezionale) tremendous

for'mina *nf* mould

for'moso *a* shapely

'formula *nf* formula. **formu'lare** *vt* formulate; (esprimere) express

for'nace *nf* furnace; (per laterizi) kiln

for'naio *nm* baker; (negozio) bakery

for'nello *nm* stove; (di pipa) bowl

for'ni|re *vt* supply (**di** with). **~'tore** *nm* supplier. **~'tura** *nf* supply

'forno *nm* oven; (panetteria) bakery; **al ~** roast. **~ a microonde** microwave [oven]

'foro *nm* hole; (romano) forum; (tribunale) [law] court

'forse *adv* perhaps, maybe; **essere in ~** be in doubt

forsen'nato, -a *a* mad ● *nmf* madman; madwoman

'forte *a* strong; ⟨colore⟩ bright; ⟨suono⟩ loud; (resistente) tough; ⟨spesa⟩ considerable; ⟨dolore⟩ severe; ⟨pioggia⟩ heavy; (a tennis, calcio) good; (fam: simpatico) great; ⟨taglia⟩ large ● *adv* strongly; ⟨parlare⟩ loudly; (velocemente) fast; ⟨piovere⟩ heavily ● *nm* (fortezza) fort; (specialità) strong point

for'tezza *nf* fortress; (forza morale) fortitude

fortifi'care *vt* fortify

for'tino *nm Mil* blockhouse

for'tuito *a* fortuitous; **incontro ~** chance encounter

for'tuna *nf* fortune; (successo) success; (buona sorte) luck. **atterraggio di ~** forced landing; **aver ~** be lucky; **buona ~!** good luck!; **di ~** makeshift; **per ~** luckily. **fortu'nato** *a* lucky, fortunate; (impresa) successful. **~ta'mente** *adv* fortunately

fo'runcolo *nm* pimple; (grosso) boil

'forza *nf* strength; (potenza) power;

(*fisica*) force; **di ~** by force; **a ~ di** by dint of; **con ~** hard; **~!** come on!; **~ di volontà** will-power; **~ maggiore** circumstances beyond one's control; **la ~ pubblica** the police; **per ~** against one's will; (*naturalmente*) of course; **farsi ~** bear up; **mare ~ 8** force 8 gale; **bella ~!** *fam* big deal!. **~ di gravità** [force of] gravity. **le forze armate** the armed forces

for'za|re *vt* force; (*scassare*) break open; (*sforzare*) strain. **~to** *a* forced; ⟨*sorriso*⟩ strained ● *nm* convict

forzi'ere *nm* coffer

for'zuto *a* strong

fo'schia *nf* haze

'fosco *a* dark

fo'sfato *nm* phosphate

'fosforo *nm* phosphorus

'fossa *nf* pit; (*tomba*) grave. **~ biologica** cesspool. **fos'sato** *nm* (*di fortificazione*) moat

fos'setta *nf* dimple

'fossile *nm* fossil

'fosso *nm* ditch; *Mil* trench

'foto *nf inv fam* photo; **fare delle ~** take some photos

foto'cellula *nf* photocell

fotocomposizi'one *nf* filmsetting, photocomposition

foto'copi|a *nf* photocopy. **~'are** *vt* photocopy. **~a'trice** *nf* photocopier

foto'finish *nm inv* photo finish

foto'genico *a* photogenic

fotogra|'fare *vt* photograph. **~'fia** *nf* (*arte*) photography; (*immagine*) photograph; **fare ~fie** take photographs. **foto'grafico** *a* photographic; **macchina fotografica** camera. **fo'tografo, -a** *nmf* photographer

foto'gramma *nm* frame

fotomo'dello *nm* [photographer's] model

fotomon'taggio *nm* photomontage

fotoro'manzo *nm* photo story

'fotter|e *vt* (*fam: rubare*) nick; *vulg* fuck, screw. **~sene** *vr vulg* not give a fuck

fot'tuto *a* (*fam: maledetto*) bloody

fou'lard *nm inv* scarf

fra *prep* (*in mezzo a due*) between; (*in un insieme*) among; (*tempo, distanza*) in; **detto ~ noi** between you and me; **~ sé e sé** to oneself; **~ l'altro** what's more; **~ breve** soon; **~ quindici giorni** in two weeks' time; **~ tutti, siamo in venti** there are twenty of us altogether

fracas'sar|e *vt* smash. **~si** *vr* shatter

fra'casso *nm* din; (*di cose che cadono*) crash

'fradicio *a* (*bagnato*) soaked; (*guasto*) rotten; **ubriaco ~** blind drunk

'fragil|e *a* fragile; *fig* frail. **~ità** *nf* fragility; *fig* frailty

'fragola *nf* strawberry

fra'go|re *nm* uproar; (*di cose rotte*) clatter; (*di tuono*) rumble. **~'roso** *a* uproarious; ⟨*tuono*⟩ rumbling; ⟨*suono*⟩ clanging

fra'gran|te *a* fragrant. **~za** *nf* fragrance

frain'te|ndere *vt* misunderstand. **~ndersi** *vr* be at cross-purposes. **~so** *pp di* **fraintendere**

frammen'tario *a* fragmentary. **fram'mento** *nm* fragment

'frana *nf* landslide; (*fam: persona*) walking disaster area. **fra'nare** *vi* slide down

franca'mente *adv* frankly

fran'cese *a* French ● *nmf* Frenchman; Frenchwoman ● *nm* (*lingua*) French

fran'chezza *nf* frankness

'Francia *nf* France

'franco¹ *a* frank; *Comm* free; **farla franca** get away with sth

'franco² *nm* (*moneta*) franc

franco'bollo *nm* stamp

fran'gente *nm* (*onda*) breaker; (*scoglio*) reef; (*fig: momento difficile*) crisis; **in quel ~** given the situation

'frangia *nf* fringe

fra'noso *a* subject to landslides

fran'toio *nm* olive-press

frantu'mar|e *vt*, **~si** *vr* shatter. **fran'tumi** *nmpl* splinters; **andare in frantumi** be smashed to smithereens

frappé *nm inv* milkshake

frap'por|re *vt* interpose. **~si** *vr* intervene

fra'sario *nm* vocabulary; (*libro*) phrase book

'frase *nf* sentence; (*espressione*) phrase. **~ fatta** cliché

'frassino *nm* ash[-tree]

frastagli'a|re *vt* make jagged. **~to** *a* jagged

frastor'na|re *vt* daze. **~to** *a* dazed

frastu'ono *nm* racket

'frate *nm* friar; (*monaco*) monk

fratel'la|nza *nf* brotherhood. **~stro** *nm* half-brother

fra'tell|i *nmpl* (*fratello e sorella*) brother and sister. **~o** *nm* brother

fraterniz'zare *vi* fraternize. **fra'terno** *a* brotherly

frat'taglie *nfpl* (*di pollo ecc*) giblets

frat'tanto *adv* in the meantime

frat'tempo *nm* **nel ~** meanwhile, in the meantime

frat'tu|ra *nf* fracture. **~'rare** *vt*, **~'rarsi** *vr* break

fraudo'lento *a* fraudulent

frazi'one *nf* fraction; (*borgata*) hamlet

'frecci|a *nf* arrow; *Auto* indicator. **~'ata** *nf* (*osservazione pungente*) cutting remark

fredda'mente *adv* coldly

fred'dare *vt* cool; (*fig: con sguardo, battuta*) cut down; (*uccidere*) kill

fred'dezza *nf* coldness

'freddo *a & nm* cold; **aver ~** be cold; **fa ~** it's cold

freddo'loso *a* sensitive to cold, chilly

fred'dura *nf* pun

fre'ga|re *vt* rub; (*fam: truffare*) cheat; (*fam: rubare*) swipe. **~rsene** *fam* not give a damn; **chi se ne frega!** what the heck!. **~si** *vr* rub (*occhi*). **~ta** *nf* rub. **~'tura** *nf fam* (*truffa*) swindle; (*delusione*) letdown

'fregio *nm Archit* frieze; (*ornamento*) decoration

fre'mente *a* quivering

'frem|ere *vi* quiver. **~ito** *nm* quiver

fre'na|re *vt* brake; *fig* restrain; hold back (*lacrime, impazienza*) ● *vi* brake. **~rsi** *vr* check oneself. **~ta** *nf* **fare una ~ta brusca** hit the brakes

frene'sia *nf* frenzy; (*desiderio smodato*) craze. **fre'netico** *a* frenzied

'freno *nm* brake; *fig* check; **togliere il ~** release the brake; **usare il ~** apply the brake; **tenere a ~** restrain. **~ a mano** handbrake

frequen'tare *vt* frequent; attend (*scuola ecc*); mix with (*persone*)

fre'quen|te *a* frequent; **di ~te** frequently. **~za** *nf* frequency; (*assiduità*) attendance

fre'schezza *nf* freshness; (*di temperatura*) coolness

'fresco *a* fresh; (*temperatura*) cool; **stai ~!** you're for it! ● *nm* coolness; **far ~** be cool; **mettere/tenere in ~** put/keep in a cool place

'fretta *nf* hurry, haste; **aver ~** be in a hurry; **far ~ a qcno** hurry sb; **in ~ e furia** in a great hurry. **fretto'loso** *a* (*persona*) in a hurry; (*lavoro*) rushed, hurried

fri'abile *a* crumbly

'friggere *vt* fry; **vai a farti ~!** get lost! ● *vi* sizzle

friggi'trice *nf* chip pan

frigidità *nf* frigidity. **'frigido** *a* frigid

fri'gnare *vi* whine

'frigo *nm* fridge

frigo'bar *nm inv* minibar

frigo'rifero *a* refrigerating ● *nm* refrigerator

fringu'ello *nm* chaffinch

frit'tata *nf* omelette

frit'tella *nf* fritter; (*fam: macchia d'unto*) grease stain

'fritto *pp di* **friggere** ● *a* fried; **essere ~** be done for ● *nm* fried food. **~ misto** mixed fried fish/vegetables. **frit'tura** *nf* (*pietanza*) fried dish

frivo'lezza *nf* frivolity. **'frivolo** *a* frivolous

frizio'nare *vt* rub. **frizi'one** *nf* friction; *Mech* clutch; (*di pelle*) rub

friz'zante *a* fizzy; (*vino*) sparkling; (*aria*) bracing

'frizzo *nm* gibe

fro'dare *vt* defraud

'frode *nf* fraud. **~ fiscale** tax evasion

'frollo *a* tender; (*selvaggina*) high; (*persona*) spineless; **pasta frolla** short[crust] pastry

'fronda *nf* [leafy] branch; *fig* rebellion. **fron'doso** *a* leafy

fron'tale *a* frontal; (*scontro*) head-on

'fronte *nf* forehead; (*di edificio*) front; **di ~** opposite; **di ~ a** opposite, facing; (*a paragone*) compared with; **far ~ a** face ● *nm Mil, Pol* front. **~ggi'are** *vt* face

fronte'spizio *nm* title page

fronti'era *nf* frontier, border

fron'tone *nm* pediment

'fronzolo *nm* frill

'frotta *nf* swarm; (*di animali*) flock

'frottola *nf* fib; **frottole** *pl* nonsense *sg*

fru'gale *a* frugal

fru'gare *vi* rummage ● *vt* search

frul'la|re *vt Culin* whisk ● *vi* (*ali:*) whirr. **~to** *nm* **~to di frutta** *fruit* drink with milk and crushed ice. **~'tore** *nm* [electric] mixer. **frul'lino** *nm* whisk

fru'mento *nm* wheat

frusci'are *vi* rustle

fru'scio *nm* rustle; (*radio, giradischi*) background noise; (*di acque*) murmur

'frusta *nf* whip; (*frullino*) whisk

fru'sta|re *vt* whip. **~ta** *nf* lash. **fru'stino** *nm* riding crop

fru'stra|re *vt* frustrate. **~to** *a* frustrated. **~zi'one** *nf* frustration

'frutt|a *nf* fruit; (*portata*) dessert. **frut-'tare** *vi* bear fruit ● *vt* yield. **frut'teto**

nm orchard. **~i'vendolo, -a** *nmf* green-grocer. **~o** *nm anche fig* fruit; *Fin* yield; **~i di bosco** fruits of the forest. **~i di mare** seafood *sg*. **~u'oso** *a* profitable

f.to *abbr* (**firmato**) signed

fu *a* (*defunto*) late; **il ~ signor Rossi** the late Mr Rossi

fuci'la|re *vt* shoot. **~ta** *nf* shot

fu'cile *nm* rifle

fu'cina *nf* forge

'fucsia *nf* fuchsia

'fuga *nf* escape; (*perdita*) leak; *Mus* fugue; **darsi alla ~** take to flight

fu'gace *a* fleeting

fug'gevole *a* short-lived

fuggi'asco, -a *nmf* fugitive

fuggi'fuggi *nm* stampede

fug'gi|re *vi* flee; ⟨*innamorati:*⟩ elope; *fig* fly. **~'tivo, -a** *nmf* fugitive

'fulcro *nm* fulcrum

ful'gore *nm* splendour

fu'liggine *nf* soot

fulmi'nar|e *vt* strike by lightning; (*con sguardo*) look daggers at; (*con scarica elettrica*) electrocute. **~si** *vr* burn out. **'fulmine** *nm* lightning. **ful'mineo** *a* rapid

'fulvo *a* tawny

fumai'olo *nm* funnel; (*di casa*) chimney

fu'ma|re *vt/i* smoke; (*in ebollizione*) steam. **~'tore, ~'trice** *nmf* smoker; **non fumatori** non-smoker, non-smoking

fu'metto *nm* comic strip; **fumetti** *pl* comics

'fumo *nm* smoke; (*vapore*) steam; *fig* hot air; **andare in ~** vanish. **fu'moso** *a* ⟨*ambiente*⟩ smoky; ⟨*discorso*⟩ vague

fu'nambolo, -a *nmf* tightrope walker

'fune *nf* rope; (*cavo*) cable

'funebre *a* funeral; (*cupa*) gloomy

fune'rale *nm* funeral

fu'nereo *a* ⟨*aria*⟩ funereal

fu'nesto *a* sad

'fungere *vi* **~ da** act as

'fungo *nm* mushroom; *Bot, Med* fungus

funico'lare *nf* funicular [railway]

funi'via *nf* cableway

funzio'nal|e *a* functional. **~ità** *nf* functionality

funziona'mento *nm* functioning

funzio'nare *vi* work, function; **~ da** (*fungere da*) act as

funzio'nario *nm* official

funzi'one *nf* function; (*carica*) office; *Relig* service; **entrare in ~** take up office

fu'oco *nm* fire; (*fisica, fotografia*) focus; **far ~** fire; **dar ~ a** set fire to; **prendere ~** catch fire. **fuochi** *pl* **d'artificio** fireworks. **~ di paglia** nine-days' wonder

fuorché *prep* except

fu'ori *adv* out; (*all'esterno*) outside; (*all'aperto*) outdoors; **andare di ~** (*traboccare*) spill over; **essere ~ di sé** be beside oneself; **essere in ~** (*sporgere*) stick out; **far ~** *fam* do in; **~ mano** out of the way; **~ moda** old-fashioned; **~ pasto** between meals; **~ pericolo** out of danger; **~ questione** out of the question; **~ uso** out of use ● *nm* outside

fuori'bordo *nm* speedboat (*with outboard motor*)

fuori'classe *nmf inv* champion

fuorigi'oco *nm & adv* offside

fuori'legge *nmf* outlaw

fuori'serie *a* custom-made ● *nf* custom-built model

fuori'strada *nm* off-road vehicle

fuorvi'are *vt* lead astray ● *vi* go astray

furbacchi'one *nm* crafty old devil

furbe'ria *nf* cunning. **fur'bizia** *nf* cunning

'furbo *a* cunning; (*intelligente*) clever; (*astuto*) shrewd; **bravo ~!** nice one!; **fare il ~** try to be clever

fu'rente *a* furious

fur'fante *nm* scoundrel

furgon'cino *nm* delivery van. **fur'gone** *nm* van

'furi|a *nf* fury; (*fretta*) haste; **a ~a di** by dint of. **~'bondo, ~'oso** *a* furious

fu'rore *nm* fury; (*veemenza*) frenzy; **far ~** be all the rage. **~ggi'are** *vi* be a great success

furtiva'mente *adv* covertly. **fur'tivo** *a* furtive

'furto *nm* theft; (*con scasso*) burglary

'fusa *nfpl* **fare le ~** purr

fu'scello *nm* (*di legno*) twig; (*di paglia*) straw; **sei un ~** you're as light as a feather

fu'seaux *mpl* leggings

fu'sibile *nm* fuse

fusi'one *nf* fusion; *Comm* merger

'fuso *pp di* **fondere** ● *a* melted ● *nm* spindle. **~ orario** time zone

fusoli'era *nf* fuselage

fu'stagno *nm* corduroy

fu'stino *nm* (*di detersivo*) box

'fusto *nm* stem; (*tronco*) trunk; (*di metallo*) drum; (*di legno*) barrel

'futile *a* futile

fu'turo *a & nm* future

Gg

gab'bar|e *vt* cheat. **~si** *vr* **~si di** make fun of

'gabbia *nf* cage; (*da imballaggio*) crate. **~ degli imputati** dock. **~ toracica** rib cage

gabbi'ano *nm* [sea]gull

gabi'netto *nm* (*di medico*) consulting room; *Pol* cabinet; (*toletta*) lavatory; (*laboratorio*) laboratory

'gaffe *nf inv* blunder

gagli'ardo *a* vigorous

gai'ezza *nf* gaiety. **'gaio** *a* cheerful

'gala *nf* gala

ga'lante *a* gallant. **~'ria** *nf* gallantry. **galantu'omo** *nm* (*pl* **galantuomini**) gentleman

ga'lassia *nf* galaxy

gala'teo *nm* [good] manners *pl*; (*trattato*) book of etiquette

gale'otto *nm* (*rematore*) galley-slave; (*condannato*) convict

ga'lera *nf* (*nave*) galley; *fam* prison

'galla *nf Bot* gall; **a ~** *adv* afloat; **venire a ~** surface

galleggi'ante *a* floating ● *nm* craft; (*boa*) float

galleggi'are *vi* float

galle'ria *nf* (*traforo*) tunnel; (*d'arte*) gallery; *Theat* circle; (*arcata*) arcade. **~ d'arte** art gallery

'Galles *nm* Wales. **gal'lese** *a* welsh ● *nm* Welshman; (*lingua*) Welsh ● *nf* Welshwoman

gal'letto *nm* cockerel; **fare il ~** show off

gal'lina *nf* hen

gal'lismo *nm* machismo

'gallo *nm* cock

gal'lone *nm* stripe; (*misura*) gallon

galop'pare *vi* gallop. **ga'loppo** *nm* gallop; **al galoppo** at a gallop

galvaniz'zare *vt* galvanize

'gamba *nf* leg; (*di lettera*) stem; **a quattro gambe** on all fours; **darsela a gambe** take to one's heels; **essere in ~** (*essere forte*) be strong; (*capace*) be smart

gamba'letto *nm* pop sock

gambe'retto *nm* shrimp. **'gambero** *nm* prawn; (*di fiume*) crayfish

'gambo *nm* stem; (*di pianta*) stalk

'gamma *nf Mus* scale; *fig* range

ga'nascia *nf* jaw; **ganasce** *pl* **del freno** brake shoes

'gancio *nm* hook

'ganghero *nm* **uscire dai gangheri** *fig* get into a temper

'gara *nf* competition; (*di velocità*) race; **fare a ~** compete. **~ d'appalto** call for tenders

ga'rage *nm inv* garage

ga'ran|te *nmf* guarantor. **~'tire** *vt* guarantee; (*rendersi garante*) vouch for; (*assicurare*) assure. **~'zia** *nf* guarantee; **in ~zia** under guarantee

gar'ba|re *vi* like; **non mi garba** I don't like it. **~to** *a* courteous

'garbo *nm* courtesy; (*grazia*) grace; **con ~** graciously

gareggi'are *vi* compete

garga'nella *nf* **a ~** from the bottle

garga'rismo *nm* gargle; **fare i gargarismi** gargle

ga'rofano *nm* carnation

gar'rire *vi* chirp

'garza *nf* gauze

gar'zone *nm* boy. **~ di stalla** stable-boy

gas *nm inv* gas; **dare ~** *Auto* accelerate; **a tutto ~** flat out. **~ lacrimogeno** tear gas. **~ di scarico** *pl* exhaust fumes

gas'dotto *nm* natural gas pipeline

ga'solio *nm* diesel oil

ga'sometro *nm* gasometer

gas's|are *vt* aerate; (*uccidere col gas*) gas. **~ato** *a* gassy. **~oso, -a** *a* gassy; (*bevanda*) fizzy ● *nf* lemonade

'gastrico *a* gastric. **ga'strite** *nf* gastritis

gastro|no'mia *nf* gastronomy. **~'no-mico** *a* gastronomic. **ga'stronomo, -a** *nmf* gourmet

'gatta *nf* **una ~ da pelare** a headache

gatta'buia *nf hum* clink

gat'tino, -a *nmf* kitten

'gatto, -a *nmf* cat. **~ delle nevi** snowmobile

gat'toni *adv* on all fours

ga'vetta *nf* mess tin; **fare la ~** rise through the ranks

gay *a inv* gay

'gazza *nf* magpie

gaz'zarra *nf* racket

gaz'zella *nf* gazelle; *Auto* police car

gaz'zetta *nf* gazette

gaz'zosa *nf* clear lemonade

'geco *nm* gecko

ge'la|re *vt/i* freeze. **~ta** *nf* frost

gela't|aio, -a *nmf* ice-cream seller; *(negozio)* ice-cream shop. **~e'ria** *nf* ice-cream parlour. **~i'era** *nf* ice-cream maker

gela'ti|na *nf* gelatine; *(dolce)* jelly. **~na di frutta** fruit jelly. **~'noso** *a* gelatinous

ge'lato *a* frozen ● *nm* ice-cream

'gelido *a* freezing

'gelo *nm* *(freddo intenso)* freezing cold; *(brina)* frost; *fig* chill

ge'lone *nm* chilblain

gelosa'mente *adv* jealously

gelo'sia *nf* jealousy. **ge'loso** *a* jealous

'gelso *nm* mulberry[-tree]

gelso'mino *nm* jasmine

gemel'laggio *nm* twinning

ge'mello, -a *a & nmf* twin; *(di polsino)* cuff-link; **Gemelli** *pl Astr* Gemini *sg*

'gem|ere *vi* groan; *(tubare)* coo. **~ito** *nm* groan

'gemma *nf* gem; *Bot* bud

'gene *nm* gene

genealo'gia *nf* genealogy

gene'ral|e[1] *a* general; **spese ~i** overheads

gene'rale[2] *nm* Mil general

generalità *nf* *(qualità)* generality, general nature; **~** *pl (dati personali)* particulars

generaliz'za|re *vt* generalize. **~zi'one** *nf* generalization. **general'mente** *adv* generally

gene'ra|re *vt* give birth to; *(causare)* breed; *Techn* generate. **~'tore** *nm Techn* generator. **~zi'one** *nf* generation

'genere *nm* kind; *Biol* genus; *Gram* gender; *(letterario, artistico)* genre; *(prodotto)* product; **il ~ umano** mankind; **in ~** generally. **generi** *pl* **alimentari** provisions

generica'mente *adv* generically. **ge'nerico** *a* generic; **medico generico** general practitioner

'genero *nm* son-in-law

generosità *nf* generosity. **gene'roso** *a* generous

'genesi *nf* genesis

ge'netico, -a *a* genetic ● *nf* genetics *sg*

gen'giva *nf* gum

geni'ale *a* ingenious; *(congeniale)* congenial

'genio *nm* genius; **andare a ~** be to one's taste. **~ civile** civil engineering. **~ [militare]** Engineers

geni'tale *a* genital. **genitali** *nmpl* genitals

geni'tore *nm* parent

gen'naio *nm* January

'Genova *nf* Genoa

gen'taglia *nf* rabble

'gente *nf* people *pl*

gen'til|e *a* kind; **G~e Signore** Dear Sir. **genti'lezza** *nf* kindness; **per gentilezza** *(per favore)* please. **~'mente** *adv* kindly. **~u'omo** *(pl ~u'omini) nm* gentleman

genu'ino *a* genuine; *(cibo, prodotto)* natural

geogra'fia *nf* geography. **geo'grafico** *a* geographical. **ge'ografo** *nm* geographer

geolo'gia *nf* geology. **geo'logico** *a* geological. **ge'ologo, -a** *nmf* geologist

ge'ometra *nmf* surveyor

geom|e'tria *nf* geometry. **geo'metrico** *a* geometric[al]

ge'ranio *nm* geranium

gerar'chia *nf* hierarchy. **ge'rarchico** *a* hierarchic[al]

ge'rente *nm* manager ● *nf* manageress

'gergo *nm* slang; *(di professione ecc)* jargon

geria'tria *nf* geriatrics *sg*

Ger'mania *nf* Germany

'germe *nm* germ; *(fig: principio)* seed

germogli'are *vi* sprout. **ger'moglio** *nm* sprout

gero'glifico *nm* hieroglyph

'gesso *nm* chalk; *(Med, scultura)* plaster

gestazi'one *nf* gestation

gestico'lare *vi* gesticulate

gesti'one *nf* management

ge'stir|e *vi* manage. **~si** *vr* budget one's time and money

'gesto *nm* gesture; *(azione pl nf gesta)* deed

ge'store *nm* manager

Gesù *nm* Jesus. **~ bambino** baby Jesus

gesu'ita *nm* Jesuit

get'ta|re *vt* throw; (*scagliare*) fling; (*emettere*) spout; *Techn, fig* cast; **~re via** throw away. **~rsi** *vr* throw oneself; **~rsi in** ⟨*fiume:*⟩ flow into. **~ta** *nf* throw; *Techn* casting

get'tito *nm* **~ fiscale** tax revenue

'getto *nm* throw; (*di liquidi, gas*) jet; **a ~ continuo** in a continuous stream; **di ~** straight off

getto'nato *a* ⟨*canzone*⟩ popular. **get-'tone** *nm* token; (*per giochi*) counter

ghe'pardo *nm* cheetah

ghettiz'zare *vt* ghettoize. **'ghetto** *nm* ghetto

ghiacci'aio *nm* glacier

ghiacci'a|re *vt/i* freeze. **~to** *a* frozen; (*freddissimo*) ice-cold

ghi'acci|o *nm* ice; *Auto* black ice. **~'olo** *nm* icicle; (*gelato*) ice lolly

ghi'aia *nf* gravel

ghi'anda *nf* acorn

ghi'andola *nf* gland

ghigliot'tina *nf* guillotine

ghi'gnare *vi* sneer. **'ghigno** *nm* sneer

ghi'ot|to *a* greedy, gluttonous; (*appetitoso*) appetizing. **~'tone, -a** *nmf* glutton. **~tone'ria** *nf* (*qualità*) gluttony; (*cibo*) tasty morsel

ghir'landa *nf* (*corona*) wreath; (*di fiori*) garland

'ghiro *nm* dormouse; **dormire come un ~** sleep like a log

'ghisa *nf* cast iron

già *adv* already; (*un tempo*) formerly; **~!** indeed!; **~ da ieri** since yesterday

gi'acca *nf* jacket. **~ a vento** windcheater

giacché *conj* since

giac'cone *nm* jacket

gia'cere *vi* lie

giaci'mento *nm* deposit. **~ di petrolio** oil deposit

gia'cinto *nm* hyacinth

gi'ada *nf* jade

giaggi'olo *nm* iris

giagu'aro *nm* jaguar

gial'lastro *a* yellowish

gi'allo *a & nm* yellow; [**libro**] **~** thriller

Giap'pone *nm* Japan. **giappo'nese** *a & nmf* Japanese

giardi'n|aggio *nm* gardening. **~i'ere, -a** *nmf* gardener ● *nf Auto* estate car; (*sottaceti*) pickles *pl*

giar'dino *nm* garden. **~ d'infanzia** kindergarten. **~ pensile** roof-garden. **~ zoologico** zoo

giarretti'era *nf* garter

giavel'lotto *nm* javelin

gi'gan|te *a* gigantic ● *nm* giant. **~'tesco** *a* gigantic

gigantogra'fia *nf* blow-up

'giglio *nm* lily

gilè *nm inv* waistcoat

gin *nm inv* gin

gineco'lo'gia *nf* gynaecology. **~'logico** *a* gynaecological. **gine'cologo, -a** *nmf* gynaecologist

gi'nepro *nm* juniper

gi'nestra *nf* broom

gingil'larsi *vr* fiddle; (*perder tempo*) potter. **gin'gillo** *nm* plaything; (*ninnolo*) knick-knack

gin'nasio *nm* (*scuola*) ≈ grammar school

gin'nast|a *nmf* gymnast. **~ica** *nf* gymnastics; (*esercizi*) exercises *pl*

ginocchi'ata *nf* **prendere una ~** bang one's knee

gi'nocchi|o *nm* (*pl nm* **ginocchi** *o nf* **ginocchia**) knee; **in ~o** on one's knees; **mettersi in ~o** kneel down; (*per supplicare*) go down on one's knees; **al ~o** ⟨*gonna*⟩ knee-length. **~'oni** *adv* kneeling

gio'ca|re *vt/i* play; (*giocherellare*) toy; (*d'azzardo*) gamble; (*puntare*) stake; (*ingannare*) trick. **~rsi la carriera** throw one's career away. **~'tore, ~'trice** *nmf* player; (*d'azzardo*) gambler

gio'cattolo *nm* toy

giocherel'l|are *vi* toy; (*nervosamente*) fiddle. **~one** *a* skittish

gi'oco *nm* game; (*di bambini, Techn*) play; (*d'azzardo*) gambling; (*scherzo*) joke; (*insieme di pezzi ecc*) set; **essere in ~** be at stake; **fare il doppio ~ con** qcno double-cross sb

giocoli'ere *nm* juggler

glo'coso *a* playful

gi'ogo *nm* yoke

gi'oia *nf* joy; (*gioiello*) jewel; (*appellativo*) sweetie

gioiell'e'ria *nf* jeweller's [shop]. **~i'ere, -a** *nmf* jeweller; (*negozio*) jeweller's. **gioi'ello** *nm* jewel; **gioielli** *pl* jewellery

gioi'oso *a* joyous

gio'ire *vi* **~ per** rejoice at

Gior'dania *nf* Jordan

giorna'laio, -a *nmf* newsagent, newsdealer

gior'nale *nm* [news]paper; (*diario*) journal. **~ di bordo** logbook. **~ radio** news bulletin

giornali'ero *a* daily ● *nm* (*per sciare*) day pass

giorna'lino *nm* comic

giorna'lis|mo *nm* journalism. **~ta** *nmf* journalist

giornal'mente *adv* daily

gior'nata *nf* day; **in ~** today; **vivere alla ~** live from day to day

gi'orno *nm* day; **al ~** per day; **al ~ d'oggi** nowadays; **di ~** by day; **in pieno ~** in broad daylight; **un ~ sì, un ~ no** every other day

gi'ostra *nf* merry-go-round

giova'mento *nm* **trarre ~ da** derive benefit from

gi'ova|ne *a* young; (*giovanile*) youthful ● *nm* youth, young man ● *nf* girl, young woman. **~'nile** *a* youthful. **~'notto** *nm* young man

gio'var|e *vi* **~e a** be useful to; (*far bene*) be good for. **~si** *vr* **~si di** avail oneself of

giovedì *nm inv* Thursday. **~ grasso** *last Thursday before Lent*

gioventù *nf* youth; (*i giovani*) young people *pl*

giovi'ale *a* jovial

giovi'nezza *nf* youth

gira'dischi *nm inv* record-player

gi'raffa *nf* giraffe; *Cinema* boom

gi'randola *nf* (*fuoco d'artificio*) Catherine wheel; (*giocattolo*) windmill; (*banderuola*) weathercock

gi'ra|re *vt* turn; (*andare intorno, visitare*) go round; *Comm* endorse; *Cinema* shoot ● *vi* turn; (*aerei, uccelli:*) circle; (*andare in giro*) wander; **far ~re le scatole a qcno** *fam* drive sb round the twist; **~re al largo** steer clear. **~rsi** *vr* turn [round]; **mi gira la testa** I feel dizzy

girar'rosto *nm* spit

gira'sole *nm* sunflower

gi'rata *nf* turn; *Comm* endorsement; (*in macchina ecc*) ride; **fare una ~** (*a piedi*) go for a walk; (*in macchina*) go for a ride

gira'volta *nf* spin; *fig* U-turn

gi'rello *nm* (*per bambini*) babywalker; *Culin* topside

gi'revole *a* revolving

gi'rino *nm* tadpole

'giro *nm* turn; (*circolo*) circle; (*percorso*) round; (*viaggio*) tour; (*passeggiata*) short walk; (*in macchina*) drive; (*in bicicletta*) ride; (*circolazione di denaro*) circulation; **nel ~ di un mese** within a month; **prendere in ~ qcno** pull sb's

leg; **senza giri di parole** without beating about the bush; **a ~ di posta** by return mail. **~ d'affari** *Comm* turnover. **~ [della] manica** armhole. **giri** *pl* **al minuto** rpm. **~ turistico** sightseeing tour. **~ vita** waist measurement

giro'collo *nm* choker; **a ~** crewneck

gi'rone *nm* round

gironzo'lare *vi* wander about

giro'tondo *nm* ring-a-ring-o'-roses

girova'gare *vi* wander about. **giro'vago** *nm* wanderer

'gita *nf* trip; **andare in ~** go on a trip. **~ scolastica** school trip. **gi'tante** *nmf* tripper

giù *adv* down; (*sotto*) below; (*dabbasso*) downstairs; **a testa in ~** (*a capofitto*) headlong; **essere ~** be down; (*di salute*) be run down; **~ di corda** down; **~ di lì, su per ~** more or less; **non andare ~ a qcno** stick in sb's craw

gi'ub|ba *nf* jacket; *Mil* tunic. **~'botto** *nm* bomber jacket, jerkin

giudi'care *vt* judge; (*ritenere*) consider

gi'udice *nm* judge. **~ conciliatore** justice of the peace. **~ di gara** umpire. **~ di linea** linesman

giu'dizi|o *nm* judg[e]ment; (*opinione*) opinion; (*senno*) wisdom; (*processo*) trial; (*sentenza*) sentence; **mettere ~o** become wise. **~'oso** *a* sensible

gi'ugno *nm* June

giu'menta *nf* mare

gi'unco *nm* reed

gi'ungere *vi* arrive; **~ a** (*riuscire*) succeed in ● *vt* (*unire*) join

gi'ungla *nf* jungle

gi'unta *nf* addition; *Mil* junta; **per ~** in addition. **~ comunale** district council

gi'unto *pp di* giungere ● *nm Mech* joint

giun'tura *nf* joint

giuo'care, giuo'co = **giocare, gioco**

giura'mento *nm* oath; **prestare ~** take the oath

giu'ra|re *vt/i* swear. **~to, -a** *a* sworn ● *nmf* juror

giu'ria *nf* jury

giu'ridico *a* legal

giurisdizi'one *nf* jurisdiction

giurispru'denza *nf* jurisprudence

giu'rista *nmf* jurist

giustifi'ca|re *vt* justify. **~zi'one** *nf* justification

giu'stizi|a *nf* justice. **~'are** *vt* execute. **~'ere** *nm* executioner

gi'usto *a* just, fair; (*adatto*) right; (*esatto*) exact ● *nm* (*uomo retto*) just man; (*cosa giusta*) right ● *adv* exactly; **~ ora** just now

glaci'ale *a* glacial

gla'diolo *nm* gladiolus

'glassa *nf* Culin icing

gli *def art mpl* (*before vowel and s + consonant, gn, ps, z*) the; *vedi* **il** ● *pron* (*a lui*) [to] him; (*a esso*) [to] it; (*a loro*) [to] them

glice'rina *nf* glycerine

'glicine *nm* wisteria

gli'e|lo, -a *pron* [to] him/her/them; (*forma di cortesia*) [to] you; **~ chiedo** I'll ask him/her/them/you; **gliel'ho prestato** I've lent it to him/her/them/you. **~ne** *pron* (*di ciò*) [of] it; **~ne ho dato un po'** I gave him/her/them/you some

glo'bal|e *a* global; *fig* overall. **~izza'zione** *f* globalization. **~'mente** *adv* globally

'globo *nm* globe. **~ oculare** eyeball. **~ terrestre** globe

'globulo *nm* globule; *Med* corpuscle. **~ rosso** red cell, red corpuscle

'glori|a *nf* glory. **~'arsi** *vr* **~arsi di** be proud of. **~'oso** *a* glorious

glos'sario *nm* glossary

glu'cosio *nm* glucose

'gluteo *nm* buttock

'gnomo *nm* gnome

'gnorri *nm* **fare lo ~** play dumb

'gobb|a *nf* hump. **~o, -a** *a* hunchbacked ● *nmf* hunchback

'gocci|a *nf* drop; (*di sudore*) bead; **è stata l'ultima ~a** it was the last straw. **~o'lare** *vi* drip. **~o'lio** *nm* dripping

go'der|e *vi* (*sessualmente*) come; **~e di** enjoy. **~sela** have a good time. **~si** *vr* **~si qcsa** enjoy sth

godi'mento *nm* enjoyment

goffa'mente *adv* awkwardly. **'goffo** *a* awkward

'gola *nf* throat; (*ingordigia*) gluttony; *Geog* gorge; (*di camino*) flue; **avere mal di ~** have a sore throat; **far ~ a qcno** tempt sb

golf *nm inv* jersey; *Sport* golf

'golfo *nm* gulf

golosità *nf inv* greediness; (*cibo*) tasty morsel. **go'loso** *a* greedy

'golpe *nm inv* coup

gomi'tata *nf* nudge

'gomito *nm* elbow; **alzare il ~** raise one's elbow

go'mitolo *nm* ball

'gomma *nf* rubber; (*colla, da mastica-*

re) gum; (*pneumatico*) tyre. **~ da masticare** chewing gum

gommapi'uma *nf* foam rubber

gom'mista *nm* tyre specialist

gom'mone *nm* [rubber] dinghy

gom'moso *a* chewy

'gondol|a *nf* gondola. **~i'ere** *nm* gondolier

gonfa'lone *nm* banner

gonfi'abile *a* inflatable

gonfi'ar|e *vi* swell ● *vt* blow up; pump up (*pneumatico*); (*esagerare*) exaggerate. **~si** *vr* swell; (*acque:*) rise. **'gonfio** *a* swollen; (*pneumatico*) inflated; **a gonfie vele** splendidly. **gonfi'ore** *nm* swelling

gongo'la|nte *a* overjoyed. **~re** *vi* be overjoyed

'gonna *nf* skirt. **~ pantalone** culottes *pl*

gorgheggi'are *vi* warble. **gor'gheggio** *nm* warble

'gorgo *nm* whirlpool

gorgogli'are *vi* gurgle

go'rilla *nm inv* gorilla; (*guardia del corpo*) bodyguard, minder

'gotico *a & nm* Gothic

gover'nante *nf* housekeeper

gover'na|re *vt* govern; (*dominare*) rule; (*dirigere*) manage; (*curare*) look after. **~'tivo** *a* government. **~'tore** *nm* governor

go'verno *nm* government; (*dominio*) rule; **al ~** in power

gracchi'are *vi* caw; (*persona:*) screech

graci'dare *vi* croak

'gracile *a* delicate

gra'dasso *nm* braggart

gradata'mente *adv* gradually

gradazi'one *nf* gradation. **~ alcoolica** alcohol[ic] content

gra'devol|e *a* agreeable. **~'mente** *adv* pleasantly, agreeably

gradi'mento *nm* liking; **indice di ~** *Radio, TV* popularity rating; **non è di mio ~** it's not to my liking

gradi'nata *nf* flight of steps; (*di stadio*) stand; (*di teatro*) tiers *pl*

gra'dino *nm* step

gra'di|re *vt* like; (*desiderare*) wish. **~to** *a* pleasant; (*bene accetto*) welcome

'grado *nm* degree; (*rango*) rank; **di buon ~** willingly; **essere in ~ di fare qcsa** be in a position to do sth; (*essere capace a*) be able to do sth

gradu'ale *a* gradual

gradu'a|re *vt* graduate. **~to** *a* graded; (*provvisto di scala graduata*) graduated

● *nm Mil* noncommissioned officer. **~'toria** *nf* list. **~zi'one** *nf* graduation

'graffa *nf* clip; (*segno grafico*) brace

graf'fetta *nf* staple

graffi'a|re *vt* scratch. **~'tura** *nf* scratch

'graffio *nm* scratch

gra'fia *nf* [hand]writing; (*ortografia*) spelling

'grafic|a *nf* graphics; **~a pubblicitaria** commercial art. **~a'mente** *adv* in graphics, graphically. **~o** *a* graphic ● *nm* graph; (*persona*) graphic designer

gra'migna *nf* weed

gram'mati|ca *nf* grammar. **~'cale** *a* grammatical

'grammo *nm* gram[me]

gran *a vedi* **grande**

'grana *nf* grain; (*formaggio*) parmesan; (*fam: seccatura*) trouble; (*fam: soldi*) readies *pl*

gra'naio *nm* barn

gra'nat|a *nf Mil* grenade; (*frutto*) pomegranate. **~i'ere** *nm Mil* grenadier

Gran Bre'tagna *nf* Great Britain

'granchio *nm* crab; (*fig: errore*) blunder; **prendere un ~** make a blunder

grandango'lare *nm* wide-angle lens

'grande (*a volte* **gran**) *a* (*ampio*) large; (*grosso*) big; (*alto*) tall; (*largo*) wide; (*fig: senso morale*) great; (*grandioso*) grand; (*adulto*) grown-up; **ho una gran fame** I'm very hungry; **fa un gran caldo** it is very hot; **in ~** on a large scale; **in gran parte** to a great extent; **non è un gran che** it is nothing much; **un gran ballo** a grand ball ● *nmf* (*persona adulta*) grown-up; (*persona eminente*) great man/woman. **~ggi'are** *vi* **~ggiare su** tower over; (*darsi arie*) show off

gran'dezza *nf* greatness; (*ampiezza*) largeness; (*larghezza*) width, breadth; (*dimensione*) size; (*fasto*) grandeur; (*prodigalità*) lavishness; **a ~ naturale** life-size

grandi'nare *vi* hail; **grandina** it's hailing. **'grandine** *nf* hail

grandiosità *nf* grandeur. **grandi'oso** *a* grand

gran'duca *nm* grand duke

gra'nello *nm* grain; (*di frutta*) pip

gra'nita *nf* crushed ice drink

gra'nito *nm* granite

'grano *nm* grain; (*frumento*) wheat

gran'turco *nm* maize

'granulo *nm* granule

'grappa *nf* grappa; (*morsa*) cramp

'grappolo *nm* bunch. **~ d'uva** bunch of grapes

gras'setto *nm* bold [type]

gras'sezza *nf* fatness

'gras|so *a* fat; (*cibo*) fatty; (*unto*) greasy; (*terreno*) rich; (*grossolano*) coarse ● *nm* fat; (*sostanza*) grease. **~'soccio** *a* plump

'grata *nf* grating. **gra'tella, gra'ticola** *nf Culin* grill

gra'tifica *nf* bonus. **~zi'one** *nf* satisfaction

grati'na|re *vt* cook au gratin. **~to** *a* au gratin

'gratis *adv* free

grati'tudine *nf* gratitude. **'grato** *a* grateful; (*gradito*) pleasant

gratta'capo *nm* trouble

grattaci'elo *nm* skyscraper

gratta e 'vinci *nm inv* scratch card

grat'tar|e *vt* scratch; (*raschiare*) scrape; (*grattugiare*) grate; (*fam: rubare*) pinch ● *vi* grate. **~si** *vr* scratch oneself

grat'tugi|a *nf* grater. **~'are** *vt* grate

gratuita'mente *adv* free [of charge]. **gra'tuito** *a* free [of charge]; (*ingiustificato*) gratuitous

gra'vare *vt* burden ● *vi* **~ su** weigh on

'grave *a* (*pesante*) heavy; (*serio*) serious; (*difficile*) hard; (*voce, suono*) low; (*fonetica*) grave; **essere ~** (*gravemente ammalato*) be seriously ill. **~'mente** *adv* seriously, gravely

gravi'danza *nf* pregnancy. **'gravido** *a* pregnant

gravità *nf* seriousness; *Phys* gravity

gravi'tare *vi* gravitate

gra'voso *a* onerous

'grazi|a *nf* grace; (*favore*) favour; *Jur* pardon; **entrare nelle ~e di qcno** get into sb's good books. **~'are** *vt* pardon

'grazie *int* thank you!, thanks!; **~ mille!** many thanks!, thanks a lot!

grazi'oso *a* charming; (*carino*) pretty

'Grec|ia *nf* Greece. **g~o, -a** *a & nmf* Greek

'gregge *nm* flock

'greggio *a* raw ● *nm* (*petrolio*) crude [oil]

grembi'ale, grembi'ule *nm* apron

'grembo *nm* lap; (*utero*) womb; *fig* bosom

gre'mi|re *vt* pack. **~rsi** *vr* become crowded (**di** with). **~to** *a* packed

'gretto *a* stingy; (*di vedute ristrette*) narrow-minded

'grezzo *a* = **greggio**

gri'dare vi shout; (di dolore) scream; ⟨animale:⟩ cry ● vt shout

'grido nm (pl m gridi o f grida) shout, cry; (di animale) cry; **l'ultimo ~** the latest fashion; **scrittore di ~** celebrated writer

'grigio a & nm grey

'griglia nf grill; **alla ~** grilled

gril'letto nm trigger

'grillo nm cricket; (fig: capriccio) whim

grimal'dello nm picklock

'grinfia nf fig clutch

'grin|ta nf grit. **~'toso** a determined

'grinza nf wrinkle; (di stoffa) crease

grip'pare vi Mech seize

gris'sino nm bread-stick

'gronda nf eaves pl

gron'daia nf gutter

gron'dare vi pour; (essere bagnato fradicio) be dripping

'groppa nf back

'groppo nm knot; **avere un ~ alla gola** have a lump in one's throat

gros'sezza nf size; (spessore) thickness

gros'sista nmf wholesaler

'grosso a big, large; (spesso) thick; (grossolano) coarse; (grave) serious ● nm big part; (massa) bulk; **farla grossa** do a stupid thing

grosso|lanità nf inv (qualità) coarseness; (di errore) grossness; (azione, parola) coarse thing. **~'lano** a coarse; ⟨errore⟩ gross

grosso'modo adv roughly

'grotta nf cave, grotto

grot'tesco a & nm grotesque

grovi'era nmf Gruyère

gro'viglio nm tangle; fig muddle

gru nf inv (uccello, edilizia) crane

'gruccia nf (stampella) crutch; (per vestito) hanger

gru'gni|re vi grunt. **~to** nm grunt

'grugno nm snout

'grullo a silly

'grumo nm clot; (di farina ecc) lump. **gru'moso** a lumpy

'gruppo nm group; (comitiva) party. **~ sanguigno** blood group

gruvi'era nmf Gruyère

'gruzzolo nm nest-egg

guada'gnare vt earn; gain ⟨tempo, forza ecc⟩. **gua'dagno** nm gain; (profitto) profit; (entrate) earnings pl

gu'ado nm ford; **passare a ~** ford

gua'ina nf sheath; (busto) girdle

gu'aio nm trouble; **che ~!** that's just brilliant!; **essere nei guai** be in a fix;

guai a te se lo tocchi! don't you dare touch it!

gua'i|re vi yelp. **~to** nm yelp

gu'anci|a nf cheek. **~'ale** nm pillow

gu'anto nm glove. **guantoni** pl [da boxe] boxing gloves

guarda'coste nm inv coastguard

guarda'linee nm inv Sport linesman

guar'dar|e vt look at; (osservare) watch; (badare a) look after; (dare su) look out on ● vi look; (essere orientato verso) face. **~si** vr look at oneself; **~si da** beware of; (astenersi) refrain from

guarda'rob|a nm inv wardrobe; (di locale pubblico) cloakroom. **~i'ere, -a** nmf cloakroom attendant

gu'ardia nf guard; (poliziotto) policeman; (vigilanza) watch; **essere di ~** be on guard; ⟨medico:⟩ be on duty; **fare la ~ a** keep guard over; **mettere in ~ qcno** warn sb; **stare in ~** be on one's guard. **~ carceraria** prison warder. **~ del corpo** bodyguard, minder. **~ di finanza** ≈ Fraud Squad. **~ forestale** forest ranger. **~ medica** duty doctor

guardi'ano, -a nmf caretaker. **~ notturno** night watchman

guar'dingo a cautious

guardi'ola nf gatekeeper's lodge

guarigi'one nf recovery

gua'rire vt cure ● vi recover; ⟨ferita:⟩ heal [up]

guarnigi'one nf garrison

guarni|re vt trim; Culin garnish. **~zi'one** nf trimming; Culin garnish; Mech gasket

guasta'feste nmf inv spoilsport

gua'star|e vt spoil; (rovinare) ruin; break ⟨meccanismo⟩. **~si** vr spoil; (andare a male) go bad; ⟨tempo:⟩ change for the worse; ⟨meccanismo:⟩ break down. **gu'asto** a broken; ⟨ascensore, telefono⟩ out of order; ⟨auto⟩ broken down; ⟨cibo, dente⟩ bad ● nm breakdown; (danno) damage

guazza'buglio nm muddle

guaz'zare vi wallow

gu'ercio a cross-eyed

gu'err|a nf war; (tecnica bellica) warfare. **~ fredda** Cold War. **~ mondiale** world war. **~afon'daio** nm warmonger. **~eggi'are** vi wage war. **guer'resco** a (di guerra) war; (bellicoso) warlike. **~'i'ero** nm warrior

guer'rigli|a nf guerrilla warfare. **~'ero, -a** nmf guerrilla

'gufo nm owl

'guglia nf spire

gu'id|a *nf* guide; (*direzione*) guidance; (*comando*) leadership; *Auto* driving; (*tappeto*) runner; **~a a destra/sinistra** right-/left-hand drive. **~a telefonica** telephone directory. **~a turistica** tourist guide. **gui'dare** *vt* guide; *Auto* drive; steer (*nave*). **~a'tore, ~a'trice** *nmf* driver

guin'zaglio *nm* leash

guiz'zare *vi* dart; (*luce:*) flash. **gu'izzo** *nm* dart; (*di luce*) flash

'guscio *nm* shell

gu'stare *vt* taste ● *vi* like. **'gusto** *nm* taste; (*piacere*) liking; **mangiare di gusto** eat heartily; **prenderci gusto** come to enjoy it, develop a taste for it. **gu'stoso** *a* tasty; *fig* delightful

guttu'rale *a* guttural

---

habitué *nmf inv* regular [customer]
ham'burger *nm inv* hamburger
'handicap *nm inv Sport* handicap
handicap'pa|re *vt* handicap. **~to, -a** *nmf* disabled person ● *a* disabled
'harem *nm inv* harem
'hascisc *nm* hashish

henné *nm* henna
hi-fi *nm inv* hi-fi
'hippy *a* hippy
hockey *nm* hockey. **~ su ghiaccio** ice hockey. **~ su prato** hockey
hollywoodi'ano *a* Hollywood *attrib*
ho'tel *nm inv* hotel

---

i *def art mpl* the; *vedi* **il**
i'ato *nm* hiatus
iber'na|re *vi* hibernate. **~zi'one** *nf* hibernation
i'bisco *nm* hibiscus
'ibrido *a & nm* hybrid
'iceberg *nm inv* iceberg
i'cona *nf* icon
Id'dio *nm* God
i'dea *nf* idea; (*opinione*) opinion; (*ideale*) ideal; (*indizio*) inkling; (*piccola quantità*) hint; (*intenzione*) intention; **cambiare ~** change one's mind; **neanche per ~!** not on your life!; **chiarirsi le idee** get one's ideas straight. **~ fissa** obsession
ide'a|le *a & nm* ideal. **~'lista** *nmf* idealist. **~liz'zare** *vt* idealize
ide'a|re *vt* conceive. **~'tore, ~'trice** *nmf* originator
'idem *adv* the same
i'dentico *a* identical

identifi'cabile *a* identifiable
identifi'ca|re *vt* identify. **~zi'one** *nf* identification
identi'kit *nm inv* identikit®
identità *nf inv* identity
ideolo'gia *nf* ideology. **ideo'logico** *a* ideological
i'dilli|co *a* idyllic. **~o** *nm* idyll
idi'oma *nm* idiom. **idio'matico** *a* idiomatic
idi'ota *a* idiotic ● *nmf* idiot. **idio'zia** *nf* (*cosa stupida*) idiocy
idola'trare *vt* worship
idoleggi'are *vt* idolize. **'idolo** *nm* idol
idoneità *nf* suitability; *Mil* fitness; **esame di ~** qualifying examination. **i'doneo** *a* **idoneo a** suitable for; *Mil* fit for
i'drante *nm* hydrant
idra'ta|re *vt* hydrate; (*cosmetico:*) moisturize. **~nte** *a* (*crema, gel*) moisturizing. **~zi'one** *nf* moisturizing

i'draulico *a* hydraulic ● *nm* plumber

'idrico *a* water *attrib*

idrocar'buro *nm* hydrocarbon

idroe'lettrico *a* hydroelectric

i'drofilo *a vedi* **cotone**

i'drogeno *nm* hydrogen

idromas'saggio *nm* (*sistema*) whirl-pool bath

idrovo'lante *nm* seaplane

i'ella *nf* bad luck; **portare ~** be bad luck. **iel'lato** *a* plagued by bad luck

i'ena *nf* hyena

i'eri *adv* yesterday; **~ l'altro, l'altro ~** the day before yesterday; **~ pomeriggio** yesterday afternoon; **il giornale di ~** yesterday's paper

ietta|'tore, -'trice *nmf* jinx. **~'tura** *nf* (*sfortuna*) bad luck

igi'en|e *nf* hygiene. **~ico** *a* hygienic. **igie'nista** *nmf* hygienist

i'gnaro *a* unaware

i'gnobile *a* base; (*non onorevole*) dishonourable

igno'ran|te *a* ignorant ● *nmf* ignoramus. **~za** *nf* ignorance

igno'rare *vt* (*non sapere*) be unaware of; (*trascurare*) ignore

i'gnoto *a* unknown

il *def art m* the; **il latte fa bene** milk is good for you; **il signor Magnetti** Mr Magnetti; **il dottor Piazza** Dr Piazza; **ha il naso storto** he has a bent nose; **mettiti il cappello** put your hat on; **il lunedì** on Mondays; **il 1986** 1986; **5 000 lire il chilo** 5,000 lire the *o* a kilo

'ilar|e *a* merry. **~ità** *nf* hilarity

illazi'one *nf* inference

illecita'mente *adv* illicitly. **il'lecito** *a* illicit

ille'gal|e *a* illegal. **~ità** *nf* illegality. **~'mente** *adv* illegally

illeg'gibile *a* illegible; (*libro*) unreadable

illegittimità *nf* illegitimacy. **ille'gittimo** *a* illegitimate

il'leso *a* unhurt

illette'rato, -a *a & nmf* illiterate

illi'bato *a* chaste

illimi'tato *a* unlimited

illivi'dire *vt* bruise ● *vi* (*per rabbia*) turn livid

il'logico *a* illogical

il'luder|e *vt* deceive. **~si** *vr* deceive oneself

illumi'na|re *vt* light [up]; *fig* enlighten; **~re a giorno** floodlight. **~rsi** *vr* light up. **~zi'one** *nf* lighting; *fig* enlightenment

Illumi'nismo *nm* Enlightenment

illusi'one *nf* illusion; **farsi illusioni** delude oneself

illusio'nis|mo *nm* conjuring. **~ta** *nmf* conjurer

il'lu|so, -a *pp di* **illudere** ● *a* deluded ● *nmf* day-dreamer. **~'sorio** *a* illusory

illu'stra|re *vt* illustrate. **~'tivo** *a* illustrative. **~'tore, ~'trice** *nmf* illustrator. **~zi'one** *nf* illustration

il'lustre *a* distinguished

imbacuc'ca|re *vt*, **~rsi** *vr* wrap up. **~to** *a* wrapped up

imbal'la|ggio *nm* packing. **~re** *vt* pack; *Auto* race

imbalsa'ma|re *vt* embalm; stuff (*animale*). **~to** *a* embalmed; (*animale*) stuffed

imbambo'lato *a* vacant

imbaraz'zante *a* embarrassing

imbaraz'za|re *vt* embarrass; (*ostacolare*) encumber. **~rsi** *vr* be embarrassed

imba'razzo *nm* embarrassment; (*ostacolo*) hindrance; **trarre qcno d'~** help sb out of a difficulty; **avere l'~ della scelta** be spoilt for choice. **~ di stomaco** indigestion

imbarca'dero *nm* landing-stage

imbar'ca|re *vt* embark; (*fam: rimorchiare*) score. **~rsi** *vr* embark, go on board. **~zi'one** *nf* boat. **~zione di salvataggio** lifeboat. **im'barco** *nm* embarkation, boarding; (*banchina*) landing-stage

imba'sti|re *vt* tack; *fig* sketch. **~'tura** *nf* tacking, basting

im'battersi *vr* **~ in** run into

imbat't|ibile *a* unbeatable. **~uto** *a* unbeaten

imbavagli'are *vt* gag

imbec'cata *nf* *Theat* prompt

imbe'cille *a* stupid ● *nmf* *Med* imbecile

imbel'lire *vt* embellish

im'berbe *a* beardless; *fig* inexperienced

imbestia'li|re *vi*, **~rsi** *vr* fly into a rage. **~to** *a* enraged

im'bever|e *vt* imbue (**di** with). **~si** *vr* absorb

imbe'v|ibile *a* undrinkable. **~uto** *a* **~uto di** (*acqua*) soaked in; (*nozioni*) imbued with

imbian'c|are *vt* whiten ● *vi* turn white. **~hino** *nm* house painter

imbizzar'rir|e *vi*, **~si** *vr* become restless; (*arrabbiarsi*) become angry

imboc'ca|re *vt* feed; (*entrare*) enter;

fig prompt. **~'tura** *nf* opening; (*ingresso*) entrance; (*Mus: di strumento*) mouthpiece. **im'bocco** *nm* entrance

imbo'scar|e *vt* hide. **~si** *vr Mil* shirk military service

imbo'scata *nf* ambush

imbottigli'a|re *vt* bottle. **~rsi** *vr* get snarled up in a traffic jam. **~to** ‹*vino, acqua*› bottled

imbot'ti|re *vt* stuff; pad ‹*giacca*›; *Culin* fill. **~rsi** *vr* **~rsi di** (*fig: di pasticche*) stuff oneself with. **~ta** *nf* quilt. **~to** ‹*spalle*› padded; ‹*cuscino*› stuffed; ‹*panino*› filled. **~'tura** *nf* stuffing; (*di giacca*) padding; *Culin* filling

imbracci'are *vt* shoulder ‹*fucile*›

imbra'nato *a* clumsy

imbrat'tar|e *vt* mark. **~si** *vr* dirty oneself

imbroc'car|e *vt* hit; **~la giusta** hit the nail on the head

imbrogli'are *vt* muddle; (*raggirare*) cheat. **~arsi** *vr* get tangled; (*confondersi*) get confused. **im'broglio** *nm* tangle; (*pasticcio*) mess; (*inganno*) trick. **~'one, -a** *nmf* cheat

imbronci'a|re *vi*, **~rsi** *vr* sulk. **~to** *a* sulky

imbru'nire *vi* get dark; **all'~** at dusk

imbrut'tire *vt* make ugly ● *vi* become ugly

imbu'care *vt* post, mail; (*nel biliardo*) pot

imbur'rare *vt* butter

im'buto *nm* funnel

imi'ta|re *vt* imitate. **~'tore**, **~'trice** *nmf* imitator, impersonator. **~zi'one** *nf* imitation

immaco'lato *a* immaculate, spotless

immagazzi'nare *vt* store

immagi'na|re *vt* imagine; (*supporre*) suppose; **s'immagini!** imagine that!. **~rio** *a* imaginary. **~zi'one** *nf* imagination. **im'magine** *nf* image; (*rappresentazione, idea*) picture

imman'cabil|e *a* unfailing. **~'mente** *adv* without fail

im'mane *a* huge; (*orribile*) terrible

imma'nente *a* immanent

immangi'abile *a* inedible

immatrico'la|re *vt* register. **~rsi** *vr* ‹*studente:*› matriculate. **~zi'one** *nf* registration; (*di studente*) matriculation

immaturità *nf* immaturity. **imma'turo** *a* unripe; ‹*persona*› immature; (*precoce*) premature

immedesima|rsi *vr* **~rsi in** identify oneself with. **~zi'one** *nf* identification

immedia|ta'mente *adv* immediately. **~'tezza** *nf* immediacy. **immedi'ato** *a* immediate

immemo'rabile *a* immemorial

immens|a'mente *adv* enormously. **~ità** *nf* immensity. **im'menso** *a* immense

immensu'rabile *a* immeasurable

im'merger|e *vt* immerse. **~si** *vr* plunge; ‹*sommergibile:*› dive; **~si in** immerse oneself in

immeri't|ato *a* undeserved. **~evole** *a* undeserving

immersi'one *nf* immersion; (*di sommergibile*) dive. **im'merso** *pp di* **immergere**

immi'gra|nte *a & nmf* immigrant. **~re** *vi* immigrate. **~to, -a** *nmf* immigrant. **~zi'one** *nf* immigration

immi'nen|te *a* imminent. **~za** *nf* imminence

immischi'ar|e *vt* involve. **~si** *vr* **~si in** meddle in

immis'sario *nm* tributary

immissi'one *nf* insertion

im'mobile *a* motionless

im'mobili *nmpl* real estate. **~'are** *a* **società ~are** building society, savings and loan *Am*

immobili|tà *nf* immobility. **~z'zare** *vt* immobilize; *Comm* tie up

immo'desto *a* immodest

immo'lare *vt* sacrifice

immondez'zaio *nm* rubbish tip. **immon'dizia** *nf* filth; (*spazzatura*) rubbish. **im'mondo** *a* filthy

immo'ral|e *a* immoral. **~ità** *nf* immorality

immorta'lare *vt* immortalize. **immor'tale** *a* immortal

immoti'vato *a* ‹*gesto*› unjustified

im'mun|e *a* exempt; *Med* immune. **~ità** *nf* immunity. **~iz'zare** *vt* immunize. **~izzazi'one** *nf* immunization

immunodefici'enza *nf* immunodeficiency

immuso'ni|rsi *vr* sulk. **~to** *a* sulky

immu'ta|bile *a* unchangeable. **~to** *a* unchanging

impacchet'tare *vt* wrap up

impacci'a|re *vt* hamper; (*disturbare*) inconvenience; (*imbarazzare*) embarrass. **~to** *a* embarrassed; (*goffo*) awkward. **im'paccio** *nm* embarrassment; (*ostacolo*) hindrance; (*situazione difficile*) awkward situation

im'pacco *nm* compress

impadronirsi | impiegare

impadro'nirsi vr ~ **di** take possession of; ⟨fig: imparare⟩ master

impa'gabile a priceless

impagi'na|re vt paginate. **~zi'one** nf pagination

impagli'are vt stuff ⟨animale⟩

impa'lato a fig stiff

impalca'tura nf scaffolding; fig structure

impalli'dire vi turn pale; ⟨fig: perdere d'importanza⟩ pale into insignificance

impa'nare vt Culin roll in breadcrumbs

impan'tanarsi vr get bogged down

impape'rarsi vr, **impappi'narsi** vr falter, stammer

impa'rare vt learn

impareggi'abile a incomparable

imparen'ta|rsi vr ~ **con** become related to. **~to** a related

'impari a unequal; ⟨dispari⟩ odd

impar'tire vt impart

imparzi'al|e a impartial. **~ità** nf impartiality

impas'sibile a impassive

impa'sta|re vt Culin knead; blend ⟨colori⟩. **~'tura** nf kneading. **im'pasto** nm Culin dough; ⟨miscuglio⟩ mixture

impastic'carsi vr pop pills

im'patto nm impact

impau'rir|e vt frighten. **~si** vr become frightened

im'pavido a fearless

impazi'en|te a impatient; **~te di fare qcsa** eager to do sth. **~'tirsi** vr lose patience. **~za** nf impatience

impaz'zata nf **all'~** at breakneck speed

impaz'zire vi go mad; ⟨maionese:⟩ separate; **far ~ qcno** drive sb mad; **~ per** be crazy about; **da ~** ⟨mal di testa⟩ blinding

impec'cabile a impeccable

impedi'mento nm hindrance; ⟨ostacolo⟩ obstacle

impe'dire vt ~ **di** prevent from; ⟨impacciare⟩ hinder; ⟨ostruire⟩ obstruct; **~ a qcno di fare qcsa** prevent sb [from] doing sth

impe'gna|re vt ⟨dare in pegno⟩ pawn; ⟨vincolare⟩ bind; ⟨prenotare⟩ reserve; ⟨assorbire⟩ take up. **~rsi** vr apply oneself; **~rsi a fare qcsa** commit oneself to doing sth. **~'tiva** nf referral. **~'tivo** a binding; ⟨lavoro⟩ demanding. **~ato** a engaged; Pol committed. **im'pegno** nm engagement; Comm commitment; ⟨zelo⟩ care

impel'lente a pressing

impene'trabile a impenetrable

impen'na|rsi vr ⟨cavallo:⟩ rear; fig bristle. **~ta** nf ⟨di prezzi⟩ sharp rise; ⟨di cavallo⟩ rearing; ⟨di moto⟩ wheelie

impen'sa|bile a unthinkable. **~to** a unexpected

impensie'rir|e vt, **~si** vr worry

impe'ra|nte a prevailing. **~re** vi reign; ⟨tendenza:⟩ prevail, hold sway

impera'tivo a & nm imperative

impera'tore, -'trice nm emperor ● nf empress

impercet'tibile a imperceptible

imperdo'nabile a unforgivable

imper'fe|tto a & nm imperfect. **~zi'one** nf imperfection

imperi'a|le a imperial. **~'lismo** nm imperialism. **~'lista** a imperialist. **~'listico** a imperialistic

imperi'oso a imperious; ⟨impellente⟩ urgent

impe'rizia nf lack of skill

imperme'abile a waterproof ● nm raincoat

imperni'ar|e vt pivot; ⟨fondare⟩ base. **~si** vr **~si su** be based on

im'pero nm empire; ⟨potere⟩ rule

imperscru'tabile a inscrutable

imperso'nale a impersonal

imperso'nare vt personify; ⟨interpretare⟩ act [the part of]

imper'territo a undaunted

imperti'nen|te a impertinent. **~za** nf impertinence

impertur'ba|bile a imperturbable. **~to** a unperturbed

imperver'sare vi rage

im'pervio a inaccessible

'impet|o nm impetus; ⟨impulso⟩ impulse; ⟨slancio⟩ transport. **~u'oso** a impetuous; ⟨vento⟩ blustering

impet'tito a stiff

impian'tare vt install; set up ⟨azienda⟩

impi'anto nm plant; ⟨sistema⟩ system; ⟨operazione⟩ installation. **~ radio** Auto car stereo system

impia'strare vt plaster; ⟨sporcare⟩ dirty. **impi'astro** nm poultice; ⟨persona noiosa⟩ bore; ⟨pasticcione⟩ cack-handed person

impic'car|e vt hang. **~si** vr hang oneself

impicci'|arsi vr meddle. **im'piccio** nm hindrance; ⟨seccatura⟩ bother. **~'one, -a** nmf nosey parker

impie'ga|re vt employ; ⟨usare⟩ use; spend ⟨tempo, denaro⟩; Fin invest;

l'autobus ha ~to un'ora it took the bus an hour. **~rsi** vr get [oneself] a job

impiega'tizio a clerical

impie'gato, -a nmf employee. **~ di banca** bank clerk. **impi'ego** nm employment; (posto) job; Fin investment

impieto'sir|e vt move to pity. **~si** vr be moved to pity

impie'trito a petrified

impigli'ar|e vt entangle. **~si** vr get entangled

impi'grir|e vt make lazy. **~si** vr get lazy

impla'cabile a implacable

impli'ca|re vt implicate; (sottintendere) imply. **~rsi** vr become involved. **~zi'one** nf implication

implicita'mente adv implicitly. **im'plicito** a implicit

implo'ra|re vt implore. **~zi'one** nf entreaty

impolve'ra|re vt cover with dust. **~rsi** vr get covered with dust. **~to** a dusty

imponde'rabile a imponderable; (causa, evento) unpredictable

impo'nen|te a imposing. **~za** nf impressiveness

impo'nibile a taxable ● nm taxable income

impopo'lar|e a unpopular. **~ità** nf unpopularity

im'por|re vt impose; (ordinare) order. **~si** vr assert oneself; (aver successo) be successful; **~si di** (prefiggersi) set oneself the task of

impor'tan|te a important ● nm important thing. **~za** nf importance

impor'ta|re vt Comm, Comput import; (comportare) cause ● vi matter; (essere necessario) be necessary. **non ~!** it doesn't matter!; **non me ne ~ niente!** I couldn't care less!. **~'tore, ~'trice** nmf importer. **~zi'one** nf importation; (merce importata) import

im'porto nm amount

importu'nare vt pester. **impor'tuno** a troublesome; (inopportuno) untimely

imposizi'one nf imposition; (imposta) tax

imposses'sarsi vr **~ di** seize

impos'sibil|e a impossible ● nm **fare l'~e** do absolutely all one can. **~ità** nf impossibility

im'posta¹ nf tax; **~ sul reddito** income tax; **~ sul valore aggiunto** value added tax

im'posta² nf (di finestra) shutter

impo'sta|re vt (progettare) plan; (basare) base; Mus pitch; (imbucare) post, mail; set out (domanda, problema). **~zi'one** nf planning; (di voce) pitching

im'posto pp di **imporre**

impo'store, -a nmf impostor

impo'ten|te a powerless; Med impotent. **~za** nf powerlessness; Med impotence

impove'rir|e vt impoverish. **~si** vr become poor

imprati'cabile a impracticable; (strada) impassable

imprati'chir|e vt train. **~si** vr **~si in o a** get practice in

impre'ca|re vi curse. **~zi'one** nf curse

impreci's|abile a indeterminable. **~ato** a indeterminate. **~i'one** nf inaccuracy. **impre'ciso** a inaccurate

impre'gnar|e vt impregnate; (imbevere) soak; fig imbue. **~si** vr become impregnated with

imprendi'tor|e, -'trice nmf entrepreneur. **~i'ale** a entrepreneurial

imprepa'rato a unprepared

im'presa nf undertaking; (gesta) exploit; (azienda) firm

impre'sario nm impresario; (appaltatore) contractor

imprescin'dibile a inescapable

impressio'na|bile a impressionable. **~nte** a impressive; (spaventoso) frightening

impressi|o'nare vt impress; (spaventare) frighten; expose (foto). **~o'narsi** vr be affected; (spaventarsi) be frightened. **~'one** nf impression; (sensazione) sensation; (impronta) mark; **far ~one a qcno** upset sb

impressio'nis|mo nm impressionism. **~ta** nmf impressionist

im'presso pp di **imprimere** ● a printed

impre'stare vt lend

impreve'dibile a unforeseeable; (persona) unpredictable

imprevi'dente a improvident

impre'visto a unforeseen ● nm unforeseen event; **salvo imprevisti** all being well

imprigio|na'mento nm imprisonment. **~'nare** vt imprison

im'primere vt impress; (stampare) print; (comunicare) impart

impro'babil|e a unlikely, improbable. **~ità** nf improbability

improdut'tivo a unproductive

im'pronta *nf* impression; *fig* mark. **~ digitale** fingerprint. **~ del piede** footprint

impro'perio *nm* insult; **improperi** *pl* abuse *sg*

im'proprio *a* improper

improvvisa'mente *adv* suddenly

improvvi'sa|re *vt/i* improvise. **~rsi** *vr* turn oneself into a. **~ta** *nf* surprise. **~to** *a* ⟨*discorso*⟩ unrehearsed. **~zi'one** *nf* improvisation

improv'viso *a* sudden; **all'~** unexpectedly

impru'den|te *a* imprudent. **~za** *nf* imprudence

impu'gna|re *vt* grasp; *Jur* contest. **~'tura** *nf* grip; ⟨*manico*⟩ handle

impulsività *nf* impulsiveness. **impul'sivo** *a* impulsive

im'pulso *nm* impulse; **agire d'~** act on impulse

impune'mente *adv* with impunity. **impu'nito** *a* unpunished

impun'tarsi *vr* dig one's heels in

impun'tura *nf* stitching

impurità *nf inv* impurity. **im'puro** *a* impure

impu'tabile *a* attributable (**a** to)

impu'ta|re *vt* attribute; ⟨*accusare*⟩ charge. **~to, -a** *nmf* accused. **~zi'one** *nf* charge

imputri'dire *vi* rot

in *prep* in; ⟨*moto a luogo*⟩ to; ⟨*su*⟩ on; ⟨*entro*⟩ within; ⟨*mezzo*⟩ by; ⟨*con materiale*⟩ made of; **essere in casa/ufficio** be at home/at the office; **in mano/tasca** in one's hand/pocket; **andare in Francia/campagna** go to France/the country; **salire in treno** get on the train; **versa la birra nel bicchiere** pour the beer into the glass; **in alto** up there; **in giornata** within the day; **nel 1997** in 1997; **una borsa in pelle** a bag made of leather, a leather bag; **in macchina** ⟨*viaggiare, venire*⟩ by car; **in contanti** [in] cash; **in vacanza** on holiday; **di giorno in giorno** from day to day; **se fossi in te** if I were you; **siamo in sette** there are seven of us

inabbor'dabile *a* unapproachable

i'nabil|e *a* incapable; ⟨*fisicamente*⟩ unfit. **~ità** *nf* incapacity

inabi'tabile *a* uninhabitable

inacces'sibile *a* inaccessible; ⟨*persona*⟩ unapproachable

inaccet'tabil|e *a* unacceptable. **~ità** *nf* unacceptability

inacer'bi|re *vt* embitter; exacerbate ⟨*rapporto*⟩. **~si** *vr* grow bitter

inaci'dir|e *vt* turn sour. **~si** *vr* go sour; ⟨*persona:*⟩ become embittered

ina'datto *a* unsuitable

inadegu'ato *a* inadequate

inadempi'|ente *nmf* defaulter. **~'mento** *nm* non-fulfilment

inaffer'rabile *a* elusive

ina'la|re *vt* inhale. **~'tore** *nm* inhaler. **~zi'one** *nf* inhalation

inalbe'rar|e *vt* hoist. **~si** *vr* ⟨*cavallo:*⟩ rear [up]; ⟨*adirarsi*⟩ lose one's temper

inalte'ra|bile *a* unchangeable; ⟨*colore*⟩ fast. **~to** *a* unchanged

inami'da|re *vt* starch. **~to** *a* starched

inammis'sibile *a* inadmissible

inamovi'bile *a* irremovable

inani'mato *a* inanimate; ⟨*senza vita*⟩ lifeless

inappa'ga|bile *a* unsatisfiable. **~to** *a* unfulfilled

inappel'labile *a* final

inappe'tenza *nf* lack of appetite

inappli'cabile *a* inapplicable

inappun'tabile *a* faultless

inar'car|e *vt* arch; raise ⟨*sopracciglia*⟩. **~si** *vr* ⟨*legno:*⟩ warp; ⟨*ripiano:*⟩ sag; ⟨*linea:*⟩ curve

inari'dir|e *vt* parch; empty of feelings ⟨*persona*⟩. **~si** *vr* dry up; ⟨*persona:*⟩ become empty of feelings

inartico'lato *a* inarticulate

inaspetta'mente *adv* unexpectedly. **inaspet'tato** *a* unexpected

inaspri'mento *nm* ⟨*di carattere*⟩ embitterment; ⟨*di conflitto*⟩ worsening

ina'sprir|e *vt* embitter. **~si** *vr* become embittered

inattac'cabile *a* unassailable; ⟨*irreprensibile*⟩ irreproachable

inatten'dibile *a* unreliable. **inat'teso** *a* unexpected

inattività *nf* inactivity. **inat'tivo** *a* inactive

inattu'abile *a* impracticable

inau'dito *a* unheard of

inaugu'rale *a* inaugural; **viaggio ~** maiden voyage

inaugu'ra|re *vt* inaugurate; open ⟨*mostra*⟩; unveil ⟨*statua*⟩; christen ⟨*lavastoviglie*⟩. **~zi'one** *nf* inauguration; ⟨*di mostra*⟩ opening; ⟨*di statua*⟩ unveiling

inavver't|enza *nf* inadvertence. **~ita'mente** *adv* inadvertently

incagli'ar|e *vi* ground ● *vt* hinder. **~si** *vr* run aground

incalco'labile *a* incalculable

incal'li|rsi *vr* grow callous; *(abituarsi)* become hardened. **~to** *a* callous; *(abituato)* hardened

incal'za|nte *a* ⟨*ritmo*⟩ driving; ⟨*richiesta*⟩ urgent. **~re** *vt* pursue; *fig* press

incame'rare *vt* appropriate

incammi'nar|e *vt* get going; *(fig: guidare)* set off. **~si** *vr* set out

incana'lar|e *vt* canalize; *fig* channel. **~si** *vr* converge on

incande'scen|te *a* incandescent; ⟨*discussione*⟩ burning. **~za** *nf* incandescence

incan'ta|re *vt* enchant. **~rsi** *vr* stand spellbound; *(incepparsi)* jam. **~'tore, ~'trice** *nm* enchanter ● *nf* enchantress

incan'tesimo *nm* spell

incan'tevole *a* enchanting

in'canto *nm* spell; *fig* delight; ⟨*asta*⟩ auction; **come per ~** as if by magic

incanu'ti|re *vt* turn white. **~to** *a* white

inca'pac|e *a* incapable. **~ità** *nf* incapability

incapo'nirsi *vr* be set

incap'pare *vi* **~ in** run into

incappucci'arsi *vr* wrap up

incapricci'arsi *vr* **~ di** take a fancy to

incapsu'lare *vt* seal; crown ⟨*dente*⟩

incarce'ra|re *vt* imprison. **~zi'one** *nf* imprisonment

incari'ca|re *vt* charge. **~rsi** *vr* take upon oneself; **me ne incarico io** I will see to it. **~to, -a** *a* in charge ● *nmf* representative. **in'carico** *nm* charge; **per incarico di** on behalf of

incar'na|re *vt* embody. **~rsi** *vr* become incarnate. **~zi'one** *nf* incarnation

incarta'mento *nm* documents *pl*. **incar'tare** *vt* wrap [in paper]

incasi'nato *a fam* ⟨*vita*⟩ screwed up; ⟨*stanza*⟩ messed up

incas'sa|re *vt* pack; *Mech* embed; box in ⟨*mobile, frigo*⟩; *(riscuotere)* cash; take ⟨*colpo*⟩. **~to** *a* set; ⟨*fiume*⟩ deeply embanked. **in'casso** *nm* collection; *(introito)* takings *pl*

incasto'na|re *vt* set. **~'tura** *nf* setting. **~to** *a* embedded; ⟨*anello*⟩ inset (**di** with)

inca'strar|e *vt* fit in; *(fam: in situazione)* corner. **~si** *vr* fit. **in'castro** *nm* joint; **a incastro** ⟨*pezzi*⟩ interlocking

incate'nare *vt* chain

incatra'mare *vt* tar

incatti'vire *vt* turn nasty

in'cauto *a* imprudent

inca'va|re *vt* hollow out. **~to** *a* hollow. **~'tura** *nf* hollow. **in'cavo** *nm* hollow; *(scanalatura)* groove

incavo'la|rsi *vr fam* get shirty. **~to** *a fam* shirty

incendi'ar|e *vt* set fire to; *fig* inflame. **~si** *vr* catch fire. **~io, -a** *a* incendiary; ⟨*fig: discorso*⟩ inflammatory; ⟨*fig: bellezza*⟩ sultry ● *nmf* arsonist. **in'cendio** *nm* fire. **incendio doloso** arson

incene'ri|re *vt* burn to ashes; *(cremare)* cremate. **~rsi** *vr* be burnt to ashes. **~'tore** *nm* incinerator

in'censo *nm* incense

incensu'rato *a* blameless; **essere ~** *Jur* have a clean record

incenti'vare *vt* motivate. **incen'tivo** *nm* incentive

incen'trarsi *vr* **~ su** centre on

incep'par|e *vt* block; *fig* hamper. **~si** *vr* jam

ince'rata *nf* oilcloth

incerot'tato *a* with a plaster on

incer'tezza *nf* uncertainty. **in'certo** *a* uncertain ● *nm* uncertainty

inces'sante *a* unceasing. **~'mente** *adv* incessantly

in'cest|o *nm* incest. **~u'oso** *a* incestuous

in'cetta *nf* buying up; **fare ~ di** stockpile

inchi'esta *nf* investigation

inchi'nar|e *vt*, **~si** *vr* bow. **in'chino** *nm* bow; *(di donna)* curtsy

inchio'dare *vt* nail; nail down ⟨*coperchio*⟩; **~ a letto** ⟨*malattia:*⟩ confine to bed

inchi'ostro *nm* ink

inciam'pare *vi* stumble; **~ in** *(imbattersi)* run into. **inci'ampo** *nm* hindrance

inciden'tale *a* incidental

inci'den|te *nm* *(episodio)* incident; *(infortunio)* accident. **~za** *nf* incidence

in'cidere *vt* cut; ⟨*arte*⟩ engrave; *(registrare)* record ● *vi* **~ su** *(gravare)* weigh upon

in'cinta *a* pregnant

incipi'ente *a* incipient

incipri'ar|e *vt* powder. **~si** *vr* powder one's face

in'circa *adv* **all'~** more or less

incisi'one *nf* incision; ⟨*arte*⟩ engraving; *(acquaforte)* etching; *(registrazione)* recording

inci'sivo *a* incisive ● *nm* *(dente)* incisor

in'ciso nm per ~ incidentally

incita'mento nm incitement. **inci'tare** vt incite

inci'vil|e a uncivilized; (maleducato) impolite. **~tà** nf barbarism; (maleducazione) rudeness

incle'men|te a harsh. **~za** nf harshness

incli'nabile a reclining

incli'na|re vt tilt ● vi **~re a** be inclined to. **~rsi** vr list. **~to** a tilted; ⟨terreno⟩ sloping. **~zi'one** nf slope, inclination. **in'cline** a inclined

in'clu|dere vt include; (allegare) enclose. **~si'one** nf inclusion. **~'sivo** a inclusive. **~so** pp di **includere** ● a included; (compreso) inclusive; (allegato) enclosed

incoe'ren|te a (contraddittorio) inconsistent. **~za** nf inconsistency

in'cognit|a nf unknown quantity. **~o** a unknown ● nm **in ~o** incognito

incol'lar|e vt stick; (con colla liquida) glue. **~si** vr stick to; **~si a qcno** stick close to sb

incolle'ri|rsi vr lose one's temper. **~to** a enraged

incol'mabile a ⟨differenza⟩ unbridgeable; ⟨vuoto⟩ unfillable

incolon'nare vt line up

inco'lore a colourless

incol'pare vt blame

in'colto a uncultivated; ⟨persona⟩ uneducated

in'colume a unhurt

incom'ben|te a impending. **~za** nf task

in'combere vi ~ **su** hang over; ~ **a** (spettare) be incumbent on

incominci'are vt/i begin, start

incomo'dar|e vt inconvenience. **~si** vr trouble. **in'comodo** a uncomfortable; (inopportuno) inconvenient ● nm inconvenience

incompa'rabile a incomparable

incompa'tibil|e a incompatible. **~ità** nf incompatibility

incompe'ten|te a incompetent. **~za** nf incompetence

incompi'uto a unfinished

incom'pleto a incomplete

incompren'si|bile a incomprehensible. **~'one** nf lack of understanding; (malinteso) misunderstanding. **incom'preso** a misunderstood

inconce'pibile a inconceivable

inconcili'abile a irreconcilable

inconclu'dente a inconclusive; ⟨persona⟩ ineffectual

incondizio|nata'mente adv unconditionally. **~'nato** a unconditional

inconfes'sabile a unmentionable

inconfon'dibile a unmistakable

inconfu'tabile a irrefutable

incongru'ente a inconsistent

in'congruo a inadequate

inconsa'pevol|e a unaware; (inconscio) unconscious. **~'mente** adv unwittingly

inconscia'mente adv unconsciously. **in'conscio** a & nm Psych unconscious

inconsi'sten|te a insubstantial; ⟨notizia ecc⟩ unfounded. **~za** nf (di ragionamento, prove) flimsiness

inconso'labile a inconsolable

inconsu'eto a unusual

incon'sulto a rash

incontami'nato a uncontaminated

inconte'nibile a irrepressible

inconten'tabile a insatiable; (esigente) hard to please

inconte'stabile a indisputable

inconti'nen|te a incontinent. **~za** nf incontinence

incon'trar|e vt meet; encounter, meet with ⟨difficoltà⟩. **~si** vr meet (**con qcno** sb)

incon'trario: all'~ adv the other way around; (in modo sbagliato) the wrong way around

incontra'sta|bile a incontrovertible. **~to** a undisputed

in'contro nm meeting; Sport match. ~ **al vertice** summit meeting ● prep ~ **a** towards; **andare ~ a qn** go to meet sb; fig meet sb half way

inconveni'ente nm drawback

incoraggi|a'mento nm encouragement. **~'ante** a encouraging. **~'are** vt encourage

incornici'a|re vt frame. **~'tura** nf framing

incoro'na|re vt crown. **~zi'one** nf coronation

incorpo'rar|e vt incorporate; (mescolare) blend. **~si** vr blend; ⟨territori:⟩ merge

incorreg'gibile a incorrigible

in'correre vt ~ **in** incur; ~ **nel pericolo di...** run the risk of...

incorrut'tibile a incorruptible

incosci'en|te a unconscious; (irresponsabile) reckless ● nmf irresponsible person. **~za** *nf* unconsciousness; recklessness

inco'stan|te *a* changeable; ⟨*persona*⟩ fickle. **~za** *nf* changeableness; (*di persona*) fickleness

incostituzio'nale *a* unconstitutional

incre'dibile *a* unbelievable, incredible

incredulità *nf* incredulity. **in'credulo** *a* incredulous

incremen'tare *vt* increase; (*intensificare*) step up. **incre'mento** *nm* increase. **incremento demografico** population growth

incresci'oso *a* regrettable

incre'spar|e *vt* ruffle; wrinkle ⟨*tessuto*⟩; make frizzy ⟨*capelli*⟩; **~e la fronte** frown. **~si** *vr* ⟨*acqua:*⟩ ripple; ⟨*tessuto:*⟩ wrinkle; ⟨*capelli:*⟩ go frizzy

incrimi'na|re *vt* indict; *fig* incriminate. **~zi'one** *nf* indictment

incri'na|re *vt* crack; *fig* affect ⟨*amicizia*⟩. **~rsi** *vr* crack; ⟨*amicizia:*⟩ be affected. **~'tura** *nf* crack

incroci'a|re *vt* cross ● *vi* Naut, Aeron cruise. **~rsi** *vr* cross. **~'tore** *nm* cruiser

in'crocio *nm* crossing; (*di strade*) crossroads *sg*

incrol'labile *a* indestructible

incro'sta|re *vt* encrust. **~zi'one** *nf* encrustation

incuba'|trice *nf* incubator. **~zi'one** *nf* incubation

'incubo *nm* nightmare

in'cudine *nf* anvil

incu'rabile *a* incurable

incu'rante *a* careless

incurio'sir|e *vt* make curious. **~si** *vr* become curious

incursi'one *nf* raid. **~ aerea** air raid

incurva'mento *nm* bending

incur'va|re *vt*, **~rsi** *vr* bend. **~'tura** *nf* bending

in'cusso *pp di* **incutere**

incusto'dito *a* unguarded

in'cutere *vt* arouse; **~ spavento a qcno** strike fear into sb

'indaco *nm* indigo

indaffa'rato *a* busy

inda'gare *vt/i* investigate

in'dagine *nf* research; (*giudiziaria*) investigation. **~ di mercato** market survey

indebi'tar|e *vt*, **~si** *vr* get into debt

in'debito *a* undue

indeboli'mento *nm* weakening

indebo'lir|e *vt*, **~si** *vr* weaken

inde'cen|te *a* indecent. **~za** *nf* indecency; (*vergogna*) disgrace

indeci'frabile *a* indecipherable

indecisi'one *nf* indecision. **inde'ciso** *a* undecided

inde'fesso *a* tireless

indefi'ni|bile *a* indefinable. **~to** *a* indefinite

indefor'mabile *a* crushproof

in'degno *a* unworthy

inde'lebile *a* indelible

indelica'tezza *nf* indelicacy; (*azione*) tactless act. **indeli'cato** *a* indiscreet; (*grossolano*) indelicate

indemoni'ato *a* possessed

in'denn|e *a* uninjured; (*da malattia*) unaffected. **~ità** *nf inv* allowance; (*per danni*) compensation. **~ità di trasferta** travel allowance. **~iz'zare** *vt* compensate. **inden'nizzo** *nm* compensation

indero'gabile *a* binding

indescri'vibile *a* indescribable

indeside'ra|bile *a* undesirable. **~to** *a* ⟨*figlio, ospite*⟩ unwanted

indetermi'na|bile *a* indeterminable. **~'tezza** *nf* vagueness. **~to** *a* indeterminate

'Indi|a *nf* India. **i~'ano, -a** *a & nmf* Indian; **in fila i~ana** in single file

indiavo'lato *a* possessed; (*vivace*) wild

indi'ca|re *vt* show, indicate; (*col dito*) point at; (*far notare*) point out; (*consigliare*) advise. **~'tivo** *a* indicative ● *nm* Gram indicative. **~'tore** *nm* indicator; Techn gauge; (*prontuario*) directory. **~zi'one** *nf* indication; (*istruzione*) direction

'indice *nm* (*dito*) forefinger; (*lancetta*) pointer; (*di libro, statistica*) index; (*fig: segno*) sign

indi'cibile *a* inexpressible

indietreggi'are *vi* draw back; *Mil* retreat

indi'etro *adv* back, behind; **all'~** backwards; **avanti e ~** back and forth; **essere ~** be behind; (*mentalmente*) be backward; (*con pagamenti*) be in arrears; (*di orologio*) be slow; **fare marcia ~** reverse; **rimandare ~** send back; **rimanere ~** be left behind; **torna ~!** come back!

indi'feso *a* undefended; (*inerme*) helpless

indiffe'ren|te *a* indifferent; **mi è ~te** it is all the same to me. **~za** *nf* indifference

in'digeno, -a a indigenous. ● nmf native

indi'gen|te a needy. **~za** nf poverty

indigesti'one nf indigestion. **indi'gesto** a indigestible

indi'gna|re vt make indignant. **~rsi** vr be indignant. **~to** a indignant. **~zi'one** nf indignation

indimenti'cabile a unforgettable

indipen'den|te a independent. **~te-'mente** adv independently; **~temente dal tempo** regardless of the weather, whatever the weather. **~za** nf independence

in'dire vt announce

indiretta'mente adv indirectly. **indi-'retto** a indirect

indiriz'zar|e vt address; (mandare) send; (dirigere) direct. **~si** vr direct one's steps. **indi'rizzo** nm address; (direzione) direction

indisci'pli|na nf lack of discipline. **~'nato** a undisciplined

indi'scre|to a indiscreet. **~zi'one** nf indiscretion

indiscrimi|nata'mente adv indiscriminately. **~'nato** a indiscriminate

indi'scusso a unquestioned

indiscu'tibil|e a unquestionable. **~'mente** adv unquestionably

indispen'sabile a essential, indispensable

indispet'tir|e vt irritate. **~si** vr get irritated

indi'spo|rre vt antagonize. **~sto** pp di **indisporre** ● a indisposed. **~sizi'one** nf indisposition

indisso'lubile a indissoluble

indissolubil'mente adv indissolubly

indistin'guibile a indiscernible

indistinta'mente adv without exception. **indi'stinto** a indistinct

indistrut'tibile a indestructible

indistur'bato a undisturbed

in'divia nf endive

individu'a|le a individual. **~'lista** nmf individualist. **~'lità** nf individuality. **~re** vt individualize; (localizzare) locate; (riconoscere) single out

indi'viduo nm individual

indivi'sibile a indivisible. **indi'viso** a undivided

indizi'a|re vt throw suspicion on. **~to, -a** a suspected ● nmf suspect. **in'dizio** nm sign; Jur circumstantial evidence

'indole nf nature

indo'len|te a indolent. **~za** nf indolence

indolenzi'mento nm stiffness

indolen'zi|rsi vr go stiff. **~to** a stiff

indo'lore a painless

indo'mani nm **l'~** the following day

Indo'nesia nf Indonesia

indo'rare vt gild

indos'sa|re vt wear; (mettere addosso) put on. **~'tore, ~'trice** nmf model

in'dotto pp di **indurre**

indottri'nare vt indoctrinate

indovi'n|are vt guess; (predire) foretell. **~ato** a successful; (scelta) well-chosen. **~ello** nm riddle. **indo'vino, -a** nmf fortune-teller

indubbia'mente adv undoubtedly. **in'dubbio** a undoubted

indugi'ar|e vi, **~si** vr linger. **in'dugio** nm delay

indul'gen|te a indulgent. **~za** nf indulgence

in'dul|gere vi **~gere a** indulge in. **~to** pp di **indulgere** ● nm Jur pardon

indu'mento nm garment; **indumenti** pl clothes

induri'mento nm hardening

indu'rir|e vt, **~si** vr harden

in'durre vt induce

in'dustri|a nf industry. **~'ale** a industrial ● nm industrialist

industrializ'za|re vt industrialize. **~to** a industrialized. **~zi'one** nf industrialization

industrial'mente adv industrially

industri'|arsi vr try one's hardest. **~'oso** a industrious

induzi'one nf induction

inebe'tito a stunned

inebri'ante a intoxicating, exciting

inecce'pibile a unexceptionable

i'nedia nf starvation

i'nedito a unpublished

ineffi'cace a ineffective

ineffici'en|te a inefficient. **~za** nf inefficiency

ineguagli'abile a incomparable

inegu'ale a unequal; (superficie) uneven

inelut'tabile a inescapable

ine'rente a **~ a** concerning

i'nerme a unarmed; fig defenceless

inerpi'carsi vr **~ su** clamber up; (pianta:) climb up

i'ner|te a inactive; Phys inert. **~zia** nf inactivity; Phys inertia

inesat'tezza nf inaccuracy. **ine'satto**

a inaccurate; (*erroneo*) incorrect; (*non riscosso*) uncollected

inesau'ribile *a* inexhaustible

inesi'sten|te *a* non-existent. **~za** *nf* non-existence

ineso'rabile *a* inexorable

inesperi'enza *nf* inexperience. **ine-'sperto** *a* inexperienced

inespli'cabile *a* inexplicable

ine'sploso *a* unexploded

inespri'mibile *a* inexpressible

inesti'mabile *a* inestimable

inetti'tudine *nf* ineptitude. **i'netto** *a* inept; **inetto a** unsuited to

ine'vaso *a* ⟨*pratiche*⟩ pending; ⟨*corrispondenza*⟩ unanswered

inevi'tabil|e *a* inevitable. **~'mente** *adv* inevitably

i'nezia *nf* trifle

infagot'tar|e *vt* wrap up. **~si** *vr* wrap [oneself] up

infal'libile *a* infallible

infa'ma|re *vt* defame. **~'torio** *a* defamatory

in'fam|e *a* infamous; (*fam: orrendo*) awful, shocking. **~ia** *nf* infamy

infan'garsi *vr* get muddy

infan'tile *a* ⟨*letteratura, abbigliamento*⟩ children's; ⟨*ingenuità*⟩ childlike; *pej* childish

in'fanzia *nf* childhood; (*bambini*) children *pl*; **prima ~** infancy

infar'cire *vi* pepper ⟨*discorso*⟩ (**di** with)

infari'na|re *vt* flour; **~re di** sprinkle with. **~'tura** *nf fig* smattering

in'farto *nm* coronary

infasti'dir|e *vt* irritate. **~si** *vr* get irritated

infati'cabile *a* untiring

in'fatti *conj* as a matter of fact; (*veramente*) indeed

infatu'a|rsi *vr* become infatuated (**di** with). **~to** *a* infatuated. **~zi'one** *nf* infatuation

in'fausto *a* ill-omened

infe'condo *a* infertile

infe'del|e *a* unfaithful. **~tà** *nf* unfaithfulness; **~ pl** affairs

infe'lic|e *a* unhappy; (*inappropriato*) unfortunate; (*cattivo*) bad. **~ità** *nf* unhappiness

infel'tri|rsi *vr* get matted. **~to** *a* matted

inferi'or|e *a* (*più basso*) lower; ⟨*qualità*⟩ inferior ● *nmf* inferior. **~ità** *nf* inferiority

inferme'ria *nf* infirmary; (*di nave*) sick-bay

infermi'er|a *nf* nurse. **~e** *nm* [male] nurse

infermità *nf* sickness. **~ mentale** mental illness. **in'fermo, -a** *a* sick ● *nmf* invalid

infer'nale *a* infernal; (*spaventoso*) hellish

in'ferno *nm* hell; **va all'~!** go to hell!

infero'cirsi *vr* become fierce

inferri'ata *nf* grating

infervo'rar|e *vt* arouse enthusiasm in. **~si** *vr* get excited

infe'stare *vt* infest

infet't|are *vt* infect. **~arsi** *vr* become infected. **~ivo** *a* infectious. **in'fetto** *a* infected. **infezi'one** *nf* infection

infiac'chir|e *vt/i*, **~si** *vr* weaken

infiam'mabile *a* [in]flammable

infiam'ma|re *vt* set on fire; *Med, fig* inflame. **~rsi** *vr* catch fire; *Med* become inflamed. **~zi'one** *nf Med* inflammation

in'fido *a* treacherous

infie'rire *vi* (*imperversare*) rage; **~ su** attack furiously

in'figger|e *vt* drive. **~si** *vr* **~si in** penetrate

infi'lar|e *vt* thread; (*mettere*) insert; (*indossare*) put on. **~si** *vr* slip on ⟨*vestito*⟩; **~si in** (*introdursi*) slip into

infil'tra|rsi *vr* infiltrate. **~zi'one** *nf* infiltration; (*d'acqua*) seepage; (*Med: iniezione*) injection

infil'zare *vt* pierce; (*infilare*) string; (*conficcare*) stick

'infimo *a* lowest

in'fine *adv* finally; (*insomma*) in short

infinità *nf* infinity; **un'~ di** masses of. **~'mente** *adv* infinitely. **infi'nito** *a* infinite; *Gram* infinitive ● *nm* infinite; *Gram* infinitive; *Math* infinity; **all'infinito** endlessly

infinocchi'are *vt fam* hoodwink

infischi'arsi *vr* **~ di** not care about; **me ne infischio** *fam* I couldn't care less

in'fisso *pp di* **infiggere** ● *nm* fixture; (*di porta, finestra*) frame

inflazi'one *nf* inflation

infles'sibil|e *a* inflexible. **~ità** *nf* inflexibility

inflessi'one *nf* inflexion

in'fli|ggere *vt* inflict. **~tto** *pp di* **infliggere**

influ'en|te *a* influential. **~za** *nf* influence; *Med* influenza

influen'za|bile *a* ⟨*mente, opinione*⟩ impressionable. **~re** *vt* influence. **~to** *a* ⟨*malato*⟩ with the flu

influ'ire *vi* **~ su** influence

in'flusso *nm* influence

info'carsi *vr* catch fire; ⟨*viso:*⟩ go red; ⟨*discussione:*⟩ become heated

info'gnarsi *vr fam* get into a mess

infol'tire *vt/i* thicken

infon'dato *a* unfounded

in'fondere *vt* instil

infor'care *vt* fork up; get on ⟨*bici*⟩; put on ⟨*occhiali*⟩

infor'male *a* informal

infor'ma|re *vt* inform. **~rsi** *vr* inquire (di about). **~'tivo** *a* informative.

infor'matic|a *nf* computing, IT. **~o** *a* computer *attrib*

infor'ma|tivo *a* informative. **infor'mato** *a* informed; **male informa** ill-informed. **~'tore, ~'trice** *nmf* ⟨*di polizia*⟩ informer. **~zi'one** *nf* information (*solo sg*); **un'~zione** a piece of information

in'forme *a* shapeless

infor'nare *vt* put into the oven

infortu'narsi *vr* have an accident.

infor'tu|nio *nm* accident. **~nio sul lavoro** industrial accident. **~'nistica** *nf* study of industrial accidents

infos'sa|rsi *vr* sink; ⟨*guance, occhi:*⟩ become hollow. **~to** *a* sunken, hollow

infradici'ar|e *vt* drench. **~si** *vr* get drenched; ⟨*diventare marcio*⟩ rot

infra'dito *nm inv* ⟨*scarpa*⟩ flip-flop

in'frang|ere *vt* break; (*in mille pezzi*) shatter. **~ersi** *vr* break. **~'gibile** *a* unbreakable

in'franto *pp di* **infrangere** ● *a* shattered; ⟨*fig: cuore*⟩ broken

infra'rosso *a* infra-red

infrastrut'tura *nf* infrastructure

infrazi'one *nf* offence

infredda'tura *nf* cold

infreddo'li|rsi *vr* feel cold. **~to** *a* cold

infruttu'oso *a* fruitless

infuo'ca|re *vt* make red-hot. **~to** *a* burning

infu'ori *adv* **all'~** outwards; **all'~ di** except

infuri'a|re *vi* rage. **~rsi** *vr* fly into a rage. **~to** *a* blustering

infusi'one *nf* infusion. **in'fuso** *pp di* **infondere** ● *nm* infusion

Ing. *abbr* **ingegnere**

ingabbi'are *vt* cage; ⟨*fig: mettere in prigione*⟩ jail

ingaggi'are *vt* engage; sign up ⟨*calciatori ecc*⟩; begin ⟨*lotta, battaglia*⟩. **in'gaggio** *nm* engagement; ⟨*di calciatore*⟩ signing [up]

ingan'nar|e *vt* deceive; ⟨*essere infedele a*⟩ be unfaithful to. **~si** *vr* deceive oneself; **se non m'inganno** if I am not mistaken

ingan'nevole *a* deceptive. **in'ganno** *nm* deceit; ⟨*frode*⟩ fraud

ingarbugli'a|re *vt* entangle; ⟨*confondere*⟩ confuse. **~rsi** *vr* get entangled; ⟨*confondersi*⟩ become confused. **~to** *a* confused

inge'gnarsi *vr* do one's best

inge'gnere *nm* engineer. **ingegne'ria** *nf* engineering

in'gegno *nm* brains *pl*; ⟨*genio*⟩ genius; ⟨*abilità*⟩ ingenuity. **~sa'mente** *adv* ingeniously

ingegnosità *nf* ingenuity. **inge'gnoso** *a* ingenious

ingelo'sir|e *vt* make jealous. **~si** *vr* become jealous

in'gente *a* huge

ingenu|a'mente *adv* artlessly. **~ità** *nf* ingenuousness. **in'genuo** *a* ingenuous; ⟨*credulone*⟩ naïve

inge'renza *nf* interference

inge'rire *vt* swallow

inges'sa|re *vt* put in plaster. **~'tura** *nf* plaster

Inghil'terra *nf* England

inghiot'tire *vt* swallow

in'ghippo *nm* trick

ingial'li|re *vi*, **~rsi** *vr* turn yellow. **~to** *a* yellowed

ingigan'tir|e *vt* magnify ● *vi*, **~si** *vr* grow to enormous proportions

inginocchi'a|rsi *vr* kneel [down]. **~to** *a* kneeling. **~'toio** *nm* prie-dieu

ingioiel'larsi *vr* put on one's jewels

ingiù *adv* down; **all'~** downwards; **a testa ~** head downwards

ingi'un|gere *vt* order. **~zi'one** *nf* injunction. **~zione di pagamento** final demand

ingi'uri|a *nf* insult; ⟨*torto*⟩ wrong; ⟨*danno*⟩ damage. **~'are** *vt* insult; ⟨*fare un torto a*⟩ wrong. **~'oso** *a* insulting

ingiusta'mente *adv* unjustly, unfairly. **ingiu'stizia** *nf* injustice. **ingi'u-sto** *a* unjust, unfair

in'glese *a* English ● *nm* Englishman; ⟨*lingua*⟩ English ● *nf* Englishwoman

ingoi'are *vt* swallow

ingol'far|e *vt* flood ‹*motore*›. **~si** *vr fig* get involved; ‹*motore:*› flood

ingom'bra|nte *a* cumbersome. **~re** *vt* clutter up; *fig* cram ‹*mente*›

in'gombro *nm* encumbrance; **essere d'~** be in the way

ingor'digia *nf* greed. **in'gordo** *a* greedy

ingor'gar|e *vt* block. **~si** *vr* be blocked [up]. **in'gorgo** *nm* blockage; ‹*del traffico*› jam

ingoz'zar|e *vt* gobble up; (*nutrire eccessivamente*) stuff; fatten ‹*animali*›. **~si** *vr* stuff oneself (**di** with)

ingra'na|ggio *nm* gear; *fig* mechanism. **~re** *vt* engage ● *vi* be in gear

ingrandi'mento *nm* enlargement

ingran'di|re *vt* enlarge; (*esagerare*) magnify. **~rsi** *vr* become larger; (*aumentare*) increase

ingras'sar|e *vt* fatten up; *Mech* grease ● *vi*, **~si** *vr* put on weight

ingrati'tudine *nf* ingratitude. **in'grato** *a* ungrateful; (*sgradevole*) thankless

ingrazi'arsi *vr* ingratiate oneself with

ingredi'ente *nm* ingredient

in'gresso *nm* entrance; (*accesso*) admittance; (*sala*) hall; **~ gratuito/libero** admission free; **vietato l'~** no entry; no admittance

ingros'sar|e *vt* make big; (*gonfiare*) swell ● *vi*, **~si** *vr* grow big; (*gonfiare*) swell

in'grosso *adv* **all'~** wholesale; (*pressappoco*) roughly

ingua'ribile *a* incurable

'inguine *nm* groin

ingurgi'tare *vt* gulp down

ini'bi|re *vt* inhibit; (*vietare*) forbid. **~to** *a* inhibited. **~zi'one** *nf* inhibition; (*divieto*) prohibition

iniet'tar|e *vt* inject. **~si** *vr* **~si di sangue** ‹*occhi:*› become bloodshot. **iniezi'one** *nf* injection

inimic'arsi *vr* make an enemy of. **inimi'cizia** *nf* enmity

inimi'tabile *a* inimitable

ininter|rotta'mente *adv* continuously. **~'rotto** *a* continuous

iniquità *nf* iniquity. **i'niquo** *a* iniquitous

inizi'al|e *a & nf* initial. **~'mente** *adv* initially

inizi'are *vt* begin; (*avviare*) open; **~ qcno a qcsa** initiate sb in sth ● *vi* begin

inizia'tiva *nf* initiative; **prendere l'~** take the initiative

inizi'a|to, -a *a* initiated ● *nmf* initiate; **gli ~ti** the initiated. **~'tore, ~'trice** *nmf* initiator. **~zi'one** *nf* initiation

i'nizio *nm* beginning, start; **dare ~ a** start; **avere ~** get under way

innaffi'a|re *vt* water. **~'toio** *nm* watering-can

innal'zar|e *vt* raise; (*erigere*) erect. **~si** *vr* rise

innamo'ra|rsi *vr* fall in love (**di** with). **~ta** *nf* girl-friend. **~to** *a* in love ● *nm* boy-friend

in'nanzi *adv* (*stato in luogo*) in front; (*di tempo*) ahead; (*avanti*) forward; (*prima*) before; **d'ora ~** from now on ● *prep* (*prima*) before; **~ a** in front of. **~'tutto** *adv* first of all; (*soprattutto*) above all

in'nato *a* innate

innatu'rale *a* unnatural

inne'gabile *a* undeniable

innervo'sir|e *vt* make nervous. **~si** *vr* get irritated

inne'scare *vt* prime. **in'nesco** *nm* primer

inne'stare *vt* graft; *Mech* engage; (*inserire*) insert. **in'nesto** *nm* graft; *Mech* clutch; *Electr* connection

inne'vato *a* covered in snow

'inno *nm* hymn. **~ nazionale** national anthem

inno'cen|te *a* innocent **~te'mente** *adv* innocently. **~za** *nf* innocence.

in'nocuo *a* innocuous

inno'va|re *vt* make changes in. **~'tivo** *a* innovative. **~'tore** *a* trail-blazing. **~zi'one** *nf* innovation

innume'revole *a* innumerable

ino'doro *a* odourless

inoffen'sivo *a* harmless

inol'trar|e *vt* forward. **~si** *vr* advance

inol'trato *a* late

i'noltre *adv* besides

inon'da|re *vt* flood. **~zi'one** *nf* flood

inope'roso *a* idle

inoppor'tuno *a* untimely

inorgo'glir|e *vt* make proud. **~si** *vr* become proud

inorri'dire *vt* horrify ● *vi* be horrified

inospi'tale *a* inhospitable

inosser'vato *a* unobserved; (*non rispettato*) disregarded; **passare ~** go unnoticed

inossi'dabile *a* stainless

'inox *a inv* ‹*acciaio*› stainless

inqua'dra|re *vt* frame; *fig* put in context ‹scrittore, problema›. **~rsi** vr fit into. **~'tura** nf framing

inqualifi'cabile a unspeakable

inquie'tar|e vt worry. **~si** get worried; (impazientirsi) get cross. **inqui'eto** a restless; (preoccupato) worried. **inquie'tudine** nf anxiety

inqui'lino, -a nmf tenant

inquina'mento nm pollution

inqui'na|re vt pollute. **~to** a polluted

inqui'rente a Jur ‹magistrato› examining; **commissione ~** commission of enquiry

inqui'si|re vt/i investigate. **~to** a under investigation. **~'tore**, **~'trice** a inquiring ● nmf inquisitor. **~zi'one** nf inquisition

insabbi'are vt shelve

insa'lat|a nf salad. **~a belga** endive. **~i'era** nf salad bowl

insa'lubre a unhealthy

insa'nabile a incurable

insangui'na|re vt cover with blood. **~to** a bloody

insapo'nare vt soap

insa'po|re a tasteless. **~'rire** vt flavour

insa'puta nf all'~ di unknown to

insazi'abile a insatiable

insce'nare vt stage

inscin'dibile a inseparable

insedia'mento nm installation

insedi'ar|e vt install. **~si** vr install oneself

in'segna nf sign; (bandiera) flag; (decorazione) decoration; (emblema) insignia pl; (stemma) symbol. **~ luminosa** neon sign

insegna'mento nm teaching. **inse'gnante** a teaching ● nmf teacher

inse'gnare vt/i teach; **~ qcsa a qcno** teach sb sth

insegui'mento nmf pursuit

insegu'i|re vt pursue. **~'tore**, **~'trice** nmf pursuer

inselvati'chir|e vt make wild ● vi, **~si** vr grow wild

insemi'na|re vt inseminate. **~zi'one** nf insemination. **~zione artificiale** artificial insemination

insena'tura nf inlet

insen'sato a senseless; (folle) crazy

insen'sibil|e a insensitive; ‹braccio ecc› numb. **~ità** nf insensitivity

insepa'rabile a inseparable

inseri'mento nm insertion

inse'rir|e vt insert; place ‹annuncio›;

Electr connect. **~si** vr **~si in** get into. **in'serto** nm file; (in un film ecc) insert

inservi'ente nmf attendant

inserzi'o|ne nf insertion; (avviso) advertisement. **~'nista** nmf advertiser

insetti'cida nm insecticide

in'setto nm insect

insicu'rezza nf insecurity. **insi'curo** a insecure

in'sidi|a nf trick; (tranello) snare. **~'are** vt/i lay a trap for. **~'oso** a insidious

insi'eme adv together; (contemporaneamente) at the same time ● prep **~ a** [together] with ● nm whole; (completo) outfit; Theat ensemble; Math set; **nell'~** as a whole; **tutto ~** all together; ‹bere› at one go

in'signe a renowned

insignifi'cante a insignificant

insi'gnire vt decorate

insinda'cabile a final

insinu'ante a insinuating

insinu'a|re vt insinuate. **~rsi** vr penetrate; **~rsi in** fig creep into. **~zi'one** nf insinuation

in'sipido a insipid

insi'sten|te a insistent. **~te'mente** adv repeatedly. **~za** nf insistence. **in'sistere** vi insist; (perseverare) persevere

insoddisfa'cente a unsatisfactory

insoddi'sfa|tto a unsatisfied; (scontento) dissatisfied. **~zi'one** nf dissatisfaction

insoffe'ren|te a intolerant. **~za** nf intolerance

insolazi'one nf sunstroke

inso'len|te a rude, insolent. **~za** nf rudeness, insolence; (commento) insolent remark

in'solito a unusual

inso'lubile a insoluble

inso'luto a unsolved; (non pagato) unpaid

insol'v|enza nf insolvency

in'somma adv in short; **~!** well really!; (così così) so so

in'sonne a sleepless. **~ia** nf insomnia

insonno'lito a sleepy

insonoriz'zato a soundproofed

insoppor'tabile a unbearable

insor'genza nf onset

in'sorgere vi revolt, rise up; (sorgere) arise; ‹difficoltà› crop up

insormon'tabile a ‹ostacolo, difficoltà› insurmountable

in'sorto *pp di* **insorgere** ● *a* rebellious ● *nm* rebel

insospet'tabile *a* unsuspected

insospet'tir|e *vt* make suspicious ● *vi*, **~si** *vr* become suspicious

insoste'nibile *a* untenable; (*insopportabile*) unbearable

insostitu'ibile *a* irreplaceable

inspe'ra|bile *a* **una sua vittoria è ~bile** there is no hope of him winning. **~to** *a* unhoped-for

inspie'gabile *a* inexplicable

inspi'rare *vt* breathe in

in'stabile *a* unstable; ⟨*tempo*⟩ changeable. **~ità** *nf* instability; (*di tempo*) changeability

instal'la|re *vt* install. **~rsi** *vr* settle in. **~zi'one** *nf* installation

instan'cabile *a* untiring

instau'ra|re *vt* found. **~rsi** *vr* become established. **~zi'one** *nf* foundation

instra'dare *vt* direct

insù *adv* **all'~** upwards

insubordinazi'one *nf* insubordination

insuc'cesso *nm* failure

insudici'ar|e *vt* dirty. **~si** *vr* get dirty

insuffici'en|te *a* insufficient; (*inadeguato*) inadequate ● *nf Sch* fail. **~za** *nf* insufficiency; (*inadeguatezza*) inadequacy; *Sch* fail. **~za cardiaca** heart failure. **~za di prove** lack of evidence

insu'lare *a* insular

insu'lina *nf* insulin

in'sulso *a* insipid; (*sciocco*) silly

insul'tare *vt* insult. **in'sulto** *nm* insult

insupe'rabile *a* insuperable; (*eccezionale*) incomparable

insurrezi'one *nf* insurrection

insussi'stente *a* groundless

intac'care *vt* nick; (*corrodere*) corrode; draw o ⟨*un capitale*⟩; (*danneggiare*) damage

intagli'are *vt* carve. **in'taglio** *nm* carving

intan'gibile *a* untouchable

in'tanto *adv* meanwhile; (*per ora*) for the moment; (*avversativo*) but; **~ che** while

intarsi'a|re *vt* inlay. **~to** *a* **~to di** inset with. **in'tarsio** *nm* inlay

inta'sa|re *vt* clog; block ⟨*traffico*⟩. **~rsi** *vr* get blocked. **~to** *a* blocked

inta'scare *vt* pocket

in'tatto *a* intact

intavo'lare *vt* start

inte'gra|le *a* whole; **edizione ~le** unabridged edition; **pane ~le** whole-

meal bread. **~l'mente** *adv* fully. **~nte** *a* integral. **'integro** *a* complete; (*retto*) upright

inte'gra|re *vt* integrate; (*aggiungere*) supplement. **~rsi** *vr* integrate. **~'tivo** *a* ⟨*corso*⟩ supplementary. **~zi'one** *nf* integration

integrità *nf* integrity

intelaia'tura *nf* framework

intel'letto *nm* intellect

intellettu'al|e *a & nmf* intellectual. **~'mente** *adv* intellectually

intelli'gen|te *a* intelligent. **~te'mente** *adv* intelligently. **~za** *nf* intelligence

intelli'gibil|e *a* intelligible. **~'mente** *adv* intelligibly

intempe'ranza *nf* intemperance

intem'perie *nfpl* bad weather

inten'den|te *nm* superintendent. **~za** *nf* **~za di finanza** inland revenue office

in'tender|e *vt* (*comprendere*) understand; (*udire*) hear; (*avere intenzione*) intend; (*significare*) mean. **~sela con** have an understanding with; **~si** *vr* (*capirsi*) understand each other; **~si di** (*essere esperto*) have a good knowledge of

intendi|'mento *nm* understanding; (*intenzione*) intention. **~'tore,** **~'trice** *nmf* connoisseur

intene'rir|e *vt* soften; (*commuovere*) touch. **~si** *vr* be touched

intensa'mente *adv* intensely

intensifi'car|e *vt*, **~si** *vr* intensify

intensità *nf inv* intensity. **inten'sivo** *a* intensive. **in'tenso** *a* intense

inten'tare *vt* start up; **~ causa contro qcno** bring o institute proceedings against sb

in'tento *a* engrossed (**a** in) ● *nm* purpose

intenzio'nato *a* **essere ~ a fare qcsa** have the intention of doing sth

intenzio|'nale *a* intentional. **inten-zi'one** *nf* intention; **senza ~ne** unintentionally; **avere ~ne di fare qcsa** intend to do sth, have the intention of doing sth.

intera'gire *vi* interact

intera'mente *adv* completely, entirely

intera|t'tivo *a* interactive. **~zi'one** *nf* interaction

interca'lare[1] *nm* stock phrase

interca'lare[2] *vt* insert

intercambi'abile *a* interchangeable

interca'pedine *nf* cavity

inter'ce|dere *vi* intercede. **~ssi'one**
nf intercession

intercet'ta|re *vt* intercept; tap ⟨*tele-
fono*⟩. **~zi'one** *nf* interception. **~zione
telefonica** telephone tapping

inter'city *nm inv* inter-city

intercontinen'tale *a* interconti-
nental

inter'correre *vi* ⟨*tempo:*⟩ elapse; (*esistere*) exist

interco'stale *a* intercostal

inter'detto *pp di* **interdire** ● *a* astonished; (*proibito*) forbidden; **rimanere
~** be taken aback

inter'di|re *vt* forbid; *Jur* deprive of
civil rights. **~zi'one** *nf* prohibition

interessa'mento *nm* interest

interes'sante *a* interesting; **essere
in stato ~** be pregnant

interes'sa|re *vt* interest; (*riguardare*)
concern ● *vi* **~re a** matter to. **~rsi** *vr*
~rsi a take an interest in. **~rsi di** take
care of. **~to, -a** *nmf* interested party
● *a* interested; **essere ~to** *pej* have an
interest

inte'resse *nm* interest; **fare qcsa per
~** do sth out of self-interest

inter'faccia *nf Comput* interface

interfe'renza *nf* interference

interfe'r|ire *vi* interfere

interiezi'one *nf* interjection

interi'ora *nfpl* entrails

interi'ore *a* interior

inter'ludio *nm* interlude

intermedi'ario, -a *a & nmf* intermediary

inter'medio *a* in-between

inter'mezzo *nm Theat, Mus* inter-
mezzo

intermi'nabile *a* interminable

intermit'ten|te *a* intermittent; ⟨*luce*⟩
flashing. **~za** *nf* **luce a ~za** flashing
light

interna'mento *nm* internment; (*in
manicomio*) committal

inter'nare *vt* intern; (*in manicomio*)
commit [to a mental institution]

internazio'nale *a* international

'Internet *nf inv* Internet

in'terno *a* internal; *Geog* inland; (*interiore*) inner; ⟨*politica*⟩ national; **alunno
~** boarder ● *nm* interior; (*di condominio*) flat; *Teleph* extension; *Cinema*
interior shot; **all'~** inside

in'tero *a* whole, entire; (*intatto*) intact;
(*completo*) complete; **per ~** in full

interpel'lare *vt* consult

inter'por|re *vt* place ⟨*ostacolo*⟩. **~si** *vr*
come between

interpre'ta|re *vt* interpret; *Mus* per-
form. **~zi'one** *nf* interpretation; *Mus*
performance. **in'terprete** *nmf* inter-
preter; *Mus* performer

inter'ra|re *vt* (*seppellire*) bury; plant
⟨*pianta, seme*⟩. **~to** *nm* basement

interro'ga|re *vt* question; *Sch* test; ex-
amine ⟨*studenti*⟩. **~tiva'mente** *adv*
questioningly. **~'tivo** *a* interrogative;
⟨*sguardo*⟩ questioning; **punto ~tivo**
question mark ● *nm* question **~'torio** *a*
& *nm* questioning. **~zi'one** *nf* question;
Sch oral [test]

inter'romper|e *vt* interrupt; (*sospen-
dere*) stop; cut off ⟨*collegamento*⟩. **~si** *vr*
break off

interrut'tore *nm* switch

interruzi'one *nf* interruption; **senza
~** non-stop. **~ di gravidanza** termination of pregnancy

interse'care *vt*, **~'carsi** *vr* intersect.
~zi'one *nf* intersection

inter'stizio *nm* interstice

interur'ban|a *nf* long-distance call.
~o *a* inter-city

interval'lare *vt* space out. **inter'vallo**
nm interval; (*spazio*) space; *Sch* break.
intervallo pubblicitario commercial
break

interve'nire *vi* intervene; (*Med: operare*) operate; **~ a** take part in. **inter-
'vento** *nm* intervention; (*presenza*)
presence; (*chirurgico*) operation; **pronto intervento** emergency services

inter'vista *nf* interview

intervi'sta|re *vt* interview. **~'tore,
~'trice** *nmf* interviewer

in'tes|a *nf* understanding; **cenno
d'~a** acknowledgement. **~o** *pp di* **intendere** ● *a* **resta ~o che...** needless
to say,...; **~i!** agreed!; **~o a** meant to;
non darsi per ~o refuse to understand

inte'sta|re *vt* head; write one's name
and address at the top of ⟨*lettera*⟩;
Comm register. **~rsi** *vr* **~rsi a fare
qcsa** take it into one's head to do sth.
~'tario, -a *nmf* holder. **~zi'one** *nf*
heading; ⟨*su carta da lettere*⟩ letterhead

intesti'nale *a* intestinal

inte'stino *a* ⟨*lotte*⟩ internal ● *nm* in-
testine

intima'mente *adv* intimately

inti'ma|re *vt* order; **~re l'alt a qcno**
order sb to stop. **~zi'one** *nf* order

intimida|'torio *a* threatening.
~zi'one *nf* intimidation

intimi'dire *vt* intimidate

intimità *nf* cosiness. **'intimo** *a* intimate; (*interno*) innermost; (*amico*) close ● *nm* (*amico*) close friend; (*dell'animo*) heart

intimo'ri|re *vt* frighten. **~rsi** *vr* get frightened. **~to** *a* frightened

in'tingere *vt* dip

in'tingolo *nm* sauce; (*pietanza*) stew

intiriz'zi|re *vt* numb. **~rsi** *vr* grow numb. **~to** *a* **essere ~to** (*dal freddo*) be perished

intito'lar|e *vt* entitle; (*dedicare*) dedicate. **~si** *vr* be called

intolle'rabile *a* intolerable

intona'care *vt* plaster. **in'tonaco** *nm* plaster

into'na|re *vt* start to sing; tune (*strumento*); (*accordare*) match. **~rsi** *vr* match. **~to** *a* (*persona*) able to sing in tune; (*colore*) matching

intonazi'one *nf* (*inflessione*) intonation; (*ironico*) tone

inton'ti|re *vt* daze; (*gas:*) make dizzy ● *vi* be dazed. **~to** *a* dazed

intop'pare *vi* **~ in** run into

in'toppo *nm* obstacle

in'torno *adv* around ● *prep* **~ a** around; (*circa*) about

intorpi'di|re *vt* numb. **~rsi** *vr* become numb. **~to** *a* torpid

intossi'ca|re *vt* poison. **~rsi** *vr* be poisoned. **~zi'one** *nf* poisoning

intralci'are *vt* hamper

in'tralcio *nm* hitch; **essere d'~** be a hindrance (**a** to)

intrallaz'zare *vi* intrigue. **intral'lazzo** *nm* racket

intramon'tabile *a* timeless

intramusco'lare *a* intramuscular

intransi'gen|te *a* intransigent, uncompromising. **~za** *nf* intransigence

intransi'tivo *a* intransitive

intrappo'lato *a* **rimanere ~** be trapped

intrapren'den|te *a* enterprising. **~za** *nf* initiative

intra'prendere *vt* undertake

intrat'tabile *a* very difficult

intratte'n|ere *vt* entertain. **~ersi** *vr* linger. **~i'mento** *nm* entertainment

intrave'dere *vt* catch a glimpse of; (*presagire*) foresee

intrecci'ar|e *vt* interweave; plait (*capelli, corda*). **~si** *vr* intertwine; (*aggrovigliarsi*) become tangled; **~e le mani** clasp one's hands

in'treccio *nm* (*trama*) plot

in'trepido *a* intrepid

intri'cato *a* tangled

intri'gante *a* scheming; (*affascinante*) intriguing

intri'ga|re *vt* entangle; (*incuriosire*) intrigue ● *vi* intrigue, scheme. **~rsi** *vr* meddle. **in'trigo** *nm* plot; **intrighi** *pl* intrigues

in'trinseco *a* intrinsic

in'triso *a* **~ di** soaked in

intri'stirsi *vr* grow sad

intro'du|rre *vt* introduce; (*inserire*) insert; **~rre a** (*iniziare a*) introduce to. **~rsi** *vr* get in (**in** to). **~t'tivo** *a* (*pagine, discorso*) introductory. **~zi'one** *nf* introduction

in'troito *nm* income, revenue; (*incasso*) takings *pl*

intro'metter|e *vt* introduce. **~si** *vr* interfere; (*interporsi*) intervene. **intromissi'one** *nf* intervention

intro'vabile *a* that can't be found; (*prodotto*) unobtainable

intro'verso, -a *a* introverted ● *nmf* introvert

intrufo'larsi *vr* sneak in

in'truglio *nm* concoction

intrusi'one *nf* intrusion. **in'truso, -a** *nmf* intruder

intu'i|re *vt* perceive

intui'tiva'mente *adv* intuitively. **~'tivo** *a* intuitive. **in'tuito** *nm* intuition. **~zi'one** *nf* intuition

inuguagli'anza *nf* inequality

inu'mano *a* inhuman

inu'mare *vt* inter

inumi'dir|e *vt* dampen; moisten (*labbra*). **~si** *vr* become damp

i'nutil|e *a* useless; (*superfluo*) unnecessary. **~ità** *nf* uselessness

inutiliz'za|bile *a* unusable. **~to** *a* unused

inutil'mente *adv* fruitlessly

inva'dente *a* intrusive

in'vadere *vt* invade; (*affollare*) overrun

invali'd|are *vt* invalidate. **~ità** *nf* disability; *Jur* invalidity. **in'valido, -a** *a* invalid; (*handicappato*) disabled ● *nmf* disabled person

in'vano *adv* in vain

invari'abil|e *a* invariable

invari'ato *a* unchanged

invasi'one *nf* invasion. **in'vaso** *pp di* **invadere**. **inva'sore** *a* invading ● *nm* invader

invecchia'mento *nm* (*di vino*) maturation

invecchi'are *vt/i* age

in'vece *adv* instead; *(anzi)* but; ~ **di** instead of

inve'ire *vi* ~ **contro** inveigh against

inven'd|ibile *a* unsaleable. ~**uto** *a* unsold

inven'tare *vt* invent

inventari'are *vt* make an inventory of. **inven'tario** *nm* inventory

inven|'tivo, -a *a* inventive ● *nf* inventiveness. ~**-'tore**, ~**'trice** *nmf* inventor. ~**zi'one** *nf* invention

inver'nale *a* wintry. **in'verno** *nm* winter

invero'simile *a* improbable

inversa'mente *adv* inversely; ~ **proporzionale** in inverse proportion

inversi'one *nf* inversion; *Mech* reversal. **in'verso** *a* inverse; *(opposto)* opposite ● *nm* opposite

inverte'brato *a* & *nm* invertebrate

inver'ti|re *vt* reverse; *(capovolgere)* turn upside down. ~**to, -a** *nmf* homosexual

investi'ga|re *vt* investigate. ~**'tore** *nm* investigator. ~**zi'one** *nf* investigation

investi'mento *nm* investment; *(incidente)* crash

inve'sti|re *vt* invest; *(urtare)* collide with; *(travolgere)* run over; ~**re qcno di** invest sb with. ~**'tura** *nf* investiture

invet'tiva *nf* invective

invi'a|re *vt* send. ~**to, -a** *nmf* envoy; *(di giornale)* correspondent

invidi|a *nf* envy. ~**'are** *vt* envy. ~**'oso** *a* envious

invigo'rir|e *vt* invigorate. ~**si** *vr* become strong

invin'cibile *a* invincible

in'vio *nm* dispatch; *Comput* enter

invio'labile *a* inviolable

invipe'ri|rsi *vr* get nasty. ~**to** *a* furious

invi'sibil|e *a* invisible. ~**ità** *nf* invisibility

invi'tante *a* *(piatto, profumo)* enticing

invi'ta|re *vt* invite. ~**to, -a** *nmf* guest. **in'vito** *nm* invitation

invo'ca|re *vt* invoke; *(implorare)* beg. ~**zi'one** *nf* invocation

invogli'ar|e *vt* tempt; *(indurre)* induce. ~**si** *vr* ~**si di** take a fancy to

involon|taria'mente *adv* involuntarily. ~**'tario** *a* involuntary

invol'tino *nm* Culin beef olive

in'volto *nm* parcel; *(fagotto)* bundle

in'volucro *nm* wrapping

invulne'rabile *a* invulnerable

inzacche'rare *vt* splash with mud

inzup'par|e *vt* soak; *(intingere)* dip. ~**si** *vr* get soaked

'io *pron* I; **chi è? – [sono] io** who is it? – [it's] me; **l'ho fatto io [stesso]** I did it myself ● *nm* **l'~** the ego

i'odio *nm* iodine

I'onio *nm* **lo** ~ the Ionian [Sea]

i'osa: a ~ *adv* in abundance

iperat'tivo *a* hyperactive

ipermer'cato *nm* hypermarket

iper'metrope *a* long-sighted

ipersen'sibile *a* hypersensitive

ipertensi'one *nf* high blood pressure

ip'no|si *nf* hypnosis. ~**tico** *a* hypnotic. ~**'tismo** *nm* hypnotism. ~**tiz'zare** *vt* hypnotize

ipoca'lorico *a* low-calorie

ipocon'driaco, -a *a* & *nmf* hypochondriac

ipocri'sia *nf* hypocrisy. **i'pocrita** *a* hypocritical ● *nmf* hypocrite

ipo'te|ca *nf* mortgage. ~**'care** *vt* mortgage

i'potesi *nf inv* hypothesis; *(caso, eventualità)* eventuality. **ipo'tetico** *a* hypothetical. **ipotiz'zare** *vt* hypothesize

'ippico, -a *a* horse *attrib* ● *nf* riding

ippoca'stano *nm* horse-chestnut

ip'podromo *nm* racecourse

ippo'potamo *nm* hippopotamus

'ira *nf* anger. ~**'scibile** *a* irascible

i'rato *a* irate

'iride *nf Anat* iris; *(arcobaleno)* rainbow

Ir'lan|da *nf* Ireland. ~**da del Nord** Northern Ireland. **i~'dese** *a* Irish ● *nm* Irishman; *(lingua)* Irish ● *nf* Irishwoman

iro'nia *nf* irony. **i'ronico** *a* ironic[al]

irradi'a|re *vt/i* radiate. ~**zi'one** *nf* radiation

irraggiun'gibile *a* unattainable

irragio'nevole *a* unreasonable; *(speranza, timore)* irrational; *(assurdo)* absurd

irrazio'nal|e *a* irrational. ~**ità** *a* irrationality. ~**'mente** *adv* irrationally

irre'a|le *a* unreal. ~**'listico** *a* unrealistic. ~**liz'zabile** *a* unattainable. ~**ltà** *nf* unreality

irrecupe'rabile *a* irrecoverable

irrego'lar|e *a* irregular. ~**ità** *nf inv* irregularity

irremo'vibile *a fig* adamant

irrepa'rabile *a* irreparable

irrepe'ribile *a* not to be found; **sarò** ~ I won't be contactable

irrepren'sibile *a* irreproachable

irrepri'mibile *a* irrepressible

irrequi'eto *a* restless
irresi'stibile *a* irresistible
irrespon'sabil|e *a* irresponsible. **~ità** *nf* irresponsibility
irrever'sibile *a* irreversible
irrevo'cabile *a* irrevocable
irricono'scibile *a* unrecognizable
irri'ga|re *vt* irrigate; ⟨*fiume:*⟩ flow through. **~zi'one** *nf* irrigation
irrigidi'mento *nm* stiffening
irrigi'dir|e *vt*, **~si** *vr* stiffen
irrile'vante *a* unimportant
irrimedi'abile *a* irreparable
irripe'tibile *a* unrepeatable
irri'sorio *a* derisive; ⟨*differenza, particolare, somma*⟩ insignificant
irri'ta|bile *a* irritable. **~nte** *a* aggravating
irri'ta|re *vt* irritate. **~rsi** *vr* get annoyed. **~to** *a* irritated; ⟨*gola*⟩ sore. **~zi'one** *nf* irritation
irrobu'stir|e *vt* fortify. **~si** *vr* get stronger
ir'rompere *vi* burst (**in** into)
irro'rare *vt* sprinkle
irru'ente *a* impetuous
irruzi'one *nf* fare **~ in** burst into
i'scritto, -a *pp di* iscrivere ● *a* registered ● *nmf* member; **per ~** in writing
i'scriver|e *vt* register. **~si** *vr* **~si a** register at, enrol at ⟨*scuola*⟩; join ⟨*circolo ecc*⟩. **iscrizi'one** *nf* registration; (*epigrafe*) inscription
i'sla|mico *a* Islamic. **~'mismo** *nm* Islam
I'slan|da *nf* Iceland. **i~'dese** *a* Icelandic ● *nmf* Icelander
'isola *nf* island. **le isole britanniche** the British Isles. **~ pedonale** pedestrian precinct. **~ spartitraffico** traffic island. **iso'lano, -a** *a* insular ● *nmf* islander
iso'lante *a* insulating ● *nm* insulator
iso'la|re *vt* isolate; *Mech, Electr* insulate; (*acusticamente*) soundproof. **~to** *a* isolated *nm* (*di appartamenti*) block
ispes'sir|e *vt*, **~si** *vr* thicken
ispetto'rato *nm* inspectorate. **ispet-**

'tore *nm* inspector. **ispezio'nare** *vt* inspect. **ispezi'one** *nf* inspection
'ispido *a* bristly
ispi'ra|re *vt* inspire; suggest ⟨*idea, soluzione*⟩. **~rsi** *vr* **~rsi a** be based on. **~to** *a* inspired. **~zi'one** *nf* inspiration; (*idea*) idea
Isra'el|e *nm* Israel. **i~i'ano, -a** *a* & *nmf* Israeli
is'sare *vt* hoist
istan'taneo, -a *a* instantaneous ● *nf* snapshot
i'stante *nm* instant; **all'~** instantly
i'stanza *nf* petition
i'sterico *a* hysterical. **iste'rismo** *nm* hysteria
isti'ga|re *vt* instigate; **~re qcno al male** incite sb to evil. **~'tore, ~'trice** *nmf* instigator. **~zi'one** *nf* instigation
istin|tiva'mente *adv* instinctively. **~'tivo** *a* instinctive. **i'stinto** *nm* instinct; **d'istinto** instinctively
istitu'ire *vt* institute; (*fondare*) found; initiate ⟨*manifestazione*⟩
isti'tu|to *nm* institute; (*universitario*) department; *Sch* secondary school. **~to di bellezza** beauty salon. **~'tore, ~'trice** *nmf* (*insegnante*) tutor; (*fondatore*) founder
istituzio'nale *a* institutional. **istituzi'one** *nf* institution
'istmo *nm* isthmus
'istrice *nm* porcupine
istru'i|re *vt* instruct; (*addestrare*) train; (*informare*) inform; *Jur* prepare. **~to** *a* educated
istrut't|ivo *a* instructive. **~ore, ~rice** *nmf* instructor; **giudice ~ore** examining magistrate. **~oria** *nf Jur* investigation. **istruzi'one** *nf* education; (*indicazione*) instruction
l'tali|a *nf* Italy. **i~'ano, -a** *a* & *nmf* Italian
itine'rario *nm* route, itinerary
itte'rizia *nf* jaundice
'ittico *a* fishing *attrib*
I.V.A. *nf abbr* (**imposta sul valore aggiunto**) VAT

Jj

jack *nm inv* jack
jazz *nm* jazz. **jaz'zista** *nmf* jazz player
jeep *nf inv* jeep
'jolly *nm inv* (*carta da gioco*) joker

Jugo'slav|ia *nf* Yugoslavia. **j~o, -a** *a* & *nmf* Yugoslav[ian]
ju'niores *nmfpl Sport* juniors

Kk

ka'jal *nm inv* kohl
kara'oke *nm inv* karaoke
ka'rate *nm* karate

kg *abbr* (**chilogrammo**) kg
km *abbr* (**chilometro**) km

Ll

l' *def art mf* (*before vowel*) the; *vedi* **il**
la *def art f* the; *vedi* **il** ● *pron* (*oggetto, riferito a persona*) her; (*riferito a cosa, animale*) it; (*forma di cortesia*) you ● *nm inv Mus* (*chiave, nota*) A
là *adv* there; **di là** (*in quel luogo*) in there; (*da quella parte*) that way; **eccolo là!** there he is!; **farsi più in là** (*far largo*) make way; **là dentro** in there; **là fuori** out there; **[ma] va là!** come off it!; **più in là** (*nel tempo*) later on; (*nello spazio*) further on
'labbro *nm* (*pl nf Anat* **labbra**) lip
labi'rinto *nm* labyrinth; (*di sentieri ecc*) maze
labora'torio *nm* laboratory; (*di negozio, officina ecc*) workshop
labori'oso *a* (*operoso*) industrious; (*faticoso*) laborious
labu'rista *a* Labour ● *nmf* member of the Labour Party

'lacca *nf* lacquer; (*per capelli*) hairspray, lacquer. **lac'care** *vt* lacquer
'laccio *nm* noose; (*lazo*) lasso; (*trappola*) snare; (*stringa*) lace
lace'rante *a* ⟨*grido*⟩ earsplitting
lace'ra|re *vt* tear; lacerate ⟨*carne*⟩. **~rsi** *vr* tear. **~zi'one** *nf* laceration. **'lacero** *a* torn; (*cencioso*) ragged
la'conico *a* laconic
'lacri|ma *nf* tear; (*goccia*) drop. **~'mare** *vi* weep. **~'mevole** *a* tear-jerking
lacri'mogeno *a* gas ~ tear gas
lacri'moso *a* tearful
la'cuna *nf* gap. **lacu'noso** *a* ⟨*preparazione, resoconto*⟩ incomplete
la'custre *a* lake *attrib*
lad'dove *conj* whereas
'ladro, -a *nmf* thief; **al ~!** stop thief! **~'cinio** *nm* theft. **la'druncolo** *nm* petty thief
'lager *nm inv* concentration camp

laggiù *adv* down there; (*lontano*) over there

'lagna *nf* (*fam: persona*) moaning Minnie; (*film*) bore

la'gna|nza *nf* complaint. **~rsi** *vr* moan; (*protestare*) complain (**di** about). **la'gnoso** *a* (*persona*) moaning

'lago *nm* lake

la'guna *nf* lagoon

'laico, -a *a* lay; (*vita*) secular ● *nm* layman ● *nf* laywoman

'lama *nf* blade ● *nm inv* (*animale*) llama

lambic'carsi *vr* **~ il cervello** rack one's brains

lam'bire *vt* lap

lamé *nm inv* lamé

lamen'tar|e *vt* lament. **~si** *vr* moan. **~si di** (*lagnarsi*) complain about

lamen'te|la *nf* complaint. **~vole** *a* mournful; (*pietoso*) pitiful. **la'mento** *nm* moan

la'metta *nf* **~ [da barba]** razor blade

lami'era *nf* sheet metal

'lamina *nf* foil. **~ d'oro** gold leaf

lami'na|re *vt* laminate. **~to** *a* laminated ● *nm* laminate; (*tessuto*) lamé

'lampa|da *nf* lamp. **~da abbronzante** sunlamp. **~da a pila** torch. **~'dario** *nm* chandelier. **~'dina** *nf* light bulb

lam'pante *a* clear

lampeggi'a|re *vi* flash. **~'tore** *nm* *Auto* indicator

lampi'one *nm* street lamp

'lampo *nm* flash of lightning; (*luce*) flash; **lampi** *pl* lightning *sg*. **~ di genio** stroke of genius. **[cerniera] ~** zip [fastener], zipper *Am*

lam'pone *nm* raspberry

'lana *nf* wool; **di ~** woollen. **~ d'acciaio** steel wool. **~ vergine** new wool. **~ di vetro** glass wool

lan'cetta *nf* pointer; (*di orologio*) hand

'lancia *nf* (*arma*) spear, lance; *Naut* launch

lanci'ar|e *vt* throw; (*da un aereo*) drop; launch (*missile, prodotto*); give (*grido*); **~e uno sguardo a** glance at. **~si** *vr* fling oneself; (*intraprendere*) launch out

lanci'nante *a* piercing

'lancio *nm* throwing; (*da aereo*) drop; (*di missile, prodotto*) launch. **~ del disco** discus [throwing]. **~ del giavellotto** javelin [throwing]. **~ del peso** putting the shot

'landa *nf* heath

'languido *a* languid

lani'ero *a* wool

lani'ficio *nm* woollen mill

lan'terna *nf* lantern; (*faro*) lighthouse

la'nugine *nf* down

lapi'dare *vt* stone; *fig* demolish

lapi'dario *a* (*conciso*) terse

'lapide *nf* tombstone; (*commemorativa*) memorial tablet

'lapis *nm inv* pencil

'lapsus *nm inv* lapse, error

'lardo *nm* lard

larga'mente *adv* (*ampiamente*) widely

lar'ghezza *nf* width, breadth; *fig* liberality. **~ di vedute** broadmindedness

'largo *a* wide; (*ampio*) broad; (*abito*) loose; (*liberale*) liberal; (*abbondante*) generous; **stare alla larga** keep away; **~ di manica** generous; **essere ~ di spalle/vedute** be broad-shouldered/minded ● *nm* width; **andare al ~** *Naut* go out to sea; **fare ~** make room; **farsi ~** make one's way; **al ~ di** off the coast of

'larice *nm* larch

la'ringe *nf* larynx. **larin'gite** *nf* laryngitis

'larva *nf* larva; (*persona emaciata*) shadow

la'sagne *nfpl* lasagna *sg*

lasciapas'sare *nm inv* pass

lasci'ar|e *vt* leave; (*rinunciare*) give up; (*rimetterci*) lose; (*smettere di tenere*) let go [of]; (*concedere*) let; **~e di fare qcsa** (*smettere*) stop doing sth; **lascia perdere!** forget it!; **lascialo venire, lascia che venga** let him come. **~si** *vr* (*reciproco*) leave each other, split up; **~si andare** let oneself go

'lascito *nm* legacy

'laser *a & nm inv* **[raggio] ~** laser [beam]

lassa'tivo *a & nm* laxative

'lasso *nm* **~ di tempo** period of time

lassù *adv* up there

'lastra *nf* slab; (*di ghiaccio*) sheet; (*di metallo, Phot*) plate; (*radiografia*) X-ray [plate]

lastri'ca|re *vt* pave. **~to, 'lastrico** *nm* pavement; **sul lastrico** on one's beam-ends

la'tente *a* latent

late'rale *a* side *attrib*; *Med, Techn ecc* lateral; **via ~** side street

late'rizi *nmpl* bricks

lati'fondo *nm* large estate

la'tino *a & nm* Latin

lati'tan|te *a* in hiding ● *nmf* fugitive [from justice]

lati'tudine *nf* latitude

'lato *a* (*ampio*) broad; **in senso ~** broadly speaking ● *nm* side; (*aspetto*) aspect; **a ~ di** beside; **dal ~ mio** (*punto di vista*) for my part; **d'altro ~** *fig* on the other hand

la'tra|re *vi* bark. **~to** *nm* barking

la'trina *nf* latrine

'latta *nf* tin, can

lat'taio *nm* milkman

lat'tante *a* breast-fed ● *nmf* suckling

'latt|e *nm* milk. **~e acido** sour milk. **~e condensato** condensed milk. **~e detergente** cleansing milk. **~e in polvere** powdered milk. **~e scremato** skimmed milk. **~eo** *a* milky. **~e'ria** *nf* dairy. **~i'cini** *nmpl* dairy products. **~i'era** *nf* milk jug

lat'tina *nf* can

lat'tuga *nf* lettuce

'laure|a *nf* degree; **prendere la ~a** graduate. **~'ando, -a** *nmf* final-year student

laure'a|rsi *vr* graduate. **~to, -a** *a & nmf* graduate

'lauro *nm* laurel

'lauto *a* lavish; **~ guadagno** handsome profit

'lava *nf* lava

la'vabile *a* washable

la'vabo *nm* wash-basin

la'vaggio *nm* washing. **~ automatico** (*per auto*) carwash. **~ del cervello** brainwashing. **~ a secco** dry-cleaning

la'vagna *nf* slate; *Sch* blackboard

la'van|da *nf* wash; *Bot* lavender; **fare una ~da gastrica** have one's stomach pumped. **~'daia** *nf* washerwoman. **~de'ria** *nf* laundry. **~deria automatica** launderette

lavan'dino *nm* sink; (*hum: persona*) bottomless pit

lavapi'atti *nmf inv* dishwasher

la'var|e *vt* wash; **~e i piatti** wash up. **~si** *vr* wash, have a wash; **~si i denti** brush one's teeth; **~si le mani** wash one's hands

lava'secco *nmf inv* dry-cleaner's

lavasto'viglie *nf inv* dishwasher

la'vata *nf* wash; **darsi una ~** have a wash; **~ di capo** *fig* scolding

lava'tivo, -a *nmf* idler

lava'trice *nf* washing-machine

lavo'rante *nmf* worker

lavo'ra|re *vi* work ● *vt* work; knead ⟨*pasta ecc*⟩; till ⟨*la terra*⟩; **~re a maglia** knit. **~'tivo** *a* working. **~to** *a* ⟨*pietra, legno*⟩ carved; ⟨*cuoio*⟩ tooled; ⟨*metallo*⟩ wrought. **~'tore, ~'trice** *nmf* worker

● *a* working. **~zi'one** *nf* manufacture; (*di terra*) working; (*artigianale*) workmanship; (*del terreno*) cultivation.

lavo'rio *nm* intense activity

la'voro *nm* work; (*faticoso, sociale*) labour; (*impiego*) job; *Theat* play; **mettersi al ~** set to work (**su** on). **~ a maglia** knitting. **~ nero** moonlighting. **~ straordinario** overtime. **~ a tempo pieno** full-time job. **lavori** *pl* **di casa** housework. **lavori** *pl* **in corso** roadworks. **lavori** *pl* **forzati** hard labour. **lavori** *pl* **stradali** roadworks

le *def art fpl* the; *vedi* **il** ● *pron* (*oggetto*) them; (*a lei*) her; (*forma di cortesia*) you

le'al|e *a* loyal. **~'mente** *adv* loyally. **~tà** *nf* loyalty

'lebbra *nf* leprosy

'lecca 'lecca *nm inv* lollipop

leccapi'edi *nmf inv pej* bootlicker

lec'ca|re *vt* lick; *fig* suck up to. **~rsi** *vr* lick; (*fig: agghindarsi*) doll oneself up; **da ~rsi i baffi** mouth-watering. **~ta** *nf* lick

leccor'nia *nf* delicacy

'lecito *a* lawful; (*permesso*) permissibile

'ledere *vt* damage; *Med* injure

'lega *nf* league; (*di metalli*) alloy; **far ~ con qcno** take up with sb

le'gaccio *nm* string; (*delle scarpe*) shoelace

le'gal|e *a* legal ● *nm* lawyer. **~ità** *nf* legality. **~iz'zare** *vt* authenticate; (*rendere legale*) legalize. **~'mente** *adv* legally

le'game *nm* tie; (*amoroso*) liaison; (*connessione*) link

lega'mento *nm Med* ligament

le'gar|e *vt* tie; tie up ⟨*persona*⟩; tie together ⟨*due cose*⟩; (*unire, rilegare*) bind; alloy ⟨*metalli*⟩; (*connettere*) connect; **~sela al dito** bear a grudge ● *vi* (*far lega*) get on well. **~si** *vr* bind oneself; **~si a qcno** become attached to sb

le'gato *nm* legacy; *Relig* legate

lega'tura *nf* tying; (*di libro*) binding

le'genda *nf* legend

'legge *nf* law; (*parlamentare*) act; **a norma di ~** by law

leg'genda *nf* legend; (*didascalia*) caption. **leggen'dario** *a* legendary

'leggere *vt/i* read

legge'r|ezza *nf* lightness; (*frivolezza*) frivolity; (*incostanza*) fickleness. **~'mente** *adv* slightly

leg'gero *a* light; ⟨*bevanda*⟩ weak; (*lieve*) slight; (*frivolo*) frivolous; (*incostante*) fickle; **alla leggera** frivolously

leg'gibile *a* ⟨*scrittura*⟩ legible; ⟨*stile*⟩ readable

leg'gio *nm* lectern; *Mus* music stand

legife'rare *vi* legislate

legio'nario *nm* legionary. **legi'one** *nf* legion

legisla'tivo *a* legislative. **~'tore** *nm* legislator. **~'tura** *nf* legislature. **~zi'one** *nf* legislation

legittimità *nf* legitimacy. **le'gittimo** *a* legitimate; ⟨*giusto*⟩ proper; **legittima difesa** self-defence

'legna *nf* firewood

le'gname *nm* timber

le'gnata *nf* blow with a stick

'legno *nm* wood; **di ~** wooden. **~ compensato** plywood. **le'gnoso** *a* woody

le'gume *nm* pod

'lei *pron* ⟨*soggetto*⟩ she; ⟨*oggetto, con prep*⟩ her; ⟨*forma di cortesia*⟩ you; **lo ha fatto ~ stessa** she did it herself

'lembo *nm* edge; ⟨*di terra*⟩ strip

'lemma *nm* headword

'lena *nf* vigour

le'nire *vt* soothe

lenta'mente *adv* slowly

'lente *nf* lens. **~ a contatto** contact lens. **~ d'ingrandimento** magnifying glass

len'tezza *nf* slowness

len'ticchia *nf* lentil

len'tiggine *nf* freckle

'lento *a* slow; ⟨*allentato*⟩ slack; ⟨*abito*⟩ loose

'lenza *nf* fishing-line

len'zuolo *nm* (*pl f* **lenzuola**) *nm* sheet

le'one *nm* lion; *Astr* Leo

leo'pardo *nm* leopard

'lepre *nf* hare

'lercio *a* filthy

'lesbica *nf* lesbian

lesi'nare *vt* grudge ● *vi* be stingy

lesio'nare *vt* damage. **lesi'one** *nf* lesion

'leso *pp di* **ledere** ● *a* injured

les'sare *vt* boil

'lessico *nm* vocabulary

'lesso *a* boiled ● *nm* boiled meat

'lesto *a* quick; ⟨*mente*⟩ sharp

le'tale *a* lethal

leta'maio *nm* dunghill; *fig* pigsty. **le'tame** *nm* dung

le'targ|ico *a* lethargic. **~o** *nm* lethargy; ⟨*di animali*⟩ hibernation

le'tizia *nf* joy

'lettera *nf* letter; **alla ~** literally; **~ maiuscola** capital letter; **~ minuscola** small letter; **lettere** *pl* ⟨*letteratura*⟩

literature *sg*; *Univ* Arts; **dottore in lettere** BA, Bachelor of Arts

lette'rale *a* literal

lette'rario *a* literary

lette'rato *a* well-read

lettera'tura *nf* literature

let'tiga *nf* stretcher

let'tino *nm* cot; *Med* couch

'letto *nm* bed. **~ a castello** bunkbed. **~ a una piazza** single bed. **~ a due piazze** double bed. **~ matrimoniale** double bed

letto'rato *nm* ⟨*corso*⟩ ≈ tutorial

let'tore, -'trice *nmf* reader; *Univ* language assistant ● *nm* *Comput* disk drive. **~ di CD-ROM** CD-Rom drive

let'tura *nf* reading

leuce'mia *nf* leukaemia

'leva *nf* lever; *Mil* call-up; **far ~** lever. **~ del cambio** gear lever

le'vante *nm* East; ⟨*vento*⟩ east wind

le'va|re *vt* ⟨*alzare*⟩ raise; ⟨*togliere*⟩ take away; ⟨*rimuovere*⟩ take off; ⟨*estrarre*⟩ pull out; **~re di mezzo** qcsa get sth out of the way. **~rsi** *vr* rise; ⟨*da letto*⟩ get up; **~rsi di mezzo**, **~rsi dai piedi** get out of the way. **~ta** *nf* rising; ⟨*di posta*⟩ collection

leva'taccia *nf* **fare una ~** get up at the crack of dawn

leva'toio *a* **ponte ~** drawbridge

levi'ga|re *vt* smooth; ⟨*con carta vetro*⟩ rub down. **~to** *a* ⟨*superficie*⟩ polished

levri'ero *nm* greyhound

lezi'one *nf* lesson; *Univ* lecture; ⟨*rimprovero*⟩ rebuke

lezi'oso *a* ⟨*stile, modi*⟩ affected

li *pron mpl* them

lì *adv* there; **fin lì** as far as there; **giù di lì** thereabouts; **lì per lì** there and then

Li'bano *nm* Lebanon

'libbra *nf* ⟨*peso*⟩ pound

li'beccio *nm* south-west wind

li'bellula *nf* dragon-fly

libe'rale *a* liberal; ⟨*generoso*⟩ generous ● *nmf* liberal

libe'ra|re *vt* free; release ⟨*prigioniero*⟩; vacate ⟨*stanza*⟩; ⟨*salvare*⟩ rescue. **~rsi** *vr* ⟨*stanza:*⟩ become vacant; *Teleph* become free; ⟨*da impegno*⟩ get out of it; **~rsi di** get rid of. **~'tore**, **~'trice** *a* liberating ● *nmf* liberator. **~'torio** *a* liberating. **~zi'one** *nf* liberation; **la L~zione** ⟨*ricorrenza*⟩ Liberation Day

'liber|o *a* free; ⟨*strada*⟩ clear. **~o docente** qualified university lecturer. **~o professionista** self-employed person. **~tà** *nf inv* freedom; ⟨*di pri-*⟩

gioniero) release. **~tà provvisoria** *Jur*
bail; **~tà** *pl (confidenze)* liberties
'liberty *nm & a inv* Art Nouveau
'Libi|a *nf* Libya. **l~co, -a** *a & nmf*
Libyan
li'bidi|ne *nf* lust. **~'noso** *a* lustful.
li'bido *nf* libido
libra'io *nm* bookseller
libre'ria *nf (negozio)* bookshop; *(mobile)* bookcase; *(biblioteca)* library
li'bretto *nm* booklet; *Mus* libretto. **~ degli assegni** cheque book. **~ di circolazione** logbook. **~ d'istruzioni** instruction booklet. **~ di risparmio** bankbook. **~ universitario** *book held by students which records details of their exam performances*
'libro *nm* book. **~ giallo** thriller. **~ paga** payroll
lice'ale *nmf* secondary-school student ● *a* secondary-school *attrib*
li'cenza *nf* licence; *(permesso)* permission; *Mil* leave; *Sch* school-leaving certificate; **essere in ~** be on leave
licenzia'mento *nm* dismissal
licenzi'a|re *vt* dismiss, sack *fam.* **~rsi** *vr (da un impiego)* resign; *(accomiatarsi)* take one's leave
li'ceo *nm* secondary school, high school. **~ classico** *secondary school with an emphasis on humanities.* **~ scientifico** *secondary school with an emphasis on sciences*
li'chene *nm* lichen
'lido *nm* beach
li'eto *a* glad; *(evento)* happy; **molto ~!** pleased to meet you!
li'eve *a* light; *(debole)* faint; *(trascurabile)* slight
lievi'tare *vi* rise ● *vt* leaven. **li'evito** *nm* yeast. **lievito in polvere** baking powder
'lifting *nm inv* face-lift
'ligio *a* **essere ~ al dovere** have a sense of duty
'lilla *nf Bot* lilac ● *nm (colore)* lilac
'lima *nf* file
limacci'oso *a* slimy
li'mare *vt* file
'limbo *nm* limbo
li'metta *nf* nail-file
limi'ta|re *nm* threshold ● *vt* limit. **~rsi** *vr* **~rsi a fare qcsa** restrict oneself to doing sth; **~rsi in qcsa** cut down on sth. **~'tivo** *a* limiting. **~to** *a* limited. **~zi'one** *nf* limitation
'limite *nm* limit; *(confine)* boundary. **~ di velocità** speed limit

li'mitrofo *a* neighbouring
limo'nata *nf (bibita)* lemonade; *(succo)* lemon juice
li'mone *nm* lemon; *(albero)* lemon tree
'limpido *a* clear; *(occhi)* limpid
'lince *nf* lynx
linci'are *vt* lynch
'lindo *a* neat; *(pulito)* clean
'linea *nf* line; *(di autobus, aereo)* route; *(di metro)* line; *(di abito)* cut; *(di auto, mobile)* design; *(fisico)* figure; **in ~ d'aria** as the crow flies; **è caduta la ~** I've been cut off; **in ~ di massima** as a rule; **a grandi linee** in outline; **mantenere la ~** keep one's figure; **in prima ~** in the front line; **mettersi in ~** line up; **nave di ~** liner; **volo di ~** scheduled flight. **~ d'arrivo** finishing line. **~ continua** unbroken line
linea'menti *nmpl* features
line'are *a* linear; *(discorso)* to the point; *(ragionamento)* consistent
line'etta *nf (tratto lungo)* dash; *(d'unione)* hyphen
lin'gotto *nm* ingot
'lingu|a *nf* tongue; *(linguaggio)* language. **~'accia** *nf (persona)* backbiter. **~'aggio** *nm* language. **~'etta** *nf (di scarpa)* tongue; *(di strumento)* reed; *(di busta)* flap
lingu'ist|a *nmf* linguist. **~ica** *nf* linguistics *sg.* **~ico** *a* linguistic
'lino *nm Bot* flax; *(tessuto)* linen
li'noleum *nm* linoleum
liofiliz'za|re *vt* freeze-dry. **~to** *a* freeze-dried
liposuzi'one *nf* liposuction
lique'far|e *vt,* **~si** *vr* liquefy; *(sciogliersi)* melt
liqui'da|re *vt* liquidate; settle *(conto)*; pay off *(debiti)*; clear *(merce)*; *(fam: uccidere)* get rid of. **~zi'one** *nf* liquidation; *(di conti)* settling; *(di merce)* clearance sale
'liquido *a & nm* liquid
liqui'rizia *nf* liquorice
li'quore *nm* liqueur; **liquori** *pl (bevande alcooliche)* liquors
'lira *nf* lira; *Mus* lyre
'lirico, -a *a* lyrical; *(poesia)* lyric; *(cantante, musica)* opera *attrib* ● *nf* lyric poetry; *Mus* opera
'lisca *nf* fishbone; **avere la ~** *(fam: nel parlare)* have a lisp
lisci'are *vt* smooth; *(accarezzare)* stroke. **'liscio** *a* smooth; *(capelli)* straight; *(liquore)* neat; *(non gassato)* still; **passarla liscia** get away with it

'liso *a* worn [out]

'lista *nf* list; (*striscia*) strip. **~ di attesa** waiting list; **in ~ di attesa** *Aeron* stand-by. **~ elettorale** electoral register. **~ di nozze** wedding list. **li'stare** *vt* edge; *Comput* list

li'stino *nm* list. **~ prezzi** price list

Lit. *abbr* (**lire italiane**) Italian lire

'lite *nf* quarrel; (*baruffa*) row; *Jur* lawsuit

liti'gare *vi* quarrel. **li'tigio** *nm* quarrel. **litigi'oso** *a* quarrelsome

lito'rale *a* coastal ● *nm* coast

'litro *nm* litre

li'turgico *a* liturgical

li'vella *nf* level. **~ a bolla d'aria** spirit level

livel'lar|e *vt* level. **~si** *vr* level out

li'vello *nm* level; **passaggio a ~** level crossing; **sotto/sul ~ del mare** below/above sea level

'livido *a* livid; (*per il freddo*) blue; (*per una botta*) black and blue ● *nm* bruise

Li'vorno *nf* Leghorn

'lizza *nf* lists *pl*; **essere in ~ per qcsa** be in the running for sth

lo *def art m* (*before s + consonant, gn, ps, z*) the; *vedi* **il** ● *pron* (*riferito a persona*) him; (*riferito a cosa*) it; **non lo so** I don't know

'lobo *nm* lobe

lo'cal|e *a* local ● *nm* (*stanza*) room; (*treno*) local train; **~i** *pl* (*edifici*) premises. **~e notturno** night-club. **~ità** *nf inv* locality

localiz'zare *vt* localize; (*trovare*) locate

lo'cand|a *nf* inn

locan'dina *nf* bill, poster

loca|'tario, -a *nmf* tenant. **~'tore, ~'trice** *nm* landlord ● *nf* landlady. **~zi'one** *nf* tenancy

locomo|'tiva *nf* locomotive. **~zi'one** *nf* locomotion; **mezzi di ~zione** means of transport

'loculo *nm* burial niche

lo'custa *nf* locust

locuzi'one *nf* expression

lo'dare *vt* praise. **'lode** *nf* praise; **laurea con lode** first-class degree

'loden *nm inv* (*cappotto*) loden coat

lo'devole *a* praiseworthy

'lodola *nf* lark

'loggia *nf* loggia; (*massonica*) lodge

loggi'one *nm* gallery, the gods

'logica *nf* logic

logica'mente *adv* (*in modo logico*) logically; (*ovviamente*) of course

'logico *a* logical

lo'gistica *nf* logistics *sg*

logo'rante *a* (*esperienza*) wearing

logo'ra|re *vt* wear out; (*sciupare*) waste. **~rsi** *vr* wear out; (*persona:*) wear oneself out. **logo'rio** *nm* wear and tear. **'logoro** *a* worn-out

lom'baggine *nf* lumbago

Lombar'dia *nf* Lombardy

lom'bata *nf* loin. **'lombo** *nm* *Anat* loin

lom'brico *nm* earthworm

'Londra *nf* London

lon'gevo *a* long-lived

longi'lineo *a* tall and slim

longi'tudine *nf* longitude

lontana'mente *adv* distantly; (*vagamente*) vaguely; **neanche ~** not for a moment

lonta'nanza *nf* distance; (*separazione*) separation; **in ~** in the distance

lon'tano *a* far; (*distante*) distant; (*nel tempo*) far-off, distant; (*parente*) distant; (*vago*) vague; (*assente*) absent; **più ~** further ● *adv* far [away]; **da ~** from a distance; **tenersi ~ da** keep away from

'lontra *nf* otter

lo'quace *a* talkative

'lordo *a* dirty; (*somma, peso*) gross

'loro[1] *pron pl* (*soggetto*) they; (*oggetto*) them; (*forma di cortesia*) you; **sta a ~** it is up to them

'loro[2] (**il ~** *m*, **la ~** *f*, **i ~** *mpl*, **le ~** *fpl*) *a* their; (*forma di cortesia*) your; **un ~ amico** a friend of theirs; (*forma di cortesia*) a friend of yours ● *pron* theirs; (*forma di cortesia*) yours; **i ~** their folk

lo'sanga *nf* lozenge; **a losanghe** diamond-shaped

'losco *a* suspicious

'loto *nm* lotus

'lott|a *nf* fight, struggle; (*contrasto*) conflict; *Sport* wrestling. **lot'tare** *vi* fight, struggle; *Sport*, *fig* wrestle. **~a'tore** *nm* wrestler

lotte'ria *nf* lottery

'lotto *nm* [national] lottery; (*porzione*) lot; (*di terreno*) plot

lozi'one *nf* lotion

lubrifi'ca|nte *a* lubricating ● *nm* lubricant. **~re** *vt* lubricate

luc'chetto *nm* padlock

lucci'ca|nte *a* sparkling. **~re** *vi* sparkle. **lucci'chio** *nm* sparkle

'luccio *nm* pike

'lucciola *nf* glow-worm

'luce *nf* light; **far ~ su** shed light on; **dare alla ~** give birth to. **~ della luna** moonlight. **luci** *pl* **di posizione** sidelights. **~ del sole** sunlight

lu'cen|te *a* shining. **~'tezza** *nf* shine

lucer'nario *nm* skylight

lu'certola *nf* lizard

lucida'labbra *nm inv* lip gloss

luci'da|re *vt* polish. **~'trice** *nf* [floor-]polisher. **'lucido** *a* shiny; ⟨*pavimento, scarpe*⟩ polished; ⟨*chiaro*⟩ clear; ⟨*persona, mente*⟩ lucid; ⟨*occhi*⟩ watery ● *nm* shine. **lucido [da scarpe]** [shoe] polish

lucra'tivo *a* lucrative. **'lucro** *nm* lucre

'luglio *nm* July

'lugubre *a* gloomy

'lui *pron* ⟨*soggetto*⟩ he; ⟨*oggetto, con prep*⟩ him; **lo ha fatto ~ stesso** he did it himself

lu'maca *nf* ⟨*mollusco*⟩ slug; *fig* slowcoach

'lume *nm* lamp; ⟨*luce*⟩ light; **a ~ di candela** by candlelight

luminosità *nf* brightness. **lumi'noso** *a* luminous; ⟨*stanza, cielo ecc*⟩ bright

'luna *nf* moon; **chiaro di ~** moonlight; **avere la ~ storta** be in a bad mood. **~ di miele** honeymoon

luna park *nm inv* fairground

lu'nare *a* lunar

lu'nario *nm* almanac; **sbarcare il ~** make both ends meet

lu'natico *a* moody

lunedì *nm inv* Monday

lu'netta *nf* half-moon [shape]

lun'gaggine *nf* slowness

lun'ghezza *nf* length. **~ d'onda** wavelength

'lungi *adv* ero [ben] **~ dall'immaginare che...** I never dreamt for a moment that...

lungimi'rante *a* far-seeing

'lungo *a* long; ⟨*diluito*⟩ weak; ⟨*lento*⟩ slow; **saperla lunga** be shrewd ● *nm* length; **di gran lunga** by far; **andare per le lunghe** drag on ● *prep* ⟨*durante*⟩ throughout; ⟨*per la lunghezza di*⟩ along

lungofi'ume *nm* riverside

lungo'lago *nm* lakeside

lungo'mare *nm* sea front

lungome'traggio *nm* feature film

lu'notto *nm* rear window

lu'ogo *nm* place; ⟨*punto preciso*⟩ spot; ⟨*passo d'autore*⟩ passage; **aver ~** take place; **dar ~ a** give rise to; **del ~** ⟨*usanze*⟩ local. **~ comune** platitude. **~ pubblico** public place

luogote'nente *nm* Mil lieutenant

lu'petto *nm* Cub [Scout]

'lupo *nm* wolf

'luppolo *nm* hop

'lurido *a* filthy. **luri'dume** *nm* filth

lu'singa *nf* flattery

lusin'g|are *vt* flatter. **~arsi** *vr* flatter oneself; ⟨*illudersi*⟩ fool oneself. **~hi'ero** *a* flattering

lus'sa|re *vt*, **~rsi** *vr* dislocate. **~zi'one** *nf* dislocation

Lussem'burgo *nm* Luxembourg

'lusso *nm* luxury; **di ~** luxury *attrib*

lussu'oso *a* luxurious

lussureggi'ante *a* luxuriant

lus'suria *nf* lust

lu'strare *vt* polish

lu'strino *nm* sequin

'lustro *a* shiny ● *nm* sheen; *fig* prestige; ⟨*quinquennio*⟩ five-year period

'lutt|o *nm* mourning; **~o stretto** deep mourning. **~u'oso** *a* mournful

Mm

m *abbr* (**metro**) m

ma *conj* but; ⟨*eppure*⟩ yet; **ma!** ⟨*dubbio*⟩ I don't know; ⟨*indignazione*⟩ really!; **ma davvero?** really?; ⟨*certo che sì*⟩ of course!

'macabro *a* macabre

macché *int* of course not!

macche'roni *nmpl* macaroni *sg*

macche'ronico *a* ⟨*italiano*⟩ broken

'macchia[1] *nf* stain; ⟨*di diverso colore*⟩ spot; ⟨*piccola*⟩ speck; **senza ~** spotless

'macchia[2] *nf* ⟨*boscaglia*⟩ scrub; **darsi alla ~** take to the woods

macchi'a|re *vt*, **~rsi** *vr* stain. **~to a** ⟨*caffè*⟩ with a dash of milk; **~to di** ⟨*sporco*⟩ stained with

'macchina *nf* machine; ⟨*motore*⟩ engine; ⟨*automobile*⟩ car. **~ da cucire** sewing machine. **~ da presa** cine camera, movie camera. **~ da scrivere** typewriter

macchinal'mente *adv* mechanically

macchi'nare *vt* plot

macchi'nario *nm* machinery

macchi'netta *nf* (*per i denti*) brace

macchi'nista *nm* Rail engine-driver; *Naut* engineer; *Theat* stagehand

macchi'noso *a* complicated

Mace'donia *nf* Macedonia

mace'donia *nf* fruit salad

macel'la|io *nm* butcher. **~re** *vt* slaughter. **macelle'ria** *nf* butcher's [shop]. **ma'cello** *nm* slaughterhouse; *fig* shambles *sg*; **andare al macello** *fig* go to the slaughter; **mandare al macello** *fig* send to his/her death

mace'rar|e *vt* macerate; *fig* distress. **~si** *vr* be consumed

ma'cerie *nfpl* rubble *sg*; (*rottami*) debris *sg*

ma'cigno *nm* boulder

'macina *nf* millstone

macinacaffè *nm inv* coffee mill

macina'pepe *nm inv* pepper mill

maci'na|re *vt* mill. **~to** *a* ground ● *nm* (*carne*) mince. **maci'nino** *nm* mill; (*hum: macchina*) old banger

maciul'lare *vt* (*stritolare*) crush

macrobiotic|a *nf* **negozio di ~a** health-food shop. **~o** *a* macrobiotic

macro'scopico *a* macroscopic

macu'lato *a* spotted

'madido *a* **~ di** moist with

Ma'donna *nf* Our Lady

mador'nale *a* gross

'madre *nf* mother. **~'lingua** *a inv* inglese **~'lingua** English native speaker. **~'patria** *nf* native land. **~'perla** *nf* mother-of-pearl

ma'drina *nf* godmother

maestà *nf* majesty

maestosità *nf* majesty. **mae'stoso** *a* majestic

mae'strale *nm* northwest wind

mae'stranza *nf* workers *pl*

mae'stria *nf* mastery

ma'estro, -a *nmf* teacher ● *nm* master; *Mus* maestro. **~ di cerimonie** master of ceremonies ● *a* (*principale*) chief; (*di grande abilità*) skilful

'mafi|a *nf* Mafia. **~'oso** *a* of the Mafia ● *nm* member of the Mafia, Mafioso

'maga *nf* sorceress

ma'gagna *nf* fault

ma'gari *adv* (*forse*) maybe ● *int* I wish! ● *conj* (*per esprimere desiderio*) if only; (*anche se*) even if

magazzini'ere *nm* storesman, warehouseman. **magaz'zino** *nm* warehouse; (*emporio*) shop; **grande magazzino** department store

'maggio *nm* May

maggio'lino *nm* May bug

maggio'rana *nf* marjoram

maggio'ranza *nf* majority

maggio'rare *vt* increase

maggior'domo *nm* butler

maggi'ore *a* (*di dimensioni, numero*) bigger, larger; (*superlativo*) biggest, largest; (*di età*) older; (*superlativo*) oldest; (*di importanza, Mus*) major; (*superlativo*) greatest; **la maggior parte di** most; **la maggior parte del tempo** most of the time ● *pron* (*di dimensioni*) the bigger, the larger; (*superlativo*) the biggest, the largest; (*di età*) the older; (*superlativo*) the oldest; (*di importanza*) the major; (*superlativo*) the greatest ● *nm* Mil major; Aeron squadron leader. **maggio'renne** *a* of age ● *nmf* adult

maggior|i'tario *a* (*sistema*) first-past-the-post *attrib*. **~'mente** *adv* [all] the more; (*più di tutto*) most

'Magi *nmpl* **i re ~** the Magi

ma'gia *nf* magic; (*trucco*) magic trick **magica'mente** *adv* magically. **'magico** *a* magic

magi'stero *nm* (*insegnamento*) teaching; (*maestria*) skill; **facoltà di ~** arts faculty

magi'strale *a* masterly; **istituto ~e** teachers' training college

magi'stra|to *nm* magistrate. **~'tura** *nf* magistrature. **la ~tura** the Bench

'magli|a *nf* stitch; (*lavoro ai ferri*) knitting; (*tessuto*) jersey; (*di rete*) mesh; (*di catena*) link; (*indumento*) vest; **fare la ~a** knit. **~a diritta** knit. **~a rosa** (*ciclismo*) ≈ yellow jersey. **~a rovescia** purl. **~e'ria** *nf* knitwear. **~'etta** *nf* **~etta** [**a maniche corte**] tee-shirt. **~'ficio** *nm* knitwear factory. **ma'glina** *nf* (*tessuto*) jersey

magli'one *nm* sweater

'magma *nm* magma

ma'gnanimo *a* magnanimous

ma'gnate *nm* magnate

ma'gnesi|a *nf* magnesia. **~o** *nm* magnesium

ma'gne|te *nm* magnet. **~tico** *a* magnetic. **~tismo** *nm* magnetism

magne'tofono *nm* tape recorder

magnifi|ca'mente *adv* magnificently. **~'cenza** *nf* magnificence;

magnolia | malloppo

(*generosità*) munificence. **ma'gnifico** *a* magnificent; (*generoso*) munificent

ma'gnolia *nf* magnolia

'mago *nm* magician

ma'gone *nm* **avere il ~** be down; **mi è venuto il ~** I've got a lump in my throat

'magr|a *nf* low water. **ma'grezza** *nf* thinness. **~o** *a* thin; ⟨*carne*⟩ lean; (*scarso*) meagre

'mai *adv* never; (*inter, talvolta*) ever; **caso ~** if anything; **caso ~ tornasse** in case he comes back; **come ~?** why?; **cosa ~?** what on earth?; **~ più** never again; **più che ~** more than ever; **quando ~?** whenever?; **quasi ~** hardly ever

mai'ale *nm* pig; (*carne*) pork

mai'olica *nf* majolica

maio'nese *nf* mayonnaise

'mais *nm* maize

mai'uscol|a *nf* capital [letter]. **~o** *a* capital

mal *vedi* **male**

'mala *nf* **la ~** *sl* the underworld

mala'fede *nf* bad faith

malaf'fare *nm* **gente di ~** shady characters *pl*

mala'lingua *nf* backbiter

mala'mente *adv* ⟨*ridotto*⟩ badly

malan'dato *a* in bad shape; (*di salute*) in poor health

ma'lanimo *nm* ill will

ma'lanno *nm* misfortune; (*malattia*) illness; **prendersi un ~** catch something

mala'pena: a ~ *adv* hardly

ma'laria *nf* malaria

mala'ticcio *a* sickly

ma'lato, -a *a* ill, sick; ⟨*pianta*⟩ diseased ● *nmf* sick person. **~ di mente** mentally ill person. **malat'tia** *nf* disease, illness; **ho preso due giorni di malattia** I had two days off sick. **malattia venerea** venereal disease

malaugu'rato *a* ill-omened. **malau'gurio** *nm* bad *o* ill omen

mala'vita *nf* underworld

mala'voglia *nf* unwillingness; **di ~** unwillingly

malcapi'tato *a* wretched

malce'lato *a* ill-concealed

mal'concio *a* battered

malcon'tento *nm* discontent

malco'stume *nm* immorality

mal'destro *a* awkward; (*inesperto*) inexperienced

maldi'cen|te *a* slanderous. **~za** *nf* slander

maldi'sposto *a* ill-disposed

'male *adv* badly; **funzionare ~** not work properly; **star ~** be ill; **star ~ a qcno** ⟨*vestito ecc:*⟩ not suit sb; **rimanerci ~** be hurt; **non c'è ~!** not bad at all! ● *nm* evil; (*dolore*) pain; (*malattia*) illness; (*danno*) harm. **distinguere il bene dal ~** know right from wrong; **andare a ~** go off; **aver ~ a** have a pain in; **dove hai ~?** where does it hurt?; **far ~ a qcno** (*provocare dolore*) hurt sb; ⟨*cibo:*⟩ be bad for sb; **le cipolle mi fanno ~** onions don't agree with me; **mi fa ~ la schiena** my back is hurting; **mal d'auto** car-sickness. **mal di denti** toothache. **mal di gola** sore throat. **mal di mare** sea-sickness; **avere il mal di mare** be sea-sick. **mal di pancia** stomach ache. **mal di testa** headache

male'detto *a* cursed; (*orribile*) awful

male'di|re *vt* curse. **~zi'one** *nf* curse; **~zione!** damn!

maledu|cata'mente *adv* rudely. **~'cato** *a* ill-mannered. **~cazi'one** *nf* rudeness

male'fatta *nf* misdeed

male'ficio *nm* witchcraft. **ma'lefico** *a* ⟨*azione*⟩ evil; (*nocivo*) harmful

maleodo'rante *a* foul-smelling

ma'lessere *nm* indisposition; *fig* uneasiness

ma'levolo *a* malevolent

malfa'mato *a* of ill repute

mal'fat|to *a* badly done; (*malformato*) ill-shaped. **~'tore** *nm* wrongdoer

mal'fermo *a* unsteady; ⟨*salute*⟩ poor

malfor'ma|to *a* misshapen. **~zi'one** *nf* malformation

malgo'verno *nm* misgovernment

mal'grado *prep* in spite of ● *conj* although

ma'lia *nf* spell

mali'gn|are *vi* malign. **~ità** *nf* malice; *Med* malignancy. **ma'ligno** *a* malicious; (*perfido*) evil; *Med* malignant

malinco'ni|a *nf* melancholy. **~ca'mente** *adv* melancholically. **malin'conico** *a* melancholy

malincu'ore: a ~ *adv* unwillingly, reluctantly

malinfor'mato *a* misinformed

malintenzio'nato, -a *nmf* miscreant

malin'teso *a* mistaken ● *nm* misunderstanding

ma'lizi|a *nf* malice; (*astuzia*) cunning; (*espediente*) trick. **~'oso** *a* malicious; (*birichino*) mischievous

malle'abile *a* malleable

mal'loppo *nm fam* loot

malme'nare *vt* ill-treat

mal'messo *a* (*vestito male*) shabbily dressed; (*casa*) poorly furnished; (*fig: senza soldi*) hard up

malnu'tri|to *a* undernourished. **~zi'one** *nf* malnutrition

'malo *a* **in ~ modo** badly

ma'locchio *nm* evil eye

ma'lora *nf* ruin; **della ~** awful; **andare in ~** go to ruin

ma'lore *nm* illness; **essere colto da ~** be suddenly taken ill

malri'dotto *a* (*persona*) in a sorry state

mal'sano *a* unhealthy

'malta *nf* mortar

mal'tempo *nm* bad weather

'malto *nm* malt

maltrat|ta'mento *nm* ill-treatment. **~'tare** *vt* ill-treat

malu'more *nm* bad mood; **di ~** in a bad mood

mal'vagi|o *a* wicked. **~tà** *nf* wickedness

malversazi'one *nf* embezzlement

mal'visto *a* unpopular (**da** with)

malvi'vente *nm* criminal

malvolenti'eri *adv* unwillingly

malvo'lere *vt* **farsi ~** make oneself unpopular

'mamma *nf* mummy, mum; **~ mia!** good gracious!

mam'mella *nf* breast

mam'mifero *nm* mammal

'mammola *nf* violet

ma'nata *nf* handful; (*colpo*) slap

'manca *nf* vedi **manco**

manca'mento *nm* **avere un ~** faint

man'can|te *a* missing. **~za** *nf* lack; (*assenza*) absence; (*insufficienza*) shortage; (*fallo*) fault; (*imperfezione*) defect; **in ~za d'altro** failing all else; **sento la sua ~za** I miss him

man'care *vi* be lacking; (*essere assente*) be missing; (*venir meno*) fail; (*morire*) pass away; **~ di** be lacking in; **~ a** fail to keep (*promessa*); **mi manca casa** I miss home; **mi manchi** I miss you; **mi è mancato il tempo** I didn't have [the] time; **mi mancano 1000 lire** I'm 1,000 lire short; **quanto manca alla partenza?** how long before we leave?; **è mancata la corrente** there was a power failure; **sentirsi ~ le forze** feel faint; **sentirsi ~ il respiro** be unable to breathe [properly] ● *vt* miss (*bersaglio*); **è mancato poco che cadesse** he nearly fell

'manche *nf inv* heat

man'chevole *a* defective

'mancia *nf* tip

manci'ata *nf* handful

man'cino *a* left-handed

'manco, -a *a* left ● *nf* left hand ● *adv* (*nemmeno*) not even

man'dante *nmf* (*di delitto*) instigator

manda'rancio *nm* clementine

man'dare *vt* send; (*emettere*) give off; utter (*suono*); **~ a chiamare** send for; **~ avanti la casa** run the house; **~ giù** (*ingoiare*) swallow

manda'rino *nm* Bot mandarin

man'data *nf* consignment; (*di serratura*) turn; **chiudere a doppia ~** double lock

man'dato *nm* (*incarico*) mandate; *Jur* warrant; (*di pagamento*) money order. **~ di comparizione [in giudizio]** subpoena. **~ di perquisizione** search warrant

man'dibola *nf* jaw

mando'lino *nm* mandolin

'mandor|la *nf* almond; **a ~la** (*occhi*) almond-shaped. **~'lato** *nm* nut brittle (*type of nougat*). **~lo** *nm* almond[-tree]

'mandria *nf* herd

maneg'gevole *a* easy to handle. **maneggi'are** *vt* handle

ma'neggio *nm* handling; (*intrigo*) plot; (*scuola di equitazione*) riding school

ma'nesco *a* quick to hit out

ma'netta *nf* hand lever; **manette** *pl* handcuffs

man'forte *nm* **dare ~ a qcno** support sb

manga'nello *nm* truncheon

manga'nese *nm* manganese

mange'reccio *a* edible

mangia'dischi® *nm inv* type of portable record player

mangia'fumo *a inv* **candela** *nf* **~** air-purifying candle

mangia'nastri *nm inv* cassette player

mangi'a|re *vt/i* eat; (*consumare*) eat up; (*corrodere*) eat away; take (*scacchi, carte ecc*) ● *nm* eating; (*cibo*) food; (*pasto*) meal. **~rsi** *vr* **~rsi le parole** mumble; **~rsi le unghie** bite one's nails

mangi'ata *nf* big meal; **farsi una bella ~ di…** feast on…

mangia'toia *nf* manger

man'gime *nm* fodder

mangi'one, -a *nmf fam* glutton

mangiucchi'are *vt* nibble

'mango *nm* mango

ma'nia *nf* mania. **~ di grandezza** delu-

sions of grandeur. **~co, -a** *a* maniacal
● *nmf* maniac

'manica *nf* sleeve; (*fam: gruppo*) band;
a maniche lunghe long-sleeved; **essere in maniche di camicia** be in shirt
sleeves; **essere di ~ larga** be free with
one's money. **~ a vento** wind sock

'Manica *nf* **la ~** the [English] Channel

manica'retto *nm* tasty dish

mani'chetta *nf* hose

mani'chino *nm* (*da sarto, vetrina*)
dummy

'manico *nm* handle; *Mus* neck

mani'comio *nm* mental home; (*fam:
confusione*) tip

mani'cotto *nm* muff; *Mech* sleeve

mani'cure *nf* manicure ● *nmf inv* (*persona*) manicurist

mani'e|ra *nf* manner; **in ~ra che** so
that. **~'rato** *a* affected; (*stile*) mannered. **~'rismo** *nm* mannerism

manifat'tura *nf* manufacture;
(*fabbrica*) factory

manife'stante *nmf* demonstrator

manife'sta|re *vt* show; (*esprimere*) ex-
press ● *vi* demonstrate. **~rsi** *vr* show
oneself. **~zi'one** *nf* show; (*espressione*)
expression; (*sintomo*) manifestation;
(*dimostrazione pubblica*) demonstration

mani'festo *a* evident ● *nm* poster;
(*dichiarazione pubblica*) manifesto

ma'niglia *nf* handle; (*sostegno, in autobus ecc*) strap

manipo'la|re *vt* handle; (*massaggiare*)
massage; (*alterare*) adulterate; *fig* manipulate. **~'tore, ~'trice** *nmf* manipu-
lator. **~zi'one** *nf* handling; (*massaggio*)
massage; (*alterazione*) adulteration; *fig*
manipulation

mani'scalco *nm* smith

man'naia *nf* (*scure*) axe; (*da macelleria*)
cleaver

man'naro *a* **lupo** *nm* **~** werewolf

'mano *nf* hand; (*strato di vernice ecc*)
coat; **alla ~** informal; **fuori ~** out of the
way; **man ~** little by little; **man ~ che**
as; **sotto ~** to hand

mano'dopera *nf* labour

ma'nometro *nm* gauge

mano'mettere *vt* tamper with; (*viola-
re*) violate

ma'nopola *nf* (*di apparecchio*) knob;
(*guanto*) mitten; (*su pullman*) handle

mano'scritto *a* handwritten ● *nm*
manuscript

mano'vale *nm* labourer

mano'vella *nf* handle; *Techn* crank

ma'no|vra *nf* manoeuvre; *Rail* shunt-
ing; **fare le ~vre** manoeuvre. **~'vra-
bile** *a fig* easy to manipulate. **~'vrare** *vt*
(*azionare*) operate; *fig* manipulate
(*persona*) ● *vi* manoeuvre

manro'vescio *nm* slap

man'sarda *nf* attic

mansi'one *nf* task; (*dovere*) duty

mansu'eto *a* meek; (*animale*) do-cile

man'tell|a *nf* cape. **~o** *nm* cloak; (*so-
prabito, di animale*) coat; (*di neve*)
mantle

mante'ner|e *vt* (*conservare*) keep; (*in
buono stato, sostentare*) maintain. **~si**
vr **~si in forma** keep fit. **manteni-
'mento** *nm* maintenance

'mantice *nm* bellows *pl*; (*di automobile*) hood

'manto *nm* cloak; (*coltre*) mantle

manto'vana *nf* pelmet

manu'al|e *a & nm* manual. **~e d'uso**
user manual. **~'mente** *adv* manually

ma'nubrio *nm* handle; (*di bicicletta*)
handlebars *pl*; (*per ginnastica*) dumb-
bell

manu'fatto *a* manufactured

manutenzi'one *nf* maintenance

'manzo *nm* steer; (*carne*) beef

'mappa *nf* map

mappa'mondo *nm* globe

mar *vedi* **mare**

ma'rasma *nm fig* decline

mara'to|na *nf* marathon. **~'neta** *nmf*
marathon runner

'marca *nf* mark; *Comm* brand; (*fabbricazione*) make; (*scontrino*) ticket. **~
da bollo** revenue stamp

mar'ca|re *vt* mark; *Sport* score. **~ta-
'mente** *adv* markedly. **~to** *a* (*tratto,
accento*) strong, marked. **~'tore** *nm* (*nel
calcio*) scorer

mar'chese, -a *nm* marquis ● *nf* mar-
chioness

marchi'are *vt* brand

'marchio *nm* brand; (*caratteristica*)
mark. **~ di fabbrica** trademark. **~
registrato** registered trademark

'marcia *nf* march; *Auto* gear; *Sport*
walk; **mettere in ~** put into gear;
mettersi in ~ start off. **~ funebre** funeral march. **~ indietro** reverse gear;
fare ~ indietro reverse; *fig* back-pedal.
~ nuziale wedding march

marciapi'ede *nm* pavement; (*di stazione*) platform

marci'a|re *vi* march; (*funzionare*) go,
work. **~'tore, ~'trice** *nmf* walker

'marcio *a* rotten ● *nm* rotten part; *fig*
corruption. **mar'cire** *vi* go bad, rot

'**marco** *nm* (*moneta*) mark

'**mare** *nm* sea; (*luogo di mare*) seaside; **sul ~** (*casa*) at the seaside; (*città*) on the sea; **in alto ~** on the high seas; **essere in alto ~** *fig* not know which way to turn. **~ Adriatico** Adriatic Sea. **mar Ionio** Ionian Sea. **mar Mediterraneo** Mediterranean. **mar Tirreno** Tyrrhenian Sea

ma'rea *nf* tide; (**una ~ di** hundreds of; **alta/bassa ~** high/low tide

mareggi'ata *nf* [sea] storm

mare'moto *nm* tidal wave, seaquake

maresci'allo *nm* (*ufficiale*) marshal; (*sottufficiale*) warrant-officer

marga'rina *nf* margarine

marghe'rita *nf* marguerite. **margheri'tina** *nf* daisy

margi'nal|e *a* marginal. **~'mente** *adv* marginally

'**margine** *nm* margin; (*orlo*) brink; (*bordo*) border. **~ di errore** margin of error. **~ di sicurezza** safety margin

ma'rina *nf* navy; (*costa*) seashore; (*quadro*) seascape. **~ mercantile** merchant navy. **~ militare** navy

mari'naio *nm* sailor

mari'na|re *vt* marinate; **~re la scuola** play truant. **~ta** *nf* marinade. **~to** *a* *Culin* marinated

ma'rino *a* sea *attrib*, marine

mario'netta *nf* puppet

ma'rito *nm* husband

ma'rittimo *a* maritime

mar'maglia *nf* rabble

marmel'lata *nf* jam; (*di agrumi*) marmalade

mar'mitta *nf* pot; *Auto* silencer. **~ catalitica** catalytic converter

'**marmo** *nm* marble

mar'mocchio *nm* *fam* brat

mar'mor|eo *a* marble. **~iz'zato** *a* marbled

mar'motta *nf* marmot

Ma'rocco *nm* Morocco

ma'roso *nm* breaker

mar'rone *a* brown ● *nm* brown; (*castagna*) chestnut; **marroni** *pl* **canditi** marrons glacés

mar'sina *nf* tails *pl*

mar'supio *nm* (*borsa*) bumbag

martedì *nm inv* Tuesday. **~ grasso** Shrove Tuesday

martel'lante *a* (*mal di testa*) pounding

martel'la|re *vt* hammer ● *vi* throb. **~ta** *nf* hammer blow

martel'letto *nm* (*di giudice*) gavel

mar'tello *nm* hammer; (*di battente*) knocker. **~ pneumatico** pneumatic drill

marti'netto *nm* *Mech* jack

'**martire** *nmf* martyr. **mar'tirio** *nm* martyrdom

'**martora** *nf* marten

martori'are *vt* torment

mar'xis|mo *nm* Marxism. **~ta** *a* & *nmf* Marxist

marza'pane *nm* marzipan

marzi'ale *a* martial

marzi'ano, -a *nmf* Martian

'**marzo** *nm* March

mascal'zone *nm* rascal

ma'scara *nm inv* mascara

mascar'pone *nm* *full-fat cream cheese often used for desserts*

ma'scella *nf* jaw

'**mascher|a** *nf* mask; (*costume*) fancy dress; *Cinema*, *Theat* usher *m*, usherette *f*; (*nella commedia dell'arte*) stock character. **~a antigas** gas mask. **~a di bellezza** face pack. **~a ad ossigeno** oxygen mask. **~a'mento** *nm* masking; *Mil* camouflage. **masche'rare** *vt* mask; *fig* camouflage. **~arsi** *vr* put on a mask; **~arsi da** dress up as. **~ata** *nf* masquerade

maschi'accio *nm* (*ragazza*) tomboy

ma'schi|le *a* masculine; (*sesso*) male ● *nm* masculine [gender]. **~'lista** *a* sexist. '**maschio** *a* male; (*virile*) manly ● *nm* male; (*figlio*) son. **masco'lino** *a* masculine

ma'scotte *nf inv* mascot

maso'chis|mo *nm* masochism. **~ta** *a* & *nmf* masochist

'**massa** *nf* mass; *Electr* earth, ground *Am*; **communicazioni di ~** mass media

massa'cra|nte *a* gruelling. **~re** *vt* massacre. **mas'sacro** *nm* massacre; *fig* mess

massaggi'a|re *vt* massage. **mas'saggio** *nm* massage. **~'tore**, **~'trice** *nm* masseur ● *nf* masseuse

mas'saia *nf* housewife

masse'rizie *nfpl* household effects

mas'siccio *a* massive; (*oro ecc*) solid; (*corporatura*) heavy ● *nm* massif

'**massim|a** *nf* maxim; (*temperatura*) maximum. **~o** *a* greatest; (*quantità*) maximum, greatest ● *nm* **il ~o** the maximum; **al ~o** at [the] most, as a maximum

'**masso** *nm* rock

mas'sone *nm* [Free]mason. **~'ria** Freemasonry

ma'stello *nm wooden box for the grape or olive harvest*

masti'care *vt* chew; (*borbottare*) mumble

'**mastice** *nm* mastic; (*per vetri*) putty

ma'stino *nm* mastiff

masto'dontico *a* gigantic

'**mastro** *nm* master; **libro ~** ledger

mastur'ba|rsi *vr* masturbate. **~zi'one** *nf* masturbation

ma'tassa *nf* skein

mate'matic|a *nf* mathematics, maths. **~o, -a** *a* mathematical ● *nmf* mathematician

materas'sino *nm* **~ gonfiabile** air bed

mate'rasso *nm* mattress. **~ a molle** spring mattress

ma'teria *nf* matter; (*materiale*) material; (*di studio*) subject. **~ prima** raw material

materi'a|le *a* material; (*grossolano*) coarse ● *nm* material. **~'lismo** *nm* materialism. **~'lista** *a* materialistic ● *nmf* materialist. **~liz'zarsi** *vr* materialize. **~l'mente** *adv* physically

maternità *nf* motherhood; **ospedale di ~** maternity hospital

ma'terno *a* maternal; **lingua materna** mother tongue

ma'tita *nf* pencil

ma'trice *nf* matrix; (*origini*) roots *pl*; *Comm* counterfoil

ma'tricola *nf* (*registro*) register; *Univ* fresher

ma'trigna *nf* stepmother

matrimoni'ale *a* matrimonial; **vita ~** married life. **matri'monio** *nm* marriage; (*cerimonia*) wedding

ma'trona *nf* matron

'**matta** *nf* (*nelle carte*) joker

mattacchi'one, -a *nmf* rascal

matta'toio *nm* slaughterhouse

matte'rello *nm* rolling-pin

mat'ti|na *nf* morning; **la ~na** in the morning. **~'nata** *nf* morning; *Theat* matinée. **~nie'ro a essere ~niero** be an early riser. **~no** *nm* morning

'**matto, -a** *a* mad, crazy; *Med* insane; (*falso*) false; (*opaco*) matt; **~ da legare** barking mad; **avere una voglia matta di** be dying for ● *nmf* madman; madwoman

mat'tone *nm* brick; (*libro*) bore

matto'nella *nf* tile

mattu'tino *a* morning *attrib*

matu'rare *vt* ripen. **maturità** *nf* maturity; *Sch* school-leaving certificate. **ma'turo** *a* mature; (*frutto*) ripe

ma'tusa *nm* old fogey

mauso'leo *nm* mausoleum

maxi+ *pref* maxi+

'**mazza** *nf* club; (*martello*) hammer; (*da baseball, cricket*) bat. **~ da golf** golf-club. **maz'zata** *nf* blow

maz'zetta *nf* (*di banconote*) bundle

'**mazzo** *nm* bunch; (*carte da gioco*) pack

me *pers pron* me; **me lo ha dato** he gave it to me; **fai come me** do as I do; **è più veloce di me** he is faster than me *o* faster than I am

me'andro *nm* meander

M.E.C. *nm abbr* (**Mercato Comune Europeo**) EEC

mec'canica *nf* mechanics *sg*

meccanica'mente *adv* mechanically

mec'canico *a* mechanical ● *nm* mechanic. **mecca'nismo** *nm* mechanism

mèche *nfpl* [*farsi*] **fare le ~** have one's hair streaked

me'dagli|a *nf* medal. **~'one** *nm* medallion; (*gioiello*) locket

me'desimo *a* same

'**medi|a** *nf* average; *Sch* average mark; *Math* mean; **essere nella ~a** be in the mid-range. **~'ano** *a* middle ● *nm* (*calcio*) half-back

medi'ante *prep* by

medi'a|re *vt* act as intermediary in. **~'tore, ~'trice** *nmf* mediator; *Comm* middleman. **~zi'one** *nf* mediation

medica'mento *nm* medicine

medi'ca|re *vt* treat; dress (*ferita*). **~zi'one** *nf* medication; (*di ferita*) dressing

medi'c|ina *nf* medicine. **~ina legale** forensic medicine. **~i'nale** *a* medicinal ● *nm* medicine

'**medico** *a* medical ● *nm* doctor. **~ generico** general practitioner. **~ legale** forensic scientist. **~ di turno** duty doctor

medie'vale *a* medieval

'**medio** *a* average; (*punto*) middle; (*statura*) medium ● *nm* (*dito*) middle finger

medi'ocre *a* mediocre; (*scadente*) poor

medio'evo *nm* Middle Ages *pl*

medi'ta|re *vt* meditate; (*progettare*) plan; (*considerare attentamente*) think over ● *vi* meditate. **~zi'one** *nf* meditation

mediter'raneo *a* Mediterranean; **il [mar] M~** the Mediterranean [Sea]

me'dusa *nf* jellyfish

me'gafono *nm* megaphone

megaga'lattico *a fam* gigantic

mega'lomane *nmf* megalomaniac

me'gera *nf* hag

'meglio *adv* better; **tanto ~, ~ così** so much the better ● *a* better; *(superlativo)* best ● *nmf* best ● *nf* **avere la ~ su** have the better of; **fare qcsa alla [bell'e] ~** do sth as best one can ● *nm* **fare del proprio ~** do one's best; **fare qcsa il ~ possibile** make an excellent job of sth; **al ~** to the best of one's ability; **per il ~** for the best

'mela *nf* apple. **~ cotogna** quince

mela'grana *nf* pomegranate

mela'nina *nf* melanin

melan'zana *nf* aubergine, eggplant *Am*

me'lassa *nf* molasses *sg*

me'lenso *a* ⟨*persona, film*⟩ dull

mel'lifluo *a* ⟨*parole*⟩ honeyed; ⟨*voce*⟩ sugary

'melma *nf* slime. **mel'moso** *a* slimy

melo *nm* apple[-tree]

melo'di|a *nf* melody. **me'lodico** *a* melodic. **~'oso** *a* melodious

melo'dram|ma *nm* melodrama. **~'matico** *a* melodramatic

melo'grano *nm* pomegranate tree

me'lone *nm* melon

mem'brana *nf* membrane

'membro *nm* member; (*pl nf* **membra** *Anat*) limb

memo'rabile *a* memorable

'memore *a* mindful; *(riconoscente)* grateful

me'mori|a *nf* memory; *(oggetto ricordo)* souvenir. **imparare a ~a** learn by heart. **~a permanente** *Comput* nonvolatile memory. **~a tampone** *Comput* buffer. **~a volatile** *Comput* volatile memory; **memorie** *pl (biografiche)* memoirs. **~'ale** *nm* memorial. **~z'zare** *vt* memorize; *Comput* save, store

mena'dito: a ~ *adv* perfectly

me'nare *vt* lead; *(fam: picchiare)* hit

mendi'ca|nte *nmf* beggar. **~re** *vt/i* beg

menefre'ghista *a* devil-may-care

me'ningi *nfpl* **spremersi le ~** rack one's brains

menin'gite *nf* meningitis

me'nisco *nm* meniscus

'meno *adv* less; *(superlativo)* least; *(in operazioni, con temperatura)* minus; **far qcsa alla ~ peggio** do sth as best one can; **fare a ~ di qcsa** do without sth;

non posso fare a ~ di ridere I can't help laughing; **~ male!** thank goodness!; **sempre ~** less and less; **venir ~** *(svenire)* faint; **venir ~ a qcno** ⟨*coraggio:*⟩ fail sb; **sono le tre ~ un quarto** it's a quarter to three; **che tu venga o ~** whether you're coming or not; **quanto ~** at least ● *a inv* less; *(con nomi plurali)* fewer ● *nm* least; *Math* minus sign; **il ~ possibile** as little as possible; **per lo ~** at least ● *prep* except [for] ● *conj* **a ~ che** unless

meno'ma|re *vt* ⟨*incidente:*⟩ maim. **~to** *a* disabled

meno'pausa *nf* menopause

'mensa *nf* table; *Mil* mess; *Sch, Univ* refectory

men'sil|e *a* monthly ● *nm (stipendio)* [monthly] salary; *(rivista)* monthly. **~ità** *nf inv* monthly salary. **~'mente** *adv* monthly

'mensola *nf* bracket; *(scaffale)* shelf

'menta *nf* mint. **~ peperita** peppermint

men'tal|e *a* mental. **~ità** *nf inv* mentality

'mente *nf* mind; **a ~ fredda** in cold blood; **venire in ~ a qcno** occur to sb; **mi è uscito di ~** it slipped my mind

men'tina *nf* mint

men'tire *vi* lie

'mento *nm* chin

'mentre *conj (temporale)* while; *(invece)* whereas

menù *nm inv* menu. **~ fisso** set menu. **~ a tendina** *Comput* pulldown menu

menzio'nare *vt* mention. **menzi'one** *nf* mention

men'zogna *nf* lie

mera'viglia *nf* wonder; **a ~** marvellously; **che ~!** how wonderful!; **con mia grande ~** much to my amazement; **mi fa ~ che...** I am surprised that...

meravigli'ar|e *vt* surprise. **~si** *vr* **~si di** be surprised at

meravigli|osa'mente *adv* marvellously. **~'oso** *a* marvellous

mer'can|te *nm* merchant. **~teggi'are** *vi* trade; *(sul prezzo)* bargain. **~'tile** *a* mercantile ● *nm* merchant ship. **~'zia** *nf* merchandise, goods *pl*

mer'cato *nm* market; *Fin* market [-place]. **a buon ~** ⟨*comprare*⟩ cheap[ly]; ⟨*articolo*⟩ cheap. **~ dei cambi** foreign exchange market. **M~ Comune [Europeo]** [European] Common Market. **~ coperto** covered market. **~ libero** free market. **~ nero** black market

'**merce** *nf* goods *pl*

mercé *nf* **alla ~ di** at the mercy of

merce'nario *a & nm* mercenary

merce'ria *nf* haberdashery; (*negozio*) haberdasher's

mercoledì *nm inv* Wednesday. **~ delle Ceneri** Ash Wednesday

mer'curio *nm* mercury

me'renda *nf* afternoon snack; **far ~** have an afternoon snack

meridi'ana *nf* sundial

meridi'ano *a* midday ● *nm* meridian

meridio'nale *a* southern ● *nmf* southerner. **meridi'one** *nm* south

me'rin|ga *nf* meringue. **~'gata** *nf* meringue pie

meri'tare *vt* deserve. **meri'tevole** *a* deserving

'**meri|to** *nm* merit; (*valore*) worth; **in ~to a** as to; **per ~to di** thanks to. **~'torio** *a* meritorious

mer'letto *nm* lace

'**merlo** *nm* blackbird

mer'luzzo *nm* cod

'**mero** *a* mere

meschine'ria *nf* meanness. **me'schino** *a* wretched; (*gretto*) mean ● *nm* wretch

mesco|la'mento *nm* mixing. **~'lanza** *nf* mixture

mesco'la|re *vt* mix; shuffle ⟨*carte*⟩; (*confondere*) mix up; blend ⟨*tè, tabacco ecc*⟩. **~rsi** *vr* mix; (*immischiarsi*) meddle. **~ta** *nf* (*a carte*) shuffle; *Culin* stir

'**mese** *nm* month

me'setto *nm* **un ~** about a month

'**messa¹** *nf* Mass

'**messa²** *nf* (*il mettere*) putting. **~ in moto** *Auto* starting. **~ in piega** (*di capelli*) set. **~ a punto** adjustment. **~ in scena** production. **~ a terra** earthing, grounding *Am*

messag'gero *nm* messenger. **mes'saggio** *nm* message

mes'sale *nm* missal

'**messe** *nf* harvest

Mes'sia *nm* Messiah

messi'cano, -a *a & nmf* Mexican

'**Messico** *nm* Mexico

messin'scena *nf* staging; *fig* act

'**messo** *pp di* **mettere** ● *nm* messenger

mesti'ere *nm* trade; (*lavoro*) job; **essere del ~** be an expert, know one's trade

'**mesto** *a* sad

'**mestola** *nf* (*di cuoco*) ladle

mestru'a|le *a* menstrual. **~zi'one** *nf* menstruation. **~zi'oni** *pl* period

'**meta** *nf* destination; *fig* aim

metà *nf inv* half; (*centro*) middle; **a ~ strada** half-way; **fare a ~ con qcno** go halves with sb

metabo'lismo *nm* metabolism

meta'done *nm* methadone

meta'fisico *a* metaphysical

me'tafora *nf* metaphor. **meta'forico** *a* metaphorical

me'talli|co *a* metallic. **~z'zato** *a* ⟨*grigio*⟩ metallic

me'tall|o *nm* metal. **~ur'gia** *nf* metallurgy

metalmec'canico *a* engineering ● *nm* engineering worker

meta'morfosi *nf* metamorphosis

me'tano *nm* methane. **~'dotto** *nm* methane pipeline

meta'nolo *nm* methanol

me'teora *nf* meteor. **meteo'rite** *nm* meteorite

meteoro|lo'gia *nf* meteorology. **~'logico** *a* meteorological

me'ticcio, -a *nmf* half-caste

metico'loso *a* meticulous

me'tod|ico *a* methodical. '**metodo** *nm* method. **~olo'gia** *nf* methodology

me'traggio *nm* length (*in metres*)

'**metrico, -a** *a* metric; (*in poesia*) metrical ● *nf* metrics *sg*

'**metro** *nm* metre; (*nastro*) tape measure ● *nf* (*fam: metropolitana*) tube *Br*, subway

me'tronomo *nm* metronome

metro'notte *nmf inv* night security guard

me'tropoli *nf inv* metropolis. **~'tana** *nf* subway, underground *Br*. **~'tano** *a* metropolitan

'**metter|e** *vt* put; (*indossare*) put on; (*fam: installare*) put in; **~e al mondo** bring into the world; **~e da parte** set aside; **~e fiducia** inspire trust; **~e qcsa in chiaro** make sth clear; **~e in mostra** display; **~e a posto** tidy up; **~e in vendita** put up for sale; **~e su** set up ⟨*casa, azienda*⟩; **metter su famiglia** start a family; **ci ho messo un'ora** it took me an hour; **mettiamo che...** let's suppose that... **~si** *vr* (*indossare*) put on; (*diventare*) turn out; **~si a** start to; **~si con qcno** (*fam: formare una coppia*) start to go out with sb; **~si a letto** go to bed; **~si a sedere** sit down; **~si in viaggio** set out

'**mezza** *nf* **è la ~** it's half past twelve; **sono le quattro e ~** it's half past four

mezza'luna *nf* half moon; (*simbolo*)

islamico) crescent; (*coltello*) two-handled chopping knife; **a ~** half-moon shaped

mezza'manica *nf* **a ~** ⟨*maglia*⟩ short-sleeved

mez'zano *a* middle

mezza'notte *nf* midnight

mezz'asta: a ~ *adv* at half mast

'**mezzo** *a* half; **di mezza età** middle-aged; **~ bicchiere** half a glass; **una mezza idea** a vague idea; **siamo mezzi morti** we're half dead; **sono le quattro e ~** it's half past four. **mezz'ora** *nf* half an hour. **mezza pensione** *nf* half board. **mezza stagione** *nf* **una giacca di mezza stagione** a spring/autumn jacket ● *adv* (*a metà*) half ● *nm* (*metà*) half; (*centro*) middle; (*per raggiungere un fine*) means *sg*; **uno e ~** one and a half; **tre anni e ~** three and a half years; **in ~ a** in the middle of; **il giusto ~** the happy medium; **levare di ~** clear away; **per ~ di** by means of; **a ~ posta** by mail; **via di ~** *fig* halfway house; (*soluzione*) middle way. **mezzi** *pl* (*denaro*) means *pl*. **mezzi** *pl* **pubblici** public transport. **mezzi** *pl* **di trasporto** [means of] transport.

mezzo'busto: a ~ *a* ⟨*foto, ritratto*⟩ half-length

mezzo'fondo *nm* middle-distance running

mezzogi'orno *nm* midday; (*sud*) South. **il M~** Southern Italy. **~ in punto** high noon

mi *pers pron* me; (*refl*) myself; **mi ha dato un libro** he gave me a book; **mi lavo le mani** I wash my hands; **eccomi** here I am ● *nm Mus* (*chiave, nota*) E

miago'l|are *vi* miaow. **~io** *nm* miaowing

'**mica**[1] *nf* mica

'**mica**[2] *adv fam* (*per caso*) by any chance; **hai ~ visto Paolo?** have you seen Paul, by any chance?; **non è ~ bello** it is not at all nice; **~ male** not bad

'**miccia** *nf* fuse

micidi'ale *a* deadly

'**micio** *nm* pussy-cat

'**microbo** *nm* microbe

micro'cosmo *nm* microcosm

micro'fiche *nf inv* microfiche

micro'film *nm inv* microfilm

mi'crofono *nm* microphone

microorga'nismo *nm* microorganism

microproces'sore *nm* microprocessor

micro'scopi|o *nm* microscope. **~co** *a* microscopic

micro'solco *nm* long-playing record

mi'dollo *nm* (*pl nf* **midolla**, *Anat*) marrow; **fino al ~** through and through. **~ osseo** bone marrow. **~ spinale** spinal cord

'**mie, mi'ei** *vedi* **mio**

mi'ele *nm* honey

mi'et|ere *vt* reap. **~i'trice** *nf Mech* harvester. **~i'tura** *nf* harvest

migli'aio *nm* (*pl nf* **migliaia**) thousand. **a migliaia** in thousands

'**miglio** *nm Bot* millet; (*pl nf* **miglia**: *misura*) mile

migliora'mento *nm* improvement

miglio'rare *vt/i* improve

migli'ore *a* better; (*superlativo*) the best ● *nmf* **il/la ~** the best

'**mignolo** *nm* little finger; (*del piede*) little toe

mi'gra|re *vi* migrate. **~zi'one** *nf* migration

'**mila** *vedi* **mille**

Mi'lano *nf* Milan

miliar'dario, -a *nm* millionaire; (*plurimiliardario*) billionaire ● *nf* millionairess; billionairess. **mili'ardo** *nm* billion

mili'are *a* **pietra** *nf* **~** milestone

milio'nario, -a *nm* millionaire ● *nf* millionairess

mili'one *nm* million

milio'nesimo *a* millionth

mili'tante *a* & *nmf* militant

mili'tare *vi* **~ in** be a member of ⟨*partito ecc*⟩ ● *a* military ● *nm* soldier; **fare il ~** do one's military service. **~ di leva** National Serviceman

'**milite** *nm* soldier. **mil'izia** *nf* militia

'**mille** *a* & *nm* (*pl* **mila**) a o one thousand; **due/tre mila** two/three thousand; **~ grazie!** thanks a lot!

mille'foglie *nm inv Culin* vanilla slice

mil'lennio *nm* millennium

millepi'edi *nm inv* centipede

mil'lesimo *a* & *nm* thousandth

milli'grammo *nm* milligram

mil'limetro *nm* millimetre

milza *nf* spleen

mi'mare *vt* mimic ⟨*persona*⟩ ● *vi* mime

mi'metico *a* camouflage *attrib*

mimetiz'zar|e *vt* camouflage. **~si** *vr* camouflage oneself

'**mim|ica** *nf* mime. **~ico** *a* mimic. **~o** *nm* mime

mi'mosa *nf* mimosa

'**mina** *nf* mine; (*di matita*) lead

mi'naccia *nf* threat

minacci|'are *vt* threaten. **~'oso** *a* threatening

mi'nare *vt* mine; *fig* undermine

mina'tor|e *nm* miner. **~io** *a* threatening

mine'ra|le *a & nm* mineral. **~rio** *a* mining *attrib*

mi'nestra *nf* soup. **mine'strone** *nm* vegetable soup; *(fam: insieme confuso)* hotchpotch

mingher'lino *a* skinny

mini+ *pref* mini+

minia'tura *nf* miniature. **miniaturiz-'zato** *a* miniaturized

mini'era *nf* mine

mini'golf *nm* miniature golf

mini'gonna *nf* miniskirt

minima'mente *adv* minimally

mini'market *nm inv* minimarket

minimiz'zare *vt* minimize

'minimo *a* least, slightest; *(il più basso)* lowest; *⟨salario, quantità ecc⟩* minimum ● *nm* minimum; **girare al ~** *Auto* idle

mini'stero *nm* ministry; *(governo)* government

mi'nistro *nm* minister. **M~ del Tesoro** Finance Minister, Chancellor of the Exchequer *Br*

mino'ranza *nf* minority *attrib*

mino'rato, -a *a* disabled ● *nmf* disabled person

mi'nore *a* *⟨gruppo, numero⟩* smaller; *(superlativo)* smallest; *⟨distanza⟩* shorter; *(superlativo)* shortest; *⟨prezzo⟩* lower; *(superlativo)* lowest; *(di età)* younger; *(superlativo)* youngest; *(di importanza)* minor; *(superlativo)* least important ● *nmf* younger; *(superlativo)* youngest; *Jur* minor; **il ~ dei mali** the lesser of two evils; **i minori di 14 anni** children under 14. **mino'renne** *a* under age ● *nmf* minor

minori'tario *a* minority *attrib*

minu'etto *nm* minuet

mi'nuscolo, -a *a* tiny ● *nf* small letter

mi'nuta *nf* rough copy

mi'nuto¹ *a* minute; *⟨persona⟩* delicate; *⟨ricerca⟩* detailed; *⟨pioggia, neve⟩* fine; **al ~** *Comm* retail

mi'nuto² *nm* *(di tempo)* minute; **spaccare il ~** be dead on time

mi'nuzi|a *nf* trifle. **~'oso** *a* detailed; *⟨persona⟩* meticulous

'mio *(il mio m, la mia f, i miei mpl, le mie fpl) a poss* my; **questa macchina è mia** this car is mine; **~ padre** my fa-

ther; **un ~ amico** a friend of mine ● *poss pron* mine; **i miei** *(genitori ecc)* my folks

'miope *a* short-sighted. **mio'pia** *nf* short-sightedness

'mira *nf* aim; *(bersaglio)* target; **prendere la ~** take aim; **prendere di ~ qcno** *fig* have it in for sb

mi'racolo *nm* miracle. **~sa'mente** *adv* miraculously. **miraco'loso** *a* miraculous

mi'raggio *nm* mirage

mi'rar|e *vi* [take] aim. **~si** *vr* *(guardarsi)* look at oneself

mi'riade *nf* myriad

mi'rino *nm* sight; *Phot* view-finder

mir'tillo *nm* blueberry

mi'santropo, -a *nmf* misanthropist

mi'scela *nf* mixture; *(di caffè, tabacco)* blend. **~'tore** *nm* *(di acqua)* mixer tap

miscel'lanea *nf* miscellany

'mischia *nf* scuffle; *(nel rugby)* scrum

mischi'ar|e *vt* mix; shuffle *⟨carte da gioco⟩*. **~si** *vr* *(immischiarsi)* interfere

misco'noscere *vt* not appreciate

mi'scuglio *nm* mixture; *fig* medley

mise'rabile *a* wretched

misera'mente *adv* *⟨finire⟩* miserably; *⟨vivere⟩* in abject poverty

mi'seria *nf* poverty; *(infelicità)* misery; **guadagnare una ~** earn a pittance; **porca ~!** hell!; **miserie** *pl* *(disgrazie)* misfortunes

miseri'cordi|a *nf* mercy. **~'oso** *a* merciful

'misero *a* *(miserabile)* wretched; *(povero)* poor; *(scarso)* paltry

mi'sfatto *nm* misdeed

mi'sogino *nm* misogynist

mis'saggio *nm* vision mixer

'missile *nm* missile

missio'nario, -a *nmf* missionary. **missi'one** *nf* mission

misteri|osa'mente *adv* mysteriously. **~'oso** *a* mysterious. **mi'stero** *nm* mystery

'misti|ca *nf* mysticism. **~'cismo** *nm* mysticism. **~co** *a* mystic[al] ● *nm* mystic

mistifi'ca|re *vt* distort *⟨verità⟩*. **~zi'one** *nf* *(della verità)* distortion

'misto *a* mixed; **~ lana/cotone** wool/cotton-mix; **scuola mista** mixed *o* co-educational school ● *nm* mixture

mi'sura *nf* measure; *(dimensione)* measurement; *(taglia)* size; *(limite)* limit; **su ~** *⟨abiti⟩* made to measure;

⟨*mobile*⟩ custom-made; **a ~** ⟨*andare, calzare*⟩ perfectly; **a ~ che** as. **~ di sicurezza** safety measure. **misu'rare** *vt* measure; try on ⟨*indumenti*⟩; ⟨*limitare*⟩ limit. **misu'rarsi** *vr* **misurarsi con** ⟨*gareggiare*⟩ compete with. **misu'rato** *a* measured. **misu'rino** *nm* measuring spoon

'**mite** *a* mild; ⟨*prezzo*⟩ moderate

'**mitico** *a* mythical

miti'gar|e *vt* mitigate. **~si** *vr* calm down; ⟨*clima:*⟩ become mild

mitiz'zare *vt* mythicize

'**mito** *nm* myth. **~lo'gia** *nf* mythology. **~'logico** *a* mythological

mi'tomane *nmf* compulsive liar

'**mitra** *nf* *Relig* mitre ● *nm inv* *Mil* machine-gun

mitragli'a|re *vt* machine-gun; **~re di domande** fire questions at. **~'trice** *nf* machine-gun

mit'tente *nmf* sender

mne'monico *a* mnemonic

mo' *nm* **a ~ di** by way of ⟨*esempio, consolazione*⟩

'**mobile**[1] *a* mobile; ⟨*volubile*⟩ fickle; ⟨*che si può muovere*⟩ movable; **beni mobili** personal estate; **squadra ~** flying squad

'**mobi|le**[2] *nm* piece of furniture; **mobili** *pl* furniture *sg*. **mo'bilia** *nf* furniture. **~li'ficio** *nm* furniture factory

mo'bilio *nm* furniture

mobilità *nf* mobility

mobili'ta|re *vt* mobilize. **~zi'one** *nf* mobilization

mocas'sino *nm* moccasin

mocci'oso, -a *nmf* brat

'**moccolo** *nm* ⟨*di candela*⟩ candle-end; ⟨*moccio*⟩ snot

'**moda** *nf* fashion; **di ~** in fashion; **alla ~** ⟨*musica, vestiti*⟩ up-to-date; **fuori ~** unfashionable

modalità *nf inv* formality; **~ d'uso** instruction

mo'della *nf* model. **model'lare** *vt* model

model'li|no *nm* model. **~sta** *nmf* designer

mo'dello *nm* model; ⟨*stampo*⟩ mould; ⟨*di carta*⟩ pattern; ⟨*modulo*⟩ form

'**modem** *nm inv* modem; **mandare per ~** modem, send by modem

mode'ra|re *vt* moderate; ⟨*diminuire*⟩ reduce. **~rsi** *vr* control oneself. **~ta'mente** *adv* moderately **~to** *a* moderate. **~'tore, ~'trice** *nmf* (*in tavola rotonda*) moderator. **~zi'one** *nf* moderation

modern|a'mente *adv* (*in modo moderno*) in a modern style. **~iz'zare** *vt* modernize. **mo'derno** *a* modern

mo'dest|ia *nf* modesty. **~o** *a* modest

'**modico** *a* reasonable

mo'difica *nf* modification

modifi'ca|re *vt* modify. **~zi'one** *nf* modification

mo'dista *nf* milliner

'**modo** *nm* way; ⟨*garbo*⟩ manners *pl*; ⟨*occasione*⟩ chance; *Gram* mood; **ad ogni ~** anyhow; **di ~ che** so that; **fare in ~ di** try to; **in che ~** (*inter*) how; **in qualche ~** somehow; **in questo ~** like this; **~ di dire** idiom; **per ~ di dire** so to speak

modu'la|re *vt* modulate. **~zi'one** *nf* modulation. **~zione di frequenza** frequency modulation. **~'tore** *nm* **~tore di frequenza** frequency modulator

'**modulo** *nm* form; ⟨*lunare, di comando*⟩ module. **~ continuo** continuous paper

'**mogano** *nm* mahogany

'**mogio** *a* dejected

'**moglie** *nf* wife

'**mola** *nf* millstone; *Mech* grindstone

mo'lare *nm* molar

'**mole** *nf* mass; ⟨*dimensione*⟩ size

mo'lecola *nf* molecule

mole'stare *vt* bother; ⟨*più forte*⟩ molest. **mo'lestia** *nf* nuisance. **mo'lesto** *a* bothersome

'**molla** *nf* spring; **molle** *pl* tongs

mol'lare *vt* let go; ⟨*fam: lasciare*⟩ leave; *fam* give ⟨*ceffone*⟩; *Naut* cast off ● *vi* cease; **mollala!** *fam* stop that!

'**molle** *a* soft; ⟨*bagnato*⟩ wet

mol'letta *nf* ⟨*per capelli*⟩ hair-grip; ⟨*per bucato*⟩ clothes-peg; **mollette** *pl* ⟨*per ghiaccio ecc*⟩ tongs

mol'lezz|a *nf* softness; **~e** *pl* *fig* luxury

mol'lica *nf* crumb

mol'lusco *nm* mollusc

'**molo** *nm* pier; ⟨*banchina*⟩ dock

mol'teplic|e *a* manifold; ⟨*numeroso*⟩ numerous. **~ità** *nf* multiplicity

moltipli'ca|re *vt*, **~rsi** *vr* multiply. **~'tore** *nm* multiplier. **~'trice** *nf* calculating machine. **~zi'one** *nf* multiplication

molti'tudine *nf* multitude

'**molto** *a* a lot of; ⟨*con negazione e interrogazione*⟩ much, a lot of; ⟨*con nomi plurali*⟩ many, a lot of; **non ~ tempo** not much time, not a lot of time ● *adv* very; ⟨*con verbi*⟩ a lot; ⟨*con avverbi*⟩ much; **~ stupido** very stupid; **mangiare ~** eat a lot; **~ più veloce** much faster; **non mangiare ~** not eat a lot, not eat much ● *pron* a lot; (*molto tempo*) a lot of time; (*con negazione e interrogazione*) much, a lot; (*plurale*) many; **non ne ho ~** I don't have much, I don't have a lot; **non ne ho molti** I don't have many, I don't have a lot; **non ci metterò ~** I won't be long; **fra non ~** before long; **molti** (*persone*) a lot of people; **eravamo in molti** there were a lot of us

momentanea'mente *adv* momentarily; **è ~ assente** he's not here at the moment. **momen'taneo** *a* momentary

mo'mento *nm* moment; **a momenti** (*a volte*) sometimes; (*fra un momento*) in a moment; **dal ~ che** since; **per il ~** for the time being; **da un ~ all'altro** (*cambiare idea ecc*) from one moment to the next; (*aspettare qcno ecc*) at any moment

'**monac|a** *nf* nun. **~o** *nm* monk

'**Monaco** *nm* Monaco ● *nf* (*di Baviera*) Munich

mo'narc|a *nm* monarch. **monar'chia** *nf* monarchy. **~hico, -a** *a* monarchic ● *nmf* monarchist

mona'stero *nm* (*di monaci*) monastery; (*di monache*) convent. **mo'nastico** *a* monastic.

monche'rino *nm* stump

'**monco** *a* maimed; (*fig: troncato*) truncated; **~ di un braccio** one-armed

mon'dano *a* worldly; **vita mondana** social life

mondi'ale *a* world *attrib*; **di fama ~** world-famous

'**mondo** *nm* world; **il bel ~** fashionable society; **un ~** (*molto*) a lot

mondovisi'one *nf* **in ~** transmitted worldwide

mo'nello, -a *nmf* urchin

mo'neta *nf* coin; (*denaro*) money; (*denaro spicciolo*) [small] change. **~ estera** foreign currency. **~ legale** legal tender. **~ unica** single currency. **mone'tario** *a* monetary

mongolfi'era *nf* hot air balloon

mo'nile *nm* jewel

'**monito** *nm* warning

moni'tore *nm* monitor

mo'nocolo *nm* monocle

monoco'lore *a* *Pol* one-party

mono'dose *a inv* individually packaged

monogra'fia *nf* monograph

mono'gramma *nm* monogram

mono'kini *nm inv* monokini

mono'lingue *a* monolingual

monolo'cale *nm* studio flat, studio apartment *Am*

mo'nologo *nm* monologue

mono'pattino *nm* [child's] scooter

mono'poli|o *nm* monopoly. **~z'zare** *vt* monopolize

mono'sci *nm inv* monoski

monosil'labico *a* monosyllabic. **mono'sillabo** *nm* monosyllable

mono'nia *nf* monotony. **mo'notono** *a* monotonous

mono'uso *a* disposable

monou'tente *a inv* single-user *attrib*

monsi'gnore *nm* monsignor

mon'sone *nm* monsoon

monta'carichi *nm inv* hoist

mon'taggio *nm* *Mech* assembly; *Cinema* editing; **catena di ~** production line

mon'ta|gna *nf* mountain; (*zona*) mountains *pl*; **montagne** *pl* **russe** big dipper. **~'gnoso** *a* mountainous. **~'naro, -a** *nmf* highlander. **~no** *a* mountain *attrib*

mon'tante *nm* (*di finestra, porta*) upright

mon'ta|re *vt/i* mount; get on (*veicolo*); (*aumentare*) rise; *Mech* assemble; frame (*quadro*); *Culin* whip; edit (*film*); (*a cavallo*) ride; *fig* blow up; **~rsi la testa** get big-headed. **~to, -a** *nmf* poser. **~'tura** *nf Mech* assembling; (*di occhiali*) frame; (*di gioiello*) mounting; *fig* exaggeration

'**monte** *nm anche fig* mountain; **a ~** upstream; **andare a ~** be ruined; **mandare a ~ qcsa** ruin sth. **~ di pietà** pawnshop

Monte'negro *nm* Montenegro

monte'premi *nm inv* jackpot

mont'gomery *nm inv* duffle coat

mon'tone *nm* ram; **carne di ~** mutton

montu'oso *a* mountainous

monumen'tale *a* monumental. **monu'mento** *nm* monument

mo'quette *nf* (*tappeto*) fitted carpet

'**mora** *nf* (*del gelso*) mulberry; (*del rovo*) blackberry

mo'ral|e *a* moral ● *nf* morals *pl*; (*di storia*) moral ● *nm* morale. **mora'lista** *nmf* moralist. **~ità** *nf* morality; (*condotta*) morals *pl*. **~iz'zare** *vt/i* moralize. **~'mente** *adv* morally

morbi'dezza *nf* softness

'**morbido** *a* soft

mor'billo *nm* measles *sg*

'**morbo** *nm* disease. **~sità** *nf* (*qualità*) morbidity

mor'boso *a* morbid

mor'dace *a* cutting

mor'dente *a* biting. **'mordere** *vt* bite; (*corrodere*) bite into. **mordicchi'are** *vt* gnaw

mor'fina *nf* morphine. **morfi'nomane** *nmf* morphine addict

mori'bondo *a* dying; ⟨*istituzione*⟩ moribund

morige'rato *a* moderate

mo'rire *vi* die; *fig* die out; **fa un freddo da ~** it's freezing cold, it's perishing; **~ di noia** be bored to death; **c'era da ~ dal ridere** it was hilariously funny

mor'mone *nmf* Mormon

mormo'r|are *vt/i* murmur; (*brontolare*) mutter. **~io** *nm* murmuring; (*lamentela*) grumbling

'moro *a* dark ● *nm* Moor

mo'roso *a* in arrears

'morsa *nf* vice; *fig* grip

'morse *a* alfabeto **~** Morse code

mor'setto *nm* clamp

morsi'care *vt* bite. **'morso** *nm* bite; (*di cibo, briglia*) bit; **i morsi della fame** hunger pangs

morta'della *nf* mortadella (*type of salted pork*)

mor'taio *nm* mortar

mor'tal|e *a* mortal; (*simile a morte*) deadly; **di una noia ~e** deadly. **~ità** *nf* mortality. **~'mente** *adv* ⟨*ferito*⟩ fatally; ⟨*offeso*⟩ mortally

morta'retto *nm* firecracker

'morte *nf* death

mortifi'cante *a* mortifying

mortifi'ca|re *vt* mortify. **~rsi** *vr* be mortified. **~to** *a* mortified. **~zi'one** *nf* mortification

'morto, -a *pp di* **morire** ● *a* dead; **~ di freddo** frozen to death; **stanco ~** dead tired ● *nm* dead man ● *nf* dead woman

mor'torio *nm* funeral

mo'saico *nm* mosaic

'Mosca *nf* Moscow

'mosca *nf* fly; (*barba*) goatee. **~ cieca** blindman's buff

mo'scato *a* muscat; **noce moscata** nutmeg ● *nm* muscatel

mosce'rino *nm* midge; (*fam: persona*) midget

mo'schea *nf* mosque

moschi'cida *a* fly *attrib*

'moscio *a* limp; **avere l'erre moscia** not be able to say one's r's properly

mo'scone *nm* bluebottle; (*barca*) pedalo

'moss|a *nf* movement; (*passo*) move.

~o *pp di* **muovere** ● *a* ⟨*mare*⟩ rough; ⟨*capelli*⟩ wavy; ⟨*fotografia*⟩ blurred

mo'starda *nf* mustard

'mostra *nf* show; (*d'arte*) exhibition; **far ~ di** pretend; **in ~** on show; **mettersi in ~** make oneself conspicuous

mo'stra|re *vt* show; (*indicare*) point out; (*spiegare*) explain. **~rsi** *vr* show oneself; (*apparire*) appear

'mostro *nm* monster; (*fig: persona*) genius; **~ sacro** *fig* sacred cow

mostru|osa'mente *adv* tremendously. **~'oso** *a* monstrous; (*incredibile*) enormous

mo'tel *nm inv* motel

moti'va|re *vt* cause; *Jur* justify. **~to** *a* ⟨*persona*⟩ motivated. **~zi'one** *nf* motivation; (*giustificazione*) justification

mo'tivo *nm* reason; (*movente*) motive; (*in musica, letteratura*) theme; (*disegno*) motif

'moto *nm* motion; (*esercizio*) exercise; (*gesto*) movement; (*sommossa*) rising ● *nf inv* (*motocicletta*) motor bike; **mettere in ~** start ⟨*motore*⟩

moto'carro *nm* three-wheeler

motoci'cl|etta *nf* motor cycle. **~ismo** *nm* motorcycling. **~ista** *nmf* motor-cyclist

moto'cros|s *nm* motocross. **~'sista** *nmf* scrambler

moto'lancia *nf* motor launch

moto'nave *nf* motor vessel

mo'tore *a* motor ● *nm* motor, engine. **moto'retta** *nf* motor scooter. **moto'rino** *nm* moped. **motorino d'avviamento** starter

motoriz'za|to *a Mil* motorized. **~zi'one** *nf* (*ufficio*) vehicle licensing office

moto'scafo *nm* motorboat

motove'detta *nf* patrol vessel

'motto *nm* motto; (*facezia*) witticism; (*massima*) saying

mountain bike *nf inv* mountain bike

mouse *nm inv Comput* mouse

mo'vente *nm* motive

movimen'ta|re *vt* enliven. **~to** *a* lively. **movi'mento** *nm* movement; **essere sempre in movimento** be always on the go

mozi'one *nf* motion

mozzafi'ato *a inv* nail-biting

moz'zare *vt* cut off; dock ⟨*coda*⟩; **~ il fiato a** qcno take sb's breath away

mozza'rella *nf* mozzarella, *mild, white cheese*

mozzi'cone *nm* (*di sigaretta*) stub

'mozzo nm Mech hub; Naut ship's boy
● a ‹coda› truncated; ‹testa› severed

'mucca nf cow. **morbo della ~ pazza**
mad cow disease

'mucchio nm heap, pile; **un ~ di** fig
lots of

'muco nm mucus

'muffa nf mould; **fare la ~** go mouldy.
muf'fire vi go mouldy

muf'fole nfpl mittens

mug'gi|re vi ‹mucca:› moo, low; ‹toro:›
bellow. **~to** nm moo; bellow; ‹azione›
mooing; bellowing

mu'ghetto nm lily of the valley

mugo'lare vi whine; ‹persona:› moan.
mugo'lio nm whining

mugu'gnare vt fam mumble

mulatti'era nf mule track

mu'latto, -a nmf mulatto

muli'nello nm ‹d'acqua› whirl-pool; ‹di
vento› eddy; ‹giocattolo› windmill

mu'lino nm mill. **~ a vento** windmill

'mulo nm mule

'multa nf fine. **mul'tare** vt fine

multico'lore a multicoloured

multi'lingue a multilingual

multi'media mpl multimedia

multimedi'ale a multimedia attrib

multimiliar'dario, -a nmf multi-mil-
lionaire

multinazio'nale nf multinational

'multiplo a & nm multiple

multiproprietà nf inv time-share

multi'uso a ‹utensile› all-purpose

'mummia nf mummy

'mungere vt milk

mungi'tura nf milking

munici'pal|e a municipal. **~ità** nf inv
town council. **muni'cipio** nm town hall

mu'nifico a munificent

mu'nire vt fortify; **~ di** ‹provvedere›
supply with

munizi'oni nfpl ammunition sg

'munto pp di **mungere**

mu'over|e vt move; ‹suscitare› arouse.
~si vr move; **muoviti!** hurry up!, come
on!

mura nfpl ‹cinta di città› walls

mu'raglia nf wall

mu'rale a mural; ‹pittura› wall attrib

mur'a|re vt wall up. **~'tore** nm brick-
layer; ‹con pietre› mason; ‹operaio edile›
builder. **~'tura** nf ‹di pietra› masonry,
stonework; ‹di mattoni› brickwork

mu'rena nf moray eel

'muro nm wall; ‹di nebbia› bank; **a ~**
‹armadio› built-in. **~ portante** load-
bearing wall. **~ del suono** sound barrier

'muschio nm Bot moss

musco'la|re a muscular. **~'tura** nf
muscles pl. **'muscolo** nm muscle

mu'seo nm museum

museru'ola nf muzzle

'musi|ca nf music. **~cal** nm inv musi-
cal. **~'cale** a musical. **~'cista** nmf musician

'muso nm muzzle; ‹pej: di persona›
mug; ‹di aeroplano› nose; **fare il ~** sulk.
mu'sone, -a nmf sulker

'mussola nf muslin

musul'mano, -a nmf Moslem

'muta nf ‹cambio› change; ‹di penne›
moult; ‹di cani› pack; ‹per immersione
subacquea› wetsuit

muta'mento nm change

mu'tan|de nfpl pants; ‹da donna›
knickers. **~'doni** nmpl ‹da uomo› long
johns; ‹da donna› bloomers

mu'tare vt change

mu'tevole a changeable

muti'la|re vt mutilate. **~to, -a** nmf
disabled person. **~to di guerra** disabled ex-serviceman. **~zi'one** nf mutila-
tion

mu'tismo nm dumbness; fig obstinate
silence

'muto a dumb; ‹silenzioso› silent; ‹fonetica› mute

'mutu|a nf [**cassa** nf] **~** sickness ben-
efit fund. **~'ato, -a** nmf NHS patient

'mutuo[1]

'mutuo[2] nm loan; ‹per la casa› mortgage; **fare un ~** take out a mortgage. **~
ipotecario** mortgage

Nn

'**nacchera** *nf* castanet

'**nafta** *nf* naphtha; (*per motori*) diesel oil

'**naia** *nf* cobra; (*sl: servizio militare*) national service

'**nailon** *nm* nylon

'**nanna** *nf* (*sl: infantile*) byebyes; **andare a ~** go byebyes; **fare la ~** sleep

'**nano, -a** *a & nmf* dwarf

napole'tano, -a *a & nmf* Neapolitan

'**Napoli** *nf* Naples

'**nappa** *nf* tassel; (*pelle*) soft leather

narci'sis|mo *nm* narcissism. ~**ta** *a & nmf* narcissist

nar'ciso *nm* narcissus

nar'cotico *a & nm* narcotic

na'rice *nf* nostril

nar'ra|re *vt* tell. ~'**tivo, -a** *a* narrative ● *nf* fiction. ~'**tore**, ~'**trice** *nmf* narrator. ~**zi'one** *nf* narration; (*racconto*) story

na'sale *a* nasal

'**nasc|ere** *vi* (*venire al mondo*) be born; (*germogliare*) sprout; (*sorgere*) rise; ~**ere da** *fig* arise from. ~**ita** *nf* birth. ~**i'turo** *nm* unborn child

na'sconder|e *vt* hide. ~**si** *vr* hide

nascon'di|glio *nm* hiding-place. ~**no** *nm* hide-and-seek. na'**scosto** *pp di* na-scondere ● *a* hidden; **di nascosto** secretly

na'sello *nm* (*pesce*) hake

'**naso** *nm* nose

'**nastro** *nm* ribbon; (*di registratore ecc*) tape. ~ **adesivo** adhesive tape. ~ **iso-lante** insulating tape. ~ **trasportatore** conveyor belt

na'tal|e *a* (*paese*) of one's birth. **N~e** *nm* Christmas; ~**i** *pl* parentage. ~**ità** *nf* [number of] births. nata'**lizio** *a* (*del Natale*) Christmas *attrib*; (*di nascita*) of one's birth

na'tante *a* floating ● *nm* craft

'**natica** *nf* buttock

na'tio *a* native

Natività *nf* Nativity. na'**tivo, -a** *a & nmf* native

'**nato** *pp di* **nascere** ● *a* born; **uno** **scrittore ~** a born writer; **nata Rossi** née Rossi

NATO *nf* Nato, NATO

na'tura *nf* nature; **pagare in ~** pay in kind. **~ morta** still life

natu'ra|le *a* natural; **al ~le** (*alimento*) plain, natural; **~le!** naturally, of course. ~'**lezza** *nf* naturalness. ~**liz'zare** *vt* naturalize. ~**l'mente** *adv* (*ovviamente*) naturally, of course

natu'rista *nmf* naturalist

naufra'gare *vi* be wrecked; (*persona:*) be shipwrecked. **nau'fragio** *nm* shipwreck; *fig* wreck. '**naufrago, -a** *nmf* survivor

'**nause|a** *nf* nausea; **avere la ~a** feel sick. ~**a'bondo** *a* nauseating. ~'**ante** *a* nauseating. ~'**are** *vt* nauseate

'**nautic|a** *nf* navigation. ~**o** *a* nautical

na'vale *a* naval

na'vata *nf* (*centrale*) nave; (*laterale*) aisle

'**nave** *nf* ship. ~ **cisterna** tanker. ~ **da** **guerra** warship. ~ **spaziale** spaceship

na'vetta *nf* shuttle

navicella *nf* ~ **spaziale** nose cone

navi'gabile *a* navigable

navi'ga|re *vi* sail; ~**re in Internet** surf the Net. ~'**tore**, ~'**trice** *mf* navigator. ~**zi'one** *nf* navigation

na'viglio *nm* fleet; (*canale*) canal

nazio'na|le *a* national ● *nf Sport* national team. ~'**lismo** *nm* nationalism. ~'**lista** *nmf* nationalist ~**lità** *nf inv* nationality. ~**liz'zare** *vt* nationalize. na-zi'**one** *nf* nation

na'zista *a nmf* Nazi

N.B. *abbr* (**nota bene**) N.B.

ne *pers pron* (*di lui*) about him; (*di lei*) about her; (*di loro*) about them; (*di ciò*) about it; (*da ciò*) from that; (*di un insieme*) of it; (*di un gruppo*) of them; **non ne conosco nessuno** I don't know any of them; **ne ho** I have some; **non ne ho più** I don't have any left ● *adv* from there; **ne vengo ora** I've just come from there; **me ne vado** I'm off

né *conj* **né... né...** neither... nor...; **non**

ne ho il tempo né la voglia I don't have either the time or the inclination; **né tu né io vogliamo andare** neither you nor I want to go; **né l'uno né l'altro** neither [of them/us]

ne'anche adv (neppure) not even; (senza neppure) without even ● conj (e neppure) neither... nor; **non parlo inglese, e lui ~** I don't speak English, neither does he o and he doesn't either

'nebbi|a nf mist; (in città, su strada) fog. **~'oso** a misty; foggy

necessaria'mente adv necessarily. **neces'sario** a necessary

necessità nf inv necessity; (bisogno) need

necessi'tare vi **~ di** need; (essere necessario) be necessary

necro'logio nm obituary

ne'cropoli nf inv necropolis

ne'fando a wicked

ne'fasto a ill-omened

ne'ga|re vt deny; (rifiutare) refuse; **essere ~to per qcsa** be no good at sth. **~'tivo, -a** a negative ● nf negative. **~zi'one** nf negation; (diniego) denial; Gram negative

ne'gletto a neglected

'negli = in + gli

negli'gen|te a negligent. **~za** nf negligence

negozi'abile a negotiable

negozi'ante nmf dealer; (bottegaio) shopkeeper

negozi'a|re vt negotiate ● vi **~re in** trade in. **~ti** nmpl negotiations

ne'gozio nm shop

'negro, -a a Negro, black ● nmf Negro, black; (scrittore) ghost writer

'nei = in + i. **nel** = in + il. **'nella** = in + la. **'nelle** = in + le. **'nello** = in + lo

'nembo nm nimbus

ne'mico, -a a hostile ● nmf enemy

nem'meno conj not even

'nenia nf dirge; (per bambini) lullaby; (piagnucolio) wail

'neo nm mole; (applicato) beauty spot

'neo+ pref neo+

neofa'scismo nm neofascism

neo'litico a Neolithic

neolo'gismo nm neologism

'neon nm neon

neo'nato, -a a newborn ● nmf newborn baby

neozelan'dese a New Zealand ● nmf New Zealander

nep'pure conj not even

'nerb|o nm (forza) strength; fig backbone. **~o'ruto** a brawny

ne'retto nm Typ bold [type]

'nero a black; (fam: arrabbiato) fuming ● nm black; **mettere ~ su bianco** put in writing

nerva'tura nf nerves pl; Bot veining; (di libro) band

'nervo nm nerve; Bot vein; **avere i nervi** be bad-tempered; **dare ai nervi a qcno** get on sb's nerves. **~'sismo** nm nerviness

ner'voso a nervous; (irritabile) badtempered; **avere il ~** be irritable; **esaurimento** Typ **~** nervous breakdown

'nespol|a nf medlar. **~o** nm medlar[-tree]

'nesso nm link

nes'suno a no, not... any; (qualche) any; **non ho nessun problema** I don't have any problems, I have no problems; **non lo trovo da nessuna parte** I can't find it anywhere; **in nessun modo** on no account; **nessuna notizia?** any news? ● pron nobody, no one, not... anybody, not... anyone; (qualcuno) anybody, anyone; **hai delle domande? – nessuna** do you have any questions? – none; **~ di voi** none of you; **~ dei due** (di voi due) neither of you; **non ho visto ~ dei tuoi amici** I haven't seen any of your friends; **c'è ~?** is anybody there?

'nettare¹ nm nectar

net'tare² vt clean

net'tezza nf cleanliness. **~ urbana** cleansing department

'netto a clean; (chiaro) clear; Comm net; **di ~** just like that

nettur'bino nm dustman

neu'tral|e a & nm neutral. **~ità** nf neutrality. **~iz'zare** vt neutralize. **'neutro** a neutral; Gram neuter ● nm Gram neuter

neu'trone nm neutron

'neve nf snow

nevi'|care vi snow; **~ca** it is snowing. **~'cata** nf snowfall. **ne'vischio** nm sleet. **ne'voso** a snowy

nevral'gia nf neuralgia. **ne'vralgico** a neuralgic

ne'vro|si nf inv neurosis. **~tico** a neurotic

'nibbio nm kite

'nicchia nf niche

nicchi'are vi shilly-shally

'nichel nm nickel

nichi'lista a & nmf nihilist

nico'tina *nf* nicotine

nidi'ata *nf* brood. **'nido** *nm* nest; (*giardino d'infanzia*) crèche

ni'ente *pron* nothing, not... anything; (*qualcosa*) anything; **non ho fatto ~ di male** I didn't do anything wrong, I did nothing wrong; **grazie! – di ~!** thank you! – don't mention it!; **non serve a ~** it is no use; **vuoi ~?** do you want anything?; **da ~** (*poco importante*) minor; (*di poco valore*) worthless ● *a inv fam* **non ho ~ fame** I'm not in the slightest bit hungry ● *adv* **non fa ~** (*non importa*) it doesn't matter; **per ~** at all; ‹*litigare*› over nothing; **~ affatto!** no way! ● *nm* **un bel ~** absolutely nothing

nientedi'meno, niente'meno *adv* **~ che** no less than ● *int* fancy that!

'ninfa *nf* nymph

nin'fea *nf* water-lily

ninna'nanna *nf* lullaby

'ninnolo *nm* plaything; (*fronzolo*) knick-knack

ni'pote *nm* (*di zii*) nephew; (*di nonni*) grandson, grandchild ● *nf* (*di zii*) niece; (*di nonni*) granddaughter, grandchild

'nisba *pron* (*sl: niente*) zilch

'nitido *a* neat; (*chiaro*) clear

ni'trato *nm* nitrate

ni'tri|re *vi* neigh. **~to** *nm* (*di cavallo*) neigh

n° *abbr* (**numero**) No

no *adv* no; (*con congiunzione*) not; **dire di no** say no; **credo di no** I don't think so; **perché no?** why not?; **io no** not me; **ha detto così, no?** he said so, didn't he?; **fa freddo, no?** it's cold, isn't it?

'nobil|e *a* noble ● *nm* noble, nobleman ● *nf* noble, noblewoman. **~i'are** *a* noble. **~tà** *nf* nobility

'nocca *nf* knuckle

nocci'ol|a *nf* hazel-nut. **~o** *nm* (*albero*) hazel

'nocciolo *nm* stone; *fig* heart

'noce *nf* walnut ● *nm* (*albero, legno*) walnut. **~ moscata** nutmeg. **~'pesca** *nf* nectarine

no'civo *a* harmful

'nodo *nm* knot; *fig* lump; *Comput* node; **fare il ~ della cravatta** do up one's tie. **~ alla gola** lump in the throat. **no'do-so** *a* knotty. **'nodulo** *nm* nodule

'noi *pers pron* (*soggetto*) we; (*oggetto, con prep*) us; **chi è? – siamo ~** who is it? – it's us

'noia *nf* boredom; (*fastidio*) bother; (*persona*) bore; **dar ~** annoy

noi'altri *pers pron* we

noi'oso *a* boring; (*fastidioso*) tiresome

noleggi'are *vt* hire; (*dare a noleggio*) hire out; charter ‹*nave, aereo*›. **no'leggio** *nm* hire; (*di macchina, aereo*) charter. **'nolo** *nm* hire; *Naut* freight; **a nolo** for hire

'nomade *a* nomadic ● *nmf* nomad

'nome *nm* name; *Gram* noun; **a ~ di** in the name of; **di ~** by name; **farsi un ~** make a name for oneself. **~ di famiglia** surname. **~ da ragazza** maiden name.

no'mea *nf* reputation

nomencla'tura *nf* nomenclature

no'mignolo *nm* nickname

no'mina *nf* appointment. **nomi'nale** *a* nominal; *Gram* noun *attrib*

nomi'na|re *vt* name; (*menzionare*) mention; (*eleggere*) appoint. **~'tivo** *a* nominative; *Comm* registered ● *nm* nominative; (*nome*) name

non *adv* not; **~ ti amo** I do not *o* don't love you; **~ c'è di che** not at all

nonché *conj* (*tanto meno*) let alone; (*e anche*) as well as

noncu'ran|te *a* nonchalant; (*negligente*) indifferent. **~za** *nf* nonchalance; (*negligenza*) indifference

nondi'meno *conj* nevertheless

'nonna *nf* grandmother, grandma *fam*

'nonno *nm* grandfather, grandpa *fam*; **nonni** *pl* grandparents

non'nulla *nm inv* trifle

'nono *a & nm* ninth

nono'stante *prep* in spite of ● *conj* although

nontiscordardimé *nm inv* forget-me-not

nonvio'lento *a* nonviolent

nord *nm* north; **del ~** northern

nor'd-est *nm* northeast; **a ~** northeasterly

'nordico *a* northern

nordocciden'tale *a* northwestern

nordorien'tale *a* northeastern

nor'd-ovest *nm* northwest; **a ~** northwesterly

'norma *nf* rule; (*istruzione*) instruction; **a ~ di legge** according to law; **è buona ~** it's advisable

nor'mal|e *a* normal. **~ità** *nf* normality. **~iz'zare** *vt* normalize. **~'mente** *adv* normally

norve'gese *a & nmf* Norwegian. **Nor'vegia** *nf* Norway

nossi'gnore *adv* no way

nostal'gia *nf* (*di casa, patria*) homesickness; (*del passato*) nostalgia; **aver ~** be homesick; **aver ~ di qcno** miss sb.

no'stalgico, -a *a* nostalgic ● *nmf* reactionary

no'strano *a* local; (*fatto in casa*) homemade

'nostro (**il nostro** *m*, **la nostra** *f*, **i nostri** *mpl*, **le nostre** *fpl*) *poss a* our; **quella macchina è nostra** that car is ours; **~ padre** our father; **un ~ amico** a friend of ours ● *poss pron* ours

'nota *nf* (*segno*) sign; (*comunicazione, commento, Mus*) note; (*conto*) bill; (*lista*) list; **degno di ~** noteworthy; **prendere ~** take note. **note** *pl* **caratteristiche** distinguishing marks

no'tabile *a & nm* notable

no'taio *nm* notary

no'ta|re *vt* (*segnare*) mark; (*annotare*) note down; (*osservare*) notice; **far ~ qcsa** point sth out; **farsi ~re** get oneself noticed. **~zi'one** *nf* marking; (*annotazione*) notation

'notes *nm inv* notepad

no'tevole *a* (*degno di nota*) remarkable; (*grande*) considerable

no'tifica *nf* notification. **notifi'care** *vt* notify; *Comm* advise. **~zi'one** *nf* notification

no'tizi|a *nf* **una ~a** a piece of news, some news; (*informazione*) a piece of information, some information; **le ~e** the news *sg*. **~'ario** *nm* news *sg*

'noto *a* [well-]known; **rendere ~** (*far sapere*) announce

notorietà *nf* fame; **raggiungere la ~** become famous. **no'torio** *a* well-known; *pej* notorious

not'tambulo *nm* night-bird

not'tata *nf* night; **far ~** stay up all night

'notte *nf* night; **di ~** at night; **~ bianca** sleepless night; **peggio che andar di ~** worse than ever. **~'tempo** *adv* at night

not'turno *a* nocturnal; ⟨*servizio ecc*⟩ night

no'vanta *a & nm* ninety

novan't|enne *a & nmf* ninety-year-old. **~esimo** *a* ninetieth. **~ina** *nf* about ninety. **'nove** *a & nm* nine. **nove'cento** *a & nm* nine hundred. **il N~cento** the twentieth century

no'vella *nf* short story

novel'lino, -a *a* inexperienced ● *nmf* novice, beginner. **no'vello** *a* new

no'vembre *nm* November

novità *nf inv* novelty; (*notizie*) news *sg*; **l'ultima ~** (*moda*) the latest fashion

novizi'ato *nm Relig* novitiate; (*tirocinio*) apprenticeship

nozi'one *nf* notion; **nozioni** *pl* rudiments

'nozze *nfpl* marriage *sg*; (*cerimonia*) wedding *sg*. **~ d'argento/d'oro** silver/golden wedding [anniversary]

'nub|e *nf* cloud. **~e tossica** toxic cloud. **~i'fragio** *nm* cloudburst

'nubile *a* unmarried ● *nf* unmarried woman

'nuca *nf* nape

nucle'are *a* nuclear

'nucleo *nm* nucleus; (*unità*) unit

nu'di|smo *nm* nudism. **~sta** *nmf* nudist. **~tà** *nf inv* nudity, nakedness

'nudo *a* naked; ⟨*spoglio*⟩ bare; **a occhio ~** to the naked eye

'nugolo *nm* large number

'nulla *pron* = **niente**; **da ~** worthless

nulla'osta *nm inv* permit

nullate'nente *nm* **i nullatenenti** the have-nots

nullità *nf inv* (*persona*) nonentity

'nullo *a Jur* null and void

nume'ra|bile *a* countable. **~le** *a & nm* numeral

nume'ra|re *vt* number. **~zi'one** *nf* numbering. **nu'merico** *a* numerical

'numero *nm* number; (*romano, arabo*) numeral; (*di scarpe ecc*) size; **dare i numeri** be off one's head. **~ cardinale** cardinal [number]. **~ decimale** decimal. **~ ordinale** ordinal [number]. **~ di telefono** phone number. **~ verde** Freephone®. **nume'roso** *a* numerous

'nunzio *nm* nuncio

nu'ocere *vi* **~ a** harm

nu'ora *nf* daughter-in-law

nuo'ta|re *vi* swim; *fig* wallow; **~re nell'oro** be stinking rich, be rolling in it. **nu'oto** *nm* swimming. **~'tore, ~'trice** *nmf* swimmer

nu'ov|a *nf* (*notizia*) news *sg*. **~a'mente** *adv* again. **~o** *a* new; **di ~o** again; **rimettere a ~o** give a new lease of life to

nutri'|ente *a* nourishing. **~'mento** *nm* nourishment

nu'tri|re *vt* nourish; harbour ⟨*sentimenti*⟩. **~rsi** eat; **~rsi di** *fig* live on. **~'tivo** *a* nourishing. **~zi'one** *nf* nutrition

'nuvola *nf* cloud. **nuvo'loso** *a* cloudy

nuzi'ale *a* nuptial; ⟨*vestito, anello ecc*⟩ wedding *attrib*

Oo

O *abbr* (**ovest**) W

o *conj* or; ~ **l'uno** ○ **l'altro** one or the other, either

'oasi *nf inv* oasis

obbedi'ente ecc = **ubbidiente** ecc

obbli'ga|re *vt* force, oblige; **~rsi** *vr* **~rsi a** undertake to. **~to to** *a* obliged. **~'torio** *a* compulsory. **~zi'one** *nf* obligation; *Comm* bond. **'obbligo** *nm* obligation; (*dovere*) duty; **avere obblighi verso** be under an obligation to; **d'obbligo** obligatory

obbligatoria'mente *adv* **fare qcsa ~** be obliged to do sth; **bisogna ~ farlo** you absolutely have to do it

ob'bro|brio *nm* disgrace. **~'brioso** *a* disgraceful

obe'lisco *nm* obelisk

obe'rare *vt* overburden

obesità *nf* obesity. **o'beso** *a* obese

obiet'tare *vt/i* object; **~ su** object to

obietti|va'mente *adv* objectively. **~vità** *nf* objectivity. **obiet'tivo** *a* objective ● *nm* objective; (*scopo*) object

obie|t'tore *nm* objector. **~ttore di coscienza** conscientious objector. **~zi'one** *nf* objection

obi'torio *nm* mortuary

o'blio *nm* oblivion

o'bliquo *a* oblique; *fig* underhand

oblite'rare *vt* obliterate

oblò *nm inv* porthole

'oboe *nm* oboe

obso'leto *a* obsolete

'oca *nf* (*pl* **oche**) goose; (*donna*) silly girl

occasio'nal|e *a* occasional. **~'mente** *adv* occasionally

occasi'one *nf* occasion; (*buon affare*) bargain; (*motivo*) cause; (*opportunità*) chance; **d'~** secondhand

occhi'aia *nf* eye socket; **occhiaie** *pl* shadows under the eyes

occhi'ali *nmpl* glasses, spectacles. **~ da sole** sunglasses. **~ da vista** glasses, spectacles

occhi'ata *nf* look; **dare un'~ a** have a look at

occhieggi'are *vt* ogle ● *vi* (*far capolino*) peep

occhi'ello *nm* buttonhole; (*asola*) eyelet

'occhio *nm* eye; **~!** watch out!; **a quattr'occhi** in private; **tenere d'~ qcno** keep an eye on sb; **a ~ [e croce]** roughly; **chiudere un'~** turn a blind eye; **dare nell'~** attract attention; **pagare** ○ **spendere un ~ [della testa]** pay an arm and a leg; **saltare agli occhi** be blindingly obvious. **~ nero** (*pesto*) black eye. **~ di pernice** (*callo*) corn. **~'lino** *nm* **fare l'~lino a qcno** wink at sb

occiden'tale *a* western ● *nmf* westerner. **occi'dente** *nm* west

oc'clu|dere *vt* obstruct. **~si'one** *nf* occlusion

occor'ren|te *a* necessary ● *nm* the necessary. **~za** *nf* need; **all'~za** if need be

oc'correre *vi* be necessary

occulta'mento *nm* **~ di prove** concealment of evidence

occul't|are *vt* hide. **~ismo** *nm* occult. **oc'culto** *a* hidden; (*magico*) occult

occu'pante *nmf* occupier; (*abusivo*) squatter

occu'pa|re *vt* occupy; spend (*tempo*); take up (*spazio*); (*dar lavoro a*) employ. **~rsi** *vr* occupy oneself; (*trovare lavoro*) find a job; **~rsi di** (*badare*) look after. **~to** *a* engaged; (*persona*) busy; (*posto*) taken. **~zi'one** *nf* occupation; **trovarsi un'~zione** (*interesse*) find oneself something to do

o'ceano *nm* ocean. **~ Atlantico** Atlantic [Ocean]. **~ Pacifico** Pacific [Ocean]

'ocra *nf* ochre

ocu'lare *a* ocular; (*testimone, bagno*) eye *attrib*

ocula'tezza *nf* care. **ocu'lato** *a* (*scelta*) wise

ocu'lista *nmf* optician; (*per malattie*) ophthalmologist

od *conj* or

'ode *nf* ode

odi'are *vt* hate

odi'erno *a* of today; (*attuale*) present

'odi|o *nm* hatred; **avere in ~o** hate. **~'oso** *a* hateful

odo'ra|re *vt* smell; (*profumare*) perfume ● *vi* **~re di** smell of. **~to** *nm* sense of smell. **o'dore** *nm* smell; (*profumo*) scent; (*profumo*) **c'è odore di...** there's a smell of...; **sentire odore di** smell; **odori** *pl Culin* herbs. **odo'roso** *a* fragrant

of'fender|e *vt* offend; (*ferire*) injure. **~si** *vr* take offence

offen'siv|a *nf Mil* offensive. **~o** *a* offensive

offe'rente *nmf* offerer; (*in aste*) bidder

offer'ta *nf* offer; (*donazione*) donation; *Comm* supply; (*nelle aste*) bid; **in ~a speciale** on special offer. **~o** *pp di* **offrire**

of'fes|a *nf* offence. **~o** *pp di* **offendere** ● *a* offended

offi'ciare *vt* officiate

offi'cina *nf* workshop; **~ [meccanica]** garage

of'frir|e *vt* offer. **~si** *vr* offer oneself; (*occasione:*) present itself; **~si di fare qcsa** offer to do sth

offu'scar|e *vt* darken; *fig* dull (*memoria, bellezza*); blur (*vista*). **~si** *vr* darken; (*fig: memoria, bellezza:*) fade away; (*vista:*) become blurred

of'talmico *a* ophthalmic

oggettività *nf* objectivity. **ogget'tivo** *a* objective

og'getto *nm* object; (*argomento*) subject; **oggetti** *pl* **smarriti** lost property, lost and found *Am*

'oggi *adv & nm* today; (*al giorno d'oggi*) nowadays; **da ~ in poi** from today on; **~ a otto** a week today; **dall'~ al domani** overnight; **il giornale di ~** today's paper; **al giorno d'~** these days, nowadays. **~gl'orno** *adv* nowadays

'ogni *a inv* every; (*qualsiasi*) any; **~ tre giorni** every three days; **ad ~ costo** at any cost; **ad ~ modo** anyway; **~ cosa** everything; **~ tanto** now and then; **~ volta che** every time, whenever

o'gnuno *pron* everyone, everybody; **~ di voi** each of you

ohimè *int* oh dear!

'ola *nf inv* Mexican wave

O'lan|da *nf* Holland. **o~'dese** *a* Dutch ● *nm* Dutchman; (*lingua*) Dutch ● *nf* Dutchwoman

ole'andro *nm* oleander

ole'at|o *a* oiled; **carta ~a** grease-proof paper

oleo'dotto *nm* oil pipeline. **ole'oso** *a* oily

ol'fatto *nm* sense of smell

oli'are *vt* oil

olim'piadi *nfpl* Olympic Games. **o'limpico** *a* Olympic. **olim'pionico** *a* (*primato, squadra*) Olympic

'olio *nm* oil; **sott'~** in oil; **colori a ~** oils; **quadro a ~** oil painting. **~ d'oliva** olive oil. **~ di semi** vegetable oil. **~ solare** sun-tan oil

o'liv|a *nf* olive. **oli'vastro** *a* olive. **oli'veto** *nm* olive grove. **~o** *nm* olive tree

'olmo *nm* elm

olo'gramma *nm* hologram

oltraggi'are *vt* offend. **ol'traggio** *nm* offence

ol'tranza *nf* **ad ~** to the bitter end

'oltre *adv* (*di luogo*) further; (*di tempo*) longer ● *prep* (*di luogo*) over; (*di tempo*) later than; (*più di*) more than; (*in aggiunta*) besides; **~ a** (*eccetto*) except, apart from; **per ~ due settimane** for more than two weeks; **una settimana e ~** a week and more. **~'mare** *adv* overseas. **~'modo** *adv* extremely

oltrepas'sare *vt* go beyond; (*eccedere*) exceed

o'maggio *nm* homage; (*dono*) gift; **in ~ con** free with; **omaggi** *pl* (*saluti*) respects

ombeli'cale *a* umbilical; **cordone ~** umbilical cord. **ombe'lico** *nm* navel

'ombr|a *nf* (*zona*) shade; (*immagine oscura*) shadow; **all'~a** in the shade. **~eggi'are** *vt* shade

om'brello *nm* umbrella. **ombrel'lone** *nm* beach umbrella

om'bretto *nm* eye-shadow

om'broso *a* shady; (*cavallo*) skittish

ome'lette *nf inv* omelette

ome'lia *nf Relig* sermon

omeopa'tia *nf* homoeopathy. **omeo'patico** *a* homoeopathic ● *nm* homoeopath

omertà *nf* conspiracy of silence

o'messo *pp di* **omettere**

o'mettere *vt* omit

OMG *nm abbr* (**organismo modificato geneticamente**) GMO

omi'cid|a *a* murderous ● *nmf* murderer. **~io** *nm* murder. **~io colposo** manslaughter

omissi'one *nf* omission

omogeneiz'zato *a* homogenized. **omo'geneo** *a* homogeneous

omolo'gare *vt* approve

o'monimo, -a *nmf* namesake ● *nm* (*parola*) homonym

omosessu'al|e *a* & *nmf* homosexual. **~ità** *nf* homosexuality

On. *abbr* (**onorevole**) M.P.

'oncia *nf* ounce

'onda *nf* wave; **andare in ~** *Radio* go on the air. **a ondate** in waves. **onde** *pl* **corte** short wave. **onde** *pl* **lunghe** long wave. **onde** *pl* **medie** medium wave. **on'data** *nf* wave

'onde *conj* so that ● *pron* whereby

ondeggi'are *vi* wave; ⟨*barca:*⟩ roll

ondula'torio *a* undulating. **~zi'one** *nf* undulation; (*di capelli*) wave

'oner|e *nm* burden. **~'oso** *a* onerous

onestà *nf* honesty; (*rettitudine*) integrity. **o'nesto** *a* honest; (*giusto*) just

'onice *nf* onyx

onnipo'tente *a* omnipotent

onnipre'sente *a* ubiquitous; *Rel* omnipresent

ono'mastico *nm* name-day

ono'ra|bile *a* honourable. **~re** *vt* (*fare onore a*) be a credit to; honour ⟨*promessa*⟩. **~rio** *a* honorary ● *nm* fee. **~rsi** *vr* **~rsi di** be proud of

o'nore *nm* honour; **in ~ di** ⟨*festa, ricevimento*⟩ in honour of; **fare ~ a** do justice to ⟨*pranzo*⟩; **farsi ~ in** excel in; **fare gli onori di casa** do the honours

ono'revole *a* honourable ● *nmf* Member of Parliament

onorifi'cenza *nf* honour; (*decorazione*) decoration. **ono'rifico** *a* honorary

'onta *nf* shame

O.N.U. *nf abbr* (**Organizzazione delle Nazioni Unite**) UN

o'paco *a* opaque; ⟨*colori ecc*⟩ dull; ⟨*fotografia, rossetto*⟩ matt

o'pale *nf* opal

'opera *nf* (*lavoro*) work; (*azione*) deed; *Mus* opera; (*teatro*) opera house; (*ente*) institution; **mettere in ~** put into effect; **mettersi all'~** get to work; **opere** *pl* **pubbliche** public works. **~ d'arte** work of art. **~ lirica** opera

ope'raio, -a *a* working ● *nmf* worker; **~ specializzato** skilled worker

ope'ra|re *vt Med* operate on; **farsi ~re** have an operation ● *vi* operate; (*agire*) work. **~'tivo**, **~'torio** *a* operating *attrib.* **~'tore**, **~'trice** *nmf* operator; *TV* cameraman. **~tore turistico** tour operator. **~zi'one** *nf* operation; *Comm* transaction

ope'retta *nf* operetta

ope'roso *a* industrious

opini'one *nf* opinion; **rimanere della propria ~** still feel the same way. **~ pubblica** public opinion, vox pop

'oppio *nm* opium

oppo'nente *a* opposing ● *nmf* opponent

op'por|re *vt* oppose; (*obiettare*) object; **~re resistenza** offer resistance. **~si** *vr* **~si a** oppose

opportu'ni|smo *nm* expediency. **~sta** *nmf* opportunist. **~tà** *nf inv* opportunity; (*l'essere opportuno*) timeliness. **oppor'tuno** *a* opportune; (*adeguato*) appropriate; **ritenere opportuno fare qcsa** think it appropriate to do sth; **il momento opportuno** the right moment

opposi'tore *nm* opposer. **~zi'one** *nf* opposition; **d'~zione** ⟨*giornale, partito*⟩ opposition

op'posto *pp di* **opporre** ● *a* opposite; ⟨*opinioni*⟩ opposing ● *nm* opposite; **all'~** on the contrary

oppres|si'one *nf* oppression. **~'sivo** *a* oppressive. **op'presso** *pp di* **opprimere** ● *a* oppressed. **~'sore** *nm* oppressor

oppri'me|nte *a* oppressive. **op'primere** *vt* oppress; (*gravare*) weigh down

op'pure *conj* otherwise, or [else]; **lunedì ~ martedì** Monday or Tuesday

op'tare *vi* **~ per** opt for

opu'lento *a* opulent

o'puscolo *nm* booklet; (*pubblicitario*) brochure

opzio'nale *a* optional. **opzi'one** *nf* option

'ora¹ *nf* time; (*unità*) hour; **di buon'~** early; **che ~ è?, che ore sono?** what time is it?; **mezz'~** half an hour; **a ore** ⟨*lavorare, pagare*⟩ by the hour; **50 km all'~** 50 km an hour; **a un'~ di macchina** one hour by car; **non vedo l'~ di vederti** I can't wait to see you; **fare le ore piccole** stay up until the small hours. **~ d'arrivo** arrival time. **l'~ esatta** *Teleph* speaking clock. **~ legale** daylight saving time. **~ di punta, ore** *pl* **di punta** peak time; (*per il traffico*) rush hour

'ora² *adv* now; (*tra poco*) presently; **~ come ~** just now, at the moment; **d'~ in poi** from now on; **per ~** for the time being, for now; **è ~ di finirla!** that's enough now! ● *conj* (*dunque*) now [then]; **~ che ci penso,...** now that I come to think about it,...

o'racolo nm oracle

'orafo nm goldsmith

o'rale a & nm oral; **per via ~** by mouth

ora'mai adv = **ormai**

o'rario a ⟨tariffa⟩ hourly; ⟨segnale⟩ time attrib; ⟨velocità⟩ per hour ● nm time; ⟨tabella dell'orario⟩ timetable, schedule Am; **essere in ~** be on time; **in senso ~** clockwise. **~ di chiusura** closing time. **~ flessibile** flexitime. **~ d'ufficio** business hours. **~ di visita** Med consulting hours

o'rata nf gilthead

ora'tore, -'trice nmf speaker

ora'torio, -a a oratorical ● nm Mus oratorio ● nmf oratory. **orazi'one** nf Relig prayer

'orbita nf orbit; Anat [eye-]socket

or'chestra nf orchestra; ⟨parte del teatro⟩ pit

orche'stra|le a orchestral ● nmf member of an/the orchestra. **~re** vt orchestrate

orchi'dea nf orchid

'orco nm ogre

'orda nf horde

or'digno nm device; ⟨arnese⟩ tool. **~ esplosivo** explosive device

ordi'nale a & nm ordinal

ordina'mento nm order; ⟨leggi⟩ rules pl.

ordi'nanza nf ⟨del sindaco⟩ bylaw; **d'~** ⟨soldato⟩ on duty

ordi'na|re vt ⟨sistemare⟩ arrange; ⟨comandare⟩ order; ⟨prescrivere⟩ prescribe; Relig ordain

ordi'nario a ordinary; ⟨grossolano⟩ common; ⟨professore⟩ with a permanent position; **di ordinaria amministrazione** routine ● nm ordinary; Univ professor

ordi'nato a ⟨in ordine⟩ tidy

ordinazi'one nf order; **fare un'~** place an order

'ordine nm order; ⟨di avvocati, medici⟩ association; **mettere in ~** put in order; tidy up ⟨appartamento ecc⟩; **di prim'~** first-class; **di terz'~e** ⟨film, albergo⟩ third- rate; **di ~ pratico/economico** ⟨problema⟩ of a practical/economic nature; **fino a nuovo ~** until further notice; **parola d'~** password. **~ del giorno** agenda. **ordini sacri** pl Holy Orders

or'dire vt ⟨tramare⟩ plot

orec'chino nm ear-ring

o'recchi|o nm (pl nf **orecchie**) ear; **avere ~o** have a good ear; **mi è giunto all'~o che...** I've heard that...; **parlare all'~o a qcno** whisper in sb's ear; **suonare a ~o** play by ear; **~'oni** pl Med mumps sg

o'refice nm jeweller. **~'ria** nf ⟨arte⟩ goldsmith's art; ⟨negozio⟩ goldsmith's [shop]

'orfano, -a a orphan ● nmf orphan. **~'trofio** nm orphanage

orga'netto nm barrel-organ; ⟨a bocca⟩ mouth-organ; ⟨fisarmonica⟩ accordion

or'ganico a organic ● nm personnel

orga'nismo nm organism; ⟨corpo umano⟩ body

orga'nista nmf organist

organiz'za|re vt organize. **~rsi** vr get organized. **~'tore, ~'trice** nmf organizer. **~zi'one** nf organization

'organo nm organ

or'gasmo nm orgasm; fig agitation

'orgia nf orgy

or'gogli|o nm pride. **~'oso** a proud

orien'tale a eastern; ⟨cinese ecc⟩ oriental

orienta'mento nm orientation; **perdere l'~** lose one's bearings; **senso dell'~** sense of direction

orien'ta|re vt orientate. **~rsi** vr find one's bearings; ⟨tendere⟩ tend

ori'ente nm east. **l'Estremo O~** the Far East. **il Medio O~** the Middle East

o'rigano nm oregano

origi'na|le a original; ⟨eccentrico⟩ odd ● nm original. **~lità** nf originality. **~re** vt/i originate. **~rio** a ⟨nativo⟩ native

o'rigine nf origin; **in ~** originally; **aver ~ da** originate from; **dare ~ a** give rise to

origli'are vi eavesdrop

o'rina nf urine. **ori'nale** nm chamberpot. **ori'nare** vi urinate

orl'undo a native

orizzon'tale a horizontal

orizzon'tare vt = **orientare**. **oriz'zonte** nm horizon

or'la|re vt hem. **~'tura** nf hem. **'orlo** nm edge; ⟨di vestito ecc⟩ hem

'orma nf track; ⟨di piede⟩ footprint; ⟨impronta⟩ mark

or'mai adv by now; ⟨passato⟩ by then; ⟨quasi⟩ almost

ormegg'iare vt moor. **or'meggio** nm mooring

ormo'nale a hormonal. **or'mone** nm hormone

ornamen'tale a ornamental. **orna'mento** nm ornament

or'na|re vt decorate. **~rsi** vr deck oneself. **~to** a ⟨stile⟩ ornate

ornitolo'gia nf ornithology

'oro nm gold; **d'~** gold; fig golden; **una persona d'~** a wonderful person

orologi'aio, -a nmf clockmaker, watchmaker

oro'logio nm (portatile) watch; (da tavolo, muro ecc) clock. **~ a pendolo** grandfather clock. **~ da polso** wristwatch. **~ a sveglia** alarm clock

o'roscopo nm horoscope

or'rendo a awful, dreadful

or'ribile a horrible

orripi'lante a horrifying

or'rore nm horror; **avere qcsa in ~** hate sth

orsacchi'otto nm teddy bear

'orso nm bear; (persona scontrosa) hermit. **~ bianco** polar bear

or'taggio nm vegetable

or'tensia nf hydrangea

or'tica nf nettle. **orti'caria** nf nettle-rash

orticol'tura nf horticulture. **'orto** nm vegetable plot

orto'dosso a orthodox

ortogo'nale a perpendicular

orto|gra'fia nf spelling. **~'grafico** a spelling attrib

orto'lano nm market gardener; (negozio) greengrocer's

orto|pe'dia nf orthopaedics sg. **~'pedico** a orthopaedic ● nm orthopaedist

orzai'olo nm sty

or'zata nf barley-water

osan'nato a praised to the skies

o'sare vt/i dare; (avere audacia) be daring

oscenità nf inv obscenity. **o'sceno** a obscene

oscil'la|re vi swing; ⟨prezzi ecc⟩ fluctuate; Tech oscillate; (fig: essere indeciso) vacillate. **~zi'one** nf swinging; (di prezzi) fluctuation; Tech oscillation

oscura'mento nm darkening; (fig: di vista, mente) dimming; (totale) black-out

oscu'r|are vt darken; fig obscure. **~arsi** vr get dark. **~ità** nf darkness. **o'scuro** a dark; (triste) gloomy; (incomprensibile) obscure

ospe'dal|e nm hospital. **~i'ero** a hospital attrib

ospi'ta|le a hospitable. **~lità** nf hospitality. **~re** vt give hospitality to. **'ospite** nm (chi ospita) host; (chi viene ospitato) guest ● nf hostess; guest

o'spizio nm (per vecchi) [old people's] home

ossa'tura nf bone structure; (di romanzo) structure, framework. **'osseo** a bone attrib

ossequi'|are vt pay one's respects to. **os'sequio** nm homage; **ossequi** pl respects. **~'oso** a obsequious

osser'van|te a ⟨cattolico⟩ practising. **~za** nf observance

osser'va|re vt observe; (notare) notice; keep ⟨ordine, silenzio⟩. **~'tore**, **~'trice** nmf observer. **~'torio** nm Astr observatory; Mil observation post. **~zi'one** nf observation; (rimprovero) reproach

ossessio'na|nte a haunting; ⟨persona⟩ nagging. **~re** vt obsess; (infastidire) nag. **ossessi'one** nf obsession; (assillo) pain in the neck. **osses'sivo** a obsessive. **os'sesso** a obsessed

os'sia conj that is

ossi'dabile a liable to tarnish

ossi'dar|e vt, **~si** vr oxidize

'ossido nm oxide. **~ di carbonio** carbon monoxide

os'sidrico a **fiamma ossidrica** blowlamp

ossige'nar|e vt oxygenate; (decolorare) bleach; fig put back on its feet ⟨azienda⟩. **~si** vr **~si i capelli** dye one's hair blonde. **os'sigeno** nm oxygen

'osso nm (Anat: pl nf **ossa**) bone; (di frutto) stone

osso'buco nm marrowbone

os'suto a bony

ostaco'lare vt hinder, obstruct. **o'stacolo** nm obstacle; Sport hurdle

o'staggio nm hostage; **prendere in ~** take hostage

o'stello nm **~ della gioventù** youth hostel

osten'ta|re vt show off; **~re indifferenza** pretend to be indifferent. **~zi'one** nf ostentation

oste'ria nf inn

o'stetrico, -a a obstetric ● nmf obstetrician

'ostia nf host; (cialda) wafer

'ostico a tough

o'stil|e a hostile. **~ità** nf inv hostility

osti'na|rsi vr persist (**a** in). **~to** a obstinate. **~zi'one** nf obstinacy

ostra'cismo nm ostracism

'ostrica nf oyster

ostro'goto nm **parlare ~** talk double Dutch

ostru|'ire *vt* obstruct. **~zi'one** *nf* obstruction

otorinolaringoi'atra *nmf* ear, nose and throat specialist

ottago'nale *a* octagonal. **ot'tagono** *nm* octagon

ot'tan|ta *a & nm* eighty. **~'tenne** *a & nmf* eighty-year-old. **~'tesimo** *a* eightieth. **~'tina** *nf* about eighty

ot'tav|a *nf* octave. **~o** *a* eighth

otte'nere *vt* obtain; *(più comune)* get; *(conseguire)* achieve

'ottico, -a *a* optic[al] ● *nmf* optician ● *nf (scienza)* optics *sg*; *(di lenti ecc)* optics *pl*

otti'ma|le *a* optimum. **~'mente** *adv* very well

otti'mis|mo *nm* optimism. **~ta** *nmf* optimist. **~tico** *a* optimistic

'ottimo *a* very good ● *nm* optimum

'otto *a & nm* eight

ot'tobre *nm* October

otto'cento *a & nm* eight hundred; **l'O~** the nineteenth century

ot'tone *nm* brass

ottuage'nario, -a *a & nmf* octogenarian

ottu'ra|re *vt* block; fill ⟨*dente*⟩. **~rsi** *vr* clog. **~'tore** *nm* Phot shutter. **~zi'one** *nf* stopping; *(di dente)* filling

ot'tuso *pp di* **ottundere** ● *a* obtuse

o'vaia *nf* ovary

o'vale *a & nm* oval

o'vat|ta *nf* cotton wool. **~'tato** *a* ⟨*suono, passi*⟩ muffled

ovazi'one *nf* ovation

over'dose *nf inv* overdose

'ovest *nm* west

o'vi|le *nm* sheep-fold. **~no** *a* sheep *attrib*

ovo'via *nf* two-seater cable car

ovulazi'one *nf* ovulation

o'vunque *adv* = **dovunque**

ov'vero *conj* or; *(cioè)* that is

ovvia'mente *adv* obviously

ovvi'are *vi* **~ a** *qcsa* counter sth. **'ovvio** *a* obvious

ozi'are *vi* laze around. **'ozio** *nm* idleness; **stare in ozio** idle about. **ozi'oso** *a* idle; ⟨*questione*⟩ pointless

o'zono *nm* ozone; **buco nell'~** hole in the ozone layer

Pp

pa'ca|re *vt* quieten. **~to** *a* quiet

pac'chetto *nm* packet; *(postale)* parcel, package; *(di sigarette)* pack, packet. **~ software** software package

'pacchia *nf (fam: situazione)* bed of roses

pacchia'nata *nf* **è una ~** it's so garish. **pacchi'ano** *a* garish

'pacco *nm* parcel; *(involto)* bundle. **~ regalo** gift-wrapped package

paccot'tiglia *nf (roba scadente)* junk, rubbish

'pace *nf* peace; **darsi ~** forget it; **fare ~ con** *qcno* make it up with sb; **lasciare in ~** *qcno* leave sb in peace

pachi'derma *nm (animale)* pachyderm

pachi'stano, -a *nmf & a* Pakistani

pacifi'ca|re *vt* reconcile; *(mettere pace)* pacify. **~zi'one** *nf* reconciliation

pa'cifico *a* pacific; *(calmo)* peaceful; **il P~** the Pacific

paci'fis|mo *nm* pacifism. **~ta** *nmf* pacifist

pacioc'cone, -a *nmf fam* chubby-chops

pa'dano *a* **pianura** *nf* **padana** Po Valley

pa'del|la *nf* frying-pan; *(per malati)* bedpan. **~'lata** *nf* **una ~lata di** a frying-panful of

padigli'one *nm* pavilion

'padr|e *nm* father; **~i** *pl (antenati)* forefathers. **pa'drino** *nm* godfather. **~e'nostro** *nm* **il ~enostro** the Lord's Prayer. **~e'terno** *nm* God Almighty

padro'nanza *nf* mastery. **~ di sé** self-control

pa'drone, -a *nmf* master; mistress; *(datore di lavoro)* boss; *(proprietario)* owner. **~ggi'are** *vt* master

pae'sag|gio *nm* scenery; *(pittura)* landscape. **~'gista** *nmf* landscape architect

149

paesano | panchetto

pae'sano, -a *a* country ● *nmf* villager

pa'ese *nm* (*nazione*) country; (*territorio*) land; (*villaggio*) village; **il Bel P~** Italy; **va' a quel ~!** get lost!; **Paesi** *pl* **Bassi** Netherlands

paf'futo *a* plump

'paga *nf* pay, wages *pl*

pa'gabile *a* payable

pa'gaia *nf* paddle

paga'mento *nm* payment; **a ~** (*parcheggio*) which you have to pay to use. **~ anticipato** *Comm* advance payment. **~ alla consegna** cash on delivery, COD

paga'nesimo *nm* paganism

pa'gano, -a *a* & *nmf* pagan

pa'gare *vt/i* pay; **~ da bere a qcno** buy sb a drink; **te la faccio ~** you'll pay for this

pa'gella *nf* [school] report

'pagina *nf* page. **Pagine** *pl* **Gialle** Yellow Pages. **~ web** *Comput* web page

'paglia *nf* straw

pagliac'cetto *nm* (*per bambini*) rompers *pl*

pagliac'ciata *nf* farce

pagli'accio *nm* clown

pagli'aio *nm* haystack

paglie'riccio *nm* straw mattress

pagli'etta *nf* (*cappello*) boater; (*per pentole*) steel wool

pagli'uzza *nf* wisp of straw; (*di metallo*) particle

pa'gnotta *nf* [round] loaf

pa'goda *nf* pagoda

pail'lette *nf inv* sequin

'paio *nm* (*pl nf* **paia**) pair; **un ~** (*circa due*) a couple; **un ~ di** (*scarpe, forbici*) a pair of

'Pakistan *nm* Pakistan

'pala *nf* shovel; (*di remo, elica*) blade; (*di ruota*) paddle

pala'fitta *nf* pile-dwelling

pala'sport *nm inv* indoor sports arena

pa'late *nfpl* **a ~** (*fare soldi*) hand over fist

pa'lato *nm* palate

palaz'zetto *nm* **~ dello sport** indoor sports arena

palaz'zina *nf* villa

pa'lazzo *nm* palace; (*edificio*) building. **~ delle esposizioni** exhibition centre. **~ di giustizia** law courts *pl*, courthouse. **~ dello sport** indoor sports arena

'palco *nm* (*pedana*) platform; *Theat* box. **~**['**scenico**] *nm* stage

pale'sar|e *vt* disclose. **~si** *vr* reveal oneself. **pa'lese** *a* evident

Pale'sti|na *nf* Palestine. **~'nese** *nmf* Palestinian

pa'lestra *nf* gymnasium, gym; (*ginnastica*) gymnastics *pl*

pa'letta *nf* spade; (*per focolare*) shovel. **~** [**della spazzatura**] dustpan

pa'letto *nm* peg

'palio *nm* (*premio*) prize. **il P~** horse-race held at Siena

paliz'zata *nf* fence

'palla *nf* ball; (*proiettile*) bullet; (*fam: bugia*) porkie; **che palle!** *vulg* this is a pain in the arse!. **~ di neve** snowball. **~ al piede** *fig* millstone round one's neck

pallaca'nestro *nf* basketball

palla'mano *nf* handball

pallanu'oto *nf* water polo

palla'volo *nf* volley-ball

palleggi'are *vi* (*calcio*) practise ball control; *Tennis* knock up

pallia'tivo *nm* palliative

'pallido *a* pale; **non ne ho la più pallida idea** I don't have the faintest idea

pal'lina *nf* (*di vetro*) marble

pal'lino *nm* **avere il ~ del calcio** be crazy about football

pallon'cino *nm* balloon; (*lanterna*) Chinese lantern; (*fam: etilometro*) Breathalyzer®

pal'lone *nm* ball; (*calcio*) football; (*aerostato*) balloon

pal'lore *nm* pallor

pal'loso *a sl* boring

pal'lottola *nf* pellet; (*proiettile*) bullet

'palm|a *nf Bot* palm. **~o** *nm Anat* palm; (*misura*) hand's-breadth; **restare con un ~o di naso** feel disappointed

'palo *nm* pole; (*di sostegno*) stake; (*in calcio*) goalpost; **fare il ~** (*ladro:*) keep a lookout. **~ della luce** lamppost

palom'baro *nm* diver

pal'pare *vt* feel

'palpebra *nf* eyelid

palpi'ta|re *vi* throb; (*fremere*) quiver. **~zi'one** *nf* palpitation. **'palpito** *nm* throb; (*del cuore*) beat

pa'lude *nf* marsh, swamp

palu'doso *a* marshy

pa'lustre *a* marshy; (*piante, uccelli*) marsh *attrib*

'pampino *nm* vine leaf

pana'cea *nf* panacea

'panca *nf* bench; (*in chiesa*) pew

pancar'ré *nm* sliced bread

pan'cetta *nf Culin* bacon; (*di una certa età*) paunch

pan'chetto *nm* [foot]stool

pan'china *nf* garden seat; (*in calcio*) bench

'**pancia** *nf* belly, tummy *fam*; **mal di ~** stomach-ache; **metter su ~** develop a paunch; **a ~ in giù** lying face down. **panci'era** *nf* corset

panci'olle: **stare in ~** lounge about

panci'one *nm* (*persona*) pot belly

panci'otto *nm* waistcoat

pande'monio *nm* pandemonium

pan'doro *nm* *kind of sponge cake eaten at Christmas*

'**pane** *nm* bread; (*pagnotta*) loaf; (*di burro*) block. **~ a cassetta** sliced bread. **pan grattato** breadcrumbs *pl.* **~ di segale** rye bread. **pan di Spagna** sponge cake. **~ tostato** toast

panett|e'ria *nf* bakery; (*negozio*) baker's [shop]. **~i'ere, -a** *nmf* baker

panet'tone *nf* *dome-shaped cake with sultanas and candied fruit eaten at Christmas*

'**panfilo** *nm* yacht

pan'forte *nm* *nougat-like spicy delicacy from Siena*

'**panico** *nm* panic; **lasciarsi prendere dal ~** panic

pani'ere *nm* basket; (*cesta*) hamper

pani'ficio *nm* bakery; (*negozio*) baker's [shop]

pani'naro *nm* *sl* ≈ preppie

pa'nino *nm* [bread] roll. **~ imbottito** filled roll. **~ al prosciutto** ham roll. **~'teca** *nf* sandwich bar

'**panna** *nf* cream. **~ da cucina** [single] cream. **~ montata** whipped cream

'**panne** *nf* *Mech* **in ~** broken down; **restare in ~** break down

pan'nello *nm* panel. **~ solare** solar panel

'**panno** *nm* cloth; **panni** *pl* (*abiti*) clothes; **mettersi nei panni di qcno** *fig* put oneself in sb's shoes

pan'nocchia *nf* (*di granoturco*) cob

panno'lino *nm* (*per bambini*) nappy; (*da donna*) sanitary towel

pano'ram|a *nm* panorama; *fig* overview. **~ico** *a* panoramic

pantacol'lant *nmpl* leggings

pantalon'cini *nmpl* **~** [**corti**] shorts

panta'loni *nmpl* trousers, pants *Am*

pan'tano *nm* bog

pan'tera *nf* panther; (*auto della polizia*) high-speed police car

pan'tofo|la *nf* slipper. **~'laio, -a** *nmf* *fig* stay-at-home

pan'zana *nf* fib

pao'nazzo *a* purple

'**papa** *nm* Pope

papà *nm inv* dad[dy]

pa'pale *a* papal

papa'lina *nf* skull-cap

papa'razzo *nm* paparazzo

pa'pato *nm* papacy

pa'pavero *nm* poppy

'**paper|a** *nf* (*errore*) slip of the tongue. **~o** *nm* gosling

papil'lon *nm inv* bow tie

pa'piro *nm* papyrus

'**pappa** *nf* (*per bambini*) pap

pappa'gallo *nm* parrot

pappa'molle *nmf* wimp

'**para** *nf* suede; **suole di ~** crêpe soles

pa'rabola *nf* parable; (*curva*) parabola

para'bolico *a* parabolic

para'brezza *nm inv* windscreen, windshield *Am*

paracadu'tar|e *vt* parachute. **~si** *vr* parachute

paraca'du|te *nm inv* parachute. **~'tismo** *nm* parachuting. **~'tista** *nmf* parachutist

para'carro *nm* roadside post

paradi'siaco *a* heavenly

para'diso *nm* paradise. **~ terrestre** Eden, earthly paradise

parados'sale *a* paradoxical. **para'dosso** *nm* paradox

para'fango *nm* mudguard

paraf'fina *nf* paraffin

parafra'sare *vt* paraphrase

para'fulmine *nm* lightning-conductor

pa'raggi *nmpl* neighbourhood *sg*

parago'na|bile *a* comparable (**a** to). **~re** *vt* compare. **para'gone** *nm* comparison; **a paragone di** in comparison with

pa'ragrafo *nm* paragraph

pa'ra|lisi *nf inv* paralysis. **~'litico, -a** *a & nmf* paralytic. **~liz'zare** *vt* paralyse. **~liz'zato** *a* (*dalla paura*) transfixed

paral'lel|a *nf* parallel line. **~a'mente** *adv* in parallel. **~o** *a & nm* parallel; **~e** *pl* parallel bars. **~o'gramma** *nm* parallelogram

para'lume *nm* lampshade

para'medico *nm* paramedic

pa'rametro *nm* parameter

para'noi|a *nf* paranoia. **~co, -a** *a & nmf* paranoid

paranor'male *a* (*fenomeno, facoltà*) paranormal

para'occhi *nmpl* blinkers. **parao'recchie** *nm* earmuffs

para'petto *nm* parapet

151   **parapiglia | parte**

para'piglia *nm* turmoil
para'plegico, -a *a* & *nmf* paraplegic
pa'rar|e *vt* (*addobbare*) adorn; (*ripara-re*) shield; save (*tiro, pallone*); ward off, parry (*schiaffo, pugno*) ● *vi* (*mirare*) lead up to. **~si** *vr* (*abbigliarsi*) dress up; (*da pioggia, pugni*) protect oneself; **~si dinanzi a qcno** appear in front of sb
para'sole *nm inv* parasol
paras'sita *a* parasitic ● *nm* parasite
parasta'tale *a* government-controlled
pa'rata *nf* parade; (*in calcio*) save; (*in scherma, pugilato*) parry
para'urti *nm inv Auto* bumper, fender *Am*
para'vento *nm* screen
par'cella *nf* bill
parcheggi'a|re *vt* park. **~'tore, ~'trice** *nmf* parking attendant. **~tore abusivo** *person who illegally earns money by looking after parked cars*
par'cheggio *nm* parking; (*posteggio*) carpark, parking lot *Am*
par'chimetro *nm* parking-meter
'parco[1] *a* sparing; (*moderato*) moderate
'parco[2] *nm* park. **~ di divertimenti** fun-fair. **~ giochi** playground. **~ naturale** wildlife park. **~ nazionale** national park. **~ regionale** [regional] wildlife park
pa'recchi *a* a good many ● *pron* several
pa'recchio *a* quite a lot of ● *pron* quite a lot ● *adv* rather; (*parecchio tempo*) quite a time
pareggi'are *vt* level; (*eguagliare*) equal; *Comm* balance ● *vi* draw
pa'reggio *nm Comm* balance; *Sport* draw
paren'tado *nm* relatives *pl*; (*vincolo di sangue*) relationship
pa'rente *nmf* relative. **~ stretto** close relation
paren'tela *nf* relatives *pl*; (*vincolo di sangue*) relationship
pa'rentesi *nf inv* parenthesis; (*segno grafico*) bracket; (*fig: pausa*) break. **~ pl graffe** curly brackets. **~ quadre** square brackets. **~ tonde** round brackets
pa'reo *nm* (*copricostume*) sarong; **a ~** (*gonna*) wrap-around
pa'rere[1] *nm* opinion; **a mio ~** in my opinion
pa'rere[2] *vi* seem; (*pensare*) think; **che te ne pare?** what do you think of it?; **pare di sì** it seems so

pa'rete *nf* wall; (*in alpinismo*) face. **~ divisoria** partition wall
'pari *a inv* equal; (*numero*) even; **andare di ~ passo** keep pace; **essere ~** be even *o* quits; **arrivare ~** draw; **~ ~** (*copiare, ripetere*) word for word; **fare ~ o dispari** ≈ toss a coin ● *nmf inv* equal, peer; **ragazza alla ~** au pair [girl]; **mettersi in ~ con qcsa** catch up with sth ● *nm* (*titolo nobiliare*) peer
Pa'rigi *nf* Paris
pa'riglia *nf* pair
pari|tà *nf* equality; *Tennis* deuce. **~'tario** *a* parity attrib
parlamen'tare *a* parliamentary ● *nmf* Member of Parliament ● *vi* discuss. **parla'mento** *nm* Parliament. **il Parlamento europeo** the European Parliament
parlan'tina *nf* **avere la ~** be a chatterbox
par'la|re *vt/i* speak, talk; (*confessare*) talk; **~ bene/male di qcno** speak well/ill of somebody; **non parliamone più** let's forget about it; **non se ne parla nemmeno!** don't even mention it!. **~to** *a* (*lingua*) spoken. **~'torio** *nm* parlour; (*in prigione*) visiting room
parlot'tare *vi* mutter. **parlot'tio** *nm* muttering
parmigi'ano *nm* Parmesan
paro'dia *nf* parody
pa'rola *nf* word; (*facoltà*) speech; **è una ~!** it is easier said than done!; **parole** *pl* (*di canzone*) words, lyrics; **rivolgere la ~ a** address; **dare a qcno la propria ~** give sb one's word; **in parole povere** crudely speaking. **parole** *pl* **incrociate** crossword [puzzle] *sg*. **~ d'onore** word of honour. **~ d'ordine** password. **paro'laccia** *nf* swear-word
par'quet *nm inv* (*pavimento*) parquet flooring
par'rocchi|a *nf* parish. **~'ale** *a* parish attrib. **~'ano, -a** *nmf* parishioner. **'parr|oco** *nm* parish priest
par'rucca *nf* wig
parrucchi'ere, -a *nmf* hairdresser
parruc'chino *nm* toupée, hairpiece
parsi'moni|a *nf* thrift. **~'oso** *a* thrifty
'parso *pp di* parere
'parte *nf* part; (*lato*) side; (*partito*) party; (*porzione*) share; **è gentile da** ...; **in ~** in part; **la maggior ~ di** the majority of; **d'altra ~** on the other hand; **da ~** aside; (*in disparte*) to one side; **farsi da ~** stand aside; **da ~ di** from; (*per conto di*) on behalf of; **è gentile da**

~ **tua** it is kind of you; **fare una brutta** ~ **a qcno** behave badly towards sb; **da che** ~ **è...?** whereabouts is...?; **da una** ~**..., dall'altra...** on the one hand..., on the other hand...; **dall'altra** ~ **di** on the other side of; **da nessuna** ~ nowhere; **da tutte le parti** (*essere*) everywhere; **da questa** ~ (*in questa direzione*) this way; **da un anno a questa** ~ for about a year now; **essere dalla** ~ **di qcno** be on sb's side; **prendere le parti di qcno** take sb's side; **essere** ~ **in causa** be involved; **fare** ~ **di** (*appartenere a*) be a member of; **rendere** ~ **a** take part in. ~ **civile** plaintiff

parteci'pante *nmf* participant

parteci'pa|re *vi* ~**re a** participate in, take part in; (*condividere*) share in. ~**zi'one** *nf* participation; (*annuncio*) announcement; *Fin* shareholding; (*presenza*) presence. **par'tecipe** *a* participating

parteggi'are *vi* ~ **per** side with

par'tenza *nf* departure; *Sport* start; **in** ~ **per** leaving for

parti'cella *nf* particle

parti'cipio *nm* participle

partico'lar|e *a* particular; (*privato*) private ● *nm* detail, particular; **fin nei minimi** ~**i** down to the smallest detail. ~**eggi'ato** *a* detailed. ~**ità** *nf inv* particularity; (*dettaglio*) detail

partigi'ano, -a *a & nmf* partisan

par'tire *vi* leave; (*aver inizio*) start; **a** ~ **da** [beginning] from

par'tita *nf* game; (*incontro*) match; *Comm* lot; (*contabilità*) entry. ~ **di calcio** football match. ~ **a carte** game of cards

par'tito *nm* party; (*scelta*) choice; (*occasione di matrimonio*) match; **per** ~ **preso** out of sheer pig-headedness

'parto *nm* childbirth; **un** ~ **facile** an easy birth *o* labour; **dolori** *pl* **del** ~ labour pains. ~ **cesareo** Caesarian section. ~**'rire** *vt* give birth to

par'venza *nf* appearance

parzi'al|e *a* partial. ~**ità** *nf* partiality. ~**'mente** *adv* (*non completamente*) partially; ~**mente scremato** semi-skimmed

pasco'lare *vt* graze. **'pascolo** *nm* pasture

'Pasqua *nf* Easter. **pa'squale** *a* Easter *attrib*

'passa: e ~ *adv* (*e oltre*) plus

pas'sabile *a* passable

pas'saggio *nm* passage; (*traversata*) crossing; *Sport* pass; (*su veicolo*) lift; **essere di** ~ be passing through. ~ **a livello** level crossing, grade crossing *Am*. ~ **pedonale** pedestrian crossing

passamon'tagna *nm inv* balaclava

pas'sante *nmf* passer-by ● *nm* (*di cintura*) loop ● *a* Tennis passing

passa'porto *nm* passport

pas'sa|re *vi* pass; (*attraversare*) pass through; (*far visita*) call; (*andare*) go; (*essere approvato*) be passed; ~**re alla storia** go down in history; **mi è** ~**to di mente** it slipped my mind; ~**re per un genio/idiota** be taken for a genius/an idiot; **farsi** ~**re per qcno** pass oneself off as sb ● *vt* (*far scorrere*) pass over; (*sopportare*) go through; (*al telefono*) put through; *Culin* strain; ~**re di moda** go out of fashion; **le passo il signor Rossi** I'll put you through to Mr Rossi; ~**rsela bene** be well off; **come te la passi?** how are you doing?. ~**ta** *nf* (*di vernice*) coat; (*spolverata*) dusting; (*occhiata*) look

passa'tempo *nm* pastime

pas'sato *a* past; **l'anno** ~ last year; **sono le tre passate** it's past *o* after three o'clock ● *nm* past; *Culin* purée; *Gram* past tense. ~ **prossimo** *Gram* present perfect. ~ **remoto** *Gram* [simple] past. ~ **di verdure** cream of vegetable soup

passaver'dure *nm inv* food mill

passeg'gero, -a *a* passing ● *nmf* passenger

passeggi'a|re *vi* walk, stroll. ~**ta** *nf* walk, stroll; (*luogo*) public walk; (*in bicicletta*) ride; **fare una** ~**ta** go for a walk

passeg'gino *nm* pushchair, stroller *Am*

pas'seggio *nm* walk; (*luogo*) promenade; **andare a** ~ go for a walk; **scarpe da** ~ walking shoes

passe-partout *nm inv* master-key

passe'rella *nf* gangway; *Aeron* boarding bridge; (*per sfilate*) catwalk

'passero *nm* sparrow. **passe'rotto** *nm* (*passero*) sparrow

pas'sibile *a* ~ **di** liable to

passio'nale *a* passionate. **passi'one** *nf* passion

pas'sivo *a* passive ● *nm* passive; *Comm* liabilities *pl*; **in** ~ (*bilancio*) loss-making

'passo *nm* step; (*orma*) footprint; (*andatura*) pace; (*brano*) passage; (*valico*) pass; **a due passi da qui** a stone's throw away; **a ~ d'uomo** at walking pace; **di buon ~** at a spanking pace; **fare due passi** go for a stroll; **di pari ~** *fig* hand in hand. **~ carrabile, ~ carraio** driveway

'**past|a** *nf* (*impasto per pane ecc*) dough; (*per dolci, pasticcino*) pastry; (*pastasciutta*) pasta; (*massa molle*) paste; *fig* nature. **~a frolla** shortcrust pastry. **pa'stella** *nf* batter

pastasci'utta *nf* pasta

pa'stello *nm* pastel

pa'sticca *nf* pastille; (*fam: pastiglia*) pill

pasticc|e'ria *nf* cake shop, patisserie; (*pasticcini*) pastries *pl*; (*arte*) confectionery

pasticci'are *vi* make a mess ● *vt* make a mess of

pasticci'ere, -a *nmf* confectioner

pastic'cino *nm* little cake

pa'sticci|o *nm Culin* pie; (*lavoro disordinato*) mess; **mettersi nei pasticci** get into trouble. **~'one, -a** *nmf* bungler ● *a* bungling

pasti'ficio *nm* pasta factory

pa'stiglia *nf Med* pill, tablet; (*di menta*) sweet. **~ dei freni** brake pad

'**pasto** *nm* meal

pasto'rale *a* pastoral. **pa'store** *nm* shepherd; *Relig* pastor. **pastore tedesco** German shepherd, Alsatian

pastoriz'za|re *vt* pasteurize. **~to** *a* pasteurized. **~zi'one** *nf* pasteurization

pa'stoso *a* doughy; *fig* mellow

pa'stura *nf* pasture; (*per pesci*) bait

pa'tacca *nf* (*macchia*) stain; (*fig: oggetto senza valore*) piece of junk

pa'tata *nf* potato. **patate** *pl* **fritte** chips *Br*, French fries. **pata'tine** *nfpl* [potato] crisps, chips *Am*

pata'trac *nm inv* (*crollo*) crash

pâté *nm inv* pâté

pa'tella *nf* limpet

pa'tema *nm* anxiety

pa'tente *nf* licence. **~ di guida** driving licence, driver's license *Am*

pater'na|le *nf* scolding. **~'lista** *nm* paternalist

paternità *nf* paternity. **pa'terno** *a* paternal; (*affetto ecc*) fatherly

pa'tetico *a* pathetic. '**pathos** *nm* pathos

pa'tibolo *nm* gallows *sg*

'**patina** *nf* patina; (*sulla lingua*) coating

pa'ti|re *vt/i* suffer. **~to, -a** *a* suffering ● *nmf* fanatic. **~to della musica** music lover

patolo'gia *nf* pathology. **pato'logico** *a* pathological

'**patria** *nf* native land

patri'arca *nm* patriarch

pa'trigno *nm* stepfather

patrimoni'ale *a* property *attrib*. **patri'monio** *nm* estate

patri'o|ta *nmf* patriot. **~tico** *a* patriotic. **~'tismo** *nm* patriotism

pa'trizio, -a *a* & *nmf* patrician

patro|ci'nare *vt* support. **~'cinio** *nm* support

patro'nato *nm* patronage. **pa'trono** *nm Relig* patron saint; *Jur* counsel

'**patta¹** *nf* (*di tasca*) flap

'**patta²** *nf* (*pareggio*) draw

patteggi|a'mento *nm* bargaining. **~'are** *vt/i* negotiate

patti'naggio *nm* skating. **~ su ghiaccio** ice skating. **~ a rotelle** roller skating

patti'na|re *vi* skate; (*auto:*) skid. **~'tore, ~'trice** *nmf* skater. '**pattino** *nm* skate; *Aeron* skid. **pattino da ghiaccio** iceskate. **pattino a rotelle** roller-skate

'**patto** *nm* deal; *Pol* pact; **a ~ che** on condition that

pat'tuglia *nf* patrol. **~ stradale** ≈ patrol car; police motorbike, highway patrol *Am*

pattu'ire *vt* negotiate

pattumi'era *nf* dustbin, trashcan *Am*

pa'ura *nf* fear; (*spavento*) fright; **aver ~** be afraid; **mettere ~ a** frighten. **pau'roso** *a* (*che fa paura*) frightening; (*che ha paura*) fearful; (*fam: enorme*) awesome

'**pausa** *nf* pause; (*nel lavoro*) break; **fare una ~** pause; (*nel lavoro*) have a break

pavimen'ta|re *vt* pave (*strada*). **~zi'one** *nf* (*operazione*) paving. **pavi'mento** *nm* floor

pa'vone *nm* peacock. **~ggi'arsi** *vr* strut

pazien'tare *vi* be patient

pazi'ente *a* & *nmf* patient. **~'mente** *adv* patiently. **pazi'enza** *nf* patience; **pazienza!** never mind!

'**pazza** *nf* madwoman. **~'mente** *adv* madly

paz'z|esco *a* foolish; (*esagerato*) crazy. **~ia** *nf* madness; (*azione*) [act of] folly. '**pazzo** *a* mad; *fig* crazy ● *nm* madman; **essere pazzo di/per** be crazy about; **pazzo di gioia** mad with joy; **da pazzi** *fam* crackpot; **darsi alla pazza gioia** live it up. **paz'zoide** *a* whacky

'**pecca** *nf* fault; **senza** ~ flawless.
  peccami'noso *a* sinful
pec'ca|re *vi* sin; ~**re di** be guilty of
  ‹*ingratitudine*›. ~**to** *nm* sin; ~**to che...**
  it's a pity that...; [**che**] ~**to!** [what a]
  pity!. ~'**tore**, ~'**trice** *nmf* sinner
'**pece** *nf* pitch
'**peco|ra** *nf* sheep. ~**ra nera** black
  sheep. ~'**raio** *nm* shepherd. ~'**rella** *nf*
  cielo a ~**relle** sky full of fluffy white
  clouds. ~'**rino** *nm* (*formaggio*) sheep's
  milk cheese
peculi'ar|e *a* ~ **di** peculiar to. ~**ità** *nf*
  inv peculiarity
pe'daggio *nm* toll
pedago'gia *nf* pedagogy. **peda'gogi-**
  co *a* pedagogical
peda'lare *vi* pedal. **pe'dale** *nm* pedal.
  pedalò *nm inv* pedalo
pe'dana *nf* footrest; *Sport* springboard
pe'dante *a* pedantic. ~'**ria** *nf* pedantry.
  pedan'tesco *a* pedantic
pe'data *nf* (*in calcio*) kick; (*impronta*)
  footprint
pede'rasta *nm* pederast
pe'destre *a* pedestrian
pedi'atra *nmf* paediatrician. **pedia-**
  '**tria** *nf* paediatrics *sg*
pedi'cure *nmf inv* chiropodist, podia-
  trist *Am* • *nm* (*cura dei piedi*) pedicure
pedi'gree *nm inv* pedigree
pe'dina *nf* (*alla dama*) piece; *fig* pawn.
  ~'**mento** *nm* shadowing. **pedi'nare** *vt*
  shadow
pe'dofilo, -a *nmf* paedophile
pedo'nale *a* pedestrian. **pe'done, -a**
  nmf pedestrian
peeling *nm inv* exfoliation treatment
'**peggio** *adv* worse; ~ **per te!** too bad!;
  ~ **di così** any worse; **la persona** ~
  vestita the worst dressed person • *a*
  worse; **niente di** ~ nothing worse per
  il ~ **è che...** the worst of it is that...;
  pensare al ~ think the worst • *nf* **alla**
  ~ at worst; **avere la** ~ get the worst of
  it; **alla meno** ~ as best I can
peggiora'mento *nm* worsening
peggiora're *vt* make worse, worsen
  • *vi* get worse, worsen. ~'**tivo** *a* pejorative
peggi'ore *a* worse; (*superlativo*) worst;
  nella ~ **delle ipotesi** if the worst
  comes to the worst • *nmf* **il/la** ~ the
  worst
'**pegno** *nm* pledge; (*nei giochi di società*)
  forfeit; *fig* token
pelan'drone *nm* slob
pe'la|re *vt* (*spennare*) pluck; (*spellare*)

skin; (*sbucciare*) peel; (*fam: spillare
  denaro*) fleece. ~**rsi** *vr fam* lose one's
  hair. ~**to** *a* bald. ~**ti** *nmpl* (*pomodori*)
  peeled tomatoes
pel'lame *nm* skins *pl*
'**pelle** *nf* skin; (*cuoio*) leather; (*buccia*)
  peel; **avere la** ~ **d'oca** have goose-flesh
pellegri'naggio *nm* pilgrimage.
  pelle'grino, -a *nmf* pilgrim
pelle'rossa *nmf* Red Indian, Redskin
pellette'ria *nf* leather goods *pl*
pelli'cano *nm* pelican
pellicc|e'ria *nf* furrier's [shop].
  pel'licc|ia *nf* fur; (*indumento*) fur coat.
  ~**i'aio, -a** *nmf* furrier
pel'licola *nf* Phot, Cinema film. ~
  [**trasparente**] cling film
'**pelo** *nm* hair; (*di animale*) coat; (*di
  lana*) pile; **per un** ~ by the skin of one's
  teeth; **cavarsela per un** ~ have a narrow escape. **pe'loso** *a* hairy
'**peltro** *nm* pewter
pe'luche *nm inv* **giocattolo di** ~ soft
  toy
pe'luria *nf* down
'**pelvico** *a* pelvic
'**pena** *nf* (*punizione*) punishment; (*sofferenza*) pain; (*dispiacere*) sorrow; (*disturbo*) trouble; **a mala** ~ hardly; **mi fa**
  ~ I pity him; **vale la** ~ **andare** it is
  worth [while] going. ~ **di morte** death
  sentence
pe'nal|e *a* criminal; **diritto** *nm* ~**e**
  criminal law. ~**ità** *nf inv* penalty
penaliz'za|re *vt* penalize. ~**zi'one** *nf*
  (*penalità*) penalty
pe'nare *vi* suffer; (*faticare*) find it difficult
pen'daglio *nm* pendant
pen'dant *nm inv* **fare** ~ [**con**] match
pen'den|te *a* hanging; *Comm* out-
  standing • *nm* (*ciondolo*) pendant; ~**ti**
  pl drop earrings; ~**za** *nf* slope; *Comm*
  outstanding account
'**pendere** *vi* hang; ‹*superficie:*› slope;
  (*essere inclinato*) lean
pen'dio *nm* slope; **in** ~ sloping
pendo'l|are *a* pendulum • *nmf* com-
  muter. ~**ino** *nm* (*treno*) special, first
  class only, fast train
'**pendolo** *nm* pendulum
'**pene** *nm* penis
pene'trante *a* penetrating; ‹*freddo*›
  biting
pene'tra|re *vt/i* penetrate; (*trafiggere*)
  pierce • *vt* ‹*odore:*› get into • *vi* (*entrare
  furtivamente*) steal in. ~**zi'one** *nf* pen-
  etration

penicil'lina *nf* penicillin

pe'nisola *nf* peninsula

peni'ten|te *a & nmf* penitent. **~za** *nf* penitence; (*punizione*) penance; (*in gioco*) forfeit. **~zi'ario** *nm* penitentiary

'penna *nf* (*da scrivere*) pen; (*di uccello*) feather. **~ a feltro** felt-tip[ped pen]. **~ a sfera** ball-point [pen]. **~ stilografica** fountain-pen

pen'nacchio *nm* plume

penna'rello *nm* felt-tip[ped pen]

pennel'la|re *vt* paint. **~ta** *nf* brushstroke. **pen'nello** *nm* brush; **a pennello** (*a perfezione*) perfectly

pen'nino *nm* nib

pen'none *nm* (*di bandiera*) flagpole

pen'nuto *a* feathered

pe'nombra *nf* half-light

pe'noso *a* (*fam: pessimo*) painful

pen'sa|re *vi* think; **penso di sì** I think so; **~re** a think of; remember to ⟨*chiudere il gas ecc*⟩; **pensa ai fatti tuoi!** mind your own business!; **ci penso io** I'll take care of it; **~re di fare qcsa** think of doing sth; **~re tra sé e sé** think to oneself ● *vt* think. **~ta** *nf* idea

pensi'e|ro *nm* thought; (*mente*) mind; (*preoccupazione*) worry; **stare in ~ro per** be anxious about. **~'roso** *a* pensive

'pensi|le *a* hanging; **giardino ~le** roof-garden ● *nm* (*mobile*) wall unit. **~'lina** *nf* (*di fermata d'autobus*) bus shelter

pensio'nante *nmf* boarder; (*ospite pagante*) lodger

pensio'nato, -a *nmf* pensioner ● *nm* (*per anziani*) [old folks'] home; (*per studenti*) hostel. **pensi'one** *nf* pension; (*albergo*) boarding-house; (*vitto e alloggio*) board and lodging; **andare in pensione** retire; **mezza pensione** half board. **pensione completa** full board

pen'soso *a* pensive

pen'tagono *nm* pentagon

Pente'coste *nf* Whitsun

penti'mento *nm* repentance

pen'ti|rsi *vr* **~rsi di** repent of; (*rammaricarsi*) regret. **~'tismo** *nm* turning informant. **~to** *nm* Mafioso turned informant

'pentola *nf* saucepan; (*contenuto*) potful. **~ a pressione** pressure cooker

pe'nultimo *a* last but one

pe'nuria *nf* shortage

penzo'l|are *vi* dangle. **~oni** *adv* dangling

pe'pa|re *vt* pepper. **~to** *a* peppery

'pepe *nm* pepper; **grano di ~** peppercorn. **~ in grani** whole peppercorns. **~ macinato** ground pepper

pepero'n|ata *nf* peppers cooked in olive oil with onion, tomato and garlic. **~'cino** *nm* chilli pepper. **pepe'rone** *nm* pepper. **peperone verde** green pepper

pe'pita *nf* nugget

per *prep* for; (*attraverso*) through; (*stato in luogo*) in, on; (*distributivo*) per; (*mezzo, entro*) by; (*causa*) with; (*in qualità di*) as; **~ strada** on the street; **~ la fine del mese** by the end of the month; **in fila ~ due** in double file; **l'ho sentito ~ telefono** I spoke to him on the phone; **~ iscritto** in writing; **~ caso** by chance; **ho aspettato ~ ore** I've been waiting for hours; **~ tempo** in time; **~ sempre** forever; **~ scherzo** as a joke; **gridare ~ il dolore** scream with pain; **vendere ~ 10 milioni** sell for 10 million; **uno ~ volta** one at a time; **uno ~ uno** one by one; **venti ~ cento** twenty per cent; **~ fare qcsa** [in order to] do sth; **stare ~** be about to; **è troppo bello ~ essere vero** it's too good to be true

'pera *nf* pear; **farsi una ~** (*sl: di eroina*) shoot up

perbe'nis|mo *nm* prissiness. **~ta** *a inv* prissy

per'cento *adv* per cent. **percentu'ale** *nf* percentage

perce'pibile *a* perceivable; ⟨*somma*⟩ payable

perce'pi|re *vt* perceive; (*riscuotere*) cash

perce't'tibile *a* perceptible. **~zi'one** *nf* perception

perché *conj* (*in interrogazioni*) why; (*per il fatto che*) because; (*affinché*) so that; **~ non vieni?** why don't you come?; **dimmi ~** tell me why; **~ no/sì!** because!; **la ragione ~ l'ho fatto** the reason [that] I did it, the reason why I did it; **è troppo difficile ~ lo possa capire** it's too difficult for me to understand ● *nm inv* reason [why]; **senza un ~** without any reason

perciò *conj* so

per'correre *vt* cover ⟨*distanza*⟩; (*viaggiare*) travel. **per'corso** *pp di* **percorrere** ● *nm* (*tragitto*) course, route; (*distanza*) distance; (*viaggio*) journey

per'coss|a *nf* blow. **~o** *pp di* **percuotere. percu'otere** *vt* strike

percussi'o|ne *nf* percussion; **strumenti a ~ne** percussion instruments. **~'nista** *nmf* percussionist

per'dente *nmf* loser

'perder|e vt lose; (sprecare) waste; (non prendere) miss; ⟨fig: vizio:⟩ ruin; **~e tempo** waste time ● vi lose; ⟨recipiente:⟩ leak; **lascia ~e!** forget it!. **~si** vr get lost; (reciproco) lose touch

perdifi'ato: **a ~** adv ⟨gridare⟩ at the top of one's voice

perdigi'orno nmf inv idler

'perdita nf loss; (spreco) waste; (falla) leak; **a ~ d'occhio** as far as the eye can see. **~ di tempo** waste of time. **perdi'tempo** nm waste of time

perdo'nare vt forgive; (scusare) excuse. **per'dono** nm forgiveness; Jur pardon

perdu'rare vi last; (perseverare) persist

perduta'mente adv hopelessly. **per'duto** pp di **perdere** ● a lost; (rovinato) ruined

pe'renne a everlasting; Bot perennial; **nevi perenni** perpetual snow. **~'mente** adv perpetually

peren'torio a peremptory

per'fetto a perfect ● nm Gram perfect [tense]

perfezio'nar|e vt perfect; (migliorare) improve. **~si** vr improve oneself; (specializzarsi) specialize

perfezi'o|ne nf perfection; **alla ~ne** to perfection. **~'nismo** nm perfectionism. **~'nista** nmf perfectionist

per'fidia nf wickedness; (atto) wicked act. **'perfido** a treacherous; (malvagio) perverse

per'fino adv even

perfo'ra|re vt pierce; punch ⟨schede⟩; Mech drill. **~'tore**, **~'trice** nmf punch-card operator ● nm perforator. **~zi'one** nf perforation; (di schede) punching

per'formance nf inv performance

perga'mena nf parchment

perico'lante a precarious; ⟨azienda⟩ shaky

pe'rico|lo nm danger; (rischio) risk; **mettere in ~lo** endanger. **~lo pubblico** danger to society. **~'loso** a dangerous

perife'ria nf periphery; (di città) outskirts pl; fig fringes pl

peri'feric|a nf peripheral; (strada) ring road. **~o** a ⟨quartiere⟩ outlying

pe'rifrasi nf inv circumlocution

pe'rimetro nm perimeter

peri'odico nm periodical ● a periodical; ⟨vento, mal di testa, Math⟩ recurring. **pe'riodo** nm period; Gram sentence. **periodo di prova** trial period

peripe'zie nfpl misadventures

pe'rire vi perish

peri'scopio nm periscope

pe'ri|to, -a a skilled ● nmf expert

perito'nite nf peritonitis

pe'rizia nf skill; (valutazione) survey

'perla nf pearl. **per'lina** nf bead

perlo'meno adv at least

perlu'stra|re vt patrol. **~zi'one** nf patrol; **andare in ~zione** go on patrol

perma'loso a touchy

perma'ne|nte a permanent ● nf perm; **farsi [fare] la ~nte** have a perm. **~nza** nf permanence; (soggiorno) stay; **in ~nza** permanently. **~re** vi remain

perme'are vt permeate

per'messo pp di **permettere** ● nm permission; (autorizzazione) permit; Mil leave; **[è] ~?** (posso entrare?) may I come in?; (posso passare?) excuse me. **~ di lavoro** work permit

per'mettere vt allow, permit; **potersi ~** qcsa (finanziariamente) be able to afford sth; **come si permette?** how dare you?. **permis'sivo** a permissive

permutazi'one nf exchange; Math permutation

per'nacchia nf ⟨sl: con la bocca⟩ raspberry sl

per'nic|e nf partridge. **~i'oso** a pernicious

'perno nm pivot

pernot'tare vi stay overnight

'pero nm pear-tree

però conj but; (tuttavia) however

pero'rare vt plead

perpendico'lare a & nf perpendicular

perpe'trare vt perpetrate

perpetu'are vt perpetuate. **per'petuo** a perpetual

perplessità nf inv perplexity; (dubbio) doubt. **per'plesso** a perplexed

perqui'si|re vt search. **~zi'one** nf search. **~zione domiciliare** search of the premises

persecu'tore, -'trice nmf persecutor. **~zi'one** nf persecution

persegu'ire vt pursue

persegui'tare vt persecute

perseve'ra|nte a persevering. **~nza** nf perseverance. **~re** vi persevere

persi'ano, -a a Persian ● nf (di finestra) shutter. **'persico** a Persian

per'sino adv = **perfino**

persi'sten|te a persistent. **~za** nf persistence. **per'sistere** vi persist

'**perso** *pp di* **perdere** ● *a* lost; **a tempo** ~ in one's spare time

per'sona *nf* person; (*un tale*) somebody; **di ~, in ~** in person, personally; **per ~** per person, a head; **per interposta ~** through an intermediary; **persone** *pl* people

perso'naggio *nm* (*persona di riguardo*) personality; *Theat ecc* character

perso'nal|e *a* personal ● *nm* staff. **~e di terra** ground crew. **~ità** *nf inv* personality. **~iz'zare** *vt* customize (*auto ecc*); personalize (*penna ecc*)

personifi'ca|re *vt* personify. **~zi'one** *nf* personification

perspi'cac|e *a* shrewd. **~ia** *nf* shrewdness

persua|'dere *vt* convince; impress (*critici*); **~dere qcno a fare qcsa** persuade sb to do sth. **~si'one** *nf* persuasion. **~'sivo** *a* persuasive. **persu'aso** *pp di* **persuadere**

per'tanto *conj* therefore

'**pertica** *nf* pole

perti'nente *a* relevant

per'tosse *nf* whooping cough

pertur'ba|re *vt* perturb. **~zi'one** *nf* disturbance. **~zione atmosferica** atmospheric disturbance

per'va|dere *vt* pervade. **~so** *pp di* **pervadere**

perven'ire *vi* reach; **far ~ qcsa a qcno** send sth to sb

pervers|'ione *nf* perversion. **~ità** *nf* perversity. **per'verso** *a* perverse

perver'ti|re *vt* pervert. **~to** *a* perverted ● *nm* pervert

per'vinca *nm* (*colore*) blue with a touch of purple

p. es. *abbr* (**per esempio**) e.g.

pesa *nf* weighing; (*bilancia*) weighing machine; (*per veicoli*) weighbridge

pe'sante *a* heavy; (*stomaco*) overfull ● *adv* (*vestirsi*) warmly. **~'mente** *adv* (*cadere*) heavily. **pesan'tezza** *nf* heaviness

pe'sar|e *vt/i* weigh; **~e su** *fig* lie heavy on; **~e le parole** weigh one's words. **~si** *vr* weigh oneself

'**pesca**[1] *nf* (*frutto*) peach

'**pesca**[2] *nf* fishing; **andare a ~** go fishing. **~ subaquea** underwater fishing. **pe'scare** *vt* (*andare a pesca di*) fish for; (*prendere*) catch; (*fig: trovare*) fish out. **~'tore** *nm* fisherman

'**pesce** *nm* fish. **~ d'aprile!** April Fool!. ~ **grosso** *fig* big fish. ~ **piccolo** *fig* small fry. ~ **rosso** goldfish. ~ **spada** swordfish. **Pesci** *Astr* Pisces

pesce'cane *nm* shark

pesche'reccio *nm* fishing boat

pesc|he'ria *nf* fishmonger's [shop]. **~hi'era** *nf* fish-pond. **~i'vendolo** *nm* fishmonger

'**pesco** *nm* peach-tree

'**peso** *nm* weight; **essere di ~ per qcno** be a burden to sb; **di poco ~** (*senza importanza*) not very important; **non dare ~ a qcsa** not attach any importance to sth

pessi'mis|mo *nm* pessimism. **~ta** *nmf* pessimist ● *a* pessimistic. '**pessimo** *a* very bad

pe'staggio *nm* beating-up. **pe'stare** *vt* tread on; (*schiacciare*) crush; (*picchiare*) beat; crush (*aglio, prezzemolo*)

'**peste** *nf* plague; (*persona*) pest

pe'stello *nm* pestle

pesti'cida *nm* pesticide. **pe'stifero** *a* (*fastidioso*) pestilential

pesti'len|za *nf* pestilence; (*fetore*) stench. **~zi'ale** *a* (*odore aria*) noxious

'**pesto** *a* ground; **occhio** *nm* ~ black eye ● *nm* basil and garlic sauce

'**petalo** *nm* petal

pe'tardo *nm* banger

petizi'one *nf* petition; **fare una ~** draw up a petition

petro|li'era *nf* [oil] tanker. **~'lifero** *a* oil-bearing. **pe'trolio** *nm* oil

pettego|'lare *vi* gossip. **~'lezzo** *nm* piece of gossip; **far ~lezzi** gossip

pet'tegolo, -a *a* gossipy ● *nmf* gossip

petti'na|re *vt* comb. **~rsi** *vr* comb one's hair. **~'tura** *nf* combing; (*acconciatura*) hair-style. '**pettine** *nm* comb

'**petting** *nm* petting

petti'nino *nm* (*fermaglio*) comb

petti'rosso *nm* robin [redbreast]

'**petto** *nm* chest; (*seno*) breast; **a doppio ~** double-breasted

petto|'rale *nm* (*in gare sportive*) number.. **~'rina** *nf* (*di salopette*) bib. **~'ruto** *a* (*donna*) full-breasted; (*uomo*) broad-chested

petu'lante *a* impertinent

'**pezza** *nf* cloth; (*toppa*) patch; (*rotolo di tessuto*) roll

pez'zente *nmf* tramp; (*avaro*) miser

'**pezzo** *nm* piece; (*parte*) part; **un bel ~ d'uomo** a fine figure of a man; **un ~** (*di tempo*) some time; (*di spazio*) a long way; **al ~** (*costare*) each; **essere a pezzi** (*stanco*) be shattered; **fare a pezzi** tear to shreds. ~ **grosso** bigwig

pia'cente *a* attractive

pia'ce|re *nm* pleasure; (*favore*) favour; **a ~re** as much as one likes; **per ~re!** please!; **~re [di conoscerla]!** pleased to meet you!; **con ~re** with pleasure ● *vi* **la Scozia mi piace** I like Scotland; **mi piacciono i dolci** I like sweets; **faccio come mi pare e piace** I do as I please; **ti piace?** do you like it?; **lo spettacolo è piaciuto** the show was a success. **~vole** *a* pleasant

piaci'mento *nm* **a ~** as much as you like

pia'dina *nf* unleavened focaccia bread

pi'aga *nf* sore; *fig* scourge; (*fig: persona noiosa*) pain; (*fig: ricordo doloroso*) wound

piagni'steo *nm* whining

piagnuco'lare *vi* whimper

pi'alla *nf* plane. **pial'lare** *vt* plane

pi'ana *nf* (*pianura*) plane. **pianeggi'ante** *a* level

piane'rottolo *nm* landing

pia'neta *nm* planet

pi'angere *vi* cry; (*disperatamente*) weep ● *vt* (*lamentare*) lament; (*per un lutto*) mourn

pianifi'ca|re *vt* plan. **~zi'one** *nf* planning

pia'nista *nmf* *Mus* pianist

pi'ano *a* flat; (*a livello*) flush; (*regolare*) smooth; (*facile*) easy ● *adv* slowly; (*con cautela*) gently; **andarci ~** go carefully ● *nm* plain; (*di edificio*) floor; (*livello*) plane; (*progetto*) plan; *Mus* piano; **di primo ~** first-rate; **primo ~** *Phot* close-up; **in primo ~** in the foreground. **~ regolatore** town plan. **~ di studi** syllabus

piano'forte *nm* piano. **~ a coda** grand piano

piano'terra *nm inv* ground floor, first floor *Am*

pi'anta *nf* plant; (*del piede*) sole; (*disegno*) plan; **di sana ~** (*totalmente*) entirely; **in ~ stabile** permanently. **~ stradale** road map. **~gi'one** *nf* plantation

piantagrane *nmf* *fam* **è un/una ~** he's/she's bolshie

pian'tar|e *vt* plant; (*conficcare*) drive; (*fam: abbandonare*) dump; **piantala!** *fam* stop it!. **~si** *vr* plant oneself; (*fam: lasciarsi*) leave each other

pianter'reno *nm* ground floor, first floor *Am*

pi'anto *pp di* piangere ● *nm* crying; (*disperato*) weeping; (*lacrime*) tears *pl*

pian|to'nare *vt* guard. **~'tone** *nm* guard

pia'nura *nf* plain

p'iastra *nf* plate; (*lastra*) slab; *Culin* griddle. **~ elettronica** circuit board. **~ madre** *Comput* motherboard

pia'strella *nf* tile

pia'strina *nf* *Mil* identity disc; *Med* platelet; *Comput* chip

piatta'forma *nf* platform. **~ di lancio** launch pad

piat'tino *nm* saucer

pi'atto *a* flat ● *nm* plate; (*da portata, vivanda*) dish; (*portata*) course; (*parte piatta*) flat; (*di giradischi*) turntable; **piatti** *pl* *Mus* cymbals; **lavare i piatti** do the dishes, do the washing-up. **~ fondo** soup plate. **~ piano** [ordinary] plate

pi'azza *nf* square; *Comm* market; **letto a una ~** single bed; **letto a due piazze** double bed; **far ~ pulita** make a clean sweep. **~'forte** *nf* stronghold. **piaz'zale** *nm* large square. **~'mento** *nm* (*in classifica*) placing

piaz'za|re *vt* place. **~rsi** *vr* *Sport* be placed; **~rsi secondo** come second. **~to** *a* ⟨*cavallo*⟩ placed; **ben ~to** (*robusto*) well built

piaz'zista *nm* salesman

piaz'zuola *nf* **~ di sosta** pull-in

pic'cante *a* hot; (*pungente*) sharp; (*salace*) spicy

pic'carsi *vr* (*risentirsi*) take offence; **~ di** (*vantarsi di*) claim to

'picche *nfpl* (*in carte*) spades

picchet'tare *vt* stake; ⟨*scioperanti:*⟩ picket. **pic'chetto** *nm* picket

picchi'a|re *vt* beat, hit ● *vi* (*bussare*) knock; *Aeron* nosedive; **~re in testa** ⟨*motore:*⟩ knock. **~ta** *nf* beating; *Aeron* nosedive; **scendere in ~ta** nosedive

picchiet'tare *vt* tap; (*punteggiare*) spot

picchiet'tio *nm* tapping

'picchio *nm* woodpecker

pic'cino *a* tiny; (*gretto*) mean; (*di poca importanza*) petty ● *nm* little one, child

picci'one *nm* pigeon

'picco *nm* peak; **a ~** vertically; **colare a ~** sink

'piccolo, -a *a* small, little; (*di età*) young; (*di statura*) short; (*gretto*) petty ● *nmf* child, little one; **da ~** as a child

pic'co|ne *nm* pickaxe. **~zza** *nf* ice axe

pic'nic *nm inv* picnic

pi'docchio *nm* louse

piè *nm inv* **a ~ di pagina** at the foot of the page; **saltare a ~ pari** skip

pi'ede *nm* foot; **a piedi** on foot; **andare a piedi** walk; **a piedi nudi** barefoot; **a ~ libero** free; **in piedi** standing; **alzarsi in piedi** stand up; **in punta di piedi** on tiptoe; **ai piedi di** ⟨*montagna*⟩ at the foot of; **prendere ~** *fig* gain ground; ⟨*moda:*⟩ catch on; **mettere in piedi** ⟨*allestire*⟩ set up; **togliti dai piedi!** get out of the way!. **~ di porco** ⟨*strumento*⟩ jemmy

pie'dino *nm* **fare ~ a qcno** *fam* play footsie with sb

piedi'stallo *nm* pedestal

pi'ega *nf* ⟨*piegatura*⟩ fold; ⟨*di gonna*⟩ pleat; ⟨*di pantaloni*⟩ crease; ⟨*grinza*⟩ wrinkle; ⟨*andamento*⟩ turn; **non fare una ~** ⟨*ragionamento:*⟩ be flawless

pie'ga|re *vt* fold; ⟨*flettere*⟩ bend ● *vi* bend. **~rsi** *vr* bend. **~rsi a** *fig* yield to. **~'tura** *nf* folding

pieghet'ta|re *vt* pleat. **~to** *a* pleated. **pie'ghevole** *a* pliable; ⟨*tavolo*⟩ folding ● *nm* leaflet

piemon'tese *a* Piedmontese

pi'en|a *nf* ⟨*di fiume*⟩ flood; ⟨*folla*⟩ crowd. **~o** *a* full; ⟨*massiccio*⟩ solid; **in ~a estate** in the middle of summer; **a ~i voti** ⟨*diplomarsi*⟩ with A-grades, with first class honours ● *nm* ⟨*colmo*⟩ height; ⟨*carico*⟩ full load; **in ~o** ⟨*completamente*⟩ fully; **fare il ~o** ⟨*di benzina*⟩ fill up

pie'none *nm* **c'era il ~** the place was packed

'piercing *nm inv* body piercing

pietà *nf* pity; ⟨*misericordia*⟩ mercy; **senza ~** ⟨*persona*⟩ pitiless; ⟨*spietatamente*⟩ pitilessly; **avere ~ di qcno** take pity on sb; **far ~** ⟨*far pena*⟩ be pitiful

pie'tanza *nf* dish

pie'toso *a* pitiful, merciful; ⟨*fam: pessimo*⟩ terrible

pi'etr|a *nf* stone. **~a dura** semi-precious stone. **~a preziosa** precious stone. **~a dello scandalo** cause of the scandal. **pie'trame** *nm* stones *pl*. **~ifi'care** *vt* petrify. **pie'trina** *nf* ⟨*di accendino*⟩ flint. **pie'troso** *a* stony

pigi'ama *nm* pyjamas *pl*

'pigia 'pigia *nm inv* crowd, crush. **pigi'are** *vt* press

pigi'one *nf* rent; **dare a ~** let, rent out; **prendere a ~** rent

pigli'are *vt* ⟨*fam: afferrare*⟩ catch. **'piglio** *nm* air

pig'mento *nm* pigment

pig'meo, -a *a & nmf* pygmy

'pigna *nf* cone

pi'gnolo *a* pedantic

pigo'lare *vi* chirp. **pigo'lio** *nm* chirping

pi'grizia *nf* laziness. **'pigro** *a* lazy; ⟨*intelletto*⟩ slow

'pila *nf* pile; *Electr* battery; ⟨*fam: lampadina tascabile*⟩ torch; ⟨*vasca*⟩ basin; **a pile** battery operated, battery powered

pi'lastro *nm* pillar

'pillola *nf* pill; **prendere la ~** be on the pill

pi'lone *nm* pylon; ⟨*di ponte*⟩ pier

pi'lota *nmf* pilot ● *nm* *Auto* driver. **pilo'tare** *vt* pilot; drive ⟨*auto*⟩

pinaco'teca *nf* art gallery

'Pinco Pallino *nm* so-and-so

pi'neta *nf* pine-wood

ping-'pong *nm* table tennis, ping-pong *fam*

'pingu|e *a* fat. **~'edine** *nf* fatness

pingu'ino *nm* penguin; ⟨*gelato*⟩ choc ice on a stick

'pinna *nf* fin; ⟨*per nuotare*⟩ flipper

'pino *nm* pine[-tree]. **pi'nolo** *nm* pine kernel. **~ marittimo** cluster pine

'pinta *nf* pint

'pinza *nf* pliers *pl*; *Med* forceps *pl*

pin'za|re *vt* ⟨*con pinzatrice*⟩ staple. **~'trice** *nf* stapler

pin'zette *nfpl* tweezers *pl*

pinzi'monio *nm* sauce for crudités

'pio *a* pious; ⟨*benefico*⟩ charitable

pi'oggia *nf* rain; ⟨*fig: di pietre, insulti*⟩ hail, shower; **sotto la ~** in the rain. **~ acida** acid rain

pi'olo *nm* ⟨*di scala*⟩ rung

piom'ba|re *vi* fall heavily; **~re su** fall upon ● *vt* fill ⟨*dente*⟩. **~'tura** *nf* ⟨*di dente*⟩ filling. **piom'bino** *nm* ⟨*sigillo*⟩ [lead] seal; ⟨*da pesca*⟩ sinker; ⟨*in gonne*⟩ weight

pi'ombo *nm* lead; ⟨*sigillo*⟩ [lead] seal; **a ~** plumb; **senza ~** ⟨*benzina*⟩ lead-free

pioni'ere, -a *nmf* pioneer

pi'oppo *nm* poplar

pio'vano *a* **acqua piovana** rainwater

pi'ov|ere *vi* rain; **~e** it's raining; **~iggi'nare** *vi* drizzle. **pio'voso** *a* rainy

'pipa *nf* pipe

pipì *nf* **fare [la] ~** pee, piddle; **andare a fare [la] ~** go for a pee

pipi'strello *nm* bat

pi'ramide *nf* pyramid

pi'ranha *nm inv* piranha

pi'rat|a *nm* pirate. **~a della strada** road-hog ● *a inv* pirate. **~e'ria** *nf* piracy

piro'etta *nf* pirouette

pi'rofil|a *nf* ⟨*tegame*⟩ oven-proof dish. **~o** *a* heat-resistant

pi'romane *nmf* pyromaniac

pi'roscafo *nm* steamer. ~ **di linea** liner

pisci'are *vi vulg* piss

pi'scina *nf* swimming pool. ~ **coperta** indoor swimming pool. ~ **scoperta** outdoor swimming pool

pi'sello *nm* pea; (*fam: pene*) willie

piso'lino *nm* nap; **fare un** ~ have a nap

'pista *nf* track; *Aeron* runway; (*orma*) footprint; (*sci*) slope, piste. ~ **d'atterraggio** airstrip. ~ **da ballo** dance floor. ~ **ciclabile** cycle track

pi'stacchio *nm* pistachio

pi'stola *nf* pistol; (*per spruzzare*) spray-gun. ~ **a spruzzo** paint spray

pi'stone *nm* piston

pi'tone *nm* python

pit'to|re, -'trice *nmf* painter. ~'**resco** *a* picturesque. **pit'torico** *a* pictorial

pit'tu|ra *nf* painting. ~'**rare** *vt* paint

più *adv* more; (*superlativo*) most; *Math* plus; ~ **importante** more important; **il** ~ **importante** the most important; ~ **caro** dearer; **il** ~ **caro** the dearest; **di** ~ more; **una coperta in** ~ an extra blanket; **non ho** ~ **soldi** I don't have any more money; **non vive** ~ **a Milano** he no longer lives in Milan, he doesn't live in Milan any longer; ~ **o meno** more or less; **il** ~ **lentamente possibile** as slow as possible; **per di** ~ what's more; **mai** ~! never again!; ~ **di** more than; **sempre** ~ more and more ● *a* more; (*superlativo*) most; ~ **tempo** more time; **la classe con** ~ **alunni** the class with most pupils; ~ **volte** several times ● *nm* most; *Math* plus sign; **il** ~ **è fatto** the worst is over; **parlare del** ~ **e del meno** make small talk; **i** ~ **the** majority

piuccheper'fetto *nm* pluperfect

pi'uma *nf* feather. **piu'maggio** *nm* plumage. **piu'mino** *nm* (*di cigni*) down; (*copriletto*) eiderdown; (*per cipria*) powder-puff; (*per spolverare*) feather duster; (*giacca*) down jacket. **piu'mone**® *nm* duvet, continental quilt

piut'tosto *adv* rather; (*invece*) instead

pi'vello *nm fam* greenhorn

'pizza *nf* pizza; *Cinema* reel.

pizzai'ola *nf* slices of beef in tomato sauce, oregano and anchovies

pizze'ria *nf* pizza restaurant, pizzeria

pizzi'c|are *vt* pinch; (*pungere*) sting; (*di sapore*) taste sharp; (*fam: sorprendere*) catch; *Mus* pluck ● *vi* scratch; (*cibo:*) be spicy **'pizzico** *nm*, ~**otto** *nm* pinch

'pizzo *nm* lace; (*di montagna*) peak

pla'car|e *vt* placate; assuage (*fame, dolore*). ~**si** *vr* calm down

'placca *nf* plate; (*commemorativa, dentale*) plaque; *Med* patch

plac'ca|re *vt* plate. ~**to** *a* ~**to d'argento** silver-plated. ~**to d'oro** gold-plated. ~'**tura** *nf* plating

pla'centa *nf* placenta

'placido *a* placid

plagi'are *vt* plagiarize; pressure (*persona*). **'plagio** *nm* plagiarism

plaid *nm inv* tartan rug

pla'nare *vi* glide

'plancia *nf Naut* bridge; (*passerella*) gangplank

plane'tario *a* planetary ● *nm* planetarium

pla'smare *vt* mould

'plastic|a *nf* (*arte*) plastic art; *Med* plastic surgery; (*materia*) plastic. ~**o** *a* plastic ● *nm* plastic model

'platano *nm* plane[-tree]

pla'tea *nf* stalls *pl*; (*pubblico*) audience

'platino *nm* platinum

pla'tonico *a* platonic

plau'sibil|e *a* plausible. ~**ità** *nf* plausibility

ple'baglia *nf pej* mob

pleni'lunio *nm* full moon

'plettro *nm* plectrum

pleu'rite *nf* pleurisy

'plico *nm* packet; **in** ~ **a parte** under separate cover

plissé *a inv* plissé; (*gonna*) accordeon-pleated

plo'tone *nm* platoon; (*di ciclisti*) group. ~ **d'esecuzione** firing-squad

'plumbeo *a* leaden

plu'ral|e *a & nm* plural; **al** ~**e** in the plural. ~**ità** *nf* (*maggioranza*) majority

pluridiscipli'nare *a* multi-disciplinary

plurien'nale *a* ~ **esperienza** many years' experience

pluripar'titico *a Pol* multi-party

plu'tonio *nm* plutonium

pluvi'ale *a* rain *attrib*

pneu'matico *a* pneumatic ● *nm* tyre

pneu'monia *nf* pneumonia

po' *vedi* poco

po'chette *nf inv* clutch bag

po'chino *nm* **un** ~ a little bit

'poco *a little:* (*tempo*) short: (*con nomi plurali*) few ● *pron* little; (*poco tempo*) a short time; (*plurale*) few ● *nm* little; **un po'** a little [bit]; **un po' di** a little, some; (*con nomi plurali*) a few; **a** ~ **a** ~ little by little; **fra ~** soon; **per ~** (*a poco prezzo*) cheap; (*quasi*) nearly; **~ fa** a little while ago; **sono arrivato da ~** I have just arrived; **un bel po'** quite a lot; **un ~ di buono** a shady character ● *adv* (*con verbi*) not much; (*con avverbi*) not very; **parla ~** he doesn't speak much; **lo conosco ~** I don't know him very well; **~ spesso** not very often

po'dere *nm* farm

pode'roso *a* powerful

'podio *nm* dais; *Mus* podium

po'dis|mo *nm* walking. **~ta** *nmf* walker

po'e|ma *nm* poem. **~'sia** *nf* poetry; (*componimento*) poem. **~ta** *nm* poet. **~'tessa** *nf* poetess. **~tico** *a* poetic

poggiapi'edi *nm inv* footrest

poggi'a|re *vt* lean; (*posare*) place ● *vi* **~re su** to be based on. **~'testa** *nm inv* head-rest

'poggio *nm* hillock

poggi'olo *nm* balcony

poi *adv* (*dopo*) then; (*più tardi*) later [on]; (*finalmente*) finally. **d'ora in ~** from now on; **questa ~!** well!

poiché *conj* since

pois *nm inv* **a ~** polka-dot

'poker *nm* poker

po'lacco, -a *a* Polish ● *nmf* Pole ● *nm* (*lingua*) Polish

po'lar|e *a* polar. **~iz'zare** *vt* polarize

'polca *nf* polka

po'lemi|ca *nf* controversy. **~ca'mente** *adv* controversially. **~co** *a* controversial. **~z'zare** *vi* engage in controversy

po'lenta *nf* cornmeal porridge

poli'clinico *nm* general hospital

poli'estere *nm* polyester

poliga'mia *nf* polygamy. **po'ligamo** *a* polygamous

polio[mie'lite] *nf* polio[myelitis]

'polipo *nm* polyp

polisti'rolo *nm* polystyrene

poli'tecnico *nm* polytechnic

po'litic|a *nf* politics *sg*; (*linea di condotta*) policy. **fare ~a** be in politics. **~iz'zare** *vt* politicize. **~o, -a** *a* political ● *nmf* politician

poliva'lente *a* catch-all

poli'zi|a *nf* police. **~a giudiziaria** ≈ Criminal Investigation Department, CID. **~a stradale** traffic police. **~'esco** *a* police *attrib*; (*romanzo, film*) detective *attrib*. **~'otto** *nm* policeman

po'lizza *nf* policy

pol'la|io *nm* chicken run; (*fam: luogo chiassoso*) mad house. **~me** *nm* poultry.

~'strello *nm* spring chicken. **~stro** *nm* cockerel

'pollice *nm* thumb; (*unità di misura*) inch

'polline *nm* pollen; **allergia al ~** hay fever

polli'vendolo, -a *nmf* poulterer

'pollo *nm* chicken; (*fam: semplicione*) simpleton. **~ arrosto** roast chicken

polmo|'nare *a* pulmonary. **pol'mone** *nm* lung. **polmone d'acciaio** iron lung. **~'nite** *nf* pneumonia

'polo *nm* pole; *Sport* polo; (*maglietta*) polo top. **~ nord** North Pole. **~ sud** South Pole

Po'lonia *nf* Poland

'polpa *nf* pulp

pol'paccio *nm* calf

polpa'strello *nm* fingertip

pol'pet|ta *nf* meatball. **~'tone** *nm* meat loaf

'polpo *nm* octopus

pol'poso *a* fleshy

pol'sino *nm* cuff

'polso *nm* pulse; *Anat* wrist; *fig* authority; **avere ~** be strict

pol'tiglia *nf* mush

pol'trire *vi* lie around

pol'tron|a *nf* armchair; *Theat* seat in the stalls. **~e** *a* lazy

'polve|re *nf* dust; (*sostanza polverizzata*) powder; **in ~re** powdered; **sapone in ~re** soap powder. **~re da sparo** gun powder. **~'rina** *nf* (*medicina*) powder. **~riz'zare** *vt* pulverize; (*nebulizzare*) atomize. **~'rone** *nm* cloud of dust. **~'roso** *a* dusty

po'mata *nf* ointment, cream

po'mello *nm* knob; (*guancia*) cheek

pomeridi'ano *a* afternoon *attrib*; **alle tre pomeridiane** at three in the afternoon, at three p.m. **pome'riggio** *nm* afternoon

'pomice *nf* pumice

'pomo *nm* (*oggetto*) knob. **~ d'Adamo** Adam's apple

pomo'doro *nm* tomato

'pompa *nf* pump; (*sfarzo*) pomp. **pompe** *pl* **funebri** (*funzione*) funeral. **pom'pare** *vt* pump; (*gonfiare d'aria*) pump up; (*fig: esagerare*) exaggerate; **pompare fuori** pump out

pom'pelmo *nm* grapefruit

pompi'ere *nm* fireman; **i pompieri** the fire brigade

pom'pon *nm inv* pompom

pom'poso *a* pompous

ponde'rare *vt* ponder

po'nente *nm* west

'ponte *nm* bridge; *Naut* deck; (*impalcatura*) scaffolding; **fare il ~** *fig* make a long weekend of it

pon'tefice *nm* pontiff

pontifi'ca|re *vi* pontificate. **~to** *nm* pontificate

ponti'ficio *a* papal

pon'tile *nm* jetty

popò *nf inv fam* pooh

popo'lano *a* of the [common] people

popo'la|re *a* popular; (*comune*) common ● *vt* populate. **~rsi** *vr* get crowded. **~rità** *nf* popularity. **~zi'one** *nf* population. **'popolo** *nm* people. **popo'loso** *a* populous

'poppa *nf Naut* stern; (*mammella*) breast; **a ~** astern

pop'pa|re *vt* suck. **~ta** *nf* (*pasto*) feed. **~'toio** *nm* [feeding-]bottle

popu'lista *nmf* populist

por'cata *nf* load of rubbish; **porcate** *pl* (*fam: cibo*) junk food

porcel'lana *nf* porcelain, china

porcel'lino *nm* piglet. **~ d'India** guinea-pig

porche'ria *nf* dirt; (*fig: cosa orrenda*) piece of filth; (*fam: robaccia*) rubbish

por'ci|le *nm* pigsty. **~no** *a* pig *attrib* ● *nm* (*fungo*) edible mushroom. **'porco** *nm* pig; (*carne*) pork

porco'spino *nm* porcupine

'porgere *vt* give; (*offrire*) offer; **porgo distinti saluti** (*in lettera*) I remain, yours sincerely

porno'gra'fia *nf* pornography. **~'grafico** *a* pornographic

'poro *nm* pore. **po'roso** *a* porous

'porpora *nf* purple

'por|re *vt* put; (*collocare*) place; (*supporre*) suppose; ask ⟨*domanda*⟩; present ⟨*candidatura*⟩; **poniamo il caso che...** let us suppose that...; **~re fine** *o* **termine a** put an end to. **~si** *vr* put oneself; **~si a sedere** sit down; **~si in cammino** set out

'porro *nm Bot* leek; (*verruca*) wart

'porta *nf* door; *Sport* goal; (*di città*) gate; *Comput* port. **~ a ~** door-to-door; **mettere alla ~** show sb the door. **~ di servizio** tradesmen's entrance

portaba'gagli *nm inv* (*facchino*) porter; (*di treno ecc*) luggage rack; *Auto* boot, trunk *Am*; (*sul tetto di un'auto*) roof rack

portabot'tiglie *nm inv* bottle rack, wine rack

porta'cenere *nm inv* ashtray

portachi'avi *nm inv* keyring

porta'cipria *nm inv* compact

portadocu'menti *nm inv* document wallet

porta'erei *nf inv* aircraft carrier

portafi'nestra *nf* French window

porta'foglio *nm* wallet; (*per documenti*) portfolio; (*ministero*) ministry

portafor'tuna *nm inv* lucky charm ● *a inv* lucky

portagi'oie *nm inv* jewellery box

por'tale *nm* door

portama'tite *nm inv* pencil case

porta'mento *nm* carriage; (*condotta*) behaviour

porta'mina *nm inv* propelling pencil

portamo'nete *nm inv* purse

por'tante *a* bearing *attrib*

portaom'brelli *nm inv* umbrella stand

porta'pacchi *nm inv* roof rack; (*su bicicletta*) luggage rack

porta'penne *nm inv* pencil case

por'ta|re *vt* (*verso chi parla*) bring; (*lontano da chi parla*) take; (*sorreggere, Math*) carry; (*condurre*) lead; (*indossare*) wear; (*avere*) bear. **~rsi** *vr* (*trasferirsi*) move; (*comportarsi*) behave; **~rsi bene/male gli anni** look young/old for one's age

portari'viste *nm inv* magazine rack

porta'sci *nm inv* ski rack

portasiga'rette *nm inv* cigarette-case

porta'spilli *nm inv* pin-cushion

por'ta|ta *nf* (*di pranzo*) course; *Auto* carrying capacity; (*di arma*) range; (*fig: abilità*) capability; **a ~ta di mano** within reach; **alla ~ta di tutti** accessible to all; (*finanziariamente*) within everybody's reach. **por'tatile** *a* & *nm* portable. **~to** *a* ⟨*indumento*⟩ worn; ⟨*dotato*⟩ gifted; **essere ~to per qcsa** have a gift for sth; **essere ~to a** (*tendere a*) be inclined to. **~'tore, ~'trice** *nmf* bearer; **al ~tore** to the bearer. **~tore di handicap** disabled person

portatovagli'olo *nm* napkin ring

portau'ovo *nm inv* egg-cup

porta'voce *nm inv* spokesman ● *nf inv* spokeswoman

por'tento *nm* marvel; (*persona dotata*) prodigy

'portico *nm* portico

porti'er|a *nf* door; (*tendaggio*) door curtain. **~e** *nm* porter, doorman; *Sport* goalkeeper. **~e di notte** night porter

porti'n|aio, -a *nmf* caretaker, concierge. **~e'ria** nf concierge's room; (di ospedale) porter's lodge

'porto pp di **porgere** ● nm harbour; (complesso) port; (vino) port [wine]; (spesa di trasporto) carriage; **andare in ~** succeed. **~ d'armi** gun licence

Porto'g|allo nm Portugal. **p~hese** a & nmf Portuguese

por'tone nm main door

portu'ale nm dockworker, docker

porzi'one nf portion

'posa nf laying; (riposo) rest; Phot exposure; (atteggiamento) pose; **mettersi in ~** pose

po'sa|re vt put; (giù) put [down] ● vi (poggiare) rest; (per un ritratto) pose. **~rsi** vr alight; (sostare) rest; Aeron land. **~ta** nf piece of cutlery; **~te** pl cutlery sg. **~to** a sedate

po'scritto nm postscript

posi'tivo a positive

posizio'nare vt position

posizi'one nf position; **farsi una ~** get ahead

posolo'gia nf dosage

po'spo|rre vt place after; (posticipare) postpone. **~sto** pp di **posporre**

posse'd|ere vt possess, own. **~i'men-to** nm possession

posses|'sivo a possessive. **pos'sesso** nm ownership; (bene) possession. **~'so-re** nm owner

pos'sibil|e a possible; **il più presto ~e** as soon as possible ● nm **fare [tutto] il ~e** do one's best. **~ità** nf inv possibility; (occasione) chance ● nfpl (mezzi) means

possi'dente nmf land-owner

'posta nf post, mail; (ufficio postale) post office; (al gioco) stake; **spese di ~** postage; **per ~** by post, by mail; **la ~ in gioco è...** fig what's at stake is...; **a bella ~** on purpose; **Poste e Telecomunicazioni** pl [Italian] Post Office. **~ elettronica** electronic mail, e-mail. **~ prioritaria** ≈ first-class mail. **~ vocale** voice-mail

posta'giro nm postal giro

po'stale a postal

postazi'one nf position

postda'tare vt postdate ⟨assegno⟩

posteggi'a|re vt/i park. **~'tore**, **~'trice** nmf parking attendant. **po'steggio** nm car-park, parking lot Am; (di taxi) taxi-rank

'posteri nmpl descendants. **~'ore** a rear; (nel tempo) later ● nm fam posterior, behind. **~tà** nf posterity

po'sticcio a artificial; ⟨baffi, barba⟩ false ● nm hair-piece

postici'pare vt postpone

po'stilla nf note; Jur rider

po'stino nm postman, mailman Am

'posto pp di **porre** ● nm place; (spazio) room; (impiego) job; Mil post; (sedile) seat; **a/fuori ~** in/out of place; **prende-re ~** take up room; **sul ~** on-site; **esse-re a ~** ⟨casa, libri⟩ be tidy; **mettere a ~** tidy ⟨stanza⟩; **fare ~ a** make room for; **al ~ di** (invece di) in place of, instead of. **~ di blocco** checkpoint. **~ di guida** driving seat. **~ di lavoro** workstation. **~ di polizia** police station. **posti** pl **in piedi** standing room. **posti** pl **a sedere** seating

post-partum a post-natal

'postumo a posthumous ● nm after-effect

po'tabile a drinkable; **acqua ~** drinking water

po'tare vt prune

po'tassio nm potassium

po'ten|te a powerful; (efficace) potent. **~za** nf power; (efficacia) potency. **~zi'ale** a & nm potential

po'tere nm power; **al ~** in power ● vi can, be able to; **posso entrare?** can I come in?; (formale) may I come in?; **posso fare qualche cosa?** can I do something?; **che tu possa essere felice!** may you be happy!; **non ne posso più** (sono stanco) I can't go on; (sono stufo) I can't take any more; **può darsi** perhaps; **può darsi che sia vero** perhaps it's true; **potrebbe aver ragione** he could be right, he might be right; **avresti potuto telefonare** you could have phoned, you might have phoned; **spero di poter venire** I hope to be able to come; **senza poter telefonare** without being able to phone

potestà nf inv power

'pover|o, -a a poor; (semplice) plain ● nm poor man ● nf poor woman; **i ~i** the poor. **~tà** nf poverty

'pozza nf pool. **poz'zanghera** nf puddle

'pozzo nm well; (minerario) pit. **~ petrolifero** oil-well

PP.TT. abbr (Poste e Telegrafi) [Italian] Post Office

prag'matico a pragmatic

prali'nato a ⟨mandorla, gelato⟩ praline-coated

pram'matica nf **essere di ~** be customary

pran'zare vi dine; (a mezzogiorno)

lunch. 'pranzo nm dinner; (a mezzo-giorno) lunch. pranzo di nozze wedding breakfast

'prassi nf standard procedure

prate'ria nf grassland

'prati|ca nf practice; (esperienza) experience; (documentazione) file; avere ~ca di qcsa be familiar with sth; far ~ca gain experience; fare le pratiche per gather the necessary papers for. ~'cabile a practicable; (strada) passable. ~ca'mente adv practically. ~'cante nmf apprentice; Relig [regular] church-goer

prati'ca|re vt practise; (frequentare) associate with; (fare) make

praticità nf practicality. 'pratico a practical; (esperto) experienced; essere pratico di qcsa know about sth

'prato nm meadow; (di giardino) lawn

pre'ambolo nm preamble

preannunci'are vt give advance notice of

preavvi'sare vt forewarn. preav'viso nm warning

pre'cario a precarious

precauzi'one nf precaution; (cautela) care

prece'den|te a previous ● nm precedent. ~te'mente adv previously. ~za nf precedence; (di veicoli) right of way; dare la ~za give way. pre'cedere vt precede

pre'cetto nm precept

precipi'ta|re vt ~re le cose precipitate events; ~re qcno nella disperazione cast sb into a state of despair ● vi fall headlong; ⟨situazione, eventi:⟩ come to a head. ~rsi vr (gettarsi) throw oneself; (affrettarsi) rush; ~rsi a fare qcsa rush to do sth. ~zi'one nf (fretta) haste, (atmosferica) precipitation. precipi'toso a hasty; (avventato) reckless; ⟨caduta⟩ headlong

preci'pizio nm precipice; a ~ headlong

precisa'mente adv precisely

preci'sa|re vt specify; (spiegare) clarify. ~zi'one nf clarification

precisi'one nf precision. pre'ciso a precise; ⟨ore⟩ sharp; (identico) identical

pre'clu|dere vt preclude. ~so pp di precludere

pre'coc|e a precocious; (prematuro) premature. ~ità nf precociousness

precon'cetto a preconceived ● nm prejudice

pre'corr|ere vt ~ere i tempi be ahead of one's time

precur'sore nm forerunner, precursor

'preda nf prey; (bottino) booty; essere in ~ al panico be panic-stricken; in ~ alle fiamme engulfed in flames. pre'dare vt plunder. ~'tore nm predator

predeces'sore nmf predecessor

pre'del|la nf platform. ~'lino nm step

predesti'na|re vt predestine. ~to a Relig predestined, preordained

predetermi'nato a predetermined, preordained

pre'detto pp di predire

'predica nf sermon; fig lecture

predi'ca|re vt preach. ~to nm predicate

predi'le|tto, -a pp di prediligere ● a favourite ● nmf pet. ~zi'one nf predilection. predi'ligere vt prefer

pre'di|re vt foretell

predi'spo|rre vt arrange. ~rsi vr ~rsi a prepare oneself for. ~sizi'one nf predisposition; (al disegno ecc) bent (a for). ~sto pp di predisporre

predizi'one nf prediction

predomi'na|nte a predominant. ~re vi predominate. predo'minio nm predominance

pre'done nm robber

prefabbri'cato a prefabricated ● nm prefabricated building

prefazi'one nf preface

prefe'renz|a nf preference; di ~a preferably. ~i'ale a preferential; corsia ~iale bus and taxi lane

prefe'ribil|e a preferable. ~'mente adv preferably

prefe'ri|re vt prefer. ~to, -a a & nmf favourite

pre'fet|to nm prefect. ~'tura nf prefecture

pre'figgersi vr be determined

pre'fisso pp di prefiggere ● nm prefix; Teleph [dialling] code

pre'gare vt/i pray; (supplicare) beg; farsi ~ need persuading

pre'gevole a valuable

preghi'era nf prayer; (richiesta) request

pregi'ato a esteemed; (prezioso) valuable. 'pregio nm esteem; (valore) value; (di persona) good point; di pregio valuable

pregiudi'ca|re vt prejudice; (danneggiare) harm. ~to a prejudiced ● nm Jur previous offender

pregiu'dizio *nm* prejudice; (*danno*) detriment

'prego *int* (*non c'è di che*) don't mention it!; (*per favore*) please; **~?** I beg your pardon?

pregu'stare *vt* look forward to

prei'storia *nf* prehistory. **prei'storico** *a* prehistoric

pre'lato *nm* prelate

prela'vaggio *nm* prewash

preleva'mento *nm* withdrawal. **pre-le'vare** *vt* withdraw (*denaro*); collect (*merci*); *Med* take. **preli'evo** *nm* (*di soldi*) withdrawal. **prelievo di sangue** blood sample

prelimi'nare *a* preliminary ● *nm* preliminari *pl* preliminaries

pre'ludio *nm* prelude

prema'man *nm inv* maternity dress ● *a* maternity *attrib*

prematrimoni'ale *a* premarital

prema'turo, -a *a* premature ● *nmf* premature baby

premedi'ta|re *vt* premeditate. **~zi'one** *nf* premeditation

'premere *vt* press; *Comput* hit (*tasto*) ● *vi* **~ a** (*importare*) matter to; **mi preme sapere** I need to know; **~ su** press on; push (*pulsante*)

pre'messa *nf* introduction

pre'me|sso *pp di* premettere. **~sso che** bearing in mind that. **~ttere** *vt* put forward; (*mettere prima*) put before.

premi'a|re *vt* give a prize to; (*ricompensare*) reward. **~zi'one** *nf* prize giving

premi'nente *a* pre-eminent

'premio *nm* prize; (*ricompensa*) reward; *Comm* premium. **~ di consolazione** booby prize

premoni'|tore *a* (*sogno, segno*) premonitory. **~zi'one** *nf* premonition

premu'nir|e *vt* fortify. **~si** *vr* take protective measures; **~si di** provide oneself with; **~si contro** protect oneself against

pre'mu|ra *nf* (*fretta*) hurry; (*cura*) care. **~'roso** *a* thoughtful

prena'tale *a* antenatal

'prender|e *vt* take; (*afferrare*) seize; catch (*treno, malattia, ladro, pesce*); have (*cibo, bevanda*); (*far pagare*) charge; (*assumere*) take on; (*ottenere*) get; (*occupare*) take up; **~e informazioni** make inquiries; **~e a calci/pugni** kick/punch; **che ti prende?** what's got into you?; **~e una persona per un'altra** mistake one person for some-

body else ● *vi* (*voltare*) turn; (*attecchire*) take root; (*rapprendersi*) set; **~e a destra/sinistra** turn right/left; **~e a fare qcsa** start doing sth. **~si** *vr* **~si a pugni** come to blows; **~si cura di** take care of (*ammalato*); **~sela** take it to heart

prendi'sole *nm* sundress

preno'ta|re *vt* book, reserve. **~to** *a* booked, reserved **~zi'one** *nf* booking, reservation

'prensile *a* prehensile

preoccu'pante *a* alarming

preoccu'pa|re *vt* worry. **~rsi** *vr* **~rsi** worry (**di** about); **~rsi di fare qcsa** take the trouble to do sth. **~to** *a* (*ansioso*) worried. **~zi'one** *nf* worry; (*apprensione*) concern

prepa'gato *a* prepaid

prepa'ra|re *vt* prepare. **~rsi** *vr* get ready. **~'tivi** *nmpl* preparations. **~to** *nm* (*prodotto*) preparation. **~'torio** *a* preparatory. **~zi'one** *nf* preparation

prepensiona'mento *nm* early retirement

preponde'ran|te *a* predominant. **~za** *nf* prevalence

pre'porre *vt* place before

preposizi'one *nf* preposition

pre'posto *pp di* preporre ● *a* **~ a** (*addetto a*) in charge of

prepo'ten|te *a* overbearing ● *nmf* bully. **~za** *nf* high-handedness

preroga'tiva *nf* prerogative

'presa *nf* taking; (*conquista*) capture; (*stretta*) hold; (*di cemento ecc*) setting; *Electr* socket; (*pizzico*) pinch; **essere alle prese con** be struggling *o* grappling with; **a ~ rapida** (*cemento, colla*) quick-setting; **fare ~ su** qcno influence sb. **~ d'aria** air vent. **~ in giro** leg-pull. **~ multipla** adaptor

pre'sagio *nm* omen. **presa'gire** *vt* foretell

'presbite *a* long-sighted

presbiteri'ano, -a *a & nmf* Presbyterian. **presbi'terio** *nm* presbytery

pre'scelto *a* selected

pre'scindere *vi* **~ da** leave aside; **a ~ da** apart from

presco'lare *a* **in età ~** preschool

pre'scri|tto *pp di* prescrivere

pre'scri|vere *vt* prescribe. **~zi'one** *nf* prescription; (*norma*) rule

preselezi'one *nf* **chiamare** qcno **in ~** call sb via the operator

presen'ta|re *vt* present; (*far conoscere*) introduce; show (*documento*); (*inoltrare*) submit. **~rsi** *vr* present oneself;

(*farsi conoscere*) introduce oneself; (*a ufficio*) attend; (*alla polizia ecc*) report; (*come candidato*) stand, run; (*occasione:*) occur; ~**rsi bene/male** ⟨*persona:*⟩ make a good/bad impression; ⟨*situazione:*⟩ look good/bad. ~'**tore**, ~'**trice** *nmf* presenter; (*di notizie*) announcer. ~**zi'one** *nf* presentation; (*per conoscersi*) introduction

pre'sente *a* present; (*attuale*) current; (*questo*) this; **aver** ~ remember ● *nm* present; **i presenti** those present ● *nf* **allegato alla** ~ (*in lettera*) enclosed

presenti'mento *nm* foreboding

pre'senza *nf* presence; (*aspetto*) appearance; **in** ~ **di, alla** ~ **di** in the presence of; **di bella** ~ personable. ~ **di spirito** presence of mind

presenzi'are *vi* ~ **a** attend

pre'sepe *nm,* **pre'sepio** *nm* crib

preser'va|re *vt* preserve; (*proteggere*) protect (**da** from). ~'**tivo** *nm* condom. ~**zi'one** *nf* preservation

'**preside** *nm* headmaster; *Univ* dean ● *nf* headmistress; *Univ* dean

presi'den|te *nm* chairman; *Pol* president ● *nf* chairwoman; *Pol* president. ~ **del consiglio** [**dei ministri**] Prime Minister. ~ **della repubblica** President of the Republic. ~**za** *nf* presidency; (*di assemblea*) chairmanship. ~**zi'ale** *a* presidential

presidi'are *vt* garrison. **pre'sidio** *nm* garrison

presi'edere *vt* preside over

'**preso** *pp di* **prendere**

'**pressa** *nf Mech* press

pres'sante *a* urgent

pressap'poco *adv* about

pres'sare *vt* press

pressi'one *nf* pressure; **far** ~ **su** put pressure on. ~ **del sangue** blood pressure

'**presso** *prep* near; (*a casa di*) with; (*negli indirizzi*) care of, c/o; ⟨*lavorare*⟩ for ● **pressi** *nmpl*: **nei pressi di...** in the neighbourhood *o* vicinity of...

pressoché *adv* almost

pressuriz'za|re *vt* pressurize. ~**to** *a* pressurized

prestabi'li|re *vt* arrange in advance. ~**to** *a* agreed

prestam'pato *a* printed ● *nm* (*modulo*) form

pre'stante *a* good-looking

pre'star|e *vt* lend; ~**e attenzione** pay attention; ~**e aiuto** lend a hand; **farsi**

~**e** borrow (**da** from). ~**si** *vr* ⟨*frase:*⟩ lend itself; ⟨*persona:*⟩ offer

prestazi'one *nf* performance; **prestazioni** *pl* (*servizi*) services

prestigia'tore, -'**trice** *nmf* conjurer

pre'stigi|o *nm* prestige; **gioco di** ~**o** conjuring trick. ~'**oso** *nm* prestigious

'**prestito** *nm* loan; **dare in** ~ lend; **prendere in** ~ borrow

'**presto** *adv* soon; (*di buon'ora*) early; (*in fretta*) quickly; **a** ~ see you soon; **al più** ~ as soon as possible; ~ **o tardi** sooner or later; **far** ~ be quick

pre'sumere *vt* presume; (*credere*) think

presu'mibile *a* **è** ~ **che...** presumably,...

pre'sunto *a* ⟨*colpevole*⟩ presumed

presun|tu'oso *a* presumptuous ● *nmf* presumptuous person. ~**zi'one** *nf* presumption

presup'po|rre *vt* suppose; (*richiedere*) presuppose. ~**sizi'one** *nf* presupposition. ~**sto** *nm* essential requirement

'**prete** *nm* priest

preten'dente *nmf* pretender ● *nm* (*corteggiatore*) suitor

pre'ten|dere *vt* (*sostenere*) claim; (*esigere*) demand ● *vi* ~**dere a** claim to; ~**dere di** (*esigere*) demand to. ~**si'one** *nf* pretension. ~**zi'oso** *a* pretentious

pre'tes|a *nf* pretension; (*esigenza*) claim; **senza** ~**e** unpretentious. ~**o** *pp di* **pretendere**

pre'testo *nm* pretext

pre'tore *nm* magistrate

pretta'mente *adv* decidedly

pre'tura *nf* magistrate's court

preva'le|nte *a* prevalent. ~**nte-'mente** *adv* primarily. ~**nza** *nf* prevalence. ~**re** *vi* prevail

pre'valso *pp di* **prevalere**

preve'dere *vt* foresee; forecast ⟨*tempo*⟩; ⟨*legge ecc:*⟩ provide for

preve'nire *vt* precede; (*evitare*) prevent; (*avvertire*) forewarn

preven|ti'vare *vt* estimate; (*aspettarsi*) budget for. ~'**tivo** *a* preventive ● *nm Comm* estimate

preve'n|uto *a* forewarned; (*mal disposto*) prejudiced. ~**zi'one** *nf* prevention; (*preconcetto*) prejudice

previ'den|te *a* provident. ~**za** *nf* foresight. ~**za sociale** social security, welfare *Am.* ~**zi'ale** *a* provident

'**previo** *a* ~ **pagamento** on payment

previsi'one *nf* forecast; **in** ~ **di** in anticipation of

pre'visto pp di **prevedere** ● a foreseen ● nm **più/meno/prima del ~** more/less/earlier than expected

prezi'oso a precious

prez'zemolo nm parsley

'prezzo nm price. **~ di fabbrica** factory price. **~ all'ingrosso** wholesale price. **[a] metà ~** half price

prigi'on|e nf prison; (pena) imprisonment. **prigio'nia** nf imprisonment. **~i'ero, -a** a imprisoned ● nmf prisoner

'prima adv before; (più presto) earlier; (in primo luogo) first; **~, finiamo questo** let's finish this first; **puoi venire ~?** (di giorni) can't you come any sooner?; (di ore) can't you come any earlier?; **~ o poi** sooner or later; **quanto ~** as soon as possible ● prep **~ di** before; **~ d'ora** before now ● conj **~ che** before ● nf first class; Theat first night; Auto first [gear]

pri'mario a primary; (principale) principal

pri'mat|e nm primate. **~o** nm supremacy; Sport record

prima've|ra nf spring. **~'rile** a spring attrib

primeggi'are vi excel

primi'tivo a primitive; (originario) original

pri'mizie nfpl early produce sg

'primo a first; (fondamentale) principal; (precedente di due) former; (iniziale) early; (migliore) best ● nm first; **primi** pl (i primi giorni) the beginning; **in un ~ tempo** at first. **prima copia** master copy

primo'genito, -a a & nmf first-born

primordi'ale a primordial

'primula nf primrose

princi'pale a main ● nm head, boss fam

princi'|pato nm principality. **'principe** nm prince. **principe ereditario** crown prince. **~'pesco** a princely. **~'pessa** nf princess

principi'ante nmf beginner

prin'cipio nm beginning; (concetto) principle; (causa) cause; **per ~** on principle

pri'ore nm prior

priori|tà nf inv priority. **~'tario** a having priority

'prisma nm prism

pri'va|re vt deprive. **~rsi** vr deprive oneself

privatizzazi'one nf privatization.

pri'vato, -a a private ● nmf private citizen

privazi'one nf deprivation

privilegi'are vt privilege; (considerare più importante) favour. **privi'legio** nm privilege

'privo a **~ di** devoid of; (mancante) lacking in

pro prep for ● nm advantage; **a che ~?** what's the point?; **il ~ e il contro** the pros and cons

pro'babil|e a probable. **~ità** nf inv probability. **~'mente** adv probably

pro'ble|ma nm problem. **~'matico** a problematic

pro'boscide nf trunk

procacci'ar|e vt, **~si** vr obtain

pro'cace a (ragazza) provocative

pro'ced|ere vi proceed; (iniziare) start; **~ere contro** Jur start legal proceedings against. **~i'mento** nm process; Jur proceedings pl. **proce'dura** nf procedure

proces'sare vt Jur try

processi'one nf procession

pro'cesso nm process; Jur trial

proces'sore nm Comput processor

processu'ale a a trial

pro'cinto nm **essere in ~ di** be about to

pro'clama nm proclamation

procla'ma|re vt proclaim. **~zi'one** nf proclamation

procrasti'na|re vt liter postpone

procreazi'one nf procreation

pro'cura nf power of attorney; **per ~** by proxy

procu'ra|re vt/i procure; (causare) cause; (cercare) try. **~'tore** nm attorney. **P~tore Generale** Attorney General. **~tore legale** lawyer. **~tore della repubblica** public prosecutor

'prode a brave. **pro'dezza** nf bravery

prodi'gar|e vt lavish. **~si** vr do one's best

pro'digi|o nm prodigy. **~'oso** a prodigious

pro'dotto pp di **produrre** ● nm product. **prodotti agricoli** farm produce sg. **~ derivato** by-product. **~ interno lordo** gross domestic product. **~ nazionale lordo** gross national product

pro'du|rre vt produce. **~rsi** vr (attore:) play; (accadere) happen. **~ttività** nf productivity. **~t'tivo** a productive. **~t'tore, ~t'trice** nmf producer. **~zi'one** nf production

profa'na|re vt desecrate. **~zi'one** nf desecration. **pro'fano** a profane

profe'rire vt utter

Prof.essa abbr (**Professoressa**) Prof.

profes'sare vt profess; practise ⟨professione⟩

professio'nale a professional

professi'o|ne nf profession; **libera ~ne** profession. **~'nismo** nm professionalism. **~'nista** nmf professional

profes'sor|e, **-'essa** nmf Sch teacher; Univ lecturer; (titolare di cattedra) professor

pro'fe|ta nm prophet. **~tico** a prophetic. **~tiz'zare** vt prophesy. **~'zia** nf prophecy

pro'ficuo a profitable

profi'lar|e vt outline; (ornare) border; Aeron streamline. **~si** vr stand out

profi'lattico a prophylactic ● nm condom

pro'filo nm profile; (breve studio) outline; **di ~** in profile

profit'tare vi **~ di** (avvantaggiarsi) profit by; (approfittare) take advantage of. **pro'fitto** nm profit; (vantaggio) advantage

profond|a'mente adv deeply, profoundly. **~ità** nf inv depth

pro'fondo a deep; fig profound; ⟨cultura⟩ great

'profugo, -a nmf refugee

profu'mar|e vt perfume. **~si** vr put on perfume

profumata'mente adv **pagare ~** pay through the nose

profu'mato a ⟨fiore⟩ fragrant; ⟨fazzoletto ecc⟩ scented

profume'ria nf perfumery. **pro'fumo** nm perfume, scent

profusi'one nf profusion; **a ~** in profusion. **pro'fuso** pp di **profondere** ● a profuse

proget|'tare vt plan. **~'tista** nmf designer. **pro'getto** nm plan; (di lavoro importante) project. **progetto di legge** bill

prog'nosi nf inv prognosis; **in ~ riservata** on the danger list

pro'gramma nm programme; Comput program. **~ scolastico** syllabus

program'ma|re vt programme; Comput program. **~'tore**, **~'trice** nmf [computer] programmer. **~zi'one** nf programming

progre'dire vi [make] progress

progres|si'one nf progression.

~'sivo a progressive. **pro'gresso** nm progress

proi'bi|re vt forbid. **~'tivo** a prohibitive. **~to** a forbidden. **~zi'one** nf prohibition

proie|t'tare vt project; show ⟨film⟩. **~t'tore** nm projector; Auto headlight

proi'ettile nm bullet

proiezi'one nf projection

'prole nf offspring. **proletari'ato** nm proletariat. **prole'tario** a & nm proletarian

prolife'rare vi proliferate. **pro'lifico** a prolific

pro'lisso a verbose, prolix

'prologo nm prologue

pro'lunga nf Electr extension

prolun'gar|e vt prolong; (allungare) lengthen; extend ⟨contratto, scadenza⟩. **~si** vr continue; **~si su** (dilungarsi) dwell upon

prome'moria nm memo; (per se stessi) reminder, note; (formale) memorandum

pro'me|ssa nf promise. **~sso** pp di **promettere. ~ttere** vt/i promise

promet'tente a promising

promi'nente a prominent

promiscuità nf promiscuity. **pro'miscuo** a promiscuous

promon'torio nm promontory

pro'mo|sso pp di **promuovere** ● a Sch who has gone up a year; Univ who has passed an exam. **~'tore**, **~'trice** nmf promoter

promozio'nale a promotional. **promozi'one** nf promotion

promul'gare vt promulgate

promu'overe vt promote; Sch move up a class

proni'pote nm (di bisnonno) great-grandson; (di prozio) great-nephew ● nf (di bisnonno) great-granddaughter; (di prozio) great-niece

pro'nome nm pronoun

pronosti'care vt forecast, predict. **pro'nostico** nm forecast

pron'tezza nf readiness; (rapidità) quickness

'pronto a ready; (rapido) quick; **~!** Teleph hallo!; **tenersi ~** be ready (**per** for); **pronti, via!** (in gare) ready! steady! go!. **~ soccorso** first aid; (in ospedale) accident and emergency

prontu'ario nm handbook

pro'nuncia nf pronunciation

pronunci'a|re vt pronounce; (dire) utter; deliver ⟨discorso⟩. **~rsi** vr (su un *argomento*) give one's opinion. **~to** *a* pronounced; (*prominente*) prominent

pro'nunzia *ecc* = **pronuncia** *ecc*

propa'ganda *nf* propaganda

propa'ga|re *vt* propagate. **~rsi** *vr* spread. **~zi'one** *nf* propagation

prope'deutico *a* introductory

pro'pen|dere *vi* **~dere per** be in favour of. **~si'one** *nf* inclination, propensity. **~so** *pp di* **propendere ● ** *a* **essere ~so a fare qcsa** be inclined to do sth

propi'nare *vt* administer

pro'pizio *a* favourable

proponi'mento *nm* resolution

pro'por|re *vt* propose; (*suggerire*) suggest. **~si** *vr* set oneself ⟨*obiettivo, meta*⟩; **~si di** intend to

proporzio'na|le *a* proportional. **~re** *vt* proportion. **~to** *a* proportioned. **proporzi'one** *nf* proportion

pro'posito *nm* purpose; **a ~** by the way; **a ~ di** with regard to; **di ~** (*apposta*) on purpose; **capitare a ~**, **giungere a ~** come at just the right time

proposizi'one *nf* clause; (*frase*) sentence

pro'post|a *nf* proposal. **~o** *pp di* **proporre**

proprietà *nf inv* property; (*diritto*) ownership; (*correttezza*) propriety. **~ immobiliare** property. **~ privata** private property. **proprie'taria** *nf* owner; (*di casa affittata*) landlady. **proprie'tario** *nm* owner; (*di casa affittata*) landlord

'proprio *a* one's [own]; (*caratteristico*) typical; (*appropriato*) proper **●** *adv* just; (*veramente*) really; **non ~** not really, not exactly; (*affatto*) not... at all **●** *pron* one's own **●** *nm* one's [own]; **lavorare in ~** be one's own boss; **mettersi in ~** set up on one's own

propul|si'one *nf* propulsion. **~'sore** *nm* propeller

'proroga *nf* extension

proro'ga|bile *a* extendable. **~re** *vt* extend

pro'rompere *vi* burst out

'prosa *nf* prose. **pro'saico** *a* prosaic

pro'scio|gliere *vt* release; *Jur* acquit. **~lto** *pp di* **prosciogliere**

prosciu'gar|e *vt* dry up; (*bonificare*) reclaim. **~si** *vr* dry up

prosci'utto *nm* ham. **~ cotto** cooked ham. **~ crudo** type of dry-cured ham, Parma ham

pro'scri|tto, -a *pp di* **proscrivere ●** *nmf* exile

prosecuzi'one *nf* continuation

prosegui'mento *nm* continuation; **buon ~!** (*viaggio*) have a good journey!; (*festa*) enjoy the rest of the party!

prosegu'ire *vt* continue **●** *vi* go on, continue

prospe'r|are *vi* prosper. **~ità** *nf* prosperity. **'prospero** *a* prosperous; (*favorevole*) favourable. **~oso** *a* flourishing; ⟨*ragazza*⟩ buxom

prospet'tar|e *vt* show. **~si** *vr* seem

prospet'tiva *nf* perspective; (*panorama*) view; *fig* prospect. **pro'spetto** *nm* (*vista*) view; (*facciata*) façade; (*tabella*) table

prospici'ente *a* facing

prossima'mente *adv* soon

prossimità *nf* proximity

'prossimo, -a *a* near; (*seguente*) next; (*molto vicino*) close; **l'anno ~** next year **●** *nmf* neighbour

prosti'tu|ta *nf* prostitute. **~zi'one** *nf* prostitution

pro'stra|re *vt* prostrate. **~rsi** *vr* prostrate oneself. **~to** *a* prostrate

protago'nista *nmf* protagonist

pro'te|ggere *vt* protect; (*favorire*) favour

prote'ina *nf* protein

pro'tender|e *vt* stretch out. **~si** *vr* (*in avanti*) lean out. **pro'teso** *pp di* **protendere**

pro'te|sta *nf* protest; (*dichiarazione*) protestation. **~'stante** *a & nmf* Protestant. **~'stare** *vt/i* protest

prote|t'tivo *a* protective. **~tto** *pp di* **proteggere**. **~t'tore, ~t'trice** *nmf* protector; (*sostenitore*) patron **●** *nm* (*di prostituta*) pimp. **~zi'one** *nf* protection

protocol'lare *a* ⟨*visita*⟩ protocol **●** *vt* register

proto'collo *nm* protocol; (*registro*) register; **carta ~** official stamped paper

pro'totipo *nm* prototype

pro'tra|rre *vt* protract; (*differire*) postpone. **~rsi** *vr* go on, continue. **~tto** *pp di* **protrarre**

protube'ran|te *a* protuberant. **~za** *nf* protuberance

'prova *nf* test; (*dimostrazione*) proof; (*tentativo*) try; (*di abito*) fitting; *Sport* heat; *Theat* rehearsal; (*bozza*) proof; **fino a ~ contraria** until I'm told otherwise; **in ~** (*assumere*) for a trial period;

mettere alla ~ put to the test. **~ generale** dress rehearsal

pro'var|e vt test; (dimostrare) prove; (tentare) try; try on ‹abiti ecc›; (sentire) feel; Theat rehearse. **~si** vr try

proveni'enza nf origin. **prove'nire** vi **provenire da** come from

pro'vento nm proceeds pl

prove'nuto pp di **provenire**

pro'verbio nm proverb

pro'vetta nf test-tube; **bambino in ~** test-tube baby

pro'vetto a skilled

pro'vinci|a nf province; (strada) B road, secondary road. **~'ale** a provincial; **strada ~ale** B road, secondary road

pro'vino nm specimen; Cinema screen test

provo'ca|nte a provocative. **~re** vt provoke; (causare) cause. **~'tore**, **~'trice** nmf trouble-maker. **~'torio** a provocative. **~zi'one** nf provocation

provve'd|ere vi **~ere a** provide for. **~i'mento** nm measure; (previdenza) precaution

provvi'denz|a nf providence. **~i'ale** a providential

provvigi'one nf Comm commission

provvi'sorio a provisional

prov'vista nf supply

pro'zio, -a nm great-uncle ● nf great-aunt

'prua nf prow

pru'den|te a prudent. **~za** nf prudence; **per ~za** as a precaution

'prudere vi itch

'prugn|a nf plum. **~a secca** prune. **~o** nm plum[-tree]

prurigi'noso a itchy. **pru'rito** nm itch

pseu'donimo nm pseudonym

psica'na|lisi nf psychoanalysis. **~'lista** nmf psychoanalyst. **~liz'zare** vt psychoanalyse

'psiche nf psyche

psichi'a|tra nmf psychiatrist. **~'tria** nf psychiatry. **~trico** a psychiatric

'psichico a mental

psico|lo'gia nf psychology. **~'logico** a psychological. **psi'cologo, -a** nmf psychologist

psico'patico, -a a psychopathic ● nmf psychopath

PT abbr (Posta e Telecomunicazioni) PO

pubbli'ca|re vt publish. **~zi'one** nf publication. **~zioni** pl (di matrimonio) banns

pubbli'cista nmf Journ correspondent

pubblicità nf inv publicity, advertising; (annuncio) advertisement, advert; **fare ~ a qcsa** advertise sth; **piccola ~** small advertisements. **pubblici'tario** a advertising

'pubblico a public; **scuola pubblica** state school ● nm public; (spettatori) audience; **grande ~** general public. **Pubblica Sicurezza** Police. **~ ufficiale** civil servant

'pube nm pubis

pubertà nf puberty

pu'dico a modest. **pu'dore** nm modesty

pue'rile a children's; pej childish

pugi'lato nm boxing. **'pugile** nm boxer

pugna'la|re vt stab. **~ta** nf stab. **pu'gnale** nm dagger

'pugno nm fist; (colpo) punch; (manciata) fistful; (fig: numero limitato) handful; **dare un ~ a** punch

'pulce nf flea; (microfono) bug

pul'cino nm chick; (nel calcio) junior

pu'ledra nf filly

pu'ledro nm colt

pu'li|re vt clean. **~re a secco** dry-clean. **~to** a clean. **~'tura** nf cleaning. **~'zia** nf (il pulire) cleaning; (l'essere pulito) cleanliness; **~zie** pl housework; **fare le ~zie** do the cleaning

'pullman nm inv bus, coach; (urbano) bus

pul'mino nm minibus

'pulpito nm pulpit

pul'sante nm button; Electr [push-]button. **~ di accensione** on/off switch

pul'sa|re vi pulsate. **~zi'one** nf pulsation

pul'viscolo nm dust

'puma nm inv puma

pun'gente a prickly; ‹insetto› stinging; ‹odore ecc› sharp

'punger|e vt prick; ‹insetto:› sting. **~si** vr **~si un dito** prick one's finger

pungigli'one nm sting

pu'ni|re vt punish. **~'tivo** a punitive. **~zi'one** nf punishment; Sport free kick

'punta nf point; (estremità) tip; (di monte) peak; (un po') pinch; Sport forward; **doppie punte** (di capelli) split ends

pun'tare vt point; (spingere con forza) push; (scommettere) bet; (fam: appuntare) fasten ● vi **~ su** fig rely on; **~ verso** (dirigersi) head for; **~ a** aspire to

punta'spilli nm inv pincushion

pun'tat|a nf (di una storia) instalment;

(*televisiva*) episode; (*al gioco*) stake, bet; (*breve visita*) flying visit; **a puntate** serialized, in instalments; **fare una ~ a/in** pop over to ⟨*luogo*⟩

punteggia'tura *nf* punctuation

pun'teggio *nm* score

puntel'lare *vt* prop. **pun'tello** *nm* prop

pun'tigli|o *nm* spite; (*ostinazione*) obstinacy. **~'oso** *a* punctilious, pernickety *pej*

pun'tin|a *nf* (*da disegno*) drawing pin, thumb tack *Am*; (*di giradischi*) stylus. **~o** *nm* dot; **a ~o** perfectly; ⟨*cotto*⟩ to a T

'punto *nm* point; (*in cucito, Med*) stitch; (*in punteggiatura*) full stop; **in che ~?** where, exactly?; **di ~ in bianco** all of a sudden; **due punti** colon; **in ~** sharp; **mettere a ~** put right; *fig* fine tune; tune up ⟨*motore*⟩; **essere sul ~ di fare qcsa** be about to do sth, be on the point of doing sth. **punti** *pl* **cardinali** points of the compass. **~ debole** blind spot. **~ esclamativo** exclamation mark. **~ interrogativo** question mark. **~ nero** *Med* blackhead. **~ di riferimento** landmark; (*per la qualità*) benchmark. **~ di vendita** point of sale. **~ e virgola** semicolon. **~ di vista** point of view

puntu'al|e *a* punctual. **~ità** *nf* punctuality. **~'mente** *adv* punctually, on time

pun'tura *nf* (*di insetto*) sting; (*di ago ecc*) prick; *Med* puncture; (*iniezione*) injection; (*fitta*) stabbing pain

punzecchi'are *vt* prick; *fig* tease

'pupa *nf* doll. **pu'pazzo** *nm* puppet. **pupazzo di neve** snowman

pup'illa *nf Anat* pupil

pu'pillo, -a *nmf* (*di professore*) favourite

purché *conj* provided

'pure *adv* too, also; (*concessivo*) **fate ~!** please do! ● *conj* (*tuttavia*) yet; (*anche se*) even if; **pur di** just to

purè *nm inv* purée. **~ di patate** mashed potatoes, creamed potatoes

pu'rezza *nf* purity

'purga *nf* purge. **pur'gante** *nm* laxative. **pur'gare** *vt* purge

purga'torio *nm* purgatory

purifi'care *vt* purify

puri'tano, -a *a & nmf* Puritan

'puro *a* pure; (*vino ecc*) undiluted; **per ~ caso** by sheer chance, purely by chance

puro'sangue *a & nm* thoroughbred

pur'troppo *adv* unfortunately

pus *nm* pus. **'pustola** *nf* pimple

puti'ferio *nm* uproar

putre'far|e *vi*, **~si** *vr* putrefy

'putrido *a* putrid

put'tana *nf vulg* whore

'puzza *nf* = **puzzo**

puz'zare *vi* stink; **~ di bruciato** *fig* smell fishy

'puzzo *nm* stink, bad smell. **~la** *nf* polecat. **~'lente** *a* stinking

p.zza *abbr* (**piazza**) Sq.

Qq

qua *adv* here; **da un anno in ~** for the last year; **da quando in ~?** since when?; **di ~** this way; **di ~ di** on this side of; **~ dentro** in here; **~ sotto** under here; **~ vicino** near here; **~ e là** here and there

qua'derno *nm* exercise book; (*per appunti*) notebook

quadrango'lare *a* ⟨*forma*⟩ quadrangular. **qua'drangolo** *nm* quadrangle

qua'drante *nm* quadrant; (*di orologio*) dial

qua'dra|re *vt* square; (*contabilità*) balance. ● *vi* fit in. **~to** *a* square;

(*equilibrato*) levelheaded ● *nm* square; (*pugilato*) ring; **al ~to** squared

quadret'tato *a* squared; ⟨*carta*⟩ graph *attrib*. **qua'dretto** *nm* square; (*piccolo quadro*) small picture; **a quadretti** ⟨*tessuto*⟩ check

quadricro'mia *nf* four-colour printing

quadrien'nale *a* (*che dura quattro anni*) four-year

quadri'foglio *nm* four-leaf clover

quadri'latero *nm* quadrilateral

quadri'mestre *nm* (*periodo*) four-month period

'quadro *nm* picture, painting; *(quadrato)* square; *(fig: scena)* sight; *(tabella)* table; *Theat* scene; *Comm* executive **quadri** *pl* *(carte)* diamonds; **a quadri** *(tessuto, giacca, motivo)* check. **quadri** *pl* direttivi senior management

qua'drupede *nm* quadruped

quaggiù *adv* down here

'quaglia *nf* quail

'qualche *a* *(alcuni)* a few, some; *(un certo)* some; *(in interrogazioni)* any; **ho ~ problema** I have a few problems, I have some problems; **~ tempo fa** some time ago; **hai ~ libro italiano?** have you any Italian books?; **posso prendere ~ libro?** can I take some books?; **in ~ modo** somehow; **in ~ posto** somewhere; **~ volta** sometimes; **~ cosa = qualcosa**

qual'cos|a *pron* something; *(in interrogazioni)* anything; **~'altro** something else; **vuoi ~'altro?** would you like anything else?; **~a di strano** something strange; **vuoi ~a da mangiare?** would you like something to eat?

qual'cuno *pron* someone, somebody; *(in interrogazioni)* anyone, anybody; *(alcuni)* some; *(in interrogazioni)* any; **c'è ~?** is anybody in?; **qualcun altro** someone else, somebody else; **c'è qualcun altro che aspetta?** is anybody else waiting?; **ho letto ~ dei suoi libri** I've read some of his books; **conosci ~ dei suoi amici?** do you know any of his friends?

'quale *a* which; *(indeterminato)* what; *(come)* as, like; **~ macchina è la tua?** which car is yours?; **~ motivo avrà di parlare così?** what reason would he have to speak like that?; **~ onore!** what an honour!; **città quali Venezia** towns like Venice; **~ che sia la tua opinione** whatever you may think ● *pron inter* which [one]; **~ preferisci?** which [one] do you prefer? ● *pron rel* **il/la ~** *(persona)* who; *(animale, cosa)* that, which; *(oggetto: con prep)* whom; *(animale, cosa)* which; **ho incontrato tua madre, la ~ mi ha detto...** I met your mother, who told me...; **l'ufficio nel ~ lavoro** the office in which I work; **l'uomo con il ~ parlavo** the man to whom I was speaking ● *adv (come)* as

qua'lifica *nf* qualification; *(titolo)* title

qualifi'ca|re *vt* qualify; *(definire)* define. **~rsi** *vr* be placed. **~'tivo** *a* qualifying. **~to** *a* *(operaio)* semiskilled. **~zi'one** *nf* qualification

qualità *nf inv* quality; *(specie)* kind; **in ~ di** in one's capacity as. **~tiva'mente** *adv* qualitatively. **~'tivo** *a* qualitative

qua'lora *conj* in case

qual'siasi, qua'lunque *a* any; *(non importa quale)* whatever; *(ordinario)* ordinary; **dammi una penna ~** give me any pen [whatsoever]; **farei ~ cosa** I would do anything; **~ cosa io faccia** whatever I do; **~ persona** anyone; **in ~ caso** in any case; **uno ~** any one, whichever; **l'uomo qualunque** the man in the street; **vivo in una casa ~** I live in an ordinary house

qualunqu'ismo *nm* lack of political views

'quando *conj & adv* when; **da ~ ti ho visto** since I saw you; **da ~ esci con lui?** how long have you been going out with him?; **da ~ in qua?** since when?; **~ ... ~ ...** sometimes..., sometimes...

quantifi'care *vt* quantify

quantità *nf inv* quantity; **una ~ di** *(gran numero)* a great deal of. **~tiva'mente** *adv* quantitatively. **~'tivo** *nm* amount ● *a* quantitative

'quanto *a inter* how much; *(con nomi plurali)* how many; *(in esclamazione)* what a lot of; *(tempo)* how long; **quanti anni hai?** how old are you? ● *a rel* as much... as; *(tempo)* as long as; *(con nomi plurali)* as many... as; **prendi ~ denaro ti serve** take as much money as you need; **prendi quanti libri vuoi** take as many books as you like ● *pron inter* how much; *(quanto tempo)* how long; *(plurale)* how many; **quanti ne abbiamo oggi?** what date is it today? ● *pron rel* as much as; *(quanto tempo)* as long as; *(plurale)* as many as; **prendine ~/quanti ne vuoi** take as much/as many as you like; **stai ~ vuoi** stay as long as you like; **questo è ~** that's it ● *adv inter* how much; *(quanto tempo)* how long; **~ sei alto?** how tall are you?; **~ hai aspettato?** how long did you wait for?; **~ costa?** how much is it?; **~ mi dispiace!** I'm so sorry!; **~ è bello!** how nice! ● *adv rel* as much as; **lavoro ~ posso** I work as much as I can; **è tanto intelligente ~ bello** he's as intelligent as he's good-looking; **in ~** *(in qualità di)* as; *(poiché)* since; **in ~ a me** as far as I'm concerned; **per ~** however; **per ~ ne sappia** as far as I know; **per ~ mi riguarda** as far as I'm concerned; **per ~ mi sia simpatico** much as I like him; **~ a** as for; **~ prima** (*al più presto*) as soon as possible

quan'tunque *conj* although

qua'ranta *a & nm* forty

quaran'tena *nf* quarantine

quaran'tenn|e *a* forty-year-old. **~io** *nm* period of forty years

quaran't|esimo *a* fortieth. **~ina** *nf* una **~ina** about forty

qua'resima *nf* Lent

quar'tetto *nm* quartet

quarti'ere *nm* district; *Mil* quarters *pl*. **~ generale** headquarters

quarto *a* fourth ● *nm* fourth; (*quarta parte*) quarter; **le sette e un ~** a quarter past seven. **quarti** *pl* **di finale** quarterfinals. **~ d'ora** quarter of an hour. **quar'tultimo, -a** *nmf* fourth from the end, fourth last

'quarzo *nm* quartz

'quasi *adv* almost, nearly; **~ mai** hardly ever ● *conj* (*come se*) as if; **~ ~ sto a casa** I'm tempted to stay home

quassù *adv* up here

'quatto *a* crouching; (*silenzioso*) silent; **starsene ~** keep very quiet

quat'tordici *a & nm* fourteen

quat'trini *nmpl* money *sg*, dosh *sg fam*

'quattro *a & nm* four; **dirne ~ a qcno** give sb a piece of one's mind; **farsi in ~** (**per qcno/per fare qcsa**) go to a lot of trouble (for sb/to do sth); **in ~ e quattr'otto** in a flash. **~ per ~** *nm inv Auto* four-wheel drive [vehicle]

quat'trocchi: a ~ *adv* in private

quattro|'cento *a & nm* four hundred; **il ~cento** the fifteenth century

quattro'mila *a & nm* four thousand

'quell|o *a* that (*pl* those); **quell'albero** that tree; **quegli alberi** those trees; **quel cane** that dog; **quei cani** those dogs ● *pron* that [one] (*pl* those [ones]); **~o lì** that one over there; **~o che** the one that; (*ciò che*) what; **quelli che** the ones that, those that; **~o a destra** the one on the right

'quercia *nf* oak

que'rela *nf* [legal] action

quere'lare *vt* bring an action against

que'sito *nm* question

questio'nario *nm* questionnaire

quest'ione *nf* question; (*faccenda*)

matter; (*litigio*) quarrel; **in ~** in doubt; **è fuori ~** it's out of the question; **è ~ di vita o di morte** it's a matter of life and death

'quest|o *a* this (*pl* these) ● *pron* this [one] (*pl* these [ones]); **~o qui, ~o qua** this one here; **~o è quello che a detto** that's what he said; **per ~o** for this *or* that reason. **quest'oggi** today

que'store *nm* chief of police

que'stura *nf* police headquarters

qui *adv* here; **da ~ in poi** from now on; **fin ~** (*di tempo*) up till now, until now; **~ dentro** in here; **~ sotto** under here; **~ vicino** near here ● *nm* **~ pro quo** misunderstanding

quie'scienza *nf* **trattamento di ~** retirement package

quie'tanza *nf* receipt

quie'tar|e *vt* calm. **~si** *vr* quieten down

qui'et|e *nf* quiet; **disturbo della ~e pubblica** breach of the peace. **~o** *a* quiet

'quindi *adv* then ● *conj* therefore

'quindi|ci *a & nm* fifteen. **~'cina** *nf* una **~cina** about fifteen; **una ~cina di giorni** a fortnight *Br*, two weeks

quinquen'nale *a* (*che dura cinque anni*) five-year. **quin'quennio** *nm* [period of] five years

quin'tale *nm* a hundred kilograms

'quinte *nfpl Theat* wings

quin'tetto *nm* quintet

'quinto *a* fifth

quin'tuplo *a* quintuple

qui'squiglia *nf* **perdersi in quisquiglie** get bogged down in details

'quota *nf* quota; (*rata*) instalment; (*altitudine*) height; *Aeron* altitude, height; (*ippica*) odds *pl*; **perdere ~** lose altitude; **prendere ~** gain altitude. **~ di iscrizione** entry fee

quo'ta|re *vt Comm* quote. **~to** *a* quoted; **essere ~to in Borsa** be quoted on the Stock Exchange. **~zi'one** *nf* quotation

quotidi|ana'mente *adv* daily. **~'ano** *a* daily; (*ordinario*) everyday ● *nm* daily [paper]

quozi'ente *nm* quotient. **~ d'intelligenza** intelligence quotient, IQ

Rr

ra'barbaro *nm* rhubarb

'rabbia *nf* rage; (*ira*) anger; *Med* rabies *sg*; **che ~!** what a nuisance!; **mi fa ~** it makes me angry

rab'bino *nm* rabbi

rabbiosa'mente *adv* furiously. **rabbi'oso** *a* hot-tempered; *Med* rabid; (*violento*) violent

rabbo'nir|e *vt* pacify. **~si** *vr* calm down

rabbrivi'dire *vi* shudder; (*di freddo*) shiver

rabbui'arsi *vr* become dark

raccapez'zar|e *vt* put together. **~si** *vr* see one's way ahead

raccapricci'ante *a* horrifying

raccatta'palle *nm inv* ball boy ● *nf inv* ball girl

raccat'tare *vt* pick up

rac'chetta *nf* racket. **~ da ping pong** table-tennis bat. **~ da sci** ski stick, ski pole. **~ da tennis** tennis racket

'racchio *a fam* ugly

racchi'udere *vt* contain

rac'cogli|ere *vt* pick; (*da terra*) pick up; (*mietere*) harvest; (*collezionare*) collect; (*radunare*) gather; win (*voti ecc*); (*dare asilo a*) take in. **~ersi** *vr* gather; (*concentrarsi*) collect one's thoughts. **~'mento** *nm* concentration. **~'tore**, **~'trice** *nmf* collector ● *nm* (*cartella*) ring-binder

rac'colto, **-a** *pp di* **raccogliere** ● *a* (*rannicchiato*) hunched; (*intimo*) cosy; (*concentrato*) engrossed ● *nm* (*mietitura*) harvest ● *nf* collection; (*di scritti*) compilation; (*del grano ecc*) harvesting; (*adunata*) gathering

raccoman'dabile *a* recommendable; **poco ~** (*persona*) shady

raccoman'da|re *vt* recommend; (*affidare*) entrust. **~rsi** *vr* (*implorare*) beg. **~ta** *nf* registered letter; **~ta con ricevuta di ritorno** recorded delivery. **~-espresso** *nf* guaranteed next-day delivery of recorded items. **~zi'one** *nf* recommendation

raccon'tare *vt* tell. **rac'conto** *nm* story

raccorci'are *vt* shorten

raccor'dare *vt* join. **rac'cordo** *nm* connection; (*stradale*) feeder. **raccordo anulare** ring road. **raccordo ferro-viario** siding

ra'chitico *a* rickety; (*poco sviluppato*) stunted

racimo'lare *vt* scrape together

racket *nm inv* racket

'radar *nm* radar

raddol'cir|e *vt* sweeten; *fig* soften. **~si** *vr* become milder; (*carattere:*) mellow

raddoppi'are *vt* double. **rad'doppio** *nm* doubling

raddriz'zare *vt* straighten

'rader|e *vt* shave; graze (*muro*); **~e al suolo** raze [to the ground]. **~si** *vr* shave

radi'are *vt* strike off; **~ dall'albo** strike off

radia|'tore *nm* radiator. **~zi'one** *nf* radiation

'radica *nf* briar

radi'cale *a* radical ● *nm Gram* root; *Pol* radical

ra'dicchio *nm* chicory

ra'dice *nf* root; **mettere [le] radici** *fig* put down roots. **~ quadrata** square root

'radio *nf inv* radio; **via ~** by radio. **~ transistor** transistor radio ● *nm Chem* radium.

radioama'tore, **-'trice** *nmf* [radio] ham

radioascolta'tore, **-'trice** *nmf* listener

radioat|tività *nf* radioactivity. **~'tivo** *a* radioactive

radio'cro|naca *nf* radio commentary; **fare la ~naca di** commentate on. **~'nista** *nmf* radio reporter

radiodiffusi'one *nf* broadcasting

radiogra|'fare *vt* X-ray. **~'fia** *nf* X-ray [photograph]; (*radiologia*) radiography; **fare una ~fia** (*paziente:*) have an X-ray; (*dottore:*) take an X-ray

radio'fonico *a* radio *attrib*

radio'lina *nf* transistor

radi'ologo, **-a** *nmf* radiologist

radi'oso *a* radiant

radio'sveglia *nf* radio alarm

radio'taxi *nm inv* radio taxi

radiote'lefono *nm* radio-telephone; (*privato*) cordless [phone]

radiotelevi'sivo *a* broadcasting *attrib*

'**rado** *a* sparse; (*non frequente*) rare; **di** ~ seldom

radu'nar|e *vt*, ~**si** *vr* gather [together]. **ra'duno** *nm* meeting; *Sport* rally

ra'dura *nf* clearing

'**rafano** *nm* horseradish

raffazzo'nato *a* ⟨*discorso, lavoro*⟩ botched

raf'fermo *a* stale

'**raffica** *nf* gust; (*di armi da fuoco*) burst; (*di domande*) barrage

raffigu'ra|re *vt* represent. ~**zi'one** *nf* representation

raffi'na|re *vt* refine. ~**ta'mente** *adv* elegantly. ~'**tezza** *nf* refinement. ~**to** *a* refined. **raffine'ria** *nf* refinery

rafforza|'mento *nm* reinforcement; (*di muscolatura*) strengthening. ~**re** *vt* reinforce. ~'**tivo** *nm* Gram intensifier

raffredda'mento *nm* (*processo*) cooling

raffred'd|are *vt* cool. ~**arsi** *vr* get cold; (*prendere un raffreddore*) catch a cold. ~**ore** *nm* cold. ~**ore da fieno** hay fever

raf'fronto *nm* comparison

'**rafia** *nf* raffia

Rag. *abbr* **ragioniere**

ra'gaz|za *nf* girl; (*fidanzata*) girlfriend. ~**za alla pari** au pair [girl]. ~'**zata** *nf* prank. ~**zo** *nm* boy; (*fidanzato*) boyfriend; **da** ~**zo** (*da giovane*) as a boy

ragge'lar|e *vt fig* freeze. ~**si** *vr fig* turn to ice

raggi'ante *a* radiant; ~ **di successo** flushed with success

raggi'era *nf* **a** ~ with a pattern like spokes radiating from a centre

'**raggio** *nm* ray; *Math* radius; (*di ruota*) spoke; ~ **d'azione** range. ~ **laser** laser beam

raggi'rare *vt* trick. **rag'giro** *nm* trick

raggi'un|gere *vt* reach; (*conseguire*) achieve. ~'**gibile** *a* ⟨*luogo*⟩ within reach

raggomito'lar|e *vt* wind. ~**si** *vr* curl up

raggranel'lare *vt* scrape together

raggrin'zir|e *vt*, ~**si** *vr* wrinkle

raggrup|pa'mento *nm* (*gruppo*) group; (*azione*) grouping. ~'**pare** *vt* group together

ragguagli'are *vt* compare; (*informare*) inform. **raggu'aglio** *nm* comparison; (*informazione*) information

ragguar'devole *a* considerable

'**ragia** *nf* resin; **acqua** *nf* ~ turpentine

ragiona'mento *nm* reasoning; (*discussione*) discussion. **ragio'nare** *vi* reason; (*discutere*) discuss

ragi'one *nf* reason; (*ciò che è giusto*) right; **a** ~ **o a torto** rightly or wrongly; **aver** ~ be right; **perdere la** ~ go out of one's mind; **a ragion veduta** after due consideration

ragione'ria *nf* accountancy

ragio'nevol|e *a* reasonable. ~'**mente** *adv* reasonably

ragioni'ere, -a *nmf* accountant

ragli'are *vi* bray

ragna'tela *nf* cobweb. '**ragno** *nm* spider

ragù *nm inv* meat sauce

RAI *nf abbr* (**Radio Audizioni Italiane**) *Italian public broadcasting company*

ralle'gra|re *vt* gladden. ~**rsi** *vr* rejoice; ~**rsi con qcno** congratulate sb. ~'**menti** *nmpl* congratulations

rallenta'mento *nm* slowing down

rallen'ta|re *vt/i* slow down; (*allentare*) slacken. ~**rsi** *vr* slow down. ~'**tore** *nm* (*su strada*) speed bump; **al** ~**tore** in slow motion

raman'zina *nf* reprimand

ra'marro *nm type of* lizard

ra'mato *a* ⟨*capelli*⟩ copper[-coloured]

'**rame** *nm* copper

ramifi'ca|re *vi*, ~**rsi** *vr* branch out; ⟨*strada:*⟩ branch. ~**zi'one** *nf* ramification

rammari'carsi *vr* ~ **di** regret; (*lamentarsi*) complain (**di** about). **ram'marico** *nm* regret

rammen'dare *vt* darn. **ram'mendo** *nm* darning

rammen'tar|e *vt* remember; ~**e qcsa a qcno** (*richiamare alla memoria*) remind sb of sth. ~**si** *vr* remember

rammol'li|re *vt* soften. ~**rsi** *vr* go soft. ~**to, -a** *nmf* wimp

'**ramo** *nm* branch. ~'**scello** *nm* twig

'**rampa** *nf* (*di scale*) flight. ~ **d'accesso** slip road. ~ **di lancio** launch[ing] pad

ram'pante *a* **giovane** ~ yuppie

rampi'cante *a* climbing ● *nm* Bot creeper

ram'pollo *nm hum* brat; ⟨*discendente*⟩ descendant

ram'pone *nm* harpoon; ⟨*per scarpe*⟩ crampon

'rana *nf* frog; ⟨*nel nuoto*⟩ breaststroke; **uomo ~** frogman

'rancido *a* rancid

ran'core *nm* resentment

ran'dagio *a* stray

'rango *nm* rank

rannicchi'arsi *vr* huddle up

rannuvola'mento *nm* clouding over. **rannuvo'larsi** *vr* cloud over

ra'nocchio *nm* frog

ranto'lare *vi* wheeze. **'rantolo** *nm* wheeze; ⟨*di moribondo*⟩ death-rattle

'rapa *nf* turnip

ra'pace *a* rapacious; ⟨*uccello*⟩ predatory

ra'pare *vt* crop

'rapida *nf* rapids *pl.* **~'mente** *adv* rapidly

rapidità *nf* speed

'rapido *a* swift ● *nm* ⟨*treno*⟩ express [train]

rapi'mento *nm* ⟨*crimine*⟩ kidnapping

ra'pina *nf* robbery; **~ a mano armata** armed robbery. **~ in banca** bank robbery. **rapi'nare** *vt* rob. **~'tore** *nm* robber

ra'pi|re *vt* abduct; ⟨*a scopo di riscatto*⟩ kidnap; ⟨*estasiare*⟩ ravish. **~'tore**, **~'trice** *nmf* kidnapper

rappacifi'ca|re *vt* pacify. **~rsi** *vr* be reconciled, make it up. **~zi'one** *nf* reconciliation

rappor'tare *vt* reproduce ⟨*disegno*⟩; ⟨*confrontare*⟩ compare

rap'porto *nm* report; ⟨*connessione*⟩ relation; ⟨*legame*⟩ relationship; *Math*, *Techn* ratio; **rapporti** *pl* relationship; **essere in buoni rapporti** be on good terms. **~ di amicizia** friendship. **~ di lavoro** working relationship. **rapporti** *pl* **sessuali** sexual intercourse

rap'prendersi *vr* set; ⟨*latte:*⟩ curdle

rappre'saglia *nf* reprisal

rappresen'tan|te *nmf* representative. **~te di classe** class representative. **~te di commercio** sales representative, [sales] rep *fam*. **~za** *nf* delegation; *Comm* agency; **spese** *nfpl* **di ~za** entertainment expenses; **di ~za** ⟨*appartamento ecc*⟩ representative

rappresen'ta|re *vt* represent; *Theat* perform. **~'tivo** *a* representative. **~zi'one** *nf* representation; ⟨*spettacolo*⟩ performance

rap'preso *pp di* **rapprendersi**

rapso'dia *nf* rhapsody

'raptus *nm inv* fit of madness

rara'mente *adv* rarely, seldom

rare'fa|re *vt*, **~rsi** *vr* rarefy. **~tto** *a* rarefied

rarità *nf inv* rarity. **'raro** *a* rare

ra'sar|e *vt* shave; trim ⟨*siepe ecc*⟩. **~si** *vr* shave

raschia'mento *nm Med* curettage

raschi'are *vt* scrape; ⟨*togliere*⟩ scrape off

rasen'tare *vt* go close to. **ra'sente** *prep* very close to

'raso *pp di* **radere** ● *a* smooth; ⟨*colmo*⟩ full to the brim; ⟨*barba*⟩ close-cropped; **~ terra** close to the ground; **un cucchiaio ~** a level spoonful ● *nm* satin

ra'soio *nm* razor

ras'segna *nf* review; ⟨*mostra*⟩ exhibition; ⟨*musicale, cinematografica*⟩ festival; **passare in ~** review; *Mil* inspect

rasse'gna|re *vt* present. **~rsi** *vr* resign oneself. **~to** *a* ⟨*persona, aria, tono*⟩ resigned. **~zi'one** *nf* resignation

rassere'nar|e *vt* clear; *fig* cheer up. **~si** *vr* become clear; *fig* cheer up

rasset'tare *vt* tidy up; ⟨*riparare*⟩ mend

rassicu'ra|nte *a* ⟨*persona, parole, presenza*⟩ reassuring. **~re** *vt* reassure. **~zi'one** *nf* reassurance

rasso'dare *vt* harden; *fig* strengthen

rassomigli'a|nza *nf* resemblance. **~re** *vi* **~re a** resemble

rastrella'mento *nm* ⟨*di fieno*⟩ raking; ⟨*perlustrazione*⟩ combing. **rastrel'lare** *vt* rake; ⟨*perlustrare*⟩ comb

rastrelli'era *nf* rack; ⟨*per biciclette*⟩ bicycle rack; ⟨*scolapiatti*⟩ [plate] rack. **ra'strello** *nm* rake

'rata *nf* instalment; **pagare a rate** pay by instalments; **comprare qcsa a rate** buy sth on hire purchase, buy sth on the installment plan *Am*. **rate'ale** *a* by instalments; **pagamento rateale** payment by instalments

rate'are, **rateiz'zare** *vt* divide into instalments

ra'tifica *nf Jur* ratification

ratifi'care *vt Jur* ratify

'ratto *nm* abduction; ⟨*roditore*⟩ rat

rattop'pare *vt* patch. **rat'toppo** *nm* patch

rattrap'pir|e *vt* make stiff. **~si** *vr* become stiff

rattri'star|e *vt* sadden. **~si** *vr* become sad

rau'cedine *nf* hoarseness. **'rauco** *a* hoarse

rava'nello *nm* radish

ravi'oli *nmpl* ravioli *sg*

ravve'dersi *vr* mend one's ways

ravvicina'mento *nm* (*tra persone*) reconciliation; *Pol* rapprochement

ravvici'nar|e *vt* bring closer; (*riconciliare*) reconcile. **~si** *vr* be reconciled

ravvi'sare *vt* recognize

ravvi'var|e *vt* revive; *fig* brighten up. **~si** *vr* revive

'rayon *nm* rayon

razio'cinio *nm* rational thought; (*buon senso*) common sense

razio'nal|e *a* rational. **~ità** *nf* (*raziocinio*) rationality; (*di ambiente*) functional nature. **~iz'zare** *vt* rationalize (*programmi, metodi, spazio*). **~'mente** *adv* (*con raziocinio*) rationally

razio'nare *vt* ration. **razi'one** *nf* ration

'razza *nf* race; (*di cani ecc*) breed; (*genere*) kind; **che ~ di idiota!** *fam* what an idiot!

raz'zia *nf* raid

razzi'ale *a* racial

raz'zis|mo *nm* racism. **~ta** *a & nmf* racist

'razzo *nm* rocket. **~ da segnalazione** flare

razzo'lare *vi* (*polli:*) scratch about

re *nm inv* king; *Mus* (*chiave, nota*) D

rea'gire *vi* react

re'ale *a* real; (*di re*) royal

rea'lis|mo *nm* realism. **~ta** *nmf* realist; (*fautore del re*) royalist

realistica'mente *adv* realistically. **rea'listico** *a* realistic

realiz'zabile *a* (*programma*) feasible

realiz'za|re *vt* (*attuare*) carry out, realize; *Comm* make; score (*gol, canestro*); (*rendersi conto di*) realize. **~rsi** *vr* come true; (*nel lavoro ecc*) fulfil oneself. **~zi'one** *nf* realization; (*di sogno, persona*) fulfilment. **~zione scenica** production

rea'lizzo *nm* (*vendita*) proceeds *pl*; (*riscossione*) yield

real'mente *adv* really

realtà *nf inv* reality. **~ virtuale** virtual reality

re'ato *nm* crime, criminal offence

reat'tivo *a* reactive

reat'tore *nm* reactor; *Aeron* jet [aircraft]

reazio'nario, -a *a & nmf* reactionary

reazi'one *nf* reaction. **~ a catena** chain reaction

'rebus *nm inv* rebus; (*enigma*) puzzle

recapi'tare *vt* deliver. **re'capito** *nm* address; (*consegna*) delivery. **recapito a domicilio** home delivery. **recapito telefonico** contact telephone number

re'car|e *vt* bear; (*produrre*) cause. **~si** *vr* go

re'cedere *vi* recede; *fig* give up

recensi'one *nf* review

recen's|ire *vt* review. **~ore** *nm* reviewer

re'cente *a* recent; **di ~** recently. **~'mente** *adv* recently

reces'sione *nf* recession

reces'sivo *a* *Biol* recessive. **re'cesso** *nm* recess

re'cidere *vt* cut off

reci'divo, -a *a* *Med* recurrent ● *nmf* repeat offender

recin|'tare *vt* close off. **re'cinto** *nm* enclosure; (*per animali*) pen; (*per bambini*) play-pen. **~zi'one** *nf* (*muro*) wall; (*rete*) wire fence; (*cancellata*) railings *pl*

recipi'ente *nm* container

re'ciproco *a* reciprocal

re'ciso *pp di* recidere

'recita *nf* performance. **reci'tare** *vt* recite; *Theat* act; play (*ruolo*). **~zi'one** *nf* recitation; *Theat* acting

recla'mare *vi* protest ● *vt* claim

ré'clame *nf inv* advertising; (*avviso pubblicitario*) advertisement

re'clamo *nm* complaint; **ufficio reclami** complaints department

recli'na|bile *a* reclining; **sedile ~bile** reclining seat. **~re** *vt* tilt (*sedile*); lean (*capo*)

reclusi'one *nf* imprisonment. **re'cluso, -a** *a* secluded ● *nmf* prisoner

'recluta *nf* recruit

reclu|ta'mento *nm* recruitment. **~'tare** *vt* recruit

'record *nm inv* record ● *a inv* (*cifra*) record *attrib*

recrimi'na|re *vi* recriminate. **~zi'one** *nf* recrimination

recupe'rare *vt* recover. **re'cupero** *nm* recovery; **corso di recupero** additional classes; **minuti di recupero** *Sport* injury time

redargu'ire *vt* rebuke

re'datto *pp di* redigere

redat'tore, -'trice *nmf* editor; *(di testo)* writer. **redazi'one** *nf (ufficio)* editorial office; *(di testi)* editing

reddi'tizio *a* profitable

'reddito *nm* income. **~ imponibile** taxable income

re'den|to *pp di* **redimere**. **~'tore** *nm* redeemer. **~zi'one** *nf* redemption

re'digere *vt* write; draw up *(documento)*

re'dimer|e *vt* redeem. **~si** *vr* redeem oneself

'redini *nfpl* reins

'reduce *a* **~ da** back from ● *nmf* survivor

refe'rendum *nm inv* referendum

refe'renza *nf* reference

refet'torio *nm* refectory

refrat'tario *a* refractory; **essere ~ a** have no aptitude for

refrige'ra|re *vt* refrigerate. **~zi'one** *nf* refrigeration

refur'tiva *nf* stolen goods *pl*

rega'lare *vt* give

re'gale *a* regal

re'galo *nm* present, gift

re'gata *nf* regatta

reg'gen|te *nmf* regent. **~za** *nf* regency

'regger|e *vt (sorreggere)* bear; *(tenere in mano)* hold; *(dirigere)* run; *(governare)* govern; *Gram* take ● *vi (resistere)* hold out; *(durare)* last; *fig* stand. **~si** *vr* stand

'reggia *nf* royal palace

reggi'calze *nm inv* suspender belt

reggi'mento *nm* regiment; *(fig: molte persone)* army

reggi'petto, reggi'seno *nm* bra

re'gia *nf Cinema* direction; *Theat* production

re'gime *nm* regime; *(dieta)* diet; *Mech* speed. **~ militare** military regime

re'gina *nf* queen

'regio *a* royal

regio'na|le *a* regional. **~'lismo** *nm (parola)* regionalism

regi'one *nf* region

re'gista *nmf Cinema* director; *Theat, TV* producer

regi'stra|re *vt* register; *Comm* enter; *(incidere su nastro)* tape, record; *(su disco)* record. **~'tore** *nm* recorder; *(magnetofono)* tape-recorder. **~tore di cassa** cash register. **~zi'one** *nf* registration; *Comm* entry; *(di programma)* recording

re'gistro *nm* register; *(ufficio)* registry. **~ di cassa** ledger

re'gnare *vi* reign

'regno *nm* kingdom; *(sovranità)* reign. **R~ Unito** United Kingdom

'regola *nf* rule; **essere in ~** be in order; *(persona:)* have one's papers in order. **rego'labile** *a (meccanismo)* adjustable. **~'mento** *nm* regulation; *Comm* settlement. **~mento di conti** settling of scores

rego'lar|e *a* regular ● *vt* regulate; *(ridurre, moderare)* limit; *(sistemare)* settle. **~si** *vr (agire)* act; *(moderarsi)* control oneself. **~ità** *nf inv* regularity. **~iz'zare** *vt* settle *(debito)*

rego'la|ta *nf* **darsi una ~ta** pull oneself together. **~'tore, ~'trice** *a* **piano ~tore** urban development plan

'regolo *nm* ruler

regre'dire *vi Biol, Psych* regress

regres|si'one *nf* regression. **~'sivo** *a* regressive. **re'gresso** *nm* decline

reinseri'mento *nm (di persona)* reintegration

reinser'irsi *vr (in ambiente)* reintegrate

reinte'grare *vt* restore

relativa'mente *adv* relatively; **~ a** as regards. **relatività** *nf* relativity. **rela'tivo** *a* relative

rela'tore, -'trice *nmf (in una conferenza)* speaker

re'lax *nm* relaxation

relazi'one *nf* relation[ship]; *(rapporto amoroso)* [love] affair; *(resoconto)* report; **pubbliche relazioni** *pl* public relations

rele'gare *vt* relegate

religi'o|ne *nf* religion. **~so, -a** *a* religious ● *nm* monk ● *nf* nun

re'liqui|a *nf* relic. **~'ario** *nm* reliquary

re'litto *nm* wreck

re'ma|re *vi* row. **~'tore, ~'trice** *nmf* rower

remini'scenza *nf* reminiscence

remissi'one *nf* remission; *(sottomissione)* submissiveness. **remis'sivo** *a* submissive

'remo *nm* oar

'remora *nf* **senza remore** without hesitation

re'moto *a* remote

remune'ra|re *vt* remunerate. **~'tivo** *a* remunerative. **~zi'one** *nf* remuneration

'render|e *vt (restituire)* return; *(esprimere)* render; *(fruttare)* yield; *(far diventare)* make. **~si** *vr* become; **~si**

179

rendi'conto nm report

rendi'mento nm rendering; (produzione) yield

'rendita nf income; (dello Stato) revenue; vivere di ~ fig rest on one's laurels

'rene nm kidney. ~ artificiale kidney machine

'reni nfpl (schiena) back

reni'tente a essere ~ a ⟨consigli di qcno⟩ be unwilling to accept

'renna nf reindeer (pl inv); (pelle) buckskin

'Reno nm Rhine

'reo, -a a guilty ● nmf offender

re'parto nm department; Mil unit

repel'lente a repulsive

repen'taglio nm mettere a ~ risk

repen'tino a sudden

reper'ibile a available; non è ~ (perduto) it's not to be found

repe'rire vt trace ⟨fondi⟩

re'perto nm ~ archeologico find

reper'torio nm repertory; (elenco) index; immagini pl di ~ archive footage

'replica nf reply; (obiezione) objection; (copia) replica; Theat repeat performance. repli'care vt reply; Theat repeat

repor'tage nm inv report

repres|si'one nf repression. ~'sivo a repressive. re'presso pp di reprimere. re'primere vt repress

re'pubbli|ca nf republic. ~'cano, -a a & nmf republican

repu'tare vt consider

reputazi'one nf reputation

requi'si|re vt requisition. ~to nm requirement

requisi'toria nf (arringa) closing speech

requisizi'one nf requisition

'resa nf surrender; Comm rendering. ~ dei conti rendering of accounts

'residence nm inv residential hotel

resi'den|te a & nmf resident. ~za nf residence; (soggiorno) stay. ~zi'ale a residential; zona ~ziale residential district

re'siduo a residual ● nm remainder

'resina nf resin

resi'sten|te a resistant; ~te all'acqua water-resistant. ~za nf resistance; (fisica) stamina; Electr resistor; la R~za the Resistance

re'sistere vi ~ [a] resist; (a colpi,

scosse) stand up to; ~ alla pioggia/al vento be rain-/wind-resistant

'reso pp di rendere

reso'conto nm report

respin'gente nm Rail buffer

re'spin|gere vt repel; (rifiutare) reject; (bocciare) fail. ~to pp di respingere

respi'ra|re vt/i breathe. ~'tore nm respirator. ~tore [a tubo] snorkel ~'torio a respiratory. ~zi'one nf breathing; Med respiration. ~zione bocca a bocca mouth-to-mouth rescuscitation, kiss of life. re'spiro nm breath; (il respirare) breathing; fig respite

respon'sabil|e a responsible (di for); Jur liable ● nm person responsible; ~ della produzione production manager. ~ità nf inv responsibility; Jur liability. ~ità civile Jur civil liability. ~iz'zare vt give responsibility to ⟨dipendente⟩

re'sponso nm response

'ressa nf crowd

re'stante a remaining ● nm remainder

re'stare vi = rimanere

restau'ra|re vt restore. ~'tore, ~'trice nmf restorer. ~zi'one nf restoration. re'stauro nm (riparazione) repair

re'stio a restive; ~ a reluctant to

restitu|'ire vt return; (reintegrare) restore. ~zi'one nf return; Jur restitution

'resto nm remainder; (saldo) balance; (denaro) change; resti pl (avanzi) remains; del ~ besides

re'string|ere vt contract; take in ⟨vestiti⟩; (limitare) restrict; shrink ⟨stoffa⟩. ~si vr contract; (farsi più vicini) close up; ⟨stoffa:⟩ shrink. restringi'mento nm (di tessuto) shrinkage

restri|'t'tivo a ⟨legge, clausola⟩ restrictive. ~zi'one nf restriction

resurrezi'one nf resurrection

resusci'tare vt/i revive

re'tata nf round-up

'rete nf net; (sistema) network; (televisiva) channel; (in calcio, hockey) goal; fig trap; (per la spesa) string bag. ~ locale Comput local [area] network, LAN. ~ stradale road network. ~ televisiva television channel

reti'cen|te a reticent. ~za nf reticence

retico'lato nm grid; (rete metallica) wire netting. re'ticolo nm network

'retina *nf* retina

re'tina *nf* (*per capelli*) hair net

re'torico, -a *a* rhetorical; **domanda retorica** rhetorical question ● *nf* rhetoric

retribu'|ire *vt* remunerate. **~zi'one** *nf* remuneration

'retro *adv* behind; **vedi ~** see over ● *nm inv* back. **~ di copertina** outside back cover

retroat'tivo *a* retroactive

retro'ce|dere *vi* retreat ● *vt Mil* demote; *Sport* relegate. **~ssi'one** *nf Sport* relegation

retroda'tare *vt* backdate

re'trogrado *a* retrograde; *fig* old-fashioned; *Pol* reactionary

retrogu'ardia *nf Mil* rearguard

retro'marcia *nf* reverse [gear]

retro'scena *nm inv Theat* backstage; *fig* background details *pl*

retrospet'tivo *a* retrospective

retro'stante *a* **il palazzo ~** the building behind

retrovi'sore *nm* rear-view mirror

'retta[1] *nf Math* straight line; (*di collegio, pensionato*) fee

'retta[2] *nf* **dar ~ a qcno** take sb's advice

rettango'lare *a* rectangular. **ret'tangolo** *a* right-angled ● *nm* rectangle

ret'tifi|ca *nf* rectification. **~'care** *vt* rectify

'rettile *nm* reptile

retti'lineo *a* rectilinear; (*retto*) upright ● *nm Sport* back straight

retti'tudine *nf* rectitude

'retto *pp di* **reggere** ● *a* straight; *fig* upright; (*giusto*) correct; **angolo ~** right angle

ret'tore *nm Relig* rector; *Univ* chancellor

reu'matico *a* rheumatic

reuma'tismi *nmpl* rheumatism

reve'rendo *a* reverend

rever'sibile *a* reversible

revisio'nare *vt* revise; *Comm* audit; *Auto* overhaul. **revisi'one** *nf* revision; *Comm* audit; *Auto* overhaul. **revi'sore** *nm* (*di conti*) auditor; (*di bozze*) proofreader; (*di traduzioni*) revisor

re'vival *nm inv* revival

'revoca *nf* repeal. **revo'care** *vt* repeal

riabili'ta|re *vt* rehabilitate. **~zi'one** *nf* rehabilitation

riabitu'ar|e *vt* reaccustom. **~si** *vr* reaccustom oneself

riac'cender|e *vt* rekindle ⟨*fuoco*⟩. **~si** *vr* ⟨*luce:*⟩ come back on

riacqui'stare *vt* buy back; regain ⟨*libertà, prestigio*⟩; recover ⟨*vista, udito*⟩

riagganci'are *vt* replace ⟨*ricevitore*⟩; **~ la cornetta** hang up ● *vi* hang up

riallac'ciare *vt* refasten; reconnect ⟨*corrente*⟩; renew ⟨*amicizia*⟩

rial'zare *vt* raise ● *vi* rise. **ri'alzo** *nm* rise

riani'mar|e *vt Med* resuscitate; (*ridare forza a*) revive; (*ridare coraggio a*) cheer up. **~si** *vr* regain consciousness; (*riprendere forza*) revive; (*riprendere coraggio*) cheer up

riaper'tura *nf* reopening

ria'prir|e *vt,* **~si** *vr* reopen

ri'armo *nm* rearmament

rias'sumere *vt* (*ricapitolare*) resume

riassun'tivo *a* summarizing.
rias'sunto *pp di* **riassumere** ● *nm* summary

ria'ver|e *vt* get back; regain ⟨*salute, vista*⟩. **~si** *vr* recover

riavvicina'mento *nm* (*tra persone*) reconciliation

riavvici'nar|e *vt* reconcile ⟨*paesi, persone*⟩. **~si** *vr* (*riconciliarsi*) be reconciled, make it up

riba'dire *vt* (*confermare*) reaffirm

ri'balta *nf* flap; *Theat* footlights *pl*; *fig* limelight

ribal'tabile *a* tip-up

ribal'tar|e *vt/i,* **~si** *vr* tip over; *Naut* capsize

ribas'sare *vt* lower ● *vi* fall. **ri'basso** *nm* fall; (*sconto*) discount

ri'battere *vt* (*a macchina*) retype; (*controbattere*) deny ● *vi* answer back

ribel'l|arsi *vr* rebel. **ri'belle** *a* rebellious ● *nmf* rebel. **~'ione** *nf* rebellion

'ribes *nm inv* (*rosso*) redcurrant; (*nero*) blackcurrant

ribol'lire *vi* (*fermentare*) ferment; *fig* seethe

ri'brezzo *nm* disgust; **far ~ a** disgust

rica'dere *vi* fall back; (*nel peccato ecc*) lapse; (*pendere*) hang [down]; **~ su** (*riversarsi*) fall on. **rica'duta** *nf* relapse

rical'care *vt* trace

ricalci'trante *a* recalcitrant

rica'ma|re *vt* embroider. **~to** *a* embroidered

ri'cambi *nmpl* spare parts

ricambi'are *vt* return; reciprocate ⟨*sentimento*⟩; **~ qcsa a qcno** repay sb for sth. **ri'cambio** *nm* replacement; *Biol* metabolism; **pezzo di ricambio** spare [part]

ri'camo *nm* embroidery

ricapito'la|re *vt* sum up. **~zi'one** *nf* summary, recap *fam*

ri'carica *nf* (*di sveglia*) rewinding; *Teleph* top-up card

ricari'care *vt* reload (*macchina fotografica, fucile, camion*); recharge (*batteria*); *Comput* reboot

ricat'ta|re *vt* blackmail. **~'tore**, **~'trice** *nmf* blackmailer. **ri'catto** *nm* blackmail

rica'va|re *vt* get; (*ottenere*) obtain; (*dedurre*) draw. **~to** *nm* proceeds *pl*. **ri'cavo** *nm* proceeds *pl*

'ricca *nf* rich woman. **~'mente** *adv* lavishly

ric'chezza *nf* wealth; *fig* richness; **ricchezze** *pl* riches

'riccio *a* curly ● *nm* curl; (*animale*) hedgehog. **~ di mare** sea-urchin. **~lo** *nm* curl. **~'luto** *a* curly. **ricci'uto** *a* (*barba*) curly

'ricco *a* rich ● *nm* rich man

ri'cerca *nf* search; (*indagine*) investigation; (*scientifica*) research; *Sch* project

ricer'ca|re *vt* search for; (*fare ricerche su*) research. **~ta** *nf* wanted woman. **~'tezza** *nf* refinement. **~to** *a* sought-after; (*raffinato*) refined; (*affettato*) affected ● *nm* (*polizia*) wanted man

ricetrasmit'tente *nf* transceiver

ri'cetta *nf Med* prescription; *Culin* recipe

ricet'tacolo *nm* receptacle

ricet'tario *nm* (*di cucina*) recipe book

ricetta'|tore, -'trice *nmf* fence, receiver of stolen goods. **~zi'one** *nf* receiving [stolen goods]

rice'vente *a* (*apparecchio, stazione*) receiving ● *nmf* receiver

ri'cev|ere *vt* receive; (*dare il benvenuto*) welcome; (*di albergo*) accommodate. **~i'mento** *nm* receiving; (*accoglienza*) welcome; (*trattenimento*) reception

ricevi'tor|e *nm* receiver. **~'ia** *nf* **~ia del lotto** agency authorized to sell lottery tickets

rice'vuta *nf* receipt. **~ fiscale** tax receipt

ricezi'one *nf Radio, TV* reception

richia'mare *vt* (*al telefono*) call back; (*far tornare*) recall; (*rimproverare*) rebuke; (*attirare*) draw; **~ alla mente** call

to mind. **richi'amo** *nm* recall; (*attrazione*) call

richi'edere *vt* ask for; (*di nuovo*) ask again for; **~ a qcno di fare qcsa** ask *o* request sb to do sth. **richi'esta** *nf* request; *Comm* demand

ri'chiuder|e *vt* shut again, close again. **~si** *vr* (*ferita:*) heal

rici'claggio *nm* recycling

rici'clar|e *vt* recycle (*carta, vetro*); launder (*denaro sporco*)

'ricino *nm* **olio di ~** castor oil

ricognizi'one *nf Mil* reconnaissance

ri'colmo *a* full

ricomin'ci'are *vt/i* start again

ricompa'rire *vi* reappear

ricom'pen|sa *nf* reward. **~'sare** *vt* reward

ricom'por|re *vt* (*riscrivere*) rewrite; (*ricostruire*) reform; *Typ* reset. **~si** *vr* regain one's composure

riconcili'a|re *vt* reconcile. **~rsi** *vr* be reconciled. **~zi'one** *nf* reconciliation

ricono'scen|te *a* grateful. **~za** *nf* gratitude

rico'nosc|ere *vt* recognize; (*ammettere*) acknowledge. **~i'mento** *nm* recognition; (*ammissione*) acknowledgement; (*per la polizia*) identification. **~i'uto** *a* recognized

riconqui'stare *vt* retake, reconquer

riconside'rare *vt* rethink

rico'prire *vt* recover; (*rivestire*) coat; (*di insulti*) shower (**di** with); hold (*carica*)

ricor'dar|e *vt* remember; (*richiamare alla memoria*) recall; (*far ricordare*) remind; (*rassomigliare*) look like. **~si** *vr* **~ [di]** remember. **ri'cordo** *nm* memory; (*oggetto*) memento; (*di viaggio*) souvenir; **ricordi** *pl* (*memorie*) memoirs

ricor'ren|te *a* recurrent. **~za** *nf* recurrence; (*anniversario*) anniversary

ri'correre *vi* recur; (*accadere*) occur; (*data:*) fall; **~ a** have recourse to; (*rivolgersi a*) turn to. **ri'corso** *pp di* **ricorrere** ● *nm* recourse; *Jur* appeal

ricostitu'ente *nm* tonic

ricostitu'ire *vt* re-establish

ricostru'|ire *vt* reconstruct. **~zi'one** *nf* reconstruction

ricove'ra|re *vt* give shelter to; **~re in ospedale** admit to hospital, hospitalize. **~to, -a** *nmf* hospital patient. **ri'covero** *nm* shelter; (*ospizio*) home

ricre'a|re *vt* re-create; (*ristorare*) restore. **~rsi** *vr* amuse oneself. **~'tivo** *a*

recreational. **~zi'one** nf recreation; Sch
break

ri'credersi vr change one's mind

ricupe'rare vt recover; rehabilitate
⟨tossicodipendente⟩; **~ il tempo
perduto** make up for lost time.
ri'cupero nm recovery; (di tossicodipendente) rehabilitation; (salvataggio) rescue; [**minuti nmpl di**]
ricupero injury time

ri'curvo a bent

ridacchi'are vi giggle

ri'dare vt give back, return

ri'dente a (piacevole) pleasant

'ridere vi laugh; **~ di** (deridere) laugh at

ri'detto pp di **ridire**

ridicoliz'zare vt ridicule. **ri'dicolo** a
ridiculous

ridimensio'nare vt reshape; fig see in
the right perspective

ri'dire vt repeat; (criticare) find fault
with; **trova sempre da ~** he's always
finding fault

ridon'dante a redundant

ri'dotto pp di **ridurre** ● nm Theat foyer
● a reduced

ri'du|**rre** vt reduce. **~rsi** vr diminish.
~rsi a be reduced to. **~t'tivo** a
reductive. **~zi'one** nf reduction; (per
cinema, teatro) adaptation

rieducazi'one nf (di malato) rehabilitation

riem'pi|**re** vt fill [up]; fill in ⟨moduli
ecc⟩. **~rsi** vr fill [up]. **~'tivo** a filling
● nm filler

rien'tranza nf recess

rien'trare vi go/come back in;
(tornare) return; (piegare indentro) recede; **~ in** (far parte) fall within.
ri'entro nm return; (di astronave) re-en-
try

riepilo'gare vt recapitulate.
rie'pilogo nm roundup

riesami'nare vt reappraise

ri'essere vi **ci risiamo!** here we go
again!

riesu'mare vt exhume

rievo'ca|**re** vt (commemorare) com-
memorate. **~zi'one** nf (commemo-
razione) commemoration

rifaci'mento nm remake

ri'fa|**re** vt do again; (creare) make again;
(riparare) repair; (imitare) imitate;
make ⟨letto⟩. **~rsi** vr (rimettersi) recover; (vendicarsi) get even; **~rsi una
vita/carriera** make a new life/career
for oneself; **~rsi il trucco** touch up

one's makeup; **~rsi di** make up for.
~tto pp di **rifare**

riferi'mento nm reference

rife'rir|**e** vt report; **~e a** attribute to
● vi make a report. **~si** vr **~si a** refer to

rifi'lare vt (tagliare a filo) trim; (fam:
affibbiare) saddle

rifi'ni|**re** vt finish off. **~'tura** nf finish

rifio'rire vi blossom again; fig flourish
again

rifiu'tare vt refuse. **rifi'uto** nm refusal;
rifiuti pl (immondizie) rubbish. **rifiuti**
pl **urbani** urban waste

riflessi'one nf reflection; (osservazione) remark. **rifles'sivo** a thought-
ful; Gram reflexive

ri'flesso pp di **riflettere** ● nm (luce)
reflection; Med reflex; **per ~** indirectly

ri'fletter|**e** vt reflect ● vi think. **~si** vr
be reflected

riflet'tore nm reflector; (proiettore)
searchlight

ri'flusso nm ebb

rifocil'lar|**e** vt restore. **~si** vr liter,
hum take some refreshment

ri'fondere vt (rimborsare) refund

ri'forma nf reform; Relig reformation;
Mil exemption on medical grounds

rifor'ma|**re** vt reform; (migliorare) re-
form; Mil declare unfit for military
service. **~to a** ⟨chiesa⟩ Reformed.
~'tore, **~'trice** nmf reformer. **~'torio**
nm reformatory. **rifor'mista** a reform-
ist

riforni'mento nm supply; (scorta)
stock; (di combustibile) refuelling;
stazione nf **di ~** petrol station

rifor'nir|**e** vt **~e di** provide with. **~si**
vr restock, stock up (**di** with)

ri'fra|**ngere** vt refract. **~tto** pp di
rifangere. **~zi'one** nf refraction

rifug'gire vi **~ da** fig shun

rifugi'a|**rsi** vr take refuge. **~to, -a** nmf
refugee

ri'fugio nm shelter; (nascondiglio)
hideaway

'riga nf line; (fila) row; (striscia) stripe;
(scriminatura) parting; (regolo) rule; **a
righe** ⟨stoffa⟩ striped; ⟨quaderno⟩ ruled;
mettersi in ~ line up

ri'gagnolo nm rivulet

ri'gare vt rule ⟨foglio⟩ ● vi **~ dritto** behave well

rigatti'ere nm junk dealer

rigene'rare vt regenerate

riget'tare vt (gettare indietro) throw
back; (respingere) reject; (vomitare)
throw up. **ri'getto** nm rejection

ri'ghello *nm* ruler

rigid|a'mente *adv* rigidly. **~ità** *nf* rigidity; *(di clima)* severity; *(severità)* strictness. **'rigido** *a* rigid; *(freddo)* severe; *(severo)* strict

rigi'rar|e *vt* turn again; *(ripercorrere)* go round; ~'**roso** *a* luxuriant twist *(argomentazione)* ● *vi* walk about. **~si** *vr* turn round; *(nel letto)* turn over. **ri'giro** *nm* *(imbroglio)* trick

'rigo *nm* line; *Mus* staff

ri'gogli|o *nm* bloom. ~'**oso** *a* luxuriant

ri'gonfio *a* swollen

ri'gore *nm* rigours *pl*; **a ~** strictly speaking; **calcio di ~** penalty [kick]; **area di ~** penalty area; **essere di ~** be compulsory

rigo|rosa'mente *adv* ⟨giudicare⟩ severely. ~'**roso** *a* *(severo)* strict; *(scrupoloso)* rigorous.

riguada'gnare *vt* regain ⟨quota, velocità⟩

riguar'dar|e *vt* look at again; *(considerare)* regard; *(concernere)* concern; **per quanto riguarda** with regard to. **~si** *vr* take care of oneself. **rigu'ardo** *nm* care; *(considerazione)* consideration; **nei riguardi di** towards; **riguardo a** with regard to

ri'gurgito *nm* regurgitation

rilanci'are *vt* throw back ⟨palla⟩; *(di nuovo)* throw again; increase ⟨offerta⟩; revive ⟨moda⟩; relaunch ⟨prodotto⟩ ● *vi* ⟨a carte⟩ raise the stakes

rilasci'ar|e *vt* *(concedere)* grant; *(liberare)* release; issue ⟨documento⟩. **~si** *vr* relax. **ri'lascio** *nm* release; *(di documento)* issue

rilassa'mento *nm* *(relax)* relaxation

rilas'sa|re *vt*, **~rsi** *vr* relax. **~to** *a* ⟨ambiente⟩ relaxed

rile'ga|re *vt* bind ⟨libro⟩. **~to** *a* bound. ~'**tura** *nf* binding

ri'leggere *vt* reread

ri'lento: a ~ *adv* slowly

rileva'mento *nm* survey; *Comm* buyout

rile'van|te *a* considerable

rile'va|re *vt* *(trarre)* get; *(mettere in evidenza)* point out; *(notare)* notice; *(topografia)* survey; *Comm* take over; *Mil* relieve. **~zi'one** *nf* *(statistica)* survey

rili'evo *nm* relief; *Geog* elevation; *(topografia)* survey; *(importanza)* importance; *(osservazione)* remark; **mettere in ~** qcsa point sth out

rilut'tan|te *a* reluctant. **~za** *nf* reluctance

'rima *nf* rhyme; **far ~ con** qcsa rhyme with sth

riman'dare *vt* *(posporre)* postpone; *(mandare indietro)* send back; *(mandare di nuovo)* send again; *(far ridare un esame)* make resit an examination. **ri'mando** *nm* return; *(in un libro)* cross-reference

rima'nen|te *a* remaining ● *nm* remainder. **~za** *nf* remainder; **~ze** *pl* remnants

rima'ne|re *vi* stay, remain; *(essere d'avanzo)* be left; *(venirsi a trovare)* be; *(restare stupito)* be astonished; *(restare d'accordo)* agree

rimar'chevole *a* remarkable

ri'mare *vt/i* rhyme

rimargi'nar|e *vt*, **~si** *vr* heal

ri'masto *pp di* **rimanere**

rima'sugli *nmpl* *(di cibo)* leftovers

rimbal'zare *vi* rebound; ⟨proiettile:⟩ ricochet; **far ~** bounce. **rim'balzo** *nm* rebound; *(di proiettile)* ricochet

rimbam'bi|re *vi* be in one's dotage ● *vt* stun. **~to** *a* in one's dotage

rimboc'care *vt* turn up; roll up ⟨maniche⟩; tuck in ⟨coperte⟩

rimbom'bare *vi* resound

rimbor'sare *vt* reimburse, repay. **rim'borso** *nm* reimbursement, repayment. **rimborso spese** reimbursement of expenses

rimedi'are *vi* **~ a** remedy; make up for ⟨errore⟩; *(procurare)* scrape up. **ri'medio** *nm* remedy

rimesco'lare *vt* mix [up]; shuffle ⟨carte⟩; *(rivangare)* rake up

ri'messa *nf* *(locale per veicoli)* garage; *(per aerei)* hangar; *(per autobus)* depot; *(di denaro)* remittance; *(di merci)* consignment

ri'messo *pp di* **rimettere**

ri'metter|e *vt* *(a posto)* put back; *(restituire)* return; *(affidare)* entrust; *(perdonare)* remit; *(rimandare)* put off; *(vomitare)* bring up; **~ci** *(fam: perdere)* lose [out]. **~si** *vr* *(ristabilirsi)* recover; ⟨tempo:⟩ clear up; **~si a** start again

'rimmel® *nm inv* mascara

rimoder'nare *vt* modernize

rimon'tare *vt* *(risalire)* go up; *Mech* reassemble ● *vi* remount; **~ a** *(risalire)* go back to

rimorchi'a|re *vt* tow; *fam* pick up ⟨ragazza⟩. **~'tore** *nm* tug[boat]. **ri'morchio** *nm* tow; *(veicolo)* trailer

ri'morso *nm* remorse

rimo'stranza *nf* complaint

rimozi'one *nf* removal; (*da un incarico*) dismissal. **~ forzata** *illegally parked vehicles removed at owner's expense*

rim'pasto *nm* Pol reshuffle

rimpatri'are *vt/i* repatriate. **rim'patrio** *nm* repatriation

rim'pian|gere *vt* regret. **~to** *pp di* **rimpiangere ● nm** regret

rimpiat'tino *nm* hide-and-seek

rimpiaz'zare *vt* replace

rimpiccio'lire *vi* become smaller

rimpinz'ar|e *vt* **~e di** stuff with. **~si** *vr* stuff oneself

rimprove'rare *vt* reproach; **~ qcsa a qcno** reproach sb for sth. **rim'provero** *nm* reproach

rimugi'nare *vt* rummage; *fig* **~ su** brood over

rimune'ra|re *vt* remunerate. **~'tivo** *a* remunerative. **~zi'one** *nf* remuneration

ri'muovere *vt* remove

ri'nascere *vi* be reborn, be born again

rinascimen'tale *a* Renaissance. **Rinasci'mento** *nm* Renaissance

ri'nascita *nf* rebirth

rincal'zare *vt* (*sostenere*) support; (*rimboccare*) tuck in. **rin'calzo** *nm* support; **rincalzi** *pl* Mil reserves

rincantucci'arsi *vr* hide oneself away in a corner

rinca'rare *vt* increase the price of **● vi** become more expensive. **rin'caro** *nm* price increase

rinca'sare *vi* return home

rinchi'uder|e *vt* shut up. **~si** *vr* shut oneself up

rin'correre *vt* run after

rin'cors|a *nf* run-up. **~o** *pp di* **rincorrere**

rin'cresc|ere *vi* **mi rincresce di non...** I'm sorry *o* I regret that I can't...; **se non ti ~e** if you don't mind. **~i'mento** *nm* regret. **~i'uto** *pp di* **rincrescere**

rincreti'nire *vi* be stupid

rincu'lare *vi* ⟨*arma:*⟩ recoil; ⟨*cavallo:*⟩ shy. **rin'culo** *nm* recoil

rincuo'rar|e *vt* encourage. **~si** *vr* take heart

rinfacci'are *vt* **~ qcsa a qcno** throw sth in sb's face

rinfor'zar|e *vt* strengthen; (*rendere più saldo*) reinforce. **~si** *vr* become

stronger. **rin'forzo** *nm* reinforcement; *fig* support

rinfran'care *vt* reassure

rinfre'scante *a* cooling

rinfre'scar|e *vt* cool; (*rinnovare*) freshen up **● vi** get cooler. **~si** *vr* freshen [oneself] up. **rin'fresco** *nm* light refreshment; (*ricevimento*) party

rin'fusa *nf* **alla ~** at random

ringhi'are *vi* snarl

ringhi'era *nf* railing; (*di scala*) banisters *pl*

ringiova'nire *vt* rejuvenate ⟨*pelle, persona*⟩; ⟨*vestito:*⟩ make look younger **● vi** become young again; (*sembrare*) look young again

ringrazi|a'mento *nm* thanks *pl*. **~'are** *vt* thank

rinne'ga|re *vt* disown. **~to, -a** *nmf* renegade

rinnova'mento *nm* renewal; (*di edifici*) renovation

rinno'var|e *vt* renew; renovate ⟨*edifici*⟩. **~si** *vr* be renewed; (*ripetersi*) recur, happen again. **rin'novo** *nm* renewal

rinoce'ronte *nm* rhinoceros

rino'mato *a* renowned

rinsal'dare *vt* consolidate

rinsa'vire *vi* come to one's senses

rinsec'chi|re *vi* shrivel up. **~to** *a* shrivelled up

rinta'narsi *vr* hide oneself away; ⟨*animale:*⟩ retreat into its den

rintoc'care *vi* ⟨*campana:*⟩ toll; ⟨*orologio:*⟩ strike. **rin'tocco** *nm* toll; (*di orologio*) stroke

rinton'ti|re *vt anche fig* stun. **~to** *a* (*stordito*) dazed

rintracci'are *vt* trace

rintro'nare *vt* stun **● vi** boom

ri'nuncia *nf* renunciation

rinunci'a|re *vi* **~re a** renounce, give up. **~'tario** *a* defeatist

ri'nunzia, rinunzi'are = **rinuncia, rinunciare**

rinveni'mento *nm* (*di reperti*) discovery; (*di refurtiva*) recovery. **rinve'nire** *vt* find **● vi** (*riprendere i sensi*) come round; (*ridiventare fresco*) revive

rinvi'are *vt* put off; (*mandare indietro*) return; (*in libro*) refer; **~ a giudizio** indict

rin'vio *nm* Sport goal kick; (*in libro*) cross-reference; (*di appuntamento*) postponement; (*di merce*) return

rio'nale *a* local. **ri'one** *nm* district

riordi'nare *vt* tidy [up]; (*ordinare di*

nuovo) reorder; (*riorganizzare*) reorganize

riorganiz'zare *vt* reorganize

ripa'gare *vt* repay

ripa'ra|re *vt* (*proteggere*) shelter, protect; (*aggiustare*) repair; (*porre rimedio*) remedy ● *vi* **~re a** make up for. **~rsi** *vr* take shelter. **~to** *a* (*luogo*) sheltered. **~zi'one** *nf* repair; *fig* reparation. **ri'paro** *nm* shelter; (*rimedio*) remedy

ripar'ti|re *vt* (*dividere*) divide ● *vi* leave again. **~zi'one** *nf* division

ripas'sa|re *vt* recross; (*rivedere*) revise ● *vi* pass again. **~ta** *nf* (*di vernice*) second coat. **ri'passo** *nm* (*di lezione*) revision

ripensa'mento *nm* second thoughts *pl*

ripen'sare *vi* (*cambiare idea*) change one's mind; **~ a** a think of; **ripensaci!** think again!

riper'correre *vt* (*con la memoria*) go back over

riper'cosso *pp di* **ripercuotere**

ripercu'oter|e *vt* strike again. **~si** *vr* (*suono:*) reverberate; **~si su** (*fig: avere conseguenze*) impact on. **ripercussi'one** *nf* repercussion

ripe'scare *vt* fish out (*oggetti*)

ripe'tente *nmf* student repeating a year

ri'pet|ere *vt* repeat. **~ersi** *vr* (*evento:*) recur. **~izi'one** *nf* repetition; (*di lezione*) revision; (*lezione privata*) private lesson. **~uta'mente** *adv* repeatedly

ri'piano *nm* (*di scaffale*) shelf; (*terreno pianeggiante*) terrace

ri'picc|a *nf* **fare qcsa per ~a** do sth out of spite. **~o** *nm* spite

'ripido *a* steep

ripie'gar|e *vt* refold; (*abbassare*) lower ● *vi* (*indietreggiare*) retreat. **~si** *vr* bend; (*sedile:*) fold. **ripi'ego** *nm* expedient; (*via d'uscita*) way out

ripi'eno *a* full; *Culin* stuffed ● *nm* filling; *Culin* stuffing

ripopo'lar|e *vt* repopulate. **~si** *vr* be repopulated

ri'porre *vt* put back; (*mettere da parte*) put away; (*collocare*) place; repeat (*domanda*)

ripor'tar|e *vt* (*restituire*) bring/take back; (*riferire*) report; (*subire*) suffer; *Math* carry; win (*vittoria*); transfer (*disegno*). **~si** *vr* go back; (*riferirsi*) refer. **ri'porto** *nm* **cane da riporto** gun dog

ripo'sante *a* (*colore*) restful, soothing

ripo'sa|re *vi* rest ● *vt* put back. **~rsi** *vr* rest. **~to** *a* (*mente*) fresh. **ri'poso** *nm* rest; **andare a riposo** retire; **riposo!** *Mil* at ease!; **giorno di riposo** day off

ripo'stiglio *nm* cupboard

ri'posto *pp di* **riporre**

ri'prender|e *vt* take again; (*prendere indietro*) take back; (*riconquistare*) recapture; (*ricuperare*) recover; (*ricominciare*) resume; (*rimproverare*) reprimand; take in (*cucitura*); *Cinema* shoot. **~si** *vr* recover; (*correggersi*) correct oneself

ri'presa *nf* resumption; (*ricupero*) recovery; *Theat* revival; *Cinema* shot; *Auto* acceleration; *Mus* repeat. **~ aerea** bird's-eye view

ripresen'tar|e *vt* resubmit (*domanda, certificato*). **~si** *vr* (*a ufficio*) go/come back again; (*come candidato*) stand *o* run again; (*occasione:*) arise again

ri'preso *pp di* **riprendere**

ripristi'nare *vt* restore

ripro'dotto *pp di* **riprodurre**

ripro'du|rre *vt*, **~rsi** *vr* reproduce. **~t'tivo** *a* reproductive. **~zi'one** *nf* reproduction

ripro'mettersi *vr* (*intendere*) intend

ri'prova *nf* confirmation

ripudi'are *vt* repudiate

ripu'gnan|te *a* repugnant. **~za** *nf* disgust. **ripu'gnare** *vi* **ripugnare a** disgust

ripu'li|re *vt* clean [up]; *fig* polish. **~ta** *nf* **darsi una ~ta** have a wash and brushup

ripuls|i'one *nf* repulsion. **~'ivo** *a* repulsive

ri'quadro *nm* square; (*pannello*) panel

ri'sacca *nf* undertow

ri'saia *nf* rice field, paddy field

risa'lire *vt* go back up ● *vi* **~ a** (*nel tempo*) go back to; (*essere datato a*) date back to, go back to

risal'tare *vi* (*emergere*) stand out. **ri'salto** *nm* prominence; (*rilievo*) relief

risa'nare *vt* heal; (*bonificare*) reclaim

risa'puto *a* well-known

risarci'mento *nm* compensation. **risar'cire** *vt* indemnify

ri'sata *nf* laugh

riscalda'mento *nm* heating. **~ autonomo** central heating (*for one apartment*)

riscal'dar|e *vt* heat; warm (*persona*). **~si** *vr* warm up

riscat'tar|e *vt* ransom. **~si** *vr* redeem

oneself. **ri'scatto** *nm* ransom; (*morale*) redemption

rischia'rar|e *vt* light up; brighten ⟨*colore*⟩. **~si** *vr* light up; ⟨*cielo:*⟩ clear up

rischi|'are *vt* risk ●*vi* run the risk. **'rischio** *nm* risk. **~'oso** *a* risky

risciac'quare *vt* rinse. **risci'acquo** *nm* rinse

riscon'trare *vt* (*confrontare*) compare; (*verificare*) check; (*rilevare*) find. **ri'scontro** *nm* comparison; check; (*Comm: risposta*) reply

ri'scossa *nf* revolt; (*riconquista*) recovery

riscossi'one *nf* collection

ri'scosso *pp di* **riscuotere**

riscu'oter|e *vt* shake; (*percepire*) draw; (*ottenere*) gain; cash ⟨*assegno*⟩. **~si** *vr* rouse oneself

risen'ti|re *vt* hear again; (*provare*) feel ●*vi* **~re di** feel the effect of. **~rsi** *vr* (*offendersi*) take offence. **~to** *a* resentful

ri'serbo *nm* reserve; **mantenere il ~** remain tight-lipped

ri'serva *nf* reserve; (*di caccia, pesca*) preserve; *Sport* substitute, reserve. **~ di caccia** game reserve. **~ indiana** Indian reservation. **~ naturale** wildlife reserve

riser'va|re *vt* reserve; (*prenotare*) book; (*per occasione*) keep. **~rsi** *vr* (*ripromettersi*) plan for oneself ⟨*cambiamento*⟩. **~'tezza** *nf* reserve. **~to** *a* reserved

ri'siedere *vi* **~ a** reside in

'riso[1] *pp di* **ridere** ●*nm* (*pl nf* **risa**) laughter; (*singolo*) laugh. **~'lino** *nm* giggle

'riso[2] *nm* (*cereale*) rice

ri'solto *pp di* **risolvere**

risolu|'tezza *nf* determination. **riso'luto** *a* resolute, determined. **~zi'one** *nf* resolution

ri'solver|e *vt* resolve; *Math* solve. **~si** *vr* (*decidersi*) decide; **~si in** turn into

riso'na|nza *nf* resonance; **aver ~nza** *fig* arouse great interest. **~re** *vi* resound; (*rimbombare*) echo

ri'sorgere *vi* rise again

risorgi'mento *nm* revival; (*storico*) Risorgimento

ri'sorsa *nf* resource; (*espediente*) resort

ri'sorto *pp di* **risorgere**

ri'sotto *nm* risotto

ri'sparmi *nmpl* (*soldi*) savings

risparmi'a|re *vt* save; (*salvare*) spare. **~'tore, ~'trice** *nmf* saver **ri'sparmio** *nm* saving

rispecchi'are *vt* reflect

rispet'tabil|e *a* respectable. **~ità** *nf* respectability

rispet'tare *vt* respect; **farsi ~** command respect

rispet'tivo *a* respective

ri'spetto *nm* respect; **~ a** as regards; (*in paragone a*) compared to

rispet|tosa'mente *adv* respectfully. **~'toso** *a* respectful

risplen'dente *a* shining. **ri'splendere** *vi* shine

rispon'den|te *a* **~te a** in keeping with. **~za** *nf* correspondence

ri'spondere *vi* answer; (*rimbeccare*) answer back; (*obbedire*) respond; **~ a** reply to; **~ di** (*rendersi responsabile*) answer for

ri'spost|a *nf* answer, reply; (*reazione*) response. **~o** *pp di* **rispondere**

'rissa *nf* brawl. **ris'soso** *a* pugnacious

ristabi'lir|e *vt* re-establish. **~si** *vr* (*in salute*) recover

rista'gnare *vi* stagnate; ⟨*sangue:*⟩ coagulate. **ri'stagno** *nm* stagnation

ri'stampa *nf* reprint; (*azione*) reprinting. **ristam'pare** *vt* reprint

risto'rante *nm* restaurant

risto'ra|re *vt* refresh. **~rsi** *vr liter* take some refreshment; (*riposarsi*) take a rest. **~'tore, ~'trice** *nmf* (*proprietario di ristorante*) restaurateur; (*fornitore*) caterer ●*a* refreshing. **ri'storo** *nm* refreshment; (*sollievo*) relief

ristret'tezza *nf* narrowness; (*povertà*) poverty; **vivere in ristrettezze** live in straitened circumstances

ri'stretto *pp di* **restringere** ●*a* narrow; (*condensato*) condensed; (*limitato*) restricted; **di idee ristrette** narrow-minded

ristruttu'rare *vt* restructure, reorganize ⟨*ditta*⟩; refurbish ⟨*casa*⟩

risucchi'are *vt* suck in. **ri'succhio** *nm* whirlpool; (*di corrente*) undertow

risul'ta|re *vi* result; (*riuscire*) turn out. **~to** *nm* result

risuo'nare *vi* ⟨*grida, parola:*⟩ echo; *Phys* resonate

risurrezi'one *nf* resurrection

risusci'tare *vt* resuscitate; *fig* revive ●*vi* return to life

risvegli'ar|e *vt* reawaken ⟨*interesse*⟩. **~si** *vr* wake up; ⟨*natura:*⟩ awake; ⟨*desiderio:*⟩ be aroused. **ri'sveglio** *nm* waking up; (*dell'interesse*) revival; (*del desiderio*) arousal

ri'svolto *nm* (*di giacca*) lapel; (*di pantaloni*) turn-up, cuff *Am*; (*di manica*) cuff; (*di tasca*) flap; (*di libro*) inside flap

ritagli'are *vt* cut out. **ri'taglio** *nm* cutting; (*di stoffa*) scrap

ritar'da|re *vi* be late; ⟨*orologio:*⟩ be slow ● *vt* delay; slow down ⟨*progresso*⟩; (*differire*) postpone. **~'tario, -a** *nmf* late-comer. **~to** *a* *Psych* retarded

ri'tardo *nm* delay; **essere in ~** be late; ⟨*volo:*⟩ be delayed

ri'tegno *nm* reserve

rite'n|ere *vt* retain; deduct ⟨*somma*⟩; (*credere*) believe. **~uta** *nf* (*sul salario*) deduction

riti'ra|re *vt* throw back ⟨*palla*⟩; (*prelevare*) withdraw; (*riscuotere*) draw; collect ⟨*pacco*⟩. **~rsi** *vr* withdraw; ⟨*stoffa:*⟩ shrink; (*da attività*) retire; ⟨*marea:*⟩ recede. **~ta** *nf* retreat; (*WC*) toilet. **ri'tiro** *nm* withdrawal; *Relig* retreat; (*da attività*) retirement. **ritiro bagagli** baggage reclaim

'ritmo *nm* rhythm

'rito *nm* rite; **di ~** customary

ritoc'care *vt* (*correggere*) touch up. **ri'tocco** *nm* retouch

ritor'nare *vi* return; (*andare/venire indietro*) go/come back; (*ricorrere*) recur; (*ridiventare*) become again

ritor'nello *nm* refrain

ri'torno *nm* return

ritorsi'one *nf* retaliation

ri'trarre *vt* (*ritirare*) withdraw; (*distogliere*) turn away; (*rappresentare*) portray

ritrat'ta|re *vt* deal with again; retract ⟨*dichiarazione*⟩. **~zi'one** *nf* withdrawal, retraction

ritrat'tista *nmf* portrait painter. **ri'tratto** *pp di* **ritrarre** ● *nm* portrait

ritro'sia *nf* shyness. **ri'troso** *a* backward; (*timido*) shy; **a ritroso** backwards; **ritroso a** reluctant to

ritrova'mento *nm* (*azione*) finding

ritro'va|re *vt* find [again]; regain ⟨*salute*⟩. **~rsi** *vr* meet; (*di nuovo*) meet again; (*capitare*) find oneself; (*raccapezzarsi*) see one's way. **~to** *nm* discovery. **ri'trovo** *nm* meeting-place; (*notturno*) night-club

'ritto *a* upright; (*diritto*) straight

ritu'ale *a & nm* ritual

riunifi'ca|re *vt* reunify. **~rsi** *vr* be reunited. **~zi'one** *nf* reunification

riuni'one *nf* meeting; (*fra amici*) reunion

riu'nir|e *vt* (*unire*) join together; (*radunare*) gather. **~si** *vr* be reunited; (*adunarsi*) meet

riusc'i|re *vi* (*aver successo*) succeed; (*in matematica ecc*) be good (**in** at); (*aver esito*) turn out; **le è riuscito simpatico** she found him likeable. **~ta** *nf* (*esito*) result; (*successo*) success

'riva *nf* (*di mare, lago*) shore; (*di fiume*) bank

ri'val|e *nmf* rival. **~ità** *nf inv* rivalry

rivalutazi'one *nf* revaluation

rivan'gare *vt* dig up again

rive'dere *vt* see again; revise ⟨*lezione*⟩; (*verificare*) check

rive'la|re *vt* reveal. **~rsi** *vr* (*dimostrarsi*) turn out. **~'tore** *a* revealing ● *nm Techn* detector. **~zi'one** *nf* revelation

ri'vendere *vt* resell

rivendi'ca|re *vt* claim. **~zi'one** *nf* claim

ri'vendi|ta *nf* (*negozio*) shop. **~'tore, ~'trice** *nmf* retailer. **~tore autorizzato** authorized dealer

ri'verbero *nm* reverberation; (*bagliore*) glare

rive'renza *nf* reverence; (*inchino*) curtsy; (*di uomo*) bow

rive'rire *vt* respect; (*ossequiare*) pay one's respects to

river'sar|e *vt* pour. **~si** *vr* ⟨*fiume:*⟩ flow

river'sibile *a* reversible

rivesti'mento *nm* covering

rive'sti|re *vt* (*rifornire di abiti*) clothe; (*ricoprire*) cover; (*internamente*) line; hold ⟨*carica*⟩. **~rsi** *vr* get dressed again; (*per una festa*) dress up

rivi'era *nf* coast; **la ~ ligure** the Italian Riviera

ri'vincita *nf Sport* return match; (*vendetta*) revenge

rivis'suto *pp di* **rivivere**

ri'vista *nf* review; (*pubblicazione*) magazine; *Theat* revue; **passare in ~** review

ri'vivere *vi* come to life again; (*riprendere le forze*) revive ● *vt* relive

ri'volger|e *vt* turn; (*indirizzare*) address; **~e da** (*distogliere*) turn away from. **~si** *vr* turn round; **~si a** (*indirizzarsi*) turn to

ri'volta *nf* revolt

rivol'tante *a* disgusting

rivol'tar|e *vt* turn [over]; (*mettendo l'interno verso l'esterno*) turn inside out; (*sconvolgere*) upset. **~si** *vr* (*ribellarsi*) revolt

rivol'tella *nf* revolver

ri'volto *pp di* **rivolgere**

rivoluzio'nar|e *vt* revolutionize. **~io, -a** *a & nmf* revolutionary. **rivoluzi'one** *nf* revolution; (*fig: disordine*) chaos

riz'zar|e *vt* raise; (*innalzare*) erect; prick up ⟨*orecchie*⟩. **~si** *vr* stand up; ⟨*capelli:*⟩ stand on end; ⟨*orecchie:*⟩ prick up

'roaming *nm inv* Teleph ~ [**internazionale**] roaming

'roba *nf* stuff; (*personale*) belongings *pl*, stuff; (*faccenda*) thing; (*sl: droga*) drugs *pl*; ~ **da matti!** absolute madness!. ~ **da mangiare** food, things to eat

ro'baccia *nf* rubbish

ro'bot *nm inv* robot. **~iz'zato** *a* robotic

robu'stezza *nf* sturdiness, robustness; (*forza*) strength. **ro'busto** *a* sturdy, robust; (*forte*) strong

'rocca *nf* fortress. **~'forte** *nf* stronghold

roc'chetto *nm* reel

'roccia *nf* rock

ro'da|ggio *nm* running in. **~re** *vt* run in

'roder|e *vt* gnaw; (*corrodere*) corrode. **~si** *vr* **~si da** (*logorarsi*) be consumed with. **rodi'tore** *nm* rodent

'rogna *nf* scabies *sg; fig* nuisance

ro'gnone *nm* Culin kidney

'rogo *nm* (*supplizio*) stake; (*per cadaveri*) pyre

'Roma *nf* Rome

Roma'nia *nf* Romania

ro'manico *a* Romanesque

ro'mano, -a *a & nmf* Roman

romanti'cismo *nm* romanticism. **ro'mantico** *a* romantic

ro'man|za *nf* romance. **~'zato** *a* romanticized. **~'zesco** *a* fictional; (*stravagante*) wild, unrealistic. **~zi'ere** *nm* novelist

ro'manzo *a* Romance ● *nm* novel. ~ **d'appendice** serial story. ~ **giallo** thriller

'rombo *nm* rumble; *Math* rhombus; (*pesce*) turbot

'romper|e *vt* break; break off ⟨*relazione*⟩; **non ~e** [**le scatole**]! (*fam: seccare*) don't be a pain [in the neck]!. **~si** *vr* break; **~si una gamba** break one's leg

rompi'capo *nm* nuisance; (*indovinello*) puzzle

rompi'collo *nm* daredevil; **a ~** at breakneck speed

rompighi'accio *nm* ice-breaker

rompi'scatole *nmf inv fam* pain

'ronda *nf* rounds *pl*

ron'della *nf* washer

'rondine *nf* swallow

ron'done *nm* swift

ron'fare *vi* (*russare*) snore

ron'zare *vi* buzz; ~ **attorno a qcno** *fig* hang about sb

ron'zino *nm* jade

ron'zio *nm* buzz

'rosa *nf* rose. ~ **dei venti** wind rose ● *a & nm* (*colore*) pink. **ro'saio** *nm* rose-bush

ro'sario *nm* rosary

ro'sato *a* rosy ● *nm* (*vino*) rosé

'roseo *a* pink

ro'seto *nm* rose garden

rosicchi'are *vt* nibble; (*rodere*) gnaw

rosma'rino *nm* rosemary

'roso *pp di* **rodere**

roso'lare *vt* brown

roso'lia *nf* German measles

ro'sone *nm* rosette; (*apertura*) rose-window

'rospo *nm* toad

ros'setto *nm* (*per labbra*) lipstick

'rosso *a & nm* red; **passare con il ~** jump a red light. ~ **d'uovo** [egg] yolk. **ros'sore** *nm* redness; (*della pelle*) flush

rosticce'ria *nf* shop selling cooked meat and other prepared food

ro'tabile *a* **strada ~** carriageway

ro'taia *nf* rail; (*solco*) rut

ro'ta|re *vt/i* rotate. **~zi'one** *nf* rotation

rote'are *vt/i* roll

ro'tella *nf* small wheel; (*di mobile*) castor

roto'lar|e *vt/i* roll. **~si** *vr* roll [about]. **'rotolo** *nm* roll; **andare a rotoli** go to rack and ruin

rotondità *nf* (*qualità*) roundness; ~ *pl* (*curve femminili*) curves. **ro'tondo, -a** *a* round ● *nf* (*spiazzo*) terrace

ro'tore *nm* rotor

'rotta¹ *nf* Naut, Aeron course; **far ~ per** make course for; **fuori ~** off course

'rotta² *nf* **a ~ di collo** at breakneck speed; **essere in ~ con** be on bad terms with

rot'tame *nm* scrap; *fig* wreck

'rotto *pp di* **rompere** ● *a* broken; (*stracciato*) torn

rot'tura *nf* break; **che ~ di scatole!** *fam* what a pain!

'rotula *nf* kneecap

rou'lette *nf inv* roulette

rou'lotte *nf inv* caravan, trailer *Am*

rou'tine *nf inv* routine; **di ~** ⟨*operazioni, controlli*⟩ routine

ro'vente *a* scorching

'rovere nm (legno) oak

rovesci'ar|e vt (buttare a terra) knock over; (sottosopra) turn upside down; (rivoltare) turn inside out; spill ⟨liquido⟩; overthrow ⟨governo⟩; reverse ⟨situazione⟩. **~si** vr (capovolgersi) overturn; (riversarsi) pour. **ro'vescio** a (contrario) reverse; **alla rovescia** (capovolto) upside down; (con l'interno all'esterno) inside out ● nm reverse; (nella maglia) purl; (di pioggia) downpour; Tennis backhand

ro'vina nf ruin; (crollo) collapse

rovi'na|re vt ruin; (guastare) spoil ● vi crash. **~rsi** vr be ruined. **~to** a ⟨oggetto⟩ ruined. **rovi'noso** a ruinous

rovi'stare vt ransack

'rovo nm bramble

'rozzo a rough

R.R. abbr (ricevuta di ritorno) return receipt for registered mail

'ruba nf andare a ~ sell like hot cakes

ru'bare vt steal

rubi'netto nm tap, faucet Am

ru'bino nm ruby

ru'brica nf (in giornale) column; (in programma televisivo) TV report; (quaderno con indice) address book. ~ **telefonica** telephone and address book

'rude a rough

'rudere nm ruin

rudimen'tale a rudimentary. **rudi'menti** nmpl rudiments

ruffi'an|a nf procuress. **~o** nm pimp; (adulatore) bootlicker

'ruga nf wrinkle

'ruggine nf rust; **fare la ~** go rusty

rug'gi|re vi roar. **~to** nm roar

rugi'ada nf dew

ru'goso a wrinkled

rul'lare vi roll; Aeron taxi

rul'lino nm film

rul'lio nm rolling; Aeron taxiing

'rullo nm roll; Techn roller

rum nm inv rum

ru'meno, -a a & nmf Romanian

rumi'nare vt ruminate

ru'mor|e nm noise; fig rumour. **~eggi'are** vi rumble. **rumo'roso** a noisy; (sonoro) loud

ru'olo nm roll; Theat role; **di ~** on the staff

ru'ota nf wheel; **andare a ~ libera** free-wheel. **~ di scorta** spare wheel

'rupe nf cliff

ru'rale a rural

ru'scello nm stream

'ruspa nf bulldozer

rus'sare vi snore

'Russ|ia nf Russia. **r~o, -a** a & nmf Russian; (lingua) Russian

'rustico a rural; ⟨carattere⟩ rough

rut'tare vi belch. **'rutto** nm belch

'ruvido a coarse

ruzzo'l|are vi tumble down. **~one** nm tumble; **cadere ruzzoloni** tumble down

Ss

'sabato nm Saturday

'sabbi|a nf sand. **~e** pl **mobili** quicksand. **~'oso** a sandy

sabo'ta|ggio nm sabotage. **~re** vt sabotage. **~'tore**, **~'trice** nmf saboteur

'sacca nf bag. **~ da viaggio** travelling-bag

sacca'rina nf saccharin

sac'cente a pretentious ● nmf know-all

saccheggi'a|re vt sack; hum raid ⟨frigo⟩. **~'tore**, **~'trice** nmf plunderer. **sac'cheggio** nm sack

sac'chetto nm bag

'sacco nm sack; Anat sac; **mettere nel ~** fig swindle; **un ~** (moltissimo) a lot; **un ~ di** (gran quantità) lots of. **~ a pelo** sleeping-bag

sacer'do|te nm priest. **~zio** nm priesthood

sacra'mento nm sacrament

sacrifi'ca|re vt sacrifice. **~rsi** vr sacrifice oneself. **~to** a (non valorizzato) wasted. **sacri'ficio** nm sacrifice

sacri'legio nm sacrilege. **sa'crilego** a sacrilegious

'sacro a sacred ● nm Anat sacrum

sacro'santo a sacrosanct

'**sadico, -a** _a_ sadistic ● _nmf_ sadist. **sa'dismo** _nm_ sadism

sa'etta _nf_ arrow

sa'fari _nm inv_ safari

'**saga** _nf_ saga

sa'gace _a_ shrewd

sag'gezza _nf_ wisdom

saggi'are _vt_ test

'**saggio**[1] _nm_ (_scritto_) essay; (_prova_) proof; (_di metallo_) assay; (_campione_) sample; (_esempio_) example

'**saggio**[2] _a_ wise ● _nm_ (_persona_) sage

sag'gistica _nf_ non-fiction

Sagit'tario _nm Astr_ Sagittarius

sa'goma _nf_ shape; (_profilo_) outline; **che ~!** _fam_ what a character!. **sa-go'mato** _a_ shaped

'**sagra** _nf_ festival

sagre|'stano _nm_ sacristan. **~'stia** _nf_ sacristy

'**sala** _nf_ hall; (_stanza_) room; (_salotto_) living room. **~ d'attesa** waiting room. **~ da ballo** ballroom. **~ d'imbarco** departure lounge. **~ macchine** engine room. **~ operatoria** operating theatre _Br_, operating room _Am_. **~ parto** delivery room. **~ da pranzo** dining room

sa'lame _nm_ salami

sala'moia _nf_ brine

sa'lare _vt_ salt

sa'lario _nm_ wages _pl_

sa'lasso _nm_ **essere un ~** _fig_ cost a fortune

sala'tini _nmpl_ savouries (_eaten with aperitifs_)

sa'lato _a_ salty; (_costoso_) dear

sal'ciccia _nf_ = **salsiccia**

sal'dar|e _vt_ weld; set (_osso_); pay off (_debito_); settle (_conto_); **~e a stagno** solder. **~si** _vr_ (_Med: osso:_) knit

salda'trice _nf_ welder; (_a stagno_) soldering iron

salda'tura _nf_ weld; (_azione_) welding; (_di osso_) knitting

'**saldo** _a_ firm; (_resistente_) strong ● _nm_ (_di conto_) settlement; (_svendita_) sale; _Comm_ balance

'**sale** _nm_ salt; **restare di ~** be struck dumb [with astonishment]. **~ fine** table salt. **~ grosso** cooking salt. **sali** _pl_ **e tabacchi** tobacconist's shop

'**salice** _nm_ willow. **~ piangente** weeping willow

sali'ente _a_ outstanding; **i punti salienti di un discorso** the main points of a speech

sali'era _nf_ salt-cellar

sa'lina _nf_ salt-works _sg_

sa'li|re _vi_ go/come up; (_levarsi_) rise; (_su treno ecc_) get on; (_in macchina_) get in ● _vt_ go/come up (_scale_). **~ta** _nf_ climb; (_aumento_) rise; **in ~ta** uphill

sa'liva _nf_ saliva

'**salma** _nf_ corpse

'**salmo** _nm_ psalm

sal'mone _nm_ & _a inv_ salmon

sa'lone _nm_ hall; (_salotto_) living room; (_di parrucchiere_) salon. **~ di bellezza** beauty parlour

salo'pette _nf inv_ dungarees _pl_

salot'tino _nm_ bower

sa'lotto _nm_ drawing room; (_soggiorno_) sitting room; (_mobili_) [three-piece] suite; **fare ~** chat

sal'pare _vt/i_ sail; **~ l'ancora** weigh anchor

'**salsa** _nf_ sauce. **~ di pomodoro** tomato sauce

sal'sedine _nf_ saltiness

sal'siccia _nf_ sausage

salsi'era _nf_ sauce-boat

sal'ta|re _vi_ jump; (_venir via_) come off; (_balzare_) leap; (_esplodere_) blow up; **~r fuori** spring from nowhere; (_oggetto cercato:_) turn up; **è ~to fuori che...** it emerged that...; **~re fuori con...** come out with...; **~re in aria** blow up; **~re in mente** spring to mind ● _vt_ jump [over]; skip (_pasti, lezioni_); _Culin_ sauté. **~to a** _Culin_ sautéed

saltel'lare _vi_ hop; (_di gioia_) skip

saltim'banco _nm_ acrobat

'**salto** _nm_ jump; (_balzo_) leap; (_dislivello_) drop; (_fig: omissione, lacuna_) gap; **fare un ~ da** (_visitare_) drop in on; **in un ~** _fig_ in a jiffy. **~ in alto** high jump. **~ con l'asta** pole-vault. **~ in lungo** long jump. **~ pagina** _Comput_ page down

saltuaria'mente _adv_ occasionally. **saltu'ario** _a_ desultory; **lavoro saltuario** casual work

sa'lubre _a_ healthy

salume'ria _nf_ ≈ delicatessen. **sa'lumi** _nmpl_ cold cuts

salu'tare _vt_ greet; (_congedandosi_) say goodbye to; (_portare i saluti a_) give one's regards to; _Mil_ salute ● _a_ healthy

sa'lute _nf_ health; **~!** (_dopo uno starnuto_) bless you!; (_a un brindisi_) cheers!

sa'luto _nm_ greeting; (_di addio_) goodbye; _Mil_ salute; **saluti** _pl_ (_ossequi_) regards '**salva** *nf* salvo; **sparare a salve** fire blanks

salvada'naio *nm* money box

salva'gente *nm* lifebelt; (*a giubbotto*) life-jacket; (*ciambella*) rubber ring; (*spartitraffico*) traffic island

salvaguar'dare *vt* safeguard. **salvagu'ardia** *nf* safeguard

sal'var|e *vt* save; (*proteggere*) protect. **~si** *vr* save oneself

salva'slip *nm inv* panty-liner

salva|'taggio *nm* rescue; *Naut* salvage; *Comput* saving; **battello di ~taggio** lifeboat. **~'tore, ~'trice** *nmf* saviour

sal'vezza *nf* safety; *Relig* salvation

'**salvia** *nf* sage

salvi'etta *nf* serviette

'**salvo** *a* safe ● *prep* except [for] ● *conj* **~ che** (*a meno che*) unless; (*eccetto che*) except that

samari'tano, -a *a & nmf* Samaritan

sam'buco *nm* elder

san *nm* S~ **Francesco** Saint Francis

sa'nare *vt* heal

sana'torio *nm* sanatorium

san'cire *vt* sanction

'**sandalo** *nm* sandal; *Bot* sandalwood

'**sangu|e** *nm* blood; **al ~e** (*carne*) rare; **farsi cattivo ~e per** worry about; **occhi iniettati di ~e** bloodshot eyes. **~e freddo** composure; **a ~e freddo** in cold blood. **~'igno** *a* blood

sangui'naccio *nm* Culin black pudding

sangui'nante *a* bleeding

sangui'nar|e *vi* bleed. **~io** *a* bloodthirsty

sangui'noso *a* bloody

sangui'suga *nf* leech

sanità *nf* soundness; (*salute*) health. **~ mentale** sanity, mental health

sani'tario *a* sanitary; **Servizio S~** National Health Service

'**sano** *a* sound; (*salutare*) healthy; **~ di mente** sane; **~ come un pesce** as fit as a fiddle

San Sil'vestro *nm* New Year's Eve

santifi'care *vt* sanctify

'**santo** *a* holy; (*con nome proprio*) saint ● *nm* saint. **san'tone** *nm* guru. **santu'ario** *nm* sanctuary

sanzi'one *nf* sanction

sa'pere *vt* know; (*essere capace di*) be able to; (*venire a sapere*) hear; **saperla lunga** know a thing or two ● *vi* **~ di** know about; (*aver sapore di*) taste of;

(*aver odore di*) smell of; **saperci fare** have the know-how ● *nm* knowledge

sapi'en|te *a* wise; (*esperto*) expert ● *nm* (*uomo colto*) sage. **~za** *nf* wisdom

sa'pone *nm* soap. **~ da bucato** washing soap. **sapo'netta** *nf* bar of soap

sa'pore *nm* taste. **saporita'mente** *adv* (*dormire*) soundly. **sapo'rito** *a* tasty

sapu'tello, -a *a & nm sl* know-all, know-it-all *Am*

saraci'nesca *nf* roller shutter

sar'cas|mo *nm* sarcasm. **~tico** *a* sarcastic

Sar'degna *nf* Sardinia

sar'dina *nf* sardine

'**sardo, -a** *a & nmf* Sardinian

sar'donico *a* sardonic

'**sarto, -a** *nm* tailor ● *nf* dressmaker. **~'ria** *nf* tailor's; dressmaker's; (*arte*) couture

sas'sata *nf* blow with a stone; **prendere a sassate** stone. '**sasso** *nm* stone; (*ciottolo*) pebble

sassofo'nista *nmf* saxophonist. **sas'sofono** *nm* saxophone

sas'soso *a* stony

'**Satana** *nm* Satan. **sa'tanico** *a* satanic

sa'tellite *a inv & nm* satellite

sati'nato *a* glossy

'**satira** *nf* satire. **sa'tirico** *a* satirical

satu'ra|re *vt* saturate. **~zi'one** *nf* saturation. '**saturo** *a* saturated; (*pieno*) full

'**sauna** *nf* sauna

savoi'ardo *nm* (*biscotto*) sponge finger

sazi'ar|e *vt* satiate. **~si** *vr* **~si di** *fig* grow tired of

sazietà *nf* **mangiare a ~** eat one's fill. '**sazio** *a* satiated

sbaciucchi'ar|e *vt* smother with kisses. **~si** *vr* kiss and cuddle

sbada'ta|ggine *nf* carelessness; **è stata una ~ggine** it was careless. **~'mente** *adv* carelessly. **sba'dato** *a* careless

sbadigli'are *vi* yawn. **sba'diglio** *nm* yawn

sba'fa|re *vt* sponge. **~ta** *nf sl* nosh

'**sbafo** *nm* sponging; **a ~** (*gratis*) without paying

sbagli'ar|e *vi* make a mistake; (*aver torto*) be wrong ● *vt* make a mistake in; **~e strada** go the wrong way; **~e numero** get the number wrong; *Teleph* dial a wrong number. **~si** *vr* make a mistake. '**sbaglio** *nm* mistake; **per sbaglio** by mistake

sbal'l|are *vt* unpack; *fam* screw up (*conti*) ● *vi fam* go crazy. **~ato** *a* (*squilibrato*) unbalanced. '**sballo** *nm fam* scream; (*per droga*) trip; **da sballo** *sl* terrific

sballot'tare *vt* toss about

sbalor'di|re *vt* stun ● *vi* be stunned. ~'**tivo** *a* amazing. ~**to** *a* stunned

sbal'zare *vt* throw; (*da una carica*) dismiss ● *vi* bounce; (*saltare*) leap. '**sbalzo** *nm* bounce; (*sussulto*) jolt; (*di temperatura*) sudden change; **a sbalzi** in spurts; **a sbalzo** (*lavoro a rilievo*) embossed

sban'care *vt* bankrupt; ~ **il banco** break the bank

sbanda'mento *nm Auto* skid; *Naut* list; *fig* going off the rails

sban'da|re *vi Auto* skid; *Naut* list. ~**rsi** *vr* (*disperdersi*) disperse. ~**ta** *nf* skid; *Naut* list; **prendere una ~ta per** get a crush on. ~**to, -a** *a* mixed-up ● *nmf* mixed-up person

sbandie'rare *vt* wave; *fig* display

sbarac'care *vt/i* clear up

sbaragli'are *vt* rout. **sba'raglio** *nm* rout; **mettere allo sbaraglio** rout

sbaraz'zar|e *vt* clear. ~**si** *vr* ~**si di** get rid of

sbaraz'zino, -a *a* mischievous ● *nmf* scamp

sbar'bar|e *vt*, ~**si** *vr* shave

sbar'care *vt/i* disembark; ~ **il lunario** make ends meet. '**sbarco** *nm* landing; (*di merci*) unloading

'**sbarra** *nf* bar; (*di passaggio a livello*) barrier. ~'**mento** *nm* barricade.

sbar'rare *vt* bar; (*ostruire*) block; cross (*assegno*); (*spalancare*) open wide

sbatacchi'are *vt/i sl* bang, slam

'**sbatter|e** *vt* bang; slam, bang (*porta*); (*urtare*) knock; *Culin* beat; flap (*ali*); shake (*tappeto*) ● *vi* bang; (*porta:*) slam, bang. ~**si** *vr sl* rush around; ~**sene di qcsa** not give a damn about sth. **sbat'tuto** *a* tossed; *Culin* beaten; *fig* run down

sba'va|re *vi* dribble; (*colore:*) smear. ~'**tura** *nf* smear; **senza ~ture** *fig* faultless

sbelli'carsi *vr* ~ **dalle risa** split one's sides [with laughter]

'**sberla** *nf* slap

sbia'di|re *vt/i*, ~**rsi** *vr* fade. ~**to** *a* faded; *fig* colourless

sbian'car|e *vt/i*, ~**si** *vr* whiten

sbi'eco *a* slanting; **di ~** on the slant; (*guardare*) sidelong; **guardare qcno di ~** look askance at sb; **tagliare di ~** cut on the bias

sbigot'ti|re *vt* dismay ● *vi*, ~**rsi** *vr* be dismayed. ~**to** *a* dismayed

sbilanci'ar|e *vt* unbalance ● *vi* (*perdere l'equilibrio*) overbalance. ~**si** *vr* lose one's balance

sbirci'a|re *vt* cast sidelong glances at. ~**ta** *nf* furtive glance. ~'**tina** *nf* **dare una ~tina a** sneak a glance at

sbizzar'rirsi *vr* satisfy one's whims

sbloc'care *vt* unblock; *Mech* release; decontrol (*prezzi*)

sboc'care *vi* ~ **in** (*fiume:*) flow into; (*strada:*) lead to; (*folla:*) pour into

sboc'cato *a* foul-mouthed

sbocci'are *vi* blossom

'**sbocco** *nm* flowing; (*foce*) mouth; *Comm* outlet

sbolo'gnare *vt fam* get rid of

'**sbornia** *nf* **prendere una ~** get drunk

sbor'sare *vt* pay out

sbot'tare *vi* burst out

sbotto'nar|e *vt* unbutton. ~**si** *vr* (*fam: confidarsi*) open up; ~**si la camicia** unbutton one's shirt

sbra'carsi *vr* put on something more comfortable; ~ **dalle risate** *fam* kill oneself laughing

sbracci'a|rsi *vr* wave one's arms. ~**to** *a* bare-armed; (*abito*) sleeveless

sbrai'tare *vi* bawl

sbra'nare *vt* tear to pieces

sbricio'lar|e *vt*, ~**si** *vr* crumble

sbri'ga|re *vt* expedite; (*occuparsi di*) attend to. ~**rsi** *vr* be quick. ~'**tivo** *a* quick

sbrindel'la|re *vt* tear to shreds. ~**to** *a* in rags

sbrodo'l|are *vt* stain. ~**one** *nm* messy eater, dribbler

'**sbronz|a** *nf* **prendersi una ~a** get tight. **sbron'zarsi** *vr* get tight. ~**o** *a* (*ubriaco*) tight

sbruffo'nata *nf* boast. **sbruf'fone, -a** *nmf* boaster

sbu'care *vi* come out

sbucci'ar|e *vt* peel; shell (*piselli*). ~**si** *vr* graze oneself

sbuf'fare *vi* snort; (*per impazienza*) fume. '**sbuffo** *nm* puff

'**scabbia** *nf* scabies *sg*

sca'broso *a* rough; *fig* difficult; (*scena*) indecent

scacci'are *vt* chase away

'**scacc|o** *nm* check; ~**hi** *pl* (*gioco*) chess; (*pezzi*) chessmen; **dare ~o matto** checkmate; **a ~hi** (*tessuto*) checked. ~**hi'era** *nf* chess-board

sca'dente *a* shoddy

sca'de|nza *nf* (*di contratto*) expiry;

Comm maturity; (*di progetto*) deadline; **a breve/lunga ~nza** short-/long-term. **~re** *vi* expire; ⟨*valore:*⟩ decline; ⟨*debito:*⟩ be due. **sca'duto** *a* ⟨*biglietto*⟩ out-of-date

sca'fandro *nm* diving suit; (*di astronauta*) spacesuit

scaf'fale *nm* shelf; (*libreria*) bookshelf

'scafo *nm* hull

scagion'are *vt* exonerate

'scaglia *nf* scale; (*di sapone*) flake; (*scheggia*) chip

scagli'ar|e *vt* fling. **~si** *vr* fling oneself; **~si contro** *fig* rail against

scagli|o'nare *vt* space out. **~'one** *nm* group; **a ~oni** in groups. **~one di reddito** tax bracket

'scala *nf* staircase; (*portatile*) ladder; (*Mus, misura, fig*) scale; **scale** *pl* stairs. **~ mobile** escalator; (*dei salari*) cost of living index

sca'la|re *vt* climb; layer ⟨*capelli*⟩; (*detrarre*) deduct. **~ta** *nf* climb; (*dell'Everest ecc*) ascent; **fare delle ~te** go climbing. **~'tore**, **~'trice** *nmf* climber

scalca'gnato *a* down at heel

scalci'are *vi* kick

scalci'nato *a* shabby

scalda'bagno *nm* water heater

scalda'muscoli *nm inv* leg-warmer

scal'dar|e *vt* heat. **~si** *vr* warm up; (*eccitarsi*) get excited

scal'fi|re *vt* scratch. **~t'tura** *nf* scratch

scali'nata *nf* flight of steps. **sca'lino** *nm* step; (*di scala a pioli*) rung

scalma'narsi *vr* get worked up

'scalo *nm* slipway; *Aeron, Naut* port of call; **fare ~** a call at; *Aeron* land at

sca'lo|gna *nf* bad luck. **~'gnato** *a* unlucky

scalop'pina *nf* escalope

scal'pello *nm* chisel

scalpi'tare *vi* paw the ground; *fig* champ at the bit

'scalpo *nm* scalp

scal'pore *nm* noise; **far ~** *fig* cause a sensation

scal'trezza *nf* shrewdness. **scal'trirsi** *vr* get shrewder. **'scaltro** *a* shrewd

scal'zare *vt* bare the roots of ⟨*albero*⟩; *fig* undermine; (*da una carica*) oust

'scalzo *a & adv* barefoot

scambi|'are *vt* exchange; **~are qcno per qualcun altro** mistake sb for somebody else. **~'evole** *a* reciprocal

'scambio *nm* exchange; *Comm* trade; **libero ~** free trade

scamosci'ato *a* suede

scampa'gnata *nf* trip to the country

scampa'nato *a* ⟨*gonna*⟩ flared

scampanel'lata *nf* [loud] ring

scam'pare *vt* save; (*evitare*) escape; **scamparla bella** have a lucky escape. **'scampo** *nm* escape

'scampolo *nm* remnant

scanala'tura *nf* groove

scandagli'are *vt* sound

scanda'listico *a* sensational

scandal|iz'zare *vt* scandalize. **~iz'zarsi** *vr* be scandalized

'scanda|lo *nm* scandal. **~'loso** *a* ⟨*somma ecc*⟩ scandalous; ⟨*fortuna*⟩ outrageous

Scandi'navia *nf* Scandinavia. **scan'dinavo, -a** *a & nmf* Scandinavian

scan'dire *vt* scan ⟨*verso*⟩; pronounce clearly ⟨*parole*⟩

scan'nare *vt* slaughter

scanneriz'zare *vt* *Comput* scan

scansafa'tiche *nmf inv* lazybones *sg*

scan'sar|e *vt* shift; (*evitare*) avoid. **~si** *vr* get out of the way

scansi'one *nf* *Comput* scanning

'scanso *nm* **a ~ di** in order to avoid; **a ~ di equivoci** to avoid any misunderstanding

scanti'nato *nm* basement

scanto'nare *vi* turn the corner; (*svignarsela*) sneak off

scanzo'nato *a* easy-going

scapacci'one *nm* smack

scape'strato *a* dissolute

'scapito *nm* loss; **a ~ di** to the detriment of

'scapola *nf* shoulder-blade

'scapolo *nm* bachelor

scappa'mento *nm* *Auto* exhaust

scap'pa|re *vi* escape; (*andarsene*) dash [off]; (*sfuggire*) slip; **mi ~ da ridere!** I want to burst out laughing; **mi ~ la pipì** I'm bursting, I need a pee. **~ta** *nf* short visit. **~'tella** *nf* escapade; (*infedeltà*) fling. **~'toia** *nf* way out

scappel'lotto *nm* cuff

scara'bocchio *nm* scribble

scara'faggio *nm* cockroach

scara'mantico *a* ⟨*gesto*⟩ to ward off the evil eye

scara'muccia *nf* skirmish

scarabocchi'are *vt* scribble

scaraven'tare *vt* hurl

scarce'rare *vt* release [from prison]

scardi'nare *vt* unhinge

'scarica *nf* discharge; (*di arma da fuoco*) volley; *fig* shower

scari'ca|re *vt* discharge; unload ‹*arma, merci*›; *Comput* download; *fig* unburden. **~rsi** *vr* ‹*fiume:*› flow; ‹*orologio, batteria:*› run down; *fig* unwind. **~'tore** *nm* loader; (*di porto*) docker. **'scarico** *a* unloaded; ‹*vuoto*› empty; ‹*orologio*› rundown; ‹*batteria*› flat; *fig* untroubled ● *nm* unloading; (*di rifiuti*) dumping; (*di acqua*) draining; (*di sostanze inquinanti*) discharge; (*luogo*) [rubbish] dump; *Auto* exhaust; (*idraulico*) drain; (*tubo*) waste pipe

scarlat'tina *nf* scarlet fever

scar'latto *a* scarlet

'scarno *a* thin; ‹*fig: stile*› bare

sca'ro|gna *nf fam* bad luck. **~'gnato** *a fam* unlucky

'scarpa *nf* shoe; (*fam: persona*) dead loss. **scarpe** *pl* **da ginnastica** trainers, gym shoes

scar'pata *nf* slope; (*burrone*) escarpment

scarpi'nare *vi* hike

scar'pone *nm* boot. **scarponi** *pl* **da sci** ski boot. **scarponi** *pl* **da trekking** walking boots

scarroz'zare *vt/i* drive around

scarseggi'are *vi* be scarce; **~ di** (*mancare*) be short of

scar'sezza *nf* scarcity, shortage. **scarsità** *nf* shortage. **'scarso** *a* scarce; (*manchevole*) short

scarta'mento *nm Rail* gauge. **~ ridotto** narrow gauge

scar'tare *vt* discard; unwrap ‹*pacco*›; (*respingere*) reject ● *vi* (*deviare*) swerve. **'scarto** *nm* scrap; (*in carte*) discard; (*deviazione*) swerve; (*distacco*) gap

scar'toffie *nfpl* bumf, bumph

scas'sa|re *vt* break. **~to** *a fam* clapped out

scassi'nare *vt* force open

scassina'tore, -'trice *nmf* burglar. **'scasso** *nm* (*furto*) house-breaking

scate'na|re *vt fig* stir up. **~rsi** *vr* break out; ‹*fig: temporale:*› break; (*fam: infiammarsi*) get excited. **~to** *a* crazy

'scatola *nf* box; (*di latta*) can, tin *Br*; **in ~** ‹*cibo*› canned, tinned *Br*; **rompere le scatole a qcno** *fam* get on sb's nerves

scat'tare *vi* go off; (*balzare*) spring up; (*adirarsi*) lose one's temper ● *vt* take ‹*foto*›. **'scatto** *nm* (*balzo*) spring; (*d'ira*) outburst; (*di telefono*) unit; (*dispositivo*) release; **a scatti** jerkily; **di scatto** suddenly

scatu'rire *vi* spring

scaval'care *vt* jump over ‹*muretto*›;

climb over ‹*muro*›; (*fig: superare*) overtake

sca'vare *vt* dig ‹*buca*›; dig up ‹*tesoro*›; excavate ‹*città sepolta*›. **'scavo** *nm* excavation

scazzot'tata *nf fam* punch-up

'scegliere *vt* choose, select

scelle'rato *a* wicked

'scelt|a *nf* choice; (*di articoli*) range; **...a ~a** (*in menù*) choice of...; **prendine uno a ~a** take your choice *o* pick; **di prima ~a** top-grade, choice. **~o** *pp di* **scegliere** ● *a* select; (*merce ecc*) choice

sce'mare *vt/i* diminish

sce'menza *nf* silliness; (*azione*) silly thing to do/say. **'scemo** *a* silly

'scempio *nm* havoc; ‹*fig: di paesaggio*› ruination; **fare ~ di** play havoc with

'scena *nf* scene; (*palcoscenico*) stage; **entrare in ~** go/come on; *fig* enter the scene; **fare ~** put on an act; **fare una ~** make a scene; **andare in ~** *Theat* be staged, be put on. **sce'nario** *nm* scenery

sce'nata *nf* row, scene

'scendere *vi* go/come down; (*da treno, autobus*) get off; (*da macchina*) get out; ‹*strada:*› slope; ‹*notte, prezzi:*› fall ● *vt* go/come down ‹*scale*›

sceneggi'a|re *vt* dramatize. **~to** *nm* television serial. **~'tura** *nf* screenplay

'scenico *a* scenic

scervel'la|rsi *vr* rack one's brains. **~to** *a* brainless

'sceso *pp di* **scendere**

scetti'cismo *nm* scepticism. **'scettico, -a** *a* sceptical ● *nmf* sceptic

'scettro *nm* sceptre

'scheda *nf* card. **~ elettorale** ballot-paper. **~ di espansione** *Comput* expansion card. **~ perforata** punch card. **~ telefonica** phonecard. **sche'dare** *vt* file. **sche'dario** *nm* file; (*mobile*) filing cabinet

sche'dina *nf* pools coupon; **giocare la ~** do the pools

scheggi|a *nf* fragment; (*di legno*) splinter. **~'arsi** *vr* chip; ‹*legno:*› splinter

'scheletro *nm* skeleton

'schema *nm* diagram; (*abbozzo*) outline. **sche'matico** *a* schematic. **~tiz'zare** *vt* schematize

'scherma *nf* fencing

scher'mirsi *vr* protect oneself

'schermo *nm* screen; **grande ~** big screen

scher'nire *vt* mock. **'scherno** *nm* mockery

scher'zare *vi* joke; *(giocare)* play

'scherzo *nm* joke; *(trucco)* trick; *(effetto)* play; *Mus* scherzo; **fare uno ~ a qcno** play a joke on sb; **per ~** for fun; **stare allo ~** take a joke. **scher'zoso** *a* playful

schiaccia'noci *nm inv* nutcrackers *pl*

schiacci'ante *a* damning

schiacci'are *vt* crush; *Sport* smash; press *(pulsante)*; crack *(noce)*; **~ un pisolino** grab forty winks

schiaffeggi'are *vt* slap. **schi'affo** *nm* slap; **dare uno schiaffo a** slap

schiamaz'zare *vi* make a racket; *(galline:)* cackle

schian'tar|e *vt* break. **~si** *vr* crash ● *vi* **schianto dalla fatica** I'm wiped out. **'schianto** *nm* crash; *fam* knock-out; *(divertente)* scream

schia'rir|e *vt* clear; *(sbiadire)* fade ● *vi*, **~si** *vr* brighten up; **~si la gola** clear one's throat

schiavitù *nf* slavery. **schi'avo, -a** *nmf* slave

schi'ena *nf* back; **mal di ~** backache. **schie'nale** *nm* *(di sedia)* back

schi'er|a *nf* *Mil* rank; *(moltitudine)* crowd. **~a'mento** *nm* lining up

schie'rar|e *vt* draw up. **~si** *vr* draw up; **~si con** *(parteggiare)* side with

schiet'tezza *nf* frankness. **schi'etto** *a* frank; *(puro)* pure

schi'fezza *nf* **una ~** rubbish. **schi-fil'toso** *a* fussy. **schifo** *nm* disgust; **mi fa schifo** it makes me sick. **schi'foso** *a* disgusting; *(di cattiva qualità)* rubbishy

schioc'care *vt* crack; snap *(dita)*. **schi'occo** *nm* *(di frusta)* crack; *(di bacio)* smack; *(di dita, lingua)* click

schi'oppo *nm* **ad un tiro di ~** a stone's throw away

schi'uder|e *vt*, **~si** *vr* open

schi'u|ma *nf* foam; *(di sapone)* lather; *(feccia)* scum. **~ma da barba** shaving foam. **~'mare** *vt* skim ● *vi* foam

schi'uso *pp di* **schiudere**

schi'vare *vt* avoid. **'schivo** *a* bashful

schizo'frenico *a* schizophrenic

schiz'zare *vt* squirt; *(inzaccherare)* splash; *(abbozzare)* sketch ● *vi* spurt; **~ via** scurry away

schiz'zato, -a *a & nmf sl* loony

schizzi'noso *a* squeamish

'schizzo *nm* squirt; *(di fango)* splash; *(abbozzo)* sketch

sci *nm inv* ski; *(sport)* skiing. **~ d'acqua** water-skiing

'scia *nf* wake; *(di fumo ecc)* trail

sci'abola *nf* sabre

sciabor'dare *vt/i* lap

scia'callo *nm* jackal; *fig* profiteer

sciac'quar|e *vt* rinse. **~si** *vr* rinse oneself. **sci'acquo** *nm* mouthwash

scia'gu|ra *nf* disaster. **~'rato** *a* unfortunate; *(scellerato)* wicked

scialac'quare *vt* squander

scia'lare *vi* spend money like water

sci'albo *a* pale; *fig* dull

sci'alle *nm* shawl

scia'luppa *nf* dinghy. **~ di salva-taggio** lifeboat

sci'ame *nm* swarm

sci'ampo *nm* shampoo

scian'cato *a* lame

sci'are *vi* ski

sci'arpa *nf* scarf

sci'atica *nf* *Med* sciatica

scia'tore, -'trice *nmf* skier

sci'atto *a* slovenly; *(stile)* careless. **sciat'tone, -a** *nmf* slovenly person

scienti'fico *a* scientific

sci'enz|a *nf* science; *(sapere)* knowledge. **~i'ato, -a** *nmf* scientist

'scimmi|a *nf* monkey. **~ot'tare** *vt* ape

scimpanzé *nm inv* chimpanzee, chimp

scimu'nito *a* idiotic

'scinder|e *vt*, **~si** *vr* split

scin'tilla *nf* spark. **scintil'lante** *a* sparkling. **scintil'lare** *vi* sparkle

scioc'ca|nte *a* shocking. **~re** *vt* shock

scioc'chezza *nf* foolishness; *(assurdità)* nonsense. **sci'occo** *a* foolish

sci'oglier|e *vt* untie; undo, untie *(nodo)*; *(liberare)* release; *(liquefare)* melt; dissolve *(contratto, qcsa nell'acqua)*; loosen up *(muscoli)*. **~si** *vr* release oneself; *(liquefarsi)* melt; *(contratto:)* be dissolved; *(pastiglia:)* dissolve

sciogli'lingua *nm inv* tongue-twister

scio'lina *nf* wax

sciol'tezza *nf* agility; *(disinvoltura)* ease

sci'olto *pp di* **sciogliere** ● *a* loose; *(agile)* agile; *(disinvolto)* easy; **versi sciolti** blank verse

sciope'ra|nte *nmf* striker. **~re** *vi* go on strike, strike. **sci'opero** *nm* strike. **sciopero a singhiozzo** on-off strike

sciori'nare *vt fig* show off

sci'pito *a* insipid

scip'pa|re *vt fam* snatch. **~'tore, ~'trice** *nmf* bag snatcher. **'scippo** *nm* bag-snatching

sci'rocco *nm* sirocco

scirop'pato *a* ⟨frutta⟩ in syrup. **sci'roppo** *nm* syrup

'scisma *nm* schism

scissi'one *nf* division

'scisso *pp di* **scindere**

sciu'par|e *vt* spoil; ⟨sperperare⟩ waste. **~si** *vr* get spoiled; ⟨deperire⟩ wear oneself out. **sciu'pio** *nm* waste

scivo'l|are *vi* slide; ⟨involontariamente⟩ slip. **'scivolo** *nm* slide; *Techn* chute. **~oso** *a* slippery

scle'rosi *nf* sclerosis

scoc'care *vt* shoot ● *vi* ⟨scintilla:⟩ shoot out; ⟨ora:⟩ strike

scocci'a|re *vt* ⟨dare noia a⟩ bother. **~rsi** *vr* be bothered. **~to** *a fam* narked. **~'tore, ~'trice** *nmf* bore. **~'tura** *nf* nuisance

sco'della *nf* bowl

scodinzo'lare *vi* wag its tail

scogli'era *nf* cliff; ⟨a fior d'acqua⟩ reef. **'scoglio** *nm* rock; ⟨fig: ostacolo⟩ stumbling block

scoi'attolo *nm* squirrel

scola|'pasta *nm inv* colander. **~pi'atti** *nm inv* dish drainer

sco'lara *nf* schoolgirl

sco'lare *vt* drain; strain ⟨pasta, verdura⟩ ● *vi* drip

sco'la|ro *nm* schoolboy. **~'resca** *nf* pupils *pl.* **~stico** *a* school *attrib*

scoli'osi *nf* curvature of the spine

scol'la|re *vt* cut away the neck of ⟨abito⟩; ⟨staccare⟩ unstick. **~to** *a* ⟨abito⟩ low-necked. **~'tura** *nf* neckline

'scolo *nm* drainage

scolo'ri|re *vt*, **~rsi** *vr* fade. **~to** *a* faded

scol'pire *vt* carve; ⟨imprimere⟩ engrave

scombi'nare *vt* upset

scombusso'lare *vt* muddle up

scom'mess|a *nf* bet. **~o** *pp di* **scommettere. scom'mettere** *vt* bet

scomo'dar|e *vt*, **~si** *vr* trouble. **scomodità** *nf* discomfort. **'scomodo** *a* uncomfortable ● *nm* **essere di scomodo a qcno** be a trouble to sb

scompa'rire *vi* disappear; ⟨morire⟩ pass on. **scom'parsa** *nf* disappearance; ⟨morte⟩ passing, death. **scom'parso, -a** *pp di* **scomparire** ● *nmf* departed

scomparti'mento *nm* compartment. **scom'parto** *nf* compartment

scom'penso *nm* imbalance

scompigli'are *vt* disarrange. **scom'piglio** *nm* confusion

scom'po|rre *vt* take to pieces; ⟨fig:*

⟨turbare⟩ upset. **~rsi** *vr* get flustered, lose one's composure. **~sto** *pp di* **scomporre** ● *a* ⟨sguaiato⟩ unseemly; ⟨disordinato⟩ untidy

sco'muni|ca *nf* excommunication. **~'care** *vt* excommunicate

sconcer'ta|re *vt* disconcert; ⟨rendere perplesso⟩ bewilder. **~to** *a* disconcerted; bewildered

scon'cezza *nf* obscenity. **'sconcio** *a* ⟨osceno⟩ dirty ● *nm* **è uno sconcio che...** it's a disgrace that...

sconclusio'nato *a* incoherent

scon'dito *a* unseasoned; ⟨insalata⟩ with no dressing

sconfes'sare *vt* disown

scon'figgere *vt* defeat

sconfi'na|re *vi* cross the border; ⟨in proprietà privata⟩ trespass. **~to** *a* unlimited

scon'fitt|a *nf* defeat. **~o** *pp di* **sconfiggere**

scon'forto *nm* dejection

sconge'lare *vt* thaw out ⟨cibo⟩, defrost

scongi|u'rare *vt* beseech; ⟨evitare⟩ avert. **~'uro** *nm* **fare gli scongiuri** ≈ touch wood, knock on wood *Am*

scon'nesso *pp di* **sconnettere** ● *a fig* incoherent. **scon'nettere** *vt* disconnect

sconosci'uto, -a *a* unknown ● *nmf* stranger

sconquas'sare *vt* smash; ⟨sconvolgere⟩ upset

sconside'rato *a* inconsiderate

sconsigli'a|bile *a* not advisable. **~re** *vt* advise against

sconso'lato *a* disconsolate

scon'ta|re *vt* discount; ⟨dedurre⟩ deduct; ⟨pagare⟩ pay off; serve ⟨pena⟩. **~to** *a* discount; ⟨ovvio⟩ expected; **~to del 10%** with 10% discount; **dare qcsa per ~to** take sth for granted

scon'tento *a* displeased ● *nm* discontent

'sconto *nm* discount; **fare uno ~** give a discount

scon'trarsi *vr* clash; ⟨urtare⟩ collide

scon'trino *nm* ticket; ⟨di cassa⟩ receipt

'scontro *nm* clash; ⟨urto⟩ collision

scon'troso *a* unsociable

sconveni'ente *a* unprofitable; ⟨scorretto⟩ unseemly

sconvol'gente *a* mind-blowing

scon'vol|gere *vt* upset; ⟨mettere in disordine⟩ disarrange. **~gi'mento** *nm* upheaval. **~to** *pp di* **sconvolgere** ● *a* distraught

'scopa *nf* broom. **sco'pare** *vt* sweep; *vulg* shag, screw

scoperchi'are *vt* take the lid off ⟨*pentola*⟩; take the roof off ⟨*casa*⟩

sco'pert|a *nf* discovery. **~o** *pp di* **scoprire** ● *a* uncovered; (*senza riparo*) exposed; (*conto*) overdrawn; (*spoglio*) bare

'scopo *nm* aim; **allo ~ di** in order to

scoppi'are *vi* burst; *fig* break out. **scoppiet'tare** *vi* crackle. **'scoppio** *nm* burst; (*di guerra*) outbreak; (*esplosione*) explosion

sco'prire *vt* discover; (*togliere la copertura a*) uncover

scoraggi'ante *a* discouraging

scoraggi'a|re *vt* discourage. **~rsi** *vr* lose heart

scor'butico *a* peevish

scorcia'toia *nf* short cut

'scorcio *nm* (*di epoca*) end; (*di cielo*) patch; (*in arte*) foreshortening; **di ~** ⟨*vedere*⟩ from an angle. **~ panoramico** panoramic view

scor'da|re *vt*, **~rsi** *vr* forget. **~to a** *Mus* out of tune

sco'reggi|a *nf fam* fart. **~'are** *vi fam* fart

'scorgere *vt* make out; (*notare*) notice

scoria *nf* waste; (*di metallo, carbone*) slag; **scorie** *pl* **radioattive** radioactive waste

scor'nato *a fig* hangdog. **'scorno** *nm* humiliation

scorpacci'ata *nf* bellyful; **fare una ~ di** stuff oneself with

scorpi'one *nm* scorpion; *Astr* Scorpio

scorraz'zare *vi* run about

'scorrere *vt* (*dare un'occhiata*) glance through ● *vi* run; (*scivolare*) slide; (*fluire*) flow; *Comput* scroll. **scor're-vole** *a* **porta scorrevole** sliding door

scorre'ria *nf* raid

scorret'tezza *nf* (*mancanza di educazione*) bad manners *pl*. **scor'retto** *a* incorrect; (*sconveniente*) improper

scorri'banda *nf* raid; *fig* excursion

'scors|a *nf* glance. **~o** *pp di* **scorrere** ● *a* last

scor'soio *a* **nodo ~** noose

'scor|ta *nf* escort; (*provvista*) supply. **~'tare** *vt* escort

scor'te|se *a* discourteous. **~'sia** *nf* discourtesy

scorti'ca|re *vt* skin. **~'tura** *nf* graze

'scorto *pp di* **scorgere**

'scorza *nf* peel; (*crosta*) crust; (*corteccia*) bark

sco'sceso *a* steep

'scossa *nf* shake; *Electr, fig* shock; **prendere la ~** get an electric shock. **~ elettrica** electric shock. **~ sismica** earth tremor

'scosso *pp di* **scuotere** ● *a* shaken; (*sconvolto*) upset

sco'stante *a* off-putting

sco'sta|re *vt* push away. **~rsi** *vr* stand aside

scostu'mato *a* dissolute; (*maleducato*) ill-mannered

scot'tante *a* ⟨*argomento*⟩ dangerous

scot'ta|re *vt* scald ● *vi* burn; ⟨*bevanda:*⟩ be too hot; ⟨*sole, pentola:*⟩ be very hot. **~rsi** *vr* burn oneself; (*al sole*) get sunburnt; *fig* get one's fingers burnt. **~'tura** *nf* burn; (*da liquido*) scald; **~tura solare** sunburn; *fig* painful experience

'scotto *a* overcooked

sco'vare *vt* (*scoprire*) discover

'Scoz|ia *nf* Scotland. **~'zese** *a* Scottish ● *nmf* Scot

scredi'tare *vt* discredit

scre'mare *vt* skim

screpo'la|re *vt*, **~rsi** *vr* crack. **~to** *a* ⟨*labbra*⟩ chapped. **~'tura** *nf* crack

screzi'ato *a* speckled

'screzio *nm* disagreement

scribac|chi'are *vt* scribble. **~'chino, -a** *nmf* scribbler; (*impiegato*) penpusher

scricchio'l|are *vi* creak. **~io** *nm* creaking

'scricciolo *nm* wren

'scrigno *nm* casket

scrimina'tura *nf* parting

'scrit|ta *nf* writing; (*su muro*) graffiti. **~to** *pp di* **scrivere** ● *a* written ● *nm* writing; (*lettera*) letter. **~'toio** *nm* writing-desk. **~'tore**, **~'trice** *nmf* writer. **~'tura** *nf* writing; *Relig* scripture

scrittu'rare *vt* engage

scriva'nia *nf* desk

'scrivere *vt* write; (*descrivere*) write about; **~ a macchina** type

scroc'c|are *vt* **~are a** sponge off. **'scrocco** *nm fam* **a scrocco** *fam* without paying; **vivere a scrocco** sponge off other people. **~one, -a** *nmf* sponger

'scrofa *nf* sow

scrol'lar|e *vt* shake; **~e le spalle** shrug one's shoulders. **~si** *vr* shake oneself; **~si qcsa di dosso** shake sth off

scrosci'are *vi* roar; ⟨*pioggia:*⟩ pelt down. **'scroscio** *nm* roar; (*di pioggia*) pelting; **uno scroscio di applausi** thunderous applause

scro'star|e vt scrape. **~si** vr peel off

'scrupo|lo nm scruple; (diligenza) care; **senza scrupoli** unscrupulous, without scruples. **~'loso** a scrupulous

scru'ta|re vt scan; (indagare) search. **~'tore** nm (alle elezioni) returning officer

scruti'nare vt scrutinize. **scru'tinio** nm (di voti alle elezioni) poll; Sch assessment of progress

scu'cire vt unstitch; **scuci i soldi!** fam cough up [the money]!

scude'ria nf stable

scu'detto nm Sport championship shield

'scudo nm shield

sculacci|'are vt spank. **~'ata** nf spanking. **~'one** nm spanking

sculet'tare vi wiggle one's hips

scul|'tore, -'trice nm sculptor ● nf sculptress. **~'tura** nf sculpture

scu'ola nf school. **~ elementare** primary school. **~ guida** driving school. **~ materna** day nursery. **~ media** secondary school. **~ media [inferiore]** secondary school (10-13). **~ [media] superiore** secondary school (13-18). **~ dell'obbligo** compulsory education

scu'oter|e vt shake. **~si** vr (destarsi) rouse oneself; **~si di dosso** shake off

'scure nf axe

scu'reggia nf fam fart. **scureggi'are** vi fam fart

scu'rire vt/i darken

'scuro a dark ● nm darkness; (imposta) shutter

scur'rile a scurrilous

'scusa nf excuse; (giustificazione) apology; **chiedere ~** apologize; **chiedo ~!** I'm sorry!

scu'sar|e vt excuse. **~si** vr **~si** apologize (**di** for); **[mi] scusi!** excuse me!; (chiedendo perdono) [I'm] sorry!

sdebi'tarsi vr (disobbligarsi) repay a kindness

sde'gna|re vt despise. **~rsi** vr get angry. **~to** a indignant. **'sdegno** nm disdain. **sde'gnoso** a disdainful

sden'tato a toothless

sdolci'nato a sentimental, schmaltzy

sdoppi'are vt halve

sdrai'arsi vr lie down. **'sdraio** nm [sedia a] sdraio deckchair

sdrammatiz'zare vi provide some comic relief

se conj if; (interrogativo) whether, if; **se mai** (caso mai) if need be; **se mai telefonasse,...** should he call,..., if he calls,...; **se no** otherwise, or else; **se non altro** at least, if nothing else; **se pure** (sebbene) even though; (anche se) even if; **non so se sia vero** I don't know whether it's true, I don't know if it's true; **come se** as if; **se lo avessi saputo prima!** if only I had known before!; **e se andassimo fuori a cena?** how about going out for dinner? ● nm inv if

sé pron oneself; (lui) himself; (lei) herself; (esso, essa) itself; (loro) themselves; **l'ha fatto da sé** he did it himself; **ha preso i soldi con sé** he took the money with him; **si sono tenuti le notizie per sé** they kept the news to themselves

seb'bene conj although

'secca nf shallows pl; **in ~** (nave) aground

sec'cante a annoying

sec'ca|re vt dry; (importunare) annoy ● vi dry up. **~rsi** vr dry up; (irritarsi) get annoyed; (annoiarsi) get bored. **~'tore, ~'trice** nmf nuisance. **~'tura** nf bother

secchi'ello nm pail

'secchio nm bucket. **~ della spazzatura** rubbish bin, trash can Am

'secco, -a a dry; (dissecato) dried; (magro) thin; (brusco) curt; (preciso) sharp; **restare a ~** be left penniless; **restarci ~** (fam: morire di colpo) be killed on the spot ● nm (siccità) drought; **lavare a ~** dry-clean

secessi'one nf secession

seco'lare a age-old; (laico) secular. **'secolo** nm century; (epoca) age; **è un secolo che non lo vedo** fam I haven't seen him for ages o yonks

se'cond|a nf Sch, Rail second class; Auto second [gear]. **~o** a second ● nm second; (secondo piatto) main course ● prep according to; **~o me** in my opinion

secondo'genito, -a a & nm secondborn

secrezi'one nf secretion

'sedano nm celery

seda'tivo a & nm sedative

'sede nf seat; (centro) centre; Relig see; Comm head office. **~ sociale** registered office

seden'tario a sedentary

se'der|e *vi* sit. **~si** *vr* sit down ● *nm* (*deretano*) bottom

'sedia *nf* chair. **~ a dondolo** rocking chair. **~ a rotelle** wheelchair

sedi'cente *a* self-styled

'sedici *a & nm* sixteen

se'dile *nm* seat

sedizi'o|ne *nf* sedition. **~so** *a* seditious

se'dotto *pp di* sedurre

sedu'cente *a* seductive; (*allettante*) enticing

se'durre *vt* seduce

se'duta *nf* session; (*di posa*) sitting. **~ stante** *adv* here and now

seduzi'one *nf* seduction

'sega *nf* saw; *vulg* wank

'segala *nf* rye

se'gare *vt* saw

sega'tura *nf* sawdust

'seggio *nm* seat. **~ elettorale** polling station

seg'gio|la *nf* chair. **~'lino** *nm* seat; (*da bambino*) child's seat. **~'lone** *nm* (*per bambini*) high chair

seggio'via *nf* chair lift

seghe'ria *nf* sawmill

se'ghetto *nm* hacksaw

seg'mento *nm* segment

segna'lar|e *vt* signal; (*annunciare*) announce; (*indicare*) point out. **~si** *vr* distinguish oneself

se'gna|le *nm* signal; (*stradale*) sign. **~le acustico** beep. **~le orario** time signal. **~'letica** *nf* signals *pl*. **~letica stradale** road signs *pl*

segna'libro *nm* bookmark

se'gnar|e *vt* mark; (*prendere nota*) note; (*indicare*) indicate; *Sport* score. **~si** *vr* cross oneself. **'segno** *nm* sign; (*traccia, limite*) mark; (*bersaglio*) target; **far segno** (*col capo*) nod; (*con la mano*) beckon. **segno zodiacale** birth sign

segre'ga|re *vt* segregate. **~zi'one** *nf* segregation

segretari'ato *nm* secretariat

segre'tario, -a *nmf* secretary. **~ comunale** town clerk

segrete'ria *nf* (*uffico*) [administrative] office; (*segretariato*) secretariat. **~ telefonica** answering machine, answerphone

segre'tezza *nf* secrecy

se'greto *a & nm* secret; **in ~** in secret

segu'ace *nmf* follower

segu'ente *a* following, next

se'gugio *nm* bloodhound

segu'ire *vt/i* follow; (*continuare*) continue

segui'tare *vt/i* continue

'seguito *nm* retinue; (*sequela*) series; (*continuazione*) continuation; **di ~** in succession; **in ~** later on; **in ~ a** following; **al ~** in his/her wake; (*a causa di*) owing to; **fare ~ a** *Comm* follow up

'sei *a & nm* six. **sei'cento** *a & nm* six hundred; **il Seicento** the seventeenth century. **sei'mila** *a & nm* six thousand

sel'ciato *nm* paving

selet'tivo *a* selective. **selezio'nare** *vt* select. **selezi'one** *nf* selection

'sella *nf* saddle. **sel'lare** *vt* saddle

seltz *nm* soda water

'selva *nf* forest

selvag'gina *nf* game

sel'vaggio, -a *a* wild; (*primitivo*) savage ● *nmf* savage

sel'vatico *a* wild

se'maforo *nm* traffic lights *pl*

se'mantica *nf* semantics *sg*

sem'brare *vi* seem; (*assomigliare*) look like; **che te ne sembra?** what do you think?; **mi sembra che...** I think...

'seme *nm* seed; (*di mela*) pip; (*di carte*) suit; (*sperma*) semen

se'mestre *nm* half-year

semi'cerchio *nm* semicircle

semifi'nale *nf* semifinal

semi'freddo *nm* ice cream and sponge dessert

'semina *nf* sowing

semi'nare *vt* sow; *fam* shake off (*inseguitori*)

semi'nario *nm* seminar; *Relig* seminary

seminter'rato *nm* basement

se'mitico *a* Semitic

sem'mai *conj* in case ● *adv* è lui, ~, che... if anyone, it's him who...

'semola *nf* bran. **semo'lino** *nm* semolina

'sempli|ce *a* simple; **in parole semplici** in plain words. **~'cemente** *adv* simply. **~ci'otto, -a** *nmf* simpleton. **~'cistico** *a* simplistic. **~cità** *nf* simplicity. **~fi'care** *vt* simplify

'sempre *adv* always; (*ancora*) still; **per ~** for ever

sempre'verde *a & nm* evergreen

'senape *nf* mustard

se'nato *nm* senate. **sena'tore** *nm* senator

se'nil|e *a* senile. **~ità** *nf* senility

'senno *nm* sense

'seno *nm* (*petto*) breast; *Math* sine; **in ~ a** in the bosom of

sen'sato *a* sensible

sensazi|o'nale *a* sensational. **~'one** *nf* sensation

sen'sibil|e *a* sensitive; (*percepibile*) perceptible; (*notevole*) considerable. **~ità** *nf* sensitivity. **~iz'zare** *vt* make more aware (**a** of)

sensi'tivo, -a *a* sensory ● *nmf* sensitive person; (*medium*) medium

'senso *nm* sense; (*significato*) meaning; (*direzione*) direction; **far ~ a qcno** make sb shudder; **non ha ~** it doesn't make sense; **senza ~** meaningless; **perdere i sensi** lose consciousness. **~ dell'umorismo** sense of humour. **~ unico** (*strada*) one-way; **~ vietato** no entry

sensu'al|e *a* sensual. **~ità** *nf* sensuality

sen'tenz|a *nf* sentence; (*massima*) saying. **~i'are** *vi Jur* pass judgment

senti'ero *nm* path

sentimen'tale *a* sentimental. **senti'mento** *nm* feeling

senti'nella *nf* sentry

sen'ti|re *vt* feel; (*udire*) hear; (*ascoltare*) listen to; (*gustare*) taste; (*odorare*) smell ● *vi* feel; (*udire*) hear; **~re caldo/freddo** feel hot/cold. **~rsi** *vr* feel; **~rsi di fare qcsa** feel like doing sth; **~rsi bene** feel well; **~rsi poco bene** feel unwell; **~rsela di fare qcsa** feel up to doing sth. **~to** *a* (*sincero*) sincere; **per ~to dire** by hearsay

sen'tore *nm* inkling

'senza *prep* without; **~ correre** without running; **senz'altro** certainly; **~ ombrello** without an umbrella

senza'tetto *nm inv* **i ~** the homeless

sepa'ra|re *vt* separate. **~rsi** *vr* separate; (*amici:*) part; **~rsi da** be separated from. **~ta'mente** *adv* separately. **~zi'one** *nf* separation

se'pol|cro *nm* sepulchre. **~to** *pp di* **seppellire**. **~tura** *nf* burial

seppel'lire *vt* bury

'seppia *nf* cuttle fish; **nero di ~** sepia

sep'pure *conj* even if

se'quenza *nf* sequence

seque'strare *vt* (*rapire*) kidnap; *Jur* impound; (*confiscare*) confiscate. **se'questro** *nm Jur* impounding; (*di persona*) kidnap[ping]

'sera *nf* evening; **di ~** in the evening. **se'rale** *a* evening. **se'rata** *nf* evening; (*ricevimento*) party

ser'bare *vt* keep; harbour (*odio*); cherish (*speranza*)

serba'toio *nm* tank. **~ d'acqua** water tank; (*per una città*) reservoir

'Serbia *nf* Serbia

'serbo, -a *a & nmf* Serbian ● *nm* (*lingua*) Serbian; **mettere in ~** put aside

sere'nata *nf* serenade

serenità *nf* serenity. **se'reno** *a* serene; (*cielo*) clear

ser'gente *nm* sergeant

seria'mente *adv* seriously

'serie *nf inv* series; (*complesso*) set; *Sport* division; **fuori ~** custom-built; **produzione in ~** mass production; **di ~ B** second-rate

serietà *nf* seriousness. **'serio** *a* serious; (*degno di fiducia*) reliable; **sul serio** seriously; (*davvero*) really

ser'mone *nm* sermon

'serpe *nf liter* viper. **~ggi'are** *vi* meander; (*diffondersi*) spread

ser'pente *nm* snake. **~ a sonagli** rattlesnake

'serra *nf* greenhouse; **effetto ~** greenhouse effect

ser'randa *nf* shutter

ser'ra|re *vt* shut; (*stringere*) tighten; (*incalzare*) press on. **~tura** *nf* lock

ser'vir|e *vt* serve; (*al ristorante*) wait on ● *vi* serve; (*essere utile*) be of use; **non serve** it's no good. **~si** *vr* (*di cibo*) help oneself; **~si da** buy from; **~si di** use

servitù *nf inv* servitude; (*personale di servizio*) servants *pl*

servizi'evole *a* obliging

ser'vizio *nm* service; (*da caffè ecc*) set; (*di cronaca, sportivo*) report; **servizi** *pl* bathroom; **essere di ~** be on duty; **fare ~** (*autobus ecc:*) run; **fuori ~** (*bus*) not in service; (*ascensore*) out of order; **~ compreso** service charge included. **~ in camera** room service. **~ civile** civilian duties done instead of national service. **~ militare** military service. **~ pubblico** utility company

'servo, -a *nmf* servant

servo'sterzo *nm* power steering

ses'san|ta *a & nm* sixty. **~'tina** *nf* **una ~tina** about sixty

sessi'one *nf* session

'sesso *nm* sex

sessu'al|e *a* sexual. **~ità** *nf* sexuality

'sesto¹ *a* sixth

'sesto² *nm* (*ordine*) order

'seta *nf* silk

setacci'are vt sieve. **se'taccio** nm sieve

'sete nf thirst; **avere ~** be thirsty

'setola nf bristle

'setta nf sect

set'tan|ta a & nm seventy. **~'tina** nf una **~tina** about seventy

'sette a & nm seven. **~'cento** a & nm seven hundred; **il S~cento** the eighteenth century

set'tembre nm September

settentri|o'nale a northern ● nmf northerner. **~'one** nm north

setti'ma|na nf week. **~'nale** a & nm weekly

'settimo a seventh

set'tore nm sector

severità nf severity. **se'vero** a severe; (rigoroso) strict

se'vizi|a nf torture; **se'vizie** pl torture sg. **~'are** vt torture

sezio'nare vt divide; Med dissect. **sezi'one** nf section; (reparto) department; Med dissection

sfaccen'dato a idle

sfacchi'na|re vi toil. **~ta** nf drudgery

sfacci|a'taggine nf cheek, insolence. **~'ato** a cheeky, fresh Am

sfa'celo nm ruin; **in ~** in ruins

sfal'darsi vr flake off

sfa'mar|e vt feed. **~si** vr satisfy one's hunger, eat one's fill

'sfar|zo nm pomp. **~'zoso** a sumptuous

sfa'sato a fam confused; (motore) which needs tuning

sfasci'a|re vt unbandage; (fracassare) smash. **~rsi** vr fall to pieces. **~to** a beat-up

sfa'tare vt explode

sfati'cato a lazy

sfavil'la|nte a sparkling. **~re** vi sparkle

sfavo'revole a unfavourable

sfavo'rire vt disadvantage, put at a disadvantage

'sfer|a nf sphere. **~ico** a spherical

sfer'rare vt unshoe (cavallo); (scagliare) land

sfer'zare vt whip

sfian'carsi vr wear oneself out

sfi'bra|re vt exhaust. **~to** a exhausted

'sfida nf challenge. **sfi'dare** vt challenge

sfi'duci|a nf mistrust. **~'ato** a discouraged

'sfiga nf vulg bloody bad luck

sfigu'rare vt disfigure ● vi (far cattiva figura) look out of place

sfilacci'ar|e vt, **~si** vr fray

sfi'la|re vt unthread; (togliere di dosso) take off ● vi (truppe:) march past; (in parata) parade. **~rsi** vr come unthreaded; (collant:) ladder; take off (pantaloni). **~ta** nf parade; (sfilza) series. **~ta di moda** fashion show

'sfilza nf (di errori, domande) string

'sfinge nf sphinx

sfi'nito a worn out

sfio'rare vt skim; touch on (argomento)

sfio'rire vi wither; (bellezza:) fade

'sfitto a vacant

'sfizio nm whim, fancy; **togliersi uno ~** satisfy a whim

sfo'cato a out of focus

sfoci'are vi **~ in** flow into

sfode'ra|re vt draw (pistola, spada). **~to** a unlined

sfo'gar|e vt vent. **~si** vr give vent to one's feelings

sfoggi'are vt/i show off. **'sfoggio** nm show, display; **fare sfoggio di** show off

'sfoglia nf sheet of pastry; **pasta ~** puff pastry

sfogli'are vt leaf through

'sfogo nm outlet; fig outburst; Med rash; **dare ~ a** give vent to

sfolgo'ra|nte a blazing. **~re** vi blaze

sfol'lare vt clear ● vi Mil be evacuated

sfol'tire vt thin [out]

sfon'dare vt break down ● vi (aver successo) make a name for oneself

'sfondo nm background

sfor'ma|re vt pull out of shape (tasche). **~rsi** vr lose its shape; (persona:) lose one's figure. **~to** nm Culin flan

sfor'nito a **~ di** (negozio) out of stock

sfor'tuna nf bad luck. **~ta'mente** adv unfortunately. **sfortu'nato** a unlucky

sfor'zar|e vt force. **~si** vr try hard. **'sforzo** nm effort; (tensione) strain

'sfottere vt sl tease

sfracel'larsi vr smash

sfrat'tare vt evict. **'sfratto** nm eviction

sfrecci'are vi flash past

sfregi'a|re vt slash. **~to** a scarred

'sfregio nm slash

sfre'na|rsi vr run wild. **~to** a wild

sfron'tato a shameless

sfrutta'mento nm exploitation. **sfrut'tare** vt exploit

sfug'gente a elusive; (mento) receding

sfug'gi|re vi escape; **~re a** escape [from]; **mi sfugge** it escapes me; **mi è**

sfuggito di mano I lost hold of it ● vt avoid. **~ta** nf di **~ta** in passing

sfu'ma|re vi (svanire) vanish; ‹colore:› shade off ● vt soften ‹colore›. **~'tura** nf shade

sfuri'ata nf outburst [of anger]

sga'bello nm stool

sgabuz'zino nm cupboard

sgam'bato a ‹costume da bagno› high-cut

sgambet'tare vi kick one's legs; (camminare) trot. **sgam'betto** nm **fare lo sgambetto a qcno** trip sb up

sganasci'arsi vr **~ dalle risa** roar with laughter

sganci'ar|e vt unhook; Rail uncouple; drop ‹bombe›; fam cough up ‹denaro›. **~si** vr become unhooked; fig get away

sganghe'rato a ramshackle

sgar'bato a rude. **'sgarbo** nm discourtesy; **fare uno sgarbo** be rude

sgargi'ante a garish

sgar'rare vi be wrong; (da regola) stray from the straight and narrow. **'sgarro** nm mistake, slip

sgattaio'lare vi sneak away; **~ via** decamp

sghignaz'zare vi laugh scornfully, sneer

sgob'b|are vi slog; (fam: studente:) swot. **~one, -a** nmf slogger; (fam: studente) swot

sgoccio'lare vi drip

sgo'larsi vr shout oneself hoarse

sgomb[e]'rare vt clear [out]. **'sgombro** a clear ● nm (trasloco) removal; (pesce) mackerel

sgomen'tar|e vt dismay. **~si** vr be dismayed. **sgo'mento** nm dismay

sgomi'nare vt defeat

sgom'mata nf screech of tyres

sgonfi'ar|e vt deflate. **~si** vr go down. **'sgonfio** a flat

'sgorbio nm scrawl; (fig: vista sgradevole) sight

sgor'gare vi gush [out] ● vt flush out, unblock ‹lavandino›

sgoz'zare vt **~ qcno** cut sb's throat

sgra'd|evole a disagreeable. **~ito** a unwelcome

sgrammati'cato a ungrammatical

sgra'nare vt shell ‹piselli›; open wide ‹occhi›

sgran'chir|e vt, **~si** vr stretch

sgranocchi'are vt munch

sgras'sare vt remove the grease from

sgrazi'ato a ungainly

sgreto'lar|e vt, **~si** vr crumble

sgri'da|re vt scold. **~ta** nf scolding

sgros'sare vt rough-hew ‹marmo›; fig polish

sguai'ato a coarse

sgual'cire vt crumple

sgual'drina nf slut

sgu'ardo nm look; (breve) glance

'sguattero, -a nmf skivvy

sguaz'zare vi splash; (nel fango) wallow

sguinzagli'are vt unleash

sgusci'are vt shell ● vi (sfuggire) slip away; **~ fuori** slip out

shake'rare vt shake

si pron (riflessivo) oneself; (lui) himself; (lei) herself; (esso, essa) itself; (loro) themselves; (reciproco) each other; (tra più di due) one another; (impersonale) you, one; **lavarsi** wash [oneself]; **si è lavata** she washed [herself]; **lavarsi le mani** wash one's hands; **si è lavata le mani** she washed her hands; **si è mangiato un pollo intero** he ate an entire chicken by himself; **incontrarsi** meet each other; **la gente si aiuta a vicenda** people help one another; **non si sa mai** you never know, one never knows; **queste cose si dimenticano facilmente** these things are easily forgotten ● nm (chiave, nota) B

sì adv yes

'sia¹ vedi **essere**

'sia² conj **~...~...** (entrambi) both... and...; (o l'uno o l'altro) either...or...**~ che venga, ~ che non venga** whether he comes or not; **scegli ~ questo ~ quello** choose either this one or that one; **voglio ~ questo che quello** I want both this one and that one

sia'mese a Siamese

sibi'lare vi hiss. **'sibilo** nm hiss

si'cario nm hired killer

sicché conj (perciò) so [that]; (allora) then

siccità nf drought

sic'come conj as

Si'cili|a nf Sicily. **s~'ano, -a** a & nmf Sicilian

si'cura nf safety catch; (di portiera) child-proof lock. **~'mente** adv definitely

sicu'rezza nf (certezza) certainty; (salvezza) safety; **uscita di ~** emergency exit

si'curo a (non pericoloso) safe; (certo) sure; ‹saldo› steady; Comm sound ● adv certainly ● nm safety; **al ~** safe; **andare sul ~** play [it] safe; **di ~** definitely; **di ~, sarà arrivato** he must have arrived

siderur'gia *nf* iron and steel industry. **side'rurgico** *a* iron and steel *attrib*

'sidro *nm* cider

si'epe *nf* hedge

si'ero *nm* serum

sieroposi'tivo, -a *a* HIV positive ● *nmf* person who is HIV positive

si'esta *nf* afternoon nap, siesta

si'fone *nm* siphon

Sig. *abbr* (**signore**) Mr

Sig.a *abbr* (**signora**) Mrs, Ms

siga'retta *nf* cigarette; **pantaloni a ~** drainpipes

'sigaro *nm* cigar

Sigg. *abbr* (**signori**) Messrs

sigil'lare *vt* seal. **si'gillo** *nm* seal

'sigla *nf* initials *pl*. **~ musicale** signature tune. **si'glare** *vt* initial

Sig.na *abbr* (**signorina**) Miss, Ms

signifi'ca|re *vt* mean. **~'tivo** *a* significant. **~to** *nm* meaning

si'gnora *nf* lady; (*davanti a nome proprio*) Mrs; (*non sposata*) Miss; (*in lettere ufficiali*) Dear Madam; **il signor Vené e ~** Mr and Mrs Vené

si'gnore *nm* gentleman; *Relig* lord; (*davanti a nome proprio*) Mr; (*in lettere ufficiali*) Dear Sir. **signo'rile** *a* gentlemanly; (*di lusso*) luxury

signo'rina *nf* young lady; (*seguito da nome proprio*) Miss

silenzia'tore *nm* silencer

si'lenzi|o *nm* silence. **~'oso** *a* silent

silhou'ette *nf* silhouette, outline

si'licio *nm* **piastrina di ~** silicon chip

sili'cone *nm* silicone

'sillaba *nf* syllable

silu'rare *vt* torpedo. **si'luro** *nm* torpedo

simboleggi'are *vt* symbolize

sim'bolico *a* symbolic[al]

'simbolo *nm* symbol

similarità *nf inv* similarity

'simil|e *a* similar; (*tale*) such; **~e a** like ● *nm* (*il prossimo*) fellow man. **~'mente** *adv* similarly. **~'pelle** *nf* Leatherette®

simme'tria *nf* symmetry. **sim'metrico** *a* symmetric[al]

simpa'ti|a *nf* liking; (*compenetrazione*) sympathy; **prendere qcno in ~a** take a liking to sb. **sim'patico** *a* nice. **~iz'zante** *nmf* well-wisher. **~iz'zare** *vt* **~izzare con** take a liking to; **~izzare per qcsa/qcno** lean towards sth/sb

sim'posio *nm* symposium

simu'la|re *vt* simulate; feign (*amicizia, interesse*). **~zi'one** *nf* simulation

simul'tane|a *nf* in **~a** simultaneously. **~o** *a* simultaneous

sina'goga *nf* synagogue

sincerità *nf* sincerity. **sin'cero** *a* sincere

'sincope *nf* syncopation; *Med* fainting fit

sincron'ia *nf* synchronization; **in ~** with synchronized timing

sincroniz'za|re *vt* synchronize. **~zi'one** *nf* synchronization

sinda'ca|le *a* [trade] union, [labor] union *Am.* **~'lista** *nmf* trade unionist, labor union member *Am.* **~re** *vt* inspect. **~to** *nm* [trade] union, [labor] union *Am*; (*associazione*) syndicate

'sindaco *nm* mayor

'sindrome *nf* syndrome

sinfo'nia *nf* symphony. **sin'fonico** *a* symphonic

singhi|oz'zare *vi* (*di pianto*) sob. **~'ozzo** *nm* hiccup; (*di pianto*) sob; **avere il ~ozzo** have the hiccups

singo'lar|e *a* singular ● *nm* singular. **~'mente** *adv* individually; (*stranamente*) peculiarly

'singolo *a* single ● *nm* individual; *Tennis* singles *pl*

si'nistra *nf* left; **a ~** on the left; **girare a ~** turn to the left; **con la guida a ~** (*auto*) with left-hand drive

sini'strato *a* injured

si'nistr|o, -a *a* left[-hand]; (*avverso*) sinister ● *nm* accident ● *nf* left [hand]; *Pol* left [wing]

'sino *prep* = **fino¹**

si'nonimo *a* synonymous ● *nm* synonym

sin'ta|ssi *nf* syntax. **~ttico** *a* syntactic[al]

'sintesi *nf* synthesis; (*riassunto*) summary

sin'teti|co *a* synthetic; (*conciso*) summary. **~z'zare** *vt* summarize

sintetizza'tore *nm* synthesizer

sinto'matico *a* symptomatic. **'sintomo** *nm* symptom

sinto'nia *nf* tuning; **in ~** on the same wavelength

sinu'oso *a* (*strada*) winding

sinu'site *nf* sinusitis

si'pario *nm* curtain

si'rena *nf* siren

'Siri|a *nf* Syria. **s~'ano, -a** *a & nmf* Syrian

si'ringa *nf* syringe

'**sismico** *a* seismic

si'**stem|a** *nm* system. **S~a Monetario Europeo** European Monetary System. **~a operativo** *Comput* operating system

siste'**ma|re** *vt* (*mettere*) put; tidy up ⟨*casa, camera*⟩; (*risolvere*) sort out; (*procurare lavoro a*) fix up with a job; (*trovare alloggio a*) find accommodation for; (*sposare*) marry off; (*fam: punire*) sort out. **~rsi** *vr* settle down; (*trovare un lavoro*) find a job; (*trovare alloggio*) find accommodation; (*sposarsi*) marry. **~tico** *a* systematic. **~zi'one** *nf* arrangement; (*di questione*) settlement; (*lavoro*) job; (*alloggio*) accommodation; (*matrimonio*) marriage

'**sito** *nm* site. **~ web** *Comput* web site

situ'**are** *vt* place

situazi'**one** *nf* situation

ski-'**lift** *nm* ski tow

slacci'**are** *vt* unfasten

slanci'**a|rsi** *vr* hurl oneself. **~to** *a* slender. '**slancio** *nm* impetus; (*impulso*) impulse

sla'**vato** *a* ⟨*carnagione, capelli*⟩ fair

'**slavo** *a* Slav[onic]

sle'**al|e** *a* disloyal. **~tà** *nf* disloyalty

sle'**gare** *vt* untie

'**slitta** *nf* sledge, sleigh. **~'mento** *nm* (*di macchina*) skid; (*fig: di riunione*) postponement

slit'**ta|re** *vi* *Auto* skid; ⟨*riunione:*⟩ be put off. **~ta** *nf* skid

slit'**tino** *nm* toboggan

'**slogan** *nm inv* slogan

slo'**ga|re** *vt* dislocate. **~rsi** *vr* **~rsi una caviglia** sprain one's ankle. **~'tura** *nf* dislocation

sloggi'**are** *vt* dislodge ● *vi* move out

Slo'**vacchia** *nf* Slovakia

Slo'**venia** *nf* Slovenia

smacchi'**a|re** *vt* clean. **~'tore** *nm* stain remover

'**smacco** *nm* humiliating defeat

smagli'**ante** *a* dazzling

smagli'**a|rsi** *vr* ⟨*calza:*⟩ ladder *Br*, run. **~'tura** *nf* ladder *Br*, run

smalizi'**ato** *a* cunning

smal'**ta|re** *vt* enamel; glaze ⟨*ceramica*⟩; varnish ⟨*unghie*⟩. **~to a** enamelled

smalti'**mento** *nm* disposal; (*di merce*) selling off. **~ rifiuti** waste disposal; (*di grassi*) burning off

smal'**tire** *vt* burn off; (*merce*) sell off; *fig* get through ⟨*corrispondenza*⟩

'**smalto** *nm* enamel; (*di ceramica*) glaze; (*per le unghie*) nail varnish

'**smani|a** *nf* fidgets *pl*; (*desiderio*) long-ing. **~'are** *vi* have the fidgets; **~are per** long for. **~'oso** *a* restless

smantel|la'**mento** *nm* dismantling. **~'lare** *vt* dismantle

smarri'**mento** *nm* loss; (*psicologico*) bewilderment

smar'**ri|re** *vt* lose; (*temporaneamente*) mislay. **~rsi** *vr* get lost; (*turbarsi*) be bewildered

smasche'**rar|e** *vt* unmask. **~si** *vr* (*tradirsi*) give oneself away

SME *nm abbr* (**Sistema Monetario Europeo**) EMS

smemo'**rato** *a* forgetful

smen'**ti|re** *vt* deny. **~ta** *nf* denial

sme'**raldo** *nm* & *a* emerald

smerci'**are** *vt* sell off

smerigli'**ato** *a* emery; **vetro ~** frosted glass. **sme'riglio** *nm* emery

'**smesso** *pp di* **smettere** ● *a* ⟨*abiti*⟩ cast-off

'**smett|ere** *vt* stop; stop wearing ⟨*abiti*⟩; **~ila!** stop it!

smidol'**lato** *a* spineless

sminu'**ir|e** *vt* diminish. **~si** *vr fig* belittle oneself

sminuz'**zare** *vt* crumble; (*fig: analizzare*) analyse in detail

smista'**mento** *nm* clearing; (*postale*) sorting. **smi'stare** *vt* sort; *Mil* post

smisu'**rato** *a* boundless; (*esorbitante*) excessive

smobili'**ta|re** *vt* demobilize. **~zi'one** *nf* demobilization

smo'**dato** *a* immoderate

smog *nm* smog

smoking *nm inv* dinner jacket, tuxedo *Am*

smon'**tabile** *a* jointed

smon'**tar|e** *vt* take to pieces; (*scoraggiare*) dishearten ● *vi* (*da veicolo*) get off; (*da cavallo*) dismount; (*dal servizio*) go off duty. **~si** *vr* lose heart

'**smorfi|a** *nf* grimace; (*moina*) simper; **fare ~e** make faces. **~'oso** *a* affected

'**smorto** *a* pale; ⟨*colore*⟩ dull

smor'**zare** *vt* dim ⟨*luce*⟩; tone down ⟨*colori*⟩; deaden ⟨*suoni*⟩; quench ⟨*sete*⟩

'**smosso** *pp di* **smuovere**

smotta'**mento** *nm* landslide

sms *nm abbr* (**short message service**) text message

'**smunto** *a* emaciated

smu'**over|e** *vt* shift; (*commuovere*) move. **~si** *vr* move; (*commuoversi*) be moved

smus'**sar|e** *vt* round off; (*fig: attenuare*) tone down. **~si** *vr* go blunt

snatu'rato *a* inhuman

snel'lir|e *vt* slim down. **~si** *vr* slim [down]. **'snello** *a* slim

sner'vante *a* enervating

sner'va|re *vt* enervate. **~rsi** *vr* get exhausted

sni'dare *vt* drive out

snif'fare *vt* snort

snob'bare *vt* snub. **sno'bismo** *nm* snobbery

snoccio'lare *vt* stone; *fig* blurt out

sno'da|re *vt* untie; *(sciogliere)* loosen. **~rsi** *vr* come untied; *(strada:)* wind. **~to** *a* *(persona)* double-jointed; *(dita)* flexible

so'ave *a* gentle

sobbal'zare *vi* jerk; *(trasalire)* start. **sob'balzo** *nm* jerk; *(trasalimento)* start

sobbar'carsi *vr* **~ a** undertake

sob'borgo *nm* suburb

sobil'la|re *vt* stir up

'sobrio *a* sober

socchi'u|dere *vt* half-close. **~so** *pp di* **socchiudere** ● *a* *(occhi)* half-closed; *(porta)* ajar

soc'combere *vi* succumb

soc'cor|rere *vt* assist. **~so** *pp di* **soccorrere** ● *nm* assistance; **soccorsi** *pl* rescuers; *(dopo disastro)* relief workers. **~so stradale** breakdown service

socialdemo'cra|tico, -a *a* Social Democratic ● *nmf* Social Democrat. **~'zia** *nf* Social Democracy

soci'ale *a* social

socia'li|smo *nm* Socialism. **~sta** *a & nmf* Socialist. **~z'zare** *vi* socialize

società *nf inv* society; *Comm* company. **~ per azioni** plc. **~ a responsabilità limitata** limited liability company

soci'evole *a* sociable

'socio, -a *nmf* member; *Comm* partner

sociolo'gia *nf* sociology. **socio'logico** *a* sociological

'soda *nf* soda

soddisfa'cente *a* satisfactory

soddi'sfa|re *vt/i* satisfy; meet *(richiesta)*; make amends for *(offesa)*. **~tto** *pp di* **soddisfare** ● *a* satisfied. **~zi'one** *nf* satisfaction

'sodo *a* hard; *fig* firm; *(uovo)* hard-boiled ● *adv* hard; **dormire ~** sleep soundly ● *nm* **venire al ~** get to the point

sofà *nm inv* sofa

soffe'ren|te *a* *(malato)* ill. **~za** *nf* suffering

soffer'marsi *vr* pause; **~ su** dwell on

sof'ferto *pp di* **soffrire**

soffi'a|re *vt* blow; reveal *(segreto)*; *(rubare)* pinch *fam* ● *vi* blow. **~ta** *nf fig* sl tip-off

'soffice *a* soft

'soffio *nm* puff; *Med* murmur

sof'fitt|a *nf* attic. **~o** *nm* ceiling

soffo|ca'mento *nm* suffocation

soffo'ca|nte *a* suffocating. **~re** *vt/i* suffocate; *(con cibo)* choke; *fig* stifle

sof'friggere *vt* fry lightly

sof'frire *vt/i* suffer; *(sopportare)* bear; **~ di** suffer from

sof'fritto *pp di* **soffriggere**

sof'fuso *a* *(luce)* soft

sofisti'ca|re *vt* *(adulterare)* adulterate ● *vi* *(sottilizzare)* quibble. **~to** *a* sophisticated

sogget|tiva'mente *adv* subjectively. **~'tivo** *a* subjective

sog'getto *nm* subject ● *a* subject; **essere ~ a** be subject to

soggezi'one *nf* subjection; *(rispetto)* awe

sogghi'gnare *vi* sneer. **sog'ghigno** *nm* sneer

soggio'gare *vt* subdue

soggior'nare *vi* stay. **soggi'orno** *nm* stay; *(stanza)* living room

soggi'ungere *vt* add

'soglia *nf* threshold

sogli'ola *nf* sole

so'gna|re *vt/i* dream; **~re a occhi aperti** daydream. **~'tore**, **~'trice** *nmf* dreamer. **'sogno** *nm* dream; **fare un sogno** have a dream; **neanche per sogno!** not at all!

'soia *nf* soya

sol *nm Mus* *(chiave, nota)* G

so'laio *nm* attic

sola'mente *adv* only

so'lar|e *a* *(energia, raggi)* solar; *(crema)* sun *attrib*. **~ium** *nm inv* solarium

sol'care *vt* plough. **'solco** *nm* furrow; *(di ruota)* track; *(di nave)* wake; *(di disco)* groove

sol'dato *nm* soldier

'soldo *nm* **non ha un ~** he hasn't got a penny to his name; **senza un ~** penniless; **soldi** *pl* *(denaro)* money *sg*

'sole *nm* sun; *(luce del sole)* sun[light]; **al ~** in the sun; **prendere il ~** sunbathe

soleggi'ato *a* sunny

so'lenn|e *a* solemn. **~ità** *nf* solemnity

so'lere *vi* be in the habit of; **come si suol dire** as they say

sol'fato *nm* sulphate

soli'da|le *a* in agreement. **~rietà** *nf* solidarity

solidifi'car|e *vt/i,* **~si** *vr* solidify

solidità *nf* solidity; *(di colori)* fastness. **'solido** *a* solid; *(robusto)* sturdy; *‹colore›* fast ● *nm* solid

soli'loquio *nm* soliloquy

so'lista *a* solo ● *nmf* soloist

solita'mente *adv* usually

soli'tario *a* solitary; *(isolato)* lonely ● *nm* *(brillante)* solitaire; *(gioco di carte)* patience, solitaire

'solito *a* usual; **essere ~ fare qcsa** be in the habit of doing sth ● *nm* usual; **di ~** usually

soli'tudine *nf* solitude

solleci'ta|re *vt* speed up; urge *‹persona›*. **~zi'one** *nf* *(richiesta)* request; *(preghiera)* entreaty

sol'leci|to *a* prompt ● *nm* reminder. **~'tudine** *nf* promptness; *(interessamento)* concern

solle'one *nm* noonday sun; *(periodo)* dog days of summer

solleti'care *vt* tickle. **sol'letico** *nm* tickling; **fare il solletico a qcno** tickle sb; **soffrire il solletico** be ticklish

solleva'mento *nm* **~ pesi** weightlifting

solle'var|e *vt* lift; *(elevare)* raise; *(confortare)* comfort. **~si** *vr* rise; *(riaversi)* recover

solli'evo *nm* relief

'solo, -a *a* alone; *(isolato)* lonely; *(unico)* only; *Mus* solo; **da ~** by myself/yourself/himself etc ● *nmf* **il ~, la sola** the only one ● *nm* *Mus* solo ● *adv* only

sol'stizio *nm* solstice

sol'tanto *adv* only

so'lubile *a* soluble; *‹caffè›* instant

soluzi'one *nf* solution; *Comm* payment; **in unica ~** *Comm* as a lump sum

sol'vente *a & nm* solvent; **~ per unghie** nail polish remover

'soma *nf* **bestia da ~** beast of burden

so'maro *nm* ass; *Sch* dunce

so'matico *a* somatic

somigli'an|te *a* similar. **~za** *nf* resemblance

somigli'ar|e *vi* **~e a** resemble. **~si** *vr* be alike

'somma *nf* sum; *Math* addition

som'mare *vt* add; *(totalizzare)* add up

som'mario *a & nm* summary

som'mato *a* **tutto ~** all things considered

sommeli'er *nm inv* wine waiter

som'mer|gere *vt* submerge. **~'gibile** *nm* submarine. **~so** *pp di* **sommergere**

som'messo *a* soft

sommini'stra|re *vt* administer. **~zi'one** *nf* administration

sommità *nf inv* summit

'sommo *a* highest; *fig* supreme ● *nm* summit

som'mossa *nf* rising

sommozza'tore *nm* frogman

so'naglio *nm* bell

so'nata *nf* sonata; *fig fam* beating

'sonda *nf Mech* drill; *(spaziale, Med)* probe. **son'daggio** *nm* drilling; *(spaziale, Med)* probe; *(indagine)* survey. **sondaggio d'opinioni** opinion poll. **son'dare** *vt* sound; *(investigare)* probe

so'netto *nm* sonnet

sonnambu'lismo *nm* sleepwalking. **son'nambulo, -a** *nmf* sleepwalker

sonnecchi'are *vi* doze

son'nifero *nm* sleeping-pill

'sonno *nm* sleep; **aver ~** be sleepy. **~'lenza** *nf* sleepiness

so'noro *a* resonant; *(rumoroso)* loud; *‹onde, scheda›* sound *attrib*

sontu'oso *a* sumptuous

sopo'rifero *a* soporific

sop'palco *nm* platform

soppe'rire *vi* **~ a qcsa** provide for sth

soppe'sare *vt* weigh up *‹situazione›*

soppi'atto: di ~ *adv* furtively

soppor'ta|re *vt* support; *(tollerare)* stand; bear *‹dolore›*

soppressi'one *nf* removal; *(di legge)* abolition; *(di diritti, pubblicazione)* suppression; *(annullamento)* cancellation. **sop'presso** *pp di* **sopprimere**

sop'primere *vt* get rid of; abolish *‹legge›*; suppress *‹diritti, pubblicazione›*; *(annullare)* cancel

'sopra *adv* on top; *(più in alto)* higher [up]; *(al piano superiore)* upstairs; *(in testo)* above; **mettilo lì ~** put it up there; **di ~** upstairs; **dormirci ~** *fig* sleep on it; **pensarci ~** think about it; **vedi ~** see above ● *prep* **~ [a]** on; *(senza contatto, oltre)* over; *(riguardo a)* about; **è ~ al tavolo, è ~ il tavolo** it's on the table; **il quadro è appeso ~ al camino** the picture is hanging over the fireplace; **il ponte passa ~ all'autostrada** the bridge crosses over the motorway; **è caduto ~ il tetto** it fell on the roof; **l'uno ~ l'altro** one on top of the other; *(senza contatto)* one above the other; **abita ~ di me** he lives upstairs from me; **i bambini ~ i dieci**

anni children over ten; **20°** ~ **lo zero** 20° above zero; ~ **il livello del mare** above sea level; **rifletti** ~ **quello che è successo** think about what happened; **non ha nessuno** ~ **di sé** he has nobody above him; **al di** ~ **di** over ● *nm* **il** [**di**] ~ the top

so'prabito *nm* overcoat

soprac'ciglio *nm* (*pl nf* **sopracciglia**) eyebrow

sopracco'per|ta *nf* (*di letto*) bedspread; (*di libro*) [dust-]jacket. ~**'tina** *nf* book jacket

soprad'detto *a* above-mentioned

sopraele'vata *nf* elevated railway

sopraf'fa|re *vt* overwhelm. ~**tto** *pp di* **sopraffare**. ~**zi'one** *nf* abuse of power

sopraf'fino *a* excellent; (*gusto, udito*) highly refined

sopraggi'ungere *vi* (*persona:*) turn up; (*accadere*) happen

soprallu'ogo *nm* inspection

sopram'mobile *nm* ornament

soprannatu'rale *a & nm* supernatural

sopran'nom|e *nm* nickname. ~**i'nare** *vt* nickname

so'prano *nmf* soprano

soprappensi'ero *adv* lost in thought

sopras'salto *nm* **di** ~ with a start

soprasse'dere *vi* ~ **a** postpone

soprat'tutto *adv* above all

sopravvalu'tare *vt* overvalue

soprav|ve'nire *vi* turn up; (*accadere*) happen. ~**'vento** *nm fig* upper hand

sopravvi|s'suto *pp di* **sopravvivere**. ~**'venza** *nf* survival. **soprav'vivere** *vi* survive; **sopravvivere a** outlive (*persona*)

soprinten'den|te *nmf* supervisor; (*di museo ecc*) keeper. ~**za** *nf* supervision; (*ente*) board

so'pruso *nm* abuse of power

soq'quadro *nm* **mettere a** ~ turn upside down

sor'betto *nm* sorbet

sor'bire *vt* sip; *fig* put up with

'sordido *a* sordid; (*avaro*) stingy

sor'dina *nf* mute; **in** ~ *fig* on the quiet

sordità *nf* deafness. **'sordo, -a** *a* deaf; (*rumore, dolore*) dull ● *nmf* deaf person.

sordo'muto, -a *a* deaf-and-dumb ● *nmf* deaf mute

so'rel|la *nf* sister. ~**'lastra** *nf* stepsister

sor'gente *nf* spring; (*fonte*) source

'sorgere *vi* rise; *fig* arise

sormon'tare *vt* surmount

sorni'one *a* sly

sorpas'sa|re *vt* surpass; (*eccedere*) exceed; overtake, pass *Am* (*veicolo*). ~**to** *a* old-fashioned. **sor'passo** *nm* overtaking, passing *Am*

sorpren'dente *a* surprising; (*straordinario*) remarkable

sor'prendere *vt* surprise; (*cogliere in flagrante*) catch

sor'pres|a *nf* surprise; **di** ~**a** by surprise. ~**o** *pp di* **sorprendere**

sor're|ggere *vt* support; (*tenere*) hold up. ~**ggersi** *vr* support oneself. ~**tto** *pp di* **sorreggere**

sorri'dente *a* smiling

sor'ri|dere *vi* smile. ~**so** *pp di* **sorridere** ● *nm* smile

sorseggi'are *vt* sip. **'sorso** *nm* sip; (*piccola quantità*) drop

'sorta *nf* sort; **di** ~ whatever; **ogni** ~ **di** all sorts of

'sorte *nf* fate; (*caso imprevisto*) chance; **tirare a** ~ draw lots. ~**ggi'are** *vt* draw lots for. **sor'teggio** *nm* draw

sorti'legio *nm* witchcraft

sor'ti|re *vi* come out. ~**ta** *nf Mil* sortie; (*battuta*) witticism

'sorto *pp di* **sorgere**

sorvegli'an|te *nmf* keeper; (*controllore*) overseer. ~**za** *nf* watch; *Mil ecc* surveillance

sorvegli'are *vt* watch over; (*controllare*) oversee; (*polizia:*) watch, keep under surveillance

sorvo'lare *vt* fly over; *fig* skip

'sosia *nm inv* double

so'spen|dere *vt* hang; (*interrompere*) stop; (*privare di una carica*) suspend. ~**si'one** *nf* suspension. ~**'sorio** *nm Sport* jockstrap

so'speso *pp di* **sospendere** ● *a* (*impiegato, alunno*) suspended; ~ **a** hanging from; ~ **a un filo** *fig* hanging by a thread ● *nm* **in** ~ pending; (*emozionato*) in suspense

sospet|'tare *vt* suspect. **so'spetto** *a* suspicious ● *nm* suspicion; (*persona*) suspect. ~**'toso** *a* suspicious

so'spin|gere *vt* drive. ~**to** *pp di* **sospingere**

sospi'rare *vi* sigh ● *vt* long for. **so'spiro** *nm* sigh

'sosta *nf* stop; (*pausa*) pause; **senza** ~ non-stop; **"divieto di** ~**"** "no parking"

sostan'tivo *nm* noun

so'stanz|a *nf* substance; ~**e** *pl* (*patrimonio*) property *sg*; **in** ~**a** to sum up. **~i'oso** *a* substantial; ⟨*cibo*⟩ nourishing

so'stare *vi* stop; (*fare una pausa*) pause

so'stegno *nm* support

soste'ner|e *vt* support; (*sopportare*) bear; (*resistere*) withstand; (*affermare*) maintain; (*nutrire*) sustain; sit ⟨*esame*⟩; **~e le spese** meet the costs. **~si** *vr* support oneself

sosteni'tore, -'trice *nmf* supporter

sostenta'mento *nm* maintenance

soste'nuto *a* ⟨*stile*⟩ formal; ⟨*prezzi, velocità*⟩ high

sostitu'ir|e *vt* substitute (**a** for), replace (**con** with). **~si** *vr* **~si a** replace

sosti'tu|to, -a *nmf* replacement, stand-in ● *nm* (*surrogato*) substitute. **~zi'one** *nf* substitution

sotta'ceto *a* pickled; **sottaceti** *pl* pickles

sot'tana *nf* petticoat; (*di prete*) cassock

sotter'fugio *nm* subterfuge; **di ~** secretly

sotter'raneo *a* underground ● *nm* cellar

sotter'rare *vt* bury

sottigli'ezza *nf* slimness; *fig* subtlety

sot'til|e *a* thin; ⟨*udito, odorato*⟩ keen; ⟨*osservazione, distinzione*⟩ subtle. **~iz-'zare** *vi* split hairs

sottin'te|ndere *vt* imply. **~so** *pp di* **sottintendere** ● *nm* allusion; **senza ~si** openly ● *a* implied

'sotto *adv* below; (*più in basso*) lower [down]; (*al di sotto*) underneath; (*al piano di sotto*) downstairs; **è lì ~** it's underneath; **~** deep down; (*di nascosto*) on the quiet; **di ~** downstairs; **mettersi ~** *fig* get down to it; **mettere ~** (*fam: investire*) knock down; **fatti ~!** *fam* get stuck in! ● *prep* ~ [**a**] under; (*al di sotto di*) under[neath]; **abita ~ di me** he lives downstairs from me; **i bambini ~ i dieci anni** children under ten; **20° ~ zero** 20° below zero; **~ il livello del mare** below sea level; **~ la pioggia** in the rain; **~ Elisabetta I** under Elizabeth I; **~ calmante** under sedation; **~ condizione che...** on condition that...; **~ giuramento** under oath; **~ sorveglianza** under surveillance; **~ Natale/gli esami** around Christmas/ exam time; **al di ~ di** under; **andare ~ i 50 all'ora** do less than 50km an hour ● *nm* **il** [**di**] **~** the bottom

sotto'banco *adv* under the counter

sottobicchi'ere *nm* coaster

sotto'bosco *nm* undergrowth

sotto'braccio *adv* arm in arm

sotto'fondo *nm* background

sottoline'are *vt* underline; *fig* stress

sot'tolio *adv* in oil

sotto'mano *adv* within reach

sottoma'rino *a & nm* submarine

sotto'messo *pp di* **sottomettere** ● *a* (*remissivo*) submissive

sotto'metter|e *vt* submit; subdue ⟨*popolo*⟩. **~si** *vr* submit. **sotto-missi'one** *nf* submission

sottopa'gare *vt* underpay

sottopas'saggio *nm* underpass; (*pedonale*) subway

sotto'por|re *vt* submit; (*costringere*) subject. **~si** *vr* submit oneself; **~si a** undergo. **sotto'posto** *pp di* **sottoporre**

sotto'scala *nm* cupboard under the stairs

sotto'scritto *pp di* **sottoscrivere** ● *nm* undersigned

sotto'scri|vere *vt* sign; (*approvare*) sanction, subscribe to. **~zi'one** *nf* (*petizione*) petition; (*approvazione*) sanction; (*raccolta di denaro*) appeal

sottosegre'tario *nm* undersecretary

sotto'sopra *adv* upside down

sotto'stante *a* **la strada ~** the road below

sottosu'olo *nm* subsoil

sottosvi|lup'pato *a* underdeveloped. **~'luppo** *nm* underdevelopment

sotto'terra *adv* underground

sotto'titolo *nm* subtitle

sottovalu'tare *vt* underestimate

sotto'veste *nf* slip

sotto'voce *adv* in a low voice

sottovu'oto *a* vacuum-packed

sot'tra|rre *vt* remove; embezzle ⟨*fondi*⟩; *Math* subtract. **~rsi** *vr* **~rsi a** escape from; avoid ⟨*responsabilità*⟩. **~tto** *pp di* **sottrarre**. **~zi'one** *nf* removal; (*di fondi*) embezzlement; *Math* subtraction

sottuffici'ale *nm* non-commissioned officer; *Naut* petty officer

sou'brette *nf inv* showgirl

so'vietico, -a *a & nmf* Soviet

sovraccari'care *vt* overload. **sovrac'carico** *a* overloaded (**di** with) ● *nm* overload

sovraffati'carsi *vr* overexert oneself

sovrannatu'rale *a & nm* = **soprannaturale**

so'vrano, -a *a* sovereign; *fig* supreme ● *nmf* sovereign

209

sovrapporre | specchiarsi

sovrap'por|re *vt* superimpose. **~si** *vr* overlap. **sovrapposizi'one** *nf* superimposition

sovra'stare *vt* dominate; ⟨*fig: pericolo:*⟩ hang over

sovrinten'den|te, **~za** = **soprintendente, soprintendenza**

sovru'mano *a* superhuman

sovvenzi'one *nf* subsidy

sovver'sivo *a* subversive

'sozzo *a* filthy

S.p.A. *abbr* (**società per azioni**) plc

spac'ca|re *vt* split; chop ⟨*legna*⟩. **~rsi** *vr* split. **~'tura** *nf* split

spacci'a|re *vt* deal in, push ⟨*droga*⟩; **~re qcsa per qcsa** pass sth off as sth; **essere ~to** be done for, be a goner. **~rsi** *vr* **~rsi per** pass oneself off as. **~'tore**, **~'trice** *nmf* (*di droga*) pusher; (*di denaro falso*) distributor of forged bank notes. **'spaccio** *nm* (*di droga*) dealer, pusher; (*negozio*) shop

'spacco *nm* split

spac'cone, -a *nmf* boaster

'spada *nf* sword. **~c'cino** *nm* swordsman

spadroneggi'are *vi* act the boss

spae'sato *a* disorientated

spa'ghetti *nmpl* spaghetti *sg*

spa'ghetto *nm* (*fam: spavento*) fright

'Spagna *nf* Spain

spa'gnolo, -a *a* Spanish ● *nmf* Spaniard ● *nm* (*lingua*) Spanish

'spago *nm* string; **dare ~ a qcno** encourage sb

spai'ato *a* odd

spalan'ca|re *vt*, **~rsi** *vr* open wide. **~to** *a* wide open

spa'lare *vt* shovel

'spall|a *nf* shoulder; (*di comico*) straight man; **~e** *pl* (*schiena*) back; **alle ~e di qcno** ⟨*ridere*⟩ behind sb's back. **~eggi'are** *vt* back up

spal'letta *nf* parapet

spalli'era *nf* back; (*di letto*) headboard; (*ginnastica*) wall bars *pl*

spal'lina *nf* strap; (*imbottitura*) shoulder pad

spal'mare *vt* spread

'spander|e *vt* spread; (*versare*) spill. **~si** *vr* spread

spappo'lare *vt* crush

spa'ra|re *vt/i* shoot; **~rle grosse** talk big. **~ta** *nf fam* tall story. **~'toria** *nf* shooting

sparecchi'are *vt* clear

spa'reggio *nm Comm* deficit; *Sport* play-off

'sparg|ere *vt* scatter; (*diffondere*) spread; shed ⟨*lacrime, sangue*⟩. **~ersi** *vr* spread. **~i'mento** *nm* scattering; (*di lacrime, sangue*) shedding; **~imento di sangue** bloodshed

spa'ri|re *vi* disappear; **~sci!** get lost!. **~zi'one** *nf* disappearance

spar'lare *vi* **~ di** run down

'sparo *nm* shot

sparpagli'ar|e *vt*, **~si** *vr* scatter

'sparso *pp di* **spargere** ● *a* scattered; (*sciolto*) loose

spar'tire *vt* share out; (*separare*) separate

sparti'traffico *nm inv* traffic island; (*di autostrada*) central reservation, median strip *Am*

spartizi'one *nf* division

spa'ruto *a* gaunt; ⟨*gruppo*⟩ small; ⟨*peli, capelli*⟩ sparse

sparvi'ero *nm* sparrow-hawk

spasi'ma|nte *nm hum* admirer. **~re** *vi* suffer agonies

'spasimo *nm* spasm

spa'smodico *a* spasmodic

spas'sar|si *vr* amuse oneself; **~sela** have a good time

spassio'nato *a* ⟨*osservatore*⟩ dispassionate, impartial

'spasso *nm* fun; **essere uno ~** be hilarious; **andare a ~** go for a walk. **spas'soso** *a* hilarious

'spatola *nf* spatula

spau'racchio *nm* scarecrow; *fig* bugbear. **spau'rire** *vt* frighten

spa'valdo *a* defiant

spaventa'passeri *nm inv* scarecrow

spaven'tar|e *vt* frighten, scare. **~si** *vr* be frightened, be scared. **spa'vento** *nm* fright. **spaven'toso** *a* frightening; (*fam: enorme*) incredible

spazi'ale *a* spatial; (*cosmico*) space *attrib*

spazi'are *vt* space out ● *vi* range

spazien'tirsi *vr* lose [one's] patience

'spazi|o *nm* space. **~'oso** *a* spacious

spazzaca'mino *nm* chimney sweep

spaz'z|are *vt* sweep; **~are via** sweep away; (*fam: mangiare*) devour. **~a'tura** *nf* (*immondizia*) rubbish. **~ino** *nm* road sweeper; (*netturbino*) dustman

'spazzo|la *nf* brush; (*di tergicristallo*) blade. **~'lare** *vt* brush. **~'lino** *nm* small brush. **~lino da denti** toothbrush. **~'lone** *nm* scrubbing brush

specchi'arsi *vr* look at oneself in a/ the mirror; (*riflettersi*) be mirrored; **~ in qcno** model oneself on sb

specchi'etto nm ~ **retrovisore** driving mirror, rearview mirror

'specchio nm mirror

speci'a|le a special ● nm TV special [programme]. ~'**lista** nmf specialist. ~**lità** nf inv speciality, specialty Am

specializ'za|re vt, ~**rsi** vr specialize. ~**to** ⟨operaio⟩ skilled

special'mente adv especially

'specie nf inv ⟨scientifico⟩ species; ⟨tipo⟩ kind; **fare la ~ a** surprise

specifi'care vt specify. **spe'cifico** a specific

specu'lare[1] vi speculate; ~ **su** ⟨indagare⟩ speculate on; Fin speculate in

specu'lare[2] a mirror attrib

specula|'tore, -'trice nmf speculator. ~**zi'one** nf speculation

spe'di|re vt send. ~**to** pp di spedire ● a quick; ⟨parlata⟩ fluent. ~**zi'one** nf ⟨di lettere ecc⟩ dispatch; Comm consignment; ⟨scientifica⟩ expedition

'spegner|e vt put out; turn off ⟨gas, luce⟩; switch off ⟨motore⟩; slake ⟨sete⟩. ~**si** vr go out; ⟨morire⟩ pass away

spelacchi'ato a ⟨tappeto⟩ threadbare; ⟨cane⟩ mangy

spe'lar|e vt skin ⟨coniglio⟩. ~**si** vr ⟨cane:⟩ moult

speleolo'gia nf potholing, speleology

spel'lar|e vt skin; fig fleece. ~**si** vr peel off

spe'lonca nf cave; fig dingy hole

spendacci'one, -a nmf spendthrift

'spendere vt spend; ~ **fiato** waste one's breath

spen'nare vt pluck; fam fleece ⟨cliente⟩

spennel'lare vt brush

spensie|ra'tezza nf lightheartedness. ~'**rato** a carefree

'spento pp di spegnere ● a off; ⟨gas⟩ out; ⟨smorto⟩ dull

spe'ranza nf hope; **pieno di ~** hopeful; **senza ~** hopeless

spe'rare vt hope for; ⟨aspettarsi⟩ expect ● vi ~ **in** trust in; **spero di sì** I hope so

'sper|dersi vr get lost. ~'**duto** a lost; ⟨isolato⟩ secluded

spergi'uro, -a nmf perjurer ● nm perjury

sperico'lato a swashbuckling

sperimen'ta|le a experimental. ~**re** vt experiment with; test ⟨resistenza, capacità, teoria⟩. ~**zi'one** nf experimentation

'sperma nm sperm

spe'rone nm spur

sperpe'rare vt squander. **'sperpero** nm waste

'spes|a nf expense; ⟨acquisto⟩ purchase; **andare a far ~e** go shopping; **fare la ~a** do the shopping; **fare le ~e di** pay for. ~**e** pl **bancarie** bank charges. ~**e a carico del destinatario** carriage forward. ~**e di spedizione** shipping costs. **spe'sato** a all-expenses-paid. ~**o** pp di spendere

'spesso[1] a thick

'spesso[2] adv often

spes'sore nm thickness; ⟨fig: consistenza⟩ substance

spet'tabile a ⟨Comm abbr **Spett.**⟩ **S~ ditta Rossi** Messrs Rossi

spettaco|'lare a spectacular. **spet'tacolo** nm spectacle; ⟨rappresentazione⟩ show. ~**loso** a spectacular

spet'tare vi ~ **a** be up to; ⟨diritto:⟩ be due to

spetta|'tore, -'trice nmf spectator; **spettatori** pl ⟨di cinema ecc⟩ audience sg

spettego'lare vi gossip

spetti'nar|e vt ~**e qcno** ruffle sb's hair. ~**si** vr ruffle one's hair

spet'trale a ghostly. **'spettro** nm ghost; Phys spectrum

'spezie nfpl spices

spez'zar|e vt, ~**si** vr break

spezza'tino nm stew

spez'zato nm coordinated jacket and trousers

spezzet'tare vt break into small pieces

'spia nf spy; ⟨della polizia⟩ informer; ⟨di porta⟩ peep-hole; **fare la ~** sneak. ~ **[luminosa]** light. ~ **dell'olio** oil [warning] light

spiacci'care vt squash

spia'ce|nte a sorry. ~**vole** a unpleasant

spi'aggia nf beach

spia'nare vt level; ⟨rendere liscio⟩ smooth; roll out ⟨pasta⟩; raze to the ground ⟨edificio⟩

spi'ano nm **a tutto ~** flat out

spian'tato a fig penniless

spi'are vt spy on; wait for ⟨occasione ecc⟩

spiattel'lare vt blurt out; shove ⟨oggetto⟩

spiaz'zare vt wrong-foot

spi'azzo nm ⟨radura⟩ clearing

spic'ca|re vt ~**re un salto** jump; ~**re il volo** take flight ● vi stand out. ~**to** a marked '**spicchio** *nm* (*di agrumi*) segment; (*di aglio*) clove

spicci'a|rsi *vr* hurry up. **~'tivo** *a* speedy

'**spicciolo** *a* (*comune*) banal; ⟨*denaro, 10 000 lire*⟩ in change. **spiccioli** *pl* change *sg*

'**spicco** *nm* relief; **fare ~** stand out

'**spider** *nmf inv* open-top sports car

spie'dino *nm* kebab. **spi'edo** *nm* spit; **allo spiedo** on a spit, spit-roasted

spie'ga|re *vt* explain; open out ⟨*cartina*⟩; unfurl ⟨*vele*⟩. **~rsi** *vr* explain oneself; ⟨*vele, bandiere:*⟩ unfurl. **~zi'one** *nf* explanation

spiegaz'zato *a* crumpled

spie'tato *a* ruthless

spiffe'rare *vt* blurt out ● *vi* (*vento:*) whistle. '**spiffero** *nm* (*corrente d'aria*) draught

'**spiga** *nf* spike; *Bot* ear

spigli'ato *a* self-possessed

'**spigolo** *nm* edge; (*angolo*) corner

'**spilla** *nf* (*gioiello*) brooch. **~ da balia** safety pin. **~ di sicurezza** safety pin

spil'lare *vt* tap

'**spillo** *nm* pin. **~ di sicurezza** safety pin; (*in arma*) safety catch

spi'lorcio *a* stingy

spilun'gone, -a *nmf* beanpole

'**spina** *nf* thorn; (*di pesce*) bone; *Electr* plug. **~ dorsale** spine

spi'naci *nmpl* spinach *sg*

spi'nale *a* spinal

spi'nato *a* ⟨*filo*⟩ barbed; ⟨*pianta*⟩ thorny

spi'nello *nm fam* joint

'**spinger|e** *vt* push; *fig* drive. **~si** *vr* (*andare*) proceed

spi'noso *a* thorny

'**spint|a** *nf* push; (*violenta*) thrust; *fig* spur. **~o** *pp di* **spingere**

spio'naggio *nm* espionage, spying

spio'vente *a* ⟨*tetto*⟩ sloping

spi'overe *vi liter* stop raining; (*ricadere*) fall; (*scorrere*) flow down

'**spira** *nf* coil

spi'raglio *nm* small opening; (*soffio d'aria*) breath of air; (*raggio di luce*) gleam of light

spi'rale *a* spiral ● *nf* spiral; (*negli orologi*) hairspring; (*anticoncezionale*) coil

spi'rare *vi* (*soffiare*) blow; (*morire*) pass away

spiri't|ato *a* possessed; ⟨*espressione*⟩ wild. **~ismo** *nm* spiritualism. '**spirito** *nm* spirit; (*arguzia*) wit; (*intelletto*)

mind; **fare dello spirito** be witty; **sotto spirito** ≈ in brandy. **~o'saggine** *nf* witticism. **spiri'toso** *a* witty

spiritu'ale *a* spiritual

splen'dente *a* shining

'**splen|dere** *vi* shine. **~dido** *a* splendid. **~'dore** *nm* splendour

spode'stare *vt* dispossess; depose ⟨*re*⟩

'**spoglia** *nf* (*di animale*) skin; **spoglie** *pl* (*salma*) mortal remains; (*bottino*) spoils

spogli'a|re *vt* strip; (*svestire*) undress; (*fare lo spoglio di*) go through. **~'rello** *nm* strip-tease. **~rsi** *vr* strip, undress. **~'toio** *nm* dressing room; *Sport* changing room; (*guardaroba*) cloakroom, checkroom *Am*. '**spoglio** *a* undressed; ⟨*albero, muro*⟩ bare ● *nm* (*scrutinio*) perusal

'**spola** *nf* shuttle; **fare la ~** shuttle

spol'pare *vt* take the flesh off; *fig* fleece

spolve'rare *vt* dust; *fam* devour ⟨*cibo*⟩

'**sponda** *nf* (*di mare, lago*) shore; (*di fiume*) bank; (*bordo*) edge

sponsoriz'zare *vt* sponsor

spon'taneo *a* spontaneous

spopo'lar|e *vt* depopulate ● *vi* (*avere successo*) draw the crowds. **~si** *vr* become depopulated

sporadica'mente *adv* sporadically. **spo'radico** *a* sporadic

sporcacci'one, -a *nmf* dirty pig

spor'c|are *vt* dirty; (*macchiare*) soil. **~arsi** *vr* get dirty. **~izia** *nf* dirt. '**sporco** *a* dirty; **avere la coscienza sporca** have a guilty conscience ● *nm* dirt

spor'gen|te *a* jutting. **~za** *nf* projection

'**sporger|e** *vt* stretch out; **~e querela contro** take legal action against ● *vi* jut out. **~si** *vr* lean out

sport *nm inv* sport

'**sporta** *nf* shopping basket

spor'tello *nm* door; (*di banca ecc*) window. **~ automatico** cash dispenser

spor'tivo, -a *a* sports *attrib*; ⟨*persona*⟩ sporty ● *nm* sportsman ● *nf* sportswoman

'**sporto** *pp di* **sporgere**

'**sposa** *nf* bride. **~'lizio** *nm* wedding

spo'sa|re *vt* marry; *fig* espouse. **~rsi** *vr* get married; ⟨*vino:*⟩ go (**con** with). **~to** *a* married. '**sposo** *nm* bridegroom; **sposi** *pl* [novelli] newlyweds

spossa'tezza *nf* exhaustion. **spos'sato** *a* exhausted, worn out

spo'sta|re *vt* move; (*differire*) post-

pone; *(cambiare)* change. **~rsi** *vr* move.
~to, -a *a* ill-adjusted ● *nmf (disa-dattato)* misfit

'**spranga** *nf* bar. **spran'gare** *vt* bar

'**sprazzo** *nm (di colore)* splash; *(di luce)* flash; *fig* glimmer

spre'care *vt* waste. '**spreco** *nm* waste

spre'g|evole *a* despicable. **~ia'tivo** *a* pejorative. '**spregio** *nm* contempt

spregiudi'cato *a* unscrupulous

'**spremer|e** *vt* squeeze. **~si** *vr* **~si le meningi** rack one's brains

spremia'grumi *nm* lemon squeezer

spre'muta *nf* juice. **~ d'arancia** fresh orange [juice]

sprez'zante *a* contemptuous

sprigio'nar|e *vt* emit. **~si** *vr* burst out

spriz'zare *vt/i* spurt; be bursting with *(salute, gioia)*

sprofon'dar|e *vi* sink; *(crollare)* collapse. **~si** *vr* **~si in** sink into; *fig* be engrossed in

spro'nare *vt* spur on. '**sprone** *nm* spur; *(sartoria)* yoke

sproporzi|o'nato *a* disproportionate. **~'one** *nf* disproportion

sproposi'tato *a* full of blunders; *(enorme)* huge. **spro'posito** *nm* blunder; *(eccesso)* excessive amount; **a spro-posito** inopportunely

sprovve'duto *a* unprepared; **~ di** lacking in

sprov'visto *a* **~ di** out of; lacking in *(fantasia, pazienza)*; **alla sprovvista** unexpectedly

spruz'za|re *vt* sprinkle; *(vaporizzare)* spray; *(inzaccherare)* spatter. **~'tore** *nm* spray; '**spruzzo** *nm* spray; *(di fango)* splash

spudo|ra'tezza *nf* shamelessness. **~'rato** *a* shameless

'**spugna** *nf* sponge; *(tessuto)* towelling. **spu'gnoso** *a* spongy

'**spuma** *nf* foam; *(schiuma)* froth; *Culin* mousse. **spu'mante** *nm* sparkling wine, spumante. **spumeggi'are** *vi* foam

spun'ta|re *vt (rompere la punta di)* break the point of; trim *(capelli)*; **~rla** *fig* win ● *vi (pianta:)* sprout; *(capelli:)* begin to grow; *(sorgere)* rise; *(apparire)* appear. **~rsi** *vr* get blunt. **~ta** *nf* trim

spun'tino *nm* snack

'**spunto** *nm* cue; *fig* starting point; **dare ~** a give rise to

spur'gar|e *vt* purge. **~si** *vr* *Med* expectorate

spu'tare *vt/i* spit; **~ sentenze** pass judgment. '**sputo** *nm* spit

'**squadra** *nf (gruppo)* team, squad; *(di polizia ecc)* squad; *(da disegno)* square. **squa'drare** *vt* square; *(guardare)* look up and down

squa'dr|iglia *nf*, **~one** *nm* squadron

squagli'ar|e *vt*, **~si** *vr* melt; **~sela** *(fam:* svignarsela) steal out

squa'lifi|ca *nf* disqualification. **~'care** *vt* disqualify

'**squallido** *a* squalid. **squal'lore** *nm* squalor

'**squalo** *nm* shark

'**squama** *nf* scale; *(di pelle)* flake

squa'm|are *vt* scale. **~arsi** *vr (pelle:)* flake off. **~'moso** *a* scaly; *(pelle)* flaky

squarcia'gola: a ~ *adv* at the top of one's voice

squarci'are *vt* rip. '**squarcio** *nm* rip; *(di ferita, in nave)* gash; *(di cielo)* patch

squar'tare *vt* quarter; dismember *(animale)*

squattri'nato *a* penniless

squilib'ra|re *vt* unbalance. **~to, -a** *a* unbalanced ● *nmf* lunatic. **squi'librio** *nm* imbalance

squil'la|nte *a* shrill. **~re** *vi (campana:)* peal; *(tromba:)* blare; *(telefono:)* ring. '**squillo** *nm* blare; *Teleph* ring; *(ragazza)* call girl

squi'sito *a* exquisite

squit'tire *vi (pappagallo, fig:)* squawk; *(topo:)* squeak

sradi'care *vt* uproot; eradicate *(vizio, male)*

sragio'nare *vi* rave

srego|la'tezza *nf* dissipation. **~'lato** *a* inordinate; *(dissoluto)* dissolute

s.r.l. *abbr* (**società a responsabilità limitata**) Ltd

sroto'lare *vt* uncoil

SS *abbr* (**strada statale**) national road

'**stabile** *a* stable; *(permanente)* lasting; *(saldo)* steady; **compagnia ~** *Theat* repertory company ● *nm (edificio)* building

stabili'mento *nm* factory; *(industriale)* plant; *(edificio)* establishment. **~ balneare** lido

stabi'li|re *vt* establish; *(decidere)* decide. **~rsi** *vr* settle. **~tà** *nf* stability

stabiliz'za|re *vt* stabilize. **~rsi** *vr* stabilize. **~'tore** *nm* stabilizer

stac'car|e *vt* detach; pronounce clearly *(parole)*; *(separare)* separate; turn off *(corrente)*; **~e gli occhi da** take one's eyes off ● *vi (fam: finire di lavorare)* knock off. **~si** *vr* come off;

~si da break away from ⟨*partito, famiglia*⟩

staccio'nata *nf* fence

'stacco *nm* gap

'stadio *nm* stadium

'staffa *nf* stirrup

staf'fetta *nf* dispatch rider

stagio'nale *a* seasonal

stagio'na|re *vt* season ⟨*legno*⟩; mature ⟨*formaggio*⟩. **~to** *a* ⟨*legno*⟩ seasoned; ⟨*formaggio*⟩ matured

stagi'one *nf* season; **alta/bassa ~** high/low season

stagli'arsi *vr* stand out

sta'gna|nte *a* stagnant. **~re** *vt* ⟨*saldare*⟩ solder; ⟨*chiudere ermeticamente*⟩ seal ● *vi* ⟨*acqua:*⟩ stagnate.
'stagno *a* ⟨*a tenuta d'acqua*⟩ watertight ● *nm* ⟨*acqua ferma*⟩ pond; ⟨*metallo*⟩ tin

sta'gnola *nf* tinfoil

stalag'mite *nf* stalagmite

stalat'tite *nf* stalactite

'stall|a *nf* stable; ⟨*per buoi*⟩ cowshed. **~i'ere** *nm* groom

stal'lone *nm* stallion

sta'mani, stamat'tina *adv* this morning

stam'becco *nm* ibex

stam'berga *nf* hovel

'stampa *nf* *Typ* printing; ⟨*giornali, giornalisti*⟩ press; ⟨*riproduzione*⟩ print

stam'pa|nte *nf* printer. **~nte ad aghi** dot matrix printer. **~nte laser** laser printer. **~re** *vt* print. **~'tello** *nm* block letters *pl*

stam'pella *nf* crutch

'stampo *nm* mould; **di vecchio ~** ⟨*persona*⟩ of the old school

sta'nare *vt* drive out

stan'car|e *vt* tire; ⟨*annoiare*⟩ bore. **~si** *vr* get tired

stan'chezza *nf* tiredness. **'stanco** *a* tired; **stanco di** ⟨*stufo*⟩ fed up with. **stanco morto** dead tired, knackered *fam*

'standard *a & nm inv* standard. **~iz'zare** *vt* standardize

'stan|ga *nf* bar; ⟨*persona*⟩ beanpole. **~'gata** *nf fig* blow; ⟨*fam: nel calcio*⟩ big kick; **prendere una ~gata** ⟨*fam: agli esami, economica*⟩ come a cropper. **stan'ghetta** *nf* ⟨*di occhiali*⟩ leg

sta'notte *nf* tonight; ⟨*la notte scorsa*⟩ last night

'stante *prep* on account of; **a sé ~** separate

stan'tio *a* stale

stan'tuffo *nm* piston

'stanza *nf* room; ⟨*metrica*⟩ stanza

stanzi'are *vt* allocate

stap'pare *vt* uncork

'stare *vi* ⟨*rimanere*⟩ stay; ⟨*abitare*⟩ live; ⟨*con gerundio*⟩ be; **sto solo cinque minuti** I'll stay only five minutes; **sto in piazza Peyron** I live in Peyron Square; **sta dormendo** he's sleeping; **~ a** ⟨*attenersi*⟩ keep to; ⟨*spettare*⟩ be up to; **~ bene** ⟨*economicamente*⟩ be well off; ⟨*di salute*⟩ be well; ⟨*addirsi*⟩ suit; **~ dietro a** ⟨*seguire*⟩ follow; ⟨*sorvegliare*⟩ keep an eye on; ⟨*corteggiare*⟩ run after; **~ in piedi** stand; **~ per** be about to; **ben ti sta!** it serves you right!; **come stai/sta?** how are you?!; **lasciar ~** leave alone; **starci** ⟨*essere contenuto*⟩ go into; ⟨*essere d'accordo*⟩ agree; **il 3 nel 12 ci sta 4 volte** 3 into 12 goes 4; **non sa ~ agli scherzi** he can't take a joke; **~ su** ⟨*con la schiena*⟩ sit up straight; **~ sulle proprie** keep oneself to oneself. **starsene** *vr* ⟨*rimanere*⟩ stay

starnu'tire *vi* sneeze. **star'nuto** *nm* sneeze

sta'sera *adv* this evening, tonight

sta'tale *a* state *attrib* ● *nmf* state employee ● *nf* ⟨*strada*⟩ main road, trunk road

'statico *a* static

sta'tista *nm* statesman

sta'tistic|a *nf* statistics *sg*. **~o** *a* statistical

'stato *pp di* **essere, stare** ● *nm* state; ⟨*posizione sociale*⟩ position; *Jur* status. **~ d'animo** frame of mind. **~ civile** marital status. **S~ Maggiore** *Mil* General Staff. **Stati** *pl* **Uniti [d'America]** United States [of America]

'statua *nf* statue

statuni'tense *a* United States *attrib*, US *attrib* ● *nmf* citizen of the United States, US citizen

sta'tura *nf* height; **di alta ~** tall; **di bassa ~** short

sta'tuto *nm* statute

stazio'nario *a* stationary

stazi'one *nf* station; ⟨*città*⟩ resort. **~ balneare** seaside resort. **~ ferroviaria** railway station *Br*, train station. **~ di servizio** petrol station *Br*, service station. **~ termale** spa

'stecca *nf* stick; ⟨*di ombrello*⟩ rib; ⟨*da biliardo*⟩ cue; *Med* splint; ⟨*di sigarette*⟩ carton; ⟨*di reggiseno*⟩ stiffener

stec'cato *nm* fence

stec'chito *a* skinny; ⟨*rigido*⟩ stiff; ⟨*morto*⟩ stone cold dead

'stella *nf* star; **salire alle stelle** ⟨*prezzi:*⟩ rise skyhigh. **~ alpina** edelweiss. **~ cadente** shooting star. **~ filante** streamer. **~ di mare** starfish

stel'la|re *a* star *attrib*; ⟨*grandezza*⟩ stellar. **~to** *a* starry

'stelo *nm* stem; **lampada** *nf* **a ~** standard lamp

'stemma *nm* coat of arms

stempi'ato *a* bald at the temples

sten'dardo *nm* standard

'stender|e *vt* spread out; ⟨*appendere*⟩ hang out; ⟨*distendere*⟩ stretch [out]; ⟨*scrivere*⟩ write down. **~si** *vr* stretch out

stendibianche'ria *nm* *inv*, **stendi'toio** *nm* clothes horse

stenodatti|logra'fia *nf* shorthand typing. **~'lografo, -a** *nmf* shorthand typist

stenogra'f|are *vt* take down in shorthand. **~ia** *nf* shorthand

sten'ta|re *vi* **~re a** find it hard to. **~to** *a* laboured. **'stento** *nm* ⟨*fatica*⟩ effort; **a stento** with difficulty; **stenti** *pl* hardships, privations

'sterco *nm* dung

'stereo['fonico] *a* stereo[phonic]

stereoti'pato *a* stereotyped; ⟨*sorriso*⟩ insincere. **stere'otipo** *nm* stereotype

'steril|e *a* sterile; ⟨*terreno*⟩ barren. **~ità** *nf* sterility. **~iz'zare** *vt* sterilize. **~izzazi'one** *nf* sterilization

ster'lina *nf* pound; **lira ~** [pound] sterling

stermi'nare *vt* exterminate

stermi'nato *a* immense

ster'minio *nm* extermination

'sterno *nm* breastbone

ster'zare *vi* steer. **'sterzo** *nm* steering

'steso *pp di* **stendere**

'stesso *a* same; **io ~** myself; **tu ~** yourself; **me ~** myself; **se ~** himself; **in quel momento ~** at that very moment; **dalla stessa regina** ⟨*in persona*⟩ by the Queen herself; **tuo fratello ~ dice che hai torto** even your brother says you're wrong; **coi miei stessi occhi** with my own eyes ● *pron* **lo ~** the same one; ⟨*la stessa cosa*⟩ the same; **fa lo ~** it's all the same; **ci vado lo ~** I'll go just the same

ste'sura *nf* drawing up; ⟨*documento*⟩ draft

stick *nm* **colla a ~** glue stick; **deodorante a ~** stick deodorant

'stigma *nm* stigma. **~te** *nfpl* stigmata

sti'lare *vt* draw up

'stil|e *nm* style. **~e libero** ⟨*nel nuoto*⟩ freestyle, crawl. **sti'lista** *nmf* stylist. **~iz'zato** *a* stylized

stil'lare *vi* ooze

stilo'grafic|a *nf* fountain pen. **~o** *a* **penna ~a** fountain pen

'stima *nf* esteem; ⟨*valutazione*⟩ estimate. **sti'mare** *vt* esteem; ⟨*valutare*⟩ estimate; ⟨*ritenere*⟩ consider

stimo'la|nte *a* stimulating ● *nm* stimulant. **~re** *vt* stimulate; ⟨*incitare*⟩ incite

'stimolo *nm* stimulus; ⟨*fitta*⟩ pang

'stinco *nm* shin

'stinger|e *vt/i* fade. **~si** *vr* fade. **'stinto** *pp di* **stingere**

sti'par|e *vt* cram. **~si** *vr* crowd together

stipendi'ato *a* salaried ● *nm* salaried worker. **sti'pendio** *nm* salary

'stipite *nm* doorpost

stipu'la|re *vt* stipulate. **~zi'one** *nf* stipulation; ⟨*accordo*⟩ agreement

stira'mento *nm* sprain

sti'ra|re *vt* iron; ⟨*distendere*⟩ stretch. **~rsi** *vr* ⟨*distendersi*⟩ stretch; pull ⟨*muscolo*⟩. **~'tura** *nf* ironing. **'stiro** *nm* **ferro da stiro** iron

'stirpe *nf* stock

stiti'chezza *nf* constipation. **'stitico** *a* constipated

'stiva *nf* *Naut* hold

sti'vale *nm* boot. **stivali** *pl* **di gomma** Wellington boots, Wellingtons

'stizza *nf* anger

stiz'zi|re *vt* irritate. **~rsi** *vr* become irritated. **~to** *a* irritated. **stiz'zoso** *a* peevish

stocca'fisso *nm* stockfish

stoc'cata *nf* stab; ⟨*battuta pungente*⟩ gibe

'stoffa *nf* material; *fig* stuff

'stola *nf* stole

'stolto *a* foolish

stoma'chevole *a* revolting

'stomaco *nm* stomach; **mal di ~** stomach-ache

sto'na|re *vt/i* sing/play out of tune ● *vi* ⟨*non intonarsi*⟩ clash. **~to** *a* out of tune; ⟨*discordante*⟩ clashing; ⟨*confuso*⟩ bewildered. **~'tura** *nf* false note; ⟨*discordanza*⟩ clash

'stoppia *nf* stubble

stop'pino *nm* wick

stop'poso *a* tough

'storcer|e *vt*, **~si** *vr* twist

stor'di|re *vt* stun; ⟨*intontire*⟩ daze. **~rsi** *vr* dull one's senses. **~to** *a* stunned; ⟨*intontito*⟩ dazed; ⟨*sventato*⟩ heedless

215

'storia *nf* history; (*racconto, bugia*) story; (*pretesto*) excuse; **senza storie!** no fuss! **fare [delle] storie** make a fuss

'storico, -a *a* historical; (*di importanza storica*) historic ● *nmf* historian

stori'one *nm* sturgeon

'stormo *nm* flock

'storno *nm* starling

storpi'a|re *vt* cripple; mangle (*parole*). **~'tura** *nf* deformation. **'storpio, -a** *a* crippled ● *nmf* cripple

'stort|a *nf* (*distorsione*) sprain; **prendere una ~a alla caviglia** sprain one's ankle. **~o** *pp di* **storcere** ● *a* crooked; (*ritorto*) twisted; (*gambe*) bandy; *fig* wrong

sto'viglie *nfpl* crockery *sg*

'strabico *a* cross-eyed; **essere ~** be cross-eyed, have a squint.

strabili'ante *a* astonishing

stra'bismo *nm* squint

straboc'care *vi* overflow

stra'carico *a* overloaded

stracci|'are *vt* tear; (*fam: vincere*) thrash. **~'ato** *a* torn; (*persona*) in rags; (*prezzi*) slashed; **a un prezzo ~ato** dirt cheap. **'straccio** *a* torn ● *nm* rag; (*strofinaccio*) cloth **~'one** *nm* tramp

stra'cotto *a* overdone; (*fam: innamorato*) head over heels ● *nm* stew

'strada *nf* road; (*di città*) street; (*fig: cammino*) way; **essere fuori ~** be on the wrong track; **fare ~** lead the way; **farsi ~** make one's way. **~ maestra** main road. **~ a senso unico** one-way street. **~ senza uscita** blind alley. **stra'dale** *a* road *attrib*

strafalci'one *nm* blunder

stra'fare *vi* overdo it, overdo things

stra'foro: di ~ *adv* on the sly

strafot'ten|te *a* arrogant. **~za** *nf* arrogance

'strage *nf* slaughter

'stralcio *nm* (*parte*) extract

stralu'na|re *vt* **~re gli occhi** open one's eyes wide. **~to** *a* (*occhi*) staring; (*persona*) distraught

stramaz'zare *vi* fall heavily

strambe'ria *nf* oddity. **'strambo** *a* strange

strampa'lato *a* odd

stra'nezza *nf* strangeness

strango'lare *vt* strangle

strani'ero, -a *a* foreign ● *nmf* foreigner

'strano *a* strange

straordi|naria'mente *adv* extraordinarily. **~'nario** *a* extraordinary; (*notevole*) remarkable; (*edizione*) special; **lavoro ~nario** overtime; **treno ~nario** special train

strapaz'zar|e *vt* ill-treat; scramble (*uova*). **~si** *vr* tire oneself out.

stra'pazzo *nm* strain; **da strapazzo** *fig* worthless

strapi'eno *a* overflowing

strapi'ombo *nm* projection; **a ~** sheer

strap'par|e *vt* tear; (*per distruggere*) tear up; pull out (*dente, capelli*); (*sradicare*) pull up; (*estorcere*) wring. **~si** *vr* get torn; (*allontanarsi*) tear oneself away. **'strappo** *nm* tear; (*strattone*) jerk; (*fam: passaggio*) lift; **fare uno strappo alla regola** make an exception to the rule. **~ muscolare** muscle strain

strapun'tino *nm* folding seat

strari'pare *vi* flood

strasci'c|are *vt* trail; shuffle (*piedi*); drawl (*parole*). **'strascico** *nm* train; *fig* after-effect

strass *nm inv* rhinestone

strata'gemma *nm* stratagem

strate'gia *nf* strategy. **stra'tegico** *a* strategic

'strato *nm* layer; (*di vernice ecc*) coat, layer; (*roccioso, sociale*) stratum. **~'sfera** *nf* stratosphere. **~'sferico** *a* stratospheric; *fig* sky-high

stravac'ca|rsi *vr fam* slouch. **~to** *a* *fam* slouching

strava'gan|te *a* extravagant; (*eccentrico*) eccentric. **~za** *nf* extravagance; (*eccentricità*) eccentricity

stra'vecchio *a* ancient

strave'dere *vt* **~ per** worship

stravizi'are *vi* indulge oneself. **stra'vizio** *nm* excess

stra'volg|ere *vt* twist; (*turbare*) upset. **~i'mento** *nm* twisting. **stra'volto** *a* distraught; (*fam: stanco*) done in

strazi'a|nte *a* heartrending; (*dolore*) agonizing. **~re** *vt* grate on (*orecchie*); break (*cuore*). **'strazio** *nm* agony; **essere uno strazio** be agony; **che strazio!** *fam* it's awful!

'strega *nf* witch. **stre'gare** *vt* bewitch. **stre'gone** *nm* wizard

'stregua *nf* **alla ~ di** like

stre'ma|re *vt* exhaust. **~to** *a* exhausted

'stremo *nm* **ridotto allo ~** at the end of one's tether

'strenuo *a* strenuous

strepi|'tare *vi* make a din. **'strepito**

nm noise. **~'toso** *a* noisy; *fig* resounding

stres'sa|nte *a* ⟨*lavoro, situazione*⟩ stressful. **~to** *a* stressed [out]

'stretta *nf* grasp; ⟨*dolore*⟩ pang; **essere alle strette** be in dire straits; **mettere alle strette** qcno have sb's back up against the wall. **~ di mano** handshake

stret'tezza *nf* narrowness; **stret'tezze** *pl* ⟨*difficoltà finanziarie*⟩ financial difficulties

'stret|to *pp di* **stringere** ● *a* narrow; ⟨*serrato*⟩ tight; ⟨*vicino*⟩ close; ⟨*dialetto*⟩ broad; ⟨*rigoroso*⟩ strict; **lo ~to necessario** the bare minimum ● *nm* Geog strait. **~'toia** *nf* bottleneck; ⟨*fam: difficoltà*⟩ tight spot

stri'a|to *a* striped. **~'tura** *nf* streak

stri'dente *a* strident

'stridere *vi* squeak; *fig* clash. **stri'dore** *nm* screech

'stridulo *a* shrill

strigli'a|re *vt* groom. **~ta** *nf* grooming; *fig* dressing down

stril'l|are *vi/t* scream. **'strillo** *nm* scream

strimin'zito *a* skimpy; ⟨*magro*⟩ skinny

strimpel'lare *vt* strum

'strin|ga *nf* lace; *Comput* string. **~'gato** *a fig* terse

'stringer|e *vt* press; ⟨*serrare*⟩ squeeze; ⟨*tenere stretto*⟩ hold tight; take in ⟨*abito*⟩; ⟨*comprimere*⟩ be tight; ⟨*restringere*⟩ tighten; **~e la mano a** shake hands with ● *vi* ⟨*premere*⟩ press. **~si** *vr* ⟨*accostarsi*⟩ draw close (**a** to); ⟨*avvicinarsi*⟩ squeeze up

'striscia *nf* strip; ⟨*riga*⟩ stripe. **strisce** *pl* [pedonali] zebra crossing *sg*

strisci'ar|e *vi* crawl; ⟨*sfiorare*⟩ graze ● *vt* drag ⟨*piedi*⟩. **~si** *vr* **~si a** rub against. **'striscio** *nm* graze; *Med* smear; **colpire di striscio** graze

strisci'one *nm* banner

strito'lare *vt* grind

striz'zare *vt* squeeze; ⟨*torcere*⟩ wring [out]; **~ l'occhio** wink

'strofa *nf* strophe

strofi'naccio *nm* cloth; ⟨*per spolverare*⟩ duster. **~ da cucina** tea towel

strofi'nare *vt* rub

strombaz'zare *vt* boast about ● *vi* hoot

strombaz'zata *nf* ⟨*di clacson*⟩ hoot

stron'care *vt* cut off; ⟨*reprimere*⟩ crush; ⟨*criticare*⟩ tear to shreds

'stronzo *nm vulg* shit

stropicci'are *vt* rub; crumple ⟨*vestito*⟩

stroz'za|re *vt* strangle. **~'tura** *nf* strangling; ⟨*di strada*⟩ narrowing

strozzi'naggio *nm* loan-sharking

stroz'zino *nm pej* usurer; ⟨*truffatore*⟩ shark

strug'gente *a* all-consuming

'struggersi *vr liter* pine [away]

strumen'tale *a* instrumental

strumentaliz'zare *vt* make use of

strumentazi'one *nf* instrumentation

stru'mento *nm* instrument; ⟨*arnese*⟩ tool. **~ a corda** string instrument. **~ musicale** musical instrument

strusci'are *vt* rub

'strutto *nm* lard

strut'tura *nf* structure. **struttu'rale** *a* structural

struttu'rare *vt* structure

strutturazi'one *nf* structuring

'struzzo *nm* ostrich

stuc'ca|re *vt* stucco

stuc'chevole *a* nauseating

'stucco *nm* stucco

stu'den|te, -'essa *nmf* student; ⟨*di scuola*⟩ schoolboy; schoolgirl. **~'tesco** *a* student; ⟨*di scolaro*⟩ school *attrib*

studi'ar|e *vt* study. **~si** *vr* **~si di** try to

'studi|o *nm* studying; ⟨*stanza, ricerca*⟩ study; ⟨*di artista, TV ecc*⟩ studio; ⟨*di professionista*⟩ office. **~'oso, -a** *a* studious ● *nmf* scholar

'stufa *nf* stove. **~ elettrica** electric fire

stu'fa|re *vt Culin* stew; ⟨*dare fastidio*⟩ bore. **~rsi** *vr* get bored. **~to** *nm* stew

'stufo *a* bored; **essere ~ di** be fed up with

stu'oia *nf* mat

stupefa'cente *a* amazing ● *nm* drug

stu'pendo *a* stupendous

stupi'd|aggine *nf* ⟨*azione*⟩ stupid thing; ⟨*cosa da poco*⟩ nothing. **~ata** *nf* stupid thing. **~ità** *nf* stupidity. **'stupido** *a* stupid

stu'pir|e *vt* astonish ● *vi*, **~si** *vr* be astonished. **stu'pore** *nm* amazement

stu'pra|re *vt* rape. **~'tore** *nm* rapist. **'stupro** *nm* rape

sturalavan'dini *nm inv* plunger

stu'rare *vt* uncork; unblock ⟨*lavandino*⟩

stuzzica'denti *nm inv* toothpick

stuzzi'care *vt* prod [at]; pick ⟨*denti*⟩; poke ⟨*fuoco*⟩; ⟨*molestare*⟩ tease; whet ⟨*appetito*⟩

stuzzi'chino *nm Culin* appetizer

su *prep* on; (*senza contatto*) over; (*riguardo a*) about; (*circa, intorno a*) about, around; **le chiavi sono sul tavolo** the keys are on the table; **il quadro è appeso sul camino** the picture is hanging over the fireplace; **un libro sull'antico Egitto** a book on *o* about Ancient Egypt; **costa sulle 50 000 lire** it costs about 50,000 lire; **decidere sul momento** decide at the time; **su commissione** on commission; **su due piedi** on the spot; **uno su dieci** one out of ten ● *adv* (*sopra*) up; (*al piano di sopra*) upstairs; (*addosso*) on; **ho su il cappotto** I've got my coat on; **in su** ⟨*guardare*⟩ up; **dalla vita in su** from the waist up; **su!** come on!

su'bacqueo *a* underwater

subaffit'tare *vt* sublet. **subaf'fitto** *nm* sublet

subal'terno *a & nm* subordinate

sub'buglio *nm* turmoil

sub'conscio *a & nm* subconscious

subdola'mente *adv* deviously. **'subdolo** *a* devious, underhand

suben'trare *vi* ⟨*circostanze:*⟩ come up; **~ a** take the place of

su'bire *vt* undergo; (*patire*) suffer

subis'sare *vt fig* **~ di** overwhelm with

'subito *adv* at once; **~ dopo** straight after

su'blime *a* sublime

subodo'rare *vt* suspect

subordi'nato, -a *a & nmf* subordinate

subur'bano *a* suburban

suc'ceder|e *vi* (*accadere*) happen; **~e a** succeed; (*venire dopo*) follow; **~e al trono** succeed to the throne. **~si** *vr* happen one after the other

successi'one *nf* succession; **in ~** in succession

succes|siva'mente *adv* subsequently. **~'sivo** *a* successive

suc'ces|so *pp di* **succedere** ● *nm* success; (*esito*) outcome; (*disco ecc*) hit. **~'sone** *nm* huge success

succes'sore *nm* successor

succhi'are *vt* suck [up]

suc'cinto *a* (*conciso*) concise; ⟨*abito*⟩ scanty

'succo *nm* juice; *fig* essence; **~ di frutta** fruit juice. **suc'coso** *a* juicy

'succube *nm* **essere ~ di qcno** be totally dominated by sb

succu'lento *a* succulent

succur'sale *nf* branch [office]

sud *nm* south; **del ~** southern

su'da|re *vi* sweat, perspire; (*faticare*) sweat blood; **~re freddo** be in a cold sweat. **~ta** *nf anche fig* sweat. **~'ticcio** *a* sweaty. **~to** *a* sweaty; ⟨*vittoria*⟩ hard-won; ⟨*pane*⟩ hard-earned

sud'detto *a* above-mentioned

'suddito, -a *nmf* subject

suddi'vi|dere *vt* subdivide. **~si'one** *nf* subdivision

su'd-est *nm* southeast

'sudici|o *a* dirty, filthy. **~'ume** *nm* dirt, filth

sudorazi'one *nf* perspiring. **su'dore** *nm* sweat, perspiration; *fig* sweat

su'd-ovest *nm* southwest

suffici'en|te *a* sufficient; (*presuntuoso*) conceited ● *nm* bare essentials *pl*; *Sch* pass mark. **~za** *nf* sufficiency; (*presunzione*) conceit; *Sch* pass; **a ~za** enough

suf'fisso *nm* suffix

suf'fragio *nm* (*voto*) vote. **~ universale** universal suffrage

suggeri'mento *nm* suggestion

sugge'ri|re *vt* suggest; *Theat* prompt. **~'tore, ~'trice** *nmf Theat* prompter

suggestiona'bile *a* suggestible

suggestio'na|re *vt* influence. **~to** *a* influenced. **suggesti'one** *nf* influence

sugge'stivo *a* suggestive; ⟨*musica ecc*⟩ evocative

'sughero *nm* cork

'sugli = **su** + **gli**

'sugo *nm* (*di frutta*) juice; (*di carne*) gravy; (*salsa*) sauce; (*sostanza*) substance

'sui = **su** + **i**

sui'cid|a *a* suicidal ● *nmf* suicide. **suici'darsi** *vr* commit suicide. **~io** *nm* suicide

su'ino *a* **carne suina** pork ● *nm* swine

sul = **su** + **il**. **'sullo** = **su** + **lo**. **'sulla** = **su** + **la**. **'sulle** = **su** + **le**

sul'ta|na *nf* sultana. **~'nina** *a* **uva ~nina** sultana. **~no** *nm* sultan

'sunto *nm* summary

'suo, -a *poss a* **il ~, i suoi** his; (*di cosa, animale*) its; (*forma di cortesia*) your; **la sua, le sue** her; (*di cosa, animale*) its; (*forma di cortesia*) your; **questa macchina è sua** this car is his/hers; **~ padre** his/her/your father; **un ~ amico** a friend of his/hers/yours ● *poss pron* **il ~, i suoi** his; (*di cosa, animale*) its; (*forma di cortesia*) yours; **la sua, le sue** hers; (*di cosa animale*) its; (*forma di cortesia*) yours; **i suoi** his/her folk

su'ocera *nf* mother-in-law

su'ocero nm father-in-law

su'ola nf sole

su'olo nm ground; (terreno) soil

suo'na|re vt/i Mus play; ring ⟨campanello⟩; sound ⟨allarme, clacson⟩; ⟨orologio:⟩ strike. ~'tore, ~'trice nmf player. **suone'ria** nf alarm. **su'ono** nm sound

su'ora nf nun; **Suor Maria** Sister Maria

superal'colico nm spirit ● a **bevande superalcoliche** spirits

supera'mento nm (di timidezza) overcoming; (di esame) success (di in)

supe'rare vt surpass; (eccedere) exceed; (vincere) overcome; overtake, pass Am ⟨veicolo⟩; pass ⟨esame⟩

su'perb|ia nf haughtiness. ~o a haughty; (magnifico) superb

superdo'tato a highly gifted

superfici'al|e a superficial ● nmf superficial person. ~ità nf superficiality. **super'ficie** nf surface; (area) area

su'perfluo a superfluous

superi'or|e a superior; (di grado) senior; (più elevato) higher; (sovrastante) upper; (al di sopra) above ● nmf superior. ~ità nf superiority

superla'tivo a & nm superlative

supermer'cato nm supermarket

super'sonico a supersonic

su'perstite a surviving ● nmf survivor

superstizi'o|ne nf superstition. ~so a superstitious

super'strada nf toll-free motorway

supervi'si|one nf supervision. ~'sore nm supervisor

su'pino a supine

suppel'lettili nfpl furnishings

suppergiù adv about

supplemen'tare a additional, supplementary

supple'mento nm supplement; ~ **rapido** express train supplement

sup'plen|te a temporary ● nmf Sch supply teacher. ~za nf temporary post

'suppli|ca nf plea; (domanda) petition. ~'care vt beg. ~'chevole a imploring

sup'plire vt replace ● vi ~ **a** (compensare) make up for

sup'plizio nm torture

sup'porre vt suppose

sup'porto nm support

supposizi'one nf supposition

sup'posta nf suppository

sup'posto pp di **supporre**

suprema'zia nf supremacy. **su'premo** a supreme

sur'fare vi ~ **in Internet** surf the Net

surge'la|re vt deep-freeze. ~ti nmpl frozen food sg. ~**to** a frozen

surrea'lis|mo nm surrealism. ~ta nmf surrealist

surriscal'dare vt overheat

surro'gato nm substitute

suscet'tibil|e a touchy. ~ità nf touchiness

susci'tare vt stir up; arouse ⟨ammirazione ecc⟩

su'sin|a nf plum. ~o nm plumtree

su'spense nf suspense

sussegu'|ente a subsequent. ~'irsi vr follow one after the other

sussidi'ar|e vt subsidize. ~io a subsidiary. **sus'sidio** nm subsidy; (aiuto) aid. **sussidio di disoccupazione** unemployment benefit

sus'siego nm haughtiness

sussi'stenza nf subsistence. **sus'sistere** vi subsist; (essere valido) hold good

sussul'tare vi start. **sus'sulto** nm start

sussur'rare vt whisper. **sus'surro** nm whisper

su'tu|ra nf suture. ~'rare vt suture

sva'gar|e vt amuse. ~si vr amuse oneself. **'svago** nm relaxation; (divertimento) amusement

svaligi'are vt rob; burgle ⟨casa⟩

svalu'ta|re vt devalue; fig underestimate. ~rsi vr lose value. ~zi'one nf devaluation

svam'pito a absent-minded

sva'nire vi vanish

svantaggi'|ato a at a disadvantage; ⟨bambino, paese⟩ disadvantaged. **svan'taggio** nm disadvantage; **essere in svantaggio** Sport be losing; **in svantaggio di tre punti** three points down; ~'oso a disadvantageous

svapo'rare vi evaporate

svari'ato a varied

sva'sato a flared

'svastica nf swastika

sve'dese a & nm (lingua) Swedish ● nmf Swede

'sveglia nf (orologio) alarm [clock]; ~! get up!; **mettere la** ~ set the alarm [clock]

svegli'ar|e vt wake up; fig awaken. ~si vr wake up. **'sveglio** a awake; (di mente) quick-witted

sve'lare vt reveal

svel'tezza nf speed; fig quick-wittedness

svel'tir|e *vt* quicken. **~si** *vr* ⟨persona:⟩ liven up. **'svelto** *a* quick; (*slanciato*) svelte; **alla svelta** quickly

'svend|ere *vt* undersell. **~ita** *nf* [clear-ance] sale

sveni'mento *nm* fainting fit. **sve'nire** *vi* faint

sven'ta|re *vt* foil. **~to** *a* thoughtless ● *nmf* thoughtless person

'sventola *nf* slap; **orecchie** *nfpl* **a ~** protruding ears

svento'lare *vt/i* wave

sven'trare *vt* disembowel; *fig* demol-ish ⟨edificio⟩

sven'tura *nf* misfortune. **sventu'rato** *a* unfortunate

sve'nuto *pp di* svenire

svergo'gnato *a* shameless

sver'nare *vi* winter

sve'stir|e *vt* undress. **~si** *vr* undress, get undressed

'Svezia *nf* Sweden

svezza'mento *nm* weaning. **svez'zare** *vt* wean

svi'ar|e *vt* divert; (*corrompere*) lead astray. **~si** *vr fig* go astray

svico'lare *vi* turn down a side street; (*fig: dalla questione ecc*) evade the issue; (*fig: da una persona*) dodge out of the way

svi'gnarsela *vr* slip away

svi'lire *vt* debase

svilup'par|e *vt*, **~si** *vr* develop. **svi'luppo** *nm* development; **paese in via di sviluppo** developing country

svinco'lar|e *vt* release; clear ⟨merce⟩. **~si** *vr* free oneself. **'svincolo** *nm* clear-ance; (*di autostrada*) exit

svisce'ra|re *vt* gut; *fig* dissect. **~to** *a* ⟨amore⟩ passionate; (*ossequioso*) obse-quious

'svista *nf* oversight

svi'ta|re *vt* unscrew. **~to** *a* (*fam: matto*) cracked, nutty

'Svizzer|a *nf* Switzerland. **s~o, -a** *a* & *nmf* Swiss

svogli|a'tezza *nf* half-heartedness. **~'ato** *a* lazy

svolaz'za|nte *a* ⟨capelli⟩ wind-swept. **~re** *vi* flutter

'svolger|e *vt* unwind; unwrap ⟨pacco⟩; (*risolvere*) solve; (*portare a termine*) carry out; (*sviluppare*) develop. **~si** *vr* (*accadere*) take place. **svolgi'mento** *nm* course; (*sviluppo*) development

'svolta *nf* turning; *fig* turning-point. **svol'tare** *vi* turn

'svolto *pp di* svolgere

svuo'tare *vt* empty [out]

Tt

tabac'c|aio, -a *nmf* tobacconist. **~he'ria** *nf* tobacconist's (*which also sells stamps, postcards etc*). **ta'bacco** *nm* tobacco

ta'bel|la *nf* table; (*lista*) list. **~la dei prezzi** price list. **~'lina** *nf Math* multi-plication table. **~'lone** *nm* wall chart. **~lone del canestro** backboard

taber'nacolo *nm* tabernacle

tabù *a* & *nm inv* taboo

tabu'lato *nm Comput* [data] printout

'tacca *nf* notch; **di mezza ~** ⟨attore, giornalista⟩ second-rate

tac'cagno *a fam* stingy

tac'cheggio *nm* shoplifting

tac'chetto *nm Sport* stud

tac'chino *nm* turkey

tacci'are *vt* **~ qcno di qcsa** accuse sb of sth

'tacco *nm* heel; **alzare i tacchi** take to one's heels; **scarpe senza ~** flat shoes. **tacchi** *pl* **a spillo** stiletto heels

tac'cuino *nm* notebook

ta'cere *vi* be silent ● *vt* say nothing about; **mettere a ~ qcsa** ⟨scandalo⟩ hush sth up; **mettere a ~ qcno** silence sb

ta'chimetro *nm* speedometer

'tacito *a* silent; (*inespresso*) tacit. **taci'turno** *a* taciturn

ta'fano *nm* horsefly

taffe'ruglio *nm* scuffle

'taglia *nf* (*riscatto*) ransom; (*ricom-pensa*) reward; (*statura*) height; (*misu-ra*) size. **~ unica** one size

tagliacarte | tappo

220

taglia'carte *nm inv* paperknife
taglia'erba *nm inv* lawn-mower
tagliafu'oco *a inv* **porta ~** fire door; **striscia ~** fire break
tagli'ando *nm* coupon; **fare il ~** ≈ put one's car in for its MOT
tagli'ar|e *vt* cut; (*attraversare*) cut across; (*interrompere*) cut off; (*togliere*) cut out; carve ‹carne›; mow ‹erba›; **farsi ~e i capelli** have a haircut ● *vi* cut. **~si** *vr* cut oneself; **~si i capelli** have a haircut
taglia'telle *nfpl* tagliatelle *sg, thin, flat strips of egg pasta*
taglieggi'are *vt* extort money from
tagli'e|nte *a* sharp ● *nm* cutting edge. **~re** *nm* chopping board
'taglio *nm* cut; (*il tagliare*) cutting; (*di stoffa*) length; (*parte tagliente*) edge; **a doppio ~** double-edged. **~ cesareo** Caesarean section
tagli'ola *nf* trap
tagli'one *nm* **legge del ~** an eye for an eye and a tooth for a tooth
tagliuz'zare *vt* cut into small pieces
tail'leur *nm inv* [lady's] suit
talassotera'pia *nf* thalassotherapy
'talco *nm* talcum powder
'tale *a* such a; (*con nomi plurali*) such; **c'è un ~ disordine** there is such a mess; **non accetto tali scuse** I won't accept such excuses; **il rumore era ~ che non si sentiva nulla** there was so much noise you couldn't hear yourself think; **il ~ giorno** on such and such a day; **quel tal signore** that gentleman; **~ quale** just like ● *pron* **un ~** someone; **quel ~** that man; **il tal dei tali** such and such a person
ta'lento *nm* talent
tali'smano *nm* talisman
tallo'nare *vt* be hot on the heels of
tallon'cino *nm* coupon
tal'lone *nm* heel
tal'mente *adv* so
ta'lora *adv* = **talvolta**
'talpa *nf* mole
tal'volta *adv* sometimes
tamburel'lare *vi* (*con le dita*) drum; ‹pioggia:› beat, drum. **tambu'rello** *nm* tambourine. **tambu'rino** *nm* drummer. **tam'buro** *nm* drum
Ta'migi *nm* Thames
tampona'mento *nm* Auto collision; (*di ferita*) dressing; (*di falla*) plugging. **~ a catena** pile-up. **tampo'nare** *vt* (*urtare*) crash into; (*otturare*) plug. **tam'pone** *nm* swab; (*per timbri*) pad;

(*per mestruazioni*) tampon; (*per treni, Comput*) buffer
'tana *nf* den
'tanfo *nm* stench
'tanga *nm inv* tanga
tan'gen|te *a* tangent ● *nf* tangent; (*somma*) bribe. **~'topoli** *nf* widespread corruption in Italy in the early 90s. **~zi'ale** *nf* orbital road
tan'gibile *a* tangible
'tango *nm* tango
tan'tino: un ~ *adv* a little [bit]
'tanto *a* [so] much; (*con nomi plurali*) [so] many, [such] a lot of; **~ tempo** [such] a long time; **non ha tanta pazienza** he doesn't have much patience; **~ tempo quanto ti serve** as much time as you need; **non è ~ intelligente quanto suo padre** he's not as intelligent as his father; **tanti amici quanti parenti** as many friends as relatives ● *pron* much; (*plurale*) many; (*tanto tempo*) a long time; **è un uomo come tanti** he's just an ordinary man; **tanti** (*molte persone*) many people; **non ci vuole così ~** it doesn't take that long; **~ quanto** as much as; **tanti quanti** as many as ● *conj* (*comunque*) anyway, in any case ● *adv* (*così*) so; (*con verbi*) so much; **~ debole** so weak; **è ~ ingenuo da crederle** he's naive enough to believe her; **di ~ in ~** every now and then; **~ l'uno come l'altro** both; **~ quanto** as much as; **tre volte ~** three times as much; **una volta ~** once in a while; **~ meglio così!** so much the better!; **tant'è** so much so; **~ per cambiare** for a change
'tappa *nf* stop; (*parte di viaggio*) stage
tappa'buchi *nm inv* stopgap
tap'par|e *vt* plug; cork ‹bottiglia›; **~e la bocca a qcno** *fam* shut sb up. **~si** *vr* **~si gli occhi** cover one's eyes; **~si il naso** hold one's nose; **~si le orecchie** put one's fingers in one's ears
tappa'rella *nf fam* roller blind
tappe'tino *nm* mat; Comput mouse mat. **~ antiscivolo** safety bathmat
tap'peto *nm* carpet; (*piccolo*) rug; **andare al ~** ‹pugilato:› hit the canvas; **mandare qcno al ~** knock sb down
tappez'z|are *vt* paper ‹pareti›; (*rivestire*) cover. **~e'ria** *nf* tapestry; (*di carta*) wallpaper; (*arte*) upholstery. **~i'ere** *nm* upholsterer; (*imbianchino*) decorator
'tappo *nm* plug; (*di sughero*) cork; (*di*

metallo, per penna) top; (*fam: persona piccola*) dwarf. **~ di sughero** cork

'tara *nf* (*difetto*) flaw; (*ereditaria*) hereditary defect; (*peso*) tare

ta'rantola *nf* tarantula

ta'ra|re *vt* calibrate ‹*strumento*›. **~to** *a Comm* discounted; *Techn* calibrated; *Med* with a hereditary defect; *fam* crazy

tarchi'ato *a* stocky

tar'dare *vi* be late ● *vt* delay

'tard|i *adv* late; **al più ~i** at the latest; **più ~i** later [on]; **sul ~i** late in the day; **far ~i** (*essere in ritardo*) be late; (*con gli amici*) stay up late; **a più ~i** I see you later. **tar'divo** *a* late; ‹*bambino*› retarded. **~o** *a* slow; (*tempo*) late

'targ|a *nf* plate; *Auto* numberplate. **~a di circolazione** numberplate. **tar'gato** *a* **un'auto targata...** a car with the registration number.... **~'hetta** *nf* (*su porta*) nameplate; (*sulla valigia*) name tag

ta'rif|fa *nf* rate, tariff. **~'fario** *nm* price list

tar'larsi *vr* get wormeaten. **'tarlo** *nm* woodworm

'tarma *nf* moth. **tar'marsi** *vr* get motheaten

ta'rocco *nm* tarot; **ta'rocchi** *pl* tarot

tartagli'are *vi* stutter

'tartaro *a & nm* tartar

tarta'ruga *nf* tortoise; (*di mare*) turtle; (*per pettine ecc*) tortoiseshell

tartas'sare *vt* (*angariare*) harass

tar'tina *nf* canapé

tar'tufo *nm* truffle

'tasca *nf* pocket; (*in borsa*) compartment; **da ~** pocket *attrib*; **avere le tasche piene di qcsa** *fam* have had a bellyful of sth. **~ da pasticciere** icing bag

ta'scabile *a* pocket *attrib* ● *nm* paperback

tasca'pane *nm inv* haversack

ta'schino *nm* breast pocket

'tassa *nf* tax; (*discrizione ecc*) fee; (*doganale*) duty. **~ di circolazione** road tax. **~ d'iscrizione** registration fee

tas'sametro *nm* taximeter

tas'sare *vt* tax

tassa|tiva'mente *adv* without question. **~'tivo** *a* peremptory

tassazi'one *nf* taxation

tas'sello *nm* wedge; (*di stoffa*) gusset

tassì *nm inv* taxi. **tas'sista** *nmf* taxi driver

'tasso¹ *nm Bot* yew; (*animale*) badger

'tasso² *nm Comm* rate. **~ di cambio** exchange rate. **~ di interesse** interest rate

ta'stare *vt* feel; (*sondare*) sound; **~ il terreno** *fig* test the water *or* ground, feel one's way

tasti'e|ra *nf* keyboard. **~'rista** *nmf* keyboarder

'tasto *nm* key; (*tatto*) touch. **~ delicato** *fig* touchy subject. **~ funzione** *Comput* function key. **~ tabulatore** tab key

ta'stoni: a ~ *adv* gropingly

'tattica *nf* tactics *pl*

'tattico *a* tactical

'tatto *nm* (*senso*) touch; (*accortezza*) tact; **aver ~** be tactful

tatu'a|ggio *nm* tattoo. **~re** *vt* tattoo

'tavola *nf* table; (*illustrazione*) plate; (*asse*) plank. **~ calda** snackbar

tavo'lato *nm* boarding; (*pavimento*) wood floor

tavo'letta *nf* bar; (*medicinale*) tablet; **andare a ~** *Auto* drive flat out

tavo'lino *nm* small table

'tavolo *nm* table. **~ operatorio** *Med* operating table

tavo'lozza *nf* palette

'tazza *nf* cup; (*del water*) bowl. **~ da caffè/tè** coffee-cup/teacup

taz'zina *nf* **~ da caffè** espresso coffee cup

T.C.I. *abbr* (**Touring Club Italiano**) Italian Touring Club

te *pers pron* you; **te l'ho dato** I gave it to you

tè *nm inv* tea

tea'trale *a* theatrical

te'atro *nm* theatre. **~ all'aperto** open-air theatre. **~ di posa** *Cinema* set. **~ tenda** *marquee for theatre performances*

'tecnico, -a *a* technical ● *nmf* technician ● *nf* technique

tec'nigrafo *nm* drawing board

tecno|lo'gia *nf* technology. **~'logico** *a* technological

te'desco, -a *a & nmf* German

'tedi|o *nm* tedium. **~'oso** *a* tedious

te'game *nm* saucepan

'teglia *nf* baking tin

'tegola *nf* tile; *fig* blow

tei'era *nf* teapot

tek *nm* teak

'tela *nf* cloth; (*per quadri, vele*) canvas; *Theat* curtain. **~ cerata** oilcloth. **~ di lino** linen

te'laio *nm* (*di bicicletta, finestra*) frame; *Auto* chassis; (*per tessere*) loom

tele'camera *nf* television camera

teleco|man'dato *a* remote-controlled, remote control *attrib*. **~'mando** *nm* remote control

Telecom Italia *nf* Italian State telephone company

telecomunicazi'oni *nfpl* telecommunications

tele'cro|naca *nf* [television] commentary. **~naca diretta** live [television] coverage. **~naca registrata** recording. **~'nista** *nmf* television commentator

tele'ferica *nf* cableway

telefo'na|re *vt/i* [tele]phone, ring. **~ta** *nf* call. **~ta interurbana** long-distance call

telefonica'mente *adv* by [tele]phone

tele'fonico *a* [tele]phone *attrib*.

telefo'nino *nm* mobile [phone]

telefo'nista *nmf* operator

te'lefono *nm* [tele]phone. **~ senza filo** cordless [phone]. **~ a gettoni** pay phone, coin-box. **~ interno** internal telephone. **~ a schede** cardphone

telegior'nale *nm* television news *sg*

telegra'fare *vt* telegraph. **tele'grafico** *a* telegraphic; ⟨*risposta*⟩ monosyllabic; **sii telegrafico** keep it brief

tele'gramma *nm* telegram

tele'lavoro *nm* teleworking

tele'matica *nf* data communications, telematics

teleno'vela *nf* soap opera

teleobiet'tivo *nm* telephoto lens

telepa'tia *nf* telepathy

telero'manzo *nm* television serial

tele'schermo *nm* television screen

tele'scopio *nm* telescope

teleselezi'one *nf* subscriber trunk dialling, STD; **chiamare in ~** dial direct

telespetta'tore, -'trice *nmf* viewer

tele'text® *nm* Teletext®

televisi'one *nf* television; **guardare la ~** watch television

televi'sivo *a* television *attrib*; **operatore ~** television cameraman; **apparecchio ~** television set

televi'sore *nm* television [set]

'tema *nm* theme; *Sch* essay. **te'matica** *nf* main theme

teme'rario *a* reckless

te'mere *vt* be afraid of, fear ● *vi* be afraid, fear

tem'paccio *nm* filthy weather

temperama'tite *nm inv* pencil-sharpener

tempera'mento *nm* temperament

tempe'ra|re *vt* temper; sharpen ⟨*matita*⟩. **~to** *a* temperate. **~'tura** *nf* temperature. **~tura ambiente** room temperature

tempe'rino *nm* penknife

tem'pe|sta *nf* storm. **~sta di neve** snowstorm. **~sta di sabbia** sandstorm

tempe|stiva'mente *adv* quickly. **~'stivo** *a* timely. **~'stoso** *a* stormy

'tempia *nf Anat* temple

'tempio *nm Relig* temple

tem'pismo *nm* timing

'tempo *nm* time; (*atmosferico*) weather; *Mus* tempo; *Gram* tense; (*di film*) part; (*di partita*) half; **a suo ~** in due course; **~ fa** some time ago; **un ~** once; **ha fatto il suo ~** it's superannuated. **~ reale** real time. **~ supplementare** *Sport* extra time, overtime *Am*. **~'rale** *a* temporal ● *nm* [thunder]storm. **~ranea'mente** *adv* temporarily. **~'raneo** *a* temporary. **~reggi'are** *vi* play for time

tem'prare *vt* temper

te'nac|e *a* tenacious. **~ia** *nf* tenacity

te'naglia *nf* pincers *pl*

'tenda *nf* curtain; (*per campeggio*) tent; (*tendone*) awning. **~ a ossigeno** oxygen tent

ten'denz|a *nf* tendency. **~ial'mente** *adv* by nature. **~i'oso** *a* tendentious

'tendere *vt* (*allargare*) stretch [out]; (*tirare*) tighten; (*porgere*) hold out; *fig* lay ⟨*trappola*⟩ ● *vi* **~ a** aim at; (*essere portato a*) tend to

'tendine *nm* tendon

ten'do|ne *nm* awning; (*di circo*) tent. **~poli** *nf inv* tent city

'tenebre *nfpl* darkness. **tene'broso** *a* gloomy

te'nente *nm* lieutenant

tenera'mente *adv* tenderly

te'ner|e *vt* hold; (*mantenere*) keep; (*gestire*) run; (*prendere*) take; (*seguire*) follow; (*considerare*) consider ● *vi* hold; **~ci a**, **~e a** be keen on; **~e per** support ⟨*squadra*⟩. **~si** *vr* hold on (**a** to); (*in una condizione*) keep oneself; (*seguire*) stick to; **~si indietro** stand back

tene'rezza *nf* tenderness. **'tenero** *a* tender

'tenia *nf* tapeworm

'tennis *nm* tennis. **~ da tavolo** table tennis. **ten'nista** *nmf* tennis player

te'nore *nm* standard; *Mus* tenor; **a ~ di**

223

legge by law. ~ **di vita** standard of living

tensi'one *nf* tension; *Electr* voltage; **alta ~** high voltage

ten'tacolo *nm* tentacle

ten'ta|re *vt* attempt; (*sperimentare*) try; (*indurre in tentazione*) tempt. ~**'tivo** *nm* attempt. ~**zi'one** *nf* temptation

tenten|na'mento *nm* wavering. ~**'nare** *vi* waver

'tenue *a* fine; (*debole*) weak; (*esiguo*) small; (*leggero*) slight

te'nuta *nf* (*capacità*) capacity; (*Sport: resistenza*) stamina; (*possedimento*) estate; (*divisa*) uniform; (*abbigliamento*) clothes *pl*; **a ~ d'aria** airtight. **~ di strada** road holding

teolo'gia *nf* theology. **teo'logico** *a* theological. **te'ologo** *nm* theologian

teo'rema *nm* theorem

teo'ria *nf* theory

teorica'mente *adv* theoretically. **te'orico** *a* theoretical

te'pore *nm* warmth

'teppa *nf* mob. **tep'pismo** *nm* hooliganism. **tep'pista** *nm* hooligan

tera'peutico *a* therapeutic. **tera'pia** *nf* therapy

tergicri'stallo *nm* windscreen wiper, windshield wiper *Am*

tergilu'notto *nm* rear windscreen wiper

tergiver'sare *vi* hesitate

'tergo *nm* **a ~** behind; **segue a ~** please turn over, PTO

ter'male *a* thermal; **stazione ~** spa. **'terme** *nfpl* thermal baths

'termico *a* thermal

termi'na|le *a & nm* terminal; **malato ~le** terminally ill person. **~re** *vt/i* finish, end. **'termine** *nm* (*limite*) limit; (*fine*) end; (*condizione, espressione*) term

terminolo'gia *nf* terminology

'termite *nf* termite

termoco'perta *nf* electric blanket

ter'mometro *nm* thermometer

'termos *nm inv* thermos®

termosi'fone *nm* radiator; (*sistema*) central heating

ter'mostato *nm* thermostat

'terra *nf* earth; (*regione*) land; (*terreno*) ground; (*argilla*) clay; (*cosmetico*) dark face powder (*which gives the impression of a tan*); **a ~** (*sulla costa*) ashore; (*installazioni*) onshore; **per ~** on the ground; **sotto ~** underground. ~**'cot-**

ta *nf* terracotta; **vasellame di ~cotta** earthenware. ~**'ferma** *nf* dry land. ~**pi'eno** *nm* embankment

ter'razz|a *nf,* ~**o** *nm* balcony

terremo'tato, -a *a* (*zona*) affected by an earthquake ● *nmf* earthquake victim. **terre'moto** *nm* earthquake

ter'reno *a* earthly ● *nm* ground; (*suolo*) soil; (*proprietà terriera*) land; **perdere/guadagnare ~** lose/gain ground. **~ di gioco** playing field

ter'restre *a* terrestrial; **esercito ~** land forces *pl*

ter'ribil|e *a* terrible. ~**'mente** *adv* terribly

ter'riccio *nm* potting compost

terrifi'cante *a* terrifying

territori'ale *a* territorial. **terri'torio** *nm* territory

ter'rore *nm* terror

terro'ris|mo *nm* terrorism. ~**ta** *nmf* terrorist

terroriz'zare *vt* terrorize

'terso *a* clear

ter'zetto *nm* trio

terzi'ario *a* tertiary

'terzo *a* third; **di terz'ordine** (*locale, servizio*) third-rate; **fare il ~ grado a qn** give sb the third degree; **la terza età** the third age ● *nm* third; **terzi** *pl Jur* third party *sg*. **ter'zultimo, -a** *a & nmf* third from last

'tesa *nf* brim

'teschio *nm* skull

'tesi *nf inv* thesis

'teso *pp di* **tendere** ● *a* taut; *fig* tense

tesor|e'ria *nf* treasury. ~**i'ere** *nm* treasurer

te'soro *nm* treasure; (*tesoreria*) treasury

'tessera *nf* card; (*abbonamento all'autobus*) season ticket

'tessere *vt* weave; hatch (*complotto*)

tesse'rino *nm* travel card

'tessile *a* textile. **tessili** *nmpl* textiles; (*operai*) textile workers

tessi|'tore, -'trice *nmf* weaver. ~**'tura** *nf* weaving

tes'suto *nm* fabric; *Anat* tissue

'testa *nf* head; (*cervello*) brain; **essere in ~ a** be ahead of; **in ~** *Sport* in the lead; ~ **o croce?** heads or tails?; **fare ~ o croce** have a toss-up to decide

'testa-'coda *nm inv* **fare un ~** spin right round

testa'mento *nm* will; **T~** *Relig* Testament

testar'daggine *nf* stubbornness. **te'stardo** *a* stubborn

te'stata *nf* head; (*intestazione*) heading; (*colpo*) butt

'teste *nmf* witness

te'sticolo *nm* testicle

testi'mon|e *nmf* witness. **~e oculare** eye witness

testi'monial *nmf inv* celebrity who promotes a brand of cosmetics

testimoni|'anza *nf* testimony; **falsa ~anza** *Jur* perjury. **~'are** *vt* testify to ● *vi* testify, give evidence

'testo *nm* text; **far ~** be an authority

te'stone, -a *nmf* blockhead

testu'ale *a* textual

'tetano *nm* tetanus

'tetro *a* gloomy

tetta'rella *nf* teat

'tetto *nm* roof. **~ apribile** (*di auto*) sunshine roof. **tet'toia** *nf* roofing. **tet'tuccio** *nm* **tettuccio apribile** sunroof

'Tevere *nm* Tiber

ti *pers pron* you; (*riflessivo*) yourself; **ti ha dato un libro** he gave you a book; **lavati le mani** wash your hands; **eccoti!** here you are!; **sbrigati!** hurry up!

ti'ara *nf* tiara

tic *nm inv* tic

ticchet't|are *vi* tick. **~io** *nm* ticking

'ticchio *nm* tic; (*ghiribizzo*) whim

'ticket *nm inv* (*per farmaco, esame*) amount paid by National Health patients

tiepida'mente *adv* halfheartedly. **ti'epido** *a anche fig* lukewarm

ti'fare *vi* **~ per** shout for. **'tifo** *nm Med* typhus; **fare il tifo per** *fig* be a fan of

tifoi'dea *nf* typhoid

ti'fone *nm* typhoon

ti'foso, -a *nmf* fan

'tiglio *nm* lime

ti'grato *a* **gatto ~** tabby [cat]

'tigre *nf* tiger

'tilde *nmf* tilde

tim'ballo *nm Culin* pie

tim'brare *vt* stamp; **~ il cartellino** clock in/out

'timbro *nm* stamp; (*di voce*) tone

timida'mente *adv* timidly, shyly. **timi'dezza** *nf* timidity, shyness. **'timido** *a* timid, shy

'timo *nm* thyme

ti'mon|e *nm* rudder. **~i'ere** *nm* helmsman

ti'more *nm* fear; (*soggezione*) awe. **timo'roso** *a* timorous

'timpano *nm* eardrum; *Mus* kettledrum

ti'nello *nm* dining room

'tinger|e *vt* dye; (*macchiare*) stain. **~si** *vi* (*viso, cielo:*) be tinged (**di** with); **~si i capelli** have one's hair dyed; (*da solo*) dye one's hair

'tino *nm*, **ti'nozza** *nf* tub

'tint|a *nf* dye; (*colore*) colour; **in ~a unita** plain. **~a'rella** *nf fam* suntan

tintin'nare *vi* tinkle

'tinto *pp di* **tingere**. **~'ria** *nf* (*negozio*) cleaner's. **tin'tura** *nf* dyeing; (*colorante*) dye.

'tipico *a* typical

'tipo *nm* type; (*fam: individuo*) chap, guy

tipogra'fia *nf* printery; (*arte*) typography. **tipo'grafico** *a* typographic[al]. **ti'pografo** *nm* printer

tip tap *nm* tap dancing

ti'raggio *nm* draught

tiramisù *nm inv* dessert made of coffee-soaked sponge, eggs, Marsala, cream and cocoa powder

tiran|neggi'are *vt* tyrannize. **~'nia** *nf* tyranny. **ti'ranno, -a** *a* tyrannical ● *nmf* tyrant

tirapi'edi *nm inv pej* hanger-on

ti'rar|e *vt* pull; (*gettare*) throw; kick (*palla*); (*sparare*) fire; (*tracciare*) draw; (*stampare*) print ● *vi* pull; (*vento:*) blow; (*abito:*) be tight; (*sparare*) fire; **~e avanti** get by; **~e su** (*crescere*) bring up; (*da terra*) pick up; **tirar su col naso** sniffle. **~si** *vr* **~si indietro** *fig* back out, pull out

tiras'segno *nm* target shooting; (*alla fiera*) rifle range

ti'rata *nf* (*strattone*) pull, tug; **in una ~** in one go

tira'tore *nm* shot. **~ scelto** marksman

tira'tura *nf* printing; (*di giornali*) circulation; (*di libri*) [print] run

tirchie'ria *nf* meanness. **'tirchio** *a* mean

tiri'tera *nf* spiel

'tiro *nm* (*traino*) draught; (*lancio*) throw; (*sparo*) shot; (*scherzo*) trick. **~ con l'arco** archery. **~ alla fune** tug-of-war. **~ a segno** rifle-range

tiro'cinio *nm* apprenticeship

ti'roide *nf* thyroid

Tir'reno *nm* **il [mar] ~** the Tyrrhenian Sea

ti'sana *nf* herb[al] tea

225 | **titolare | tortino**

tito'lare *a* regular ● *nmf* principal; (*proprietario*) owner; (*calcio*) regular player

'titolo *nm* title; (*accademico*) qualification; *Comm* security; **a ~ di** as; **a ~ di favore** as a favour. **titoli** *pl* **di studio** qualifications

titu'ba|nte *a* hesitant. **~nza** *nf* hesitation. **~re** *vi* hesitate

tivù *nf inv fam* TV, telly

'tizio *nm* fellow

tiz'zone *nm* brand

toc'cante *a* touching

toc'ca|re *vt* touch; touch on (*argomento*); (*tastare*) feel; (*riguardare*) concern ● *vi* **~re a** (*capitare*) happen to; **mi tocca aspettare** I'll have to wait; **tocca a te** it's your turn; (*da pagare da bere*) it's your round

tocca'sana *nm inv* cure-all

'tocco *nm* touch; (*di pennello, orologio*) stroke; (*di pane ecc*) chunk ● *a fam* crazy, touched

'toga *nf* toga; (*accademica, di magistrato*) gown

'toglier|e *vt* take off (*coperta*); take away (*bambino da scuola, sete, Math*); take out, remove (*dente*); **~e qcsa di mano a qcno** take sth away from sb; **~e qcno dei guai** get sb out of trouble; **ciò non toglie che...** nevertheless... **~si** *vr* take off (*abito*); **~si la vita** take one's [own] life; **togliti dai piedi!** get out of here!

toilette *nf inv*, **to'letta** *nf* toilet; (*mobile*) dressing table

tolle'ra|nte *a* tolerant. **~nza** *nf* tolerance. **~re** *vt* tolerate

'tolto *pp di* **togliere**

to'maia *nf* upper

'tomba *nf* grave, tomb

tom'bino *nm* manhole cover

'tombola *nf* bingo; (*caduta*) tumble

'tomo *nm* tome

'tonaca *nf* habit

tonalità *nf inv Mus* tonality

'tondo *a* round ● *nm* circle

'tonfo *nm* thud; (*in acqua*) splash

'tonico *a & nm* tonic

tonifi'care *vt* brace

tonnel'la|ggio *nm* tonnage. **~ta** *nf* ton

'tonno *nm* tuna [fish]

'tono *nm* tone

ton'sil|la *nf* tonsil. **~'lite** *nf* tonsillitis

'tonto *a fam* thick

top *nm inv* (*indumento*) sun-top

to'pazio *nm* topaz

'topless *nm inv* **in ~** topless

'topo *nm* mouse. **~ di biblioteca** *fig* bookworm

topogra'fia *nf* topography. **topo'grafico** *a* topographic[al]

to'ponimo *nm* place name

'toppa *nf* (*rattoppo*) patch; (*serratura*) keyhole

to'race *nm* chest. **to'racico** *a* thoracic; **gabbia toracica** rib cage

'torba *nf* peat

'torbido *a* cloudy; *fig* troubled

'torcer|e *vt* twist; wring [out] (*biancheria*). **~si** *vr* twist

'torchio *nm* press

'torcia *nf* torch

torci'collo *nm* stiff neck

'tordo *nm* thrush

to'rero *nm* bullfighter

To'rino *nf* Turin

tor'menta *nf* snowstorm

tormen'tare *vt* torment. **tor'mento** *nm* torment

torna'conto *nm* benefit

tor'nado *nm* tornado

tor'nante *nm* hairpin bend

tor'nare *vi* return, go/come back; (*ridiventare*) become again; (*conto:*) add up; **~ a sorridere** become happy again

tor'neo *nm* tournament

'tornio *nm* lathe

'torno *nm* **togliersi di ~** get out of the way

'toro *nm* bull; *Astr* Taurus

tor'pedin|e *nf* torpedo. **~i'era** *nf* torpedo boat

tor'pore *nm* torpor

'torre *nf* tower; (*scacchi*) castle. **~ di controllo** control tower

torrefazi'one *nf* roasting

tor'ren|te *nm* torrent, mountain stream; (*fig: di lacrime*) flood. **~zi'ale** *a* torrential

tor'retta *nf* turret

'torrido *a* torrid

torri'one *nm* keep

tor'rone *nm* nougat

'torso *nm* torso; (*di mela, pera*) core; **a ~ nudo** bare-chested

'torsolo *nm* core

'torta *nf* cake; (*crostata*) tart

tortel'lini *nmpl* tortellini, *small packets of pasta stuffed with pork, ham, Parmesan and nutmeg*

torti'era *nf* baking tin

tor'tino *nm* pie

'torto *pp di* **torcere ●** *a* twisted **●** *nm* wrong; (*colpa*) fault; **aver ~** be wrong; **a ~** wrongly

'tortora *nf* turtle-dove

tortu'oso *a* winding; (*ambiguo*) tortuous

tor'tu|ra *nf* torture. **~'rare** *vt* torture

'torvo *a* grim

to'sare *vt* shear

tosa'tura *nf* shearing

To'scana *nf* Tuscany

'tosse *nf* cough

'tossico *a* toxic **●** *nm* poison. **tossi'comane** *nmf* drug addict, drug user

tos'sire *vi* cough

tosta'pane *nm inv* toaster

to'stare *vt* toast ⟨*pane*⟩; roast ⟨*caffè*⟩

'tosto *adv* (*subito*) soon **●** *a fam* cool

tot *a inv* **una cifra ~** such and such a figure **●** *nm* **un ~** so much

to'tal|e *a & nm* total. **~ità** *nf* entirety; **la ~ità dei presenti** all those present

totali'tario *a* totalitarian

totaliz'zare *vt* total; score ⟨*punti*⟩

total'mente *adv* totally

'totano *nm* squid

toto'calcio *nm* ≈ [football] pools *pl*

tournée *nf inv* tour

to'vagli|a *nf* tablecloth. **~'etta** *nf* ~**etta [all'americana]** place mat. **~'olo** *nm* napkin

'tozzo *a* squat **●** *nm* **~ di pane** stale piece of bread

tra = **fra**

trabal'la|nte *a* staggering; ⟨*sedia*⟩ rickety, wonky. **~re** *vi* stagger; ⟨*veicolo:*⟩ jolt

tra'biccolo *nm fam* contraption; (*auto*) jalopy

traboc'care *vi* overflow

traboc'chetto *nm* trap

tracan'nare *vt* gulp down

'tracci|a *nf* track; (*orma*) footstep; (*striscia*) trail; (*residuo*) trace; *fig* sign. **~'are** *vt* trace; sketch out ⟨*schema*⟩; draw ⟨*linea*⟩. **~'ato** *nm* (*schema*) layout

tra'chea *nf* windpipe

tra'colla *nf* shoulder-strap; **borsa a ~** shoulder-bag

tra'collo *nm* collapse

tradi'mento *nm* betrayal; *Pol* treason

tra'di|re *vt* betray; be unfaithful to ⟨*moglie, marito*⟩. **~'tore, ~'trice** *nmf* traitor

tradizio'na|le *a* traditional. **~'lista** *nmf* traditionalist. **~l'mente** *adv* traditionally. **tradizi'one** *nf* tradition

tra'dotto *pp di* **tradurre**

tra'du|rre *vt* translate. **~t'tore, ~t'trice** *nmf* translator. **~ttore elettronico** electronic phrasebook. **~zi'one** *nf* translation

tra'ente *nmf Comm* drawer

trafe'lato *a* breathless

traffi'ca|nte *nmf* dealer. **~nte di droga** [drug] pusher. **~re** *vi* (*affaccendarsi*) busy oneself; **~re in** *pej* traffic in. **'traffico** *nm* traffic; *Comm* trade

tra'figgere *vt* stab; (*straziare*) pierce

tra'fila *nf fig* rigmarole

trafo'rare *vt* bore, drill. **tra'foro** *nm* boring; (*galleria*) tunnel

trafu'gare *vt* steal

tra'gedia *nf* tragedy

traghet'tare *vt* ferry. **tra'ghetto** *nm* ferrying; (*nave*) ferry

tragica'mente *adv* tragically. **'tragico** *a* tragic **●** *nm* (*autore*) tragedian

tra'gitto *nm* journey; (*per mare*) crossing

tragu'ardo *nm* finishing post; (*meta*) goal

traiet'toria *nf* trajectory

trai'nare *vt* drag; (*rimorchiare*) tow

tralasci'are *vt* interrupt; (*omettere*) leave out

'tralcio *nm Bot* shoot

tra'liccio *nm* (*graticcio*) trellis

tram *nm inv* tram, streetcar *Am*

'trama *nf* weft; (*di film ecc*) plot

traman'dare *vt* hand down

tra'mare *vt* weave; (*macchinare*) plot

tram'busto *nm* turmoil, hullabaloo

trame'stio *nm* bustle

tramez'zino *nm* sandwich

tra'mezzo *nm* partition

'tramite *prep* through **●** *nm* link; **fare da ~** act as go-between

tramon'tana *nf* north wind

tramon'tare *vi* set; (*declinare*) decline. **tra'monto** *nm* sunset; (*declino*) decline

tramor'tire *vt* stun **●** *vi* faint

trampo'lino *nm* springboard; (*per lo sci*) ski-jump

'trampolo *nm* stilt

tramu'tare *vt* transform

'trancia *nf* shears *pl*; (*fetta*) slice

tra'nello *nm* trap

trangugi'are *vt* gulp down, gobble up

'tranne *prep* except

tranquilla'mente *adv* peacefully

tranquil'lante *nm* tranquillizer

tranquilli'tà *nf* calm; (*di spirito*) tranquillity. **~z'zare** *vt* reassure.

tran'quillo *a* quiet; (*pacifico*) peaceful; (*coscienza*) easy

transat'lantico *a* transatlantic ● *nm* ocean liner

tran'sa|tto *pp di* transigere. **~zi'one** *nf Comm* transaction

tran'senna *nf* (*barriera*) barrier

tran'sigere *vi* reach an agreement; (*cedere*) yield

transi'ta|bile *a* passable. **~re** *vi* pass

transi'tivo *a* transitive

'transi|to *nm* transit; **diritto di ~to** right of way; **"divieto di ~to"** "no thoroughfare". **~torio** *a* transitory. **~zi'one** *nf* transition

tran'tran *nm fam* routine

tranvi'ere *nm* tram driver; streetcar driver *Am*

'trapano *nm* drill

trapas'sare *vt* go [right] through ● *vi* (*morire*) pass away

tra'passo *nm* passage

trape'lare *vi* ⟨*liquido, fig:*⟩ leak out

tra'pezio *nm* trapeze; *Math* trapezium

trapi|an'tare *vt* transplant. **~'anto** *nm* transplant

'trappola *nf* trap

tra'punta *nf* quilt

'trarre *vt* draw; (*ricavare*) obtain; **~ in inganno** deceive

trasa'lire *vi* start

trasan'dato *a* shabby

trasbor'dare *vt* transfer; *Naut* tran[s]ship ● *vi* change. **tra'sbordo** *nm* trans[s]hipment

tra'scendere *vt* transcend ● *vi* (*eccedere*) go too far

trasci'nar|e *vt* drag; ⟨*fig: entusiasmo:*⟩ carry away. **~si** *vr* drag oneself

tra'scorrere *vt* spend ● *vi* pass

tra'scri|tto *pp di* trascrivere. **~vere** *vt* transcribe. **~zi'one** *nf* transcription

trascu'ra|bile *a* negligible. **~re** *vt* neglect; (*non tenere conto di*) disregard. **~'tezza** *nf* negligence. **~to** *a* negligent; (*curato male*) neglected; (*nel vestire*) slovenly

traseco'lato *a* amazed

trasferi'mento *nm* transfer; (*trasloco*) move

trasfe'ri|re *vt* transfer. **~rsi** *vr* move

tra'sferta *nf* transfer; (*indennità*) subsistence allowance; *Sport* away match; **in ~** ⟨*impiegato:*⟩ on secondment; **giocare in ~** play away

trasfigu'rare *vt* transfigure

trasfor'ma|re *vt* transform; (*in rugby*) convert. **~'tore** *nm* transformer.

~zi'one *nf* transformation; (*in rugby*) conversion

trasfor'mista *nmf* (*artista*) quick-change artist

trasfusi'one *nf* transfusion

trasgre'dire *vt* disobey; *Jur* infringe

trasgredi'trice *nf* transgressor

trasgres|si'one *nf* infringement. **~'sivo** *a* intended to shock. **~'sore** *nm* transgressor

tra'slato *a* metaphorical

traslo'car|e *vt* move ● *vi*, **~si** *vr* move house. **tra'sloco** *nm* removal

tra'smesso *pp di* trasmettere

tra'smett|ere *vt* pass on; *TV, Radio* broadcast; *Techn, Med* transmit. **~i'tore** *nm* transmitter

trasmis'si|bile *a* transmissible. **~'one** *nf* transmission; *TV, Radio* programme

trasmit'tente *nm* transmitter ● *nf* broadcasting station

traso'gna|re *vi* day-dream. **~to** *a* dreamy

traspa'ren|te *a* transparent. **~za** *nf* transparency; **in ~za** against the light. **traspa'rire** *vi* show [through]

traspi'ra|re *vi* perspire; *fig* transpire. **~zi'one** *nf* perspiration

tra'sporre *vt* transpose

traspor'tare *vt* transport; **lasciarsi ~ da** get carried away by. **tra'sporto** *nm* transport; (*passione*) passion

trastul'lar|e *vt* amuse. **~si** *vr* amuse oneself

trasu'dare *vt* ooze with ● *vi* sweat

trasver'sale *a* transverse

trasvo'la|re *vt* fly over ● *vi* **~re su** *fig* skim over. **~ta** *nf* crossing [by air]

'tratta *nf* (*traffico illegale*) trade; *Comm* draft

trat'tabile *a* or nearest offer, o.n.o.

tratta'mento *nm* treatment. **~ di riguardo** special treatment

trat'ta|re *vt* treat; (*commerciare in*) deal in; (*negoziare*) negotiate ● *vi* **~re di** deal with. **~rsi** *vr* **di che si tratta?** what is it about?; **si tratta di...** it's about... **~'tive** *nfpl* negotiations. **~to** *nm* treaty; (*opera scritta*) treatise

tratteggi'are *vt* outline; (*descrivere*) sketch

tratte'ner|e *vt* (*far restare*) keep; hold ⟨*respiro, in questura*⟩; hold back ⟨*lacrime, riso*⟩; (*frenare*) restrain; (*da paga*) withhold; **sono stato trattenuto** (*ritardato*) I was o got held up. **~si** *vr* restrain oneself; (*fermarsi*) stay;

~si su (*indugiare*) dwell on. **tratteni'mento** nm entertainment; (*ricevimento*) party

tratte'nuta nf deduction

trat'tino nm dash; (*in parole composte*) hyphen

'tratto pp di **trarre** ● nm (*di spazio, tempo*) stretch; (*di penna*) stroke; (*linea*) line; (*brano*) passage; **tratti** pl (*lineamenti*) features; **a tratti** at intervals; **ad un ~** suddenly

trat'tore nm tractor

tratto'ria nf restaurant

'trauma nm trauma. **trau'matico** a traumatic. **~tiz'zare** vt traumatize

tra'vaglio nm labour; (*angoscia*) anguish

trava'sare vt decant

'trave nf beam

tra'veggole nfpl **avere le ~** be seeing things

tra'versa nf crossbar; **è una ~ di Via Roma** it's off Via Roma, it crosses via Roma

traver'sa|re vt cross. **~ta** nf crossing

traver'sie nfpl misfortunes

traver'sina nf Rail sleeper

tra'vers|o a crosswise ● adv **di ~o** crossways; **andare di ~o** (*cibo:*) go down the wrong way; **camminare di ~o** not walk in a straight line; **guardare qcno di ~o** look askance at sb. **~one** nm (*in calcio*) cross

travesti'mento nm disguise

trave'sti|re vt disguise. **~rsi** vr disguise oneself. **~to** a disguised ● nm transvestite

travi'are vt lead astray

travi'sare vt distort

travol'gente a overwhelming

tra'vol|gere vt sweep away; (*sopraffare*) overwhelm. **~to** pp di **travolgere**

trazi'one nf traction. **~ anteriore/ posteriore** front-/rear-wheel drive

tre a & nm three

trebbi'a|re vt thresh

'treccia nf plait, braid

tre'cento a & nm three hundred; **il T~** the fourteenth century

tredi'cesima nf extra month's salary paid as a Christmas bonus

'tredici a & nm thirteen

'tregua nf truce; fig respite

tre'mare vi tremble; (*di freddo*) shiver. **trema'rella** nf fam jitters pl

tremenda'mente adv terribly.

tre'mendo a terrible; **ho una fame tremenda** I'm terribly hungry

tremen'tina nf turpentine

tre'mila a & nm three thousand

'tremito nm tremble

tremo'lare vi shake; (*luce:*) flicker. **tre'more** nm trembling

tre'nino nm miniature railway

'treno nm train

'tren|ta a & nm thirty; **~ta e lode** top marks. **~tatré giri** nm inv LP. **~'tenne** a & nmf thirty-year-old. **~'tesimo** a & nm thirtieth. **~'tina** nf **una ~tina di** about thirty

trepi'dare vi be anxious. **'trepido** a anxious

treppi'ede nm tripod

'tresca nf intrigue; (*amorosa*) affair

'trespolo nm perch

triango'lare a triangular. **tri'angolo** nm triangle

tri'bale a tribal

tribo'la|re vi (*soffrire*) suffer; (*fare fatica*) go through all kinds of trials and tribulations. **~zi'one** nf tribulation

tribù nf inv tribe

tri'buna nf tribune; (*per uditori*) gallery; Sport stand. **~ coperta** stand

tribu'nale nm court

tribu'tare vt bestow

tribu'tario a tax attrib. **tri'buto** nm tribute; (*tassa*) tax

tri'checo nm walrus

tri'ciclo nm tricycle

trico'lore a three-coloured ● nm (*bandiera*) tricolour

tri'dente nm trident

trien'nale a (*ogni tre anni*) three-yearly; (*lungo tre anni*) three-year. **tri'ennio** nm three-year period

tri'foglio nm clover

trifo'lato a sliced thinly and cooked with olive oil, parsley and garlic

'triglia nf mullet

trigonome'tria nf trigonometry

tril'lare vi trill

trilo'gia nf trilogy

tri'mestre nm quarter; Sch term

'trina nf lace

trin'ce|a nf trench. **~'rare** vt entrench

trincia'pollo nm inv poultry shears pl

trinci'are vt cut up

Trinità nf Trinity

'trio nm trio

trion'fa|le a triumphal. **~nte** a triumphant. **~re** vi triumph; **~re su** triumph over. **tri'onfo** nm triumph

tripli'care vt triple. **'triplice** a triple;

in triplice [copia] in triplicate. **'triplo** *a* treble ● *nm* **il triplo (di)** three times as much (as)

'trippa *nf* tripe; (*fam: pancia*) belly

'trist|e *a* sad; ⟨*luogo*⟩ gloomy. **tri'stezza** *nf* sadness. **~o** *a* wicked; (*meschino*) miserable

trita|'carne *nm inv* mincer. **~ghi'accio** *nm inv* ice-crusher

tri'ta|re *vt* mince. **'trito** *a* **trito e ritrito** well-worn, trite

'trittico *nm* triptych

tritu'rare *vt* chop finely

triumvi'rato *nm* triumvirate

tri'vella *nf* drill. **trivel'lare** *vt* drill

trivi'ale *a* vulgar

tro'feo *nm* trophy

'trogolo *nm* (*per maiali*) trough

'troia *nf* sow; *vulg* bitch; (*sessuale*) whore

'tromba *nf* trumpet; *Auto* horn; (*delle scale*) well. **~ d'aria** whirlwind

trom'bare *vt vulg* screw; (*fam: in esame*) fail

trom'b|etta *nm* toy trumpet. **~one** *nm* trombone

trom'bosi *nf* thrombosis

tron'care *vt* sever; truncate ⟨*parola*⟩

'tronco *a* truncated; **licenziare in ~** fire on the spot ● *nm* trunk; (*di strada*) section. **tron'cone** *nm* stump

troneggi'are *vi* **~ su** tower over

'trono *nm* throne

tropi'cale *a* tropical. **'tropico** *nm* tropic

'troppo *a* too much; (*con nomi plurali*) too many ● *pron* too much; (*plurale*) too many; (*troppo tempo*) too long; **troppi** (*troppa gente*) too many people ● *adv* too; (*con verbi*) too much; **~ stanco** too tired; **ho mangiato ~** I ate too much; **hai fame? – non ~** are you hungry? – not very; **sentirsi di ~** feel unwanted

'trota *nf* trout

trot'tare *vi* trot. **trotterel'lare** *vi* trot along; ⟨*bimbo:*⟩ toddle

'trotto *nm* trot; **andare al ~** trot

'trottola *nf* [spinning] top; (*movimento*) spin

troupe *nf inv* **~ televisiva** camera crew

tro'va|re *vt* find; (*scoprire*) find out; (*incontrare*) meet; (*ritenere*) think; **andare a ~re** go and see. **~rsi** *vr* find oneself; ⟨*luogo:*⟩ be; (*sentirsi*) feel. **~ta** *nf* bright idea. **~ta pubblicitaria** advertising gimmick

truc'ca|re *vt* make up; (*falsificare*) fix

sl. **~rsi** *vr* make up. **~tore, ~'trice** *nmf* make-up artist

'trucco *nm* (*cosmetico*) make-up; (*imbroglio*) trick

'truce *a* fierce; ⟨*delitto*⟩ appalling

truci'dare *vt* slay

truciolo *nm* shaving

trucu'lento *a* truculent

'truffa *nf* fraud. **truf'fare** *vt* swindle. **~'tore, ~'trice** *nmf* swindler

'truppa *nf* troops *pl*; (*gruppo*) group

tu *pers pron* you; **sei tu?** is that you?; **l'hai fatto tu?** did you do it yourself?; **a tu per tu** in private; **darsi del tu** *use the familiar tu*

'tuba *nf Mus* tuba; (*cappello*) top hat

tu'bare *vi* coo

tuba'tura, tubazi'one *nf* piping

tubazi'oni *nfpl* piping *sg*, pipes

tuberco'losi *nf* tuberculosis

tu'betto *nm* tube

tu'bino *nm* (*vestito*) shift

'tubo *nm* pipe; *Anat* canal; **non ho capito un ~** *fam* I understood zilch. **~ di scappamento** exhaust [pipe]

tubo'lare *a* tubular

tuf'fa|re *vt* plunge. **~rsi** *vr* dive. **~'tore, ~'trice** *nmf* diver

'tuffo *nm* dive; (*bagno*) dip; **ho avuto un ~ al cuore** my heart missed a beat. **~ di testa** dive

'tufo *nm* tufa

tu'gurio *nm* hovel

tuli'pano *nm* tulip

'tulle *nm* tulle

tume'fa|tto *a* swollen. **~zi'one** *nf* swelling. **'tumido** *a* swollen

tu'more *nm* tumour

tumulazi'one *nf* burial

tu'mult|o *nm* turmoil; (*sommossa*) riot. **~u'oso** *a* uproarious

'tunica *nf* tunic

Tuni'sia *nf* Tunisia

'tunnel *nm inv* tunnel

'tuo (**il ~** *m*, **la tua** *f*, **i ~i** *mpl*, **le tue** *fpl*) *poss a* your; **è tua questa macchina?** is this car yours?; **un ~ amico** a friend of yours; **~ padre** your father ● *poss pron* yours; **i tuoi** your folks

tuo'nare *vi* thunder. **tu'ono** *nm* thunder

tu'orlo *nm* yolk

tu'racciolo *nm* stopper; (*di sughero*) cork

tu'rar|e *vt* stop; cork ⟨*bottiglia*⟩. **~si** *vr* become blocked; **~si le orecchie** stick one's fingers in one's ears; **~si il naso** hold one's nose

turba'mento *nm* disturbance; *(sconvolgimento)* upsetting. **~ della quiete pubblica** breach of the peace

tur'bante *nm* turban

tur'ba|re *vt* upset. **~rsi** *vr* get upset. **~to** *a* upset

tur'bina *nf* turbine

turbi'nare *vi* whirl. **'turbine** *nm* whirl. **turbine di vento** whirlwind

turbo'len|to *a* turbulent. **~za** *nf* turbulence

turboreat'tore *nm* turbo-jet

tur'chese *a & nmf* turquoise

Tur'chia *nf* Turkey

tur'chino *a & nm* deep blue

'turco, -a *a* Turkish ● *nmf* Turk ● *nm* *(lingua)* Turkish; *fig* double Dutch; **fumare come un ~** smoke like a chimney; **bestemmiare come un ~** swear like a trooper

tu'ris|mo *nm* tourism. **~ta** *nmf* tourist. **~tico** *a* tourist *attrib*

'turno *nm* turn; **a ~** in turn; **di ~** on duty; **fare a ~** take turns. **~ di notte** night shift

'turp|e *a* base. **~i'loquio** *nm* foul language

'tuta *nf* overalls *pl*; *Sport* tracksuit. **~ da ginnastica** tracksuit. **~ da lavoro** overalls. **~ mimetica** camouflage. **~ spaziale** spacesuit. **~ subacquea** wetsuit

tu'tela *nf* *Jur* guardianship; *(pro-*

tezione) protection. **tute'lare** *vt* protect

tu'tina *nf* sleepsuit; *(da danza)* leotard

tu'tore, -'trice *nmf* guardian

'tutta *nf* **mettercela ~ per fare qcsa** go flat out for sth

tutta'via *conj* nevertheless, still

'tutto *a* whole; *(con nomi plurali)* all; *(ogni)* every; **tutta la classe** the whole class, all the class; **tutti gli alunni** all the pupils; **a tutta velocità** at full speed; **ho aspettato ~ il giorno** I waited all day [long]; **in ~ il mondo** all over the world; **noi tutti** all of us; **era tutta contenta** she was delighted; **tutti e due** both; **tutti e tre** all three ● *pron* all; *(tutta la gente)* everybody; *(tutte le cose)* everything; *(qualunque cosa)* anything; **l'ho mangiato ~** I ate it all; **le ho lavate tutte** I washed them all; **raccontami ~** tell me everything; **lo sanno tutti** everybody knows; **è capace di ~** he's capable of anything; **~ compreso** all in; **del ~** quite; **in ~** altogether ● *adv* completely; **tutt'a un tratto** all at once; **tutt'altro** not at all; **tutt'altro che** anything but ● *nm* whole; **tentare il ~ per ~** go for broke. **~'fare** *a inv & nmf* [impiegato] **~** general handyman; **donna ~** general maid

tut'tora *adv* still

tutù *nm inv* tutu, ballet dress

tv *nf inv* TV

Uu

ubbidi'en|te *a* obedient. **~za** *nf* obedience. **ubbi'dire** *vi* **~ (a)** obey

ubi'ca|to *a* located. **~zi'one** *nf* location

ubria'car|e *vt* get drunk. **~si** *vr* get drunk; **~si di** *fig* become intoxicated with

ubria'chezza *nf* drunkenness; **in stato di ~** inebriated

ubri'aco, -a *a* drunk; **~ fradicio** dead *o* blind drunk ● *nmf* drunk

ubria'cone *nm* drunkard

uccelli'era *nf* aviary. **uc'cello** *nm* bird; *(vulg: pene)* cock

uc'cider|e *vt* kill. **~si** *vr* kill oneself

ucci|si'one *nf* killing. **uc'ciso** *pp di* **uccidere. ~'sore** *nm* killer

u'dente *a* **i non udenti** the hearing impaired

u'dibile *a* audible

udi'enza *nf* audience; *(colloquio)* interview; *Jur* hearing

u'di|re *vt* hear. **~'tivo** *a* auditory. **~to** *nm* hearing. **~'tore, ~'trice** *nmf* listener; *Sch* unregistered student *(allowed to sit in on lectures)*. **~'torio** *nm* audience

'uffa *int* *(con impazienza)* come on!; *(con tono seccato)* damn!

uffici'al|e *a* official ● *nm* officer;

(*funzionario*) official; **pubblico ~e** public official. **~e giudiziario** clerk of the court. **~iz'zare** vt make official, officialize

uf'ficio nm office; (*dovere*) duty. **~ di collocamento** employment office. **~ informazioni** information office. **~ del personale** personnel department. **~sa'mente** adv unofficially. **uffici'oso** a unofficial

'ufo[1] nm inv UFO

'ufo[2]: **a ~** adv without paying

uggi'oso a boring

uguagli'a|nza nf equality. **~re** vt make equal; (*essere uguale*) equal; (*livellare*) level. **~rsi** vr **~rsi a** compare oneself to

ugu'al|e a equal; (*lo stesso*) the same; (*simile*) like. **~'mente** adv equally; (*malgrado tutto*) all the same

'ulcera nf ulcer

uli'veto nm olive grove

ulteri'or|e a further. **~'mente** adv further

ultima'mente adv lately

ulti'ma|re vt complete. **~tum** nm inv ultimatum

ulti'missime nfpl Journ stop press, latest news sg

'ultimo a last; (*notizie ecc*) latest; (*più lontano*) farthest; fig ultimate ● nm last; **fino all'~** to the last; **per ~** at the end; **l'~ piano** the top floor

ultrà nmf inv Sport fanatical supporter

ultramo'derno a ultramodern

ultra'rapido a extra-fast

ultrasen'sibile a ultrasensitive

ultra's|onico a ultrasonic. **~u'ono** nm ultrasound

ultrater'reno a (*vita*) after death

ultravio'letto a ultraviolet

ulu'la|re vi howl. **~to** nm howling; **gli ~ti** the howls, the howling

umana'mente adv (*trattare*) humanely; **~ impossibile** not humanly possible

uma'nesimo nm humanism

umani'tà nf humanity. **~'tario** a humanitarian. **u'mano** a human; (*benevolo*) humane

umidifica'tore nm humidifier

umidità nf dampness; (*di clima*) humidity. **'umido** a damp; (*clima*) humid; (*mani, occhi*) moist ● nm dampness; **in umido** Culin stewed

'umile a humble

umili'a|nte a humiliating. **~re** vt humiliate. **~rsi** vr humble oneself.

~zi'one nf humiliation. **umiltà** nf humility. **umil'mente** adv humbly

u'more nm humour; (*stato d'animo*) mood; **di cattivo/buon ~** in a bad/good mood

umo'ris|mo nm humour. **~ta** nmf humorist. **~tico** a humorous

un indef art a; (*davanti a vocale o h muta*) an; vedi **uno**

una indef art f a; vedi **un**

u'nanim|e a unanimous. **~e'mente** adv unanimously. **~ità** nf unanimity; **all'~ità** unanimously

unci'nato a hooked; (*parentesi*) angle

unci'netto nm crochet hook

un'cino nm hook

'undici a & nm eleven

'unger|e vt grease; (*sporcare*) get greasy; Relig anoint; (*blandire*) flatter. **~si** vr (*con olio solare*) oil oneself; **~si le mani** get one's hands greasy

unghe'rese a & nmf Hungarian. **Unghe'ria** nf Hungary; (*lingua*) Hungarian

'unghi|a nf nail; (*di animale*) claw. **~'ata** nf (*graffio*) scratch

ungu'ento nm ointment

unica'mente adv only. **'unico** a only; (*singolo*) single; (*incomparabile*) unique

unifi'ca|re vt unify. **~zi'one** nf unification

unifor'mar|e vt level. **~si** vr conform (**a** to)

uni'form|e a & nf uniform. **~ità** nf uniformity

unilate'rale a unilateral

uni'one nf union; (*armonia*) unity. **U~ Europea** European Union. **U~ Monetaria Europea** European Monetary Union. **~ sindacale** trade union, labor union Am. **U~ Sovietica** Soviet Union

u'ni|re vt unite; (*collegare*) join; blend (*colori ecc*). **~rsi** vr unite; (*collegarsi*) join

'unisex a inv unisex

unità nf inv unity; Math, Mil unit; Comput drive. **~ di misura** unit of measurement. **~rio** a unitary

u'nito a united; (*tinta*) plain

univer'sal|e a universal. **~iz'zare** vt universalize. **~'mente** adv universally

università nf inv university. **~rio, -a** a university attrib ● nmf (*insegnante*) university lecturer; (*studente*) undergraduate

uni'verso nm universe

uno, -a indef art (*before s + consonant,*)

gn, ps, z) a ●*pron* one; **a ~ a ~** one by one; **l'~ e l'altro** both [of them]; **né l'~ né l'altro** neither [of them]; **~ di noi** one of us; **~ fa quello che può** you do what you can ●*a* a, one ●*nm* (*numerale*) one; (*un tale*) some man ●*nf* some woman

'unt|o *pp di* ungere ●*a* greasy ●*nm* grease. **~u'oso** *a* greasy. **unzi'one** *nf* **l'Estrema Unzione** Extreme Unction

u'omo *nm* (*pl* uomini) man. **~ d'affari** business man. **~ di fiducia** right-hand man. **~ di Stato** statesman

u'ovo *nm* (*pl nf* uova) egg. **~ in camicia** poached egg. **~ alla coque** boiled egg. **~ di Pasqua** Easter egg. **~ sodo** hard-boiled egg. **~ strapazzato** scrambled egg

ura'gano *nm* hurricane

u'ranio *nm* uranium

urba'n|esimo *nm* urbanization. **~ista** *nmf* town planner. **~istica** *nf* town planning. **~istico** *a* urban. **urbanizzazi'one** *nf* urbanization. **ur'bano** *a* urban; (*cortese*) urbane

ur'gen|te *a* urgent. **~te'mente** *adv* urgently. **~za** *nf* urgency; **in caso d'~za** in an emergency; **d'~za** (*misura, chiamata*) emergency

'urgere *vi* be urgent

u'rina *nf* urine. **uri'nare** *vi* urinate

ur'lare *vi* shout, yell; (*cane, vento:*) howl. 'urlo *nm* (*pl nm* urli, *nf* urla) shout; (*di cane, vento*) howling

'urna *nf* urn; (*elettorale*) ballot box; **andare alle urne** go to the polls

urrà *int* hurrah!

U.R.S.S. *nf abbr* (**Unione delle Repubbliche Socialiste Sovietiche**) USSR

ur'tar|e *vt* knock against; (*scontrarsi*) bump into; *fig* irritate. **~si** *vr* collide; *fig* clash

'urto *nm* knock; (*scontro*) crash; (*contrasto*) conflict; *fig* clash; **d'~** (*misure, terapia*) shock

usa e getta *a inv* (*rasoio, siringa*) throw-away, disposable

u'sanza *nf* custom; (*moda*) fashion

u'sa|re *vt* use; (*impiegare*) employ; (*esercitare*) exercise; **~re fare qcsa** be in the habit of doing sth ●*vi* (*essere di moda*) be fashionable; **non si usa più** it is out of fashion; (*attrezzatura, espressione:*) it's not used any more. **~to** *a* used; (*non nuovo*) second-hand

U.S.A. *nmpl* US[A] *sg*

u'scente *a* (*presidente*) outgoing

usci'ere *nm* usher. 'uscio *nm* door

u'sci|re *vi* come out; (*andare fuori*) go out; (*sfuggire*) get out; (*essere sorteggiato*) come up; (*giornale:*) come out; **~re da** *Comput* exit from, quit; **~re di strada** leave the road. **~ta** *nf* exit, way out; (*spesa*) outlay; (*di auto-strada*) junction; (*battuta*) witty remark; **essere in libera ~ta** be off duty. **~ta di servizio** back door. **~ta di sicurezza** emergency exit

usi'gnolo *nm* nightingale

'uso *nm* use; (*abitudine*) custom; (*usanza*) usage; **fuori ~** out of use; **per ~ esterno** (*medicina*) for external use only

U.S.S.L. *nf abbr* (**Unità Socio-Sanitaria Locale**) local health centre

ustio'na|rsi *vr* burn oneself. **~to, -a** *nmf* burns case ●*a* burnt. **usti'one** *nf* burn

usu'ale *a* usual

usufru'ire *vi* **~ di** take advantage of

u'sura *nf* usury. **usu'raio** *nm* usurer

usur'pare *vt* usurp

u'tensile *nm* tool; *Culin* utensil; **cassetta degli utensili** tool box

u'tente *nmf* user. **~ finale** end user

u'tenza *nf* use; (*utenti*) users *pl*

ute'rino *a* uterine. 'utero *nm* womb

'util|e *a* useful ●*nm* *Comm* profit. **~ità** *nf* usefulness, utility; *Comput* utility. **~i'taria** *nf* *Auto* small car. **~i'tario** *a* utilitarian

utiliz'za|re *vt* utilize. **~zi'one** *nf* utilization. **uti'lizzo** *nm* (*utilizzazione*) use

uto'pistico *a* Utopian

'uva *nf* grapes *pl*; **chicco d'~** grape. **~ passa** raisins *pl*. **~ sultanina** currants *pl*

Vv

va'cante *a* vacant

va'canza *nf* holiday; (*posto vacante*) vacancy. **essere in ~** be on holiday

'vacca *nf* cow. **~ da latte** dairy cow

vacc|i'nare *vt* vaccinate. **~inazi'one** *nf* vaccination. **vac'cino** *nm* vaccine

vacil'la|nte *a* tottering; (*oggetto*) wobbly; (*luce*) flickering; *fig* wavering. **~re** *vi* totter; (*oggetto:*) wobble; (*luce:*) flicker; *fig* waver

'vacuo *a* (*vano*) vain; *fig* empty ● *nm* vacuum

vagabon'dare *vi* wander. **vaga'bondo, -a** *a* (*cane*) stray; **gente vagabonda** tramps *pl* ● *nmf* tramp

va'gare *vi* wander

vagheggi'are *vt* long for

va'gi|na *nf* vagina. **~'nale** *a* vaginal

va'gi|re *vi* whimper. **~to** *nm* whimper

'vaglia *nm inv* money order. **~ bancario** bank draft. **~ postale** postal order

vagli'are *vt* sift; *fig* weigh

'vago *a* vague

vagon'cino *nm* (*di funivia*) car

va'gone *nm* (*per passeggeri*) carriage; (*per merci*) wagon. **~ letto** sleeper. **~ ristorante** restaurant car

vai'olo *nm* smallpox

va'langa *nf* avalanche

va'lente *a* skilful

va'ler|e *vi* be worth; (*contare*) count; (*regola:*) apply (**per** to); (*essere valido*) be valid; **far ~e i propri diritti** assert one's rights; **farsi ~e** assert oneself; **non vale!** that's not fair!; **tanto vale che me ne vada** I might as well go ● *vt* **~re qcsa a qcno** (*procurare*) earn sb sth; **~ne la pena** be worth it; **vale la pena di vederlo** it's worth seeing; **~si di** avail oneself of

valeri'ana *nf* valerian

va'levole *a* valid

vali'care *vt* cross. **'valico** *nm* pass

validità *nf* validity; **con ~ illimitata** valid indefinitely

'valido *a* valid; (*efficace*) efficient; (*contributo*) valuable

valige'ria *nf* (*fabbrica*) leather factory; (*negozio*) leather goods shop

va'ligia *nf* suitcase; **fare le valigie** pack; *fig* pack one's bags. **~ diplomatica** diplomatic bag

val'lata *nf* valley. **'valle** *nf* valley; **a valle** downstream

val'lett|a *nf TV* assistant. **~o** *nm* valet; *TV* assistant

val'lone *nm* (*valle*) deep valley

va'lor|e *nm* value, worth; (*merito*) merit; (*coraggio*) valour; **~i** *pl Comm* securities; **di ~e** (*oggetto*) valuable; **oggetti** *nmpl* **di ~e** valuables; **senza ~e** worthless. **~iz'zare** *vt* (*mettere in valore*) use to advantage; (*aumentare di valore*) increase the value of; (*migliorare l'aspetto di*) enhance

valo'roso *a* courageous

'valso *pp di* **valere**

va'luta *nf* currency. **~ estera** foreign currency

valu'ta|re *vt* value; weigh up (*situazione*). **~rio** *a* (*mercato, norme*) currency. **~zi'one** *nf* valuation

'valva *nf* valve. **'valvola** *nf* valve; *Electr* fuse

'valzer *nm inv* waltz

vam'pata *nf* blaze; (*di calore*) blast; (*al viso*) flush

vam'piro *nm* vampire; *fig* blood-sucker

vana'mente *adv* (*inutilmente*) in vain

van'da|lico *a* atto **~lico** act of vandalism. **~'lismo** *nm* vandalism. **'vandalo** *nm* vandal

vaneggi'are *vi* rave

'vanga *nf* spade. **van'gare** *vt* dig

van'gelo *nm* Gospel; (*fam: verità*) gospel [truth]

vanifi'care *vt* nullify

va'nigli|a *nf* vanilla. **~'ato** *a* (*zucchero*) vanilla *attrib*

vanil'lina *nf* vanillin

vanità *nf* vanity. **vani'toso** *a* vain

'vano *a* vain ● *nm* (*stanza*) room; (*spazio vuoto*) hollow

van'taggi|o *nm* advantage; *Sport* lead; *Tennis* advantage; **trarre ~o da qcsa**

derive benefit from sth. **~'oso** *a* advantageous

van't|are *vt* praise; (*possedere*) boast. **~arsi** *vr* boast. **~e'ria** *nf* boasting. **'vanto** *nm* boast

'vanvera *nf* **a ~** at random; **parlare a ~** talk nonsense

va'por|e *nm* steam; (*di benzina, cascata*) vapour; **a ~e** steam *attrib*; **al ~e** *Culin* steamed. **~e acqueo** steam, water vapour; **battello a ~e** steamboat. **vapo'retto** *nm* ferry. **~i'era** *nf* steam engine

vaporiz'za|re *vt* vaporize. **~'tore** *nm* spray

vapo'roso *a* (*vestito*) filmy; **capelli vaporosi** big hair *sg*

va'rare *vt* launch

var'care *vt* cross. **'varco** *nm* passage; **aspettare al varco** lie in wait

vari'abil|e *a* changeable, variable ● *nf* variable. **~ità** *nf* changeableness, variability

vari'a|nte *nf* variant. **~re** *vt/i* vary; **~re di umore** change one's mood. **~zi'one** *nf* variation

va'rice *nf* varicose vein

vari'cella *nf* chickenpox

vari'coso *a* varicose

varie'gato *a* variegated

varietà *nf inv* variety ● *nm inv* variety show

'vario *a* varied; (*al pl, parecchi*) various; **vari** *pl* (*molti*) several; **varie ed eventuali** any other business

vario'pinto *a* multicoloured

'varo *nm* launch

va'saio *nm* potter

'vasca *nf* tub; (*piscina*) pool; (*lunghezza*) length. **~ da bagno** bath

va'scello *nm* vessel

va'schetta *nf* tub

vase'lina *nf* Vaseline®

vasel'lame *nm* china. **~ d'oro/d'argento** gold/silver plate

'vaso *nm* pot; (*da fiori*) vase; *Anat* vessel; (*per cibi*) jar. **~ da notte** chamber pot

vas'soio *nm* tray

vastità *nf* vastness. **'vasto** *a* vast; **di vaste vedute** broad-minded

Vati'cano *nm* Vatican

vattela'pesca *adv fam* God knows!

ve *pers pron* you; **ve l'ho dato** I gave it to you

vecchia *nf* old woman. **vecchi'aia** *nf* old age. **'vecchio** *a* old ● *nmf* old man; **i vecchi** old people

'vece *nf* **in ~ di** in place of; **fare le veci di qcno** take sb's place

ve'dente *a* **i non vedenti** the visually handicapped

ve'der|e *vt/i* see; **far ~e** show; **farsi ~e** show one's face; **non vedo l'ora di ...** I can't wait to... **~si** *vr* see oneself; (*reciproco*) see each other

ve'detta *nf* (*luogo*) lookout; *Naut* patrol vessel

'vedovo, -a *nm* widower ● *nf* widow

ve'duta *nf* view

vee'mente *a* vehement

vege'ta|le *a & nm* vegetable. **~li'ano** *a & nmf* vegan. **~re** *vi* vegetate. **~ri'ano, -a** *a & nmf* vegetarian. **~zi'one** *nf* vegetation

'vegeto *a* vedi **vivo**

veg'gente *nmf* clairvoyant

'veglia *nf* watch; **fare la ~** keep watch. **~ funebre** vigil

vegli|'are *vi* be awake; **~are su** watch over. **~'one** *nm* **~one di capodanno** New Year's Eve celebration

ve'icolo *nm* vehicle

'vela *nf* sail; *Sport* sailing; **far ~** set sail

ve'la|re *vt* veil; (*fig: nascondere*) hide. **~rsi** *vr* (*vista:*) mist over; (*voce:*) go husky. **~ta'mente** *adv* indirectly. **~to** *a* veiled; (*occhi*) misty; (*collant*) sheer

'velcro® *nm* velcro®

veleggi'are *vi* sail

ve'leno *nm* poison. **vele'noso** *a* poisonous

veli'ero *nm* sailing ship

ve'lina *nf* (*carta*) **~** tissue paper; (*copia*) carbon copy

ve'lista *nm* yachtsman ● *nf* yachtswoman

ve'livolo *nm* aircraft

vellei'tà *nf inv* foolish ambition. **~'tario** *a* unrealistic

'vello *nm* fleece

vellu'tato *a* velvety. **vel'luto** *nm* velvet. **velluto a coste** corduroy

'velo *nm* veil; (*di zucchero, cipria*) dusting; (*tessuto*) voile

ve'loc|e *a* fast. **~e'mente** *adv* quickly. **velo'cista** *nmf Sport* sprinter. **~ità** *nf inv* speed; (*Auto: marcia*) gear. **~ità di crociera** cruising speed. **~iz'zare** *vt* speed up

ve'lodromo *nm* cycle track

'vena *nf* vein; **essere in ~ di** be in the mood for

ve'nale *a* venal; (*persona*) mercenary, venal

ve'nato *a* grainy

vena'torio a hunting attrib

vena'tura nf (di legno) grain; (di foglia, marmo) vein

ven'demmi|a nf grape harvest. **~'are** vt harvest

'vender|e vt sell. **~si** vr sell oneself; **vendesi** for sale

ven'detta nf revenge

vendi'ca|re vt avenge. **~rsi** vr get one's revenge. **~'tivo** a vindictive

'vendi|ta nf sale; **in ~ta** on sale. **~ta all'asta** sale by auction. **~ta al dettaglio** retailing. **~ta all'ingrosso** wholesaling. **~ta al minuto** retailing. **~ta porta a porta** door-to-door selling. **~'tore, ~'trice** nmf seller. **~tore ambulante** hawker, pedlar

vene'ra|bile, ~ndo a venerable

vene'ra|re vt revere

venerdì nm inv Friday. **V~ Santo** Good Friday

'Venere nf Venus. **ve'nereo** a venereal

Ve'nezi|a nf Venice. **v~'ano, -a** a & nmf Venetian ● nf (persiana) Venetian blind; Culin sweet bun

veni'ale a venial

ve'nire vi come; (riuscire) turn out; (costare) cost; (in passivi) be; **~ a sapere** learn; **~ in mente** occur; **~ meno** (svenire) faint; **~ meno a un contratto** go back on a contract; **~ via** come away; (staccarsi) come off; **mi viene da piangere** I feel like crying; **vieni a prendermi** come and pick me up

ven'taglio nm fan

ven'tata nf gust [of wind]; fig breath

ven'te|nne a & nmf twenty-year-old. **~simo** a & nm twentieth. **'venti** a & nm twenty

venti'la|re vt air. **~'tore** nm fan. **~zi'one** nf ventilation

ven'tina nf una **~** (circa venti) about twenty

ventiquat'trore nf inv (valigia) overnight case

'vento nm wind; **farsi ~** fan oneself

ven'tosa nf sucker

ven'toso a windy

'ventre nm stomach. **ven'triloquo** nm ventriloquist

ven'tura nf fortune; **andare alla ~** trust to luck

ven'turo a next

ve'nuta nf coming

vera'mente adv really

ve'randa nf veranda

ver'bal|e a verbal ● nm (di riunione) minutes pl. **~'mente** adv verbally

'verbo nm verb. **~ ausiliare** auxiliary [verb]

'verde a green ● nm green; (vegetazione) greenery; (semaforo) green light; **essere al ~** be broke. **~ oliva** olive green. **~ pisello** pea green. **~'rame** nm verdigris

ver'detto nm verdict

ver'dura nf vegetables pl; **una ~** a vegetable

'verga nf rod

vergi'n|ale a virginal. **'vergine** nf virgin; Astr Virgo ● a virgin; (cassetta) blank. **~ità** nf virginity

ver'gogna nf shame; (timidezza) shyness

vergo'gn|arsi vr feel ashamed; (essere timido) feel shy. **~oso** a ashamed; (timido) shy; (disonorevole) shameful

ve'rifica nf check. **verifi'cabile** a verifiable

verifi'car|e vt check. **~si** vr come true

ve'rismo nm realism

verit|à nf truth. **~i'ero** a truthful

'verme nm worm. **~ solitario** tapeworm

ver'miglio a & nm vermilion

'vermut nm inv vermouth

ver'nacolo nm vernacular

ver'nic|e nf paint; (trasparente) varnish; (pelle) patent leather; fig veneer; **"vernice fresca"** "wet paint". **~i'are** vt paint; (con vernice trasparente) varnish. **~ia'tura** nf painting; (strato) paintwork; fig veneer

'vero a true; (autentico) real; (perfetto) perfect; **è ~?** is that so?; **~ e proprio** full-blown; **sei stanca, ~?** you're tired, aren't you? ● nm truth; (realtà) life

verosimigli'anza nf probability. **vero'simile** a probable

ver'ruca nf wart; (sotto la pianta del piede) verruca

versa'mento nm (pagamento) payment; (in banca) deposit

ver'sante nm slope

ver'sa|re vt pour; (spargere) shed; (rovesciare) spill; pay (denaro). **~rsi** vr spill; (sfociare) flow

ver'satil|e a versatile. **~ità** nf versatility

ver'setto nm verse

versi'one nf version; (traduzione) translation; **"~ integrale"** "unabridged version"; **"~ ridotta"** "abridged version"

'verso[1] nm verse; (grido) cry; (gesto) gesture; (senso) direction; (modo) man-

ner; **fare il ~ a qcno** ape sb; **non c'è ~ di** there is no way of
'verso² *prep* towards; (*nei pressi di*) round about; **~ dove?** which way?
'vertebra *nf* vertebra
'vertere *vi* **~ su** focus on
verti'cal|e *a* vertical; (*in parole crociate*) down ● *nm* vertical ● *nf* handstand. **~'mente** *adv* vertically
'vertice *nm* summit; *Math* vertex; **conferenza al ~** summit conference
ver'tigine *nf* dizziness; *Med* vertigo; **vertigini** *pl* giddy spells; **aver le vertigini** feel dizzy
vertigi|nosa'mente *adv* dizzily. **~'noso** *a* dizzy; (*velocità*) breakneck; (*prezzi*) sky-high; (*scollatura*) plunging
ve'scica *nf* bladder; (*sulla pelle*) blister
'vescovo *nm* bishop
'vespa *nf* wasp
vespasi'ano *nm* urinal
'vespro *nm* vespers *pl*
ves'sillo *nm* standard
ve'staglia *nf* dressing gown
'vest|e *nf* dress; (*rivestimento*) covering; **in ~e di** in the capacity of; **in ~e ufficiale** in an official capacity. **~i'ario** *nm* clothing
ve'stibolo *nm* hall
ve'stigio *nm* (*pl nm* **vestigi**, *pl nf* **vestigia**) trace
ve'sti|re *vt* dress. **~rsi** *vr* get dressed. **~ti** *pl* clothes. **~to** *a* dressed ● *nm* (*da uomo*) suit; (*da donna*) dress
vete'rano, -a *a & nmf* veteran
veteri'naria *nf* veterinary science
veteri'nario *a* veterinary ● *nm* veterinary surgeon
'veto *nm inv* veto
ve'tra|io *nm* glazier. **~ta** *nf* big window; (*in chiesa*) stained glass window; (*porta*) glass door. **~to** *a* glazed. **vetre'ria** *nf* glass works
ve'tri|na *nf* [shop-]window; (*mobile*) display cabinet. **~'nista** *nmf* window dresser
vetri'olo *nm* vitriol
'vetro *nm* glass; (*di finestra, porta*) pane. **~'resina** *nf* fibreglass
'vetta *nf* peak
vet'tore *nm* vector
vetto'vaglie *nfpl* provisions
vet'tura *nf* coach; (*ferroviaria*) carriage; *Auto* car. **vettu'rino** *nm* coachman
vezzeggia're *vt* fondle. **~'tivo** *nm* pet name. **'vezzo** *nm* habit; (*attrattiva*) charm; **vezzi** *pl* (*moine*) affectation *sg*.
vez'zoso *a* charming; *pej* affected

vi *pers pron* you; (*riflessivo*) yourselves; (*reciproco*) each other; (*tra più persone*) one another; **vi ho dato un libro** I gave you a book; **lavatevi le mani** wash your hands; **eccovi** here you are! ● *adv* = **ci**
'via¹ *nf* street, road; *fig* way; *Anat* tract; **in ~ di** in the course of; **per ~ di** on account of; **~ ~ che** as; **per ~ aerea** by airmail
'via² *adv* away; (*fuori*) out; **andar ~** go away; **e così ~** and so on; **e ~ dicendo** and whatnot ● *int* **~!** go away!; *Sport* go!; (*andiamo*) come on! ● *nm* starting signal
viabilità *nf* road conditions *pl*; (*rete*) road network; (*norme*) road and traffic laws *pl*
via'card *nf inv* motorway card
via'dotto *nm* viaduct
viaggi'a|re *vi* travel. **~'tore, ~'trice** *nmf* traveller
vi'aggio *nm* journey; (*breve*) trip; **buon ~!** safe journey!, have a good trip!; **fare un ~** go on a journey. **~ di nozze** honeymoon
vi'ale *nm* avenue; (*privato*) drive
via'vai *nm* coming and going
vi'bra|nte *a* vibrant. **~re** *vi* vibrate; (*fremere*) quiver. **~zi'one** *nf* vibration
vi'cario *nm* vicar
'vice+ *pref* vice+
'vice *nmf* deputy. **~diret'tore** *nm* assistant manager
vi'cenda *nf* event; **a ~** (*fra due*) each other; (*a turno*) in turn[s]
vice'versa *adv* vice versa
vici'na|nza *nf* nearness; **~nze** *pl* (*paraggi*) neighbourhood. **~to** *nm* neighbourhood; (*vicini*) neighbours *pl*
vi'cino, -a *a* near; (*accanto*) next ● *adv* near, close. **~ a** *prep* near [to] ● *nmf* neighbour. **~ di casa** nextdoor neighbour
vicissi'tudine *nf* vicissitude
'vicolo *nm* alley
'video *nm* video. **~'camera** *nf* camcorder. **~cas'setta** *nf* video cassette
videoci'tofono *nm* video entry phone
video'clip *nm inv* video clip
videogi'oco *nm* video game
videoregistra'tore *nm* videorecorder
video'teca *nf* video library
video'tel® *nm* ≈ Videotex®
videotermi'nale *nm* visual display unit, VDU
vidi'mare *vt* authenticate
vie'ta|re *vt* forbid; **sosta ~ta** no parking; **~to fumare** no smoking; **~to ai**

minori di 18 anni prohibited to children under the age of 18

vi'gente a in force. **'vigere** vi be in force

vigi'la|nte a vigilant. **~nza** nf vigilance. **~re** vt keep an eye on ● vi keep watch

'vigile a watchful ● nm ~ [urbano] policeman. **~ del fuoco** fireman

vi'gilia nf eve

vigliacche'ria nf cowardice. **vigli'acco, -a** a cowardly ● nmf coward

'vigna nf, **vi'gneto** nm vineyard

vi'gnetta nf cartoon

vi'gore nm vigour; **entrare in ~** come into force. **vigo'roso** a vigorous

'vile a cowardly; (abietto) vile

'villa nf villa

vil'laggio nm village. **~ turistico** holiday village

vil'lano a rude ● nm boor; (contadino) peasant

villeggi'a|nte nmf holiday-maker. **~re** vi spend one's holidays. **~'tura** nf holiday[s] [pl], vacation Am

vil'l|etta nf small detached house. **~ino** nm detached house

viltà nf cowardice

'vimine nm wicker

'vinc|ere vt win; (sconfiggere) beat; (superare) overcome. **~ita** nf win; (somma vinta) winnings pl. **~i'tore, ~i'trice** nmf winner

vinco'la|nte a binding. **~re** vt bind; Comm tie up. **'vincolo** nm bond

vi'nicolo a wine attrib

vinil'pelle® nm Leatherette®

'vino nm wine. **~ spumante** sparkling wine. **~ da taglio** blending wine. **~ da tavola** table wine

'vinto pp di vincere

vi'ola nf Bot violet; Mus viola. **vio'laceo** a purplish; (labbra) blue

vio'la|re vt violate. **~zi'one** nf violation. **~zione di domicilio** breaking and entering

violen'tare vt rape

violente'mente adv violently

vio'len|to a violent. **~za** nf violence. **~za carnale** rape

vio'letta nf violet

vio'letto a & nm (colore) violet

violi'nista nmf violinist. **vio'lino** nm violin. **violon'cello** nm cello

vi'ottolo nm path

'vipera nf viper

vi'ra|ggio nm Phot toning; Naut, Aeron turn. **~re** vi turn; **~re di bordo** veer

'virgol|a nf comma. **~ette** nfpl inverted commas

vi'ril|e a virile; (da uomo) manly. **~ità** nf virility; manliness

virtù nf inv virtue; **in ~ di** (legge) under. **~'ale** a virtual. **~'oso** a virtuous ● nm virtuoso

viru'lento a virulent

'virus nm inv virus

visa'gista nmf beautician

visce'rale a visceral; (odio) deep-seated; (reazione) gut

'viscere nm internal organ ● nfpl guts

'vischi|o nm mistletoe. **~'oso** a viscous; (appiccicoso) sticky

'viscido a slimy

vi'scont|e nm viscount. **~'essa** nf viscountess

vi'scoso a viscous

vi'sibile a visible

visi'bilio nm profusion; **andare in ~** go into ecstasies

visibilità nf visibility

visi'era nf (di elmo) visor; (di berretto) peak

visio'nare vt examine; Cinema screen. **visi'one** nf vision; **prima visione** Cinema first showing

'visit|a nf visit; (breve) call; Med examination; **fare ~a a qcno** pay sb a visit. **~a di controllo** Med checkup. **visi'tare** vt visit; (brevemente) call on; Med examine; **~a'tore, ~a'trice** nmf visitor

vi'sivo a visual

'viso nm face

vi'sone nm mink

'vispo a lively

vis'suto pp di vivere ● a experienced

'vist|a nf sight; (veduta) view; **a ~a d'occhio** (crescere) visibly; (estendersi) as far as the eye can see; **in ~a di** in view of; **perdere di ~a qcno** lose sight of sb; fig lose touch with sb. **~o** pp di vedere ● nm visa. **vi'stoso** a showy; (notevole) considerable

visu'al|e a visual. **~izza'tore** nm Comput display, VDU. **~izzazi'one** nf Comput display

'vita nf life; (durata della vita) lifetime; Anat waist; **a ~** for life; **essere in fin di ~** be at death's door; **essere in ~** be alive

vi'tal|e a vital. **~ità** nf vitality

vita'lizio a life attrib ● nm [life] annuity

vita'min|a nf vitamin. **~iz'zato** a vitamin-enriched

'vite nf Mech screw; Bot vine

vi'tello nm calf; Culin veal; (pelle) calfskin

vi'ticcio *nm* tendril

viticol't|ore *nm* wine grower. **~ura** *nf* wine growing

'vitreo *a* vitreous; ⟨*sguardo*⟩ glassy

'vittima *nf* victim

'vitto *nm* food; (*pasti*) board. **~ e alloggio** board and lodging

vit'toria *nf* victory

vittori'ano *a* Victorian

vittori'oso *a* victorious

vi'uzza *nf* narrow lane

'viva *int* hurrah!; **~ la Regina!** long live the Queen!

vi'vac|e *a* vivacious; ⟨*mente*⟩ lively; ⟨*colore*⟩ bright. **~ità** *nf* vivacity; (*di mente*) liveliness; (*di colore*) brightness. **~iz'zare** *vt* liven up

vi'vaio *nm* nursery; (*per pesci*) pond; *fig* breeding ground

viva'mente *adv* ⟨*ringraziare*⟩ warmly

vi'vanda *nf* food; (*piatto*) dish

vi'vente *a* living ● *nmpl* **i viventi** the living

'vivere *vi* live; **~ di** live on ● *vt* (*passare*) go through ● *nm* life

'viveri *nmpl* provisions

'vivido *a* vivid

vivisezi'one *nf* vivisection

'vivo *a* alive; (*vivente*) living; (*vivace*) lively; ⟨*colore*⟩ bright; **~ e vegeto** alive and kicking; **farsi ~** keep in touch; (*arrivare*) turn up ● *nm* **colpire qcno sul ~** cut sb to the quick; **dal ~** ⟨*trasmissione*⟩ live; ⟨*disegnare*⟩ from life; **i vivi** the living

vizi|'are *vt* spoil ⟨*bambino ecc*⟩; (*guastare*) vitiate. **~'ato** *a* spoilt; ⟨*aria*⟩ stale. **'vizio** *nm* vice; (*cattiva abitudine*) bad habit; (*difetto*) flaw. **~'oso** *a* dissolute; (*difettoso*) faulty; **circolo ~oso** vicious circle

vocabo'lario *nm* dictionary; (*lessico*) vocabulary. **vo'cabolo** *nm* word

vo'cale *a* vocal ● *nf* vowel. **vo'calico** *a* ⟨*corde*⟩ vocal; ⟨*suono*⟩ vowel *attrib*

vocazi'one *nf* vocation

'voce *nf* voice; (*diceria*) rumour; (*di bilancio, dizionario*) entry

voci'are *vi* (*spettegolare*) gossip ● *nm* buzz of conversation

vocife'rare *vi* shout; **si vocifera che...** it is rumoured that...

'vog|a *nf* rowing; (*lena*) enthusiasm; (*moda*) vogue; **essere in ~a** be in fashion. **vo'gare** *vi* row. **~a'tore** *nm* oarsman; (*attrezzo*) rowing machine

'vogli|a *nf* desire; (*volontà*) will; (*della pelle*) birthmark; **aver ~a di fare qcsa**

feel like doing sth. **~'oso** *a* ⟨*occhi, persona*⟩ covetous

'voi *pers pron* you; **siete ~?** is that you?; **l'avete fatto ~?** did you do it yourself?. **~a'ltri** *pers pron* you

vo'lano *nm* shuttlecock; *Mech* flywheel

vo'lante *a* flying; ⟨*foglio*⟩ loose ● *nm* steering-wheel

volan'tino *nm* leaflet

vo'la|re *vi* fly. **~ta** *nf* *Sport* final sprint; **di ~ta** in a rush

vo'latile *a* ⟨*liquido*⟩ volatile ● *nm* bird

volée *nf inv* *Tennis* volley

vo'lente *a* **~ o nolente** whether you like it or not

volente'roso *a* willing

volenti'eri *adv* willingly; **~!** with pleasure!

vo'lere *vt* want; (*chiedere di*) ask for; (*aver bisogno di*) need; **vuole che lo faccia io** he wants me to do it; **fai come vuoi** do as you like; **se tuo padre vuole, ti porto al cinema** if your father agrees, I'll take you to the cinema; **vorrei un caffè** I'd like a coffee; **la leggenda vuole che...** legend has it that...; **la vuoi smettere?** will you stop that!; **senza ~** without meaning to; **voler bene/male a qcno** love/hate something against sb; **voler dire** mean; **ci vuole il latte** we need milk; **ci vuole tempo/pazienza** it takes time/patience; **volerne a** have a grudge against; **vuoi...vuoi...** either...or... ● *nm* will; **voleri** *pl* wishes

vol'gar|e *a* vulgar; (*popolare*) common. **~ità** *nf inv* vulgarity. **~iz'zare** *vt* popularize. **~'mente** *adv* (*grossolanamente*) vulgarly, coarsely; (*comunemente*) commonly

'volger|e *vt/i* turn. **~si** *vr* turn [round]; **~si a** (*dedicarsi*) take up

voli'era *nf* aviary

voli'tivo *a* strong-minded

'volo *nm* flight; **al ~** ⟨*fare qcsa*⟩ quickly; ⟨*prendere qcsa*⟩ in mid-air; **alzarsi in ~** ⟨*uccello:*⟩ take off; **in ~** airborne. **~ di linea** scheduled flight. **~ nazionale** domestic flight. **~ a vela** gliding.

volontà *nf inv* will; (*desiderio*) wish; **a ~** ⟨*mangiare*⟩ as much as you like. **~ria'mente** *adv* voluntarily. **volon'tario** *a* voluntary ● *nm* volunteer

volonte'roso *a* willing

'volpe *nf* fox

volt *nm inv* volt

'volta *nf* time; (*turno*) turn; (*curva*) bend; *Archit* vault; **4 volte 4** 4 times 4; **a volte** sometimes; **c'era una ~...** once upon a time, there was...; **una ~** once; **due volte** twice; **tre/quattro volte** three/four times; **una ~ per tutte** once and for all; **uno per ~** one at a time; **uno alla ~** one at a time; **alla ~ di** in the direction of

volta'faccia *nm inv* volte-face

vol'taggio *nm* voltage

vol'ta|re *vt/i* turn; (*rigirare*) turn round; (*rivoltare*) turn over; **~re pagina** *fig* forget the past. **~rsi** *vr* turn [round]

volta'stomaco *nm* nausea; *fig* disgust

volteggi'are *vi* circle; (*ginnastica*) vault

'volto *pp di* volgere ● *nm* face; **mi ha mostrato il suo vero ~** he revealed his true colours

vo'lubile *a* fickle

vo'lum|e *nm* volume. **~i'noso** *a* voluminous

voluta'mente *adv* deliberately

voluttu|osità *nf* voluptuousness. **~'oso** *a* voluptuous

vomi'tare *vt* vomit, be sick. **vomi'tevole** *a* nauseating. **'vomito** *nm* vomit.

'vongola *nf* clam

vo'race *a* voracious. **~'mente** *adv* voraciously

vo'ragine *nf* abyss

'vortice *nm* whirl; (*gorgo*) whirlpool; (*di vento*) whirlwind

'vostro (**il ~** *m*, **la vostra** *f*, **i vostri** *mpl*, **le vostre** *fpl*) *poss a* your; **è vostra questa macchina?** is this car yours?; **un ~ amico** a friend of yours; **~ padre** your father ● *poss pron* yours; **i vostri** your folks

vo'ta|nte *nmf* voter. **~re** *vi* vote. **~zi'one** *nf* voting; *Sch* marks *pl.* **'voto** *nm* vote; *Sch* mark; *Relig* vow

vs. *abbr Comm* (**vostro**) yours

vul'canico *a* volcanic. **vul'cano** *nm* volcano

vulne'rabil|e *a* vulnerable. **~ità** *nf* vulnerability

vuo'tare *vt*, **vuo'tarsi** *vr* empty

vu'oto *a* empty; (*non occupato*) vacant; **~ di** (*sprovvisto*) devoid of ● *nm* empty space; *Phys* vacuum; *fig* void; **assegno a ~** dud cheque; **sotto ~** ⟨*prodotto*⟩ vacuum-packed; **~ a perdere** no deposit. **~ d'aria** air pocket

WwXxYy

W *abbr* (**viva**) long live

'wafer *nm inv* (*biscotto*) wafer

walkie-'talkie *nm inv* walkie-talkie

water *nm inv* toilet, loo *fam*

watt *nm inv* watt

wat'tora *nm inv Phys* watt-hour

WC *nm* WC

Web *nm inv* Web

'western *a inv* cowboy *attrib* ● *nm Cinema* western

X, x *a* **raggi** *nmpl* **X** X-rays; **il giorno X** D-day

xenofo'bia *nf* xenophobia. **xe'nofobo,**

-a *a* xenophobic ● *nmf* xenophobe

xe'res *nm inv* sherry

xi'lofono *nm* xylophone

yacht *nm inv* yacht

yen *nm inv Fin* yen

'yeti *nm inv* yeti

'yoga *nm* yoga; (*praticante*) yogi

'yogurt *nm inv* yoghurt. **~i'era** *nf* yoghurt-maker

'yorkshire *nm inv* (*cane*) Yorkshire terrier

yo-yo *nm inv* yoyo®

Zz

zaba[gl]i'one *nm* zabaglione (*dessert made from eggs, wine or marsala and sugar*)

'zacchera *nf* (*schizzo*) splash of mud

zaf'fata *nf* whiff; (*di fumo*) cloud

zaffe'rano *nm* saffron

zaf'firo *nm* sapphire

'zaino *nm* rucksack

'zampa *nf* leg; **a quattro zampe** ⟨*animale*⟩ four-legged; (*carponi*) on all fours. **zampe** *pl* **di gallina** crow's feet

zampil'la|nte *a* spurting. **~re** *vi* spurt. **zam'pillo** *nm* spurt

zam'pogna *nf* bagpipe. **zampo'gnaro** *nm* piper

'zanna *nf* fang; (*di elefante*) tusk

zan'zar|a *nf* mosquito. **~i'era** *nf* (*velo*) mosquito net; (*su finestra*) insect screen

'zappa *nf* hoe. **zap'pare** *vt* hoe

'zattera *nf* raft

za'vorra *nf* ballast; *fig* dead wood

'zazzera *nf* mop of hair

'zebra *nf* zebra; **zebre** *pl* (*passaggio pedonale*) zebra crossing

'zecca[1] *nf* mint; **nuovo di ~** brand-new

'zecca[2] *nf* (*parassita*) tick

zec'chino *nm* sequin; **oro ~** pure gold

ze'lante *a* zealous. **'zelo** *nm* zeal

'zenit *nm* zenith

'zenzero *nm* ginger

'zeppa *nf* wedge

'zeppo *a* packed full; **pieno ~ di** crammed *o* packed with

zer'bino *nm* doormat

'zero *nm* zero, nought; (*in calcio*) nil; *Tennis* love; **due a ~** (*in partite*) two nil; **ricominciare da ~** *fig* start again from scratch

'zeta *nf* zed, zee *Am*

'zia *nf* aunt

zibel'lino *nm* sable

'zigomo *nm* cheek-bone

zigri'nato *a* ⟨*pelle*⟩ grained; ⟨*metallo*⟩ milled

zig'zag *nm inv* zigzag

zim'bello *nm* decoy; (*oggetto di scherno*) laughing-stock

'zinco *nm* zinc

'zingaro, -a *nmf* gypsy

'zio *nm* uncle

zi'tel|la *nf* spinster; *pej* old maid. **~'lona** *nf pej* old maid

zit'tire *vi* fall silent ● *vt* silence. **'zitto** *a* silent; **sta' zitto!** keep quiet!

ziz'zania *nf* (*discordia*) discord; **seminare ~** cause trouble

'zoccolo *nm* clog; (*di cavallo*) hoof; (*di terra*) clump; (*di parete*) skirting board, baseboard *Am*; (*di colonna*) base

zodia'cale *a* of the zodiac. **zo'diaco** *nm* zodiac

'zolfo *nm* sulphur

'zolla *nf* clod; (*di zucchero*) lump

zol'letta *nf* sugar cube, sugar lump

'zombi *nmf inv fig* zombi

'zona *nf* zone; (*area*) area. **~ di depressione** area of low pressure. **~ disco** area for parking discs only. **~ pedonale** pedestrian precinct. **~ verde** green belt

'zonzo *adv* **andare a ~** stroll about

zoo *nm inv* zoo

zoolo'gia *nf* zoology. **zoo'logico** *a* zoological. **zo'ologo, -a** *nmf* zoologist

zoo sa'fari *nm inv* safari park

zoppi'ca|nte *a* limping; *fig* shaky. **~re** *vi* limp; (*essere debole*) be shaky. **'zoppo, -a** *a* lame ● *nmf* cripple

zoti'cone *nm* boor

zu'ava *nf* **calzoni alla ~** plus-fours

'zucca *nf* marrow; (*fam: testa*) head; (*fam: persona*) thickie

zucche'r|are *vt* sugar. **~i'era** *nf* sugar bowl. **~i'ficio** *nm* sugar refinery. **zucche'rino** *a* sugary ● *nm* sugar lump

'zucchero *nm* sugar. **~ di canna** cane sugar. **~ a velo** icing sugar. **zucche'roso** *a fig* honeyed

zuc'chin|a *nf*, **~o** *nm* courgette, zucchini *Am*

zuc'cone *nm* blockhead

'zuffa *nf* scuffle

zufo'lare *vt/i* whistle

zu'mare *vi* zoom

'zuppa *nf* soup. **~ inglese** trifle

zup'petta *nf* **fare ~** [**con**] dunk

zuppi'era *nf* soup tureen

'zuppo *a* soaked

Aa

A /eɪ/ n Mus la m inv

a /ə/, accentato /eɪ/ (davanti a una vocale **an**) indef art un m, una f; (before s + consonant, gn, ps and z) uno; (before feminine noun starting with a vowel) un'; (each) a; **I am a lawyer** sono avvocato; **a tiger is a feline** la tigre è un felino; **a knife and fork** un coltello e una forchetta; **a Mr Smith is looking for you** un certo signor Smith ti sta cercando; **£2 a kilo/a head** due sterline al chilo/a testa

aback /ə'bæk/ adv **be taken ~** essere preso in contropiede

abandon /ə'bændən/ vt abbandonare; (give up) rinunciare a ● n abbandono m. **~ed** a abbandonato

abashed /ə'bæʃt/ a imbarazzato

abate /ə'beɪt/ vi calmarsi

abattoir /'æbətwɑ:(r)/ n mattatoio m

abbey /'æbɪ/ n abbazia f

abbreviat|e /ə'bri:vɪeɪt/ vt abbreviare. **~ion** /-'eɪʃn/ n abbreviazione f

abdicat|e /'æbdɪkeɪt/ vi abdicare. ● vt rinunciare a. **~ion** /-'keɪʃn/ n abdicazione f

abdom|en /'æbdəmən/ n addome m. **~inal** /-'dɒmɪnl/ a addominale

abduct /əb'dʌkt/ vt rapire. **~ion** /-'ʌkʃn/ n rapimento m

aberration /æbə'reɪʃn/ n aberrazione f

abet /ə'bet/ vt (pt/pp abetted) **aid and ~** Jur essere complice di

abeyance /ə'beɪəns/ n **in ~** in sospeso; **fall into ~** cadere in disuso

abhor /əb'hɔ:(r)/ vt (pt/pp abhorred) aborrire. **~rence** /-'hɒrəns/ n orrore m

abid|e /ə'baɪd/ vt (pt/pp abided) (tolerate) sopportare ● **abide by** vi rispettare. **~ing** a perpetuo

ability /ə'bɪlətɪ/ n capacità f inv

abject /'æbdʒekt/ a (poverty) degradante; (apology) umile; (coward) abietto

ablaze /ə'bleɪz/ a in fiamme; **be ~ with light** risplendere di luci

able /'eɪbl/ a capace, abile; **be ~ to do sth** poter fare qcsa; **were you ~ to...?** sei riuscito a...? **~-'bodied** a robusto; Mil abile

ably /'eɪblɪ/ adv abilmente

abnormal /æb'nɔ:ml/ a anormale. **~ity** /-'mælətɪ/ n anormalità f inv. **~ly** adv in modo anormale

aboard /ə'bɔ:d/ adv & prep a bordo

abol|ish /ə'bɒlɪʃ/ vt abolire. **~ition** /æbə'lɪʃn/ n abolizione f

abomina|ble /ə'bɒmɪnəbl/ a abominevole

Aborigine /æbə'rɪdʒənɪ/ n aborigeno, -a mf d'Australia

abort /ə'bɔ:t/ vt fare abortire; fig annullare. **~ion** /-'ɔ:ʃn/ n aborto m; **have an ~ion** abortire. **~ive** /-tɪv/ a (attempt) infruttuoso

abound /ə'baʊnd/ vi abbondare; **~ in** abbondare di

about /ə'baʊt/ adv (here and there) [di] qua e [di] là; (approximately) circa; **be ~** (illness, tourists:) essere in giro; **be up and ~** essere alzato; **leave sth lying ~** lasciare in giro qcsa ● prep (concerning) su; (in the region of) intorno a; (here and there in) per; **what is the book/the film ~?** di cosa parla il libro/il film?; **he wants to see you - what ~?** ti vuole vedere - a che proposito?; **talk/know ~** parlare/sapere di; **I know nothing ~ it** non ne so niente; **~ 5 o'clock** intorno alle 5; **travel ~ the world** viaggiare per il mondo; **be ~ to do sth** stare per fare qcsa; **how going to the cinema?** e se andassimo al cinema?

about: **~-'face** n, **~-'turn** n dietro front m inv

above /ə'bʌv/ adv & prep sopra; **~ all** soprattutto

above: **~-'board** a onesto. **~-'mentioned** a suddetto

abrasive /ə'breɪsɪv/ a abrasivo; (remark) caustico ● n abrasivo m

abreast /ə'brest/ adv fianco a fianco; **come ~ of** allinearsi con; **keep ~ of** tenersi al corrente di

abridged /ə'brɪdʒd/ a ridotto

abroad /ə'brɔ:d/ adv all'estero

abrupt /ə'brʌpt/ a brusco

abscess /'æbsɪs/ n ascesso m

abscond /əb'skɒnd/ vi fuggire

absence /'æbsəns/ n assenza f; (lack) mancanza f

absent[1] /'æbsənt/ a assente

absent[2] /æb'sent/ vt ~ oneself essere assente

absentee /æbsən'ti:/ n assente mf

absent-minded /æbsənt'maɪndɪd/ a distratto

absolute /'æbsəlu:t/ a assoluto; **an ~ idiot** un perfetto idiota. **~ly** adv assolutamente; (fam: indicating agreement) esattamente

absolution /æbsə'lu:ʃn/ n assoluzione f

absolve /əb'zɒlv/ vt assolvere

absorb /əb'sɔ:b/ vt assorbire; **~ed in** assorto in. **~ent** /-ənt/ a assorbente

absorption /əb'sɔ:pʃn/ n assorbimento m; (in activity) concentrazione f

abstain /əb'steɪn/ vi astenersi (**from** da)

abstemious /əb'sti:mɪəs/ a moderato

abstention /əb'stenʃn/ n Pol astensione f

abstinence /'æbstɪnəns/ n astinenza f

abstract /'æbstrækt/ a astratto ● n astratto m; (summary) estratto m

absurd /əb'sɜ:d/ a assurdo. **~ity** n assurdità f inv

abundan|ce /ə'bʌndəns/ n abbondanza f. **~t** a abbondante

abuse[1] /ə'bju:z/ vt (misuse) abusare di; (insult) insultare; (ill-treat) maltrattare

abus|e[2] /ə'bju:s/ n abuso m; (verbal) insulti mpl; (ill-treatment) maltrattamento m. **~ive** /-ɪv/ a offensivo

abut /ə'bʌt/ vi (pt/pp abutted) confinare (**onto** con)

abysmal /ə'bɪzml/ a fam pessimo; (ignorance) abissale

abyss /ə'bɪs/ n abisso m

academic /æə'demɪk/ a teorico; (qualifications, system) scolastico; **be ~** (person:) avere predisposizione allo studio ● n docente mf universitario, -a

academy /ə'kædəmɪ/ n accademia f; (of music) conservatorio m

accede /ək'si:d/ vi ~ **to** accedere a (request); salire a (throne)

accelerat|e /ək'seləreɪt/ vt/i accelerare. **~ion** /-'reɪʃn/ n accelerazione f. **~or** n Auto acceleratore m

accent /'æksənt/ n accento m

accentuate /ək'sentjʊeɪt/ vt accentuare

accept /ək'sept/ vt accettare. **~able** /-əbl/ a accettabile. **~ance** n accettazione f

access /'ækses/ n accesso m. **~ible** /ək'sesɪbl/ a accessibile

accession /ək'seʃn/ n (to throne) ascesa f al trono

accessory /ək'sesərɪ/ n accessorio m; Jur complice mf

accident /'æksɪdənt/ n incidente m; (chance) caso m; **by ~** per caso; (unintentionally) senza volere; **I'm sorry, it was an ~** mi dispiace, non l'ho fatto apposta. **~al** /-'dentl/ a (meeting) casuale; (death) incidentale; (unintentional) involontario. **~ally** adv per caso; (unintentionally) inavvertitamente

acclaim /ə'kleɪm/ n acclamazione f ● vt acclamare (**as** come)

acclimatize /ə'klaɪmətaɪz/ vt **become ~d** acclimatarsi

accolade /'ækəleɪd/ n riconoscimento m

accommodat|e /ə'kɒmədeɪt/ vt ospitare; (oblige) favorire. **~ing** a accomodante. **~ion** /-'deɪʃn/ n (place to stay) sistemazione f

accompan|iment /ə'kʌmpənɪmənt/ n accompagnamento m. **~ist** n Mus accompagnatore, -trice mf

accompany /ə'kʌmpənɪ/ vt (pt/pp -ied) accompagnare

accomplice /ə'kʌmplɪs/ n complice mf

accomplish /ə'kʌmplɪʃ/ vt (achieve) concludere; realizzare (aim). **~ed** a dotato; (fact) compiuto. **~ment** n realizzazione f; (achievement) risultato m; (talent) talento m

accord /ə'kɔ:d/ n (treaty) accordo m; **with one ~** tutti d'accordo; **of his own ~** di sua spontanea volontà. **~ance** n **in ~ance with** in conformità di o a

according /ə'kɔ:dɪŋ/ adv ~ **to** secondo. **~ly** adv di conseguenza

accordion /ə'kɔ:dɪən/ n fisarmonica f

accost /ə'kɒst/ vt abbordare

account /ə'kaʊnt/ n conto m; (report) descrizione f; (of eye-witness) resoconto m; **~s** pl Comm conti mpl; **on ~ of** a causa di; **on no ~** per nessun motivo; **on this ~** per questo motivo; **on my ~** per causa mia; **of no ~** di nessuna importanza; **take into ~** tener conto di ● **account for** vi (explain) spiegare; (person:) render conto di; (constitute) costituire. **~ability** n responsabilità f inv. **~able** a responsabile (**for** di)

3

accountant /əˈkaʊntənt/ n (*book-keeper*) contabile *mf*; (*consultant*) commercialista *mf*

accredited /əˈkredɪtɪd/ a accreditato

accrue /əˈkruː/ vi (*interest:*) maturare

accumulat|e /əˈkjuːmjʊleɪt/ vt accumulare ● vi accumularsi. **~ion** /-ˈleɪʃn/ n accumulazione *f*

accura|cy /ˈækjʊrəsɪ/ n precisione *f*. **~te** /-rət/ a preciso. **~tely** adv con precisione

accusation /ækjʊˈzeɪʃn/ n accusa *f*

accusative /əˈkjuːzətɪv/ a & n **~ [case]** Gram accusativo *m*

accuse /əˈkjuːz/ vt accusare; **~ sb of doing sth** accusare qcno di fare qcsa. **~d** n **the ~d** l'accusato *m*, l'accusata *f*

accustom /əˈkʌstəm/ vt abituare (**to** a); **grow** or **get ~ed to** abituarsi a. **~ed** a abituato

ace /eɪs/ n Cards asso *m*; (*tennis*) ace *m inv*

ache /eɪk/ n dolore *m* ● vi dolere, far male; **~ all over** essere tutto indolenzito

achieve /əˈtʃiːv/ vt ottenere (*success*); realizzare (*goal, ambition*). **~ment** n (*feat*) successo *m*

acid /ˈæsɪd/ a acido ● n acido *m*. **~ity** /əˈsɪdətɪ/ n acidità *f*. **~ 'rain** n pioggia *f* acida

acknowledge /əkˈnɒlɪdʒ/ vt riconoscere; rispondere a (*greeting*); far cenno di aver notato (*sb's presence*); **~ receipt of** accusare ricevuta di. **~ment** n riconoscimento *m*; **send an ~ment of a letter** confermare il ricevimento di una lettera

acne /ˈæknɪ/ n acne *f*

acorn /ˈeɪkɔːn/ n ghianda *f*

acoustic /əˈkuːstɪk/ a acustico. **~s** npl acustica *fsg*

acquaint /əˈkweɪnt/ vt **~ sb with** metter qcno al corrente di; **be ~ed with** conoscere (*person*); essere a conoscenza di (*fact*). **~ance** n (*person*) conoscente *mf*; **make sb's ~ance** fare la conoscenza di qcno

acquiesce /ækwɪˈes/ vi acconsentire (**to, in** a). **~nce** n acquiescenza *f*

acquire /əˈkwaɪə(r)/ vt acquisire

acquisit|ion /ækwɪˈzɪʃn/ n acquisizione *f*. **~ive** /əˈkwɪzətɪv/ a avido

acquit /əˈkwɪt/ vt (pt/pp **acquitted**) assolvere; **~ oneself well** cavarsela bene. **~tal** n assoluzione *f*

acre /ˈeɪkə(r)/ n acro *m* (= 4 047 *m²*)

acrid /ˈækrɪd/ a acre

acrimon|ious /ækrɪˈməʊnɪəs/ a aspro. **~y** /ˈækrɪmənɪ/ n asprezza *f*

acrobat /ˈækrəbæt/ n acrobata *mf*. **~ic** /-ˈbætɪk/ a acrobatico

across /əˈkrɒs/ adv dall'altra parte; (*wide*) in larghezza; (*not lengthwise*) attraverso; (*in crossword*) orizzontale; **come ~ sth** imbattersi in qcsa; **go ~** attraversare ● prep (*crosswise*) di traverso su; (*on the other side of*) dall'altra parte di

act /ækt/ n atto *m*; (*in variety show*) numero *m*; **put on an ~** fam fare scena ● vi agire; (*behave*) comportarsi; Theat recitare; (*pretend*) fingere; **~ as** fare da ● vt recitare (*role*). **~ing** a (*deputy*) provvisorio ● n Theat recitazione *f*; (*profession*) teatro *m*. **~ing profession** n professione *f* dell'attore

action /ˈækʃn/ n azione *f*; Mil combattimento *m*; Jur azione *f* legale; **out of ~** (*machine:*) fuori uso; **take ~** agire. **~ 'replay** n replay *m inv*

activ|e /ˈæktɪv/ a attivo. **~ely** adv attivamente. **~ity** /-ˈtɪvətɪ/ n attività *f inv*

act|or /ˈæktə(r)/ n attore *m*. **~ress** n attrice *f*

actual /ˈæktʃʊəl/ a (*real*) reale. **~ly** adv in realtà

acumen /ˈækjʊmən/ n acume *m*

acupuncture /ˈækjʊ-/ n agopuntura *f*

acute /əˈkjuːt/ a acuto; (*shortage, hardship*) estremo

ad /æd/ n fam pubblicità *f inv;* (*in paper*) inserzione *f.* annuncio *m*

AD abbr (**Anno Domini**) d.C.

adamant /ˈædəmənt/ a categorico (**that** sul fatto che)

adapt /əˈdæpt/ vt adattare (*play*) ● vi adattarsi. **~ability** /-əˈbɪlətɪ/ n adattabilità *f*. **~able** /-əbl/ a adattabile

adaptation /ædæpˈteɪʃn/ n Theat adattamento *m*

adapter, adaptor /əˈdæptə(r)/ n adattatore *m*; (*two-way*) presa *f* multipla

add /æd/ vt aggiungere; Math addizionare ● vi addizionare; **~ to** (*fig: increase*) aggravare. **add up** vt addizionare (*figures*) ● vi addizionare; **~ up to** ammontare a; **it doesn't ~ up** fig non quadra

adder /ˈædə(r)/ n vipera *f*

addict /ˈædɪkt/ n tossicodipendente *mf*; fig fanatico, -a *mf*

addict|ed /əˈdɪktɪd/ a assuefatto (**to** a); **~ed to drugs** tossicodipendente; **he's ~ed to television** è videodipendente. **~ion** /-ɪkʃn/ n dipendenza *f*; (*to drugs*) tossicodipendenza *f*. **~ive** /-ɪv/ *a* **be ~ive** dare assuefazione

addition /ə'dɪʃn/ *n* Math addizione *f*; (*thing added*) aggiunta *f*; **in ~** in aggiunta. **~al** *a* supplementare. **~ally** *adv* in più

additive /'ædɪtɪv/ *n* additivo *m*

address /ə'dres/ *n* indirizzo *m*; (*speech*) discorso *m*; **form of ~** formula *f* di cortesia ● *vt* indirizzare; (*speak to*) rivolgersi a ⟨*person*⟩; tenere un discorso a ⟨*meeting*⟩. **~ee** /ædre'si:/ *n* destinatario, -a *mf*

adenoids /'ædənɔɪdz/ *npl* adenoidi *fpl*

adept /'ædept/ *a* & *n* esperto, -a *mf* (**at in**)

adequate /'ædɪkwət/ *a* adeguato. **~ly** *adv* adeguatamente

adhere /əd'hɪə(r)/ *vi* aderire; **~ to** attenersi a ⟨*principles, rules*⟩

adhesive /əd'hi:sɪv/ *a* adesivo ● *n* adesivo *m*

adjacent /ə'dʒeɪsənt/ *a* adiacente

adjective /'ædʒɪktɪv/ *n* aggettivo *m*

adjoin /ə'dʒɔɪn/ *vt* essere adiacente a. **~ing** *a* adiacente

adjourn /ə'dʒɜ:n/ *vt/i* aggiornare (**until** a). **~ment** *n* aggiornamento *m*

adjudicate /ə'dʒu:dɪkeɪt/ *vi* decidere; (*in competition*) giudicare

adjust /ə'dʒʌst/ *vt* modificare; regolare ⟨*focus, sound etc*⟩ ● *vi* adattarsi. **~able** /-əbl/ *a* regolabile. **~ment** *n* adattamento *m*; Techn regolamento *m*

ad lib /æd'lɪb/ *a* improvvisato ● *adv* a piacere ● *vi* (*pt/pp* **ad libbed**) *fam* improvvisare

administer /əd'mɪnɪstə(r)/ *vt* amministrare; somministrare ⟨*medicine*⟩

administrat|ion /ədmɪnɪ'streɪʃn/ *n* amministrazione *f*; Pol governo *m*. **~or** /əd'mɪnɪstreɪtə(r)/ *n* amministratore, -trice *mf*

admirable /'ædmərəbl/ *a* ammirevole

admiral /'ædmərəl/ *n* ammiraglio *m*

admiration /ædmə'reɪʃn/ *n* ammirazione *f*

admire /əd'maɪə(r)/ *vt* ammirare. **~r** *n* ammiratore, -trice *mf*

admissible /əd'mɪsəbl/ *a* ammissibile

admission /əd'mɪʃn/ *n* ammissione *f*; (*to hospital*) ricovero *m*; (*entry*) ingresso *m*

admit /əd'mɪt/ *vt* (*pt/pp* **admitted**) (*let in*) far entrare; (*to hospital*) ricoverare; (*acknowledge*) ammettere ● *vi* **~ to sth** ammettere qcsa. **~tance** *n* ammissione

f; **'no ~tance'** 'vietato l'ingresso'. **~tedly** *adv* bisogna riconoscerlo

admonish /əd'mɒnɪʃ/ *vt* ammonire

ado /ə'du:/ *n* **without more ~** senza ulteriori indugi

adolescen|ce /ædə'lesns/ *n* adolescenza *f*. **~t** *a* & *n* adolescente *mf*

adopt /ə'dɒpt/ *vt* adottare; Pol scegliere ⟨*candidate*⟩. **~ion** /-ɒpʃn/ *n* adozione *f*. **~ive** /-ɪv/ *a* adottivo

ador|able /ə'dɔ:rəbl/ *a* adorabile. **~ation** /ædə'reɪʃn/ *n* adorazione *f*

adore /ə'dɔ:(r)/ *vt* adorare

adrenalin /ə'drenəlɪn/ *n* adrenalina *f*

Adriatic /eɪdrɪ'ætɪk/ *a* & *n* **the ~ [Sea]** il mare Adriatico, l'Adriatico *m*

adrift /ə'drɪft/ *a* alla deriva; **be ~** andare alla deriva; **come ~** staccarsi

adroit /ə'drɔɪt/ *a* abile

adulation /ædju'leɪʃn/ *n* adulazione *f*

adult /'ædʌlt/ *n* adulto, -a *mf*

adulterate /ə'dʌltəreɪt/ *vt* adulterare ⟨*wine*⟩

adultery /ə'dʌltərɪ/ *n* adulterio *m*

advance /əd'vɑ:ns/ *n* avanzamento *m*; Mil avanzata *f*; (*payment*) anticipo *m*; **in ~** in anticipo ● *vi* avanzare; (*make progress*) fare progressi ● *vt* avanzare ⟨*theory*⟩; promuovere ⟨*cause*⟩; anticipare ⟨*money*⟩. **~ booking** *n* prenotazione *f* [in anticipo]. **~d** *a* avanzato. **~ment** *n* promozione *f*

advantage /əd'vɑ:ntɪdʒ/ *n* vantaggio *m*; **take ~ of** approfittare di. **~ous** /ædvən'teɪdʒəs/ *a* vantaggioso

advent /'ædvent/ *n* avvento *m*

adventur|e /əd'ventʃə(r)/ *n* avventura *f*. **~ous** /-rəs/ *a* avventuroso

adverb /'ædvɜ:b/ *n* avverbio *m*

adversary /'ædvəsərɪ/ *n* avversario, -a *mf*

advers|e /'ædvɜ:s/ *a* avverso. **~ity** /əd'vɜ:sətɪ/ *n* avversità *f*

advert /'ædvɜ:t/ *n* *fam* = **advertisement**

advertise /'ædvətaɪz/ *vt* reclamizzare; mettere un annuncio per ⟨*job, flat*⟩ ● *vi* fare pubblicità; (*for job, flat*) mettere un annuncio

advertisement /əd'vɜ:tɪsmənt/ *n* pubblicità *f* inv; (*in paper*) inserzione *f*, annuncio *m*

advertis|er /'ædvətaɪzə(r)/ *n* (*in newspaper*) inserzionista *mf*. **~ing** *n* pubblicità *f* ● *attrib* pubblicitario

advice /əd'vaɪs/ *n* consigli *mpl*; **piece of ~** consiglio *m*

advisable /əd'vaɪzəbl/ *a* consigliabile

advis|e /əd'vaɪz/ *vt* consigliare; (*inform*) avvisare; **~e sb to do sth** consigliare a qcno di fare qcsa; **~e sb against sth** sconsigliare qcsa a qcno. **~er** *n* consulente *mf*. **~ory** *a* consultivo

advocate[1] /'ædvəkət/ *n* (*supporter*) fautore, -trice *mf*

advocate[2] /'ædvəkeɪt/ *vt* propugnare

aerial /'eərɪəl/ *a* aereo ● *n* antenna *f*

aerobics /eə'rəʊbɪks/ *n* aerobica *fsg*

aero|drome /'eərədrəʊm/ *n* aerodromo *m*. **~plane** *n* aeroplano *m*

aerosol /'eərəsɒl/ *n* bomboletta *f* spray

aesthetic /iːs'θetɪk/ *a* estetico

afar /ə'fɑː(r)/ *adv* **from ~** da lontano

affable /'æfəbl/ *a* affabile

affair /ə'feə(r)/ *n* affare *m*; (*scandal*) caso *m*; (*sexual*) relazione *f*

affect /ə'fekt/ *vt* influire su; (*emotionally*) colpire; (*concern*) riguardare. **~ation** /æfek'teɪʃn/ *n* affettazione *f*. **~ed** *a* affettato

affection /ə'fekʃn/ *n* affetto *m*. **~ate** /-ət/ *a* affettuoso

affiliated /ə'fɪlɪeɪtɪd/ *a* affiliato

affinity /ə'fɪnəti/ *n* affinità *f inv*

affirm /ə'fɜːm/ *vt* affermare; *Jur* dichiarare solennemente

affirmative /ə'fɜːmətɪv/ *a* affermativo ● *n* **in the ~** affermativamente

afflict /ə'flɪkt/ *vt* affliggere. **~ion** /-ɪkʃn/ *n* afflizione *f*

afflue|nce /'æflʊəns/ *n* agiatezza *f*. **~t** *a* agiato

afford /ə'fɔːd/ *vt* **be able to ~ sth** potersi permettere qcsa. **~able** /-əbl/ *a* abbordabile

affray /ə'freɪ/ *n* rissa *f*

affront /ə'frʌnt/ *n* affronto *m*

afield /ə'fiːld/ *adv* **further ~** più lontano

afloat /ə'fləʊt/ *a* a galla

afoot /ə'fʊt/ *a* **there's something ~** si sta preparando qualcosa

aforesaid /ə'fɔːsed/ *a Jur* suddetto

afraid /ə'freɪd/ *a* **be ~** aver paura; **I'm ~ not** purtroppo no; **I'm ~ so** temo di sì; **I'm ~ I can't help you** mi dispiace, ma non posso esserle d'aiuto

afresh /ə'freʃ/ *adv* da capo

Africa /'æfrɪkə/ *n* Africa *f*. **~n** *a* & *n* africano, -a *mf*

after /'ɑːftə(r)/ *adv* dopo; **the day ~** il giorno dopo; **be ~** cercare ● *prep* dopo; **~ all** dopotutto; **the day ~ tomorrow** dopodomani ● *conj* dopo che

after: ~-effect *n* conseguenza *f*. **~math** /-mɑːθ/ *n* conseguenze *fpl*; **the**

~math of war il dopoguerra; **in the ~math of** nel periodo successivo a. **~'noon** *n* pomeriggio *m*; **good ~noon!** buon giorno! **~-sales service** *n* servizio *m* assistenza clienti. **~shave** *n* [lozione *f*] dopobarba *m inv*. **~thought** *n* added as an **~thought** aggiunto in un secondo momento; **~wards** *adv* in seguito

again /ə'gem/ *adv* di nuovo; [*then*] **~** (*besides*) inoltre; (*on the other hand*) d'altra parte; **~ and ~** continuamente

against /ə'gemst/ *prep* contro

age /eɪdʒ/ *n* età *f inv*; (*era*) era *f*; **~s** *fam* secoli; **what ~ are you?** quanti anni hai?; **be under ~** non avere l'età richiesta; **he's two years of ~** ha due anni ● *vt/i* (*pres p* **ageing**) invecchiare

aged[1] /eɪdʒd/ *a* **~ two** di due anni

aged[2] /'eɪdʒɪd/ *a* anziano ● *npl* **the ~** gli anziani

ageless /'eɪdʒlɪs/ *a* senza età

agency /'eɪdʒənsɪ/ *n* agenzia *f*; **have the ~ for** essere il concessionario di

agenda /ə'dʒendə/ *n* ordine *m* del giorno; **on the ~** all'ordine del giorno; *fig* in programma

agent /'eɪdʒənt/ *n* agente *mf*

aggravat|e /'ægrəveɪt/ *vt* aggravare; (*annoy*) esasperare. **~ion** /-'veɪʃn/ *n* aggravamento *m*; (*annoyance*) esasperazione *f*

aggregate /'ægrɪgət/ *a* totale ● *n* totale *m*; **on ~** nel complesso

aggress|ion /ə'greʃn/ *n* aggressione *f*. **~ive** /-sɪv/ *a* aggressivo. **~iveness** *n* aggressività *f*. **~or** *n* aggressore *m*

aggro /'ægrəʊ/ *n fam* aggressività *f*; (*problems*) grane *fpl*

aghast /ə'gɑːst/ *a* inorridito

agil|e /'ædʒaɪl/ *a* agile. **~ity** /ə'dʒɪləti/ *n* agilità *f*

agitat|e /'ædʒɪteɪt/ *vt* mettere in agitazione; (*shake*) agitare ● *vi fig* **~e for** creare delle agitazioni per. **~ed** *a* agitato. **~ion** /-'teɪʃn/ *n* agitazione *f*. **~or** *n* agitatore, -trice *mf*

agnostic /æg'nɒstɪk/ *n* agnostico, -a *mf*

ago /ə'gəʊ/ *adv* fa; **a long time/a month ~** molto tempo/un mese fa

agog /ə'gɒg/ *a* eccitato

agoniz|e /'ægənaɪz/ *vi* angosciarsi (*over* per). **~ing** *a* angosciante

agony /'ægənɪ/ *n* (*mental*) angoscia *f*; **be in ~** avere dei dolori atroci

agree /ə'griː/ *vt* accordarsi su; **~ to do sth** accettare di fare qcsa; **~ that** essere d'accordo [sul fatto] che ● *vi* essere d'accordo; ⟨*figures:*⟩ concordare; (*reach agreement*) mettersi d'accordo; (*get on*) andare d'accordo; (*consent*) acconsentire (**to** a); **it doesn't ~ with me** mi fa male; **~ with sth** (*approve of*) approvare qcsa

agreeable /ə'griːəbl/ *a* gradevole; (*willing*) d'accordo

agreed /ə'griːd/ *a* convenuto

agreement /ə'griːmənt/ *n* accordo *m*; **in ~** d'accordo

agricultur|al /ægrɪ'kʌltʃərəl/ *a* agricolo. **~e** /'ægrɪkʌltʃə(r)/ *n* agricoltura *f*

aground /ə'graʊnd/ *adv* **run ~** ⟨*ship:*⟩ arenarsi

ahead /ə'hed/ *adv* avanti; **be ~ of** essere davanti a; *fig* essere avanti rispetto a; **draw ~** passare davanti (**of** a); **get ~** (*in life*) riuscire; **go ~!** fai pure!; **look ~** pensare all'avvenire; **plan ~** fare progetti per l'avvenire

aid /eɪd/ *n* aiuto *m*; **in ~ of** a favore di ● *vt* aiutare

aide /eɪd/ *n* assistente *mf*

Aids /eɪdz/ *n* AIDS *m*

ail|ing /'eɪlɪŋ/ *a* malato. **~ment** *n* disturbo *m*

aim /eɪm/ *n* mira *f*; *fig* scopo *m*; **take ~** prendere la mira ● *vt* puntare ⟨*gun*⟩ (**at** contro) ● *vi* mirare; **~ to do sth** aspirare a fare qcsa. **~less** *a*, **~lessly** *adv* senza scopo

air /eə(r)/ *n* aria *f*; **be on the ~** ⟨*programme:*⟩ essere in onda; **put on ~s** darsi delle arie; **by ~** in aereo; (*airmail*) per via aerea ● *vt* arieggiare; far conoscere ⟨*views*⟩

air: **~-bed** *n* materassino *m* [gonfiabile]. **~-conditioned** *a* con aria condizionata. **~-conditioning** *n* aria *f* condizionata. **~craft** *n* aereo *m*. **~craft carrier** *n* portaerei *f inv*. **~fare** *n* tariffa *f* aerea. **~field** *n* campo *m* d'aviazione. **~ force** *n* aviazione *f*. **~ freshener** *n* deodorante *m* per l'ambiente. **~gun** *n* fucile *m* pneumatico. **~ hostess** *n* hostess *f inv*. **~ letter** *n* aerogramma *m*. **~line** *n* compagnia *f* aerea. **~lock** *n* bolla *f* d'aria. **~mail** *n* posta *f* aerea. **~plane** *n Am* aereo *m*. **~ pocket** *n* vuoto *m* d'aria. **~port** *n* aeroporto *m*. **~-raid** *n* incursione *f* aerea. **~-raid shelter** *n* rifugio *m* antiaereo. **~ship** *n* dirigibile *m*. **~tight** *a* ermetico. **~ traffic** *n* traffico *m* aereo. **~-traffic controller** *n* controllore *m* di volo. **~worthy** *a* idoneo al volo

airy /'eərɪ/ *a* (**-ier, -iest**) arieggiato; ⟨*manner*⟩ noncurante

aisle /aɪl/ *n* corridoio *m*; (*in supermarket*) corsia *f*; (*in church*) navata *f*

ajar /ə'dʒɑː(r)/ *a* socchiuso

akin /ə'kɪn/ *a* **~ to** simile a

alarm /ə'lɑːm/ *n* allarme *m*; **set the ~** (*of alarm clock*) mettere la sveglia ● *vt* allarmare. **~ clock** *n* sveglia *f*

alas /ə'læs/ *int* ahimè

Albania /æl'beɪnɪə/ *n* Albania *f*

album /'ælbəm/ *n* album *m inv*

alcohol /'ælkəhɒl/ *n* alcol *m*. **~ic** /-'hɒlɪk/ *a* alcolico ● *n* alcolizzato, -a *mf*. **~ism** *n* alcolismo *m*

alcove /'ælkəʊv/ *n* alcova *f*

alert /ə'lɜːt/ *a* sveglio; (*watchful*) vigile ● *n* segnale *m* d'allarme; **be on the ~** stare allerta ● *vt* allertare

algae /'ældʒiː/ *npl* alghe *fpl*

algebra /'ældʒɪbrə/ *n* algebra *f*

Algeria /æl'dʒɪərɪə/ *n* Algeria *f*. **~n** *a* & *n* algerino, -a *mf*

alias /'eɪlɪəs/ *n* pseudonimo *m* ● *adv* alias

alibi /'ælɪbaɪ/ *n* alibi *m inv*

alien /'eɪlɪən/ *a* straniero; *fig* estraneo ● *n* straniero, -a *mf*; (*from space*) alieno, -a *mf*

alienat|e /'eɪlɪəneɪt/ *vt* alienare. **~ion** /-'neɪʃn/ *n* alienazione *f*

alight¹ /ə'laɪt/ *vi* scendere; ⟨*bird:*⟩ posarsi

alight² /ə'laɪt/ **be ~** essere in fiamme; **set ~** dar fuoco a

align /ə'laɪn/ *vt* allineare. **~ment** *n* allineamento *m*; **out of ~ment** non allineato

alike /ə'laɪk/ *a* simile; **be ~** rassomigliarsi ● *adv* in modo simile; **look ~** rassomigliarsi; **summer and winter ~** sia d'estate che d'inverno

alimony /'ælɪmənɪ/ *n* alimenti *mpl*

alive /ə'laɪv/ *a* vivo; **~ with** brulicante di; **~ to** sensibile a

alkali /'ælkəlaɪ/ *n* alcali *m*

all /ɔːl/ *a* tutto; **~ the children, ~ children** tutti i bambini; **~ day** tutto il giorno; **he refused ~ help** ha rifiutato qualsiasi aiuto; **for ~ that** (*nevertheless*) ciononostante; **in ~ sincerity** in tutta sincerità; **be ~ for** essere favorevole a ● *pron* tutto; **~ of you/ them** tutti voi/loro; **~ of it** tutto; **~ of the town** tutta la città; **in ~** in tutto; **in ~** tutto sommato; **most of ~** più di ogni altra cosa; **once and for ~** una volta per tutte ● *adv* completamente; **~ but** quasi; **~ at once** (*at the same time*) tutto in una volta; **~ at once, ~ of a sudden** all'improvviso; **~ too soon** troppo presto; **~ the same** (*nevertheless*) ciononostante; **~ the better** meglio ancora; **she's not ~ that good an actress** non è poi così brava come attrice; **~ in** in tutto; *fam* esausto; **thirty/three ~** (*in sport*) trenta/tre pari; **~ over** (*finished*) tutto finito; (*everywhere*) dappertutto; **it's ~ right** (*I don't mind*) non fa niente; **I'm ~ right** (*not hurt*) non ho niente; **~ right!** va bene!

allay /ə'leɪ/ *vt* placare ‹suspicions, anger›

allegation /ælɪ'geɪʃn/ *n* accusa *f*

allege /ə'ledʒ/ *vt* dichiarare. **~d** a presunto. **~dly** /-ɪdlɪ/ *adv* a quanto si dice

allegiance /ə'li:dʒəns/ *n* fedeltà *f*

allegor|ical /ælɪ'ɡɒrɪkl/ *a* allegorico. **~y** /'ælɪɡərɪ/ *n* allegoria *f*

allerg|ic /ə'lɜːdʒɪk/ *a* allergico. **~y** /'ælədʒɪ/ *n* allergia *f*

alleviate /ə'liːvɪeɪt/ *vt* alleviare

alley /'ælɪ/ *n* vicolo *m*; (*for bowling*) corsia *f*

alliance /ə'laɪəns/ *n* alleanza *f*

allied /'ælaɪd/ *a* alleato; (*fig: related*) connesso (**to** a)

alligator /'ælɪɡeɪtə(r)/ *n* alligatore *m*

allocat|e /'æləkeɪt/ *vt* assegnare; distribuire ‹resources›. **~ion** /-'keɪʃn/ *n* assegnazione *f*; (*of resources*) distribuzione *f*

allot /ə'lɒt/ *vt* (*pt/pp* **allotted**) distribuire. **~ment** *n* distribuzione *f*; (*share*) parte *f*; (*land*) piccolo lotto *m* di terreno

allow /ə'laʊ/ *vt* permettere; (*grant*) accordare; (*reckon on*) contare; (*agree*) ammettere; **~ for** tener conto di; **~ sb to do sth** permettere a qcno di fare qcsa; **you are not ~ed to...** è vietato...

allowance /ə'laʊəns/ *n* sussidio *m*; (*Am: pocket money*) paghetta *f*; (*for petrol etc*) indennità *f inv*; (*of luggage, duty free*) limite *m*; **make ~s for** essere indulgente verso ‹sb›; tener conto di ‹sth›

alloy /'ælɔɪ/ *n* lega *f*

allude /ə'lu:d/ *vi* alludere

allusion /ə'lu:ʒn/ *n* allusione *f*

ally[1] /'ælaɪ/ *n* alleato, -a *mf*

ally[2] /ə'laɪ/ *vt* (*pt/pp* **-ied**) alleare; **~ oneself with** allearsi con

almighty /ɔ:l'maɪtɪ/ *a* (*fam: big*) mega *inv* ● *n* **the A~** l'Onnipotente *m*

almond /'ɑ:mənd/ *n* mandorla *f*; (*tree*) mandorlo *m*

almost /'ɔ:lməʊst/ *adv* quasi

alone /ə'ləʊn/ *a* solo; **leave me ~!** lasciami in pace!; **let ~** (*not to mention*) figurarsi ● *adv* da solo

along /ə'lɒŋ/ *prep* lungo ● *adv* **~ with** assieme a; **all ~** tutto il tempo; **come ~!** (*hurry up*) vieni qui!; **I'll be ~ in a minute** arrivo tra un attimo; **move ~** spostarsi; **move ~!** circolare!

along'side *adv* lungo bordo ● *prep* lungo; **work ~ sb** lavorare fianco a fianco con qcno

aloof /ə'lu:f/ *a* distante

aloud /ə'laʊd/ *adv* ad alta voce

alphabet /'ælfəbet/ *n* alfabeto *m*. **~ical** /-'betɪkl/ *a* alfabetico

alpine /'ælpaɪn/ *a* alpino

Alps /ælps/ *npl* Alpi *fpl*

already /ɔ:l'redɪ/ *adv* già

Alsatian /æl'seɪʃn/ *n* (*dog*) pastore *m* tedesco

also /'ɔ:lsəʊ/ *adv* anche; **~, I need...** [e] inoltre, ho bisogno di...

altar /'ɔ:ltə(r)/ *n* altare *m*

alter /'ɔ:ltə(r)/ *vt* cambiare; aggiustare ‹clothes› ● *vi* cambiare. **~ation** /-'reɪʃn/ *n* modifica *f*

alternate[1] /'ɔ:ltəneɪt/ *vi* alternarsi ● *vt* alternare

alternate[2] /ɔ:l'tɜ:nət/ *a* alterno; **on ~ days** a giorni alterni

'alternating current *n* corrente *f* alternata

alternative /ɔ:l'tɜ:nətɪv/ *a* alternativo ● *n* alternativa *f*. **~ly** *adv* alternativamente

although /ɔ:l'ðəʊ/ *conj* benché, sebbene

altitude /'æltɪtju:d/ *n* altitudine *f*

altogether /ɔ:ltə'ɡeðə(r)/ *adv* (*in all*) in tutto; (*completely*) completamente; **I'm not ~ sure** non sono del tutto sicuro

altruistic /æltrʊ'ɪstɪk/ *a* altruistico

aluminium /æljʊ'mɪnɪəm/ *n*, *Am* **aluminum** /ə'lu:mɪnəm/ *n* alluminio *m*

always /'ɔ:lweɪz/ *adv* sempre

am /æm/ *see* **be**

a.m. *abbr* (**ante meridiem**) del mattino

amalgamate /ə'mælɡəmeɪt/ *vt* fondere ● *vi* fondersi

amass /ə'mæs/ *vt* accumulare

amateur /'æmətə(r)/ *n* non professionista *mf*; *pej* dilettante *mf* ● *attrib* dilet-

tante; ~ **dramatics** filodrammatica *f*.
~**ish** *a* dilettantesco

amaze /əˈmeɪz/ *vt* stupire. ~**d** *a* stupito. ~**ment** *n* stupore *m*

amazing /əˈmeɪzɪŋ/ *a* incredibile

ambassador /æmˈbæsədə(r)/ *n* ambasciatore, -trice *mf*

amber /ˈæmbə(r)/ *n* ambra *f* ● *a* (*colour*) ambra *inv*

ambidextrous /æmbɪˈdekstrəs/ *a* ambidestro

ambience /ˈæmbɪəns/ *n* atmosfera *f*

ambigu|ity /æmbɪˈgjuːətɪ/ *n* ambiguità *f inv*. ~**ous** /-ˈbɪgjʊəs/ *a* ambiguo

ambiti|on /æmˈbɪʃn/ *n* ambizione *f*; (*aim*) aspirazione *f*. ~**ous** /-ʃəs/ *a* ambizioso

ambivalent /æmˈbɪvələnt/ *a* ambivalente

amble /ˈæmbl/ *vi* camminare senza fretta

ambulance /ˈæmbjʊləns/ *n* ambulanza *f*

ambush /ˈæmbʊʃ/ *n* imboscata *f* ● *vt* tendere un'imboscata a

amenable /əˈmiːnəbl/ *a* conciliante; ~ **to** sensibile a

amend /əˈmend/ *vt* modificare. ~**ment** *n* modifica *f*. ~**s** *npl* **make** ~**s** fare ammenda (**for** di, per)

amenities /əˈmiːnətɪz/ *npl* comodità *fpl*

America /əˈmerɪkə/ *n* America *f*. ~**n** *a* & *n* americano, -a *mf*

amiable /ˈeɪmɪəbl/ *a* amabile

amicable /ˈæmɪkəbl/ *a* amichevole

amiss /əˈmɪs/ *a* **there's something** ~ c'è qualcosa che non va ● *adv* **take sth** ~ prendersela [a male]; **it won't come** ~ non sarebbe sgradito

ammonia /əˈməʊnɪə/ *n* ammoniaca *f*

ammunition /æmjʊˈnɪʃn/ *n* munizioni *fpl*

amnesia /æmˈniːzɪə/ *n* amnesia *f*

amnesty /ˈæmnəstɪ/ *n* amnistia *f*

among[st] /əˈmʌŋ[st]/ *prep* tra, fra

amoral /erˈmɒrəl/ *a* amorale

amorous /ˈæmərəs/ *a* amoroso

amount /əˈmaʊnt/ *n* quantità *f inv*; (*sum of money*) importo *m* ● *vi* ~ **to** ammontare a; *fig* equivalere a

amp /æmp/ *n* ampère *m inv*

amphibi|an /æmˈfɪbɪən/ *n* anfibio *m*. ~**ous** /-ɪəs/ *a* anfibio

amphitheatre /ˈæmfɪ-/ *n* anfiteatro *m*

ampl|e /ˈæmpl/ *a* (*large*) grande; (*proportions*) ampio; (*enough*) largamente sufficiente

amplif|ier /ˈæmplɪfaɪə(r)/ *n* amplificatore *m*. ~**y** /-faɪ/ *vt* (*pt/pp* -**ied**) amplificare ⟨*sound*⟩

amputat|e /ˈæmpjʊteɪt/ *vt* amputare. ~**ion** /-ˈteɪʃn/ *n* amputazione *f*

amuse /əˈmjuːz/ *vt* divertire. ~**ment** *n* divertimento *m*. ~**ment arcade** *n* sala *f* giochi

amusing /əˈmjuːzɪŋ/ *a* divertente

an /ən/, *accentato* /æn/ *see* **a**

anaem|ia /əˈniːmɪə/ *n* anemia *f*. ~**ic** *a* anemico

anaesthetic /ænəsˈθetɪk/ *n* anestesia *f*

anaesthet|ist /əˈniːsθətɪst/ *n* anestesista *mf*

analog[ue] /ˈænəlɒg/ *a* analogico

analogy /əˈnælədʒɪ/ *n* analogia *f*

analyse /ˈænəlaɪz/ *vt* analizzare

analysis /əˈnæləsɪs/ *n* analisi *f inv*

analyst /ˈænəlɪst/ *n* analista *mf*

analytical /ænəˈlɪtɪkl/ *a* analitico

anarch|ist /ˈænəkɪst/ *n* anarchico, -a *mf*. ~**y** *n* anarchia *f*

anatom|ical /ænəˈtɒmɪkl/ *a* anatomico. ~**ically** *adv* anatomicamente. ~**y** /əˈnætəmɪ/ *n* anatomia *f*

ancest|or /ˈænsestə(r)/ *n* antenato, -a *mf*. ~**ry** *n* antenati *mpl*

anchor /ˈæŋkə(r)/ *n* ancora *f* ● *vi* gettar l'ancora ● *vt* ancorare

anchovy /ˈæntʃəvɪ/ *n* acciuga *f*

ancient /ˈeɪnʃənt/ *a* antico; *fam* vecchio

ancillary /ænˈsɪlərɪ/ *a* ausiliario

and /ənd/, *accentato* /ænd/ *conj* e; **two** ~ **two** due più due; **six hundred** ~ **two** seicentodue; **more** ~ **more** sempre più; **nice** ~ **warm** bello caldo; **try** ~ **come** cerca di venire; **go** ~ **get** vai a prendere

anecdote /ˈænɪkdəʊt/ *n* aneddoto *m*

anew /əˈnjuː/ *adv* di nuovo

angel /ˈeɪndʒl/ *n* angelo *m*. ~**ic** /ænˈdʒelɪk/ *a* angelico

anger /ˈæŋgə(r)/ *n* rabbia *f* ● *vt* far arrabbiare

angle¹ /ˈæŋgl/ *n* angolo *m*; *fig* angolazione *f*; **at an** ~ storto

angle² *vi* pescare con la lenza; ~ **for** *fig* cercare di ottenere. ~**r** *n* pescatore, -trice *mf*

Anglican /ˈæŋglɪkən/ *a* & *n* anglicano, -a *mf*

Anglo-Saxon /æŋgləʊˈsæksn/ *a* & *n* anglo-sassone *mf*

angr|y /ˈæŋgrɪ/ *a* (-**ier**, -**iest**) arrabbiato; **get** ~**y** arrabbiarsi; ~**y with** *or* **sb** arrabbiato con qcno; ~**y at** *or*

about sth arrabbiato per qcsa. **~ily** *adv* rabbiosamente

anguish /'æŋgwɪʃ/ *n* angoscia *f*

angular /'æŋgjʊlə(r)/ *a* angolare

animal /'ænɪml/ *a & n* animale *m*

animate[1] /'ænɪmət/ *a* animato

animat|e[2] /'ænɪmeɪt/ *vt* animare. **~ed** *a* animato; ⟨person⟩ vivace. **~ion** /-'meɪʃn/ *n* animazione *f*

animosity /ænɪ'mɒsətɪ/ *n* animosità *f inv*

ankle /'æŋkl/ *n* caviglia *f*

annex /ə'neks/ *vt* annettere

annex[e] /'æneks/ *n* annesso *m*

annihilat|e /ə'naɪəleɪt/ *vt* annientare. **~ion** /-'leɪʃn/ *n* annientamento *m*

anniversary /ænɪ'vɜːsərɪ/ *n* anniversario *m*

announce /ə'naʊns/ *vt* annunciare. **~ment** *n* annuncio *m*. **~r** *n* annunciatore, -trice *mf*

annoy /ə'nɔɪ/ *vt* dare fastidio a; **get ~ed** essere infastidito. **~ance** *n* seccatura *f*; ⟨anger⟩ irritazione *f*. **~ing** *a* fastidioso

annual /'ænjʊəl/ *a* annuale; ⟨income⟩ annuo ● *n Bot* pianta *f* annua; ⟨children's book⟩ almanacco *m*

annuity /ə'njuːətɪ/ *n* annualità *f inv*

annul /ə'nʌl/ *vt* (*pt/pp* **annulled**) annullare

anomaly /ə'nɒməlɪ/ *n* anomalia *f*

anonymous /ə'nɒnɪməs/ *a* anonimo

anorak /'ænəræk/ *n* giacca *f* a vento

anorex|ia /ænə'reksɪə/ *n* anoressia *f*. **~ic** *a* anoressico

another /ə'nʌðə(r)/ *a & pron*; **~ [one]** un altro, un'altra; **in ~ way** diversamente; **one ~** l'un l'altro

answer /'ɑːnsə(r)/ *n* risposta *f*; ⟨solution⟩ soluzione *f* ● *vt* rispondere a ⟨person, question, letter⟩; esaudire ⟨prayer⟩; **~ the door** aprire la porta; **~ the telephone** rispondere al telefono ● *vi* rispondere; **~ back** ribattere; **~ for** rispondere di. **~able** /-əbl/ *a* responsabile; **be ~able to sb** rispondere a qcno. **~ing machine** *n Teleph* segreteria *f* telefonica

ant /ænt/ *n* formica *f*

antagonis|m /æn'tægənɪzm/ *n* antagonismo *m*. **~tic** /-'nɪstɪk/ *a* antagonistico

antagonize /æn'tægənaɪz/ *vt* provocare l'ostilità di

Antarctic /æn'tɑːktɪk/ *n* Antartico *m* ● *a* antartico

antenatal /æntɪ'neɪtl/ *a* prenatale

antenna /æn'tenə/ *n* antenna *f*

anthem /'ænθəm/ *n* inno *m*

anthology /æn'θɒlədʒɪ/ *n* antologia *f*

anthropology /ænθrə'pɒlədʒɪ/ *n* antropologia *f*

anti-'aircraft /æntɪ-/ *a* antiaereo

antibiotic /æntɪbaɪ'ɒtɪk/ *n* antibiotico *m*

'antibody *n* anticorpo *m*

anticipat|e /æn'tɪsɪpeɪt/ *vt* prevedere; ⟨forestall⟩ anticipare. **~ion** /-'peɪʃn/ *n* anticipo *m*; ⟨excitement⟩ attesa *f*

anti'climax *n* delusione *f*

anti'clockwise *a & adv* in senso antiorario

antics /'æntɪks/ *npl* gesti *mpl* buffi

anti'cyclone *n* anticiclone *m*

antidote /'æntɪdəʊt/ *n* antidoto *m*

'antifreeze *n* antigelo *m*

antipathy /æn'tɪpəθɪ/ *n* antipatia *f*

antiquated /'æntɪkweɪtɪd/ *a* antiquato

antique /æn'tiːk/ *a* antico ● *n* antichità *f inv*. **~ dealer** *n* antiquario, -a *mf*

antiquity /æn'tɪkwətɪ/ *n* antichità *f*

anti-Semitic /æntɪsɪ'mɪtɪk/ *a* antisemita

anti'septic *a & n* antisettico *m*

anti'social *a* ⟨behaviour⟩ antisociale; ⟨person⟩ asociale

anti'virus program *n Comput* programma *m* di antivirus

antlers /'æntləz/ *npl* corna *fpl*

anus /'eɪnəs/ *n* ano *m*

anxiety /æŋ'zaɪətɪ/ *n* ansia *f*

anxious /'æŋkʃəs/ *a* ansioso. **~ly** *adv* con ansia

any /'enɪ/ *a* ⟨no matter which⟩ qualsiasi, qualunque; **have we ~ wine/ biscuits?** abbiamo del vino/dei biscotti?; **have we ~ jam/apples?** abbiamo della marmellata/delle mele?; **~ colour/number you like** qualsiasi colore/numero ti piaccia; **we don't have ~ wine/biscuits** non abbiamo vino/biscotti; **I don't have ~ reason to lie** non ho nessun motivo per mentire; **for ~ reason** per qualsiasi ragione ● *pron* ⟨some⟩ ne; ⟨no matter which⟩ uno qualsiasi; **I don't want ~ [of it]** non ne voglio [nessuno]; **there aren't ~** non ce ne sono; **have we ~?** ne abbiamo?; **have you read ~ of her books?** hai letto qualcuno dei suoi libri? ● *adv* **I can't go ~ quicker** non posso andare più in fretta; **is ~ better?** va un po' meglio?; **would you like ~ more?** ne vuoi ancora?; **I can't eat ~ more** non posso mangiare più niente

'anybody *pron* chiunque; *(after negative)* nessuno; **I haven't seen ~** non ho visto nessuno

'anyhow *adv* ad ogni modo, comunque; *(badly)* non importa come

'anyone *pron* = **anybody**

'anything *pron* qualche cosa, qualcosa; *(no matter what)* qualsiasi cosa; *(after negative)* niente; **take/ buy ~ you like** prendi/compra quello che vuoi; **I don't remember ~** non mi ricordo niente; **he's ~ but stupid** è tutto, ma non stupido; **I'll do ~ but that** farò qualsiasi cosa, tranne quello

'anyway *adv* ad ogni modo, comunque

'anywhere *adv* dovunque; *(after negative)* da nessuna parte; **put it ~** mettilo dove vuoi; **I can't find it ~** non lo trovo da nessuna parte; **~ else** da qualch'altra parte; *(after negative)* da nessun'altra parte; **I don't want to go ~ else** non voglio andare da nessun'altra parte

apart /ə'pɑːt/ *adv* lontano; **live ~** vivere separati; **100 miles ~** lontani 100 miglia; **~ from** a parte; **you can't tell them ~** non si possono distinguere; **joking ~** scherzi a parte

apartment /ə'pɑːtmənt/ *n (Am: flat)* appartamento *m*; **in my ~** a casa mia

apathy /'æpəθɪ/ *n* apatia *f*

ape /eɪp/ *n* scimmia *f* ● *vt* scimmiottare

aperitif /ə'perətiːf/ *n* aperitivo *m*

aperture /'æpətʃə(r)/ *n* apertura *f*

apex /'eɪpeks/ *n* vertice *m*

apiece /ə'piːs/ *adv* ciascuno

apologetic /əpɒlə'dʒetɪk/ *a* ⟨air, remark⟩ di scusa; **be ~** essere spiacente

apologize /ə'pɒlədʒaɪz/ *vi* scusarsi (**for** per)

apology /ə'pɒlədʒɪ/ *n* scusa *f*; *fig* **an ~ for a dinner** una sottospecie di cena

apostle /ə'pɒsl/ *n* apostolo *m*

apostrophe /ə'pɒstrəfɪ/ *n* apostrofo *m*

appal /ə'pɔːl/ *vt* (*pt/pp* **appalled**) sconvolgere. **~ling** *a* sconvolgente

apparatus /æpə'reɪtəs/ *n* apparato *m*

apparent /ə'pærənt/ *a* evidente; *(seeming)* apparente. **~ly** *adv* apparentemente

apparition /æpə'rɪʃn/ *n* apparizione *f*

appeal /ə'piːl/ *n* appello *m*; *(attraction)* attrattiva *f* ● *vi* fare appello; **~ to** (*be attractive to*) attrarre. **~ing** *a* attraente

appear /ə'pɪə(r)/ *vi* apparire; *(seem)* sembrare; ⟨*publication:*⟩ uscire; *Theat* esibirsi. **~ance** *n* apparizione *f*; *(look)* aspetto *m*; **to all ~ances** a giudicare

dalle apparenze; **keep up ~ances** salvare le apparenze

appease /ə'piːz/ *vt* placare

appendicitis /əpendɪ'saɪtɪs/ *n* appendicite *f*

appendix /ə'pendɪks/ *n* (*pl* **-ices** /-ɪsiːz/) *(of book)* appendice *f*; (*pl* **-es**) *Anat* appendice *f*

appetite /'æpɪtaɪt/ *n* appetito *m*

appetiz|er /'æpɪtaɪzə(r)/ *n* stuzzichino *m*. **~ing** *a* appetitoso

applau|d /ə'plɔːd/ *vt/i* applaudire. **~se** *n* applauso *m*

apple /'æpl/ *n* mela *f*. **~-tree** *n* melo *m*

appliance /ə'plaɪəns/ *n* attrezzo *m*; **[electrical] ~** elettrodomestico *m*

applicable /ə'plɪkəbl/ *a* **be ~ to** essere valido per; **not ~** *(on form)* non applicabile

applicant /'æplɪkənt/ *n* candidato, -a *mf*

application /æplɪ'keɪʃn/ *n* applicazione *f*; *(request)* domanda *f*; *(for job)* candidatura *f*. **~ form** *n* modulo *m* di domanda

applied /ə'plaɪd/ *a* applicato

apply /ə'plaɪ/ *vt* (*pt/pp* **-ied**) applicare; **~ oneself** applicarsi ● *vi* applicarsi; ⟨*law:*⟩ essere applicabile; **~ to** *(ask)* rivolgersi a; **~ for** fare domanda per ⟨*job etc*⟩

appoint /ə'pɔɪnt/ *vt* nominare; fissare ⟨*time*⟩. **~ment** *n* appuntamento *m*; *(to job)* nomina *f*; *(job)* posto *m*

appraisal /ə'preɪz(ə)l/ *n* valutazione *f*

appreciable /ə'priːʃəbl/ *a* sensibile

appreciat|e /ə'priːʃɪeɪt/ *vt* apprezzare; *(understand)* comprendere ● *vi* *(increase in value)* aumentare di valore. **~ion** /-'eɪʃn/ *n* *(gratitude)* riconoscenza *f*; *(enjoyment)* apprezzamento *m*; *(understanding)* comprensione *f*; *(in value)* aumento *m*. **~ive** /-ətɪv/ *a* riconoscente

apprehend /æprɪ'hend/ *vt* arrestare

apprehens|ion /æprɪ'henʃn/ *n* arresto *m*; *(fear)* apprensione *f*. **~ive** /-sɪv/ *a* apprensivo

apprentice /ə'prentɪs/ *n* apprendista *mf*. **~ship** *n* apprendistato *m*

approach /ə'prəʊtʃ/ *n* avvicinamento *m*; *(to problem)* approccio *m*; *(access)* accesso *m*; **make ~es to** fare degli approcci con ● *vi* avvicinarsi ● *vt* avvicinarsi a; *(with request)* rivolgersi a; affrontare ⟨*problem*⟩. **~able** /-əbl/ *a* accessibile

appropriate¹ /ə'prəʊprɪət/ *a* appropriato

appropriate² /ə'prəʊprɪeɪt/ *vt* appropriarsi di

approval /ə'pru:vl/ *n* approvazione *f*; **on ~** in prova

approv|e /ə'pru:v/ *vt* approvare ● *vi* **~e of** approvare ⟨*sth*⟩; avere una buona opinione di ⟨*sb*⟩. **~ing** *a* ⟨*smile, nod*⟩ d'approvazione

approximate /ə'prɒksɪmət/ *a* approssimativo. **~ly** *adv* approssimativamente

approximation /əprɒksɪ'meɪʃn/ *n* approssimazione *f*

apricot /'eɪprɪkɒt/ *n* albicocca *f*

April /'eɪprəl/ *n* aprile *m*; **~ Fool's Day** il primo d'aprile

apron /'eɪprən/ *n* grembiule *m*

apt /æpt/ *a* appropriato; **be ~ to do sth** avere tendenza a fare qcsa

aptitude /'æptɪtjuːd/ *n* disposizione *f*. **~ test** *n* test *m inv* attitudinale

aqualung /'ækwəlʌŋ/ *n* autorespiratore *m*

aquarium /ə'kweərɪəm/ *n* acquario *m*

Aquarius /ə'kweərɪəs/ *n Astr* Acquario *m*

aquatic /ə'kwætɪk/ *a* acquatico

Arab /'ærəb/ *a & n* arabo, -a *mf*. **~ian** /ə'reɪbɪən/ *a* arabo

Arabic /'ærəbɪk/ *a* arabo; **~ numerals** numeri *mpl* arabici ● *n* arabo *m*

arable /'ærəbl/ *a* coltivabile

arbitrary /'ɑːbɪtrərɪ/ *a* arbitrario

arbitrat|e /'ɑːbɪtreɪt/ *vi* arbitrare. **~ion** /-'treɪʃn/ *n* arbitraggio *m*

arc /ɑːk/ *n* arco *m*

arcade /ɑː'keɪd/ *n* portico *m*; ⟨*shops*⟩ galleria *f*

arch /ɑːtʃ/ *n* arco *m*; ⟨*of foot*⟩ dorso *m* del piede

archaeological /ɑːkɪə'lɒdʒɪkl/ *a* archeologico

archaeolog|ist /ɑːkɪ'ɒlədʒɪst/ *n* archeologo, -a *mf*. **~y** *n* archeologia *f*

archaic /ɑː'keɪɪk/ *a* arcaico

arch'bishop /ɑːtʃ-/ *n* arcivescovo *m*

arch-'enemy *n* acerrimo nemico *m*

architect /'ɑːkɪtekt/ *n* architetto *m*. **~ural** /ɑːkɪ'tektʃərəl/ *a* architettonico

architecture /'ɑːkɪtektʃə(r)/ *n* architettura *f*

archives /'ɑːkaɪvz/ *npl* archivi *mpl*

archiving /'ɑːkaɪvɪŋ/ *n Comput* archiviazione *f*

archway /'ɑːtʃweɪ/ *n* arco *m*

Arctic /'ɑːktɪk/ *a* artico ● *n* **the ~** l'Artico

ardent /'ɑːdənt/ *a* ardente

arduous /'ɑːdjʊəs/ *a* arduo

are /ɑː(r)/ *see* **be**

area /'eərɪə/ *n* area *f*; ⟨*region*⟩ zona *f*; ⟨*fig: field*⟩ campo *m*. **~ code** *n* prefisso *m* [telefonico]

arena /ə'riːnə/ *n* arena *f*

aren't /ɑːnt/ = **are not** *see* **be**

Argentina /ɑːdʒən'tiːnə/ *n* Argentina *f*

Argentinian /-'tɪnɪən/ *a & n* argentino, -a *mf*

argue /'ɑːgjuː/ *vi* litigare (**about** su); ⟨*debate*⟩ dibattere; **don't ~!** non discutere! ● *vt* ⟨*debate*⟩ dibattere; ⟨*reason*⟩ **~ that** sostenere che

argument /'ɑːgjʊmənt/ *n* argomento *m*; ⟨*reasoning*⟩ ragionamento *m*; **have an ~** litigare. **~ative** /-'mentətɪv/ *a* polemico

aria /'ɑːrɪə/ *n* aria *f*

arid /'ærɪd/ *a* arido

Aries /'eəriːz/ *n Astr* Ariete *m*

arise /ə'raɪz/ *vi* (*pt* **arose**, *pp* **arisen**) ⟨*opportunity, need, problem:*⟩ presentarsi; ⟨*result*⟩ derivare

aristocracy /ærɪ'stɒkrəsɪ/ *n* aristocrazia *f*

aristocrat /'ærɪstəkræt/ *n* aristocratico, -a *mf*. **~ic** /-'krætɪk/ *a* aristocratico

arithmetic /ə'rɪθmətɪk/ *n* aritmetica *f*

arm /ɑːm/ *n* braccio *m*; ⟨*of chair*⟩ bracciolo *m*; **~s** *pl* ⟨*weapons*⟩ armi *fpl*; **~ in ~** a braccetto; **up in ~s** *fam* furioso (**about** per) ● *vt* armare

armaments /'ɑːməmənts/ *npl* armamenti *mpl*

'armchair *n* poltrona *f*

armed /ɑːmd/ *a* armato; **~ forces** forze *fpl* armate; **~ robbery** rapina *f* a mano armata

armistice /'ɑːmɪstɪs/ *n* armistizio *m*

armour /'ɑːmə(r)/ *n* armatura *f*. **~ed** *a* ⟨*vehicle*⟩ blindato

'armpit *n* ascella *f*

army /'ɑːmɪ/ *n* esercito *m*; **join the ~** arruolarsi

aroma /ə'rəʊmə/ *n* aroma *f*. **~tic** /ærə'mætɪk/ *a* aromatico

arose /ə'rəʊz/ *see* **arise**

around /ə'raʊnd/ *adv* intorno; **all ~** tutt'intorno; **I'm not from ~ here** non sono di qui; **he's not ~** non c'è ● *prep* intorno a; in giro per ⟨*room, shops, world*⟩

arouse /ə'raʊz/ *vt* svegliare; ⟨*sexually*⟩ eccitare

arrange /ə'reɪndʒ/ vt sistemare ⟨furniture, books⟩; organizzare ⟨meeting⟩; fissare ⟨date, time⟩; ~ **to do sth** combinare di fare qcsa. ~**ment** n (of furniture) sistemazione f; Mus arrangiamento m; (agreement) accordo; (of flowers) composizione f; **make ~ments** prendere disposizioni

arrears /ə'rɪəz/ npl arretrati mpl; **be in ~** essere in arretrato; **paid in ~** pagato a lavoro eseguito

arrest /ə'rest/ n arresto m; **under ~** in stato d'arresto ● vt arrestare

arrival /ə'raɪvl/ n arrivo m; **new ~s** pl nuovi arrivati mpl

arrive /ə'raɪv/ vi arrivare; ~ **at** fig raggiungere

arrogan|ce /'ærəgəns/ n arroganza f. ~**t** a arrogante

arrow /'ærəʊ/ n freccia f

arse /ɑːs/ n vulg culo m

arsenic /'ɑːsənɪk/ n arsenico m

arson /'ɑːsn/ n incendio m doloso. ~**ist** /-sənɪst/ n incendiario, -a mf

art /ɑːt/ n arte f; ~**s and crafts** pl artigianato m; **the A~s** pl l'arte f; **A~s degree** Univ laurea f in Lettere

artery /'ɑːtərɪ/ n arteria f

artful /'ɑːtfl/ a scaltro

'**art gallery** n galleria f d'arte

arthritis /ɑː'θraɪtɪs/ n artrite f

artichoke /'ɑːtɪtʃəʊk/ n carciofo m

article /'ɑːtɪkl/ n articolo m; ~ **of clothing** capo m d'abbigliamento

articulate[1] /ɑː'tɪkjʊlət/ a ⟨speech⟩ chiaro; **be ~** esprimersi bene

articulate[2] /ɑː'tɪkjʊleɪt/ vt scandire ⟨words⟩. ~**d lorry** n autotreno m

artifice /'ɑːtɪfɪs/ n artificio m

artificial /ɑːtɪ'fɪʃl/ a artificiale. ~**ly** adv artificialmente; ⟨smile⟩ artificiosamente

artillery /ɑː'tɪlərɪ/ n artiglieria f

artist /'ɑːtɪst/ n artista mf

artiste /ɑː'tiːst/ n Theat artista mf

artistic /ɑː'tɪstɪk/ a artistico

as /æz/ conj come; (since) siccome; (while) mentre; **as he grew older** diventando vecchio; **as you get to know her** conoscendola meglio; **young as she is** per quanto sia giovane ● prep come; **as a friend** come amico; **as a child** da bambino; **as a foreigner** in quanto straniero; **disguised as** travestito da ● adv **as well** (also) anche; **as soon as I get home** [non] appena arrivo a casa; **as quick as you** veloce quanto te; **as quick as you can** più

veloce che puoi; **as far as** (distance) fino a; **as far as I'm concerned** per quanto mi riguarda; **as long as** finché; (provided that) purché

asbestos /æz'bestɒs/ n amianto m

ascend /ə'send/ vi salire ● vt salire a ⟨throne⟩

Ascension /ə'senʃn/ n Relig Ascensione f

ascent /ə'sent/ n ascesa f

ascertain /æsə'teɪn/ vt accertare

ascribe /ə'skraɪb/ vt attribuire

ash[1] /æʃ/ n (tree) frassino m

ash[2] n cenere f

ashamed /ə'ʃeɪmd/ a **be/feel ~** vergognarsi

ashore /ə'ʃɔː(r)/ adv a terra; **go ~** sbarcare

ash: ~**tray** n portacenere m. **A~ 'Wednesday** n mercoledì m inv delle Ceneri

Asia /'eɪʒə/ n Asia f. ~**n** a & n asiatico, -a mf. ~**tic** /eɪʒɪ'ætɪk/ a asiatico

aside /ə'saɪd/ adv **take sb ~** prendere qcno a parte; **put sth ~** mettere qcsa da parte; ~ **from you** Am a parte te

ask /ɑːsk/ vt fare ⟨question⟩; (invite) invitare; ~ **sb sth** domandare or chiedere qcsa a qcno; ~ **sb to do sth** domandare or chiedere a qcno di fare qcsa ● vi ~ **about sth** informarsi su qcsa; ~ **after** chiedere [notizie] di; ~ **for** chiedere ⟨sth⟩; chiedere di ⟨sb⟩; ~ **for trouble** fam andare in cerca di guai. **ask in** vt ~ **sb in** invitare qcno ad entrare. **ask out** vt ~ **sb out** chiedere a qcno di uscire

askance /ə'skɑːns/ adv **look ~ at sb/sth** guardare qcno/qcsa di traverso

askew /ə'skjuː/ a & adv di traverso

asleep /ə'sliːp/ a **be ~** dormire; **fall ~** addormentarsi

asparagus /ə'spærəgəs/ n asparagi mpl

aspect /'æspekt/ n aspetto m

aspersions /ə'spɜːʃnz/ npl **cast ~ on** diffamare

asphalt /'æsfælt/ n asfalto m

asphyxia /əs'fɪksɪə/ n asfissia f. ~**te** /əs'fɪksɪeɪt/ vt asfissiare. ~**tion** /-'eɪʃn/ n asfissia f

aspirations /æspə'reɪʃnz/ npl aspirazioni fpl

aspire /ə'spaɪə(r)/ vi ~ **to** aspirare a

ass /æs/ n asino m

assailant /ə'seɪlənt/ n assalitore, -trice mf

assassin /ə'sæsɪn/ n assassino, -a mf.

~ate *vt* assassinare. **~ation** /-'neɪʃn/ *n* assassinio *m*

assault /ə'sɔ:lt/ *n Mil* assalto *m*; *Jur* aggressione *f* ● *vt* aggredire

assemble /ə'sembl/ *vi* radunarsi ● *vt* radunare; *Techn* montare

assembly /ə'semblɪ/ *n* assemblea *f*; *Sch* assemblea *f* giornaliera di alunni e professori di una scuola; *Techn* montaggio *m*. **~ line** *n* catena *f* di montaggio

assent /ə'sent/ *n* assenso *m* ● *vi* acconsentire

assert /ə'sɜ:t/ *vt* asserire; far valere ⟨one's rights⟩; **~ oneself** farsi valere. **~ion** /-ɜ:ʃn/ *n* asserzione *f*. **~ive** /-tɪv/ *a* **be ~ive** farsi valere

assess /ə'ses/ *vt* valutare; ⟨for tax purposes⟩ stabilire l'imponibile di. **~ment** *n* valutazione *f*; (of tax) accertamento *m*

asset /'æset/ *n* ⟨advantage⟩ vantaggio *m*; ⟨person⟩ elemento *m* prezioso. **~s** *pl* beni *mpl*; ⟨on balance sheet⟩ attivo *msg*

assign /ə'sam/ *vt* assegnare. **~ment** *n* ⟨task⟩ incarico *m*

assimilate /ə'sɪmɪleɪt/ *vt* assimilare; integrare ⟨person⟩

assist /ə'sɪst/ *vt/i* assistere; **~ sb to do sth** assistere qcno nel fare qcsa. **~ance** *n* assistenza *f*. **~ant** *a* **~ant manager** vicedirettore, -trice *mf* ● *n* assistente *mf*; ⟨in shop⟩ commesso, -a *mf*

associat|e¹ /ə'səʊʃɪeɪt/ *vt* associare (**with** a); **be ~ed with sth** ⟨involved in⟩ essere coinvolto in qcsa ● *vi* **~e with** frequentare. **~ion** /-'eɪʃn/ *n* associazione *f*. **A~ion 'Football** *n* [gioco *m* del] calcio *m*

associate² /ə'səʊʃɪət/ *a* associato ● *n* collega *mf*; ⟨member⟩ socio, -a *mf*

assort|ed /ə'sɔ:tɪd/ *a* assortito. **~ment** *n* assortimento *m*

assum|e /ə'sju:m/ *vt* presumere; assumere ⟨control⟩; **~e office** entrare in carica; **~ing that you're right,...** ammettendo che tu abbia ragione,...

assumption /ə'sʌmpʃn/ *n* supposizione *f*; **on the ~ that** partendo dal presupposto che; **the A~** *Relig* l'Assunzione *f*

assurance /ə'ʃʊərəns/ *n* assicurazione *f*; ⟨confidence⟩ sicurezza *f*

assure /ə'ʃʊə(r)/ *vt* assicurare. **~d** *a* sicuro

asterisk /'æstərɪsk/ *n* asterisco *m*

astern /ə'stɜ:n/ *adv* a poppa

asthma /'æsmə/ *n* asma *f*. **~tic** /-'mætɪk/ *a* asmatico

astonish /ə'stɒnɪʃ/ *vt* stupire. **~ing** *a* stupefacente. **~ment** *n* stupore *m*

astound /ə'staʊnd/ *vt* stupire

astray /ə'streɪ/ *adv* **go ~** smarrirsi; ⟨morally⟩ uscire dalla retta via; **lead ~** traviare

astride /ə'straɪd/ *adv* [a] cavalcioni ● *prep* a cavalcioni di

astrolog|er /ə'strɒlədʒə(r)/ *n* astrologo, -a *mf*. **~y** *n* astrologia *f*

astronaut /'æstrənɔ:t/ *n* astronauta *mf*

astronom|er /ə'strɒnəmə(r)/ *n* astronomo, -a *mf*. **~ical** /æstrə'nɒmɪkl/ *a* astronomico. **~y** *n* astronomia *f*

astute /ə'stju:t/ *a* astuto

asylum /ə'saɪləm/ *n* [**political**] **~** asilo *m* politico; [**lunatic**] **~** manicomio *m*

at /ət/, *accentato* /æt/ *prep* a; **at the station/the market** alla stazione/al mercato; **at the office/the bank** in ufficio/banca; **at the beginning** all'inizio; **at John's** da John; **at the hairdresser's** dal parrucchiere; **at home** a casa; **at work** al lavoro; **at school** a scuola; **at a party/wedding** a una festa/un matrimonio; **at 1 o'clock** all'una; **at 50 km an hour** ai 50 all'ora; **at Christmas/Easter** a Natale/Pasqua; **at times** talvolta; **two at a time** due alla volta; **good at languages** bravo nelle lingue; **at sb's request** su richiesta di qcno; **are you at all worried?** sei preoccupato?

ate /et/ *see* eat

atheist /'eɪθɪɪst/ *n* ateo, -a *mf*

athlet|e /'æθli:t/ *n* atleta *mf*. **~ic** /-'letɪk/ *a* atletico. **~ics** /-'letɪks/ *n* atletica *fsg*

Atlantic /ət'læntɪk/ *a & n* **the ~ [Ocean]** l'[Oceano *m*] Atlantico *m*

atlas /'ætləs/ *n* atlante *m*

atmospher|e /'ætməsfɪə(r)/ *n* atmosfera *f*. **~ic** /-'ferɪk/ *a* atmosferico

atom /'ætəm/ *n* atomo *m*. **~ bomb** *n* bomba *f* atomica

atomic /ə'tɒmɪk/ *a* atomico

atone /ə'təʊn/ *vi* **~ for** pagare per

atrocious /ə'trəʊʃəs/ *a* atroce; ⟨fam: meal, weather⟩ abominevole

atrocity /ə'trɒsətɪ/ *n* atrocità *f inv*

at sign /'ætsaɪn/ *n Comput* chiocciola *f*

attach /ə'tætʃ/ *vt* attaccare; attribuire ⟨importance⟩; **be ~ed to** *fig* essere attaccato a

attachê /ə'tæʃeɪ/ *n* addetto *m*. **~ case** *n* ventiquattrore *f inv*

attachment /əˈtætʃmənt/ n (affection) attaccamento m; (accessory) accessorio m

attack /əˈtæk/ n attacco m; (physical) aggressione f ● vt attaccare; (physically) aggredire. **~er** n assalitore, -trice mf; (critic) detrattore, -trice mf

attain /əˈteɪn/ vt realizzare (ambition); raggiungere (success, age, goal)

attempt /əˈtempt/ n tentativo m ● vt tentare

attend /əˈtend/ vt essere presente a; (go regularly to) frequentare; (doctor:) avere in cura ● vi essere presente; (pay attention) prestare attenzione. **attend to** vt occuparsi di; (in shop) servire. **~ance** n presenza f. **~ant** n guardiano, -a mf

attention /əˈtenʃn/ n attenzione f; **~!** Mil attenti!; **pay ~** prestare attenzione; **need ~** aver bisogno di attenzioni; (skin, hair, plant:) dover essere curato; (car, tyres:) dover essere riparato; **for the ~ of** all'attenzione di

attentive /əˈtentɪv/ a (pupil, audience) attento

attest /əˈtest/ vt/i attestare

attic /ˈætɪk/ n soffitta f

attitude /ˈætɪtjuːd/ n atteggiamento m

attorney /əˈtɜːnɪ/ n (Am: lawyer) avvocato m; **power of ~** delega f

attract /əˈtrækt/ vt attirare. **~ion** /-ˈækʃn/ n attrazione f; (feature) attrattiva f. **~ive** /-tɪv/ a (person) attraente; (proposal, price) allettante

attribute[1] /ˈætrɪbjuːt/ n attributo m

attribute[2] /əˈtrɪbjuːt/ vt attribuire

attrition /əˈtrɪʃn/ n **war of ~** guerra f di logoramento

aubergine /ˈəʊbəʒiːn/ n melanzana f

auburn /ˈɔːbən/ a castano ramato

auction /ˈɔːkʃn/ n asta f ● vt vendere all'asta. **~eer** /-ʃəˈnɪə(r)/ n banditore m

audacious /ɔːˈdeɪʃəs/ a sfacciato; (daring) audace. **~ty** /-ˈdæsətɪ/ n sfacciataggine f; (daring) audacia f

audible /ˈɔːdəbl/ a udibile

audience /ˈɔːdɪəns/ n Theat pubblico m; TV telespettatori mpl; Radio ascoltatori mpl; (meeting) udienza f

audio /ˈɔːdɪəʊ/: **~tape** n audiocassetta f. **~ typist** n dattilografo, -a mf (che trascrive registrazioni). **~'visual** a audiovisivo

audit /ˈɔːdɪt/ n verifica f del bilancio ● vt verificare

audition /ɔːˈdɪʃn/ n audizione f ● vi fare un'audizione

auditor /ˈɔːdɪtə(r)/ n revisore m di conti

auditorium /ɔːdɪˈtɔːrɪəm/ n sala f

augment /ɔːgˈment/ vt aumentare

augur /ˈɔːgə(r)/ vi **~ well/ill** essere di buon/cattivo augurio

August /ˈɔːgəst/ n agosto m

aunt /ɑːnt/ n zia f

au pair /əʊˈpeə(r)/ n **~ [girl]** ragazza f alla pari

aura /ˈɔːrə/ n aura f

auspices /ˈɔːspɪsɪz/ npl **under the ~ of** sotto l'egida di

auspicious /ɔːˈspɪʃəs/ a di buon augurio

auster|e /ɒˈstɪə(r)/ a austero. **~ity** /-terətɪ/ n austerità f

Australia /ɒˈstreɪlɪə/ n Australia f. **~n** a & n australiano, -a mf

Austria /ˈɒstrɪə/ n Austria f. **~n** a & n austriaco, -a mf

authentic /ɔːˈθentɪk/ a autentico. **~ate** vt autenticare. **~ity** /-ˈtɪsətɪ/ n autenticità f

author /ˈɔːθə(r)/ n autore m

authoritarian /ɔːθɒrɪˈteərɪən/ a autoritario

authoritative /ɔːˈθɒrɪtətɪv/ a autorevole; (manner) autoritario

authority /ɔːˈθɒrətɪ/ n autorità f; (permission) autorizzazione f; **be in ~ over** avere autorità su

authorization /ɔːθəraɪˈzeɪʃn/ n autorizzazione f

authorize /ˈɔːθəraɪz/ vt autorizzare

autobi'ography /ɔːtə-/ n autobiografia f

autocratic /ɔːtəˈkrætɪk/ a autocratico

autograph /ˈɔːtəgrɑːf/ n autografo m

automate /ˈɔːtəmeɪt/ vt automatizzare

automatic /ɔːtəˈmætɪk/ a automatico ● n (car) macchina f col cambio automatico; (washing machine) lavatrice f automatica. **~ally** adv automaticamente

automation /ɔːtəˈmeɪʃn/ n automazione f

automobile /ˈɔːtəməbiːl/ n automobile f

autonom|ous /ɔːˈtɒnəməs/ a autonomo. **~y** n autonomia f

autopsy /ˈɔːtɒpsɪ/ n autopsia f

autumn /ˈɔːtəm/ n autunno m. **~al** /-ˈtʌmnl/ a autunnale

auxiliary /ɔːgˈzɪlɪərɪ/ a ausiliario ● n ausiliare m

avail /əˈveɪl/ n **to no ~** invano ● vi **~ oneself of** approfittare di

available /ə'veɪləbl/ *a* disponibile; ⟨*book, record etc*⟩ in vendita

avalanche /'ævəlɑ:nʃ/ *n* valanga *f*

avarice /'ævərɪs/ *n* avidità *f*

avenge /ə'vendʒ/ *vt* vendicare

avenue /'ævənju:/ *n* viale *m*; *fig* strada *f*

average /'ævərɪdʒ/ *a* medio; ⟨*mediocre*⟩ mediocre ● *n* media *f*; **on ~** in media ● *vt* ⟨*sales, attendance etc:*⟩ raggiungere una media di. **average out at** *vt* risultare in media

aversl|e /ə'vɜ:s/ *a* not be ~e to sth non essere contro qcsa. **~ion** /-ɜ:ʃn/ *n* avversione *f* (**to** per)

avert /ə'vɜ:t/ *vt* evitare ⟨*crisis*⟩; distogliere ⟨*eyes*⟩

aviary /'eɪvɪərɪ/ *n* uccelliera *f*

aviation /eɪvɪ'eɪʃn/ *n* aviazione *f*

avid /'ævɪd/ *a* avido (**for** di); ⟨*reader*⟩ appassionato

avocado /ævə'kɑ:dəʊ/ *n* avocado *m*

avoid /ə'vɔɪd/ *vt* evitare. **~able** /-əbl/ *a* evitabile

await /ə'weɪt/ *vt* attendere

awake /ə'weɪk/ *a* sveglio; **wide ~** completamente sveglio ● *vi* (*pt* **awoke**, *pp* **awoken**) svegliarsi

awaken /ə'weɪkn/ *vt* svegliare. **~ing** *n* risveglio *m*

award /ə'wɔ:d/ *n* premio *m*; ⟨*medal*⟩ riconoscimento *m*; ⟨*of prize*⟩ assegnazione *f* ● *vt* assegnare; ⟨*hand over*⟩ consegnare

aware /ə'weə(r)/ *a* be ~ of ⟨*sense*⟩ percepire; ⟨*know*⟩ essere conscio di; **become ~ of** accorgersi di; ⟨*learn*⟩ venire a sapere di; **be ~ that** rendersi conto che. **~ness** *n* percezione *f*; ⟨*knowledge*⟩ consapevolezza *f*

awash /ə'wɒʃ/ *a* inondato (**with** di)

away /ə'weɪ/ *adv* via; **go/stay ~** andare/stare via; **he's ~ from his desk/the office** non è alla sua scrivania/in ufficio; **four kilometres ~** a quattro chilometri; **play ~** *Sport* giocare fuori casa. **~ game** *n* partita *f* fuori casa

awe /ɔ:/ *n* soggezione *f*

awful /'ɔ:fl/ *a* terribile. **~ly** *adv* /'ɔ:f(ʊ)lɪ/ terribilmente; ⟨*pretty*⟩ estremamente

awhile /ə'waɪl/ *adv* per un po'

awkward /'ɔ:kwəd/ *a* ⟨*movement*⟩ goffo; ⟨*moment, situation*⟩ imbarazzante; ⟨*time*⟩ scomodo. **~ly** *adv* ⟨*move*⟩ goffamente; ⟨*say*⟩ con imbarazzo

awning /'ɔ:nɪŋ/ *n* tendone *m*

awoke(n) /ə'wəʊk(ən)/ *see* **awake**

awry /ə'raɪ/ *adv* storto

axe /æks/ *n* scure *f*; **have an ~ to grind** avere il proprio tornaconto ● *vt* (*pres p* **axing**) fare dei tagli a ⟨*budget*⟩; sopprimere ⟨*jobs*⟩; annullare ⟨*project*⟩

axis /'æksɪs/ *n* (*pl* **axes** /-si:z/) asse *m*

axle /'æksl/ *n* *Techn* asse *m*

ay[e] /aɪ/ *adv* sì ● *n* sì *m* *inv*

Bb

B /bi:/ *n Mus* si *m* *inv*

BA *n abbr* **Bachelor of Arts**

babble /'bæbl/ *vi* farfugliare; ⟨*stream:*⟩ gorgogliare

baby /'beɪbɪ/ *n* bambino, -a *mf*; ⟨*fam: darling*⟩ tesoro *m*

baby: **~ carriage** *n Am* carrozzina *f*. **~ish** *a* bambinesco. **~-sit** *vi* fare il/la baby-sitter. **~-sitter** *n* baby-sitter *mf*

bachelor /'bætʃələ(r)/ *n* scapolo *m*; **B~ of Arts/Science** laureato, -a *mf* in lettere/in scienze

back /bæk/ *n* schiena *f*; ⟨*of horse, hand*⟩ dorso *m*; ⟨*of chair*⟩ schienale *m*; ⟨*of house, cheque, page*⟩ retro *m*; ⟨*in football*⟩ difesa *f*; **at the ~** in fondo; **in the ~** *Auto* dietro; **~ to front** ⟨*sweater*⟩ il davanti di dietro; **the ~ of beyond** in un posto sperduto ● *a* posteriore; ⟨*taxes, payments*⟩ arretrato ● *adv* indietro; ⟨*returned*⟩ di ritorno; **turn/move ~** tornare/spostarsi indietro; **put it ~ here/there** rimettilo qui/là; **~ at home** di ritorno a casa; **I'll be ~ in five minutes** torno fra cinque minuti; **I'm just ~** sono appena tornato; **when do you want the book ~?** quando rivuoi il libro?; **pay ~** ripagare ⟨*sb*⟩; restituire ⟨*money*⟩; **~ in power** di nuovo al potere ● *vt* ⟨*support*⟩ sostene-

re; (*with money*) finanziare; puntare su ⟨*horse*⟩; (*cover the back of*) rivestire il retro di ● *vi Auto* fare retromarcia.
back down *vi* battere in ritirata. **back in** *vi Auto* entrare in retromarcia; ⟨*person:*⟩ entrare camminando all'indietro. **back out** *vi Auto* uscire in retromarcia; ⟨*person:*⟩ uscire camminando all'indietro; *fig* tirarsi indietro (**of** da). **back up** *vt* sostenere; confermare ⟨*person's alibi*⟩; *Comput* fare una copia di salvataggio di; **be ~ed up** ⟨*traffic:*⟩ essere congestionato ● *vi Auto* fare retromarcia

back: **~ache** *n* mal *m* di schiena. **~bencher** *n* parlamentare *mf* ordinario, -a. **~biting** *n* maldicenza *f*. **~bone** *n* spina *f* dorsale. **~chat** *n* risposta *f* impertinente. **~date** *vt* retrodatare ⟨*cheque*⟩; **~dated to** valido a partire da. **~ 'door** *n* porta *f* di servizio
backer /'bækə(r)/ *n* sostenitore, -trice *mf*; (*with money*) finanziatore, -trice *mf*
back: **~'fire** *vi Auto* avere un ritorno di fiamma; ⟨*fig: plan*⟩ fallire. **~ground** *n* sfondo *m*; (*environment*) ambiente *m*. **~hand** *n* ⟨*tennis*⟩ rovescio *m*. **~'handed** *a* ⟨*compliment*⟩ implicito. **~'hander** *n* (*fam: bribe*) bustarella *f*
backing /'bækɪŋ/ *n* (*support*) supporto *m*; (*material*) riserva *f*; *Mus* accompagnamento *m*; **~ group** gruppo *m* d'accompagnamento
back: **~lash** *n fig* reazione *f* opposta. **~log** *n* **~log of work** lavoro *m* arretrato. **~ 'seat** *n* sedile *m* posteriore. **~side** *n fam* fondoschiena *m inv*. **~slash** *n Typ* barra *f* retroversa. **~stage** *a & adv* dietro le quinte. **~stroke** *n* dorso *m*. **~-up** *n* rinforzi *mpl*; *Comput* riserva *f*. **~-up copy** *n Comput* copia *f* di riserva
backward /'bækwəd/ *a* ⟨*step*⟩ indietro; ⟨*child*⟩ lento nell'apprendimento; ⟨*country*⟩ arretrato ● *adv* **~s** (*also Am:* **~**) indietro; ⟨*fall, walk*⟩ all'indietro; **~s and forwards** avanti e indietro
back: **~water** *n fig* luogo *m* allo scarto. **~ 'yard** *n* cortile *m*
bacon /'beɪkn/ *n* ≈ pancetta *f*
bacteria /bæk'tɪərɪə/ *npl* batteri *mpl*
bad /bæd/ *a* (**worse, worst**) cattivo; ⟨*weather, habit, news, accident*⟩ brutto; ⟨*apple etc*⟩ marcio; **the light is ~** non c'è una buona luce; **use ~ language** dire delle parolacce; **feel ~** sentirsi male; (*feel guilty*) sentirsi in colpa; **have a ~ back** avere dei problemi alla schiena; **smoking is ~ for you** fumare

fa male; **go ~** andare a male; **that's just too ~!** pazienza!; **not ~** niente male
bade /bæd/ *see* bid
badge /bædʒ/ *n* distintivo *m*
badger /'bædʒə(r)/ *n* tasso *m* ● *vt* tormentare
badly /'bædlɪ/ *adv* male; ⟨*hurt*⟩ gravemente; **~ off** povero; **~ behaved** maleducato; **need ~** aver estremamente bisogno di
bad-'mannered *a* maleducato
badminton /'bædmɪntən/ *n* badminton *m*
bad-'tempered *a* irascibile
baffle /'bæfl/ *vt* confondere
bag /bæg/ *n* borsa *f*; (*of paper*) sacchetto *m*; **old ~** *sl* megera *f*; **~s under the eyes** occhiaie *fpl*; **~s of** *fam* un sacco di
baggage /'bægɪdʒ/ *n* bagagli *mpl*
baggy /'bægɪ/ *a* ⟨*clothes*⟩ ampio
'bagpipes *npl* cornamusa *fsg*
Bahamas /bə'hɑːməz/ *npl* **the ~** le Bahamas
bail /beɪl/ *n* cauzione *f*; **on ~** su cauzione ● **bail out** *vt Naut* aggottare; **~ sb out** *Jur* pagare la cauzione per qcno ● *vi Aeron* paracadutarsi
bait /beɪt/ *n* esca *f* ● *vt* innescare; (*fig: torment*) tormentare
bake /beɪk/ *vt* cuocere al forno; (*make*) fare ● *vi* cuocersi al forno
baker /'beɪkə(r)/ *n* fornaio, -a *mf*, panettiere, -a *mf*; **~'s [shop]** panetteria *f*. **~y** *n* panificio *m*, forno *m*
baking /'beɪkɪŋ/ *n* cottura *f* al forno. **~-powder** *n* lievito *m* in polvere. **~-tin** *n* teglia *f*
balance /'bæləns/ *n* equilibrio *m*; *Comm* bilancio *m*; (*outstanding sum*) saldo *m*; [**bank**] **~** saldo *m*; **be** *or* **hang in the ~** *fig* essere in sospeso ● *vt* bilanciare; equilibrare ⟨*budget*⟩; *Comm* fare il bilancio di ⟨*books*⟩ ● *vi* bilanciarsi; *Comm* essere in pareggio. **~d** *a* equilibrato. **~ sheet** *n* bilancio *m* [d'esercizio]
balcony /'bælkənɪ/ *n* balcone *m*
bald /bɔːld/ *a* ⟨*person*⟩ calvo; ⟨*tyre*⟩ liscio; ⟨*statement*⟩ nudo e crudo; **go ~** perdere i capelli
bald|ing /'bɔːldɪŋ/ *a* **be ~ing** stare perdendo i capelli. **~ness** *n* calvizie *f*
bale /beɪl/ *n* balla *f*
baleful /'beɪlfl/ *a* malvagio; (*sad*) triste
balk /bɔːlk/ *vt* ostacolare ● *vi* **at**

⟨*horse:*⟩ impennarsi davanti a; *fig* tirarsi indietro davanti a

Balkans /'bɔːlknz/ *npl* Balcani *mpl*

ball[1] /bɔːl/ *n* palla *f*; (*football*) pallone *m*; (*of yarn*) gomitolo *m*; **on the ~** *fam* sveglio

ball[2] *n* (*dance*) ballo *m*

ballad /'bæləd/ *n* ballata *f*

ballast /'bæləst/ *n* zavorra *f*

ball-'bearing *n* cuscinetto *m* a sfera

ballerina /bælə'riːnə/ *n* ballerina *f* [classica]

ballet /'bæleɪ/ *n* balletto *m*; (*art form*) danza *f*; **~ dancer** *n* ballerino, -a *mf* [classico, -a]

ballistic /bə'lɪstɪk/ *a* balistico. **~s** *n* balistica *fsg*

balloon /bə'luːn/ *n* pallone *m*; Aeron mongolfiera *f*

ballot /'bælət/ *n* votazione *f*. **~-box** *n* urna *f*. **~-paper** *n* scheda *f* di votazione

ball: ~-point ['pen] *n* penna *f* a sfera. **~room** *n* sala *f* da ballo

balm /bɑːm/ *n* balsamo *m*

balmy /'bɑːmɪ/ *a* (**-ier, -iest**) mite; (*fam: crazy*) strampalato

Baltic /'bɔːltɪk/ *a* & *n* **the ~** [**Sea**] il [mar] Baltico

bamboo /bæm'buː/ *n* bambù *m inv*

bamboozle /bæm'buːzl/ *vt* (*fam: mystify*) confondere

ban /bæn/ *n* proibizione *f* ● *vt* (*pt/pp* **banned**) proibire; **~ from** espellere da ⟨*club*⟩; **she was ~ned from driving** le hanno ritirato la patente

banal /bə'nɑːl/ *a* banale. **~ity** /-'nælətɪ/ *n* banalità *f inv*

banana /bə'nɑːnə/ *n* banana *f*

band /bænd/ *n* banda *f*; (*stripe*) nastro *m*; (*Mus: pop group*) complesso *m*; (*Mus: brass ~*) banda *f*; *Mil* fanfara *f* ● **band together** *vi* riunirsi

bandage /'bændɪdʒ/ *n* benda *f* ● *vt* fasciare ⟨*limb*⟩

b. & b. *abbr* bed and breakfast

bandit /'bændɪt/ *n* bandito *m*

band: ~stand *n* palco *m* coperto [dell'orchestra]. **~wagon** *n* **jump on the ~wagon** *fig* seguire la corrente

bandy[1] /'bændɪ/ *vt* (*pt/pp* **-ied**) scambiarsi ⟨*words*⟩. **bandy about** *vt* far circolare

bandy[2] *a* (**-ier, -iest**) **be ~** avere le gambe storte

bang /bæŋ/ *n* (*noise*) fragore *m*; (*of gun, firework*) scoppio *m*; (*blow*) colpo *m* ● *adv* **~ in the middle of** *fam* proprio nel mezzo di; **go ~** ⟨*gun:*⟩ sparare;

⟨*balloon:*⟩ esplodere ● *int* bum! ● *vt* battere ⟨*fist*⟩; battere su ⟨*table*⟩; sbattere ⟨*door, head*⟩ ● *vi* scoppiare; ⟨*door:*⟩ sbattere

banger /'bæŋə(r)/ *n* (*firework*) petardo *m*; (*fam: sausage*) salsiccia *f*; **old ~** (*fam: car*) macinino *m*

bangle /'bæŋgl/ *n* braccialetto *m*

banish /'bænɪʃ/ *vt* bandire

banisters /'bænɪstəz/ *npl* ringhiera *fsg*

bank[1] /bæŋk/ *n* (*of river*) sponda *f*; (*slope*) scarpata *f* ● *vi* Aeron inclinarsi in virata

bank[2] *n* banca *f* ● *vt* depositare in banca ● *vi* **~ with** avere un conto [bancario] presso. **bank on** *vt* contare su

'bank account *n* conto *m* in banca

'bank card *n* carta *f* assegno

banker /'bæŋkə(r)/ *n* banchiere *m*

bank: ~ 'holiday *n* giorno *m* festivo. **~ing** *n* bancario *m*. **~ manager** *n* direttore, -trice *mf* di banca. **~note** *n* banconota *f*

bankrupt /'bæŋkrʌpt/ *a* fallito; **go ~** fallire ● *n* persona *f* che ha fatto fallimento ● *vt* far fallire. **~cy** *n* bancarotta *f*

banner /'bænə(r)/ *n* stendardo *m*; (*of demonstrators*) striscione *m*

banns /bænz/ *npl* Relig pubblicazioni *fpl* [di matrimonio]

banquet /'bæŋkwɪt/ *n* banchetto *m*

banter /'bæntə(r)/ *n* battute *fpl* di spirito

baptism /'bæptɪzm/ *n* battesimo *m*

Baptist /'bæptɪst/ *a* & *n* battista *mf*

baptize /bæp'taɪz/ *vt* battezzare

bar /bɑː(r)/ *n* sbarra *f*; *Jur* ordine *m* degli avvocati; (*of chocolate*) tavoletta *f*; (*café*) bar *m inv*; (*counter*) banco *m*; *Mus* battuta *f*; (*fig: obstacle*) ostacolo *m*; **~ of soap/gold** saponetta *f*/lingotto *m*; **behind ~s** *fam* dietro le sbarre ● *vt* (*pt/pp* **barred**) sbarrare ⟨*way*⟩; sprangare ⟨*door*⟩; escludere ⟨*person*⟩ ● *prep* tranne; **~ none** in assoluto

barbarian /bɑː'beərɪən/ *n* barbaro, -a *mf*

barbaric /bɑː'bærɪk/ *a* barbarico. **~ity** *n* barbarie *f inv*. **~ous** /'bɑːbərəs/ *a* barbaro

barbecue /'bɑːbɪkjuː/ *n* barbecue *m inv*; (*party*) grigliata *f*, barbecue *m inv* ● *vt* arrostire sul barbecue

barbed /bɑːbd/ *a* **~ wire** filo *m* spinato

barber /'bɑːbə(r)/ *n* barbiere *m*

barbiturate /bɑː'bɪtjʊrət/ *n* barbiturico *m*

'**bar code** n codice m a barre
bare /beə(r)/ a nudo; ⟨tree, room⟩ spoglio; ⟨floor⟩ senza moquette ● vt scoprire; mostrare ⟨teeth⟩
bare: ~**back** adv senza sella. ~**faced** a sfacciato. ~**foot** adv scalzo. ~'**headed** a a capo scoperto
barely /'beəlɪ/ adv appena
bargain /'bɑːgɪn/ n ⟨agreement⟩ patto m; ⟨good buy⟩ affare m; **into the** ~ per di più ● vi contrattare; ⟨haggle⟩ trattare. **bargain for** vt ⟨expect⟩ aspettarsi
barge /bɑːdʒ/ n barcone m ● **barge in** vi fam ⟨to room⟩ piombare dentro; ⟨into conversation⟩ interrompere bruscamente. ~ **into** vt piombare dentro a ⟨room⟩; venire addosso a ⟨person⟩
baritone /'bærɪtəʊn/ n baritono m
bark[1] /bɑːk/ n ⟨of tree⟩ corteccia f
bark[2] n abbaiamento m ● vi abbaiare
barley /'bɑːlɪ/ n orzo m
bar: ~**maid** n barista f. ~**man** n barista m
barmy /'bɑːmɪ/ a fam strampalato
barn /bɑːn/ n granaio m
barometer /bə'rɒmɪtə(r)/ n barometro m
baron /'bærn/ n barone m. ~**ess** n baronessa f
baroque /bə'rɒk/ a & n barocco m
barracks /'bærəks/ npl caserma fsg
barrage /'bærɑːʒ/ n Mil sbarramento m; ⟨fig: of criticism⟩ sfilza f
barrel /'bærl/ n barile m, botte f; ⟨of gun⟩ canna f. ~-**organ** n organetto m [a cilindro]
barren /'bærən/ a sterile; ⟨landscape⟩ brullo
barricade /bærɪ'keɪd/ n barricata f ● vt barricare
barrier /'bærɪə(r)/ n barriera f; Rail cancello m; fig ostacolo m
barring /'bɑːrɪŋ/ prep ~ **accidents** tranne imprevisti
barrister /'bærɪstə(r)/ n avvocato m
barrow /'bærəʊ/ n carretto m; ⟨wheel~⟩ carriola f
barter /'bɑːtə(r)/ vi barattare (**for** con)
base /beɪs/ n base f ● a vile ● vt basare; **be** ~**d on** basarsi su
base: ~**ball** n baseball m. ~**less** a infondato. ~**ment** n seminterrato m. ~**ment flat** n appartamento m nel seminterrato
bash /bæʃ/ n colpo m [violento] ● vt colpire [violentemente]; ⟨dent⟩ ammaccare; ~**ed in** ammaccato
bashful /'bæʃfl/ a timido

basic /'beɪsɪk/ a di base; ⟨condition, requirement⟩ basilare; ⟨living conditions⟩ povero; **my Italian is pretty** ~ il mio italiano è abbastanza rudimentale; **the** ~**s** ⟨of language, science⟩ i rudimenti; ⟨essentials⟩ l'essenziale m. ~**ally** adv fondamentalmente
basil /'bæzɪl/ n basilico m
basilica /bə'zɪlɪkə/ n basilica f
basin /'beɪsn/ n bacinella f; ⟨wash-hand ~⟩ lavabo m; ⟨for food⟩ recipiente m; Geog bacino m
basis /'beɪsɪs/ n ⟨pl -**ses** /-siːz/⟩ base f
bask /bɑːsk/ vi crogiolarsi
basket /'bɑːskɪt/ n cestino m. ~**ball** n pallacanestro f
Basle /bɑːl/ n Basilea f
bass /beɪs/ a basso; ~ **voice** voce f di basso ● n basso m
bastard /'bɑːstəd/ n ⟨illegitimate child⟩ bastardo, -a mf; sl figlio m di puttana
bastion /'bæstɪən/ n bastione m
bat[1] /bæt/ n mazza f; ⟨for table tennis⟩ racchetta f; **off one's own** ~ fam tutto da solo ● vt ⟨pt/pp batted⟩ battere; **she didn't** ~ **an eyelid** fig non ha battuto ciglio
bat[2] n Zool pipistrello m
batch /bætʃ/ n gruppo m; ⟨of goods⟩ partita f; ⟨of bread⟩ infornata f
bated /'beɪtɪd/ a **with** ~ **breath** col fiato sospeso
bath /bɑːθ/ n ⟨pl ~**s** /bɑːðz/⟩ bagno m; ⟨tub⟩ vasca f da bagno; ~**s** pl piscina f; **have a** ~ fare un bagno ● vt fare il bagno a
bathe /beɪð/ n bagno m ● vi fare il bagno ● vt lavare ⟨wound⟩. ~**r** n bagnante mf
bathing /'beɪðɪŋ/ n bagni mpl. ~-**cap** n cuffia f. ~-**costume** n costume m da bagno
bath: ~-**mat** n tappetino m da bagno. ~**robe** n accappatoio m. ~**room** n bagno m. ~-**towel** n asciugamano m da bagno
baton /'bætn/ n Mus bacchetta f
battalion /bə'tælɪən/ n battaglione m
batter /'bætə(r)/ n Culin pastella f; ~**ed** a ⟨car⟩ malandato; ⟨wife, baby⟩ maltrattato
battery /'bætərɪ/ n batteria f; ⟨of torch, radio⟩ pila f
battle /'bætl/ n battaglia f; fig lotta f ● vi fig lottare
battle: ~**field** n campo m di battaglia. ~**ship** n corazzata f
bawdy /'bɔːdɪ/ a ⟨-ier, -iest⟩ piccante

bawl /bɔːl/ *vt/i* urlare

bay[1] /beɪ/ *n Geog* baia *f*

bay[2] *n* **keep at ~** tenere a bada

bay[3] *n Bot* alloro *m*. **~-leaf** *n* foglia *f* d'alloro

bayonet /'beɪənɪt/ *n* baionetta *f*

bay 'window *n* bay window *f inv* (*grande finestra sporgente*)

bazaar /bə'zɑː(r)/ *n* bazar *m inv*

BC *abbr* (**before Christ**) a.C.

be /biː/ *vi* (*pres* **am, are, is, are**; *pt* **was, were**; *pp* **been**) essere; **he is a teacher** è insegnante, fa l'insegnante; **what do you want to be?** cosa vuoi fare?; **be quiet!** sta' zitto!; **I am cold/hot** ho freddo/caldo; **it's cold/hot, isn't it?** fa freddo/caldo, vero?; **how are you?** come stai?; **I am well** sto bene; **there is** c'è; **there are** ci sono; **I have been to Venice** sono stato a Venezia; **has the postman been?** è passato il postino?; **you're coming too, aren't you?** vieni anche tu, no?; **it's yours, is it?** è tuo, vero?; **was John there? - yes, he was** c'era John? - sì; **John wasn't there - yes he was!** John non c'era - sì che c'era!; **three and three are six** tre più tre fanno sei; **he is five** ha cinque anni; **that will be £10, please** fanno 10 sterline, per favore; **how much is it?** quanto costa?; **that's £5 you owe me** mi devi 5 sterline ● *v aux* **I am coming/reading** sto venendo/leggendo; **I'm staying** (*not leaving*) resto; **I am being lazy** sono pigro; **I was thinking of you** stavo pensando a te; **you are not to tell him** non devi dirgielo; **you are to do that immediately** devi farlo subito ● *passive* essere; **I have been robbed** sono stato derubato

beach /biːtʃ/ *n* spiaggia *f*. **~wear** *n* abbigliamento *m* da spiaggia

bead /biːd/ *n* perlina *f*

beak /biːk/ *n* becco *m*

beaker /'biːkə(r)/ *n* coppa *f*

beam /biːm/ *n* trave *f*; (*of light*) raggio *m* ● *vi* irradiare; (*person:*) essere raggiante. **~ing** *a* raggiante

bean /biːn/ *n* fagiolo *m*; (*of coffee*) chicco *m*

bear[1] /beə(r)/ *n* orso *m*

bear[2] *v* (*pt* **bore**, *pp* **borne**) ● *vt* (*endure*) sopportare; mettere al mondo (*child*); (*carry*) portare; **~ in mind** tenere presente ● *vi* **~ left/right** andare a sinistra/a destra. **bear with** *vt* aver pazienza con. **~able** /-əbl/ *a* sopportabile

beard /bɪəd/ *n* barba *f*. **~ed** *a* barbuto

bearer /'beərə(r)/ *n* portatore, -trice *mf*; (*of passport*) titolare *mf*

bearing /'beərɪŋ/ *n* portamento *m*; *Techn* cuscinetto *m* [a sfera]; **have a ~ on** avere attinenza con; **get one's ~s** orientarsi

bend /biːst/ *n* bestia *f*; (*fam: person*) animale *m*

beat /biːt/ *n* battito *m*; (*rhythm*) battuta *f*; (*of policeman*) giro *m* d'ispezione ● *v* (*pt* **beat**, *pp* **beaten**) ● *vt* battere; picchiare (*person*); **~ it!** *fam* darsela a gambe!; **it ~s me why...** *fam* non capisco proprio perché... **beat up** *vt* picchiare

beat|en /'biːtn/ *a* **off the ~en track** fuori mano. **~ing** *n* bastonata *f*; **get a ~ing** (*with fists*) essere preso a pugni; (*team, player:*) prendere una batosta

beautician /bjuː'tɪʃn/ *n* estetista *mf*

beauti|ful /'bjuːtɪfl/ *a* bello. **~fully** *adv* splendidamente

beauty /'bjuːtɪ/ *n* bellezza *f*. **~ parlour** *n* istituto *m* di bellezza. **~ spot** *n* neo *m*; (*place*) luogo *m* pittoresco

beaver /'biːvə(r)/ *n* castoro *m*

became /bɪ'keɪm/ *see* **become**

because /bɪ'kɒz/ *conj* perché; **~ you didn't tell me, I...** poiché non me lo hai detto,... ● *adv* **~ of** a causa di

beck /bek/ *n* **at the ~ and call of** a completa disposizione di

beckon /'bekn/ *vt/i* **~ [to]** chiamare con un cenno

becom|e /bɪ'kʌm/ *v* (*pt* **became**, *pp* **become**) ● *vt* diventare ● *vi* diventare; **what has ~e of her?** che ne è di lei? **~ing** *a* (*clothes*) bello

bed /bed/ *n* letto *m*; (*of sea, lake*) fondo *m*; (*layer*) strato *m*; (*of flowers*) aiuola *f*; **in ~** a letto; **go to ~** andare a letto; **~ and breakfast** pensione *f* familiare in cui il prezzo della camera comprende la prima colazione. **~clothes** *npl* lenzuola e coperte *fpl*. **~ding** *n* biancheria *f* per il letto, materasso e guanciali

bedlam /'bedləm/ *n* baraonda *f*

bedraggled /bɪ'drægld/ *a* inzaccherato

bed: **~ridden** *a* costretto a letto. **~room** *n* camera *f* da letto

'bedside *n* **at his ~** al suo capezzale. **~ 'lamp** *n* abat-jour *m inv*. **~ 'table** *n* comodino *m*

bed: **~'sit** *n*, **~'sitter** *n*, **~-'sitting-**

room n = camera f ammobiliata fornita di cucina. **~spread** n copriletto m. **~time** n l'ora f di andare a letto

bee /biː/ n ape f

beech /biːtʃ/ n faggio m

beef /biːf/ n manzo m. **~burger** n hamburger m inv

bee: **~hive** n alveare m. **~-line** n make a **~line for** fam precipitarsi verso

been /biːn/ see **be**

beer /bɪə(r)/ n birra f

beetle /ˈbiːtl/ n scarafaggio m

beetroot /ˈbiːtruːt/ n barbabietola f

before /bɪˈfɔː(r)/ prep prima di; **the day ~ yesterday** ieri l'altro; **~ long** fra poco ● adv prima; **never ~ have I seen...** non ho mai visto prima...; **~ that** prima; **~ going** prima di andare ● conj (time) prima che; **~ you go** prima che tu vada. **~hand** adv in anticipo

befriend /bɪˈfrend/ vt trattare da amico

beg /beg/ v (pt/pp **begged**) ● vi mendicare ● vt pregare; chiedere (favour, forgiveness)

began /bɪˈgæn/ see **begin**

beggar /ˈbegə(r)/ n mendicante mf; **poor ~!** povero cristo!

begin /bɪˈgɪn/ vt/i (pt **began**, pp **begun**, pres p **beginning**) cominciare. **~ner** n principiante mf. **~ning** n principio m

begonia /bɪˈgəʊnɪə/ n begonia f

begrudge /bɪˈgrʌdʒ/ vt (envy) essere invidioso di; dare malvolentieri (money)

begun /bɪˈgʌn/ see **begin**

behalf /bɪˈhɑːf/ n **on ~ of** a nome di; **on my ~** a nome mio

behave /bɪˈheɪv/ vi comportarsi; **~ [oneself]** comportarsi bene

behaviour /bɪˈheɪvjə(r)/ n comportamento m; (of prisoner, soldier) condotta f

behead /bɪˈhed/ vt decapitare

behind /bɪˈhaɪnd/ prep dietro; **be ~ sth** fig stare dietro qcsa ● adv dietro, indietro; (late) in ritardo; **a long way ~** molto indietro ● n fam didietro m. **~hand** adv indietro

beholden /bɪˈhəʊldn/ a obbligato (**to** verso)

beige /beɪʒ/ a & n beige m inv

being /ˈbiːɪŋ/ n essere m; **come into ~** nascere

belated /bɪˈleɪtɪd/ a tardivo

belch /beltʃ/ vi ruttare ● vt **~ [out]** eruttare (smoke)

belfry /ˈbelfrɪ/ n campanile m

Belgian /ˈbeldʒən/ a & n belga mf

Belgium /ˈbeldʒəm/ n Belgio m

belief /bɪˈliːf/ n fede f; (opinion) convinzione f

believable /bɪˈliːvəbl/ a credibile

believe /bɪˈliːv/ vt/i credere. **~r** n Relig credente mf; **be a great ~r in** credere fermamente in

belittle /bɪˈlɪtl/ vt sminuire (person, achievements)

bell /bel/ n campana f; (on door) campanello m

belligerent /bɪˈlɪdʒərənt/ a belligerante; (aggressive) bellicoso

bellow /ˈbeləʊ/ vi gridare a squarciagola; (animal:) muggire

bellows /ˈbeləʊz/ npl (for fire) soffietto msg

belly /ˈbelɪ/ n pancia f

belong /bɪˈlɒŋ/ vi appartenere (**to** a); (be member) essere socio (**to** di). **~ings** npl cose fpl

beloved /bɪˈlʌvɪd/ a & n amato, -a m

below /bɪˈləʊ/ prep sotto; (with numbers) al di sotto di ● adv sotto, di sotto; Naut sotto coperta; **see ~** guardare qui di seguito

belt /belt/ n cintura f; (area) zona f; Techn cinghia f ● vi **~ along** (fam: rush) filare velocemente ● vt (fam: hit) picchiare

bemused /bɪˈmjuːzd/ a confuso

bench /bentʃ/ n panchina f; (work~) piano m da lavoro; **the B~** Jur la magistratura

bend /bend/ n curva f; (of river) ansa f ● v (pt/pp **bent**) ● vt piegare ● vi piegarsi; (road:) curvare; **~ [down]** chinarsi. **bend over** vi inchinarsi

beneath /bɪˈniːθ/ prep sotto, al di sotto di; **he thinks it's ~ him** fig pensa che sia sotto al suo livello ● adv giù

benediction /benɪˈdɪkʃn/ n Relig benedizione f

benefactor /ˈbenɪfæktə(r)/ n benefattore, -trice mf

beneficial /benɪˈfɪʃl/ a benefico

beneficiary /benɪˈfɪʃərɪ/ n beneficiario, -a mf

benefit /ˈbenɪfɪt/ n vantaggio m; (allowance) indennità f inv ● v (pt/pp **-fited**, pres p **-fiting**) ● vt giovare a ● vi trarre vantaggio (**from** da)

benevolen|ce /bɪˈnevələns/ n benevolenza f. **~t** a benevolo

benign /bɪˈnaɪn/ a benevolo; Med benigno

bent /bent/ *see* **bend** ● *a* ⟨*person*⟩ ricurvo; (*distorted*) curvato; (*fam: dishonest*) corrotto; **be ~ on doing sth** essere ben deciso a fare qcsa ● *n* predisposizione *f*

be|queath /bɪˈkwiːð/ *vt* lasciare in eredità. **~quest** /-ˈkwest/ *n* lascito *m*

bereave|d /bɪˈriːvd/ *n* **the ~d** *pl* i familiari del defunto. **~ment** *n* lutto *m*

bereft /bɪˈreft/ *a* **~ of** privo di

beret /ˈbereɪ/ *n* berretto *m*

berry /ˈberɪ/ *n* bacca *f*

berserk /bəˈsɜːk/ *a* **go ~** diventare una belva

berth /bɜːθ/ *n* (*bed*) cuccetta *f*; (*for ship*) ormeggio *m* ● *vi* ormeggiare

beseech /bɪˈsiːtʃ/ *vt* (*pt/pp* **beseeched** *or* **besought**) supplicare

beside /bɪˈsaɪd/ *prep* accanto a; **~ oneself** fuori di sé

besides /bɪˈsaɪdz/ *prep* oltre a ● *adv* inoltre

besiege /bɪˈsiːdʒ/ *vt* assediare

besought /bɪˈsɔːt/ *see* **beseech**

best /best/ *a* migliore; **the ~ part of a year** la maggior parte dell'anno; **~ before** *Comm* preferibilmente prima di ● *n* **the ~** il meglio; (*person*) il/la migliore; **at ~** tutt'al più; **all the ~!** tanti auguri!; **do one's ~** fare del proprio meglio; **to the ~ of my knowledge** per quel che ne so; **make the ~ of it** cogliere il lato buono della cosa ● *adv* meglio, nel modo migliore; **as ~ I could** meglio che potevo. **~ 'man** *n* testimone *m*

bestow /bɪˈstəʊ/ *vt* conferire (**on** a)

best'seller *n* bestseller *m inv*

bet /bet/ *n* scommessa *f* ● *vt/i* (*pt/pp* **bet** *or* **betted**) scommettere

betray /bɪˈtreɪ/ *vt* tradire. **~al** *n* tradimento *m*

better /ˈbetə(r)/ *a* migliore, meglio; **get ~** migliorare; (*after illness*) rimettersi ● *adv* meglio; **~ off** meglio; (*wealthier*) più ricco; **all the ~** tanto meglio; **the sooner the ~** prima è, meglio è; **I've thought ~ of it** ci ho ripensato; **you'd ~ stay** faresti meglio a restare; **I'd ~ not** è meglio che non lo faccia ● *vt* migliorare; **~ oneself** migliorare le proprie condizioni

'betting shop *n* ricevitoria *f* (*dell'allibratore*)

between /bɪˈtwiːn/ *prep* fra, tra; **~ you and me** detto fra di noi; **~ us** (*together*) tra me e te ● *adv* [**in**] **~** in mezzo; (*time*) frattempo

beverage /ˈbevərɪdʒ/ *n* bevanda *f*

beware /bɪˈweə(r)/ *vi* guardarsi (**of** da); **~ of the dog!** attenti al cane!

bewilder /bɪˈwɪldə(r)/ *vt* disorientare; **~ed** perplesso. **~ment** *n* perplessità *f*

beyond /bɪˈjɒnd/ *prep* oltre; **~ reach** irraggiungibile; **~ doubt** senza alcun dubbio; **~ belief** da non credere; **it's ~ me** *fam* non riesco proprio a capire ● *adv* più in là

bias /ˈbaɪəs/ *n* (*preference*) preferenza *f*; *pej* pregiudizio *m* ● *vt* (*pt/pp* **biased**) (*influence*) influenzare. **~ed** *a* parziale

bib /bɪb/ *n* bavaglino *m*

Bible /ˈbaɪbl/ *n* Bibbia *f*

biblical /ˈbɪblɪkl/ *a* biblico

bicarbonate /baɪˈkɑːbəneɪt/ *n* **~ of soda** bicarbonato *m* di sodio

biceps /ˈbaɪseps/ *n* bicipite *m*

bicker /ˈbɪkə(r)/ *vi* litigare

bicycle /ˈbaɪsɪkl/ *n* bicicletta *f* ● *vi* andare in bicicletta

bid¹ /bɪd/ *n* offerta *f*; (*attempt*) tentativo *m* ● *vt/i* (*pt/pp* **bid**, *pres p* **bidding**) offrire; (*in cards*) dichiarare

bid² *vt* (*pt* **bade** *or* **bid**, *pp* **bidden** *or* **bid**, *pres p* **bidding**) *liter* (*command*) comandare; **~ sb welcome** dare il benvenuto a qcno

bidder /ˈbɪdə(r)/ *n* offerente *mf*

bide /baɪd/ *vt* **~ one's time** aspettare il momento buono

biennial /baɪˈenɪəl/ *a* biennale

bifocals /baɪˈfəʊklz/ *npl* occhiali *mpl* bifocali

big /bɪg/ *a* (**bigger, biggest**) grande; ⟨*brother, sister*⟩ più grande; (*fam: generous*) generoso ● *adv* **talk ~** *fam* sparare grosse

bigam|ist /ˈbɪgəmɪst/ *n* bigamo, -a *mf*. **~y** *n* bigamia *f*

'big-head *n fam* gasato, -a *mf*

big-'headed *a fam* gasato

bigot /ˈbɪgət/ *n* fanatico, -a *mf*. **~ed** *a* mentalità ristretta

'bigwig *n fam* pezzo *m* grosso

bike /baɪk/ *n fam* bici *f inv*

bikini /bɪˈkiːnɪ/ *n* bikini *m inv*

bile /baɪl/ *n* bile *f*

bilingual /baɪˈlɪŋgwəl/ *a* bilingue

bill¹ /bɪl/ *n* fattura *f*; (*in restaurant etc*) conto *m*; (*poster*) manifesto *m*; *Pol* progetto *m* di legge; (*Am: note*) biglietto *m* di banca ● *vt* fatturare

bill² *n* (*beak*) becco *m*

'billfold *n Am* portafoglio *m*

billiards /ˈbɪljədz/ *n* biliardo *m*

billion /ˈbɪljən/ *n* (*thousand million*)

miliardo *m*; (*old-fashioned Br: million million*) mille miliardi *mpl*

billy-goat /ˈbɪlɪ-/ *n* caprone *m*

bin /bɪn/ *n* bidone *m*

bind /baɪnd/ *vt* (*pt/pp* **bound**) legare (**to** a); (*bandage*) fasciare; *Jur* obbligare. **~ing** *a* (*promise, contract*) vincolante ● *n* (*of book*) rilegatura *f*; (*on ski*) attacco *m* [di sicurezza]

binge /bɪndʒ/ *n fam* **have a ~** fare baldoria; (*eat a lot*) abbuffarsi ● *vi* abbuffarsi (**on** di)

binoculars /brˈnɒkjʊləz/ *npl* [**pair of**] ~ binocolo *msg*

bio'chemist /baɪəʊ-/ *n* biochimico, -a *mf*. **~ry** *n* biochimica *f*

biodegradable /-dɪˈɡreɪdəbl/ *a* biodegradabile

biograph|er /barˈɒɡrəfə(r)/ *n* biografo, -a *mf*. **~y** *n* biografia *f*

biological /baɪəˈlɒdʒɪkl/ *a* biologico

biolog|ist /baɪˈɒlədʒɪst/ *n* biologo, -a *mf*. **~y** *n* biologia *f*

birch /bɜːtʃ/ *n* (*tree*) betulla *f*

bird /bɜːd/ *n* uccello *m*; (*fam: girl*) ragazza *f*

Biro® /ˈbaɪrəʊ/ *n* biro *f inv*

birth /bɜːθ/ *n* nascita *f*

birth: ~ **certificate** *n* certificato *m* di nascita. **~-control** *n* controllo *m* delle nascite. **~day** *n* compleanno *m*. **~mark** *n* voglia *f*. **~-rate** *n* natalità *f*

biscuit /ˈbɪskɪt/ *n* biscotto *m*

bisect /baɪˈsekt/ *vt* dividere in due [parti]

bishop /ˈbɪʃəp/ *n* vescovo *m*; (*in chess*) alfiere *m*

bit¹ /bɪt/ *n* pezzo *m*; (*smaller*) pezzetto *m*; (*for horse*) morso *m*; *Comput* bit *m inv*; **a ~ of** un pezzo di (*cheese, paper*); un po' di (*time, rain, silence*); ~ **by ~** poco a poco; **do one's ~** fare la propria parte

bit² *see* **bite**

bitch /bɪtʃ/ *n* cagna *f*; *sl* stronza *f*. **~y** *a* velenoso

bit|e /baɪt/ *n* morso *m*; (*insect* ~) puntura *f*; (*mouthful*) boccone *m* ● *vt* (*pt* **bit**, *pp* **bitten**) mordere; (*insect:*) pungere; **~e one's nails** mangiarsi le unghie ● *vi* mordere; (*insect:*) pungere. **~ing** *a* (*wind, criticism*) pungente; (*remark*) mordace

bitter /ˈbɪtə(r)/ *a* amaro ● *n Br* birra *f* amara. **~ly** *adv* amaramente; **it's ~ly cold** c'è un freddo pungente. **~ness** *n* amarezza *f*

bitty /ˈbɪtɪ/ *a Br fam* frammentario

bizarre /bɪˈzɑː(r)/ *a* bizzarro

blab /blæb/ *vi* (*pt/pp* **blabbed**) spifferare

black /blæk/ *a* nero; **be ~ and blue** essere pieno di lividi ● *n* negro, -a *mf* ● *vt* boicottare (*goods*). **black out** *vt* cancellare ● *vi* (*lose consciousness*) perdere coscienza

black: **~berry** *n* mora *f*. **~bird** *n* merlo *m*. **~board** *n Sch* lavagna *f*. **~'currant** *n* ribes *m inv* nero; ~ **'eye** *n* occhio *m* nero. **~ 'ice** *n* ghiaccio *m* (*sulla strada*). **~leg** *n Br* crumiro *m*. **~list** *vt* mettere sulla lista nera. **~mail** *n* ricatto *m* ● *vt* ricattare. **~mailer** *n* ricattatore, -trice *mf*. **~'market** *n* mercato *m* nero. **~-out** *n* blackout *m inv*; **have a ~-out** *Med* perdere coscienza. **~smith** *n* fabbro *m*

bladder /ˈblædə(r)/ *n Anat* vescica *f*

blade /bleɪd/ *n* lama *f*; (*of grass*) filo *m*

blame /bleɪm/ *n* colpa *f* ● *vt* dare la colpa a; ~ **sb for doing sth** dare la colpa a qcno per aver fatto qcsa; **no one is to ~** non è colpa di nessuno. **~less** *a* innocente

blanch /blɑːntʃ/ *vi* sbiancare ● *vt Culin* sbollentare

blancmange /bləˈmɒnʒ/ *n* biancomangiare *m inv*

bland /blænd/ *a* (*food*) insipido; (*person*) insulso

blank /blæŋk/ *a* bianco; (*look*) vuoto ● *n* spazio *m* vuoto; (*cartridge*) a salve. ~ **'cheque** *n* assegno *m* in bianco

blanket /ˈblæŋkɪt/ *n* coperta *f*

blank 'verse *n* versi *mpl* sciolti

blare /bleə(r)/ *vi* suonare a tutto volume. **blare out** *vt* far risuonare ● *vi* (*music, radio:*) strillare

blasé /ˈblɑːzeɪ/ *a* vissuto, blasé *inv*

blaspheme /blæsˈfiːm/ *vi* bestemmiare

blasphem|ous /ˈblæsfəməs/ *a* blasfemo. **~y** *n* bestemmia *f*

blast /blɑːst/ *n* (*gust*) raffica *f*; (*sound*) scoppio *m* ● *vt* (*with explosive*) far saltare ● *int sl* maledizione!. **~ed** *a sl* maledetto

blast: **~-furnace** *n* altoforno *m*. **~-off** *n* (*of missile*) lancio *m*

blatant /ˈbleɪtənt/ *a* sfacciato

blaze /bleɪz/ *n* incendio *m*; **a ~ of colour** un'esplosione *f* di colori ● *vi* ardere

blazer /ˈbleɪzə(r)/ *n* blazer *m inv*

bleach /bliːtʃ/ *n* decolorante *m*; (*for cleaning*) candeggina *f* ● *vt* sbiancare; ossigenare (*hair*)

bleak /bli:k/ *a* desolato; ⟨*fig: prospects, future*⟩ tetro

bleary-eyed /ˈblɪərɪˈaɪd/ *a* **look ~** avere gli occhi assonnati

bleat /bli:t/ *vi* belare ● *n* belato *m*

bleed /bli:d/ *v* (*pt/pp* **bled**) ● *vi* sanguinare ● *vt* spurgare ⟨*brakes, radiator*⟩

bleep /bli:p/ *n* bip *m* ● *vi* suonare ● *vt* chiamare (*col cercapersone*) ⟨*doctor*⟩. **~er** *n* cercapersone *m inv*

blemish /ˈblemɪʃ/ *n* macchia *f*

blend /blend/ *n* (*of tea, coffee, whisky*) miscela *f*; (*of colours*) insieme *m* ● *vt* mescolare ● *vi* ⟨*colours, sounds:*⟩ fondersi (**with** con). **~er** *n Culin* frullatore *m*

bless /bles/ *vt* benedire. **~ed** /ˈblesɪd/ *a also sl* benedetto. **~ing** *n* benedizione *f*

blew /blu:/ *see* **blow**²

blight /blaɪt/ *n Bot* ruggine *f* ● *vt* far avvizzire ⟨*plants*⟩

blind¹ /blaɪnd/ *a* cieco; **~ man/woman** cieco/cieca ● *npl* **the ~** i ciechi *mpl*; ● *vt* accecare

blind² *n* [**roller**] **~** avvolgibile *m*; [**Venetian**] **~** veneziana *f*

blind: **~ 'alley** *n* vicolo *m* cieco. **~fold** *a* **be ~fold** avere gli occhi bendati ● *n* benda *f* ● *vt* bendare gli occhi a. **~ly** *adv* ciecamente. **~ness** *n* cecità *f*

blink /blɪŋk/ *vi* sbattere le palpebre; ⟨*light:*⟩ tremolare

blinkered /ˈblɪŋkəd/ *adj fig* **be ~** avere i paraocchi

blinkers /ˈblɪŋkəz/ *npl* paraocchi *mpl*

bliss /blɪs/ *n Rel* beatitudine *f*; (*happiness*) felicità *f*. **~ful** *a* beato; (*happy*) meraviglioso

blister /ˈblɪstə(r)/ *n Med* vescica *f*; (*in paint*) bolla *f* ● *vi* ⟨*paint:*⟩ formare una bolla/delle bolle

blitz /blɪts/ *n* bombardamento *m* aereo; **have a ~ on sth** *fig* darci sotto con qcsa

blizzard /ˈblɪzəd/ *n* tormenta *f*

bloated /ˈbləʊtɪd/ *a* gonfio

blob /blɒb/ *n* goccia *f*

bloc /blɒk/ *n Pol* blocco *m*

block /blɒk/ *n* blocco *m*; (*building*) isolato *m*; (*building ~*) cubo *m* (*per giochi di costruzione*); **~ of flats** palazzo *m* ● *vt* bloccare. **block up** *vt* bloccare

blockade /blɒˈkeɪd/ *n* blocco *m* ● *vt* bloccare

blockage /ˈblɒkɪdʒ/ *n* ostruzione *f*

block: **~head** *n fam* testone, -a *mf*. **~ 'letters** *npl* stampatello *m*

bloke /bləʊk/ *n fam* tizio *m*

blonde /blɒnd/ *a* biondo ● *n* bionda *f*

blood /blʌd/ *n* sangue *m*

blood: **~ bath** *n* bagno *m* di sangue. **~ count** *n* esame *m* emocromocitometrico. **~ donor** *n* donatore *m* di sangue. **~ group** *n* gruppo *m* sanguigno. **~hound** *n* segugio *m*. **~-poisoning** *n* setticemia *f*. **~ pressure** *n* pressione *f* del sangue. **~shed** *n* spargimento *m* di sangue. **~shot** *a* iniettato di sangue. **~ sports** *npl* sport *mpl* cruenti. **~-stained** *a* macchiato di sangue. **~stream** *n* sangue *m*. **~ test** *n* analisi *f* del sangue. **~thirsty** *a* assetato di sangue. **~ transfusion** *n* trasfusione *f* del sangue

bloody /ˈblʌdɪ/ *a* (**-ier, -iest**) insanguinato; *sl* maledetto ● *adv sl* **~ easy/difficult** facile/difficile da matti. **~-'minded** *a* scorbutico

bloom /blu:m/ *n* fiore *m*; **in ~** ⟨*flower:*⟩ sbocciato; ⟨*tree:*⟩ in fiore ● *vi* fiorire; *fig* essere in forma smagliante

bloom|er /ˈblu:mə(r)/ *n fam* papera *f*. **~ing** *a fam* maledetto. **~ers** *npl* mutandoni *mpl* (*da donna*)

blossom /ˈblɒsəm/ *n* fiori *mpl* (*d'albero*); (*single one*) fiore *m* ● *vi* sbocciare

blot /blɒt/ *n also fig* macchia *f* ● **blot out** *vt* (*pt/pp* **blotted**) *fig* cancellare

blotch /blɒtʃ/ *n* macchia *f*. **~y** *a* chiazzato

'blotting-paper *n* carta *f* assorbente

blouse /blaʊz/ *n* camicetta *f*

blow² /bləʊ/ *n* colpo *m*

blow² *v* (*pt* **blew**, *pp* **blown**) ● *vi* ⟨*wind:*⟩ soffiare; ⟨*fuse:*⟩ saltare ● *vt* (*fam: squander*) sperperare; **~ one's nose** soffiarsi il naso. **blow away** *vt* far volar via ⟨*papers*⟩ ● *vi* ⟨*papers:*⟩ volare via. **blow down** *vt* abbattere ● *vi* abbattersi al suolo. **blow out** *vt* (*extinguish*) spegnere. **blow over** *vi* ⟨*storm:*⟩ passare; ⟨*fuss, trouble:*⟩ dissiparsi. **blow up** *vt* (*inflate*) gonfiare; (*enlarge*) ingrandire ⟨*photograph*⟩; (*by explosion*) far esplodere ● *vi* esplodere

blow: **~-dry** *vt* asciugare col fon. **~lamp** *n* fiamma *f* ossidrica

blown /bləʊn/ *see* **blow**²

'blowtorch *n* fiamma *f* ossidrica

blowy /ˈbləʊɪ/ *a* ventoso

blue /blu:/ *a* (*pale*) celeste; (*navy*) blu *inv*; (*royal*) azzurro; **~ with cold** livido per il freddo ● *n* blu *m inv*; **have the ~s** essere giù [di tono]; **out of the ~** inaspettatamente

blue: **~bell** *n* giacinto *m* di bosco. **~berry** *n* mirtillo *m*. **~bottle** *n* mosco-

ne *m*. ~ **film** *n* film *m inv* a luci rosse.
~**print** *n fig* riferimento *m*

bluff /blʌf/ *n* bluff *m inv* ● *vi* bluffare

blunder /'blʌndə(r)/ *n* gaffe *f inv* ● *vi* fare una/delle gaffe

blunt /blʌnt/ *a* spuntato; ⟨*person*⟩ reciso. ~**ly** *adv* schiettamente

blur /blɜ:(r)/ *n* **it's all a** ~ *fig* è tutto un insieme confuso ● *vt* (*pt/pp* **blurred**) rendere confuso. ~**red** *a* ⟨*vision, photo*⟩ sfocato

blurb /blɜ:b/ *n* soffietto *m* editoriale

blurt /blɜ:t/ *vt* ~ **out** spifferare

blush /blʌʃ/ *n* rossore *m* ● *vi* arrossire

blusher /'blʌʃə(r)/ *n* fard *m*

bluster /'blʌstə(r)/ *n* sbruffonata *f*. ~**y** *a* ⟨*wind*⟩ furioso; ⟨*day, weather*⟩ molto ventoso

boar /bɔ:(r)/ *n* cinghiale *m*

board /bɔ:d/ *n* tavola *f*; (*for notices*) tabellone *m*; (*committee*) assemblea *f*; (*of directors*) consiglio *m*; **full** ~ *Br* pensione *f* completa; **half** ~ *Br* mezza pensione *f*; ~ **and lodging** vitto e alloggio *m*; **go by the** ~ *fam* andare a monte ● *vt Naut, Aeron* salire a bordo di ● *vi* ⟨*passengers:*⟩ salire a bordo. **board up** *vt* sbarrare con delle assi. **board with** *vt* stare a pensione da.

boarder /'bɔ:də(r)/ *n* pensionante *mf*; *Sch* convittore, -trice *mf*

board: ~-**game** *n* gioco *m* da tavolo. ~**ing-house** *n* pensione *f*. ~**ing-school** *n* collegio *m*

boast /bəʊst/ *vi* vantarsi (**about** di). ~**ful** *a* vanaglorioso

boat /bəʊt/ *n* barca *f*; (*ship*) nave *f*. ~**er** *n* (*hat*) paglietta *f*

bob /bɒb/ *n* (*hairstyle*) caschetto *m* ● *vi* (*pt/pp* **bobbed**) (*also* ~ **up and down**) andare su e giù

'bob-sleigh *n* bob *m inv*

bode /bəʊd/ *vi* ~ **well/ill** essere di buono/cattivo augurio

bodily /'bɒdɪlɪ/ *a* fisico ● *adv* (*forcibly*) fisicamente

body /'bɒdɪ/ *n* corpo *m*; (*organization*) ente *m*; (*amount: of poems etc*) quantità *f*. ~**guard** *n* guardia *f* del corpo. ~**work** *n Auto* carrozzeria *f*

bog /bɒg/ *n* palude *f* ● *vt* (*pt/pp* **bogged**) **get** ~**ged down** impantanarsi

boggle /'bɒgl/ *vi* **the mind** ~**s** non posso neanche immaginarlo

bogus /'bəʊgəs/ *a* falso

boil[1] /bɔɪl/ *n Med* foruncolo *m*

boil[2] *n* **bring/come to the** ~

portare/arrivare ad ebollizione ● *vt* [far] bollire ● *vi* bollire; (*fig: with anger*) ribollire; **the water** *or* **kettle's** ~**ing** boil down to *vt fig* ridursi a. **boil over** *vi* straboccare (*bollendo*). **boil up** *vt* far bollire

boiler /'bɔɪlə(r)/ *n* caldaia *f*. ~**suit** *n* tuta *f*

'boiling point *n* punto *m* di ebollizione

boisterous /'bɔɪstərəs/ *a* chiassoso

bold /bəʊld/ *a* audace ● *n Typ* neretto *m*. ~**ness** *n* audacia *f*

bollard /'bɒlɑ:d/ *n* colonnina *m* di sbarramento al traffico

bolster /'bəʊlstə(r)/ *n* cuscino *m* (*lungo e rotondo*) ● *vt* ~ [**up**] sostenere

bolt /bəʊlt/ *n* (*for door*) catenaccio *m*; (*for fixing*) bullone *m* ● *vt* fissare (*con i bulloni*) (**to** a); chiudere col chiavistello ⟨*door*⟩; ingurgitare ⟨*food*⟩ ● *vi* svignarsela; ⟨*horse:*⟩ scappar via ● *adv* ~ **upright** diritto come un fuso

bomb /bɒm/ *n* bomba *f* ● *vt* bombardare

bombard /bɒm'bɑ:d/ *vt also fig* bombardare

bombastic /bɒm'bæstɪk/ *a* ampolloso

bomb|er /'bɒmə(r)/ *n Aeron* bombardiere *m*; (*person*) dinamitardo *m*. ~**er jacket** giubbotto *m*, bomber *m inv*. ~**shell** *n* (*fig: news*) bomba *f*

bond /bɒnd/ *n fig* legame *m*; *Comm* obbligazione *f* ● *vt* ⟨*glue:*⟩ attaccare

bondage /'bɒndɪdʒ/ *n* schiavitù *f*

bone /bəʊn/ *n* osso *m*; (*of fish*) spina *f* ● *vt* disossare ⟨*meat*⟩; togliere le spine da ⟨*fish*⟩. ~-'**dry** a secco

bonfire /'bɒn-/ *n* falò *m inv*. ~ **night** *festa celebrata la notte del 5 novembre con fuochi d'artificio e falò*

bonnet /'bɒnɪt/ *n* cuffia *f*; (*of car*) cofano *m*

bonus /'bəʊnəs/ *n* (*individual*) gratifica *f*; (*production* ~) premio *m*; (*life insurance*) dividendo *m*; **a** ~ *fig* qualcosa in più

bony /'bəʊnɪ/ *a* (-**ier**, -**iest**) ossuto; ⟨*fish*⟩ pieno di spine

boo /bu:/ *int* (*to surprise or frighten*) bu! ● *vt/i* fischiare

boob /bu:b/ *n* (*fam: mistake*) gaffe *f inv*; (*breast*) tetta *f* ● *vi fam* fare una gaffe

book /bʊk/ *n* libro *m*; (*of tickets*) blocchetto *m*; **keep the** ~**s** *Comm* tenere la contabilità; **be in sb's bad/good** ~**s** essere nel libro nero/nelle grazie di qcno ● *vt* ⟨*reserve*⟩ prenotare; ⟨*for offence*⟩ multare ● *vi* ⟨*reserve*⟩ prenotare

book: **~case** *n* libreria *f*. **~-ends** *npl* reggilibri *mpl*. **~ing-office** *n* biglietteria *f*. **~keeping** *n* contabilità *f*. **~let** *n* opuscolo *m*. **~maker** *n* allibratore *m*. **~mark** *n* segnalibro *m*. **~seller** *n* libraio, -a *mf*. **~shop** *n* libreria *f*. **~worm** *n* topo *m* di biblioteca

boom /buːm/ *n Comm* boom *m inv*; ⟨*upturn*⟩ impennata *f*; ⟨*of thunder, gun*⟩ rimbombo *m* ● *vi* ⟨*thunder, gun:*⟩ rimbombare; *fig* prosperare

boon /buːn/ *n* benedizione *f*

boor /bʊə(r)/ *n* zoticone *m*. **~ish** *a* maleducato

boost /buːst/ *n* spinta *f* ● *vt* stimolare ⟨*sales*⟩; sollevare ⟨*morale*⟩; far crescere ⟨*hopes*⟩. **~er** *n Med* dose *f* supplementare

boot /buːt/ *n* stivale *m*; ⟨*up to ankle*⟩ stivaletto *m*; ⟨*football*⟩ scarpetta *f*; ⟨*climbing*⟩ scarpone *m*; *Auto* portabagagli *m inv* ● *vt Comput* inizializzare

booth /buːð/ *n* ⟨*Teleph, voting*⟩ cabina *f*; ⟨*at market*⟩ bancarella *f*

'boot-up *n Comput* boot *m inv*

booty /ˈbuːtɪ/ *n* bottino *m*

booze /buːz/ *fam n* alcolici *mpl*

border /ˈbɔːdə(r)/ *n* bordo *m*; ⟨*frontier*⟩ frontiera *f*; ⟨*in garden*⟩ bordura *f* ● *vi* **~ on** confinare con; *fig* essere ai confini di ⟨*madness*⟩. **~line** *n* linea *f* di demarcazione; **~line case** caso *m* dubbio

bore[1] /bɔː(r)/ *see* **bear**[2]

bore[2] *vt Techn* forare

bor|e[3] *n* ⟨*of gun*⟩ calibro *m*; ⟨*person*⟩ seccatore, -trice *mf*; ⟨*thing*⟩ seccatura *f* ● *vt* annoiare. **~edom** *n* noia *f*. **be ~ed (to tears** *or* **to death)** annoiarsi (da morire). **~ing** *a* noioso

born /bɔːn/ *pp* **be ~** nascere; **I was ~ in 1966** sono nato nel 1966 ● *a* nato; **a ~ liar/actor** un bugiardo/attore nato

borne /bɔːn/ *see* **bear**[2]

borough /ˈbʌrə/ *n* municipalità *f inv*

borrow /ˈbɒrəʊ/ *vt* prendere a prestito ⟨**from** da⟩; **can I ~ your pen?** mi presti la tua penna?

Bosnia /ˈbɒznɪə/ *n* Bosnia *f*

bosom /ˈbʊzm/ *n* seno *m*

boss /bɒs/ *n* direttore, -trice *mf* ● *vt* ⟨*also* **~ about**⟩ comandare a bacchetta. **~y** *a* autoritario

botanical /bəˈtænɪkl/ *a* botanico

botan|ist /ˈbɒtənɪst/ *n* botanico, -a *mf*. **~y** *n* botanica *f*

botch /bɒtʃ/ *vt* fare un pasticcio con

both /bəʊθ/ *a & pron* tutti e due, entrambi ● *adv* **~ men and women** entrambi uomini e donne; **~ [of] the children** tutti e due i bambini; **they are ~ dead** sono morti entrambi; **~ of them** tutti e due

bother /ˈbɒðə(r)/ *n* preoccupazione *f*; ⟨*minor trouble*⟩ fastidio *m*; **it's no ~** non c'è problema ● *int fam* che seccatura! ● *vt* ⟨*annoy*⟩ dare fastidio a; ⟨*disturb*⟩ disturbare ● *vi* preoccuparsi ⟨**about** di⟩; **don't ~** lascia perdere

bottle /ˈbɒtl/ *n* bottiglia *f*; ⟨*baby's*⟩ biberon *m inv* ● *vt* imbottigliare. **bottle up** *vt fig* reprimere

bottle: **~ bank** *n* contenitore *m* per la raccolta del vetro. **~-neck** *n fig* ingorgo *m*. **~-opener** *n* apribottiglie *m inv*

bottom /ˈbɒtm/ *a* ultimo; **the ~ shelf** l'ultimo scaffale in basso ● *n* ⟨*of container*⟩ fondo *m*; ⟨*of river*⟩ fondale *m*; ⟨*of hill*⟩ piedi *mpl*; ⟨*buttocks*⟩ sedere *m*; **at the ~ of the page** in fondo alla pagina; **get to the ~ of** *fig* vedere cosa c'è sotto. **~less** *a* senza fondo

bough /baʊ/ *n* ramoscello *m*

bought /bɔːt/ *see* **buy**

boulder /ˈbəʊldə(r)/ *n* masso *m*

bounce /baʊns/ *vi* rimbalzare; ⟨*fam: cheque:*⟩ essere respinto ● *vt* far rimbalzare ⟨*ball*⟩

bouncer /ˈbaʊnsə(r)/ *n fam* buttafuori *m inv*

bound[1] /baʊnd/ *n* balzo *m* ● *vi* balzare

bound[2] *see* **bind** ● *a* **~ for** ⟨*ship*⟩ diretto a; **be ~ to do** ⟨*likely*⟩ dovere fare per forza; ⟨*obliged*⟩ essere costretto a fare

boundary /ˈbaʊndərɪ/ *n* limite *m*

'boundless *a* illimitato

bounds /baʊndz/ *npl fig* limiti *mpl*; **out of ~** fuori dai limiti

bouquet /bʊˈkeɪ/ *n* mazzo *m* di fiori; ⟨*of wine*⟩ bouquet *m*

bourgeois /ˈbʊəʒwɑː/ *a pej* borghese

bout /baʊt/ *n Med* attacco *m*; *Sport* incontro *m*

bow[1] /bəʊ/ *n* ⟨*weapon*⟩ arco *m*; *Mus* archetto *m*; ⟨*knot*⟩ nodo *m*

bow[2] /baʊ/ *n* inchino *m* ● *vi* inchinarsi ● *vt* piegare ⟨*head*⟩

bow[3] /baʊ/ *n Naut* prua *f*

bowel /ˈbaʊəl/ *n* intestino *m*; **~s** *pl* intestini *mpl*

bowl[1] /bəʊl/ *n* ⟨*for soup, cereal*⟩ scodella *f*; ⟨*of pipe*⟩ fornello *m*

bowl[2] *n* ⟨*ball*⟩ boccia *f* ● *vt* lanciare ● *vi*

Cricket servire; (*in bowls*) lanciare. **bowl over** *vt* buttar giù; (*fig: leave speechless*) lasciar senza parole

bow-legged /bəʊ'legd/ *a* dalle gambe storte

bowler¹ /'bəʊlə(r)/ *n Cricket* lanciatore *m*; *Bowls* giocatore *m* di bocce

bowler² *n* ~ [hat] bombetta *f*

bowling /'bəʊlɪŋ/ *n* gioco *m* delle bocce. ~-alley *n* pista *f* da bowling

bowls /bəʊlz/ *n* gioco *m* delle bocce

bow-'tie /bəʊ-/ *n* cravatta *f* a farfalla

box¹ /bɒks/ *n* scatola *f*; *Theat* palco *m*

box² *vi Sport* fare il pugile ● *vt* ~ **sb's ears** dare uno schiaffo a qcno

box|er /'bɒksə(r)/ *n* pugile *m*. ~**ing** *n* pugilato *m*. **B~ing Day** *n* [giorno *m* di] Santo Stefano *m*

box: ~-**office** *n Theat* botteghino *m*. ~-**room** *n Br* sgabuzzino *m*

boy /bɔɪ/ *n* ragazzo *m*; (*younger*) bambino *m*

boycott /'bɔɪkɒt/ *n* boicottaggio *m* ● *vt* boicottare

boy: ~**friend** *n* ragazzo *m*. ~**ish** *a* da ragazzino

bra /brɑː/ *n* reggiseno *m*

brace /breɪs/ *n* sostegno *m*; (*dental*) apparecchio *m*; ~**s** *npl* bretelle *fpl* ● *vt* ~ **oneself** *fig* farsi forza (**for** per affrontare)

bracelet /'breɪslɪt/ *n* braccialetto *m*

bracing /'breɪsɪŋ/ *a* tonificante

bracken /'brækn/ *n* felce *f*

bracket /'brækɪt/ *n* mensola *f*; (*group*) categoria *f*; *Typ* parentesi *f inv* ● *vt* mettere fra parentesi

brag /bræg/ *vi* (*pt/pp* **bragged**) vantarsi (**about** di)

braid /breɪd/ *n* (*edging*) passamano *m*

braille /breɪl/ *n* braille *m*

brain /breɪn/ *n* cervello *m*; ~**s** *pl fig* testa *fsg*

brain: ~**child** *n* invenzione *f* personale. ~ **dead** *a Med* celebralmente morto; *fig fam* senza cervello. ~**less** *a* senza cervello. ~**wash** *vt* fare il lavaggio del cervello a. ~**wave** *n* lampo *m* di genio

brainy /'breɪnɪ/ *a* (**-ier, -iest**) intelligente

braise /breɪz/ *vt* brasare

brake /breɪk/ *n* freno *m* ● *vi* frenare. ~-**light** *n* stop *m inv*

bramble /'bræmbl/ *n* rovo *m*; (*fruit*) mora *f*

bran /bræn/ *n* crusca *f*

branch /brɑːntʃ/ *n* also *fig* ramo *m*; *Comm* succursale *f* ● *vi* (*road:*) biforcarsi. **branch off** *vi* biforcarsi. **branch out** *vi* ~ **out into** allargare le proprie attività nel ramo di

brand /brænd/ *n* marca *f*; (*on animal*) marchio *m* ● *vt* marcare ⟨*animal*⟩; *fig* tacciare (**as** di)

brandish /'brændɪʃ/ *vt* brandire

brand-'new *a* nuovo fiammante

brandy /'brændɪ/ *n* brandy *m inv*

brash /bræʃ/ *a* sfrontato

brass /brɑːs/ *n* ottone *m*; **the** ~ *Mus* gli ottoni *mpl*; **top** ~ *fam* pezzi *mpl* grossi. ~ **band** *n* banda *f* (*di soli ottoni*)

brassiere /'bræzɪə(r)/ *n fml, Am* reggipetto *m*

brat /bræt/ *n pej* marmocchio, -a *mf*

bravado /brə'vɑːdəʊ/ *n* bravata *f*

brave /breɪv/ *a* coraggioso ● *vt* affrontare. ~**ry** /-ərɪ/ *n* coraggio *m*

brawl /brɔːl/ *n* rissa *f* ● *vi* azzuffarsi

brawn /brɔːn/ *n Culin* soppressata *f*

brawny /'brɔːnɪ/ *a* muscoloso

brazen /'breɪzn/ *a* sfrontato

brazier /'breɪzɪə(r)/ *n* braciere *m*

Brazil /brə'zɪl/ *n* Brasile *m*. ~**ian** *a & n* brasiliano, -a *mf*. ~ **nut** *n* noce *f* del Brasile

breach /briːtʃ/ *n* (*of law*) violazione *f*; (*gap*) breccia *f*; (*fig: in party*) frattura *f*; ~ **of contract** inadempienza *f* di contratto; ~ **of the peace** violazione *f* della quiete pubblica ● *vt* recedere ⟨*contract*⟩

bread /bred/ *n* pane *m*; **a slice of** ~ **and butter** una fetta di pane imburrato

bread: ~ **bin** *n* cassetta *f* portapane *inv*. ~**crumbs** *npl* briciole *fpl*; *Culin* pangrattato *m*. ~**line** *n* **be on the** ~**line** essere povero in canna

breadth /bredθ/ *n* larghezza *f*

'bread-winner *n* quello, -a *mf* che porta i soldi a casa

break /breɪk/ *n* rottura *f*; (*interval*) intervallo *m*; (*interruption*) interruzione *f*; (*fam: chance*) opportunità *f inv* ● *v* (*pt* **broke,** *pp* **broken**) ● *vt* rompere; (*interrupt*) interrompere; ~ **one's arm** rompersi un braccio ● *vi* rompersi; ⟨*day:*⟩ spuntare; ⟨*storm:*⟩ scoppiare; ⟨*news:*⟩ diffondersi; ⟨*boy's voice:*⟩ cambiare. **break away** *vi* scappare; *fig* chiudere (**from** con). **break down** *vi* ⟨*machine, car:*⟩ guastarsi; (*emotionally*) cedere (*psicologicamente*) ● *vt* sfondare ⟨*door*⟩; ripartire ⟨*figures*⟩. **break into** *vt* introdursi (*con la forza*) in; forzare ⟨*car*⟩. **break off** *vt* rompere ⟨*engagement*⟩ ● *vi* ⟨*part of whole:*⟩ rompersi. **break out** *vi* ⟨*fight,* *war.*⟩ scoppiare. **break up** *vt* far cessare ⟨*fight*⟩; disperdere ⟨*crowd*⟩ ● *vi* ⟨*crowd:*⟩ disperdersi; ⟨*couple:*⟩ separarsi; *Sch* iniziare le vacanze

'**break|able** /'breɪkəbl/ *a* fragile. **~age** /-ɪdʒ/ *n* rottura *f*. **~down** *n* (*of car, machine*) guasto *m*; *Med* esaurimento *m* nervoso; (*of figures*) analisi *f inv*. **~er** *n* (*wave*) frangente *m*

breakfast /'brekfəst/ *n* [prima] colazione *f*

break: **~through** *n* scoperta *f*. **~water** *n* frangiflutti *m inv*

breast /brest/ *n* seno *m*. **~-feed** *vt* allattare [al seno]. **~-stroke** *n* nuoto *m* a rana

breath /breθ/ *n* respiro *m*, fiato *m*; **out of ~** senza fiato

breathalyse /'breθəlaɪz/ *vt* sottoporre alla prova [etilica] del palloncino. **~r®** *n Br* alcoltest *m inv*

breathe /briːð/ *vt/i* respirare. **breathe in** *vi* inspirare ● *vt* respirare ⟨*scent, air*⟩. **breathe out** *vt/i* espirare

breath|er /'briːðə(r)/ *n* pausa *f*. **~ing** *n* respirazione *f*

breath /'breθ/: **~less** *a* senza fiato. **~-taking** *a* mozzafiato. **~ test** *n* prova [etilica] *f* del palloncino

bred /bred/ *see* **breed**

breed /briːd/ *n* razza *f* ● *v* (*pt/pp* **bred**) ● *vt* allevare; (*give rise to*) generare ● *vi* riprodursi. **~er** *n* allevatore, -trice *mf*. **~ing** *n* allevamento *m*; *fig* educazione *f*

breez|e /briːz/ *n* brezza *f*. **~y** *a* ventoso

brew /bruː/ *n* infuso *m* ● *vt* mettere in infusione ⟨*tea*⟩; produrre ⟨*beer*⟩ ● *vi fig* ⟨*trouble:*⟩ essere nell'aria. **~er** *n* birraio *m*. **~ery** *n* fabbrica *f* di birra

bribe /braɪb/ *n* (*money*) bustarella *f*; (*large sum of money*) tangente *f* ● *vt* corrompere. **~ry** /-ərɪ/ *n* corruzione *f*

brick /brɪk/ *n* mattone *m*. '**~layer** *n* muratore *m* ● **brick up** *vt* murare

bridal /'braɪdl/ *a* nuziale

bride /braɪd/ *n* sposa *f*. **~groom** *n* sposo *m*. **~smaid** *n* damigella *f* d'onore

bridge[1] /brɪdʒ/ *n* ponte *m*; (*of nose*) setto *m* nasale; (*of spectacles*) ponticello *m* ● *vt fig* colmare ⟨*gap*⟩

bridge[2] *n Cards* bridge *m*

bridle /'braɪdl/ *n* briglia *f*

brief[1] /briːf/ *a* breve

brief[2] *n* istruzioni *fpl* ⟨*Jur: case*⟩ causa *f* ● *vt* dare istruzioni a; *Jur* affidare la causa a. **~case** *n* cartella *f*

brief|ing /'briːfɪŋ/ *n* briefing *m inv*. **~ly**

adv brevemente. **~ly,...** in breve,... **~ness** *n* brevità *f*

briefs /briːfs/ *npl* slip *m inv*

brigad|e /brɪ'geɪd/ *n* brigata *f*. **~ier** /-ə'dɪə(r)/ *n* generale *m* di brigata

bright /braɪt/ *a* ⟨*metal, idea*⟩ brillante; ⟨*day, room, future*⟩ luminoso; (*clever*) intelligente; **~ red** rosso *m* acceso

bright|en /'braɪtn/ *v* **~en [up]** *vt* ravvivare; rallegrare ⟨*person*⟩ ● *vi* ⟨*weather:*⟩ schiarirsi; ⟨*face:*⟩ illuminarsi; ⟨*person:*⟩ rallegrarsi. **~ly** *adv* ⟨*shine*⟩ intensamente; ⟨*smile*⟩ allegramente. **~ness** *n* luminosità *f*; (*intelligence*) intelligenza *f*

brilliance /'brɪljəns/ *n* luminosità *f*; (*of person*) genialità *f*

brilliant /'brɪljənt/ *a* (*very good*) eccezionale; (*very intelligent*) brillante; ⟨*sunshine*⟩ splendente

brim /brɪm/ *n* bordo *m*; (*of hat*) tesa *f* ● **brim over** *vi* (*pt/pp* **brimmed**) traboccare

brine /braɪn/ *n* salamoia *f*

bring /brɪŋ/ *vt* (*pt/pp* **brought**) portare ⟨*person, object*⟩. **bring about** *vt* causare. **bring along** *vt* portare [con sé]. **bring back** *vt* restituire ⟨*sth borrowed*⟩; reintrodurre ⟨*hanging*⟩; fare ritornare in mente ⟨*memories*⟩. **bring down** *vt* portare giù; fare cadere ⟨*government*⟩; fare abbassare ⟨*price*⟩. **bring off** *vt* **~ sth off** riuscire a fare qcsa. **bring on** *vt* (*cause*) provocare. **bring out** *vt* (*emphasize*) mettere in evidenza; pubblicare ⟨*book*⟩. **bring round** *vt* portare; (*persuade*) convincere; far rinvenire ⟨*unconscious person*⟩. **bring up** *vt* (*vomit*) rimettere; allevare ⟨*children*⟩; tirare fuori ⟨*question, subject*⟩

brink /brɪŋk/ *n* orlo *m*

brisk /brɪsk/ *a* svelto; ⟨*person*⟩ sbrigativo; ⟨*trade, business*⟩ redditizio; ⟨*walk*⟩ a passo spedito

brist|le /'brɪsl/ *n* setola *f* ● *vi* **~ling with** pieno di. **~ly** *a* ⟨*chin*⟩ ispido

Brit|ain /'brɪtn/ *n* Gran Bretagna *f*. **~ish** *a* britannico; ⟨*ambassador*⟩ della Gran Bretagna ● *npl* **the ~ish** il popolo britannico. **~on** *n* cittadino, -a britannico, -a *mf*

brittle /'brɪtl/ *a* fragile

broach /brəʊtʃ/ *vt* toccare ⟨*subject*⟩

broad /brɔːd/ *a* ampio; ⟨*hint*⟩ chiaro; ⟨*accent*⟩ marcato. **two metres ~** largo due metri; **in ~ daylight** in pieno giorno. **~ beans** *npl* fave *fpl*

'**broadcast** *n* trasmissione *f* ● *vt/i*

broaden | bug

(*pt/pp* **-cast**) trasmettere. **~er** *n* giornalista *mf* radiotelevisivo, -a. **~ing** *n* diffusione *f* radiotelevisiva; **be in ~ing** lavorare per la televisione/radio

broaden /'brɔːdn/ *vt* allargare ● *vi* allargarsi

broadly /'brɔːdlɪ/ *adv* largamente; **~ [speaking]** generalmente

broad'minded *a* di larghe vedute

broccoli /'brɒkəlɪ/ *n inv* broccoli *mpl*

brochure /'brəʊʃə(r)/ *n* opuscolo *m*; (*travel ~*) dépliant *m inv*

broke /brəʊk/ *see* **break** ● *a fam* al verde

broken /'brəʊkn/ *see* **break** ● *a* rotto; (*fig: marriage*) fallito. **~ English** inglese *m* stentato. **~-hearted** *a* affranto

broker /'brəʊkə(r)/ *n* broker *m inv*

brolly /'brɒlɪ/ *n fam* ombrello *m*

bronchitis /brɒŋ'kaɪtɪs/ *n* bronchite *f*

bronze /brɒnz/ *n* bronzo *m* ● *attrib* di bronzo

brooch /brəʊtʃ/ *n* spilla *f*

brood /bruːd/ *n* covata *f*; (*hum: children*) prole *f* ● *vi fig* rimuginare

brook /brʊk/ *n* ruscello *m*

broom /bruːm/ *n* scopa *f*. **~stick** *n* manico *m* di scopa

broth /brɒθ/ *n* brodo *m*

brothel /'brɒθl/ *n* bordello *m*

brother /'brʌðə(r)/ *n* fratello *m*

brother: ~-in-law *n* (*pl* **~s-in-law**) cognato *m*. **~ly** *a* fraterno

brought /brɔːt/ *see* **bring**

brow /braʊ/ *n* fronte *f*; (*of hill*) cima *f*

'browbeat *vt* (*pt* **-beat**, *pp* **-beaten**) intimidire

brown /braʊn/ *a* marrone; castano (*hair*) ● *n* marrone *m* ● *vt* rosolare (*meat*) ● *vi* (*meat:*) rosolarsi. **~ 'paper** *n* carta *f* da pacchi

Brownie /'braʊnɪ/ *n* coccinella *f* (*negli scout*)

browse /braʊz/ *vi* (*read*) leggicchiare; (*in shop*) curiosare

bruise /bruːz/ *n* livido *m*; (*on fruit*) ammaccatura *f* ● *vt* ammaccare (*fruit*); **one's arm** farsi un livido sul braccio. **~d** *a* contuso

brunette /bruː'net/ *n* bruna *f*

brunt /brʌnt/ *n* **bear the ~ of sth** subire maggiormente qcsa

brush /brʌʃ/ *n* spazzola *f*; (*with long handle*) spazzolone *m*; (*for paint*) pennello *m*; (*bushes*) boscaglia *f*; (*fig: conflict*) breve scontro *m* ● *vt* spazzolare (*hair*); lavarsi (*teeth*); scopare (*stairs, floor*). **brush against** *vt* sfiorare. **brush**

aside *vt fig* ignorare. **brush off** *vt* spazzolare; (*with hands*) togliere; ignorare (*criticism*). **brush up** *vt/i fig* **~ up [on]** rinfrescare

brusque /brʊsk/ *a* brusco

Brussels /'brʌslz/ *n* Bruxelles *f*. **~ sprouts** *npl* cavoletti *mpl* di Bruxelles

brutal /'bruːtl/ *a* brutale. **~ity** /-'tælətɪ/ *n* brutalità *f inv*

brute /bruːt/ *n* bruto *m*. **~ force** *n* forza *f* bruta

BSc *n abbr* **Bachelor of Science**

BSE *n abbr* (**bovine spongiform encephalitis**) encefalite *f* bovina spongiforme

bubble /'bʌbl/ *n* bolla *f*; (*in drink*) bollicina *f*

buck¹ /bʌk/ *n* maschio *m* del cervo; (*rabbit*) maschio *m* del coniglio ● *vi* (*horse:*) saltare a quattro zampe. **buck up** *vi fam* tirarsi su; (*hurry*) sbrigarsi

buck² *n Am fam* dollaro *m*

buck³ *n* **pass the ~** scaricare la responsabilità

bucket /'bʌkɪt/ *n* secchio *m*

buckle /'bʌkl/ *n* fibbia *f* ● *vt* allacciare ● *vi* (*shelf:*) piegarsi; (*wheel:*) storcersi

bud /bʌd/ *n* bocciolo *m*

Buddhis|m /'bʊdɪzm/ *n* buddismo *m*. **~t** *a* & *n* buddista *mf*

buddy /'bʌdɪ/ *n fam* amico, -a *mf*

budge /bʌdʒ/ *vt* spostare ● *vi* spostarsi

budgerigar /'bʌdʒərɪɡɑː(r)/ *n* cocorita *f*

budget /'bʌdʒɪt/ *n* bilancio *m*; (*allotted to specific activity*) budget *m inv* ● *vi* (*pt/pp* **budgeted**) prevedere le spese; **~ for sth** includere qcsa nelle spese previste

buff /bʌf/ *a* (*colour*) [color] camoscio ● *n fam* fanatico, -a *mf*

buffalo /'bʌfələʊ/ *n* (*inv or pl* **-es**) bufalo *m*

buffer /'bʌfə(r)/ *n* Rail respingente *m*; **~ zone** *n* zona *f* cuscinetto

buffet¹ /'bʊfeɪ/ *n* buffet *m inv*

buffet² /'bʌfɪt/ *vt* (*pt/pp* **buffeted**) sferzare

bug /bʌɡ/ *n* (*insect*) insetto *m*; *Comput* bug *m inv*; (*fam: device*) cimice *f* ● *vt* (*pt/pp* **bugged**) *fam* installare le microspie in (*room*); mettere sotto controllo (*telephone*); (*fam: annoy*) scocciare

buggy /'bʌgɪ/ *n* [**baby**] ~ passeggino *m*

bugle /'bju:gl/ *n* tromba *f*

build /bɪld/ *n* (*of person*) corporatura *f* ● *vt/i* (*pt/pp* **built**) costruire. **build on** *vt* aggiungere 〈*extra storey*〉; sviluppare 〈*previous work*〉. **build up** *vt* ~ **up one's strength** rimettersi in forza ● *vi* 〈*pressure, traffic:*〉 aumentare; 〈*excitement, tension:*〉 crescere

builder /'bɪldə(r)/ *n* (*company*) costruttore *m*; (*worker*) muratore *m*

building /'bɪldɪŋ/ *n* edificio *m*. ~ **site** *n* cantiere *m* [di costruzione]. ~ **society** *n* istituto *m* di credito immobiliare

'**build-up** *n* (*of gas etc*) accumulo *m*; *fig* battage *m inv* pubblicitario

built /bɪlt/ *see* **build**. **~-in** *a* 〈*unit*〉 a muro; 〈*fig: feature*〉 incorporato. **~-up area** *n Auto* centro *m* abitato

bulb /bʌlb/ *n* bulbo *m*; *Electr* lampadina *f*

Bulgaria /bʌl'geərɪə/ *n* Bulgaria *f*

bulg|e /bʌldʒ/ *n* rigonfiamento *m* ● *vi* esser gonfio (**with** di); 〈*stomach, wall:*〉 sporgere; 〈*eyes, with surprise:*〉 uscire dalle orbite. **~ing** *a* gonfio; 〈*eyes*〉 sporgente

bulk /bʌlk/ *n* volume *m*; (*greater part*) grosso *m*; **in** ~ in grande quantità; (*loose*) sfuso. **~y** *a* voluminoso

bull /bʊl/ *n* toro *m*

'**bulldog** *n* bulldog *m inv*

bulldozer /'bʊldəʊzə(r)/ *n* bull-dozer *m inv*

bullet /'bʊlɪt/ *n* pallottola *f*

bulletin /'bʊlɪtɪn/ *n* bollettino *m*. ~ **board** *n Comput* bacheca *f* elettronica

'**bullet-proof** *a* antiproiettile *inv*; 〈*vehicle*〉 blindato

'**bullfight** *n* corrida *f*. **~er** *n* torero *m*

bullion /'bʊlɪən/ *n* **gold** ~ oro *m* in lingotti

bullock /'bʊlək/ *n* manzo *m*

bull: **~ring** *n* arena *f*. **~'s-eye** *n* centro *m* del bersaglio; **score a ~'s-eye** fare centro

bully /'bʊlɪ/ *n* prepotente *mf* ● *vt* fare il/la prepotente con. **~ing** *n* prepotenze *fpl*

bum¹ /bʌm/ *n sl* sedere *m*

bum² *n Am fam* vagabondo, -a *mf* ● **bum around** *vi fam* vagabondare

bumble-bee /'bʌmbl-/ *n* calabrone *m*

bump /bʌmp/ *n* botta *f*; (*swelling*) bozzo *m*, gonfiore *m*; (*in road*) protuberanza *f* ● *vt* sbattere. **bump into** *vt* sbattere contro; (*meet*) imbattersi in. **bump off** *vt fam* far fuori

bumper /'bʌmpə(r)/ *n Auto* paraurti *m inv* ● *a* abbondante

bumpkin /'bʌmpkɪn/ *n* **country** ~ zoticone, -a *mf*

bumptious /'bʌmpʃəs/ *a* presuntuoso

bumpy /'bʌmpɪ/ *a* 〈*road*〉 accidentato; 〈*flight*〉 turbolento

bun /bʌn/ *n* focaccina *f* (*dolce*); (*hair*) chignon *m inv*

bunch /bʌntʃ/ *n* (*of flowers, keys*) mazzo *m*; (*of bananas*) casco *m*; (*of people*) gruppo *m*; ~ **of grapes** grappolo *m* d'uva

bundle /'bʌndl/ *n* fascio *m*; (*of money*) mazzetta *f*; **a ~ of nerves** *fam* un fascio di nervi ● *vt* ~ [**up**] affastellare

bung /bʌŋ/ *vt fam* (*throw*) buttare. **bung up** *vt* (*block*) otturare

bungalow /'bʌŋgələʊ/ *n* bungalow *m inv*

bungle /'bʌŋgl/ *vt* fare un pasticcio di

bunion /'bʌnjən/ *n Med* callo *m* all'alluce

bunk /bʌŋk/ *n* cuccetta *f*. **~-beds** *npl* letti *mpl* a castello

bunny /'bʌnɪ/ *n fam* coniglietto *m*

buoy /bɔɪ/ *n* boa *f*

buoyan|cy /'bɔɪənsɪ/ *n* galleggiabilità *f*. **~t** *a* 〈*boat*〉 galleggiante; 〈*water*〉 che aiuta a galleggiare

burden /'bɜ:dn/ *n* carico *m* ● *vt* caricare. **~some** /-səm/ *a* gravoso

bureau /'bjʊərəʊ/ *n* (*pl* **-x** /-əʊz/ *or* **~s**) (*desk*) scrivania *f*; (*office*) ufficio *m*

bureaucracy /bjʊə'rɒkrəsɪ/ *n* burocrazia *f*

bureaucrat /'bjʊərəkræt/ *n* burocrate *mf*. **~ic** /-'krætɪk/ *a* burocratico

burger /'bɜ:gə(r)/ *n* hamburger *m inv*

burglar /'bɜ:glə(r)/ *n* svaligiatore, -trice *mf*. **~ alarm** *n* antifurto *m inv*

burglar|ize /'bɜ:gləraɪz/ *vt Am* svaligiare. **~y** *n* furto *m* con scasso

burgle /'bɜ:gl/ *vt* svaligiare

Burgundy /'bɜ:gəndɪ/ *n* Borgogna *f*

burial /'berɪəl/ *n* sepoltura *f*. ~ **ground** *n* cimitero *m*

burlesque /bɜ:'lesk/ *n* parodia *f*

burly /'bɜ:lɪ/ *a* (**-ier, -iest**) corpulento

Burm|a /'bɜ:mə/ *n* Birmania *f*. **~ese** /-'mi:z/ *a* & *n* birmano, -a *mf*

burn /bɜ:n/ *n* bruciatura *f* ● *v* (*pt/pp* **burnt** *or* **burned**) ● *vt* bruciare ● *vi* bruciare. **burn down** *vt/i* bruciare. **burn out** *vi fig* esaurirsi. **~er** *n* (*on stove*) bruciatore *m*

burnish /'bɜ:nɪʃ/ *vt* lucidare

burnt /bɜ:nt/ *see* **burn**

burp /bɜːp/ *n fam* rutto *m* ● *vi fam* ruttare

burrow /'bʌrəʊ/ *n* tana *f* ● *vt* scavare

bursar /'bɜːsə(r)/ *n* economo, -a *mf*. **~y** *n* borsa *f* di studio

burst /bɜːst/ *n* (*of gunfire, energy, laughter*) scoppio *m*; (*of speed*) scatto *m* ● *v* (*pt/pp* **burst**) ● *vt* far scoppiare ● *vi* scoppiare; **~ into tears** scoppiare in lacrime; **she ~ into the room** ha fatto irruzione nella stanza. **burst out** *vi* **~ out laughing/crying** scoppiare a ridere/piangere

bury /'berɪ/ *vt* (*pt/pp* **-ied**) seppellire; (*hide*) nascondere

bus /bʌs/ *n* autobus *m inv*, pullman *m inv*, (*long distance*) pullman *m inv*, corriera *f*

bush /bʊʃ/ *n* cespuglio *m*; (*land*) boscaglia *f*. **~y** *a* (**-ier, -iest**) folto

busily /'bɪzɪlɪ/ *adv* con grande impegno

business /'bɪznɪs/ *n* affare *m*; *Comm* affari *mpl*; (*establishment*) attività *f* di commercio; **on ~** per affari; **he has no ~ to** non ha alcun diritto di; **mind one's own ~** farsi gli affari propri; **that's none of your ~** non sono affari tuoi. **~like** *a* efficiente. **~man** *n* uomo *m* d'affari. **~woman** *n* donna *f* d'affari

busker /'bʌskə(r)/ *n* suonatore, -trice *mf* ambulante

'**bus station** *n* stazione *f* degli autobus

'**bus-stop** *n* fermata *f* d'autobus

bust[1] /bʌst/ *n* busto *m*; (*chest*) petto *m*

bust[2] *a fam* rotto; **go ~** fallire ● *v* (*pt/pp* **busted** *or* **bust**) *fam* ● *vt* far scoppiare ● *vi* scoppiare

bustl|**e** /'bʌsl/ *n* (*activity*) trambusto *m* ● **bustle about** *vi* affannarsi. **~ing** *a* animato

'**bust-up** *n fam* lite *f*

busy /'bɪzɪ/ *a* (**-ier, -iest**) occupato; ⟨*day, time*⟩ intenso; ⟨*street*⟩ affollato; (*with traffic*) pieno di traffico; **be ~ doing** essere occupato a fare ● *vt* **~ oneself** darsi da fare

'**busybody** *n* ficcanaso *mf inv*

but /bʌt/, *atono* /bət/ *conj* ma ● *prep* eccetto, tranne; **nobody ~ you** nessuno tranne te; **~ for** (*without*) se non fosse stato per; **the last ~ one** il penultimo; **the next ~ one** il secondo ● *adv* (*only*) soltanto; **there were ~ two** ce n'erano soltanto due

butcher /'bʊtʃə(r)/ *n* macellaio *m*; **~'s [shop]** macelleria *f* ● *vt* macellare; *fig* massacrare

butler /'bʌtlə(r)/ *n* maggiordomo *m*

butt /bʌt/ *n* (*of gun*) calcio *m*; (*of cigarette*) mozzicone *m*; (*for water*) barile *m*; (*fig: target*) bersaglio *m* ● *vt* dare una testata a; ⟨*goat:*⟩ dare una cornata a. **butt in** *vi* interrompere

butter /'bʌtə(r)/ *n* burro *m* ● *vt* imburrare. **butter up** *vt fam* arruffianarsi

butter: **~cup** *n* ranuncolo *m*. **~fingers** *nsg fam* **be a ~fingers** avere le mani di pasta frolla. **~fly** *n* farfalla *f*

buttocks /'bʌtəks/ *npl* natiche *fpl*

button /'bʌtn/ *n* bottone *m* ● *vt* **~ [up]** abbottonare ● *vi* **~ [up]** abbottonarsi. **~hole** *n* occhiello *m*, asola *f*

buttress /'bʌtrɪs/ *n* contrafforte *m*

buxom /'bʌksəm/ *a* formosa

buy /baɪ/ *n* **good/bad ~** buon/cattivo acquisto *m* ● *vt* (*pt/pp* **bought**) comprare; **~ sb a drink** pagare da bere a qcno; **I'll ~ this one** (*drink*) questo, lo offro io. **~er** *n* compratore, -trice *mf*

buzz /bʌz/ *n* ronzio *m*; **give sb a ~** *fam* (*on phone*) dare un colpo di telefono a qcno; (*excite*) mettere in fermento qcno ● *vi* ronzare ● *vt* **~ sb** chiamare qcno col cicalino. **buzz off** *vi fam* levarsi di torno

buzzer /'bʌzə(r)/ *n* cicalino *m*

by /baɪ/ *prep* (*near, next to*) vicino a; (*at the latest*) per; **by Mozart** di Mozart; **he was run over by a bus** è stato investito da un autobus; **by oneself** da solo; **by the sea** al mare; **by sea** via mare; **by car/bus** in macchina/autobus; **by day/ night** di giorno/notte; **by the hour/metre** a ore/metri; **six metres by four** sei metri per quattro; **he won by six metres** ha vinto di sei metri; **I missed the train by a minute** ho perso il treno per un minuto; **I'll be home by six** sarò a casa per le sei; **by this time next week** a quest'ora tra una settimana; **he rushed by me** mi è passato accanto di corsa ● *adv* **she'll be here by and by** sarà qui fra poco; **by and large** in complesso

bye[**-bye**] /baɪ['baɪ]/ *int fam* ciao

by: **~-election** *n* elezione *f* straordinaria indetta per coprire una carica rimasta vacante in Parlamento. **~gone** *a* passato. **~-law** *n* legge *f* locale. **~pass** *n* circonvallazione *f*; *Med* by-pass *m inv* ● *vt* evitare. **~-product** *n* sottoprodotto *m*. **~stander** *n* spettatore, -trice *mf*. **~word** *n* **be a ~word for** essere sinonimo di

Cc

cab /kæb/ n taxi m inv; (of lorry, train) cabina f

cabaret /'kæbəreɪ/ n cabaret m inv

cabbage /'kæbɪdʒ/ n cavolo m

cabin /'kæbɪn/ n (of plane, ship) cabina f; (hut) capanna f

cabinet /'kæbɪnɪt/ n armadietto m; [display] ~ vetrina f; C~ Pol consiglio m dei ministri. **~-maker** n ebanista mf

cable /'keɪbl/ n cavo m. ~ '**railway** n funicolare f. ~ '**television** n televisione f via cavo

cache /kæʃ/ n nascondiglio m; ~ of arms deposito m segreto di armi

cackle /'kækl/ vi ridacchiare

cactus /'kæktəs/ n (pl -ti /-taɪ/ or -tuses) cactus m inv

caddie /'kædɪ/ n portabastoni m inv

caddy /'kædɪ/ n [tea-]~ barattolo m del tè

cadet /kə'det/ n cadetto m

cadge /kædʒ/ vt/i fam scroccare

Caesarean /sɪ'zeərɪən/ n parto m cesareo

café /'kæfeɪ/ n caffè m inv

cafeteria /kæfə'tɪərɪə/ n tavola f calda

caffeine /'kæfiːn/ n caffeina f

cage /keɪdʒ/ n gabbia f

cagey /'keɪdʒɪ/ a fam riservato (about su)

cajole /kə'dʒəʊl/ vt persuadere con le lusinghe

cake /keɪk/ n torta f; (small) pasticcino m. **~d** a incrostato (with di)

calamity /kə'læmətɪ/ n calamità f inv

calcium /'kælsɪəm/ n calcio m

calculat|e /'kælkjʊleɪt/ vt calcolare. **~ing** a fig calcolatore. **~ion** /-'leɪʃn/ n calcolo m. **~or** n calcolatrice f

calendar /'kælmdə(r)/ n calendario m

calf¹ /kɑːf/ n (pl calves) vitello m

calf² n (pl calves) Anat polpaccio m

calibre /'kælɪbə(r)/ n calibro m

call /kɔːl/ n grido m; Teleph telefonata f; (visit) visita f; **be on** ~ (doctor:) essere di guardia ● vt chiamare; indire (strike); **be ~ed** chiamarsi ● vi chiamare; ~ **[in or round]** passare. **call back** vt/i richiamare. **call for** vt (ask

for) chiedere; (require) richiedere; (fetch) passare a prendere. **call off** vt richiamare (dog); disdire (meeting); revocare (strike). **call on** vt chiamare; (appeal to) fare un appello a; (visit) visitare. **call out** vt chiamare ad alta voce (names) ● vi chiamare ad alta voce. **call together** vt riunire. **call up** vt Mil chiamare alle armi; Teleph chiamare

call: **~-box** n cabina f telefonica. **~er** n visitatore, -trice mf; Teleph persona f che telefona. **~ing** n vocazione f

callous /'kæləs/ a insensibile

'**call-up** n Mil chiamata f alle armi

calm /kɑːm/ a calmo ● n calma f. **calm down** vt calmare ● vi calmarsi. **~ly** adv con calma

calorie /'kælərɪ/ n caloria f

calves /kɑːvz/ npl see **calf¹** & ²

camber /'kæmbə(r)/ n curvatura f

Cambodia /kæm'bəʊdɪə/ n Cambogia f. **~n** a & n cambogiano, -a mf

camcorder /'kæmkɔːdə(r)/ n videocamera f

came /keɪm/ see **come**

camel /'kæml/ n cammello m

camera /'kæmərə/ n macchina f fotografica; TV telecamera f. **~man** m operatore m [televisivo], cameraman m inv

camouflage /'kæməflɑːʒ/ n mimetizzazione f ● vt mimetizzare

camp /kæmp/ n campeggio f; Mil campo m ● vi campeggiare; Mil accamparsi

campaign /kæm'peɪn/ n campagna f ● vi fare una campagna

camp: **~-bed** n letto m da campo. **~er** n campeggiatore, -trice mf; Auto camper m inv. **~ing** n campeggio m. **~site** n campeggio m

campus /'kæmpəs/ n (pl -puses) Univ città f universitaria, campus m inv

can¹ /kæn/ n (for petrol) latta f; (tin) scatola f; ~ **of beer** lattina f di birra ● vt mettere in scatola

can² /kæn/, atono /kən/ v aux (pres **can**; pt **could**) (be able to) potere; (know how to) sapere; **I cannot** or **can't go** non posso andare; **he could not** or **couldn't go** non poteva andare; **she**

can't swim non sa nuotare; **I ~ smell something burning** sento odor di bruciato

Canad|a /ˈkænədə/ n Canada m. **~ian** /kəˈneɪdɪən/ a & n canadese mf

canal /kəˈnæl/ n canale m

Canaries /kəˈneərɪz/ npl Canarie fpl

canary /kəˈneərɪ/ n canarino m

cancel /ˈkænsl/ v (pt/pp **cancelled**) ● vt disdire ‹meeting, newspaper›; revocare ‹contract, order›; annullare ‹reservation, appointment, stamp›. **~lation** /-əˈleɪʃn/ n (of meeting, contract) revoca f; (in hotel, restaurant, for flight) cancellazione f

cancer /ˈkænsə(r)/ n cancro m; **C~** Astr Cancro m. **~ous** /-rəs/ a canceroso

candelabra /kændəˈlɑːbrə/ n candelabro m

candid /ˈkændɪd/ a franco

candidate /ˈkændɪdət/ n candidato, -a mf

candle /ˈkændl/ n candela f. **~stick** n portacandele m inv

candour /ˈkændə(r)/ n franchezza f

candy /ˈkændɪ/ n Am caramella f; **a [piece of] ~** una caramella. **~floss** /-flɒs/ n zucchero m filato

cane /keɪn/ n (stick) bastone m; Sch bacchetta f ● vt prendere a bacchettate ‹pupil›

canine /ˈkeɪnaɪn/ a canino. **~ tooth** n canino m

canister /ˈkænɪstə(r)/ n barattolo m (di metallo)

cannabis /ˈkænəbɪs/ n cannabis f

canned /kænd/ a in scatola; **~ music** fam musica f registrata

cannibal /ˈkænɪbl/ n cannibale m. **~ism** n cannibalismo m

cannon /ˈkænən/ n inv cannone m. **~-ball** n palla f di cannone

cannot /ˈkænɒt/ see **can²**

canny /ˈkænɪ/ a astuto

canoe /kəˈnuː/ n canoa f ● vi andare in canoa

'can-opener n apriscatole m inv

canopy /ˈkænəpɪ/ n baldacchino f; (of parachute) calotta f

can't /kɑːnt/ = **cannot** see **can²**

cantankerous /kænˈtæŋkərəs/ a stizzoso

canteen /kænˈtiːn/ n mensa f; **~ of cutlery** servizio m di posate

canter /ˈkæntə(r)/ vi andare a piccolo galoppo

canvas /ˈkænvəs/ n tela f; (painting) dipinto m su tela

canvass /ˈkænvəs/ vi Pol fare propaganda elettorale. **~ing** n sollecitazione f di voti

canyon /ˈkænjən/ n canyon m inv

cap /kæp/ n berretto m; (nurse's) cuffia f; (top, lid) tappo m ● vt (pt/pp **capped**) (fig: do better than) superare

capability /keɪpəˈbɪlətɪ/ n capacità f

capabl|e /ˈkeɪpəbl/ a capace; (skilful) abile; **be ~e of doing sth** essere capace di fare qcsa. **~y** adv con abilità

capacity /kəˈpæsətɪ/ n capacità f; (function) qualità f; **in my ~ as** in qualità di

cape¹ /keɪp/ n (cloak) cappa f

cape² n Geog capo m

caper¹ /ˈkeɪpə(r)/ vi saltellare ● n fam birichinata f

caper² n Culin cappero m

capital /ˈkæpɪtl/ n (town) capitale f; (money) capitale m; (letter) lettera f maiuscola. **~ city** n capitale f

capital|ism /ˈkæpɪtəlɪzm/ n capitalismo m. **~ist** /-ɪst/ a & n capitalista mf. **~ize** /-aɪz/ vi **~ize on** fig trarre vantaggio da. **~ 'letter** n lettera f maiuscola. **~ 'punishment** n pena f capitale

capitulat|e /kəˈpɪtjʊleɪt/ vi capitolare. **~ion** /-ˈleɪʃn/ n capitolazione f

capricious /kəˈprɪʃəs/ a capriccioso

Capricorn /ˈkæprɪkɔːn/ n Astr Capricorno m

capsize /kæpˈsaɪz/ vi capovolgersi ● vt capovolgere

capsule /ˈkæpsjʊl/ n capsula f

captain /ˈkæptɪn/ n capitano m ● vt comandare ‹team›

caption /ˈkæpʃn/ n intestazione f; (of illustration) didascalia f

captivate /ˈkæptɪveɪt/ vt incantare

captiv|e /ˈkæptɪv/ a prigioniero; **hold/take ~e** tenere/fare prigioniero ● n prigioniero, -a mf. **~ity** /-ˈtɪvətɪ/ n prigionia f; (animals) cattività f

capture /ˈkæptʃə(r)/ n cattura f ● vt catturare; attirare ‹attention›

car /kɑː(r)/ n macchina f; **by ~** in macchina

carafe /kəˈræf/ n caraffa f

caramel /ˈkærəmel/ n (sweet) caramella f al mou; Culin caramello m

carat /ˈkærət/ n carato m

caravan /ˈkærəvæn/ n roulotte f inv; (horse-drawn) carovana f

carbohydrate /kɑːbəˈhaɪdreɪt/ n carboidrato m

carbon /ˈkɑːbən/ n carbonio m

carbon: ~ copy n copia f in carta carbone; (*fig: person*) ritratto *m*. ~ **di'oxide** *n* anidride *f* carbonica. ~ **paper** *n* carta *f* carbone

carburettor /kɑːbjʊ'retə(r)/ *n* carburatore *m*

carcass /'kɑːkəs/ *n* carcassa *f*

card /kɑːd/ *n* (*for birthday, Christmas etc*) biglietto *m* di auguri; (*playing ~*) carta *f* [da gioco]; (*membership ~*) tessera *f*; (*business ~*) biglietto *m* da visita; (*credit ~*) carta *f* di credito; *Comput* scheda *f*

'**cardboard** *n* cartone *m*. ~ '**box** *n* scatola *f* di cartone; (*large*) scatolone *m*

'**card-game** *n* gioco *m* di carte

cardiac /'kɑːdiæk/ *a* cardiaco

cardigan /'kɑːdɪgən/ *n* cardigan *m inv*

cardinal /'kɑːdɪnl/ *a* cardinale; ~ **number** numero *m* cardinale ● *n Relig* cardinale *m*

card 'index *n* schedario *m*

care /keə(r)/ *n* cura *f*; (*caution*) attenzione *f*; (*worry*) preoccupazione *f*; ~ **of** (*on letter abbr* **c/o**) presso; **take ~** (*be cautious*) fare attenzione; **bye, take ~** ciao, stammi bene; **take ~ of** occuparsi di; **be taken into ~** essere preso in custodia da un ente assistenziale ● *vi* ~ **about** interessarsi di; ~ **for** (*feel affection for*) volere bene a; (*look after*) aver cura di; **I don't ~ for chocolate** non mi piace il cioccolato; **I don't ~** non me ne importa; **who ~s?** chi se ne frega?

career /kə'rɪə(r)/ *n* carriera *f*; (*profession*) professione *f* ● *vi* andare a tutta velocità

care: ~**free** *a* spensierato. ~**ful** *a* attento; (*driver*) prudente. ~**fully** *adv* con attenzione. ~**less** *a* irresponsabile; (*in work*) trascurato; (*work*) fatto con poca cura; (*driver*) distratto. ~**lessly** *adv* negligentemente. ~**lessness** *n* trascuratezza *f*. ~**r** *n* persona *f* che accudisce a un anziano o a un malato

caress /kə'res/ *n* carezza *f* ● *vt* accarezzare

'**caretaker** *n* custode *mf*; (*in school*) bidello *m*

'**car ferry** *n* traghetto *m* (*per il trasporto di auto*)

cargo /'kɑːgəʊ/ *n* (*pl* **-es**) carico *m*

Caribbean /kærɪ'biːən/ *n* **the ~** (*sea*) il Mar dei Caraibi ● *a* caraibico

caricature /'kærɪkətjʊə(r)/ *n* caricatura *f*

caring /'keərɪŋ/ *a* (*parent*) premuroso;

(*attitude*) altruista; **the ~ professions** le attività assistenziali

carnage /'kɑːnɪdʒ/ *n* carneficina *f*

carnal /'kɑːnl/ *a* carnale

carnation /kɑː'neɪʃn/ *n* garofano *m*

carnival /'kɑːnɪvl/ *n* carnevale *m*

carnivorous /kɑː'nɪvərəs/ *a* carnivoro

carol /'kærəl/ *n* [**Christmas**] ~ canzone *f* natalizia

carp¹ /kɑːp/ *n inv* carpa *f*

carp² *vi* ~ **at** trovare da ridire su

'**car park** *n* parcheggio *m*

carpent|er /'kɑːpɪntə(r)/ *n* falegname *m*. ~**ry** *n* falegnameria *f*

carpet /'kɑːpɪt/ *n* tappeto *m*; (*wall-to-wall*) moquette *f inv* ● *vt* mettere la moquette in (*room*)

'**car phone** *n* telefono *m* in macchina

carriage /'kærɪdʒ/ *n* carrozza *f*; (*of goods*) trasporto *m*; (*cost*) spese *fpl* di trasporto; (*bearing*) portamento *m*; ~**way** *n* strada *f* carrozzabile; **northbound** ~**way** carreggiata *f* nord

carrier /'kærɪə(r)/ *n* (*company*) impresa *f* di trasporti; *Aeron* compagnia *f* di trasporto aereo; (*of disease*) portatore *m*. ~ [**bag**] *n* borsa *f* [per la spesa]

carrot /'kærət/ *n* carota *f*

carry /'kærɪ/ *v* (*pt/pp* **-ied**) ● *vt* portare; (*transport*) trasportare; **get carried away** *fam* lasciarsi prender la mano ● *vi* (*sound:*) trasmettersi. **carry off** *vt* portare via; vincere (*prize*). **carry on** *vi* continuare; (*fam: make scene*) fare delle storie; ~ **on with sth** continuare qcsa; ~ **on with sb** *fam* intendersela con qcno ● *vt* mantenere (*business*). **carry out** *vt* portare fuori; eseguire (*instructions, task*); mettere in atto (*threat*); effettuare (*experiment, survey*)

'**carry-cot** *n* porte-enfant *m inv*

cart /kɑːt/ *n* carretto *m* ● *vt* (*fam: carry*) portare

cartilage /'kɑːtɪlɪdʒ/ *n Anat* cartilagine *f*

carton /'kɑːtn/ *n* scatola *f* di cartone; (*for drink*) cartone *m*; (*of cream, yoghurt*) vasetto *m*; (*of cigarettes*) stecca *f*

cartoon /kɑː'tuːn/ *n* vignetta *f*; (*strip*) vignette *fpl*; (*film*) cartone *m* animato; (*in art*) bozzetto *m*. ~**ist** *n* vignettista *mf*; (*for films*) disegnatore, -trice *mf* di cartoni animati

cartridge /'kɑːtrɪdʒ/ *n* cartuccia *f*; (*for film*) bobina *f*; (*of record player*) testina *f*

carve /kɑːv/ *vt* scolpire; tagliare (*meat*)

carving /'kɑːvɪŋ/ n scultura f. **~-knife** n trinciante m

'car wash n autolavaggio m inv

case¹ /keɪs/ n caso m; **in any ~** in ogni caso; **in that ~** in questo caso; **just in ~** per sicurezza; **in ~ he comes** nel caso in cui venisse

case² n (container) scatola f; (crate) cassa f; (for spectacles) astuccio m; (suitcase) valigia f; (for display) vetrina f

cash /kæʃ/ n denaro m contante; (fam: money) contanti mpl; **pay [in] ~** pagare in contanti; **~ on delivery** pagamento alla consegna ● vt incassare ⟨cheque⟩. **~ desk** n cassa f

cashier /kæ'ʃɪə(r)/ n cassiere, -a mf

'cash register n registratore m di cassa

casino /kə'siːnəʊ/ n casinò m inv

casket /'kɑːskɪt/ n scrigno m; (Am: coffin) bara f

casserole /'kæsərəʊl/ n casseruola f; (stew) stufato m

cassette /kə'set/ n cassetta f. **~ recorder** n registratore m (a cassette)

cast /kɑːst/ n (mould) forma f; Theat cast m inv; [plaster] **~** Med ingessatura f ● vt (pt/pp cast) dare ⟨vote⟩; Theat assegnare le parti di ⟨play⟩; fondere ⟨metal⟩; (throw) gettare; **~ an actor as** dare ad un attore il ruolo di; **~ a glance at** lanciare uno sguardo a. **cast off** vi Naut sganciare gli ormeggi ● vt (in knitting) diminuire. **cast on** vt (in knitting) avviare

castaway /'kɑːstəweɪ/ n naufrago, -a mf

caste /kɑːst/ n casta f

caster /'kɑːstə(r)/ n (wheel) rotella f. **~ sugar** n zucchero m raffinato

cast 'iron n ghisa f

cast-'iron a di ghisa; fig solido

castle /'kɑːsl/ n castello m; (in chess) torre f

'cast-offs npl abiti mpl smessi

castor /'kɑːstə(r)/ n (wheel) rotella f. **~ oil** n olio m di ricino. **~ sugar** n zucchero m raffinato

castrat|e /kæ'streɪt/ vt castrare. **~ion** /-eɪʃn/ n castrazione f

casual /'kæʒʊəl/ a (chance) casuale; ⟨remark⟩ senza importanza; ⟨glance⟩ di sfuggita; ⟨attitude, approach⟩ disinvolto; ⟨chat⟩ informale; ⟨clothes⟩ casual inv; ⟨work⟩ saltuario; **~ wear** abbigliamento m casual. **~ly** adv ⟨dress⟩ casual; ⟨meet⟩ casualmente

casualty /'kæʒʊəltɪ/ n (injured person) ferito m; (killed) vittima f. **~ [department]** n pronto soccorso m

cat /kæt/ n gatto m; pej arpia f

catalogue /'kætəlɒg/ n catalogo m ● vt catalogare

catalyst /'kætəlɪst/ n Chem & fig catalizzatore m

catalytic /kætə'lɪtɪk/ a **~ converter** Auto marmitta f catalitica

catapult /'kætəpʌlt/ n catapulta f; (child's) fionda f ● vt fig catapultare

cataract /'kætərækt/ n Med cataratta f

catarrh /kə'tɑː(r)/ n catarro m

catastroph|e /kə'tæstrəfi/ n catastrofe f. **~ic** /kætə'strɒfɪk/ a catastrofico

catch /kætʃ/ n (of fish) pesca f; (fastener) fermaglio m; (on door) fermo m; (on window) gancio m; (fam: snag) tranello m ● v (pt/pp **caught**) ● vt acchiappare ⟨ball⟩; (grab) afferrare; prendere ⟨illness, fugitive, train⟩; **~ a cold** prendersi un raffreddore; **~ sight of** scorgere; **I caught him stealing** l'ho sorpreso mentre rubava; **~ one's finger in the door** chiudersi il dito nella porta; **~ sb's eye** or **attention** attirare l'attenzione di qcno ● vi ⟨fire:⟩ prendere; (get stuck) impigliarsi. **catch on** vi fam (understand) afferrare; (become popular) diventare popolare. **catch up** vt raggiungere ● vi recuperare; ⟨runner:⟩ riguadagnare terreno; **~ up with** raggiungere ⟨sb⟩; mettersi in pari con ⟨work⟩

catching /'kætʃɪŋ/ a contagioso

catch: ~-phrase n tormentone m. **~word** n slogan m inv

catchy /'kætʃɪ/ a (-ier, -iest) orecchiabile

categor|ical /kætɪ'gɒrɪkl/ a categorico. **~y** /'kætɪgərɪ/ n categoria f

cater /'keɪtə(r)/ vi **~ for** provvedere a ⟨needs⟩; fig venire incontro alle esigenze di. **~ing** n (trade) ristorazione f; (food) rinfresco m

caterpillar /'kætəpɪlə(r)/ n bruco m

cathedral /kə'θiːdrl/ n cattedrale f

Catholic /'kæθəlɪk/ a & n cattolico, -a mf. **~ism** /kə'θɒlɪsɪzm/ n cattolicesimo m

cat's eyes npl catarifrangente msg (inserito nell'asfalto)

cattle /'kætl/ npl bestiame msg

catty /'kætɪ/ a (-ier, -iest) dispettoso

catwalk /'kætwɔːk/ n passerella f

caught /kɔːt/ see **catch**

cauliflower /'kɒlɪ-/ n cavolfiore m

cause /kɔːz/ n causa f ● vt causare; **~ sb to do sth** far fare qcsa a qcno

'causeway *n* strada *f* sopraelevata

caustic /'kɔːstɪk/ *a* caustico

caution /'kɔːʃn/ *n* cautela *f*; (*warning*) ammonizione *f* ● *vt* mettere in guardia; *Jur* ammonire

cautious /'kɔːʃəs/ *a* cauto

cavalry /'kævəlrɪ/ *n* cavalleria *f*

cave /keɪv/ *n* caverna *f* ● **cave in** *vi* ⟨*roof:*⟩ crollare; (*fig: give in*) capitolare

cavern /'kævən/ *n* caverna *f*

caviare /'kævɪɑː(r)/ *n* caviale *m*

caving /'keɪvɪŋ/ *n* speleologia *f*

cavity /'kævətɪ/ *n* cavità *f inv*; (*in tooth*) carie *f inv*

CD *n* CD *m inv.* **~ player** *n* lettore *m* [di] compact

CD-Rom /siːdiː'rɒm/ *n* CD-Rom *m inv.* **~ drive** *n* lettore *m* [di] CD-Rom

cease /siːs/ *n* **without ~** incessantemente ● *vt/i* cessare. **~-fire** *n* cessate il fuoco *m inv.* **~less** *a* incessante

cedar /'siːdə(r)/ *n* cedro *m*

cede /siːd/ *vt* cedere

ceiling /'siːlɪŋ/ *n* soffitto *m*; *fig* tetto *m* [massimo]

celebrat|e /'selɪbreɪt/ *vt* festeggiare ⟨*birthday, victory*⟩ ● *vi* far festa; celebre (**for** per). **~ion** /-'breɪʃn/ *n* celebrazione *f*

celebrity /sɪ'lebrətɪ/ *n* celebrità *f inv*

celery /'selərɪ/ *n* sedano *m*

celiba|cy /'selɪbəsɪ/ *n* celibato *m.* **~te** *a* ⟨*man*⟩ celibe; ⟨*woman*⟩ nubile

cell /sel/ *n* cella *f*; *Biol* cellula *f*

cellar /'selə(r)/ *n* scantinato *m*; (*for wine*) cantina *f*

cellist /'tʃelɪst/ *n* violoncellista *mf*

cello /'tʃeləʊ/ *n* violoncello *m*

Cellophane® /'seləfeɪn/ *n* cellofan *m inv*

cellular phone /seljʊlə'fəʊn/ *n* [telefono *m*] cellulare *m*

celluloid /'seljʊlɔɪd/ *n* celluloide *f*

Celsius /'selsɪəs/ *a* Celsius

Celt /kelt/ *n* celta *mf.* **~ic** *a* celtico

cement /sɪ'ment/ *n* cemento *m*; (*adhesive*) mastice *m* ● *vt* cementare; *fig* consolidare

cemetery /'semətrɪ/ *n* cimitero *m*

censor /'sensə(r)/ *n* censore *m* ● *vt* censurare. **~ship** *n* censura *f*

censure /'senʃə(r)/ *vt* biasimare

census /'sensəs/ *n* censimento *m*

cent /sent/ *n* (*of dollar*) centesimo *m*; (*of euro*) cent *m inv*, centesimo *m*

centenary /sen'tiːnərɪ/ *n*, *Am* **centennial** /sen'tenɪəl/ *n* centenario *m*

center /'sentə(r)/ *n Am* = **centre**

centi|grade /'sentɪ-/ *a* centigrado. **~metre** *n* centimetro *m.* **~pede** /-piːd/ *n* centopiedi *m inv*

central /'sentrəl/ *a* centrale. **~ 'heating** *n* riscaldamento *m* autonomo. **~ize** *vt* centralizzare. **~ly** *adv* al centro; **~ly heated** con riscaldamento autonomo. **~ reser'vation** *n Auto* banchina *f* spartitraffico

centre /'sentə(r)/ *n* centro *m* ● *v* (*pt/pp* **centred**) ● *vt* centrare ● *vi* **~ on** *fig* incentrarsi su. **~-'forward** *n* centravanti *m inv*

centrifugal /sentrɪ'fjuːgl/ *a* **~ force** forza *f* centrifuga

century /'sentʃərɪ/ *n* secolo *m*

ceramic /sɪ'ræmɪk/ *a* ceramico. **~s** *n* (*art*) ceramica *fsg*; (*objects*) ceramiche *fpl*

cereal /'sɪərɪəl/ *n* cereale *m*

cerebral /'serɪbrl/ *a* cerebrale

ceremon|ial /serɪ'məʊnɪəl/ *a* da cerimonia ● *n* cerimoniale *m.* **~ious** /-ɪəs/ *a* cerimonioso

ceremony /'serɪmənɪ/ *n* cerimonia *f*

certain /'sɜːtn/ *a* certo; **for ~** di sicuro; **make ~** accertarsi ; **he is ~ to win** è certo di vincere; **it's not ~ whether he'll come** non è sicuro che venga. **~ly** *adv* certamente; **~ly not!** no di certo! **~ty** *n* certezza *f*; **it's a ~ty** è una cosa certa

certificate /sə'tɪfɪkət/ *n* certificato *m*

certify /'sɜːtɪfaɪ/ *vt* (*pt/pp* **-ied**) certificare; (*declare insane*) dichiarare malato di mente

cessation /se'seɪʃn/ *n* cessazione *f*

cesspool /'ses-/ *n* pozzo *m* nero

cf *abbr* (*compare*) cf, cfr

chafe /tʃeɪf/ *vt* irritare

chain /tʃeɪn/ *n* catena *f* ● *vt* incatenare ⟨*prisoner*⟩; attaccare con la catena ⟨*dog*⟩ (**to** a). **chain up** *vt* legare alla catena ⟨*dog*⟩

chain: ~ re'action *n* reazione *f* a catena. **~-smoke** *vi* fumare una sigaretta dopo l'altra. **~-smoker** *n* fumatore, -trice *mf* accanito, -a. **~ store** *n* negozio *m* appartenente a una catena

chair /tʃeə(r)/ *n* sedia *f*; *Univ* cattedra *f* ● *vt* presiedere. **~-lift** *n* seggiovia *f.* **~man** *n* presidente *m*

chalet /'ʃæleɪ/ *n* chalet *m inv*; (*in holiday camp*) bungalow *m inv*

chalice /'tʃælɪs/ *n Relig* calice *m*

chalk /tʃɔːk/ *n* gesso *m.* **~y** *a* gessoso

challeng|e /'tʃælɪndʒ/ *n* sfida *f*; *Mil* intimazione *f* ● *vt* sfidare; *Mil* intimare il chi va là a; *fig* mettere in dubbio ⟨*statement*⟩. **~er** *n* sfidante *mf*. **~ing** *a* ⟨*job*⟩ impegnativo

chamber /'tʃeɪmbə(r)/ *n* **C~ of Commerce** camera *f* di commercio

chamber: **~maid** *n* cameriera *f* [d'albergo]. **~ music** *n* musica *f* da camera

chamois[1] /'ʃæmwɑ:/ *n inv* ⟨*animal*⟩ camoscio *m*

chamois[2] /'ʃæmɪ/ *n* **~[-leather]** [pelle *f* di] camoscio *m*

champagne /ʃæm'peɪn/ *n* champagne *m inv*

champion /'tʃæmpɪən/ *n* *Sport* campione *m*; (*of cause*) difensore, difenditrice *mf* ● *vt* (*defend*) difendere; (*fight for*) lottare per. **~ship** *n Sport* campionato *m*

chance /tʃɑ:ns/ *n* caso *m*; (*possibility*) possibilità *f inv*; (*opportunity*) occasione *f*; **by ~** per caso; **take a ~** provarci; **give sb a second ~** dare un'altra possibilità a qcno ● *attrib* fortuito ● *vt* **I'll ~ it** *fam* corro il rischio

chancellor /'tʃɑ:nsələ(r)/ *n* cancelliere *m*; *Univ* rettore *m*; **C~ of the Exchequer** ≈ ministro *m* del tesoro

chancy /'tʃɑ:nsɪ/ *a* rischioso

chandelier /ʃændə'lɪə(r)/ *n* lampadario *m*

change /tʃeɪndʒ/ *n* cambiamento *m*; (*money*) resto *m*; (*small coins*) spiccioli *mpl*; **for a ~** tanto per cambiare; **a ~ of clothes** un cambio di vestiti; **the ~ [of life]** la menopausa ● *vt* cambiare; (*substitute*) scambiare (**for** con); **~ one's clothes** cambiarsi [i vestiti]; **~ trains** cambiare treno ● *vi* cambiare; (*~ clothes*) cambiarsi; **all ~!** stazione terminale!

changeable /'tʃeɪndʒəbl/ *a* mutevole; ⟨*weather*⟩ variabile

'changing-room *n* camerino *m*; (*for sports*) spogliatoio *m*

channel /'tʃænl/ *n* canale *m*; **the [English] C~** la Manica; **the C~ Islands** le Isole del Canale ● *vt* (*pt/pp* **channelled**) **~ one's energies into sth** convogliare le proprie energie in qcsa

chant /tʃɑ:nt/ *n* cantilena *f*; (*of demonstrators*) slogan *m inv* di protesta ● *vt* cantare; ⟨*demonstrators:*⟩ gridare

chao|s /'keɪɒs/ *n* caos *m*. **~tic** /-'ɒtɪk/ *a* caotico

chap /tʃæp/ *n fam* tipo *m*

chapel /'tʃæpl/ *n* cappella *f*

chaperon /'ʃæpərəʊn/ *n* chaperon *f inv* ● *vt* fare da chaperon a ⟨*sb*⟩

chaplain /'tʃæplɪn/ *n* cappellano *m*

chapped /tʃæpt/ *a* ⟨*skin, lips*⟩ screpolato

chapter /'tʃæptə(r)/ *n* capitolo *m*

char[1] /tʃɑ:(r)/ *n fam* donna *f* delle pulizie

char[2] *vt* (*pt/pp* **charred**) (*burn*) carbonizzare

character /'kærɪktə(r)/ *n* carattere *m*; (*in novel, play*) personaggio *m*; **quite a ~** *fam* un tipo particolare

characteristic /kærɪktə'rɪstɪk/ *a* caratteristico ● *n* caratteristica *f*. **~ally** *adv* tipicamente

characterize /'kærɪktəraɪz/ *vt* caratterizzare

charade /ʃə'rɑ:d/ *n* farsa *f*

charcoal /'tʃɑ:-/ *n* carbonella *f*

charge /tʃɑ:dʒ/ *n* (*cost*) prezzo *m*; *Electr, Mil* carica *f*; *Jur* accusa *f*; **free of ~** gratuito; **be in ~** essere responsabile (**of** di); **take ~** assumersi la responsabilità; **take ~ of** occuparsi di ● *vt* far pagare ⟨*fee*⟩; far pagare a ⟨*person*⟩; *Electr, Mil* caricare; *Jur* accusare (**with** di); **~ sb for sth** far pagare qcsa a qcno; **~ it to my account** lo addebiti sul mio conto ● *vi* (*attack*) caricare

chariot /'tʃærɪət/ *n* cocchio *m*

charisma /kə'rɪzmə/ *n* carisma *m*. **~tic** /kærɪz'mætɪk/ *a* carismatico

charitable /'tʃærɪtəbl/ *a* caritatevole; (*kind*) indulgente

charity /'tʃærətɪ/ *n* carità *f*; (*organization*) associazione *f* di beneficenza; **concert given for ~** concerto *m* di beneficenza; **live on ~** vivere di elemosina

charm /tʃɑ:m/ *n* fascino *m*; (*object*) ciondolo *m* ● *vt* affascinare. **~ing** *a* affascinante

chart /tʃɑ:t/ *n* carta *f* nautica; (*table*) tabella *f*

charter /'tʃɑ:tə(r)/ *n* **~ [flight]** [volo *m*] charter *m inv* ● *vt* noleggiare. **~ed accountant** *n* commercialista *mf*

charwoman /'tʃɑ:-/ *n* donna *f* delle pulizie

chase /tʃeɪs/ *n* inseguimento *m* ● *vt* inseguire. **chase away** *or* **off** *vt* cacciare via

chasm /'kæz(ə)m/ *n* abisso *m*

chassis /'ʃæsɪ/ *n* (*pl* **chassis** /-sɪz/) telaio *m*

chaste /tʃeɪst/ *a* casto

chastity /'tʃæstətɪ/ *n* castità *f*

chat /tʃæt/ n chiacchierata f; **have a ~ with** fare quattro chiacchere con ● vi (pt/pp **chatted**) chiacchierare; Comput chattare. **~ show** n talk show m inv

chatter /'tʃætə(r)/ n chiacchiere fpl ● vi chiacchierare; ⟨teeth:⟩ battere. **~box** n fam chiacchierone, -a mf

chatty /'tʃætɪ/ a (-ier, -iest) chiacchierone; ⟨style⟩ familiare

chauffeur /'ʃəʊfə(r)/ n autista mf

chauvin|ism /'ʃəʊvɪnɪzm/ n sciovinismo m. **~ist** n sciovinista mf. **male ~ist** n fam maschilista m

cheap /tʃi:p/ a a buon mercato; ⟨rate⟩ economico; ⟨vulgar⟩ grossolano; ⟨of poor quality⟩ scadente ● adv a buon mercato. **~ly** adv a buon mercato

cheat /tʃi:t/ n imbroglione, -a mf; ⟨at cards⟩ baro m ● vt imbrogliare; **~ sb out of sth** sottrarre qcsa a qcno con l'inganno ● vi imbrogliare; ⟨at cards⟩ barare. **cheat on** vt fam tradire ⟨wife⟩

check[1] /tʃek/ a ⟨pattern⟩ a quadri ● n disegno m a quadri

check[2] n verifica f; ⟨of tickets⟩ controllo m; ⟨in chess⟩ scacco m; ⟨Am: bill⟩ conto m; ⟨Am: cheque⟩ assegno m; ⟨Am: tick⟩ segnetto m; **keep a ~ on** controllare; **keep in ~** tenere sotto controllo ● vt verificare; controllare ⟨tickets⟩; ⟨restrain⟩ contenere; ⟨stop⟩ bloccare ● vi controllare; **~ on sth** controllare qcsa. **check in** vi registrarsi all'arrivo ⟨in albergo⟩; Aeron fare il check-in ● vt registrare all'arrivo ⟨in albergo⟩. **check out** vi ⟨of hotel⟩ saldare il conto ● vt ⟨fam: investigate⟩ controllare. **check up** vi accertarsi; **~ up on** prendere informazioni su

check|ed /tʃekt/ a a quadri. **~ers** n Am dama f

check: ~-in n ⟨in airport: place⟩ banco m accettazione, check-in m inv; **~-in time** check-in m inv. **~ mark** n Am segnetto m. **~mate** int scacco matto! **~-out** n ⟨in supermarket⟩ cassa f. **~room** n Am deposito m bagagli. **~-up** n Med visita f di controllo, check-up m inv

cheek /tʃi:k/ n guancia f; ⟨impudence⟩ sfacciataggine f. **~y** a sfacciato

cheep /tʃi:p/ vi pigolare

cheer /tʃɪə(r)/ n evviva m inv; **three ~s** tre urrà; **~s!** salute!; ⟨goodbye⟩ arrivederci!; ⟨thanks⟩ grazie ● vt/i acclamare. **cheer up** vt tirare su [di morale] ● vi tirarsi su [di morale]; **~ up!** su con

la vita!. **~ful** a allegro. **~fulness** n allegria f. **~ing** n acclamazione f

cheerio /tʃɪərɪ'əʊ/ int fam arrivederci

'cheerless a triste, tetro

cheese /tʃi:z/ n formaggio m. **~cake** n dolce m al formaggio

chef /ʃef/ n cuoco, -a mf, chef mf inv

chemical /'kemɪkl/ a chimico ● n prodotto m chimico

chemist /'kemɪst/ n ⟨pharmacist⟩ farmacista mf; ⟨scientist⟩ chimico, -a mf; **~'s [shop]** farmacia f. **~ry** n chimica f

cheque /tʃek/ n assegno m. **~-book** n libretto m degli assegni. **~ card** n carta f assegni

cherish /'tʃerɪʃ/ vt curare teneramente; ⟨love⟩ avere caro; nutrire ⟨hope⟩

cherry /'tʃerɪ/ n ciliegia f; ⟨tree⟩ ciliegio m

cherub /'tʃerəb/ n cherubino m

chess /tʃes/ n scacchi mpl

chess: ~board n scacchiera f. **~-man** n pezzo m degli scacchi. **~player** n scacchista mf

chest /tʃest/ n petto m; ⟨box⟩ cassapanca f

chestnut /'tʃesnʌt/ n castagna f; ⟨tree⟩ castagno m

chest of 'drawers n cassettone m

chew /tʃu:/ vt masticare. **~ing-gum** n gomma f da masticare

chic /ʃi:k/ a chic inv

chick /tʃɪk/ n pulcino m; ⟨fam: girl⟩ ragazza f

chicken /'tʃɪkn/ n pollo m ● attrib ⟨soup, casserole⟩ di pollo ● a fam fifone ● **chicken out** vi fam he **~ed out** gli è venuta fifa. **~pox** n varicella f

chicory /'tʃɪkərɪ/ n cicoria f

chief /tʃi:f/ a principale ● n capo m. **~ly** adv principalmente

chilblain /'tʃɪlbleɪn/ n gelone m

child /tʃaɪld/ n (pl **-ren**) bambino, -a mf; ⟨son/daughter⟩ figlio, -a mf

child: ~birth n parto m. **~hood** n infanzia f. **~ish** a infantile. **~ishness** n puerilità f. **~less** a senza figli. **~like** a ingenuo. **~-minder** n baby-sitter mf inv

children /'tʃɪldrən/ see **child**

Chile /'tʃɪlɪ/ n Cile m. **~an** a & n cileno, -a mf

chill /tʃɪl/ n freddo m; ⟨illness⟩ infreddatura f ● vt raffreddare

chilli /'tʃɪlɪ/ n (pl **-es**) **~ [pepper]** peperoncino m

chilly /'tʃɪlɪ/ a freddo

chime /tʃaɪm/ vi suonare

chimney /'tʃɪmnɪ/ n camino m. **~-pot**

n comignolo *m*. **~-sweep** *n* spazzaca-
mino *m*

chimpanzee /tʃɪmpæn'zi:/ *n* scimpanzé *m inv*

chin /tʃɪn/ *n* mento *m*

china /'tʃaɪnə/ *n* porcellana *f*

Chin|a *n* Cina *f*. **~ese** /-'ni:z/ *a & n* ci-
nese *mf*; (*language*) cinese *m*; **the ~ese**
pl i cinesi

chink¹ /tʃɪŋk/ *n* (*slit*) fessura *f*

chink² *n* (*noise*) tintinnio *m*

chip /tʃɪp/ *n* (*fragment*) scheggia *f*; (*in
china, paintwork*) scheggiatura *f*;
Comput chip *m inv*; (*in gambling*) fiche *f
inv*; **~s** *pl Br Culin* patatine *fpl* fritte;
Am Culin patatine *fpl* ● *vt* (*pt/pp
chipped*) (*damage*) scheggiare. **chip in**
vi fam intromettersi; (*with money*) contribuire. **~ped** *a* (*damaged*) scheggiato

chiropod|ist /kɪ'rɒpədɪst/ *n* podiatra
mf inv. **~y** *n* podiatria *f*

chirp /tʃɜ:p/ *vi* cinguettare; ⟨*cricket:*⟩
fare cri cri. **~y** *a fam* pimpante

chisel /'tʃɪzl/ *n* scalpello *m*

chival|rous /'ʃɪvlrəs/ *a* cavalleresco.
~ry *n* cavalleria *f*

chives /tʃaɪvz/ *npl* erba *f* cipollina

chlorine /'klɔ:ri:n/ *n* cloro *m*

chloroform /'klɒrəfɔ:m/ *n* clorofor-
mio *m*

chock-a-block /tʃɒkə'blɒk/,
chock-full /tʃɒk'fʊl/ *a* pieno zeppo

chocolate /'tʃɒkələt/ *n* cioccolato *m*;
(*drink*) cioccolata *f*; **a ~** un cioccolatino

choice /tʃɔɪs/ *n* scelta *f* ● *a* scelto

choir /'kwaɪə(r)/ *n* coro *m*. **~boy** *n*
corista *m*

choke /tʃəʊk/ *n Auto* aria *f* ● *vt/i* soffocare

cholera /'kɒlərə/ *n* colera *m*

cholesterol /kə'lestərɒl/ *n* cole-
sterolo *m*

choose /tʃu:z/ *vt/i* (*pt chose*, *pp
chosen*) scegliere; **as you ~** come vuoi

choos[e]y /'tʃu:zi/ *a fam* difficile

chop /tʃɒp/ *n* (*blow*) colpo *m* (*d'ascia*);
Culin costata *f* ● *vt* (*pt/pp chopped*) tagliare. **chop down** *vt* abbattere ⟨*tree*⟩.
chop off *vt* spaccare

chop|per /'tʃɒpə(r)/ *n* accetta *f*, *fam*
elicottero *m*. **~py** *a* increspato

'chopsticks *npl* bastoncini *mpl* cinesi

choral /'kɔ:rəl/ *a* corale

chord /kɔ:d/ *n Mus* corda *f*

chore /tʃɔ:(r)/ *n* corvé *f inv*;
[**household**] **~s** faccende *fpl* domesti-
che

choreograph|er /kɒrɪ'ɒɡrəfə(r)/ *n*
coreografo, -a *mf*. **~y** /-ɪ/ *n* coreografia *f*

chortle /'tʃɔ:tl/ *vi* ridacchiare

chorus /'kɔ:rəs/ *n* coro *m*; (*of song*) ritornello *m*

chose, chosen /tʃəʊz, 'tʃəʊzn/ *see*
choose

Christ /kraɪst/ *n* Cristo *m*

christen /'krɪsn/ *vt* battezzare. **~ing** *n*
battesimo *m*

Christian /'krɪstʃən/ *a & n* cristiano, -a
mf. **~ity** /-stɪ'ænətɪ/ *n* cristianesimo *m*.
~ name *n* nome *m* di battesimo

Christmas /'krɪsməs/ *n* Natale *m*
● *attrib* di Natale. **~ card** *n* biglietto *m*
d'auguri di Natale. **~ 'Day** *n* il giorno di
Natale. **~ 'Eve** *n* la vigilia di Natale. **'~
present** *n* regalo *m* di Natale. **~
'pudding** *m* dolce *m* natalizio *a base de
frutta candita e liquore*. **'~ tree** *n* albero
m di Natale

chrome /krəʊm/ *n*, **chromium**
/'krəʊmɪəm/ *n* cromo *m*

chromosome /'krəʊməsəʊm/ *n* cro-
mosoma *m*

chronic /'krɒnɪk/ *a* cronico

chronicle /'krɒnɪkl/ *n* cronaca *f*

chronological /krɒnə'lɒdʒɪkl/ *a* cronologico. **~ly** *adv* ⟨*ordered*⟩ in ordine
cronologico

chrysanthemum /krɪ'sænθəməm/ *n*
crisantemo *m*

chubby /'tʃʌbɪ/ *a* (**-ier, -iest**) paffuto

chuck /tʃʌk/ *vt fam* buttare. **chuck
out** *vt fam* buttare via ⟨*object*⟩; buttare
fuori ⟨*person*⟩

chuckle /'tʃʌkl/ *vi* ridacchiare

chug /tʃʌɡ/ *vi* (*pt/pp chugged*) **the
train ~ged out of the station** il treno
è uscito dalla stazione sbuffando

chum /tʃʌm/ *n* amico, -a *mf*. **~my** *a fam*
be ~my with essere amico di

chunk /tʃʌŋk/ *n* grosso pezzo *m*

church /tʃɜ:tʃ/ *n* chiesa *f*. **~yard** *n* cimitero *m*

churlish /'tʃɜ:lɪʃ/ *a* sgarbato

churn /tʃɜ:n/ *vt* **churn out** sfornare

chute /ʃu:t/ *n* scivolo *m*; (*for rubbish*)
canale *m* di scarico

CID *n abbr* (**Criminal Investigation
Department**) polizia *f* giudiziaria

cider /'saɪdə(r)/ *n* sidro *m*

cigar /sɪ'ɡɑ:(r)/ *n* sigaro *m*

cigarette /sɪɡə'ret/ *n* sigaretta *f*

cine-camera /'sɪnɪ-/ *n* cinepresa *f*

cinema /'sɪnɪmə/ *n* cinema *m inv*

cinnamon /'sɪnəmən/ *n* cannella *f*

circle /'sɜ:kl/ *n* cerchio *m*; *Theat* galleria *f*; **in a ~** in cerchio ● *vt* girare intorno a; cerchiare ⟨*mistake*⟩ ● *vi* descrivere dei cerchi

circuit /'sɜːkɪt/ *n* circuito *m*; (*lap*) giro *m*; **~ board** *n* circuito *m* stampato. **~ous** /səˈkjuːɪtəs/ *a* **~ous route** percorso *m* lungo e indiretto

circular /'sɜːkjʊlə(r)/ *a* circolare ● *n* circolare *f*

circulat|e /'sɜːkjʊleɪt/ *vt* far circolare ● *vi* circolare. **~ion** /-'leɪʃn/ *n* circolazione *f*; (*of newspaper*) tiratura *f*

circumcis|e /'sɜːkəmsaɪz/ *vt* circoncidere. **~ion** /-'sɪʒn/ *n* circoncisione *f*

circumference /fəˈkʌmfərəns/ *n* conconferenza *f*

circumstance /'sɜːkəmstəns/ *n* circostanza *f*; **~s** *pl* (*financial*) condizioni *fpl* finanziarie

circus /'sɜːkəs/ *n* circo *m*

CIS *n abbr* (**Commonwealth of Independent States**) CSI *f*

cistern /'sɪstən/ *n* (*tank*) cisterna *f*; (*of WC*) serbatoio *m*

cite /saɪt/ *vt* citare

citizen /'sɪtɪzn/ *n* cittadino, -a *mf*; (*of town*) abitante *mf*. **~ship** *n* cittadinanza *f*

citrus /'sɪtrəs/ *n* ~ [**fruit**] agrume *m*

city /'sɪtɪ/ *n* città *f inv*; **the C~** la City (*di Londra*)

civic /'sɪvɪk/ *a* civico

civil /'ʃɪvl/ *a* civile

civilian /sɪˈvɪljən/ *a* civile; **in ~ clothes** in borghese ● *n* civile *mf*

civiliz|ation /sɪvɪlaɪˈzeɪʃn/ *n* civiltà *f inv*. **~e** /'sɪvɪlaɪz/ *vt* civilizzare

civil: ~ 'servant *n* impiegato, -a *mf* statale. **C~ 'Service** *n* pubblica amministrazione *f*

clad /klæd/ *a* vestito (**in** di)

claim /kleɪm/ *n* richiesta *f*; (*right*) diritto *m*; (*assertion*) dichiarazione *f*; **lay ~ to sth** rivendicare qcsa ● *vt* richiedere; reclamare ⟨*lost property*⟩; rivendicare ⟨*ownership*⟩; **~ that** sostenere che. **~ant** *n* richiedente *mf*

clairvoyant /kleəˈvɔɪənt/ *n* chiaroveggente *mf*

clam /klæm/ *n Culin* vongola *f* ● **clam up** *vi* (*pt/pp* **clammed**) zittirsi

clamber /'klæmbə(r)/ *vi* arrampicarsi

clammy /'klæmɪ/ *a* (**-ier, -iest**) appiccicaticcio

clamour /'klæmə(r)/ *n* (*protest*) rimostranza *f* ● *vi* **~ for** chiedere a gran voce

clamp /klæmp/ *n* morsa *f* ● *vt*

ammorsare; *Auto* mettere i ceppi bloccaruote a. **clamp down** *vi fam* essere duro; **~ down on** reprimere

clan /klæn/ *n* clan *m inv*

clandestine /klænˈdestɪn/ *a* clandestino

clang /klæŋ/ *n* suono *m* metallico. **~er** *n fam* gaffe *f inv*

clank /klæŋk/ *n* rumore *m* metallico

clap /klæp/ *n* **give sb a ~** applaudire qcno; **~ of thunder** tuono *m* ● *vt/i* (*pt/pp* **clapped**) applaudire; **~ one's hands** applaudire. **~ping** *n* applausi *mpl*

clari|fication /klærɪfrˈkeɪʃn/ *n* chiarimento *m*. **~fy** /'klærɪfaɪ/ *vt/i* (*pt/pp* **-ied**) chiarire

clarinet /klærɪˈnet/ *n* clarinetto *m*

clarity /'klærətɪ/ *n* chiarezza *f*

clash /klæʃ/ *n* scontro *m*; (*noise*) fragore *m* ● *vi* scontrarsi; ⟨*colours:*⟩ stonare; ⟨*events:*⟩ coincidere

clasp /klɑːsp/ *n* chiusura *f* ● *vt* agganciare; (*hold*) stringere

class /klɑːs/ *n* classe *f*; (*lesson*) corso *m* ● *vt* classificare

classic /'klæsɪk/ *a* classico ● *n* classico *m*; **~s** *pl Univ* lettere *fpl* classiche. **~al** *a* classico

classi|fication /klæsɪfrˈkeɪʃn/ *n* classificazione *f*. **~fy** /'klæsɪfaɪ/ *vt* (*pt/pp* **-ied**) classificare

classroom *n* aula *f*

classy /'klɑːsɪ/ *a* (**-ier, -iest**) *fam* d'alta classe

clatter /'klætə(r)/ *n* fracasso *m* ● *vi* far fracasso

clause /klɔːz/ *n* clausola *f*; *Gram* proposizione *f*

claustrophob|ia /klɔːstrəˈfəʊbɪə/ *n* claustrofobia *f*

claw /klɔː/ *n* artiglio *m*; (*of crab, lobster & Techn*) tenaglia *f* ● *vt* ⟨*cat:*⟩ graffiare

clay /kleɪ/ *n* argilla *f*

clean /kliːn/ *a* pulito, lindo ● *adv* completamente ● *vt* pulire ⟨*shoes, windows*⟩; **~ one's teeth** lavarsi i denti; **have a coat ~ed** portare un cappotto in lavanderia. **clean up** *vt* pulire ● *vi* far pulizia

cleaner /'kliːnə(r)/ *n* uomo *m*/donna *f* delle pulizie; (*substance*) detersivo *m*; [**dry**] **~'s** lavanderia *f*, tintoria *f*

cleanliness /'klenlɪnɪs/ *n* pulizia *f*

cleanse /klenz/ *vt* pulire. **~r** *n* detergente *m*

clean-shaven *a* sbarbato

cleansing cream /'klenz-/ n latte m detergente

clear /klɪə(r)/ a chiaro; ⟨conscience⟩ pulito; ⟨road⟩ libero; ⟨profit, advantage, majority⟩ netto; ⟨sky⟩ sereno; ⟨water⟩ limpido; ⟨glass⟩ trasparente; **make sth ~** mettere qcsa in chiaro; **have I made myself ~?** mi sono fatto capire?; **five ~ days** cinque giorni buoni ● adv **stand ~ of** allontanarsi da; **keep ~ of** tenersi alla larga da ● vt sgombrare ⟨room, street⟩; sparecchiare ⟨table⟩; ⟨acquit⟩ scagionare; ⟨authorize⟩ autorizzare; scavalcare senza toccare ⟨fence, wall⟩; guadagnare ⟨sum of money⟩; passare ⟨Customs⟩; **~ one's throat** schiarirsi la gola ● vi ⟨face, sky:⟩ rasserenarsi; ⟨fog:⟩ dissiparsi. **clear away** vt metter via. **clear off** vi fam filar via. **clear out** vt sgombrare ● vi fam filar via. **clear up** vt ⟨tidy⟩ mettere a posto; chiarire ⟨mystery⟩ ● vi ⟨weather:⟩ schiarirsi

clearance /'klɪərəns/ n ⟨space⟩ spazio m libero; ⟨authorization⟩ autorizzazione f; ⟨Customs⟩ sdoganamento m. **~ sale** n liquidazione f

clear|ing /'klɪərɪŋ/ n radura f. **~ly** adv chiaramente. **~ way** n Auto strada f con divieto di sosta

cleavage /'kli:vɪdʒ/ n ⟨woman's⟩ décolleté m inv

cleft /kleft/ n fenditura f

clench /klentʃ/ vt serrare

clergy /'klɜ:dʒɪ/ npl clero m. **~man** n ecclesiastico m

cleric /'klerɪk/ n ecclesiastico m. **~al** a impiegatizio; Relig clericale

clerk /klɑ:k/, Am /klɜ:k/ n impiegato, -a mf; (Am: in shop) commesso, -a mf

clever /'klevə(r)/ a intelligente; (skilful) abile

cliché /'kli:ʃeɪ/ n cliché m inv

click /klɪk/ vi scattare; Comput cliccare ● n Comput click m. **click on** vt Comput cliccare su

client /'klaɪənt/ n cliente mf

clientele /kli:ɒn'tel/ n clientela f

cliff /klɪf/ n scogliera f

climat|e /'klaɪmət/ n clima f. **~ic** /-'mætɪk/ a climatico

climax /'klaɪmæks/ n punto m culminante

climb /klaɪm/ n salita f ● vt scalare ⟨mountain⟩; arrampicarsi su ⟨ladder, tree⟩ ● vi arrampicarsi; ⟨rise⟩ salire; ⟨road:⟩ salire. **climb down** vi scendere; (from ladder, tree) scendere; fig tornare sui propri passi

climber /'klaɪmə(r)/ n alpinista mf; (plant) rampicante m

clinch /klɪntʃ/ vt fam concludere ⟨deal⟩ ● n (in boxing) clinch m inv

cling /klɪŋ/ vi (pt/pp **clung**) aggrapparsi; (stick) aderire. **~ film** n pellicola f trasparente

clinic /'klɪnɪk/ n ambulatorio m. **~al** a clinico

clink /klɪŋk/ n tintinnio m; (fam: prison) galera f ● vi tintinnare

clip¹ /klɪp/ n fermaglio m; (jewellery) spilla f ● vt (pt/pp **clipped**) attaccare

clip² n (extract) taglio m ● vt obliterare ⟨ticket⟩. **~board** n fermabloc m inv. **~pers** npl (for hair) rasoio m; (for hedge) tosasiepi m inv; (for nails) tronchesina f. **~ping** n (from newspaper) ritaglio m

clique /kli:k/ n cricca f

cloak /kləʊk/ n mantello m. **~room** n guardaroba m inv; (toilet) bagno m

clock /klɒk/ n orologio m; (fam: speedometer) tachimetro m ● **clock in** vi attaccare. **clock out** vi staccare

clock: ~ tower n torre f dell'orologio. **~wise** a & adv in senso orario. **~work** n meccanismo m

clod /klɒd/ n zolla f

clog /klɒg/ n zoccolo m ● vt (pt/pp **clogged**) **~ [up]** intasare ⟨drain⟩; inceppare ⟨mechanism⟩ ● vi ⟨drain:⟩ intasarsi

cloister /'klɔɪstə(r)/ n chiostro m

clone /kləʊn/ n clone m

close¹ /kləʊs/ a vicino; ⟨friend⟩ intimo; ⟨weather⟩ afoso; **have a ~ shave** fam scamparla bella; **be ~ to sb** essere unito a qcno ● adv vicino; **~ by** vicino; **it's ~ on five o'clock** sono quasi le cinque

close² /kləʊz/ n fine f ● vt chiudere ● vi chiudersi; ⟨shop:⟩ chiudere. **close down** vt chiudere ● vi ⟨TV station:⟩ interrompere la trasmissione; ⟨factory:⟩ chiudere

closely /'kləʊslɪ/ adv da vicino; ⟨watch, listen⟩ attentamente

closet /'klɒzɪt/ n Am armadio m

close-up /'kləʊs-/ n primo piano m

closure /'kləʊʒə(r)/ n chiusura f

clot /klɒt/ n grumo m; (fam: idiot) tonto, -a mf ● vi (pt/pp **clotted**) ⟨blood:⟩ coagularsi

cloth /klɒθ/ n (fabric) tessuto m; (duster etc) straccio m

clothe /kləʊð/ vt vestire

clothes /kləʊðz/ npl vestiti mpl, abiti

mpl. **~-brush** *n* spazzola *f* per abiti.
~-line *n* corda *f* stendibiancheria

clothing /'kləʊðɪŋ/ *n* abbigliamento *m*

cloud /klaʊd/ *n* nuvola *f*. ● **cloud over**
vi rannuvolarsi. **~burst** *n* acquazzone *m*

cloudy /'klaʊdɪ/ *a* (**-ier, -iest**) nuvoloso; ⟨*liquid*⟩ torbido

clout /klaʊt/ *n fam* colpo *m*; (*influence*)
impatto *m* (**with** su) ● *vt fam* colpire

clove /kləʊv/ *n* chiodo *m* di garofano; **~ of garlic** spicchio *m* d'aglio

clover /'kləʊvə(r)/ *n* trifoglio *m*

clown /klaʊn/ *n* pagliaccio *m* ● *vi* **~ [about]** fare il pagliaccio

club /klʌb/ *n* club *m inv*; (*weapon*) clava
f; *Sport* mazza *f*; **~s** *pl* (*Cards*) fiori *mpl*
● *v* (*pt/pp* **clubbed**) ● *vt* bastonare.
club together *vi* unirsi

cluck /klʌk/ *vi* chiocciare

clue /klu:/ *n* indizio *m*; (*in crossword*)
definizione *f*; **I haven't a ~** *fam* non ne
ho idea

clump /klʌmp/ *n* gruppo *m*

clumsiness /'klʌmzɪnɪs/ *n* goffaggine *f*

clumsy /'klʌmzɪ/ *a* (**-ier, -iest**) maldestro; ⟨*tool*⟩ scomodo; ⟨*remark*⟩ senza tatto

clung /klʌŋ/ *see* **cling**

cluster /'klʌstə(r)/ *n* gruppo *m* ● *vi*
raggrupparsi (**round** intorno a)

clutch /klʌtʃ/ *n* stretta *f*; *Auto* frizione
f; **be in sb's ~es** essere in balia di qcno
● *vt* stringere; (*grab*) afferrare ● *vi* **~ at** afferrare

clutter /'klʌtə(r)/ *n* caos *m* ● *vt* **~ [up]** ingombrare

c/o *abbr* (**care of**) c/o, presso

coach /kəʊtʃ/ *n* pullman *m inv*; *Rail*
vagone *m*; (*horse-drawn*) carrozza *f*;
Sport allenatore, -trice *mf* ● *vt* fare esercitare; *Sport* allenare

coagulate /kəʊ'ægjʊleɪt/ *vi* coagularsi

coal /kəʊl/ *n* carbone *m*

coalition /kəʊə'lɪʃn/ *n* coalizione *f*

'coal-mine *n* miniera *f* di carbone

coarse /kɔ:s/ *a* grossolano; ⟨*joke*⟩ spinto

coast /kəʊst/ *n* costa *f* ● *vi* (*freewheel*)
scendere a ruota libera; *Auto* scendere
in folle. **~al** *a* costiero. **~er** *n* (*mat*)
sottobicchiere *m inv*

coast: ~guard *n* guardia *f* costiera.
~line *n* litorale *m*

coat /kəʊt/ *n* cappotto *m*; (*of animal*)
manto *m*; (*of paint*) mano *f*; **~ of arms**

stemma *f* ● *vt* coprire; (*with paint*) ricoprire. **~-hanger** *n* gruccia *f*. **~-hook** *n*
gancio *m* [appendiabiti]

coating /'kəʊtɪŋ/ *n* rivestimento *m*; (*of
paint*) stato *m*

coax /kəʊks/ *vt* convincere con le moine

cob /kɒb/ *n* (*of corn*) pannocchia *f*

cobble /'kɒbl/ *vt* **~ together** raffazzonare. **~r** *n* ciabattino *m*

'cobblestones *npl* ciottolato *msg*

cobweb /'kɒb-/ *n* ragnatela *f*

cocaine /kə'keɪn/ *n* cocaina *f*

cock /kɒk/ *n* gallo *m*; (*any male bird*)
maschio *m* ● *vt* sollevare il grilletto di
⟨*gun*⟩; **~ its ears** ⟨*animal:*⟩ drizzare le
orecchie

cockerel /'kɒkərəl/ *n* galletto *m*

cock-'eyed *a fam* storto; (*absurd*) assurdo

cockle /'kɒkl/ *n* cardio *m*

cockney /'kɒknɪ/ *n* (*dialect*) dialetto *m*
londinese; (*person*) abitante *mf* dell'est
di Londra

cock: ~pit *n Aeron* cabina *f*. **~roach**
/-rəʊtʃ/ *n* scarafaggio *m*. **~tail** *n* cocktail *m inv*. **~-up** *n sl* **make a ~-up** fare
un casino (**of** con)

cocky /'kɒkɪ/ *a* (**-ier, -iest**) *fam* presuntuoso

cocoa /'kəʊkəʊ/ *n* cacao *m*

coconut /'kəʊkənʌt/ *n* noce *f* di cocco

cocoon /kə'ku:n/ *n* bozzolo *m*

cod /kɒd/ *n inv* merluzzo *m*

COD *abbr* (**cash on delivery**) pagamento *m* alla consegna

code /kəʊd/ *n* codice *m*. **~d** *a* codificato

coedu'cational /kəʊ-/ *a* misto

coerc|e /kəʊ'з:s/ *vt* costringere. **~ion** *n*
/-'з:ʃn/ *n* coercizione *f*

coe'xist *vi* coesistere. **~ence** *n*
coesistenza *f*

coffee /'kɒfɪ/ *n* caffè *m inv*

coffee: ~-grinder *n* macinacaffè *m
inv*. **~-pot** *n* caffettiera *f*. **~-table** *n* tavolino *m*

coffin /'kɒfɪn/ *n* bara *f*

cog /kɒg/ *n Techn* dente *m* (*di ruota*)

cogent /'kəʊdʒənt/ *a* convincente

cog-wheel *n* ruota *f* dentata

cohabit /kəʊ'hæbɪt/ *vi Jur* convivere

coherent /kəʊ'hɪərənt/ *a* coerente;
(*when speaking*) logico

coil /kɔɪl/ *n* rotolo *m*; *Electr* bobina *f*;
~s *pl* spire *fpl* ● *vt* **~ [up]** avvolgere

coin /kɔɪn/ *n* moneta *f* ● *vt* coniare
⟨*word*⟩

coincide /kəʊɪn'saɪd/ *vi* coincidere

coinciden|ce /kəʊˈmsɪdəns/ n coincidenza f. **~tal** /-ˈdentl/ a casuale. **~tally** adv casualmente

coke /kəʊk/ n [carbone m] coke m

Coke® n Coca[-cola]® f

cold /kəʊld/ a freddo; **I'm ~** ho freddo ● n freddo m; Med raffreddore m

cold: **~-ˈblooded** a spietato. **~-ˈhearted** a insensibile. **~ly** adv fig freddamente. **~ meat** n salumi mpl. **~ness** n freddezza f

coleslaw /ˈkəʊlslɔː/ n insalata f di cavolo crudo, cipolle e carote in maionese

colic /ˈkɒlɪk/ n colica f

collaborat|e /kəˈlæbəreɪt/ vi collaborare; **~e on sth** collaborare in qcsa. **~ion** /-ˈreɪʃn/ n collaborazione f; (with enemy) collaborazionismo m. **~or** n collaboratore, -trice mf; (with enemy) collaborazionista mf

collaps|e /kəˈlæps/ n crollo m ● vi ⟨person:⟩ svenire; ⟨roof, building:⟩ crollare. **~ible** a pieghevole

collar /ˈkɒlə(r)/ n colletto m; (for animal) collare m. **~-bone** n clavicola f

colleague /ˈkɒliːg/ n collega mf

collect /kəˈlekt/ vt andare a prendere ⟨person⟩; ritirare ⟨parcel, tickets⟩; riscuotere ⟨taxes⟩; raccogliere ⟨rubbish⟩; (as hobby) collezionare ● vi riunirsi ● adv call **~** Am telefonare a carico del destinatario. **~ed** /-ɪd/ a controllato

collection /kəˈlekʃn/ n collezione f; (in church) questua f; (of rubbish) raccolta f; (of post) levata f

collective /kəˈlektɪv/ a collettivo

collector /kəˈlektə(r)/ n (of stamps etc) collezionista mf

college /ˈkɒlɪdʒ/ n istituto m parauniversitario; **C~ of...** Scuola f di...

collide /kəˈlaɪd/ vi scontrarsi

colliery /ˈkɒlɪərɪ/ n miniera f di carbone

collision /kəˈlɪʒn/ n scontro m

colloquial /kəˈləʊkwɪəl/ a colloquiale. **~ism** n espressione f colloquiale

cologne /kəˈləʊn/ n colonia f

colon /ˈkəʊlən/ n due punti mpl; Anat colon m inv

colonel /ˈkɜːnl/ n colonnello m

colonial /kəˈləʊnɪəl/ a coloniale

colon|ize /ˈkɒlənaɪz/ vt colonizzare. **~y** n colonia f

colossal /kəˈlɒsl/ a colossale

colour /ˈkʌlə(r)/ n colore m; (complexion) colorito m; **~s** pl (flag) bandiera fsg; **off ~** fam giù di tono ● vt

colorare; **~ [in]** colorare ● vi (blush) arrossire

colour: **~ bar** n discriminazione f razziale. **~-blind** a daltonico. **~ed** a colorato; ⟨person⟩ di colore ● n (person) persona f di colore. **~-fast** a dai colori resistenti. **~ film** n film m inv a colori. **~ful** a pieno di colore. **~less** a incolore. **~ television** n televisione f a colori

colt /kəʊlt/ n puledro m

column /ˈkɒləm/ n colonna f. **~ist** /-nɪst/ n giornalista mf che cura una rubrica

coma /ˈkəʊmə/ n coma m inv

comb /kəʊm/ n pettine m; (for wearing) pettinino m ● vt pettinare; (fig: search) setacciare; **~ one's hair** pettinarsi i capelli

combat /ˈkɒmbæt/ n combattimento m ● vt (pt/pp combated) combattere

combination /kɒmbɪˈneɪʃn/ n combinazione f

combine¹ /kəmˈbaɪn/ vt unire; **~ a job with being a mother** conciliare il lavoro con il ruolo di madre ● vi ⟨chemical elements:⟩ combinarsi

combine² /ˈkɒmbaɪn/ n Comm associazione f. **~ [harvester]** n mietitrebbia f

combustion /kəmˈbʌstʃn/ n combustione f

come /kʌm/ vi (pt came, pp come) venire; **where do you ~ from?** da dove vieni?; **~ to** (reach) arrivare a; **that ~s to £10** fanno 10 sterline; **~ into money** ricevere dei soldi; **~ true/open** verificarsi/aprirsi; **~ first** arrivare primo; fig venire prima di tutto; **~ in two sizes** esistere in due misure; **the years to ~** gli anni a venire; **how ~?** fam come mai? **come about** vi succedere. **come across** vi **~ across as being** fam dare l'impressione di essere ● vt (find) imbattersi in. **come along** vi venire; ⟨job, opportunity:⟩ presentarsi; (progress) andare bene. **come apart** vi smontarsi; (break) rompersi. **come away** vi venir via; ⟨button, fastener:⟩ staccarsi. **come back** vi ritornare. **come by** vi passare ● vt (obtain) avere. **come down** vi scendere; **~ down to** (reach) arrivare a. **come in** vi entrare; (in race) arrivare; ⟨tide:⟩ salire. **come in for** vt **~ in for criticism** essere criticato. **come off** vi staccarsi; (take place) esserci; (succeed) riuscire. **come on** vi (make progress) migliorare; **~ on!** (hurry) dai!; (indicating disbelief) ma va là!. **come out** vi venir fuori; ⟨book, *sun:*⟩ uscire; ⟨*stain:*⟩ andar via. **come over** *vi* venire. **come round** *vi* venire; *(after fainting)* riaversi; *(change one's mind)* farsi convincere. **come to** *vi (after fainting)* riaversi. **come up** *vi* salire; ⟨*sun:*⟩ sorgere; ⟨*plant:*⟩ crescere; **something came up** (*I was prevented*) ho avuto un imprevisto. **come up with** *vt* tirar fuori

'**come-back** *n* ritorno *m*

comedian /kə'miːdɪən/ *n* comico *m*

'**come-down** *n* passo *m* indietro

comedy /'kɒmədɪ/ *n* commedia *f*

comet /'kɒmɪt/ *n* cometa *f*

come-uppance /kʌm'ʌpəns/ *n* **get one's ~** *fam* avere quel che si merita

comfort /'kʌmfət/ *n* benessere *m*; *(consolation)* conforto *m* ● *vt* confortare

comfortabl|e /'kʌmfətəbl/ *a* comodo; **be ~e** ⟨*person:*⟩ stare comodo; *(fig: in situation)* essere a proprio agio; *(financially)* star bene. **~y** *adv* comodamente

'**comfort station** *n Am* bagno *m* pubblico

comfy /'kʌmfɪ/ *a fam* comodo

comic /'kɒmɪk/ *a* comico ● *n* comico, -a *mf*; *(periodical)* fumetto *m*. **~al** *a* comico. **~ strip** *n* striscia *f* di fumetti

coming /'kʌmɪŋ/ *n* venuta *f*; **~s and goings** viavai *m*

comma /'kɒmə/ *n* virgola *f*

command /kə'mɑːnd/ *n* comando *m*; *(order)* ordine *m*; *(mastery)* padronanza *f* ● *vt* ordinare; comandare ⟨*army*⟩

commandeer /kɒmən'dɪə(r)/ *vt* requisire

command|er /kə'mɑːndə(r)/ *n* comandante *m*. **~ing** *a* ⟨*view*⟩ imponente; ⟨*lead*⟩ dominante. **~ing officer** *n* comandante *m*. **~ment** *n* comandamento *m*

commemorat|e /kə'meməreɪt/ *vt* commemorare. **~ion** /-'reɪʃn/ *n* commemorazione *f*. **~ive** /-ətɪv/ *a* commemorativo

commence /kə'mens/ *vt/i* cominciare. **~ment** *n* inizio *m*

commend /kə'mend/ *vt* complimentarsi con (**on** per); *(recommend)* raccomandare (**to** a). **~able** /-əbl/ *a* lodevole

commensurate /kə'menʃərət/ *a* proporzionato (**with** a)

comment /'kɒment/ *n* commento *m* ● *vi* fare commenti (**on** su)

commentary /'kɒməntrɪ/ *n* commento *m*; [**running**] **~** (*on radio, TV*) cronaca *f* diretta

commentat|e /'kɒmənteɪt/ *vt* **~e on**

TV, Radio fare la cronaca di. **~or** *n* cronista *mf*

commerce /'kɒmɜːs/ *n* commercio *m*

commercial /kə'mɜːʃl/ *a* commerciale ● *n* TV pubblicità *f inv.* **~ize** *vt* commercializzare

commiserate /kə'mɪzəreɪt/ *vi* esprimere il proprio rincrescimento (**with** a)

commission /kə'mɪʃn/ *n* commissione *f*; **receive one's ~** *Mil* essere promosso ufficiale; **out of ~** fuori uso ● *vt* commissionare

commissionaire /kəmɪʃə'neə(r)/ *n* portiere *m*

commissioner /kə'mɪʃənə(r)/ *n* commissario *m*

commit /kə'mɪt/ *vt* (*pt/pp* **committed**) commettere; *(to prison, hospital)* affidare (**to** a); impegnare ⟨*funds*⟩; **~ oneself** impegnarsi. **~ment** *n* impegno *m*; *(involvement)* compromissione *f*. **~ted** *a* impegnato

committee /kə'mɪtɪ/ *n* comitato *m*

commodity /kə'mɒdətɪ/ *n* prodotto *m*

common /'kɒmən/ *a* comune; *(vulgar)* volgare ● *n* prato *m* pubblico; **have in ~** avere in comune. **House of C~s** Camera *f* dei Comuni. **~er** *n* persona *f* non nobile

common: ~ law *n* diritto *m* consuetudinario. **~ly** *adv* comunemente. **C~ 'Market** *n* Mercato *m* Comune. **~place** *a* banale. **~room** *n* sala *f* dei professori/degli studenti. **~ 'sense** *n* buon senso *m*

commotion /kə'məʊʃn/ *n* confusione *f*

communal /'kɒmjʊnl/ *a* comune

communicate /kə'mjuːnɪkeɪt/ *vt/i* comunicare

communication /kəmjuːnɪ'keɪʃn/ *n* comunicazione *f*; *(of disease)* trasmissione *f*; **be in ~ with sb** essere in contatto (con qcno; **~s** *pl (technology)* telecomunicazioni *fpl.* **~ cord** *n* fermata *f* d'emergenza

communicative /kə'mjuːnɪkətɪv/ *a* comunicativo

Communion /kə'mjuːnɪən/ *n* [**Holy**] **~** comunione *f*

communiqué /kə'mjuːnɪkeɪ/ *n* comunicato *m* stampa

Communis|m /'kɒmjʊnɪzm/ *n* comunismo *m*. **~t** /-ɪst/ *a* & *n* comunista *mf*

community /kə'mjuːnətɪ/ *n* comunità *f*. **~ centre** *n* centro *m* sociale

commute /kə'mjuːt/ *vi* fare il pendolare ● *vt* Jur commutare. **~r** *n* pendolare *mf*

compact | compromise

compact[1] /kəm'pækt/ *a* compatto

compact[2] /'kɒmpækt/ *n* portacipria *m inv*. **~ disc** *n* compact disc *m inv*

companion /kəm'pænjən/ *n* compagno, -a *mf*. **~ship** *n* compagnia *f*

company /'kʌmpəni/ *n* compagnia *f*; (*guests*) ospiti *mpl*. **~ car** *n* macchina *f* della ditta

comparable /'kɒmpərəbl/ *a* paragonabile

comparative /kəm'pærətɪv/ *a* comparativo; (*relative*) relativo ● *n Gram* comparativo *m*. **~ly** *adv* relativamente

compare /kəm'peə(r)/ *vt* paragonare (**with/to** a) ● *vi* essere paragonato

comparison /kəm'pærɪsn/ *n* paragone *m*

compartment /kəm'pɑːtmənt/ *n* compartimento *m*; *Rail* scompartimento *m*

compass /'kʌmpəs/ *n* bussola *f*. **~es** *npl*, **pair of ~es** compasso *msg*

compassion /kəm'pæʃn/ *n* compassione *f*. **~ate** /-ʃənət/ *a* compassionevole

compatible /kəm'pætəbl/ *a* compatibile

compatriot /kəm'pætrɪət/ *n* compatriota *mf*

compel /kəm'pel/ *vt* (*pt/pp* **compelled**) costringere. **~ling** *a* (*reason*) inconfutabile

compensat|e /'kɒmpənseɪt/ *vt* risarcire ● *vi* **~e for** *fig* compensare di. **~ion** /-'seɪʃn/ *n* risarcimento *m*; (*fig: comfort*) consolazione *f*

compère /'kɒmpeə(r)/ *n* presentatore, -trice *mf*

compete /kəm'piːt/ *vi* competere; (*take part*) gareggiare

competen|ce /'kɒmpɪtəns/ *n* competenza *f*. **~t** *a* competente

competition /kɒmpə'tɪʃn/ *n* concorrenza *f*; (*contest*) gara *f*

competitive /kəm'petɪtɪv/ *a* competitivo; **~ prices** prezzi *mpl* concorrenziali

competitor /kəm'petɪtə(r)/ *n* concorrente *mf*

complacen|cy /kəm'pleɪsənsi/ *n* compiacimento *m*. **~t** *a* compiaciuto

complain /kəm'pleɪn/ *vi* lamentarsi (**about** di); (*formally*) reclamare; **~ of** *Med* accusare. **~t** *n* lamentela *f*; (*formal*) reclamo *m*; *Med* disturbo *m*

complement[1] /'kɒmplɪmənt/ *n* complemento *m*

complement[2] /'kɒmplɪment/ *vt* complementare; **~ each other** complementarsi a vicenda. **~ary** /-'mentəri/ *a* complementare

complete /kəm'pliːt/ *a* completo; (*utter*) finito ● *vt* completare; compilare (*form*). **~ly** *adv* completamente

completion /kəm'pliːʃn/ *n* fine *f*

complex /'kɒmpleks/ *a* complesso ● *n* complesso *m*

complexion /kəm'plekʃn/ *n* carnagione *f*

complexity /kəm'pleksəti/ *n* complessità *f inv*

compliance /kəm'plaɪəns/ *n* accettazione *f*; (*with rules*) osservanza *f*; **in ~ with** in osservanza a (*law*); conformemente a (*request*)

complicat|e /'kɒmplɪkeɪt/ *vt* complicare. **~ed** *a* complicato. **~ion** /-'keɪʃn/ *n* complicazione *f*

compliment /'kɒmplɪmənt/ *n* complimento *m*; **~s** *pl* omaggi *mpl* ● *vt* complimentare. **~ary** /-'mentəri/ *a* complimentoso; (*given free*) in omaggio

comply /kəm'plaɪ/ *vi* (*pt/pp* **-ied**) **~ with** conformarsi a

component /kəm'pəʊnənt/ *a* & *n* [**part**] componente *m*

compose /kəm'pəʊz/ *vt* comporre; **~ oneself** ricomporsi; **be ~d of** essere composto da. **~d** *a* (*calm*) composto. **~r** *n* compositore, -trice *mf*

composition /kɒmpə'zɪʃn/ *n* composizione *f*; (*essay*) tema *m*

compost /'kɒmpɒst/ *n* composta *f*

composure /kəm'pəʊʒə(r)/ *n* calma *f*

compound /'kɒmpaʊnd/ *a* composto. **~ fracture** *n* frattura *f* esposta. **~ 'interest** *n* interesse *m* composto ● *n Chem* composto *m*; *Gram* parola *f* composta; (*enclosure*) recinto *m*

comprehen|d /kɒmprɪ'hend/ *vt* comprendere. **~sible** /-'hensəbl/ *a* comprensibile. **~sion** /-'henʃn/ *n* comprensione *f*

comprehensive /kɒmprɪ'hensɪv/ *a* & *n* comprensivo; **~ [school]** *scuola f media in cui gli allievi hanno capacità d'apprendimento diverse*. **~ insurance** *n Auto* polizza *f* casco

compress[1] /'kɒmpres/ *n* compressa *f*

compress[2] /kəm'pres/ *vt* comprimere; **~ed air** aria *f* compressa

comprise /kəm'praɪz/ *vt* comprendere; (*form*) costituire

compromise /'kɒmprəmaɪz/ *n* compromesso *m* ● *vt* compromettere ● *vi* fare un compromesso

compuls|ion /kəm'pʌlʃn/ *n* desiderio *m* irresistibile. **~ive** /-sɪv/ *a Psych* patologico. **~ive eating** voglia *f* ossessiva di mangiare. **~ory** /-sərɪ/ *a* obbligatorio

comput|er /kəm'pju:tə(r)/ *n* computer *m inv*. **~erize** *vt* computerizzare. **~ing** *n* informatica *f*

comrade /'kɒmreɪd/ *n* camerata *m*; *Pol* compagno, -a *mf*. **~ship** *n* cameratismo *m*

con¹ /kɒn/ *see* **pro**

con² *n fam* fregatura *f* ● *vt* (*pt/pp* **conned**) *fam* fregare

concave /'kɒnkeɪv/ *a* concavo

conceal /kən'si:l/ *vt* nascondere

concede /kən'si:d/ *vt* (*admit*) ammettere; (*give up*) rinunciare a; lasciar fare (*goal*)

conceit /kən'si:t/ *n* presunzione *f*. **~ed** *a* presuntuoso

conceivable /kən'si:vəbl/ *a* concepibile

conceive /kən'si:v/ *vt Biol* concepire ● *vi* aver figli. **conceive of** *vt fig* concepire

concentrat|e /'kɒnsəntreɪt/ *vt* concentrare ● *vi* concentrarsi. **~ion** /-'treɪʃn/ *n* concentrazione *f*. **~ion camp** *n* campo *m* di concentramento

concept /'kɒnsept/ *n* concetto *m*. **~ion** /kən'sepʃn/ *n* concezione *f*; (*idea*) idea *f*

concern /kən'sɜ:n/ *n* preoccupazione *f*; *Comm* attività *f inv* ● *vt* (*be about, affect*) riguardare; (*worry*) preoccupare; **be ~ed about** essere preoccupato per; **~ oneself with** preoccuparsi di; **as far as I am ~ed** per quanto mi riguarda. **~ing** *prep* riguardo a

concert /'kɒnsət/ *n* concerto *m*. **~ed** /kən'sɜ:tɪd/ *a* collettivo

concertina /kɒnsə'ti:nə/ *n* piccola fisarmonica *f*

'concertmaster *n Am* primo violino *m*

concerto /kən'tʃeətəʊ/ *n* concerto *m*

concession /kən'seʃn/ *n* concessione *f*; (*reduction*) sconto *m*. **~ary** *a* (*reduced*) scontato

conciliation /kənsɪlɪ'eɪʃn/ *n* conciliazione *f*

concise /kən'saɪs/ *a* conciso

conclu|de /kən'klu:d/ *vt* concludere ● *vi* concludersi. **~ding** *a* finale

conclusion /kən'klu:ʒn/ *n* conclusione *f*; **in ~** per concludere

conclusive /kən'klu:sɪv/ *a* definitivo. **~ly** *adv* in modo definitivo

concoct /kən'kɒkt/ *vt* confezionare; *fig* inventare. **~ion** /-ɒkʃn/ *n* mistura *f*; (*drink*) intruglio *m*

concourse /'kɒnkɔ:s/ *n* atrio *m*

concrete /'kɒnkri:t/ *a* concreto ● *n* calcestruzzo *m*

concur /kən'kɜ:(r)/ *vi* (*pt/pp* **concurred**) essere d'accordo

concurrently /kən'kʌrəntlɪ/ *adv* contemporaneamente

concussion /kən'kʌʃn/ *n* commozione *f* cerebrale

condemn /kən'dem/ *vt* condannare; dichiarare inagibile (*building*). **~ation** /kɒndem'neɪʃn/ *n* condanna *f*

condensation /kɒnden'seɪʃn/ *n* condensazione *f*

condense /kən'dens/ *vt* condensare; *Phys* condensare ● *vi* condensarsi. **~d milk** *n* latte *m* condensato

condescend /kɒndɪ'send/ *vi* degnarsi. **~ing** *a* condiscendente

condition /kən'dɪʃn/ *n* condizione *f*; **on ~ that** a condizione che ● *vt Psych* condizionare. **~al** *a* (*acceptance*) condizionato; *Gram* condizionale ● *n Gram* condizionale *m*. **~er** *n* balsamo *m*; (*for fabrics*) ammorbidente *m*

condolences /kən'dəʊlənsɪz/ *npl* condoglianze *fpl*

condom /'kɒndəm/ *n* preservativo *m*

condo[minium] /'kɒndə('mɪnɪəm)/ *n Am* condominio *m*

condone /kən'dəʊn/ *vt* passare sopra a

conducive /kən'dju:sɪv/ *a* **be ~ to** contribuire a

conduct¹ /'kɒndʌkt/ *n* condotta *f*

conduct² /kən'dʌkt/ *vt* condurre; dirigere (*orchestra*). **~or** *n* direttore *m* d'orchestra; (*of bus*) bigliettaio *m*; *Phys* conduttore *m*. **~ress** *n* bigliettaia *f*

cone /kəʊn/ *n* cono *m*; *Bot* pigna *f*; *Auto* birillo *m* ● **cone off** *vt* **be ~d off** *Auto* essere chiuso da birilli

confectioner /kən'fekʃənə(r)/ *n* pasticciere, -a *mf*. **~y** *n* pasticceria *f*

confederation /kənfedə'reɪʃn/ *n* confederazione *f*

confer /kən'fɜ:(r)/ *v* (*pt/pp* **conferred**) ● *vt* conferire (**on** a) ● *vi* (*discuss*) conferire

conference /'kɒnfərəns/ *n* conferenza *f*

confess /kən'fes/ *vt* confessare ● *vi* confessare; *Relig* confessarsi. **~ion** /-eʃn/ *n* confessione *f*. **~ional** /-eʃənəl/ *n* confessionale *m*. **~or** *n* confessore *m*

confetti /kən'fetɪ/ *n* coriandoli *mpl*

confide /kən'faɪd/ *vt* confidare.
confide in *vt* ~ **in sb** fidarsi di qcno
confidence /'kɒnfɪdəns/ *n* (*trust*) fiducia *f*; (*self-assurance*) sicurezza *f* di sé; (*secret*) confidenza *f*; **in** ~ in confidenza.
~ **trick** *n* truffa *f*
confident /'kɒnfɪdənt/ *a* fiducioso; (*self-assured*) sicuro di sé. ~**ly** *adv* con aria fiduciosa
confidential /kɒnfɪ'denʃl/ *a* confidenziale
confine /kən'faɪn/ *vt* rinchiudere; (*limit*) limitare; **be** ~**d to bed** essere confinato a letto. ~**d** *a* (*space*) limitato.
~**ment** *n* detenzione *f*; *Med* parto *m*
confines /'kɒnfaɪnz/ *npl* confini *mpl*
confirm /kən'fɜːm/ *vt* confermare; *Relig* cresimare. ~**ation** /kɒnfə'meɪʃn/ *n* conferma *f*; *Relig* cresima *f*. ~**ed** *a* incallito; ~**ed bachelor** scapolo *m* impenitente
confiscat|e /'kɒnfɪskeɪt/ *vt* confiscare. ~**ion** /-'keɪʃn/ *n* confisca *f*
conflict[1] /'kɒnflɪkt/ *n* conflitto *m*
conflict[2] /kən'flɪkt/ *vi* essere in contraddizione. ~**ing** *a* contraddittorio
conform /kən'fɔːm/ *vi* (*person:*) conformarsi; (*thing:*) essere conforme (**to** a). ~**ist** *n* conformista *mf*
confounded /kən'faʊndɪd/ *a fam* maledetto
confront /kən'frʌnt/ *vt* affrontare; **the problems** ~**ing us** i problemi che dobbiamo affrontare. ~**ation** /kɒnfrʌn'teɪʃn/ *n* confronto *m*
confus|e /kən'fjuːz/ *vt* confondere. ~**ing** *a* che confonde. ~**ion** /-juːʒn/ *n* confusione *f*
congeal /kən'dʒiːl/ *vi* (*blood:*) coagularsi
congenial /kən'dʒiːnɪəl/ *a* congeniale
congenital /kən'dʒenɪtl/ *a* congenito
congest|ed /kən'dʒestɪd/ *a* congestionato. ~**ion** /-estʃn/ *n* congestione *f*
congratulat|e /kən'grætjʊleɪt/ *vt* congratularsi con (**on** per). ~**ions** /-'eɪʃnz/ *npl* congratulazioni *fpl*
congregat|e /'kɒŋgrɪgeɪt/ *vi* radunarsi. ~**ion** /-'geɪʃn/ *n Relig* assemblea *f*
congress /'kɒŋgres/ *n* congresso *m*. ~**man** *n Am Pol* membro *m* del congresso
conical /'kɒnɪkl/ *a* conico
conifer /'kɒnɪfə(r)/ *n* conifera *f*
conjecture /kən'dʒektʃə(r)/ *n* congettura *f*
conjugal /'kɒndʒʊgl/ *a* coniugale

conjugat|e /'kɒndʒʊgeɪt/ *vt* coniugare. ~**ion** /-'geɪʃn/ *n* coniugazione *f*
conjunction /kən'dʒʌŋkʃn/ *n* congiunzione *f*; **in** ~ **with** insieme a
conjunctivitis /kəndʒʌŋktɪ'vaɪtɪs/ *n* congiuntivite *f*
conjur|e /'kʌndʒə(r)/ *vi* ~**ing tricks** *npl* giochi *mpl* di prestigio. ~**or** *n* prestigiatore, -trice *mf*. **conjure up** *vt* evocare (*image*); tirar fuori dal nulla (*meal*)
conk /kɒŋk/ *vi* ~ **out** *fam* (*machine:*) guastarsi; (*person:*) crollare
'con-man *n fam* truffatore *m*
connect /kə'nekt/ *vt* collegare; **be** ~**ed with** avere legami con; (*be related to*) essere imparentato con; **be well** ~**ed** aver conoscenze influenti ● *vi* essere collegato (**with** a); (*train:*) fare coincidenza
connection /kə'nekʃn/ *n* (*between ideas*) nesso *m*; (*in travel*) coincidenza *f*; *Electr* collegamento *m*; **in** ~ **with** con riferimento a. ~**s** *pl* (*people*) conoscenze *fpl*
connoisseur /kɒnə'sɜː(r)/ *n* intenditore, -trice *mf*
conquer /'kɒŋkə(r)/ *vt* conquistare; *fig* superare (*fear*). ~**or** *n* conquistatore *m*
conquest /'kɒŋkwest/ *n* conquista *f*
conscience /'kɒnʃəns/ *n* coscienza *f*
conscientious /kɒnʃɪ'enʃəs/ *a* coscienzioso. ~ **ob'jector** *n* obiettore *m* di coscienza
conscious /'kɒnʃəs/ *a* conscio; (*decision*) meditato; [**fully**] ~ cosciente; **be/become** ~ **of sth** rendersi conto di qcsa. ~**ly** *adv* consapevolmente. ~**ness** *n* consapevolezza *f*; *Med* conoscenza *f*
conscript[1] /'kɒnskrɪpt/ *n* coscritto *m*
conscript[2] /kən'skrɪpt/ *vt Mil* chiamare alle armi. ~**ion** /-ɪpʃn/ *n* coscrizione *f*, leva *f*
consecrat|e /'kɒnsɪkreɪt/ *vt* consacrare. ~**ion** /-'kreɪʃn/ *n* consacrazione *f*
consecutive /kən'sekjʊtɪv/ *a* consecutivo
consensus /kən'sensəs/ *n* consenso *m*
consent /kən'sent/ *n* consenso *m* ● *vi* acconsentire
consequen|ce /'kɒnsɪkwəns/ *n* conseguenza *f*; (*importance*) importanza *f*. ~**t** *a* conseguente. ~**tly** *adv* di conseguenza
conservation /kɒnsə'veɪʃn/ *n* conservazione *f*. ~**ist** *n* fautore, -trice *mf* della tutela ambientale
conservative   /kən'sɜːvətɪv/   *a*

conservativo; ⟨*estimate*⟩ ottimistico. **C~**
Pol a conservatore ● *n* conservatore,
-trice *mf*

conservatory /kən'sɜːvətrɪ/ *n* spazio
m chiuso da vetrate adiacente alla casa

conserve /kən'sɜːv/ *vt* conservare

consider /kən'sɪdə(r)/ *vt* considerare;
~ doing sth considerare la possibilità
di fare qcsa. **~able** /-əbl/ *a* considerevo-
le. **~ably** *adv* considerevolmente

consider|ate /kən'sɪdərət/ *a* pieno di
riguardo. **~ately** *adv* con riguardo.
~ation /-'reɪʃn/ *n* considerazione *f*;
(*thoughtfulness*) attenzione *f*; (*respect*)
riguardo *m*; (*payment*) compenso *m*;
take into ~ation prendere in considerazione. **~ing** *prep* considerando

consign /kən'saɪn/ *vt* affidare. **~ment**
n consegna *f*

consist /kən'sɪst/ *vi* **~ of** consistere di

consisten|cy /kən'sɪstənsɪ/ *n* coeren-
za *f*; (*density*) consistenza *f*. **~t** *a* coerente; ⟨*loyalty*⟩ costante. **~tly** *adv* coeren-
temente; ⟨*late, loyal*⟩ costantemente

consolation /kɒnsə'leɪʃn/ *n* consolazione *f*. **~ prize** *n* premio *m* di consolazione

console /kən'səʊl/ *vt* consolare

consolidate /kən'sɒlɪdeɪt/ *vt* consolidare

consonant /'kɒnsənənt/ *n* consonante *f*

consort /kən'sɔːt/ *vi* **~ with** frequentare

consortium /kən'sɔːtɪəm/ *n* consorzio *m*

conspicuous /kən'spɪkjʊəs/ *a* facilmente distinguibile

conspiracy /kən'spɪrəsɪ/ *n* cospirazio-
ne *f*

conspire /kən'spaɪə(r)/ *vi* cospirare

constable /'kʌnstəbl/ *n* agente *m* [di
polizia]

constant /'kɒnstənt/ *a* costante. **~ly**
adv costantemente

constellation /kɒnstə'leɪʃn/ *n* costel-
lazione *f*

consternation /kɒnstə'neɪʃn/ *n* co-
sternazione *f*

constipat|ed /'kɒnstɪpeɪtɪd/ *a* stitico.
~ion /-'peɪʃn/ *n* stitichezza *f*

constituency /kən'stɪtjʊənsɪ/ *n* area *f*
elettorale di un deputato nel Regno Unito

constituent /kən'stɪtjʊənt/ *n* costi-
tuente *m*; *Pol* elettore, -trice *mf*

constitut|e /'kɒnstɪtjuːt/ *vt* costituire.
~ion /-'tjuːʃn/ *n* costituzione *f*. **~ional**
/-'tjuːʃənl/ *a* costituzionale

constrain /kən'streɪn/ *vt* costringere.

~t *n* costrizione *f*; (*restriction*) restrizione *f*; (*strained manner*) disagio *m*

construct /kən'strʌkt/ *vt* costruire.
~ion /-ʌkʃn/ *n* costruzione *f*; **under
~ion** in costruzione. **~ive** /-ɪv/ *a*
costruttivo

construe /kən'struː/ *vt* interpretare

consul /'kɒnsl/ *n* console *m*. **~ar**
/'kɒnsjʊlə(r)/ *a* consolare. **~ate**
/'kɒnsjʊlət/ *n* consolato *m*

consult /kən'sʌlt/ *vt* consultare. **~ant**
n consulente *mf*; *Med* specialista *mf*.
~ation /kɒnsl'teɪʃn/ *n* consultazione *f*;
Med consulto *m*

consume /kən'sjuːm/ *vt* consumare.
~r *n* consumatore, -trice *mf*. **~r goods**
npl beni *mpl* di consumo. **~er
organization** *n* organizzazione *f* per la
tutela dei consumatori

consumerism /kən'sjuːmərɪzm/ *n*
consumismo *m*

consummate /'kɒnsəmeɪt/ *vt* consumare

consumption /kən'sʌmpʃn/ *n* consumo *m*

contact /'kɒntækt/ *n* contatto *m*;
(*person*) conoscenza *f* ● *vt* mettersi in
contatto con. **~ 'lenses** *npl* lenti *fpl* a
contatto

contagious /kən'teɪdʒəs/ *a* contagioso

contain /kən'teɪn/ *vt* contenere; **~
oneself** controllarsi. **~er** *n* recipiente
m; (*for transport*) container *m inv*

contaminat|e /kən'tæmɪneɪt/ *vt* con-
taminare. **~ion** /-'neɪʃn/ *n* contamina-
zione *f*

contemplat|e /'kɒntəmpleɪt/ *vt* con-
templare; (*consider*) considerare; **~e
doing sth** considerare di fare qcsa.
~ion /-'pleɪʃn/ *n* contemplazione *f*

contemporary /kən'tempərərɪ/ *a* & *n*
contemporaneo, -a *mf*

contempt /kən'tempt/ *n* disprezzo *m*;
beneath ~ più che vergognoso; **~ of
court** oltraggio *m* alla Corte. **~ible**
/-əbl/ *a* spregevole. **~uous** /-tjʊəs/ *a*
sprezzante

contend /kən'tend/ *vi* **~ with** occuparsi di ● *vt* (*assert*) sostenere. **~er** *n*
concorrente *mf*

content¹ /'kɒntent/ *n* contenuto *m*

content² /kən'tent/ *a* soddisfatto ● *vt*
~ oneself accontentarsi (**with** di).
~ed *a* soddisfatto. **~edly** *adv* con aria
soddisfatta

contention /kən'tenʃn/ *n* (*assertion*)
opinione *f*

contentment /kən'tentmənt/ n soddisfazione f

contents /'kɒntents/ npl contenuto m

contest[1] /'kɒntest/ n gara f

contest[2] /kən'test/ vt contestare ⟨statement⟩; impugnare ⟨will⟩; Pol ⟨candidates:⟩ contendersi; ⟨one candidate:⟩ aspirare a. **~ant** n concorrente mf

context /'kɒntekst/ n contesto m

continent /'kɒntmənt/ n continente m; **the C~** l'Europa f continentale

continental /kɒntr'nentl/ a continentale. **~ breakfast** n prima colazione f a base di pane, burro, marmellata, croissant, ecc. **~ quilt** n piumone m

contingency /kən'tɪndʒənsɪ/ n eventualità f inv

continual /kən'tɪnjʊəl/ a continuo

continuation /kəntɪnjʊ'eɪʃn/ n continuazione f

continue /kən'tɪnju:/ vt continuare; **~ doing** or **to do sth** continuare a fare qcsa; **to be ~d** continua ● vi continuare. **~d** a continuo

continuity /kɒntr'nju:ətɪ/ n continuità f

continuous /kən'tɪnjʊəs/ a continuo

contort /kən'tɔ:t/ vt contorcere. **~ion** /-ɔ:ʃn/ n contorsione f. **~ionist** n contorsionista mf

contour /'kɒntʊə(r)/ n contorno m; ⟨line⟩ curva f di livello

contraband /'kɒntrəbænd/ n contrabbando m

contracep|tion /kɒntrə'sepʃn/ n contraccezione f. **~tive** /-tɪv/ n contraccettivo m

contract[1] /'kɒntrækt/ n contratto m

contract[2] /kən'trækt/ vi ⟨get smaller⟩ contrarsi ● vt contrarre ⟨illness⟩. **~ion** /-ækʃn/ n contrazione f. **~or** n imprenditore, -trice mf

contradict /kɒntrə'dɪkt/ vt contraddire. **~ion** /-ɪkʃn/ n contraddizione f. **~ory** a contraddittorio

contra-flow /'kɒntrəfləʊ/ n utilizzazione f di una corsia nei due sensi di marcia durante lavori stradali

contralto /kən'træltəʊ/ n contralto m

contraption /kən'træpʃn/ n fam aggeggio m

contrary[1] /'kɒntrərɪ/ a contrario ● adv **~ to** contrariamente a ● n contrario m; **on the ~** al contrario

contrary[2] /kən'treərɪ/ a disobbediente

contrast[1] /'kɒntrɑ:st/ n contrasto m

contrast[2] /kən'trɑ:st/ vt confrontare ● vi contrastare. **~ing** a contrastante

contraven|e /kɒntrə'vi:n/ vt trasgredire. **~tion** /-'venʃn/ n trasgressione f

contribut|e /kən'trɪbju:t/ vt/i contribuire. **~ion** /kɒntrɪ'bju:ʃn/ n contribuzione f; ⟨what is contributed⟩ contributo m. **~or** n contributore, -trice mf

contrive /kən'traɪv/ vt escogitare; **~ to do sth** riuscire a fare qcsa

control /kən'trəʊl/ n controllo m; **~s** pl ⟨of car, plane⟩ comandi mpl; **get out of ~** sfuggire al controllo ● vt ⟨pt/pp **controlled**⟩ controllare; **~ oneself** controllarsi

controvers|ial /kɒntrə'vɜ:ʃl/ a controverso. **~y** /'kɒntrəvɜ:sɪ/ n controversia f

conurbation /kɒnɜ:'beɪʃn/ n conurbazione f

convalesce /kɒnvə'les/ vi essere in convalescenza

convalescent /kɒnvə'lesənt/ a convalescente. **~ home** n convalescenziario m

convector /kən'vektə(r)/ n **~ [heater]** convettore m

convene /kən'vi:n/ vt convocare ● vi riunirsi

convenience /kən'vi:nɪəns/ n convenienza f; **[public] ~** gabinetti mpl pubblici; **with all modern ~s** con tutti i comfort

convenient /kən'vi:nɪənt/ a comodo; **be ~ for sb** andar bene per qcno; **if it is ~ [for you]** se ti va bene. **~ly** adv comodamente; **~ly located** in una posizione comoda

convent /'kɒnvənt/ n convento m

convention /kən'venʃn/ n convenzione f; ⟨assembly⟩ convegno m. **~al** a convenzionale

converge /kən'vɜ:dʒ/ vi convergere

conversant /kən'vɜ:sənt/ a **~ with** pratico di

conversation /kɒnvə'seɪʃn/ n conversazione f. **~al** a di conversazione. **~alist** n conversatore, -trice mf

converse[1] /kən'vɜ:s/ vi conversare

converse[2] /'kɒnvɜ:s/ n inverso m. **~ly** adv viceversa

conversion /kən'vɜ:ʃn/ n conversione f

convert[1] /'kɒnvɜ:t/ n convertito, -a mf

convert[2] /kən'vɜ:t/ vt convertire (**into** in); sconsacrare ⟨church⟩. **~ible** /-əbl/ a convertibile ● n Auto macchina f decappottabile

convex /'kɒnveks/ a convesso

convey /kən'veɪ/ vt portare; trasmettere ⟨*idea, message*⟩. **~or belt** *n* nastro *m* trasportatore

convict¹ /'kɒnvɪkt/ *n* condannato, -a *mf*

convict² /kən'vɪkt/ *vt* giudicare colpevole. **~ion** /-ɪkʃn/ *n* condanna *f*; (*belief*) convinzione *f*; **previous ~ion** precedente *m* penale

convinc|e /kən'vɪns/ *vt* convincere. **~ing** *a* convincente

convivial /kən'vɪvɪəl/ *a* conviviale

convoluted /'kɒnvəlu:tɪd/ *a* contorto

convoy /'kɒnvɔɪ/ *n* convoglio *m*

convuls|e /kən'vʌls/ *vt* sconvolgere; **be ~ed with laughter** contorcersi dalle risa. **~ion** /-ʌlʃn/ *n* convulsione *f*

coo /ku:/ *vi* tubare

cook /kʊk/ *n* cuoco, -a *mf* ● *vt* cucinare; **is it ~ed?** è cotto?; **~ the books** *fam* truccare i libri contabili ● *vi* ⟨*food:*⟩ cuocere; ⟨*person:*⟩ cucinare. **~book** *n* libro *m* di cucina

cooker /'kʊkə(r)/ *n* cucina *f*; (*apple*) mela *f* da cuocere. **~y** *n* cucina *f*. **~y book** *n* libro *m* di cucina

cookie /'kʊkɪ/ *n Am* biscotto *m*

cool /ku:l/ *a* fresco; (*calm*) calmo; (*unfriendly*) freddo ● *n* fresco *m* ● *vt* rinfrescare ● *vi* rinfrescarsi. **~-box** *n* borsa *f* termica. **~ness** *n* freddezza *f*

coop /ku:p/ *n* stia *f* ● *vt* **~ up** rinchiudere

co-operat|e /kəʊ'ɒpəreɪt/ *vi* cooperare. **~'ion** /-'reɪʃn/ *n* cooperazione *f*

co-operative /kəʊ'ɒpərətɪv/ *a* cooperativo ● *n* cooperativa *f*

co-opt /kəʊ'ɒpt/ *vt* eleggere

co-ordinat|e /kəʊ'ɔ:dɪneɪt/ *vt* coordinare. **~ion** /-'neɪʃn/ *n* coordinazione *f*

cop /kɒp/ *n fam* poliziotto *m*

cope /kəʊp/ *vi fam* farcela; **can she ~ by herself?** ce la fa da sola?; **~ with** farcela con

copious /'kəʊpɪəs/ *a* abbondante

copper¹ /'kɒpə(r)/ *n* rame *m*; **~s** *pl* monete *fpl* da uno o due pence ● *attrib* di rame

copper² *n fam* poliziotto *m*

coppice /'kɒpɪs/ *n*, **copse** /kɒps/ *n* boschetto *m*

copulat|e /'kɒpjʊleɪt/ *vi* accoppiarsi. **~ion** /-'leɪʃn/ *n* copulazione *f*

copy /'kɒpɪ/ *n* copia *f* ● *vt* (*pt/pp* **-ied**) copiare

copy: ~right *n* diritti *mpl* d'autore. **~-writer** *n* copywriter *mf inv*

coral /'kɒrəl/ *n* corallo *m*

cord /kɔ:d/ *n* corda *f*; (*thinner*) cordon-

cino *m*; (*fabric*) velluto *m* a coste; **~s** *pl* pantaloni *mpl* di velluto a coste

cordial /'kɔ:dɪəl/ *a* cordiale ● *n* analcolico *m*

cordless /'kɔ:dlɪs/ *a* **~ phone** cordless *m inv*

cordon /'kɔ:dn/ *n* cordone *m* (*di persone*) ● **cordon off** *vt* mettere un cordone (*di persone*) intorno a

corduroy /'kɔ:dərɔɪ/ *n* velluto *m* a coste

core /kɔ:(r)/ *n* (*of apple, pear*) torsolo *m*; (*fig: of organization*) cuore *m*; (*of problem, theory*) nocciolo *m*

cork /kɔ:k/ *n* sughero *m*; (*for bottle*) turacciolo *m*. **~screw** *n* cavatappi *m inv*

corn¹ /kɔ:n/ *n* grano *m*; (*Am: maize*) granturco *m*

corn² *n Med* callo *m*

cornea /'kɔ:nɪə/ *n* cornea *f*

corned beef /kɔ:nd'bi:f/ *n* manzo *m* sotto sale

corner /'kɔ:nə(r)/ *n* angolo *m*; (*football*) calcio *m* d'angolo, corner *m inv* ● *vt fig* bloccare; accaparrarsi ⟨*market*⟩

cornet /'kɔ:nɪt/ *n Mus* cornetta *f*; (*for ice-cream*) cono *m*

corn: ~flour *n*, *Am* **~starch** *n* farina *f* di granturco

corny /'kɔ:nɪ/ *a* (**-ier, -est**) ⟨*fam: joke, film*⟩ scontato; ⟨*person*⟩ banale; (*sentimental*) sdolcinato

coronary /'kɒrənərɪ/ *a* coronario ● *n* **~** [**thrombosis**] trombosi *f* coronarica

coronation /kɒrə'neɪʃn/ *n* incoronazione *f*

coroner /'kɒrənə(r)/ *n* coroner *m inv* (*nel diritto britannico, ufficiale incaricato delle indagini su morti sospette*)

corporal¹ /'kɔ:pərəl/ *n Mil* caporale *m*

corporal² *a* corporale

corporate /'kɔ:pərət/ *a* ⟨*decision, policy, image*⟩ aziendale; **~ life** la vita in un'azienda

corporation /kɔ:pə'reɪʃn/ *n* ente *m*; (*of town*) consiglio *m* comunale

corps /kɔ:(r)/ *n* (*pl* **corps** /kɔ:z/) corpo *m*

corpse /kɔ:ps/ *n* cadavere *m*

corpulent /'kɔ:pjʊlənt/ *a* corpulento

corpuscle /'kɔ:pʌsl/ *n* globulo *m*

correct /kə'rekt/ *a* corretto; **be ~** ⟨*person:*⟩ aver ragione; **~!** esatto! ● *vt* correggere. **~ion** /-ekʃn/ *n* correzione *f*. **~ly** *adv* correttamente

correlation /kɒrə'leɪʃn/ *n* correlazione *f*

correspond /kɒrɪ'spɒnd/ *vi* corrispondere (**to** a); ⟨*two things:*⟩ corrispondere; (*write*) scriversi. **~ence** *n* corrispondenza *f*. **~ent** *n* corrispondente *mf*. **~ing** *a* corrispondente. **~ingly** *adv* in modo corrispondente

corridor /'kɒrɪdɔː(r)/ *n* corridoio *m*

corroborate /kə'rɒbəreɪt/ *vt* corroborare

corro|de /kə'rəʊd/ *vt* corrodere ● *vi* corrodersi. **~sion** /-'rəʊʒn/ *n* corrosione *f*

corrugated /'kɒrəgeɪtɪd/ *a* ondulato. **~ iron** *n* lamiera *f* ondulata

corrupt /kə'rʌpt/ *a* corrotto ● *vt* corrompere. **~ion** /-ʌpʃn/ *n* corruzione *f*

corset /'kɔːsɪt/ *n* & **-s** *pl* busto *m*

Corsica /'kɔːsɪkə/ *n* Corsica *f*. **~n** *a* & *n* corso, -a *mf*

cortège /kɔː'teɪʒ/ *n* [*funeral*] **~** corteo *m* funebre

cosh /kɒʃ/ *n* randello *m*

cosmetic /kɒz'metɪk/ *a* cosmetico ● *n* **~s** *pl* cosmetici *mpl*

cosmic /'kɒzmɪk/ *a* cosmico

cosmonaut /'kɒzmənɔːt/ *n* cosmonauta *mf*

cosmopolitan /kɒzmə'pɒlɪtən/ *a* cosmopolita

cosmos /'kɒzmɒs/ *n* cosmo *m*

cosset /'kɒsɪt/ *vt* coccolare

cost /kɒst/ *n* costo *m*; **~s** *pl Jur* spese *fpl* processuali; **at all ~s** a tutti i costi; **I learnt to my ~** ho imparato a mie spese ● *vt* (*pt/pp* **cost**) costare; **it ~ me £20** mi è costato 20 sterline ● *vt* (*pt/pp* **costed**) **~** [**out**] stabilire il prezzo di

costly /'kɒstlɪ/ *a* (**-ier, -iest**) costoso

cost: **~ of 'living** *n* costo *m* della vita. **~ price** *n* prezzo *m* di costo

costume /'kɒstjuːm/ *n* costume *m*. **~ jewellery** *n* bigiotteria *f*

cosy /'kəʊzɪ/ *a* (**-ier, -iest**) ⟨*pub, chat*⟩ intimo; **it's nice and ~ in here** si sta bene qui

cot /kɒt/ *n* lettino *m*; (*Am: camp-bed*) branda *f*

cottage /'kɒtɪdʒ/ *n* casetta *f*. **~ 'cheese** *n* fiocchi *mpl* di latte

cotton /'kɒtn/ *n* cotone *m* ● *attrib* di cotone ● **cotton on** *vi fam* capire

cotton 'wool *n* cotone *m* idrofilo

couch /kaʊtʃ/ *n* divano *m*. **~ potato** *n* pantofolaio, -a *mf*

couchette /kuː'ʃet/ *n* cuccetta *f*

cough /kɒf/ *n* tosse *f* ● *vi* tossire. **cough up** *vt/i* sputare; (*fam: pay*) sborsare

'cough mixture *n* sciroppo *m* per la tosse

could /kʊd/, *atono* /kəd/ *v aux* (*see also*

can²*) **~ I have a glass of water? potrei avere un bicchier d'acqua?; **I ~n't do it even if I wanted to** non potrei farlo nemmeno se lo volessi; **I ~n't care less** non potrebbe importarmene di meno; **he ~n't have done it without help** non avrebbe potuto farlo senza aiuto; **you ~ have phoned** avresti potuto telefonare

council /'kaʊnsl/ *n* consiglio *m*. **~ house** *n* casa *f* popolare

councillor /'kaʊnsələ(r)/ *n* consigliere, -a *mf*

'council tax *n* imposta *f* locale sugli immobili

counsel /'kaʊnsl/ *n* consigli *mpl*; *Jur* avvocato *m* ● *vt* (*pt/pp* **counselled**) consigliare a ⟨*person*⟩. **~lor** *n* consigliere, -a *mf*

count¹ /kaʊnt/ *n* (*nobleman*) conte *m*

count² *n* conto *m*; **keep ~** tenere il conto ● *vt/i* contare. **count on** *vt* contare su

countdown /'kaʊntdaʊn/ *n* conto *m* alla rovescia

countenance /'kaʊntənəns/ *n* espressione *f* ● *vt* approvare

counter¹ /'kaʊntə(r)/ *n* banco *m*; (*in games*) gettone *m*

counter² *adv* **~ to** contro, in contrasto a; **go ~ to sth** andare contro qcsa ● *vt/i* opporre ⟨*measure, effect*⟩; parare ⟨*blow*⟩

counter'act *vt* neutralizzare

'counter-attack *n* contrattacco *m*

counter-'espionage *n* controspionaggio *m*

'counterfeit /-fɪt/ *a* contraffatto ● *n* contraffazione *f* ● *vt* contraffare

'counterfoil *n* matrice *f*

'counterpart *n* equivalente *mf*

counter-pro'ductive *a* controproduttivo

'countersign *vt* controfirmare

countess /'kaʊntɪs/ *n* contessa *f*

countless /'kaʊntlɪs/ *a* innumerevole

country /'kʌntrɪ/ *n* nazione *f*, paese *m*; (*native land*) patria *f*; (*countryside*) campagna *f*; **in the ~** in campagna; **go to the ~** andare in campagna; *Pol* indire le elezioni politiche. **~man** *n* uomo *m* di campagna; (*fellow ~man*) compatriota *m*. **~side** *n* campagna *f*

county /'kaʊntɪ/ *n* contea *f* (*unità amministrativa britannica*)

coup /kuː/ *n Pol* colpo *m* di stato

couple /'kʌpl/ *n* coppia *f*; **a ~ of** un paio di

coupon /'kuːpɒn/ *n* tagliando *m*; (*for discount*) buono *m* sconto

courage /'kʌrɪdʒ/ n coraggio m. **~ous** /kə'reɪdʒəs/ a coraggioso

courgette /kʊə'ʒet/ n zucchino m

courier /'kʊrɪə(r)/ n corriere m; (for tourists) guida f

course /kɔːs/ n Sch corso m; Naut rotta f; Culin portata f, (for golf) campo m; **~ of treatment** Med serie f inv di cure; **of ~** naturalmente; **in the ~ of** durante; **in due ~** a tempo debito

court /kɔːt/ n tribunale m; Sport campo m; **take sb to ~** citare qcno in giudizio ●vt fare la corte a ⟨woman⟩; sfidare ⟨danger⟩; **~ing couples** coppiette fpl

courteous /'kɜːtɪəs/ a cortese

courtesy /'kɜːtəsɪ/ n cortesia f

court: ~ 'martial n (pl **~s martial**) corte f marziale ●**~-martial** vt (pt **~-martialled**) portare davanti alla corte marziale; **~yard** n cortile m

cousin /'kʌzn/ n cugino, -a mf

cove /kəʊv/ n insenatura f

cover /'kʌvə(r)/ n copertura f; (of cushion, to protect sth) fodera f, (of book, magazine) copertina f; **take ~** mettersi al riparo; **under separate ~** a parte ●vt coprire; foderare ⟨cushion⟩; Journ fare un servizio su. **cover up** vt coprire; fig soffocare ⟨scandal⟩

coverage /'kʌvərɪdʒ/ n Journ **it got a lot of ~** i media gli hanno dedicato molto spazio

cover: ~ charge n coperto m. **~ing** n copertura f; (for floor) rivestimento m; **~ing letter** lettera f d'accompagnamento. **~-up** n messa f a tacere

covet /'kʌvɪt/ vt bramare

cow /kaʊ/ n vacca f, mucca f

coward /'kaʊəd/ n vigliacco, -a mf. **~ice** /-ɪs/ n vigliaccheria f. **~ly** a da vigliacco

'cowboy n cowboy m inv; buffone m fam

cower /'kaʊə(r)/ vi acquattarsi

'cowshed n stalla f

cox /kɒks/ n, **coxswain** /'kɒksn/ n timoniere, -a mf

coy /kɔɪ/ a falsamente timido; (flirtatiously) civettuolo; **be ~ about sth** essere evasivo su qcsa

crab /kræb/ n granchio m

crack /kræk/ n (in wall) crepa f, (in china, glass, bone) incrinatura f; (noise) scoppio m; (fam: joke) battuta f; **have a ~** (try) fare un tentativo ●a (fam: best) di prim'ordine ●vt incrinare ⟨china, glass⟩; schiacciare ⟨nut⟩; decifrare ⟨code⟩; fam risolvere ⟨problem⟩; **~ a joke** fam fare una battuta ●vi ⟨china,

glass:⟩ incrinarsi; ⟨whip:⟩ schioccare.

crack down vi fam prendere seri provvedimenti. **crack down on** vt fam prendere seri provvedimenti contro

cracked /krækt/ a ⟨plaster⟩ crepato; ⟨skin⟩ screpolato; ⟨rib⟩ incrinato; (fam: crazy) svitato

cracker /'krækə(r)/ n (biscuit) cracker m inv; (firework) petardo m; **[Christmas] ~** tubo m di cartone colorato contenente una sorpresa

crackers /'krækəz/ a fam matto

crackle /'krækl/ vi crepitare

cradle /'kreɪdl/ n culla f

craft¹ /krɑːft/ n inv (boat) imbarcazione f

craft² n mestiere m; (technique) arte f. **~sman** n artigiano m

crafty /'krɑːftɪ/ a (**-ier, -iest**) astuto

crag /kræg/ n rupe f. **~gy** a scosceso; ⟨face⟩ dai lineamenti marcati

cram /kræm/ v (pt/pp crammed) ●vt stipare (**into** in) ●vi (for exams) sgobbare

cramp /kræmp/ n crampo m. **~ed** a ⟨room⟩ stretto; ⟨handwriting⟩ appiccicato

crampon /'kræmpən/ n rampone m

cranberry /'krænbərɪ/ n Culin mirtillo m rosso

crane /kreɪn/ n (at docks, bird) gru f inv ●vt **~ one's neck** allungare il collo

crank¹ /kræŋk/ n tipo, -a mf strampalato, -a

crank² n Techn manovella f. **~shaft** n albero m a gomiti

cranky /'kræŋkɪ/ a strampalato; (Am: irritable) irritabile

cranny /'krænɪ/ n fessura f

crash /kræʃ/ n (noise) fragore m; Auto, Aeron incidente m; Comm crollo m ●vi schiantarsi (**into** contro); ⟨plane:⟩ precipitare ●vt schiantare ⟨car⟩

crash: ~ course n corso m intensivo. **~-helmet** n casco m. **~-landing** n atterraggio m di fortuna

crate /kreɪt/ n (for packing) cassa f

crater /'kreɪtə(r)/ n cratere m

crav|e /kreɪv/ vt morire dalla voglia di. **~ing** n voglia f smodata

crawl /krɔːl/ n (swimming) stile m libero; **do the ~** nuotare a stile libero; **at a ~** a passo di lumaca ●vi andare carponi; **~ with** brulicare di. **~er lane** n Auto corsia f riservata al traffico lento

crayon /'kreɪən/ n pastello m a cera; (pencil) matita f colorata

craze /kreɪz/ n mania f

crazy /'kreızı/ a (**-ier, -iest**) matto; **be ~ about** andar matto per

creak /kri:k/ n scricchiolio m ● vi scricchiolare

cream /kri:m/ n crema f; (fresh) panna f ● a (colour) [bianco] panna inv ● vt Culin sbattere. **~ 'cheese** n formaggio m cremoso. **~y** a cremoso

crease /kri:s/ n piega f ● vt stropicciare ● vi stropicciarsi. **~-resistant** a che non si stropiccia

creat|e /kri:'eıt/ vt creare. **~ion** /-'eıʃn/ n creazione f. **~ive** /-tıv/ a creativo. **~or** n creatore, -trice mf

creature /'kri:tʃə(r)/ n creatura f

crèche /kreʃ/ n asilo m nido

credentials /krı'denʃlz/ npl credenziali fpl

credibility /kredə'bılətı/ n credibilità f

credible /'kredəbl/ a credibile

credit /'kredıt/ n credito m; (honour) merito m; **take the ~ for** prendersi il merito di ● vt (pt/pp credited) accreditare; **~ sb with sth** Comm accreditare qcsa a qcno; fig attribuire qcsa a qcno. **~able** /-əbl/ a lodevole

credit: ~ card n carta f di credito. **~or** n creditore, -trice mf

creed /kri:d/ n credo m inv

creek /kri:k/ n insenatura f; (Am: stream) torrente m

creep /kri:p/ vi (pt/pp crept) muoversi furtivamente ● n fam tipo m viscido. **~er** n pianta f rampicante. **~y** a che fa venire i brividi

cremat|e /krı'meıt/ vt cremare. **~ion** /-eıʃn/ n cremazione f

crematorium /kremə'tɔ:rıəm/ n crematorio m

crêpe /kreıp/ n (fabric) crespo m

crept /krept/ see **creep**

crescent /'kresənt/ n mezzaluna f

cress /kres/ n crescione m

crest /krest/ n cresta f; (coat of arms) cimiero m

Crete /kri:t/ n Creta f

crevasse /krı'væs/ n crepaccio m

crevice /'krevıs/ n crepa f

crew /kru:/ n equipaggio m; (gang) équipe f inv. **~ cut** n capelli mpl a spazzola. **~ neck** n girocollo m

crib¹ /krıb/ n (for baby) culla f

crib² vt/i (pt/pp cribbed) fam copiare

crick /krık/ n **~ in the neck** torcicollo m

cricket¹ /'krıkıt/ n (insect) grillo m

cricket² n cricket m. **~er** n giocatore m di cricket

crime /kraım/ n crimine m; (criminality) criminalità f

criminal /'krımınl/ a criminale; (law, court) penale ● n criminale mf

crimson /'krımzn/ a cremisi inv

cringe /krındʒ/ vi (cower) acquattarsi; (at bad joke etc) fare una smorfia

crinkle /'krıŋkl/ vt spiegazzare ● vi spiegazzarsi

cripple /'krıpl/ n storpio, -a mf ● vt storpiare; fig danneggiare. **~d** a (person) storpio; (ship) danneggiato

crisis /'kraısıs/ n (pl -ses /-si:z/) crisi f inv

crisp /krısp/ a croccante; (air) frizzante; (style) incisivo. **~bread** n crostini mpl di pane. **~s** npl patatine fpl

criterion /kraı'tıərıən/ n (pl -ria /-rıə/) criterio m

critic /'krıtık/ n critico, -a mf. **~al** a critico. **~ally** adv in modo critico; **~ally ill** gravemente malato

criticism /'krıtısızm/ n critica f; **he doesn't like ~** non ama le critiche

criticize /'krıtısaız/ vt criticare

croak /krəʊk/ vi gracchiare; (frog:) gracidare

Croatia /krəʊ'eıʃə/ n Croazia f

crochet /'krəʊʃeı/ n lavoro m all'uncinetto ● vt fare all'uncinetto. **~-hook** n uncinetto m

crock /krɒk/ n fam **old ~** (person) rudere m; (car) macinino m

crockery /'krɒkərı/ n terrecotte fpl

crocodile /'krɒkədaıl/ n coccodrillo m. **~ tears** lacrime fpl di coccodrillo

crocus /'krəʊkəs/ n (pl -es) croco m

crook /krʊk/ n (fam: criminal) truffatore, -trice mf

crooked /'krʊkıd/ a storto; (limb) storpiato; (fam: dishonest) disonesto

crop /krɒp/ n raccolto m; fig quantità f inv ● v (pt/pp cropped) ● vt (cut) tagliare. **crop up** vi fam presentarsi

croquet /'krəʊkeı/ n croquet m

croquette /krəʊ'ket/ n crocchetta f

cross /krɒs/ a (annoyed) arrabbiato; **talk at ~ purposes** fraintendersi ● n croce f; Bot, Zool incrocio m ● vt sbarrare (cheque); incrociare (road, animals); **~ oneself** farsi il segno della croce; **~ one's arms** incrociare le braccia; **~ one's legs** accavallare le gambe; **keep one's fingers ~ed for sb** tenere le dita incrociate per qcno; **it ~ed my mind** mi è venuto in mente ● vi (go across) attraversare; (lines:) incrociarsi. **cross out** vt depennare

cross: ~bar n (*of goal*) traversa f; (*on bicycle*) canna f. **~-'country** n Sport corsa f campestre. **~-ex'amine** vt sottoporre a controinterrogatorio. **~-exami'nation** n controinterrogatorio m. **~-'eyed** a strabico. **~fire** n (*for pedestrians*) passaggio m pedonale; (*sea journey*) traversata f. **~-'reference** n rimando m. **~roads** n incrocio m. **~-'section** n sezione f; (*of community*) campione m. **~wise** adv in diagonale. **~word** n **~word** [**puzzle**] parole fpl crociate

crotchet /'krɒtʃɪt/ n Mus semiminima f
crotchety /'krɒtʃɪtɪ/ a irritabile
crouch /krautʃ/ vi accovacciarsi
crow /krəʊ/ n corvo m; **as the ~ flies** in linea d'aria ● vi cantare. **~bar** n piede m di porco
crowd /kraʊd/ n folla f ● vt affollare ● vi affollarsi. **~ed** /'kraʊdɪd/ a affollato
crown /kraʊn/ n corona f ● vt incoronare; incapsulare ⟨tooth⟩
crucial /'kruːʃl/ a cruciale
crucifix /'kruːsɪfɪks/ n crocifisso m
crucif|ixion /kruːsɪ'fɪkʃn/ n crocifissione f. **~y** /'kruːsɪfaɪ/ vt (pt/pp **-ied**) crocifiggere
crude /kruːd/ a ⟨oil⟩ greggio; ⟨language⟩ crudo; ⟨person⟩ rozzo
cruel /'kruːəl/ a (**crueller, cruellest**) crudele (**to** verso). **~ly** adv con crudeltà. **~ty** n crudeltà f
cruis|e /kruːz/ n crociera f ● vi fare una crociera; ⟨car:⟩ andare a velocità di crociera. **~er** n Mil incrociatore m; (*motor boat*) motoscafo m. **~ing speed** n velocità m inv di crociera
crumb /krʌm/ n briciola f
crumb|le /'krʌmbl/ vt sbriciolare ● vi sbriciolarsi; ⟨building, society:⟩ sgretolarsi. **~ly** a friabile
crumple /'krʌmpl/ vt spiegazzare ● vi spiegazzarsi
crunch /krʌntʃ/ n fam **when it comes to the ~** quando si viene al dunque ● vt sgranocchiare ● vi ⟨snow:⟩ scricchiolare
crusade /kruː'seɪd/ n crociata f. **~r** n crociato m
crush /krʌʃ/ n (*crowd*) calca f; **have a ~ on sb** essersi preso una cotta per qcno ● vt schiacciare; sgualcire ⟨clothes⟩
crust /krʌst/ n crosta f
crutch /krʌtʃ/ n gruccia f; Anat inforcatura f

crux /krʌks/ n fig punto m cruciale
cry /kraɪ/ n grido m; **have a ~** farsi un pianto; **a far ~ from** fig tutta un'altra cosa rispetto a ● vi (pt/pp **cried**) (*weep*) piangere; (*call*) gridare
crypt /krɪpt/ n cripta f. **~ic** a criptico
crystal /'krɪstl/ n cristallo m; (*glassware*) cristalli mpl. **~lize** vi (*become clear*) concretizzarsi
cub /kʌb/ n (*animal*) cucciolo m; **C~** [**Scout**] lupetto m
Cuba /'kjuːbə/ n Cuba f
cubby-hole /'kʌbɪ-/ n (*compartment*) scomparto m; (*room*) ripostiglio m
cub|e /kjuːb/ n cubo m. **~ic** a cubico
cubicle /'kjuːbɪkl/ n cabina f
cuckoo /'kʊkuː/ n cuculo m. **~ clock** n orologio m a cucù
cucumber /'kjuːkʌmbə(r)/ n cetriolo m
cuddl|e /'kʌdl/ vt coccolare ● vi **~e up to** starsene accoccolato insieme a ● n **have a ~e** ⟨child:⟩ farsi coccolare; ⟨lovers:⟩ abbracciarsi. **~y** a tenerone; (*wanting cuddles*) coccolone. **~y 'toy** n peluche m inv
cudgel /'kʌdʒl/ n randello m
cue[1] /kjuː/ n segnale m; Theat battuta f d'entrata
cue[2] n (*in billiards*) stecca f. **~ ball** n pallino m
cuff /kʌf/ n polsino m; (Am: turn-up) orlo m; (*blow*) scapaccione m; **off the ~** improvvisando ● vt dare una pacca a. **~-link** n gemello m
cul-de-sac /'kʌldəsæk/ n vicolo m cieco
culinary /'kʌlɪnərɪ/ a culinario
cull /kʌl/ vt scegliere ⟨flowers⟩; (*kill*) selezionare e uccidere
culminat|e /'kʌlmɪneɪt/ vi culminare. **~ion** /-'neɪʃn/ n culmine m
culottes /kjuː'lɒts/ npl gonna fsg pantalone
culprit /'kʌlprɪt/ n colpevole mf
cult /kʌlt/ n culto m
cultivate /'kʌltɪveɪt/ vt coltivare; fig coltivarsi ⟨person⟩
cultural /'kʌltʃərəl/ a culturale
culture /'kʌltʃə(r)/ n cultura f. **~d** a colto
cumbersome /'kʌmbəsəm/ a ingombrante
cumulative /'kjuːmjʊlətɪv/ a cumulativo
cunning /'kʌnɪŋ/ a astuto ● n astuzia f
cup /kʌp/ n tazza f; (*prize, of bra*) coppa f
cupboard /'kʌbəd/ n armadio m. **~ love** n fam amore m interessato
Cup 'Final n finale f di coppa

Cupid /'kju:pɪd/ n Cupido m
curable /'kjʊərəbl/ a curabile
curate /'kjʊərət/ n curato m
curator /kjʊə'reɪtə(r)/ n direttore, -trice mf (di museo)
curb /kɜ:b/ vt tenere a freno
curdle /'kɜ:dl/ vi coagularsi
cure /kjʊə(r)/ n cura f ● vt curare; (salt) mettere sotto sale; (smoke) affumicare
curfew /'kɜ:fju:/ n coprifuoco m
curio /'kjʊərɪəʊ/ n curiosità f inv
curiosity /kjʊərɪ'ɒsətɪ/ n curiosità f
curious /'kjʊərɪəs/ a curioso. **~ly** adv curiosamente
curl /kɜ:l/ n ricciolo m ● vt arricciare ● vi arricciarsi. **curl up** vi raggomitolarsi
curler /'kɜ:lə(r)/ n bigodino m
curly /'kɜ:lɪ/ a (-ier, -iest) riccio
currant /'kʌrənt/ n (dried) uvetta f
currency /'kʌrənsɪ/ n valuta f; (of word) ricorrenza f; **foreign ~** valuta f estera
current /'kʌrənt/ a corrente ● n corrente f. **~ affairs** or **events** npl attualità fsg. **~ly** adv attualmente
curriculum /kə'rɪkjʊləm/ n programma m di studi. **~ vitae** /'vi:taɪ/ n curriculum vitae m inv
curry /'kʌrɪ/ n curry m inv; (meal) piatto m cucinato nel curry ● vt (pt/pp -ied) **~ favour with sb** cercare d'ingraziarsi qcno
curse /kɜ:s/ n maledizione f; (oath) imprecazione f ● vt maledire ● vi imprecare
cursor /'kɜ:sə(r)/ n cursore m
cursory /'kɜ:sərɪ/ a sbrigativo
curt /kɜ:t/ a brusco
curtail /kɜ:'teɪl/ vt ridurre
curtain /'kɜ:tn/ n tenda f; Theat sipario m
curtsy /'kɜ:tsɪ/ n inchino m ● vi (pt/pp -ied) fare l'inchino
curve /kɜ:v/ n curva f ● vi curvare; **~ to the right/left** curvare a destra/ sinistra. **~d** a curvo
cushion /'kʊʃn/ n cuscino m ● vt attutire; (protect) proteggere
cushy /'kʊʃɪ/ a (-ier, -iest) fam facile
custard /'kʌstəd/ n (liquid) crema f pasticciera
custodian /kʌ'stəʊdɪən/ n custode mf
custody /'kʌstədɪ/ n (of child) custodia f; (imprisoning) detenzione f preventiva
custom /'kʌstəm/ n usanza f; Jur consuetudine f; Comm clientela f. **~ary** a

(habitual) abituale; **it's ~ to...** è consuetudine.... **~er** n cliente mf
customs /'kʌstəmz/ npl dogana f. **~ officer** n doganiere m
cut /kʌt/ n (with knife etc, of clothes) taglio m; (reduction) riduzione f; (in public spending) taglio m ● vt/i (pt/pp **cut**, pres p **cutting**) tagliare; (reduce) ridurre; **~ one's finger** tagliarsi il dito; **~ sb's hair** tagliare i capelli a qcno ● vi (with cards) alzare. **cut back** vt tagliare ⟨hair⟩; potare ⟨hedge⟩; (reduce) ridurre. **cut down** vt abbattere ⟨tree⟩; (reduce) ridurre. **cut off** vt tagliar via; (disconnect) interrompere; fig isolare; **I was ~ off** Teleph la linea è caduta. **cut out** vt ritagliare; (delete) eliminare; **be ~ out for** fam essere tagliato per; **~ it out!** fam dacci un taglio!. **cut up** vt (slice) tagliare a pezzi
'**cut-back** n riduzione f; (in government spending) taglio m
cute /kju:t/ a fam (in appearance) carino; (clever) acuto
cuticle /'kju:tɪkl/ n cuticola f
cutlery /'kʌtlərɪ/ n posate fpl
cutlet /'kʌtlɪt/ n cotoletta f
'**cut-price** a a prezzo ridotto; ⟨shop⟩ che fa prezzi ridotti
'**cut-throat** a spietato
cutting /'kʌtɪŋ/ a ⟨remark⟩ tagliente ● n (from newspaper) ritaglio m; (of plant) talea f
CV n abbr curriculum vitae
cyanide /'saɪənaɪd/ n cianuro m
cybernetics /saɪbə'netɪks/ n cibernetica f
cycl|e /'saɪkl/ n ciclo m; (bicycle) bicicletta f, bici f inv fam ● vi andare in bicicletta. **~ing** n ciclismo m. **~ist** n ciclista mf
cyclone /'saɪkləʊn/ n ciclone m
cylind|er /'sɪlɪndə(r)/ n cilindro m. **~rical** /-'lɪndrɪkl/ a cilindrico
cymbals /'sɪmblz/ npl Mus piatti mpl
cynic /'sɪnɪk/ n cinico, -a mf. **~al** a cinico. **~ism** /-sɪzm/ n cinismo m
cypress /'saɪprəs/ n cipresso m
Cypriot /'sɪprɪət/ n cipriota mf
Cyprus /'saɪprəs/ n Cipro m
cyst /sɪst/ n ciste f. **~itis** /-'staɪtɪs/ n cistite f
Czech /tʃek/ a ceco; **~ Republic** Repubblica f Ceca ● n ceco, -a mf
Czechoslovak /tʃekə'sləʊvæk/ a cecoslovacco. **~ia** /-'vækɪə/ n Cecoslovacchia f

Dd

dab /dæb/ *n* colpetto *m*; **a ~ of** un pochino di ● *vt* (*pt*/*pp* **dabbed**) toccare leggermente ⟨*eyes*⟩. **dab on** *vt* mettere un po' di ⟨*paint etc*⟩

dabble /'dæbl/ *vi* ~ **in sth** *fig* occuparsi di qcsa a tempo perso

dachshund /'dækshʊnd/ *n* bassotto *m*

dad[dy] /'dæd[ɪ]/ *n fam* papà *m inv*, babbo *m*

daddy-'long-legs *n* zanzarone *m* [dei boschi]; (*Am: spider*) ragno *m*

daffodil /'dæfədɪl/ *n* giunchiglia *f*

daft /dɑːft/ *a* sciocco

dagger /'dægə(r)/ *n* stiletto *m*

dahlia /'deɪlɪə/ *n* dalia *f*

daily /'deɪlɪ/ *a* giornaliero ● *adv* giornalmente ● *n* (*newspaper*) quotidiano *m*; (*fam: cleaner*) donna *f* delle pulizie

dairy /'deərɪ/ *n* caseificio *m*; (*shop*) latteria *f*. **~ cow** *n* mucca *f* da latte. **~ products** *npl* latticini *mpl*

dais /'deɪɪs/ *n* pedana *f*

daisy /'deɪzɪ/ *n* margheritina *f*; (*larger*) margherita *f*

dale /deɪl/ *n liter* valle *f*

dam /dæm/ *n* diga *f* ● *vt* (*pt*/*pp* **dammed**) costruire una diga su

damag|e /'dæmɪdʒ/ *n* danno *m* (**to** a); **~es** *pl Jur* risarcimento *msg* ● *vt* danneggiare; *fig* nuocere a. **~ing** *a* dannoso

dame /deɪm/ *n liter* dama *f*; *Am sl* donna *f*

damn /dæm/ *a fam* maledetto ● *adv* ⟨*lucky, late*⟩ maledettamente ● *n* **I don't care** *or* **give a ~** *fam* non me ne frega un accidente ● *vt* dannare. **~ation** /-'neɪʃn/ *n* dannazione *f* ● *int fam* accidenti!

damp /dæmp/ *a* umido ● *n* umidità *f* ● *vt* = **dampen**

damp|en /'dæmpən/ *vt* inumidire; *fig* raffreddare ⟨*enthusiasm*⟩. **~ness** *n* umidità *f*

dance /dɑːns/ *n* ballo *m* ● *vt*/*i* ballare. **~-hall** *n* sala *f* da ballo. **~ music** *n* musica *f* da ballo

dancer /'dɑːnsə(r)/ *n* ballerino, -a *mf*

dandelion /'dændɪlaɪən/ *n* dente *m* di leone

dandruff /'dændrʌf/ *n* forfora *f*

Dane /deɪn/ *n* danese *mf*; **Great ~** danese *m*

danger /'deɪndʒə(r)/ *n* pericolo *m*; **in/out of ~** in/fuori pericolo. **~ous** /-rəs/ *a* pericoloso. **~ously** *adv* pericolosamente; **~ously ill** in pericolo di vita

dangle /'dæŋgl/ *vi* penzolare ● *vt* far penzolare

Danish /'deɪnɪʃ/ *a & n* danese. **~ 'pastry** *n* dolce *m* a base di pasta sfoglia contenente pasta di mandorle, mele ecc

dank /dæŋk/ *a* umido e freddo

Danube /'dænjuːb/ *n* Danubio *m*

dare /deə(r)/ *vt*/*i* osare; (*challenge*) sfidare (**to** a); **~ [to] do sth** osare fare qcsa; **I ~ say!** molto probabilmente! ● *n* sfida *f*. **~devil** *n* spericolato, -a *mf*

daring /'deərɪŋ/ *a* audace ● *n* audacia *f*

dark /dɑːk/ *a* buio; **~ blue/brown** blu/marrone scuro; **it's getting ~** sta cominciando a fare buio; **~ horse** *fig* (*in race, contest*) vincitore *m* imprevisto; (*not much known about*) misterioso *m*; **keep sth ~** *fig* tenere qcsa nascosto ● *n* **after ~** col buio; **in the ~** al buio; **keep sb in the ~** *fig* tenere qcno all'oscuro

dark|en /'dɑːkn/ *vt* oscurare ● *vi* oscurarsi. **~ness** *n* buio *m*

'dark-room *n* camera *f* oscura

darling /'dɑːlɪŋ/ *a* adorabile; **my ~ Joan** carissima Joan ● *n* tesoro *m*

darn /dɑːn/ *vt* rammendare. **~ing-needle** *n* ago *m* da rammendo

dart /dɑːt/ *n* dardo *m*; (*in sewing*) pince *f inv*; **~s** *sg* (*game*) freccette *fpl* ● *vi* lanciarsi

dartboard /'dɑːtbɔːd/ *n* bersaglio *m* [per freccette]

dash /dæʃ/ *n Typ* trattino *m*; (*in Morse*) linea *f*; **a ~ of milk** un goccio di latte; **make a ~ for** lanciarsi verso ● *vi* **I must ~** devo scappare ● *vt* far svanire ⟨*hopes*⟩. **dash off** *vi* scappar via ● *vt* (*write quickly*) buttare giù. **dash out** *vi* uscire di corsa

'**dashboard** *n* cruscotto *m*

dashing /'dæʃɪŋ/ *a* (*bold*) ardito; (*in appearance*) affascinante

data /'deɪtə/ *npl & sg* dati *mpl*. **~base** *n* base [di] dati *f*, database *m inv*. **~comms** /'kɒmz/ *n* telematica *f*. **~ processing** *n* elaborazione *f* [di] dati

date[1] /deɪt/ *n* (*fruit*) dattero *m*

date[2] *n* data *f*; (*meeting*) appuntamento *m*; **to ~** fino ad oggi; **out of ~** (*not fashionable*) fuori moda; (*expired*) scaduto; (*information*) non aggiornato; **make a ~ with sb** dare un appuntamento a qcno; **be up to ~** essere aggiornato ● *vt/i* datare; (*go out with*) uscire con. **date back to** *vi* risalire a

dated /'deɪtɪd/ *a* fuori moda; (*language*) antiquato

'**date-line** *n* linea *f* [del cambiamento] di data

daub /dɔːb/ *vt* imbrattare (*walls*)

daughter /'dɔːtə(r)/ *n* figlia *f*. **~-in-law** *n* (*pl* **~s-in-law**) nuora *f*

daunt /dɔːnt/ *vt* scoraggiare; **nothing ~ed** per niente scoraggiato. **~less** *a* intrepido

dawdle /'dɔːdl/ *vi* bighellonare; (*over work*) cincischiarsi

dawn /dɔːn/ *n* alba *f*; **at ~** all'alba ● *vi* albeggiare; **it ~ed on me** *fig* mi è apparso chiaro

day /deɪ/ *n* giorno *m*; (*whole day*) giornata *f*; (*period*) epoca *f*; **these ~s** oggigiorno; **in those ~s** a quei tempi; **it's had its ~** *fam* ha fatto il suo tempo

day: ~break *n* **at ~break** allo spuntar del giorno. **~-dream** *n* sogno *m* ad occhi aperti ● *vi* sognare ad occhi aperti. **~light** *n* luce *f* del giorno. **~ re'turn** *n* (*ticket*) biglietto *m* di andata e ritorno con validità giornaliera. **~time** *n* giorno *m*; **in the ~time** di giorno

daze /deɪz/ *n* **in a ~** stordito; *fig* sbalordito. **~d** *a* stordito; *fig* sbalordito

dazzle /'dæzl/ *vt* abbagliare

deacon /'diːkn/ *n* diacono *m*

dead /ded/ *a* morto; (*numb*) intorpidito; **~ body** morto *m*; **~ centre** pieno centro *m* ● *adv* **~ tired** stanco morto; **~ slow/easy** lentissimo/facilissimo; **you're ~ right** hai perfettamente ragione; **stop ~** fermarsi di colpo; **be ~ on time** essere in perfetto orario ● *n* **the ~** *pl* i morti; **in the ~ of night** nel cuore della notte

deaden /'dedn/ *vt* attutire (*sound*); calmare (*pain*)

dead: ~ 'end *n* vicolo *m* cieco. **~ 'heat** *n* **it was a ~ heat** è finita a pari merito. **~line** *n* scadenza *f*. **~lock** *n* reach **~lock** *fig* giungere a un punto morto

deadly /'dedlɪ/ *a* (**-ier, -iest**) mortale; (*fam: dreary*) barboso; **~ sins** peccati *mpl* capitali

deadpan /'dedpæn/ *a* impassibile; (*humour*) all'inglese

deaf /def/ *a* sordo; **~ and dumb** sordomuto. **~-aid** *n* apparecchio *m* acustico

deaf|en /'defn/ *vt* assordare; (*permanently*) render sordo. **~ening** *a* assordante. **~ness** *n* sordità *f*

deal /diːl/ *n* (*agreement*) patto *m*; (*in business*) accordo *m*; **whose ~?** (*in cards*) a chi tocca dare le carte?; **a good or great ~** molto; **get a raw ~** *fam* ricevere un trattamento ingiusto ● *vt* (*pt/pp* **dealt** /delt/) (*in cards*) dare; **~ sb a blow** dare un colpo a qcno. **deal in** *vt* trattare in. **deal out** *vt* (*hand out*) distribuire. **deal with** *vt* (*handle*) occuparsi di; trattare con (*company*); (*be about*) trattare di; **that's been ~t with** è stato risolto

deal|er /'diːlə(r)/ *n* commerciante *mf*; (*in drugs*) spacciatore, -trice *mf*. **~ings** *npl* **have ~ings with** avere a che fare con

dean /diːn/ *n* decano *m*; *Univ* ≈ preside *mf* di facoltà

dear /dɪə(r)/ *a* caro; (*in letter*) Caro; (*formal*) Gentile ● *n* caro, -a *mf* ● *int* oh **~!** Dio mio!. **~ly** *adv* (*love*) profondamente; (*pay*) profumatamente

dearth /dɜːθ/ *n* penuria *f*

death /deθ/ *n* morte *f*. **~ certificate** *n* certificato *m* di morte. **~ duty** *n* tassa *f* di successione

deathly /'deθlɪ/ *a* **~ silence** silenzio *m* di tomba ● *adv* **~ pale** di un pallore cadaverico

death: ~ penalty *n* pena *f* di morte. **~-trap** *n* trappola *f* mortale

debar /dɪ'bɑː(r)/ *vt* (*pt/pp* **debarred**) escludere

debase /dɪ'beɪs/ *vt* degradare

debatable /dɪ'beɪtəbl/ *a* discutibile

debate /dɪ'beɪt/ *n* dibattito *m* ● *vt* discutere; (*in formal debate*) dibattere ● *vi* **~ whether to...** considerare se...

debauchery /dɪ'bɔːtʃərɪ/ *n* dissolutezza *f*

debility /dɪ'bɪlɪtɪ/ *n* debilitazione *f*

debit /'debɪt/ n debito m ● vt (pt/pp **debited**) Comm addebitare ⟨sum⟩

debris /'debri:/ n macerie fpl

debt /det/ n debito m; **be in ~** avere dei debiti. **~or** n debitore, -trice mf

début /'deɪbu:/ n debutto m

decade /'dekeɪd/ n decennio m

decaden|ce /'dekədəns/ n decadenza f. **~t** a decadente

decaffeinated /di:'kæfɪneɪtɪd/ a decaffeinato

decant /dɪ'kænt/ vt travasare. **~er** n caraffa f (di cristallo)

decapitate /dɪ'kæpɪteɪt/ vt decapitare

decay /dɪ'keɪ/ n (also fig) decadenza f; (rot) decomposizione f; (of tooth) carie f inv ● vi imputridire; (rot) decomporsi; ⟨tooth:⟩ cariarsi

deceased /dɪ'si:st/ a defunto ● n **the ~d** il defunto; la defunta

deceit /dɪ'si:t/ n inganno m. **~ful** a falso

deceive /dɪ'si:v/ vt ingannare

December /dɪ'sembə(r)/ n dicembre m

decency /'di:sənsɪ/ n decenza f

decent /'di:sənt/ a decente; (respectable) rispettabile; **very ~ of you** molto gentile da parte tua. **~ly** adv decentemente; (kindly) gentilmente

decentralize /di:'sentrəlaɪz/ vt decentrare

decept|ion /dɪ'sepʃn/ n inganno m. **~ive** /-tɪv/ a ingannevole. **~ively** adv ingannevolmente; **it looks ~ively easy** sembra facile, ma non lo è

decibel /'desɪbel/ n decibel m inv

decide /dɪ'saɪd/ vt decidere ● vi decidere (**on** di)

decided /dɪ'saɪdɪd/ a risoluto. **~ly** adv risolutamente; (without doubt) senza dubbio

deciduous /dɪ'sɪdjʊəs/ a a foglie decidue

decimal /'desɪml/ a decimale ● n numero m decimale. **~ 'point** n virgola f

decimate /'desɪmeɪt/ vt decimare

decipher /dɪ'saɪfə(r)/ vt decifrare

decision /dɪ'sɪʒn/ n decisione f

decisive /dɪ'saɪsɪv/ a decisivo

deck¹ /dek/ vt abbigliare

deck² n Naut ponte m; **on ~** in coperta; **top ~** (of bus) piano m di sopra; **~ of cards** mazzo m. **~-chair** n [sedia f a] sdraio f inv

declaration /deklə'reɪʃn/ n dichiarazione f

declare /dɪ'kleə(r)/ vt dichiarare; **anything to ~?** niente da dichiarare?

declension /dɪ'klenʃn/ n declinazione f

decline /dɪ'klaɪn/ n declino m ● vt also Gram declinare ● vi (decrease) diminuire; ⟨health:⟩ deperire; (say no) rifiutare

decode /di:'kəʊd/ vt decifrare; Comput decodificare

decompose /di:kəm'pəʊz/ vi decomporsi

décor /'deɪkɔ:(r)/ n decorazione f; (including furniture) arredamento m

decorat|e /'dekəreɪt/ vt decorare; (paint) pitturare; (wallpaper) tappezzare. **~ion** /-'reɪʃn/ n decorazione f. **~ive** /-rətɪv/ a decorativo. **~or** n **painter and ~or** imbianchino m

decorum /dɪ'kɔ:rəm/ n decoro m

decoy¹ /'di:kɔɪ/ n esca f

decoy² /dɪ'kɔɪ/ vt adescare

decrease¹ /'di:kri:s/ n diminuzione f

decrease² /dɪ'kri:s/ vt/i diminuire

decree /dɪ'kri:/ n decreto m ● vt (pt/pp **decreed**) decretare

decrepit /dɪ'krepɪt/ a decrepito

dedicat|e /'dedɪkeɪt/ vt dedicare. **~ed** a ⟨person⟩ scrupoloso. **~ion** /-'keɪʃn/ n dedizione f; (in book) dedica f

deduce /dɪ'dju:s/ vt dedurre (**from** da)

deduct /dɪ'dʌkt/ vt dedurre

deduction /dɪ'dʌkʃn/ n deduzione f

deed /di:d/ n azione f; Jur atto m di proprietà

deem /di:m/ vt ritenere

deep /di:p/ a profondo; **go off the ~ end** fam arrabbiarsi

deepen /'di:pn/ vt approfondire; scavare più profondamente ⟨trench⟩ ● vi approfondirsi; ⟨fig: mystery:⟩ infittirsi

deep-'freeze n congelatore m

deeply /'di:plɪ/ adv profondamente

deer /dɪə(r)/ n inv cervo m

deface /dɪ'feɪs/ vt sfigurare ⟨picture⟩; deturpare ⟨monument⟩

defamat|ion /defə'meɪʃn/ n diffamazione f. **~ory** /dɪ'fæmətərɪ/ a diffamatorio

default /dɪ'fɔ:lt/ n (Jur: non-payment) morosità f; (failure to appear) contumacia f; **win by ~** Sport vincere per abbandono dell'avversario; **in ~ of** per mancanza di ● a **~ drive** Comput lettore m di default ● vi (not pay) venir meno a un pagamento

defeat /dɪ'fi:t/ n sconfitta f ● vt sconfiggere; (frustrate) vanificare ⟨attempts⟩; **that ~s the object** questo fa fallire l'obiettivo

defect¹ /dɪ'fekt/ vi Pol fare defezione

defect² /'di:fekt/ n difetto m. **~ive** /dɪ'fektɪv/ a difettoso

defence /dɪ'fens/ n difesa f. **~less** a indifeso

defend /dɪ'fend/ vt difendere; (justify) giustificare. **~ant** n Jur imputato, -a mf

defensive /dɪ'fensɪv/ a difensivo ● n difensiva f; **on the ~** sulla difensiva

defer /dɪ'fɜ:(r)/ v (pt/pp **deferred**) ● vt (postpone) rinviare ● vi **~ to sb** rimettersi a qcno

deferen|ce /'defərəns/ n deferenza f. **~tial** /-'renʃl/ a deferente

defian|ce /dɪ'faɪəns/ n sfida f; **in ~ce of** sfidando. **~t** a (person) ribelle; (gesture, attitude) di sfida. **~tly** adv con aria di sfida

deficien|cy /dɪ'fɪʃənsɪ/ n insufficienza f. **~t** a insufficiente; **be ~t in** mancare di

deficit /'defɪsɪt/ n deficit m inv

defile /dɪ'faɪl/ vt fig contaminare

define /dɪ'faɪn/ vt definire

definite /'defɪnɪt/ a definito; (certain) (answer, yes) (improvement, difference) netto; **he was ~ about it** è stato chiaro in proposito. **~ly** adv sicuramente

definition /defɪ'nɪʃn/ n definizione f

definitive /dɪ'fɪnɪtɪv/ a definitivo

deflat|e /dɪ'fleɪt/ vt sgonfiare. **~ion** /-eɪʃn/ n Comm deflazione f

deflect /dɪ'flekt/ vt deflettere

deform|ed /dɪ'fɔ:md/ a deforme. **~ity** n deformità f inv

defraud /dɪ'frɔ:d/ vt defraudare

defrost /di:'frɒst/ vt sbrinare (fridge); scongelare (food)

deft /deft/ a abile

defunct /dɪ'fʌŋkt/ a morto e sepolto; (law) caduto in disuso

defuse /di:'fju:z/ vt disinnescare; calmare (situation)

defy /dɪ'faɪ/ vt (pt/pp **-ied**) (challenge) sfidare; resistere a (attempt); (not obey) disobbedire a

degenerate¹ /dɪ'dʒenəreɪt/ vi degenerare; **~ into** fig degenerare in

degenerate² /dɪ'dʒenərət/ a degenerato

degrading /dɪ'greɪdɪŋ/ a degradante

degree /dɪ'gri:/ n grado m; Univ laurea f; **20 ~s** 20 gradi; **not to the same ~** non allo stesso livello

dehydrate /di:'haɪdreɪt/ vt disidratare. **~d** /-ɪd/ a disidratato

de-ice /di:'aɪs/ vt togliere il ghiaccio da

deign /deɪn/ vi **to do sth** degnarsi di fare qcsa

deity /'di:ɪtɪ/ n divinità f inv

dejected /dɪ'dʒektɪd/ a demoralizzato

delay /dɪ'leɪ/ n ritardo m; **without ~** senza indugio ● vt ritardare; **be ~ed** (person:) essere trattenuto; (train, aircraft:) essere in ritardo ● vi indugiare

delegate¹ /'delɪgət/ n delegato, -a mf

delegat|e² /'delɪgeɪt/ vt delegare. **~ion** /-'geɪʃn/ n delegazione f

delet|e /dɪ'li:t/ vt cancellare. **~ion** /-i:ʃn/ n cancellatura f

deliberate¹ /dɪ'lɪbərət/ a deliberato; (slow) posato. **~ly** adv deliberatamente; (slowly) in modo posato

deliberat|e² /dɪ'lɪbəreɪt/ vt/i deliberare. **~ion** /-'reɪʃn/ n deliberazione f

delicacy /'delɪkəsɪ/ n delicatezza f; (food) prelibatezza f

delicate /'delɪkət/ a delicato

delicatessen /delɪkə'tesn/ n negozio m di specialità gastronomiche

delicious /dɪ'lɪʃəs/ a delizioso

delight /dɪ'laɪt/ n piacere m ● vt deliziare ● vi **~ in** dilettarsi con. **~ed** a lieto. **~ful** a delizioso

delinquen|cy /dɪ'lɪŋkwənsɪ/ n delinquenza f. **~t** a delinquente ● n delinquente mf

deli|rious /dɪ'lɪrɪəs/ a **be ~rious** delirare; (fig: very happy) essere pazzo di gioia. **~rium** /-rɪəm/ n delirio m

deliver /dɪ'lɪvə(r)/ vt consegnare; recapitare (post, newspaper); tenere (speech); dare (message); tirare (blow); (set free) liberare; **~ a baby** far nascere un bambino. **~ance** n liberazione f. **~y** n consegna f; (of post) distribuzione f; Med parto m; **cash on ~y** pagamento m alla consegna

delude /dɪ'lu:d/ vt ingannare; **~ oneself** illudersi

deluge /'delju:dʒ/ n diluvio m ● vt (fig: with requests etc) inondare

delusion /dɪ'lu:ʒn/ n illusione f

de luxe /də'lʌks/ a di lusso

delve /delv/ vi **~ into** (into pocket etc) frugare in; (into notes, the past) fare ricerche in

demand /dɪ'mɑ:nd/ n richiesta f; Comm domanda f; **in ~** richiesto; **on ~** a richiesta ● vt esigere (**of/from** da). **~ing** a esigente

demarcation /di:mɑ:'keɪʃn/ n demarcazione f

demean /dɪ'miːn/ *vt* ~ **oneself** abbassarsi (**to** a)

demeanour /dɪ'miːnə(r)/ *n* comportamento *m*

demented /dɪ'mentɪd/ *a* demente

demise /dɪ'maɪz/ *n* decesso *m*

demister /diː'mɪstə(r)/ *n* Auto sbrinatore *m*

demo /'deməʊ/ *n* (*pl* ~**s**) *fam* manifestazione *f*; ~ **disk** Comput demodisk *m inv*

democracy /dɪ'mɒkrəsɪ/ *n* democrazia *f*

democrat /'deməkræt/ *n* democratico, -a *mf*. ~**ic** /-'krætɪk/ *a* democratico

demo|lish /dɪ'mɒlɪʃ/ *vt* demolire. ~**lition** /deməˈlɪʃn/ *n* demolizione *f*

demon /'diːmən/ *n* demonio *m*

demonstrat|e /'demənstreɪt/ *vt* dimostrare; fare una dimostrazione sull'uso di ⟨appliance⟩ ● *vi* Pol manifestare. ~**ion** /-'streɪʃn/ *n* dimostrazione *f*; Pol manifestazione *f*

demonstrative /dɪ'mɒnstrətɪv/ *a* Gram dimostrativo; **be** ~ essere espansivo

demonstrator /'demənstreɪtə(r)/ *n* Pol manifestante *mf*; (*for product*) dimostratore, -trice *mf*

demoralize /dɪ'mɒrəlaɪz/ *vt* demoralizzare

demote /dɪ'məʊt/ *vt* retrocedere di grado; Mil degradare

demure /dɪ'mjʊə(r)/ *a* schivo

den /den/ *n* tana *f*; (*room*) rifugio *m*

denial /dɪ'naɪəl/ *n* smentita *f*

denim /'denɪm/ *n* [tessuto *m*] jeans *m*; ~**s** *pl* [blue]jeans *mpl*

Denmark /'denmɑːk/ *n* Danimarca *f*

denomination /dɪnɒmɪ'neɪʃn/ *n* Relig confessione *f*; (*money*) valore *f*

denounce /dɪ'naʊns/ *vt* denunciare

dens|e /dens/ *a* denso; ⟨crowd, forest⟩ fitto; (*stupid*) ottuso. ~**ely** *adv* ⟨populated⟩ densamente; ~**ely wooded** fittamente ricoperto di alberi. ~**ity** *n* densità *f* inv; (*of forest*) fittezza *f*

dent /dent/ *n* ammaccatura *f* ● *vt* ammaccare; ~**ed** *a* ammaccato

dental /'dentl/ *a* dei denti; ⟨treatment⟩ dentistico; ⟨hygiene⟩ dentale. ~ **surgeon** *n* odontoiatra *mf*, medico *m* dentista

dentist /'dentɪst/ *n* dentista *mf*. ~**ry** *n* odontoiatria *f*

dentures /'dentʃəz/ *npl* dentiera *fsg*

denunciation /dɪnʌnsɪ'eɪʃn/ *n* denuncia *f*

deny /dɪ'naɪ/ *vt* (*pt/pp* -**ied**) negare; (*officially*) smentire; ~ **sb sth** negare qcsa a qcno

deodorant /diː'əʊdərənt/ *n* deodorante *m*

depart /dɪ'pɑːt/ *vi* ⟨plane, train⟩ partire; ⟨liter: person⟩ andare via; (*deviate*) allontanarsi (**from** da)

department /dɪ'pɑːtmənt/ *n* reparto *m*; Pol ministero *m*; (*of company*) sezione *f*; Univ dipartimento *m*. ~ **store** *n* grande magazzino *m*

departure /dɪ'pɑːtʃə(r)/ *n* partenza *f*; (*from rule*) allontanamento *m*; **new** ~ svolta *f*

depend /dɪ'pend/ *vi* dipendere (**on** da); (*rely*) contare (**on** su); **it all** ~**s** dipende; ~**ing on what he says** a seconda di quello che dice. ~**able** /-əbl/ *a* fidato. ~**ant** *n* persona *f* a carico. ~**ence** *n* dipendenza *f*. ~**ent** *a* dipendente (**on** da)

depict /dɪ'pɪkt/ *vt* (*in writing*) dipingere; (*with picture*) rappresentare

depilatory /dɪ'pɪlətərɪ/ *n* (*cream*) crema *f* depilatoria

deplete /dɪ'pliːt/ *vt* ridurre; **totally** ~**d** completamente esaurito

deplor|able /dɪ'plɔːrəbl/ *a* deplorevole. ~**e** *vt* deplorare

deploy /dɪ'plɔɪ/ *vt* Mil spiegare ● *vi* schierarsi

deport /dɪ'pɔːt/ *vt* deportare. ~**ation** /diːpɔː'teɪʃn/ *n* deportazione *f*

depose /dɪ'pəʊz/ *vt* deporre

deposit /dɪ'pɒzɪt/ *n* deposito *m*; (*against damage*) cauzione *f*; (*first instalment*) acconto *m* ● *vt* (*pt/pp* **deposited**) depositare. ~ **account** *n* libretto *m* di risparmio; (*without instant access*) conto *m* vincolato

depot /'depəʊ/ *n* deposito *m*; Am Rail stazione *f* ferroviaria

deprav|e /dɪ'preɪv/ *vt* depravare. ~**ed** *a* depravato. ~**ity** /-'prævətɪ/ *n* depravazione *f*

depreciat|e /dɪ'priːʃɪeɪt/ *vi* deprezzarsi. ~**ion** /-'eɪʃn/ *n* deprezzamento *m*

depress /dɪ'pres/ *vt* deprimere; (*press down*) premere. ~**ed** *a* depresso; ~**ed area** zona *f* depressa. ~**ing** *a* deprimente. ~**ion** /-eʃn/ *n* depressione *f*

deprivation /deprɪ'veɪʃn/ *n* privazione *f*

deprive /dɪ'praɪv/ *vt* ~ **sb of sth** privare qcno di qcsa. ~**d** *a* ⟨area, childhood⟩ disagiato

depth /depθ/ *n* profondità *f* inv; **in** ~ ⟨study, analyse⟩ in modo approfondito;

in the ~s of winter in pieno inverno; **be out of one's ~** (*in water*) non toccare il fondo; *fig* sentirsi in alto mare

deputation /depjʊ'teɪʃn/ *n* deputazione *f*

deputize /'depjʊtaɪz/ *vi* ~ **for** fare le veci di

deputy /'depjʊtɪ/ *n* vice *mf*; (*temporary*) sostituto, -a *mf* ● *attrib* ~ **leader** vicesegretario, -a *mf*; ~ **chairman** vicepresidente *mf*

derail /dɪ'reɪl/ *vt* **be ~ed** (*train:*) essere deragliato. **~ment** *n* deragliamento *m*

deranged /dɪ'reɪndʒd/ *a* squilibrato

derelict /'derəlɪkt/ *a* abbandonato

deri|de /dɪ'raɪd/ *vt* deridere. **~sion** /-'rɪʒn/ *n* derisione *f*

derisory /dɪ'raɪsərɪ/ *a* (*laughter*) derisorio; (*offer*) irrisorio

derivation /derɪ'veɪʃn/ *n* derivazione *f*

derivative /dɪ'rɪvətɪv/ *a* derivato ● *n* derivato *m*

derive /dɪ'raɪv/ *vt* (*obtain*) derivare; **be ~d from** (*word:*) derivare da

dermatologist /dɜːmə'tɒlədʒɪst/ *n* dermatologo, -a *mf*

derogatory /dɪ'rɒɡətrɪ/ *a* (*comments*) peggiorativo

descend /dɪ'send/ *vi* scendere ● *vt* scendere da; **be ~ed from** discendere da. **~ant** *n* discendente *mf*

descent /dɪ'sent/ *n* discesa *f*; (*lineage*) origine *f*

describe /dɪ'skraɪb/ *vt* descrivere

descrip|tion /dɪ'skrɪpʃn/ *n* descrizione *f*; **they had no help of any ~tion** non hanno avuto proprio nessun aiuto. **~tive** /-tɪv/ *a* descrittivo; (*vivid*) vivido

desecrat|e /'desɪkreɪt/ *vt* profanare. **~ion** /-'kreɪʃn/ *n* profanazione *f*

desert¹ /'dezət/ *n* deserto *m* ● *a* deserto; ~ **island** isola *f* deserta

desert² /dɪ'zɜːt/ *vt* abbandonare ● *vi* disertare. **~ed** *a* deserto. **~er** *n* Mil disertore *m*. **~ion** /-'zɜːʃn/ *n* Mil diserzione *f*; (*of family*) abbandono *m*

deserts /dɪ'zɜːts/ *npl* **get one's just ~** ottenere ciò che ci si merita

deserve /dɪ'zɜːv/ *vt* meritare. **~ing** *a* meritevole; **~ing cause** opera *f* meritoria

design /dɪ'zaɪn/ *n* progettazione *f*; (*fashion ~, appearance*) design *m inv*; (*pattern*) modello *m*; (*aim*) proposito *m* ● *vt* progettare; disegnare (*clothes, furniture, model*); **be ~ed for** essere fatto per

designat|e /'dezɪɡneɪt/ *vt* designare. **~ion** /-'neɪʃn/ *n* designazione *f*

designer /dɪ'zaɪnə(r)/ *n* progettista *mf*; (*of clothes*) stilista *mf*; (*Theat: of set*) scenografo, -a *mf*

desirable /dɪ'zaɪərəbl/ *a* desiderabile

desire /dɪ'zaɪə(r)/ *n* desiderio *m* ● *vt* desiderare

desk /desk/ *n* scrivania *f*; (*in school*) banco *m*; (*in hotel*) reception *f inv*; (*cash ~*) cassa *f*. **~top 'publishing** *n* desktop publishing *m*, editoria *f* da tavolo

desolat|e /'desələt/ *a* desolato. **~ion** /-'leɪʃn/ *n* desolazione *f*

despair /dɪ'speə(r)/ *n* disperazione *f*; **in ~** disperato; (*say*) per disperazione ● *vi* **I ~ of that boy** quel ragazzo mi fa disperare

desperat|e /'despərət/ *a* disperato; **be ~e** (*criminal:*) essere un disperato; **be ~e for sth** morire dalla voglia di. **~ely** *adv* disperatamente; **he said ~ely** ha detto, disperato. **~ion** /-'reɪʃn/ *n* disperazione *f*; **in ~ion** per disperazione

despicable /dɪ'spɪkəbl/ *a* disprezzevole

despise /dɪ'spaɪz/ *vt* disprezzare

despite /dɪ'spaɪt/ *prep* malgrado

despondent /dɪ'spɒndənt/ *a* abbattuto

despot /'despɒt/ *n* despota *m*

dessert /dɪ'zɜːt/ *n* dolce *m*. ~ **spoon** *n* cucchiaio *m* da dolce

destination /destɪ'neɪʃn/ *n* destinazione *f*

destine /'destɪn/ *vt* destinare; **be ~d for sth** essere destinato a qcsa

destiny /'destɪnɪ/ *n* destino *m*

destitute /'destɪtjuːt/ *a* bisognoso

destroy /dɪ'strɔɪ/ *vt* distruggere. **~er** *n* Naut cacciatorpediniere *m*

destruc|tion /dɪ'strʌkʃn/ *n* distruzione *f*. **~tive** /-tɪv/ *a* distruttivo; (*fig: criticism*) negativo

detach /dɪ'tætʃ/ *vt* staccare. **~able** /-əbl/ *a* separabile. **~ed** *a fig* distaccato; **~ed house** villetta *f*

detachment /dɪ'tætʃmənt/ *n* distacco *m*; Mil distaccamento *m*

detail /'diːteɪl/ *n* particolare *m*, dettaglio *m*; **in ~** particolareggiatamente ● *vt* esporre con tutti i particolari; Mil assegnare. **~ed** *a* particolareggiato, dettagliato

detain /dɪ'teɪn/ *vt* (*police:*) trattenere; (*delay*) far ritardare. **~ee** /diːteɪ'niː/ *n* detenuto, -a *mf*

detect /dɪ'tekt/ *vt* individuare;

(*perceive*) percepire. **~ion** /-ekʃn/ *n* scoperta *f*

detective /dɪˈtektɪv/ *n* investigatore, -trice *mf*. **~ story** *n* racconto *m* poliziesco

detector /dɪˈtektə(r)/ *n* (*for metal*) metal detector *m inv*

detention /dɪˈtenʃn/ *n* detenzione *f*; *Sch* punizione *f*

deter /dɪˈtɜː(r)/ *vt* (*pt/pp* **deterred**) impedire; **~ sb from doing sth** impedire a qcno di fare qcsa

detergent /dɪˈtɜːdʒənt/ *n* detersivo *m*

deteriorat|e /dɪˈtɪərɪəreɪt/ *vi* deteriorarsi. **~ion** /-ˈreɪʃn/ *n* deterioramento *m*

determination /dɪtɜːmɪˈneɪʃn/ *n* determinazione *f*

determine /dɪˈtɜːmɪn/ *vt* (*ascertain*) determinare; **~ to** (*resolve*) decidere di. **~d** *a* deciso

deterrent /dɪˈterənt/ *n* deterrente *m*

detest /dɪˈtest/ *vt* detestare. **~able** /-əbl/ *a* detestabile

detonat|e /ˈdetəneɪt/ *vt* far detonare ● *vi* detonare. **~or** *n* detonatore *m*

detour /ˈdiːtʊə(r)/ *n* deviazione *f*

detract /dɪˈtrækt/ *vi* **~ from** sminuire (*merit*); rovinare (*pleasure, beauty*)

detriment /ˈdetrɪmənt/ *n* **to the ~ of** a danno di. **~al** /-ˈmentl/ *a* dannoso

deuce /djuːs/ *n Tennis* deuce *m inv*

devaluation /diːvæljʊˈeɪʃn/ *n* svalutazione *f*

de'value *vt* svalutare (*currency*)

devastat|e /ˈdevəsteɪt/ *vt* devastare. **~ed** *a fam* sconvolto. **~ing** *a* devastante; (*news*) sconvolgente. **~ion** /-ˈsteɪʃn/ *n* devastazione *f*

develop /dɪˈveləp/ *vt* sviluppare; contrarre (*illness*); (*add to value of*) valorizzare (*area*) ● *vi* svilupparsi; **~ into** divenire. **~er** *n* [**property**] **~er** imprenditore, -trice *mf* edile

de'veloping country *n* paese *m* in via di sviluppo

development /dɪˈveləpmənt/ *n* sviluppo *m*; (*of vaccine etc*) messa *f* a punto

deviant /ˈdiːvɪənt/ *a* deviato

deviat|e /ˈdiːvɪeɪt/ *vi* deviare. **~ion** /-ˈeɪʃn/ *n* deviazione *f*

device /dɪˈvaɪs/ *n* dispositivo *m*

devil /ˈdevl/ *n* diavolo *m*

devious /ˈdiːvɪəs/ *a* (*person*) subdolo; (*route*) tortuoso

devise /dɪˈvaɪz/ *vt* escogitare

devoid /dɪˈvɔɪd/ *a* **~ of** privo di

devolution /diːvəˈluːʃn/ *n* (*of power*) decentramento *m*

devot|e /dɪˈvəʊt/ *vt* dedicare. **~ed** *a* (*daughter etc*) affezionato; **be ~ed to sth** consacrarsi a qcsa. **~ee** /devəˈtiː/ *n* appassionato, -a *mf*

devotion /dɪˈvəʊʃn/ *n* dedizione *f*; **~s** *pl Relig* devozione *fsg*

devour /dɪˈvaʊə(r)/ *vt* divorare

devout /dɪˈvaʊt/ *a* devoto

dew /djuː/ *n* rugiada *f*

dexterity /dekˈsterətɪ/ *n* destrezza *f*

diabet|es /daɪəˈbiːtiːz/ *n* diabete *m*. **~ic** /-ˈbetɪk/ *a* diabetico ● *n* diabetico, -a *mf*

diabolical /daɪəˈbɒlɪkl/ *a* diabolico

diagnose /daɪəgˈnəʊz/ *vt* diagnosticare

diagnosis /daɪəgˈnəʊsɪs/ *n* (*pl* **-oses** /-siːz/) diagnosi *f inv*

diagonal /daɪˈægənl/ *a* diagonale ● *n* diagonale *f*

diagram /ˈdaɪəgræm/ *n* diagramma *m*

dial /ˈdaɪəl/ *n* (*of clock, machine*) quadrante *m*; *Teleph* disco *m* combinatore ● *v* (*pt/pp* **dialled**) ● *vi Teleph* fare il numero; **~ direct** chiamare in teleselezione ● *vt* fare (*number*)

dialect /ˈdaɪəlekt/ *n* dialetto *m*

dialling **~ code** *n* prefisso *m*. **~ tone** *n* segnale *m* di linea libera

dialogue /ˈdaɪəlɒg/ *n* dialogo *m*

'dial tone *n Am Teleph* segnale *m* di linea libera

diameter /daɪˈæmɪtə(r)/ *n* diametro *m*

diametrically /daɪəˈmetrɪklɪ/ *adv* **~ opposed** diametralmente opposto

diamond /ˈdaɪəmənd/ *n* diamante *m*, brillante *m*; (*shape*) losanga *f*; **~s** *pl* (*in cards*) quadri *mpl*

diaper /ˈdaɪəpə(r)/ *n Am* pannolino *m*

diaphragm /ˈdaɪəfræm/ *n* diaframma *m*

diarrhoea /daɪəˈriːə/ *n* diarrea *f*

diary /ˈdaɪərɪ/ *n* (*for appointments*) agenda *f*; (*for writing in*) diario *m*

dice /daɪs/ *n inv* dadi *mpl* ● *vt Culin* tagliare a dadini

dicey /ˈdaɪsɪ/ *a fam* rischioso

dictat|e /dɪkˈteɪt/ *vt/i* dettare. **~ion** /-eɪʃn/ *n* dettato *m*

dictator /dɪkˈteɪtə(r)/ *n* dittatore *m*. **~ial** /-təˈtɔːrɪəl/ *a* dittatoriale. **~ship** *n* dittatura *f*

dictionary /ˈdɪkʃənrɪ/ *n* dizionario *m*

did /dɪd/ *see* **do**

didactic /daɪˈdæktɪk/ *a* didattico

diddle /ˈdɪdl/ *vt fam* gabbare

didn't /ˈdɪdnt/ = **did not**

die /daɪ/ *vi* (*pres p* **dying**) morire (**of** di); **be dying to do sth** *fam* morire dalla voglia di fare qcsa. **die down** *vi* calmarsi; ⟨*fire, flames:*⟩ spegnersi. **die out** *vi* estinguersi; ⟨*custom:*⟩ morire

diesel /'diːzl/ *n* diesel *m*

diet /'daɪət/ *n* regime *m* alimentare; (*restricted*) dieta *f*; **be on a ~** essere a dieta ● *vi* essere a dieta

differ /'dɪfə(r)/ *vi* differire; (*disagree*) non essere d'accordo

difference /'dɪfrəns/ *n* differenza *f*; (*disagreement*) divergenza *f*

different /'dɪfrənt/ *a* diverso, differente; (*various*) diversi; **~ from** diverso da

differential /dɪfə'renʃl/ *a* differenziale ● *n* differenziale *m*

differentiate /dɪfə'renʃɪeɪt/ *vt* distinguere (**between** fra); (*discriminate*) discriminare (**between** fra); (*make differ*) differenziare

differently /'dɪfrəntlɪ/ *adv* in modo diverso; **~ from** diversamente da

difficult /'dɪfɪkəlt/ *a* difficile. **~y** *n* difficoltà *f inv*; **with ~y** con difficoltà

diffuse[1] /dɪ'fjuːs/ *a* diffuso; (*wordy*) prolisso

diffuse[2] /dɪ'fjuːz/ *vt Phys* diffondere

dig /dɪg/ *n* (*poke*) spinta *f*; (*remark*) frecciata *f*; *Archaeol* scavo *m*; **~s** *pl fam* camera *fsg* ammobiliata ● *vt/i* (*pt/pp* **dug**, *pres p* **digging**) scavare ⟨*hole*⟩; vangare ⟨*garden*⟩; (*thrust*) conficcare; **~ sb in the ribs** dare una gomitata a qcno. **dig out** *vt fig* tirar fuori. **dig up** *vt* scavare ⟨*garden, street, object*⟩; sradicare ⟨*tree, plant*⟩; (*fig: find*) scovare

digest[1] /'daɪdʒest/ *n* compendio *m*

digest[2] /daɪ'dʒest/ *vt* digerire. **~ible** *a* digeribile. **~ion** /-estʃn/ *n* digestione *f*

digger /'dɪgə(r)/ *n Techn* scavatrice *f*

digit /'dɪdʒɪt/ *n* cifra *f*; (*finger*) dito *m*

digital /'dɪdʒɪtl/ *a* digitale. **~ camera** fotocamera *f* digitale. **~ clock** orologio *m* digitale

dignified /'dɪgnɪfaɪd/ *a* dignitoso

dignitary /'dɪgnɪtərɪ/ *n* dignitario *m*

dignity /'dɪgnɪtɪ/ *n* dignità *f*

digress /daɪ'gres/ *vi* divagare. **~ion** /-eʃn/ *n* digressione *f*

dike /daɪk/ *n* diga *f*

dilapidated /dɪ'læpɪdeɪtɪd/ *a* cadente

dilate /daɪ'leɪt/ *vi* dilatarsi

dilemma /dɪ'lemə/ *n* dilemma *m*

dilettante /dɪlɪ'tæntɪ/ *n* dilettante *mf*

dilly-dally /'dɪlɪdælɪ/ *vi* (*pt/pp* **-ied**) *fam* tentennare

dilute /daɪ'luːt/ *vt* diluire

dim /dɪm/ *a* (**dimmer, dimmest**) debole ⟨*light*⟩; (*dark*) scuro; ⟨*prospect,*

chance⟩ scarso; (*indistinct*) impreciso; (*fam: stupid*) tonto ● *vt/i* (*pt/pp* **dimmed**) affievolire. **~ly** *adv* ⟨*see, remember*⟩ indistintamente; ⟨*shine*⟩ debolmente

dime /daɪm/ *n Am* moneta *f* da dieci centesimi

dimension /daɪ'menʃn/ *n* dimensione *f*

diminish /dɪ'mɪnɪʃ/ *vt/i* diminuire

diminutive /dɪ'mɪnjʊtɪv/ *a* minuscolo ● *n* diminutivo *m*

dimple /'dɪmpl/ *n* fossetta *f*

din /dɪn/ *n* baccano *m*

dine /daɪn/ *vi* pranzare. **~r** *n* (*Am: restaurant*) tavola *f* calda; **the last ~r in the restaurant** l'ultimo cliente nel ristorante

dinghy /'dɪŋgɪ/ *n* dinghy *m*; (*inflatable*) canotto *m* pneumatico

dingy /'dɪndʒɪ/ *a* (**-ier, -iest**) squallido e tetro

dining /'daɪnɪŋ/: **~-car** *n* carrozza *f* ristorante. **~-room** *n* sala *f* da pranzo. **~-table** *n* tavolo *m* da pranzo

dinner /'dɪnə(r)/ *n* cena *f*; (*at midday*) pranzo *m*. **~-jacket** *n* smoking *m inv*

dinosaur /'daɪnəsɔː(r)/ *n* dinosauro *m*

dint /dɪnt/ *n* **by ~ of** a forza di

diocese /'daɪəsɪs/ *n* diocesi *f inv*

dip /dɪp/ *n* (*in ground*) inclinazione *f*; *Culin* salsina *f*; **go for a ~** andare a fare una nuotata ● *v* (*pt/pp* **dipped**) ● *vt* (*in liquid*) immergere; abbassare ⟨*head, headlights*⟩ ● *vi* ⟨*land:*⟩ formare un avvallamento. **dip into** *vt* scorrere ⟨*book*⟩

diphtheria /dɪf'θɪərɪə/ *n* difterite *f*

diphthong /'dɪfθɒŋ/ *n* dittongo *m*

diploma /dɪ'pləʊmə/ *n* diploma *m*

diplomacy /dɪ'pləʊməsɪ/ *n* diplomazia *f*

diplomat /'dɪpləmæt/ *n* diplomatico, -a *mf*. **~ic** /-'mætɪk/ *a* diplomatico. **~ically** *adv* con diplomazia

'dip-stick *n Auto* astina *f* dell'olio

dire /'daɪə(r)/ *a* ⟨*situation, consequences*⟩ terribile

direct /dɪ'rekt/ *a* diretto ● *adv* direttamente ● *vt* (*aim*) rivolgere ⟨*attention, criticism*⟩; (*control*) dirigere; fare la regia di ⟨*film, play*⟩; **~ sb** (*show the way*) indicare la strada a qcno; **~ sb to do sth** ordinare a qcno di fare qcsa. **~ 'current** *n* corrente *m* continua

direction /dɪ'rekʃn/ *n* direzione *f*; (*of play, film*) regia *f*; **~s** *pl* indicazioni *fpl*

directly /dɪ'rektlɪ/ *adv* direttamente; (*at once*) immediatamente ● *conj* [non] appena

director /dɪ'rektə(r)/ n Comm direttore, -trice mf; (of play, film) regista mf

directory /dɪ'rektərɪ/ n elenco m; Teleph elenco m [telefonico]; (of streets) stradario m

dirt /dɜːt/ n sporco m; ~ **cheap** fam a [un] prezzo stracciato

dirty /'dɜːtɪ/ a (-ier, -iest) sporco; ~ **trick** brutto scherzo m; ~ **word** parolaccia ● vt (pt/pp -ied) sporcare

dis|a'bility /dɪs-/ n infermità f inv. ~**abled** /dɪ'seɪbld/ a invalido

disad'van|tage n svantaggio m; **at a ~tage** in una posizione di svantaggio. ~**taged** a svantaggiato. ~'**tageous** a svantaggioso

disa'gree vi non essere d'accordo; ~ **with** ⟨food:⟩ far male a

disa'greeable a sgradevole

disa'greement n disaccordo m; (quarrel) dissidio m

disal'low vt annullare ⟨goal⟩

disap'pear vi scomparire. ~**ance** n scomparsa f

disap'point vt deludere; **I'm ~ed** sono deluso. ~**ing** a deludente. ~**ment** n delusione f

disap'proval n disapprovazione f

disap'prove vi disapprovare; ~ **of sb/sth** disapprovare qcno/qcsa

dis'arm vt disarmare ● vi Mil disarmarsi. ~**ament** n disarmo m. ~**ing** a ⟨frankness etc⟩ disarmante

disar'ray n **in ~** in disordine

disast|er /dɪ'zɑːstə(r)/ n disastro m. ~**rous** /-rəs/ a disastroso

dis'band vt sciogliere; smobilitare ⟨troops⟩ ● vi sciogliersi; ⟨regiment:⟩ essere smobilitato

disbe'lief n incredulità f; **in ~** con incredulità

disc /dɪsk/ n disco m; (CD) compact disc m inv

discard /dɪ'skɑːd/ vt scartare; (throw away) eliminare; scaricare ⟨boyfriend⟩

discern /dɪ'sɜːn/ vt discernere. ~**ible** a discernibile. ~**ing** a perspicace

'discharge[1] n Electr scarica f; (dismissal) licenziamento m; Mil congedo m; (Med: of blood) emissione f; (of cargo) scarico m

dis'charge[2] vt scaricare ⟨battery, cargo⟩; (dismiss) licenziare; Mil congedare; Jur assolvere ⟨accused⟩; dimettere ⟨patient⟩ ● vi Electr scaricarsi

disciple /dɪ'saɪpl/ n discepolo m

disciplinary /'dɪsɪplɪnərɪ/ a disciplinare

discipline /'dɪsɪplɪn/ n disciplina f ● vt disciplinare; (punish) punire

'disc jockey n disc jockey m inv

dis'claim vt disconoscere. ~**er** n rifiuto m

dis'clos|e vt svelare. ~**ure** n rivelazione f

disco /'dɪskəʊ/ n discoteca f

dis'colour vt scolorire ● vi scolorirsi

dis'comfort n scomodità f; fig disagio m

disconcert /dɪskən'sɜːt/ vt sconcertare

discon'nect vt disconnettere

disconsolate /dɪs'kɒnsələt/ a sconsolato

discon'tent n scontentezza f. ~**ed** a scontento

discon'tinue vt cessare, smettere; Comm sospendere la produzione di; ~**d line** fine f serie

'discord n discordia f; Mus dissonanza f. ~**ant** /dɪ'skɔːdənt/ a ~**ant note** nota f discordante

discothèque /'dɪskətek/ n discoteca f

'discount[1] n sconto m

dis'count[2] vt (not believe) non credere a; (leave out of consideration) non tener conto di

dis'courage vt scoraggiare; (dissuade) dissuadere

'discourse n discorso m

dis'courteous a scortese

discover /dɪ'skʌvə(r)/ vt scoprire. ~**y** n scoperta f

dis'credit n discredito m ● vt (pt/pp **discredited**) screditare

discreet /dɪ'skriːt/ a discreto

discrepancy /dɪ'skrepənsɪ/ n discrepanza f

discretion /dɪ'skreʃn/ n discrezione f

discriminat|e /dɪ'skrɪmɪneɪt/ vi discriminare (**against** contro); ~**e between** distinguere tra. ~**ing** a esigente. ~**ion** /-'neɪʃn/ n discriminazione f; (quality) discernimento m

discus /'dɪskəs/ n disco m

discuss /dɪ'skʌs/ vt discutere; (examine critically) esaminare. ~**ion** /-ʌʃn/ n discussione f

disdain /dɪs'deɪn/ n sdegno m ● vt sdegnare. ~**ful** a sdegnoso

disease /dɪ'ziːz/ n malattia f. ~**d** a malato

disem'bark vi sbarcare

disen'chant vt disincantare. ~**ment** n disincanto m

disen'gage vt disimpegnare; disinnestare ⟨clutch⟩

disen'tangle vt districare

dis'favour n sfavore m

dis'figure vt deformare

dis'grace n vergogna f; **I am in ~** sono caduto in disgrazia; **it's a ~** è una vergogna ● vt disonorare. **~ful** a vergognoso

disgruntled /dɪs'grʌntld/ a malcontento

disguise /dɪs'gaɪz/ n travestimento m; **in ~** travestito ● vt contraffare ⟨voice⟩; dissimulare ⟨emotions⟩; **~d as** travestito da

disgust /dɪs'gʌst/ n disgusto m; **in ~** con aria disgustata ● vt disgustare. **~ing** a disgustoso

dish /dɪʃ/ n piatto m; **do the ~es** lavare i piatti ● **dish out** vt ⟨serve⟩ servire; ⟨distribute⟩ distribuire. **dish up** vt servire

'dishcloth n strofinaccio m

dis'hearten vt scoraggiare

dishevelled /dɪ'ʃevld/ a scompigliato

dis'honest a disonesto. **~y** n disonestà f

dis'honour n disonore m ● vt disonorare ⟨family⟩; non onorare ⟨cheque⟩. **~able** a disonorevole. **~ably** adv in modo disonorevole

'dishwasher n lavapiatti f inv

disil'lusion vt disilludere. **~ment** n disillusione f

disin'fect vt disinfettare. **~ant** n disinfettante m

disin'herit vt diseredare

dis'integrate vi disintegrarsi

dis'interested a disinteressato

dis'jointed a sconnesso

disk /dɪsk/ n Comput disco m; ⟨diskette⟩ dischetto m

dis'like n avversione f; **your likes and ~s** i tuoi gusti ● nt **I ~ him/it** non mi piace; **I don't ~ him/it** non mi dispiace

dislocate /'dɪsləkeɪt/ vt slogare; **~ one's shoulder** slogarsi una spalla

dis'lodge vt sloggiare

dis'loyal a sleale. **~ty** n slealtà f

dismal /'dɪzməl/ a ⟨person⟩ abbacchiato; ⟨news, weather⟩ deprimente; ⟨performance⟩ mediocre

dismantle /dɪs'mæntl/ vt smontare ⟨tent, machine⟩; fig smantellare

dis'may n sgomento m. **~ed** a sgomento

dis'miss vt licenziare ⟨employee⟩; ⟨reject⟩ scartare ⟨idea, suggestion⟩. **~al** n licenziamento m

dis'mount vi smontare

diso'bedien|ce n disubbidienza f. **~t** a disubbidiente

diso'bey vt disubbidire a ⟨rule⟩ ● vi disubbidire

dis'order n disordine m; Med disturbo m. **~ly** a disordinato; ⟨crowd⟩ turbolento; **~ly conduct** turbamento m della quiete pubblica

dis'organized a disorganizzato

dis'orientate vt disorientare

dis'own vt disconoscere

disparaging /dɪ'spærɪdʒɪŋ/ a sprezzante

disparity /dɪ'spærətɪ/ n disparità f inv

dispassionate /dɪ'spæʃənət/ a spassionato

dispatch /dɪ'spætʃ/ n Comm spedizione f; ⟨Mil, report⟩ dispaccio m; **with ~** con prontezza ● vt spedire; ⟨kill⟩ spedire al creatore

dispel /dɪ'spel/ vt (pt/pp **dispelled**) dissipare

dispensable /dɪ'spensəbl/ a dispensabile

dispensary /dɪ'spensərɪ/ n farmacia f

dispense /dɪ'spens/ vt distribuire; **~ with** fare a meno di; **dispensing chemist** farmacista mf; ⟨shop⟩ farmacia f. **~r** n ⟨device⟩ distributore m

dispers|al /dɪ'spɜ:sl/ n disperzione f. **~e** /dɪ'spɜ:s/ vt disperdere ● vi disperdersi

dispirited /dɪ'spɪrɪtɪd/ a scoraggiato

dis'place vt spostare; **~d person** profugo, -a mf

display /dɪ'spleɪ/ n mostra f; Comm esposizione f; ⟨of feelings⟩ manifestazione f; pej ostentazione f; Comput display m inv ● vt mostrare; esporre ⟨goods⟩; manifestare ⟨feelings⟩; Comput visualizzare

dis'please vt non piacere a; **be ~d with** essere scontento di

dis'pleasure n malcontento m

disposable /dɪ'spəʊzəbl/ a ⟨throwaway⟩ usa e getta; ⟨income⟩ disponibile

disposal /dɪ'spəʊzl/ n ⟨getting rid of⟩ eliminazione f; **be at sb's ~** essere a disposizione di qcno

dispose /dɪ'spəʊz/ vi **~ of** ⟨get rid of⟩ disfarsi di; **be well ~d** essere ben disposto (**to** verso)

disposition /dɪspə'zɪʃn/ n disposizione f; ⟨nature⟩ indole f

disproportionate /dɪsprə'pɔ:ʃənət/ a sproporzionato

dis'prove vt confutare

dispute /dɪ'spju:t/ n disputa f;

(industrial) contestazione *f* ● *vt* contestare ⟨*statement*⟩

disqualifi'cation *n* squalifica *f*; *(from driving)* ritiro *m* della patente

dis'qualify *vt* (*pt/pp* **-ied**) escludere; *Sport* squalificare; ~ **sb from driving** ritirare la patente a qcno

disquieting /dɪsˈkwaɪətɪŋ/ *a* allarmante

disre'gard *n* mancanza *f* di considerazione ● *vt* ignorare

disre'pair *n* **fall into** ~ deteriorarsi; **in a state of** ~ in cattivo stato

dis'reputable *a* malfamato

disre'pute *n* discredito *m*; **bring sb into** ~ rovinare la reputazione a qcno

disre'spect *n* mancanza *f* di rispetto. ~**ful** *a* irrispettoso

disrupt /dɪsˈrʌpt/ *vt* creare scompiglio in; sconvolgere ⟨*plans*⟩. ~**ion** /-ʌpʃn/ *n* scompiglio *m*; *(of plans)* sconvolgimento *m*. ~**ive** /-tɪv/ *a* ⟨*person, behaviour*⟩ indisciplinato

dissatis'faction *n* malcontento *m*

dis'satisfied *a* scontento

dissect /dɪˈsekt/ *vt* sezionare. ~**ion** /-ekʃn/ *n* dissezione *f*

dissent /dɪˈsent/ *n* dissenso *m* ● *vi* dissentire

dissertation /dɪsəˈteɪʃn/ *n* tesi *f inv*

dis'service *n* **do sb/oneself a** ~ rendere un cattivo servizio a qcno/se stesso

dissident /ˈdɪsɪdənt/ *n* dissidente *mf*

dis'similar *a* dissimile (**to** a)

dissociate /dɪˈsəʊʃɪeɪt/ *vt* dissociare; ~ **oneself from** dissociarsi da

dissolute /ˈdɪsəluːt/ *a* dissoluto

dissolution /dɪsəˈluːʃn/ *n* scioglimento *m*

dissolve /dɪˈzɒlv/ *vt* dissolvere ● *vi* dissolversi

dissuade /dɪˈsweɪd/ *vt* dissuadere

distance /ˈdɪstəns/ *n* distanza *f*; **it's a short** ~ **from here to the station** la stazione non è lontana da qui; **in the** ~ in lontananza; **from a** ~ da lontano

distant /ˈdɪstənt/ *a* distante; ⟨*relative*⟩ lontano

dis'taste *n* avversione *f*. ~**ful** *a* spiacevole

distil /dɪˈstɪl/ *vt* (*pt/pp* **distilled**) distillare. ~**lation** /-ˈleɪʃn/ *n* distillazione *f*. ~**lery** /-ərɪ/ *n* distilleria *f*

distinct /dɪˈstɪŋkt/ *a* chiaro; *(different)* distinto. ~**ion** /-ɪŋkʃn/ *n* distinzione *f*; *Sch* massimo *m* dei voti. ~**ive** /-tɪv/ *a* caratteristico. ~**ly** *adv* chiaramente

distinguish /dɪˈstɪŋgwɪʃ/ *vt/i* distinguere; ~ **oneself** distinguersi. ~**ed** *a* rinomato; ⟨*appearance*⟩ distinto; ⟨*career*⟩ brillante

distort /dɪˈstɔːt/ *vt* distorcere. ~**ion** /-ɔːʃn/ *n* distorsione *f*

distract /dɪˈstrækt/ *vt* distrarre. ~**ed** /-ɪd/ *a* assente; *(fam: worried)* preoccupato. ~**ing** *a* che distoglie. ~**ion** /-ækʃn/ *n* distrazione *f*; *(despair)* disperazione *f*; **drive sb to** ~ portare qcno alla disperazione

distraught /dɪˈstrɔːt/ *a* sconvolto

distress /dɪˈstres/ *n* angoscia *f*; *(pain)* sofferenza *f*; *(danger)* difficoltà *f* ● *vt* sconvolgere; *(sadden)* affliggere. ~**ing** *a* penoso; *(shocking)* sconvolgente. ~ **signal** *n* segnale *m* di richiesta di soccorso

distribut|e /dɪˈstrɪbjuːt/ *vt* distribuire. ~**ion** /-ˈbjuːʃn/ *n* distribuzione *f*. ~**or** *n* distributore *m*

district /ˈdɪstrɪkt/ *n* regione *f*; *Admin* distretto *m*. ~ **nurse** *n* infermiere, -a *mf* che fa visite a domicilio

dis'trust *n* sfiducia *f* ● *vt* non fidarsi di. ~**ful** *a* diffidente

disturb /dɪˈstɜːb/ *vt* disturbare; *(emotionally)* turbare; spostare ⟨*papers*⟩. ~**ance** *n* disturbo *m*; ~**ances** (*pl: rioting etc*) disordini *mpl*. ~**ed** *a* turbato; [**mentally**] ~**ed** malato di mente. ~**ing** *a* inquietante

dis'used *a* non utilizzato

ditch /dɪtʃ/ *n* fosso *m* ● *vt* *(fam: abandon)* abbandonare ⟨*plan, car*⟩; piantare ⟨*lover*⟩

dither /ˈdɪðə(r)/ *vi* titubare

divan /dɪˈvæn/ *n* divano *m*

dive /daɪv/ *n* tuffo *m*; *Aeron* picchiata *f*; *(fam: place)* bettola *f* ● *vi* tuffarsi; *(when in water)* immergersi; *Aeron* scendere in picchiata; *(fam: rush)* precipitarsi

diver /ˈdaɪvə(r)/ *n* *(from board)* tuffatore, -trice *mf*; *(scuba)* sommozzatore, -trice *mf*; *(deep sea)* palombaro *m*

diver|ge /daɪˈvɜːdʒ/ *vi* divergere. ~**gent** /-ənt/ *a* divergente

diverse /daɪˈvɜːs/ *a* vario

diversify /daɪˈvɜːsɪfaɪ/ *vt/i* (*pt/pp* **-ied**) diversificare

diversion /daɪˈvɜːʃn/ *n* deviazione *f*; *(distraction)* diversivo *m*

diversity /daɪˈvɜːsətɪ/ *n* varietà *f*

divert /daɪˈvɜːt/ *vt* deviare ⟨*traffic*⟩; distogliere ⟨*attention*⟩

divest /daɪˈvest/ *vt* privare (**of** di)

divide /dɪ'vaɪd/ *vt* dividere (**by** per); **six ~d by two** sei diviso due ● *vi* dividersi

dividend /'dɪvɪdend/ *n* dividendo *m*; **pay ~s** *fig* ripagare

divine /dɪ'vaɪn/ *a* divino

diving /'daɪvɪŋ/ *n* (*from board*) tuffi *mpl*; (*scuba*) immersione *f*. **~-board** *n* trampolino *m*. **~ mask** *n* maschera *f* [subacquea]. **~-suit** *n* muta *f*; (*deep sea*) scafandro *m*

divinity /dɪ'vɪnətɪ/ *n* divinità *f inv*; (*subject*) teologia *f*; (*at school*) religione *f*

divisible /dɪ'vɪzɪbl/ *a* divisibile (**by** per)

division /dɪ'vɪʒn/ *n* divisione *f*; (*in sports league*) serie *f*

divorce /dɪ'vɔːs/ *n* divorzio *m* ● *vt* divorziare da. **~d** *a* divorziato; **get ~d** divorziare

divorcee /dɪvɔː'siː/ *n* divorziato, -a *mf*

divulge /daɪ'vʌldʒ/ *vt* rendere pubblico

DIY *n abbr* **do-it-yourself**

dizziness /'dɪzɪnɪs/ *n* giramenti *mpl* di testa

dizzy /'dɪzɪ/ *a* (**-ier, -iest**) vertiginoso; **I feel ~** mi gira la testa

do /duː/ *n* (*pl* **dos** *or* **do's**) *fam* festa *f* ● *v* (*3 sg pres tense* **does**; *pt* **did**; *pp* **done**) ● *vt* fare; (*fam: cheat*) fregare; **be done** *Culin* essere cotto; **well done** bravo; *Culin* ben cotto; **do the flowers** sistemare i fiori; **do the washing up** lavare i piatti; **do one's hair** farsi i capelli ● *vi* (*be suitable*) andare; (*be enough*) bastare; **this will do** questo va bene; **that will do!** basta così!; **do well/badly** cavarsela bene/male; **how is he doing?** come sta? ● *v aux* **do you speak Italian?** parli italiano?; **you don't like him, do you?** non ti piace, vero?; (*expressing astonishment*) non dirmi che ti piace!; **yes, I do** sì; (*emphatic*) invece sì; **no, I don't** no; **I don't smoke** non fumo; **don't you/doesn't he?** vero?; **so do I** anch'io; **do come in, John** entra, John; **how do you do?** piacere. **do away with** *vt* abolire (*rule*). **do for** *vt* **done for** *fam* rovinato. **do in** *vt* (*fam: kill*) uccidere; farsi male a (*back*); **done in** *fam* esausto. **do up** *vt* (*fasten*) abbottonare; (*renovate*) rimettere a nuovo; (*wrap*) avvolgere. **do with** *vt* **I could do with a spanner** mi ci vorrebbe una chiave inglese. **do without** *vt* fare a meno di

docile /'dəʊsaɪl/ *a* docile

dock¹ /dɒk/ *n Jur* banco *m* degli imputati

dock² *n Naut* bacino *m* ● *vi* entrare in porto; (*spaceship:*) congiungersi. **~er** *n* portuale *m*. **~s** *npl* porto *m*. **~yard** *n* cantiere *m* navale

doctor /'dɒktə(r)/ *n* dottore *m*, dottoressa *f* ● *vt* alterare (*drink*); castrare (*cat*). **~ate** /-ət/ *n* dottorato *m*

doctrine /'dɒktrɪn/ *n* dottrina *f*

document /'dɒkjʊmənt/ *n* documento *m*. **~ary** /-'mentərɪ/ *a* documentario ● *n* documentario *m*

doddery /'dɒdərɪ/ *a fam* barcollante

dodge /dɒdʒ/ *n fam* trucco *m* ● *vt* schivare (*blow*); evitare (*person*) ● *vi* scansarsi; **~ out of the way** scansarsi

dodgems /'dɒdʒəmz/ *npl* auto-scontro *msg*

dodgy /'dɒdʒɪ/ *a* (**-ier, -iest**) (*fam: dubious*) sospetto

doe /dəʊ/ *n* femmina *f* (*di daino, renna, lepre*); (*rabbit*) coniglia *f*

does /dʌz/ *see* **do**

doesn't /'dʌznt/ = **does not**

dog /dɒg/ *n* cane *m* ● *vt* (*pt/pp* **dogged**) (*illness, bad luck:*) perseguitare

dog: **~-biscuit** *n* biscotto *m* per cani. **~-collar** *n* collare *m* (*per cani*); *Relig fam* collare *m* del prete. **~-eared** *a* con le orecchie

dogged /'dɒgɪd/ *a* ostinato

'dog house *n* **in the ~** *fam* in disgrazia

dogma /'dɒgmə/ *n* dogma *m*. **~tic** /-'mætɪk/ *a* dogmatico

'dogsbody *n fam* tirapiedi *mf inv*

doily /'dɔɪlɪ/ *n* centrino *m*

do-it-yourself /duːɪtjə'self/ *n* fai da te *m*, bricolage *m*. **~ shop** *n* negozio *m* di bricolage

doldrums /'dɒldrəmz/ *npl* **be in the ~** essere giù di corda; (*business:*) essere in fase di stasi

dole /dəʊl/ *n* sussidio *m* di disoccupazione; **be on the ~** essere disoccupato ● **dole out** *vt* distribuire

doleful /'dəʊlfl/ *a* triste

doll /dɒl/ *n* bambola *f* ● **doll oneself up** *vt fam* mettersi in ghingheri

dollar /'dɒlə(r)/ *n* dollaro *m*

dollop /'dɒləp/ *n fam* cucchiaiata *f*

dolphin /'dɒlfɪn/ *n* delfino *m*

dome /dəʊm/ *n* cupola *f*

domestic /də'mestɪk/ *a* domestico; *Pol* interno; *Comm* nazionale. **~ animal** *n* animale *m* domestico

domesticated /də'mestɪkeɪtɪd/ *a* (*animal*) addomesticato

domestic: ~ **flight** n volo m nazionale. ~ **'servant** n domestico, -a mf

dominant /'dɒmɪnənt/ a dominante

dominat|e /'dɒmmeɪt/ vt/i dominare. **~ion** /-'neɪʃn/ n dominio m

domineering /dɒmɪ'nɪərɪŋ/ a autoritario

dominion /də'mɪnjən/ n Br Pol dominion m inv

don[1] /dɒn/ vt (pt/pp donned) liter indossare

don[2] n docente mf universitario, -a

donat|e /dəʊ'neɪt/ vt donare. **~ion** /-eɪʃn/ n donazione f

done /dʌn/ see do

donkey /'dɒŋkɪ/ n asino m; ~'s **years** fam secoli mpl. **~-work** n sgobbata f

donor /'dəʊnə(r)/ n donatore, -trice mf

don't /dəʊnt/ = **do not**

doodle /'du:dl/ vi scarabocchiare

doom /du:m/ n fato m; (ruin) rovina f ● vt be ~ed [to failure] essere destinato al fallimento; ~ed ⟨ship⟩ destinato ad affondare

door /dɔ:(r)/ n porta f; (of car) portiera f; **out of** ~s all'aperto

door: ~**man** n portiere m. **~mat** n zerbino m. **~step** n gradino m della porta. **~way** n vano m della porta

dope /dəʊp/ n fam (drug) droga f leggera; (information) indiscrezioni fpl; (idiot) idiota mf ● vt drogare; Sport dopare

dopey /'dəʊpɪ/ a fam addormentato

dormant /'dɔ:mənt/ a latente; ⟨volcano⟩ inattivo

dormer /'dɔ:mə(r)/ n ~ [window] abbaino m

dormitory /'dɔ:mɪtərɪ/ n dormitorio m

dormouse /'dɔ:-/ n ghiro m

dosage /'dəʊsɪdʒ/ n dosaggio m

dose /dəʊs/ n dose f

doss /dɒs/ vi sl accamparsi. **~er** n barbone, -a mf. **~-house** n dormitorio m pubblico

dot /dɒt/ n punto m; **at 8 o'clock on the** ~ alle 8 in punto

dot-com /dɒt'kɒm/ n azienda f legata a Internet

dote /dəʊt/ vi ~ **on** stravedere per

dotted /'dɒtɪd/ a ~ **line** linea f punteggiata; **be** ~ **with** essere punteggiato di

dotty /'dɒtɪ/ a (-ier, -iest) fam tocco; ⟨idea⟩ folle

double /'dʌbl/ a doppio ● adv **cost** ~ costare il doppio; **see** ~ vedere doppio; ~ **the amount** la quantità doppia ● n doppio m; (person) sosia m inv; ~**s** pl

Tennis doppio m; **at the** ~ di corsa ● vt raddoppiare; (fold) piegare in due ● vi raddoppiare. **double up** vi (bend over) piegarsi in due (**with** per); (share) dividere una stanza

double: ~-'**bass** n contrabbasso m. ~ '**bed** n letto m matrimoniale. ~-**breasted** a a doppio petto. ~ '**chin** n doppio mento m. ~ '**click** vt/i cliccare due volte, fare doppio clic (**on** su). ~-'**cross** vt ingannare. ~-'**decker** n autobus m inv a due piani. ~ '**Dutch** n fam ostrogoto m. ~ '**glazing** n doppiovetro m. ~ '**room** n camera f doppia

doubly /'dʌblɪ/ adv doppiamente

doubt /daʊt/ n dubbio m ● vt dubitare di. **~ful** a dubbio; (having doubts) in dubbio. **~fully** adv con aria dubbiosa. **~less** adv indubbiamente

dough /dəʊ/ n pasta f; (for bread) impasto m; (fam: money) quattrini mpl. **~nut** n bombolone m, krapfen m inv

douse /daʊs/ vt spegnere

dove /dʌv/ n colomba f

dowdy /'daʊdɪ/ a (-ier, -iest) trasandato

down[1] /daʊn/ n (feathers) piumino m

down[2] adv giù; **go/come** ~ scendere; ~ **there** laggiù; **sales are** ~ le vendite sono diminuite; **£50** ~ 50 sterline d'acconto; ~ **10%** ridotto del 10%; ~ **with...!** abbasso...! ● prep **walk** ~ **the road** camminare per strada; ~ **the stairs** giù per le scale; **fall** ~ **the stairs** cadere giù dalle scale; **get that** ~ **you!** fam butta giù!; **be** ~ **the pub** fam essere al pub ● vt bere tutto d'un fiato ⟨drink⟩

down: ~-**and**-'**out** n spiantato, -a mf. ~**cast** a abbattuto. ~**fall** n caduta f; (of person) rovina f. ~-'**grade** vt (in seniority) degradare. ~-'**hearted** a scoraggiato. ~'**hill** adv in discesa; **go** ~**hill** fig essere in declino. ~'**load** vt scaricare. ~ **payment** n deposito m. ~**pour** n acquazzone m. ~**right** a (absolute) totale; ⟨lie⟩ bell'e buono; ⟨idiot⟩ perfetto ● adv (completely) completamente. ~'**stairs** adv al piano di sotto ● a /'-/ del piano di sotto. ~'**stream** adv a valle. ~-**to**-'**earth** a ⟨person⟩ con i piedi per terra. ~**town** adv Am in centro. ~**trodden** a oppresso. ~**ward**[s] a verso il basso; ⟨slope⟩ in discesa ● adv verso il basso

dowry /'daʊrɪ/ n dote f

doze /dəʊz/ n sonnellino m ● vi sonnecchiare. **doze off** vi assopirsi

dozen /'dʌzn/ n dozzina f; **~s of books** libri a dozzine

Dr abbr **doctor**

drab /dræb/ a spento

draft[1] /drɑːft/ n abbozzo m; Comm cambiale f; Am Mil leva f ● vt abbozzare; Am Mil arruolare

draft[2] n Am = **draught**

drag /dræg/ n fam scocciatura f; **in ~ fam** ⟨man⟩ travestito da donna ● vt (pt/pp **dragged**) trascinare; dragare ⟨river⟩. **drag on** vi ⟨time, meeting:⟩ trascinarsi

dragon /'drægən/ n drago m. **~-fly** n libellula f

drain /dreɪn/ n tubo m di scarico; ⟨grid⟩ tombino m; **the ~s** pl le fognature; **be a ~ on sb's finances** prosciugare le finanze di qcno ● vt drenare ⟨land, wound⟩; scolare ⟨liquid, vegetables⟩; svuotare ⟨tank, glass, person⟩ ● vi **~ [away]** andar via

drain|age /'dreɪnɪdʒ/ n ⟨system⟩ drenaggio m; ⟨of land⟩ scolo m. **~ing board** n scolapiatti m inv. **~-pipe** n tubo m di scarico

drake /dreɪk/ n maschio m dell'anatra

drama /'drɑːmə/ n arte f drammatica; ⟨play⟩ opera f teatrale; ⟨event⟩ dramma m

dramatic /drə'mætɪk/ a drammatico

dramat|ist /'dræmətɪst/ n drammaturgo, -a mf. **~ize** vt adattare per il teatro; fig drammatizzare

drank /dræŋk/ see **drink**

drape /dreɪp/ n Am tenda f ● vt appoggiare (**over** su)

drastic /'dræstɪk/ a drastico; **~ally** adv drasticamente

draught /drɑːft/ n corrente f [d'aria]; **~s** sg ⟨game⟩ [gioco m della] dama fsg

draught: ~ beer n birra f alla spina. **~sman** n disegnatore, -trice mf

draughty /'drɑːftɪ/ a pieno di correnti d'aria; **it's ~** c'è corrente

draw /drɔː/ n ⟨attraction⟩ attrazione f; Sport pareggio m; ⟨in lottery⟩ sorteggio m ● v (pt **drew**, pp **drawn**) ● vt tirare; ⟨attract⟩ attirare; disegnare ⟨picture⟩; tracciare ⟨line⟩; ritirare ⟨money⟩; **~ lots** tirare a sorte ● vi ⟨tea:⟩ essere in infusione; Sport pareggiare; **~ near** avvicinarsi. **draw back** vt tirare indietro; ritirare ⟨hand⟩; tirare ⟨curtains⟩ ● vi ⟨recoil⟩ tirarsi indietro. **draw in** vt ritrarre ⟨claws etc⟩ ● vi ⟨train:⟩ arrivare; ⟨days:⟩ accorciarsi. **draw out** vt ⟨pull out⟩ tirar fuori; ritirare ⟨money⟩ ● vi

⟨train:⟩ partire; ⟨days:⟩ allungarsi. **draw up** vt redigere ⟨document⟩; accostare ⟨chair⟩; **~ oneself up to one's full height** farsi grande ● vi ⟨stop⟩ fermarsi

draw: ~back n inconveniente m. **~bridge** n ponte m levatoio

drawer /drɔː(r)/ n cassetto m

drawing /'drɔːɪŋ/ n disegno m

drawing: ~-board n tavolo m da disegno; fig **go back to the ~-board** ricominciare da capo. **~-pin** n puntina f. **~-room** n salotto m

drawl /drɔːl/ n pronuncia f strascicata

drawn /drɔːn/ see **draw**

dread /dred/ n terrore m ● vt aver il terrore di

dreadful /'dredful/ a terribile. **~ly** adv terribilmente

dream /driːm/ n sogno m ● attrib di sogno ● vt/i (pt/pp **dreamt** /dremt/ or **dreamed**) sognare (**about/of** di)

dreary /'drɪərɪ/ a (**-ier, -iest**) tetro; ⟨boring⟩ monotono

dredge /dredʒ/ vt/i dragare

dregs /dregz/ npl feccia fsg

drench /drentʃ/ vt **get ~ed** inzupparsi; **~ed** zuppo

dress /dres/ n ⟨woman's⟩ vestito m; ⟨clothing⟩ abbigliamento m ● vt vestire; ⟨decorate⟩ adornare; Culin condire; Med fasciare; **~ oneself, get ~ed** vestirsi ● vi vestirsi. **dress up** vi mettersi elegante; ⟨in disguise⟩ travestirsi (**as** da)

dress: ~ circle n Theat prima galleria f. **~er** n ⟨furniture⟩ credenza f; ⟨Am: dressing-table⟩ toilette f inv

dressing /'dresɪŋ/ n Culin condimento m; Med fasciatura f

dressing: ~-gown n vestaglia f. **~-room** n ⟨in gym⟩ spogliatoio m; Theat camerino m. **~-table** n toilette f inv

dress: ~maker n sarta f. **~ rehearsal** n prova f generale

dressy /'dresɪ/ a (**-ier, -iest**) elegante

drew /druː/ see **draw**

dribble /'drɪbl/ vi gocciolare; ⟨baby:⟩ sbavare; Sport dribblare

dribs and drabs /drɪbzən'dræbz/ npl **in ~** alla spicciolata

dried /draɪd/ a ⟨food⟩ essiccato

drier /'draɪə(r)/ n asciugabiancheria m inv

drift /drɪft/ n movimento m lento; ⟨of snow⟩ cumulo m; ⟨meaning⟩ senso m ● vi ⟨off course⟩ andare alla deriva; ⟨snow:⟩ accumularsi; ⟨fig: person:⟩ pro-

cedere senza meta. **drift apart** *vi*
⟨*people:*⟩ allontanarsi l'uno dall'altro

drill /drɪl/ *n* trapano *m*; *Mil* esercitazione *f* ● *vt* trapanare; *Mil* fare esercitare
● *vi Mil* esercitarsi; ~ **for oil** trivellare
in cerca di petrolio

drily /'draɪlɪ/ *adv* seccamente

drink /drɪŋk/ *n* bevanda *f*; ⟨*alcoholic*⟩
bicchierino *m*; **have a ~** bere qualcosa;
a ~ of water un po' d'acqua ● *vt/i* (*pt*
drank, *pp* **drunk**) bere. **drink up** *vt* finire ● *vi* finire il bicchiere

drink|able /'drɪŋkəbl/ *a* potabile. **~er**
n bevitore, -trice *mf*

'drinking-water *n* acqua *f* potabile

drip /drɪp/ *n* gocciolamento *m*; ⟨*drop*⟩
goccia *f*; *Med* flebo *f inv*; ⟨*fam: person*⟩
mollaccione, -a *mf* ● *vi* (*pt/pp* **dripped**)
gocciolare. **~-'dry** *a* che non si stira.
~ping *n* (*from meat*) grasso *m* d'arrosto ● *a* **~ping [wet]** fradicio

drive /draɪv/ *n* (*in car*) giro *m*;
⟨*entrance*⟩ viale *m*; ⟨*energy*⟩ grinta *f*;
Psych pulsione *f*; ⟨*organized effort*⟩ operazione *f*; *Techn* motore *m*; *Comput* lettore *m* ● *v* (*pt* **drove**, *pp* **driven**) ● *vt*
portare ⟨*person by car*⟩; guidare ⟨*car*⟩;
⟨*Sport: hit*⟩ mandare; *Techn* far funzionare; ~ **sb mad** far diventare matto
qcno ● *vi* guidare. **drive at** *vt* **what are
you driving at?** dove vuoi arrivare?
drive away *vt* portare via in macchina;
⟨*chase*⟩ cacciare ● *vi* andare via in macchina. **drive in** *vt* piantare ⟨*nail*⟩ ● *vi*
arrivare [in macchina]. **drive off** *vt* portare via in macchina; ⟨*chase*⟩ cacciare
● *vi* andare via in macchina. **drive on**
vi proseguire (*in macchina*). **drive up** *vi*
arrivare (*in macchina*)

drivel /'drɪvl/ *n fam* sciocchezze *fpl*

driven /'drɪvn/ *see* **drive**

driver /'draɪvə(r)/ *n* guidatore, -trice
mf; ⟨*of train*⟩ conducente *mf*

driving /'draɪvɪŋ/ *a* ⟨*rain*⟩ violento;
⟨*force*⟩ motore ● *n* guida *f*

driving: ~ **lesson** *n* lezione *f* di guida.
~ **licence** *n* patente *f* di guida. ~
school *n* scuola *f* guida. ~ **test** *n* esame *m* di guida

drizzle /'drɪzl/ *n* pioggerella *f* ● *vi* pio-
vigginare

drone /drəʊn/ *n* ⟨*bee*⟩ fuco *m*; ⟨*sound*⟩
ronzio *m*

droop /druːp/ *vi* abbassarsi; ⟨*flowers:*⟩
afflosciarsi

drop /drɒp/ *n* ⟨*of liquid*⟩ goccia *f*; ⟨*fall*⟩
caduta *f*; ⟨*in price, temperature*⟩ calo *m*
● *v* (*pt/pp* **dropped**) ● *vt* far cadere;

sganciare ⟨*bomb*⟩; ⟨*omit*⟩ omettere;
⟨*give up*⟩ abbandonare ● *vi* cadere;
⟨*price, temperature, wind:*⟩ calare;
⟨*ground:*⟩ essere in pendenza. **drop in**
vi passare. **drop off** *vt* depositare
⟨*person*⟩ ● *vi* cadere; ⟨*fall asleep*⟩ assopirsi. **drop out** *vi* cadere; ⟨*of race,
society*⟩ ritirarsi; ~ **out of school** lasciare la scuola

'drop-out *n* persona *f* contro il sistema
sociale

droppings /'drɒpɪŋz/ *npl* sterco *m*

drought /draʊt/ *n* siccità *f*

drove /drəʊv/ *see* **drive**

droves /drəʊvz/ *npl* **in ~** in massa

drown /draʊn/ *vi* annegare ● *vt* annegare; coprire ⟨*noise*⟩; **he was ~ed** è an-
negato

drowsy /'draʊzɪ/ *a* sonnolento

drudgery /'drʌdʒərɪ/ *n* lavoro *m* pesante e noioso

drug /drʌg/ *n* droga *f*; *Med* farmaco *m*;
take ~s drogarsi ● *vt* (*pt/pp* **drugged**)
drogare

drug: ~ **addict** *n* tossicomane, -a *mf*. ~
dealer *n* spacciatore, -trice *mf* [di dro-
ga]. **~gist** *n Am* farmacista *mf*. **~store**
n Am negozio *m* di generi vari, inclusi
medicinali, *che funge anche da bar*;
⟨*dispensing*⟩ farmacia *f*

drum /drʌm/ *n* tamburo *m*; ⟨*for oil*⟩ bidone *m*; **~s** (*pl: in pop-group*) batteria *f*
● *v* (*pt/pp* **drummed**) ● *vi* suonare il
tamburo; ⟨*in pop-group*⟩ suonare la batteria ● *vt* ~ **sth into sb** *fam* ripetere
qcsa a qcno cento volte. **~mer** *n* percus-
sionista *mf*; ⟨*in pop-group*⟩ batterista
mf. **~stick** *n* bacchetta *f*; ⟨*of chicken,
turkey*⟩ coscia *f*

drunk /drʌŋk/ *see* **drink** ● *a* ubriaco;
get ~ ubriacarsi ● *n* ubriaco, -a *mf*

drunk|ard /'drʌŋkəd/ *n* ubriacone, -a
mf. **~en** *a* ubriaco; **~en driving** guida *f*
in stato di ebbrezza

dry /draɪ/ *a* (**drier, driest**) asciutto;
⟨*climate, country*⟩ secco ● *vt/i* (*pt/pp*
dried) asciugare; ~ **one's eyes** asciu-
garsi le lacrime. **dry up** *vi* seccarsi; ⟨*fig:
source:*⟩ prosciugarsi; ⟨*fam: be quiet*⟩
stare zitto; ⟨*do dishes*⟩ asciugare i piatti

dry: **~-'clean** *vt* pulire a secco.
~-'cleaner's *n* ⟨*shop*⟩ tintoria *f*. **~ness**
n secchezza *f*

DTP *n abbr* (**desktop publishing**)
desktop publishing *m*

dual /'djuːəl/ *a* doppio

dual: ~ **'carriageway** *n* strada *f* a due
carreggiate. **~-'purpose** *a* a doppio uso

dub /dʌb/ vt (pt/pp **dubbed**) doppiare ⟨film⟩; ⟨name⟩ soprannominare

dubious /'dju:brəs/ a dubbio; **be ~ about** avere dei dubbi riguardo

duchess /'dʌtʃɪs/ n duchessa f

duck /dʌk/ n anatra f ● vt (in water) immergere; **~ one's head** abbassare la testa ● vi abbassarsi. **~ling** n anatroccolo m

duct /dʌkt/ n condotto m; Anat dotto m

dud /dʌd/ fam a Mil disattivato; ⟨coin⟩ falso; ⟨cheque⟩ a vuoto ● n ⟨banknote⟩ banconota f falsa

due /dju:/ a dovuto; **be ~** ⟨train:⟩ essere previsto; **the baby is ~ next week** il bambino dovrebbe nascere la settimana prossima; **~ to** (owing to) a causa di; **be ~ to** (causally) essere dovuto a; **I'm ~ to...** dovrei...; **in ~ course** a tempo debito ● adv — **north** direttamente a nord

duel /'dju:əl/ n duello m

dues /dju:z/ npl quota f [di iscrizione]

duet /dju:'et/ n duetto m

dug /dʌg/ see **dig**

duke /dju:k/ n duca m

dull /dʌl/ a (overcast, not bright) cupo; (not shiny) opaco; ⟨sound⟩ soffocato; (boring) monotono; (stupid) ottuso ● vt intorpidire ⟨mind⟩; attenuare ⟨pain⟩

duly /'dju:lɪ/ adv debitamente

dumb /dʌm/ a muto; ⟨fam: stupid⟩ ottuso. **~founded** /dʌm'faʊndɪd/ a sbigottito

dummy /'dʌmɪ/ n (tailor's) manichino m; (for baby) succhiotto m; (model) riproduzione f

dump /dʌmp/ n (for refuse) scarico m; ⟨fam: town⟩ mortorio m; **be down in the ~s** fam essere depresso ● vt scaricare; ⟨fam: put down⟩ lasciare; ⟨fam: get rid of⟩ liberarsi di

dumpling /'dʌmplɪŋ/ n gnocco m

dunce /dʌns/ n zuccone, -a mf

dune /dju:n/ n duna f

dung /dʌŋ/ n sterco m

dungarees /dʌŋgə'ri:z/ npl tuta fsg

dungeon /'dʌndʒən/ n prigione f sotterranea

duo /'dju:əʊ/ n duo m inv; Mus duetto m

duplicate¹ /'dju:plɪkət/ a doppio ● n duplicato m; (document) copia f; **in ~** in duplicato

duplicat|e² /'dju:plɪkeɪt/ vt fare un duplicato di; ⟨research:⟩ essere una ripetizione di ⟨work⟩

durable /'djʊərəbl/ a resistente; durevole ⟨basis, institution⟩

duration /djʊə'reɪʃn/ n durata f

duress /djʊə'res/ n costrizione f; **under ~** sotto minaccia

during /'djʊərɪŋ/ prep durante

dusk /dʌsk/ n crepuscolo m

dust /dʌst/ n polvere f ● vt spolverare; (sprinkle) cospargere ⟨cake⟩ (**with** di) ● vi spolverare

dust: ~bin n pattumiera f. **~-cart** n camion m della nettezza urbana. **~er** n strofinaccio m. **~-jacket** n sopraccoperta f. **~man** n spazzino m. **~pan** n paletta f per la spazzatura

dusty /'dʌstɪ/ a (-ier, -iest) polveroso

Dutch /dʌtʃ/ a olandese; **go ~** fam fare alla romana ● n (language) olandese m; **the ~** pl gli olandesi. **~man** n olandese m

dutiable /'dju:tɪəbl/ a soggetto a imposta

dutiful /'dju:tɪfl/ a rispettoso

duty /'dju:tɪ/ n dovere m; (task) compito m; (tax) dogana f; **be on ~** essere di servizio. **~-free** a esente da dogana

duvet /'du:veɪ/ n piumone m

dwarf /dwɔ:f/ n (pl -s or **dwarves**) nano, -a mf ● vt rimpicciolire

dwell /dwel/ vi (pt/pp **dwelt**) liter dimorare. **dwell on** vt fig soffermarsi su. **~ing** n abitazione f

dwindle /'dwɪndl/ vi diminuire

dye /daɪ/ n tintura f ● vt (pres p **dyeing**) tingere

dying /'daɪŋ/ see **die²**

dynamic /daɪ'næmɪk/ a dinamico

dynamite /'daɪnəmaɪt/ n dinamite f

dynamo /'daɪnəməʊ/ n dinamo f inv

dynasty /'dɪnəstɪ/ n dinastia f

dysentery /'dɪsəntrɪ/ n dissenteria f

dyslex|ia /dɪs'leksɪə/ n dislessia f. **~ic** a dislessico

Ee

each /iːtʃ/ *a* ogni ● *pron* ognuno; **£1 ~** una sterlina ciascuno; **they love/hate ~ other** si amano/odiano; **we lend ~ other money** ci prestiamo i soldi

eager /ˈiːgə(r)/ *a* ansioso **(to do** di fare); ⟨*pupil*⟩ avido di sapere. **~ly** *adv* ⟨*wait*⟩ ansiosamente; ⟨*offer*⟩ premurosamente. **~ness** *n* premura *f*

eagle /ˈiːgl/ *n* aquila *f*

ear¹ /ɪə(r)/ *n* ⟨*of corn*⟩ spiga *f*

ear² *n* orecchio *m*. **~ache** *n* mal *m* d'orecchi. **~drum** *n* timpano *m*

earl /ɜːl/ *n* conte *m*

early /ˈɜːlɪ/ *a* **(-ier, -iest)** ⟨*before expected time*⟩ in anticipo; ⟨*spring*⟩ prematuro; ⟨*reply*⟩ pronto; ⟨*works, writings*⟩ primo; **be here ~!** sii puntuale!; **you're ~!** sei in anticipo!; **~ morning walk** passeggiata *f* mattutina; **in the ~ morning** la mattina presto; **in the ~ spring** all'inizio della primavera; **~ retirement** prepensionamento *m* ● *adv* presto; ⟨*ahead of time*⟩ in anticipo; **~ in the morning** la mattina presto

'**earmark** *vt* riservare **(for** a)

earn /ɜːn/ *vt* guadagnare; ⟨*deserve*⟩ meritare

earnest /ˈɜːnɪst/ *a* serio ● *n* **in ~** sul serio. **~ly** *adv* con aria seria

earnings /ˈɜːnɪŋz/ *npl* guadagni *mpl*; ⟨*salary*⟩ stipendio *m*

ear: ~phones *npl* cuffia *fsg*. **~ring** *n* orecchino *m*. **~shot** *n* **within ~shot** a portata d'orecchio; **he is out of ~shot** non può sentire

earth /ɜːθ/ *n* terra *f* **where/what on ~?** dove/che diavolo? ● *vt Electr* mettere a terra

earthenware /ˈɜːθn-/ *n* terraglia *f*

earthly /ˈɜːθlɪ/ *a* terrestre; **be no ~ use** *fam* essere perfettamente inutile

'**earthquake** *n* terremoto *m*

earthy /ˈɜːθɪ/ *a* terroso; ⟨*coarse*⟩ grossolano

earwig /ˈɪəwɪg/ *n* forbicina *f*

ease /iːz/ *n* **at ~** a proprio agio; **at ~!** *Mil* riposo!; **ill at ~** a disagio; **with ~** con facilità ● *vt* calmare ⟨*pain*⟩; allevia-

re ⟨*tension, shortage*⟩; ⟨*slow down*⟩ rallentare; ⟨*loosen*⟩ allentare ● *vi* ⟨*pain, situation, wind:*⟩ calmarsi

easel /ˈiːzl/ *n* cavalletto *m*

easily /ˈiːzɪlɪ/ *adv* con facilità; **~ the best** certamente il meglio

east /iːst/ *n* est *m*; **to the ~ of** a est di ● *a* dell'est ● *adv* verso est

Easter /ˈiːstə(r)/ *n* Pasqua *f*. **~ egg** uovo *m* di Pasqua

east|erly /ˈiːstəlɪ/ *a* da levante. **~ern** *a* orientale. **~ward[s]** /-wəd[z]/ *adv* verso est

easy /ˈiːzɪ/ *a* **(-ier, -iest)** facile; **take it** *or* **things ~** prendersela con calma; **take it ~!** ⟨*don't get excited*⟩ calma!; **go ~ with** andarci piano con

easy: ~ chair *n* poltrona *f*. **~'going** *a* conciliante

eat /iːt/ *vt/i* **(**pt **ate,** pp **eaten)** mangiare. **eat into** *vt* intaccare. **eat up** *vt* mangiare tutto ⟨*food*⟩; *fig* inghiottire ⟨*profits*⟩

eat|able /ˈiːtəbl/ *a* mangiabile. **~er** *n* ⟨*apple*⟩ mela *f* da tavola; **be a big ~er** ⟨*person:*⟩ essere una buona forchetta

eau-de-Cologne /əʊdəkəˈləʊn/ *n* acqua *f* di Colonia

eaves /iːvz/ *npl* cornicione *msg*. **~drop** *vi* **(**pt/pp **~dropped)** origliare; **~drop on** ascoltare di nascosto

ebb /eb/ *n* ⟨*tide*⟩ riflusso *m*; **at a low ~** *fig* a terra ● *vi* rifluire; *fig* declinare

ebony /ˈebənɪ/ *n* ebano *m*

eccentric /ɪkˈsentrɪk/ *a* & *n* eccentrico, -a *mf*

ecclesiastical /ɪkliːzɪˈæstɪkl/ *a* ecclesiastico

echo /ˈekəʊ/ *n* **(**pl **-es)** eco *f or m* ● *v* **(**pt/pp **echoed,** pres p **echoing)** ● *vt* echeggiare; ripetere ⟨*words*⟩ ● *vi* risuonare **(with** di)

eclipse /ɪˈklɪps/ *n Astr* eclissi *f inv* ● *vt* *fig* eclissare

ecolog|ical /iːkəˈlɒdʒɪkl/ *a* ecologico. **~y** /ɪˈkɒlədʒɪ/ *n* ecologia *f*

e-commerce /ˈiːkɒmɜːs/ *n* e-commerce *m inv*, commercio *m* elettronico

economic /iːkəˈnɒmɪk/ *a* economico.

~al *a* economico. **~ally** *adv* economicamente; *(thriftily)* in economia. **~s** *n* economia *f*

economist /ɪ'kɒnəmɪst/ *n* economista *mf*

economize /ɪ'kɒnəmaɪz/ *vi* economizzare **(on** su)

economy /ɪ'kɒnəmɪ/ *n* economia *f*

ecstasy /'ekstəsɪ/ *n* estasi *f inv; (drug)* ecstasy *f*

ecstatic /ɪk'stætɪk/ *a* estatico

ecu /'eɪkju:/ *n* ecu *m inv*

eczema /'eksɪmə/ *n* eczema *m*

edge /edʒ/ *n* bordo *m; (of knife)* filo *m; (of road)* ciglio *m;* **on ~** con i nervi tesi; **have the ~ on** *fam* avere un vantaggio su ● *vt* bordare. **edge forward** *vi* avanzare lentamente

edgeways /'edʒweɪz/ *adv* di fianco; **I couldn't get a word in ~** non ho potuto infilare neanche mezza parola nel discorso

edging /'edʒɪŋ/ *n* bordo *m*

edgy /'edʒɪ/ *a* nervoso

edible /'edɪbl/ *a* commestibile; **this pizza's not ~** questa pizza è immangiabile

edict /'i:dɪkt/ *n* editto *m*

edify /'edɪfaɪ/ *vt (pt/pp* **-ied)** edificare. **~ing** *a* edificante

edit /'edɪt/ *vt (pt/pp* **edited)** far la revisione di *(text)*; curare l'edizione di *(anthology, dictionary)*; dirigere *(newspaper)*; montare *(film)*; editare *(tape)*; **~ed by** *(book)* a cura di

edition /ɪ'dɪʃn/ *n* edizione *f*

editor /'edɪtə(r)/ *n (of anthology, dictionary)* curatore, -trice *mf; (of newspaper)* redattore, -trice *mf; (of film)* responsabile *mf* del montaggio

editorial /edɪ'tɔ:rɪəl/ *a* redazionale ● *n Journ* editoriale *m*

educate /'edjʊkeɪt/ *vt* istruire; educare *(public, mind)*; **be ~d at Eton** essere educato a Eton. **~d** *a* istruito

education /edjʊ'keɪʃn/ *n* istruzione *f; (culture)* cultura *f*, educazione *f*. **~al** *a* istruttivo; *(visit)* educativo; *(publishing)* didattico

eel /i:l/ *n* anguilla *f*

eerie /'ɪərɪ/ *a* **(-ier, -iest)** inquietante

effect /ɪ'fekt/ *n* effetto *m;* **in ~** in effetti; **take ~** *(law:)* entrare in vigore; *(medicine:)* fare effetto ● *vt* effettuare

effective /ɪ'fektɪv/ *a* efficace; *(striking)* che colpisce; *(actual)* di fatto; **~ from** in vigore a partire da. **~ly** *adv*

efficacemente; *(actually)* di fatto. **~ness** *n* efficacia *f*

effeminate /ɪ'femɪnət/ *a* effeminato

effervescent /efə'vesnt/ *a* effervescente

efficiency /ɪ'fɪʃənsɪ/ *n* efficienza *f; (of machine)* rendimento *m*

efficient /ɪ'fɪʃənt/ *a* efficiente. **~ly** *adv* efficientemente

effort /'efət/ *n* sforzo *m;* **make an ~** sforzarsi. **~less** *a* facile. **~lessly** *adv* con facilità

effrontery /ɪ'frʌntərɪ/ *n* sfrontatezza *f*

effusive /ɪ'fju:sɪv/ *a* espansivo; *(speech)* caloroso

e.g. *abbr* **(exempli gratia)** per es.

egalitarian /ɪgælɪ'teərɪən/ *a* egalitario

egg[1] /eg/ *vt* **~ on** *fam* incitare

egg[2] *n* uovo *m*. **~-cup** *n* portauovo *m inv*. **~shell** *n* guscio *m* d'uovo. **~-timer** *n* clessidra *f* per misurare il tempo di cottura delle uova

ego /'i:gəʊ/ *n* ego *m*. **~centric** /-'sentrɪk/ *a* egocentrico. **~ism** *n* egoismo *m*. **~ist** *n* egoista *mf*. **~tism** *n* egotismo *m*. **~tist** *n* egotista *mf*

Egypt /'i:dʒɪpt/ *n* Egitto *m*. **~ian** /ɪ'dʒɪpʃn/ *a & n* egiziano, -a *mf*

eiderdown /'aɪdə-/ *n (quilt)* piumino *m*

eigh|t /eɪt/ *a* otto ● *n* otto *m*. **~'teen** *a & n* diciotto *m*. **~'teenth** *a & n* diciottesimo, -a *mf*

eighth /eɪtθ/ *a* ottavo ● *n* ottavo *m*

eightieth /'eɪtɪɪθ/ *a & n* ottantesimo, -a *mf*

eighty /'eɪtɪ/ *a & n* ottanta *m*

either /'aɪðə(r)/ *a & pron* **~ [of them]** l'uno o l'altro; **I don't like ~ [of them]** non mi piace né l'uno né l'altro; **on ~ side** da tutte e due le parti ● *adv* **I don't ~** nemmeno io; **I don't like John or his brother ~** non mi piace John e nemmeno suo fratello ● *conj* **~ John or his brother will be there** ci saranno o John o suo fratello; **I don't like ~ John or his brother** non mi piacciono né John né suo fratello; **~ you go to bed or [else]...** o vai a letto o [altrimenti]..

eject /ɪ'dʒekt/ *vt* eiettare *(pilot)*; espellere *(tape, drunk)*

eke /i:k/ *vt* **~ out** far bastare; *(increase)* arrotondare; **~ out a living** arrangiarsi

elaborate[1] /ɪ'læbərət/ *a* elaborato

elaborate[2] /ɪ'læbəreɪt/ *vi* entrare nei particolari **(on** di)

elapse /ɪ'læps/ *vi* trascorrere

elastic /ɪ'læstɪk/ *a* elastico ● *n* elastico *m*. **~ 'band** *n* elastico *m*

elasticity /ɪlæs'tɪsətɪ/ n elasticità f

elated /ɪ'leɪtɪd/ a esultante

elbow /'elbəʊ/ n gomito m

elder[1] /'eldə(r)/ n (tree) sambuco m

eld|er[2] a maggiore ● n **the ~** il/la maggiore. **~erly** a anziano. **~est** a maggiore ● n **the ~est** il/la maggiore

elect /ɪ'lekt/ a **the president ~** il futuro presidente ● vt eleggere; **~ to do sth** decidere di fare qcsa. **~ion** /-ekʃn/ n elezione f

elector /ɪ'lektə(r)/ n elettore, -trice mf. **~al** a elettorale; **~al roll** liste fpl elettorali. **~ate** /-rət/ n elettorato m

electric /ɪ'lektrɪk/ a elettrico

electrical /ɪ'lektrɪkl/ a elettrico; **~ engineering** elettrotecnica f

electric: **~ 'blanket** n termocoperta f. **~ 'fire** n stufa f elettrica

electrician /ɪlek'trɪʃn/ n elettricista m

electricity /ɪlek'trɪsətɪ/ n elettricità f

electrify /ɪ'lektrɪfaɪ/ vt (pt/pp **-ied**) elettrificare; fig elettrizzare. **~ing** a fig elettrizzante

electrocute /ɪ'lektrəkjuːt/ vt fulminare; (execute) giustiziare sulla sedia elettrica

electrode /ɪ'lektrəʊd/ n elettrodo m

electron /ɪ'lektrɒn/ n elettrone m

electronic /ɪlek'trɒnɪk/ a elettronico. **~ mail** n posta f elettronica. **~s** n elettronica f

elegance /'elɪgəns/ n eleganza f

elegant /'elɪgənt/ a elegante

elegy /'elɪdʒɪ/ n elegia f

element /'elɪmənt/ n elemento m. **~ary** /-'mentərɪ/ a elementare

elephant /'elɪfənt/ n elefante m

elevat|e /'elɪveɪt/ vt elevare. **~ion** /-'veɪʃn/ n elevazione f; (height) altitudine f; (angle) alzo m

elevator /'elɪveɪtə(r)/ n Am ascensore m

eleven /ɪ'levn/ a undici ● n undici m. **~th** a & n undicesimo, -a mf; **at the ~th hour** fam all'ultimo momento

elf /elf/ n (pl **elves**) elfo m

elicit /ɪ'lɪsɪt/ vt ottenere

eligible /'elɪdʒəbl/ a eleggibile; **~ young man** buon partito; **be ~ for** aver diritto a

eliminate /ɪ'lɪmɪneɪt/ vt eliminare

élite /eɪ'liːt/ n fior fiore m

ellip|se /ɪ'lɪps/ n ellisse f. **~tical** a ellittico

elm /elm/ n olmo m

elocution /elə'kjuːʃn/ n elocuzione f

elope /ɪ'ləʊp/ vi fuggire [per sposarsi]

eloquen|ce /'eləkwəns/ n eloquenza f. **~t** a eloquente. **~tly** adv con eloquenza

else /els/ adv altro; **who ~?** e chi altro?; **he did of course, who ~?** l'ha fatto lui e chi, se no?; **nothing ~** nient'altro; **or ~** altrimenti; **someone ~** qualcun altro; **somewhere ~** da qualche altra parte; **anyone ~** chiunque altro; (as question) nessun'altro?; **anything ~** qualunque altra cosa; (as question) altro?. **~where** adv altrove

elucidate /ɪ'luːsɪdeɪt/ vt delucidare

elude /ɪ'luːd/ vt eludere; (avoid) evitare; **the name ~s me** il nome mi sfugge

elusive /ɪ'luːsɪv/ a elusivo

emaciated /ɪ'meɪsɪeɪtɪd/ a emaciato

e-mail /'iːmeɪl/ n posta f elettronica; **~ address** n indirizzo m e-mail ● vt spedire via posta elettronica

emanate /'eməneɪt/ vi emanare

emancipat|ed /ɪ'mænsɪpeɪtɪd/ a emancipato. **~ion** /-'peɪʃn/ n emancipazione f; (of slaves) liberazione f

embankment /ɪm'bæŋkmənt/ n argine m; Rail massicciata f

embargo /em'bɑːgəʊ/ n (pl **-es**) embargo m

embark /ɪm'bɑːk/ vi imbarcarsi; **~ on** intraprendere. **~ation** /embɑː'keɪʃn/ n imbarco m

embarrass /em'bærəs/ vt imbarazzare. **~ed** a imbarazzato. **~ing** a imbarazzante. **~ment** n imbarazzo m

embassy /'embəsɪ/ n ambasciata f

embedded /ɪm'bedɪd/ a (in concrete) cementato; (traditions) radicato

embellish /ɪm'belɪʃ/ vt abbellire

embers /'embəz/ npl braci fpl

embezzle /ɪm'bezl/ vt appropriarsi indebitamente di. **~ment** n appropriazione f indebita

embitter /ɪm'bɪtə(r)/ vt amareggiare

emblem /'embləm/ n emblema m

embody /ɪm'bɒdɪ/ vt (pt/pp **-ied**) incorporare; **~ what is best in...** rappresentare quanto c'è di meglio di...

emboss /ɪm'bɒs/ vt sbalzare (metal); stampare in rilievo (paper). **~ed** a in rilievo

embrace /ɪm'breɪs/ n abbraccio m ● vt abbracciare ● vi abbracciarsi

embroider /ɪm'brɔɪdə(r)/ vt ricamare (design); fig abbellire. **~y** n ricamo m

embryo /'embrɪəʊ/ n embrione m

emerald /'emərəld/ n smeraldo m

emer|ge /ɪ'mɜːdʒ/ vi emergere; (come into being: nation) nascere; (sun, *flowers*⟩ spuntare fuori. **~gence** /-əns/ *n* emergere *m*; (*of new country*) nascita *f*

emergency /ɪ'mɜ:dʒənsɪ/ *n* emergenza *f*; **in an ~** in caso di emergenza. **~ exit** *n* uscita *f* di sicurezza

emery /'emərɪ/: **~ board** *n* limetta *f* [per le unghie]

emigrant /'emɪgrənt/ *n* emigrante *mf*

emigrat|e /'emɪgreɪt/ *vi* emigrare. **~ion** /-'greɪʃn/ *n* emigrazione *f*

eminent /'emɪnənt/ *a* eminente. **~ly** *adv* eminentemente

emission /ɪ'mɪʃn/ *n* emissione *f*; (*of fumes*) esalazione *f*

emit /ɪ'mɪt/ *vt* (*pt/pp* emitted) emettere; esalare ⟨*fumes*⟩

emotion /ɪ'məʊʃn/ *n* emozione *f*. **~al** *a* denso di emozione; ⟨*person, reaction*⟩ emotivo; **become ~al** avere una reazione emotiva

emotive /ɪ'məʊtɪv/ *a* emotivo

empathize /'empəθaɪz/ *vi* **~ with sb** immedesimarsi nei problemi di qcno

emperor /'empərə(r)/ *n* imperatore *m*

emphasis /'emfəsɪs/ *n* enfasi *f*; **put the ~ on sth** accentuare qcsa

emphasize /'emfəsaɪz/ *vt* accentuare ⟨*word, syllable*⟩; sottolineare ⟨*need*⟩

emphatic /ɪm'fætɪk/ *a* categorico

empire /'empaɪə(r)/ *n* impero *m*

empirical /em'pɪrɪkl/ *a* empirico

employ /em'plɔɪ/ *vt* impiegare; *fig* usare ⟨*tact*⟩. **~ee** /emplɔr'i:/ *n* impiegato, -a *mf*. **~er** *n* datore *m* di lavoro. **~ment** *n* occupazione *f*; ⟨*work*⟩ lavoro *m*. **~ment agency** *n* ufficio *m* di collocamento

empower /ɪm'paʊə(r)/ *vt* autorizzare; ⟨*enable*⟩ mettere in grado

empress /'emprɪs/ *n* imperatrice *f*

empties /'emptɪz/ *npl* vuoti *mpl*

emptiness /'emptɪnɪs/ *n* vuoto *m*

empty /'emptɪ/ *a* vuoto; ⟨*promise, threat*⟩ vano ● *v* (*pt/pp* -ied) ● *vt* vuotare ⟨*container*⟩ ● *vi* vuotarsi

emulate /'emjʊleɪt/ *vt* emulare

emulsion /ɪ'mʌlʃn/ *n* emulsione *f*

enable /ɪ'neɪbl/ *vt* **~ sb to** mettere qcno in grado di

enact /ɪ'nækt/ *vt Theat* rappresentare; decretare ⟨*law*⟩

enamel /ɪ'næml/ *n* smalto *m* ● *vt* (*pt/pp* enamelled) smaltare

enchant /ɪn'tʃɑ:nt/ *vt* incantare. **~ing** *a* incantevole. **~ment** *n* incanto *m*

encircle /ɪn'sɜ:kl/ *vt* circondare

enclave /'enkleɪv/ *n* enclave *f inv*; *fig* territorio *m*

enclos|e /ɪn'kləʊz/ *vt* circondare ⟨*land*⟩; (*in letter*) allegare (**with** a). **~ed** *a* ⟨*space*⟩ chiuso; (*in letter*) allegato. **~ure** /-ʒə(r)/ *n* (*at zoo*) recinto *m*; (*in letter*) allegato *m*

encompass /ɪn'kʌmpəs/ *vt* (*include*) comprendere

encore /'ɒŋkɔ:(r)/ *n* & *int* bis *m inv*

encounter /ɪn'kaʊntə(r)/ *n* incontro *m*; (*battle*) scontro *m* ● *vt* incontrare

encourag|e /ɪn'kʌrɪdʒ/ *vt* incoraggiare; promuovere ⟨*the arts, independence*⟩. **~ement** *n* incoraggiamento *m*; (*of the arts*) promozione *f*. **~ing** *a* incoraggiante; ⟨*smile*⟩ di incoraggiamento

encroach /ɪn'krəʊtʃ/ *vt* **~ on** invadere ⟨*land, privacy*⟩; abusare di ⟨*time*⟩; interferire con ⟨*rights*⟩

encumb|er /ɪn'kʌmbə(r)/ *vt* **~ered with** essere carico di ⟨*children, suitcases*⟩; ingombro di ⟨*furniture*⟩. **~rance** /-rəns/ *n* peso *m*

encyclop[a]ed|ia /ɪnsaɪklə'pi:dɪə/ *n* enciclopedia *f*. **~ic** *a* enciclopedico

end /end/ *n* fine *f*; (*of box, table, piece of string*) estremità *f*; (*of town, room*) parte *f*; (*purpose*) fine *m*; **in the ~** alla fine; **at the ~ of May** alla fine di maggio; **at the ~ of the street/garden** in fondo alla strada/al giardino; **on ~** (*upright*) in piedi; **for days on ~** per giorni e giorni; **for six days on ~** per sei giorni di fila; **put an ~ to sth** mettere fine a qcsa; **make ~s meet** *fam* sbarcare il lunario; **no ~ of** *fam* un sacco di ● *vt/i* finire. **end up** *vi* finire; **~ up doing sth** finire col fare qcsa

endanger /ɪn'deɪndʒə(r)/ *vt* rischiare ⟨*one's life*⟩; mettere a repentaglio ⟨*sb else, success of sth*⟩

endear|ing /ɪn'dɪərɪŋ/ *a* accattivante. **~ment** *n* **term of ~ment** vezzeggiativo *m*

endeavour /ɪn'devə(r)/ *n* tentativo *m* ● *vi* sforzarsi (**to** di)

ending /'endɪŋ/ *n* fine *f*; *Gram* desinenza *f*

endive /'endaɪv/ *n* indivia *f*

endless /'endlɪs/ *a* interminabile; ⟨*patience*⟩ infinito. **~ly** *adv* continuamente; ⟨*patient*⟩ infinitamente

endorse /en'dɔ:s/ *vt* girare ⟨*cheque*⟩; ⟨*sports personality:*⟩ fare pubblicità a ⟨*product*⟩; approvare ⟨*plan*⟩. **~ment** *n* (*of cheque*) girata *f*; (*of plan*) conferma *f*; (*on driving licence*) registrazione *f* su patente di un'infrazione

endow /ɪn'daʊ/ *vt* dotare

endur|able /ɪn'djʊərəbl/ *a* sopportabile. **~ance** /-rəns/ *n* resistenza *f;* **it is beyond ~ance** è insopportabile

endur|e /ɪnˈdjʊə(r)/ *vt* sopportare ● *vi* durare. **~ing** *a* duraturo

'end user *n* utente *m* finale

enemy /ˈenəmɪ/ *n* nemico, -a *mf* ● *attrib* nemico

energetic /enəˈdʒetɪk/ *a* energico

energy /ˈenədʒɪ/ *n* energia *f*

enforce /ɪnˈfɔːs/ *vt* far rispettare ⟨law⟩. **~d** *a* forzato

engage /ɪnˈgeɪdʒ/ *vt* assumere ⟨staff⟩; *Theat* ingaggiare; *Auto* ingranare ⟨gear⟩ ● *vi Techn* ingranare; **~ in** impegnarsi in. **~d** *a* (*in use, busy*) occupato; ⟨person⟩ impegnato; (*to be married*) fidanzato; **get ~d** fidanzarsi (**to** con); **~d tone** *Teleph* segnale *m* di occupato. **~ment** *n* fidanzamento *m;* (*appointment*) appuntamento *m; Mil* combattimento *m;* **~ment ring** anello *m* di fidanzamento

engaging /ɪnˈgeɪdʒɪŋ/ *a* attraente

engender /ɪnˈdʒendə(r)/ *vt fig* generare

engine /ˈendʒɪn/ *n* motore *m; Rail* locomotrice *f.* **~-driver** *n* macchinista *m*

engineer /endʒɪˈnɪə(r)/ *n* ingegnere *m;* (*service, installation*) tecnico *m; Naut, Am Rail* macchinista *m* ● *vt fig* architettare. **~ing** *n* ingegneria *f*

England /ˈɪŋglənd/ *n* Inghilterra *f*

English /ˈɪŋglɪʃ/ *a* inglese; **the ~ Channel** la Manica ● *n* (*language*) inglese *m;* **the ~** *pl* gli inglesi. **~man** *n* inglese *m.* **~woman** *n* inglese *f*

engrav|e /ɪnˈgreɪv/ *vt* incidere. **~ing** *n* incisione *f*

engross /ɪnˈgrəʊs/ *vt* **~ed in** assorto in

engulf /ɪnˈgʌlf/ *vt* ⟨fire, waves:⟩ inghiottire

enhance /ɪnˈhɑːns/ *vt* accrescere ⟨beauty, reputation⟩; migliorare ⟨performance⟩

enigma /ɪˈnɪgmə/ *n* enigma *m.* **~tic** /enɪgˈmætɪk/ *a* enigmatico

enjoy /ɪnˈdʒɔɪ/ *vt* godere di ⟨good health⟩; **~ oneself** divertirsi; **I ~ cooking/painting** mi piace cucinare/dipingere; **~ your meal** buon appetito. **~able** /-əbl/ *a* piacevole. **~ment** *n* piacere *m*

enlarge /ɪnˈlɑːdʒ/ *vt* ingrandire ● *vi* **~ upon** dilungarsi su. **~ment** *n* ingrandimento *m*

enlighten /ɪnˈlaɪtn/ *vt* illuminare.

~ed *a* progressista. **~ment** *n* **The E~ment** l'Illuminismo *m*

enlist /ɪnˈlɪst/ *vt Mil* reclutare; **~ sb's help** farsi aiutare da qcno ● *vi Mil* arruolarsi

enliven /ɪnˈlaɪvn/ *vt* animare

enmity /ˈenmətɪ/ *n* inimicizia *f*

enormity /ɪˈnɔːmətɪ/ *n* enormità *f*

enormous /ɪˈnɔːməs/ *a* enorme. **~ly** *adv* estremamente; ⟨grateful⟩ infinitamente

enough /ɪˈnʌf/ *a & n* abbastanza; **I didn't bring ~ clothes** non ho portato abbastanza vestiti; **have you had ~?** (*to eat/drink*) hai mangiato/bevuto abbastanza?; **I've had ~!** *fam* ne ho abbastanza!; **is that ~?** basta?; **that's ~!** basta così!; **£50 isn't ~** 50 sterline non sono sufficienti ● *adv* abbastanza; **you're not working fast ~** non lavori abbastanza in fretta; **funnily ~** stranamente

enquir|e /ɪnˈkwaɪə(r)/ *vi* domandare; **~e about** chiedere informazioni su. **~y** *n* domanda *f;* (*investigation*) inchiesta *f*

enrage /ɪnˈreɪdʒ/ *vt* fare arrabbiare

enrich /ɪnˈrɪtʃ/ *vt* arricchire; (*improve*) migliorare ⟨vocabulary⟩

enrol /ɪnˈrəʊl/ *vi* (*pt/pp* **-rolled**) (*for exam, in club*) iscriversi (**for, in** a). **~ment** *n* iscrizione *f*

ensemble /ɒnˈsɒmbl/ *n* (*clothing & Mus*) complesso *m*

enslave /ɪnˈsleɪv/ *vt* render schiavo

ensu|e /ɪnˈsjuː/ *vi* seguire; **the ~ing discussion** la discussione che ne è seguita

ensure /ɪnˈʃʊə(r)/ *vt* assicurare; **~ that** ⟨person:⟩ assicurarsi che; ⟨measure:⟩ garantire che

entail /ɪnˈteɪl/ *vt* comportare; **what does it ~?** in che cosa consiste?

entangle /ɪnˈtæŋgl/ *vt* **get ~d in** rimanere impigliato in; *fig* rimanere coinvolto in

enter /ˈentə(r)/ *vt* entrare in; iscrivere ⟨horse, runner in race⟩; cominciare ⟨university⟩; partecipare a ⟨competition⟩; *Comput* immettere ⟨data⟩; (*write down*) scrivere ● *vi* entrare; *Theat* entrare in scena; (*register as competitor*) iscriversi; (*take part*) partecipare (**in** a)

enterpris|e /ˈentəpraɪz/ *n* impresa *f;* (*quality*) iniziativa *f.* **~ing** *a* intraprendente

entertain /entəˈteɪn/ *vt* intrattenere;

(*invite*) ricevere; nutrire 〈*ideas, hopes*〉; prendere in considerazione 〈*possibility*〉 ● *vi* intrattenersi; 〈*have guests*〉 ricevere. **~er** *n* artista *mf*. **~ing** *a* 〈*person*〉 di gradevole compagnia; 〈*evening, film, play*〉 divertente. **~ment** *n* (*amusement*) intrattenimento *m*

enthral /ɪnˈθrɔːl/ *vt* (*pt/pp* **enthralled**) **be ~led** essere affascinato (**by** da)

enthusias|m /ɪnˈθjuːzɪæzm/ *n* entusiasmo *m*. **~t** *n* entusiasta *mf*. **~tic** /-ˈæstɪk/ *a* entusiastico

entice /ɪnˈtaɪs/ *vt* attirare. **~ment** *n* (*incentive*) incentivo *m*

entire /ɪnˈtaɪə(r)/ *a* intero. **~ly** *adv* del tutto; **I'm not ~ly satisfied** non sono completamente soddisfatto. **~ty** / rətɪ/ *n* **in its ~ty** nell'insieme

entitled /ɪnˈtaɪtld/ *a* 〈*book*〉 intitolato; **be ~ to sth** aver diritto a qcsa

entitlement /ɪnˈtaɪtlmənt/ *n* diritto *m*

entity /ˈentɪtɪ/ *n* entità *f*

entrance[1] /ˈentrəns/ *n* entrata *f*; *Theat* entrata *f* in scena; 〈*right to enter*〉 ammissione *f*; ‘**no ~**’ ‘ingresso vietato’. **~ examination** *n* esame *m* di ammissione. **~ fee** *n* **how much is the ~ fee?** quanto costa il biglietto di ingresso?

entrance[2] /ɪnˈtrɑːns/ *vt* estasiare

entrant /ˈentrənt/ *n* concorrente *mf*

entreat /ɪnˈtriːt/ *vt* supplicare

entrenched /ɪnˈtrentʃt/ *a* 〈*ideas, views*〉 radicato

entrust /ɪnˈtrʌst/ *vt* **~ sb with sth, ~ sth to sb** affidare qcsa a qcno

entry /ˈentrɪ/ *n* ingresso *m*; (*way in*) entrata *f*; (*in directory etc*) voce *f*; (*in appointment diary*) appuntamento *m*; **no ~** ingresso vietato; *Auto* accesso vietato. **~ form** *n* modulo *m* di ammissione. **~ visa** *n* visto *m* di ingresso

enumerate /ɪˈnjuːməreɪt/ *vt* enumerare

enunciate /ɪˈnʌnsɪeɪt/ *vt* enunciare

envelop /ɪnˈveləp/ *vt* (*pt/pp* **enveloped**) avviluppare

envelope /ˈenvələʊp/ *n* busta *f*

enviable /ˈenvɪəbl/ *a* invidiabile

envious /ˈenvɪəs/ *a* invidioso. **~ly** *adv* con invidia

environment /ɪnˈvaɪrənmənt/ *n* ambiente *m*

environmental /ɪnvaɪrənˈmentl/ *a* ambientale. **~ist** *n* ambientalista *mf*. **~ly** *adv* **~ly friendly** che rispetta l'ambiente

envisage /ɪnˈvɪzɪdʒ/ *vt* prevedere

envoy /ˈenvɔɪ/ *n* inviato, -a *mf*

envy /ˈenvɪ/ *n* invidia *f* ● *vt* (*pt/pp* **-ied**) **~ sb sth** invidiare qcno per qcsa

enzyme /ˈenzaɪm/ *n* enzima *f*

epic /ˈepɪk/ *a* epico ● *n* epopea *f*

epidemic /epɪˈdemɪk/ *n* epidemia *f*

epilep|sy /ˈepɪlepsɪ/ *n* epilessia *f*. **~tic** /-ˈleptɪk/ *a* & *n* epilettico, -a *mf*

epilogue /ˈepɪlɒg/ *n* epilogo *m*

episode /ˈepɪsəʊd/ *n* episodio *m*

epitaph /ˈepɪtɑːf/ *n* epitaffio *m*

epithet /ˈepɪθet/ *n* epiteto *m*

epitom|e /ɪˈpɪtəmɪ/ *n* epitome *f*. **~ize** *vt* essere il classico esempio di

epoch /ˈiːpɒk/ *n* epoca *f*

equal /ˈiːkwl/ *a* 〈*parts, amounts*〉 uguale; **of ~ height** della stessa altezza; **be ~ to the task** essere a l'altezza del compito ● *n* pari *m inv* ● *vt* (*pt/pp* **equalled**) (*be same in quantity as*) essere pari a; (*rival*) uguagliare; **5 plus 5 ~s 10** 5 più 5 [è] uguale a 10. **~ity** /ɪˈkwɒlətɪ/ *n* uguaglianza *f*

equalize /ˈiːkwəlaɪz/ *vi Sport* pareggiare. **~r** *n Sport* pareggio *m*

equally /ˈiːkwəlɪ/ *adv* 〈*divide*〉 in parti uguali; **~ intelligent** della stessa intelligenza; **~,...** allo stesso tempo...

equanimity /ekwəˈnɪmətɪ/ *n* equanimità *f*

equat|e /ɪˈkweɪt/ *vt* **~e sth with sth** equiparare qcsa a qcsa. **~ion** /-eɪʒn/ *n Math* equazione *f*

equator /ɪˈkweɪtə(r)/ *n* equatore *m*

equestrian /ɪˈkwestrɪən/ *a* equestre

equilibrium /iːkwɪˈlɪbrɪəm/ *n* equilibrio *m*

equinox /ˈiːkwɪnɒks/ *n* equinozio *m*

equip /ɪˈkwɪp/ *vt* (*pt/pp* **equipped**) equipaggiare; attrezzare 〈*kitchen, office*〉. **~ment** *n* attrezzatura *f*

equitable /ˈekwɪtəbl/ *a* giusto

equity /ˈekwɪtɪ/ *n* (*justness*) equità *f*; *Comm* azioni *fpl*

equivalent /ɪˈkwɪvələnt/ *a* equivalente; **be ~ to** equivalere a ● *n* equivalente *m*

equivocal /ɪˈkwɪvəkl/ *a* equivoco

era /ˈɪərə/ *n* età *f*; (*geological*) era *f*

eradicate /ɪˈrædɪkeɪt/ *vt* eradicare

erase /ɪˈreɪz/ *vt* cancellare. **~r** *n* gomma *f* [da cancellare]; (*for blackboard*) cancellino *m*

erect /ɪˈrekt/ *a* eretto ● *vt* erigere. **~ion** /-ekʃn/ *n* erezione *f*

ero|de /ɪˈrəʊd/ *vt* 〈*water:*〉 erodere; 〈*acid:*〉 corrodere. **~sion** /-əʊʒn/ *n* erosione *f*; (*by acid*) corrosione *f*

erotic /ɪˈrɒtɪk/ *a* erotico. **~ism** /-tɪsɪzm/ *n* erotismo *m*

err /ɜ:(r)/ vi errare; (sin) peccare

errand /'erənd/ n commissione f

erratic /ɪ'rætɪk/ a irregolare; (person, moods) imprevedibile; (exchange rate) incostante

erroneous /ɪ'rəʊnɪəs/ a erroneo

error /'erə(r)/ n errore m; **in ~** per errore

erudit|e /'erʊdaɪt/ a erudito. **~ion** /-'dɪʃn/ n erudizione f

erupt /ɪ'rʌpt/ vi eruttare; (spots:) spuntare; (fig: in anger) dare in escandescenze. **~ion** /-ʌpʃn/ n eruzione f; fig scoppio m

escalat|e /'eskəleɪt/ vi intensificarsi ● vt intensificare. **~ion** /-'leɪʃn/ n escalation f inv. **~or** n scala f mobile

escapade /'eskəpeɪd/ n scappatella f

escape /ɪ'skeɪp/ n fuga f; (from prison) evasione f; **have a narrow ~** cavarsela per un pelo ● vi (prisoner:) evadere (from da); sfuggire (from sb alla sorveglianza di qcno); (animal:) scappare; (gas:) fuoriuscire ● vt **~ notice** passare inosservato; **the name ~s me** mi sfugge il nome

escapism /ɪ'skeɪpɪzm/ n evasione f [dalla realtà]

escort¹ /'eskɔ:t/ n (of person) accompagnatore, -trice mf; Mil etc scorta f

escort² /ɪ'skɔ:t/ vt accompagnare; Mil etc scortare

Eskimo /'eskɪməʊ/ n esquimese mf

esoteric /esə'terɪk/ a esoterico

especial /ɪ'speʃl/ a speciale. **~ly** adv specialmente; (kind) particolarmente

espionage /'espɪənɑ:ʒ/ n spionaggio m

essay /'eseɪ/ n saggio m; Sch tema f

essence /'esns/ n essenza f; **in ~** in sostanza

essential /ɪ'senʃl/ a essenziale ● n **the ~s** pl l'essenziale m. **~ly** adv essenzialmente

establish /ɪ'stæblɪʃ/ vt stabilire (contact, lead); fondare (firm); (prove) accertare; **~ oneself as** affermarsi come. **~ment** n (firm) azienda f; **the E~ment** l'ordine m costituito

estate /ɪ'steɪt/ n tenuta f; (possessions) patrimonio m; (housing) quartiere m residenziale. **~ agent** n agente m immobiliare. **~ car** n giardiniera f

esteem /ɪ'sti:m/ n stima f ● vt stimare; (consider) giudicare

estimate¹ /'estɪmət/ n valutazione f; Comm preventivo m; **at a rough ~** a occhio e croce

estimat|e² /'estɪmeɪt/ vt stimare. **~ion** /-'meɪʃn/ n (esteem) stima f; **in my ~ion** (judgement) a mio giudizio

estuary /'estjʊərɪ/ n estuario m

etc /et'setərə/ abbr (et cetera) ecc

etching /'etʃɪŋ/ n acquaforte f

eternal /ɪ'tɜ:nl/ a eterno

eternity /ɪ'tɜ:nətɪ/ n eternità f

ethic /'eθɪk/ n etica f. **~al** a etico. **~s** n etica f

Ethiopia /i:θɪ'əʊpɪə/ n Etiopia f

ethnic /'eθnɪk/ a etnico

etiquette /'etɪket/ n etichetta f

EU n abbr (European Union) UE f

eucalyptus /ju:kə'lɪptəs/ n eucalipto m

eulogy /'ju:lədʒɪ/ n elogio m

euphemis|m /'ju:fəmɪzm/ n eufemismo m. **~tic** /-'mɪstɪk/ a eufemistico

euphoria /ju:'fɔ:rɪə/ n euforia f

euro /'jʊərəʊ/ n euro m inv

Euro+ /'jʊərəʊ-/ pref. **~cheque** n eurochèque n m inv. **~dollar** n eurodollaro m

Europe /'jʊərəp/ n Europa f

European /jʊərə'pɪən/ a europeo; **~ Union** Unione f Europea ● n europeo, -a mf

Euro-sceptic /jʊərəʊ'skeptɪk/ a euroscettico ● n euroscettico, -a mf

evacuat|e /ɪ'vækjʊeɪt/ vt evacuare (building). **~ion** /-'eɪʃn/ n evacuazione f

evade /ɪ'veɪd/ vt evadere (taxes); evitare (the enemy, authorities); **~ the issue** evitare l'argomento

evaluate /ɪ'væljʊeɪt/ vt valutare

evange|lical /i:væn'dʒelɪkl/ a evangelico. **~list** /ɪ'vændʒəlɪst/ n evangelista m

evaporat|e /ɪ'væpəreɪt/ vi evaporare; fig svanire. **~ion** /-'reɪʃn/ n evaporazione f

evasion /ɪ'veɪʒn/ n evasione f

evasive /ɪ'veɪsɪv/ a evasivo

eve /i:v/ n liter vigilia f

even /'i:vn/ a (level) piatto; (same, equal) uguale; (regular) regolare; (number) pari; **get ~ with** vendicarsi di; **now we're ~** adesso siamo pari ● adv anche, ancora; **~ if** anche se; **~ so** con tutto ciò; **not ~** nemmeno; **~ bigger** ancora più grande ● vt **~ the score** Sport pareggiare. **even out** vi livellarsi. **even up** vt livellare

evening /'i:vnɪŋ/ n sera f; (whole evening) serata f; **this ~** stasera; **in the ~** la sera. **~ class** n corso m serale. **~ dress** n (man's) abito m scuro; (woman's) abito m da sera

evenly /'i:vnlɪ/ adv (distributed) uniformemente; ⟨*breathe*⟩ regolarmente; ⟨*divided*⟩ in uguali parti

event /ɪ'vent/ *n* avvenimento *m*; ⟨*function*⟩ manifestazione *f*; *Sport* gara *f*; **in the ~ of** nell'eventualità di; **in the ~ that** alla fine. **~ful** *a* movimentato

eventual /ɪ'ventjʊəl/ *a* **the ~ winner was...** alla fine il vincitore è stato.... **~ity** /-'ælətɪ/ *n* eventualità *f*. **~ly** *adv* alla fine; **~ly!** finalmente!

ever /'evə(r)/ *adv* mai; **I haven't ~...** non ho mai...; **for ~** per sempre; **hardly ~** quasi mai; **~ since** da quando; ⟨*since that time*⟩ da allora; **~ so** *fam* veramente

'evergreen *n* sempreverde *m*

ever'lasting *a* eterno

every /'evrɪ/ *a* ogni; **~ one** ciascuno; **~ other day** un giorno sì un giorno no

every: **~body** *pron* tutti *pl*. **~day** *a* quotidiano, di ogni giorno. **~one** *pron* tutti *pl*; **~one else** tutti gli altri. **~thing** *pron* tutto; **~thing else** tutto il resto. **~where** *adv* dappertutto; ⟨*wherever*⟩ dovunque

evict /ɪ'vɪkt/ *vt* sfrattare. **~ion** /-ɪkʃn/ *n* sfratto *m*

eviden|ce /'evɪdəns/ *n* evidenza *f*; *Jur* testimonianza *f*; **give ~ce** testimoniare. **~t** *a* evidente. **~tly** *adv* evidentemente

evil /'iːvl/ *a* cattivo ● *n* male *m*

evocative /ɪ'vɒkətɪv/ *a* evocativo; **be ~ of** evocare

evoke /ɪ'vəʊk/ *vt* evocare

evolution /iːvə'luːʃn/ *n* evoluzione *f*

evolve /ɪ'vɒlv/ *vt* evolvere ● *vi* evolversi

ewe /juː/ *n* pecora *f*

exacerbate /ɪg'zæsəbeɪt/ *vt* esacerbare ⟨*situation*⟩

exact /ɪg'zækt/ *a* esatto ● *vt* esigere. **~ing** *a* esigente. **~itude** /-ɪtjuːd/ *n* esattezza *f*. **~ly** *adv* esattamente; **not ~ly** non proprio. **~ness** *n* precisione *f*

exaggerat|e /ɪg'zædʒəreɪt/ *vt/i* esagerare. **~ion** /-'reɪʃn/ *n* esagerazione *f*

exam /ɪg'zæm/ *n* esame *m*

examination /ɪgzæmɪ'neɪʃn/ *n* esame *m*; ⟨*of patient*⟩ visita *f*

examine /ɪg'zæmɪn/ *vt* esaminare; visitare ⟨*patient*⟩. **~r** *n* *Sch* esaminatore, -trice *mf*

example /ɪg'zɑːmpl/ *n* esempio *m*; **for ~** per esempio; **make an ~ of sb** punire qcno per dare un esempio; **be an ~ to sb** dare il buon esempio a qcno

exasperat|e /ɪg'zæspəreɪt/ *vt* esasperare. **~ion** /-'reɪʃn/ *n* esasperazione *f*

excavat|e /'ekskəvert/ *vt* scavare; *Archaeol* fare gli scavi di. **~ion** /-'veɪʃn/ *n* scavo *m*

exceed /ɪk'siːd/ *vt* eccedere. **~ingly** *adv* estremamente

excel /ɪk'sel/ *v* (*pt/pp* **excelled**) ● *vi* eccellere ● *vt* **~ oneself** superare se stessi

excellen|ce /'eksələns/ *n* eccellenza *f*. **E~cy** *n* (*title*) Eccellenza *f*. **~t** *a* eccellente

except /ɪk'sept/ *prep* eccetto, tranne; **~ for** eccetto, tranne; **~ that...** eccetto che... ● *vt* eccettuare. **~ing** *prep* eccetto, tranne

exception /ɪk'sepʃn/ *n* eccezione *f*; **take ~ to** fare obiezioni a. **~al** *a* eccezionale. **~ally** *adv* eccezionalmente

excerpt /'eksɜːpt/ *n* estratto *m*

excess /ɪk'ses/ *n* eccesso *m*; **in ~ of** oltre. **~ baggage** *n* bagaglio *m* in eccedenza. **~ 'fare** *n* supplemento *m*

excessive /ɪk'sesɪv/ *a* eccessivo. **~ly** *adv* eccessivamente

exchange /ɪks'tʃeɪndʒ/ *n* scambio *m*; *Teleph* centrale *f*; *Comm* cambio *m*; [**stock**] **~** borsa *f* valori; **in ~** in cambio (**for** di) ● *vt* scambiare (**for** con); cambiare ⟨*money*⟩. **~ rate** *n* tasso *m* di cambio

exchequer /ɪks'tʃekə(r)/ *n* *Pol* tesoro *m*

excise[1] /'eksaɪz/ *n* dazio *m*; **~ duty** dazio *m*

excise[2] /ek'saɪz/ *vt* recidere

excitable /ɪk'saɪtəbl/ *a* eccitabile

excit|e /ɪk'saɪt/ *vt* eccitare. **~ed** *a* eccitato; **get ~ed** eccitarsi. **~edly** *adv* tutto eccitato. **~ement** *n* eccitazione *f*. **~ing** *a* eccitante; ⟨*story, film*⟩ appassionante; ⟨*holiday*⟩ entusiasmante

exclaim /ɪk'skleɪm/ *vt/i* esclamare

exclamation /eksklə'meɪʃn/ *n* esclamazione *f*. **~ mark** *n*, *Am* **~ point** *n* punto *m* esclamativo

exclu|de /ɪk'skluːd/ *vt* escludere. **~ding** *prep* escluso. **~sion** /-ʒn/ *n* esclusione *f*

exclusive /ɪk'skluːsɪv/ *a* ⟨*rights, club*⟩ esclusivo; ⟨*interview*⟩ in esclusiva; **~ of...** ...escluso. **~ly** *adv* esclusivamente

excommunicate /ekskə'mjuːnɪkeɪt/ *vt* scomunicare

excrement /'ekskrɪmənt/ *n* escremento *m*

excruciating /ɪk'skruːʃɪeɪtɪŋ/ *a* atroce ⟨*pain*⟩; ⟨*fam: very bad*⟩ spaventoso

excursion /ɪkˈskɜːʃn/ *n* escursione *f*

excusable /ɪkˈskjuːzəbl/ *a* perdonabile

excuse[1] /ɪkˈskjuːs/ *n* scusa *f*

excuse[2] /ɪkˈskjuːz/ *vt* scusare; **~ from** esonerare da; **~ me!** (*to get attention*) scusi!; (*to get past*) permesso!, scusi!; (*indignant*) come ha detto?

ex-di'rectory *a* **be ~** non figurare sull'elenco telefonico

execute /ˈeksɪkjuːt/ *vt* eseguire; (*put to death*) giustiziare; attuare ⟨plan⟩

execution /eksɪˈkjuːʃn/ *n* esecuzione *f*; (*of plan*) attuazione *f*. **~er** *n* boia *m inv*

executive /ɪgˈzekjʊtɪv/ *a* esecutivo ● *n* dirigente *mf*; *Pol* esecutivo *m*

executor /ɪgˈzekjʊtə(r)/ *n Jur* esecutore, -trice *mf*

exemplary /ɪgˈzemplərɪ/ *a* esemplare

exemplify /ɪgˈzemplɪfaɪ/ *vt* (*pt/pp* **-ied**) esemplificare

exempt /ɪgˈzempt/ *a* esente ● *vt* esentare (**from** da). **~ion** /-empʃn/ *n* esenzione *f*

exercise /ˈeksəsaɪz/ *n* esercizio *m*; *Mil* esercitazione *f*; **physical ~s** ginnastica *f*; **take ~** fare del moto ● *vt* esercitare ⟨muscles, horse⟩; portare a spasso ⟨dog⟩; mettere in pratica ⟨skills⟩ ● *vi* esercitarsi. **~ book** *n* quaderno *m*

exert /ɪgˈzɜːt/ *vt* esercitare; **~ oneself** sforzarsi. **~ion** /-ɜːʃn/ *n* sforzo *m*

exhale /eksˈheɪl/ *vt/i* esalare

exhaust /ɪgˈzɔːst/ *n Auto* scappamento *m*; (*pipe*) tubo *m* di scappamento; **~ fumes** fumi *mpl* di scarico *m* ● *vt* esaurire. **~ed** *a* esausto. **~ing** *a* estenuante; ⟨climate, person⟩ sfibrante. **~ion** /-ɔːstʃn/ *n* esaurimento *m*. **~ive** /-ɪv/ *a* fig esauriente

exhibit /ɪgˈzɪbɪt/ *n* oggetto *m* esposto; *Jur* reperto *m* ● *vt* esporre; *fig* dimostrare

exhibition /eksɪˈbɪʃn/ *n* mostra *f*; (*of strength, skill*) dimostrazione *f*. **~ist** *n* esibizionista *mf*

exhibitor /ɪgˈzɪbɪtə(r)/ *n* espositore, -trice *mf*

exhilarat|ed /ɪgˈzɪləreɪtɪd/ *a* rallegrato. **~ing** *a* stimolante; ⟨mountain air⟩ tonificante. **~ion** *n* allegria *f*

exhort /ɪgˈzɔːt/ *vt* esortare

exhume /egˈzjuːm/ *vt* esumare

exile /ˈeksaɪl/ *n* esilio *m*; (*person*) esule *mf* ● *vt* esiliare

exist /ɪgˈzɪst/ *vi* esistere. **~ence** /-əns/

n esistenza *f*; **in ~** esistente; **be in ~ence** esistere. **~ing** *a* attuale

exit /ˈeksɪt/ *n* uscita *f*; *Theat* uscita *f* di scena ● *vi Theat* uscire di scena; *Comput* uscire

exonerate /ɪgˈzɒnəreɪt/ *vt* esonerare

exorbitant /ɪgˈzɔːbɪtənt/ *a* esorbitante

exorcize /ˈeksɔːsaɪz/ *vt* esorcizzare

exotic /ɪgˈzɒtɪk/ *a* esotico

expand /ɪkˈspænd/ *vt* espandere ● *vi* espandersi; *Comm* svilupparsi; ⟨metal:⟩ dilatarsi; **~ on** (*fig: explain better*) approfondire

expans|e /ɪkˈspæns/ *n* estensione *f*. **~ion** /-ænʃn/ *n* espansione *f*; *Comm* sviluppo *m*; (*of metal*) dilatazione *f*. **~ive** /-ɪv/ *a* espansivo

expatriate /eksˈpætrɪət/ *n* espatriato, -a *mf*

expect /ɪkˈspekt/ *vt* aspettare ⟨letter, baby⟩; (*suppose*) pensare; (*demand*) esigere; **I ~ so** penso di sì; **be ~ing** essere in stato interessante

expectan|cy /ɪkˈspektənsɪ/ *n* aspettativa *f*. **~t** *a* in attesa; **~t mother** donna *f* incinta. **~tly** *adv* con impazienza

expectation /ekspekˈteɪʃn/ *n* aspettativa *f*, speranza *f*

expedient /ɪkˈspiːdɪənt/ *a* conveniente ● *n* espediente *m*

expedition /ekspɪˈdɪʃn/ *n* spedizione *f*. **~ary** *a Mil* di spedizione

expel /ɪkˈspel/ *vt* (*pt/pp* **expelled**) espellere

expend /ɪkˈspend/ *vt* consumare. **~able** /-əbl/ *a* sacrificabile

expenditure /ɪkˈspendɪtʃə(r)/ *n* spesa *f*

expense /ɪkˈspens/ *n* spesa *f*; **business ~s** *pl* spese *fpl*; **at my ~** a mie spese; **at the ~ of** *fig* a spese di

expensive /ɪkˈspensɪv/ *a* caro, costoso. **~ly** *adv* costosamente

experience /ɪkˈspɪərɪəns/ *n* esperienza *f* ● *vt* provare ⟨sensation⟩; avere ⟨problem⟩. **~d** *a* esperto

experiment /ɪkˈsperɪmənt/ *n* esperimento ● /-ment/ *vi* sperimentare. **~al** /-ˈmentl/ *a* sperimentale

expert /ˈekspɜːt/ *a & n* esperto, -a *mf*. **~ly** *adv* abilmente

expertise /ekspɜːˈtiːz/ *n* competenza *f*

expire /ɪkˈspaɪə(r)/ *vi* scadere

expiry /ɪkˈspaɪərɪ/ *n* scadenza *f*. **~ date** *n* data *f* di scadenza

explain /ɪkˈspleɪn/ *vt* spiegare

explana|tion /ekspləˈneɪʃn/ *n* spiegazione *f*. **~tory** /ɪkˈsplænətərɪ/ *a* esplicativo

expletive /ɪk'splɪːtɪv/ n imprecazione f
explicit /ɪk'splɪsɪt/ a esplicito. **~ly** adv esplicitamente
explode /ɪk'spləʊd/ vi esplodere ● vt fare esplodere
exploit¹ /'eksplɔɪt/ n impresa f
exploit² /ɪk'splɔɪt/ vt sfruttare. **~ation** /eksplɔɪ'teɪʃn/ n sfruttamento m
explora|tion /eksplə'reɪʃn/ n esplorazione f. **~tory** /ɪk'splɔrətərɪ/ a esplorativo
explore /ɪk'splɔː(r)/ vt esplorare; fig studiare ⟨implications⟩. **~r** n esploratore, -trice mf
explos|ion /ɪk'spləʊʒn/ n esplosione f. **~ive** /-sɪv/ a & n esplosivo m
exponent /ɪk'spəʊnənt/ n esponente mf
export /'ekspɔːt/ n esportazione f ● vt /-'spɔːt/ esportare. **~er** n esportatore, -trice mf
expos|e /ɪk'spəʊz/ vt esporre; (reveal) svelare; smascherare ⟨traitor etc⟩. **~ure** /-ʒə(r)/ n esposizione f; Med esposizione f prolungata al freddo/caldo; (of crimes) smascheramento m; **24 ~ures** Phot 24 pose
expound /ɪk'spaʊnd/ vt esporre
express /ɪk'spres/ a espresso ● adv ⟨send⟩ per espresso ● n (train) espresso m ● vt esprimere; **~ oneself** esprimersi. **~ion** /-ʃn/ n espressione f. **~ive** /-ɪv/ a espressivo. **~ly** adv espressamente
expulsion /ɪk'spʌlʃn/ n espulsione f
exquisite /ek'skwɪzɪt/ a squisito
ex-'serviceman n ex-combattente m
extend /ɪk'stend/ vt prolungare ⟨visit, road⟩; prorogare ⟨visa, contract⟩; ampliare ⟨building, knowledge⟩; (stretch out) allungare; tendere ⟨hand⟩ ● vi ⟨garden, knowledge:⟩ estendersi
extension /ɪk'stenʃn/ n prolungamento m; (of visa, contract) proroga f; (of treaty) ampliamento m; (part of building) annesso m; (length of cable) prolunga f; Teleph interno m; **~ 226** interno 226
extensive /ɪk'stensɪv/ a ampio, vasto. **~ly** adv ampiamente
extent /ɪk'stent/ n (scope) portata f; **to a certain ~** fino a un certo punto; **to such an ~ that...** fino al punto che...
extenuating /ɪk'stenjʊeɪtɪŋ/ a **~ circumstances** attenuanti fpl
exterior /ɪk'stɪərɪə(r)/ a & n esterno m
exterminat|e /ɪk'stɜːmɪneɪt/ vt sterminare. **~ion** /-'neɪʃn/ n sterminio m

external /ɪk'stɜːnl/ a esterno; **for ~ use only** Med per uso esterno. **~ly** adv esternamente
extinct /ɪk'stɪŋkt/ a estinto. **~ion** /-ɪŋkʃn/ n estinzione f
extinguish /ɪk'stɪŋgwɪʃ/ vt estinguere. **~er** n estintore m
extort /ɪk'stɔːt/ vt estorcere. **~ion** /-ɔːʃn/ n estorsione f
extortionate /ɪk'stɔːʃənət/ a esorbitante
extra /'ekstrə/ a in più; ⟨train⟩ straordinario; **an ~ £10** 10 sterline extra, 10 sterline in più ● adv in più; (especially) più; **pay ~** pagare in più, pagare extra; **~ strong/busy** fortissimo/occupatissimo ● n Theat comparsa f; **~s** pl extra mpl
extract¹ /'ekstrækt/ n estratto m
extract² /ɪk'strækt/ vt estrarre ⟨tooth, oil⟩; strappare ⟨secret⟩; ricavare ⟨truth⟩. **~or** [**fan**] n aspiratore m
extradit|e /'ekstrədaɪt/ Jur vt estradare. **~ion** /-'dɪʃn/ n estradizione f
extra'marital a extraconiugale
extraordinar|y /ɪk'strɔːdmərɪ/ a straordinario. **~ily** /-ɪlɪ/ adv straordinariamente
extravagan|ce /ɪk'strævəgəns/ n (with money) prodigalità f; (of behaviour) stravaganza f. **~t** a spendaccione; (bizarre) stravagante; ⟨claim⟩ esagerato
extrem|e /ɪk'striːm/ a estremo ● n estremo m; **in the ~e** al massimo. **~ely** adv estremamente. **~ist** n estremista mf
extremity /ɪk'stremətɪ/ n (end) estremità f inv
extricate /'ekstrɪkeɪt/ vt districare
extrovert /'ekstrəvɜːt/ n estroverso, -a mf
exuberant /ɪg'zjuːbərənt/ a esuberante
exude /ɪg'zjuːd/ vt also fig trasudare
exult /ɪg'zʌlt/ vi esultare
eye /aɪ/ n occhio m; (of needle) cruna f; **keep an ~ on** tener d'occhio; **see ~ to ~** aver le stesse idee ● vt (pt/pp **eyed**, pres p **ey[e]ing**) guardare
eye: **~ball** n bulbo m oculare. **~ brow** n sopracciglio m (pl sopracciglia f). **~lash** n ciglio m (pl ciglia f). **~lid** n palpebra f. **~-opener** n rivelazione f. **~-shadow** n ombretto m. **~sight** n vista f. **~sore** n fam pugno m nell'occhio. **~witness** n testimone mf oculare

Ff

fable /ˈfeɪbl/ n favola f

fabric /ˈfæbrɪk/ n also fig tessuto m

fabrication /fæbrɪˈkeɪʃn/ n invenzione f; (manufacture) fabbricazione f

fabulous /ˈfæbjʊləs/ a fam favoloso

façade /fəˈsɑːd/ n (of building, person) facciata f

face /feɪs/ n faccia f, viso m; (grimace) smorfia f; (surface) faccia f; (of clock) quadrante m; **pull ~s** far boccacce; **in the ~ of** di fronte a; **on the ~ of it** in apparenza ● vt essere di fronta a; (confront) affrontare; **~ north** (house:) dare a nord; **~ the fact that** arrendersi al fatto che. **face up to** vt accettare (facts); affrontare (person)

face: ~-flannel n guanto m di spugna. **~less** a anonimo. **~-lift** n plastica f facciale

facet /ˈfæsɪt/ n sfaccettatura f; fig aspetto m

facetious /fəˈsiːʃəs/ a spiritoso. **~ remarks** spiritosaggini mpl

'face value n (of money) valore m nominale; **take sb/sth at ~** fermarsi alle apparenze

facial /ˈfeɪʃl/ a facciale ● n trattamento m di bellezza al viso

facile /ˈfæsaɪl/ a semplicistico

facilitate /fəˈsɪlɪteɪt/ vt rendere possibile; (make easier) facilitare

facilit|y /fəˈsɪləti/ n facilità f; **~ies** pl (of area, in hotel etc) attrezzature fpl

facing /ˈfeɪsɪŋ/ prep **~ the sea** (house:) che dà sul mare; **the person ~ me** la persona di fronte a me

facsimile /fækˈsɪməli/ n facsimile m

fact /fækt/ n fatto m; **in ~** infatti

faction /ˈfækʃn/ n fazione f

factor /ˈfæktə(r)/ n fattore m

factory /ˈfæktəri/ n fabbrica f

factual /ˈfæktʃʊəl/ a **be ~** attenersi ai fatti. **~ly** adv (inaccurate) dal punto di vista dei fatti

faculty /ˈfækəlti/ n facoltà f inv

fad /fæd/ n capriccio m

fade /feɪd/ vi sbiadire; (sound, light:) affievolirsi; (flower:) appassire. **fade in** vt cominciare in dissolvenza (picture). **fade out** vt finire in dissolvenza (picture)

fag /fæg/ n (chore) fatica f; (fam: cigarette) sigaretta f; (Am sl: homosexual) frocio m. **~ end** n fam cicca f

fagged /fægd/ a **~ out** fam stanco morto

Fahrenheit /ˈfærənhaɪt/ a Fahrenheit

fail /feɪl/ n **without ~** senz'altro ● vi (attempt:) fallire; (eyesight, memory:) indebolirsi; (engine, machine:) guastarsi; (marriage:) andare a rotoli; (in exam) essere bocciato; **~ to do sth** non fare qcsa; **I tried but I ~ed** ho provato ma non ci sono riuscito ● vt non superare (exam); bocciare (candidate); (disappoint) deludere; **words ~ me** mi mancano le parole

failing /ˈfeɪlɪŋ/ n difetto m ● prep **~ that** altrimenti

failure /ˈfeɪljə(r)/ n fallimento m; (mechanical) guasto m; (person) incapace mf

faint /feɪnt/ a leggero; (memory) vago; **feel ~** sentirsi mancare ● n svenimento m ● vi svenire

faint: ~-'hearted a timido. **~ly** adv (slightly) leggermente. **~ness** n (physical) debolezza f

fair¹ /feə(r)/ n fiera f

fair² a (hair, person) biondo; (skin) chiaro; (weather) bello; (just) giusto; (quite good) discreto; Sch abbastanza bene; **a ~ amount** abbastanza ● adv **play ~** fare un gioco pulito. **~ly** adv con giustizia; (rather) discretamente, abbastanza. **~ness** n giustizia f. **~ play** n fair play m inv

fairy /ˈfeəri/ n fata f; **~ story, ~-tale** n fiaba f

faith /feɪθ/ n fede f; (trust) fiducia f; **in good/bad ~** in buona/mala fede

faithful /ˈfeɪθfl/ a fedele. **~ly** adv fedelmente; **yours ~ly** distinti saluti. **~ness** n fedeltà f

'faith-healer n guaritore, -trice mf

fake /feɪk/ a falso ● n falsificazione f;

(*person*) impostore *m* ● *vt* falsificare; (*pretend*) fingere

falcon /ˈfɔːlkən/ *n* falcone *m*

fall /fɔːl/ *n* caduta *f*; (*in prices*) ribasso *m*; (*Am: autumn*) autunno *m*; **have a ~** fare una caduta ● *vi* (*pt* fell, *pp* fallen) cadere; (*night:*) scendere; **~ in love** innamorarsi. **fall about** *vi* (*with laughter*) morire dal ridere. **fall back on** *vt* ritornare su. **fall for** *vt fam* innamorarsi di (*person*); cascarci (*sth, trick*). **fall down** *vi* cadere; (*building:*) crollare. **fall in** *vi* caderci dentro; (*collapse*) crollare; *Mil* mettersi in riga; **~ in with** concordare con (*suggestion, plan*). **fall off** *vi* cadere; (*diminish*) diminuire. **fall out** *vi* (*quarrel*) litigare; **his hair is ~ing out** perde i capelli. **fall over** *vi* cadere. **fall through** *vi* (*plan:*) andare a monte

fallacy /ˈfæləsɪ/ *n* errore *m*

fallible /ˈfæləbl/ *a* fallibile

'fall-out *n* pioggia *f* radioattiva

false /fɔːls/ *a* falso; **~ bottom** doppio fondo *m*; **~ start** *Sport* falsa partenza *f*. **~hood** *n* menzogna *f*. **~ness** *n* falsità *f*

false 'teeth *npl* dentiera *f*

falsify /ˈfɔːlsɪfaɪ/ *vt* (*pt/pp* -ied) falsificare

falter /ˈfɔːltə(r)/ *vi* vacillare; (*making speech*) esitare

fame /feɪm/ *n* fama *f*

familiar /fəˈmɪljə(r)/ *a* familiare; **be ~ with** (*know*) conoscere. **~ity** /-lɪˈærɪtɪ/ *n* familiarità *f*. **~ize** *vt* familiarizzare; **~ize oneself with** familiarizzarsi con

family /ˈfæməlɪ/ *n* famiglia *f*

family: ~ al'lowance *n* assegni *mpl* familiari. **~ 'doctor** *n* medico *m* di famiglia. **~ 'life** *n* vita *f* familiare. **~ 'planning** *n* pianificazione *f* familiare. **~ 'tree** *n* albero *m* genealogico

famine /ˈfæmɪn/ *n* carestia *f*

famished /ˈfæmɪʃt/ *a* **be ~** *fam* avere una fame da lupo

famous /ˈfeɪməs/ *a* famoso

fan[1] /fæn/ *n* ventilatore *m*; (*handheld*) ventaglio *m* ● *vt* (*pt/pp* fanned) far vento a; **~ oneself** sventagliarsi; *fig* **~ the flames** soffiare sul fuoco. **fan out** *vi* spiegarsi a ventaglio

fan[2] *n* (*admirer*) ammiratore, -trice *mf*; *Sport* tifoso *m*; (*of Verdi etc*) appassionato, -a *mf*

fanatic /fəˈnætɪk/ *n* fanatico, -a *mf*. **~al** *a* fanatico. **~ism** /-sɪzm/ *n* fanatismo *m*

'fan belt *n* cinghia *f* per ventilatore

fanciful /ˈfænsɪfl/ *a* fantasioso

fancy /ˈfænsɪ/ *n* fantasia *f*; **I've taken a real ~ to him** mi è molto simpatico; **as the ~ takes you** come ti pare ● *a* [a] fantasia ● *vt* (*pt/pp* -ied) (*believe*) credere; (*fam: want*) aver voglia di; **he fancies you** *fam* gli piaci; **~ that!** ma guarda un po'! **~ 'dress** *n* costume *m* (*per maschera*)

fanfare /ˈfænfeə(r)/ *n* fanfara *f*

fang /fæŋ/ *n* zanna *f*; (*of snake*) dente *m*

fan: ~ heater *n* termoventilatore *m*. **~light** *n* lunetta *f*

fantas|ize /ˈfæntəsaɪz/ *vi* fantasticare. **~tic** /-ˈtæstɪk/ *a* fantastico. **~y** *n* fantasia *f*

far /fɑː(r)/ *adv* lontano; (*much*) molto; **by ~** di gran lunga; **~ away** lontano; **as ~ as the church** fino alla chiesa; **how ~ is it from here?** quanto dista da qui?; **as ~ as I know** per quanto io sappia ● *a* (*end, side*) altro; **the F~ East** l'Estremo Oriente *m*

farc|e /fɑːs/ *n* farsa *f*. **~ical** *a* ridicolo

fare /feə(r)/ *n* tariffa *f*; (*food*) vitto *m*. **~-dodger** /-dɒdʒə(r)/ *n* passeggero, -a *mf* senza biglietto

farewell /feəˈwel/ *int liter* addio! ● *n* addio *m*

far-'fetched *a* improbabile

farm /fɑːm/ *n* fattoria *f* ● *vi* fare l'agricoltore ● *vt* coltivare (*land*). **~er** *n* agricoltore *m*

farm: ~house *n* casa *f* colonica. **~ing** *n* agricoltura *f*. **~yard** *n* aia *f*

far: ~-'reaching *a* di larga portata. **~-'sighted** *a* *fig* prudente; (*Am: long-sighted*) presbite

fart /fɑːt/ *fam* *n* scoreggia *f* ● *vi* scoreggiare

farther /ˈfɑːðə(r)/ *adv* più lontano ● *a* **at the ~ end of** all'altra estremità di

fascinat|e /ˈfæsɪneɪt/ *vt* affascinare. **~ing** *a* affascinante. **~ion** /-ˈneɪʃn/ *n* fascino *m*

fascis|m /ˈfæʃɪzm/ *n* fascismo *m*. **~t** *n* fascista *mf* ● *a* fascista

fashion /ˈfæʃn/ *n* moda *f*; (*manner*) maniera *f* ● *vt* modellare. **~able** /-əbl/ *a* di moda; **be ~able** essere alla moda. **~ably** *adv* alla moda

fast[1] /fɑːst/ *a* veloce; (*colour*) indelebile; **be ~** (*clock:*) andare avanti ● *adv* velocemente; (*firmly*) saldamente; **~er!** più in fretta!; **be ~ asleep** dormire profondamente

fast[2] *n* digiuno *m* ● *vi* digiunare

fasten /ˈfɑːsn/ *vt* allacciare; chiudere (*window*); (*stop flapping*) mettere un fermo a ● *vi* allacciarsi. **~er** *n*, **~ing** *n* chiusura *f*

fastidious /fə'stɪdɪəs/ *a* esigente

fat /fæt/ *a* (**fatter, fattest**) ⟨*person, cheque*⟩ grasso ● *n* grasso *m*

fatal /'feɪtl/ *a* mortale; ⟨*error*⟩ fatale. **~ism** /-təlɪzm/ *n* fatalismo *m*. **~ist** /-təlɪst/ *n* fatalista *mf*. **~ity** /fə'tælətɪ/ *n* morte *f*. **~ly** *adv* mortalmente

fate /feɪt/ *n* destino *m*. **~ful** *a* fatidico

'**fat-head** *n* *fam* zuccone, -a *mf*

father /'fɑːðə(r)/ *n* padre *m*; **F~ Christmas** Babbo *m* Natale ● *vt* generare ⟨*child*⟩

father: **~hood** *n* paternità *f*. **~-in-law** *n* (*pl* **~s-in-law**) suocero *m*. **~ly** *a* paterno

fathom /'fæð(ə)m/ *n* *Naut* braccio *m* ● *vt* **~** [**out**] comprendere

fatigue /fə'tiːg/ *n* fatica *f*

fatten /'fætn/ *vt* ingrassare ⟨*animal*⟩. **~ing** *a* **a cream is ~ing** la panna fa ingrassare

fatty /'fætɪ/ *a* grasso ● *n* *fam* ciccione, -a *mf*

fatuous /'fætjʊəs/ *a* fatuo

faucet /'fɔːsɪt/ *n* *Am* rubinetto *m*

fault /fɔːlt/ *n* difetto *m*; *Geol* faglia *f*; *Tennis* fallo *m*; **be at ~** avere torto; **find ~ with** trovare da ridire su; **it's your ~** è colpa tua ● *vt* criticare. **~less** *a* impeccabile

faulty /'fɔːltɪ/ *a* difettoso

fauna /'fɔːnə/ *n* fauna *f*

favour /'feɪvə(r)/ *n* favore *m*; **be in ~ of sth** essere a favore di qcsa; **do sb a ~** fare un piacere a qcno ● *vt* (*prefer*) preferire. **~able** /-əbl/ *a* favorevole

favourit|e /'feɪv(ə)rɪt/ *a* preferito ● *n* preferito, -a *mf*; *Sport* favorito, -a *mf*. **~ism** *n* favoritismo *m*

fawn /fɔːn/ *a* fulvo ● *n* (*animal*) cerbiatto *m*

fax /fæks/ *n* (*document, machine*) fax *m* *inv*; **by ~** per fax ● *vt* faxare. **~ machine** *n* fax *m* *inv*. **~-modem** *n* modem-fax *m* *inv*, fax-modem *m* *inv*

fear /fɪə(r)/ *n* paura *f*; **no ~!** *fam* vai tranquillo! ● *vt* temere ● *vi* **~ for sth** temere per qcsa

fear|ful /'fɪəfl/ *a* pauroso; ⟨*awful*⟩ terribile. **~less** *a* impavido. **~some** /-səm/ *a* spaventoso

feas|ibility /fiːzɪ'bɪlɪtɪ/ *n* praticabilità *f*. **~ible** *a* fattibile; (*possible*) probabile

feast /fiːst/ *n* festa *f*; (*banquet*) banchetto *m* ● *vi* banchettare; **~ on** godersi

feat /fiːt/ *n* impresa *f*

feather /'feðə(r)/ *n* piuma *f*

feature /'fiːtʃə(r)/ *n* (*quality*) caratteristica *f*; *Journ* articolo *m*; **~s** *pl* (*of face*) lineamenti *mpl* ● *vt* ⟨*film:*⟩ avere come protagonista ● *vi* (*on a list etc*) comparire. **~ film** *n* lungometraggio *m*

February /'febrʊərɪ/ *n* febbraio *m*

fed /fed/ *see* **feed** ● *a* **be ~ up** *fam* essere stufo (**with** di)

federal /'fed(ə)rəl/ *a* federale

federation /fedə'reɪʃn/ *n* federazione *f*

fee /fiː/ *n* tariffa *f*; (*lawyer's, doctor's*) onorario *m*; (*for membership, school*) quota *f*

feeble /'fiːbl/ *a* debole; ⟨*excuse*⟩ fiacco

feed /fiːd/ *n* mangiare *m*; (*for baby*) pappa *f* ● *v* (*pt/pp* **fed**) ● *vt* dar da mangiare a ⟨*animal*⟩; (*support*) nutrire; **~ sth into sth** inserire qcsa in qcsa ● *vi* mangiare

'**feedback** *n* controreazione *f*; (*of information*) reazione *f*, feedback *m*

feel /fiːl/ *v* (*pt/pp* **felt**) ● *vt* sentire; (*experience*) provare; (*think*) pensare; (*touch: searching*) tastare; (*touch: for texture*) toccare ● *vi* **~ soft/hard** essere duro/morbido al tatto; **~ hot/hungry** aver caldo/fame; **~ ill** sentirsi male; **I don't ~ like it** non ne ho voglia; **how do you ~ about it?** (*opinion*) che te ne pare?; **it doesn't ~ right** non mi sembra giusto. **~er** *n* (*of animal*) antenna *f*; **put out ~ers** *fig* tastare il terreno. **~ing** *n* sentimento *m*; (*awareness*) sensazione *f*

feet /fiːt/ *see* **foot**

feign /feɪn/ *vt* simulare

feline /'fiːlaɪn/ *a* felino

fell[1] /fel/ *vt* (*knock down*) abbattere

fell[2] *see* **fall**

fellow /'feləʊ/ *n* (*of society*) socio *m*; (*fam: man*) tipo *m*

fellow: **~-'countryman** *n* compatriota *m*. **~men** *npl* prossimi *mpl*. **~ship** *n* cameratismo *m*; (*group*) associazione *f*; *Univ* incarico *m* di ricercatore, -trice

felony /'felənɪ/ *n* delitto *m*

felt[1] /felt/ *see* **feel**

felt[2] *n* feltro *m*. **~-[tipped] 'pen** /[-tɪpt]/ *n* pennarello *m*

female /'fiːmeɪl/ *a* femminile; **the ~ antelope** l'antilope femmina ● *n* femmina *f*

femin|ine /'femɪnɪn/ *a* femminile ● *n* *Gram* femminile *m*. **~inity** /-'nɪnətɪ/ *n* femminilità *f*. **~ist** *a* & *n* femminista *mf*

fenc|e /fens/ *n* recinto *m*; (*fam: person*) ricettatore *m* ● *vi* *Sport* tirar di scherma. **fence in** *vt* chiudere in un recinto. **~er** *n* schermidore *m*. **~ing** *n* steccato *m*; *Sport* scherma *f*

fend /fend/ *vi* **~ for oneself** badare a se stesso. **fend off** *vt* parare; difendersi da ⟨*criticisms*⟩

fender /'fendə(r)/ *n* parafuoco *m inv*; (*Am: on car*) parafango *m*

fennel /'fenl/ *n* finocchio *m*

ferment[1] /'fɜ:ment/ *n* fermento *m*

ferment[2] /fə'ment/ *vi* fermentare ● *vt* far fermentare. **~ation** /fɜ:men'teɪʃn/ *n* fermentazione *f*

fern /fɜ:n/ *n* felce *f*

feroc|ious /fə'rəʊʃəs/ *a* feroce. **~ity** /-'rɒsəti/ *n* ferocia *f*

ferret /'ferɪt/ *n* furetto *m* ● **ferret out** *vt* scovare

ferry /'feri/ *n* traghetto *m* ● *vt* traghettare

fertil|e /'fɜ:taɪl/ *a* fertile. **~ity** /fɜ:'tɪləti/ *n* fertilità *f*

fertilize /'fɜ:tɪlaɪz/ *vt* fertilizzare ⟨*land, ovum*⟩. **~r** *n* fertilizzante *m*

fervent /'fɜ:vənt/ *a* fervente

fervour /'fɜ:və(r)/ *n* fervore *m*

fester /'festə(r)/ *vi* suppurare

festival /'festɪvl/ *n Mus, Theat* festival *m*; *Relig* festa *f*

festiv|e /'festɪv/ *a* festivo; **~e season** periodo *m* delle feste natalizie. **~ities** /fe'stɪvətɪz/ *npl* festeggiamenti *mpl*

festoon /fe'stu:n/ *vt* **~ with** ornare di

fetch /fetʃ/ *vt* andare/venire a prendere; (*be sold for*) raggiungere [il prezzo di]

fetching /'fetʃɪŋ/ *a* attraente

fête /feɪt/ *n* festa *f* ● *vt* festeggiare

fetish /'fetɪʃ/ *n* feticcio *m*

fetter /'fetə(r)/ *vt* incatenare

fettle /'fetl/ *n* **in fine ~** in buona forma

feud /fju:d/ *n* faida *f*

feudal /'fju:dl/ *a* feudale

fever /'fi:və(r)/ *n* febbre *f*. **~ish** *a* febbricitante; *fig* febbrile

few /fju:/ *a* pochi; **every ~ days** ogni due o tre giorni; **a ~ people** alcuni; **~er reservations** meno prenotazioni; **the ~est number** il numero più basso ● *pron* pochi; **~ of us** pochi di noi; **a ~** alcuni; **quite a ~** parecchi; **~er than last year** meno dell'anno scorso

fiancé /fɪ'ɒnseɪ/ *n* fidanzato *m*. **~e** *n* fidanzata *f*

fiasco /fɪ'æskəʊ/ *n* fiasco *m*

fib /fɪb/ *n* storia *f*; **tell a ~** raccontare una storia

fibre /'faɪbə(r)/ *n* fibra *f*. **~glass** *n* fibra *f* di vetro

fickle /'fɪkl/ *a* incostante

fiction /'fɪkʃn/ *n* [**works of**] **~** narrativa *f*; (*fabrication*) finzione *f*. **~al** *a* immaginario

fictitious /fɪk'tɪʃəs/ *a* fittizio

fiddle /'fɪdl/ *n fam* violino *m*; (*cheating*) imbroglio *m* ● *vi* gingillarsi (**with** con) ● *vt fam* truccare ⟨*accounts*⟩

fiddly /'fɪdlɪ/ *a* intricato

fidelity /fɪ'delətɪ/ *n* fedeltà *f*

fidget /'fɪdʒɪt/ *vi* agitarsi. **~y** *a* agitato

field /fi:ld/ *n* campo *m*

field: ~ events *npl* atletica *fsg* leggera. **~-glasses** *npl* binocolo *msg*. **F~ 'Marshal** *n* feldmaresciallo *m*. **~work** *n* ricerche *fpl* sul terreno

fiend /fi:nd/ *n* demonio *m*

fierce /fɪəs/ *a* feroce. **~ness** *n* ferocia *f*

fiery /'faɪərɪ/ *a* (**-ier, -iest**) focoso

fifteen /fɪf'ti:n/ *a & n* quindici *m*. **~th** *a & n* quindicesimo, -a *mf*

fifth /fɪfθ/ *a & n* quinto, -a *mf*

fiftieth /'fɪftɪɪθ/ *a & n* cinquantesimo, -a *mf*

fifty /'fɪftɪ/ *a & n* cinquanta *m*

fig /fɪg/ *n* fico *m*

fight /faɪt/ *n* lotta *f*; (*brawl*) zuffa *f*; (*argument*) litigio *m*; (*boxing*) incontro *m* ● *v* (*pt/pp* **fought**) ● *vt also fig* combattere ● *vi* combattere; (*brawl*) azzuffarsi; (*argue*) litigare. **~er** *n* combattente *mf*; *Aeron* caccia *m inv*. **~ing** *n* combattimento *m*

figment /'fɪgmənt/ *n* **it's a ~ of your imagination** questo è tutta una tua invenzione

figurative /'fɪgjərətɪv/ *a* ⟨*sense*⟩ figurato; ⟨*art*⟩ figurativo

figure /'fɪgə(r)/ *n* (*digit*) cifra *f*; (*carving, sculpture, illustration, form*) figura *f*; (*body shape*) linea *f*; **~ of speech** modo *m* di dire ● *vi* (*appear*) figurare ● *vt* (*Am: think*) pensare. **figure out** *vt* dedurre; capire ⟨*person*⟩

figure: ~-head *n* figura *f* simbolica. **~ skating** *n* pattinaggio *m* artistico

file[1] /faɪl/ *n* scheda *f*; (*set of documents*) incartamento *m*; (*folder*) cartellina *f*; *Comput* file *m inv* ● *vt* archiviare ⟨*documents*⟩

file[2] *n* (*line*) fila *f*; **in single ~** in fila

file[3] *n Techn* lima *f* ● *vt* limare

filing cabinet /'faɪlɪŋkæbɪnət/ *n* schedario *m*, classificatore *m*

filings /'faɪlɪŋz/ *npl* limatura *fsg*

fill /fɪl/ *n* **eat one's ~** mangiare a

sazietà ● *vt* riempire; otturare ⟨*tooth*⟩ ● *vi* riempirsi. **fill in** *vt* compilare ⟨*form*⟩. **fill out** *vt* compilare ⟨*form*⟩. **fill up** *vi* ⟨*room, tank:*⟩ riempirsi; *Auto* far il pieno ● *vt* riempire

fillet /'fɪlɪt/ *n* filetto *m* ● *vt* (*pt/pp* **filleted**) disossare

filling /'fɪlɪŋ/ *n* Culin ripieno *m*; ⟨*of tooth*⟩ piombatura *f*. **~ station** *n* stazione *f* di rifornimento

filly /'fɪlɪ/ *n* puledra *f*

film /fɪlm/ *n* Cinema film *m inv*; *Phot* pellicola *f*; [**cling**] **~** pellicola *f* per alimenti ● *vt/i* filmare. **~ star** *n* star *f inv*, divo, -a *mf*

filter /'fɪltə(r)/ *n* filtro *m* ● *vt* filtrare. **filter through** *vi* ⟨*news:*⟩ trapelare. **~ tip** *n* filtro *m*; ⟨*cigarette*⟩ sigaretta *f* col filtro

filth /fɪlθ/ *n* sudiciume *m*. **~y** *a* (**-ier, -iest**) sudicio; ⟨*language*⟩ sconcio

fin /fɪn/ *n* pinna *f*

final /'faɪnl/ *a* finale; ⟨*conclusive*⟩ decisivo ● *n* Sport finale *f*; **~s** *pl* Univ esami *mpl* finali

finale /fɪ'nɑ:lɪ/ *n* finale *m*

finalist /'faɪnəlɪst/ *n* finalista *mf*. **~ity** /-'næləti/ *n* finalità *f*

finalize /'faɪnəlaɪz/ *vt* mettere a punto ⟨*text*⟩; definire ⟨*agreement*⟩. **~ly** *adv* ⟨*at last*⟩ finalmente; ⟨*at the end*⟩ alla fine; ⟨*to conclude*⟩ per finire

finance /'faɪnæns/ *n* finanza *f* ● *vt* finanziare

financial /faɪ'nænʃl/ *a* finanziario

finch /fɪntʃ/ *n* fringuello *m*

find /faɪnd/ *n* scoperta *f* ● *vt* (*pt/pp* **found**) trovare; ⟨*establish*⟩ scoprire; **~ sb guilty** Jur dichiarare qcno colpevole. **find out** *vt* scoprire ● *vi* ⟨*enquire*⟩ informarsi

findings /'faɪndɪŋz/ *npl* conclusioni *fpl*

fine¹ /faɪn/ *n* ⟨*penalty*⟩ multa *f* ● *vt* multare

fine² *a* bello; ⟨*slender*⟩ fine; **he's ~** ⟨*in health*⟩ sta bene; **~ arts** belle arti *fpl* ● *adv* bene; **that's cutting it ~** non ci lascia molto tempo ● *int* [va] bene. **~ly** *adv* ⟨*cut*⟩ finemente

finery /'faɪnərɪ/ *n* splendore *m*

finesse /fɪ'nes/ *n* finezza *f*

finger /'fɪŋgə(r)/ *n* dito *m* (*pl* dita *f*) ● *vt* tastare

finger: ~-mark *n* ditata *f*. **~-nail** *n* unghia *f*. **~print** *n* impronta *f* digitale. **~tip** *n* punta *f* del dito; **have sth at one's ~tips** sapere qcsa a menadito;

⟨*close at hand*⟩ avere qcsa a portata di mano

finicky /'fɪnɪkɪ/ *a* ⟨*person*⟩ pignolo; ⟨*task*⟩ intricato

finish /'fɪnɪʃ/ *n* fine *f*; ⟨*finishing line*⟩ traguardo *m*; ⟨*of product*⟩ finitura *f*; **have a good ~** ⟨*runner:*⟩ avere un buon finale ● *vt* finire; **~ reading** finire di leggere ● *vi* finire

finite /'faɪnaɪt/ *a* limitato

Finland /'fɪnlənd/ *n* Finlandia *f*

Finn /fɪn/ *n* finlandese *mf*. **~ish** *a* finlandese ● *n* ⟨*language*⟩ finnico *m*

fiord /fjɔːd/ *n* fiordo *m*

fir /fɜː(r)/ *n* abete *m*

fire /'faɪə(r)/ *n* fuoco *m*; ⟨*forest, house*⟩ incendio *m*; **be on ~** bruciare; **catch ~** prendere fuoco; **set ~ to** dar fuoco a; **under ~** sotto il fuoco ● *vt* cuocere ⟨*pottery*⟩; sparare ⟨*shot*⟩; tirare ⟨*gun*⟩; ⟨*fam: dismiss*⟩ buttar fuori ● *vi* sparare (**at** a)

fire: ~ alarm *n* allarme *m* antincendio. **~arm** *n* arma *f* da fuoco. **~ brigade** *n* vigili *mpl* del fuoco. **~-engine** *n* autopompa *f*. **~-escape** *n* uscita *f* di sicurezza. **~ extinguisher** *n* estintore *m*. **~man** *n* pompiere *m*, vigile *m* del fuoco. **~place** *n* caminetto *m*. **~side** *n* **by** *or* **at the ~side** accanto al fuoco. **~ station** *n* caserma *f* dei pompieri. **~wood** *n* legna *f* (*da ardere*). **~work** *n* fuoco *m* d'artificio; **~works** *pl* ⟨*display*⟩ fuochi *mpl* d'artificio

'firing squad *n* plotone *m* d'esecuzione

firm¹ /fɜːm/ *n* ditta *f*, azienda *f*

firm² *a* fermo; ⟨*soil*⟩ compatto; ⟨*stable, fixed*⟩ solido; ⟨*resolute*⟩ risoluto. **~ly** *adv* ⟨*hold*⟩ stretto; ⟨*say*⟩ con fermezza

first /fɜːst/ *a & n* primo, -a *mf*; **at ~** all'inizio; **who's ~?** chi è il primo?; **from the ~** [fin] dall'inizio ● *adv* ⟨*arrive, leave*⟩ per primo; ⟨*beforehand*⟩ prima; ⟨*in listing*⟩ prima di tutto, innanzitutto

first: ~ 'aid *n* pronto soccorso *m*. **~-'aid kit** *n* cassetta *f* di pronto soccorso. **~-class** *a* di prim'ordine; *Rail* di prima classe ● *adv* ⟨*travel*⟩ in prima classe. **~ 'floor** *n* primo piano *m*; ⟨*Am: ground floor*⟩ pianterreno *m*. **~ly** *adv* in primo luogo. **~ name** *n* nome *m* di battesimo. **~-rate** *a* ottimo

fish /fɪʃ/ *n* pesce *m* ● *vt/i* pescare. **fish out** *vt* tirar fuori

fish: ~bone *n* lisca *f*. **~erman** *n* pescatore *m*. **~-farm** *n* vivaio *m*. **~ 'finger** *n* bastoncino *m* di pesce

fishing /ˈfɪʃɪŋ/ n pesca f. ~ **boat** n peschereccio m. **~-rod** n canna f da pesca

fish: ~**monger** /-mʌŋgə(r)/ n pescivendolo m. **~-slice** n paletta f per fritti. **~y** a (fam: suspicious) sospetto

fission /ˈfɪʃn/ n Phys fissione f

fist /fɪst/ n pugno m

fit[1] /fɪt/ n (attack) attacco m; (of rage) accesso m; (of generosity) slancio m

fit[2] a (**fitter, fittest**) (suitable) adatto; (healthy) in buona salute; Sport in forma; **be ~ to do sth** essere in grado di fare qcsa; **~ to eat** buono da mangiare; **keep ~** tenersi in forma

fit[3] n (of clothes) taglio m; **it's a good ~** ‹coat etc.› ti/le sta bene ● v (pt/pp **fitted**) ● vi (be the right size) andare bene; **it won't ~** (no room) non ci sta ● vt (fix) applicare (**to** a); (install) installare; **it doesn't ~ me** ‹coat etc.› non mi va bene; **~ with** fornire di. **fit in** vi ‹person.› adattarsi; **it won't ~ in** (no room) non ci sta ● vt (in schedule, vehicle) trovare un buco per

fit|ful /ˈfɪtfl/ a irregolare. **~fully** adv ‹sleep› a sprazzi. **~ments** npl (in house) impianti mpl fissi. **~ness** n (suitability) capacità f; [**physical**] **~ness** forma f, fitness m

fitted: ~ **'carpet** n moquette f inv. ~ **'cupboard** n armadio m a muro; (smaller) armadietto m a muro. ~ **'kitchen** n cucina f componibile. ~ **'sheet** n lenzuolo m con angoli

fitter /ˈfɪtə(r)/ n installatore, -trice mf

fitting /ˈfɪtɪŋ/ a appropriato ● n (of clothes) prova f; Techn montaggio m; **~s** pl accessori mpl. ~ **room** n camerino m

five /faɪv/ a & n cinque m. **~r** n fam biglietto m da cinque sterline

fix /fɪks/ n (sl: drugs) pera f; **be in a ~** fam essere nei guai ● vt fissare; (repair) aggiustare; preparare ‹meal›. **fix up** vt fissare ‹meeting›

fixation /fɪkˈseɪʃn/ n fissazione f

fixed /fɪkst/ a fisso

fixture /ˈfɪkstʃə(r)/ n Sport incontro m; **~s and fittings** impianti mpl fissi

fizz /fɪz/ vi frizzare

fizzle /ˈfɪzl/ vi ~ **out** finire in nulla

fizzy /ˈfɪzɪ/ a gassoso. ~ **drink** n bibita f gassata

flabbergasted /ˈflæbəgɑːstɪd/ a **be ~** rimanere a bocca aperta

flabby /ˈflæbɪ/ a floscio

flag[1] /flæg/ n bandiera f ● **flag down** vt (pt/pp **flagged**) far segno di fermarsi a ‹taxi›

flag[2] vi (pt/pp **flagged**) cedere

'flag-pole n asta f della bandiera

flagrant /ˈfleɪgrənt/ a flagrante

'flagship n Naut nave f ammiraglia; fig fiore m all'occhiello

'flagstone n pietra f da lastricare

flair /fleə(r)/ n (skill) talento m; (style) stile m

flake /fleɪk/ n fiocco m ● vi ~ [**off**] cadere in fiocchi

flaky /ˈfleɪkɪ/ a a scaglie. ~ **pastry** n pasta f sfoglia

flamboyant /flæmˈbɔɪənt/ a ‹personality› brillante; ‹tie› sgargiante

flame /fleɪm/ n fiamma f

flammable /ˈflæməbl/ a infiammabile

flan /flæn/ n [**fruit**] ~ crostata f

flank /flæŋk/ n fianco m ● vt fiancheggiare

flannel /ˈflæn(ə)l/ n flanella f; (for washing) guanto m di spugna; **~s** (trousers) pantaloni mpl di flanella

flannelette /flænəˈlet/ n flanella f di cotone

flap /flæp/ n (of pocket, envelope) risvolto m; (of table) ribalta f; **in a ~** fam in grande agitazione ● v (pt/pp **flapped**) ● vi sbattere; fam agitarsi ● vt ~ **its wings** battere le ali

flare /fleə(r)/ n fiammata f; (device) razzo m ● **flare up** vi ‹rash.› venire fuori; ‹fire.› fare una fiammata; ‹person, situation.› esplodere. **~d** a ‹garment› svasato

flash /flæʃ/ n lampo m; **in a ~** fam in un attimo ● vi lampeggiare; ~ **past** passare come un bolide ● vt lanciare ‹smile›; ~ **one's head-lights** lampeggiare; ~ **a torch** at puntare una torcia su

flash: **~back** n scena f retrospettiva. **~bulb** n Phot flash m inv. **~er** n Auto lampeggiatore m. **~light** n Phot flash m inv; (Am: torch) torcia f [elettrica]. **~y** a vistoso

flask /flɑːsk/ n fiasco m; (vacuum ~) termos m inv

flat /flæt/ a (**flatter, flattest**) piatto; ‹refusal› reciso; ‹beer› sgassato; ‹battery› scarico; ‹tyre› a terra; **A ~** Mus la bemolle ● n appartamento m; Mus bemolle m; (puncture) gomma f a terra

flat: ~ **'feet** npl piedi mpl piatti. **~-fish** n pesce m piatto. **~ly** adv ‹refuse› categoricamente. ~ **rate** n tariffa f unica

flatten /ˈflætn/ vt appiattire

flatter /ˈflætə(r)/ vt adulare. **~ing** a

⟨*comments*⟩ lusinghiero; ⟨*colour, dress*⟩ che fa sembrare più bello. **~y** n adulazione f

flat 'tyre n gomma f a terra

flaunt /flɔ:nt/ vt ostentare

flautist /'flɔ:tɪst/ n flautista mf

flavour /'fleɪvə(r)/ n sapore m ● vt condire; **chocolate ~ed** al sapore di cioccolato. **~ing** n condimento m

flaw /flɔ:/ n difetto m. **~less** a perfetto

flax /flæks/ n lino m. **~en** ⟨*hair*⟩ biondo platino

flea /fli:/ n pulce f. **~ market** n mercato m delle pulci

fleck /flek/ n macchiolina f

fled /fled/ see **flee**

flee /fli:/ vt/i (pt/pp **fled**) fuggire (**from** da)

fleec|e /fli:s/ n pelliccia f ● vt fam spennare. **~y** a ⟨*lining*⟩ felpato

fleet /fli:t/ n flotta f; ⟨*of cars*⟩ parco m

fleeting /'fli:tɪŋ/ a **catch a ~ glance of sth** intravedere qcsa; **for a ~ moment** per un attimo

flesh /fleʃ/ n carne f; **in the ~** in persona. **~y** a carnoso

flew /flu:/ see **fly**²

flex¹ /fleks/ vt flettere ⟨*muscle*⟩

flex² n Electr filo m

flexib|ility /fleksɪ'bɪlətɪ/ n flessibilità f. **~le** a flessibile

'flexitime /'fleksɪ-/ n orario m flessibile

flick /flɪk/ vt dare un buffetto a; **~ sth off sth** togliere qcsa da qcsa con un colpetto. **flick through** vt sfogliare

flicker /'flɪkə(r)/ vi tremolare

flier /'flaɪə(r)/ n = **flyer**

flight¹ /flaɪt/ n ⟨*fleeing*⟩ fuga f; **take ~** darsi alla fuga

flight² n ⟨*flying*⟩ volo m; **~ of stairs** rampa f

flight: ~ path n traiettoria f di volo. **~ recorder** n registratore m di volo

flighty /'flaɪtɪ/ a (**-ier, -iest**) frivolo

flimsy /'flɪmzɪ/ a (**-ier, -iest**) ⟨*material*⟩ leggero; ⟨*shelves*⟩ poco robusto; ⟨*excuse*⟩ debole

flinch /flɪntʃ/ vi ⟨*wince*⟩ sussultare; ⟨*draw back*⟩ ritirarsi; **~ from a task** fig sottrarsi a un compito

fling /flɪŋ/ n **have a ~** ⟨*fam: affair*⟩ aver un'avventura ● vt (pt/pp **flung**) gettare

flint /flɪnt/ n pietra f focaia; ⟨*for lighter*⟩ pietrina f

flip /flɪp/ v (pt/pp **flipped**) ● vt dare un colpetto a; buttare in aria ⟨*coin*⟩ ● vi

fam uscire dai gangheri; ⟨*go mad*⟩ impazzire. **flip through** vt sfogliare

flippant /'flɪpənt/ a irriverente

flipper /'flɪpə(r)/ n pinna f

flirt /flɜ:t/ n civetta f ● vi flirtare

flirtat|ion /flɜ:'teɪʃn/ n flirt m inv. **~ious** /-ʃəs/ a civettuolo

flit /flɪt/ vi (pt/pp **flitted**) volteggiare

float /fləʊt/ n galleggiante m; ⟨*in procession*⟩ carro m; ⟨*money*⟩ riserva f di cassa ● vi galleggiare; Fin fluttuare

flock /flɒk/ n gregge m; ⟨*of birds*⟩ stormo m ● vi affollarsi

flog /flɒg/ vt (pt/pp **flogged**) bastonare; ⟨*fam: sell*⟩ vendere

flood /flʌd/ n alluvione f; ⟨*of river*⟩ straripamento m; ⟨*fig: of letters, tears*⟩ diluvio m; **be in ~** ⟨*river:*⟩ essere straripato ● vt allagare ● vi ⟨*river:*⟩ straripare

'floodlight n riflettore m ● vt (pt/pp **floodlit**) illuminare con riflettori

floor /flɔ:(r)/ n pavimento m; ⟨*storey*⟩ piano m; ⟨*for dancing*⟩ pista f ● vt ⟨*baffle*⟩ confondere; ⟨*knock down*⟩ stendere ⟨*person*⟩

floor: ~ board n asse f del pavimento. **~-polish** n cera f per il pavimento. **~ show** n spettacolo m di varietà

flop /flɒp/ n fam ⟨*failure*⟩ tonfo m; Theat fiasco m ● vi (pt/pp **flopped**) ⟨*fam: fail*⟩ far fiasco. **flop down** vi accasciarsi

floppy /'flɒpɪ/ a floscio. **~ 'disk** n floppy disk m inv. **~ [disk] drive** n lettore di floppy m

flora /'flɔ:rə/ n flora f

floral /'flɔ:rəl/ a floreale

Florence /'florəns/ n Firenze f

florid /'florɪd/ a ⟨*complexion*⟩ florido; ⟨*style*⟩ troppo ricercato

florist /'florɪst/ n fioraio, -a mf

flounce /flaʊns/ n balza f ● vi **~ out** uscire con aria melodrammatica

flounder¹ /'flaʊndə(r)/ vi dibattersi; ⟨*speaker:*⟩ impappinarsi

flounder² n ⟨*fish*⟩ passera f di mare

flour /'flaʊə(r)/ n farina f

flourish /'flʌrɪʃ/ n gesto m drammatico; ⟨*scroll*⟩ ghirigoro m ● vi prosperare ● vt brandire

floury /'flaʊərɪ/ a farinoso

flout /flaʊt/ vt fregarsene di ⟨*rules*⟩

flow /fləʊ/ n flusso m ● vi scorrere; ⟨*hang loosely*⟩ ricadere

flower /'flaʊə(r)/ n fiore m ● vi fiorire

flower: ~-bed n aiuola f. **~ed** a a fiori. **~pot** n vaso m [per i fiori]. **~y** a fiorito

flown /fləʊn/ see **fly**²

flu /flu:/ n influenza f

fluctuate | fool

88

fluctuat|e /'flʌktjʊeɪt/ vi fluttuare. **~ion** /-'eɪʃn/ n fluttuazione f

fluent /'fluːənt/ a spedito; **speak ~ Italian** parlare correntemente l'italiano. **~ly** adv speditamente

fluff /flʌf/ n peluria f. **~y** a (-ier, -iest) vaporoso; ⟨toy⟩ di peluche

fluid /'fluːɪd/ a fluido ● n fluido m

fluke /fluːk/ n colpo m di fortuna

flung /flʌŋ/ see **fling**

flunk /flʌŋk/ vt Am fam essere bocciato in

fluorescent /flʊə'resnt/ a fluorescente

fluoride /'flʊəraɪd/ n fluoruro m

flurry /'flʌrɪ/ n ⟨snow⟩ raffica f; fig agitazione f

flush /flʌʃ/ n ⟨blush⟩ [vampata f di] rossore m ● vi arrossire ● vt lavare con un getto d'acqua; **~ the toilet** tirare l'acqua ● a a livello (**with** di); ⟨fam: affluent⟩ a soldi

flustered /'flʌstəd/ a in agitazione; **get ~** mettersi in agitazione

flute /fluːt/ n flauto m

flutter /'flʌtə(r)/ n battito m ● vi svolazzare

flux /flʌks/ n **in a state of ~** in uno stato di flusso

fly¹ /flaɪ/ n (pl **flies**) mosca f

fly² /flaɪ/ v (pt **flew**, pp **flown**) ● vi volare; ⟨go by plane⟩ andare in aereo; ⟨flag:⟩ sventolare; ⟨rush⟩ precipitarsi; **~ open** spalancarsi ● vt pilotare ⟨plane⟩; trasportare [in aereo] ⟨troops, supplies⟩; volare con ⟨Alitalia etc⟩

fly³ n & **flies** pl ⟨on trousers⟩ patta f

flyer /'flaɪə(r)/ n aviatore m; ⟨leaflet⟩ volantino m

flying /'flaɪɪŋ/: **~ 'buttress** n arco m rampante. **~ 'colours: with ~ colours** a pieni voti. **~ 'saucer** n disco m volante. **~ 'start** n **get off to a ~ start** fare un'ottima partenza. **~ 'visit** n visita f lampo

fly: **~ leaf** n risguardo m. **~over** n cavalcavia m inv

foal /fəʊl/ n puledro m

foam /fəʊm/ n schiuma f; ⟨synthetic⟩ gommapiuma® f ● vi spumare; **~ at the mouth** far la bava alla bocca. **~ 'rubber** n gommapiuma® f

fob /fɒb/ vt (pt/pp **fobbed**) **~ sth off** affibbiare qcsa (**on sb** a qcno); **~ sb off** liquidare qcno

focal /'fəʊkl/ a focale

focus /'fəʊkəs/ n fuoco m; **in ~** a fuoco; **out of ~** sfocato ● v (pt/pp **focused** or

focussed) ● vt fig concentrare (**on** su) ● vi Phot **~ on** mettere a fuoco; fig concentrarsi (**on** su)

fodder /'fɒdə(r)/ n foraggio m

foe /fəʊ/ n nemico, -a mf

foetus /'fiːtəs/ n (pl **-tuses**) feto m

fog /fɒg/ n nebbia f

fogey /'fəʊgɪ/ n **old ~** persona f antiquata

foggy /'fɒgɪ/ a (**foggier, foggiest**) nebbioso; **it's ~** c'è nebbia

'fog-horn n sirena f da nebbia

foil¹ /fɔɪl/ n lamina f di metallo

foil² vt ⟨thwart⟩ frustrare

foil³ n ⟨sword⟩ fioretto m

foist /fɔɪst/ vt appioppare (**on sb** a qcno)

fold¹ /fəʊld/ n ⟨for sheep⟩ ovile m

fold² n piega f ● vt piegare; **~ one's arms** incrociare le braccia ● vi piegarsi; ⟨fail⟩ crollare. **fold up** vt ripiegare ⟨chair⟩ ● vi essere pieghevole; ⟨fam: business:⟩ collassare

fold|er /'fəʊldə(r)/ n cartella f. **~ing** a pieghevole

foliage /'fəʊlɪɪdʒ/ n fogliame m

folk /fəʊk/ npl gente f; **my ~s** ⟨family⟩ i miei; **hello there ~s** ciao a tutti

folk: **~-dance** n danza f popolare. **~lore** n folclore m. **~-song** n canto m popolare

follow /'fɒləʊ/ vt/i seguire; **it doesn't ~** non è necessariamente così; **~ suit** fig fare lo stesso; **as ~s** come segue. **follow up** vt fare seguito a ⟨letter⟩

follow|er /'fɒləʊə(r)/ n seguace mf. **~ing** a seguente ● n seguito m; ⟨supporters⟩ seguaci mpl ● prep in seguito a

folly /'fɒlɪ/ n follia f

fond /fɒnd/ a affezionato; ⟨hope⟩ vivo; **be ~ of** essere appassionato di ⟨music⟩; **I'm ~ of...** ⟨food, person⟩ mi piace moltissimo...

fondle /'fɒndl/ vt coccolare

fondness /'fɒndnɪs/ n affetto m; ⟨for things⟩ amore m

font /fɒnt/ n fonte f battesimale; Typ carattere m di stampa

food /fuːd/ n cibo m; ⟨for animals, groceries⟩ mangiare m; **let's buy some ~** compriamo qualcosa da mangiare

food: **~ mixer** n frullatore m. **~ poisoning** n intossicazione f alimentare. **~ processor** n tritatutto m inv elettrico

fool¹ /fuːl/ n sciocco, -a mf; **she's no ~** non è una stupida; **make a ~ of**

oneself rendersi ridicolo ● *vt* prendere in giro ● *vi* ~ **around** giocare; ⟨*husband, wife:*⟩ avere l'amante

fool² *n Culin* crema *f*

'**fool|hardy** *a* temerario. ~**ish** *a* stolto. ~**ishly** *adv* scioccamente. ~**ishness** *n* sciocchezza *f*. ~**proof** *a* facilissimo

foot /fʊt/ *n* (*pl* **feet**) piede *m*; (*of animal*) zampa *f*; (*measure*) piede *m* (= *30,48 cm*); **on** ~ a piedi; **on one's feet** in piedi; **put one's** ~ **in it** *fam* fare una gaffe

foot: ~**-and-'mouth disease** *n* afta *f* epizootica. ~**ball** *n* calcio *m*; (*ball*) pallone *m*. ~**baller** *n* giocatore *m* di calcio. ~**ball pools** *npl* ≈ totocalcio *m*. ~**-brake** *n* freno *m* a pedale. ~**-bridge** *n* passerella *f*. ~**hills** *npl* colline *fpl* pedemontane. ~**hold** *n* punto *m* d'appoggio. ~**ing** *n* **lose one's** ~**ing** perdere l'appiglio; **on an equal** ~**ing** in condizioni di parità. ~**man** *n* valletto *m*. ~**note** *n* nota *f* a piè di pagina. ~**path** *n* sentiero *m*. ~**print** *n* orma *f*. ~**step** *n* passo *m*; **follow in sb's** ~**steps** *fig* seguire l'esempio di qcno. ~**stool** *n* sgabellino *m*. ~**wear** *n* calzature *fpl*

for /fə(r)/, *accentato* /fɔː(r)/ *prep* per; ~ **this reason** per questa ragione; **I have lived here** ~ **ten years** vivo qui da dieci anni; ~ **supper** per cena; ~ **all that** nonostante questo; **what** ~? a che scopo?; **send** ~ **a doctor** chiamare un dottore; **fight** ~ **a cause** lottare per una causa; **go** ~ **a walk** andare a fare una passeggiata; **there's no need** ~ **you to go** non c'è bisogno che tu vada; **it's not** ~ **me to say** no sta a me dirlo; **now you're** ~ **it** ora sei nei pasticci ● *conj* poiché, perché

forage /'fɒrɪdʒ/ *n* foraggio *m* ● *vi* ~ **for** cercare

forbade /fə'bæd/ *see* **forbid**

forbear|ance /fɔː'beərəns/ *n* pazienza *f*. ~**ing** *a* tollerante

forbid /fə'bɪd/ *vt* (*pt* **forbade**, *pp* **forbidden**) proibire. ~**ding** *a* ⟨*prospect*⟩ che spaventa; ⟨*stern*⟩ severo

force /fɔːs/ *n* forza *f*; **in** ~ in vigore; (*in large numbers*) in massa; **come into** ~ entrare in vigore; **the [armed]** ~**s** *pl* le forze armate ● *vt* forzare; ~ **sth on sb** ⟨*decision*⟩ imporre qcsa a qcno; ⟨*drink*⟩ costringere qcno a fare qcsa

forced /fɔːst/ *a* forzato

force: ~**-'feed** *vt* (*pt/pp* **-fed**) nutrire a forza. ~**ful** *a* energico. ~**fully** *adv* ⟨*say, argue*⟩ con forza

forceps /'fɔːseps/ *npl* forcipe *m*

forcible /'fɔːsɪbl/ *a* forzato

ford /fɔːd/ *n* guado *m* ● *vt* guadare

fore /fɔː(r)/ *n* **to the** ~ in vista; **come to the** ~ salire alla ribalta

fore: ~**arm** *n* avambraccio *m*. ~**boding** /-'bəʊdɪŋ/ *n* presentimento *m*. ~**cast** *n* previsione *f* ● *vt* (*pt/pp* ~**cast**) prevedere. ~**court** *n* cortile *m* anteriore. ~**fathers** *npl* antenati *mpl*. ~**finger** *n* [dito *m*] indice *m*. ~**front** *n* **be in the** ~**front** essere all'avanguardia. ~**gone** *a* **be a** ~**gone conclusion** essere una cosa scontata. ~**ground** *n* primo piano *m*. ~**head** /'fɔːhed, 'fɒrɪd/ *n* fronte *f*. ~**hand** *n Tennis* diritto *m*

foreign /'fɒrən/ *a* straniero; ⟨*trade*⟩ estero; (*not belonging*) estraneo; **he is** ~ è uno straniero. ~ **currency** *n* valuta *f* estera. ~**er** *n* straniero, -a *mf*. ~ **language** *n* lingua *f* straniera

Foreign: ~ **Office** *n* ministero *m* degli [affari] esteri. ~ '**Secretary** *n* ministro *m* degli esteri

fore: ~**man** *n* caporeparto *m*. ~**most** *a* principale ● *adv* **first and** ~**most** in primo luogo. ~**name** *n* nome *m* di battesimo

forensic /fə'rensɪk/ *a* ~ **medicine** medicina *f* legale

'**forerunner** *n* precursore *m*

fore'see *vt* (*pt* **-saw**, *pp* **-seen**) prevedere. ~**able** /-əbl/ *a* **in the** ~**able future** in futuro per quanto si possa prevedere

'**foresight** *n* previdenza *f*

forest /'fɒrɪst/ *n* foresta *f*. ~**er** *n* guardia *f* forestale

fore'stall *vt* prevenire

forestry /'fɒrɪstrɪ/ *n* silvicoltura *f*

'**foretaste** *n* pregustazione *f*

fore'tell *vt* (*pt/pp* **-told**) predire

forever /fə'revə(r)/ *adv* per sempre; **he's** ~ **complaining** si lamenta sempre

fore'warn *vt* avvertire

foreword /'fɔːwɜːd/ *n* prefazione *f*

forfeit /'fɔːfɪt/ *n* (*in game*) pegno *m*; *Jur* penalità *f* ● *vt* perdere

forgave /fə'geɪv/ *see* **forgive**

forge¹ /fɔːdʒ/ *vi* ~ **ahead** ⟨*runner:*⟩ lasciarsi indietro gli altri; *fig* farsi strada

forge² *n* fucina *f* ● *vt* fucinare; (*counterfeit*) contraffare. ~**r** *n* contraffattore *m*. ~**ry** *n* contraffazione *f*

forget /fə'get/ *vt/i* (*pt* **-got**, *pp* **-gotten**, *pres p* **-getting**) dimenticare; dimenticarsi di ⟨*language, skill*⟩. ~**table** /-əbl/

a ⟨*day, film*⟩ da dimenticare. **~ful** *a* smemorato. **~fulness** *n* smemoratezza *f*. **~-me-not** *n* non-ti-scordar-dimé *m inv*

forgive /fə'gɪv/ *vt* (*pt* **-gave**, *pp* **-given**) **~ sb for sth** perdonare qcno per qcsa. **~ness** *n* perdono *m*

forgo /fɔ:'gəʊ/ *vt* (*pt* **-went**, *pp* **-gone**) rinunciare a

forgot(ten) /fə'gɒt(n)/ *see* **forget**

fork /fɔ:k/ *n* forchetta *f*; (*for digging*) forca *f*; (*in road*) bivio *m* ● *vi* ⟨*road:*⟩ biforcarsi; **~ right** prendere a destra. **fork out** *vt fam* sborsare

fork-lift 'truck *n* elevatore *m*

forlorn /fə'lɔ:n/ *a* ⟨*look*⟩ perduto; ⟨*place*⟩ derelitto; **~ hope** speranza *f* vana

form /fɔ:m/ *n* forma *f*; (*document*) modulo *m*; *Sch* classe *f* ● *vt* formare; formulare ⟨*opinion*⟩ ● *vi* formarsi

formal /'fɔ:ml/ *a* formale. **~ity** /-'mælətɪ/ *n* formalità *f inv*. **~ly** *adv* in modo formale; (*officially*) ufficialmente

format /'fɔ:mæt/ *n* formato *m* ● *vt* formattare ⟨*disk, page*⟩

formation /fɔ:'meɪʃn/ *n* formazione *f*

formative /'fɔ:mətɪv/ *a* **~ years** anni *mpl* formativi

former /'fɔ:mə(r)/ *a* precedente; ⟨*PM, colleague*⟩ ex; **the ~, the latter** il primo, l'ultimo. **~ly** *adv* precedentemente; (*in olden times*) in altri tempi

formidable /'fɔ:mɪdəbl/ *a* formidabile

formula /'fɔ:mjʊlə/ *n* (*pl* **-ae** /-li:/ *or* **-s**) formula *f*

formulate /'fɔ:mjʊleɪt/ *vt* formulare

forsake /fə'seɪk/ *vt* (*pt* **-sook** /-sʊk/, *pp* **-saken**) abbandonare

fort /fɔ:t/ *n Mil* forte *m*

forte /'fɔ:teɪ/ *n* [pezzo *m*] forte *m*

forth /fɔ:θ/ *adv* **back and ~** avanti e indietro; **and so ~** e così via

forth: **~'coming** *a* prossimo; (*communicative*) communicativo; **no response was ~** non arrivava nessuna risposta. **~right** *a* schietto. **~'with** *adv* immediatamente

fortieth /'fɔ:tɪɪθ/ *a & n* quarantesimo, -a *mf*

fortification /fɔ:tɪfɪ'keɪʃn/ *n* fortificazione *f*

fortify /'fɔ:tɪfaɪ/ *vt* (*pt/pp* **-ied**) fortificare; *fig* rendere forte

fortnight /'fɔ:t-/ *Br n* quindicina *f*. **~ly** *a* bimensile ● *adv* ogni due settimane

fortress /'fɔ:trɪs/ *n* fortezza *f*

fortuitous /fɔ:'tju:ɪtəs/ *a* fortuito

fortunate /'fɔ:tʃənət/ *a* fortunato;

that's **~**! meno male!. **~ly** *adv* fortunatamente

fortune /'fɔ:tʃu:n/ *n* fortuna *f*. **~-teller** *n* indovino, -a *mf*

forty /'fɔ:tɪ/ *a & n* quaranta *m*

forum /'fɔ:rəm/ *n* foro *m*

forward /'fɔ:wəd/ *adv* avanti; (*towards the front*) in avanti ● *a* in avanti; (*presumptuous*) sfacciato ● *n Sport* attaccante *m* ● *vt* inoltrare ⟨*letter*⟩; spedire ⟨*goods*⟩. **~s** *adv* avanti

fossil /'fɒsl/ *n* fossile *m*. **~ized** *a* fossile; ⟨*ideas*⟩ fossilizzato

foster /'fɒstə(r)/ *vt* allevare ⟨*child*⟩. **~-child** *n* figlio, -a *mf* in affidamento. **~-mother** *n* madre *f* affidataria

fought /fɔ:t/ *see* **fight**

foul /faʊl/ *a* ⟨*smell, taste*⟩ cattivo; ⟨*air*⟩ viziato; ⟨*language*⟩ osceno; ⟨*mood, weather*⟩ orrendo; **~ play** *Jur* delitto *m* ● *n Sport* fallo *m* ● *vt* inquinare ⟨*water*⟩; *Sport* commettere un fallo contro; ⟨*nets, rope:*⟩ impigliarsi in. **~-smelling** *a* puzzo

found[1] /faʊnd/ *see* **find**

found[2] *vt* fondare

foundation /faʊn'deɪʃn/ *n* (*basis*) fondamento *m*; (*charitable*) fondazione *f*; **~s** *pl* (*of building*) fondamenta *fpl*; **lay the ~-stone** porre la prima pietra

founder[1] /'faʊndə(r)/ *n* fondatore, -trice *mf*

founder[2] *vi* ⟨*ship:*⟩ affondare

foundry /'faʊndrɪ/ *n* fonderia *f*

fountain /'faʊntɪn/ *n* fontana *f*. **~-pen** *n* penna *f* stilografica

four /fɔ:(r)/ *a & n* quattro *m*

four: **~-'poster** *n* letto *m* a baldacchino. **~some** /'fɔ:səm/ *n* quartetto *m*. **~'teen** *a & n* quattordici *m*. **~'teenth** *a & n* quattordicesimo, -a *mf*

fourth /fɔ:θ/ *a & n* quarto, -a *mf*

fowl /faʊl/ *n* pollame *m*

fox /fɒks/ *n* volpe *f* ● *vt* (*puzzle*) ingannare

foyer /'fɔɪeɪ/ *n Theat* ridotto *m*; (*in hotel*) salone *m* d'ingresso

fraction /'frækʃn/ *n* frazione *f*

fracture /'fræktʃə(r)/ *n* frattura *f* ● *vt* fratturare ● *vi* fratturarsi

fragile /'frædʒaɪl/ *a* fragile

fragment /'frægmənt/ *n* frammento *m*. **~ary** *a* frammentario

fragran|ce /'freɪgrəns/ *n* fragranza *f*. **~t** *a* fragrante

frail /freɪl/ *a* gracile

frame /freɪm/ *n* (*of picture, door, window*) cornice *f*; (*of spectacles*) montatura *f*; *Anat* ossatura *f*; ⟨*structure, of bike*⟩ telaio *m*; **~ of mind** stato *m* d'animo ● *vt* incorniciare ⟨*picture*⟩; *fig* formulare; ⟨*sl: incriminate*⟩ montare. **~work** *n* struttura *f*

franc /fræŋk/ *n* franco *m*

France /frɑːns/ *n* Francia *f*

franchise /ˈfræntʃaɪz/ *n Pol* diritto *m* di voto; *Comm* franchigia *f*

frank¹ /fræŋk/ *vt* affrancare ⟨*letter*⟩

frank² *a* franco. **~ly** *adv* francamente

frankfurter /ˈfræŋkfɜːtə(r)/ *n* würstel *m inv*

frantic /ˈfræntɪk/ *a* frenetico; **be ~ with worry** essere agitatissimo. **~ally** *adv* freneticamente

fraternal /frəˈtɜːnl/ *a* fraterno

fraud /frɔːd/ *n* frode *f*; ⟨*person*⟩ impostore *m*. **~ulent** /-jʊlənt/ *a* fraudolento

fraught /frɔːt/ *a* **~ with** pieno di

fray¹ /freɪ/ *n* mischia *f*

fray² *vi* sfilacciarsi

frayed /freɪd/ *a* ⟨*cuffs*⟩ sfilacciato; ⟨*nerves*⟩ a pezzi

freak /friːk/ *n* fenomeno *m*; ⟨*person*⟩ scherzo *m* di natura; ⟨*fam: weird person*⟩ tipo *m* strambo ● *a* anormale. **~ish** *a* strambo

freckle /ˈfrekl/ *n* lentiggine *f*. **~d** *a* lentigginoso

free /friː/ *a* (**freer, freest**) libero; ⟨*ticket, copy*⟩ gratuito; ⟨*lavish*⟩ generoso; **~ of charge** gratuito; **set ~** liberare ● *vt* (*pt/pp* **freed**) liberare

free: **~dom** *n* libertà *f*. **~hand** *adv* a mano libera. **~hold** *n* proprietà *f* [fondiaria] assoluta. **~ 'kick** *n* calcio *m* di punizione. **~lance** *a & adv* indipendente. **~ly** *adv* liberamente; ⟨*generously*⟩ generosamente; **I ~ly admit that...** devo ammettere che.... **F~mason** *n* massone *m*. **~-range** *a* **~-range egg** uovo *m* di gallina ruspante. **~'sample** *n* campione *m* gratuito. **~style** *n* stile *m* libero. **~way** *n Am* autostrada *f*. **~-'wheel** *vi* ⟨*car:*⟩ ⟨*in neutral*⟩ andare in folle; ⟨*with engine switched off*⟩ andare a motore spento; ⟨*bicycle:*⟩ andare a ruota libera

freez|e /friːz/ *vt* (*pt* **froze**, *pp* **frozen**) gelare; bloccare ⟨*wages*⟩ ● *vi* ⟨*water:*⟩ gelare; **it's ~ing** si gela; **my hands are ~ing** ho le mani congelate

freez|er /ˈfriːzə(r)/ *n* freezer *m inv*, congelatore *m*. **~ing** *a* gelido ● *n* **below ~ing** sotto zero

freight /freɪt/ *n* carico *m*. **~er** *n* nave *f* da carico. **~ train** *n Am* treno *m* merci

French /frentʃ/ *a* francese ● *n* ⟨*language*⟩ francese *m*; **the ~** *pl* i francesi *mpl*

French: **~ 'beans** *npl* fagiolini *mpl* [verdi]. **~ 'bread** *n* filone *m* ⟨*di pane*⟩. **~ 'fries** *npl* patate *fpl* fritte. **~man** *n* francese *m*. **~ 'window** *n* porta-finestra *f*. **~woman** *n* francese *f*

frenzied /ˈfrenzɪd/ *a* frenetico

frenzy /ˈfrenzɪ/ *n* frenesia *f*

frequency /ˈfriːkwənsɪ/ *n* frequenza *f*

frequent¹ /ˈfriːkwənt/ *a* frequente. **~ly** *adv* frequentemente

frequent² /frɪˈkwent/ *vt* frequentare

fresco /ˈfreskəʊ/ *n* affresco *m*

fresh /freʃ/ *a* fresco; ⟨*new*⟩ nuovo; ⟨*Am: cheeky*⟩ sfacciato. **~ly** *adv* di recente

freshen /ˈfreʃn/ *vi* ⟨*wind:*⟩ rinfrescare. **freshen up** *vt* dare una rinfrescata a ● *vi* rinfrescarsi

freshness /ˈfreʃnɪs/ *n* freschezza *f*

'freshwater *a* di acqua dolce

fret /fret/ *vi* (*pt/pp* **fretted**) inquietarsi. **~ful** *a* irritabile

'fretsaw *n* seghetto *m* da traforo

friar /ˈfraɪə(r)/ *n* frate *m*

friction /ˈfrɪkʃn/ *n* frizione *f*

Friday /ˈfraɪdeɪ/ *n* venerdì *m inv*

fridge /frɪdʒ/ *n* frigo *m*

fried /fraɪd/ *see* **fry** ● *a* fritto; **~ egg** uovo *m* fritto

friend /frend/ *n* amico, -a *mf*. **~ly** *a* (**-ier, -iest**) ⟨*relations, meeting, match*⟩ amichevole; ⟨*neighbourhood, smile*⟩ piacevole; ⟨*software*⟩ di facile uso; **be ~ly with** essere amico di. **~ship** *n* amicizia *f*

frieze /friːz/ *n* fregio *m*

fright /fraɪt/ *n* paura *f*; **take ~** spaventarsi

frighten /ˈfraɪtn/ *vt* spaventare. **~ed** *a* spaventato; **be ~ed** aver paura ⟨**of** di⟩. **~ing** *a* spaventoso

frightful /ˈfraɪtfʊl/ *a* terribile

frigid /ˈfrɪdʒɪd/ *a* frigido. **~ity** /-ˈdʒɪdətɪ/ *n* freddezza *f*; *Psych* frigidità *f*

frill /frɪl/ *n* volant *m inv*. **~y** *a* ⟨*dress*⟩ con tanti volant

fringe /frɪndʒ/ *n* frangia *f*; ⟨*of hair*⟩ frangetta *f*; ⟨*fig: edge*⟩ margine *m*. **~ benefits** *npl* benefici *mpl* supplementari

frisk /frɪsk/ *vt* ⟨*search*⟩ perquisire

frisky /ˈfrɪskɪ/ *a* (**-ier, -iest**) vispo

fritter /ˈfrɪtə(r)/ *n* frittella *f* ● **fritter away** *vt* sprecare

frivol|ity /frɪˈvɒlətɪ/ *n* frivolezza *f*. **~ous** /ˈfrɪvələs/ *a* frivolo

frizzy /'frɪzɪ/ a crespo

fro /frəʊ/ see **to**

frock /frɒk/ n abito m

frog /frɒg/ n rana f. **~man** n uomo m rana

frolic /'frɒlɪk/ vi (pt/pp **frolicked**) ⟨lambs:⟩ sgambettare; ⟨people:⟩ folleggiare

from /frɒm/ prep da; ~ **Monday** da lunedì; ~ **that day** da quel giorno; **he's ~ London** è di Londra; **this is a letter ~ my brother** questa è una lettera di mio fratello; **documents ~ the 16th century** documenti del XVI secolo; **made ~** fatto con; **she felt ill ~ fatigue** si sentiva male dalla stanchezza; ~ **now on** d'ora in poi

front /frʌnt/ n parte f anteriore; ⟨fig: organization etc⟩ facciata f; ⟨of garment⟩ davanti m; ⟨sea~⟩ lungomare m; Mil, Pol, Meteorol fronte m; **in ~ of** davanti a; **in** or **at the ~** davanti; **to the ~** avanti ● a davanti; ⟨page, row, wheel⟩ anteriore

frontal /'frʌntl/ a frontale

front: ~ '**door** n porta f d'entrata. ~ '**garden** n giardino m d'avanti

frontier /'frʌntɪə(r)/ n frontiera f

front-wheel 'drive n trazione f anteriore

frost /frɒst/ n gelo m; ⟨hoar~⟩ brina f. **~bite** n congelamento m. **~bitten** a congelato

frost|ed /'frɒstɪd/ a **~ed glass** vetro m smerigliato. **~ily** adv gelidamente. **~ing** n Am Culin glassa f. **~y** a also fig gelido

froth /frɒθ/ n schiuma f ● vi far schiuma. **~y** a schiumoso

frown /fraʊn/ n cipiglio m ● vi aggrottare le sopraciglia. **frown on** vt disapprovare

froze /frəʊz/ see **freeze**

frozen /'frəʊzn/ see **freeze** ● a ⟨corpse, hand⟩ congelato; ⟨wastes⟩ gelido; Culin surgelato; **I'm ~** sono gelato. ~ **food** n surgelati mpl

frugal /'fruːgl/ a frugale

fruit /fruːt/ n frutto m; ⟨collectively⟩ frutta f; **eat more ~** mangia più frutta. ~ **cake** n dolce m con frutta candita

fruit|erer /'fruːtərə(r)/ n fruttivendolo, -a mf. **~ful** a fig fruttuoso

fruition /fruː'ɪʃn/ n **come to ~** dare dei frutti

fruit: ~ **juice** n succo m di frutta. **~less** a infruttuoso. ~ **machine** n

macchinetta f mangiasoldi. ~ **'salad** n macedonia f [di frutta]

frumpy /'frʌmpɪ/ a scialbo

frustrat|e /frʌ'streɪt/ vt frustrare; rovinare ⟨plans⟩. **~ing** a frustrante. **~ion** /-eɪʃn/ n frustrazione f

fry¹ /fraɪ/ vt/i (pt/pp **fried**) friggere

fry² /fraɪ/ n inv **small ~** fig pesce m piccolo

frying pan n padella f

fuck /fʌk/ vulg vt/i scopare ● int cazzo. **~ing** a del cazzo

fuddy-duddy /'fʌdɪdʌdɪ/ n fam matusa mf inv

fudge /fʌdʒ/ n caramella f a base di zucchero, burro e latte

fuel /'fjuːəl/ n carburante m; fig nutrimento m ● vt fig alimentare

fugitive /'fjuːdʒɪtɪv/ n fuggiasco, -a mf

fugue /fjuːg/ n Mus fuga f

fulfil /fʊl'fɪl/ vt (pt/pp **-filled**) soddisfare ⟨conditions, need⟩; realizzare ⟨dream, desire⟩; ~ **oneself** realizzarsi. **~ling** a soddisfacente. **~ment** n **sense of ~ment** senso m di appagamento

full /fʊl/ a pieno ⟨of di⟩; ⟨detailed⟩ esauriente; ⟨bus, hotel⟩ completo; ⟨skirt⟩ ampio; **at ~ speed** a tutta velocità; **in ~ swing** in pieno fervore ● n **in ~** per intero

full: ~ '**moon** n luna f piena. **~-scale** a ⟨model⟩ in scala reale; ⟨alert⟩ di massima gravità. ~ '**stop** n punto m. **~-time** a & adv a tempo pieno

fully /'fʊlɪ/ adv completamente; ⟨in detail⟩ dettagliatamente; ~ **booked** ⟨hotel, restaurant⟩ tutto prenotato

fumble /'fʌmbl/ vi ~ **in** rovistare in; ~ **with** armeggiare con; ~ **for one's keys** rovistare alla ricerca delle chiavi

fume /fjuːm/ vi ⟨be angry⟩ essere furioso

fumes /fjuːmz/ npl fumi mpl; ⟨from car⟩ gas mpl di scarico

fumigate /'fjuːmɪgeɪt/ vt suffumicare

fun /fʌn/ n divertimento m; **for ~** per ridere; **make ~ of** prendere in giro; **have ~** divertirsi

function /'fʌŋkʃn/ n funzione f; ⟨event⟩ cerimonia f ● vi funzionare; ~ **as** ⟨serve as⟩ funzionare da. **~al** a funzionale

fund /fʌnd/ n fondo m; fig pozzo m; **~s** pl fondi mpl ● vt finanziare

fundamental /fʌndə'mentl/ a fondamentale

funeral /'fjuːnərəl/ n funerale m

funeral: ~ **directors** n impresa f di pompe funebri. ~ **home** Am, ~

parlour n camera f ardente. **~ march** n marcia f funebre. **~ service** n rito m funebre

'funfair n luna park m inv

fungus /'fʌŋgəs/ n (pl **-gi** /-gaɪ/) fungo m

funicular /fjuː'nɪkjʊlə(r)/ n funicolare f

funnel /'fʌnl/ n imbuto m; (on ship) ciminiera f

funnily /'fʌnɪlɪ/ adv comicamente; (oddly) stranamente; **~ enough** strano a dirsi

funny /'fʌnɪ/ a (**-ier, -iest**) buffo; (odd) strano. **~ business** n affare m losco

fur /fɜː(r)/ n pelo m; (for clothing) pelliccia f; (in kettle) deposito m. **~ 'coat** n pelliccia f

furious /'fjʊərɪəs/ a furioso

furnace /'fɜːnɪs/ n fornace f

furnish /'fɜːnɪʃ/ vt ammobiliare (flat); fornire (supplies). **~ed** a **~ed room** stanza f ammobiliata. **~ings** npl mobili mpl

furniture /'fɜːnɪtʃə(r)/ n mobili mpl

furred /fɜːd/ a (tongue) impastato

furrow /'fʌrəʊ/ n solco m

furry /'fɜːrɪ/ a (animal) peloso; (toy) di peluche

further /'fɜːðə(r)/ a (additional) ulteriore; **at the ~ end** all'altra estremità; **until ~ notice** fino a nuovo avviso ● adv più lontano; **~,...** inoltre,...; **~ off** più lontano ● vt promuovere

further: ~ edu'cation n ≈ formazione f parauniversitaria. **~'more** adv per di più

furthest /'fɜːðɪst/ a più lontano ● adv più lontano

furtive /'fɜːtɪv/ a furtivo

fury /'fjʊərɪ/ n furore m

fuse¹ /fjuːz/ n (of bomb) detonatore m; (cord) miccia f

fuse² n Electr fusibile m ● vt fondere; Electr far saltare ● vi fondersi; Electr saltare; **the lights have ~d** sono saltate le luci. **~-box** n scatola f dei fusibili

fuselage /'fjuːzəlɑːʒ/ n Aeron fusoliera f

fusion /'fjuːʒn/ n fusione f

fuss /fʌs/ n storie fpl; **make a ~** fare storie; **make a ~ of** colmare di attenzioni ● vi fare storie

fussy /'fʌsɪ/ a (**-ier, -iest**) (person) difficile da accontentare; (clothes etc) pieno di fronzoli

fusty /'fʌstɪ/ a che odora di stantio; (smell) di stantio

futil|e /'fjuːtaɪl/ a inutile. **~ity** /-'tɪlətɪ/ n futilità f

future /'fjuːtʃə(r)/ a & n futuro; **in ~** in futuro. **~ perfect** futuro m anteriore

futuristic /fjuːtʃə'rɪstɪk/ a futuristico

fuzz /fʌz/ n **the ~** (sl: police) la pula

fuzzy /'fʌzɪ/ a (**-ier, -iest**) (hair) crespo; (photo) sfuocato

Gg

gab /gæb/ n fam **have the gift of the ~** avere la parlantina

gabble /'gæb(ə)l/ vi parlare troppo in fretta

gad /gæd/ vi (pt/pp **gadded**) **~ about** andarsene in giro

gadget /'gædʒɪt/ n aggeggio m

Gaelic /'geɪlɪk/ a & n gaelico m

gaffe /gæf/ n gaffe f inv

gag /gæg/ n bavaglio m; (joke) battuta f ● vt (pt/pp **gagged**) imbavagliare

gaily /'geɪlɪ/ adv allegramente

gain /geɪn/ n guadagno m; (increase) aumento m ● vt acquisire; **~ weight** aumentare di peso; **~ access** accedere ● vi (clock:) andare avanti. **~ful** a **~ful employment** lavoro m remunerativo

gait /geɪt/ n andatura f

gala /'gɑːlə/ n gala f; **swimming ~** manifestazione f di nuoto ● attrib di gala

galaxy /'gæləksɪ/ n galassia f

gale /geɪl/ n bufera f

gall /gɔːl/ n (impudence) impudenza f

gallant /'gælənt/ a coraggioso; (chivalrous) galante. **~ry** n coraggio m

'gall-bladder n cistifellea f

gallery /'gælərɪ/ n galleria f

galley /'gælɪ/ n (ship's kitchen) cambusa f; **~ [proof]** bozza f in colonna

gallivant /'gælɪvænt/ vi fam andare in giro

gallon /'gælən/ n gallone m (= 4,5 l; Am = 3,7 l)

gallop /'gæləp/ n galoppo m • vi galoppare

gallows /'gæləʊz/ n forca f

'**gallstone** n calcolo m biliare

galore /gə'lɔ:(r)/ adv a bizzeffe

galvanize /'gælvənaɪz/ vt Techn galvanizzare; fig stimolare (**into** a)

gambit /'gæmbɪt/ n prima mossa f

gambl|e /'gæmbl/ n (risk) azzardo m • vi giocare; (on Stock Exchange) speculare; **~e on** (rely) contare su. **~er** n giocatore, -trice mf [d'azzardo]. **~ing** n gioco m [d'azzardo]

game /geɪm/ n gioco m; (match) partita f; (animals, birds) selvaggina f; **~s** Sch ≈ ginnastica f • a (brave) coraggioso; **are you ~?** ti va?; **be ~ for** essere pronto per. **~keeper** n guardacaccia m inv

gammon /'gæmən/ n coscia f di maiale

gamut /'gæmət/ n fig gamma f

gander /'gændə(r)/ n oca f maschio

gang /gæŋ/ n banda f; (of workmen) squadra f • **gang up** vi far comunella (**on** contro)

gangling /'gæŋglɪŋ/ a spilungone

gangrene /'gæŋgri:n/ n cancrena f

gangster /'gæŋstə(r)/ n gangster m inv

gangway /'gæŋweɪ/ n passaggio m; Naut, Aeron passerella f

gaol /dʒeɪl/ n carcere m • vt incarcerare. **~er** n carceriere m

gap /gæp/ n spazio m; (in ages, between teeth) scarto m; (in memory) vuoto m; (in story) punto m oscuro

gap|e /geɪp/ vi stare a bocca aperta; (be wide open) spalancarsi; **~e at** guardare a bocca aperta. **~ing** a aperto

garage /'gærɑ:ʒ/ n garage m inv; (for repairs) meccanico m; (for petrol) stazione f di servizio

garbage /'gɑ:bɪdʒ/ n immondizia f; (nonsense) idiozie fpl. **~ can** n Am bidone m dell'immondizia

garbled /'gɑ:bld/ a confuso

garden /'gɑ:dn/ n giardino m; [**public**] **~s** pl giardini mpl pubblici • vi fare giardinaggio. **~ centre** n negozio m di piante e articoli da giardinaggio. **~er** n giardiniere, -a mf. **~ing** n giardinaggio m

gargle /'gɑ:gl/ n gargarismo m • vi fare gargarismi

gargoyle /'gɑ:gɔɪl/ n gargouille f inv

garish /'geərɪʃ/ a sgargiante

garland /'gɑ:lənd/ n ghirlanda f

garlic /'gɑ:lɪk/ n aglio m. **~ bread** n pane m condito con aglio

garment /'gɑ:mənt/ n indumento m

garnish /'gɑ:nɪʃ/ n guarnizione f • vt guarnire

garrison /'gærɪsn/ n guarnigione f

garter /'gɑ:tə(r)/ n giarrettiera f; (Am: on man's sock) reggicalze m inv da uomo

gas /gæs/ n gas m inv; (Am fam: petrol) benzina f • v (pt/pp **gassed**) • vt asfissiare • vi fam blaterare. **~ cooker** n cucina f a gas. **~ 'fire** n stufa f a gas

gash /gæʃ/ n taglio m • vt tagliare

gasket /'gæskɪt/ n Techn guarnizione f

gas: ~ mask n maschera f antigas. **~-meter** n contatore m del gas

gasoline /'gæsəli:n/ n Am benzina f

gasp /gɑ:sp/ vi avere il fiato mozzato

'**gas station** n Am distributore m di benzina

gastric /'gæstrɪk/ a gastrico. **~ 'flu** n influenza f gastro-intestinale. **~ 'ulcer** n ulcera f gastrica

gastronomy /gæ'strɒnəmɪ/ n gastronomia f

gate /geɪt/ n cancello m; (at airport) uscita f

gâteau /'gætəʊ/ n torta f

gate: ~crash vt entrare senza invito a. **~crasher** n intruso, -a mf. **~way** n ingresso m

gather /'gæðə(r)/ vt raccogliere; (conclude) dedurre; (in sewing) arricciare; **~ speed** acquistare velocità; **~ together** radunare (people, belongings); (obtain gradually) acquistare • vi (people:) radunarsi. **~ing** n **family ~ing** ritrovo m di famiglia

gaudy /'gɔ:dɪ/ a (-ier, -iest) pacchiano

gauge /geɪdʒ/ n calibro m; Rail scartamento m; (device) indicatore m • vt misurare; fig stimare

gaunt /gɔ:nt/ a (thin) smunto

gauze /gɔ:z/ n garza f

gave /geɪv/ see **give**

gawky /'gɔ:kɪ/ a (-ier, -iest) sgraziato

gawp /gɔ:p/ vi **~ [at]** fam guardare con aria da ebete

gay /geɪ/ a gaio; (homosexual) omosessuale; (bar, club) gay

gaze /geɪz/ n sguardo m fisso • vi guardare; **~ at** fissare

GB abbr (**Great Britain**) GB

gear /gɪə(r)/ n equipaggiamento m; Techn ingranaggio m; Auto marcia f; **in ~** con la marcia innestata; **change ~** cambiare marcia • vt finalizzare (**to** a)

gear: ~box n Auto scatola f del cambio.

~-lever *n*, *Am* **~-shift** *n* leva *f* del cambio

geese /giːs/ *see* **goose**

geezer /'giːzə(r)/ *n sl* tipo *m*

gel /dʒel/ *n* gel *m inv*

gelatine /'dʒelətɪn/ *n* gelatina *f*

gelignite /'dʒelɪgnaɪt/ *n* gelatina *f* esplosiva

gem /dʒem/ *n* gemma *f*

Gemini /'dʒemɪnaɪ/ *n Astr* Gemelli *mpl*

gender /'dʒendə(r)/ *n Gram* genere *m*

gene /dʒiːn/ *n* gene *m*

genealogy /dʒiːnɪ'ælədʒɪ/ *n* genealogia *f*

general /'dʒenrəl/ *a* generale ● *n* generale *m*; **in ~** in generale. **~ e'lection** *n* elezioni *fpl* politiche

generaliz|ation /dʒenrəlaɪ'zeɪʃn/ *n* generalizzazione *f*. **~e** /'dʒenrəlaɪz/ *vi* generalizzare

generally /'dʒenrəlɪ/ *adv* generalmente

general prac'titioner *n* medico *m* generico

generate /'dʒenəreɪt/ *vt* generare

generation /dʒenə'reɪʃn/ *n* generazione *f*

generator /'dʒenəreɪtə(r)/ *n* generatore *m*

generic /dʒɪ'nerɪk/ *a* **~ term** termine *m* generico

generosity /dʒenə'rɒsɪtɪ/ *n* generosità *f*

generous /'dʒenərəs/ *a* generoso. **~ly** *adv* generosamente

genetic /dʒɪ'netɪk/ *a* genetico. **~ engineering** *n* ingegneria *f* genetica. **~s** *n* genetica *f*

Geneva /dʒɪ'niːvə/ *n* Ginevra *f*

genial /'dʒiːnɪəl/ *a* gioviale

genitals /'dʒenɪtlz/ *npl* genitali *mpl*

genitive /'dʒenɪtɪv/ *a & n* **~ [case]** genitivo *m*

genius /'dʒiːnɪəs/ *n* (*pl* **-uses**) genio *m*

genocide /'dʒenəsaɪd/ *n* genocidio *m*

genre /'ʒɒrə/ *n* genere *m* [letterario]

gent /dʒent/ *n fam* signore *m*; **the ~s** *sg* il bagno per uomini

genteel /dʒen'tiːl/ *a* raffinato

gentle /'dʒentl/ *a* delicato; ⟨*breeze, tap, slope*⟩ leggero

gentleman /'dʒentlmən/ *n* signore *m*; (*well-mannered*) gentiluomo *m*

gent|leness /'dʒentlnɪs/ *n* delicatezza *f*. **~ly** *adv* delicatamente

genuine /'dʒenjʊɪn/ *a* genuino. **~ly** *adv* ⟨*sorry*⟩ sinceramente

geograph|ical /dʒɪə'græfɪkl/ *a* geografico. **~y** /dʒɪ'ɒgrəfɪ/ *n* geografia *f*

geological /dʒɪə'lɒdʒɪkl/ *a* geologico

geolog|ist /dʒɪ'ɒlədʒɪst/ *n* geologo, -a *mf*. **~y** *n* geologia *f*

geometr|ic[al] /dʒɪə'metrɪk(l)/ *a* geometrico. **~y** /dʒɪ'ɒmətrɪ/ *n* geometria *f*

geranium /dʒə'reɪnɪəm/ *n* geranio *m*

geriatric /dʒerɪ'ætrɪk/ *a* geriatrico; **~ ward** *n* reparto *m* geriatria. **~s** *n* geriatria *f*

germ /dʒɜːm/ *n* germe *m*; **~s** *pl* microbi *mpl*

German /'dʒɜːmən/ *n & a* tedesco, -a *mf*; (*language*) tedesco *m*

Germanic /dʒə'mænɪk/ *a* germanico

German: ~ 'measles *n* rosolia *f*. **~ 'shepherd** *n* pastore *m* tedesco

Germany /'dʒɜːmənɪ/ *n* Germania *f*

germinate /'dʒɜːmɪneɪt/ *vi* germogliare

gesticulate /dʒe'stɪkjʊleɪt/ *vi* gesticolare

gesture /'dʒestʃə(r)/ *n* gesto *m*

get /get/ *v* (*pt/pp* **got**, *pp Am also* **gotten**, *pres p* **getting**) ● *vt* (*receive*) ricevere; (*obtain*) ottenere; trovare ⟨*job*⟩; (*buy, catch, fetch*) prendere; (*transport, deliver to airport etc*) portare; (*reach on telephone*) trovare; (*fam: understand*) comprendere; preparare ⟨*meal*⟩; **~ sb to do sth** far fare qcsa a qcno ● *vi* (*become*) **~ tired/bored/angry** stancarsi/annoiarsi/arrabbiarsi; **I'm ~ting hungry** mi sta venendo fame; **~ dressed/married** vestirsi/sposarsi; **~ sth ready** preparare qcsa; **~ nowhere** non concludere nulla; **this is ~ting us nowhere** questo non ci è di nessun aiuto; **~ to** (*reach*) arrivare a. **get at** *vi* (*criticize*) criticare; **I see what you're ~ting at** ho capito cosa vuoi dire; **what are you ~ting at?** dove vuoi andare a parare?. **get away** *vi* (*leave*) andarsene; (*escape*) scappare. **get back** *vi* tornare ● *vt* (*recover*) riavere; **~ one's own back** rifarsi. **get by** *vi* passare; (*manage*) cavarsela. **get down** *vi* scendere; **~ down to work** mettersi al lavoro ● *vt* (*depress*) buttare giù. **get in** *vi* entrare ● *vt* mettere dentro ⟨*washing*⟩; far venire ⟨*plumber*⟩. **get off** *vi* scendere; (*from work*) andarsene; *Jur* essere assolto; **~ off the bus/one's bike** scendere dal pullman/dalla bici ● *vt* (*remove*) togliere. **get on** *vi* salire; (*be on good terms*) andare d'accordo; (*make progress*) andare avanti; (*in life*) riuscire; **~ on the bus/one's bike** salire sul pullman/sulla bici; **how are you**

~ting on? come va?. **get out** *vi* uscire; *(of car)* scendere; **~ out!** fuori!; **~ out of** *(avoid doing)* evitare ● *vt* togliere ‹*cork, stain*›. **get over** *vi* andare al di là ● *vt fig* riprendersi da ‹*illness*›. **get round** *vt* aggirare ‹*rule*›; rigirare ‹*person*› ● *vi* **I never ~ round to it** non mi sono mai deciso a farlo. **get through** *vi* *(on telephone)* prendere la linea. **get up** *vi* alzarsi; *(climb)* salire; **~ up a hill** salire su una collina

get: **~away** *n* fuga *f*. **~-up** *n* tenuta *f*

geyser /'giːzə(r)/ *n* scaldabagno *m*; *Geol* geyser *m inv*

ghastly /'gɑːstlɪ/ *a* (**-ier, -iest**) terribile; **feel ~** sentirsi da cani

gherkin /'gɜːkɪn/ *n* cetriolino *m*

ghetto /'getəʊ/ *n* ghetto *m*

ghost /gəʊst/ *n* fantasma *m*. **~ly** *a* spettrale

ghoulish /'guːlɪʃ/ *a* macabro

giant /'dʒaɪənt/ *n* gigante *m* ● *a* gigante

gibberish /'dʒɪbərɪʃ/ *n* stupidaggini *fpl*

gibe /dʒaɪb/ *n* malignità *f inv*

giblets /'dʒɪblɪts/ *npl* frattaglie *fpl*

giddiness /'gɪdɪnɪs/ *n* vertigini *fpl*

giddy /'gɪdɪ/ *a* (**-ier, -iest**) vertiginoso; **feel ~** avere le vertigini

gift /gɪft/ *n* dono *m*; *(to charity)* donazione *f*. **~ed** /-ɪd/ *a* dotato. **~-wrap** *vt* impacchettare in carta da regalo

gig /gɪg/ *n* *Mus fam* concerto *m*

gigantic /dʒaɪ'gæntɪk/ *a* gigantesco

giggle /'gɪgl/ *n* risatina *f* ● *vi* ridacchiare

gild /gɪld/ *vt* dorare

gills /gɪlz/ *npl* branchia *fsg*

gilt /gɪlt/ *a* dorato ● *n* doratura *f*. **~-edged stock** *n* investimento *m* sicuro

gimmick /'gɪmɪk/ *n* trovata *f*

gin /dʒɪn/ *n* gin *m inv*

ginger /'dʒɪndʒə(r)/ *a* rosso fuoco *inv*; ‹*cat*› rosso ● *n* zenzero *m*. **~ ale** *n*, **~ beer** *n* bibita *f* allo zenzero. **~bread** *n* panpepato *m*

gingerly /'dʒɪndʒəlɪ/ *adv* con precauzione

gipsy /'dʒɪpsɪ/ *n* = **gypsy**

giraffe /dʒɪ'rɑːf/ *n* giraffa *f*

girder /'gɜːdə(r)/ *n* *Techn* trave *f*

girl /gɜːl/ *n* ragazza *f*; *(female child)* femmina *f*. **~friend** *n* amica *f*; *(of boy)* ragazza *f*. **~ish** *a* da ragazza

giro /'dʒaɪərəʊ/ *n* bancogiro *m*; *(cheque)* sussidio *m* di disoccupazione

girth /gɜːθ/ *n* circonferenza *f*

gist /dʒɪst/ *n* **the ~** la sostanza

give /gɪv/ *n* elasticità *f* ● *v* (*pt* **gave**, *pp* **given**) ● *vt* dare; *(as present)* regalare (**to** a); fare ‹*lecture, present, shriek*›; donare ‹*blood*›; **~ birth** partorire ● *vi* *(to charity)* fare delle donazioni; *(yield)* cedere. **give away** *vt* dar via; *(betray)* tradire; *(distribute)* assegnare; **~ away the bride** portare la sposa all'altare. **give back** *vt* restituire. **give in** *vt* consegnare ● *vi* *(yield)* arrendersi. **give off** *vt* emanare. **give over** *vi* **~ over!** piantala!. **give up** *vt* rinunciare a; **~ oneself up** arrendersi ● *vi* rinunciare. **give way** *vi* cedere; *Auto* dare la precedenza; *(collapse)* crollare

given /'gɪvn/ *see* **give** ● *a* **~ name** nome *m* di battesimo

glacier /'glæsɪə(r)/ *n* ghiacciaio *m*

glad /glæd/ *a* contento (**of** di). **~den** /'glædn/ *vt* rallegrare

glade /gleɪd/ *n* radura *f*

gladly /'glædlɪ/ *adv* volentieri

glamorize /'glæməraɪz/ *vt* rendere affascinante. **~ous** *a* affascinante

glamour /'glæmə(r)/ *n* fascino *m*

glance /glɑːns/ *n* sguardo *m* ● *vi* **~ at** dare un'occhiata a. **glance up** *vi* alzare gli occhi

gland /glænd/ *n* glandola *f*

glandular /'glændjʊlə(r)/ *a* ghiandolare. **~ fever** *n* mononucleosi *f*

glare /gleə(r)/ *n* bagliore *m*; *(look)* occhiataccia *f* ● *vi* **~ at** dare un'occhiataccia a

glaring /'gleərɪŋ/ *a* sfolgorante; ‹*mistake*› madornale

glass /glɑːs/ *n* vetro *m*; *(for drinking)* bicchiere *m*; **~es** *pl* *(spectacles)* occhiali *mpl*. **~y** *a* vitreo

glaze /gleɪz/ *n* smalto *m* ● *vt* mettere i vetri a ‹*door, window*›; smaltare ‹*pottery*›; *Culin* spennellare. **~d** *a* ‹*eyes*› vitreo

glazier /'gleɪzɪə(r)/ *n* vetraio *m*

gleam /gliːm/ *n* luccichio *m* ● *vi* luccicare

glean /gliːn/ *vt* racimolare ‹*information*›

glee /gliː/ *n* gioia *f*. **~ful** *a* gioioso

glen /glen/ *n* vallone *m*

glib /glɪb/ *a* *pej* insincero

glide /glaɪd/ *vi* scorrere; *(through the air)* planare. **~er** *n* aliante *m*

glimmer /'glɪmə(r)/ *n* barlume *m* ● *vi* emettere un barlume

glimpse /glɪmps/ *n* occhiata *f*; **catch a ~ of** intravedere ● *vt* intravedere

glint /glɪnt/ n luccichio m ● vi luccicare

glisten /'glɪsn/ vi luccicare

glitter /'glɪtə(r)/ vi brillare

gloat /gləʊt/ vi gongolare (**over** su)

global /'gləʊbl/ a mondiale. **~ization** /-aɪ'zeɪʃən/ n globalizzazione f

globe /gləʊb/ n globo m; (map) mappamondo m

gloom /gluːm/ n oscurità f; (sadness) tristezza f. **~ily** adv (sadly) con aria cupa

gloomy /'gluːmɪ/ a (-ier, -iest) cupo

glorif|y /'glɔːrɪfaɪ/ vt (pt/pp -ied) glorificare; **a ~ied waitress** niente più che una cameriera

glorious /'glɔːrɪəs/ a splendido; (deed, hero) glorioso

glory /'glɔːrɪ/ n gloria f; (splendour) splendore m; (cause for pride) vanto m ● vi (pt/pp -ied) **~ in** vantarsi di

gloss /glɒs/ n lucentezza f. **~ paint** n vernice f lucida ● **gloss over** vt sorvolare su

glossary /'glɒsərɪ/ n glossario m

glossy /'glɒsɪ/ a (-ier, -iest) lucido; **~ [magazine]** rivista f femminile

glove /glʌv/ n guanto m. **~ compartment** n Auto cruscotto m

glow /gləʊ/ n splendore m; (in cheeks) rossore m; (of candle) luce f soffusa ● vi risplendere; (candle:) brillare; (person:) avvampare. **~ing** a ardente; (account) entusiastico. **~-worm** n lucciola f

glucose /'gluːkəʊs/ n glucosio m

glue /gluː/ n colla f ● vt (pres p gluing) incollare

glum /glʌm/ a (glummer, glummest) tetro

glut /glʌt/ n eccesso m

glutton /'glʌtn/ n ghiottone, -a mf. **~ous** /-əs/ a ghiotto. **~y** n ghiottoneria f

GMO n abbr (**genetically modified organism**) OMG m inv

gnarled /nɑːld/ a nodoso

gnash /næʃ/ vt **~ one's teeth** digrignare i denti

gnaw /nɔː/ vt rosicchiare

go /gəʊ/ n (pl goes) energia f; (attempt) tentativo m; **on the go** in movimento; **at one go** in una sola volta; **it's your go** tocca a te; **make a go of it** riuscire ● vi (pt went, pp gone) andare; (leave) andar via; (vanish) sparire; (become) diventare; (be sold) vendersi; **go and see** andare a vedere; **go swimming/shopping** andare a nuotare/fare spese; **where's the time gone?** come ha fatto il tempo a volare così?; **it's all gone** è fi-

nito; **be going to do** stare per fare; **I'm not going to** non ne ho nessuna intenzione; **to go** ⟨Am: hamburgers etc⟩ da asporto; **a coffee to go** un caffè da portar via. **go about** vi andare in giro. **go away** vi andarsene. **go back** vi ritornare. **go by** vi passare. **go down** vi scendere; (sun:) tramontare; (ship:) affondare; (swelling:) diminuire. **go for** vt andare a prendere; andare a cercare (doctor); (choose) optare per; (fam: attack) aggredire; **he's not the kind I go for** non è il genere che mi attira. **go in** vi entrare. **go in for** vt partecipare a (competition); darsi a (tennis). **go off** vi andarsene; (alarm:) scattare; (gun, bomb:) esplodere; (food, milk:) andare a male; **go off well** riuscire. **go on** vi andare avanti; **what's going on?** cosa succede? **go on at** vt fam scocciare. **go out** vi uscire; (light, fire:) spegnersi. **go over** vi andare ● vt (check) controllare. **go round** vi andare in giro; (visit) andare; (turn) girare; **is there enough to go round?** ce n'è abbastanza per tutti? **go through** vi (bill, proposal:) passare ● vt (search) subire; (check) controllare; (read) leggere. **go under** vi passare sotto; (ship, swimmer:) andare sott'acqua; (fail) fallire. **go up** vi salire; (Theat: curtain:) aprirsi. **go with** vt accompagnare. **go without** vt fare a meno di (supper, sleep) ● vi fare senza

goad /gəʊd/ vt spingere (**into** a); (taunt) spronare

'go-ahead a (person, company) intraprendente ● n okay m

goal /gəʊl/ n porta f; (point scored) gol m inv; (in life) obiettivo m; **score a ~** segnare. **~ie** fam, **~keeper** n portiere m. **~-post** n palo m

goat /gəʊt/ n capra f

gobble /'gɒbl/ vt **~ [down, up]** trangugiare

'go-between n intermediario, -a mf

God, god /gɒd/ n Dio m, dio m

god: ~child n figlioccio, -a mf. **~-daughter** n figlioccia f. **~dess** n dea f. **~father** n padrino m. **~-fearing** a timorato di Dio. **~-forsaken** a dimenticato da Dio. **~mother** n madrina f. **~parents** npl padrino m e madrina f. **~send** n manna f. **~son** n figlioccio m

go-getter /'gəʊgetə(r)/ n ambizioso, -a mf

goggle /'gɒgl/ vi fam **~ at** fissare con gli occhi sgranati. **~s** npl occhiali mpl;

(*of swimmer*) occhialini *mpl* [da piscina]; (*of worker*) occhiali *mpl* protettivi

going /'gəʊɪŋ/ *a* ⟨*price, rate*⟩ corrente; **~ concern** azienda *f* florida ● *n* **it's hard ~** è una faticaccia; **while the ~ is good** finché si può. **~s-'on** *npl* avvenimenti *mpl*

gold /gəʊld/ *n* oro *m* ● *a* d'oro

golden /'gəʊldn/ *a* dorato. **~ 'handshake** *n* buonuscita *f* (*al termine di un rapporto di lavoro*). **~ mean** *n* giusto mezzo *m*. **~ 'wedding** *n* nozze *fpl* d'oro

gold: ~fish *n inv* pesce *m* rosso. **~-mine** *n* miniera *f* d'oro. **~-plated** *a* placcato d'oro. **~smith** *n* orefice *m*

golf /gɒlf/ *n* golf *m*

golf: ~-club *n* circolo *m* di golf; (*implement*) mazza *f* da golf. **~-course** *n* campo *m* di golf. **~er** *n* giocatore, -trice *mf* di golf

gondo|la /'gɒndələ/ *n* gondola *f*. **~lier** /-'lɪə(r)/ *n* gondoliere *m*

gone /gɒn/ *see* **go**

gong /gɒŋ/ *n* gong *m inv*

good /gʊd/ *a* (**better, best**) buono; ⟨*child, footballer, singer*⟩ bravo; ⟨*holiday, film*⟩ bello; **~ at** bravo in; **a ~ deal of anger** molta rabbia; **as ~ as** (*almost*) quasi; **~ morning, ~ afternoon** buon giorno; **~ evening** buona sera; **~ night** buonanotte; **have a ~ time** divertirsi ● *n* bene *m*; **for ~** per sempre; **do ~** far del bene; **do sb ~** far bene a qcno; **it's no ~** è inutile; **be up to no ~** combinare qualcosa

goodbye /gʊd'baɪ/ *int* arrivederci

good: ~-for-nothing *a* buono a nulla. **G~ 'Friday** *n* Venerdì *m* Santo

good: ~-'looking *a* bello. **~-'natured** *a* **be ~-natured** avere un buon carattere

goodness /'gʊdnɪs/ *n* bontà *f*; **my ~!** santo cielo!; **thank ~!** grazie al cielo!

goods /gʊdz/ *npl* prodotti *mpl*. **~ train** *n* treno *m* merci

good'will *n* buona volontà *f*; *Comm* avviamento *m*

goody /'gʊdɪ/ *n* (*fam: person*) buono *m*. **~-goody** *n* santarellino, -a *mf*

gooey /'guːɪ/ *a fam* appiccicaticcio; *fig* sdolcinato

goof /guːf/ *vi fam* cannare

goose /guːs/ *n* (*pl* **geese**) oca *f*

gooseberry /'gʊzbərɪ/ *n* uva *f* spina

goose /guːs/: **~-flesh** *n*, **~-pimples** *npl* pelle *fsg* d'oca

gore[1] /gɔː(r)/ *n* sangue *m*

gore[2] *vt* incornare

gorge /gɔːdʒ/ *n Geog* gola *f* ● *vt* **~ oneself** ingozzarsi

gorgeous /'gɔːdʒəs/ *a* stupendo

gorilla /gə'rɪlə/ *n* gorilla *m inv*

gormless /'gɔːmlɪs/ *a fam* stupido

gorse /gɔːs/ *n* ginestrone *m*

gory /'gɔːrɪ/ *a* (**-ier, -iest**) cruento

gosh /gɒʃ/ *int fam* caspita

gospel /'gɒspl/ *n* vangelo *m*. **~ truth** *n* sacrosanta verità *f*

gossip /'gɒsɪp/ *n* pettegolezzi *mpl*; (*person*) pettegolo, -a *mf* ● *vi* pettegolare. **~y** *a* pettegolo

got /gɒt/ *see* **get**; **have ~** avere; **have ~ to do sth** dover fare qcsa

Gothic /'gɒθɪk/ *a* gotico

gotten /'gɒtn/ *Am see* **get**

gouge /gaʊdʒ/ *vt* **~ out** cavare

gourmet /'gʊəmeɪ/ *n* buongustaio, -a *mf*

gout /gaʊt/ *n* gotta *f*

govern /'gʌv(ə)n/ *vt/i* governare; (*determine*) determinare

government /'gʌvnmənt/ *n* governo *m*. **~al** /-'mentl/ *a* governativo

governor /'gʌvənə(r)/ *n* governatore *m*; (*of school*) membro *m* de consiglio di istituto; (*of prison*) direttore, -trice *mf*; (*fam: boss*) capo *m*

gown /gaʊn/ *n* vestito *m*; *Univ, Jur* toga *f*

GP *n abbr* **general practitioner**

grab /græb/ *vt* (*pt/pp* **grabbed**) **~ [hold of]** afferrare

grace /greɪs/ *n* grazia *f*; (*before meal*) benedicite *m inv*; **with good ~** volentieri; **three days' ~** tre giorni di proroga. **~ful** *a* aggraziato. **~fully** *adv* con grazia

gracious /'greɪʃəs/ *a* cortese; (*elegant*) lussuoso

grade /greɪd/ *n* livello *m*; *Comm* qualità *f*; *Sch* voto *m*; (*Am Sch: class*) classe *f*; *Am* = **gradient** ● *vt Comm* classificare; *Sch* dare il voto a. **~ crossing** *n Am* passaggio *m* a livello

gradient /'greɪdɪənt/ *n* pendenza *f*

gradual /'grædʒʊəl/ *a* graduale. **~ly** *adv* gradualmente

graduate[1] /'grædʊət/ *n* laureato, -a *mf*

graduate[2] /'grædʒʊeɪt/ *vi Univ* laurearsi

graduation /grædʒʊ'eɪʃn/ *n* laurea *f*

graffiti /grə'fiːtɪ/ *npl* graffiti *mpl*

graft /grɑːft/ *n* (*Bot, Med*) innesto *m*; (*Med: organ*) trapianto *m*; (*fam: hard work*) duro lavoro *m*; (*fam: corruption*) corruzione *f* ● *vt* innestare; trapiantare ⟨*organ*⟩

grain /greɪn/ *n* (*of sand, salt*) granello *m*; (*of rice*) chicco *m*; (*cereals*) cereali *mpl*; (*in wood*) venatura *f*; **it goes against the ~** *fig* è contro la mia/sua natura

gram /græm/ *n* grammo *m*

grammar /'græmə(r)/ *n* grammatica *f*. **~ school** *n* ≈ liceo *m*

grammatical /grə'mætɪkl/ *a* grammaticale

granary /'grænərɪ/ *n* granaio *m*

grand /grænd/ *a* grandioso; *fam* eccellente

grandad /'grændæd/ *n fam* nonno *m*

'grandchild *n* nipote *mf*

'granddaughter *n* nipote *f*

grandeur /'grændʒə(r)/ *n* grandiosità *f*

'grandfather *n* nonno *m*. **~ clock** *n* pendolo *m* (*che poggia a terra*)

grandiose /'grændɪəʊs/ *a* grandioso

grand: ~mother *n* nonna *f*. **~parents** *npl* nonni *mpl*. **~ pi'ano** *n* pianoforte *m* a coda. **~son** *n* nipote *m*. **~stand** *n* tribuna *f*

granite /'grænɪt/ *n* granito *m*

granny /'grænɪ/ *n fam* nonna *f*

grant /grɑːnt/ *n* (*money*) sussidio *m*; *Univ* borsa *f* di studio ● *vt* accordare; (*admit*) ammettere; **take sth for ~ed** dare per scontato qcsa

granulated /'grænjʊleɪtɪd/ *a* **~ sugar** zucchero *m* semolato

granule /'grænjuːl/ *n* granello *m*

grape /greɪp/ *n* acino *m*; **~s** *pl* uva *fsg*

grapefruit /'greɪp-/ *n inv* pompelmo *m*

graph /grɑːf/ *n* grafico *m*

graphic /'græfɪk/ *a* grafico; (*vivid*) vivido. **~s** *n* grafica *f*

'graph paper *n* carta *f* millimetrata

grapple /'græpl/ *vi* **~ with** *also fig* essere alle prese con

grasp /grɑːsp/ *n* stretta *f*; (*understanding*) comprensione *f* ● *vt* afferrare. **~ing** *a* avido

grass /grɑːs/ *n* erba *f*; **at the ~ roots** alla base. **~hopper** *n* cavalletta *f*. **~land** *n* prateria *f*

grassy /'grɑːsɪ/ *a* erboso

grate¹ /greɪt/ *n* grata *f*

grate² *vt Culin* grattugiare ● *vi* stridere

grateful /'greɪtfl/ *a* grato. **~ly** *adv* con gratitudine

grater /'greɪtə(r)/ *n Culin* grattugia *f*

gratif|y /'grætɪfaɪ/ *vt* (*pt/pp* **-ied**) appagare. **~ied** *a* appagato. **~ying** *a* appagante

grating /'greɪtɪŋ/ *n* grata *f*

gratis /'grɑːtɪs/ *adv* gratis

gratitude /'grætɪtjuːd/ *n* gratitudine *f*

gratuitous /grə'tjuːɪtəs/ *a* gratuito

gratuity /grə'tjuːɪtɪ/ *n* gratifica *f*

grave¹ /greɪv/ *a* grave

grave² *n* tomba *f*

gravel /'grævl/ *n* ghiaia *f*

grave: ~stone *n* lapide *f*. **~yard** *n* cimitero *m*

gravitate /'grævɪteɪt/ *vi* gravitare

gravity /'grævɪtɪ/ *n* gravità *f*

gravy /'greɪvɪ/ *n* sugo *m* della carne

gray /greɪ/ *a Am* = **grey**

graze¹ /greɪz/ *vi* ⟨*animal:*⟩ pascolare

graze² *n* escoriazione *f* ● *vt* (*touch lightly*) sfiorare; (*scrape*) escoriare; sbucciarsi ⟨*knee*⟩

grease /griːs/ *n* grasso *m* ● *vt* ungere. **~-proof 'paper** *n* carta *f* oleata

greasy /'griːsɪ/ *a* (**-ier, -iest**) untuoso; ⟨*hair, skin*⟩ grasso

great /greɪt/ *a* grande; (*fam: marvellous*) eccezionale

great: ~-'aunt *n* prozia *f*. **G~ 'Britain** *n* Gran Bretagna *f*. **~-'grandchildren** *npl* pronipoti *mpl*. **~-'grandfather** *n* bisnonno *m*. **~-'grandmother** *n* bisnonna *f*

great|ly /'greɪtlɪ/ *adv* enormemente. **~ness** *n* grandezza *f*

great-'uncle *n* prozio *m*

Greece /griːs/ *n* Grecia *f*

greed /griːd/ *n* avidità *f*; (*for food*) ingordigia *f*

greedily /'griːdɪlɪ/ *adv* avidamente; ⟨*eat*⟩ con ingordigia

greedy /'griːdɪ/ *a* (**-ier, -iest**) avido; (*for food*) ingordo

Greek /griːk/ *a* & *n* greco, -a *mf*; (*language*) greco *m*

green /griːn/ *a* verde; (*fig: inexperienced*) immaturo ● *n* verde *m*; **~s** *pl* verdura *f*; **the G~s** *pl Pol* i verdi. **~ belt** *n* zona *f* verde intorno a una città. **~ card** *n Auto* carta *f* verde

greenery /'griːnərɪ/ *n* verde *m*

green fingers *npl* **have ~ ~** avere il police verde

'greenfly *n* afide *m*

green: ~grocer *n* fruttivendolo, -a *mf*. **~house** *n* serra *f*. **~house effect** *n* effetto *m* serra. **~ light** *n fam* verde *m*

greet /griːt/ *vt* salutare; (*welcome*) accogliere. **~ing** *n* saluto *m*; (*welcome*) accoglienza f. **~ings card** n biglietto m d'auguri

gregarious /grɪˈgeərɪəs/ a gregario; (person) socievole

grenade /grɪˈneɪd/ n granata f

grew /gruː/ see **grow**

grey /greɪ/ a grigio; (hair) bianco ● n grigio m. **~hound** n levriero m

grid /grɪd/ n griglia f; (on map) reticolato m; Electr rete f

grief /griːf/ n dolore m; **come to ~** (plans:) naufragare

grievance /ˈgriːvəns/ n lamentela f

grieve /griːv/ vt addolorare ● vi essere addolorato

grill /grɪl/ n graticola f; (for grilling) griglia f; **mixed ~** grigliata f mista ● vt/i cuocere alla griglia; (interrogate) sottoporre al terzo grado

grille /grɪl/ n grata f

grim /grɪm/ a (**grimmer, grimmest**) arcigno; (determination) accanito

grimace /grɪˈmeɪs/ n smorfia f ● vi fare una smorfia

grime /graɪm/ n sudiciume m

grimy /ˈgraɪmɪ/ a (**-ier, -iest**) sudicio

grin /grɪn/ n sorriso m ● vi (pt/pp **grinned**) fare un gran sorriso

grind /graɪnd/ n (fam: hard work) sfacchinata f ● vt (pt/pp **ground**) macinare; affilare (knife); (Am: mince) tritare; **~ one's teeth** digrignare i denti

grip /grɪp/ n presa f; fig controllo m; (bag) borsone m; **get a ~ of oneself** controllarsi ● vt (pt/pp **gripped**) afferrare; (tyres:) far presa su; tenere avvinto (attention)

gripe /graɪp/ vi (fam: grumble) lagnarsi

gripping /ˈgrɪpɪŋ/ a avvincente

grisly /ˈgrɪzlɪ/ a (**-ier, -iest**) raccapricciante

gristle /ˈgrɪsl/ n cartilagine f

grit /grɪt/ n graniglia f; (for roads) sabbia f; (courage) coraggio m ● vt (pt/pp **gritted**) spargere sabbia su (road); **~ one's teeth** serrare i denti

grizzle /ˈgrɪzl/ vi piagnucolare

groan /grəʊn/ n gemito m ● vi gemere

grocer /ˈgrəʊsə(r)/ n droghiere, -a mf; **~'s [shop]** drogheria f. **~ies** npl generi mpl alimentari

groggy /ˈgrɒgɪ/ a (**-ier, -iest**) stordito; (unsteady) barcollante

groin /grɔɪn/ n Anat inguine m

groom /gruːm/ n sposo m; (for horse) stalliere m ● vt strigliare (horse); fig preparare; **well-~ed** ben curato

groove /gruːv/ n scanalatura f

grope /grəʊp/ vi brancolare; **~ for** cercare a tastoni

gross /grəʊs/ a obeso; (coarse) volgare; (glaring) grossolano; (salary, weight) lordo ● n inv grossa f. **~ly** adv (very) enormemente

grotesque /grəʊˈtesk/ a grottesco

grotto /ˈgrɒtəʊ/ n (pl **-es**) grotta f

grotty /ˈgrɒtɪ/ a (**-ier, -iest**) (fam: flat, street) squallido

ground¹ /graʊnd/ see **grind**

ground² n terra f; Sport terreno m; (reason) ragione f; **~s** pl (park) giardini mpl; (of coffee) fondi mpl ● vi (ship:) arenarsi ● vt bloccare a terra (aircraft); Am Electr mettere a terra

ground: ~ floor n pianterreno m. **~ing** n base f. **~less** a infondato. **~sheet** n telone m impermeabile. **~work** n lavoro m di preparazione

group /gruːp/ n gruppo m ● vt raggruppare ● vi raggrupparsi

grouse¹ /graʊs/ n inv gallo m cedrone

grouse² vi fam brontolare

grovel /ˈgrɒvl/ vi (pt/pp **grovelled**) strisciare. **~ling** a leccapiedi inv

grow /grəʊ/ v (pt **grew**, pp **grown**) ● vi crescere; (become) diventare; (unemployment, fear:) aumentare; (town:) ingrandirsi ● vt coltivare; **~ one's hair** farsi crescere i capelli. **grow up** vi crescere; (town:) svilupparsi

growl /graʊl/ n grugnito m ● vi ringhiare

grown /grəʊn/ see **grow** ● a adulto. **~-up** a & n adulto, -a mf

growth /grəʊθ/ n crescita f; (increase) aumento m; Med tumore m

grub /grʌb/ n larva f; (fam: food) mangiare m

grubby /ˈgrʌbɪ/ a (**-ier, -iest**) sporco

grudge /grʌdʒ/ n rancore m; **bear sb a ~e** portare rancore a qcno ● vt dare a malincuore. **~ing** a reluttante. **~ingly** adv a malincuore

gruelling /ˈgruːəlɪŋ/ a estenuante

gruesome /ˈgruːsəm/ a macabro

gruff /grʌf/ a burbero

grumble /ˈgrʌmbl/ vi brontolare (at contro)

grumpy /ˈgrʌmpɪ/ a (**-ier, -iest**) scorbutico

grunt /grʌnt/ n grugnito m ● vi fare un grugnito

guarantee /gærənˈtiː/ n garanzia f ● vt garantire. **~or** n garante mf

guard /gɑːd/ n guardia f; (security) guardiano m; (on train) capotreno m;

Techn schermo *m* protettivo; **be on ~** essere di guardia ● *vt* sorvegliare; (*protect*) proteggere. **guard against** *vt* guardarsi da. **~-dog** *n* cane *m* da guardia

guarded /'gɑ:dɪd/ *a* guardingo

guardian /'gɑ:dɪən/ *n* (*of minor*) tutore, -trice *mf*

guerrilla /gə'rɪlə/ *n* guerrigliero, -a *mf*. **~ warfare** *n* guerriglia *f*

guess /ges/ *n* supposizione *f* ● *vt* indovinare ● *vi* indovinare; (*Am: suppose*) supporre. **~work** *n* supposizione *f*

guest /gest/ *n* ospite *mf*; (*in hotel*) cliente *mf*. **~-house** *n* pensione *f*

guffaw /gʌ'fɔ:/ *n* sghignazzata *f* ● *vi* sghignazzare

guidance /'gaɪdəns/ *n* guida *f*; (*advice*) consigli *mpl*

guide /gaɪd/ *n* guida *f*; [Girl] G~ giovane esploratrice *f* ● *vt* guidare. **~book** *n* guida *f* turistica

guided /'gaɪdɪd/ *a* **~ missile** missile *m* teleguidato; **~ tour** giro *m* guidato

guide: **~-dog** *n* cane *m* per ciechi. **~lines** *npl* direttive *fpl*

guild /gɪld/ *n* corporazione *f*

guile /gaɪl/ *n* astuzia *f*

guillotine /'gɪləti:n/ *n* ghigliottina *f*; (*for paper*) taglierina *f*

guilt /gɪlt/ *n* colpa *f*. **~ily** *adv* con aria colpevole

guilty /'gɪltɪ/ *a* (**-ier, -iest**) colpevole; **have a ~ conscience** avere la coscienza sporca

guinea-pig /'gɪnɪ-/ *n* porcellino *m* d'India; (*in experiments*) cavia *f*

guise /gaɪz/ *n* **in the ~ of** sotto le spoglie di

guitar /gɪ'tɑ:(r)/ *n* chitarra *f*. **~ist** *n* chitarrista *mf*

gulf /gʌlf/ *n Geog* golfo *m*; *fig* abisso *m*

gull /gʌl/ *n* gabbiano *m*

gullet /'gʌlɪt/ *n* esofago *m*; (*throat*) gola *f*

gullible /'gʌlɪbl/ *a* credulone

gully /'gʌlɪ/ *n* burrone *m*; (*drain*) canale *m* di scolo

gulp /gʌlp/ *n* azione *f* di deglutire; (*of food*) boccone *m*; (*of liquid*) sorso *m* ● *vi*

deglutire. **gulp down** *vt* tranguggiare ⟨*food*⟩; scolarsi ⟨*liquid*⟩

gum¹ /gʌm/ *n Anat* gengiva *f*

gum² *n* gomma *f*; (*chewing-gum*) gomma *f* da masticare, chewing-gum *m inv* ● *vt* (*pt/pp* **gummed**) ingommare (**to** a)

gummed /gʌmd/ *see* **gum²** ● *a* ⟨*label*⟩ adesivo

gumption /'gʌmpʃn/ *n fam* buon senso *m*

gun /gʌn/ *n* pistola *f*; (*rifle*) fucile *m*; (*cannon*) cannone *m* ● **gun down** *vt* (*pt/pp* **gunned**) freddare

gun: **~fire** *n* spari *mpl*; (*of cannon*) colpi *mpl* [di cannone]. **~man** uomo *m* armato

gun: **~powder** *n* polvere *f* da sparo. **~shot** *n* colpo *m* [di pistola]

gurgle /'gɜ:gl/ *vi* gorgogliare; ⟨*baby:*⟩ fare degli urletti

gush /gʌʃ/ *vi* sgorgare; (*enthuse*) parlare con troppo entusiasmo (**over** di). **gush out** *vi* sgorgare. **~ing** *a* eccessivamente entusiastico

gust /gʌst/ *n* (*of wind*) raffica *f*

gusto /'gʌstəʊ/ *n* **with ~** con trasporto

gusty /'gʌstɪ/ *a* ventoso

gut /gʌt/ *n* intestino *m*; **~s** *pl* pancia *f*; (*fam: courage*) fegato *m* ● *vt* (*pt/pp* **gutted**) *Culin* svuotare delle interiora; **~ted by fire** sventrato da un incendio

gutter /'gʌtə(r)/ *n* canale *m* di scolo; (*on roof*) grondaia *f*, *fig* bassifondi *mpl*

guttural /'gʌtərəl/ *a* gutturale

guy /gaɪ/ *n fam* tipo *m*, tizio *m*

guzzle /'gʌzl/ *vt* ingozzarsi con ⟨*food*⟩; **he's ~d the lot** si è sbafato tutto

gym /dʒɪm/ *n fam* palestra *f*; (*gymnastics*) ginnastica *f*

gymnasium /dʒɪm'neɪzɪəm/ *n* palestra *f*

gymnast /'dʒɪmnæst/ *n* ginnasta *mf*. **~ics** /-'næstɪks/ *n* ginnastica *f*

gym: **~ shoes** *npl* scarpe *fpl* da ginnastica. **~-slip** *n Sch* ≈ grembiule *m* (*da bambina*)

gynaecolog|ist /gaɪnɪ'kʊlədʒɪst/ *n* ginecologo, -a *mf*. **~y** *n* ginecologia *f*

gypsy /'dʒɪpsɪ/ *n* zingaro, -a *mf*

gyrate /dʒaɪ'reɪt/ *vi* roteare

Hh

haberdashery /ˈhæbəˈdæʃərɪ/ *n* merceria *f*; *Am* negozio *m* d'abbigliamento da uomo

habit /ˈhæbɪt/ *n* abitudine *f*; *(Relig: costume)* tonaca *f*; **be in the ~ of doing sth** avere l'abitudine di fare qcsa

habitable /ˈhæbɪtəbl/ *a* abitabile

habitat /ˈhæbɪtæt/ *n* habitat *m inv*

habitation /hæbɪˈteɪʃn/ *n* **unfit for human ~** inagibile

habitual /həˈbɪtjʊəl/ *a* abituale; ⟨*smoker, liar*⟩ inveterato. **~ly** *adv* regolarmente

hack[1] /hæk/ *n* *(writer)* scribacchino, -a *mf*

hack[2] *vt* tagliare; **~ to pieces** tagliare a pezzi

hackneyed /ˈhæknɪd/ *a* trito [e ritrito]

'hacksaw *n* seghetto *m*

had /hæd/ *see* **have**

haddock /ˈhædək/ *n inv* eglefino *m*

haemorrhage /ˈhemərɪdʒ/ *n* emorragia *f*

haemorrhoids /ˈhemərɔɪdz/ *npl* emorroidi *fpl*

hag /hæg/ *n* **old ~** vecchia befana *f*

haggard /ˈhægəd/ *a* sfatto

haggle /ˈhægl/ *vi* contrattare (**over** per)

hail[1] /heɪl/ *vt* salutare; far segno a ⟨*taxi*⟩ ● *vi* **~ from** provenire da

hail[2] *n* grandine *f* ● *vi* **~** grandinare. **~stone** *n* chicco *m* di grandine. **~storm** *n* grandinata *f*

hair /heə(r)/ *n* capelli *mpl*; *(on body, of animal)* pelo *m*

hair: ~brush *n* spazzola *f* per capelli. **~cut** *n* taglio *m* di capelli; **have a ~cut** farsi tagliare i capelli. **~-do** *n fam* pettinatura *f*. **~dresser** *n* parrucchiere, -a *mf*. **~dryer** *n* fon *m inv*; *(with hood)* casco *m* [asciugacapelli]. **~grip** *n* molletta *f*. **~pin** *n* forcina *f*. **~pin 'bend** *n* tornante *m*, curva *f* a gomito. **~-raising** *a* terrificante. **~-style** *n* acconciatura *f*

hairy /ˈheərɪ/ *a* (**-ier, -iest**) peloso; *(fam: frightening)* spaventoso

hale /heɪl/ *a* **~ and hearty** in piena forma

half /hɑːf/ *n* (*pl* **halves**) metà *f inv*; **cut in ~** tagliare a metà; **one and a ~** uno e mezzo; **~ a dozen** mezza dozzina; **~ an hour** mezz'ora ● *a* mezzo; [**at**] **~ price** [a] metà prezzo ● *adv* a metà; **~ past two** le due e mezza

half: ~ board *n* mezza pensione *f*. **~-'hearted** *a* esitante. **~-'hourly** *a* & *adv* ogni mezz'ora. **~ 'mast** *n* **at ~ mast** a mezz'asta. **~ measures** *npl* mezze misure *fpl*. **'~-open** *a* socchiuso. **~-'term** *n* vacanza *f* di metà trimestre. **~-'time** *n* *Sport* intervallo *m*. **~'way** *a* **the ~'way mark/stage** il livello intermedio ● *adv* a metà strada; **get ~way** *fig* arrivare a metà. **~wit** *n* idiota *mf*

hall /hɔːl/ *n* *(entrance)* ingresso *m*; *(room)* sala *f*; *(mansion)* residenza *f* di campagna; **~ of residence** *Univ* casa *f* dello studente

'hallmark *n* marchio *m* di garanzia; *fig* marchio *m*

hallo /həˈləʊ/ *int* ciao!; *(on telephone)* pronto!; **say ~ to** salutare

Hallowe'en /hæləʊˈiːn/ *n* vigilia *f* d'Ognissanti e notte delle streghe, celebrata soprattutto dai bambini

hallucination /həluːsɪˈneɪʃn/ *n* allucinazione *f*

halo /ˈheɪləʊ/ *n* (*pl* **-es**) aureola *f*; *Astr* alone *m*

halt /hɔːlt/ *n* alt *m inv*; **come to a ~** fermarsi; ⟨*traffic:*⟩ bloccarsi ● *vi* fermarsi; **~! alt!** alt! ● *vt* fermare. **~ing** *a* esitante

halve /hɑːv/ *vt* dividere a metà; *(reduce)* dimezzare

ham /hæm/ *n* prosciutto *m*; *Theat* attore, -trice *mf* da strapazzo

hamburger /ˈhæmbɜːgə(r)/ *n* hamburger *m inv*

hamlet /ˈhæmlɪt/ *n* paesino *m*

hammer /ˈhæmə(r)/ *n* martello *m* ● *vt* martellare ● *vi* **~ at/on** picchiare a

hammock /ˈhæmək/ *n* amaca *f*

hamper[1] /ˈhæmpə(r)/ *n* cesto *m*; [**gift**] **~** cestino *m*

hamper² *vt* ostacolare

hamster /'hæmstə(r)/ *n* criceto *m*

hand /hænd/ *n* mano *f*; (*of clock*) lancetta *f*; (*writing*) scrittura *f*; (*worker*) manovale *m*; **at ~, to ~** a portata di mano; **on the one ~** da un lato; **on the other ~** d'altra parte; **out of ~** incontrollabile; (*summarily*) su due piedi; **give sb a ~** dare una mano a qcno ● *vt* porgere. **hand down** *vt* tramandare. **hand in** *vt* consegnare. **hand out** *vt* distribuire. **hand over** *vt* passare; (*to police*) consegnare

hand: **~bag** *n* borsa *f* (*da signora*). **~book** *n* manuale *m*. **~brake** *n* freno *m* a mano. **~cuffs** *npl* manette *fpl*. **~ful** *n* manciata *f*; **be [quite] a ~ful** *fam* essere difficile da tenere a freno

handicap /'hændɪkæp/ *n* handicap *m inv*. **~ped** *a* **mentally/physically ~ped** mentalmente/fisicamente handicappato

handi|craft /'hændɪkrɑːft/ *n* artigianato *m*. **~work** *n* opera *f*

handkerchief /'hæŋkətʃɪf/ *n* (*pl* **~s** & **-chieves**) fazzoletto *m*

handle /'hændl/ *n* manico *m*; (*of door*) maniglia *f*; **fly off the ~** *fam* perdere le staffe ● *vt* maneggiare; occuparsi di (*problem, customer*); prendere (*difficult person*); trattare (*subject*). **~bars** *npl* manubrio *m*

hand: **~-luggage** *n* bagaglio *m* a mano. **~made** *a* fatto a mano. **~-out** *n* (*at lecture*) foglio *m* informativo; (*fam: money*) elemosina *f*. **~rail** *n* corrimano *m*. **~shake** *n* stretta *f* di mano

handsome /'hænsəm/ *a* bello; (*fig: generous*) generoso

hand: **~stand** *n* verticale *f*. **~writing** *n* calligrafia *f*. **~-'written** *a* scritto a mano

handy /'hændɪ/ *a* (**-ier, -iest**) utile; (*person*) abile; **have/keep ~** avere/tenere a portata di mano. **~man** *n* tuttofare *m inv*

hang /hæŋ/ *vt* (*pt/pp* **hung**) appendere (*picture*); (*pt/pp* **hanged**) impiccare (*criminal*); **~ oneself** impiccarsi ● *vi* (*pt/pp* **hung**) pendere; (*hair:*) scendere ● *n* **get the ~ of it** *fam* afferrare. **hang about** *vi* gironzolare. **hang on** *vi* tenersi stretto; (*fam: wait*) aspettare; *Teleph* restare in linea. **hang on to** *vt* tenersi stretto a; (*keep*) tenere. **hang out** *vi* spuntare; **where does he usually ~ out?** *fam* dove bazzica di solito? ● *vt* stendere (*washing*). **hang up** *vt* appen-

dere; *Teleph* riattaccare ● *vi* essere appeso; *Teleph* riattaccare

hangar /'hæŋə(r)/ *n* hangar *m inv*

hanger /'hæŋə(r)/ *n* gruccia *f*. **~-on** *n* leccapiedi *mf*

hang: **~-glider** *n* deltaplano *m*. **~-gliding** *n* deltaplano *m*. **~man** *n* boia *m*. **~over** *n fam* postumi *mpl* da sbornia. **~-up** *n fam* complesso *m*

hanker /'hæŋkə(r)/ *vi* **~ after sth** smaniare per qcsa

hanky /'hæŋkɪ/ *n fam* fazzoletto *m*

hanky-panky /hæŋkɪ'pæŋkɪ/ *n fam* qualcosa *m* di losco

haphazard /hæp'hæzəd/ *a* a casaccio

happen /'hæpn/ *vi* capitare, succedere; **as it ~s** per caso; **I ~ed to meet him** mi è capitato di incontrarlo; **what has ~ed to him?** cosa gli è capitato?; (*become of*) che fine ha fatto? **~ing** *n* avvenimento *m*

happi|ly /'hæpɪlɪ/ *adv* felicemente; (*fortunately*) fortunatamente. **~ness** *n* felicità *f*

happy /'hæpɪ/ *a* (**-ier, -iest**) contento, felice. **~-go-'lucky** *a* spensierato

harass /'hærəs/ *vt* perseguitare. **~ed** *a* stressato. **~ment** *n* persecuzione *f*; **sexual ~ment** molestie *fpl* sessuali

harbour /'hɑːbə(r)/ *n* porto *m* ● *vt* dare asilo a; nutrire (*grudge*)

hard /hɑːd/ *a* duro; (*question, problem*) difficile; **~ of hearing** duro d'orecchi; **be ~ on sb** (*person:*) essere duro con qcno ● *adv* (*work*) duramente; (*pull, hit, rain, snow*) forte; **~ hit by unemployment** duramente colpito dalla disoccupazione; **take sth ~** non accettare qcsa; **think ~!** pensaci bene!; **try ~** mettercela tutta; **try ~er** metterci più impegno; **~ done by** *fam* trattato ingiustamente

hard: **~back** *n* edizione *f* rilegata. **~-boiled** *a* (*egg*) sodo. **~ copy** *n* copia *f* stampata. **~ disk** *n* hard disk *m inv*, disco *m* rigido

harden /'hɑːdn/ *vi* indurirsi

hard: **~-'headed** *a* (*businessman*) dal sangue freddo. **~-'hearted** *a* dal cuore duro. **~ line** *n* linea *f* dura; **~ lines!** che sfortuna!. **~line** *a* duro. **~liner** *n* fautore, -trice *mf* della linea dura. **~ luck** *n* sfortuna *f*

hard|ly /'hɑːdlɪ/ *adv* appena; **~ly ever** quasi mai. **~ness** *n* durezza *f*. **~ship** *n* avversità *f inv*

hard: **~ 'shoulder** *n* *Auto* corsia *f* d'emergenza. **~ up** *a fam* a corto di sol-

di; ~ **up for sth** a corto di qcsa. **~ware**
n ferramenta *fpl*; *Comput* hardware *m*
inv. **~-'wearing** *a* resistente.
~-'working *a* **be ~-working** essere un
gran lavoratore

hardy /'hɑːdɪ/ *a* (**-ier, -iest**) dal fisico
resistente; ⟨*plant*⟩ che sopporta il gelo

hare /heə(r)/ *n* lepre *f*. **~-brained** *a*
fam ⟨*scheme*⟩ da scervellati

hark /hɑːk/ *vi* ~ **back to** *fig* ritornare
su

harm /hɑːm/ *n* male *m*; ⟨*damage*⟩ danni
mpl; **out of ~'s way** in un posto sicuro;
it won't do any ~ non farà certo male
● *vt* far male a; ⟨*damage*⟩ danneggiare.
~ful *a* dannoso. **~less** *a* innocuo

harmonica /hɑː'mɒnɪkə/ *n* armonica *f*
[a bocca]

harmonious /hɑː'məʊnɪəs/ *a* armo-
nioso. **~ly** *adv* in armonia

harmon|ize /'hɑːmənaɪz/ *vi fig* armo-
nizzare. **~y** *n* armonia *f*

harness /'hɑːnɪs/ *n* finimenti *mpl*; ⟨*of
parachute*⟩ imbracatura *f* ● *vt* bardare
⟨*horse*⟩; sfruttare ⟨*resources*⟩

harp /hɑːp/ *n* arpa *f* ● **harp on** *vi fam*
insistere (**about** su). **~ist** *n* arpista *mf*

harpoon /hɑː'puːn/ *n* arpione *m*

harpsichord /'hɑːpsɪkɔːd/ *n* clavicem-
balo *m*

harrowing /'hærəʊɪŋ/ *a* straziante

harsh /hɑːʃ/ *a* duro; ⟨*light*⟩ abbaglian-
te. **~ness** *n* durezza *f*

harvest /'hɑːvɪst/ *n* raccolta *f*; ⟨*of
grapes*⟩ vendemmia *f*; ⟨*crop*⟩ raccolto *m*
● *vt* raccogliere

has /hæz/ *see* **have**

hash /hæʃ/ *n* **make a ~ of** *fam* fare un
casino con

hashish /'hæʃɪʃ/ *n* hascish *m*

hassle /'hæsl/ *n fam* rottura *f* ● *vt* rompere le scatole a

haste /heɪst/ *n* fretta *f*

hast|y /'heɪstɪ/ *a* (**-ier, -iest**) frettoloso;
⟨*decision*⟩ affrettato. **~ily** *adv* frettolo-
samente

hat /hæt/ *n* cappello *m*

hatch¹ /hætʃ/ *n* ⟨*for food*⟩ sportello *m*
passavivande; *Naut* boccaporto *m*

hatch² *vi* ~[**out**] rompere il guscio;
⟨*egg:*⟩ schiudersi ● *vt* covare; tramare
⟨*plot*⟩

'hatchback *n* tre/cinque porte *m inv*;
⟨*door*⟩ porta *f* del bagagliaio

hatchet /'hætʃɪt/ *n* ascia *f*

hate /heɪt/ *n* odio *m* ● *vt* odiare. **~ful** *a*
odioso

hatred /'heɪtrɪd/ *n* odio *m*

haught|y /'hɔːtɪ/ *a* (**-ier, -iest**) altezzo-
so. **~ily** *adv* altezzosamente

haul /hɔːl/ *n* ⟨*fish*⟩ pescata *f*; ⟨*loot*⟩ bottino *m*; ⟨*pull*⟩ tirata *f* ● *vt* tirare; trasportare ⟨*goods*⟩ ● *vi* ~ **on** tirare. **~age**
/-ɪdʒ/ *n* trasporto *m*. **~ier** /-ɪə(r)/ *n*
autotrasportatore *m*

haunt /hɔːnt/ *n* ritrovo *m* ● *vt* frequentare; ⟨*linger in the mind*⟩ perseguitare;
this house is ~ed questa casa è abita-
ta da fantasmi

have /hæv/ *vt* (*3 sg pres tense* **has**; *pt/pp*
had) avere; fare ⟨*breakfast, bath, walk
etc*⟩; ~ **a drink** bere qualcosa; ~
lunch/dinner pranzare/cenare; ~ **a
rest** riposarsi; **I had my hair cut** mi
sono tagliata i capelli; **we had the
house painted** abbiamo fatto
tinteggiare la casa; **I had it made** l'ho
fatto fare; ~ **to do sth** dover fare qcsa;
~ **him telephone me tomorrow** digli
di telefonarmi domani; **he has** *or* **he's
got two houses** ha due case; **you've
got the money, ~n't you?** hai i soldi,
no? ● *v aux* avere; ⟨*with verbs of motion
& some others*⟩ essere; **I ~ seen him**
l'ho visto; **he has never been there**
non ci è mai stato. **have on** *vt* ⟨*be
wearing*⟩ portare; ⟨*dupe*⟩ prendere in
giro; **I've got something on tonight**
ho un impegno stasera. **have out** *vt* ~
it out with sb chiarire le cose con qcno
● *npl* **the ~s and the ~-nots** i ricchi e
i poveri

haven /'heɪvn/ *n fig* rifugio *m*

haversack /'hævə-/ *n* zaino *m*

havoc /'hævək/ *n* strage *f*; **play ~ with**
fig scombussolare

haw /hɔː/ *see* **hum**

hawk /hɔːk/ *n* falco *m*

hay /heɪ/ *n* fieno *m*. ~ **fever** *n* raffreddore *m* da fieno. **~stack** *n* pagliaio *m*

'haywire *a fam* **go ~** dare i numeri;
⟨*plans:*⟩ andare all'aria

hazard /'hæzəd/ *n* ⟨*risk*⟩ rischio *m* ● *vt*
rischiare; ~ **a guess** azzardare un'ipotesi. **~ous** /-əs/ *a* rischioso. ~
[**warning**] **lights** *npl Auto* luci *fpl*
d'emergenza

haze /heɪz/ *n* foschia *f*

hazel /'heɪz(ə)l/ *n* nocciolo *m*; ⟨*colour*⟩
[color *m*] nocciola *m*. **~-nut** *n* nocciola *f*

hazy /'heɪzɪ/ *a* (**-ier, -iest**) nebbioso;
⟨*fig: person*⟩ confuso; ⟨*memories*⟩ vago

he /hiː/ *pron* lui; **he's tired** è stanco;
I'm going but he's not io vengo, ma
lui no

head /hed/ *n* testa *f*; ⟨*of firm*⟩ capo *m*; ⟨*of*

primary school) direttore, -trice *mf*; (*of secondary school*) preside *mf*; (*on beer*) schiuma *f*; **be off one's** ~ essere fuori di testa; **have a good** ~ **for business** avere il senso degli affari; **have a good** ~ **for heights** non soffrire di vertigini; **10 pounds a** ~ 10 sterline a testa; **20** ~ **of cattle** 20 capi di bestiame; ~ **first** a capofitto; ~ **over heels in love** innamorato pazzo; ~**s or tails?** testa o croce? ● *vt* essere a capo di; essere in testa a ⟨*list*⟩; colpire di testa ⟨*ball*⟩ ● *vi* ~ **for** dirigersi verso.

head: ~**ache** *n* mal *m* di testa. ~**-dress** *n* acconciatura *f*. ~**er** /'hedə(r)/ *n* rinvio *m* di testa; (*dive*) tuffo *m* di testa. ~**hunter** *n* cacciatore, -trice *mf* di teste. ~**ing** *n* (*in list etc*) titolo *m*. ~**lamp** *n Auto* fanale *m*. ~**land** *n* promontorio *m*. ~**light** *n Auto* fanale *m*. ~**line** *n* titolo *m*. ~**long** *a & adv* a capofitto. ~'**master** *n* (*of primary school*) direttore *m*; (*of secondary school*) preside *m*. ~'**mistress** *n* (*of primary school*) direttrice *f*; (*of secondary school*) preside *f*. ~ **office** *n* sede *f* centrale. ~**-on** *a* frontale ● *adv* frontalmente. ~**phones** *npl* cuffie *fpl*. ~**quarters** *npl* sede *fsg*; *Mil* quartier *m* generale *msg*. ~**rest** *n* poggiatesta *m inv*. ~**room** *n* sottotetto *m*; (*of bridge*) altezza *f* libera di passaggio. ~**scarf** *n* foulard *m inv*, fazzoletto *m*. ~**strong** *a* testardo. ~ '**waiter** *n* capocameriere *m*. ~**way** *n* progresso *m*. ~**wind** *n* vento *m* di prua

heady /'hedɪ/ *a* che dà alla testa

heal /hiːl/ *vt/i* guarire

health /helθ/ *n* salute *f*

health: ~ **farm** *n* centro *m* di rimessa in forma. ~ **foods** *npl* alimenti *mpl* macrobiotici. ~**-food shop** *n* negozio *m* di macrobiotica. ~ **insurance** *n* assicurazione *f* contro malattie

health|y /'helθɪ/ *a* (**-ier, -iest**) sano. ~**ily** *adv* in modo sano

heap /hiːp/ *n* mucchio *m*; ~**s of** *fam* un sacco di ● *vt* ~ [**up**] ammucchiare; ~**ed teaspoon** un cucchiaino abbondante

hear /hɪə(r)/ *vt/i* (*pt/pp* **heard**) sentire; ~, ~! bravo! ~ **from** *vi* aver notizie di. **hear of** *vi* sentir parlare di; **he would not** ~ **of it** non ne ha voluto sentir parlare

hearing /'hɪərɪŋ/ *n* udito *m*; *Jur* udienza *f*. ~**-aid** *n* apparecchio *m* acustico

'**hearsay** *n* **from** ~ per sentito dire

hearse /hɜːs/ *n* carro *m* funebre

heart /hɑːt/ *n* cuore *m*; ~**s** *pl* (*in cards*) cuori *mpl*; **by** ~ a memoria

heart: ~**ache** *n* pena *f*. ~ **attack** *n* infarto *m*. ~**beat** *n* battito *m* cardiaco. ~**-break** *n* afflizione *f*. ~**-breaking** *a* straziante. ~**-broken** *a* **be** ~**-broken** avere il cuore spezzato. ~**burn** *n* mal *m* di stomaco. ~**en** *vt* rincuorare. ~**felt** *a* di cuore

hearth /hɑːθ/ *n* focolare *m*

heart|ily /'hɑːtɪlɪ/ *adv* di cuore; ⟨*eat*⟩ con appetito; **be** ~**ily sick of sth** non poterne più di qcsa. ~**less** *a* spietato. ~**-searching** *n* esame *m* di coscienza. ~**-to-** ~ *n* conversazione *f* a cuore aperto ● *a* a cuore aperto. ~**y** *a* caloroso; ⟨*meal*⟩ copioso; ⟨*person*⟩ gioviale

heat /hiːt/ *n* calore *m*; *Sport* prova *f* eliminatoria ● *vt* scaldare ● *vi* scaldarsi. ~**ed** *a* ⟨*swimming pool*⟩ riscaldato; ⟨*discussion*⟩ animato. ~**er** *n* (*for room*) stufa *f*; (*for water*) boiler *m inv*; *Auto* riscaldamento *m*

heath /hiːθ/ *n* brughiera *f*

heathen /'hiːðn/ *a & n* pagano, -a *mf*

heather /'heðə(r)/ *n* erica *f*

heating /'hiːtɪŋ/ *n* riscaldamento *m*

heat: ~**-stroke** *n* colpo *m* di sole. ~ **wave** *n* ondata *f* di calore

heave /hiːv/ *vt* tirare; (*lift*) tirare su; (*fam: throw*) gettare; emettere ⟨*sigh*⟩ ● *vi* tirare

heaven /'hev(ə)n/ *n* paradiso *m*; ~ **help you if...** Dio ti scampi se...; **H**~**s!** santo cielo!. ~**ly** *a* celeste; *fam* delizioso

heav|y /'hevɪ/ *a* (**-ier, -iest**) pesante; ⟨*traffic*⟩ intenso; ⟨*rain, cold*⟩ forte; **be a** ~**y smoker/drinker** essere un gran fumatore/bevitore. ~**ily** *adv* pesantemente; ⟨*smoke, drink etc*⟩ molto. ~**yweight** *n* peso *m* massimo

Hebrew /'hiːbruː/ *a* ebreo

heckle /'hekl/ *vt* interrompere di continuo. ~**r** *n* disturbatore, -trice *mf*

hectic /'hektɪk/ *a* frenetico

hedge /hedʒ/ *n* siepe *f* ● *vi fig* essere evasivo. ~**hog** *n* riccio *m*

heed /hiːd/ *n* **pay** ~ **to** prestare ascolto a ● *vt* prestare ascolto a. ~**less** *a* noncurante

heel[1] /hiːl/ *n* tallone *m*; (*of shoe*) tacco *m*; **take to one's** ~**s** *fam* darsela a gambe

heel[2] *vi* ~ **over** *Naut* inclinarsi

hefty /'heftɪ/ *a* (**-ier, -iest**) massiccio

heifer /'hefə(r)/ *n* giovenca *f*

height /haɪt/ n altezza f; (of plane) altitudine f; (of season, fame) culmine m. **~en** vt fig accrescere

heir /eə(r)/ n erede mf. **~ess** n ereditiera f. **~loom** n cimelio m di famiglia

held /held/ see **hold²**

helicopter /'helɪkɒptə(r)/ n elicottero m

hell /hel/ n inferno m; **go to ~!** sl va' al diavolo! ● int porca miseria!

hello /hə'ləu/ int & n = **hallo**

helm /helm/ n timone m; **at the ~** fig al timone

helmet /'helmɪt/ n casco m

help /help/ n aiuto m; (employee) aiuto m domestico; **that's no ~** non è d'aiuto ● vt aiutare; **~ oneself to sth** servirsi di qcsa; **~ yourself** (at table) serviti pure; **I could not ~ laughing** non ho potuto trattenermi dal ridere; **it cannot be ~ed** non c'è niente da fare; **I can't ~ it** non ci posso far niente ● vi aiutare

help|er /'helpə(r)/ n aiutante mf. **~ful** a ⟨person⟩ di aiuto; ⟨advice⟩ utile. **~ing** n porzione f. **~less** a (unable to manage) incapace; (powerless) impotente

helter-skelter /heltə'skeltə(r)/ adv in fretta e furia ● n scivolo m a spirale nei luna park

hem /hem/ n orlo m ● vt (pt/pp hemmed) orlare. **hem in** vt intrappolare

hemisphere /'hemɪ-/ n emisfero m

hemp /hemp/ n canapa f

hen /hen/ n gallina f; (any female bird) femmina f

hence /hens/ adv (for this reason) quindi. **~'forth** adv d'ora innanzi

'hen: ~-party n fam festa f di addio al celibato per sole donne. **~pecked** a tiranneggiato dalla moglie

her /hɜː(r)/ poss a il suo m, la sua f, i suoi mpl, le sue fpl; **~ mother/father** sua madre/suo padre ● pers pron (direct object) la; (indirect object) le; (after prep) lei; **I know ~** la conosco; **give ~ the money** dalle i soldi; **give it to ~** daglielo; **I came with ~** sono venuto con lei; **it's ~** è lei; **I've seen ~** l'ho vista; **I've seen ~, but not him** ho visto lei, ma non lui

herald /'herəld/ vt annunciare

herb /hɜːb/ n erba f

herbal /'hɜːb(ə)l/ a alle erbe; **~ tea** tisana f

herbs /hɜːbz/ npl (for cooking) aromi mpl [da cucina]; (medicinal) erbe fpl

herd /hɜːd/ n gregge m ● vt (tend) sorvegliare; (drive) far muovere; fig ammassare

here /hɪə(r)/ adv qui, qua; **in ~** qui dentro; **come/bring ~** vieni/porta qui; **~ is..., ~ are...** ecco...; **~ you are!** ecco qua!. **~'after** adv in futuro. **~'by** adv con la presente

heredit|ary /hə'redɪtərɪ/ a ereditario. **~y** n eredità f

here|sy /'herəsɪ/ n eresia f. **~tic** n eretico, -a mf

here'with adv Comm con la presente

heritage /'herɪtɪdʒ/ n eredità f

hermetic /hɜː'metɪk/ a ermetico. **~ally** adv ermeticamente

hermit /'hɜːmɪt/ n eremita mf

hernia /'hɜːnɪə/ n ernia f

hero /'hɪərəu/ n (pl -es) eroe m

heroic /hɪ'rəuɪk/ a eroico

heroin /'herəuɪn/ n eroina f (droga)

hero|ine /'herəuɪn/ n eroina f. **~ism** n eroismo m

heron /'herən/ n airone m

herring /'herɪŋ/ n aringa f

hers /hɜːz/ poss pron il suo m, la sua f, i suoi mpl, le sue fpl; **a friend of ~** un suo amico; **friends of ~** dei suoi amici; **that is ~** quello è suo; (as opposed to mine) quello è il suo

her'self pers pron (reflexive) si; (emphatic) lei stessa; ⟨after prep⟩ sé, se stessa; **she poured ~ a drink** si è versata da bere; **she told me so ~** me lo ha detto lei stessa; **she's proud of ~** è fiera di sé; **by ~** da sola

hesitant /'hezɪtənt/ a esitante. **~ly** adv con esitazione

hesitat|e /'hezɪteɪt/ vi esitare. **~ion** /-'teɪʃn/ n esitazione f

het /het/ a **~ up** fam agitato

hetero'sexual /hetərəu-/ a eterosessuale

hexagon /'heksəgən/ n esagono m. **~al** /hek'sægənl/ a esagonale

hey /heɪ/ int ehi

heyday /'heɪ-/ n tempi mpl d'oro

hi /haɪ/ int ciao!

hiatus /haɪ'eɪtəs/ n (pl -tuses) iato m

hibernat|e /'haɪbəneɪt/ vi andare in letargo. **~ion** /-'neɪʃn/ n letargo m

hiccup /'hɪkʌp/ n singhiozzo m; (fam: hitch) intoppo m ● vi fare un singhiozzo

hid /hɪd/, **hidden** /'hɪdn/ see **hide²**

hide¹ /haɪd/ n (leather) pelle f (di animale)

hide² *vt* (*pt* **hid,** *pp* **hidden**) nascondere ● *vi* nascondersi. **~-and-'seek** *n* **play ~-and-seek** giocare a nascondino

hideous /'hɪdɪəs/ *a* orribile

'hide-out *n* nascondiglio *m*

hiding¹ /'haɪdɪŋ/ *n* (*fam: beating*) bastonata *f*; (*defeat*) batosta *f*

hiding² *n* **go into ~** sparire dalla circolazione

hierarchy /'haɪərɑ:kɪ/ *n* gerarchia *f*

hieroglyphics /haɪərə'glɪfɪks/ *npl* geroglifici *mpl*

hi-fi /'haɪfaɪ/ *n fam* stereo *m*, hi-fi *m inv* ● *a fam* ad alta fedeltà

higgledy-piggledy /hɪgldɪ'pɪgldɪ/ *adv* alla rinfusa

high /haɪ/ *a* alto; (*meat*) che comincia ad andare a male; (*wind*) forte; (*on drugs*) fatto; **it's ~ time we did something about it** è ora di fare qualcosa in proposito ● *adv* in alto; **~ and low** in lungo e in largo ● *n* massimo *m*; (*temperature*) massima *f*; **be on a ~** *fam* essere fatto

high: ~brow *a & n* intellettuale *mf*. **~ chair** *n* seggiolone *m*. **~er education** *n* formazione *f* universitaria. **~'-handed** *a* dispotico. **~-'heeled** *a* coi tacchi alti. **~ heels** *npl* tacchi *mpl* alti. **~ jump** *n* salto *m* in alto

highlight /'haɪlaɪt/ *n fig* momento *m* clou; **~s** *pl* (*in hair*) mèche *fpl* ● *vt* (*emphasize*) evidenziare. **~er** *n* (*marker*) evidenziatore *m*

highly /'haɪlɪ/ *adv* molto; **speak ~ of** lodare; **think ~ of** avere un'alta opinione di. **~-'strung** *a* nervoso

Highness /'haɪnɪs/ *n* altezza *f*; **Your ~** Sua Altezza

high: ~-rise *a* (*building*) molto alto ● *n* edificio *m* molto alto. **~ school** *n* scuola *f* superiore. **~ season** *n* alta stagione *f*. **~ street** *n* strada *f* principale. **~ tea** *n* pasto *m* pomeridiano servito insieme al tè. **~ 'tide** *n* alta marea *f*. **~way code** *n* codice *m* stradale

hijack /'haɪdʒæk/ *vt* dirottare ● *n* dirottamento *m*. **~er** *n* dirottatore, -trice *mf*

hike /haɪk/ *n* escursione *f* a piedi ● *vi* fare un'escursione a piedi. **~r** *n* escursionista *mf*

hilarious /hɪ'leərɪəs/ *a* esilarante

hill /hɪl/ *n* collina *f*; (*mound*) collinetta *f*; (*slope*) altura *f*

hill: ~side *n* pendio *m*. **~y** *a* collinoso

hilt /hɪlt/ *n* impugnatura *f*; **to the ~** (*fam: support*) fino in fondo; (*mortgaged*) fino al collo

him /hɪm/ *pers pron* (*direct object*) lo; (*indirect object*) gli; (*with prep*) lui; **I know ~** lo conosco; **give ~ the money** dagli i soldi; **give it to ~** daglielo; **I spoke to ~** gli ho parlato; **it's ~** è lui; **she loves ~** lo ama; **she loves ~, not you** ama lui, non te. **~'self** *pers pron* (*reflexive*) si; (*emphatic*) lui stesso; (*after prep*) sé, se stesso; **he poured ~ a drink** si è versato da bere; **he told me so ~self** me lo ha detto lui stesso; **he's proud of ~self** è fiero di sé; **by ~self** da solo

hind /haɪnd/ *a* posteriore

hind|er /'hɪndə(r)/ *vt* intralciare. **~rance** /-rəns/ *n* intralcio *m*

hindsight /'haɪnd-/ *n* **with ~** con il senno del poi

Hindu /'hɪndu:/ *n* indù *mf inv* ● *a* indù. **~ism** *n* induismo *m*

hinge /hɪndʒ/ *n* cardine *m* ● *vi* **~ on** *fig* dipendere da

hint /hɪnt/ *n* (*clue*) accenno *m*; (*advice*) suggerimento *m*; (*indirect suggestion*) allusione *f*; (*trace*) tocco *m* ● *vt* **~ that...** far capire che... ● *vi* **~ at** alludere a

hip /hɪp/ *n* fianco *m*

hippie /'hɪpɪ/ *n* hippy *mf inv*

hippo /'hɪpəʊ/ *n* ippopotamo *m*

hip 'pocket *n* tasca *f* posteriore

hippopotamus /hɪpə'pɒtəməs/ *n* (*pl* -**muses** *or* -**mi** /-maɪ/) ippopotamo *m*

hire /'haɪə(r)/ *vt* affittare; assumere (*person*); **~ [out]** affittare ● *n* noleggio *m*; **'for ~'** 'affittasi'. **~ car** *n* macchina *f* a noleggio. **~ purchase** *n* acquisto *m* rateale

his /hɪz/ *poss a* il suo *m*, la sua *f*, i suoi *mpl*, le sue *fpl*; **~ mother/father** sua madre/suo padre ● *poss pron* il suo *m*, la sua *f*, i suoi *mpl*, le sue *fpl*; **a friend of ~** un suo amico; **friends of ~** dei suoi amici; **that is ~** questo è suo; (*as opposed to mine*) questo è il suo

hiss /hɪs/ *n* sibilo *m*; (*of disapproval*) fischio *m* ● *vt* fischiare ● *vi* sibilare; (*in disapproval*) fischiare

historian /hɪ'stɔ:rɪən/ *n* storico, -a *mf*

historic /hɪ'stɒrɪk/ *a* storico. **~al** *a* storico. **~ally** *adv* storicamente

history /'hɪstərɪ/ *n* storia *f*; **make ~** passare alla storia

hit /hɪt/ *n* (*blow*) colpo *m*; (*fam: success*) successo *m*; **score a direct ~** (*missile:*) colpire in pieno ● *vt/i* (*pt/pp* **hit,** *pres p*

hitting) colpire; **~ one's head on the table** battere la testa contro il tavolo; **the car ~ the wall** la macchina ha sbattuto contro il muro; **~ the roof** *fam* perdere le staffe. **hit off** *vt* **~ it off** andare d'accordo. **hit on** *vt fig* trovare

hitch /hɪtʃ/ *n* intoppo *m*; **technical ~** problema *m* tecnico ● *vt* attaccare; **~ a lift** chiedere un passaggio. **hitch up** *vt* tirarsi su ⟨*trousers*⟩. **~-hike** *vi* fare l'autostop. **~-hiker** *n* autostoppista *mf*

hit-or-'miss *a* **on a very ~ basis** all'improvvisata

hither /'hɪðə(r)/ *adv* **~ and thither** di qua e di là. **~'to** *adv* finora

hive /haɪv/ *n* alveare *m*; **~ of industry** fucina *f* di lavoro ● **hive off** *vt Comm* separare

hoard /hɔ:d/ *n* provvista *f*; (*of money*) gruzzolo *m* ● *vt* accumulare

hoarding /'hɔ:dɪŋ/ *n* palizzata *f*; (*with advertisements*) tabellone *m* per manifesti pubblicitari

hoarse /hɔ:s/ *a* rauco. **~ly** *adv* con voce rauca. **~ness** *n* raucedine *f*

hoax /həʊks/ *n* scherzo *m*; (*false alarm*) falso allarme *m*. **~er** *n* burlone, -a *mf*

hob /hɒb/ *n* piano *m* di cottura

hobble /'hɒbl/ *vi* zoppicare

hobby /'hɒbɪ/ *n* hobby *m inv*. **~-horse** *n fig* fissazione *f*

hockey /'hɒkɪ/ *n* hockey *m*

hoe /həʊ/ *n* zappa *f*

hog /hɒg/ *n* maiale *m* ● *vt* (*pt/pp* **hogged**) *fam* monopolizzare

hoist /hɔɪst/ *n* montacarichi *m inv*; (*fam: push*) spinta *f* in su ● *vt* sollevare; innalzare ⟨*flag*⟩; levare ⟨*anchor*⟩

hold¹ /həʊld/ *n Naut, Aeron* stiva *f*

hold² *n* presa *f*; (*fig: influence*) ascendente *m*; **get ~ of** trovare; procurarsi ⟨*information*⟩ ● *v* (*pt/pp* **held**) ● *vt* tenere; ⟨*container:*⟩ contenere; essere titolare di ⟨*licence, passport*⟩; trattenere ⟨*breath, suspect*⟩; mantenere vivo ⟨*interest*⟩; ⟨*civil servant etc:*⟩ occupare ⟨*position*⟩; (*retain*) mantenere; **~ sb's hand** tenere qcno per mano; **~ one's tongue** tenere la bocca chiusa; **~ sb responsible** considerare qcno responsabile; **~ that** (*believe*) ritenere che ● *vi* tenere; ⟨*weather, luck:*⟩ durare; ⟨*offer:*⟩ essere valido; *Teleph* restare in linea; **I don't ~ with the idea that** *fam* non sono d'accordo sul fatto che. **hold back** *vt* rallentare ● *vi* esitare. **hold down** *vt* tenere a bada ⟨*sb*⟩. **hold on** *vi* (*wait*) attendere; *Teleph* restare in

linea. **hold on to** *vt* aggrapparsi a; (*keep*) tenersi. **hold out** *vt* porgere ⟨*hand*⟩; *fig* offrire ⟨*possibility*⟩ ● *vi* (*resist*) resistere. **hold up** *vt* tenere su; (*delay*) rallentare; (*rob*) assalire; **~ one's head up** *fig* tenere la testa alta

'hold: ~all *n* borsone *m*. **~er** *n* titolare *mf*; (*of record*) detentore, -trice *mf*; (*container*) astuccio *m*. **~ing** *n* (*land*) terreno *m* in affitto; *Comm* azioni *fpl*. **~-up** *n* ritardo *m*; (*attack*) rapina *f* a mano armata

hole /həʊl/ *n* buco *m*

holiday /'hɒlɪdeɪ/ *n* vacanza *f*; (*public*) giorno *m* festivo; (*day off*) giorno *m* di ferie; **go on ~** andare in vacanza ● *vi* andare in vacanza. **~-maker** *n* vacanziere *mf*

holiness /'həʊlɪnɪs/ *n* santità *f*; **Your H~** Sua Santità

Holland /'hɒlənd/ *n* Olanda *f*

hollow /'hɒləʊ/ *a* cavo; (*promise*) a vuoto; (*voice*) assente; (*cheeks*) infossato ● *n* cavità *f inv*; (*in ground*) affossamento *m*

holly /'hɒlɪ/ *n* agrifoglio *m*

holocaust /'hɒləkɔ:st/ *n* olocausto *m*

hologram /'hɒləgræm/ *n* ologramma *m*

holster /'həʊlstə(r)/ *n* fondina *f*

holy /'həʊlɪ/ *a* (*-ier, -est*) santo; (*water*) benedetto. **H~ Ghost** *or* **Spirit** *n* Spirito *m* Santo. **H~ Scriptures** *npl* sacre scritture *fpl*. **H~ Week** *n* settimana *f* santa

homage /'hɒmɪdʒ/ *n* omaggio *m*; **pay ~ to** rendere omaggio a

home /həʊm/ *n* casa *f*; (*for children*) istituto *m*; (*for old people*) casa *f* di riposo; (*native land*) patria *f* ● *adv* **at ~** a casa; (*football*) in casa; **feel at ~** sentirsi a casa propria; **come/go ~** venire/andare a casa; **drive a nail ~** piantare un chiodo a fondo ● *a* domestico; (*movie, video*) casalingo; (*team*) ospitante; *Pol* nazionale

home: ~ ad'dress *n* indirizzo *m* di casa. **~ com'puter** *n* computer *m inv* da casa. **H~ Counties** *npl contee fpl* intorno a Londra. **~ game** *n* gioco *m* in casa. **~ help** *n* aiuto *m* domestico (*per persone non autosufficienti*). **~land** *n* patria *f*. **~less** *a* senza tetto

homely /'həʊmlɪ/ *a* (*-ier, -iest*) semplice; (*atmosphere*) familiare; (*Am: ugly*) bruttino

home: ~'made *a* fatto in casa. **H~ Office** *n Br* ministero *m* degli interni. **H~ 'Secretary** *n Br* ministro *m* degli interni. **~sick** *a* **be ~sick** avere no-stalgia (**for** di). **~sickness** *n* nostalgia *f* di casa. **~ 'town** *n* città *f* *inv* natia. **~ward** *a* di ritorno ● *adv* verso casa. **~work** *n* *Sch* compiti *mpl*

homicide /'hɒmɪsaɪd/ *n* (*crime*) omicidio *m*

homoeopath|ic /həʊmɪə'pæθɪk/ *a* omeopatico. **~y** /-'ɒpəθɪ/ *n* omeopatia *f*

homogeneous /hɒmə'dʒiːnɪəs/ *a* omogeneo

homo'sexual *a* & *n* omosessuale *mf*

honest /'ɒnɪst/ *a* onesto; (*frank*) sincero. **~ly** *adv* onestamente; (*frankly*) sinceramente; **~ly!** ma insomma!. **~y** *n* onestà *f*; (*frankness*) sincerità *f*

honey /'hʌnɪ/ *n* miele *m*; (*fam: darling*) tesoro *m*

honey: ~comb *n* favo *m*. **~moon** *n* luna *f* di miele. **~suckle** *n* caprifoglio *m*

honk /hɒŋk/ *vi* *Aut* clacsonare

honorary /'ɒnərərɪ/ *a* onorario

honour /'ɒnə(r)/ *n* onore *m* ● *vt* onorare. **~able** /-əbl/ *a* onorevole. **~ably** *adv* con onore. **~s degree** *n* ≈ diploma *m* di laurea

hood /hʊd/ *n* cappuccio *m*; (*of pram*) tettuccio *m*; (*over cooker*) cappa *f*; *Am Auto* cofano *m*

hoodlum /'huːdləm/ *n* teppista *m*

'hoodwink *vt* *fam* infinocchiare

hoof /huːf/ *n* (*pl* **~s** *or* **hooves**) zoccolo *m*

hook /hʊk/ *n* gancio *m*; (*for fishing*) amo *m*; **off the ~** *Teleph* staccato; *fig* fuori pericolo ● *vt* agganciare ● *vi* agganciarsi

hook|ed /hʊkt/ *a* (*nose*) adunco; **~ed on** (*fam: drugs*) dedito a; **be ~ed on skiing** essere un fanatico dello sci. **~er** *n* *Am* *sl* battona *f*

hookey /'hʊkɪ/ *n* **play ~** *Am* *fam* marinare la scuola

hooligan /'huːlɪgən/ *n* teppista *mf*. **~ism** *n* teppismo *m*

hoop /huːp/ *n* cerchio *m*

hooray /hʊ'reɪ/ *int* & *n* = **hurrah**

hoot /huːt/ *n* colpo *m* di clacson; (*of siren*) ululato *m*; (*of owl*) grido *m* ● *vi* (*owl:*) gridare; (*car:*) clacsonare; (*siren:*) ululare; (*jeer*) fischiare. **~er** *n* (*of factory*) sirena *f*; *Auto* clacson *m* *inv*

hoover® /'huːvə(r)/ *n* aspirapolvere *m* *inv* ● *vt* passare l'aspirapolvere su (*carpet*); passare l'aspirapolvere in (*room*)

hop /hɒp/ *n* saltello *m* ● *vi* (*pt/pp*

hopped) saltellare; **~ it!** *fam* tela!. **hop in** *vi* *fam* saltar su

hope /həʊp/ *n* speranza *f* ● *vi* sperare (**for** in); **I ~ so/not** spero di sì/no ● *vt* **~ that** sperare che

hope|ful /'həʊpfl/ *a* pieno di speranza; (*promising*) promettente; **be ~ful that** avere buone speranze che. **~fully** *adv* con speranza; (*it is hoped*) se tutto va bene. **~less** *a* senza speranze; (*useless*) impossibile; (*incompetent*) incapace. **~lessly** *adv* disperatamente; (*inefficient, lost*) completamente. **~lessness** *n* disperazione *f*

horde /hɔːd/ *n* orda *f*

horizon /hə'raɪzn/ *n* orizzonte *m*

horizontal /hɒrɪ'zɒntl/ *a* orizzontale

hormone /'hɔːməʊn/ *n* ormone *m*

horn /hɔːn/ *n* corno *m*; *Auto* clacson *m* *inv*

horny /'hɔːnɪ/ *a* calloso; *fam* arrapato

horoscope /'hɒrəskəʊp/ *n* oroscopo *m*

horribl|e /'hɒrɪbl/ *a* orribile. **~y** *adv* spaventosamente

horrid /'hɒrɪd/ *a* orrendo

horrific /hə'rɪfɪk/ *a* raccapricciante; (*fam: accident, prices, story*) terrificante

horrify /'hɒrɪfaɪ/ *vt* (*pt/pp* -ied) far inorridire; **I was horrified** ero sconvolto. **~ing** *a* terrificante

horror /'hɒrə(r)/ *n* orrore *m*. **~ film** *n* film *m* dell'orrore

hors-d'œuvre /ɔː'dɜːvr/ *n* antipasto *m*

horse /hɔːs/ *n* cavallo *m*

horse: ~back *n* **on ~back** a cavallo. **~man** *n* cavaliere *m*. **~play** *n* gioco *m* pesante. **~power** *n* cavallo *m* [vapore]. **~-racing** *n* corse *fpl* di cavalli. **~shoe** *n* ferro *m* di cavallo

horti'cultural /hɔːtɪ-/ *a* di orticoltura

'horticulture *n* orticoltura *f*

hose /həʊz/ *n* (*pipe*) manichetta *f* ● **hose down** *vt* lavare con la manichetta

hospice /'hɒspɪs/ *n* (*for the terminally ill*) ospedale *m* per i malati in fase terminale

hospitabl|e /hɒ'spɪtəbl/ *a* ospitale. **~y** *adv* con ospitalità

hospital /'hɒspɪtl/ *n* ospedale *m*

hospitality /hɒspɪ'tælətɪ/ *n* ospitalità *f*

host¹ /həʊst/ *n* **a ~ of** una moltitudine di

host² *n* ospite *m*

host³ *n* *Relig* ostia *f*

hostage /'hɒstɪdʒ/ *n* ostaggio *m*; **hold sb ~** tenere qcno in ostaggio

hostel /'hɒstl/ *n* ostello *m*

hostess /'həustɪs/ n padrona f di casa; *Aeron* hostess f inv

hostile /'hɒstaɪl/ a ostile

hostilit|y /hɒ'stɪlətɪ/ n ostilità f; **~ies** pl ostilità fpl

hot /hɒt/ a (**hotter, hottest**) caldo; ⟨spicy⟩ piccante; **I am** or **feel ~** ho caldo; **it is ~** fa caldo

'**hotbed** n fig focolaio m

hotchpotch /'hɒtʃpɒtʃ/ n miscuglio m

'**hot-dog** n hot dog m inv

hotel /həʊ'tel/ n albergo m. **~ier** /-ɪə(r)/ n albergatore, -trice mf

hot: ~head n persona f impetuosa. **~house** n serra f. **~ly** adv fig accanitamente. **~plate** n piastra f riscaldante. **~tap** n rubinetto m dell'acqua calda. **~-'tempered** a irascibile. **~-'water bottle** n borsa f dell'acqua calda

hound /haʊnd/ n cane m da caccia ● vt fig perseguire

hour /'aʊə(r)/ n ora f. **~ly** a ad ogni ora; ⟨pay, rate⟩ a ora ● adv ogni ora

house¹ /haʊs/ n casa f; *Pol* camera f; *Theat* sala f; **at my ~** a casa mia, da me

house² /haʊz/ vt alloggiare ⟨person⟩

house /haʊs/: **~boat** n casa f galleggiante. **~breaking** n furto m con scasso. **~hold** n casa f, famiglia f. **~holder** n capo m di famiglia. **~keeper** n governante f di casa. **~keeping** n governo m della casa; ⟨money⟩ soldi mpl per le spese di casa. **~plant** n pianta f da appartamento. **~-trained** a che non sporca in casa. **~-warming** [**party**] n festa f di inaugurazione della nuova casa. **~wife** n casalinga f. **~work** n lavoro m domestico

housing /'haʊzɪŋ/ n alloggio m. **~ estate** n zona f residenziale

hovel /'hɒvl/ n tugurio m

hover /'hɒvə(r)/ vi librarsi; ⟨linger⟩ indugiare. **~craft** n hovercraft m inv

how /haʊ/ adv come; **~ are you?** come stai?; **~ about a coffee/going on holiday?** che ne diresti di un caffè/di andare in vacanza?; **~ do you do?** molto lieto!; **~ old are you?** quanti anni hai?; **~ long** quanto tempo; **~ many** quanti; **~ much** quanto; **~ often** ogni quanto; **and ~!** eccome!; **~ odd!** che strano!

how'ever adv ⟨nevertheless⟩ comunque; **~ small** per quanto piccolo

howl /haʊl/ n ululato m ● vi ululare; ⟨cry, with laughter⟩ singhiozzare. **~er** n fam strafalcione m

HP n abbr **hire purchase**; n abbr (**horse power**) C.V.

hub /hʌb/ n mozzo m; fig centro m

hubbub /'hʌbʌb/ n baccano m

'**hub-cap** n coprimozzo m

huddle /'hʌdl/ vi **~ together** rannicchiarsi

hue¹ /hju:/ n colore m

hue² n **~ and cry** clamore m

huff /hʌf/ n **be in/go into a ~** fare il broncio

hug /hʌg/ n abbraccio m ● vt (pt/pp **hugged**) abbracciare; ⟨keep close to⟩ tenersi vicino a

huge /hju:dʒ/ a enorme

hulking /'hʌlkɪŋ/ a fam grosso

hull /hʌl/ n Naut scafo m

hullo /hə'ləʊ/ int = **hallo**

hum /hʌm/ n ronzio m ● v (pt/pp **hummed**) ● vt canticchiare ● vi ⟨motor:⟩ ronzare; fig fervere ⟨di attività⟩; **~ and haw** esitare

human /'hju:mən/ a umano ● n essere m umano. **~ 'being** n essere m umano

humane /hju:'meɪn/ a umano

humanitarian /hju:mænɪ'teərɪən/ a & n umanitario, -a mf

humanit|y /hju:'mænətɪ/ n umanità f; **~ies** pl Univ dottrine fpl umanistiche

humbl|e /'hʌmbl/ a umile ● vt umiliare

'**humdrum** a noioso

humid /'hju:mɪd/ a umido. **~ifier** /-'mɪdɪfaɪə(r)/ n umidificatore m. **~ity** /-'mɪdətɪ/ n umidità f

humiliat|e /hju:'mɪlɪeɪt/ vt umiliare. **~ion** /-'eɪʃn/ n umiliazione f

humility /hju:'mɪlətɪ/ n umiltà f

humorous /'hju:mərəs/ a umoristico. **~ly** adv con spirito

humour /'hju:mə(r)/ n umorismo m; ⟨mood⟩ umore m; **have a sense of ~** avere il senso dell'umorismo ● vt compiacere

hump /hʌmp/ n protuberanza f; ⟨of camel, hunchback⟩ gobba f

hunch /hʌntʃ/ n ⟨idea⟩ intuizione f

'**hunch|back** n gobbo, -a mf. **~ed** a **~ed up** incurvato

hundred /'hʌndrəd/ a **one/a ~** cento ● n cento m; **~s of** centinaia di. **~th** a centesimo ● n centesimo m. **~weight** n cinquanta chili m

hung /hʌŋ/ see **hang**

Hungarian /hʌŋ'geərɪən/ a & n ungherese mf; ⟨language⟩ ungherese m

Hungary /'hʌŋgərɪ/ n Ungheria f

111

hunger | icing

hunger /'hʌŋgə(r)/ n fame f. **~-strike** n sciopero m della fame m

hungr|y /'hʌŋgrɪ/ a (**-ier, -iest**) affamato; **be ~y** aver fame. **~ily** adv con appetito

hunk /hʌŋk/ n [grosso] pezzo m

hunt /hʌnt/ n caccia f ● vt andare a caccia di ‹animal›; dare la caccia a ‹criminal› ● vi andare a caccia; **~ for** cercare. **~er** n cacciatore m. **~ing** n caccia f

hurdle /'hɜːdl/ n Sport & fig ostacolo m. **~r** n ostacolista mf

hurl /hɜːl/ vt scagliare

hurrah /hʊ'rɑː/, **hurray** /hʊ'reɪ/ int urrà! ● n urrà m

hurricane /'hʌrɪkən/ n uragano m

hurried /'hʌrɪd/ a affrettato; ‹job› fatto in fretta. **~ly** adv in fretta

hurry /'hʌrɪ/ n fretta f; **be in a ~** aver fretta ● vi (pt/pp **-ied**) affrettarsi. **hurry up** vi sbrigarsi ● vt fare sbrigare ‹person›; accelerare ‹things›

hurt /hɜːt/ v (pt/pp **hurt**) ● vt far male a; ‹offend› ferire ● vi far male; **my leg ~s** mi fa male la gamba. **~ful** a fig offensivo

hurtle /'hɜːtl/ vi **~ along** andare a tutta velocità

husband /'hʌzbənd/ n marito m

hush /hʌʃ/ n silenzio m ● **hush up** vt mettere a tacere. **~ed** a ‹voice› sommesso. **~-'hush** a fam segretissimo

husky /'hʌskɪ/ a (**-ier, -iest**) ‹voice› rauco

hustle /'hʌsl/ vt affrettare ● n attività f incessante; **~ and bustle** trambusto m

hut /hʌt/ n capanna f

hybrid /'haɪbrɪd/ a ibrido ● n ibrido m

hydrant /'haɪdrənt/ n [fire] ~ idrante m

hydraulic /haɪ'drɔːlɪk/ a idraulico

hydroe'lectric /haɪdrəʊ-/ a idroelettrico

hydrofoil /'haɪdrə-/ n aliscafo m

hydrogen /'haɪdrədʒən/ n idrogeno m

hyena /haɪ'iːnə/ n iena f

hygien|e /'haɪdʒiːn/ n igiene f. **~ic** /haɪ'dʒiːnɪk/ a igienico

hymn /hɪm/ n inno m. **~-book** n libro m dei canti

hypermarket /'haɪpəmɑːkɪt/ n ipermercato m

hyphen /'haɪfn/ n lineetta f. **~ate** vt unire con lineetta

hypno|sis /hɪp'nəʊsɪs/ n ipnosi f. **~tic** /-'nɒtɪk/ a ipnotico

hypno|tism /'hɪpnətɪzm/ n ipnotismo m. **~tist** /-tɪst/ n ipnotizzatore, -trice mf. **~tize** vt ipnotizzare

hypochondriac /haɪpə'kɒndriæk/ a ipocondriaco ● n ipocondriaco, -a mf

hypocrisy /hɪ'pɒkrəsɪ/ n ipocrisia f

hypocrit|e /'hɪpəkrɪt/ n ipocrita mf. **~ical** /-'krɪtɪkl/ a ipocrita

hypodermic /haɪpə'dɜːmɪk/ a & n ~ [syringe] siringa f ipodermica

hypothe|sis /haɪ'pɒθəsɪs/ n ipotesi f inv. **~tical** /-ə'θetɪkl/ a ipotetico. **~tically** adv in teoria; ‹speak› per ipotesi

hyster|ia /hɪ'stɪərɪə/ n isterismo m. **~ical** /-'sterɪkl/ a isterico. **~ically** adv istericamente; **~ically funny** da morir dal ridere. **~ics** /hɪ'sterɪks/ npl attacco m isterico

I /aɪ/ pron io; **I'm tired** sono stanco; **he's going, but I'm not** lui va, ma io no

ice /aɪs/ n ghiaccio m ● vt glassare ‹cake›. **ice over/up** vi ghiacciarsi

ice: ~ age n era f glaciale. **~-axe** n piccozza f per il ghiaccio. **~berg** /-bɜːg/ n iceberg m inv. **~box** n Am frigorifero m. **~-'cream** n gelato m. **~-'cream parlour** n gelateria f. **~-cube** n cubetto m di ghiaccio. **~ hockey** n hockey m su ghiaccio

Iceland /'aɪslənd/ n Islanda f. **~er** n islandese mf; **~ic** /-'lændɪk/ a & n islandese m

ice: ~'lolly n ghiacciolo m. **~ rink** n pista f di pattinaggio. **~ skater** pattinatore, -trice mf sul ghiaccio. **~ skating** pattinaggio m sul ghiaccio

icicle /'aɪsɪkl/ n ghiacciolo m

icily /'aɪsɪlɪ/ adv gelidamente

icing /'aɪsɪŋ/ n glassa f. **~ sugar** n zucchero m a velo

icon /'aɪkɒn/ n icona f

icy /'aɪsɪ/ a (-ier, -iest) ghiacciato; fig gelido

idea /aɪ'dɪə/ n idea f; **I've no ~!** non ne ho idea!

ideal /aɪ'dɪəl/ a ideale ● n ideale m. **~ism** n idealismo m. **~ist** n idealista mf. **~istic** /-'lɪstɪk/ a idealistico. **~ize** vt idealizzare. **~ly** adv idealmente

identical /aɪ'dentɪkl/ a identico

identi|fication /aɪdentɪfɪ'keɪʃn/ n identificazione f; (proof of identity) documento m di riconoscimento. **~fy** /aɪ'dentɪfaɪ/ vt (pt/pp -ied) identificare

identikit® /aɪ'dentɪkɪt/ n identikit m inv

identity /aɪ'dentətɪ/ n identità f inv. **~ card** n carta f d'identità

ideolog|ical /aɪdɪə'lɒdʒɪkl/ a ideologico. **~y** /aɪdɪ'blədʒɪ/ n ideologia f

idiom /'ɪdɪəm/ n idioma f. **~atic** /-'mætɪk/ a idiomatico

idiosyncrasy /ɪdɪə'sɪŋkrəsɪ/ n idiosincrasia f

idiot /'ɪdɪət/ n idiota mf. **~ic** /-'ɒtɪk/ a idiota

idl|e /'aɪd(ə)l/ a (lazy) pigro, ozioso; (empty) vano; ‹machine› fermo ● vi oziare; ‹engine:› girare a vuoto. **~eness** n ozio m. **~y** adv oziosamente

idol /'aɪdl/ n idolo m. **~ize** /'aɪdəlaɪz/ vt idolatrare

idyllic /ɪ'dɪlɪk/ a idillico

i.e. abbr (id est) cioè

if /ɪf/ conj se; **as if** come se

ignite /ɪg'naɪt/ vt dar fuoco a ● vi prender fuoco

ignition /ɪg'nɪʃn/ n Auto accensione f. **~ key** n chiave f d'accensione

ignoramus /ɪgnə'reɪməs/ n ignorante mf

ignoran|ce /'ɪgnərəns/ n ignoranza f. **~t** a (lacking knowledge) ignaro; (rude) ignorante

ignore /ɪg'nɔ:(r)/ vt ignorare

ill /ɪl/ a ammalato; **feel ~ at ease** sentirsi a disagio ● adv male ● n male m. **~-advised** a avventato. **~-bred** a maleducato

illegal /ɪ'li:gl/ a illegale

illegib|le /ɪ'ledʒɪbl/ a illeggibile

illegitima|cy /ɪlɪ'dʒɪtɪməsɪ/ n illegittimità f. **~te** /-mət/ a illegittimo

illicit /ɪ'lɪsɪt/ a illecito

illitera|cy /ɪ'lɪtərəsɪ/ n analfabetismo m. **~te** /-rət/ a & n analfabeta mf

illness /'ɪlnɪs/ n malattia f

illogical /ɪ'lɒdʒɪkl/ a illogico

ill-treat /ɪl'tri:t/ vt maltrattare. **~ment** n maltrattamento m

illuminat|e /ɪ'lu:mɪneɪt/ vt illuminare. **~ing** a chiarificatore. **~ion** /-'neɪʃn/ n illuminazione f

illusion /ɪ'lu:ʒn/ n illusione f; **be under the ~** that avere l'illusione che

illusory /ɪ'lu:sərɪ/ a illusorio

illustrat|e /'ɪləstreɪt/ vt illustrare. **~ion** /-'streɪʃn/ n illustrazione f. **~or** n illustratore, -trice mf

illustrious /ɪ'lʌstrɪəs/ a illustre

ill 'will n malanimo m

image /'ɪmɪdʒ/ n immagine f; (exact likeness) ritratto m

imagin|able /ɪ'mædʒɪnəbl/ a immaginabile. **~ary** /-ərɪ/ a immaginario

imaginat|ion /ɪmædʒɪ'neɪʃn/ n immaginazione f, fantasia f; **it's your ~ion** è solo una tua idea. **~ive** /ɪ'mædʒɪnətɪv/ a fantasioso. **~ively** adv con fantasia or immaginazione

imagine /ɪ'mædʒɪn/ vt immaginare; (wrongly) inventare

im'balance n squilibrio m

imbecile /'ɪmbəsi:l/ n imbecille mf

imbibe /ɪm'baɪb/ vt ingerire

imbue /ɪm'bju:/ vt **~d with** impregnato di

imitat|e /'ɪmɪteɪt/ vt imitare. **~ion** /-'teɪʃn/ n imitazione f. **~or** n imitatore, -trice mf

immaculate /ɪ'mækjʊlət/ a immacolato. **~ly** adv immacolatamente

imma'terial a (unimportant) irrilevante

imma'ture a immaturo

immediate /ɪ'mi:dɪət/ a immediato; (relative) stretto; **in the ~ vicinity** nelle immediate vicinanze. **~ly** adv immediatamente; **~ly next to** subito accanto a ● conj [non] appena

immemorial /ɪmɪ'mɔ:rɪəl/ a **from time ~** da tempo immemorabile

immense /ɪ'mens/ a immenso

immers|e /ɪ'mɜ:s/ vt immergere; **be ~ed in** fig essere immerso in. **~ion** /-ɜ:ʃn/ n immersione f. **~ion heater** n scaldabagno m elettrico

immigrant /'ɪmɪgrənt/ n immigrante mf

immigrat|e /'ɪmɪgreɪt/ vi immigrare. **~ion** /-'greɪʃn/ n immigrazione f

imminent /'ɪmɪnənt/ a imminente

immobil|e /ɪ'məʊbaɪl/ a immobile. **~ize** /-bɪlaɪz/ vt immobilizzare

immoderate /ɪ'mɒdərət/ a smodato

immodest /ɪ'mɒdɪst/ a immodesto

immoral /ɪ'mɒrəl/ a immorale. **~ity**
/ɪmə'rælətɪ/ n immoralità f

immortal /ɪ'mɔːtl/ a immortale. **~ity**
/-'tælətɪ/ n immortalità f. **~ize** vt im-
mortalare

immovable /ɪ'muːvəbl/ a fig irremovi-
bile

immune /ɪ'mjuːn/ a immune (**to/from**
da). **~ system** n sistema m immuni-
tario

immunity /ɪ'mjuːnətɪ/ n immunità f

immuniz|e /'ɪmjʊnaɪz/ vt immunizzare

imp /ɪmp/ n diavoletto m

impact /'ɪmpækt/ n impatto m

impair /ɪm'peə(r)/ vt danneggiare

impale /ɪm'peɪl/ vt impalare

impart /ɪm'pɑːt/ vt impartire

im'parti|al a imparziale. **~'ality** n im-
parzialità f

im'passable a impraticabile

impasse /æm'pɑːs/ n fig impasse f inv

impassioned /ɪm'pæʃnd/ a appassionato

im'passive a impassibile

im'patien|ce n impazienza f. **~t** a im-
paziente. **~tly** adv impazientemente

impeccabl|e /ɪm'pekəbl/ a impecca-
bile. **~y** adv in modo impeccabile

impede /ɪm'piːd/ vt impedire

impediment /ɪm'pedɪmənt/ n impedimento m; (in speech) difetto m

impel /ɪm'pel/ vt (pt/pp impelled) costringere; **feel ~led to** sentire l'obbligo di

impending /ɪm'pendɪŋ/ a imminente

impenetrable /ɪm'penɪtrəbl/ a impenetrabile

imperative /ɪm'perətɪv/ a imperativo
● n Gram imperativo m

imper'ceptible a impercettibile

im'perfect a imperfetto; (faulty) difettoso ● n Gram imperfetto m. **~ion**
/-'fekʃn/ n imperfezione f

imperial /ɪm'pɪərɪəl/ a imperiale.
~ism n imperialismo m. **~ist** n
imperialista mf

imperious /ɪm'pɪərɪəs/ a imperioso

im'personal a impersonale

impersonat|e /ɪm'pɜːsəneɪt/ vt imper-
sonare. **~or** n imitatore, -trice mf

impertinen|ce /ɪm'pɜːtɪnəns/ n im-
pertinenza f. **~t** a impertinente

imperturbable /ɪmpə'tɜːbəbl/ a im-
perturbabile

impervious /ɪm'pɜːvɪəs/ a **~ to** fig in-
differente a

impetuous /ɪm'petjʊəs/ a impetuoso.
~ly adv impetuosamente

impetus /'ɪmpɪtəs/ n impeto m

implacable /ɪm'plækəbl/ a implacabi-
le

im'plant[1] vt trapiantare; fig inculcare

'implant[2] n trapianto m

implement[1] /'ɪmplɪmənt/ n attrezzo m

implement[2] /'ɪmplɪment/ vt mettere
in atto

implicat|e /'ɪmplɪkeɪt/ vt implicare.
~ion /-'keɪʃn/ n implicazione f; **by**
~ion implicitamente

implicit /ɪm'plɪsɪt/ a implicito;
(absolute) assoluto

implore /ɪm'plɔː(r)/ vt implorare

imply /ɪm'plaɪ/ vt (pt/pp -ied) implicare; **what are you ~ing?** che cosa vor-
resti insinuare?

impo'lite a sgarbato

import[1] /'ɪmpɔːt/ n Comm importazio-
ne f

import[2] /ɪm'pɔːt/ vt importare

importan|ce /ɪm'pɔːtəns/ n importan-
za f. **~t** a importante

importer /ɪm'pɔːtə(r)/ n importatore,
-trice mf

impos|e /ɪm'pəʊz/ vt imporre (**on** a)
● vi imporsi; **~e on** abusare di. **~ing** a
imponente. **~ition** /ɪmpə'zɪʃn/ n impo-
sizione f

impossi'bility n impossibilità f

im'possibl|e a impossibile

impostor /ɪm'pɒstə(r)/ n impostore,
-trice mf

impoten|ce /'ɪmpətəns/ n impotenza f.
~t a impotente

impound /ɪm'paʊnd/ vt confiscare

impoverished /ɪm'pɒvərɪʃt/ a impo-
verito

im'practicable a impraticabile

im'practical a non pratico

impre'cise a impreciso

impregnable /ɪm'pregnəbl/ a im-
prendibile

impregnate /'ɪmpregneɪt/ vt impregnare (**with** di); Biol fecondare

im'press vt imprimere; fig colpire (positivamente); **~ sth [up]on sb** fare capire qcsa a qcno

impression /ɪm'preʃn/ n impressione
f; (imitation) imitazione f. **~able** a
⟨child, mind⟩ influenzabile. **~ism** n im-
pressionismo m. **~ist** n imitatore,
-trice mf; (artist) impressionista mf

impressive /ɪm'presɪv/ a imponente

'imprint[1] n impressione f

im'print[2] vt imprimere; **~ed on my**
mind impresso nella mia memoria

imprison | include

im'prison vt incarcerare. ~**ment** n reclusione f
im'probable a improbabile
impromptu /ɪm'prɒmptjuː/ a improvvisato
im'proper a ⟨use⟩ improprio; ⟨behaviour⟩ scorretto. ~**ly** adv scorrettamente
impro'priety n scorrettezza f
improve /ɪm'pruːv/ vt/i migliorare. **improve** [up]**on** vt perfezionare. ~**ment** /-mənt/ n miglioramento m
improvis|e /'ɪmprəvaɪz/ vt/i improvvisare
im'prudent a imprudente
impuden|ce /'ɪmpjʊdəns/ n sfrontatezza f. ~**t** a sfrontato
impuls|e /'ɪmpʌls/ n impulso m; **on** [**an**] ~**e** impulsivamente. ~**ive** /-'pʌlsɪv/ a impulsivo
impunity /ɪm'pjuːnətɪ/ n **with** ~ impunemente
im'pur|e a impuro. ~**ity** n impurità f inv; ~**ities** pl impurità fpl
impute /ɪm'pjuːt/ vt imputare (**to** a)
in /ɪn/ prep in; ⟨with names of towns⟩ a; **in the garden** in giardino; **in the street** in or per strada; **in bed/hospital** a letto/all'ospedale; **in the world** nel mondo; **in the rain** sotto la pioggia; **in the sun** al sole; **in this heat** con questo caldo; **in summer/winter** in estate/inverno; **in 1995** nel 1995; **in the evening** la sera; **he's arriving in two hours' time** arriva fra due ore; **deaf in one ear** sordo da un orecchio; **in the army** nell'esercito; **in English/Italian** in inglese/italiano; **in ink/pencil** a penna/matita; **in red** ⟨dressed, circled⟩ di rosso; **the man in the raincoat** l'uomo con l'impermeabile; **in a soft/loud voice** a voce bassa/alta; **one in ten people** una persona su dieci; **in doing this, he...** nel far questo,...; **in itself** in sé; **in that** in quanto ● adv ⟨at home⟩ a casa; ⟨indoors⟩ dentro; **he's not in yet** non è ancora arrivato; **in there/here** lì/qui dentro; **ten in all** dieci in tutto; **day in, day out** giorno dopo giorno; **have it in for sb** fam avercela con qcno; **send him in** fallo entrare; **come in** entrare; **bring in the washing** portare dentro i panni ● a ⟨fam: in fashion⟩ di moda ● n **the ins and outs** i dettagli
ina'bility n incapacità f
inac'cessible a inaccessibile

in'accura|cy n inesattezza f. ~**te** a inesatto
in'ac|tive a inattivo. ~**'tivity** n inattività f
in'adequate a inadeguato. ~**ly** adv inadeguatamente
inad'missible a inammissibile
inadvertently /ɪnəd'vɜːtəntlɪ/ adv inavvertitamente
inad'visable a sconsigliabile
in'animate a esanime
in'applicable a inapplicabile
inap'propriate a inadatto
inar'ticulate a inarticolato
inat'tentive a disattento
in'audibl|e a impercettibile
inaugural /ɪ'nɔːgjʊrəl/ a inaugurale
inaugurat|e /ɪ'nɔːgjʊreɪt/ vt inaugurare. ~**ion** /-'reɪʃn/ n inaugurazione f
inau'spicious a infausto
inborn /'ɪnbɔːn/ a innato
inbred /ɪn'bred/ a congenito
incalculable /ɪn'kælkjʊləbl/ a incalcolabile
in'capable a incapace
incapacitate /ɪnkə'pæsɪteɪt/ vt rendere incapace
incarnat|e /ɪn'kɑːnət/ a **the devil** ~**e** il diavolo in carne e ossa
incendiary /ɪn'sendɪərɪ/ a incendiario
incense[1] /'ɪnsens/ n incenso m
incense[2] /ɪn'sens/ vt esasperare
incentive /ɪn'sentɪv/ n incentivo m
incessant /ɪn'sesənt/ a incessante
incest /'ɪnsest/ n incesto m
inch /ɪntʃ/ n pollice m (= 2.54 cm) ● vi ~ **forward** avanzare gradatamente
inciden|ce /'ɪnsɪdəns/ n incidenza f. ~**t** n incidente m
incidental /ɪnsɪ'dentl/ a incidentale; ~ **expenses** spese fpl accessorie. ~**ly** adv incidentalmente; ⟨by the way⟩ a proposito
incinerat|e /ɪn'sɪnəreɪt/ vt incenerire. ~**or** n inceneritore m
incision /ɪn'sɪʒn/ n incisione f
incisive /ɪn'saɪsɪv/ a incisivo
incisor /ɪn'saɪzə(r)/ n incisivo m
incite /ɪn'saɪt/ vt incitare. ~**ment** n incitamento m
inclination /ɪnklɪ'neɪʃn/ n inclinazione f
incline[1] /ɪn'klaɪn/ vt inclinare; **be** ~**d to do sth** essere propenso a fare qcsa
incline[2] /'ɪnklaɪn/ n pendio m
inclu|de /ɪn'kluːd/ vt includere. ~**ding** prep incluso. ~**sion** /-uːʒn/ n inclusione f

inclusive /ɪn'klu:sɪv/ *a* incluso; **~ of** comprendente; **be ~ of** comprendere ● *adv* incluso

incognito /ɪnkɒg'ni:təʊ/ *adv* incognito

inco'herent *a* incoerente; (*because drunk etc*) incomprensibile

income /'ɪnkʌm/ *n* reddito *m*. **~ tax** *n* imposta *f* sul reddito

'incoming *a* in arrivo. **~ tide** *n* marea *f* montante

in'comparable *a* incomparabile

incompati'bility *n* incompatibilità *f*

incom'patible *a* incompatibile

in'competen|ce *n* incompetenza *f*. **~t** *a* incompetente

incom'plete *a* incompleto

incompre'hensible *a* incomprensibile

incon'ceivable *a* inconcepibile

incon'clusive *a* inconcludente

incongruous /ɪn'kɒŋgrʊəs/ *a* contrastante

inconsequential /ɪnkɒnsɪ'kwenʃl/ *a* senza importanza

incon'siderate *a* trascurabile

incon'sistency *n* incoerenza *f*

incon'sistent *a* incoerente; **be ~ with** non essere coerente con. **~ly** *adv* in modo incoerente

inconsolable /ɪnkən'səʊləbl/ *a* inconsolabile

incon'spicuous *a* non appariscente. **~ly** *adv* modestamente

incontinen|ce /ɪn'kɒntɪnəns/ *n* incontinenza *f*. **~t** *a* incontinente

incon'venien|ce *n* scomodità *f*; (*drawback*) inconveniente *m*; **put sb to ~ce** dare disturbo a qcno. **~t** *a* scomodo; ⟨*time, place*⟩ inopportuno. **~tly** *adv* in modo inopportuno

incorporate /ɪn'kɔ:pəreɪt/ *vt* incorporare; (*contain*) comprendere

incor'rect *a* incorretto. **~ly** *adv* scorrettamente

incorrigible /ɪn'kɒrɪdʒəbl/ *a* incorreggibile

incorruptible /ɪnkə'rʌptəbl/ *a* incorruttibile

increase¹ /'ɪnkri:s/ *n* aumento *m*; **on the ~** in aumento

increas|e² /ɪn'kri:s/ *vt/i* aumentare. **~ing** *a* ⟨*impatience etc*⟩ crescente; ⟨*numbers*⟩ in aumento. **~ingly** *adv* sempre più

in'credible *a* incredibile

incredulous /ɪn'kredjʊləs/ *a* incredulo

increment /'ɪnkrɪmənt/ *n* incremento *m*

incriminate /ɪn'krɪmɪneɪt/ *vt Jur* incriminare

incubat|e /'ɪŋkjʊbeɪt/ *vt* incubare. **~ion** /-'beɪʃn/ *n* incubazione *f*. **~ion period** *m Med* periodo *m* di incubazione. **~or** *n* (*for baby*) incubatrice *f*

incumbent /ɪn'kʌmbənt/ *a* **be ~ on sb** incombere a qcno

incur /ɪn'kɜ:(r)/ *vt* (*pt/pp* **incurred**) incorrere; contrarre ⟨*debts*⟩

in'curable *a* incurabile

incursion /ɪn'kɜ:ʃn/ *n* incursione *f*

indebted /ɪn'detɪd/ *a* obbligato (**to** verso)

in'decent *a* indecente

inde'cision *n* indecisione *f*

inde'cisive *a* indeciso. **~ness** *n* indecisione *f*

indeed /ɪn'di:d/ *adv* (*in fact*) difatti; **yes ~!** sì, certamente!; **~ I am/do** veramente!; **very much ~** moltissimo; **thank you very much ~** grazie infinite; **~?** davvero?

indefatigable /ɪndɪ'fætɪgəbl/ *a* instancabile

inde'finable *a* indefinibile

in'definite *a* indefinito. **~ly** *adv* indefinitamente; ⟨*postpone*⟩ a tempo indeterminato

indelible /ɪn'delɪbl/ *a* indelebile

indemnity /ɪn'demnɪtɪ/ *n* indennità *f inv*

indent¹ /'ɪndent/ *n Typ* rientranza *f* dal margine

indent² /ɪn'dent/ *vt Typ* fare rientrare dal margine. **~ation** /-'teɪʃn/ *n* (*notch*) intaccatura *f*

inde'penden|ce *n* indipendenza *f*. **~t** *a* indipendente. **~tly** *adv* indipendentemente

indescribable /ɪndɪ'skraɪbəbl/ *a* indescrivibile

indestructible /ɪndɪ'strʌktəbl/ *a* indistruttibile

indeterminate /ɪndɪ'tɜ:mɪnət/ *a* indeterminato

index /'ɪndeks/ *n* indice *m*

index: ~ card *n* scheda *f*. **~ finger** *n* dito *m* indice. **~-'linked** *a* ⟨*pension*⟩ legato al costo della vita

India /'ɪndɪə/ *n* India *f*. **~n** *a* indiano; (*American*) indiano [d'America] ● *n* indiano, -a *mf*; (*American*) indiano, -a *mf* [d'America], pellerossa *mf inv*

indicat|e /'ɪndɪkeɪt/ *vt* indicare;

(*register*) segnare ● *vi Auto* mettere la freccia. **~ion** /-'keɪʃn/ *n* indicazione *f*

indicative /ɪn'dɪkətɪv/ *a* **be ~ of** essere indicativo di ● *n Gram* indicativo *m*

indicator /'ɪndɪkeɪtə(r)/ *n Auto* freccia *f*

indict /ɪn'daɪt/ *vt* accusare. **~ment** *n* accusa *f*

in'differen|ce *n* indifferenza *f*. **~t** *a* indifferente; (*not good*) mediocre

indigenous /ɪn'dɪdʒɪnəs/ *a* indigeno

indi'gest|ible *a* indigesto. **~ion** *n* indigestione *f*

indigna|nt /ɪn'dɪgnənt/ *a* indignato. **~ntly** *adv* con indignazione. **~tion** /-'neɪʃn/ *n* indignazione *f*

in'dignity *n* umiliazione *f*

indi'rect *a* indiretto. **~ly** *adv* indirettamente

indi'screet *a* indiscreto

indis'cretion *n* indiscrezione *f*

indiscriminate /ɪndɪ'skrɪmɪnət/ *a* indiscriminato. **~ly** *adv* senza distinzione

indi'spensable *a* indispensabile

indisposed /ɪndɪ'spəʊzd/ *a* indisposto

indisputable /ɪndɪ'spjuːtəbl/ *a* indisputabile

indi'stinct *a* indistinto

indistinguishable /ɪndɪ'stɪŋgwɪʃəbl/ *a* indistinguibile

individual /ɪndɪ'vɪdjʊəl/ *a* individuale ● *n* individuo *m*. **~ity** /-'æləti/ *n* individualità *f*

indi'visible *a* indivisibile

indoctrinate /ɪn'dɒktrɪneɪt/ *vt* indottrinare

indomitable /ɪn'dɒmɪtəbl/ *a* indomito

indoor /'ɪndɔː(r)/ *a* interno; (*shoes*) per casa; (*plant*) da appartamento; (*swimming pool etc*) coperto. **~s** /-'dɔːz/ *adv* dentro

induce /ɪn'djuːs/ *vt* indurre (**to** a); (*produce*) causare. **~ment** *n* (*incentive*) incentivo *m*

indulge /ɪn'dʌldʒ/ *vt* soddisfare; viziare (*child*) ● *vi* **~ in** concedersi. **~nce** /-əns/ *n* lusso *m*; (*leniency*) indulgenza *f*. **~nt** *a* indulgente

industrial /ɪn'dʌstrɪəl/ *a* industriale; **take ~ action** scioperare. **~ist** *n* industriale *mf*. **~ized** *a* industrializzato

industr|ious /ɪn'dʌstrɪəs/ *a* industrioso. **~y** /'ɪndəstrɪ/ *n* industria *f*; (*zeal*) operosità *f*

inebriated /ɪ'niːbrɪeɪtɪd/ *a* ebbro

in'edible *a* immangiabile

inef'fective *a* inefficace

ineffectual /ɪnɪ'fektʃʊəl/ *a* inutile; (*person*) inconcludente

inef'ficien|cy *n* inefficienza *f*. **~t** *a* inefficiente

in'eligible *a* inadatto

inept /ɪ'nept/ *a* inetto

ine'quality *n* ineguaglianza *f*

inert /ɪ'nɜːt/ *a* inerte. **~ia** /ɪ'nɜːʃə/ *n* inerzia *f*

inescapable /ɪnɪ'skeɪpəbl/ *a* inevitabile

inestimable /ɪn'estɪməbl/ *a* inestimabile

inevitabl|e /ɪn'evɪtəbl/ *a* inevitabile. **~y** *adv* inevitabilmente

ine'xact *a* inesatto

inex'cusable *a* imperdonabile

inexhaustible /ɪnɪg'zɔːstəbl/ *a* inesauribile

inexorable /ɪn'eksərəbl/ *a* inesorabile

inex'pensive *a* poco costoso

inex'perience *n* inesperienza *f*. **~d** *a* inesperto

inexplicable /ɪnɪk'splɪkəbl/ *a* inesplicabile

in'fallible *a* infallibile

infam|ous /'ɪnfəməs/ *a* infame; (*person*) famigerato. **~y** *n* infamia *f*

infan|cy /'ɪnfənsɪ/ *n* infanzia *f*; **in its ~cy** *fig* agli inizi. **~t** *n* bambino, -a *mf* piccolo, -a. **~tile** *a* infantile

infantry /'ɪnfəntrɪ/ *n* fanteria *f*

infatuat|ed /ɪn'fætʃʊeɪtɪd/ *a* infatuato (**with** di). **~ion** *n* infatuazione *f*

infect /ɪn'fekt/ *vt* infettare; **become ~ed** (*wound:*) infettarsi. **~ion** /-'fekʃn/ *n* infezione *f*. **~ious** /-'fekʃəs/ *a* infettivo

infer /ɪn'fɜː(r)/ *vt* (*pt/pp* **inferred**) dedurre (**from** da); (*imply*) implicare. **~ence** /'ɪnfərəns/ *n* deduzione *f*

inferior /ɪn'fɪərɪə(r)/ *a* inferiore; (*goods*) scadente; (*in rank*) subalterno ● *n* inferiore *mf*; (*in rank*) subalterno, -a *mf*

inferiority /ɪnfɪərɪ'ɒrətɪ/ *n* inferiorità *f*. **~ complex** *n* complesso *m* di inferiorità

infern|al /ɪn'fɜːnl/ *a* infernale. **~o** *n* inferno *m*

in'fertile *a* sterile. **~'tility** *n* sterilità *f*

infest /ɪn'fest/ *vt* **be ~ed with** essere infestato di

infi'delity *n* infedeltà *f*

infighting /'ɪnfaɪtɪŋ/ *n fig* lotta *f* per il potere

infiltrate /'ɪnfɪltreɪt/ *vt* infiltrare; *Pol* infiltrarsi in

infinite /'ɪnfɪnət/ *a* infinito

infinitive /ɪnˈfɪnətɪv/ *n Gram* infinito *m*

infinity /ɪnˈfɪnətɪ/ *n* infinità *f*

infirm /ɪnˈfɜːm/ *a* debole. **~ary** *n* infermeria *f*. **~ity** *n* debolezza *f*

inflame /ɪnˈfleɪm/ *vt* infiammare. **~d** *a* infiammato; **become ~d** infiammarsi

in'flammable *a* infiammabile

inflammation /ɪnfləˈmeɪʃn/ *n* infiammazione *f*

inflammatory /ɪnˈflæmətrɪ/ *a* incendiario

inflatable /ɪnˈfleɪtəbl/ *a* gonfiabile

inflat|e /ɪnˈfleɪt/ *vt* gonfiare. **~ion** /-eɪʃn/ *n* inflazione *f*. **~ionary** /-eɪʃənərɪ/ *a* inflazionario

in'flexible *a* inflessibile

inflexion /ɪnˈflekʃn/ *n* inflessione *f*

inflict /ɪnˈflɪkt/ *vt* infliggere (**on** a)

influen|ce /ˈɪnfluəns/ *n* influenza *f* ● *vt* influenzare. **~tial** /-ˈenʃl/ *a* influente

influenza /ɪnfluˈenzə/ *n* influenza *f*

influx /ˈɪnflʌks/ *n* affluenza *f*

inform /ɪnˈfɔːm/ *vt* informare; **keep sb ~ed** tenere qcno al corrente ● *vi* **~ against** denunziare

in'for|mal *a* informale; ⟨*agreement*⟩ ufficioso. **~mally** *adv* in modo informale. **~'mality** *n* informalità *f inv*

informant /ɪnˈfɔːmənt/ *n* informatore, -trice *mf*

informat|ion /ɪnfəˈmeɪʃn/ *n* informazioni *fpl*; **a piece of ~ion** un'informazione. **~ion highway** *n* autostrada *f* telematica. **~ion technology** *n* informatica *f*. **~ive** /ɪnˈfɔːmətɪv/ *a* informativo; ⟨*film, book*⟩ istruttivo

informer /ɪnˈfɔːmə(r)/ *n* informatore, -trice *mf*; *Pol* delatore, -trice *mf*

infra-'red /ɪnfrə-/ *a* infrarosso

infrastructure /ˈɪnfrəstrʌktʃə(r)/ *n* infrastruttura *f*

infringe /ɪnˈfrɪndʒ/ *vt* **~ on** usurpare. **~ment** *n* violazione *f*

infuriat|e /ɪnˈfjʊərɪeɪt/ *vt* infuriare. **~ing** *a* esasperante

infusion /ɪnˈfjuːʒn/ *n* ⟨*drink*⟩ infusione *f*; ⟨*of capital, new blood*⟩ afflusso *m*

ingenious /ɪnˈdʒiːnɪəs/ *a* ingegnoso

ingenuity /ɪndʒɪˈnjuːətɪ/ *n* ingegnosità *f*

ingenuous /ɪnˈdʒenjʊəs/ *a* ingenuo

ingot /ˈɪŋgət/ *n* lingotto *m*

ingrained /ɪnˈgreɪnd/ *a* ⟨*in person*⟩ radicato; ⟨*dirt*⟩ incrostato

ingratiate /ɪnˈgreɪʃɪeɪt/ *vt* **~ oneself with sb** ingraziarsi qcno

in'gratitude *n* ingratitudine *f*

ingredient /ɪnˈgriːdɪənt/ *n* ingrediente *m*

ingrowing /ˈɪngrəʊɪŋ/ *a* ⟨*nail*⟩ incarnito

inhabit /ɪnˈhæbɪt/ *vt* abitare. **~ant** *n* abitante *mf*

inhale /ɪnˈheɪl/ *vt* aspirare; *Med* inalare ● *vi* inspirare; (*when smoking*) aspirare. **~r** *n* (*device*) inalatore *m*

inherent /ɪnˈhɪərənt/ *a* inerente

inherit /ɪnˈherɪt/ *vt* ereditare. **~ance** /-əns/ *n* eredità *f inv*

inhibit /ɪnˈhɪbɪt/ *vt* inibire. **~ed** *a* inibito. **~ion** /-ˈbɪʃn/ *n* inibizione *f*

inho'spitable *a* inospitale

in'human *a* disumano

initial /ɪˈnɪʃl/ *a* iniziale ● *n* iniziale *f* ● *vt* (*pt/pp* **initialled**) siglare. **~ly** *adv* all'inizio

initiat|e /ɪˈnɪʃɪeɪt/ *vt* iniziare. **~ion** /-eɪʃn/ *n* iniziazione *f*

initiative /ɪˈnɪʃətɪv/ *n* iniziativa *f*

inject /ɪnˈdʒekt/ *vt* iniettare. **~ion** /-ekʃn/ *n* iniezione *f*

injur|e /ˈɪndʒə(r)/ *vt* ferire; (*wrong*) nuocere. **~y** *n* ferita *f*; (*wrong*) torto *m*

in'justice *n* ingiustizia *f*; **do sb an ~** giudicare qcno in modo sbagliato

ink /ɪŋk/ *n* inchiostro *m*

inkling /ˈɪŋklɪŋ/ *n* sentore *m*

inlaid /ɪnˈleɪd/ *a* intarsiato

inland /ˈɪnlənd/ *a* interno ● *adv* all'interno. **I~ Revenue** *n* fisco *m*

in-laws /ˈɪnlɔːz/ *npl fam* parenti *mpl* acquisiti

inlay /ˈɪnleɪ/ *n* intarsio *m*

inlet /ˈɪnlet/ *n* insenatura *f*; *Techn* entrata *f*

inmate /ˈɪnmeɪt/ *n* (*of hospital*) degente *mf*; (*of prison*) carcerato, -a *mf*

inn /ɪn/ *n* locanda *f*

innate /ɪˈneɪt/ *a* innato

inner /ˈɪnə(r)/ *a* interno. **~most** *a* il più profondo. **~ tube** *n* camera *f* d'aria

'innkeeper *n* locandiere, -a *mf*

innocen|ce /ˈɪnəsəns/ *n* innocenza *f*. **~t** *a* innocente

innocuous /ɪˈnɒkjʊəs/ *a* innocuo

innovat|e /ˈɪnəveɪt/ *vi* innovare. **~ion** /-ˈveɪʃn/ *n* innovazione *f*. **~ive** /ˈɪnəvətɪv/ *a* innovativo. **~or** /ˈɪnəveɪtə(r)/ *n* innovatore, -trice *mf*

innuendo /ɪnjuːˈendəʊ/ *n* (*pl* **-es**) insinuazione *f*

innumerable /ɪˈnjuːmərəbl/ *a* innumerevole

inoculat|e /ɪˈnɒkjʊleɪt/ *vt* vaccinare. **~ion** /-ˈleɪʃn/ *n* vaccinazione *f*

inof'fensive *a* inoffensivo

in'operable *a* inoperabile

in'opportune *a* inopportuno

inordinate /ɪˈnɔːdɪnət/ *a* smodato

inor'ganic *a* inorganico

'in-patient *n* degente *mf*

input /ˈɪmpʊt/ *n* input *m inv*, ingresso *m*

inquest /ˈɪnkwest/ *n* inchiesta *f*

inquir|e /ɪnˈkwaɪə(r)/ *vi* informarsi (**about** su); **~e into** far indagini su ● *vt* domandare. **~y** *n* domanda *f*; (*investigation*) inchiesta *f*

inquisitive /ɪnˈkwɪzətɪv/ *a* curioso

inroad /ˈɪnrəʊd/ *n* **make ~s into** intaccare ⟨*savings*⟩; cominciare a risolvere ⟨*problem*⟩

in'sane *a* pazzo; *fig* insensato

in'sanitary *a* malsano

in'sanity *n* pazzia *f*

insatiable /ɪnˈseɪʃəbl/ *a* insaziabile

inscri|be /ɪnˈskraɪb/ *vt* iscrivere. **~ption** /-ˈskrɪpʃn/ *n* iscrizione *f*

inscrutable /ɪnˈskruːtəbl/ *a* impenetrabile

insect /ˈɪnsekt/ *n* insetto *m*. **~icide** /-ˈsektɪsaɪd/ *n* insetticida *m*

inse'cur|e *a* malsicuro; ⟨*fig: person*⟩ insicuro. **~ity** *n* mancanza *f* di sicurezza

insemination /ɪnsemɪˈneɪʃn/ *n* inseminazione *f*

in'sensitive *a* insensibile

in'separable *a* inseparabile

insert[1] /ˈɪnsɜːt/ *n* inserto *m*

insert[2] /ɪnˈsɜːt/ *vt* inserire. **~ion** /-ɜːʃn/ *n* inserzione *f*

inside /ɪnˈsaɪd/ *n* interno *m*. **~s** *npl fam* pancia *f* ● *attrib Aut* **~ lane** *n* corsia *f* interna ● *adv* dentro; **~ out** a rovescio; (*thoroughly*) a fondo ● *prep* dentro; (*of time*) entro

insidious /ɪnˈsɪdɪəs/ *a* insidioso

insight /ˈɪnsaɪt/ *n* intuito *m* (**into** per); **an ~ into** un quadro di

insignia /ɪnˈsɪgnɪə/ *npl* insegne *fpl*

insig'nificant *a* insignificante

insin'cer|e *a* poco sincero. **~ity** /-ˈserɪtɪ/ *n* mancanza *f* di sincerità

insinuat|e /ɪnˈsɪnjʊeɪt/ *vt* insinuare. **~ion** /-ˈeɪʃn/ *n* insinuazione *f*

insipid /ɪnˈsɪpɪd/ *a* insipido

insist /ɪnˈsɪst/ *vi* insistere (**on** per) ● *vt* **~ that** insistere che. **~ence** *n* insistenza *f*. **~ent** *a* insistente

'insole *n* soletta *f*

insolen|ce /ˈɪnsələns/ *n* insolenza *f*. **~t** *a* insolente

in'soluble *a* insolubile

in'solven|cy *n* insolvenza *f*. **~t** *a* insolvente

insomnia /ɪnˈsɒmnɪə/ *n* insonnia *f*

inspect /ɪnˈspekt/ *vt* ispezionare; controllare ⟨*ticket*⟩. **~ion** /-ekʃn/ *n* ispezione *f*; (*of ticket*) controllo *m*. **~or** *n* ispettore, -trice *mf*; (*of tickets*) controllore *m*

inspiration /ɪnspəˈreɪʃn/ *n* ispirazione *f*

inspire /ɪnˈspaɪə(r)/ *vt* ispirare

insta'bility *n* instabilità *f*

install /ɪnˈstɔːl/ *vt* installare. **~ation** /-stəˈleɪʃn/ *n* installazione *f*

instalment /ɪnˈstɔːlmənt/ *n Comm* rata *f*; (*of serial*) puntata *f*; (*of publication*) fascicolo *m*

instance /ˈɪnstəns/ *n* (*case*) caso *m*; (*example*) esempio *m*; **in the first ~** in primo luogo; **for ~** per esempio

instant /ˈɪnstənt/ *a* immediato; *Culin* espresso ● *n* istante *m*. **~aneous** /-ˈteɪnɪəs/ *a* istantaneo

instant 'coffee *n* caffè *m inv* solubile

instantly /ˈɪnstəntlɪ/ *adv* immediatamente

instead /ɪnˈsted/ *adv* invece; **~ of doing** anziché fare; **~ of me** al mio posto; **~ of going** invece di andare

'instep *n* collo *m* del piede

instigat|e /ˈɪnstɪgeɪt/ *vt* istigare. **~ion** /-ˈgeɪʃn/ *n* istigazione *f*; **at his ~ion** dietro suo suggerimento. **~or** *n* istigatore, -trice *mf*

instil /ɪnˈstɪl/ *vt* (*pt/pp* **instilled**) inculcare (**into** in)

instinct /ˈɪnstɪŋkt/ *n* istinto *m*. **~ive** /ɪnˈstɪŋktɪv/ *a* istintivo

institut|e /ˈɪnstɪtjuːt/ *n* istituto *m* ● *vt* istituire ⟨*scheme*⟩; iniziare ⟨*search*⟩; intentare ⟨*legal action*⟩. **~ion** /-ˈtjuːʃn/ *n* istituzione *f*; (*home for elderly*) istituto *m* per anziani; (*for mentally ill*) istituto *m* per malati di mente

instruct /ɪnˈstrʌkt/ *vt* istruire; (*order*) ordinare. **~ion** /-ʌkʃn/ *n* istruzione *f*; **~s** (*pl: orders*) ordini *mpl*. **~ive** /-ɪv/ *a* istruttivo. **~or** *n* istruttore, -trice *mf*

instrument /ˈɪnstrəmənt/ *n* strumento *m*. **~al** /-ˈmentl/ *a* strumentale; **be ~al in** contribuire a. **~alist** *n* strumentista *mf*

insu'bordi|nate *a* insubordinato. **~nation** /-ˈneɪʃn/ *n* insubordinazione *f*

in'sufferable *a* insopportabile

insuf'ficient *a* insufficiente

insular /ˈɪnsjʊlə(r)/ *a fig* gretto

insulat|e /ˈɪnsjʊleɪt/ *vt* isolare. **~ing**

tape *n* nastro *m* isolante. **~ion** /-'leɪʃn/ *n* isolamento *m*

insulin /'ɪnsjʊlɪn/ *n* insulina *f*

insult¹ /'ɪnsʌlt/ *n* insulto *m*

insult² /ɪn'sʌlt/ *vt* insultare

insuperable /ɪn'su:pərəbl/ *a* insuperabile

insur|ance /ɪn'ʃʊərəns/ *n* assicurazione *f*. **~e** *vt* assicurare

insurrection /ɪnsə'rekʃn/ *n* insurrezione *f*

intact /ɪn'tækt/ *a* intatto

'intake *n* immissione *f*; *(of food)* consumo *m*

in'tangible *a* intangibile

integral /'ɪntɪɡrəl/ *a* integrale

integrat|e /'ɪntɪɡreɪt/ *vt* integrare ● *vi* integrarsi. **~ion** /-'ɡreɪʃn/ *n* integrazione *f*

integrity /ɪn'teɡrəti/ *n* integrità *f*

intellect /'ɪntəlekt/ *n* intelletto *m*. **~ual** /-'lektjʊəl/ *a* & *n* intellettuale *mf*

intelligen|ce /ɪn'telɪdʒəns/ *n* intelligenza *f*; *Mil* informazioni *fpl*. **~t** *a* intelligente

intelligentsia /ɪntelɪ'dʒentsɪə/ *n* intellighenzia *f*

intelligible /ɪn'telɪdʒəbl/ *a* intelligibile

intend /ɪn'tend/ *vt* destinare; *(have in mind)* aver intenzione di; **be ~ed for** essere destinato a. **~ed** *a* ⟨*effect*⟩ voluto ● *n* **my ~ed** *fam* il mio/la mia fidanzata, -a

intense /ɪn'tens/ *a* intenso; ⟨*person*⟩ dai sentimenti intensi. **~ly** *adv* intensamente; *(very)* estremamente

intensi|fication /ɪntensɪfɪ'keɪʃn/ *n* intensificazione *f*. **~fy** /-'tensɪfaɪ/ *v* (*pt/pp* **-ied**) ● *vt* intensificare ● *vi* intensificarsi

intensity /ɪn'tensəti/ *n* intensità *f*

intensive /ɪn'tensɪv/ *a* intensivo. **~ care** *(for people in coma)* rianimazione *f*; **~ care [unit]** terapia *f* intensiva

intent /ɪn'tent/ *a* intento; **~ on** *(absorbed in)* preso da; **be ~ on doing sth** essere intento a fare qcsa ● *n* intenzione *f*; **to all ~s and purposes** a tutti gli effetti. **~ly** *adv* attentamente

intention /ɪn'tenʃn/ *n* intenzione *f*. **~al** *a* intenzionale. **~ally** *adv* intenzionalmente

inter'acti|on *n* cooperazione *f*. **~ve** *a* interattivo

intercede /ɪntə'si:d/ *vi* intercedere **(on behalf of** a favore di)

intercept /ɪntə'sept/ *vt* intercettare

'interchange *n* scambio *m*; *Auto* raccordo *m* [autostradale]

inter'changeable *a* interscambiabile

intercom /'ɪntəkɒm/ *n* citofono *m*

'intercourse *n* *(sexual)* rapporti *mpl* [sessuali]

interest /'ɪntrəst/ *n* interesse *m*; **have an ~ in** *Comm* essere cointeressato in; **be of ~** essere interessante; **~ rate** *n* tasso *m* di interesse ● *vt* interessare. **~ed** *a* interessato. **~ing** *a* interessante

interface /'ɪntəfeɪs/ *n* interfaccia *f* ● *vt* interfacciare ● *vi* interfacciarsi

interfere /ɪntə'fɪə(r)/ *vi* interferire; **~ with** interferire con. **~nce** /-əns/ *n* interferenza *f*

interim /'ɪntərɪm/ *a* temporaneo; **~ payment** acconto *m* ● *n* **in the ~** nel frattempo

interior /ɪn'tɪərɪə(r)/ *a* interiore ● *n* interno *m*. **~ designer** *n* arredatore, -trice *mf*

interject /ɪntə'dʒekt/ *vt* intervenire. **~ion** /-ekʃn/ *n* *Gram* interiezione *f*; *(remark)* intervento *m*

interloper /'ɪntələʊpə(r)/ *n* intruso, -a *mf*

interlude /'ɪntəlu:d/ *n* intervallo *m*

inter'marry *vi* sposarsi tra parenti; ⟨*different groups:*⟩ contrarre matrimoni misti

intermediary /ɪntə'mi:dɪərɪ/ *n* intermediario, -a *mf*

intermediate /ɪntə'mi:dɪət/ *a* intermedio

interminable /ɪn'tɜ:mɪnəbl/ *a* interminabile

intermission /ɪntə'mɪʃn/ *n* intervallo *m*

intermittent /ɪntə'mɪtənt/ *a* intermittente

intern /ɪn'tɜ:n/ *vt* internare

internal /ɪn'tɜ:nl/ *a* interno. **~ly** *adv* internamente; ⟨*deal with*⟩ all'interno

inter'national *a* internazionale ● *n* *(game)* incontro *m* internazionale; *(player)* competitore, -trice *mf* in gare internazionali. **~ly** *adv* internazionalmente

Internet /'ɪntənet/ *n* Internet *m*

internist /ɪn'tɜ:nɪst/ *n* *Am* internista *mf*

internment /ɪn'tɜ:nmənt/ *n* internamento *m*

'interplay *n* azione *f* reciproca

interpret /ɪn'tɜ:prɪt/ *vt* interpretare

● *vi* fare l'interprete. **~ation** /-'teɪʃn/ *n* interpretazione *f*. **~er** *n* interprete *mf*

interre'lated *a* (*facts*) in correlazione

interrogat|e /ɪn'terəgeɪt/ *vt* interrogare. **~ion** /-'geɪʃn/ *n* interrogazione *f*; (*by police*) interrogatorio *m*

interrogative /ɪntə'rɒgətɪv/ *a & n* **~** [**pronoun**] interrogativo *m*

interrupt /ɪntə'rʌpt/ *vt/i* interrompere. **~ion** /-ʌpʃn/ *n* interruzione *f*

intersect /ɪntə'sekt/ *vi* intersecarsi ● *vt* intersecare. **~ion** /-ekʃn/ *n* intersezione *f*; (*of street*) incrocio *m*

interspersed /ɪntə'spɜːst/ *a* **~ with** inframmezzato di

inter'twine *vi* attorcigliarsi

interval /'ɪntəvl/ *n* intervallo *m*; **bright ~s** *pl* schiarite *fpl*

interven|e /ɪntə'viːn/ *vi* intervenire. **~tion** /-'venʃn/ *n* intervento *m*

interview /'ɪntəvjuː/ *n* Journ intervista *f*; (*for job*) colloquio *m* [di lavoro] ● *vt* intervistare. **~er** *n* intervistatore, -trice *mf*

intestin|e /ɪn'testɪn/ *n* intestino *m*. **~al** *a* intestinale

intimacy /'ɪntɪməsɪ/ *n* intimità *f*

intimate[1] /'ɪntɪmət/ *a* intimo. **~ly** *adv* intimamente

intimate[2] /'ɪntɪmeɪt/ *vt* far capire; (*imply*) suggerire

intimidat|e /ɪn'tɪmɪdeɪt/ *vt* intimidire. **~ion** /-'deɪʃn/ *n* intimidazione *f*

into /'ɪntə/, *di fronte a una vocale* /'ɪntʊ/ *prep* dentro, in; **go ~ the house** andare dentro [casa] *o* in casa; **be ~** (*fam: like*) essere appassionato di; **I'm not ~ that** questo non mi piace; **7 ~ 21 goes 3** il 7 nel 21 ci sta 3 volte; **translate ~ French** tradurre in francese; **get ~ trouble** mettersi nei guai

in'tolerable *a* intollerabile

In'toleran|ce *n* intolleranza *f*. **~t** *a* intollerante

intonation /ɪntə'neɪʃn/ *n* intonazione *f*

intoxicat|ed /ɪn'tɒksɪkeɪtɪd/ *a* inebriato. **~ion** /-'keɪʃn/ *n* ebbrezza *f*

intractable /ɪn'træktəbl/ *a* intrattabile; (*problem*) insolubile

intranet /'ɪntrənet/ *n* intranet *f* *inv*

intransigent /ɪn'trænzɪdʒənt/ *a* intransigente

in'transitive *a* intransitivo

intravenous /ɪntrə'viːnəs/ *a* endovenoso. **~ly** *adv* per via endovenosa

intricate /'ɪntrɪkət/ *a* complesso

intrigu|e /ɪn'triːg/ *n* intrigo *m* ● *vt* intrigare ● *vi* tramare. **~ing** *a* intrigante

intrinsic /ɪn'trɪnsɪk/ *a* intrinseco

introduce /ɪntrə'djuːs/ *vt* presentare; (*bring in, insert*) introdurre

introduct|ion /ɪntrə'dʌkʃn/ *n* introduzione *f*; (*to person*) presentazione *f*; (*to book*) prefazione *f*. **~ory** /-tərɪ/ *a* introduttivo

introspective /ɪntrə'spektɪv/ *a* introspettivo

introvert /'ɪntrəvɜːt/ *n* introverso, -a *mf*

intru|de /ɪn'truːd/ *vi* intromettersi. **~der** *n* intruso, -a *mf*. **~sion** /-uːʒn/ *n* intrusione *f*

intuit|ion /ɪntjʊ'ɪʃn/ *n* intuito *m*. **~ive** /-'tjuːɪtɪv/ *a* intuitivo

inundate /'ɪnəndeɪt/ *vt* *fig* inondare (**with** di)

invade /ɪn'veɪd/ *vt* invadere. **~r** *n* invasore *m*

invalid[1] /'ɪnvəlɪd/ *n* invalido, -a *mf*

invalid[2] /ɪn'vælɪd/ *a* non valido. **~ate** *vt* invalidare

in'valuable *a* prezioso; (*priceless*) inestimabile

in'variabl|e *a* invariabile. **~y** *adv* invariabilmente

invasion /ɪn'veɪʒn/ *n* invasione *f*

invective /ɪn'vektɪv/ *n* invettiva *f*

invent /ɪn'vent/ *vt* inventare. **~ion** /-enʃn/ *n* invenzione *f*. **~ive** /-tɪv/ *a* inventivo. **~or** *n* inventore, -trice *mf*

inventory /'ɪnvəntrɪ/ *n* inventario *m*

inverse /ɪn'vɜːs/ *a* inverso ● *n* inverso *m*

invert /ɪn'vɜːt/ *vt* invertire; **in ~ed commas** tra virgolette

invest /ɪn'vest/ *vt* investire ● *vi* fare investimenti; **~ in** (*fam: buy*) comprarsi

investigat|e /ɪn'vestɪgeɪt/ *vt* investigare. **~ion** /-'geɪʃn/ *n* investigazione *f*

invest|ment /ɪn'vestmənt/ *n* investimento *m*. **~or** *n* investitore, -trice *mf*

inveterate /ɪn'vetərət/ *a* inveterato

invidious /ɪn'vɪdɪəs/ *a* ingiusto; ⟨*position*⟩ antipatico

invigilat|e /ɪn'vɪdʒɪleɪt/ *vi* Sch sorvegliare lo svolgimento di un esame. **~or** *n* persona *f* che sorveglia lo svolgimento di un esame

invigorate /ɪn'vɪgəreɪt/ *vt* rinvigorire

invigorating /ɪn'vɪgəreɪtɪŋ/ *a* tonificante

invincible /ɪn'vɪnsəbl/ *a* invincibile

inviolable /ɪn'vaɪələbl/ *a* inviolabile

in'visible *a* invisibile

invitation /ɪnvɪ'teɪʃn/ *n* invito *m*

invit|e /ɪn'vaɪt/ *vt* invitare; (*attract*) attirare. **~ing** *a* invitante

invoice /'ɪnvɔɪs/ n fattura f ● vt ~ sb emettere una fattura a qcno

invoke /ɪn'vəʊk/ vt invocare

in'voluntar|y a involontario

involve /ɪn'vɒlv/ vt comportare; (*affect, include*) coinvolgere; (*entail*) implicare; **get ~d with sb** legarsi a qcno; (*romantically*) legarsi sentimentalmente a qcno. **~d** a complesso. **~ment** n coinvolgimento m

in'vulnerable a invulnerabile; ⟨*position*⟩ inattaccabile

inward /'ɪnwəd/ a interno; ⟨*thoughts etc*⟩ interiore; **~ investment** Comm investimento m di capitali stranieri. **~ly** adv interiormente. **~[s]** adv verso l'interno

iodine /'aɪədi:n/ n iodio m

iota /aɪ'əʊtə/ n briciolo m

IOU n abbr (**I owe you**) pagherò m inv

IQ n abbr (**intelligence quotient**) Q.I.

IRA n abbr (**Irish Republican Army**) I.R.A.f

Iran /ɪ'rɑ:n/ n Iran m. **~ian** /ɪ'reɪnɪən/ a & n iraniano, -a mf

Iraq /ɪ'rɑ:k/ n Iraq m. **~i** /ɪ'rɑ:kɪ/ a & n iracheno, -a mf

irascible /ɪ'ræsəbl/ a irascibile

irate /aɪ'reɪt/ a adirato

Ireland /'aɪələnd/ n Irlanda f

iris /'aɪrɪs/ n Anat iride f; Bot iris f inv

Irish /'aɪrɪʃ/ a irlandese ● npl **the ~** gli irlandesi. **~man** n irlandese m. **~woman** n irlandese f

iron /'aɪən/ a di ferro. **I~ Curtain** n cortina f di ferro ● n ferro m; (*appliance*) ferro m [da stiro] ● vt/i stirare. **iron out** vt eliminare stirando; fig appianare

ironic[al] /aɪ'rɒnɪk[l]/ a ironico

ironing /'aɪənɪŋ/ n stirare m; (*articles*) roba f da stirare; **do the ~** stirare. **~-board** n asse f da stiro

ironmonger /-mʌŋgə(r)/ n **~'s** [**shop**] negozio m di ferramenta

irony /'aɪrənɪ/ n ironia f

irradiate /ɪ'reɪdɪeɪt/ vt irradiare

irrational /ɪ'ræʃənl/ a irrazionale

irreconcilable /ɪ'rekənsaɪləbl/ a irreconciliabile

irrefutable /ɪrɪ'fju:təbl/ a irrefutabile

irregular /ɪ'regjʊlə(r)/ a irregolare. **~ity** /-'lærətɪ/ n irregolarità f inv

irrelevant /ɪ'reləvənt/ a non pertinente

irreparabl|e /ɪ'repərəbl/ a irreparabile. **~y** adv irreparabilmente

irreplaceable /ɪrɪ'pleɪsəbl/ a insostituibile

irrepressible /ɪrɪ'presəbl/ a irrefrenabile; ⟨*person*⟩ incontenibile

irresistible /ɪrɪ'zɪstəbl/ a irresistibile

irresolute /ɪ'rezəlu:t/ a irresoluto

irrespective /ɪrɪ'spektɪv/ a **~ of** senza riguardo per

irresponsible /ɪrɪ'spɒnsɪbl/ a irresponsabile

irreverent /ɪ'revərənt/ a irreverente

irreversible /ɪrɪ'vɜ:səbl/ a irreversibile

irrevocabl|e /ɪ'revəkəbl/ a irrevocabile. **~y** adv irrevocabilmente

irrigat|e /'ɪrɪgeɪt/ vt irrigare. **~ion** /-'geɪʃn/ n irrigazione f

irritability /ɪrɪtə'bɪlətɪ/ n irritabilità f

irritable /'ɪrɪtəbl/ a irritabile

irritant /'ɪrɪtənt/ n sostanza f irritante

irritat|e /'ɪrɪteɪt/ vt irritare. **~ing** a irritante. **~ion** /-'teɪʃn/ n irritazione f

is /ɪz/ see be

Islam /'ɪzlɑ:m/ n Islam m. **~ic** /-'læmɪk/ a islamico

island /'aɪlənd/ n isola f; (*in road*) isola f spartitraffico. **~er** n isolano, -a mf

isle /aɪl/ n liter isola f

isolat|e /'aɪsəleɪt/ vt isolare. **~ed** a isolato. **~ion** /-'leɪʃn/ n isolamento m

Israel /'ɪzreɪl/ n Israele m. **~i** /ɪz'reɪlɪ/ a & n israeliano, -a mf

issue /'ɪʃu:/ n (*outcome*) risultato m; (*of magazine*) numero m; (*of stamps etc*) emissione f; (*offspring*) figli mpl; (*matter, question*) questione f; **at ~** in questione; **take ~ with sb** prendere posizione contro qcno ● vt distribuire ⟨*supplies*⟩; rilasciare ⟨*passport*⟩; emettere ⟨*stamps, order*⟩; pubblicare ⟨*book*⟩; **be ~d with sth** ricevere qcsa ● vi **~ from** uscire da

isthmus /'ɪsməs/ n (pl **-muses**) istmo m

it /ɪt/ pron (*direct object*) lo m, la f; (*indirect object*) gli m, le f; **it's broken** è rotto/rotta; **will it be enough?** basterà?; **it's hot** fa caldo; **it's raining** piove; **it's me** sono io; **who is it?** chi è?; **it's two o'clock** sono le due; **I doubt it** ne dubito; **take it with you** prendilo con te; **give it a wipe** dagli una pulita

Italian /ɪ'tæljən/ a & n italiano, -a mf; (*language*) italiano m

italic /ɪ'tælɪk/ a in corsivo. **~s** npl corsivo msg

Italy /'ɪtəlɪ/ n Italia f

itch /ɪtʃ/ n prurito m ● vi avere prurito, prudere; **be ~ing to** fam avere una voglia matta di. **~y** a che prude; **my foot is ~y** ho prurito al piede

item /'aɪtəm/ n articolo m; (on agenda, programme) punto m; (on invoice) voce f; ~ [of news] notizia f. ~ize vt dettagliare ‹bill›

itinerant /aɪ'tɪnərənt/ a itinerante

itinerary /aɪ'tɪnərərɪ/ n itinerario m

its /ɪts/ poss pron suo m, sua f, suoi mpl, sue fpl; ~ mother/cage sua madre/la sua gabbia

it's = it is, it has

itself /ɪt'self/ pron (reflexive) si; (emphatic) essa stessa; **the baby looked at ~ in the mirror** il bambino si è guardato nello specchio; **by ~** da solo; **the machine in ~ is simple** la macchina di per sé è semplice

ITV n abbr (Independent Television) stazione f televisiva privata britannica

ivory /'aɪvərɪ/ n avorio m

ivy /'aɪvɪ/ n edera f

Jj

jab /dʒæb/ n colpo m secco; (fam: injection) puntura f ● vt (pt/pp jabbed) punzecchiare

jabber /'dʒæbə(r)/ vi borbottare

jack /dʒæk/ n Auto cric m inv; (in cards) fante m, jack m inv ● jack up vt Auto sollevare [con il cric]

jackdaw /'dʒækdɔ:/ n taccola f

jacket /'dʒækɪt/ n giacca f; (of book) sopraccoperta f. ~ po'tato n patata f cotta al forno con la buccia

'jackpot n premio m (di una lotteria); **win the ~** vincere alla lotteria; **hit the ~** fig fare un colpo grosso

jade /dʒeɪd/ n giada f ● attrib di giada

jaded /'dʒeɪdɪd/ a spossato

jagged /'dʒægɪd/ a dentellato

jail /dʒeɪl/ = gaol

jalopy /dʒə'lɒpɪ/ n fam vecchia carretta f

jam¹ /dʒæm/ n marmellata f

jam² n Auto ingorgo m; (fam: difficulty) guaio m ● v (pt/pp jammed) ● vt (cram) pigiare; disturbare ‹broadcast›; inceppare ‹mechanism, drawer etc›; **be ~med** ‹roads:› essere congestionato ● vi ‹mechanism:› incepparsi; ‹window, drawer:› incastrarsi

Jamaica /dʒə'meɪkə/ n Giamaica f. ~n a & n giamaicano, -a mf

jam-'packed a fam pieno zeppo

jangle /'dʒæŋgl/ vt far squillare ● vi squillare

janitor /'dʒænɪtə(r)/ n (caretaker) custode m; (in school) bidello, -a mf

January /'dʒænjʊərɪ/ n gennaio m

Japan /dʒə'pæn/ n Giappone m. ~ese /dʒæpə'ni:z/ a & n giapponese mf; (language) giapponese m

jar¹ /dʒɑ:(r)/ n (glass) barattolo m

jar² vi (pt/pp jarred) ‹sound:› stridere

jargon /'dʒɑ:gən/ n gergo m

jaundice /'dʒɔ:ndɪs/ n itterizia f. ~d a fig inacidito

jaunt /dʒɔ:nt/ n gita f

jaunty /'dʒɔ:ntɪ/ a (-ier, -iest) sbarazzino

javelin /'dʒævlɪn/ n giavellotto m

jaw /dʒɔ:/ n mascella f; (bone) mandibola f

jay-walker /'dʒeɪwɔ:kə(r)/ n pedone m indisciplinato

jazz /dʒæz/ n jazz m ● jazz up vt ravvivare. ~y a vistoso

jealous /'dʒeləs/ a geloso. ~y n gelosia f

jeans /dʒi:nz/ npl [blue] jeans mpl

jeep /dʒi:p/ n jeep f inv

jeer /dʒɪə(r)/ n scherno m ● vi schernire; ~ at prendersi gioco di ● vt (boo) fischiare

jell /dʒel/ vi concretarsi

jelly /'dʒelɪ/ n gelatina f. ~fish n medusa f

jeopar|dize /'dʒepədaɪz/ vt mettere in pericolo. ~dy /-dɪ/ n in ~dy in pericolo

jerk /dʒɜ:k/ n scatto m, scossa f ● vt scattare ● vi sobbalzare; ‹limb, muscle:› muoversi a scatti. ~ily adv a scatti. ~y a traballante

jersey /'dʒɜ:zɪ/ n maglia f; Sport maglietta f; (fabric) jersey m

jest /dʒest/ n scherzo m; **in ~** per scherzo ● vi scherzare

Jesus /'dʒi:zəs/ n Gesù m

jet¹ /dʒet/ n (stone) giaietto m

jet² n (of water) getto m; (nozzle) becco m; (plane) aviogetto m, jet m inv

jet: ~-'**black** a nero ebano. ~**lag** n scombussolamento m da fuso orario. ~-**pro'pelled** a a reazione

jettison /'dʒetɪsn/ vt gettare a mare; fig abbandonare

jetty /'dʒetɪ/ n molo m

Jew /dʒuː/ n ebreo m

jewel /'dʒuːəl/ n gioiello m. ~**ler** n gioielliere m; ~**ler's** [**shop**] gioielleria f. ~**lery** n gioielli mpl

Jew|ess /'dʒuːɪs/ n ebrea f. ~**ish** a ebreo

jiffy /'dʒɪfɪ/ n fam **in a** ~ in un batter d'occhio

jigsaw /'dʒɪgsɔː/ n ~ [**puzzle**] puzzle m inv

jilt /dʒɪlt/ vt piantare

jingle /'dʒɪŋgl/ n (rhyme) canzoncina f pubblicitaria ● vi tintinnare

jinx /dʒɪŋks/ n (person) iettatore, -trice mf; **it's got a** ~ **on it** è iellato

jitter|s /'dʒɪtəz/ npl fam **have the** ~**s** aver una gran fifa. ~**y** a fam in preda alla fifa

job /dʒɒb/ n lavoro m; **this is going to be quite a** ~ fam [questa] non sarà un'impresa facile; **it's a good** ~ **that...** meno male che.... ~ **centre** n ufficio m statale di collocamento. ~**less** a senza lavoro

jockey /'dʒɒkɪ/ n fantino m

jocular /'dʒɒkjʊlə(r)/ a scherzoso

jog /dʒɒg/ n colpetto m; **at a** ~ in un balzo; Sport **go for a** ~ andare a fare jogging ● v (pt/pp **jogged**) ● vt (hit) urtare; ~ **sb's memory** farlo ritornare in mente a qcno ● vi Sport fare jogging. ~**ging** n jogging m

john /dʒɒn/ n (Am fam: toilet) gabinetto m

join /dʒɔɪn/ n giuntura f ● vt raggiungere, unire; raggiungere (person); (become member of) iscriversi a; entrare in (firm) ● vi (roads:) congiungersi. **join in** vi partecipare. **join up** vi Mil arruolarsi ● vt unire

joiner /'dʒɔɪnə(r)/ n falegname m

joint /dʒɔɪnt/ a comune ● n articolazione f; (in wood, brickwork) giuntura f; Culin arrosto m; (fam: bar) bettola f; (sl:drug) spinello m. ~**ly** adv unitamente

joist /dʒɔɪst/ n travetto m

joke /dʒəʊk/ n (trick) scherzo m; (funny story) barzelletta f ● vi scherzare. ~**er** n burlone, -a mf; (in cards) jolly m inv. ~**ing** n ~**ing apart** scherzi a parte. ~**ingly** adv per scherzo

jolly /'dʒɒlɪ/ a (-**ier**, -**iest**) allegro ● adv fam molto

jolt /dʒəʊlt/ n scossa f, sobbalzo m ● vt far sobbalzare ● vi sobbalzare

Jordan /'dʒɔːdn/ n Giordania f; (river) Giordano m. ~**ian** /-'deɪnɪən/ a & n giordano, -a mf

jostle /'dʒɒsl/ vt spingere

jot /dʒɒt/ n nulla f ● **jot down** vt (pt/pp **jotted**) annotare. ~**ter** n taccuino m; (with a spine) quaderno m

journal /'dʒɜːnl/ n giornale m; (diary) diario m. ~**ese** /-ə'liːz/ n gergo m giornalistico. ~**ism** n giornalismo m. ~**ist** n giornalista mf

journey /'dʒɜːnɪ/ n viaggio m

jovial /'dʒəʊvɪəl/ a gioviale

joy /dʒɔɪ/ n gioia f. ~**ful** a gioioso. ~**ride** n fam giro m con una macchina rubata. ~**stick** n Comput joystick m inv

jubil|ant /'dʒuːbɪlənt/ a giubilante. ~**ation** /-'leɪʃn/ n giubilo m

jubilee /'dʒuːbɪliː/ n giubileo m

judder /'dʒʌdə(r)/ vi vibrare violentemente

judge /dʒʌdʒ/ n giudice m ● vt giudicare; (estimate) valutare; (consider) ritenere ● vi giudicare (**by** da). ~**ment** n giudizio m; Jur sentenza f

judic|ial /dʒuː'dɪʃl/ a giudiziario. ~**iary** /-ʃərɪ/ n magistratura f. ~**ious** /-ʃəs/ a giudizioso

judo /'dʒuːdəʊ/ n judo m

jug /dʒʌg/ n brocca f; (small) bricco m

juggernaut /'dʒʌgənɔːt/ n fam grosso autotreno m

juggle /'dʒʌgl/ vi fare giochi di destrezza. ~ n giocoliere, -a mf

juice /dʒuːs/ n succo m

juicy /'dʒuːsɪ/ a (-**ier**, -**iest**) succoso; (fam: story) piccante

juke-box /'dʒuːk-/ n juke-box m inv

July /dʒʊ'laɪ/ n luglio m

jumble /'dʒʌmbl/ n accozzaglia f ● vt ~ [**up**] mischiare. ~ **sale** n vendita f di beneficenza

jumbo /'dʒʌmbəʊ/ n ~ [**jet**] jumbo jet m inv

jump /dʒʌmp/ n salto m; (in prices) balzo m; (in horse racing) ostacolo m ● vi saltare; (with fright) sussultare; (prices:) salire rapidamente; ~ **to conclusions** saltare alle conclusioni ● vt saltare; ~ **the gun** fig precipitarsi; ~ **the queue** non rispettare la fila. **jump at** vt fig accettare con entusiasmo (offer). **jump up** vi rizzarsi in piedi

jumper /'dʒʌmpə(r)/ n (sweater) golf m inv

jumpy /'dʒʌmpɪ/ a nervoso

junction /'dʒʌŋkʃn/ n (of roads) incrocio m; (of motorway) uscita f; Rail nodo m ferroviario

juncture /'dʒʌŋktʃə(r)/ n at this ~ a questo punto

June /dʒuːn/ n giugno m

jungle /'dʒʌŋgl/ n giungla f

junior /'dʒuːnɪə(r)/ a giovane; (in rank) subalterno; Sport junior inv ● npl the ~s Sch i più giovani. ~ school n scuola f elementare

junk /dʒʌŋk/ n cianfrusaglie fpl. ~ food n fam cibo m poco sano, porcherie fpl. ~ mail posta f spazzatura

junkie /'dʒʌŋkɪ/ n sl tossico, -a mf

'**junk-shop** n negozio m di rigattiere

jurisdiction /dʒʊərɪs'dɪkʃn/ n giurisdizione f

juror /'dʒʊərə(r)/ n giurato, -a mf

jury /'dʒʊərɪ/ n giuria f; Jur giuria f [popolare]

just /dʒʌst/ a giusto ● adv (barely) appena; (simply) solo; (exactly) esattamente; ~ as tall altrettanto alto; ~ as I was leaving proprio quando stavo andando via; I've ~ seen her l'ho appena vista; it's ~ as well meno male; ~ at that moment proprio in quel momento; ~ listen! ascolta!; I'm ~ going sto andando proprio ora

justice /'dʒʌstɪs/ n giustizia f; do ~ to rendere giustizia a; J~ of the Peace giudice m conciliatore

justifiabl|e /'dʒʌstɪfaɪəbl/ a giustificabile

justi|fication /dʒʌstɪfɪ'keɪʃn/ n giustificazione f. ~fy /'dʒʌstɪfaɪ/ vt (pt/pp -ied) giustificare

justly /'dʒʌstlɪ/ adv giustamente

jut /dʒʌt/ vi (pt/pp jutted) ~ out sporgere

juvenile /'dʒuːvənaɪl/ a giovanile; (childish) infantile; (for the young) per i giovani ● n giovane mf. ~ delinquency n delinquenza f giovanile

juxtapose /dʒʌkstə'pəʊz/ vt giustapporre

Kk

kangaroo /kæŋgə'ruː/ n canguro m

karate /kə'rɑːtɪ/ n karate m

kebab /kɪ'bæb/ n Culin spiedino m di carne

keel /kiːl/ n chiglia f ● keel over vi capovolgersi

keen /kiːn/ a (intense) acuto; (interest) vivo; (eager) entusiastico; (competition) feroce; (wind, knife) tagliente; ~ on entusiasta di; she's ~ on him le piace molto; be ~ to do sth avere voglia di fare qcsa. ~ness n entusiasmo m

keep /kiːp/ n (maintenance) mantenimento m; (of castle) maschio m; for ~s per sempre ● v (pt/pp kept) ● vt tenere; (not throw away) conservare; (detain) trattenere; mantenere (family, promise); avere (shop); allevare (animals); rispettare (law, rules); ~ sth hot tenere qcsa in caldo; ~ sb from doing sth impedire a qcno di fare qcsa; ~ sb waiting far aspettare qcno; ~ sth to oneself tenere qcsa per sé; ~ sth from sb tenere nascosto qcsa a qcno ● vi (remain) rimanere; (food:) conservarsi; ~ calm rimanere calmo; ~ left/right tenere la sinistra/destra; ~ [on] doing sth continuare a fare qcsa. **keep back** vt trattenere (person); ~ sth back from sb tenere nascosto qcsa a qcno ● vi tenersi indietro. **keep in with** vt mantenersi in buoni rapporti con. **keep on** vi fam assillare (at sb qcno). **keep up** vi stare al passo ● vt (continue) continuare

keep|er /'kiːpə(r)/ n custode mf. ~-fit n ginnastica f. ~ing n custodia f; be in ~ing with essere in armonia con. ~sake n ricordo m

keg /keg/ n barilotto m

kennel /'kenl/ n canile m; ~s pl (boarding) canile m; (breeding) allevamento m di cani

Kenya /'kenjə/ n Kenia m. ~n a & n keniota mf

kept /kept/ *see* **keep**

kerb /kɜːb/ *n* bordo *m* del marciapiede

kernel /ˈkɜːnl/ *n* nocciolo *m*

kerosene /ˈkerəsiːn/ *n Am* cherosene *m*

ketchup /ˈketʃʌp/ *n* ketchup *m*

kettle /ˈket(ə)l/ *n* bollitore *m*; **put the ~ on** mettere l'acqua a bollire

key /kiː/ *n also Mus* chiave *f*; *(of piano, typewriter)* tasto *m* ● *vt* **~ [in]** digitare ⟨*character*⟩; **could you ~ this?** puoi battere questo?

key: **~board** *n Comput, Mus* tastiera *f*. **~boarder** *n* tastierista *mf*. **~ed-up** *a (anxious)* estremamente agitato; *(ready to act)* psicologicamente preparato. **~hole** *n* buco *m* della serratura. **~-ring** *n* portachiavi *m inv*

khaki /ˈkɑːkɪ/ *a* cachi *inv* ● *n* cachi *m*

kick /kɪk/ *n* calcio *m*; *(fam: thrill)* piacere *m*; **for ~s** *fam* per spasso ● *vt* dar calci a; **~ the bucket** *fam* crepare ● *vi* ⟨*animal:*⟩ scalciare; ⟨*person:*⟩ dare calci. **kick off** *vi Sport* dare il calcio d'inizio; *fam* iniziare. **kick up** *vt* **~ up a row** fare una scenata

ˈkickback *n (fam: percentage)* tangente *f*

ˈkick-off *n Sport* calcio *m* d'inizio

kid /kɪd/ *n* capretto *m*; *(fam: child)* ragazzino, -a *mf* ● *v (pt/pp* **kidded)** ● *vt fam* prendere in giro ● *vi fam* scherzare

kidnap /ˈkɪdnæp/ *vt (pt/pp* **-napped)** rapire, sequestrare. **~per** *n* sequestratore, -trice *mf*, rapitore, -trice *mf*. **~ping** *n* rapimento *m*, sequestro *m* [di persona]

kidney /ˈkɪdnɪ/ *n* rene *m*; *Culin* rognone *m*. **~ machine** *n* rene *m* artificiale

kill /kɪl/ *vt* uccidere; *fig* metter fine a; ammazzare ⟨*time*⟩. **~er** *n* assassino, -a *mf*. **~ing** *n* uccisione *f*; *(murder)* omicidio *m*; **make a ~ing** *fig* fare un colpo grosso

ˈkilljoy *n* guastafeste *mf inv*

kiln /kɪln/ *n* fornace *f*

kilo /ˈkiːləʊ/ *n* chilo *m*

kilo /ˈkɪlə/: **~byte** *n* kilobyte *m inv*. **~gram** *n* chilogrammo *m*. **~metre** /kɪˈlɒmɪtə(r)/ *n* chilometro *m*. **~watt** *n* chilowatt *m inv*

kilt /kɪlt/ *n* kilt *m inv (gonnellino degli scozzesi)*

kin /kɪn/ *n* congiunti *mpl*; **next of ~** parente *m* stretto; **parenti** *mpl* stretti

kind¹ /kaɪnd/ *n* genere *m*, specie *f*; *(brand, type)* tipo *m*; **~ of** *fam* alquanto; **two of a ~** due della stessa specie

kind² *a* gentile, buono; **~ to animals** amante degli animali; **~ regards** cordiali saluti

kindergarten /ˈkɪndəɡɑːtn/ *n* asilo *m* infantile

kindle /ˈkɪndl/ *vt* accendere

kind|ly /ˈkaɪndlɪ/ *a* **(-ier, -iest)** benevolo ● *adv* gentilmente; *(if you please)* per favore. **~ness** *n* gentilezza *f*

kindred /ˈkɪndrɪd/ *a* **she's a ~ spirit** è la mia/sua/tua anima gemella

kinetic /kɪˈnetɪk/ *a* cinetico

king /kɪŋ/ *n* re *m inv*. **~dom** *n* regno *m*

king: **~fisher** *n* martin *m inv* pescatore. **~-sized** *a* ⟨*cigarette*⟩ king-size *inv*, lungo; ⟨*bed*⟩ matrimoniale grande

kink /kɪŋk/ *n* attorcigliamento *m*. **~y** *a fam* bizzarro

kiosk /ˈkiːɒsk/ *n* chiosco *m*; *Teleph* cabina *f* telefonica

kip /kɪp/ *n fam* pisolino *m*; **have a ~** schiacciare un pisolino ● *vi (pt/pp* **kipped)** *fam* dormire

kipper /ˈkɪpə(r)/ *n* aringa *f* affumicata

kiss /kɪs/ *n* bacio *m*; **~ of life** respirazione *f* bocca a bocca ● *vt* baciare ● *vi* baciarsi

kit /kɪt/ *n* equipaggiamento *m*, kit *m inv*; *(tools)* attrezzi *mpl*; *(construction ~)* pezzi *mpl* da montare, kit *m inv* ● **kit out** *(pt/pp* **kitted)** equipaggiare. **~bag** *n* sacco *m* a spalla

kitchen /ˈkɪtʃɪn/ *n* cucina *f* ● *attrib* di cucina. **~ette** /kɪtʃɪˈnet/ *n* cucinino *m*

kitchen: **~ ˈgarden** *n* orto *m*. **~ roll** *or* **towel** Scottex® *m inv*. **~ˈsink** *n* lavello *m*

kite /kaɪt/ *n* aquilone *m*

kitten /ˈkɪtn/ *n* gattino *m*

kitty /ˈkɪtɪ/ *n (money)* cassa *f* comune

kleptomaniac /ˈkleptəˈmeɪnɪæk/ *n* cleptomane *mf*

knack /næk/ *n* tecnica *f*; **have the ~ for doing sth** avere la capacità di fare qcsa

knead /niːd/ *vt* impastare

knee /niː/ *n* ginocchio *m*. **~cap** *n* rotula *f*

kneel /niːl/ *vi (pt/pp* **knelt) ~ [down]** inginocchiarsi; **be ~ing** essere inginocchiato

knelt /nelt/ *see* **kneel**

knew /njuː/ *see* **know**

knickers /ˈnɪkəz/ *npl* mutandine *fpl*

knick-knacks /ˈnɪknæks/ *npl* ninnoli *mpl*

knife /naɪf/ *n (pl* **knives)** coltello *m* ● *vt fam* accoltellare

knight /naɪt/ n cavaliere m; (in chess) cavallo m ● vt nominare cavaliere

knit /nɪt/ vt/i (pt/pp **knitted**) lavorare a maglia; **~ one, purl one** un diritto, un rovescio. **~ting** n lavorare m a maglia; (product) lavoro m a maglia. **~ting-needle** n ferro m da calza. **~wear** n maglieria f

knives /naɪvz/ see **knife**

knob /nɒb/ n pomello m; (of stick) pomo m; (of butter) noce f. **~bly** a nodoso; (bony) spigoloso

knock /nɒk/ n colpo m; **there was a ~ at the door** hanno bussato alla porta ● vt bussare a ⟨door⟩; (fam: criticize) denigrare; **~ a hole in sth** fare un buco in qcsa; **~ one's head** battere la testa (**on** contro) ● vi (at door) bussare. **knock about** vt malmenare ● vi fam girovagare. **knock down** vt far cadere; (with fist) stendere con un pugno; (in car) investire; (demolish) abbattere; (fam: reduce) ribassare ⟨price⟩. **knock off** vt (fam: steal) fregare; (fam: complete quickly) fare alla bell'e meglio ● vi (fam: cease work) staccare. **knock out** vt eliminare; (make unconscious) mettere K.O.; (fam: anaesthetize) addormentare. **knock over** vt rovesciare; (in car) investire

knock: **~-down** a **~-down price** prezzo m stracciato. **~er** n battente m. **~-kneed** /-'niːd/ a con gambe storte. **~-out** n (in boxing) knock-out m inv

knot /nɒt/ n nodo m ● vt (pt/pp **knotted**) annodare

know /nəʊ/ v (pt **knew**, pp **known**) ● vt sapere; conoscere ⟨person, place⟩; (recognize) riconoscere; **get to ~ sb** conoscere qcno; **~ how to swim** sapere nuotare ● vi sapere; **did you ~ about this?** lo sapevi? ● n **in the ~** fam al corrente

know: **~-all** n fam sapiente, -a mf. **~-how** n abilità f. **~-ing** a d'intesa. **~ingly** adv (intentionally) consapevolmente; ⟨smile etc⟩ con un'aria d'intesa

knowledge /'nɒlɪdʒ/ n conoscenza f. **~able** /-əbl/ a ben informato

known /nəʊn/ see **know** ● a noto

knuckle /'nʌkl/ n nocca f ● **knuckle down** vi darci sotto (**to** con). **knuckle under** vi sottomettersi

Koran /kə'rɑːn/ n Corano m

Korea /kə'rɪə/ n Corea f. **~n** a & n coreano, -a mf

kosher /'kəʊʃə(r)/ a kasher inv

Kosovo /'kɒsəvəʊ/ n Kosovo m

kowtow /kaʊ'taʊ/ vi piegarsi

kudos /'kjuːdɒs/ n fam gloria f

Ll

lab /læb/ n fam laboratorio m

label /'leɪbl/ n etichetta f ● vt (pt/pp **labelled**) mettere un'etichetta a; fig etichettare ⟨person⟩

laboratory /lə'bɒrətrɪ/ n laboratorio m

laborious /lə'bɔːrɪəs/ a laborioso

labour /'leɪbə(r)/ n lavoro m; (workers) manodopera f; Med doglie fpl; **be in ~** avere le doglie; **L~** Pol partito m laburista ● attrib Pol laburista ● vi lavorare ● vt **~ the point** fig ribadire il concetto. **~er** n manovale m

'labour-saving a che fa risparmiare lavoro e fatica

labyrinth /'læbərɪnθ/ n labirinto m

lace /leɪs/ n pizzo m; (of shoe) laccio m ● attrib di pizzo ● vt allacciare ⟨shoes⟩; correggere ⟨drink⟩

lacerate /'læsəreɪt/ vt lacerare

lack /læk/ n mancanza f ● vt mancare di; **I ~ the time** mi manca il tempo ● vi **be ~ing** mancare; **be ~ing in sth** mancare di qcsa

lackadaisical /lækə'deɪzɪkl/ a senza entusiasmo

laconic /lə'kɒnɪk/ a laconico

lacquer /'lækə(r)/ n lacca f

lad /læd/ n ragazzo m

ladder /'lædə(r)/ n scala f; (in tights) sfilatura f

laden /'leɪdn/ a carico (**with** di)

ladle /'leɪdl/ n mestolo m ● vt **~ [out]** versare ⟨col mestolo⟩

lady /'leɪdɪ/ n signora f; (title) Lady f; **ladies [room]** bagno m per donne

lady: ~**bird** n, Am ~**bug** n coccinella f. ~**like** a signorile

lag¹ /læg/ vi (pt/pp **lagged**) ~ **behind** restare indietro

lag² vt (pt/pp **lagged**) isolare ⟨pipes⟩

lager /ˈlɑːgə(r)/ n birra f chiara

lagoon /ləˈguːn/ n laguna f

laid /leɪd/ see **lay³**

lain /leɪn/ see **lie²**

lair /leə(r)/ n tana f

lake /leɪk/ n lago m

lamb /læm/ n agnello m

lame /leɪm/ a zoppo; fig ⟨argument⟩ zoppicante; ⟨excuse⟩ traballante

lament /ləˈment/ n lamento m ● vt lamentare ● vi lamentarsi

lamentable /ˈlæməntəbl/ a deplorevole

laminated /ˈlæmɪneɪtɪd/ a laminato

lamp /læmp/ n lampada f; (in street) lampione m. ~**post** n lampione m. ~**shade** n paralume m

lance /lɑːns/ n lancia f ● vt Med incidere. ~-ˈcorporal n appuntato m

land /lænd/ n terreno m; ⟨country⟩ paese m; (as opposed to sea) terra f; **plot of** ~ pezzo m di terreno ● vt Naut sbarcare; ⟨fam: obtain⟩ assicurarsi; **be ~ed with sth** fam ritrovarsi fra capo e collo qcsa ● vi Aeron atterrare; (fall) cadere. **land up** vi fam finire

landing /ˈlændɪŋ/ n Naut sbarco m; Aeron atterraggio m; (top of stairs) pianerottolo m. ~**-stage** n pontile m da sbarco. ~ **strip** n pista f d'atterraggio

land: ~**lady** n proprietaria f; (of flat) padrona f di casa. ~**-locked** a privo di sbocco sul mare. ~**lord** n proprietario m; (of flat) padrone m di casa. ~**mark** n punto m di riferimento; fig pietra f miliare. ~**owner** n proprietario, -a mf terriero, -a. ~**scape** /-skeɪp/ n paesaggio m. ~**slide** n frana f; Pol valanga f di voti

lane /leɪn/ n sentiero m; Auto, Sport corsia f

language /ˈlæŋgwɪdʒ/ n lingua f; (speech, style) linguaggio m. ~ **laboratory** n laboratorio m linguistico

languid /ˈlæŋgwɪd/ a languido

languish /ˈlæŋgwɪʃ/ vi languire

lank /læŋk/ a ⟨hair⟩ diritto

lanky /ˈlæŋkɪ/ a (-**ier**, -**iest**) allampanato

lantern /ˈlæntən/ n lanterna f

lap¹ /læp/ n grembo m

lap² n (of journey) tappa f; Sport giro m ● v (pt/pp **lapped**) ● vi ⟨water:⟩ ~ **against** lambire ● vt Sport doppiare

lap³ vt (pt/pp **lapped**) ~ **up** bere avidamente; bersi completamente ⟨lies⟩; credere ciecamente a ⟨praise⟩

lapel /ləˈpel/ n bavero m

lapse /læps/ n sbaglio m; (moral) sbandamento m [morale]; (of time) intervallo m ● vi (expire) scadere; (morally) scivolare; ~ **into** cadere in

laptop /ˈlæptɒp/ n ~ [**computer**] computer m inv portabile, laptop m inv

larceny /ˈlɑːsənɪ/ n furto m

lard /lɑːd/ n strutto m

larder /ˈlɑːdə(r)/ n dispensa f

large /lɑːdʒ/ a grande; ⟨number, amount⟩ grande, grosso; **by and** ~ in complesso; **at** ~ in libertà; (in general) ampiamente; ~**ly** adv ampiamente; ~**ly because of** in gran parte a causa di

lark¹ /lɑːk/ n ⟨bird⟩ allodola f

lark² n (joke) burla f ● **lark about** vi giocherellare

larva /ˈlɑːvə/ n (pl **-vae** /-viː/) larva f

laryngitis /lærɪnˈdʒaɪtɪs/ n laringite f

larynx /ˈlærɪŋks/ n laringe f

lascivious /ləˈsɪvɪəs/ a lascivo

laser /ˈleɪzə(r)/ n laser m inv. ~ [**printer**] n stampante f laser

lash /læʃ/ n frustata f; (eyelash) ciglio m ● vt (whip) frustare; (tie) legare fermamente. **lash out** vi attaccare; (spend) sperperare (**on** in)

lashings /ˈlæʃɪŋz/ npl ~ **of** fam una marea di

lass /læs/ n ragazzina f

lasso /ləˈsuː/ n lazo m

last /lɑːst/ a (final) ultimo; (recent) scorso; ~ **year** l'anno scorso; ~ **night** ieri sera; **at** ~ alla fine; **at** ~! finalmente!; **that's the** ~ **straw** fam questa è l'ultima goccia ● n ultimo, -a mf; **the** ~ **but one** il penultimo ● adv per ultimo; (last time) l'ultima volta ● vi durare. ~**ing** a durevole. ~**ly** adv infine

late /leɪt/ a (delayed) in ritardo; (at a late hour) tardo; (deceased) defunto; **it's** ~ (at night) è tardi; **in** ~ **November** alla fine di Novembre ● adv tardi; **stay up** ~ stare alzati fino a tardi. ~**comer** n ritardatario, -a mf; (to political party etc) nuovo, -a arrivato, -a mf. ~**ly** adv recentemente. ~**ness** n ora f tarda; (delay) ritardo m

latent /ˈleɪtnt/ a latente

later /ˈleɪtə(r)/ a ⟨train⟩ che parte più tardi; ⟨edition⟩ più recente ● adv più tardi; ~ **on** più tardi, dopo

lateral /'lætərəl/ *a* laterale

latest /'leɪtɪst/ *a* ultimo; (*most recent*) più recente; **the ~ [news]** le ultime notizie ● *n* **six o'clock at the ~** alle sei al più tardi

lathe /leɪð/ *n* tornio *m*

lather /'lɑːðə(r)/ *n* schiuma *f* ● *vt* insaponare ● *vi* far schiuma

Latin /'lætɪn/ *a* latino ● *n* latino *m*. **~ A'merica** *n* America *f* Latina. **~ A'merican** *a & n* latino-americano, -a *mf*

latitude /'lætɪtjuːd/ *n Geog* latitudine *f*; *fig* libertà *f* d'azione

latter /'lætə(r)/ *a* ultimo ● *n* **the ~** quest'ultimo. **~ly** *adv* ultimamente

lattice /'lætɪs/ *n* traliccio *m*

Latvia /'lætvɪə/ *n* Lettonia *f*. **~n** *a & n* lettone *mf*

laudable /'lɔːdəbl/ *a* lodevole

laugh /lɑːf/ *n* risata *f* ● *vi* ridere (**at/about** di); **~ at sb** (*mock*) prendere in giro qcno. **~able** /-əbl/ *a* ridicolo. **~ing-stock** *n* zimbello *m*

laughter /'lɑːftə(r)/ *n* risata *f*

launch¹ /lɔːntʃ/ *n* (*boat*) lancia *f*

launch² *n* lancio *m*; (*of ship*) varo *m* ● *vt* lanciare (*rocket, product*); varare (*ship*); sferrare (*attack*)

launder /'lɔːndə(r)/ *vt* lavare e stirare; **~ money** *fig* riciclare denaro sporco. **~ette** /-'dret/ *n* lavanderia *f* automatica

laundry /'lɔːndrɪ/ *n* lavanderia *f*; (*clothes*) bucato *m*

laurel /'lɒrəl/ *n* lauro *m*; **rest on one's ~s** *fig* dormire sugli allori

lava /'lɑːvə/ *n* lava *f*

lavatory /'lævətrɪ/ *n* gabinetto *m*

lavender /'lævəndə(r)/ *n* lavanda *f*

lavish /'lævɪʃ/ *a* copioso; (*wasteful*) prodigo, su **a ~ scale** su vasta scala ● *vt* **~ sth on sb** ricoprire qcno di qcsa. **~ly** *adv* copiosamente

law /lɔː/ *n* legge *f*; **study ~** studiare giurisprudenza, studiare legge; **~ and order** ordine *m* pubblico

law: ~-abiding *a* che rispetta la legge. **~court** *n* tribunale *m*. **~ful** *a* legittimo. **~less** *a* senza legge. **~ school** *n* facoltà *f* di giurisprudenza

lawn /lɔːn/ *n* prato *m* [all'inglese]. **~-mower** *n* tosaerba *m inv*

'law suit *n* causa *f*

lawyer /'lɔːjə(r)/ *n* avvocato *m*

lax /læks/ *a* negligente; (*morals etc*) lassista

laxative /'læksətɪv/ *n* lassativo *m*

laxity /'læksətɪ/ *n* lassismo *m*

lay¹ /leɪ/ *a* laico; *fig* profano

lay² *see* **lie²**

lay³ *vt* (*pt/pp* **laid**) porre, mettere; apparecchiare (*table*) ● *vi* (*hen:*) fare le uova. **lay down** *vt* posare; stabilire (*rules, conditions*). **lay off** *vt* licenziare (*workers*) ● *vi* (*fam: stop*) **~ off!** smettila! **lay out** *vt* (*display, set forth*) esporre; (*plan*) pianificare (*garden*); (*spend*) sborsare; *Typ* impaginare

lay: ~about *n* fannullone, -a *mf*. **~-by** *n* piazzola *f* di sosta

layer /'leɪə(r)/ *n* strato *m*

lay: ~man *n* profano *m*. **~out** *n* disposizione *f*; *Typ* impaginazione *f*, layout *m inv*

laze /leɪz/ *vi* **~ [about]** oziare

laziness /'leɪzɪnɪs/ *n* pigrizia *f*

lazy /'leɪzɪ/ *a* (**-ier**, **-iest**) pigro. **~-bones** *n* poltrone, -a *mf*

lb *abbr* (**pound**) libbra

lead¹ /led/ *n* piombo *m*; (*of pencil*) mina *f*

lead² /liːd/ *n* guida *f*; (*leash*) guinzaglio *m*; (*flex*) filo *m*; (*clue*) indizio *m*; *Theat* parte *f* principale; (*distance ahead*) distanza *f* (**over** su); **in the ~** in testa ● *v* (*pt/pp* **led**) ● *vt* condurre; dirigere (*expedition, party etc*); (*induce*) indurre; **~ the way** mettersi in testa ● *vi* (*be in front*) condurre; (*in race, competition*) essere in testa; (*at cards*) giocare (*per primo*). **lead away** *vt* portar via. **lead to** *vt* portare a. **lead up to** *vt* preludere; **what's this ~ing up to?** dove porta questo?

leaded /'ledɪd/ *a* con piombo

leader /'liːdə(r)/ *n* capo *m*; (*of orchestra*) primo violino *m*; (*in newspaper*) articolo *m* di fondo. **~ship** *n* direzione *f*, leadership *f inv*; **show ~ship** mostrare capacità di comando

lead-'free *a* senza piombo

leading /'liːdɪŋ/ *a* principale; **~ lady/man** attrice *f*/attore *m* principale; **~ question** domanda *f* tendenziosa

leaf /liːf/ *n* (*pl* **leaves**) foglia *f*; (*of table*) asse *f* ● **leaf through** *vt* sfogliare. **~let** *n* dépliant *m inv*; (*advertising*) dépliant *m inv* pubblicitario; (*political*) manifestino *m*

league /liːg/ *n* lega *f*; *Sport* campionato *m*; **be in ~ with** essere in combutta con

leak /liːk/ *n* (*hole*) fessura *f*; *Naut* falla *f*; (*of gas & fig*) fuga ● *vi* colare; (*ship:*) fare acqua; (*liquid, gas:*) fuoriuscire ● *vt* **~ sth to sb** *fig* far trapelare qcsa a qcno. **~y** *a* che perde; *Naut* che fa acqua

lean¹ /li:n/ *a* magro

lean² *v* (*pt/pp* **leaned** *or* **leant** /lent/) ● *vt* appoggiare (**against/on** contro/su) ● *vi* appoggiarsi (**against/on** contro/su); (*not be straight*) pendere; **be ~ing against** essere appoggiato contro; **~ on sb** (*depend on*) appoggiarsi a qcno; (*fam: exert pressure on*) stare alle calcagne di qcno. **lean back** *vi* sporgersi indietro. **lean forward** *vi* piegarsi in avanti. **lean out** *vi* sporgersi. **lean over** *vi* piegarsi

leaning /'li:nɪŋ/ *a* pendente; **the L~ Tower of Pisa** la torre di Pisa, la torre pendente ● *n* tendenza *f*

leap /li:p/ *n* salto *m* ● *vi* (*pt/pp* **leapt** /lept/ *or* **leaped**) saltare; **he leapt at it** *fam* l'ha preso al volo. **~-frog** *n* cavallina *f*. **~ year** *n* anno *m* bisestile

learn /lɜ:n/ *v* (*pt/pp* **learnt** *or* **learned**) ● *vt* imparare; **~ to swim** imparare a nuotare; **I have ~ed that...** (*heard*) sono venuto a sapere che... ● *vi* imparare

learn|ed /'lɜ:nɪd/ *a* colto. **~er** *n also Auto* principiante *mf*. **~ing** *n* cultura *f*

lease /li:s/ *n* contratto *m* d'affitto; (*rental*) affitto *m* ● *vt* affittare

leash /li:ʃ/ *n* guinzaglio *m*

least /li:st/ *a* più piccolo; ⟨*amount*⟩ minore; **you've got ~ luggage** hai meno bagagli di tutti ● *n* **the ~** il meno; **at ~** almeno; **not in the ~** niente affatto ● *adv* meno; **the ~ expensive wine** il vino meno caro

leather /'leðə(r)/ *n* pelle *f*; (*of soles*) cuoio *m* ● *attrib* di pelle/cuoio. **~y** *a* ⟨*meat, skin*⟩ duro

leave /li:v/ *n* (*holiday*) congedo *m*; *Mil* licenza *f*; **on ~** in congedo/licenza ● *v* (*pt/pp* **left**) ● *vt* lasciare; uscire da ⟨*house, office*⟩; (*forget*) dimenticare; **there is nothing left** non è rimasto niente ● *vi* andare via; ⟨*train, bus:*⟩ partire. **leave behind** *vt* lasciare; (*forget*) dimenticare. **leave out** *vt* omettere; (*not put away*) lasciare fuori

leaves /li:vz/ *see* **leaf**

Leban|on /'lebənən/ *n* Libano *m* **~ese** /-'ni:z/ *a* & *n* libanese *mf*

lecherous /'letʃərəs/ *a* lascivo

lectern /'lektɜ:n/ *n* leggio *m*

lecture /'lektʃə(r)/ *n* conferenza *f*; *Univ* lezione *f*; (*reproof*) ramanzina *f* ● *vi* fare una conferenza (**on** su); *Univ* insegnare (**on sth** qcsa) ● *vt* **~ sb** rimproverare qcno. **~r** *n* conferenziere, -a *mf*; *Univ* docente *mf* universitario, -a

led /led/ *see* **lead²**

ledge /ledʒ/ *n* cornice *f*; (*of window*) davanzale *m*

ledger /'ledʒə(r)/ *n* libro *m* mastro

leech /li:tʃ/ *n* sanguisuga *f*

leek /li:k/ *n* porro *m*

leer /lɪə(r)/ *n* sguardo *m* libidinoso ● *vi* **~** [**at**] guardare in modo libidinoso

leeway /'li:weɪ/ *n fig* libertà *f* di azione

left¹ /left/ *see* **leave**

left² /left/ *a* sinistro ● *adv* a sinistra ● *n also Pol* sinistra *f*; **on the ~** a sinistra;

left: **~-'handed** *a* mancino. **~-'luggage** [**office**] *n* deposito *m* bagagli. **~overs** *npl* rimasugli *mpl*. **~-'wing** *a Pol* di sinistra

leg /leg/ *n* gamba *f*; (*of animal*) zampa *f*; (*of journey*) tappa *f*; *Culin* (*of chicken*) coscia *f*; (*of lamb*) cosciotto *m*

legacy /'legəsɪ/ *n* lascito *m*

legal /'li:gl/ *a* legale; **take ~ action** intentare un'azione legale. **~ly** *adv* legalmente

legality /lɪ'gælətɪ/ *n* legalità *f*

legalize /'li:gəlaɪz/ *vt* legalizzare

legend /'ledʒənd/ *n* leggenda *f*. **~ary** *a* leggendario

legib|le /'ledʒəbl/ *a* leggibile. **~ly** *adv* in modo leggibile

legislat|e /'ledʒɪsleɪt/ *vi* legiferare. **~ion** /-'leɪʃn/ *n* legislazione *f*

legislat|ive /'ledʒɪslətɪv/ *a* legislativo. **~ure** /-leɪtʃə(r)/ *n* legislatura *f*

legitima|te /lɪ'dʒɪtɪmət/ *a* legittimo; ⟨*excuse*⟩ valido

leisure /'leʒə(r)/ *n* tempo *m* libero; **at your ~** con comodo. **~ly** *a* senza fretta

lemon /'lemən/ *n* limone *m*. **~ade** /-'neɪd/ *n* limonata *f*

lend /lend/ *vt* (*pt/pp* **lent**) prestare; **~ a hand** *fig* dare una mano. **~ing library** *n* biblioteca *f* per il prestito

length /leŋθ/ *n* lunghezza *f*; (*piece*) pezzo *m*; (*of wallpaper*) parte *f*; (*of visit*) durata *f*; **at ~** a lungo; (*at last*) alla fine

length|en /'leŋθən/ *vt* allungare ● *vi* allungarsi. **~ways** *adv* per lungo

lengthy /'leŋθɪ/ *a* (**-ier, -iest**) lungo

lenien|ce /'li:nɪəns/ *n* indulgenza *f*. **~t** *a* indulgente

lens /lenz/ *n* lente *f*; *Phot* obiettivo *m*; (*of eye*) cristallino *m*

Lent /lent/ *n* Quaresima *f*

lent *see* **lend**

lentil /'lentl/ *n Bot* lenticchia *f*

Leo /'li:əʊ/ *n Astr* Leone *m*

leopard /'lepəd/ *n* leopardo *m*

leotard /'li:əta:d/ *n* body *m inv*

leprosy /'leprəsɪ/ n lebbra f

lesbian /'lezbɪən/ a lesbico ● n lesbica f

less /les/ a meno di; ~ **and** ~ sempre meno ● adv & prep meno ● n meno m

lessen /'lesn/ vt/i diminuire

lesser /'lesə(r)/ a minore

lesson /'lesn/ n lezione f

lest /lest/ conj liter per timore che

let /let/ vt (pt/pp **let**, pres p **letting**) lasciare, permettere; (rent) affittare; ~ **alone** (not to mention) tanto meno; **'to** ~' 'affittasi'; ~ **us go** andiamo; ~ **sb do sth** lasciare fare qcsa a qcno, permettere a qcno di fare qcsa; ~ **me know** fammi sapere; **just** ~ **him try!** che ci provi solamente!; ~ **oneself in for sth** fam impelagarsi in qcsa. **let down** vt sciogliersi ⟨hair⟩; abbassare ⟨blinds⟩; (lengthen) allungare; (disappoint) deludere; **don't** ~ **me down** conto su di te. **let in** vt far entrare. **let off** vt far partire; (not punish) perdonare; ~ **sb off doing sth** abbonare qcsa a qcno. **let out** vt far uscire; (make larger) allargare; emettere ⟨scream, groan⟩. **let through** vt far passare. **let up** vi fam diminuire

'let-down n delusione f

lethal /'li:θl/ a letale

letharg|ic /lɪ'θɑ:dʒɪk/ a apatico. ~**y** /'leθədʒɪ/ n apatia f

letter /'letə(r)/ n lettera f. ~**-box** n buca f per le lettere. ~**head** n carta f intestata. ~**ing** n caratteri mpl

lettuce /'letɪs/ n lattuga f

'let-up n fam pausa f

leukaemia /lu:'ki:mɪə/ n leucemia f

level /'levl/ a piano; (in height, competition) allo stesso livello; ⟨spoonful⟩ raso; **draw** ~ **with sb** affiancare qcno ● n livello m; **on the** ~ fam giusto ● vt (pt/pp **levelled**) livellare; (aim) puntare (**at** su)

level: ~ **'crossing** n passaggio m a livello. ~**-headed** a posato

lever /'li:və(r)/ n leva f ● **lever up** vt sollevare (con una leva). ~**age** /-rɪdʒ/ n azione f di una leva; fig influenza f

levy /'levɪ/ vt (pt/pp **levied**) imporre ⟨tax⟩

lewd /lju:d/ a osceno

liabilit|y /laɪə'bɪlətɪ/ n responsabilità f; (fam: burden) peso m; ~**ies** pl debiti mpl

liable /'laɪəbl/ a responsabile (**for** di); **be** ~ **to** ⟨rain, break etc⟩ rischiare di; (tend to) tendere a

liaise /lɪ'eɪz/ vi fam essere in contatto

liaison /lɪ'eɪzɒn/ n contatti mpl; Mil collegamento m; (affair) relazione f

liar /'laɪə(r)/ n bugiardo, -a mf

libel /'laɪbl/ n diffamazione f ● vt (pt/pp **libelled**) diffamare. ~**lous** a diffamatorio

liberal /'lɪb(ə)rəl/ a (tolerant) di larghe vedute; (generous) generoso. **L~** a Pol liberale ● n liberale mf

liberat|e /'lɪbəreɪt/ vt liberare. ~**ed** a ⟨woman⟩ emancipata. ~**ion** /-'reɪʃn/ n liberazione f; (of women) emancipazione f. ~**or** n liberatore, -trice mf

liberty /'lɪbətɪ/ n libertà f; **take the** ~ **of doing sth** prendersi la libertà di fare qcsa; **be at** ~ **to do sth** essere libero di fare qcsa

Libra /'li:brə/ n Astr Bilancia f

librarian /laɪ'breərɪən/ n bibliotecario, -a mf

library /'laɪbrərɪ/ n biblioteca f

Libya /'lɪbɪə/ n Libia f. ~**n** a & n libico, -a mf

lice /laɪs/ see **louse**

licence /'laɪsns/ n licenza f; (for TV) canone m televisivo; (for driving) patente f; (freedom) sregolatezza f. ~**-plate** n targa f

license /'laɪsns/ vt autorizzare; **be** ~**d** ⟨car:⟩ avere il bollo; ⟨restaurant:⟩ essere autorizzato alla vendita di alcolici

licentious /laɪ'senʃəs/ a licenzioso

lick /lɪk/ n leccata f; **a** ~ **of paint** una passata leggera di pittura ● vt leccare; (fam: defeat) battere; leccarsi ⟨lips⟩

lid /lɪd/ n coperchio m; (of eye) palpebra f

lie¹ /laɪ/ n bugia f; **tell a** ~ mentire ● vi (pt/pp **lied**, pres p **lying**) mentire

lie² vi (pt **lay**, pp **lain**, pres p **lying**) ⟨person:⟩ sdraiarsi; ⟨object:⟩ stare; (remain) rimanere; **leave sth lying about** or **around** lasciare qcsa in giro. **lie down** vi sdraiarsi

'lie: ~**-down** n **have a** ~**-down** fare un riposino. ~**-in** n fam **have a** ~**-in** restare a letto fino a tardi

lieu /lju:/ n **in** ~ **of** in luogo di

lieutenant /lef'tenənt/ n tenente m

life /laɪf/ n (pl **lives**) vita f

life: ~**-belt** n salvagente m. ~**-boat** n lancia f di salvataggio; (on ship) scialuppa f di salvataggio. ~**buoy** n salvagente m. ~**-guard** n bagnino m. ~**insurance** n assicurazione f sulla vita. ~**-jacket** n giubbotto m di salvataggio. ~**less** a inanimato. ~**like** a realistico. ~**long** a di tutta la vita. ~**-size[d]** a in grandezza naturale. ~**time** n vita f; **the**

chance of a ~time un'occasione unica

lift /lɪft/ n ascensore m; *Auto* passaggio m ● vt sollevare; revocare ⟨*restrictions*⟩; (*fam: steal*) rubare ● vi ⟨*fog:*⟩ alzarsi. **lift up** vt sollevare

'lift-off n decollo m (*di razzo*)

ligament /'lɪɡəmənt/ n *Anat* legamento m

light¹ /laɪt/ a (*not dark*) luminoso; **~ green** verde chiaro ● n luce f; (*lamp*) lampada f; **in the ~ of** *fig* alla luce di; **have you got a ~?** ha da accendere?; **come to ~** essere rivelato ● vt (*pt/pp* **lit** or **lighted**) accendere; (*illuminate*) illuminare. **light up** vi ⟨*face:*⟩ illuminarsi

light² a (*not heavy*) leggero ● adv **travel ~** viaggiare con poco bagaglio

'light-bulb n lampadina f

lighten¹ /'laɪtn/ vt illuminare

lighten² vt alleggerire ⟨*load*⟩

lighter /'laɪtə(r)/ n accendino m

light: ~-'fingered a svelto di mano. **~-'headed** a sventato. **~-'hearted** a spensierato. **~house** n faro m. **~ing** n illuminazione f. **~ly** adv leggermente; ⟨*accuse*⟩ con leggerezza; (*without concern*) senza dare importanza alla cosa; **get off ~ly** cavarsela a buon mercato. **~ness** n leggerezza f

lightning /'laɪtnɪŋ/ n lampo m, fulmine m. **~-conductor** n parafulmine m

light: ~weight a leggero ● n (*in boxing*) peso m leggero. **~ year** n anno m luce

like¹ /laɪk/ a simile ● prep come; **~ this/that** così; **what's he ~?** com'è? ● conj (*fam: as*) come; (*Am: as if*) come se

like² vt piacere, gradire; **I should** or **would ~** vorrei, gradirei; **I ~ him** mi piace; **I ~ this car** mi piace questa macchina; **I ~ dancing** mi piace ballare; **I ~ that!** *fam* questa mi è piaciuta! ● n **~s and dislikes** pl gusti mpl

like|able /'laɪkəbl/ a simpatico. **~lihood** /-lɪhʊd/ n probabilità f. **~ly** a (**-ier, -iest**) probabile ● adv probabilmente; **not ~ly!** *fam* neanche per sogno!

like-'minded a con gusti affini

liken /'laɪkən/ vt paragonare (**to** a)

like|ness /'laɪknɪs/ n somiglianza f. **'~wise** adv lo stesso

liking /'laɪkɪŋ/ n gusto m; **is it to your**

~? è di suo gusto?; **take a ~ to sb** prendere qcno in simpatia

lilac /'laɪlək/ n lillà m ● a color lillà

lily /'lɪlɪ/ n giglio m. **~ of the valley** n mughetto m

limb /lɪm/ n arto m

limber /'lɪmbə(r)/ vi **~ up** sciogliersi i muscoli

lime¹ /laɪm/ n (*fruit*) cedro m; (*tree*) tiglio m

lime² n calce f. **'~light** n **be in the ~light** essere molto in vista. **'~stone** n calcare m

limit /'lɪmɪt/ n limite m; **that's the ~!** *fam* questo è troppo! ● vt limitare (**to** a). **~ation** /-ɪ'teɪʃn/ n limite m. **~ed** a ristretto; **~ed company** società f inv a responsabilità limitata

limousine /'lɪməzi:n/ n limousine f inv

limp¹ /lɪmp/ n andatura f zoppicante; **have a ~** zoppicare ● vi zoppicare

limp² a floscio

line¹ /laɪn/ n linea f; (*length of rope, cord*) filo m; (*of writing*) riga f; (*of poem*) verso m; (*row*) fila f; (*wrinkle*) ruga f; (*of business*) settore m; (*Am: queue*) coda f; **in ~ with** in conformità con ● vt segnare; fiancheggiare ⟨*street*⟩. **line up** vi allinearsi ● vt allineare

line² vt foderare ⟨*garment*⟩

linear /'lɪnɪə(r)/ a lineare

lined¹ /laɪnd/ a ⟨*face*⟩ rugoso; ⟨*paper*⟩ a righe

lined² a ⟨*garment*⟩ foderato

linen /'lɪnɪn/ n lino m; (*articles*) biancheria f ● attrib di lino

liner /'laɪnə(r)/ n nave f di linea

'linesman n *Sport* guardalinee m inv

linger /'lɪŋɡə(r)/ vi indugiare

lingerie /'lɒ̃ʒərɪ/ n biancheria f intima (*da donna*)

linguist /'lɪŋɡwɪst/ n linguista mf

linguistic /lɪŋ'ɡwɪstɪk/ a linguistico. **~s** n linguistica fsg

lining /'laɪnɪŋ/ n (*of garment*) fodera f; (*of brakes*) guarnizione f

link /lɪŋk/ n (*of chain*) anello m; *fig* legame m ● vt collegare. **link up** vi unirsi (**with** a); *TV* collegarsi

lino /'laɪnəʊ/ n, **linoleum** /lɪ'nəʊlɪəm/ n linoleum m

lint /lɪnt/ n garza f

lion /'laɪən/ n leone m. **~ess** n leonessa f

lip /lɪp/ n labbro m (*pl* labbra f); (*edge*) bordo m

lip: ~-read vi leggere le labbra; **~-reading** n lettura f delle labbra. **~-service** n **pay ~-service to** approvare soltanto a parole. **~salve** *n* burro *m* [di] cacao. **~stick** *n* rossetto *m*

liqueur /lɪˈkjʊə(r)/ *n* liquore *m*

liquid /ˈlɪkwɪd/ *n* liquido *m* ● *a* liquido

liquidat|e /ˈlɪkwɪdeɪt/ *vt* liquidare. **~ion** /-ˈdeɪʃn/ *n* liquidazione *f*; **go into ~ion** *Comm* andare in liquidazione

liquidize /ˈlɪkwɪdaɪz/ *vt* rendere liquido. **~r** *n Culin* frullatore *m*

liquor /ˈlɪkə(r)/ *n* bevanda *f* alcoolica

liquorice /ˈlɪkərɪs/ *n* liquirizia *f*

liquor store *n Am* negozio *m* di alcolici

lisp /lɪsp/ *n* pronuncia *f* con la lisca ● *vi* parlare con la lisca

list¹ /lɪst/ *n* lista *f* ● *vt* elencare

list² *vi* ⟨ship:⟩ inclinarsi

listen /ˈlɪsn/ *vi* ascoltare; **~ to** ascoltare. **~er** *n* ascoltatore, -trice *mf*

listings /ˈlɪstɪŋz/ *npl TV* programma *m* tv

listless /ˈlɪstlɪs/ *a* svogliato

lit /lɪt/ *see* **light¹**

literacy /ˈlɪtərəsɪ/ *n* alfabetizzazione *f*

literal /ˈlɪtərəl/ *a* letterale. **~ly** *adv* letteralmente

literary /ˈlɪtərərɪ/ *a* letterario

literate /ˈlɪtərət/ *a* **be ~** saper leggere e scrivere

literature /ˈlɪtrətʃə(r)/ *n* letteratura *f*

Lithuania /lɪθjʊˈeɪnɪə/ *n* Lituania *f*. **~n** *a* & *n* lituano, -a *mf*

litigation /lɪtɪˈgeɪʃn/ *n* causa *f* [giudiziaria]

litre /ˈliːtə(r)/ *n* litro *m*

litter /ˈlɪtə(r)/ *n* immondizie *fpl*; *Zool* figliata *f* ● *vt* **be ~ed with** essere ingombrato di. **~-bin** *n* bidone *m* della spazzatura

little /ˈlɪtl/ *a* piccolo; (*not much*) poco ● *adv* & *n* poco *m*; **a ~** un po'; **a ~ water** un po' d'acqua; **a ~ better** un po' meglio; **~ by ~** a poco a poco

liturgy /ˈlɪtədʒɪ/ *n* liturgia *f*

live¹ /laɪv/ *a* vivo; ⟨ammunition⟩ carico; **~ broadcast** trasmissione *f* in diretta; **be ~** *Electr* essere sotto tensione; **~ wire** *n fig* persona *f* dinamica ● *adv* ⟨broadcast⟩ in diretta

live² /lɪv/ *vi* vivere; (*reside*) abitare; **~ with** convivere con. **live down** *vt* far dimenticare. **live off** *vt* vivere alle spalle di. **live on** *vt* vivere di ● *vi* sopravvivere. **live up** *vt* **~ it up** far la bella vita. **live up to** *vt* essere all'altezza di

liveli|hood /ˈlaɪvlɪhʊd/ *n* mezzi *mpl* di sostentamento. **~ness** *n* vivacità *f*

lively /ˈlaɪvlɪ/ *a* (-ier, -iest) vivace

liven /ˈlaɪvn/ *vt* **~ up** vivacizzare ● *vi* vivacizzarsi

liver /ˈlɪvə(r)/ *n* fegato *m*

lives /laɪvz/ *see* **life**

livestock /ˈlaɪv-/ *n* bestiame *m*

livid /ˈlɪvɪd/ *a fam* livido

living /ˈlɪvɪŋ/ *a* vivo ● *n* **earn one's ~** guadagnarsi da vivere; **the ~** *pl* i vivi. **~-room** *n* soggiorno *m*

lizard /ˈlɪzəd/ *n* lucertola *f*

load /ləʊd/ *n* carico *m*; **~s of** *fam* un sacco di ● *vt* caricare. **~ed** *a* carico; (*fam: rich*) ricchissimo

loaf¹ /ləʊf/ *n* (*pl* **loaves**) pagnotta *f*

loaf² *vi* oziare

loan /ləʊn/ *n* prestito *m*; **on ~** in prestito ● *vt* prestare

loath /ləʊθ/ *a* **be ~ to do sth** essere restio a fare qcsa

loath|e /ləʊð/ *vt* detestare. **~ing** *n* disgusto *m*. **~some** *a* disgustoso

loaves /ləʊvz/ *see* **loaf**

lobby /ˈlɒbɪ/ *n* atrio *m*; *Pol* gruppo *m* di pressione, lobby *m inv*

lobster /ˈlɒbstə(r)/ *n* aragosta *f*

local /ˈləʊkl/ *a* locale; **I'm not ~** non sono del posto ● *n* abitante *mf* del luogo; (*fam: public house*) pub *m inv* locale. **~ au'thority** *n* autorità *f* locale. **~ call** *n Teleph* telefonata *f* urbana. **~ government** *n* autorità *f inv* locale

locality /ləʊˈkælətɪ/ *n* zona *f*

localized /ˈləʊkəlaɪzd/ *a* localizzato

locally /ˈləʊkəlɪ/ *adv* localmente; ⟨live, work⟩ nei paraggi

'local network *n Comput* rete *f* locale

locat|e /ləʊˈkeɪt/ *vt* situare; trovare ⟨person⟩; **be ~ed** essere situato. **~ion** /-ˈkeɪʃn/ *n* posizione *f*; **filmed on ~ion** girato in esterni

lock¹ /lɒk/ *n* (*of hair*) ciocca *f*

lock² /lɒk/ *n* (*on door*) serratura *f*; (*on canal*) chiusa *f* ● *vt* chiudere a chiave; bloccare ⟨wheels⟩ ● *vi* chiudersi. **lock in** *vt* chiudere dentro. **lock out** *vt* chiudere fuori. **lock up** *vt* (*in prison*) mettere dentro ● *vi* chiudere

locker /ˈlɒkə(r)/ *n* armadietto *m*

locket /ˈlɒkɪt/ *n* medaglione *m*

lock: ~-out *n* serrata *f*. **~smith** *n* fabbro *m*

locomotive /ləʊkəˈməʊtɪv/ *n* locomotiva *f*

locum /ˈləʊkəm/ *n* sostituto, -a *mf*

locust /ˈləʊkəst/ *n* locusta *f*

lodge /lɒdʒ/ *n* (*porter's*) portineria *f*; (*masonic*) loggia *f* ● *vt* presentare ⟨claim, complaint⟩; (*with bank, solicitor*) depositare; **be ~d** essersi conficcato ● *vi* essere a pensione (**with** da); (*become fixed*) conficcarsi. **~r** *n* inquilino, -a *mf*

lodgings /'lɒdʒɪŋz/ *npl* camere *fpl* in affitto

loft /lɒft/ *n* soffitta *f*

lofty /'lɒftɪ/ *a* (**-ier, -iest**) alto; (*haughty*) altezzoso

log /lɒg/ *n* ceppo *m*; *Auto* libretto *m* di circolazione; *Naut* giornale *m* di bordo ● *vt* (*pt/pp* **logged**) registrare. **log on to** *vt Comput* connettersi a

logarithm /'lɒgərɪðm/ *n* logaritmo *m*

'log-book *n Naut* giornale *m* di bordo; *Auto* libretto *m* di circolazione

loggerheads /'lɒgə-/ *npl* **be at ~** *fam* essere in totale disaccordo

logic /'lɒdʒɪk/ *n* logica *f*. **~al** *a* logico. **~ally** *adv* logicamente

logistics /lə'dʒɪstɪks/ *npl* logistica *f*

logo /'ləʊgəʊ/ *n* logo *m inv*

loin /lɔɪn/ *n Culin* lombata *f*

loiter /'lɔɪtə(r)/ *vi* gironzolare

loll|ipop /'lɒlɪpɒp/ *n* lecca-lecca *m inv*. **~y** *n* lecca-lecca *m inv*; (*fam: money*) quattrini *mpl*

London /'lʌndən/ *n* Londra *f* ● *attrib* londinese, di Londra. **~er** *n* londinese *mf*

lone /ləʊn/ *a* solitario. **~liness** *n* solitudine *f*

lonely /'ləʊnlɪ/ *a* (**-ier, -iest**) solitario; (*person*) solo

lone|r /'ləʊnə(r)/ *n* persona *f* solitaria. **~some** *a* solo

long[1] /lɒŋ/ *a* lungo; **a ~ time** molto tempo; **a ~ way** distante; **in the ~ run** a lungo andare; (*in the end*) alla fin fine ● *adv* a lungo, lungamente; **how ~ is it?** quanto è lungo?; (*in time*) quanto dura?; **all day ~** tutto il giorno; **not ~ ago** non molto tempo fa; **before ~** fra breve; **he's no ~er here** non è più qui; **as** *or* **so ~as** finché; (*provided that*) purché; **so ~!** *fam* ciao!; **will you be ~?** [ti] ci vuole molto?

long[2] *vi* **~ for** desiderare ardentemente

long-'distance *a* a grande distanza; *Sport* di fondo; (*call*) interurbano

'longhand *n* **in ~** in scrittura ordinaria

longing /'lɒŋɪŋ/ *a* desideroso ● *n* brama *f*. **~ly** *adv* con desiderio

longitude /'lɒŋgɪtjuːd/ *n Geog* longitudine *f*

long: ~ jump *n* salto *m* in lungo. **~-life 'milk** *n* latte *m* a lunga conservazione.

~-lived /-lɪvd/ *a* longevo. **~-range** *a Mil, Aeron* a lunga portata; (*forecast*) a lungo termine. **~-sighted** *a* presbite. **~-sleeved** *a* a maniche lunghe. **~-suffering** *a* infinitamente paziente. **~-term** *a* a lunga scadenza. **~ wave** *n* onde *fpl* lunghe. **~-winded** /-'wɪndɪd/ *a* prolisso

loo /luː/ *n fam* gabinetto *m*

look /lʊk/ *n* occhiata *f*; (*appearance*) aspetto *m*; [**good**] **~s** *pl* bellezza *f*; **have a ~ at** dare un'occhiata a ● *vi* guardare; (*seem*) sembrare; **~ here!** mi ascolti bene!; **~ at** guardare; **~ for** cercare; **~ like** (*resemble*) assomigliare a. **look after** *vt* badare a. **look down** *vi* guardare in basso; **~ down on sb** *fig* guardare dall'alto in basso qcno. **look forward to** *vt* essere impaziente di. **look in on** *vt* passare da. **look into** *vt* (*examine*) esaminare. **look out** *vi* guardare fuori; (*take care*) fare attenzione; **~ out for** cercare; **~ out!** attento! **look round** *vi* girarsi; (*in shop, town etc*) dare un'occhiata. **look through** *vt* dare un'occhiata a (*script, notes*). **look up** *vi* guardare in alto; **~ up to sb** *fig* rispettare qcno ● *vt* cercare [nel dizionario] (*word*); (*visit*) andare a trovare

'look-out /'lʊkaʊt/ *n* guardia *f*; (*prospect*) prospettiva *f*; **be on the ~ for** tenere gli occhi aperti per

loom /luːm/ *vi* apparire; *fig* profilarsi

loony /'luːnɪ/ *a & n fam* matto, -a *mf*. **~ bin** *n* manicomio *m*

loop /luːp/ *n* cappio *m*; (*on garment*) passante *m*. **~hole** *n* (*in the law*) scappatoia *f*

loose /luːs/ *a* libero; (*knot*) allentato; (*page*) staccato; (*clothes*) largo; (*morals*) dissoluto; (*inexact*) vago; **be at a ~ end** non sapere cosa fare; **come ~** (*knot:*) sciogliersi; **set ~** liberare. **~ 'change** *n* spiccioli *mpl*. **~ly** *adv* scorrevolmente; (*defined*) vagamente

loosen /'luːsn/ *vt* sciogliere

loot /luːt/ *n* bottino *m* ● *vt/i* depredare. **~er** *n* predatore, -trice *mf*. **~ing** *n* saccheggio *m*

lop /lɒp/ **~ off** *vt* (*pt/pp* **lopped**) potare

lop'sided *a* sbilenco

lord /lɔːd/ *n* signore *m*; (*title*) Lord *m*; **House of L~s** Camera *f* dei Lords; **the L~'s Prayer** il Padrenostro; **good L~!** Dio mio!

lore /lɔː(r)/ *n* tradizioni *fpl*

lorry /'lɒrɪ/ *n* camion *m inv*; **~ driver** camionista *m*

lose /luːz/ *v* (*pt/pp* **lost**) ● *vt* perdere ● *vi* perdere; (*clock:*) essere indietro; **get lost** perdersi; **get lost!** *fam* va a quel paese! **~r** *n* perdente *mf*

loss /lɒs/ n perdita f; **~es** pl Comm perdite fpl; **be at a ~** essere perplesso; **be at a ~ for words** non trovare le parole

lost /lɒst/ see **lose** ● a perduto. ~ 'property office n ufficio m oggetti smarriti

lot¹ /lɒt/ n (at auction) lotto m; **draw ~s** tirare a sorte

lot² n **the ~** il tutto; **a ~ of, ~s of** molto/i; **the ~ of you** tutti voi; **it has changed a ~** è cambiato molto

lotion /'ləʊʃn/ n lozione f

lottery /'lɒtərɪ/ n lotteria f. **~ ticket** n biglietto m della lotteria

loud /laʊd/ a sonoro, alto; ⟨colours⟩ sgargiante ● adv forte; **out ~** ad alta voce. **~ 'hailer** n megafono m. **~ly** adv forte. **~ 'speaker** n altoparlante m

lounge /laʊndʒ/ n salotto m; (in hotel) salone m ● vi poltrire. **~ suit** n vestito m da uomo, completo m da uomo

louse /laʊs/ n (pl **lice**) pidocchio m

lousy /'laʊzɪ/ a (**-ier, -iest**) fam schifoso

lout /laʊt/ n zoticone m. **~ish** a rozzo

lovable /'lʌvəbl/ a adorabile

love /lʌv/ n amore m; Tennis zero m; **in ~** innamorato (**with** di) ● vt amare ⟨person, country⟩; **I ~ watching tennis** mi piace molto guardare il tennis. **~-affair** n relazione f [sentimentale]. **~ letter** n lettera f d'amore

lovely /'lʌvlɪ/ a (**-ier, -iest**) bello; (in looks) bello, attraente; (in character) piacevole; ⟨meal⟩ delizioso; **have a ~ time** divertirsi molto

lover /'lʌvə(r)/ n amante mf

love: ~ song n canzone f d'amore. **~ story** n storia f d'amore

loving /'lʌvɪŋ/ a affettuoso

low /ləʊ/ a basso; (depressed) giù inv ● adv basso; **feel ~** sentirsi giù ● n minimo m; Meteorol depressione f; **at an all-time ~** ⟨prices etc⟩ al livello minimo

low: ~brow a di scarsa cultura. **~-cut** a ⟨dress⟩ scollato

lower /'ləʊə(r)/ a & adv see **low** ● vt abbassare; **~ oneself** abbassarsi

low: ~-'fat a magro. **~-'grade** a di qualità inferiore. **~-key** fig moderato. **~lands** /-ləndz/ npl pianure fpl. **~ 'tide** n bassa marea f

loyal /'lɔɪəl/ a leale. **~ty** n lealtà f

lozenge /'lɒzɪndʒ/ n losanga f; ⟨tablet⟩ pastiglia f

LP n abbr **long-playing record**

Ltd abbr (**Limited**) s.r.l.

lubricant /'lu:brɪkənt/ n lubrificante m

lubricat|e /'lu:brɪkeɪt/ vt lubrificare. **~ion** /-'keɪʃn/ n lubrificazione f

lucid /'lu:sɪd/ a ⟨explanation⟩ chiaro; (sane) lucido. **~ity** /-'sɪdətɪ/ n lucidità f; (of explanation) chiarezza f

luck /lʌk/ n fortuna f; **bad ~** sfortuna f; **good ~!** buona fortuna! **~ily** adv fortunatamente

lucky /'lʌkɪ/ a (**-ier, -iest**) fortunato; **be ~** essere fortunato; ⟨thing:⟩ portare fortuna. **~ 'charm** n portafortuna m inv

lucrative /'lu:krətɪv/ a lucrativo

ludicrous /'lu:dɪkrəs/ a ridicolo. **~ly** adv ⟨expensive, complex⟩ eccessivamente

lug /lʌg/ vt (pt/pp **lugged**) fam trascinare

luggage /'lʌgɪdʒ/ n bagaglio m; **~-rack** n portabagagli m inv. **~ trolley** n carrello m portabagagli. **~-van** n bagagliaio m

lukewarm /'lu:k-/ a tiepido; fig poco entusiasta

lull /lʌl/ n pausa f ● vt **~ to sleep** cullare

lullaby /'lʌləbaɪ/ n ninnananna f

lumbago /lʌm'beɪgəʊ/ n lombaggine f

lumber /'lʌmbə(r)/ n cianfrusaglie fpl; (Am: timber) legname m ● vt fam **~ sb with sth** affibbiare qcsa a qcno. **~ jack** n tagliaboschi m inv

luminous /'lu:mɪnəs/ a luminoso

lump¹ /lʌmp/ n (of sugar) zolletta f; (swelling) gonfiore m; (in breast) nodulo m; (in sauce) grumo m ● vt **~ together** ammucchiare

lump² vt **~ it** fam **you'll just have to ~ it** che ti piaccia o no è così

lump sum n somma f globale

lumpy /'lʌmpɪ/ a (**-ier, -iest**) grumoso

lunacy /'lu:nəsɪ/ n follia f

lunar /'lu:nə(r)/ a lunare

lunatic /'lu:nətɪk/ n pazzo, -a mf

lunch /lʌntʃ/ n pranzo m ● vi pranzare

luncheon /'lʌntʃn/ n (formal) pranzo m. **~ meat** n carne f in scatola. **~ voucher** n buono m pasto

lunch: ~-hour n intervallo m per il pranzo. **~-time** n ora f di pranzo

lung /lʌŋ/ n polmone m. **~ cancer** n cancro m al polmone

lunge /lʌndʒ/ vi lanciarsi (**at** su)

lurch¹ /lɜ:tʃ/ n **leave in the ~** fam lasciare nei guai

lurch² vi barcollare

lure /lʊə(r)/ n esca f; fig lusinga f ● vt adescare

lurid /'lʊərɪd/ a (*gaudy*) sgargiante; (*sensational*) sensazionalistico

lurk /lɜːk/ vi appostarsi

luscious /'lʌʃəs/ a saporito; *fig* sexy *inv*

lush /lʌʃ/ a lussureggiante

lust /lʌst/ n lussuria f ● vi ~ **after** desiderare [fortemente]. ~**ful** a lussurioso

lusty /'lʌstɪ/ a (-ier, -iest) vigoroso

lute /luːt/ n liuto m

luxuriant /lʌg'ʒʊərɪənt/ a lussureg-giante

luxurious /lʌg'ʒʊərɪəs/ a lussuoso

luxury /'lʌkʃərɪ/ n lusso m ● *attrib* di lusso

lying /'laɪɪŋ/ *see* **lie**[1] & [2] ● n mentire m

lymph gland /'lɪmf/ n linfoghiandola f

lynch /lɪmtʃ/ vt linciare

lynx /lɪŋks/ n lince f

lyric /'lɪrɪk/ a lirico. ~**al** a lirico; (*fam: enthusiastic*) entusiasta. ~**s** npl parole fpl

....

Mm

....

mac /mæk/ n fam impermeabile m

macabre /mə'kɑːbr/ a macabro

macaroni /mækə'rəʊnɪ/ n maccheroni mpl

mace[1] /meɪs/ n (*staff*) mazza f

mace[2] n (*spice*) macis m o f

Macedonia /mæsɪ'dəʊnɪə/ n Macedonia f

machinations /mækɪ'neɪʃnz/ npl macchinazioni fpl

machine /mə'ʃiːn/ n macchina f ● vt (*sew*) cucire a macchina; *Techn* lavorare a macchina. ~**-gun** n mitragliatrice f

machinery /mə'ʃiːnərɪ/ n macchinario m

machinist /mə'ʃiːnɪst/ n macchinista mf

macho /'mætʃəʊ/ a macho inv

mackerel /'mækr(ə)l/ n inv sgombro m

mackintosh /'mækɪntɒʃ/ n impermeabile m

mad /mæd/ a (**madder, maddest**) pazzo, matto; (*fam: angry*) furioso (**at** con); **like ~** fam come un pazzo; **be ~ about** (*fam: keen on*) andare matto per

madam /'mædəm/ n signora f

mad 'cow disease n morbo m della mucca pazza

madden /'mædən/ vt (*make angry*) far diventare matto

made /meɪd/ *see* **make**; ~ **to measure** [fatto] su misura

Madeira cake /mə'dɪərə/ n dolce m di pan di Spagna

mad|ly /'mædlɪ/ adv fam follemente; ~**ly in love** innamorato follemente. ~**man** n pazzo m. ~**ness** n pazzia f

madonna /mə'dɒnə/ n madonna f

magazine /mægə'ziːn/ n rivista f; *Mil, Phot* magazzino m

maggot /'mægət/ n verme m

Magi /'meɪdʒaɪ/ npl **the ~** i Re Magi

magic /'mædʒɪk/ n magia f; (*tricks*) giochi mpl di prestigio ● a magico; (*trick*) di prestigio. ~**al** a magico

magician /mə'dʒɪʃn/ n mago, -a mf; (*entertainer*) prestigiatore, -trice mf

magistrate /'mædʒɪstreɪt/ n magistrato m

magnanim|ity /mægnə'nɪmətɪ/ n magnanimità f. ~**ous** /-'nænɪməs/ a magnanimo

magnet /'mægnɪt/ n magnete m, calamita f. ~**ic** /-'netɪk/ a magnetico. ~**ism** n magnetismo m

magnification /mægnɪfɪ'keɪʃn/ n ingrandimento m

magnificen|ce /mæg'nɪfɪsəns/ n magnificenza f. ~**t** a magnifico

magnify /'mægnɪfaɪ/ vt (pt/pp -ied) ingrandire; (*exaggerate*) ingigantire. ~**ing glass** n lente f d'ingrandimento

magnitude /'mægnɪtjuːd/ n grandezza f; (*importance*) importanza f

magpie /'mægpaɪ/ n gazza f

mahogany /mə'hɒgənɪ/ n mogano m ● a di mogano

maid /meɪd/ n cameriera f; **old ~** pej zitella f

maiden /'meɪdn/ n liter fanciulla f ● a (*speech*) inaugurale. ~ '**aunt** n zia f zitella. ~ **name** n nome m da ragazza

mail /meɪl/ n posta f ● vt impostare

mail: ~**-bag** n sacco m postale. ~**box** n

Am cassetta *f* delle lettere; (*e-mail*) casella *f* di posta elettronica. **~ing list** *n* elenco *m* d'indirizzi per un mailing. **~man** *n Am* postino *m*. **~ order** *n* vendita *f* per corrispondenza. **~-order firm** *n* ditta *f* di vendita per corrispondenza

mailshot /'meɪlʃɒt/ *n* mailing *m inv*

maim /meɪm/ *vt* menomare

main[1] /meɪn/ *n* (*water, gas, electricity*) conduttura *f* principale

main[2] *a* principale; **the ~ thing is to...** la cosa essenziale è di... ● *n* **in the ~** in complesso

main: ~land /-lənd/ *n* continente *m*. **~ly** *adv* principalmente. **~stay** *n fig* pilastro *m*. **~ street** *n* via *f* principale

maintain /meɪn'teɪn/ *vt* mantenere; (*keep in repair*) curare la manutenzione di; (*claim*) sostenere

maintenance /'meɪntənəns/ *n* mantenimento *m*; (*care*) manutenzione *f*; (*allowance*) alimenti *mpl*

maisonette /meɪzə'net/ *n* appartamento *m* a due piani

majestic /mə'dʒestɪk/ *a* maestoso

majesty /'mædʒəstɪ/ *n* maestà *f inv*; **His/Her M~** Sua Maestà

major /'meɪdʒə(r)/ *a* maggiore; **~ road** strada *f* con diritto di precedenza ● *n Mil, Mus* maggiore *m* ● *vi Am* **~ in** specializzarsi in

Majorca /mə'jɔːkə/ *n* Maiorca *f*

majority /mə'dʒɒrətɪ/ *n* maggioranza *f*; **be in the ~** avere la maggioranza

make /meɪk/ *n* (*brand*) marca *f* ● *v* (*pt/pp* **made**) ● *vt* fare; (*earn*) guadagnare; rendere (*happy, clear*); prendere (*decision*); **~ sb laugh** far ridere qcno; **~ sb do sth** far fare qcsa a qcno; **~ it** (*to party, top of hill etc*) farcela; **what time do you ~ it?** che ore fai? ● *vi* **~ as if to** fare per. **make do** *vi* arrangiarsi. **make for** *vt* dirigersi verso. **make off** *vi* fuggire. **make out** *vt* (*distinguish*) distinguere; (*write out*) rilasciare (*cheque*); compilare (*list*); (*claim*) far credere. **make over** *vt* cedere. **make up** *vt* (*constitute*) comporre; (*complete*) completare; (*invent*) inventare; (*apply cosmetics to*) truccare; fare (*parcel*); **~ up one's mind** decidersi; **~ it up** (*after quarrel*) riconciliarsi ● *vi* (*after quarrel*) fare la pace; **~ up for** compensare; **~ up for lost time** recuperare il tempo perso

'make-believe *n* finzione *f*

maker /'meɪkə(r)/ *n* fabbricante *mf*; **M~** *Relig* Creatore *m*

make: ~ shift *a* di fortuna ● *n* espediente *m*. **~-up** *n* trucco *m*; (*character*) natura *f*

making /'meɪkɪŋ/ *n* **have the ~s of** aver la stoffa di

maladjust|ed /mælə'dʒʌstɪd/ *a* disadattato

malaise /mə'leɪz/ *n fig* malessere *m*

malaria /mə'leərɪə/ *n* malaria *f*

Malaysia /mə'leɪzɪə/ *n* Malesia *f*

male /meɪl/ *a* maschile ● *n* maschio *m*. **~ nurse** *n* infermiere *m*

malevolen|ce /mə'levələns/ *n* malevolenza *f*. **~t** *a* malevolo

malfunction /mæl'fʌŋkʃn/ *n* funzionamento *m* imperfetto ● *vi* funzionare male

malice /'mælɪs/ *n* malignità *f*; **bear sb ~** voler del male a qcno

malicious /mə'lɪʃəs/ *a* maligno

malign /mə'laɪn/ *vt* malignare su

malignan|cy /mə'lɪgnənsɪ/ *n* malignità *f*. **~t** *a* maligno

malinger /mə'lɪŋgə(r)/ *vi* fingersi malato. **~er** *n* scansafatiche *mf inv*

malleable /'mælɪəbl/ *a* malleabile

mallet /'mælɪt/ *n* martello *m* di legno

malnu'trition /mæl-/ *n* malnutrizione *f*

mal'practice *n* negligenza *f*

malt /mɔːlt/ *n* malto *m*

Malta /'mɔːltə/ *n* Malta *f*. **~ese** /-iːz/ *a* & *n* maltese *mf*

mal'treat /mæl-/ *vt* maltrattare. **~ment** *n* maltrattamento *m*

mammal /'mæml/ *n* mammifero *m*

mammoth /'mæməθ/ *a* mastodontico ● *n* mammut *m inv*

man /mæn/ *n* (*pl* **men**) uomo *m*; (*chess, draughts*) pedina *f* ● *vt* (*pt/pp* **manned**) equipaggiare; essere di servizio a (*counter, telephones*)

manage /'mænɪdʒ/ *vt* dirigere; gestire (*shop, affairs*); (*cope with*) farcela; **~ to do sth** riuscire a fare qcsa ● *vi* riuscire; (*cope*) farcela (**on** con). **~able** /-əbl/ *a* (*hair*) docile; (*size*) maneggevole. **~ment** /-mənt/ *n* gestione *f*; **the ~ment** la direzione

manager /'mænɪdʒə(r)/ *n* direttore *m*; (*of shop, bar*) gestore *m*; *Sport* manager *m inv*. **~ess** /-'res/ *n* direttrice *f*. **~ial** /-'dʒɪərɪəl/ *a* **~ial staff** personale *m* direttivo

managing /'mænɪdʒɪŋ/ *a* **~ director** direttore, -trice *mf* generale

mandarin /'mændərɪn/ *n* ~ **[orange]** mandarino *m*

mandat|e /'mændeɪt/ *n* mandato *m*.
~ory /-dətrɪ/ *a* obbligatorio

mane /meɪn/ *n* criniera *f*

mangle /'mæŋgl/ *vt* (*damage*)
maciullare

mango /'mæŋgəʊ/ *n* (*pl* -es) mango *m*

mangy /'meɪndʒɪ/ *a* (*dog*) rognoso

man: **~'handle** *vt* malmenare. **~hole** *n*
botola *f*. **~hole cover** *n* tombino *m*.
~hood *n* età *f* adulta; (*quality*) virilità *f*.
~-hour *n* ora *f* lavorativa. **~-hunt** *n*
caccia *f* all'uomo

man|ia /'meɪnɪə/ *n* mania *f*. **~iac** /-ɪæk/
n maniaco, -a *mf*

manicure /'mænɪkjʊə(r)/ *n* manicure *f*
inv ● *vt* fare la manicure a

manifest /'mænɪfest/ *a* manifesto ● *vt*
~ itself manifestarsi. **~ly** *adv* palese-
mente

manifesto /mænɪ'festəʊ/ *n* manifesto *m*

manifold /'mænɪfəʊld/ *a* molteplice

manipulat|e /mə'nɪpjuleɪt/ *vt* manipo-
lare. **~ion** /-'leɪʃn/ *n* manipolazione *f*

man'kind *n* genere *m* umano

manly /'mænlɪ/ *a* virile

'man-made *a* artificiale. **~ fibre** *n* fibra *f* sintetica

manner /'mænə(r)/ *n* maniera *f*; **in
this ~** in questo modo; **have no ~s**
avere dei pessimi modi; **good/bad ~s**
buone/cattive maniere *fpl*. **~ism** *n* affettazione *f*

manœuvre /mə'nu:və(r)/ *n* manovra *f*
● *vt* fare manovra con (*vehicle*); manovrare (*person*)

manor /'mænə(r)/ *n* maniero *m*

'manpower *n* manodopera *f*

mansion /'mænʃn/ *n* palazzo *m*

'manslaughter *n* omicidio *m* colposo

mantelpiece /'mæntl-/ *n* mensola *f* di
caminetto

manual /'mænjʊəl/ *a* manuale ● *n* manuale *m*

manufacture /mænjʊ'fæktʃə(r)/ *vt*
fabbricare ● *n* manifattura *f*. **~r** *n* fabbricante *m*

manure /mə'njʊə(r)/ *n* concime *m*

manuscript /'mænjʊskrɪpt/ *n* mano-
scritto *m*

many /'menɪ/ *a & pron* molti; **there
are as ~ boys as girls** ci sono tanti
ragazzi quante ragazze; **as ~ as 500**
ben 500; **as ~ as that** così tanti; **as ~**
altrettanti; **very ~**, **a good/great ~**
moltissimi; **~ a time** molte volte

map /mæp/ *n* carta *f* geografica; (*of
town*) mappa *f* ● **map out** *vt* (*pt/pp
mapped*) *fig* programmare

maple /'meɪpl/ *n* acero *m*

mar /mɑ:(r)/ *vt* (*pt/pp* **marred**) rovinare

marathon /'mærəθən/ *n* maratona *f*

marble /'mɑ:bl/ *n* marmo *m*; (*for game*)
pallina *f* ● *attrib* di marmo

March /mɑ:tʃ/ *n* marzo *m*

march *n* marcia *f*; (*protest*) dimostrazione *f* ● *vi* marciare ● *vt* far marciare;
~ sb off scortare qcno fuori

mare /meə(r)/ *n* giumenta *f*

margarine /mɑ:dʒə'ri:n/ *n* margarina *f*

margin /'mɑ:dʒɪn/ *n* margine *m*. **~al** *a*
marginale. **~ally** *adv* marginalmente

marigold /'mærɪɡəʊld/ *n* calendula *f*

marijuana /mærʊ'wɑ:nə/ *n* marijuana *f*

marina /mə'ri:nə/ *n* porticciolo *m*

marinade /mærɪ'neɪd/ *n* marinata *f*
● *vt* marinare

marine /mə'ri:n/ *a* marino ● *n* (*sailor*)
soldato *m* di fanteria marina

marionette /mærɪə'net/ *n* marionetta *f*

marital /'mærɪtl/ *a* coniugale. **~
status** stato *m* civile

maritime /'mærɪtaɪm/ *a* marittimo

mark[1] /mɑ:k/ *n* (*currency*) marco *m*

mark[2] *n* (*stain*) macchia *f*; (*sign,
indication*) segno *m*; *Sch* voto *m* ● *vt* segnare; (*stain*) macchiare; *Sch* correggere; *Sport* marcare; **~ time** *Mil* segnare
il passo; *fig* non far progressi; **~ my
words** ricordati quello che dico. **mark
out** *vt* delimitare; *fig* designare

marked /mɑ:kt/ *a* marcato. **~ly** /-kɪdlɪ/
adv notevolmente

marker /'mɑ:kə(r)/ *n* (*for highlighting*)
evidenziatore *m*; *Sport* marcatore *m*; (*of
exam*) esaminatore, -trice *mf*

market /'mɑ:kɪt/ *n* mercato *m* ● *vt* vendere al mercato; (*launch*) commercializzare; **on the ~** sul mercato. **~ing**
n marketing *m*. **~ re'search** *n* ricerca *f*
di mercato

marksman /'mɑ:ksmən/ *n* tiratore *m*
scelto

marmalade /'mɑ:məleɪd/ *n* marmellata *f* d'arance

maroon /mə'ru:n/ *a* marrone rossastro

marooned /mə'ru:nd/ *a* abbandonato

marquee /mɑ:'ki:/ *n* tendone *m*

marquis /'mɑ:kwɪs/ *n* marchese *m*

marriage /'mærɪdʒ/ *n* matrimonio *m*

married /'mærɪd/ *a* sposato; (*life*) coniugale

marrow /'mærəʊ/ n *Anat* midollo m; (*vegetable*) zucca f

marr|y /'mæri/ vt (*pt/pp* **-ied**) sposare; **get ~ied** sposarsi ● vi sposarsi

marsh /mɑːʃ/ n palude f

marshal /'mɑːʃl/ n (*steward*) cerimoniere m ● vt (*pt/pp* **marshalled**) *fig* organizzare ⟨*arguments*⟩

marshy /'mɑːʃi/ a paludoso

marsupial /mɑː'suːpɪəl/ n marsupiale m

martial /'mɑːʃl/ a marziale

martyr /'mɑːtə(r)/ n martire mf ● vt martirizzare. **~dom** /-dəm/ n martirio m. **~ed** a *fam* da martire

marvel /'mɑːvl/ n meraviglia f ● vi (*pt/pp* **marvelled**) meravigliarsi (**at** di). **~lous** /-vələs/ a meraviglioso

Marxis|m /'mɑːksɪzm/ n marxismo m. **~t** a & n marxista mf

marzipan /'mɑːzɪpæn/ n marzapane m

mascara /mæ'skɑːrə/ n mascara m inv

mascot /'mæskət/ n mascotte f inv

masculin|e /'mæskjʊlm/ a maschile ● n *Gram* maschile m. **~ity** /-'lɪnəti/ n mascolinità f

mash /mæʃ/ vt impastare. **~ed potatoes** npl purè m inv di patate

mask /mɑːsk/ n maschera f ● vt mascherare

masochis|m /'mæsəkɪzm/ n masochismo m. **~t** /-ɪst/ n masochista mf

mason /'meɪsn/ n muratore m

Mason n massone m. **~ic** /mə'sɒnɪk/ a massonico

masonry /'meɪsnri/ n massoneria f

masquerade /mæskə'reɪd/ n *fig* mascherata f ● vi **~ as** (*pose*) farsi passare per

mass¹ /mæs/ n *Relig* messa f

mass² n massa f; **~es of** *fam* un sacco di ● vi ammassarsi

massacre /'mæsəkə(r)/ n massacro m ● vt massacrare

massage /'mæsɑːʒ/ n massaggio m ● vt massaggiare; *fig* manipolare ⟨*statistics*⟩

masseu|r /mæ'sɜː(r)/ n massaggiatore m. **~se** /-'sɜːz/ n massaggiatrice f

massive /'mæsɪv/ a enorme

mass: **~ media** npl mezzi mpl di comunicazione di massa, mass media mpl. **~-pro'duce** vt produrre in serie. **~-pro'duction** n produzione f in serie

mast /mɑːst/ n *Naut* albero m; (*for radio*) antenna f

master /'mɑːstə(r)/ n maestro m, padrone m; (*teacher*) professore m; (*of ship*) capitano m; **M~** (*boy*) signorino m

master: **~-key** n passe-partout m inv. **~ly** a magistrale. **~-mind** n cervello m ● vt ideare e dirigere. **~piece** n capolavoro m. **~-stroke** n colpo m da maestro. **~y** n (*of subject*) padronanza f

masturbat|e /'mæstəbeɪt/ vi masturbarsi. **~ion** /-'beɪʃn/ n masturbazione f

mat /mæt/ n stuoia f; (*on table*) sottopiatto m

match¹ /mætʃ/ n *Sport* partita f; (*equal*) uguale mf; (*marriage*) matrimonio m; (*person to marry*) partito m; **be a good ~** ⟨*colours:*⟩ intonarsi bene; **be no ~ for** non essere dello stesso livello di ● vt (*equal*) uguagliare; (*be like*) andare bene con ● vi intonarsi

match² n fiammifero m. **~box** n scatola f di fiammiferi

matching /'mætʃɪŋ/ a intonato

mate¹ /meɪt/ n compagno, -a mf; (*assistant*) aiuto m; *Naut* secondo m; (*fam: friend*) amico, -a mf ● vi accoppiarsi ● vt accoppiare

mate² n (*in chess*) scacco m matto

material /mə'tɪərɪəl/ n materiale m; (*fabric*) stoffa f; **raw ~s** pl materie fpl prime ● a materiale

material|ism /mə'tɪərɪəlɪzm/ n materialismo m. **~istic** /-'lɪstɪk/ a materialistico. **~ize** /-laɪz/ vi materializzarsi

maternal /mə'tɜːnl/ a materno

maternity /mə'tɜːnəti/ n maternità f. **~ clothes** npl abiti mpl pre-maman. **~ ward** n maternità f inv

matey /'meɪti/ a *fam* amichevole

mathematic|al /mæθə'mætɪkl/ a matematico. **~ian** /-mə'tɪʃn/ n matematico, -a mf

mathematics /mæθ'mætɪks/ n matematica fsg

maths /mæθs/ n *fam* matematica fsg

matinée /'mætɪneɪ/ n *Theat* matinée f inv

mating /'meɪtɪŋ/ n accoppiamento m; **~ season** stagione f degli amori

matriculat|e /mə'trɪkjʊleɪt/ vi immatricolarsi. **~ion** /-'leɪʃn/ n immatricolazione f

matrix /'meɪtrɪks/ n (*pl* **matrices** /-siːz/) n matrice f

matted /'mætɪd/ a **~ hair** capelli mpl tutti appiccicati tra loro

matter /'mætə(r)/ n (*affair*) faccenda f; (*question*) questione f; (*pus*) pus m; (*phys: substance*) materia f; **as a ~ of fact** a dire la verità; **what is the ~?** che cosa c'è? ● vi importare; **~ to sb**

essere importante per qcno; **it doesn't ~** non importa. **~-of-fact** *a* pratico

mattress /ˈmætrɪs/ *n* materasso *m*

matur|e /məˈtʃʊə(r)/ *a* maturo; *Comm* in scadenza ● *vi* maturare ● *vt* far maturare. **~ity** *n* maturità *f*; *Fin* maturazione *f*

maul /mɔːl/ *vt* malmenare

Maundy /ˈmɔːndɪ/ *n* **~ Thursday** giovedì *m* santo

mauve /məʊv/ *a* malva

maxim /ˈmæksɪm/ *n* massima *f*

maximum /ˈmæksɪməm/ *a* massimo; **ten minutes ~** dieci minuti al massimo ● *n* (*pl* **-ima**) massimo *m*

May /meɪ/ *n* maggio *m*

may /meɪ/ *v aux* (*solo al presente*) potere; **~ I come in?** posso entrare?; **if I ~ say so** se mi posso permettere; **~ you both be very happy** siate felici; **I ~ as well stay** potrei anche rimanere; **it ~ be true** potrebbe esser vero; **she ~ be old, but...** sarà anche vecchia, ma...

maybe /ˈmeɪbiː/ *adv* forse, può darsi

May Day *n* il primo maggio

mayonnaise /meɪəˈneɪz/ *n* maionese *f*

mayor /ˈmeə(r)/ *n* sindaco *m*. **~ess** *n* sindaco *m*; (*wife of mayor*) moglie *f* del sindaco

maze /meɪz/ *n* labirinto *m*

me /miː/ *pron* (*object*) mi; (*with preposition*) me; **she called me** mi ha chiamato; **she called me, not you** ha chiamato me, non te; **give me the money** dammi i soldi; **give it to me** dammelo; **he gave it to me** me lo ha dato; **it's ~** sono io

meadow /ˈmedəʊ/ *n* prato *m*

meagre /ˈmiːɡə(r)/ *a* scarso

meal¹ /miːl/ *n* pasto *m*

meal² *n* (*grain*) farina *f*

mealy-mouthed /miːlɪˈmaʊðd/ *a* ambiguo

mean¹ /miːn/ *a* avaro; (*unkind*) meschino

mean² *a* medio ● *n* (*average*) media *f*; **Greenwich ~ time** ora *f* media di Greenwich

mean³ *vt* (*pt/pp* **meant**) voler dire; (*signify*) significare; (*intend*) intendere; **I ~ it** lo dico seriamente; **~ well** avere buone intenzioni; **be ~t for** ⟨*present:*⟩ essere destinato a; ⟨*remark:*⟩ essere riferito a

meander /mɪˈændə(r)/ *vi* vagare

meaning /ˈmiːnɪŋ/ *n* significato *m*. **~ful** *a* significativo. **~less** *a* senza senso

means /miːnz/ *n* mezzo *m*; **~ of transport** mezzo *m* di trasporto; **by ~ of** per mezzo di; **by all ~!** certamente!; **by no ~** niente affatto ● *npl* (*resources*) mezzi *mpl*

meant /ment/ *see* **mean³**

meantime *n* **in the ~** nel frattempo ● *adv* intanto

meanwhile *adv* intanto

measles /ˈmiːzlz/ *nsg* morbillo *m*

measly /ˈmiːzlɪ/ *a fam* misero

measurable /ˈmeʒərəbl/ *a* misurabile

measure /ˈmeʒə(r)/ *n* misura *f* ● *vt/i* misurare. **measure up to** *vt fig* essere all'altezza di. **~d** *a* misurato. **~ment** /-mənt/ *n* misura *f*

meat /miːt/ *n* carne *f*. **~ ball** *n Culin* polpetta *f* di carne. **~ loaf** *n* polpettone *m*

mechan|ic /mɪˈkænɪk/ *n* meccanico *m*. **~ical** *a* meccanico; **~ical engineering** ingegneria *f* meccanica. **~ically** *adv* meccanicamente. **~ics** *n* meccanica *f* ● *npl* meccanismo *msg*

mechan|ism /ˈmekənɪzm/ *n* meccanismo *m*. **~ize** *vt* meccanizzare

medal /medl/ *n* medaglia *f*

medallion /mɪˈdælɪən/ *n* medaglione *m*

medallist /ˈmedəlɪst/ *n* vincitore, -trice *mf* di una medaglia

meddle /medl/ *vi* immischiarsi (**in** di); (*tinker*) armeggiare (**with** con)

media /ˈmiːdɪə/ *npl* **the ~** i mass media. **~ studies** *npl* scienze *fpl* della comunicazione

median /ˈmiːdɪən/ *a* **~ strip** *Am* banchina *f* spartitraffico

mediat|e /ˈmiːdɪeɪt/ *vi* fare da mediatore. **~ion** /-ˈeɪʃn/ *n* mediazione *f*. **~or** *n* mediatore, -trice *mf*

medical /ˈmedɪkl/ *a* medico ● *n* visita *f* medica. **~ insurance** *n* assicurazione *f* sanitaria. **~ student** *n* studente, -essa *mf* di medicina

medicat|ed /ˈmedɪkeɪtɪd/ *a* medicato. **~ion** /-ˈkeɪʃn/ *n* (*drugs*) medicinali *mpl*

medicinal /mɪˈdɪsɪnl/ *a* medicinale

medicine /ˈmedsən/ *n* medicina *f*

medieval /medɪˈiːvl/ *a* medievale

mediocr|e /miːdɪˈəʊkə(r)/ *a* mediocre. **~ity** /-ˈɒkrətɪ/ *n* mediocrità *f*

meditat|e /ˈmedɪteɪt/ *vi* meditare (**on** su). **~ion** /-ˈteɪʃn/ *n* meditazione *f*

Mediterranean /medɪtəˈreɪnɪən/ *n* **the ~ [Sea]** il [mare] Mediterraneo ● *a* mediterraneo

medium /ˈmiːdɪəm/ *a* medio; *Culin* di media cottura ● *n* (*pl* **media**) mezzo *m*; (*pl* **-s**) (*person*) medium *mf inv*

medium: ~**-sized** *a* di taglia media. ~ **wave** *n* onde *fpl* medie

medley /'medlı/ *n* miscuglio *m*; *Mus* miscellanea *f*

meek /miːk/ *a* mite, mansueto. ~**ly** *adv* docilmente

meet /miːt/ *v* (*pt/pp* met) ● *vt* incontrare; (*at station, airport*) andare incontro a; (*for first time*) far la conoscenza di; pagare (*bill*); soddisfare (*requirements*) ● *vi* incontrarsi; (*committee:*) riunirsi; ~ **with** incontrare (*problem*); incontrarsi con (*person*) ● *n* raduno *m* [sportivo]

meeting /'miːtıŋ/ *n* riunione *f*, meeting *m inv*; (*large*) assemblea *f*; (*by chance*) incontro *m*

megabyte /'megəbaıt/ *n* megabyte *m*

megalomania /megələ'meınıə/ *n* megalomania *f*

megaphone /'megəfəʊn/ *n* megafono *m*

melancholy /'melənkəlı/ *a* malinconico ● *n* malinconia *f*

mellow /'meləʊ/ *a* (*wine*) generoso; (*sound, colour*) caldo; (*person*) dolce ● *vi* (*person:*) addolcirsi

melodic /mı'lɒdık/ *a* melodico

melodrama /'melə-/ *n* melodramma *m*. ~**tic** /-drə'mætık/ *a* melodrammatico

melody /'melədı/ *n* melodia *f*

melon /'melən/ *n* melone *m*

melt /melt/ *vt* sciogliere ● *vi* sciogliersi. **melt down** *vt* fondere. ~**ing-pot** *n fig* crogiuolo *m*

member /'membə(r)/ *n* membro *m*; ~ **countries** paesi *mpl* membri; **M~ of Parliament** deputato, -a *mf*; **M~ of the European Parliament** eurodeputato, -a *mf*. ~**ship** *n* iscrizione *f*; (*members*) soci *mpl*

membrane /'membreın/ *n* membrana *f*

memo /'meməʊ/ *n* promemoria *m inv*

memoirs /'memwɑːz/ *npl* ricordi *mpl*

memorable /'memərəbl/ *a* memorabile

memorandum /memə'rændəm/ *n* promemoria *m inv*

memorial /mı'mɔːrıəl/ *n* monumento *m*. ~ **service** *n* funzione *f* commemorativa

memorize /'meməraız/ *vt* memorizzare

memory /'memərı/ *n also Comput* memoria *f*; (*thing remembered*) ricordo *m*; **from** ~ a memoria; **in** ~ **of** in ricordo di

men /men/ *see* **man**

menac|e /'menəs/ *n* minaccia *f*; (*nuisance*) piaga *f* ● *vt* minacciare. ~**ing** *a* minaccioso

mend /mend/ *vt* riparare; (*darn*) rammendare ● *n* **on the** ~ in via di guarigione

'menfolk *n* uomini *mpl*

menial /'miːnıəl/ *a* umile

meningitis /menın'dʒaıtıs/ *n* meningite *f*

menopause /'menə-/ *n* menopausa *f*

menstruat|e /'menstrʊeıt/ *vi* mestruare. ~**ion** /-'eıʃn/ *n* mestruazione *f*

mental /'mentl/ *a* mentale; (*fam: mad*) pazzo. ~ **a'rithmetic** *n* calcolo *m* mentale. ~ '**illness** *n* malattia *f* mentale

mental|ity /men'tælətı/ *n* mentalità *f inv*. ~**ly** *adv* mentalmente; ~**ly ill** malato di mente

mention /'menʃn/ *n* menzione *f* ● *vt* menzionare; **don't** ~ **it** non c'è di che

menu /'menjuː/ *n* menu *m inv*

MEP *n abbr* **Member of the European Parliament**

mercenary /'mɜːsınərı/ *a* mercenario ● *n* mercenario *m*

merchandise /'mɜːtʃəndaız/ *n* merce *f*

merchant /'mɜːtʃənt/ *n* commerciante *mf*. ~ **bank** *n* banca *f* d'affari. ~ '**navy** *n* marina *f* mercantile

merci|ful /'mɜːsıfl/ *a* misericordioso. ~**fully** *adv fam* grazie a Dio. ~**less** *a* spietato

mercury /'mɜːkjʊrı/ *n* mercurio *m*

mercy /'mɜːsı/ *n* misericordia *f*; **be at sb's** ~ essere alla mercé di qcno, essere in balia di qcno

mere /mıə(r)/ *a* solo. ~**ly** *adv* solamente

merest /'mıərıst/ *a* minimo

merge /mɜːdʒ/ *vi* fondersi

merger /'mɜːdʒə(r)/ *n* fusione *f*

meringue /mə'ræŋ/ *n* meringa *f*

merit /'merıt/ *n* merito *m*; (*advantage*) qualità *f inv* ● *vt* meritare

mermaid /'mɜːmeıd/ *n* sirena *f*

merri|ly /'merılı/ *adv* allegramente. ~**ment** /-mənt/ *n* baldoria *f*

merry /'merı/ *a* (**-ier, -iest**) allegro; ~ **Christmas!** Buon Natale!

merry: ~**-go-round** *n* giostra *f*. ~**-making** *n* festa *f*

mesh /meʃ/ *n* maglia *f*

mesmerize /'mezməraız/ *vt* ipnotizzare. ~**d** *a fig* ipnotizzato

mess /mes/ *n* disordine *m*, casino *m fam*; (*trouble*) guaio *m*; (*something spilt*) sporco *m*; *Mil* mensa *f*; **make a** ~ **of**

(botch) fare un pasticcio di ● **mess about** *vi* perder tempo; **~ about with** armeggiare con ● *vt* prendere in giro ⟨*person*⟩. **mess up** *vt* mettere in disordine, incasinare *fam*; *(botch)* mandare all'aria

message /ˈmesɪdʒ/ *n* messaggio *m*

messenger /ˈmesɪndʒə(r)/ *n* messaggero *m*

Messiah /mɪˈsaɪə/ *n* Messia *m*

Messrs /ˈmesəz/ *npl* *(on letter)* **~ Smith** Spett. ditta Smith

messy /ˈmesɪ/ *a* **(-ier, -iest)** disordinato; *(in dress)* sciatto

met /met/ *see* **meet**

metal /ˈmetl/ *n* metallo *m* ● *a* di metallo. **~lic** /mɪˈtælɪk/ *a* metallico

metamorphosis /metəˈmɔːfəsɪs/ *n* *(pl* **-phoses** /-siːz/*)* metamorfosi *f inv*

metaphor /ˈmetəfə(r)/ *n* metafora *f*. **~ical** /-ˈfɒrɪkl/ *a* metaforico

meteor /ˈmiːtɪə(r)/ *n* meteora *f*. **~ic** /-ˈɒrɪk/ *a fig* fulmineo

meteorological /miːtɪərəˈlɒdʒɪkl/ *a* meteorologico

meteorolog|ist /miːtɪəˈrɒlədʒɪst/ *n* meteorologo, -a *mf*. **~y** *n* meteorologia *f*

meter[1] /ˈmiːtə(r)/ *n* contatore *m*

meter[2] *n Am* = **metre**

method /ˈmeθəd/ *n* metodo *m*

methodical /mɪˈθɒdɪkl/ *a* metodico. **~ly** *adv* metodicamente

Methodist /ˈmeθədɪst/ *n* metodista *mf*

meths /meθs/ *n fam* alcol *m* denaturato

methylated /ˈmeθɪleɪtɪd/ *a* **~ spirit[s]** alcol *m* denaturato

meticulous /mɪˈtɪkjʊləs/ *a* meticoloso. **~ly** *adv* meticolosamente

metre /ˈmiːtə(r)/ *n* metro *m*

metric /ˈmetrɪk/ *a* metrico

metropolis /mɪˈtrɒpəlɪs/ *n* metropoli *f inv*

metropolitan /metrəˈpɒlɪtən/ *a* metropolitano

mew /mjuː/ *n* miao *m* ● *vi* miagolare

Mexican /ˈmeksɪkən/ *a & n* messicano, -a *mf*. **'Mexico** *n* Messico *m*

miaow /mɪˈaʊ/ *n* miao *m* ● *vi* miagolare

mice /maɪs/ *see* **mouse**

mickey /ˈmɪkɪ/ *n* **take the ~ out of** prendere in giro

microbe /ˈmaɪkrəʊb/ *n* microbo *m*

micro /ˈmaɪkrəʊ/: **~chip** *n* microchip *m inv*. **~computer** *n* microcomputer *m inv* . **~film** *n* microfilm *m inv*. **~phone** microfono *m*. **~processor** *n* microprocessore *m*. **~scope** *n* microscopio *m*. **~scopic** /-ˈskɒpɪk/ *a* microscopico.

~wave *n* microonda *f*; *(oven)* forno *m* a microonde

mid /mɪd/ *a* **~ May** metà maggio; **in ~ air** a mezz'aria

midday /mɪdˈdeɪ/ *n* mezzogiorno *m*

middle /ˈmɪdl/ *a* di centro; **the M~ Ages** il medioevo; **the ~ class[es]** la classe media; **the M~ East** il Medio Oriente ● *n* mezzo *m*; **in the ~ of** ⟨*room, floor etc*⟩ in mezzo a; **in the ~ of the night** nel pieno della notte, a notte piena

middle: **~-aged** *a* di mezza età. **~-class** *a* borghese. **~man** *n* *Comm* intermediario *m*

middling /ˈmɪdlɪŋ/ *a* discreto

midge /mɪdʒ/ *n* moscerino *m*

midget /ˈmɪdʒɪt/ *n* nano, -a *mf*

Midlands /ˈmɪdləndz/ *npl* **the ~** l'Inghilterra *fsg* centrale

'midnight *n* mezzanotte *f*

midriff /ˈmɪdrɪf/ *n* diaframma *m*

midst /mɪdst/ *n* **in the ~ of** in mezzo a; **in our ~** fra di noi, in mezzo a noi

mid: **~summer** *n* mezza estate *f* **~way** *adv* a metà strada. **~wife** *n* ostetrica *f*. **~wifery** /-ˈwɪfrɪ/ *n* ostetricia *f*. **~'winter** *n* pieno inverno *m*

might[1] /maɪt/ *v aux* **I ~** potrei; **will you come? - I ~** vieni? - può darsi; **it ~ be true** potrebbe essere vero; **I ~ as well stay** potrei anche restare; **you ~ have drowned** avresti potuto affogare; **you ~ have said so!** avresti potuto dirlo!

might[2] *n* potere *m*

mighty /ˈmaɪtɪ/ *a* **(-ier, -iest)** potente ● *adv fam* molto

migraine /ˈmiːgreɪn/ *n* emicrania *f*

migrant /ˈmaɪgrənt/ *a* migratore ● *n* *(bird)* migratore, -trice *mf*; *(person: for work)* emigrante *mf*

migrat|e /maɪˈgreɪt/ *vi* migrare. **~ion** /-ˈgreɪʃn/ *n* migrazione *f*

mike /maɪk/ *n fam* microfono *m*

Milan /mɪˈlæn/ *n* Milano *f*

mild /maɪld/ *a* ⟨*weather*⟩ mite; ⟨*person*⟩ dolce; ⟨*flavour*⟩ delicato; ⟨*illness*⟩ leggero

mildew /ˈmɪldjuː/ *n* muffa *f*

mild|ly /ˈmaɪldlɪ/ *adv* moderatamente; ⟨*say*⟩ dolcemente; **to put it ~** a dir poco, senza esagerazione. **~ness** *n* *(of person, words)* dolcezza *f*; *(of weather)* mitezza *f*

mile /maɪl/ *n* miglio *m* (*= 1,6 km*); **~s nicer** *fam* molto più bello

mile|age /-ɪdʒ/ *n* chilometraggio *m*. **~stone** *n* pietra *f* miliare

militant /'mɪlɪtənt/ *a & n* militante *mf*

military /'mɪlɪtrɪ/ *a* militare. **~ service** *n* servizio *m* militare

militate /'mɪlɪteɪt/ *vi* **~ against** opporsi a

militia /mɪ'lɪʃə/ *n* milizia *f*

milk /mɪlk/ *n* latte *m* ● *vt* mungere

milk: ~man *n* lattaio *m*. **~ shake** *n* frappé *m inv*

milky /'mɪlkɪ/ *a* (**-ier, -iest**) latteo; ‹*tea etc*› con molto latte. **M~ Way** *n Astr* Via *f* Lattea

mill /mɪl/ *n* mulino *m*; ‹*factory*› fabbrica *f*; ‹*for coffee etc*› macinino *m* ● *vt* macinare ‹*grain*›. **mill about, mill around** *vi* brulicare

millennium /mɪ'lenɪəm/ *n* millennio *m*

miller /'mɪlə(r)/ *n* mugnaio *m*

milli|gram /'mɪlɪ-/ *n* milligrammo *m*. **~metre** *n* millimetro *m*

million /'mɪljən/ *a & n* milione *m*; **a ~ pounds** un milione di sterline. **~aire** /-'neə(r)/ *n* miliardario, -a *mf*

'millstone *n fig* peso *m*

mime /maɪm/ *n* mimo *m* ● *vt* mimare

mimic /'mɪmɪk/ *n* imitatore, -trice *mf* ● *vt* (*pt/pp* **mimicked**) imitare. **~ry** *n* mimetismo *m*

mimosa /mɪ'məʊzə/ *n* mimosa *f*

mince /mɪns/ *n* carne *f* tritata ● *vt Culin* tritare; **not ~ one's words** parlare senza mezzi termini

mince: ~meat *n* miscuglio *m* di frutta secca; **make ~meat of** *fig* demolire. **~'pie** *n* pasticcino *m* a base di frutta secca

mincer /'mɪnsə(r)/ *n* tritacarne *m inv*

mind /maɪnd/ *n* mente *f*; ‹*sanity*› ragione *f*; **to my ~** a mio parere; **give sb a piece of one's ~** dire chiaro e tondo a qcno quello che si pensa; **make up one's ~** decidersi; **have sth in ~** avere qcsa in mente; **bear sth in ~** tenere presente qcsa; **have something on one's ~** essere preoccupato; **have a good ~ to** avere una grande voglia di; **I have changed my ~** ho cambiato idea; **in two ~s** indeciso; **are you out of your ~?** sei diventato matto? ● *vt* ‹*look after*› occuparsi di; **I don't ~ the noise** il rumore non mi dà fastidio; **I don't ~ what we do** non mi importa quello che facciamo; **~ the step!** attenzione al gradino! ● *vi* **I don't ~** non mi importa; **never ~!** non importa!; **do**

you ~ if...? ti dispiace se...? **mind out** *vi* **~ out!** [fai] attenzione!

minder /'maɪndə(r)/ *n* (*Br: bodyguard*) gorilla *m inv*; (*for child*) baby-sitter *mf inv*

mind|ful *a* **~ful of** attento a. **~less** *a* noncurante

mine¹ /maɪn/ *poss pron* il mio *m*, la mia *f*, i miei *mpl*, le mie *fpl*; **a friend of ~** un mio amico; **friends of ~** dei miei amici; **that is ~** questo è mio; (*as opposed to yours*) questo è il mio

mine² *n* miniera *f*; (*explosive*) mina *f* ● *vt* estrarre; *Mil* minare. **~ detector** *n* rivelatore *m* di mine. **~field** *n* campo *m* minato

miner /'maɪnə(r)/ *n* minatore *m*

mineral /'mɪnərəl/ *n* minerale *m* ● *a* minerale. **~ water** *n* acqua *f* minerale

minesweeper /'maɪn-/ *n* dragamine *m inv*

mingle /'mɪŋgl/ *vi* **~ with** mescolarsi a

mini /'mɪnɪ/ *n* (*skirt*) mini *f*

miniature /'mɪnɪtʃə(r)/ *a* in miniatura ● *n* miniatura *f*

mini|bus /'mɪnɪ-/ *n* minibus *m inv*, pulmino *m*. **~cab** *n* taxi *m inv*

minim /'mɪnɪm/ *n Mus* minima *f*

minim|al /'mɪnɪməl/ *a* minimo. **~ize** *vt* minimizzare. **~um** *n* (*pl* **-ima**) minimo *m* ● *a* minimo; **ten minutes ~um** minimo dieci minuti

mining /'maɪnɪŋ/ *n* estrazione *f* ● *a* estrattivo

miniskirt /'mɪnɪ-/ *n* minigonna *f*

minist|er /'mɪnɪstə(r)/ *n* ministro *m*; *Relig* pastore *m*. **~erial** /-'stɪərɪəl/ *a* ministeriale

ministry /'mɪnɪstrɪ/ *n Pol* ministero *m*; **the ~** *Relig* il ministero sacerdotale

mink /mɪŋk/ *n* visone *m*

minor /'maɪnə(r)/ *a* minore ● *n* minorenne *mf*

minority /maɪ'nɒrətɪ/ *n* minoranza *f*; (*age*) minore età *f*

minor road *n* strada *f* secondaria

mint¹ /mɪnt/ *n fam* patrimonio *m* ● *a* **in ~ condition** in condizione perfetta

mint² *n* (*herb*) menta *f*

minus /'maɪnəs/ *prep* meno; (*fam: without*) senza ● *n* **~ [sign]** meno *m*

minute¹ /'mɪnɪt/ *n* minuto *m*; **in a ~** (*shortly*) in un minuto; **~s** *pl* (*of meeting*) verbale *msg*

minute² /maɪ'njuːt/ *a* minuto; (*precise*) minuzioso

mirac|le /'mɪrəkl/ *n* miracolo *m*. **~ulous** /-'rækjʊləs/ *a* miracoloso

mirage /'mɪrɑːʒ/ n miraggio m

mirror /'mɪrə(r)/ n specchio m ● vt rispecchiare

mirth /mɜːθ/ n ilarità f

misad'venture /mɪs-/ n disavventura f

misanthropist /mɪ'zænθrəpɪst/ n misantropo, -a mf

misappre'hension n malinteso m; **be under a ~** avere frainteso

misbe'have vi comportarsi male

mis'calcu|late vt/i calcolare male. **~'lation** n calcolo m sbagliato

'miscarriage n aborto m spontaneo; **~ of justice** errore m giudiziario. **mis'carry** vi abortire

miscellaneous /mɪsə'leɪnɪəs/ a assortito

mischief /'mɪstʃɪf/ n malefatta f; (harm) danno m

mischievous /'mɪstʃɪvəs/ a (naughty) birichino; (malicious) dannoso

miscon'ception n concetto m erroneo

mis'conduct n cattiva condotta f

misde'meanour n reato m

miser /'maɪzə(r)/ n avaro m

miserabl|e /'mɪzrəbl/ a (unhappy) infelice; (wretched) miserabile; (fig: weather) deprimente. **~y** adv (live, fail) miseramente; (say) tristemente

miserly /'maɪzəlɪ/ a avaro; (amount) ridicolo

misery /'mɪzərɪ/ n miseria f; (fam: person) piagnone, -a mf

mis'fire vi (gun:) far cilecca; (plan etc:) non riuscire

'misfit n disadattato, -a mf

mis'fortune n sfortuna f

mis'givings npl dubbi mpl

mis'guided a fuorviato

mishap /'mɪshæp/ n disavventura f

misin'terpret vt fraintendere

mis'judge vt giudicar male; (estimate wrongly) valutare male

mis'lay vt (pt/pp -laid) smarrire

mis'lead vt (pt/pp -led) fuorviare. **~ing** a fuorviante

mis'manage vt amministrare male. **~ment** n cattiva amministrazione f

misnomer /mɪs'nəʊmə(r)/ n termine m improprio

'misprint n errore m di stampa

mis'quote vt citare erroneamente

misrepre'sent vt rappresentare male

miss /mɪs/ n colpo m mancato ● vt (fail to hit or find) mancare; perdere (train, bus, class); (feel the loss of) sentire la mancanza di; **I ~ed that part** (failed to notice) mi è sfuggita quella parte ● vi **but he ~ed** (failed to hit) ma l'ha mancato. **miss out** vt saltare, omettere

Miss n (pl -es) signorina f

misshapen /mɪs'ʃeɪpən/ a malformato

missile /'mɪsaɪl/ n missile m

missing /'mɪsɪŋ/ a mancante; (person) scomparso; Mil disperso; **be ~** essere introvabile

mission /'mɪʃn/ n missione f

missionary /'mɪʃənrɪ/ n missionario, -a mf

mis'spell vt (pt/pp -spelled, -spelt) sbagliare l'ortografia di

mist /mɪst/ n (fog) foschia f ● **mist up** vi appannarsi, annebbiarsi

mistake /mɪ'steɪk/ n sbaglio m; **by ~** per sbaglio ● vt (pt mistook, pp mistaken) sbagliare (road, house); fraintendere (meaning, words); **~ for** prendere per

mistaken /mɪ'steɪkən/ a sbagliato; **be ~** sbagliarsi; **~ identity** errore m di persona. **~ly** adv erroneamente

mistletoe /'mɪsltəʊ/ n vischio m

mistress /'mɪstrɪs/ n padrona f; (teacher) maestra f; (lover) amante f

mis'trust n sfiducia f ● vt non aver fiducia in

misty /'mɪstɪ/ a (-ier, -iest) nebbioso

misunder'stand vt (pt/pp -stood) fraintendere. **~ing** n malinteso m

misuse[1] /mɪs'juːz/ vt usare male

misuse[2] /mɪs'juːs/ n cattivo uso m

mite /maɪt/ n (child) piccino, -a mf

mitigat|e /'mɪtɪgeɪt/ vt attenuare. **~ing** a attenuante

mitten /'mɪtn/ n manopola f, muffola f

mix /mɪks/ n (combination) mescolanza f; Culin miscuglio m; (ready-made) preparato m ● vt mischiare ● vi mischiarsi; (person:) inserirsi; **~ with** (associate with) frequentare. **mix up** vt mescolare (papers); (confuse, mistake for) confondere

mixed /mɪkst/ a misto; **~ up** (person) confuso

mixer /'mɪksə(r)/ n Culin frullatore m, mixer m inv; **he's a good ~** è un tipo socievole

mixture /'mɪkstʃə(r)/ n mescolanza f; (medicine) sciroppo m; Culin miscela f

'mix-up n (confusion) confusione f; (mistake) pasticcio m

moan /məʊn/ n lamento m ● vi lamentarsi; (complain) lagnarsi

moat /məʊt/ n fossato m

mob /mɒb/ n folla f; (*rabble*) gentaglia f; (*fam: gang*) banda f ● vt (*pt/pp* **mobbed**) assalire

mobile /'məʊbaɪl/ a mobile ● n composizione f mobile. **~ 'home** n casa f roulotte. **~ [phone]** n [telefono m] cellulare m, telefonino m

mobility /mə'bɪlətɪ/ n mobilità f

mock /mɒk/ a finto ● vt canzonare. **~ery** n derisione f

'mock-up n modello m in scala

mode /məʊd/ n modo m; *Comput* modalità f

model /'mɒdl/ n modello m; **[fashion] ~** indossatore, -trice mf, modello, -a mf ● a ⟨yacht, plane⟩ in miniatura; ⟨pupil, husband⟩ esemplare, modello ● v (*pt/pp* **modelled**) ● vt indossare ⟨clothes⟩ ● vi fare l'indossatore, -trice mf; (*for artist*) posare

modem /'məʊdem/ n modem m inv

moderate¹ /'mɒdəreɪt/ vt moderare ● vi moderarsi

moderate² /'mɒdərət/ a moderato ● n *Pol* moderato, -a mf. **~ly** adv ⟨drink, speak etc⟩ moderatamente; ⟨good, bad etc⟩ relativamente

moderation /mɒdə'reɪʃn/ n moderazione f; **in ~** con moderazione

modern /'mɒdn/ a moderno. **~ize** vt modernizzare

modest /'mɒdɪst/ a modesto. **~y** n modestia f

modicum /'mɒdɪkəm/ n **a ~ of** un po' di

modif|ication /mɒdɪfɪ'keɪʃn/ n modificazione f. **~y** /'mɒdɪfaɪ/ vt (*pt/pp* **-fied**) modificare

module /'mɒdjuːl/ n modulo m

moist /mɔɪst/ a umido

moisten /'mɔɪsn/ vt inumidire

moistur|e /'mɔɪstʃə(r)/ n umidità f. **~izer** n [crema f] idratante m

molar /'məʊlə(r)/ n molare m

molasses /mə'læsɪz/ n Am melassa f

mole¹ /məʊl/ n (*on face etc*) neo m

mole² n *Zool* talpa f

molecule /'mɒlɪkjuːl/ n molecola f

mollycoddle /'mɒlɪkɒdl/ vt tenere nella bambagia

mom /mɒm/ n Am fam mamma f

moment /'məʊmənt/ n momento m; **at the ~** in questo momento. **~arily** adv momentaneamente. **~ary** a momentaneo

momentous /mə'mentəs/ a molto importante

momentum /mə'mentəm/ n impeto m

monarch /'mɒnək/ n monarca m. **~y** n monarchia f

monast|ery /'mɒnəstrɪ/ n monastero m. **~ic** /mə'næstɪk/ a monastico

Monday /'mʌndeɪ/ n lunedì m inv

monetary /'mʌnɪtrɪ/ a monetario

money /'mʌnɪ/ n denaro m

money: **~-box** n salvadanaio m. **~-lender** n usuraio m

mongrel /'mʌŋgrəl/ n bastardo m

monitor /'mɒnɪtə(r)/ n *Techn* monitor m inv ● vt controllare

monk /mʌŋk/ n monaco m

monkey /'mʌŋkɪ/ n scimmia f. **~-nut** n nocciolina f americana. **~-wrench** n chiave f inglese a rullino

mono /'mɒnəʊ/ n mono m

monogram /'mɒnəgræm/ n monogramma m

monologue /'mɒnəlɒg/ n monologo m

monopol|ize /mə'nɒpəlaɪz/ vt monopolizzare. **~y** n monopolio m

monosyllabic /mɒnəsɪ'læbɪk/ a monosillabico

monotone /'mɒnətəʊn/ n **speak in a ~** parlare con tono monotono

monoton|ous /mə'nɒtənəs/ a monotono. **~y** n monotonia f

monsoon /mɒn'suːn/ n monsone m

monster /'mɒnstə(r)/ n mostro m

monstrosity /mɒn'strɒsətɪ/ n mostruosità f

monstrous /'mɒnstrəs/ a mostruoso

Montenegro /mɒntɪ'niːgrəʊ/ n Montenegro m

month /mʌnθ/ n mese m. **~ly** a mensile ● adv mensilmente ● n (*periodical*) mensile m

monument /'mɒnjʊmənt/ n monumento m. **~al** /-'mentl/ a fig monumentale

moo /muː/ n muggito m ● vi (*pt/pp* **mooed**) muggire

mooch /muːtʃ/ vi **~ about** fam gironzolare (**the house** per casa)

mood /muːd/ n umore m; **be in a good/bad ~** essere di buon/cattivo umore; **be in the ~ for** essere in vena di

moody /'muːdɪ/ a (**-ier, -iest**) (*variable*) lunatico; (*bad-tempered*) di malumore

moon /muːn/ n luna f; **over the ~** fam al settimo cielo

moon: **~light** n chiaro m di luna ● vi fam lavorare in nero. **~lit** a illuminato dalla luna

moor¹ /mʊə(r)/ n brughiera f

145

moor[2] *vt Naut* ormeggiare

moose /muːs/ *n* (*pl* **moose**) alce *m*

moot /muːt/ *a* **it's a ~ point** è un punto controverso

mop /mɒp/ *n* mocio® *m* ; **~ of hair** zazzera *f* ● *vt* (*pt/pp* **mopped**) lavare con il mocio. **mop up** *vt* (*dry*) asciugare con lo straccio; (*clean*) pulire con lo straccio

mope /məʊp/ *vi* essere depresso

moped /ˈməʊped/ *n* ciclomotore *m*

moral /ˈmɒrəl/ *a* morale ● *n* morale *f*. **~ly** *adv* moralmente. **~s** *pl* moralità *f*

morale /məˈrɑːl/ *n* morale *m*

morality /məˈrælətɪ/ *n* moralità *f*

morbid /ˈmɔːbɪd/ *a* morboso

more /mɔː(r)/ *a* più; **a few ~ books** un po' più di libri; **some ~ tea?** ancora un po' di tè?; **there's no ~ bread** non c'è più pane; **there are no ~ apples** non ci sono più mele; **one ~ word and…** ancora una parola e… ● *pron* di più; **would you like some ~?** ne vuoi ancora?; **no ~, thank you** non ne voglio più, grazie ● *adv* più; **~ interesting** più interessante; **~ [and ~] quickly** [sempre] più veloce; **~ than** più di; **I don't love him any ~** non lo amo più; **once ~** ancora una volta; **~ or less** più o meno; **the ~ I see him, the ~ I like him** più lo vedo, più mi piace

moreover /mɔːrˈəʊvə(r)/ *adv* inoltre

morgue /mɔːg/ *n* obitorio *m*

moribund /ˈmɒrɪbʌnd/ *a* moribondo

morning /ˈmɔːnɪŋ/ *n* mattino *m*, mattina *f*; **in the ~** del mattino; (*tomorrow*) domani mattina

Morocc|o /məˈrɒkəʊ/ *n* Marocco *m* ● *a* **~an** *a* & *n* marocchino, -a *mf*

moron /ˈmɔːrɒn/ *n fam* deficiente *mf*

morose /məˈrəʊs/ *a* scontroso

morphine /ˈmɔːfiːn/ *n* morfina *f*

Morse /mɔːs/ *n* **~ [code]** [codice *m*] Morse *m*

morsel /ˈmɔːsl/ *n* (*food*) boccone *m*

mortal /ˈmɔːtl/ *a* & *n* mortale *mf*. **~ity** /mɔːˈtælətɪ/ *n* mortalità *f*. **~ly** *adv* (*wounded, offended*) a morte; (*afraid*) da morire

mortar /ˈmɔːtə(r)/ *n* mortaio *m*

mortgage /ˈmɔːgɪdʒ/ *n* mutuo *m*; (*on property*) ipoteca *f* ● *vt* ipotecare

mortuary /ˈmɔːtjʊərɪ/ *n* camera *f* mortuaria

mosaic /məʊˈzeɪɪk/ *n* mosaico *m*

Moscow /ˈmɒskəʊ/ *n* Mosca *f*

Moslem /ˈmɒzlɪm/ *a* & *n* musulmano, -a *mf*

mosque /mɒsk/ *n* moschea *f*

mosquito /mɒsˈkiːtəʊ/ *n* (*pl* **-es**) zanzara *f*

moss /mɒs/ *n* muschio *m*. **~y** *a* muschioso

most /məʊst/ *a* (*majority*) la maggior parte di; **for the ~ part** per lo più ● *adv* più, maggiormente; (*very*) estremamente, molto; **the ~ interesting day** la giornata più interessante; **a ~ interesting day** una giornata estremamente interessante; **the ~ beautiful woman in the world** la donna più bella del mondo; **~ unlikely** veramente improbabile ● *pron* **~ of them** la maggior parte di loro; **at [the] ~** al massimo; **make the ~ of** sfruttare al massimo; **~ of the time** la maggior parte del tempo. **~ly** *adv* per lo più

MOT *n Br* revisione *f* obbligatoria di autoveicoli

motel /məʊˈtel/ *n* motel *m inv*

moth /mɒθ/ *n* falena *f*; **[clothes-] ~** tarma *f*

moth: ~ball *n* pallina *f* di naftalina. **~-eaten** *a* tarmato

mother /ˈmʌðə(r)/ *n* madre *f*; **M~'s Day** la festa della mamma ● *vt* fare da madre a

mother: ~board *n Comput* scheda *f* madre. **~hood** *n* maternità *f*. **~-in-law** *n* (*pl* **~s-in-law**) suocera *f*. **~ly** *a* materno. **~-of-pearl** *n* madreperla *f*. **~-to-be** *n* futura mamma *f*. **~ tongue** *n* madrelingua *f*

mothproof /ˈmɒθ-/ *a* antitarmico

motif /məʊˈtiːf/ *n* motivo *m*

motion /ˈməʊʃn/ *n* moto *m*; (*proposal*) mozione *f*; (*gesture*) gesto *m* ● *vt/i* **~ [to] sb to come in** fare segno a qcno di entrare. **~less** *a* immobile. **~lessly** *adv* senza alcun movimento

motivat|e /ˈməʊtɪveɪt/ *vt* motivare. **~ion** /-ˈveɪʃn/ *n* motivazione *f*

motive /ˈməʊtɪv/ *n* motivo *m*

motley /ˈmɒtlɪ/ *a* disparato

motor /ˈməʊtə(r)/ *n* motore *m*; (*car*) macchina *f* ● *a* a motore; *Anat* motore ● *vi* andare in macchina

Motorail /ˈməʊtəreɪl/ *n* treno *m* per trasporto auto

motor: ~ bike *n fam* moto *f inv*. **~ boat** *n* motoscafo *m*. **~cade** /-keɪd/ *n Am* corteo *m* di auto. **~ car** *n* automobile *f*. **~ cycle** *n* motocicletta *f*. **~-cyclist** *n* motociclista *mf*. **~ing** *n* automobilismo *m*. **~ist** *n* automobilista *mf*. **~ racing** *n* corse *fpl* automobilistiche. **~**

vehicle n autoveicolo m. **~way** n autostrada f

mottled /'mɒtld/ a chiazzato

motto /'mɒtəʊ/ n (pl **-es**) motto m

mould[1] /məʊld/ n (fungus) muffa f

mould[2] n stampo m ● vt foggiare; fig formare. **~ing** n Archit cornice f

mouldy /'məʊldɪ/ a ammuffito; (fam: worthless) ridicolo

moult /məʊlt/ vi ⟨bird:⟩ fare la muta; ⟨animal:⟩ perdere il pelo

mound /maʊnd/ n mucchio m; (hill) collinetta f

mount /maʊnt/ n ⟨horse⟩ cavalcatura f; (of jewel, photo, picture) montatura f ● vt montare a ⟨horse⟩; salire su ⟨bicycle⟩; incastonare ⟨jewel⟩; incorniciare ⟨photo, picture⟩ ● vi aumentare. **mount up** vi aumentare

mountain /'maʊntɪn/ n montagna f. **~ bike** n mountain bike f inv

mountaineer /maʊntɪˈnɪə(r)/ n alpinista mf. **~ing** n alpinismo m

mountainous /'maʊntɪnəs/ a montagnoso

mourn /mɔːn/ vt lamentare ● vi **~ for** piangere la morte di. **~er** n persona f che participa a un funerale. **~ful** a triste. **~ing** n **in ~ing** in lutto

mouse /maʊs/ n (pl **mice**) topo m; Comput mouse m inv. **~trap** n trappola f [per topi]

mousse /muːs/ n Culin mousse f inv

moustache /məˈstɑːʃ/ n baffi mpl

mousy /'maʊsɪ/ a ⟨colour⟩ grigio topo

mouth[1] /maʊð/ vt **~ sth** dire qcsa silenziosamente muovendo solamente le labbra

mouth[2] /maʊθ/ n bocca f; (of river) foce f

mouth: **~ful** n boccone m. **~-organ** n armonica f [a bocca]. **~piece** n imboccatura f; (fig: person) portavoce m inv. **~wash** n acqua f dentifricia. **~watering** a che fa venire l'acquolina in bocca

movable /'muːvəbl/ a movibile

move /muːv/ n mossa f; (moving house) trasloco m; **on the ~** in movimento; **get a ~ on** fam darsi una mossa ● vt muovere; (emotionally) commuovere; spostare ⟨car, furniture⟩; (transfer) trasferire; (propose) proporre; **~ house** traslocare ● vi muoversi; (move house) traslocare. **move along** vi andare avanti ● vt muovere in avanti. **move away** vi allontanarsi; (move house) trasferirsi ● vt allontanare. **move forward** vi avanzare ● vt spostare avanti. **move in**

vi (to a house) trasferirsi. **move off** vi ⟨vehicle:⟩ muoversi. **move out** vi (of house) andare via. **move over** vi spostarsi ● vt spostare. **move up** vi muoversi; (advance, increase) avanzare

movement /'muːvmənt/ n movimento m

movie /'muːvɪ/ n film m inv; **go to the ~s** andare al cinema

moving /'muːvɪŋ/ a mobile; (touching) commovente

mow /məʊ/ vt (pt **mowed**, pp **mown** or **mowed**) tagliare ⟨lawn⟩. **mow down** vt (destroy) sterminare

mower /'məʊə(r)/ n tosaerba m inv

MP n abbr **Member of Parliament**

Mr /'mɪstə(r)/ n (pl **Messrs**) Signor m

Mrs /'mɪsɪz/ n Signora f

Ms /mɪz/ n Signora f (modo m formale di rivolgersi ad una donna quando non si vuole connotarla come sposata o nubile)

much /mʌtʃ/ a, adv & pron molto; **~ as** per quanto; **I love you just as ~ as before/him** ti amo quanto prima/lui; **as ~ as £5 million** ben cinque milioni di sterline; **as ~ as that** così tanto; **very ~** tantissimo, moltissimo; **~ the same** quasi uguale

muck /mʌk/ n (dirt) sporcizia f; (farming) letame m; (fam: filth) porcheria f. **muck about** vi fam perder tempo; **~ about with** trafficare con. **muck up** vt fam rovinare; (make dirty) sporcare

mucky /'mʌkɪ/ a (**-ier**, **-iest**) sudicio

mucus /'mjuːkəs/ n muco m

mud /mʌd/ n fango m

muddle /'mʌdl/ n disordine m; (mixup) confusione f ● vt **~ [up]** confondere ⟨dates⟩

muddy /'mʌdɪ/ a (**-ier**, **-iest**) ⟨path⟩ fangoso; ⟨shoes⟩ infangato

'mudguard n parafango m

muesli /'muːzlɪ/ n muesli m inv

muffle /'mʌfl/ vt smorzare ⟨sound⟩. **muffle [up]** vt (for warmth) imbacuccare

muffler /'mʌflə(r)/ n sciarpa f; Am Auto marmitta f

mug[1] /mʌg/ n tazza f; (for beer) boccale m; (fam: face) muso m; (fam: simpleton) pollo m

mug[2] vt (pt/pp **mugged**) aggredire e derubare. **~ger** n assalitore, -trice mf. **~ging** n aggressione f per furto

muggy /'mʌgɪ/ a (**-ier**, **-iest**) afoso

mule /mjuːl/ n mulo m

mull /mʌl/ vt **~ over** rimuginare su

mulled /mʌld/ *a* ~ **wine** vin brûlé *m inv*

multi /'mʌltɪ/: ~**coloured** *a* variopinto. ~**lingual** /-'lɪŋgwəl/ *a* multilingue *inv.* ~'**media** *n* multimedia *mpl* ●*a* multimediale. ~'**national** *a* multinazionale ●*n* multinazionale *f*

multiple /'mʌltɪpl/ *a* multiplo

multiplication /mʌltɪplɪ'keɪʃn/ *n* moltiplicazione *f*

multiply /'mʌltɪplaɪ/ *v* (*pt/pp* -**ied**) ●*vt* moltiplicare (**by** per) ●*vi* moltiplicarsi

multi'storey *a* ~ **car park** parcheggio *m* a più piani

mum[1] /mʌm/ *a* **keep** ~ *fam* non aprire bocca

mum[2] *n fam* mamma *f*

mumble /'mʌmbl/ *vt/i* borbottare

mummy[1] /'mʌmɪ/ *n fam* mamma *f*

mummy[2] *n Archaeol* mummia *f*

mumps /mʌmps/ *n* orecchioni *mpl*

munch /mʌntʃ/ *vt/i* sgranocchiare

mundane /mʌn'deɪn/ *a* (*everyday*) banale

municipal /mjʊ'nɪsɪpl/ *a* municipale

mural /'mjʊərəl/ *n* dipinto *m* murale

murder /'mɜːdə(r)/ *n* assassinio *m* ●*vt* assassinare; (*fam: ruin*) massacrare. ~**er** *n* assassino, -a *mf*. ~**ous** /-rəs/ *a* omicida

murky /'mɜːkɪ/ *a* (-**ier**, -**iest**) oscuro

murmur /'mɜːmə(r)/ *n* mormorio *m* ●*vt/i* mormorare

muscle /'mʌsl/ *n* muscolo *m* ●**muscle in** *vi sl* intromettersi (**on** in)

muscular /'mʌskjʊlə(r)/ *a* muscolare; (*strong*) muscoloso

muse /mjuːz/ *vi* meditare (**on** su)

museum /mjuː'zɪəm/ *n* museo *m*

mushroom /'mʌʃrʊm/ *n* fungo *m* ●*vi fig* spuntare come funghi

music /'mjuːzɪk/ *n* musica *f*; (*written*) spartito *m*.

musical /'mjuːzɪkl/ *a* musicale; 〈*person*〉 dotato di senso musicale ●*n* commedia *f* musicale. ~ **box** *n* carillon *m inv.* ~ **instrument** *n* strumento *m* musicale

music: ~ **box** *n* carillon *m inv.* ~ **centre** *n* impianto *m* stereo; '~-**hall** *n* teatro *m* di varietà

musician /mjuː'zɪʃn/ *n* musicista *mf*

Muslim /'mʊzlɪm/ *a & n* musulmano, -a *mf*

mussel /'mʌsl/ *n* cozza *f*

must /mʌst/ *v aux* (*solo al presente*) dovere; **you** ~ **not be late** non devi essere in ritardo; **she** ~ **have finished by now** (*probability*) deve aver finito ormai ●*n* **a** ~ *fam* una cosa da non perdere

mustard /'mʌstəd/ *n* senape *f*

musty /'mʌstɪ/ *a* (-**ier**, -**iest**) stantio

mutation /mjuː'teɪʃn/ *n Biol* mutazione *f*

mute /mjuːt/ *a* muto

muted /'mjuːtɪd/ *a* smorzato

mutilat|e /'mjuːtɪleɪt/ *vt* mutilare. ~**ion** /-'leɪʃn/ *n* mutilazione *f*

mutin|ous /'mjuːtɪnəs/ *a* ammutinato. ~**y** *n* ammutinamento *m* ●*vi* (*pt/pp* -**ied**) ammutinarsi

mutter /'mʌtə(r)/ *vt/i* borbottare

mutton /'mʌtn/ *n* carne *f* di montone

mutual /'mjuːtjʊəl/ *a* reciproco; (*fam: common*) comune. ~**ly** *adv* reciprocamente

muzzle /'mʌzl/ *n* (*of animal*) muso *m*; (*of firearm*) bocca *f*; (*for dog*) museruola *f* ●*vt fig* mettere il bavaglio a

my /maɪ/ *poss a* il mio *m*, la mia *f*, i miei *mpl*, le mie *fpl*; **my mother/father** mia madre/mio padre

myself /maɪ'self/ *pers pron* (*reflexive*) mi; (*emphatic*) me stesso; (*after prep*) me; **I've seen it** ~ l'ho visto io stesso; **by** ~ da solo; **I thought to** ~ ho pensato tra me e me; **I'm proud of** ~ sono fiero di me

mysterious /mɪ'stɪərɪəs/ *a* misterioso. ~**ly** *adv* misteriosamente

mystery /'mɪstərɪ/ *n* mistero *m*; ~ [**story**] racconto *m* del mistero

mysti|c[al] /'mɪstɪk[l]/ *a* mistico. ~**cism** /-sɪzm/ *n* misticismo *m*

mystified /'mɪstɪfaɪd/ *a* disorientato

mystify /'mɪstɪfaɪ/ *vt* (*pt/pp* -**ied**) disorientare

mystique /mɪ'stiːk/ *n* mistica *f*

myth /mɪθ/ *n* mito *m*. ~**ical** *a* mitico

mythology /mɪ'θɒlədʒɪ/ *n* mitologia *f*

Nn

nab /næb/ *vt* ⟨*pt/pp* **nabbed**⟩ *fam* beccare

naff /næf/ *a Br fam* banale

nag¹ /næg/ *n* ⟨*horse*⟩ ronzino *m*

nag² *v* ⟨*pt/pp* **nagged**⟩ ● *vt* assillare ● *vi* essere insistente ● *n* ⟨*person*⟩ brontolone, -a *mf*. **~ging** *a* ⟨*pain*⟩ persistente

nail /neɪl/ *n* chiodo *m*; ⟨*of finger, toe*⟩ unghia *f* ● **nail down** *vt* inchiodare; **~ sb down to a time/price** far fissare a qcno un'ora/un prezzo

nail: **~-brush** *n* spazzolino *m* da unghie. **~-file** *n* limetta *f* da unghie. **~ polish** *n* smalto *m* [per unghie]. **~ scissors** *npl* forbicine *fpl* da unghie. **~ varnish** *n* smalto *m* [per unghie]

naïve /naɪ'iːv/ *a* ingenuo. **~ty** /-ətɪ/ *n* ingenuità *f*

naked /'neɪkɪd/ *a* nudo; **with the ~ eye** a occhio nudo

name /neɪm/ *n* nome *m*; **what's your ~?** come ti chiami?; **my ~ is Matthew** mi chiamo Matthew; **I know her by ~** la conosco di nome; **by the ~ of Bates** di nome Bates; **call sb ~s** *fam* insultare qcno ● *vt* ⟨*to position*⟩ nominare; chiamare ⟨*baby*⟩; ⟨*identify*⟩ citare; **be ~d after** essere chiamato col nome di. **~less** *a* senza nome. **~ly** *adv* cioè

name: **~-plate** *n* targhetta *f*. **~sake** *n* omonimo, -a *mf*

nanny /'nænɪ/ *n* bambinaia *f*. **~-goat** *n* capra *f*

nap /næp/ *n* pisolino *m*; **have a ~** fare un pisolino ● *vi* ⟨*pt/pp* **napped**⟩ **catch sb ~ping** cogliere qcno alla sprovvista

nape /neɪp/ *n* **~ [of the neck]** nuca *f*

napkin /'næpkɪn/ *n* tovagliolo *m*

Naples /'neɪplz/ *n* Napoli *f*

nappy /'næpɪ/ *n* pannolino *m*

narcotic /naː'kɒtɪk/ *a & n* narcotico *m*

narrat|e /nə'reɪt/ *vt* narrare. **~ion** /-eɪʃn/ *n* narrazione *f*

narrative /'nærətɪv/ *a* narrativo ● *n* narrazione *f*

narrator /nə'reɪtə(r)/ *n* narratore, -trice *mf*

narrow /'nærəʊ/ *a* stretto; ⟨*fig: views*⟩ ristretto; ⟨*margin, majority*⟩ scarso ● *vi* restringersi. **~ly** *adv* **~ly escape death** evitare la morte per un pelo. **~-minded** *a* di idee ristrette

nasal /'neɪzl/ *a* nasale

nastily /'naːstɪlɪ/ *adv* ⟨*spitefully*⟩ con cattiveria

nasty /'naːstɪ/ *a* ⟨**-ier, -iest**⟩ ⟨*smell, person, remark*⟩ cattivo; ⟨*injury, situation, weather*⟩ brutto; **turn ~** ⟨*person:*⟩ diventare cattivo

nation /'neɪʃn/ *n* nazione *f*

national /'næʃənl/ *a* nazionale ● *n* cittadino, -a *mf*

national: **~ 'anthem** *n* inno *m* nazionale. **N~ 'Health Service** *n* servizio *m* sanitario britannico. **N~ In'surance** *n* Previdenza *f* sociale

nationalism /'næʃənəlɪzm/ *n* nazionalismo *m*

nationality /næʃə'nælətɪ/ *n* nazionalità *f* *inv*

national|ization /næʃənəlaɪ'zeɪʃn/ *n* nazionalizzazione. **~ize** /'næʃənəlaɪz/ *vt* nazionalizzare. **~ly** /'næʃənəlɪ/ *adv* a livello nazionale

'nation-wide *a* su scala nazionale

native /'neɪtɪv/ *a* nativo; ⟨*innate*⟩ innato ● *n* nativo, -a *mf*; ⟨*local inhabitant*⟩ abitante *mf* del posto; ⟨*outside Europe*⟩ indigeno, -a *mf*; **she's a ~ of Venice** è originaria di Venezia

native: **~ 'land** *n* paese *m* nativo. **~ 'language** *n* lingua *f* madre

Nativity /nə'tɪvətɪ/ *n* **the ~** la Natività *f*. **~ play** *n* rappresentazione *f* sulla nascita di Gesù

natter /'nætə(r)/ *vi fam* chiacchierare

natural /'nætʃrəl/ *a* naturale

natural: **~ 'gas** *n* metano *m*. **~ 'history** *n* storia *f* naturale

naturalist /'nætʃ(ə)rəlɪst/ *n* naturalista *m*

natural|ization /nætʃ(ə)rəlaɪ'zeɪʃn/ *n* naturalizzazione *f*. **~ize** /'nætʃ(ə)rəlaɪz/ *vt* naturalizzare

naturally /'nætʃ(ə)rəlɪ/ *adv* ⟨*of course*⟩ naturalmente; ⟨*by nature*⟩ per natura

nature /'neɪtʃə(r)/ n natura f; **by ~** per natura. **~ reserve** n riserva f naturale

naughtily /'nɔːtɪlɪ/ adv male

naughty /'nɔːtɪ/ a (**-ier, -iest**) monello; (slightly indecent) spinto

nausea /'nɔːzɪə/ n nausea f

nause|ate /'nɔːzɪeɪt/ vt nauseare. **~ating** a nauseante. **~ous** /-ɪəs/ a **I feel ~ous** ho la nausea

nautical /'nɔːtɪkl/ a nautico. **~ mile** n miglio m marino

naval /'neɪvl/ a navale

nave /neɪv/ n navata f centrale

navel /'neɪvl/ n ombelico m

navigable /'nævɪɡəbl/ a navigabile

navigat|e /'nævɪɡeɪt/ vi navigare; Auto fare da navigatore ● vt navigare su ⟨river⟩. **~ion** /-'ɡeɪʃn/ n navigazione f. **~or** n navigatore m

navy /'neɪvɪ/ n marina f ● **~ [blue]** a blu scuro inv ● n blu m inv scuro

Neapolitan /nɪə'pɒlɪtən/ a & n napoletano, -a mf

near /nɪə(r)/ a vicino; ⟨future⟩ prossimo; **the ~est bank** la banca più vicina ● adv vicino; **draw ~** avvicinarsi; **~ at hand** a portata di mano ● prep vicino a; **he was ~ to tears** aveva le lacrime agli occhi ● vt avvicinarsi a

near: ~by a & adv vicino. **~ly** adv quasi; **it's not ~ly enough** non è per niente sufficiente. **~ness** n vicinanza f. **~ side** a Auto ⟨wheel⟩ ⟨left⟩ sinistro; ⟨right⟩ destro. **~-sighted** a Am miope

neat /niːt/ a (tidy) ordinato; (clever) efficace; (undiluted) liscio. **~ly** adv ordinatamente; (cleverly) efficacemente. **~ness** n (tidiness) ordine m

necessarily /nesə'serɪlɪ/ adv necessariamente

necessary /'nesəsərɪ/ a necessario

necessit|ate /nɪ'sesɪteɪt/ vt rendere necessario. **~y** n necessità f inv

neck /nek/ n collo m; (of dress) colletto m; **~ and ~** a testa a testa

necklace /'neklɪs/ n collana f

neck: ~line n scollatura f. **~tie** n cravatta f

neé /neɪ/ a **~ Brett** nata Brett

need /niːd/ n bisogno m; **be in ~ of** avere bisogno di; **if ~ be** se ce ne fosse bisogno; **there is a ~ for** c'è bisogno di; **there is no ~ for** non ce n'è bisogno; **there is no ~ for you to go** non c'è bisogno che tu vada ● vt aver bisogno di; **I ~ to know** devo saperlo; **it ~s to be done** bisogna farlo ● v aux

you ~ not go non c'è bisogno che tu vada; **~ I come?** devo [proprio] venire?

needle /'niːdl/ n ago m; (for knitting) uncinetto m; (of record player) puntina f ● vt (fam: annoy) punzecchiare

needless /'niːdlɪs/ a inutile

'needlework n cucito m

needy /'niːdɪ/ a (**-ier, -iest**) bisognoso

negation /nɪ'ɡeɪʃn/ n negazione f

negative /'neɡətɪv/ a negativo ● n negazione f; Phot negativo m; **in the ~** Gram alla forma negativa

neglect /nɪ'ɡlekt/ n trascuratezza f; **state of ~** stato m di abbandono ● vt trascurare; **he ~ed to write** non si è curato di scrivere. **~ed** a trascurato. **~ful** a negligente; **be ~ful of** trascurare

négligée /'neɡlɪʒeɪ/ n négligé m inv

negligen|ce /'neɡlɪdʒəns/ n negligenza f. **~t** a negligente

negligible /'neɡlɪdʒəbl/ a trascurabile

negotiable /nɪ'ɡəʊʃəbl/ a ⟨road⟩ transitabile; Comm negoziabile; **not ~** ⟨cheque⟩ non trasferibile

negotiat|e /nɪ'ɡəʊʃɪeɪt/ vt negoziare; Auto prendere ⟨bend⟩ ● vi negoziare. **~ion** /-'eɪʃn/ n negoziato m. **~or** n negoziatore, -trice mf

Negro /'niːɡrəʊ/ a & n (pl **-es**) negro, -a mf

neigh /neɪ/ vi nitrire

neighbour /'neɪbə(r)/ n vicino, -a mf. **~hood** n vicinato m; **in the ~hood of** nei dintorni di; fig circa. **~ing** a vicino. **~ly** a amichevole

neither /'naɪðə(r)/ a & pron nessuno dei due, né l'uno né l'altro ● adv **~... nor** né... né ● conj nemmeno, neanche; **~ do/did I** nemmeno io

neon /'niːɒn/ n neon m. **~ light** n luce f al neon

nephew /'nevjuː/ n nipote m

nerve /nɜːv/ n nervo m; (fam: courage) coraggio m; (fam: impudence) faccia f tosta. **lose one's ~** perdersi d'animo. **~-racking** a logorante

nervous /'nɜːvəs/ a nervoso; **he makes me ~** mi mette in agitazione; **be a ~ wreck** avere i nervi a pezzi. **~ 'breakdown** n esaurimento m nervoso. **~ly** adv nervosamente. **~ness** n nervosismo m; (before important event) tensione f

nervy /'nɜːvɪ/ a (**-ier, -iest**) nervoso; (Am: impudent) sfacciato

nest /nest/ n nido m ● vi fare il nido. **~-egg** n gruzzolo m

nestle /'nesl/ *vi* accoccolarsi

net[1] /net/ *n* rete *f* ● *vt* (*pt/pp* **netted**) (*catch*) prendere (*con la rete*)

net[2] *a* netto ● *vt* (*pt/pp* **netted**) incassare un utile netto di

'**netball** *n* sport *m inv* femminile, simile a pallacanestro

Netherlands /'neðələndz/ *npl* the ~ i Paesi Bassi

netting /'netɪŋ/ *n* [wire] ~ reticolato *m*

nettle /'netl/ *n* ortica *f*

'**network** *n* rete *f*

neuralgia /njʊə'rældʒə/ *n* nevralgia *f*

neurolog|ist /njʊə'rɒlədʒɪst/ *n* neurologo, -a *mf*

neur|osis /njʊə'rəʊsɪs/ *n* (*pl* -**oses** /-si:z/) nevrosi *f inv.* ~**otic** /-'rɒtɪk/ *a* nevrotico

neuter /'nju:tə(r)/ *a Gram* neutro ● *n Gram* neutro *m* ● *vt* sterilizzare

neutral /'nju:trəl/ *a* neutro; (*country, person*) neutrale ● *n* in ~ Auto in folle. ~**ity** /-'træləti/ *n* neutralità *f.* ~**ize** *vt* neutralizzare

never /'nevə(r)/ *adv* [non...] mai; (*fam: expressing disbelief*) ma va; ~ **again** mai più; **well I ~!** chi l'avrebbe detto!. ~**-ending** *a* interminabile

nevertheless /nevəðə'les/ *adv* tuttavia

new /nju:/ *a* nuovo

new: ~**born** *a* neonato. ~**comer** *n* nuovo, -a arrivato, -a *mf.* ~**fangled** /-'fæŋgld/ *a pej* modernizzante. ~**-laid** *a* fresco

'**newly** *adv* (*recently*) di recente; ~**-built** costruito di recente. ~**-weds** *npl* sposini *mpl*

new: ~'**moon** *n* luna *f* nuova. ~**ness** *n* novità *f*

news /nju:z/ *n* notizie *fpl*; *TV* telegiornale *m*; *Radio* giornale *m* radio; **piece of** ~ notizia *f*

news: ~**agent** *n* giornalaio, -a *mf.* ~**bulletin** *n* notiziario *m.* ~**caster** *n* giornalista *mf* televisivo, -a/radiofonico, -a. ~**flash** *n* notizia *f* flash. ~**letter** *n* bollettino *m* d'informazione. ~**paper** *n* giornale *m*; (*material*) carta *f* di giornale. ~**reader** *n* giornalista *mf* televisivo, -a/radiofonico, -a

new: ~ **year** *n* (*next year*) anno *m* nuovo; N~ **Year's Day** *n* Capodanno *m.* N~ **Year's 'Eve** *n* vigilia *f* di Capodanno. N~ **Zealand** /-'zi:lənd/ *n* Nuova Zelanda *f.* N~ **Zealander** *n* neozelandese *mf*

next /nekst/ *a* prossimo; (*adjoining*) vicino; **who's ~?** a chi tocca?; ~ **door** accanto; ~ **to nothing** quasi niente; **the ~ day** il giorno dopo; ~ **week** la settimana prossima; **the week after ~** fra due settimane ● *adv* dopo; **when will you see him ~?** quando lo rivedi la prossima volta?; ~ **to** accanto a ● *n* seguente *mf*; ~ **of kin** parente *m* prossimo

NHS *n abbr* **National Health Service**

nib /nɪb/ *n* pennino *m*

nibble /'nɪbl/ *vt/i* mordicchiare

nice /naɪs/ *a* (*day, weather, holiday*) bello; (*person*) gentile, simpatico; (*food*) buono; **it was** ~ **meeting you** è stato un piacere conoscerla. ~**ly** *adv* gentilmente; (*well*) bene. ~**ties** /'naɪsətɪz/ *npl* finezze *fpl*

niche /ni:ʃ/ *n* nicchia *f*

nick /nɪk/ *n* tacca *f*; (*on chin etc*) taglietto *m*; (*fam: prison*) galera *f*; (*fam: police station*) centrale *f* [di polizia]; **in the ~ of time** *fam* appena in tempo ● *vt* intaccare; (*fam: steal*) fregare; (*fam: arrest*) beccare; ~ **one's chin** farsi un taglietto nel mento

nickel /'nɪkl/ *n* nichel *m*; *Am* moneta *f* da cinque centesimi

'**nickname** *n* soprannome *m* ● *vt* soprannominare

nicotine /'nɪkəti:n/ *n* nicotina *f*

niece /ni:s/ *n* nipote *f*

Nigeria /naɪ'dʒɪərɪə/ *n* Nigeria *f.* ~**n** *a* & *n* nigeriano, -a *mf*

niggling /'nɪglɪŋ/ *a* (*detail*) insignificante; (*pain*) fastidioso; (*doubt*) persistente

night /naɪt/ *n* notte *f*; (*evening*) sera *f*; **at ~** la notte, di notte; (*in the evening*) la sera, di sera; **Monday ~** lunedì notte/sera ● *a* di notte

night: ~**cap** *n* papalina *f*; (*drink*) bicchierino *m* bevuto prima di andare a letto. ~**-club** *n* locale *m* notturno, night[-club] *m inv.* ~**-dress** *n* camicia *f* da notte. ~**fall** *n* crepuscolo *m.* ~**-gown**, *fam* ~**ie** /'naɪtɪ/ *n* camicia *f* da notte

nightingale /'naɪtɪŋgeɪl/ *n* usignolo *m*

night: ~**-life** *n* vita *f* notturna. ~**ly** *a* di notte, di sera ● *adv* ogni notte, ogni sera. ~**mare** *n* incubo *m.* ~**-school** scuola *f* serale. ~**-time** *n* at ~**-time** di notte, la notte. ~**-'watchman** *n* guardiano *m* notturno

nil /nɪl/ *n* nulla *m*; *Sport* zero *m*

nimb|le /'nɪmbl/ *a* agile. ~**y** *adv* agilmente

nine /naɪn/ *a* nove *inv* ● *n* nove *m*. **~'teen** *a* diciannove *inv* ● *n* diciannove *m*. **~'teenth** *a* & *n* diciannovesimo, -a *mf*

ninetieth /'naɪntɪɪθ/ *a* & *n* novantesimo, -a *mf*

ninety /'naɪntɪ/ *a* novanta *inv* ● *n* novanta *m*

ninth /naɪnθ/ *a* & *n* nono, -a *mf*

nip /nɪp/ *n* pizzicotto *m*; (*bite*) morso *m* ● *vt* pizzicare; (*bite*) mordere; **~ in the bud** *fig* stroncare sul nascere ● *vi* (*fam: run*) fare un salto

nipple /'nɪpl/ *n* capezzolo *m*; (*Am: on bottle*) tettarella *f*

nippy /'nɪpɪ/ *a* (**-ier, -iest**) *fam* (*cold*) pungente; (*quick*) svelto

nitrogen /'naɪtrədʒn/ *n* azoto *m*

nitwit /'nɪtwɪt/ *n fam* imbecille *mf*

no /nəʊ/ *adv* no ● *n* (*pl* **noes**) no *m inv* ● *a* nessuno; **I have no time** non ho tempo; **in no time** in un baleno; **'no parking'** 'sosta vietata'; **'no smoking'** 'vietato fumare'; **no one** = **nobody**

nobility /nəʊ'bɪlətɪ/ *n* nobiltà *f*

noble /'nəʊbl/ *a* nobile. **~man** *n* nobile *m*

nobody /'nəʊbədɪ/ *pron* nessuno; **he knows ~** non conosce nessuno ● *n* **he's a ~** non è nessuno

nocturnal /nɒk'tɜːnl/ *a* notturno

nod /nɒd/ *n* cenno del capo● *v* (*pt/pp* **nodded**) ● *vi* fare un cenno col capo; (*in agreement*) fare di sì col capo ● *vt* **~ one's head** fare di sì col capo. **nod off** *vi* assopirsi

nodule /'nɒdjuːl/ *n* nodulo *m*

noise /nɔɪz/ *n* rumore *m*; (*loud*) rumore *m*, chiasso *m*. **~less** *a* silenzioso. **~lessly** *adv* silenziosamente

noisy /'nɔɪzɪ/ *a* (**-ier, -iest**) rumoroso

nomad /'nəʊmæd/ *n* nomade *mf*. **~ic** /-'mædɪk/ *a* nomade

nominal /'nɒmɪnl/ *a* nominale

nominat|e /'nɒmɪneɪt/ *vt* proporre come candidato; (*appoint*) designare. **~ion** /-'neɪʃn/ *n* nomina *f*; (*person nominated*) candidato, -a *mf*

nominative /'nɒmɪnətɪv/ *a* & *n Gram* **~ [case]** nominativo *m*

nominee /nɒmɪ'niː/ *n* persona *f* nominata

nonchalant /'nɒnʃələnt/ *a* disinvolto

non-com'missioned /nɒn-/ *a* **~ officer** sottufficiale *m*

non-com'mittal *a* che non si sbilancia

nondescript /'nɒndɪskrɪpt/ *a* qualunque

none /nʌn/ *pron* (*person*) nessuno; (*thing*) niente; **~ of us** nessuno di noi; **~ of this** niente di questo; **there's ~ left** non ce n'è più ● *adv* **she's ~ too pleased** non è per niente soddisfatta; **I'm ~ the wiser** non ne so più di prima

nonentity /nɒ'nentəti/ *n* nullità *f inv*

non-event *n* delusione *f*

non-ex'istent *a* inesistente

non-'fiction *n* saggistica *f*

non-'iron *a* che non si stira

nonplussed /nɒn'plʌst/ *a* perplesso

nonsens|e /'nɒnsəns/ *n* sciocchezze *fpl*. **~ical** /-'sensɪkl/ *a* assurdo

non-'smoker *n* non fumatore, -trice *mf*; (*compartment*) scompartimento *m* non fumatori

non-'stick *a* antiaderente

non-'stop *a* ~ **'flight** volo *m* diretto ● *adv* senza sosta; (*fly*) senza scalo

non-'violent *a* non violento

noodles /'nuːdlz/ *npl* taglierini *mpl*

nook /nʊk/ *n* cantuccio *m*

noon /nuːn/ *n* mezzogiorno *m*; **at ~** a mezzogiorno

noose /nuːs/ *n* nodo *m* scorsoio

nor /nɔː(r)/ *adv* & *conj* né; **~ do I** neppure io

Nordic /'nɔːdɪk/ *a* nordico

norm /nɔːm/ *n* norma *f*

normal /'nɔːml/ *a* normale. **~ity** /-'mælətɪ/ *n* normalità *f*. **~ly** *adv* (*usually*) normalmente

north /nɔːθ/ *n* nord *m*; **to the ~ of** a nord di ● *a* del nord, settentrionale ● *adv* a nord

north: N~ America *n* America *f* del Nord. **~-bound** *a Auto* in direzione nord. **~-east** *a* di nord-est, nordorientale ● *n* nord-est *m* ● *adv* a nord-est; (*travel*) verso nord-est

norther|ly /'nɔːðəlɪ/ *a* (*direction*) nord; (*wind*) del nord. **~n** *a* del nord, settentrionale. **N~n Ireland** *n* Irlanda *f* del Nord

north: N~ 'Pole *n* polo *m* nord. **N~ 'Sea** *n* Mare *m* del Nord. **~ward[s]** /-wəd[z]/ *adv* verso nord. **~-west** *a* di nord-ovest, nordoccidentale ● *n* nord-ovest *m* ● *adv* a nord-ovest; (*travel*) verso nord-ovest

Nor|way /'nɔːweɪ/ *n* Norvegia *f*. **~wegian** /-'wiːdʒn/ *a* & *n* norvegese *mf*

nose /nəʊz/ *n* naso *m*

nose: ~bleed *n* emorragia *f* nasale. **~dive** *n Aeron* picchiata *f*

nostalg|ia /nɒ'stældʒɪə/ *n* nostalgia *f*. **~ic** *a* nostalgico

nostril /'nɒstrəl/ n narice f

nosy /'nəʊzɪ/ a (-ier, -iest) fam ficcanaso inv

not /nɒt/ adv non; **he is ~ Italian** non è italiano; **I hope ~** spero di no; **~ all of us have been invited** non siamo stati tutti invitati; **if ~** se no; **~ at all** niente affatto; **~ a bit** per niente; **~ even** neanche; **~ yet** non ancora; **~ only... but also...** non solo... ma anche...

notabl|e /'nəʊtəbl/ a (remarkable) notevole. **~y** adv (in particular) in particolare

notary /'nəʊtərɪ/ n notaio m; **~ 'public** notaio m

notch /nɒtʃ/ n tacca f ● **notch up** vt (score) segnare

note /nəʊt/ n nota f; (short letter, banknote) biglietto m; (memo, written comment etc) appunto m; **of ~** (person) di spicco; (comments, event) degno di nota; **make a ~ of** prendere nota di; **take ~ of** (notice) prendere nota di ● vt (notice) notare; (write) annotare. **note down** vt annotare.

'notebook n taccuino m; Comput notebook m inv

noted /'nəʊtɪd/ a noto, celebre (**for** per)

note: ~paper n carta f da lettere. **~worthy** a degno di nota

nothing /'nʌθɪŋ/ pron niente, nulla ● adv niente affatto; **for ~** (free, in vain) per niente; (with no reason) senza motivo; **~ but** nient'altro che; **~ much** poco o nulla; **~ interesting** niente di interessante; **it's ~ to do with you** non ti riguarda

notice /'nəʊtɪs/ n (on board) avviso m; (review) recensione f; (termination of employment) licenziamento m; [advance] **~** preavviso m; **two months' ~** due mesi di preavviso; **at short ~** con breve preavviso; **until further ~** fino nuovo avviso; **give [in one's] ~** (employee:) dare le dimissioni; **give an employee ~** dare il preavviso a un impiegato; **take no ~ of** non fare caso a; **take no ~!** non farci caso! ● vt notare. **~able** /-əbl/ a evidente. **~ably** adv sensibilmente. **~-board** n bacheca f

noti|fication /nəʊtɪfɪ'keɪʃn/ n notifica f. **~fy** /'nəʊtɪfaɪ/ vt (pt/pp -ied) notificare

notion /'nəʊʃn/ n idea f, nozione f; **~s** pl (Am: haberdashery) merceria f

notoriety /nəʊtə'raɪətɪ/ n notorietà f

notorious /nəʊ'tɔ:rɪəs/ a famigerato; **be ~ for** essere tristemente famoso per

notwith'standing prep malgrado ● adv ciononostante

nougat /'nu:gɑ:/ n torrone m

nought /nɔ:t/ n zero m

noun /naʊn/ n nome m, sostantivo m

nourish /'nʌrɪʃ/ vt nutrire. **~ing** a nutriente. **~ment** n nutrimento m

novel /'nɒvl/ a insolito ● n romanzo m. **~ist** n romanziere, -a mf. **~ty** n novità f; **~ties** pl (objects) oggettini mpl

November /nəʊ'vembə(r)/ n novembre m

novice /'nɒvɪs/ n novizio, -a mf

now /naʊ/ adv ora, adesso; **by ~** ormai; **just ~** proprio ora; **right ~** subito; **~ and again**, **~ and then** ogni tanto; **~, ~!** su! ● conj **~ [that]** ora che, adesso che

'nowadays adv oggigiorno

nowhere /'nəʊ-/ adv in nessun posto, da nessuna parte

noxious /'nɒkʃəs/ a nocivo

nozzle /'nɒzl/ n bocchetta f

nuance /'nju:ɒ̃s/ n sfumatura f

nuclear /'nju:klɪə(r)/ a nucleare

nucleus /'nju:klɪəs/ n (pl -lei /-lɪaɪ/) nucleo m

nude /nju:d/ a nudo ● n nudo m; **in the ~** nudo

nudge /nʌdʒ/ n colpetto m di gomito ● vt dare un colpetto col gomito a

nudism /'nju:dɪzm/ n nudismo m

nud|ist /'nju:dɪst/ n nudista mf. **~ity** n nudità f

nugget /'nʌgɪt/ n pepita f

nuisance /'nju:sns/ n seccatura f; (person) piaga f; **what a ~!** che seccatura!

null /nʌl/ a **~ and void** nullo

numb /nʌm/ a intorpidito; **~ with cold** intirizzito dal freddo

number /'nʌmbə(r)/ n numero m; **a ~ of people** un certo numero di persone ● vt numerare; (include) annoverare. **~-plate** n targa f

numeral /'nju:mərəl/ n numero m, cifra f

numerate /'nju:mərət/ a **be ~** saper fare i calcoli

numerical /nju:'merɪkl/ a numerico; **in ~ order** in ordine numerico

numerous /'nju:mərəs/ a numeroso

nun /nʌn/ n suora f

nurse /nɜ:s/ n infermiere, -a mf; **children's ~** bambinaia f ● vt curare

nursery /'nɜ:sərɪ/ n stanza f dei bambini; (for plants) vivaio m; [day] **~** asilo *m.* **~ rhyme** *n* filastrocca *f.* **~ school** *n* scuola *f* materna

nursing /'nɜːsɪŋ/ *n* professione *f* d'infermiere. **~ home** *n* casa *f* di cura per anziani

nurture /'nɜːtʃə(r)/ *vt* allevare; *fig* coltivare

nut /nʌt/ *n* noce *f; Techn* dado *m;* (*fam:* *head*) zucca *f;* **~s** *npl* frutta *f* secca; **be ~s** *fam* essere svitato. **~crackers** *npl* schiaccianoci *m inv.* **~meg** *n* noce *f* moscata

nutrit|ion /nju:'trɪʃn/ *n* nutrizione *f.* **~ious** /-ʃəs/ *a* nutriente

'nutshell *n* **in a ~** *fig* in parole povere

nuzzle /'nʌzl/ *vt* ⟨*horse, dog:*⟩ strofinare il muso contro

nylon /'naɪlɒn/ *n* nailon *m;* **~s** *pl* calze *fpl* di nailon ● *a* di nailon

....

Oo

....

O /əʊ/ *n Teleph* zero *m*

oaf /əʊf/ *n* (*pl* **oafs**) zoticone, -a *mf*

oak /əʊk/ *n* quercia *f* ● *attrib* di quercia

OAP *n abbr* (**old-age pensioner**) pensionato, -a *mf*

oar /ɔː(r)/ *n* remo *m.* **~sman** *n* vogatore *m*

oasis /əʊ'eɪsɪs/ *n* (*pl* **oases** /-siːz/) oasi *f inv*

oath /əʊθ/ *n* giuramento *m;* (*swearword*) bestemmia *f*

oatmeal /'əʊt-/ *n* farina *f* d'avena

oats /əʊts/ *npl* avena *fsg; Culin* [**rolled**] **~** fiocchi *mpl* di avena

obedien|ce /ə'biːdɪəns/ *n* ubbidienza *f.* **~t** *a* ubbidiente

obes|e /ə'biːs/ *a* obeso. **~ity** *n* obesità *f*

obey /ə'beɪ/ *vt* ubbidire a; osservare ⟨*instructions, rules*⟩ ● *vi* ubbidire

obituary /ə'bɪtjʊərɪ/ *n* necrologio *m*

object[1] /'ɒbdʒɪkt/ *n* oggetto *m; Gram* complemento *m* oggetto; **money is no ~** i soldi non sono un problema

object[2] /əb'dʒekt/ *vi* (*be against*) opporsi (**to** a); **~ that...** obiettare che...

objection /əb'dʒekʃn/ *n* obiezione *f;* **have no ~** non avere niente in contrario. **~able** /-əbl/ *a* discutibile; ⟨*person*⟩ sgradevole

objectiv|e /əb'dʒektɪv/ *a* oggettivo ● *n* obiettivo *m.* **~ely** *adv* obiettivamente. **~ity** /-'tɪvətɪ/ *n* oggettività *f*

obligation /ɒblɪ'geɪʃn/ *n* obbligo *m;* **be under an ~** avere un obbligo; **without ~** senza impegno

obligatory /ə'blɪgətrɪ/ *a* obbligatorio

oblig|e /ə'blaɪdʒ/ *vt* (*compel*) obbligare; much **~ed** grazie mille. **~ing** *a* disponibile

oblique /ə'bliːk/ *a* obliquo; *fig* indiretto ● *n* ~ [**stroke**] barra *f*

obliterate /ə'blɪtəreɪt/ *vt* obliterare

oblivion /ə'blɪvɪən/ *n* oblio *m*

oblivious /ə'blɪvɪəs/ *a* **be ~** essere dimentico (**of, to** di)

oblong /'ɒblɒŋ/ *a* oblungo ● *n* rettangolo *m*

obnoxious /əb'nɒkʃəs/ *a* detestabile

oboe /'əʊbəʊ/ *n* oboe *m inv*

obscen|e /əb'siːn/ *a* osceno; ⟨*profits, wealth*⟩ vergognoso. **~ity** /-'senətɪ/ *n* oscenità *f inv*

obscur|e /əb'skjʊə(r)/ *a* oscuro ● *vt* oscurare; (*confuse*) mettere in ombra. **~ity** *n* oscurità *f*

obsequious /əb'siːkwɪəs/ *a* ossequioso

observa|nce /əb'zɜːvəns/ *n* (*of custom*) osservanza *f.* **~nt** *a* attento. **~tion** /ɒbzə'veɪʃn/ *n* osservazione *f*

observatory /əb'zɜːvətrɪ/ *n* osservatorio *m*

observe /əb'zɜːv/ *vt* osservare; (*notice*) notare; (*keep, celebrate*) celebrare. **~r** *n* osservatore, -trice *mf*

obsess /əb'ses/ *vt* **be ~ed by** essere fissato con. **~ion** /-eʃn/ *n* fissazione *f.* **~ive** /-ɪv/ *a* ossessivo

obsolete /'ɒbsəliːt/ *a* obsoleto; ⟨*word*⟩ desueto

obstacle /'ɒbstəkl/ *n* ostacolo *m*

obstetrician /ɒbstə'trɪʃn/ *n* ostetrico, -a *mf.* **obstetrics** /əb'stetrɪks/ *n* ostetricia *f*

obstinacy | offer

obstina|cy /'ɒbstɪnəsɪ/ n ostinazione f. **~te** /-nət/ a ostinato

obstreperous /əb'strepərəs/ a turbolento

obstruct /əb'strʌkt/ vt ostruire; (hinder) ostacolare. **~ion** /-ʌkʃn/ n ostruzione f; (obstacle) ostacolo m. **~ive** /-ɪv/ a **be ~ive** ⟨person:⟩ creare dei problemi

obtain /əb'teɪn/ vt ottenere. **~able** /-əbl/ a ottenibile

obtrusive /əb'truːsɪv/ a ⟨object⟩ stonato

obtuse /əb'tjuːs/ a ottuso

obvious /'ɒbvɪəs/ a ovvio. **~ly** adv ovviamente

occasion /ə'keɪʒn/ n occasione f; (event) evento m; **on ~** talvolta; **on the ~ of** in occasione di

occasional /ə'keɪʒənl/ a saltuario; **he has the ~ glass of wine** ogni tanto beve un bicchiere di vino. **~ly** adv ogni tanto

occult /ɒ'kʌlt/ a occulto

occupant /'ɒkjʊpənt/ n occupante mf; (of vehicle) persona f a bordo

occupation /ɒkjʊ'peɪʃn/ n occupazione f; (job) professione f **~al** a professionale

occupier /'ɒkjʊpaɪə(r)/ n residente mf

occupy /'ɒkjʊpaɪ/ vt (pt/pp occupied) occupare; (keep busy) tenere occupato

occur /ə'kɜː(r)/ vi (pt/pp occurred) accadere; (exist) trovarsi; **it ~red to me that** mi è venuto in mente che. **~rence** /ə'kʌrəns/ n (event) fatto m

ocean /'əʊʃn/ n oceano m

o'clock /ə'klɒk/ adv **it's 7 ~** sono le sette; **at 7 ~** alle sette;

octave /'ɒktɪv/ n Mus ottava f

October /ɒk'təʊbə(r)/ n ottobre m

octopus /'ɒktəpəs/ n (pl **-puses**) polpo m

odd /ɒd/ a ⟨number⟩ dispari; (not of set) scompagnato; (strange) strano; **forty ~** quaranta e rotti; **~ jobs** lavoretti mpl; **the ~ one out** l'eccezione f; **at ~ moments** a tempo perso; **have the ~ glass of wine** avere un bicchiere di vino ogni tanto

odd|ity /'ɒdɪtɪ/ n stranezza f. **~ly** adv stranamente; **~ly enough** stranamente. **~ment** n (of fabric) scampolo m

odds /ɒdz/ npl (chances) probabilità fpl; **at ~** in disaccordo; **~ and ends** cianfrusaglie fpl; **it makes no ~** non fa alcuna differenza

ode /əʊd/ n ode f

odour /'əʊdə(r)/ n odore m. **~less** a inodore

of /ɒv/, /əv/ prep di; **a cup of tea/coffee** una tazza di tè/caffè; **the hem of my skirt** l'orlo della mia gonna; **the summer of 1989** l'estate del 1989; **the two of us** noi due; **made of** di; **that's very kind of you** è molto gentile da parte tua; **a friend of mine** un mio amico; **a child of three** un bambino di tre anni; **the fourth of January** il quattro gennaio; **within a year of their divorce** a circa un anno dal loro divorzio; **half of it** la metà; **the whole of the room** tutta la stanza

off /ɒf/ prep da; (distant from) lontano da; **take £10 ~ the price** ridurre il prezzo di 10 sterline; **~ the coast** presso la costa; **a street ~ the main road** una traversa della via principale; (near) una strada vicino alla via principale; **get ~ the ladder** scendere dalla scala; **get ~ the bus** uscire dall'autobus; **leave the lid ~ the saucepan** lasciare la pentola senza il coperchio ● adv ⟨button, handle⟩ staccato; ⟨light, machine⟩ spento; ⟨brake⟩ tolto; ⟨tap⟩ chiuso; **'off'** (on appliance) 'off'; **2 kilometres ~** a due kilometri di distanza; **a long way ~** molto distante; (time) lontano; **~ and on** di tanto in tanto; **with his hat/coat ~** senza il cappello/cappotto; **with the light ~** a luce spenta; **20% ~** 20% di sconto; **be ~** (leave) andar via; Sport essere partito; ⟨food:⟩ essere andato a male; (all gone) essere finito; ⟨wedding, engagement:⟩ essere cancellato; **I'm ~ alcohol** ho smesso di bere; **be ~ one's food** non avere appetito; **she's ~ today** (on holiday) è in ferie oggi; (ill) è malata oggi; **I'm ~ home** vado a casa; **you'd be better ~ doing...** faresti meglio a fare...; **have a day ~** avere un giorno di vacanza; **drive/sail ~** andare via

offal /'ɒfl/ n Culin frattaglie fpl

'off-beat a insolito

'off-chance n possibilità f remota

off-'colour a (not well) giù di forma; ⟨joke, story⟩ sporco

offence /ə'fens/ n (illegal act) reato m; **give ~** offendere; **take ~** offendersi (**at** per)

offend /ə'fend/ vt offendere. **~er** n Jur colpevole mf

offensive /ə'fensɪv/ a offensivo ● n offensiva f

offer /'ɒfə(r)/ n offerta f ● vt offrire; opporre ⟨*resistance*⟩; **~ sb sth** offrire qcsa a qcno; **~ to do sth** offrirsi di fare qcsa. **~ing** n offerta f

off'hand a (*casual*) spiccio ● *adv* su due piedi

office /'ɒfɪs/ n ufficio m; (*post, job*) carica f. **~ hours** pl orario m di ufficio

officer /'ɒfɪsə(r)/ n ufficiale m; (*police*) agente m [di polizia]

official /ə'fɪʃl/ a ufficiale ● n funzionario, -a mf; *Sport* dirigente m. **~ly** adv ufficialmente

officiate /ə'fɪʃɪeɪt/ vi officiare

'offing n **in the ~** in vista

'off-licence n negozio m per la vendita di alcolici

off-'load vt scaricare

'off-putting a fam scoraggiante

'offset vt (*pt/pp* -set, *pres p* -setting) controbilanciare

'offshoot n ramo m; fig diramazione f

'offshore a ⟨*wind*⟩ di terra; ⟨*company, investment*⟩ offshore inv. **~ rig** n piattaforma f petrolifera, off-shore m inv

off'side a *Sport* [in] fuori gioco; ⟨*wheel etc*⟩ (*left*) sinistro; (*right*) destro

'offspring n prole m

off'stage adv dietro le quinte

off-'white a bianco sporco

often /'ɒfn/ adv spesso; **how ~** ogni quanto; **every so ~** una volta ogni tanto

ogle /'əʊgl/ vt mangiarsi con gli occhi

oh /əʊ/ int oh!; **~ dear** oh Dio!

oil /ɔɪl/ n olio m; (*petroleum*) petrolio m; (*for heating*) nafta f ● vt oliare

oil: **~field** n giacimento m di petrolio. **~-painting** n pittura f a olio. **~ refinery** n raffineria f di petrolio. **~ rig** piattaforma f petrolifera. **~skins** npl vestiti mpl di tela cerata. **~-slick** n chiazza f di petrolio. **~-tanker** n petroliera f. **~ well** n pozzo m petrolifero

oily /'ɔɪlɪ/ a (-ier, -iest) unto; fig untuoso

ointment /'ɔɪntmənt/ n pomata f

OK /əʊ'keɪ/ int va bene, o.k. ● a **if that's OK with you** se ti va bene; **she's OK** (*well*) sta bene; **is the milk still OK?** il latte è ancora buono? ● adv (*well*) bene ● vt (*anche* **okay**) (*pt/pp* **OK'd, okayed**) dare l'o.k. a

old /əʊld/ a vecchio; ⟨*girlfriend*⟩ ex; **how ~ is she?** quanti anni ha?; **she is ten years ~** ha dieci anni

old: **~ 'age** n vecchiaia f. **~-age 'pensioner** n pensionato, -a mf. **~ boy** n *Sch* ex-allievo m. **~'fashioned** a anti-

quato. **~ girl** n *Sch* ex-allieva f. **~ 'maid** n zitella f

olive /'ɒlɪv/ n (*fruit, colour*) oliva f; (*tree*) olivo m ● a d'oliva; (*colour*) olivastro. **~ branch** n fig ramoscello m d'olivo. **~ 'oil** n olio m di oliva

Olympic /ə'lɪmpɪk/ a olimpico; **~s, ~ Games** Olimpiadi fpl

omelette /'ɒmlɪt/ n omelette f inv

omen /'əʊmən/ n presagio m

ominous /'ɒmɪnəs/ a sinistro

omission /ə'mɪʃn/ n omissione f

omit /ə'mɪt/ vt (*pt/pp* **omitted**) omettere; **~ to do sth** tralasciare di fare qcsa

omnipotent /ɒm'nɪpətənt/ a onnipotente

on /ɒn/ prep su; (*on horizontal surface*) su, sopra; **on Monday** lunedì; **on Mondays** di lunedì; **on the first of May** il primo di maggio; **on arriving** all'arrivo; **on one's finger** ⟨*cut*⟩ nel dito; ⟨*ring*⟩ al dito; **on foot** a piedi; **on the right/left** a destra/sinistra; **on the Rhine/Thames** sul Reno/Tamigi; **on the radio/television** alla radio/televisione; **on the bus/train** in autobus/treno; **go on the bus/train** andare in autobus/treno; **get on the bus/train** salire sull'autobus/sul treno; **on me** (*with me*) con me; **it's on me** fam tocca a me ● adv (*further on*) dopo; (*switched on*) acceso; ⟨*brake*⟩ inserito; (*in operation*) in funzione; **'on'** (*on machine*) 'on'; **he had his hat/coat on** portava il cappello/cappotto; **without his hat/coat on** senza cappello/cappotto; **with/without the lid on** con/senza coperchio; **be on** ⟨*film, programme, event*⟩ esserci; **it's not on** fam non è giusto; **be on at** fam tormentare (**to** per); **on and on** senza sosta; **on and off** a intervalli; **and so on** e così via; **go on** continuare; **drive on** spostarsi (*con la macchina*); **stick on** attaccare; **sew on** cucire

once /wʌns/ adv una volta; (*formerly*) un tempo; **~ upon a time there was** c'era una volta; **at ~** subito; (*at the same time*) contemporaneamente; **~ and for all** una volta per tutte ● conj [non] appena. **~-over** n fam **give sb/sth the ~-over** (*look, check*) dare un'occhiata veloce a qcno/qcsa

'oncoming a che si avvicina dalla direzione opposta

one /wʌn/ a uno, una; **not ~ person** nemmeno una persona ● n uno m ● pron uno; (*impersonal*) si; **~ another**

l'un l'altro; **~ by ~** [a] uno a uno; **~ never knows** non si sa mai

one: ~-eyed *a* con un occhio solo. **~-off** *a* unico. **~-parent 'family** *n* famiglia *f* con un solo genitore. **~self** *pron* (*reflexive*) si; (*emphatic*) sé, se stesso; **by ~self** da solo; **be proud of ~self** essere fieri di sé. **~-sided** *a* unilaterale. **~-way** *a* ⟨*street*⟩ a senso unico; ⟨*ticket*⟩ di sola andata

onion /ˈʌnjən/ *n* cipolla *f*

'onlooker *n* spettatore, -trice *mf*

only /ˈəʊnlɪ/ *a* solo; **~ child** figlio, -a *mf* unico, -a ● *adv & conj* solo, solamente; **~ just** appena

on/'off switch *n* pulsante *m* di accensione

'onset *n* (*beginning*) inizio *m*

onslaught /ˈɒnslɔːt/ *n* attacco *m*

onus /ˈəʊnəs/ *n* **the ~ is on me** spetta a me la responsabilità (**to** di)

onward[s] /ˈɒnwəd[z]/ *adv* in avanti; **from then ~** da allora [in poi]

ooze /uːz/ *vi* fluire

opal /ˈəʊpl/ *n* opale *f*

opaque /əʊˈpeɪk/ *a* opaco

open /ˈəʊpən/ *a* aperto; (*free to all*) pubblico; ⟨*job*⟩ vacante; **in the ~ air** all'aperto ● *n* **in the ~** all'aperto; *fig* alla luce del sole ● *vt* aprire ● *vi* aprirsi; ⟨*shop:*⟩ aprire; ⟨*flower:*⟩ sbocciare. **open up** *vt* aprire ● *vi* aprirsi

open: ~-air 'swimming pool *n* piscina *f* all'aperto. **~ day** *n* giorno *m* di apertura al pubblico

opener /ˈəʊpənə(r)/ *n* (*for tins*) apriscatole *m inv*; (*for bottles*) apribottiglie *m inv*

opening /ˈəʊpənɪŋ/ *n* apertura *f*; (*beginning*) inizio *m*; (*job*) posto *m* libero; **~ hours** *npl* orario *m* d'apertura

openly /ˈəʊpənlɪ/ *adv* apertamente

open: ~-'minded *a* aperto; (*broadminded*) di vedute larghe. **~-plan** *a* pianta aperta. **~ 'sandwich** *n* tartina *f*. **~ secret** *n* segreto *m* di Pulcinella. **~ ticket** *n* biglietto *m* aperto. **O~ University** corsi *mpl* universitari per corrispondenza

opera /ˈɒpərə/ *n* opera *f*

operable /ˈɒpərəbl/ *a* operabile

opera: ~-glasses *npl* binocolo *msg* da teatro. **~-house** *n* teatro *m* lirico. **~-singer** *n* cantante *mf* lirico, -a

operate /ˈɒpəreɪt/ *vt* far funzionare ⟨*machine, lift*⟩; azionare ⟨*lever, brake*⟩; mandare avanti ⟨*business*⟩ ● *vi Techn* funzionare; (*be in action*) essere in funzione; *Mil, fig* operare; **~ on** *Med* operare

operatic /ɒpəˈrætɪk/ *a* lirico, operistico

operation /ɒpəˈreɪʃn/ *n* operazione *f*; *Tech* funzionamento *m*; **in ~** *Techn* in funzione; **come into ~** *fig* entrare in funzione; ⟨*law:*⟩ entrare in vigore; **have an ~** *Med* subire un'operazione. **~al** *a* operativo; ⟨*law etc*⟩ in vigore

operative /ˈɒpərətɪv/ *a* operativo

operator /ˈɒpəreɪtə(r)/ *n* (*user*) operatore, -trice *mf*; *Teleph* centralinista *mf*

operetta /ɒpəˈretə/ *n* operetta *f*

opinion /əˈpɪnjən/ *n* opinione *f*; **in my ~** secondo me. **~ated** *a* dogmatico

opponent /əˈpəʊnənt/ *n* avversario, -a *mf*

opportun|e /ˈɒpətjuːn/ *a* opportuno. **~ist** /-ˈtjuːnɪst/ *n* opportunista *mf*. **~istic** *a* opportunistico

opportunity /ɒpəˈtjuːnətɪ/ *n* opportunità *f inv*

oppos|e /əˈpəʊz/ *vt* opporsi a; **be ~ed to sth** esssere contrario a qcsa; **as ~ed to** al contrario di. **~ing** *a* avversario; (*opposite*) opposto

opposite /ˈɒpəzɪt/ *a* opposto; ⟨*house*⟩ di fronte; **~ number** *fig* controparte *f*; **the ~ sex** l'altro sesso ● *n* contrario *m* ● *adv* di fronte ● *prep* di fronte a

opposition /ɒpəˈzɪʃn/ *n* opposizione *f*

oppress /əˈpres/ *vt* opprimere. **~ion** /-eʃn/ *n* oppressione *f*. **~ive** /-ɪv/ *a* oppressivo; ⟨*heat*⟩ opprimente. **~or** *n* oppressore *m*

opt /ɒpt/ *vi* **~ for** optare per; **~ out** dissociarsi (**of** da)

optical /ˈɒptɪkl/ *a* ottico; **~ illusion** illusione *f* ottica

optician /ɒpˈtɪʃn/ *n* ottico, -a *mf*

optimis|m /ˈɒptɪmɪzm/ *n* ottimismo *m*. **~t** /-mɪst/ *n* ottimista *mf*. **~tic** /-ˈmɪstɪk/ *a* ottimistico

optimum /ˈɒptɪməm/ *a* ottimale ● *n* (*pl* **-ima**) optimum *m*

option /ˈɒpʃn/ *n* scelta *f*; *Comm* opzione *f*. **~al** *a* facoltativo; **~al extras** optional *m inv*

opulen|ce /ˈɒpjʊləns/ *n* opulenza *f*. **~t** *a* opulento

or /ɔː(r)/ *conj* o, oppure; (*after negative*) né; **or [else]** se no; **in a year or two** fra un anno o due

oracle /ˈɒrəkl/ *n* oracolo *m*

oral /ˈɔːrəl/ *a* orale ● *n fam* esame *m* orale. **~ly** *adv* oralmente

orange /ˈɒrɪndʒ/ *n* arancia *f*; (*colour*)

arancione *m* ● *a* arancione. **~ade** /-'dʒeɪd/ *n* aranciata *f*. **~ juice** *n* succo *m* d'arancia

orator /'ɒrətə(r)/ *n* oratore, -trice *mf*

oratorio /ɒrə'tɔːrɪəʊ/ *n* oratorio *m*

oratory /'ɒrətərɪ/ *n* oratorio *m*

orbit /'ɔːbɪt/ *n* orbita *f* ● *vt* orbitare. **~al** *a* **~al road** tangenziale *f*

orchard /'ɔːtʃəd/ *n* frutteto *m*

orches|tra /'ɔːkɪstrə/ *n* orchestra *f*. **~tral** /-'kestrəl/ *a* orchestrale. **~trate** *vt* orchestrare

orchid /'ɔːkɪd/ *n* orchidea *f*

ordain /ɔː'deɪn/ *vt* decretare; *Relig* ordinare

ordeal /ɔː'diːl/ *n fig* terribile esperienza *f*

order /'ɔːdə(r)/ *n* ordine *m*; *Comm* ordinazione *f*; **out of ~** ⟨*machine*⟩ fuori servizio; **in ~ that** affinché; **in ~ to** per ● *vt* ordinare

orderly /'ɔːdəlɪ/ *a* ordinato ● *n Mil* attendente *m*; *Med* inserviente *m*

ordinary /'ɔːdɪnərɪ/ *a* ordinario

ordination /ɔːdɪ'neɪʃn/ *n Relig* ordinazione *f*

ore /ɔː(r)/ *n* minerale *m* grezzo

organ /'ɔːgən/ *n Anat, Mus* organo *m*

organic /ɔː'gænɪk/ *a* organico; ⟨*without chemicals*⟩ biologico. **~ally** *adv* organicamente; **~ally grown** coltivato biologicamente

organism /'ɔːgənɪzm/ *n* organismo *m*

organist /'ɔːgənɪst/ *n* organista *mf*

organization /ɔːgənaɪ'zeɪʃn/ *n* organizzazione *f*

organize /'ɔːgənaɪz/ *vt* organizzare. **~r** *n* organizzatore, -trice *mf*

orgasm /'ɔːgæzm/ *n* orgasmo *m*

orgy /'ɔːdʒɪ/ *n* orgia *f*

Orient /'ɔːrɪənt/ *n* Oriente *m*. **o~al** /-'entl/ *a* orientale ● *n* orientale *mf*

orient|ate /'ɔːrɪənteɪt/ *vt* **~ate oneself** orientarsi. **~ation** /-'teɪʃn/ *n* orientamento *m*

origin /'ɒrɪdʒɪn/ *n* origine *f*

original /ə'rɪdʒɪn(ə)l/ *a* originario; ⟨*not copied, new*⟩ originale ● *n* originale *m*; **in the ~** in versione originale. **~ity** /-'nælətɪ/ *n* originalità *f*. **~ly** *adv* originariamente

originat|e /ə'rɪdʒɪneɪt/ *vi* **~e in** avere origine in. **~or** *n* ideatore, -trice *mf*

ornament /'ɔːnəmənt/ *n* ornamento *m*; ⟨*on mantelpiece etc*⟩ soprammobile *m*. **~al** /-'mentl/ *a* ornamentale. **~ation** /-'teɪʃn/ *n* decorazione *f*

ornate /ɔː'neɪt/ *a* ornato

orphan /'ɔːfn/ *n* orfano, -a *mf* ● *vt* rendere orfano; **be ~ed** rimanere orfano. **~age** /-ɪdʒ/ *n* orfanotrofio *m*

orthodox /'ɔːθədɒks/ *a* ortodosso

orthopaedic /ɔːθə'piːdɪk/ *a* ortopedico

oscillate /'ɒsɪleɪt/ *vi* oscillare

ostensibl|e /ɒ'stensəbl/ *a* apparente. **~y** *adv* apparentemente

ostentat|ion /ɒsten'teɪʃn/ *n* ostentazione *f*. **~ious** /-ʃəs/ *a* ostentato

osteopath /'ɒstɪəpæθ/ *n* osteopata *mf*

ostracize /'ɒstrəsaɪz/ *vt* bandire

ostrich /'ɒstrɪtʃ/ *n* struzzo *m*

other /'ʌðə(r)/ *a, pron & n* altro, -a *mf*; **the ~** [one] l'altro, -a *mf*; **the ~ two** gli altri due; **two ~s** altri due; **~ people** gli altri; **any ~ questions?** altre domande?; **every ~ day** ⟨*alternate days*⟩ a giorni alterni; **the ~ day** l'altro giorno; **the ~ evening** l'altra sera; **someone/something or ~** qualcuno/qualcosa ● *adv* **~ than him** tranne lui; **somehow or ~** in qualche modo; **somewhere or ~** da qualche parte

'otherwise *adv* altrimenti; ⟨*differently*⟩ diversamente

otter /'ɒtə(r)/ *n* lontra *f*

ouch /aʊtʃ/ *int* ahi!

ought /ɔːt/ *v aux* **I/we ~ to stay** dovrei/dovremmo rimanere; **he ~ not to have done it** non avrebbe dovuto farlo; **that ~ to be enough** questo dovrebbe bastare

ounce /aʊns/ *n* oncia *f* (= 28, 35 g)

our /'aʊə(r)/ *poss a* il nostro *m*, la nostra *f*, i nostri *mpl*, le nostre *fpl*; **~ mother/father** nostra madre/nostro padre

ours /'aʊəz/ *poss pron* il nostro *m*, la nostra *f*, i nostri *mpl*, le nostre *fpl*; **a friend of ~** un nostro amico; **friends of ~** dei nostri amici; **that is ~** quello è nostro; ⟨*as opposed to yours*⟩ quello è il nostro

ourselves /aʊə'selvz/ *pers pron* ⟨*reflexive*⟩ ci; ⟨*emphatic*⟩ noi, noi stessi; **we poured ~ a drink** ci siamo versati da bere; **we heard it ~** l'abbiamo sentito noi stessi; **we are proud of ~** siamo fieri di noi; **by ~** da soli

out /aʊt/ *adv* fuori; ⟨*not alight*⟩ spento; **be ~** ⟨*flower:*⟩ essere sbocciato; ⟨*workers:*⟩ essere in sciopero; ⟨*calculation:*⟩ essere sbagliato; *Sport* essere fuori; ⟨*unconscious*⟩ aver perso i sensi; ⟨*fig: not feasible*⟩ fuori questione; **the sun is ~** è uscito il sole; **~ and about** in piedi; **get ~!** *fam* fuori!; **you should get**

~ more dovresti uscire più spesso; **~ with it!** *fam* sputa il rospo!; ● *prep* **~ of** fuori da; **~ of date** non aggiornato; ⟨*passport*⟩ scaduto; **~ of order** guasto; **~ of print/stock** esaurito; **be ~ of bed/the room** fuori dal letto/dalla stanza; **~ of breath** senza fiato; **~ of danger** fuori pericolo; **~ of work** disoccupato; **nine ~ of ten** nove su dieci; **be ~ of sugar/bread** rimanere senza zucchero/pane; **go ~ of the room** uscire dalla stanza

out'bid *vt* (*pt/pp* **-bid**, *pres p* **-bidding**) **~ sb** rilanciare l'offerta di qcno

'outboard *a* **~ motor** motore *m*

'outbreak *n* (*of war*) scoppio *m*; (*of disease*) insorgenza *f*

'outbuilding *n* costruzione *f* annessa

'outburst *n* esplosione *f*

'outcome *n* risultato *m*

'outcry *n* protesta *f*

out'dated *a* sorpassato

out'do *vt* (*pt* **-did**, *pp* **-done**) superare

'outdoor *a* ⟨*life, sports*⟩ all'aperto; **~ clothes** *pl* vestiti per uscire; **~ swimming pool** piscina *f* scoperta

out'doors *adv* all'aria aperta; **go ~** uscire [all'aria aperta]

'outer *a* esterno

'outfit *n* equipaggiamento *m*; (*clothes*) completo *m*; (*fam: organization*) organizzazione *f*. **~ter** *n* **men's ~ter's** negozio *m* di abbigliamento maschile

'outgoing *a* (*president*) uscente; ⟨*mail*⟩ in partenza; (*sociable*) estroverso ● *npl* **~s** uscite *fpl*

out'grow *vi* (*pt* **-grew**, *pp* **-grown**) diventare troppo grande per

'outhouse *n* costruzione *f* annessa

outing /'aʊtɪŋ/ *n* gita *f*

outlandish /aʊt'lændɪʃ/ *a* stravagante

'outlaw *n* fuorilegge *mf inv* ● *vt* dichiarare illegale

'outlay *n* spesa *f*

'outlet *n* sbocco *m*; *fig* sfogo *m*; *Comm* punto *m* [di] vendita

'outline *n* contorno *m*; (*summary*) sommario *m* ● *vt* tracciare il contorno di; (*describe*) descrivere

out'live *vt* sopravvivere a

'outlook *n* vista *f*; (*future prospect*) prospettiva *f*; (*attitude*) visione *f*

'outlying *a* **~ areas** zone *fpl* periferiche

out'number *vt* superare in numero

'out-patient *n* paziente *mf* esterno, -a; **~s' department** ambulatorio *m*

'output *n* produzione *f*

'outrage *n* oltraggio *m* ● *vt* oltraggiare. **~ous** /-'reɪdʒəs/ *a* oltraggioso; ⟨*price*⟩ scandaloso

'outright[1] *a* completo; ⟨*refusal*⟩ netto

out'right[2] *adv* completamente; (*at once*) immediatamente; (*frankly*) francamente

'outset *n* inizio *m*; **from the ~** fin dall'inizio

'outside[1] *a* esterno ● *n* esterno *m*; **from the ~** dall'esterno; **at the ~** al massimo

out'side[2] *adv* all'esterno, fuori; (*out of doors*) fuori; **go ~** andare fuori ● *prep* fuori da; (*in front of*) davanti a

out'sider *n* estraneo, -a *mf*

'outskirts *npl* sobborghi *mpl*

out'spoken *a* schietto

out'standing *a* eccezionale; ⟨*landmark*⟩ prominente; (*not settled*) in sospeso

out'stretched *a* allungato

out'strip *vt* (*pt/pp* **-stripped**) superare

out'vote *vt* mettere in minoranza

'outward /-wəd/ *a* esterno; (*journey*) di andata ● *adv* verso l'esterno. **~ly** *adv* esternamente. **~s** *adv* verso l'esterno

out'weigh *vt* aver maggior peso di

out'wit *vt* (*pt/pp* **-witted**) battere in astuzia

oval /'əʊvl/ *a* ovale ● *n* ovale *m*

ovary /'əʊvərɪ/ *n Anat* ovaia *f*

ovation /əʊ'veɪʃn/ *n* ovazione *f*

oven /'ʌvn/ *n* forno *m*. **~-ready** *a* pronto da mettere in forno

over /'əʊvə(r)/ *prep* sopra; (*across*) al di là di; (*during*) durante; (*more than*) più di; **~ the phone** al telefono; **~ the page** alla pagina seguente; **all ~ Italy** in tutta [l']Italia; ⟨*travel*⟩ per l'Italia ● *adv Math* col resto di; (*ended*) finito; **~ again** un'altra volta; **~ and ~** più volte; **~ and above** oltre a; **~ here/there** qui/là; **all ~** (*everywhere*) dappertutto; **it's all ~** è tutto finito; **I ache all ~** ho male dappertutto; **come/bring ~** venire/portare; **turn ~** girare

over- *pref* (*too*) troppo

overall[1] /'əʊvərɔːl/ *n* grembiule *m*; **~s** *pl* tuta *fsg* [da lavoro]

overall[2] /əʊvər'ɔːl/ *a* complessivo; (*general*) generale ● *adv* complessivamente

over'balance *vi* perdere l'equilibrio

over'bearing *a* prepotente

'overboard *adv Naut* in mare

'overcast *a* coperto

over'charge *vt* **~ sb** far pagare più

del dovuto a qcno ● *vi* far pagare più del dovuto

'**overcoat** *n* cappotto *m*

over'come *vt* (*pt* **-came**, *pp* **-come**) vincere; **be ~ by** essere sopraffatto da

over'crowded *a* sovraffollato

over'do *vt* (*pt* **-did**, *pp* **-done**) esagerare; (*cook too long*) stracuocere; **~ it** (*fam: do too much*) strafare

'**overdose** *n* overdose *f inv*

'**overdraft** *n* scoperto *m*; **have an ~** avere il conto scoperto

over'draw *vt* (*pt* **-drew**, *pp* **-drawn**) **~ one's account** andare allo scoperto; **be ~n by** (*account:*) essere [allo] scoperto di

over'due *a* in ritardo

over'estimate *vt* sopravvalutare

'**overflow**[1] *n* (*water*) acqua *f* che deborda; (*people*) pubblico *m* in eccesso; (*outlet*) scarico *m*

over'flow[2] *vi* debordare

over'grown *a* (*garden*) coperto di erbacce

'**overhaul**[1] *n* revisione *f*

over'haul[2] *vt Techn* revisionare

over'head[1] *adv* in alto

'**overhead**[2] *a* aereo; (*railway*) sopraelevato; (*lights*) da soffitto ● *npl* **~s** spese *fpl* generali

over'hear *vt* (*pt/pp* **-heard**) sentire per caso (*conversation*)

over'heat *vi Auto* surriscaldarsi ● *vt* surriscaldare

over'joyed *a* felicissimo

'**overland** *a & adv* via terra; **~ route** via *f* terrestre

over'lap *v* (*pt/pp* **-lapped**) ● *vi* sovrapporsi ● *vt* sovrapporre

over'leaf *adv* sul retro

over'load *vt* sovraccaricare

over'look *vt* dominare; (*fail to see, ignore*) lasciarsi sfuggire

overly /'əʊvəlɪ/ *adv* eccessivamente

over'night[1] *adv* per la notte; **stay ~** fermarsi a dormire

'**overnight**[2] *a* notturno; **~ bag** piccola borsa *f* da viaggio; **~ stay** sosta *f* per la notte

'**overpass** *n* cavalcavia *m inv*

over'pay *vt* (*pt/pp* **-paid**) strapagare

over'populated *a* sovrappopolato

over'power *vt* sopraffare. **~ing** *a* insostenibile

over'priced *a* troppo caro

overpro'duce *vt* produrre in eccesso

over'rate *vt* sopravvalutare. **~d** *a* sopravvalutato

over'reach *vt* **~ oneself** puntare troppo in alto

overre'act *vi* avere una reazione eccessiva. **~ion** *n* reazione *f* eccessiva

over'rid|e *vt* (*pt* **-rode**, *pp* **-ridden**) passare sopra a. **~ing** *a* prevalente

over'rule *vt* annullare (*decision*)

over'run *vt* (*pt* **-ran**, *pp* **-run**, *pres p* **-running**) invadere; oltrepassare (*time*); **be ~ with** essere invaso da

over'seas[1] *adv* oltremare

'**overseas**[2] *a* d'oltremare

over'see *vt* (*pt* **-saw**, *pp* **-seen**) sorvegliare

over'shadow *vt* adombrare

over'shoot *vt* (*pt/pp* **-shot**) oltrepassare

'**oversight** *n* disattenzione *f*; **an ~** una svista

over'sleep *vi* (*pt/pp* **-slept**) svegliarsi troppo tardi

over'step *vt* (*pt/pp* **-stepped**) **~ the mark** oltrepassare ogni limite

overt /əʊ'vɜːt/ *a* palese

over'tak|e *vt/i* (*pt* **-took**, *pp* **-taken**) sorpassare. **~ing** *n* sorpasso *m*; **no ~ing** divieto di sorpasso

over'tax *vt fig* abusare di

'**overthrow**[1] *n Pol* rovesciamento *m*

over'throw[2] *vt* (*pt* **-threw**, *pp* **-thrown**) *Pol* rovesciare

'**overtime** *n* lavoro *m* straordinario ● *adv* **work ~** fare lo straordinario

over'tired *a* sovraffaticato

'**overtone** *n fig* sfumatura *f*

overture /'əʊvətjʊə(r)/ *n Mus* preludio *m*; **~s** *pl fig* approccio *msg*

over'turn *vt* ribaltare ● *vi* ribaltarsi

over'weight *a* sovrappeso

overwhelm /-'welm/ *vt* sommergere (**with** di); (*with emotion*) confondere. **~ing** *a* travolgente; (*victory, majority*) schiacciante

over'work *n* lavoro *m* eccessivo ● *vt* far lavorare eccessivamente ● *vi* lavorare eccessivamente

ow|e /əʊ/ *vt also fig* dovere ([**to**] **sb** a qcno); **~e sb sth** dovere qcsa a qcno. **~ing** *a* **be ~ing** (*money:*) essere da pagare ● *prep* **~ing to** a causa di

owl /aʊl/ *n* gufo *m*

own[1] /əʊn/ *a* proprio ● *pron* **a car of my ~** una macchina per conto mio; **on one's ~** da solo; **hold one's ~ with** tener testa a; **get one's ~ back** *fam* prendersi una rivincita

own[2] *vt* possedere; (*confess*) ammettere;

I don't ~ it non mi appartiene. **own up** *vi* confessare **(to sth** qcsa)

owner /'əʊnə(r)/ *n* proprietario, -a *mf*. **~ship** *n* proprietà *f*

ox /ɒks/ *n* (*pl* **oxen**) bue *m* (*pl* buoi)

oxide /'ɒksaɪd/ *n* ossido *m*

oxygen /'ɒksɪdʒən/ *n* ossigeno *m*. **~ mask** *n* maschera *f* a ossigeno

oyster /'ɔɪstə(r)/ *n* ostrica *f*

ozone /'əʊzəʊn/ *n* ozono *m*. **~-'friendly** *a* che non danneggia l'ozono. **~ layer** *n* fascia *f* d'ozono

---

Pp

PA *abbr* (**per annum**) all'anno

pace /peɪs/ *n* passo *m*; (*speed*) ritmo *m*; **keep ~ with** camminare di pari passo con ● *vi* **~ up and down** camminare avanti e indietro. **~-maker** *n* *Med* pacemaker *m*; (*runner*) battistrada *m*

Pacific /pə'sɪfɪk/ *a* & *n* **the ~** [**Ocean**] l'oceano *m* Pacifico, il Pacifico

pacifier /'pæsɪfaɪə(r)/ *n* *Am* ciuccio *m*, succhiotto *m*

pacifist /'pæsɪfɪst/ *n* pacifista *mf*

pacify /'pæsɪfaɪ/ *vt* (*pt/pp* **-ied**) placare ⟨*person*⟩; pacificare ⟨*country*⟩

pack /pæk/ *n* (*of cards*) mazzo *m*; (*of hounds*) muta *f*; (*of wolves, thieves*) branco *m*; (*of cigarettes etc*) pacchetto *m*; **a ~ of lies** un mucchio di bugie ● *vt* impacchettare ⟨*article*⟩; fare ⟨*suitcase*⟩; mettere in valigia ⟨*swimsuit etc*⟩; (*press down*) comprimere; **~ed** [**out**] (*crowded*) pieno zeppo ● *vi* fare i bagagli; **send sb ~ing** *fam* mandare qcno a stendere. **pack up** *vt* impacchettare ● *vi fam* ⟨*machine*⟩ piantare in asso

package /'pækɪdʒ/ *n* pacco *m* ● *vt* impacchettare. **~ deal** offerta *f* tutto compreso. **~ holiday** *n* vacanza *f* organizzata. **~ tour** viaggio *m* organizzato

packaging /'pækɪdʒɪŋ/ *n* confezione *f*

packed 'lunch *n* pranzo *m* al sacco

packet /'pækɪt/ *n* pacchetto *m*; **cost a ~** *fam* costare un sacco

packing /'pækɪŋ/ *n* imballaggio *m*

pact /pækt/ *n* patto *m*

pad¹ /pæd/ *n* imbottitura *f*; (*for writing*) bloc-notes *m inv*, taccuino *m*; (*fam: home*) [piccolo] appartamento *m* ● *vt* (*pt/pp* **padded**) imbottire. **pad out** *vt* gonfiare

pad² *vi* (*pt/pp* **padded**) camminare con passo felpato

padded /'pædɪd/ *a* **~ bra** reggiseno *m* imbottito

padding /'pædɪŋ/ *n* imbottitura *f*; (*in written work*) fronzoli *mpl*

paddle¹ /'pæd(ə)l/ *n* pagaia *f* ● *vt* (*row*) spingere remando

paddle² *vi* (*wade*) sguazzare

paddock /'pædək/ *n* recinto *m*

padlock /'pædlɒk/ *n* lucchetto *m* ● *vt* chiudere con lucchetto

paediatrician /pi:dɪə'trɪʃn/ *n* pediatra *mf*

paediatrics /pi:dɪ'ætrɪks/ *n* pediatria *f*

page¹ /peɪdʒ/ *n* pagina *f*

page² *n* (*boy*) paggetto *m*; (*in hotel*) fattorino *m* ● *vt* far chiamare ⟨*person*⟩

pageant /'pædʒənt/ *n* parata *f*. **~ry** *n* cerimoniale *m*

pager /'peɪdʒə(r)/ *n* cercapersone *m inv*

paid /peɪd/ *see* **pay** ● *a* **~ employment** lavoro *m* remunerato; **put ~ to** mettere un termine a

pail /peɪl/ *n* secchio *m*

pain /peɪn/ *n* dolore *m*; **be in ~** soffrire; **take ~s to** fare il possibile per; **~ in the neck** *fam* spina *f* nel fianco

pain: **~ful** *a* doloroso; (*laborious*) penoso.. **~-killer** *n* calmante *m*. **~less** *a* indolore

painstaking /'peɪnzteɪkɪŋ/ *a* minuzioso

paint /peɪnt/ *n* pittura *f*; **~s** *pl* colori *mpl* ● *vt/i* pitturare; ⟨*artist:*⟩ dipingere. **~-brush** *n* pennello *m*. **~er** *n* pittore, -trice *mf*; (*decorator*) imbianchino *m*. **~ing** *n* pittura *f*; (*picture*) dipinto *m*. **~work** *n* pittura *f*

pair /peə(r)/ *n* paio *m*; (*of people*) coppia *f*; **~ of trousers** paio *m* di pantaloni; **~ of scissors** paio *m* di forbici

pajamas /pə'dʒɑːməz/ *npl Am* pigiama *msg*

Pakistan /pɑːkɪˈstɑːn/ n Pakistan m.
~i a pakistano ● n pakistano, -a mf

pal /pæl/ n fam amico, -a mf

palace /ˈpælɪs/ n palazzo m

palatable /ˈpælətəbl/ a gradevole (al gusto)

palate /ˈpælət/ n palato m

palatial /pəˈleɪʃl/ a sontuoso

palaver /pəˈlɑːvə(r)/ n (fam: fuss) storie fpl

pale /peɪl/ a pallido

Palestin|e /ˈpælɪstaɪn/ n Palestina f.
~ian /pælɪˈstɪnɪən/ a palestinese ● n palestinese mf

palette /ˈpælɪt/ n tavolozza f

pall|id /ˈpælɪd/ a pallido. **~or** n pallore m

palm /pɑːm/ n palmo m; (tree) palma f;
P**~** '**Sunday** n Domenica f delle Palme
● **palm off** vt **~ sth off on sb** rifilare qcsa a qcno

palpable /ˈpælpəbl/ a palpabile;
(perceptible) tangibile

palpitat|e /ˈpælpɪteɪt/ vi palpitare.
~ions /-ˈteɪʃnz/ npl palpitazioni fpl

paltry /ˈpɔːltrɪ/ a (-ier, -iest) insignificante

pamper /ˈpæmpə(r)/ vt viziare

pamphlet /ˈpæmflɪt/ n opuscolo m

pan /pæn/ n tegame m, pentola f; (for frying) padella f; (of scales) piatto m ● vt (pt/pp **panned**) (fam: criticize) stroncare

panache /pəˈnæʃ/ n stile m

'**pancake** n crêpe f inv, frittella f

pancreas /ˈpæŋkrɪəs/ n pancreas m inv

panda /ˈpændə/ n panda m inv. **~ car** n macchina f della polizia

pandemonium /pændɪˈməʊnɪəm/ n pandemonio m

pander /ˈpændə(r)/ vi **~ to sb** compiacere qcno

pane /peɪn/ n **~ [of glass]** vetro m

panel /ˈpænl/ n pannello m; (group of people) giuria f; **~ of experts** gruppo m di esperti. **~ling** n pannelli mpl

pang /pæŋ/ n **~s of hunger** morsi mpl della fame; **~s of conscience** rimorsi mpl di coscienza

panic /ˈpænɪk/ n panico m ● vi (pt/pp **panicked**) lasciarsi prendere dal panico. **~-stricken** a in preda al panico

panoram|a /pænəˈrɑːmə/ n panorama m. **~ic** /-ˈræmɪk/ a panoramico

pansy /ˈpænzɪ/ n viola f del pensiero;
(fam: effeminate man) finocchio m

pant /pænt/ vi ansimare

panther /ˈpænθə(r)/ n pantera f

panties /ˈpæntɪz/ npl mutandine fpl

pantomime /ˈpæntəmaɪm/ n pantomima f

pantry /ˈpæntrɪ/ n dispensa f

pants /pænts/ npl (underwear) mutande fpl; (woman's) mutandine fpl;
(trousers) pantaloni mpl

'**pantyhose** n Am collant m inv

papal /ˈpeɪpl/ a papale

paper /ˈpeɪpə(r)/ n carta f; (wallpaper) carta f da parati; (newspaper) giornale m; (exam) esame m; (treatise) saggio m;
~s pl (documents) documenti mpl; (for identification) documento m [d'identità]; **on ~** in teoria; **put down on ~** mettere per iscritto ● attrib di carta
● vt tappezzare

paper: ~back n edizione f economica.
~-clip n graffetta f. **~-knife** n tagliacarte m inv. **~weight** n fermacarte m inv. **~work** n lavoro m d'ufficio

par /pɑː(r)/ n (in golf) par m inv; **on a ~ with** alla pari con; **feel below ~** essere un po' giù di tono

parable /ˈpærəbl/ n parabola f

parachut|e /ˈpærəʃuːt/ n paracadute m inv ● vi lanciarsi col paracadute.
~ist n paracadutista mf

parade /pəˈreɪd/ n (military) parata f militare ● vi sfilare ● vt (show off) far sfoggio di

paradise /ˈpærədaɪs/ n paradiso m

paradox /ˈpærədɒks/ n paradosso m.
~ical /-ˈdɒksɪkl/ a paradossale.
~ically adv paradossalmente

paraffin /ˈpærəfɪn/ n paraffina f

paragon /ˈpærəgən/ n **~ of virtue** modello m di virtù

paragraph /ˈpærəgrɑːf/ n paragrafo m

parallel /ˈpærəlel/ a & adv parallelo. **~ bars** npl parallele fpl. **~ port** n Comput porta f parallela ● n Geog, fig parallelo m; (line) parallela f ● vt essere paragonabile a

paralyse /ˈpærəlaɪz/ vt also fig paralizzare

paralysis /pəˈræləsɪs/ n (pl -ses)
/-siːz/ paralisi f inv

parameter /pəˈræmɪtə(r)/ n parametro m

paramount /ˈpærəmaʊnt/ a supremo;
be ~ essere essenziale

paranoia /pærəˈnɔɪə/ n paranoia f

paranoid /ˈpærənɔɪd/ a paranoico

paraphernalia /pærəfəˈneɪlɪə/ n armamentario m

paraphrase /ˈpærəfreɪz/ n parafrasi f inv ● vt parafrasare

paraplegic /pærə'pli:dʒɪk/ *a* paraplegico ● *n* paraplegico, -a *mf*

parasite /'pærəsaɪt/ *n* parassita *mf*

parasol /'pærəsɒl/ *n* parasole *m*

paratrooper /'pærətruːpə(r)/ *n* paracadutista *m*

parcel /'pɑːsl/ *n* pacco *m*

parch /pɑːtʃ/ *vt* disseccare; **be ~ed** ⟨*person:*⟩ morire dalla sete

pardon /'pɑːdn/ *n* perdono *m*; *Jur* grazia *f*; **~?** prego?; **I beg your ~?** *fml* chiedo scusa?; **I do beg your ~** ⟨*sorry*⟩ chiedo scusa! ● *vt* perdonare; *Jur* graziare

pare /peə(r)/ *vt* ⟨*peel*⟩ pelare

parent /'peərənt/ *n* genitore, -trice *mf*; **~s** *pl* genitori *mpl*. **~al** /pə'rentl/ *a* dei genitori

parenthesis /pə'renθəsɪs/ *n* (*pl* **-ses** /-siːz/) parentesi *m inv*

Paris /'pærɪs/ *n* Parigi *f*

parish /'pærɪʃ/ *n* parrocchia *f*. **~ioner** /pə'rɪʃənə(r)/ *n* parrocchiano, -a *mf*

Parisian /pə'rɪzɪən/ *a & n* parigino, -a *mf*

parity /'pærətɪ/ *n* parità *f*

park /pɑːk/ *n* parco *m* ● *vt/i Auto* posteggiare, parcheggiare; **~ oneself** *fam* installarsi

parka /'pɑːkə/ *n* parka *m inv*

parking /'pɑːkɪŋ/ *n* parcheggio *m*, posteggio *m*; **'no ~'** 'divieto di sosta'. **~-lot** *n Am* posteggio *m*, parcheggio *m*. **~-meter** *n* parchimetro *m*. **~ space** *n* posteggio *m*, parcheggio *m*

parliament /'pɑːləmənt/ *n* parlamento *m*. **~ary** /-'mentərɪ/ *a* parlamentare

parlour /'pɑːlə(r)/ *n* salotto *m*

parochial /pə'rəʊkɪəl/ *a* parrocchiale; *fig* ristretto

parody /'pærədɪ/ *n* parodia *f* ● *vt* (*pt/pp* **-ied**) parodiare

parole /pə'rəʊl/ *n* **on ~** in libertà condizionale ● *vt* mettere in libertà condizionale

parquet /'pɑːkeɪ/ *n* **~ floor** parquet *m inv*

parrot /'pærət/ *n* pappagallo *m*

parry /'pærɪ/ *vt* (*pt/pp* **-ied**) parare ⟨*blow*⟩; (*in fencing*) eludere

parsimonious /pɑːsɪ'məʊnɪəs/ *a* parsimonioso

parsley /'pɑːslɪ/ *n* prezzemolo *m*

parsnip /'pɑːsnɪp/ *n* pastinaca *f*

parson /'pɑːsn/ *n* pastore *m*

part /pɑːt/ *n* parte *f*; (*of machine*) pezzo *m*; **for my ~** per quanto mi riguarda; **on the ~ of** da parte di; **take sb's ~**

prendere le parti di qcno; **take ~ in** prendere parte a ● *adv* in parte ● *vt* **~ one's hair** farsi la riga ● *vi* ⟨*people:*⟩ separare; **~ with** separarsi da

part-ex'change *n* take in **~** prendere indietro

partial /'pɑːʃl/ *a* parziale; **be ~ to** aver un debole per. **~ly** *adv* parzialmente

particip|ant /pɑː'tɪsɪpənt/ *n* partecipante *mf*. **~ate** /-peɪt/ *vi* partecipare (**in** a). **~ation** /-'peɪʃn/ *n* partecipazione *f*

participle /'pɑːtɪsɪpl/ *n* participio *m*; **present/past ~** participio *m* presente/passato

particle /'pɑːtɪkl/ *n Phys, Gram* particella *f*

particular /pə'tɪkjʊlə(r)/ *a* particolare; (*precise*) meticoloso; *pej* noioso; **in ~** in particolare. **~ly** *adv* particolarmente. **~s** *npl* particolari *mpl*

parting /'pɑːtɪŋ/ *n* separazione *f*; (*in hair*) scriminatura *f* ● *attrib* di commiato

partisan /pɑːtɪ'zæn/ *n* partigiano, -a *mf*

partition /pɑː'tɪʃn/ *n* (*wall*) parete *f* divisoria; *Pol* divisione *f* ● *vt* dividere (*in parti*). **partition off** *vt* separare

partly /'pɑːtlɪ/ *adv* in parte

partner /'pɑːtnə(r)/ *n Comm* socio, -a *mf*; (*sport, in relationship*) compagno, -a *mf*. **~ship** *n Comm* società *f inv*

partridge /'pɑːtrɪdʒ/ *n* pernice *f*

part-'time *a & adv* part time; **be** *or* **work ~** lavorare part time

party /'pɑːtɪ/ *n* ricevimento *m*, festa *f*; (*group*) gruppo *m*; *Pol* partito *m*; *Jur* parte *f* [in causa]; **be ~ to** essere parte attiva in

'party line¹ *n Teleph* duplex *m inv*

party 'line² *n Pol* linea *f* del partito

pass /pɑːs/ *n* lasciapassare *m inv*; (*in mountains*) passo *m*; *Sport* passaggio *m*; *Sch* (*mark*) [voto *m*] sufficiente *m*; **make a ~ at** *fam* fare delle avances a ● *vt* passare; (*overtake*) sorpassare; (*approve*) far passare; fare ⟨*remark*⟩; *Jur* pronunciare ⟨*sentence*⟩; **~ the time** passare il tempo ● *vi* passare; (*in exam*) essere promosso. **pass away** *vi* mancare. **pass down** *vt* passare; *fig* trasmettere. **pass out** *vi fam* svenire. **pass round** *vt* far passare. **pass through** *vt* attraversare. **pass up** *vt* passare; (*fam: miss*) lasciarsi scappare

passable /'pɑːsəbl/ *a* ⟨*road*⟩ praticabile; (*satisfactory*) passabile

passage /'pæsɪdʒ/ *n* passaggio *m*;

(*corridor*) corridoio *m*; (*voyage*) traversata *f*

passenger /'pæsɪndʒə(r)/ *n* passeggero, -a *mf*. **~ seat** *n* posto *m* accanto al guidatore

passer-by /pɑː'sə'baɪ/ *n* (*pl* ~**s-by**) passante *mf*

'passing place *n* piazzola *f* di sosta *per consentire il transito dei veicoli nei due sensi*

passion /'pæʃn/ *n* passione *f*. **~ate** /-ət/ *a* appassionato

passive /'pæsɪv/ *a* passivo ● *n* passivo *m*. **~ness** *n* passività *f*

'pass-mark *n Sch* [voto *m*] sufficiente *m*

Passover /'pɑːsəʊvə(r)/ *n* Pasqua *f* ebraica

pass: ~**port** *n* passaporto *m*. ~**word** *n* parola *f* d'ordine

past /pɑːst/ *a* passato; (*former*) ex; **in the ~ few days** nei giorni scorsi; **that's all ~** tutto questo è passato; **the ~ week** la settimana scorsa ● *n* passato *m* ● *prep* oltre; **at ten ~ two** alle due e dieci ● *adv* oltre; **go/come ~** passare

pasta /'pæstə/ *n* pasta[sciutta] *f*

paste /peɪst/ *n* pasta *f*; (*dough*) impasto *m*; (*adhesive*) colla *f* ● *vt* incollare

pastel /'pæstl/ *n* pastello *m* ● *attrib* pastello

pasteurize /'pɑːstʃəraɪz/ *vt* pastorizzare

pastille /'pæstɪl/ *n* pastiglia *f*

pastime /'pɑːstaɪm/ *n* passatempo *m*

pastoral /'pɑːstərəl/ *a* pastorale

pastrami /pæ'strɑːmɪ/ *n* carne *f* di manzo affumicata

pastr|y /'peɪstrɪ/ *n* pasta *f*; **~ies** *pl* pasticcini *mpl*

pasture /'pɑːstʃə(r)/ *n* pascolo *m*

pasty[1] /'pæstɪ/ *n* pasticcio *m*

pasty[2] /'peɪstɪ/ *a* smorto

pat /pæt/ *n* buffetto *m*; (*of butter*) pezzetto *m* ● *adv* **have sth off ~** conoscere qcsa a menadito ● *vt* (*pt/pp* **patted**) dare un buffetto a; **~ sb on the back** *fig* congratularsi con qcno

patch /pætʃ/ *n* toppa *f*; (*spot*) chiazza *f*; (*period*) periodo *m*; **not a ~ on** *fam* molto inferiore a ● *vt* mettere una toppa su. **patch up** *vt* riparare alla bell'e meglio; appianare ⟨*quarrel*⟩

patchy /'pætʃɪ/ *a* incostante

pâté /'pæteɪ/ *n* pâté *m inv*

patent /'peɪtnt/ *a* palese ● *n* brevetto *m* ● *vt* brevettare. **~ leather shoes** *npl* scarpe *fpl* di vernice. **~ly** *adv* in modo palese

patern|al /pə'tɜːnl/ *a* paterno. **~ity** *n* paternità *f*

path /pɑːθ/ *n* (*pl* ~**s** /pɑːðz/) sentiero *m*; (*orbit*) traiettoria *m*; *fig* strada *f*

pathetic /pə'θetɪk/ *a* patetico; (*fam: very bad*) penoso

patholog|ical /pæθə'lɒdʒɪkl/ *a* patologico. **~ist** /pə'θɒlədʒɪst/ *n* patologo, -a *mf*. **~y** patologia *f*

pathos /'peɪθɒs/ *n* pathos *m*

patience /'peɪʃns/ *n* pazienza *f*; (*game*) solitario *m*

patient /'peɪʃnt/ *a* paziente ● *n* paziente *mf*. **~ly** *adv* pazientemente

patio /'pætɪəʊ/ *n* terrazza *f*

patriot /'pætrɪət/ *n* patriota *mf*. **~ic** /-'ɒtɪk/ *a* patriottico. **~ism** *n* patriottismo *m*

patrol /pə'trəʊl/ *n* pattuglia *f* ● *vt/i* pattugliare. **~ car** *n* autopattuglia *f*

patron /'peɪtrən/ *n* patrono *m*; (*of charity*) benefattore, -trice *mf*; (*of the arts*) mecenate *mf*; (*customer*) cliente *mf*

patroniz|e /'pætrənaɪz/ *vt* frequentare abitualmente; *fig* trattare con condiscendenza. **~ing** *a* condiscendente. **~ingly** *adv* con condiscendenza

patter[1] /'pætə(r)/ *n* picchiettio *m* ● *vi* picchiettare

patter[2] *n* (*of salesman*) chiacchiere *fpl*

pattern /'pætn/ *n* disegno *m* (*stampato*); (*for knitting, sewing*) modello *m*

paunch /pɔːntʃ/ *n* pancia *f*

pause /pɔːz/ *n* pausa *f* ● *vi* fare una pausa

pave /peɪv/ *vt* pavimentare; **~ the way** preparare la strada (**for** a). **~ment** *n* marciapiede *m*

pavilion /pə'vɪljən/ *n* padiglione *m*

paw /pɔː/ *n* zampa *f* ● *vt fam* mettere le zampe addosso a

pawn[1] /pɔːn/ *n* (*in chess*) pedone *m*; *fig* pedina *f*

pawn[2] *vt* impegnare ● *n* **in ~** in pegno. **~broker** *n* prestatore, -trice *mf* su pegno. **~shop** *n* monte *m* di pietà

pay /peɪ/ *n* paga *f*; **in the ~ of** al soldo di ● *v* (*pt/pp* **paid**) ● *vt* pagare; prestare ⟨*attention*⟩; fare ⟨*compliment, visit*⟩; **~ cash** pagare in contanti ● *vi* pagare; (*be profitable*) rendere; **it doesn't ~ to...** *fig* è fatica sprecata...; **~ for sth** pagare per qcsa. **pay back** *vt* ripagare. **pay in** *vt* versare. **pay off** *vt* saldare ⟨*debt*⟩ ● *vi fig* dare dei frutti. **pay up** *vi* pagare

payable /'peɪəbl/ *a* pagabile; **make ~ to** intestare a

payee /per'i:/ n beneficiario m (di una somma)

payment /'peɪmənt/ n pagamento m

pay: ~ packet n busta f paga. **~ phone** n telefono m pubblico

PC n abbr (**personal computer**) PC m inv

pea /pi:/ n pisello m

peace /pi:s/ n pace f; **~ of mind** tranquillità f

peace|able /'pi:səbl/ a pacifico. **~ful** a calmo, sereno. **~fully** adv in pace. **~maker** n mediatore, -trice mf

peach /pi:tʃ/ n pesca f; (tree) pesco m

peacock /'pi:kɒk/ n pavone m

peak /pi:k/ n picco m; fig culmine m. **~ed 'cap** n berretto m a punta. **~ hours** npl ore fpl di punta

peaky /'pi:kɪ/ a malaticcio

peal /pi:l/ n (of bells) scampanio m; **~s of laughter** pl fragore m di risate

'peanut n nocciolina f [americana]; **~s** pl fam miseria f

pear /peə(r)/ n pera f; (tree) pero m

pearl /pɜ:l/ n perla f

peasant /'peznt/ n contadino, -a mf

pebble /'pebl/ n ciottolo m

peck /pek/ n beccata f; (kiss) bacetto m ● vt beccare; (kiss) dare un bacetto a. **~ing order** n gerarchia f. **peck at** vt beccare

peckish /'pekɪʃ/ a **be ~** fam avere un languorino [allo stomaco]

peculiar /pɪ'kju:lɪə(r)/ a strano; (special) particolare; **~ to** tipico di. **~ity** /-'ærətɪ/ n stranezza f, (feature) particolarità f inv

pedal /'pedl/ n pedale m ● vi pedalare. **~ bin** n pattumiera f a pedale

pedantic /pɪ'dæntɪk/ a pedante

pedestal /'pedɪstl/ n piedistallo m

pedestrian /pɪ'destrɪən/ n pedone m ● a fig scadente. **~ 'crossing** n passaggio m pedonale. **~ 'precinct** n zona f pedonale

pedicure /'pedɪkjʊə(r)/ n pedicure f inv

pedigree /'pedɪgri:/ n pedigree m inv; (of person) lignaggio m ● attrib ⟨animal⟩ di razza, con pedigree

pee /pi:/ vi (pt/pp peed) fam fare [la] pipì

peek /pi:k/ vi fam sbirciare

peel /pi:l/ n buccia f ● vt sbucciare ● vi ⟨nose etc:⟩ spellarsi; ⟨paint:⟩ staccarsi

peep /pi:p/ n sbirciata f ● vi sbirciare

peer¹ /pɪə(r)/ vi **~ at** scrutare

peer² n nobile m; **his ~s** pl (in rank) i suoi pari; (in age) i suoi coetanei. **~age** n nobiltà f

peeved /pi:vd/ a fam irritato

peg /peg/ n (hook) piolo m; (for tent) picchetto m; (for clothes) molletta f; **off the ~** fam prêt-à-porter

pejorative /pɪ'dʒɒrətɪv/ a peggiorativo

pelican /'pelɪkən/ n pellicano m

pellet /'pelɪt/ n pallottola f

pelt /pelt/ vt bombardare ● vi (fam: run fast) catapultarsi; **~ [down]** ⟨rain:⟩ venir giù a fiotti

pelvis /'pelvɪs/ n Anat bacino m

pen¹ /pen/ n (for animals) recinto m

pen² n penna f; (ball-point) penna f a sfera

penal /'pi:nl/ a penale. **~ize** vt penalizzare

penalty /'penltɪ/ n sanzione f, (fine) multa f; (in football) **~ [kick]** [calcio m di] rigore m; **~ area** or **box** area f di rigore

penance /'penəns/ n penitenza f

pence /pens/ see penny

pencil /'pensl/ n matita f. **~-sharpener** n temperamatite m inv

pendant /'pendənt/ n ciondolo m

pending /'pendɪŋ/ a in sospeso ● prep in attesa di

pendulum /'pendjʊləm/ n pendolo m

penetrat|e /'penɪtreɪt/ vt/i penetrare. **~ing** a acuto; (sound, stare) penetrante. **~ion** /-'treɪʃn/ n penetrazione f

'penfriend n amico, -a mf di penna

penguin /'peŋgwɪn/ n pinguino m

penicillin /penɪ'sɪlɪn/ n penicillina f

peninsula /pɪ'nɪnsjʊlə/ n penisola f

penis /'pi:nɪs/ n pene m

peniten|ce /'penɪtəns/ n penitenza f. **~t** a penitente ● n penitente mf

penitentiary /penɪ'tenʃərɪ/ n Am penitenziario m

pen: ~knife n temperino m. **~-name** n pseudonimo m

pennant /'penənt/ n bandiera f

penniless /'penɪlɪs/ a senza un soldo

penny /'penɪ/ n (pl pence; single coins pennies) penny m; Am centesimo m; **spend a ~** fam andare in bagno

pension /'penʃn/ n pensione f. **~er** n pensionato, -a mf

pensive /'pensɪv/ a pensoso

Pentecost /'pentɪkɒst/ n Pentecoste f

pent-up /'pentʌp/ a represso

penultimate /pɪ'nʌltɪmət/ a penultimo

people /'pi:pl/ npl persone fpl, gente

fsg; *(citizens)* popolo *msg*; **a lot of ~** una marea di gente; **the ~** la gente; **English ~** gli inglesi; **~ say** si dice; **for four ~** per quattro ● *vt* popolare

pepper /'pepə(r)/ *n* pepe *m*; *(vegetable)* peperone *m* ● *vt* *(season)* pepare

pepper: ~corn *n* grano *m* di pepe. **~ mill** macinapepe *m inv.* **~mint** *n* menta *f* peperita; *(sweet)* caramella *f* alla menta. **~pot** *n* pepiera *f*

per /pɜː(r)/ *prep* per; **~ annum** all'anno; **~ cent** percento

perceive /pə'siːv/ *vt* percepire; *(interpret)* interpretare

percentage /pə'sentɪdʒ/ *n* percentuale *f*

perceptible /pə'septəbl/ *a* percettibile; *(difference)* sensibile

percept|ion /pə'sepʃn/ *n* percezione *f*. **~ive** /-tɪv/ *a* perspicace

perch /pɜːtʃ/ *n* pertica *f* ● *vi* *(bird:)* appollaiarsi

percolator /'pɜːkəleɪtə(r)/ *n* caffettiera *f* a filtro

percussion /pə'kʌʃn/ *n* percussione *f*. **~ instrument** *n* strumento *m* a percussione

peremptory /pə'remptərɪ/ *a* perentorio

perennial /pə'renɪəl/ *a* perenne ● *n* pianta *f* perenne

perfect[1] /'pɜːfɪkt/ *a* perfetto ● *n* Gram passato *m* prossimo

perfect[2] /pə'fekt/ *vt* perfezionare. **~ion** /-ekʃn/ *n* perfezione *f*; **to ~ion** alla perfezione. **~ionist** *n* perfezionista *mf*

perfectly /'pɜːfɪktlɪ/ *adv* perfettamente

perforat|e /'pɜːfəreɪt/ *vt* perforare. **~ed** *a* perforato; *(ulcer)* perforante. **~ion** *n* perforazione *f*

perform /pə'fɔːm/ *vt* compiere, fare; eseguire *(operation, sonata)*; recitare *(role)*; mettere in scena *(play)* ● *vi* Theat recitare; Techn funzionare. **~ance** *n* esecuzione *f*; *(at theatre, cinema)* rappresentazione *f*; Techn rendimento *m*. **~er** *n* artista *mf*

perfume /'pɜːfjuːm/ *n* profumo *m*

perfunctory /pə'fʌŋktərɪ/ *a* superficiale

perhaps /pə'hæps/ *adv* forse

peril /'perɪl/ *n* pericolo *m*. **~ous** /-əs/ *a* pericoloso

perimeter /pə'rɪmɪtə(r)/ *n* perimetro *m*

period /'pɪərɪəd/ *n* periodo *m*; *(menstruation)* mestruazioni *fpl*; Sch

ora *f* di lezione; *(full stop)* punto *m* fermo ● *attrib* *(costume)* d'epoca; *(furniture)* in stile. **~ic** /-'ɒdɪk/ *a* periodico. **~ical** /-'ɒdɪkl/ *n* periodico *m*, rivista *f*

peripher|al /pə'rɪfərəl/ *a* periferico. **~y** *n* periferia *f*

periscope /'perɪskəʊp/ *n* periscopio *m*

perish /'perɪʃ/ *vi* *(rot)* deteriorarsi; *(die)* perire. **~able** /-əbl/ *a* deteriorabile

perjur|e /'pɜːdʒə(r)/ *vt* **~e oneself** spergiurare. **~y** *n* spergiuro *m*

perk /pɜːk/ *n fam* vantaggio *m*

perk up *vt* tirare su ● *vi* tirarsi su

perky /'pɜːkɪ/ *a* allegro

perm /pɜːm/ *n* permanente *f* ● *vt* **~ sb's hair** fare la permanente a qno

permanent /'pɜːmənənt/ *a* permanente; *(job, address)* stabile. **~ly** *adv* stabilmente

permeate /'pɜːmɪeɪt/ *vt* impregnare

permissible /pə'mɪsəbl/ *a* ammissibile

permission /pə'mɪʃn/ *n* permesso *m*

permissive /pə'mɪsɪv/ *a* permissivo

permit[1] /pə'mɪt/ *vt* *(pt/pp* -mitted) permettere; **~ sb to do sth** permettere a qcno di fare qcsa

permit[2] /'pɜːmɪt/ *n* autorizzazione *f*

perpendicular /pɜːpən'dɪkjʊlə(r)/ *a* perpendicolare ● *n* perpendicolare *f*

perpetual /pə'petjʊəl/ *a* perenne. **~ly** *adv* perennemente

perpetuate /pə'petjʊeɪt/ *vt* perpetuare

perplex /pə'pleks/ *vt* lasciare perplesso. **~ed** *a* perplesso. **~ity** *n* perplessità *f inv*

persecut|e /'pɜːsɪkjuːt/ *vt* perseguitare. **~ion** /-'kjuːʃn/ *n* persecuzione *f*

perseverance /pɜːsɪ'vɪərəns/ *n* perseveranza *f*

persever|e /pɜːsɪ'vɪə(r)/ *vi* perseverare. **~ing** *a* assiduo

Persian /'pɜːʃn/ *a* persiano

persist /pə'sɪst/ *vi* persistere; **~ in doing sth** persistere nel fare qcsa. **~ence** *n* persistenza *f*. **~ent** *a* persistente. **~ently** *adv* persistentemente

person /'pɜːsn/ *n* persona *f*; **in ~** di persona

personal /'pɜːsənl/ *a* personale. **~ 'hygiene** *n* igiene *f* personale. **~ly** *adv* personalmente. **~ organizer** *n* Comput agenda *f* elettronica

personality /pɜːsə'nælətɪ/ *n* personalità *f inv*; *(on TV)* personaggio *m*

personnel /pɜ:sə'nel/ n personale m

perspective /pə'spektɪv/ n prospettiva f

persp|iration /pɜ:spɪ'reɪʃn/ n sudore m. **~ire** /-'spaɪə(r)/ vi sudare

persua|de /pə'sweɪd/ vt persuadere. **~sion** /-eɪʒn/ n persuasione f; (belief) convinzione f

persuasive /pə'sweɪsɪv/ a persuasivo. **~ly** adv in modo persuasivo

pertinent /'pɜ:tɪnənt/ a pertinente (**to** a)

perturb /pə'tɜ:b/ vt perturbare

peruse /pə'ru:z/ vt leggere

perva|de /pə'veɪd/ vt pervadere. **~sive** /-sɪv/ a pervasivo

pervers|e /pə'vɜ:s/ a irragionevole. **~ion** /-ɜ:ʃn/ n perversione f

pervert /'pɜ:vɜ:t/ n pervertito, -a mf

perverted /pə'vɜ:tɪd/ a perverso

pessimis|m /'pesɪmɪzm/ n pessimismo m. **~t** /-mɪst/ n pessimista mf. **~tic** /-'mɪstɪk/ a pessimistico. **~tically** adv in modo pessimistico

pest /pest/ n piaga f, (fam: person) peste f

pester /'pestə(r)/ vt molestare

pesticide /'pestɪsaɪd/ n pesticida m

pet /pet/ n animale m domestico; (favourite) cocco, -a mf ● a prediletto ● v (pt/pp **petted**) ● vt coccolare ● vi ⟨couple:⟩ praticare il petting

petal /'petl/ n petalo m

peter /'pi:tə(r)/ vi **~ out** finire

petite /pə'ti:t/ a minuto

petition /pə'tɪʃn/ n petizione f

pet 'name n vezzeggiativo m

petrif|y /'petrɪfaɪ/ vt (pt/pp **-ied**) pietrificare. **~ied** a (frightened) pietrificato

petrol /'petrəl/ n benzina f

petroleum /pɪ'trəʊliəm/ n petrolio m

petrol: **~-pump** n pompa f di benzina. **~ station** n stazione f di servizio. **~ tank** n serbatoio m della benzina

'pet shop n negozio m di animali [domestici]

petticoat /'petɪkəʊt/ n sottoveste f

petty /'petɪ/ a (**-ier, -iest**) insignificante; (mean) meschino. **~ 'cash** n cassa f per piccole spese

petulant /'petjʊlənt/ a petulante

pew /pju:/ n banco m (di chiesa)

pewter /'pju:tə(r)/ n peltro m

phallic /'fælɪk/ a fallico

phantom /'fæntəm/ n fantasma m

pharmaceutical /fɑ:mə'sju:tɪkl/ a farmaceutico

pharmac|ist /'fɑ:məsɪst/ n farmacista mf. **~y** n farmacia f

phase /feɪz/ n fase f ● vt **phase in/out** introdurre/eliminare gradualmente

Ph.D. n abbr (**Doctor of Philosophy**) dottorato m di ricerca

pheasant /'feznt/ n fagiano m

phenomen|al /fɪ'nɒmɪnl/ a fenomenale; (incredible) incredibile. **~ally** adv incredibilmente. **~on** n (pl **-na**) fenomeno m

philanderer /fɪ'lændərə(r)/ n donnaiolo m

philanthrop|ic /fɪlən'θrɒpɪk/ a filantropico. **~ist** /fɪ'lænθrəpɪst/ n filantropo, -a mf

philatel|y /fɪ'lætəlɪ/ n filatelia f. **~ist** n filatelico, -a mf

philharmonic /fɪlhɑ:'mɒnɪk/ n (orchestra) orchestra f filarmonica ● a filarmonico

Philippines /'fɪlɪpi:nz/ npl Filippine fpl

philistine /'fɪlɪstaɪm/ n filisteo, -a mf

philosoph|er /fɪ'lɒsəfə(r)/ n filosofo, -a mf. **~ical** /fɪlə'sɒfɪkl/ a filosofico. **~ically** adv con filosofia. **~y** n filosofia f

phlegm /flem/ n Med flemma f

phlegmatic /fleg'mætɪk/ a flemmatico

phobia /'fəʊbɪə/ n fobia f

phone /fəʊn/ n telefono m; **be on the ~** avere il telefono; (be phoning) essere al telefono ● vt telefonare a ● vi telefonare. **phone back** vt/i richiamare. **~ book** n guida f del telefono. **~ box** n cabina f telefonica. **~ card** n scheda f telefonica. **~ call** n telefonata f. **~-in** n trasmissione f con chiamate in diretta. **~ number** n numero m telefonico

phonetic /fə'netɪk/ a fonetico. **~s** n fonetica f

phoney /'fəʊnɪ/ a (**-ier, -iest**) fasullo

phosphorus /'fɒsfərəs/ n fosforo m

photo /'fəʊtəʊ/ n foto f; **~ album** album m inv di fotografie. **~copier** n fotocopiatrice f. **~copy** n fotocopia f ● vt fotocopiare

photogenic /fəʊtəʊ'dʒenɪk/ a fotogenico

photograph /'fəʊtəgrɑ:f/ n fotografia f ● vt fotografare

photograph|er /fə'tɒgrəfə(r)/ n fotografo, -a mf. **~ic** /fəʊtə'græfɪk/ a fotografico. **~y** n fotografia f

phrase /freɪz/ n espressione f ● vt esprimere. **~-book** n libro m di fraseologia

physical /'fɪzɪkl/ *a* fisico. **~ edu'cation** *n* educazione *f* fisica. **~ly** *adv* fisicamente

physician /fɪ'zɪʃn/ *n* medico *m*

physic|ist /'fɪzɪsɪst/ *n* fisico, -a *mf.* **~s** *n* fisica *f*

physiology /fɪzɪ'ɒlədʒɪ/ *n* fisiologia *f*

physio'therap|ist /fɪzɪəʊ-/ *n* fisiote-rapista *mf.* **~y** *n* fisioterapia *f*

physique /fɪ'ziːk/ *n* fisico *m*

pianist /'pɪənɪst/ *n* pianista *mf*

piano /pɪ'ænəʊ/ *n* piano *m*

pick¹ /pɪk/ *n* (*tool*) piccone *m*

pick² *n* scelta *f;* **take your ~** prendi quello che vuoi ● *vt* (*select*) scegliere; cogliere ⟨*flowers*⟩; scassinare ⟨*lock*⟩; borseggiare ⟨*pockets*⟩; **~ and choose** fare il difficile; **~ one's nose** mettersi le dita nel naso; **~ a quarrel** attaccar briga; **~ holes in** *fam* criticare; **~ at one's food** spilluzzicare. **pick on** *vt* (*fam: nag*) assillare; **he always ~s on me** ce l'ha con me. **pick out** *vt* (*identify*) individuare. **pick up** *vt* sollevare; (*off the ground, information*) raccogliere; prendere in braccio ⟨*baby*⟩; (*learn*) im-parare; prendersi ⟨*illness*⟩; (*buy*) com-prare; captare ⟨*signal*⟩; (*collect*) andare/venire a prendere; prendere ⟨*passengers, habit*⟩; ⟨*police:*⟩ arrestare ⟨*criminal*⟩; *fam* rimorchiare ⟨*girl*⟩; **~ oneself up** riprendersi ● *vi* (*improve*) recuperare; ⟨*weather:*⟩ rimettersi

'pickaxe *n* piccone *m*

picket /'pɪkɪt/ *n* picchettista *mf* ● *vt* picchettare. **~ line** *n* picchetto *m*

pickle /'pɪkl/ *n* **~s** *pl* sottaceti *mpl;* **in a ~** *fig* nei pasticci ● *vt* mettere sottaceto

pick: ~pocket *n* borsaiolo *m.* **~-up** *n* (*truck*) furgone *m;* (*on record-player*) pickup *m inv*

picnic /'pɪknɪk/ *n* picnic *m* ● *vi* (*pt/pp* **-nicked**) fare un picnic

picture /'pɪktʃə(r)/ *n* (*painting*) qua-dro *m;* (*photo*) fotografia *f;* (*drawing*) di-segno *m;* (*film*) film *m inv;* **put sb in the ~** *fig* mettere qcno al corrente; **the ~s** il cinema ● *vt* (*imagine*) immagina-re

picturesque /pɪktʃə'resk/ *a* pittore-sco

pie /paɪ/ *n* torta *f*

piece /piːs/ *n* pezzo *m;* (*in game*) pedina *f;* **a ~ of bread/paper** un pezzo di pane/carta; **a ~ of news/advice** una notizia/un consiglio; **take to ~s** smon-tare. **~meal** *adv* un po' alla volta.

~-work *n* lavoro *m* a cottimo ● **piece together** *vt* montare; *fig* ricostruire

pier /pɪə(r)/ *n* molo *m;* (*pillar*) pilastro *m*

pierc|e /pɪəs/ *vt* perforare; **~e a hole in sth** fare un buco in qcsa. **~ing** *n* [**body**] **~** piercing *m inv* ● *a* penetrante

pig /pɪg/ *n* maiale *m*

pigeon /'pɪdʒɪn/ *n* piccione *m.* **~-hole** *n* casella *f*

piggy /'pɪgɪ/ **~back** *n* **give sb a ~back** portare qcno sulle spalle. **~ bank** *n* salvadanaio *m*

pig'headed *a fam* cocciuto

pig: ~skin *n* pelle *f* di cinghiale. **~tail** *n* (*plait*) treccina *f*

pile *n* (*heap*) pila *f* ● *vt* **~ sth on to sth** appilare qcsa su qcsa. **pile up** *vt* accata-stare ● *vi* ammucchiarsi

piles /paɪlz/ *npl* emorroidi *fpl*

'pile-up *n* tamponamento *m* a catena

pilfering /'pɪlfərɪŋ/ *n* piccoli furti *mpl*

pilgrim /'pɪlgrɪm/ *n* pellegrino, -a *mf.* **~age** /-ɪdʒ/ *n* pellegrinaggio *m*

pill /pɪl/ *n* pillola *f*

pillage /'pɪlɪdʒ/ *vt* saccheggiare

pillar /'pɪlə(r)/ *n* pilastro *m.* **~-box** *n* buca *f* delle lettere

pillion /'pɪlJən/ *n* sellino *m* posteriore; **ride ~** viaggiare dietro

pillory /'pɪlərɪ/ *vt* (*pt/pp* -ied) *fig* mette-re alla berlina

pillow /'pɪləʊ/ *n* guanciale *m.* **~case** *n* federa *f*

pilot /'paɪlət/ *n* pilota *mf* ● *vt* pilotare. **~-light** *n* fiamma *f* di sicurezza

pimp /pɪmp/ *n* protettore *m*

pimple /'pɪmpl/ *n* foruncolo *m*

pin /pɪn/ *n* spillo *m; Electr* spinotto *m; Med* chiodo *m;* **I have ~s and needles in my leg** *fam* mi formicola una gamba ● *vt* (*pt/pp* **pinned**) appuntare (**to/on** su); (*sewing*) fissare con gli spilli; (*hold down*) immobilizzare; **~ sb down to a date** ottenere un appuntamento da qcno; **~ sth on sb** *fam* addossare a qcno la colpa di qcsa. **pin up** *vt* appunta-re; (*on wall*) affiggere

pinafore /'pɪnəfɔː(r)/ *n* grembiule *m.* **~ dress** *n* scamiciato *m*

pincers /'pɪnsəz/ *npl* tenaglie *fpl*

pinch /pɪntʃ/ *n* pizzicotto *m;* (*of salt*) presa *f;* **at a ~** *fam* in caso di bisogno ● *vt* pizzicare; (*fam: steal*) fregare ● *vi* ⟨*shoe:*⟩ stringere

'pincushion *n* puntaspilli *m inv*

pine¹ /paɪn/ *n* (*tree*) pino *m*

pine² *vi* **she is pining for you** le man-chi molto. **pine away** *vi* deperire

pineapple /'paɪn-/ n ananas m inv
ping /pɪŋ/ n rumore m metallico
'ping-pong n ping-pong m
pink /pɪŋk/ a rosa inv
pinnacle /'pɪnəkl/ n guglia f
PIN number n codice m segreto
pin: ~**point** vt definire con precisione. ~**stripe** a gessato
pint /paɪnt/ n pinta f (= 0,571, Am: 0,47 l); **a** ~ fam una birra media
'pin-up n ragazza f da copertina, pin-up f inv
pioneer /paɪə'nɪə(r)/ n pioniere, -a mf ● vt essere un pioniere di
pious /'paɪəs/ a pio
pip /pɪp/ n (seed) seme m
pipe /paɪp/ n tubo m; (for smoking) pipa f; **the** ~**s** Mus la cornamusa ● vt far arrivare con tubature (water, gas etc). **pipe down** vi fam abbassare la voce
pipe: ~**-cleaner** n scovolino m. ~**-dream** n illusione f. ~**line** n conduttura f; **in the** ~**line** fam in cantiere
piper /'paɪpə(r)/ n suonatore m di cornamusa
piping /'paɪpɪŋ/ a ~ **hot** bollente
pirate /'paɪrət/ n pirata m
Pisces /'paɪsi:z/ n Astr Pesci mpl
piss /pɪs/ vi sl pisciare
pistol /'pɪstl/ n pistola f
piston /'pɪstn/ n Techn pistone m
pit /pɪt/ n fossa f; (mine) miniera f; (for orchestra) orchestra f ● vt (pt/pp **pitted**) fig opporre (**against** a)
pitch[1] /pɪtʃ/ n (tone) tono m; (level) altezza f; (in sport) campo m; (fig: degree) grado m ● vt montare (tent). **pitch in** vi fam mettersi sotto
pitch[2] n ~**-'black** a nero come la pece. ~**-'dark** a buio pesto
'pitchfork n forca f
piteous /'pɪtɪəs/ a pietoso
'pitfall n fig trabocchetto m
pith /pɪθ/ n (of lemon, orange) interno m della buccia
pithy /'pɪθɪ/ a (-ier, -iest) fig conciso
piti|ful /'pɪtɪfl/ a pietoso. ~**less** a spietato
pittance /'pɪtns/ n miseria f
pity /'pɪtɪ/ n pietà f; [**what a**] ~**!** che peccato!; **take** ~ **on** avere compassione di ● vt aver pietà di
pivot /'pɪvət/ n perno m; fig fulcro m ● vi imperniarsi (**on** su)
pizza /'pi:tsə/ n pizza f
placard /'plækɑ:d/ n cartellone m
placate /plə'keɪt/ vt placare

place /pleɪs/ n posto m; (fam: house) casa f; (in book) segno m; **feel out of** ~ sentirsi fuori posto; **take** ~ aver luogo; **all over the** ~ dappertutto ● vt collocare; (remember) identificare; ~ **an order** fare un'ordinazione; **be** ~**d** (in race) piazzarsi. ~**-mat** n sottopiatto m
placid /'plæsɪd/ a placido
plagiar|ism /'pleɪdʒərɪzm/ n plagio m. ~**ize** vt plagiare
plague /pleɪg/ n peste f
plaice /pleɪs/ n inv platessa f
plain /pleɪn/ a chiaro; (simple) semplice; (not pretty) scialbo; (not patterned) normale; (chocolate) fondente; **in** ~ **clothes** in borghese ● adv (simply) semplicemente ● n pianura f. ~**ly** adv francamente; (simply) semplicemente; (obviously) chiaramente
plaintiff /'pleɪntɪf/ n Jur parte f lesa
plaintive /'pleɪntɪv/ a lamentoso
plait /plæt/ n treccia f ● vt intrecciare
plan /plæn/ n progetto m, piano m ● vt (pt/pp **planned**) progettare; (intend) prevedere
plane[1] /pleɪn/ n (tree) platano m
plane[2] n aeroplano m
plane[3] n (tool) pialla f ● vt piallare
planet /'plænɪt/ n pianeta m
plank /plæŋk/ n asse f
planning /'plænɪŋ/ n pianificazione f. ~ **permission** n licenza f edilizia
plant /plɑ:nt/ n pianta f; (machinery) impianto m; (factory) stabilimento m ● vt piantare. ~**ation** /plæn'teɪʃn/ n piantagione f
plaque /plɑ:k/ n placca f
plasma /'plæzmə/ n plasma m
plaster /'plɑ:stə(r)/ n intonaco m; Med gesso m; (sticking ~) cerotto m; ~ **of Paris** gesso m ● vt intonacare (wall); (cover) ricoprire. ~**ed** a sl sbronzo. ~**er** n intonacatore m
plastic /'plæstɪk/ n plastica f ● a plastico
Plasticine® /'plæstɪsi:n/ n plastilina® f
plastic: ~ '**surgeon** n chirurgo m plastico. ~ **surgery** n chirurgia f plastica
plate /pleɪt/ n piatto m; (flat sheet) placca f; (gold and silverware) argenteria f; (in book) tavola f [fuori testo] ● vt (cover with metal) placcare
plateau /'plætəʊ/ n (pl ~**x** /-əʊz/) altopiano m
platform /'plætfɔ:m/ n (stage) palco m; Rail marciapiede m; Pol piattaforma f; ~ **5** binario 5

platinum /'plætɪnəm/ n platino m ● a di platino

platitude /'plætɪtjuːd/ n luogo m comune

platonic /plə'tɒnɪk/ a platonico

platoon /plə'tuːn/ n Mil plotone m

platter /'plætə(r)/ n piatto m da portata

plausible /'plɔːzəbl/ a plausibile

play /pleɪ/ n gioco m; Theat, TV rappresentazione f; Radio sceneggiato m radiofonico; **~ on words** gioco m di parole ● vt giocare a; (act) recitare; suonare ⟨instrument⟩; giocare ⟨card⟩ ● vi giocare; Mus suonare; **~ safe** non prendere rischi. **play down** vt minimizzare. **play up** vi fam fare i capricci

play: ~boy n playboy m inv. **~er** n giocatore, -trice mf. **~ful** a scherzoso. **~ground** n Sch cortile m (per la ricreazione). **~group** n asilo m

playing: ~-card n carta f da gioco. **~-field** n campo m da gioco

play: ~mate n compagno, -a mf di gioco. **~-pen** n box m inv. **~thing** n giocattolo m. **~wright** /-raɪt/ n drammaturgo, -a mf

plc n abbr (**public limited company**) s.r.l.

plea /pliː/ n richiesta f; **make a ~ for** fare un appello a

plead /pliːd/ vi fare appello (**for** a); **~ guilty** dichiararsi colpevole; **~ with sb** implorare qcno

pleasant /'plez(ə)nt/ a piacevole. **~ly** adv piacevolmente; ⟨say, smile⟩ cordialmente

please /pliːz/ adv per favore; **~e do** prego ● vt far contento; **~e oneself** fare il proprio comodo; **~e yourself!** come vuoi!; pej fai come ti pare!. **~ed** a lieto; **~ed with/about** contento di. **~ing** a gradevole

pleasurable /'pleʒərəbl/ a gradevole

pleasure /'pleʒə(r)/ n piacere m; **with ~** con piacere, volentieri

pleat /pliːt/ n piega f ● vt pieghettare. **~ed 'skirt** n gonna f a pieghe

pledge /pledʒ/ n pegno m; (promise) promessa f ● vt impegnarsi a; (pawn) impegnare

plentiful /'plentɪfl/ a abbondante

plenty /'plentɪ/ n abbondanza f; **~ of money** molti soldi; **~ of people** molta gente; **I've got ~** ne ho in abbondanza

pliable /'plaɪəbl/ a flessibile

pliers /'plaɪəz/ npl pinze fpl

plight /plaɪt/ n condizione f

plimsolls /'plɪmsəlz/ npl scarpe fpl da ginnastica

plinth /plɪnθ/ n plinto m

plod /plɒd/ vi (pt/pp **plodded**) trascinarsi; (work hard) sgobbare

plonk /plɒŋk/ n fam vino m mediocre

plot /plɒt/ n complotto m; (of novel) trama f; **~ of land** appezzamento m [di terreno] ● vt/i (pt/pp **plotted**) complottare

plough /plaʊ/ n aratro m ● vt/i arare. **~man's [lunch]** piatto m di formaggi e sottaceti, servito con pane. **plough back** vt Comm reinvestire

ploy /plɔɪ/ n fam manovra f

pluck /plʌk/ n fegato m ● vt strappare; depilare ⟨eyebrows⟩; spennare ⟨bird⟩; cogliere ⟨flower⟩. **pluck up** vt **~ up courage** farsi coraggio

plucky /'plʌkɪ/ a (**-ier, -iest**) coraggioso

plug /plʌg/ n tappo m; Electr spina f; Auto candela f; (fam: advertisement) pubblicità f inv ● vt (pt/pp **plugged**) tappare; (fam: advertise) pubblicizzare con insistenza. **plug in** vt Electr inserire la spina di

plum /plʌm/ n prugna f; (tree) prugno m

plumage /'pluːmɪdʒ/ n piumaggio m

plumb /plʌm/ a verticale ● adv esattamente ● **plumb in** vt collegare

plumb|er /'plʌmə(r)/ n idraulico m. **~ing** n impianto m idraulico

'plumb-line n filo m a piombo

plume /pluːm/ n piuma f

plummet /'plʌmɪt/ vi precipitare

plump /plʌmp/ a paffuto ● **plump for** vt scegliere

plunge /plʌndʒ/ n tuffo m; **take the ~** fam buttarsi ● vt tuffare; fig sprofondare ● vi tuffarsi

plunging /'plʌndʒɪŋ/ a ⟨neckline⟩ profondo

plu'perfect /pluː-/ n trapassato m prossimo

plural /'plʊərəl/ a plurale ● n plurale m

plus /plʌs/ prep più ● a in più; **500 ~** più di 500 ● n più m; (advantage) extra m inv

plush /'plʌʃ[ɪ]/ a lussuoso

plutonium /pluː'təʊnɪəm/ n plutonio m

ply /plaɪ/ vt (pt/pp **plied**) **~ sb with drink** continuare a offrire da bere a qcno. **~wood** n compensato m

p.m. abbr (**post meridiem**) del pomeriggio

PM n abbr **Prime Minister**

pneumatic /njuːˈmætɪk/ a pneumatico. ~ 'drill n martello m pneumatico

pneumonia /njuːˈməʊnɪə/ n polmonite f

P.O. abbr **Post Office**

poach /pəʊtʃ/ vt Culin bollire; cacciare di frodo ⟨deer⟩; pescare di frodo ⟨salmon⟩; ~ed egg uovo m in camicia. ~er n bracconiere m

pocket /ˈpɒkɪt/ n tasca f; be out of ~ rimetterci ● vt intascare. ~-book n taccuino m; ⟨wallet⟩ portafoglio m. ~-money n denaro m per le piccole spese

pod /pɒd/ n baccello m

podgy /ˈpɒdʒɪ/ a (-ier, -iest) grassoccio

poem /ˈpəʊɪm/ n poesia f

poet /ˈpəʊɪt/ n poeta m. ~ic /-ˈetɪk/ a poetico

poetry /ˈpəʊɪtrɪ/ n poesia f

poignant /ˈpɔɪnjənt/ a emozionante

point /pɔɪnt/ n punto m; ⟨sharp end⟩ punta f; ⟨meaning, purpose⟩ senso m; Electr presa f [di corrente]; ~s pl Rail scambio m; ~ of view punto m di vista; good/bad ~s aspetti mpl positivi/negativi; what is the ~? a che scopo?; the ~ is il fatto è; I don't see the ~ non vedo il senso; up to a ~ fino a un certo punto; be on the ~ of doing sth essere sul punto di fare qcsa ● vt puntare ⟨at verso⟩ ● vi ⟨with finger⟩ puntare il dito; ~ at/to ⟨person:⟩ mostrare col dito; ⟨indicator:⟩ indicare. point out vt far notare ⟨fact⟩; ~ sth out to sb far notare qcsa a qcno

point-'blank a a bruciapelo

point|ed /ˈpɔɪntɪd/ a appuntito; ⟨question⟩ diretto. ~ers npl ⟨advice⟩ consigli mpl. ~less a inutile

poise /pɔɪz/ n padronanza f. ~d a in equilibrio; ~d to sul punto di

poison /ˈpɔɪzn/ n veleno m ● vt avvelenare. ~ous a velenoso

poke /pəʊk/ n [piccola] spinta f ● vt spingere; ⟨fire⟩ attizzare; ⟨put⟩ ficcare; ~ fun at prendere in giro. poke about vi frugare

poker¹ /ˈpəʊkə(r)/ n attizzatoio m

poker² n ⟨Cards⟩ poker m

poky /ˈpəʊkɪ/ a (-ier, -iest) angusto

Poland /ˈpəʊlənd/ n Polonia f

polar /ˈpəʊlə(r)/ a polare. ~ 'bear n orso m bianco. ~ize vt polarizzare

Pole /pəʊl/ n polacco, -a mf

pole¹ n palo m

pole² n ⟨Geog, Electr⟩ polo m

'pole-star n stella f polare

'pole-vault n salto m con l'asta

police /pəˈliːs/ npl polizia f ● vt pattugliare ⟨area⟩

police: ~man n poliziotto m. ~ state n stato m militarista. ~ station n commissariato m. ~woman n donna f poliziotto

policy¹ /ˈpɒlɪsɪ/ n politica f

policy² n ⟨insurance⟩ polizza f

polio /ˈpəʊlɪəʊ/ n polio f

Polish /ˈpəʊlɪʃ/ a polacco ● n ⟨language⟩ polacco m

polish /ˈpɒlɪʃ/ n ⟨shine⟩ lucentezza f; ⟨substance⟩ lucido m; ⟨for nails⟩ smalto m; fig raffinatezza f ● vt lucidare; fig smussare. **polish off** vt fam finire; far fuori ⟨food⟩

polished /ˈpɒlɪʃt/ a ⟨manner⟩ raffinato; ⟨performance⟩ senza sbavature

polite /pəˈlaɪt/ a cortese. ~ly adv cortesemente. ~ness n cortesia f

politic /ˈpɒlɪtɪk/ a prudente

politic|al /pəˈlɪtɪkl/ a politico. ~ally adv dal punto di vista politico. ~ian /pɒlɪˈtɪʃn/ n politico m

politics /ˈpɒlɪtɪks/ n politica f

poll /pəʊl/ n votazione f; ⟨election⟩ elezioni fpl; [opinion] ~ sondaggio m d'opinione; go to the ~s andare alle urne ● vt ottenere ⟨votes⟩

pollen /ˈpɒlən/ n polline m

polling /ˈpəʊlɪŋ/: ~-booth n cabina f elettorale. ~-station n seggio m elettorale

'poll tax n imposta f locale sulle persone fisiche

pollutant /pəˈluːtənt/ n sostanza f inquinante

pollut|e /pəˈluːt/ vt inquinare. ~ion /-uːʃn/ n inquinamento m

polo /ˈpəʊləʊ/ n polo m. ~-neck n collo m alto. ~ shirt n dolcevita f

polyester /pɒlɪˈestə(r)/ n poliestere m

polystyrene® /pɒlɪˈstaɪriːn/ n polistirolo m

polytechnic /pɒlɪˈteknɪk/ n politecnico m

polythene /ˈpɒlɪθiːn/ n politene m. ~ bag n sacchetto m di plastica

polyun'saturated a polinsaturo

pomegranate /ˈpɒmɪɡrænɪt/ n melagrana f

pomp /pɒmp/ n pompa f

pompon /ˈpɒmpɒn/ n pompon m

pompous /ˈpɒmpəs/ a pomposo

pond /pɒnd/ n stagno m

ponder /ˈpɒndə(r)/ vt/i ponderare

pong /pɒŋ/ *n fam* puzzo *m*

pontiff /'pɒntɪf/ *n* pontefice *m*

pony /'pəʊnɪ/ *n* pony *m inv*. **~-tail** *n* coda *f* di cavallo. **~-trekking** *n* escursioni *fpl* col pony

poodle /'puːdl/ *n* barboncino *m*

pool[1] /puːl/ *n* (*of water, blood*) pozza *f*; [swimming] ~ piscina *f*

pool[2] *n* (*common fund*) cassa *f* comune; (*in cards*) piatto *m*; (*game*) biliardo *m* a buca. **~s** *npl* ≈ totocalcio *msg* ● *vt* mettere insieme

poor /pʊə(r)/ *a* povero; (*not good*) scadente; **in ~ health** in cattiva salute ● *npl* **the ~** i poveri. **~ly** *a* **be ~ly** non stare bene ● *adv* male

pop[1] /pɒp/ *n* botto *m*; (*drink*) bibita *f* gasata ● *v* (*pt/pp* **popped**) ● *vt* (*fam: put*) mettere; (*burst*) far scoppiare ● *vi* (*burst*) scoppiare. **pop in/out** *vi fam* fare un salto/un salto fuori

pop[2] *n fam* musica *f* pop ● *attrib* pop *inv*

'popcorn *n* popcorn *m inv*

pope /pəʊp/ *n* papa *m*

poplar /'pɒplə(r)/ *n* pioppo *m*

poppy /'pɒpɪ/ *n* papavero *m*

popular /'pɒpjʊlə(r)/ *a* popolare; (*belief*) diffuso. **~ity** /-'lærətɪ/ *n* popolarità *f*

populat|e /'pɒpjʊleɪt/ *vt* popolare. **~ion** /-'leɪʃn/ *n* popolazione *f*

porcelain /'pɔːsəlɪn/ *n* porcellana *f*

porch /pɔːtʃ/ *n* portico *m*; *Am* veranda *f*

porcupine /'pɔːkjʊpaɪn/ *n* porcospino *m*

pore[1] /pɔː(r)/ *n* poro *m*

pore[2] *vi* ~ **over** immergersi in

pork /pɔːk/ *n* carne *f* di maiale

porn /pɔːn/ *n fam* porno *m*. **~o** *a fam* porno *inv*

pornograph|ic /pɔːnə'græfɪk/ *a* pornografico. **~y** /-'nɒgrəfɪ/ *n* pornografia *f*

porous /'pɔːrəs/ *a* poroso

porpoise /'pɔːpəs/ *n* focena *f*

porridge /'pɒrɪdʒ/ *n* farinata *f* di fiocchi d'avena

port[1] /pɔːt/ *n* porto *m*

port[2] *n* (*Naut: side*) babordo *m*

port[3] *n* (*wine*) porto *m*

portable /'pɔːtəbl/ *a* portatile

porter /'pɔːtə(r)/ *n* portiere *m*; (*for luggage*) facchino *m*

portfolio /pɔːt'fəʊlɪəʊ/ *n* cartella *f*; *Comm* portafoglio *m*

'porthole *n* oblò *m inv*

portion /'pɔːʃn/ *n* parte *f*; (*of food*) porzione *f*

portly /'pɔːtlɪ/ *a* (**-ier, -iest**) corpulento

portrait /'pɔːtrɪt/ *n* ritratto *m*

portray /pɔː'treɪ/ *vt* ritrarre; (*represent*) descrivere; (*actor:*) impersonare. **~al** *n* ritratto *m*

Portug|al /'pɔːtjʊgl/ *n* Portogallo *m*. **~uese** /-'giːz/ *a* portoghese ● *n* portoghese *mf*; (*language*) portoghese *m*

pose /pəʊz/ *n* posa *f* ● *vt* porre (*problem, question*) ● *vi* (*for painter*) posare; ~ **as** atteggiarsi a

posh /pɒʃ/ *a fam* lussuoso; (*people*) danaroso

position /pə'zɪʃn/ *n* posizione *f*; (*job*) posto *m*; (*status*) ceto *m* [sociale] ● *vt* posizionare

positive /'pɒzɪtɪv/ *a* positivo; (*certain*) sicuro; (*progress*) concreto ● *n* positivo *m*. **~ly** *adv* positivamente; (*decidedly*) decisamente

possess /pə'zes/ *vt* possedere. **~ion** /pə'zeʃn/ *n* possesso *m*; **~ions** *pl* beni *mpl*

possess|ive /pə'zesɪv/ *a* possessivo. **~iveness** *n* carattere *m* possessivo. **~or** *n* possessore, -ditrice *mf*

possibility /pɒsə'bɪlətɪ/ *n* possibilità *f inv*

possib|le /'pɒsɪbl/ *a* possibile. **~ly** *adv* possibilmente; **I couldn't ~ly accept** non mi è possibile accettare; **he can't ~ly be right** non è possibile che abbia ragione; **could you ~ly...?** potrebbe per favore...?

post[1] /pəʊst/ *n* (*pole*) palo *m* ● *vt* affiggere (*notice*)

post[2] *n* (*place of duty*) posto *m* ● *vt* appostare; (*transfer*) assegnare

post[3] *n* (*mail*) posta *f*; **by ~** per posta ● *vt* spedire; (*put in letter-box*) imbucare; (*as opposed to fax*) mandare per posta; **keep sb ~ed** tenere qcno al corrente

post- *pref* dopo

postage /'pəʊstɪdʒ/ *n* affrancatura *f*. ~ **stamp** *n* francobollo *m*

postal /'pəʊstl/ *a* postale. ~ **order** *n* vaglia *m inv* postale

post: **~-box** *n* cassetta *f* delle lettere. **~card** *n* cartolina *f*. **~code** *n* codice *m* postale. **~-'date** *vt* postdatare

poster /'pəʊstə(r)/ *n* poster *m inv*; (*advertising, election*) cartellone *m*

posterior /pɒ'stɪərɪə(r)/ *n fam* posteriore *m*

posterity /pɒ'sterətɪ/ *n* posterità *f*

posthumous /'pɒstjʊməs/ *a* postumo. **~ly** *adv* dopo la morte

postman | predator

post: ~**man** n postino m. ~**mark** n timbro m postale

post-mortem /-'mɔːtəm/ n autopsia f

'post office n ufficio m postale

postpone /pəʊst'pəʊn/ vt rimandare. ~**ment** n rinvio m

posture /'pɒstʃə(r)/ n posizione f

post-'war n del dopoguerra

pot /pɒt/ n vaso m; (for tea) teiera f; (for coffee) caffettiera f; (for cooking) pentola f; ~**s of money** fam un sacco di soldi; **go to** ~ fam andare in malora

potassium /pə'tæsɪəm/ n potassio m

potato /pə'teɪtəʊ/ n (pl -es) patata f

poten|t /'pəʊtənt/ a potente. ~**tate** n potentato m

potential /pə'tenʃl/ a potenziale ● n potenziale m. ~**ly** adv potenzialmente

pot: ~**-hole** n cavità f inv; (in road) buca f. ~**-holer** n speleologo, -a mf. ~**-luck** n **take** ~**-luck** affidarsi alla sorte. ~ **plant** n pianta f da appartamento. ~**-shot** n **take a** ~**-shot at** sparare a casaccio a

potted /'pɒtɪd/ a conservato; (shortened) condensato. ~ **plant** n pianta f da appartamento

potter¹ /'pɒtə(r)/ vi ~ [**about**] gingillarsi

potter² n vasaio, -a mf. ~**y** n lavorazione f della ceramica; (articles) ceramiche fpl; (place) laboratorio m di ceramiche

potty /'pɒtɪ/ a (-ier, -iest) fam matto ● n vasino m

pouch /paʊtʃ/ n marsupio m

pouffe /puːf/ n pouf m inv

poultry /'pəʊltrɪ/ n pollame m

pounce /paʊns/ vi balzare; ~ **on** saltare su

pound¹ /paʊnd/ n libbra f (= 0,454 kg); (money) sterlina f

pound² vt battere ● vi ⟨heart:⟩ battere forte; (run heavily) correre pesantemente

pour /pɔː(r)/ vt versare ● vi riversarsi; (with rain) piovere a dirotto. **pour out** vi riversarsi fuori ● vt versare ⟨drink⟩; sfogare ⟨troubles⟩

pout /paʊt/ vi fare il broncio ● n broncio m

poverty /'pɒvətɪ/ n povertà f

powder /'paʊdə(r)/ n polvere f; (cosmetic) cipria f ● vt polverizzare; (face) incipriare. ~**y** a polveroso

power /'paʊə(r)/ n potere m; Electr corrente f [elettrica]; Math potenza f. ~**cut** n interruzione f di corrente. ~**ed** a ~**ed by electricity** dotato di corrente

[elettrica]. ~**ful** a potente. ~**less** a impotente. ~**-station** n centrale f elettrica

PR n abbr **public relations**

practicable /'præktɪkəbl/ a praticabile

practical /'præktɪkl/ a pratico. ~ '**joke** n burla f. ~**ly** adv praticamente

practice /'præktɪs/ n pratica f; (custom) usanza f; (habit) abitudine f; (exercise) esercizio m; Sport allenamento m; **in** ~ (in reality) in pratica; **out of** ~ fuori esercizio; **put into** ~ mettere in pratica

practise /'præktɪs/ vt fare pratica in; (carry out) mettere in pratica; esercitare ⟨profession⟩ ● vi esercitarsi; ⟨doctor:⟩ praticare. ~**d** a esperto

pragmatic /præg'mætɪk/ a pragmatico

praise /preɪz/ n lode f ● vt lodare. ~**worthy** a lodevole

pram /præm/ n carrozzella f

prance /prɑːns/ vi saltellare

prank /præŋk/ n tiro m

prattle /'prætl/ vi parlottare

prawn /prɔːn/ n gambero m. ~ '**cocktail** n cocktail m inv di gamberetti

pray /preɪ/ vi pregare. ~**er** /preə(r)/ n preghiera f

preach /priːtʃ/ vt/i predicare. ~**er** n predicatore, -trice mf

preamble /priː'æmbl/ n preambolo m

pre-ar'range /priː-/ vt predisporre

precarious /prɪ'keərɪəs/ a precario. ~**ly** adv in modo precario

precaution /prɪ'kɔːʃn/ n precauzione f; **as a** ~ per precauzione. ~**ary** a preventivo

precede /prɪ'siːd/ vt precedere

preceden|ce /'presɪdəns/ n precedenza f. ~**t** n precedente m

preceding /prɪ'siːdɪŋ/ a precedente

precinct /'priːsɪŋkt/ n (traffic-free) zona f pedonale; (Am: district) circoscrizione f

precious /'preʃəs/ a prezioso; ⟨style⟩ ricercato ● adv fam ~ **little** ben poco

precipice /'presɪpɪs/ n precipizio m

precipitate /prɪ'sɪpɪteɪt/ vt precipitare

précis /'preɪsiː/ n (pl précis /-siːz/) sunto m

precis|e /prɪ'saɪs/ a preciso. ~**ely** adv precisamente. ~**ion** /-'sɪʒn/ n precisione f

precursor /priː'kɜːsə(r)/ n precursore m

predator /'predətə(r)/ n predatore, -trice mf. ~**y** a rapace

predecessor /'pri:dɪsesə(r)/ n predecessore, -a mf

predicament /prɪ'dɪkəmənt/ n situazione f difficile

predicat|e /'predɪkət/ n Gram predicato m. **~ive** /prɪ'dɪkətɪv/ a predicativo

predict /prɪ'dɪkt/ vt predire. **~able** /-əbl/ a prevedibile. **~ion** /-'dɪkʃn/ n previsione f

pre'domin|ant /prɪ-/ a predominante. **~ate** vi predominare

pre-'eminent /pri:-/ a preminente

preen /pri:n/ vt lisciarsi; **~ oneself** fig farsi bello

pre|fab /'pri:fæb/ n fam casa f prefabbricata. **~'fabricated** a prefabbricato

preface /'prefɪs/ n prefazione f

prefect /'pri:fekt/ n Sch studente, -tessa mf della scuola superiore con responsabilità disciplinari ecc

prefer /prɪ'fɜ:(r)/ vt (pt/pp **preferred**) preferire

prefera|ble /'prefərəbl/ a preferibile (**to** a). **~bly** adv preferibilmente

preferen|ce /'prefərəns/ n preferenza f. **~tial** /-'renʃl/ a preferenziale

prefix /'pri:fɪks/ n prefisso m

pregnan|cy /'pregnənsɪ/ n gravidanza f. **~t** a incinta

prehi'storic /pri:-/ a preistorico

prejudice /'predʒʊdɪs/ n pregiudizio m ● vt influenzare (**against** contro); (harm) danneggiare. **~d** a prevenuto

preliminary /prɪ'lɪmɪnərɪ/ a preliminare

prelude /'prelju:d/ n preludio m

pre-'marital a prematrimoniale

premature /'premətjʊə(r)/ a prematuro

pre'meditated /pri:-/ a premeditato

premier /'premɪə(r)/ a primario ● n Pol primo ministro m, premier m inv

première /'premɪeə(r)/ n prima f

premises /'premɪsɪz/ npl locali mpl; **on the ~** sul posto

premium /'pri:mɪəm/ n premio m; **be at a ~** essere una cosa rara

premonition /premə'nɪʃn/ n presentimento m

preoccupied /pri:'ɒkjʊpaɪd/ a preoccupato

prep /prep/ n Sch compiti mpl

preparation /prepə'reɪʃn/ n preparazione f. **~s** pl preparativi mpl

preparatory /prɪ'pærətrɪ/ a preparatorio ● adv **~ to** per

prepare /prɪ'peə(r)/ vt preparare ● vi prepararsi (**for** per); **~d to** disposto a

pre'pay /pri:-/ vt (pt/pp **-paid**) pagare in anticipo

preposition /prepə'zɪʃn/ n preposizione f

prepossessing /pri:pə'zesɪŋ/ a attraente

preposterous /prɪ'pɒstərəs/ a assurdo

prerequisite /pri:'rekwɪzɪt/ n condizione f sine qua non

prescribe /prɪ'skraɪb/ vt prescrivere

prescription /prɪ'skrɪpʃn/ n Med ricetta f

presence /'prezns/ n presenza f; **~ of mind** presenza f di spirito

present¹ /'preznt/ a presente ● n presente m; **at ~** attualmente

present² n (gift) regalo m; **give sb sth as a ~** regalare qcsa a qcno

present³ /prɪ'zent/ vt presentare; **~ sb with an award** consegnare un premio a qcno. **~able** /-əbl/ a **be ~able** essere presentabile

presentation /prezn'teɪʃn/ n presentazione f

presently /'prezntlɪ/ adv fra poco; (Am: now) attualmente

preservation /prezə'veɪʃn/ n conservazione f

preservative /prɪ'zɜ:vətɪv/ n conservante m

preserve /prɪ'zɜ:v/ vt preservare; (maintain, Culin) conservare ● n (in hunting & fig) riserva f; (jam) marmellata f

preside /prɪ'zaɪd/ vi presiedere (**over** a)

presidency /'prezɪdənsɪ/ n presidenza f

president /'prezɪdənt/ n presidente m. **~ial** /-'denʃl/ a presidenziale

press /pres/ n (machine) pressa f; (newspapers) stampa f ● vt premere; pressare (flower); (iron) stirare; (squeeze) stringere ● vi (urge) incalzare. **press for** vi fare pressione per; **be ~ed for** essere a corto di. **press on** vi andare avanti

press: ~ conference n conferenza f stampa. **~ cutting** n ritaglio m di giornale. **~ing** a urgente. **~-stud** n [bottone m] automatico m. **~-up** n flessione f

pressure /'preʃə(r)/ n pressione f ● vt = **pressurize**. **~-cooker** n pentola f a pressione. **~ group** n gruppo m di pressione

pressurize /'preʃəraɪz/ vt far pressione su. **~d** a pressurizzato

prestig|e /pre'sti:ʒ/ *n* prestigio *m*. **~ious** /-'stɪdʒəs/ *a* prestigioso

presumably /prɪ'zju:məblɪ/ *adv* presumibilmente

presume /prɪ'zju:m/ *vt* presumere; **~ to do sth** permettersi di fare qcsa

presumpt|ion /prɪ'zʌmpʃn/ *n* presunzione *f*; *(boldness)* impertinenza *f*. **~uous** /-'zʌmptjʊəs/ *a* impertinente

presup'pose /pri:-/ *vt* presupporre

pretence /prɪ'tens/ *n* finzione *f*; *(pretext)* pretesto *m*; **it's all ~** è tutta una scena

pretend /prɪ'tend/ *vt* fingere; *(claim)* pretendere ● *vi* fare finta

pretentious /prɪ'tenʃəs/ *a* pretenzioso

pretext /'pri:tekst/ *n* pretesto *m*

pretty /'prɪtɪ/ *a* (**-ier, -iest**) carino ● *adv (fam: fairly)* abbastanza

prevail /prɪ'veɪl/ *vi* prevalere; **~ on sb to do sth** convincere qcno a fare qcsa. **~ing** *a* prevalente

prevalen|ce /'prevələns/ *n* diffusione *f*. **~t** *a* diffuso

prevent /prɪ'vent/ *vt* impedire; **~ sb [from] doing sth** impedire a qcno di fare qcsa. **~ion** /-enʃn/ *n* prevenzione *f*. **~ive** /-ɪv/ *a* preventivo

preview /'pri:vju:/ *n* anteprima *f*

previous /'pri:vɪəs/ *a* precedente. **~ly** *adv* precedentemente

pre-'war /pri:-/ *a* anteguerra

prey /preɪ/ *n* preda *f*; **bird of ~** uccello *m* rapace ● *vi* **~ on** far preda di; **~ on sb's mind** attanagliare qcno

price /praɪs/ *n* prezzo *m* ● *vt Comm* fissare il prezzo di. **~less** *a* inestimabile; *(fam: amusing)* spassosissimo. **~y** *a* *fam* caro

prick /prɪk/ *n* puntura *f* ● *vt* pungere; **prick up** *vt* **~ up one's ears** rizzare le orecchie

prickl|e /'prɪkl/ *n* spina *f*; *(sensation)* formicolio *m*. **~y** *a* pungente; *(person)* irritabile

pride /praɪd/ *n* orgoglio *m* ● *vt* **~ oneself on** vantarsi di

priest /pri:st/ *n* prete *m*

prim /prɪm/ *a* (**primmer, primmest**) perbenino

primarily /'praɪmərɪlɪ/ *adv* in primo luogo

primary /'praɪmərɪ/ *a* primario; *(chief)* principale. **~ school** *n* scuola *f* elementare

prime[1] /praɪm/ *a* principale, primo;

(first-rate) eccellente ● *n* **be in one's ~** essere nel fiore degli anni

prime[2] *vt* preparare ⟨*surface, person*⟩

Prime Minister *n* Primo Ministro *m*

primeval /praɪ'mi:vl/ *a* primitivo

primitive /'prɪmɪtɪv/ *a* primitivo

primrose /'prɪmrəʊz/ *n* primula *f*

prince /prɪns/ *n* principe *m*

princess /prɪn'ses/ *n* principessa *f*

principal /'prɪnsəpl/ *a* principale ● *n Sch* preside *m*

principality /prɪnsɪ'pælətɪ/ *n* principato *m*

principally /'prɪnsəplɪ/ *adv* principalmente

principle /'prɪnsəpl/ *n* principio *m*; **in ~** in teoria; **on ~** per principio

print /prɪnt/ *n* *(mark, trace)* impronta *f*; *Phot* copia *f*; *(picture)* stampa *f*; **in ~** *(printed out)* stampato; ⟨*book*⟩ in commercio; **out of ~** esaurito ● *vt* stampare; *(write in capitals)* scrivere in stampatello. **~ed matter** *n* stampe *fpl*

print|er /'prɪntə(r)/ *n* stampante *f*; *Typ* tipografo, -a *mf*. **~er port** *n Comput* porta *f* per la stampante. **~ing** *n* tipografia *f*

'printout *n Comput* stampa *f*

prior /'praɪə(r)/ *a* precedente. **~ to** *prep* prima di

priority /praɪ'ɒrətɪ/ *n* precedenza *f*; *(matter)* priorità *f inv*

prise /praɪz/ *vt* **~ open/up** forzare

prison /'prɪz(ə)n/ *n* prigione *f*. **~er** *n* prigioniero, -a *mf*

privacy /'prɪvəsɪ/ *n* privacy *f*

private /'praɪvət/ *a* privato; ⟨*car, secretary, letter*⟩ personale ● *n Mil* soldato *m* semplice; **in ~** in privato. **~ly** *adv* ⟨*funded, educated etc*⟩ privatamente; *(in secret)* in segreto; *(confidentially)* in privato; *(inwardly)* interiormente

privation /praɪ'veɪʃn/ *n* privazione *f*; **~s** *pl* stenti *mpl*

privatize /'praɪvətaɪz/ *vt* privatizzare

privilege /'prɪvəlɪdʒ/ *n* privilegio *m*. **~d** *a* privilegiato

privy /'prɪvɪ/ *a* **be ~ to** essere al corrente di

prize /praɪz/ *n* premio *m* ● *a (idiot etc)* perfetto ● *vt* apprezzare. **~-giving** *n* premiazione *f*. **~-winner** *n* vincitore, -trice *mf*. **~-winning** *a* vincente

pro /prəʊ/ *n (fam: professional)* professionista *mf*; **the ~s and cons** il pro e il contro

probability /prɒbə'bɪlətɪ/ *n* probabilità *f inv*

175

probabl|e /'prɒbəbl/ *a* probabile. **~y**
adv probabilmente

probation /prəˈbeɪʃn/ *n* prova *f*; *Jur* libertà *f* vigilata. **~ary** *a* in prova; **~ary period** periodo *m* di prova

probe /prəʊb/ *n* sonda *f*; ⟨*fig: investigation*⟩ indagine *f* ● *vt* sondare; (*investigate*) esaminare a fondo

problem /'prɒbləm/ *n* problema *m* ● *a* difficile. **~atic** /-'mætɪk/ *a* problematico

procedure /prəˈsiːdʒə(r)/ *n* procedimento *m*

proceed /prəˈsiːd/ *vi* procedere ● *vt* **~ to do sth** proseguire facendo qcsa

proceedings /prəˈsiːdɪŋz/ *npl* (*report*) atti *mpl*; *Jur* azione *fsg* legale

proceeds /'prəʊsiːdz/ *npl* ricavato *msg*

process /'prəʊses/ *n* processo *m*; (*procedure*) procedimento *m*; **in the ~** nel far ciò ● *vt* trattare; *Admin* occuparsi di; *Phot* sviluppare

procession /prəˈseʃn/ *n* processione *f*

proclaim /prəˈkleɪm/ *vt* proclamare

procure /prəˈkjʊə(r)/ *vt* ottenere

prod /prɒd/ *n* colpetto *m* ● *vt* (*pt/pp* **prodded**) punzecchiare; *fig* incitare

prodigal /'prɒdɪgl/ *a* prodigo

prodigious /prəˈdɪdʒəs/ *a* prodigioso

prodigy /'prɒdɪdʒɪ/ *n* [**infant**] **~** bambino *m* prodigio

produce¹ /'prɒdjuːs/ *n* prodotti *mpl*; **~ of Italy** prodotto in Italia

produce² /prəˈdjuːs/ *vt* produrre; (*bring out*) tirar fuori; (*cause*) causare; (*fam: give birth to*) fare. **~r** *n* produttore *m*

product /'prɒdʌkt/ *n* prodotto *m*. **~ion** /prəˈdʌkʃn/ *n* produzione *f*; *Theat* spettacolo *m*

productiv|e /prəˈdʌktɪv/ *a* produttivo. **~ity** /-'tɪvətɪ/ *n* produttività *f*

profan|e /prəˈfeɪm/ *a* profano; (*blasphemous*) blasfemo. **~ity** /-'fænətɪ/ *n* (*oath*) bestemmia *f*

profession /prəˈfeʃn/ *n* professione *f*. **~al** *a* professionale; (*not amateur*) professionista; (*piece of work*) da professionista; (*man*) di professione ● *n* professionista *mf*. **~ally** *adv* professionalmente

professor /prəˈfesə(r)/ *n* professore *m* [universitario]

proficien|cy /prəˈfɪʃnsɪ/ *n* competenza *f*. **~t** *a* **be ~t in** essere competente in

profile /'prəʊfaɪl/ *n* profilo *m*

profit /'prɒfɪt/ *n* profitto *m* ● *vi* **~ from** trarre profitto da. **~able** /-əbl/ *a* proficuo. **~ably** *adv* in modo proficuo

profound /prəˈfaʊnd/ *a* profondo. **~ly** *adv* profondamente

profus|e /prəˈfjuːs/ *a* **~e apologies** una profusione di scuse. **~ion** /-juːʒn/ *n* profusione *f*; **in ~ion** in abbondanza

progeny /'prɒdʒənɪ/ *n* progenie *f inv*

prognosis /prɒgˈnəʊsɪs/ *n* (*pl* **-oses**) prognosi *f inv*

program /'prəʊgræm/ *n* programma *m* ● *vt* (*pt/pp* **programmed**) programmare

programme /'prəʊgræm/ *n* *Br* programma *m*. **~r** *n* *Comput* programmatore, -trice *mf*

progress¹ /'prəʊgres/ *n* progresso *m*; **in ~** in corso; **make ~** *fig* fare progressi

progress² /prəˈgres/ *vi* progredire; *fig* fare progressi

progressive /prəˈgresɪv/ *a* progressivo; (*reforming*) progressista. **~ly** *adv* progressivamente

prohibit /prəˈhɪbɪt/ *vt* proibire. **~ive** /-ɪv/ *a* proibitivo

project¹ /'prɒdʒekt/ *n* progetto *m*; *Sch* ricerca *f*

project² /prəˈdʒekt/ *vt* proiettare ⟨*film, image*⟩ ● *vi* (*jut out*) sporgere

projectile /prəˈdʒektaɪl/ *n* proiettile *m*

projector /prəˈdʒektə(r)/ *n* proiettore *m*

prolific /prəˈlɪfɪk/ *a* prolifico

prologue /'prəʊlɒg/ *n* prologo *m*

prolong /prəˈlɒŋ/ *vt* prolungare

promenade /prɒməˈnɑːd/ *n* lungomare *m inv*

prominent /'prɒmɪnənt/ *a* prominente; (*conspicuous*) di rilievo

promiscu|ity /prɒmɪˈskjuːətɪ/ *n* promiscuità *f*. **~ous** /prəˈmɪskjʊəs/ *a* promiscuo

promis|e /'prɒmɪs/ *n* promessa *f* ● *vt* promettere; **~e sb that** promettere a qcno che; **I ~ed** lo l'ho promesso. **~ing** *a* promettente

promot|e /prəˈməʊt/ *vt* promuovere; **be ~ed** *Sport* essere promosso. **~ion** /-əʊʃn/ *n* promozione *f*

prompt /prɒmpt/ *a* immediato; (*punctual*) puntuale ● *adv* in punto ● *vt* incitare (**to** a); *Theat* suggerire a ● *vi* suggerire. **~er** *n* suggeritore, -trice *mf*. **~ly** *adv* puntualmente

Proms /prɒmz/ *npl rassegna f di concerti estivi di musica classica presso l'Albert Hall a Londra*

prone /prəʊn/ *a* be ~ to do sth essere
incline a fare qcsa

prong /prɒŋ/ *n* dente *m (di forchetta)*

pronoun /'prəʊnaʊn/ *n* pronome *m*

pronounce /prə'naʊns/ *vt* pronunciare; *(declare)* dichiarare. **~d** *a*
(noticeable) pronunciato

pronunciation /prənʌnsɪ'eɪʃn/ *n* pronuncia *f*

proof /pru:f/ *n* prova *f*; *Typ* bozza *f*, prova *f* ● *a* ~ **against** a prova di

prop[1] /prɒp/ *n* puntello *m* ● *vt* *(pt/pp*
propped) ~ **open** tenere aperto; ~
against *(lean)* appoggiare a. **prop up** *vt*
sostenere

prop[2] *n* *Theat, fam* accessorio *m* di scena

propaganda /prɒpə'gændə/ *n* propaganda *f*

propel /prə'pel/ *vt* *(pt/pp* **propelled)**
spingere. **~ler** *n* elica *f*

proper /'prɒpə(r)/ *a* corretto; *(suitable)*
adatto; *(fam: real)* vero [e proprio]. **~ly**
adv correttamente. ~ **'name**, ~ **'noun**
n nome *m* proprio

property /'prɒpətɪ/ *n* proprietà *f inv*. ~
developer *n* agente *m* immobiliare. ~
market *n* mercato *m* immobiliare

prophecy /'prɒfəsɪ/ *n* profezia *f*

prophesy /'prɒfɪsaɪ/ *vt* *(pt/pp* **-ied)**
profetizzare

prophet /'prɒfɪt/ *n* profeta *m*. **~ic**
/prə'fetɪk/ *a* profetico

proportion /prə'pɔ:ʃn/ *n* proporzione
f; *(share)* parte *f*; **~s** *pl* *(dimensions)*
proporzioni *fpl*. **~al** *a* proporzionale.
~ally *adv* in proporzione

proposal /prə'pəʊzl/ *n* proposta *f*; *(of
marriage)* proposta *f* di matrimonio

propose /prə'pəʊz/ *vt* proporre;
(intend) proporsi ● *vi* fare una proposta
di matrimonio

proposition /prɒpə'zɪʃn/ *n* proposta *f*;
(fam: task) impresa *f*

proprietor /prə'praɪətə(r)/ *n* proprietario, -a *mf*

prosaic /prə'zeɪɪk/ *a* prosaico

prose /prəʊz/ *n* prosa *f*

prosecut|e /'prɒsɪkju:t/ *vt* intentare
azione contro. **~ion** /-'kju:ʃn/ *n* azione *f*
giudiziaria; **the ~ion** l'accusa *f*. **~or** *n*
[**Public**] **P~or** Pubblico Ministero *m*

prospect[1] /'prɒspekt/ *n* *(expectation)*
prospettiva *f*

prospect[2] /prə'spekt/ *vi* ~ **for** cercare

prospect|ive /prə'spektɪv/ *a* *(future)*
futuro; *(possible)* potenziale. **~or** *n*
cercatore *m*

prospectus /prə'spektəs/ *n* prospetto *m*

prosper /'prɒspə(r)/ *vi* prosperare;
(person:) stare bene finanziariamente.
~ity /-'sperətɪ/ *n* prosperità *f*

prosperous /'prɒspərəs/ *a* prospero

prostitut|e /'prɒstɪtju:t/ *n* prostituta *f*.
~ion /-'tju:ʃn/ *n* prostituzione *f*

prostrate /'prɒstreɪt/ *a* prostrato; ~
with grief *fig* prostrato dal dolore

protagonist /prəʊ'tægənɪst/ *n* protagonista *mf*

protect /prə'tekt/ *vt* proteggere (**from**
da). **~ion** /-ekʃn/ *n* protezione *f*. **~ive**
/-ɪv/ *a* protettivo. **~or** *n* protettore,
-trice *mf*

protégé /'prɒtɪʒeɪ/ *n* protetto *m*

protein /'prəʊti:n/ *n* proteina *f*

protest[1] /'prəʊtest/ *n* protesta *f*

protest[2] /prə'test/ *vt/i* protestare

Protestant /'prɒtɪstənt/ *a* protestante
● *n* protestante *mf*

protester /prə'testə(r)/ *n* contestato-
re, -trice *mf*

protocol /'prəʊtəkɒl/ *n* protocollo *m*

prototype /'prəʊtə-/ *n* prototipo *m*

protract /prə'trækt/ *vt* protrarre

protrude /prə'tru:d/ *vi* sporgere

proud /praʊd/ *a* fiero (**of** di). **~ly** *adv*
fieramente

prove /pru:v/ *vt* provare ● *vi* ~ **to be a
lie** rivelarsi una bugia. **~n** *a* dimostrato

proverb /'prɒvɜ:b/ *n* proverbio *m*. **~ial**
/prə'vɜ:bɪəl/ *a* proverbiale

provide /prə'vaɪd/ *vt* fornire; ~ **sb
with sth** fornire qcsa a qcno ● *vi* ~ **for**
(law:) prevedere

provided /prə'vaɪdɪd/ *conj* ~ [**that**]
purché

providen|ce /'prɒvɪdəns/ *n* provvi-
denza *f*. **~tial** /-'denʃl/ *a* provvidenziale

providing /prə'vaɪdɪŋ/ *conj* =
provided

provinc|e /'prɒvɪns/ *n* provincia *f*; *fig*
campo *m*. **~ial** /prə'vɪnʃl/ *a* provinciale

provision /prə'vɪʒn/ *n* *(of food, water)*
approvvigionamento *m* (**of** di); *(of law)*
disposizione *f*; **~s** *pl* provviste *fpl*. **~al**
a provvisorio

proviso /prə'vaɪzəʊ/ *n* condizione *f*

provocat|ion /prɒvə'keɪʃn/ *n* provo-
cazione *f*. **~ive** /prə'vɒkətɪv/ *a* provocatorio; *(sexually)* provocante. **~ively** *adv*
in modo provocatorio

provoke /prə'vəʊk/ *vt* provocare

prow /praʊ/ *n* prua *f*

prowess /'praʊɪs/ *n* abilità *f inv*

prowl /praʊl/ *vi* aggirarsi ● *n* **on the ~** in cerca di preda. **~er** *n* tipo *m* sospetto

proximity /prɒkˈsɪmətɪ/ *n* prossimità *f*

proxy /ˈprɒksɪ/ *n* procura *f*; (*person*) persona *f* che agisce per procura

prude /pruːd/ *n* **be a ~** essere eccessivamente pudico

pruden|ce /ˈpruːdəns/ *n* prudenza *f*. **~t** *a* prudente; (*wise*) oculatezza *f*

prudish /ˈpruːdɪʃ/ *a* eccessivamente pudico

prune[1] /pruːn/ *n* prugna *f* secca

prune[2] *vt* potare

pry /praɪ/ *vi* (*pt/pp* **pried**) ficcare il naso

psalm /sɑːm/ *n* salmo *m*

pseudonym /ˈsjuːdənɪm/ *n* pseudonimo *m*

psychiatric /saɪkɪˈætrɪk/ *a* psichiatrico

psychiatr|ist /saɪˈkaɪətrɪst/ *n* psichiatra *mf*. **~y** *n* psichiatria *f*

psychic /ˈsaɪkɪk/ *a* psichico; **I'm not ~** non sono un indovino

psycho|'analyse /saɪkəʊ-/ *vt* psicanalizzare. **~a'nalysis** *n* psicanalisi *f*. **~'analyst** *n* psicanalista *mf*

psychological /saɪkəˈlɒdʒɪkl/ *a* psicologico

psycholog|ist /saɪˈkɒlədʒɪst/ *n* psicologo, -a *mf*. **~y** *n* psicologia *f*

psychopath /ˈsaɪkəpæθ/ *n* psicopatico, -a *mf*

P.T.O. *abbr* (**please turn over**) vedi retro

pub /pʌb/ *n fam* pub *m inv*

puberty /ˈpjuːbətɪ/ *n* pubertà *f*

public /ˈpʌblɪk/ *a* pubblico ● *n* **the ~** il pubblico; **in ~** in pubblico. **~ly** *adv* pubblicamente

publican /ˈpʌblɪkən/ *n* gestore, -trice *mf*/proprietario, -a *mf* di un pub

publication /pʌblɪˈkeɪʃn/ *n* pubblicazione *f*

public: ~ con'venience *n* gabinetti *mpl* pubblici. **~ 'holiday** *n* festa *f* nazionale. **~ 'house** *n* pub *m inv*

publicity /pʌbˈlɪsətɪ/ *n* pubblicità *f*

publicize /ˈpʌblɪsaɪz/ *vt* pubblicizzare

public: ~ 'library *n* biblioteca *f* pubblica. **~ re'lations** pubbliche relazioni *fpl*. **~ school** *n* scuola *f* privata; *Am* scuola *f* pubblica. **~-'spirited** *a* **be ~spirited** essere dotato di senso civico. **~ 'transport** *n* mezzi *mpl* pubblici

publish /ˈpʌblɪʃ/ *vt* pubblicare. **~er** *n* editore *m*; (*firm*) editore *m*, casa *f* editrice. **~ing** *n* editoria *f*

pudding /ˈpʊdɪŋ/ *n* dolce *m* cotto al vapore; (*course*) dolce *m*

puddle /ˈpʌdl/ *n* pozzanghera *f*

pudgy /ˈpʌdʒɪ/ *a* (**-ier**, **-iest**) grassoccio

puff /pʌf/ *n* (*of wind*) soffio *m*; (*of smoke*) tirata *f*; (*for powder*) piumino *m* ● *vt* sbuffare. **puff at** *vt* tirare boccate da (*pipe*). **puff out** *vt* lasciare senza fiato (*person*); spegnere (*candle*). **~ed** *a* (*out of breath*) senza fiato. **~ pastry** *n* pasta *f* sfoglia

puffy /ˈpʌfɪ/ *a* gonfio

pull /pʊl/ *n* trazione *f*; (*fig: attraction*) attrazione *f*; (*fam: influence*) influenza *f* ● *vt* tirare; estrarre (*tooth*); stirarsi (*muscle*); **~ faces** far boccace; **~ oneself together** cercare di controllarsi; **~ one's weight** mettercela tutta; **~ sb's leg** *fam* prendere in giro qcno. **pull down** *vt* (*demolish*) demolire. **pull in** *vi Auto* accostare. **pull off** *vt* togliere; *fam* azzeccare. **pull out** *vt* tirar fuori ● *vi Auto* spostarsi; (*of competition*) ritirarsi. **pull through** *vi* (*recover*) farcela. **pull up** *vt* sradicare (*plant*); (*reprimand*) rimproverare ● *vi Auto* fermarsi

pulley /ˈpʊlɪ/ *n Techn* puleggia *f*

pullover /ˈpʊləʊvə(r)/ *n* pullover *m inv*

pulp /pʌlp/ *n* poltiglia *f*; (*of fruit*) polpa *f*; (*for paper*) pasta *f*

pulpit /ˈpʊlpɪt/ *n* pulpito *m*

pulsate /pʌlˈseɪt/ *vi* pulsare

pulse /pʌls/ *n* polso *m*

pulses /ˈpʌlsɪz/ *npl* legumi *mpl* secchi

pulverize /ˈpʌlvəraɪz/ *vt* polverizzare

pumice /ˈpʌmɪs/ *n* pomice *f*

pummel /ˈpʌml/ *vt* (*pt/pp* **pummelled**) prendere a pugni

pump /pʌmp/ *n* pompa *f* ● *vt* pompare; **~ sb for sth** *fam* cercare di estorcere qcsa da qcno. **pump up** *vt* (*inflate*) gonfiare

pumpkin /ˈpʌmpkɪn/ *n* zucca *f*

pun /pʌn/ *n* gioco *m* di parole

punch[1] /pʌntʃ/ *n* pugno *m*; (*device*) pinza *f* per forare ● *vt* dare un pugno a; forare (*ticket*); perforare (*hole*)

punch[2] *n* (*drink*) ponce *m inv*

punch: ~ line *n* battuta *f* finale. **~-up** *n* rissa *f*

punctual /ˈpʌŋktjʊəl/ *a* puntuale. **~ity** /-ˈælətɪ/ *n* puntualità *f*. **~ly** *adv* puntualmente

punctuat|e /ˈpʌŋktjʊeɪt/ *vt* punteggiare. **~ion** /-ˈeɪʃn/ *n* punteggiatura *f*. **~ion mark** *n* segno *m* di interpunzione

puncture /ˈpʌŋktʃə(r)/ *n* foro *m*; (*tyre*) foratura *f* ● *vt* forare

pungent /'pʌndʒənt/ a acre

punish /'pʌnɪʃ/ vt punire. **~able** /-əbl/ a punibile. **~ment** n punizione f

punitive /'pju:nɪtɪv/ a punitivo

punk /pʌŋk/ n punk m inv

punnet /'pʌnɪt/ n cestello m (per frutta)

punt /pʌnt/ n (boat) barchino m

punter /'pʌntə(r)/ n (gambler) scommettitore, -trice mf; (client) consumatore, -trice mf

puny /'pju:nɪ/ a (-ier, -iest) striminzito

pup /pʌp/ n = **puppy**

pupil /'pju:pl/ n alluno, -a mf; (of eye) pupilla f

puppet /'pʌpɪt/ n marionetta f; (glove ~, fig) burattino m

puppy /'pʌpɪ/ n cucciolo m

purchase /'pɜ:tʃəs/ n acquisto m; (leverage) presa f ● vt acquistare. **~r** n acquirente mf

pure /pjʊə(r)/ a puro. **~ly** adv puramente

purée /'pjʊəreɪ/ n purè m inv

purgatory /'pɜ:gətrɪ/ n purgatorio m

purge /pɜ:dʒ/ Pol n epurazione f ● vt epurare

puri|fication /pjʊərɪfɪ'keɪʃn/ n purificazione f. **~fy** /'pjʊərɪfaɪ/ vt (pt/pp -ied) purificare

puritan /'pjʊərɪtən/ n puritano, -a mf. **~ical** a puritano

purity /'pjʊərɪtɪ/ n purità f

purple /'pɜ:pl/ a viola inv

purpose /'pɜ:pəs/ n scopo m; (determination) fermezza f; **on ~** apposta. **~-built** a costruito ad hoc. **~ful** a deciso. **~fully** adv con decisione. **~ly** adv apposta

purr /pɜ:(r)/ vi ‹cat:› fare le fusa

purse /pɜ:s/ n borsellino m; (Am: handbag) borsa f ● vt increspare ‹lips›

pursue /pə'sju:/ vt inseguire; fig proseguire. **~r** /-ə(r)/ n inseguitore, -trice mf

pursuit /pə'sju:t/ n inseguimento m; (fig: of happiness) ricerca f; (pastime) attività f inv; **in ~** all'inseguimento

pus /pʌs/ n pus m

push /pʊʃ/ n spinta f; (fig: effort) sforzo m; (drive) iniziativa f; **at a ~** in caso di bisogno; **get the ~** fam essere licenziato ● vt spingere; premere ‹button›; (pressurize) far pressione su; **be ~ed for time** fam non avere tempo ● vi spingere. **push aside** vt scostare. **push back** vt respingere. **push off** vt togliere

● vi (fam: leave) levarsi dai piedi. **push on** vi (continue) continuare. **push up** vt alzare ‹price›

push: ~-button n pulsante m. **~-chair** n passeggino m. **~-over** n fam bazzecola f. **~-up** n flessione f

pushy /'pʊʃɪ/ a fam troppo intraprendente

puss /pʊs/ n, **pussy** /'pʊsɪ/ n micio m

put /pʊt/ vt (pt/pp put, pres p **putting**) mettere; **~ the cost of sth at** valutare il costo di qcsa ● vi **~ to sea** salpare. **put aside** vt mettere da parte. **put away** vt mettere via. **put back** vt rimettere; mettere indietro ‹clock›. **put by** vt mettere da parte. **put down** vt mettere giù; (suppress) reprimere; (kill) sopprimere; (write) annotare; **~ one's foot down** fam essere fermo; Auto dare un'accelerata; **~ down to** (attribute) attribuire. **put forward** vt avanzare; mettere avanti ‹clock›. **put in** vt (insert) introdurre; (submit) presentare ● vi **~ in for** far domanda di. **put off** vt spegnere ‹light›; (postpone) rimandare; **~ sb off** tenere a bada qcno; (deter) smontare qcno; (disconcert) distrarre qcno; **~ sb off sth** (disgust) disgustare qcno di qcsa. **put on** vt mettersi ‹clothes›; mettere ‹brake›; Culin mettere su; accendere ‹light›; mettere in scena ‹play›; prendere ‹accent›; **~ on weight** mettere su qualche chilo. **put out** vt spegnere ‹fire, light›; tendere ‹hand›; (inconvenience) creare degli inconvenienti a. **put through** vt far passare; Teleph **I'll ~ you through to him** glielo passo. **put up** vt alzare; erigere ‹building›; montare ‹tent›; aprire ‹umbrella›; affiggere ‹notice›; aumentare ‹price›; ospitare ‹guest›; **~ sb up to sth** mettere qcsa in testa a qcno ● vi (at hotel) stare; **~ up with** sopportare ● a **stay ~!** rimani lì!

putty /'pʌtɪ/ n mastice m

put-up /'pʊtʌp/ a **~ job** truffa f

puzz|le /'pʌzl/ n enigma m; (jigsaw) puzzle m inv ● vt lasciare perplesso ● vi **~e over** scervellarsi su. **~ing** a inspiegabile

pygmy /'pɪgmɪ/ n pigmeo, -a mf

pyjamas /pə'dʒɑ:məz/ npl pigiama msg

pylon /'paɪlən/ n pilone m

pyramid /'pɪrəmɪd/ n piramide f

python /'paɪθn/ n pitone m

Qq

quack[1] /kwæk/ *n* qua qua *m inv* ● *vi* fare qua qua

quack[2] *n* (*doctor*) ciarlatano *m*

quad /kwɒd/ *n* (*fam: court*) = **quadrangle**. **~s** *pl* = **quadruplets**

quadrangle /'kwɒdræŋgl/ *n* quadrangolo *m*; (*court*) cortile *m* quadrangolare

quadruped /'kwɒdrʊped/ *n* quadrupede *m*

quadruple /'kwɒdrʊpl/ *a* quadruplo ● *vt* quadruplicare ● *vi* quadruplicarsi. **~ts** /-plɪts/ *npl* quattro gemelli *mpl*

quagmire /'kwɒgmaɪə(r)/ *n* pantano *m*

quaint /kweɪnt/ *a* pittoresco; (*odd*) bizzarro

quake /kweɪk/ *n fam* terremoto *m* ● *vi* tremare

qualif|ication /kwɒlɪfɪ'keɪʃn/ *n* qualifica *f*. **~ied** /-faɪd/ *a* qualificato; (*limited*) con riserva

qualify /'kwɒlɪfaɪ/ *v* (*pt/pp* **-ied**) ● *vt* ⟨*course:*⟩ dare la qualifica a (**as** di); (*entitle*) dare diritto a; (*limit*) precisare ● *vi* ottenere la qualifica; *Sport* qualificarsi

quality /'kwɒlətɪ/ *n* qualità *f inv*

qualm /kwɑːm/ *n* scrupolo *m*

quandary /'kwɒndərɪ/ *n* dilemma *m*

quantity /'kwɒntətɪ/ *n* quantità *f inv*; **in ~** in grande quantità

quarantine /'kwɒrəntiːn/ *n* quarantena *f*

quarrel /'kwɒrəl/ *n* lite *f* ● *vi* (*pt/pp* **quarrelled**) litigare. **~some** *a* litigioso

quarry[1] /'kwɒrɪ/ *n* (*prey*) preda *f*

quarry[2] *n* cava *f*

quart /kwɔːt/ *n* 1.14 litro

quarter /'kwɔːtə(r)/ *n* quarto *m*; (*of year*) trimestre *m*; *Am* 25 centesimi *mpl*; **~s** *pl Mil* quartiere *msg*; **at** [**a**] **~ to six** alle sei meno un quarto ● *vt* dividere in quattro. **~-'final** *n* quarto *m* di finale

quarterly /'kwɔːtəlɪ/ *a* trimestrale ● *adv* trimestralmente

quartet /kwɔː'tet/ *n* quartetto *m*

quartz /kwɔːts/ *n* quarzo *m*. **~ watch** *n* orologio *m* al quarzo

quash /kwɒʃ/ *vt* annullare; soffocare ⟨*rebellion*⟩

quaver /'kweɪvə(r)/ *vi* tremolare

quay /kiː/ *n* banchina *f*

queasy /'kwiːzɪ/ *a* **I feel ~** ho la nausea

queen /kwiːn/ *n* regina *f*. **~ mother** *n* regina *f* madre

queer /kwɪə(r)/ *a* strano; (*dubious*) sospetto; (*fam: homosexual*) finocchio ● *n fam* finocchio *m*

quell /kwel/ *vt* reprimere

quench /kwentʃ/ *vt* **~ one's thirst** dissetarsi

query /'kwɪərɪ/ *n* domanda *f*; (*question mark*) punto *m* interrogativo ● *vt* (*pt/pp* **-ied**) interrogare; (*doubt*) mettere in dubbio

quest /kwest/ *n* ricerca *f* (**for** di)

question /'kwestʃn/ *n* domanda *f*; (*for discussion*) questione *f*; **out of the ~** fuori discussione; **without ~** senza dubbio; **in ~** in questione ● *vt* interrogare; (*doubt*) mettere in dubbio. **~able** /-əbl/ *a* discutibile. **~ mark** *n* punto *m* interrogativo

questionnaire /kwestʃə'neə(r)/ *n* questionario *m*

queue /kjuː/ *n* coda *f*, fila *f* ● *vi* **~ [up]** mettersi in coda (**for** per)

quick /kwɪk/ *a* veloce; **be ~!** sbrigati!; **have a ~ meal** fare uno spuntino ● *adv* in fretta ● *n* **be cut to the ~** *fig* essere punto sul vivo. **~ly** *adv* in fretta. **~-tempered** *a* collerico

quid /kwɪd/ *n inv fam* sterlina *f*

quiet /'kwaɪət/ *a* (*calm*) tranquillo; (*silent*) silenzioso; (*voice, music*) basso; **keep ~ about** *fam* non raccontare a nessuno ● *n* quiete *f*; **on the ~** di nascosto. **~ly** *adv* (*peacefully*) tranquillamente; ⟨*say*⟩ a bassa voce

quiet|en /'kwaɪətn/ *vt* calmare. **quieten down** *vi* calmarsi. **~ness** *n* quiete *f*

quilt /kwɪlt/ *n* piumino *m*. **~ed** *a* trapuntato

quins /kwɪnz/ *npl fam* = **quintuplets**

quintet /kwɪn'tet/ *n* quintetto *m*

quintuplets /'kwɪntjʊplɪts/ *npl* cinque gemelli *mpl*

quip /kwɪp/ *n* battuta *f*

quirk /kwɜːk/ *n* stranezza *f*

quit /kwɪt/ *v* (*pt*/*pp* **quitted, quit**) ● *vt* lasciare; (*give up*) smettere (**doing** di fare) ● *vi* (*fam: resign*) andarsene; *Comput* uscire; **give sb notice to ~** ⟨*landlord:*⟩ dare a qcno il preavviso di sfratto

quite /kwaɪt/ *adv* (*fairly*) abbastanza; (*completely*) completamente; (*really*)
veramente; **~ [so]!** proprio così!; **~ a few** parecchi

quits /kwɪts/ *a* pari

quiver /'kwɪvə(r)/ *vi* tremare

quiz /kwɪz/ *n* (*game*) quiz *m inv* ● *vt* (*pt*/*pp* **quizzed**) interrogare

quota /'kwəʊtə/ *n* quota *f*

quotation /kwəʊ'teɪʃn/ *n* citazione *f*; (*price*) preventivo *m*; (*of shares*) quota *f*. **~ marks** *npl* virgolette *fpl*

quote /kwəʊt/ *n fam* = **quotation; in ~s** tra virgolette ● *vt* citare; quotare ⟨*price*⟩

Rr

rabbi /'ræbaɪ/ *n* rabbino *m*; (*title*) rabbi

rabbit /'ræbɪt/ *n* coniglio *m*

rabble /'ræbl/ *n* **the ~** la plebaglia

rabies /'reɪbiːz/ *n* rabbia *f*

race[1] /reɪs/ *n* (*people*) razza *f*

race[2] *n* corsa *f* ● *vi* correre ● *vt* gareggiare con; fare correre ⟨*horse*⟩

race: ~course *n* ippodromo *m*. **~horse** *n* cavallo *m* da corsa. **~-track** *n* pista *f*

racial /'reɪʃl/ *a* razziale. **~ism** *n* razzismo *m*

racing /'reɪsɪŋ/ *n* corse *fpl*; (*horse-*) corse *fpl* dei cavalli. **~ car** *n* macchina *f* da corsa. **~ driver** *n* corridore *m* automobilistico

racis|m /'reɪsɪzm/ *n* razzismo *m*. **~t** /-ɪst/ *a* razzista ● *n* razzista *mf*

rack[1] /ræk/ *n* (*for bikes*) rastrelliera *f*; (*for luggage*) portabagagli *m inv*; (*for plates*) scolapiatti *m inv* ● *vt* **~ one's brains** scervellarsi

rack[2] *n* **go to ~ and ruin** andare in rovina

racket[1] /'rækɪt/ *n Sport* racchetta *f*

racket[2] *n* (*din*) chiasso *m*; (*swindle*) truffa *f*; (*crime*) racket *m inv*, giro *m*

radar /'reɪdɑː(r)/ *n* radar *m*

radian|ce /'reɪdɪəns/ *n* radiosità *f*. **~t** *a* raggiante

radiat|e /'reɪdɪeɪt/ *vt* irradiare ● *vi* ⟨*heat:*⟩ irradiarsi. **~ion** /-'eɪʃn/ *n* radiazione *f*

radiator /'reɪdɪeɪtə(r)/ *n* radiatore *m*

radical /'rædɪkl/ *a* radicale ● *n* radicale *mf*. **~ly** *adv* radicalmente

radio /'reɪdɪəʊ/ *n* radio *f inv*

radio|'active *a* radioattivo. **~ac'tivity** *n* radioattività *f*

radiograph|er /reɪdɪ'ɒɡrəfə(r)/ *n* radiologo, *a mf*. **~y** *n* radiografia *f*

radio'therapy *n* radioterapia *f*

radish /'rædɪʃ/ *n* ravanello *m*

radius /'reɪdɪəs/ *n* (*pl* **-dii** /-dɪaɪ/) raggio *m*

raffle /'ræfl/ *n* lotteria *f*

raft /rɑːft/ *n* zattera *f*

rafter /'rɑːftə(r)/ *n* trave *f*

rag /ræɡ/ *n* straccio *m*; (*pej: newspaper*) giornalaccio *m*; **in ~s** stracciato

rage /reɪdʒ/ *n* rabbia *f*; **all the ~** *fam* all'ultima moda ● *vi* infuriarsi; ⟨*storm:*⟩ infuriare; ⟨*epidemic:*⟩ imperversare

ragged /'ræɡɪd/ *a* logoro; ⟨*edge*⟩ frastagliato

raid /reɪd/ *n* (*by thieves*) rapina *f*; *Mil* incursione *f*, raid *m inv*; (*police*) irruzione *f* ● *vt Mil* fare un'incursione in; ⟨*police, burglars:*⟩ fare irruzione in. **~er** *n* (*of bank*) rapinatore, -trice *mf*

rail /reɪl/ *n* ringhiera *f*; (*hand~*) ringhiera *f*; *Naut* parapetto *m*; **by ~** per ferrovia

'railroad *n Am* = **railway**

'railway *n* ferrovia *f*. **~man** *n* ferroviere *m*. **~ station** *n* stazione *f* ferroviaria

rain /reɪn/ *n* pioggia *f* ● *vi* piovere

rain: ~bow *n* arcobaleno *m*. **~coat** *n* impermeabile *m*. **~fall** *n* precipitazione *f* [atmosferica]

rainy /'reɪnɪ/ *a* (**-ier, -iest**) piovoso

raise /reɪz/ *n Am* aumento *m* ● *vt* alzare; levarsi ⟨hat⟩; allevare ⟨children, animals⟩; sollevare ⟨question⟩; ottenere ⟨money⟩

raisin /ˈreɪzn/ n uva f passa

rake /reɪk/ n rastrello m ● vt rastrellare. **rake up** vt raccogliere col rastrello; fam rivangare

rally /ˈrælɪ/ n raduno m; Auto rally m inv; Tennis scambio m ● v (pt/pp -ied) ● vt radunare ● vi radunarsi; (recover strength) riprendersi

ram /ræm/ n montone m; Astr Ariete m ● vt (pt/pp rammed) cozzare contro

RAM /ræm/ n [memoria f] RAM f

rambl|e /ˈræmbl/ n escursione f ● vi gironzolare; (in speech) divagare. **~er** n escursionista mf; (rose) rosa f rampicante. **~ing** a (in speech) sconnesso; ⟨club⟩ escursionistico

ramp /ræmp/ n rampa f; Aeron scaletta f mobile (di aerei)

rampage /ˈræmpeɪdʒ/ n be/go on the ~ scatenarsi ● vi ~ through the streets scatenarsi per le strade

rampant /ˈræmpənt/ a dilagante

rampart /ˈræmpɑːt/ n bastione f

ramshackle /ˈræmʃækl/ a sgangherato

ran /ræn/ see run

ranch /rɑːntʃ/ n ranch m inv

rancid /ˈrænsɪd/ a rancido

rancour /ˈræŋkə(r)/ n rancore m

random /ˈrændəm/ a casuale; ~ sample campione m a caso ● n at ~ a casaccio

randy /ˈrændɪ/ a (-ier, -iest) fam eccitato

rang /ræŋ/ see ring²

range /reɪndʒ/ n serie f; Comm, Mus gamma f; (of mountains) catena f; (distance) raggio m; (for shooting) portata f; (stove) cucina f economica; at a ~ of a una distanza di ● vi estendersi; ~ from... to... andare da... a.... ~r n guardia f forestale

rank /ræŋk/ n (row) riga f; Mil grado m; (social position) rango m; the ~ and file la base; the ~s pl Mil i soldati semplici ● vt (place) annoverare (among tra) ● vi (be placed) collocarsi

rankle /ˈræŋkl/ vi fig bruciare

ransack /ˈrænsæk/ vt rovistare; (pillage) saccheggiare

ransom /ˈrænsəm/ n riscatto m; hold sb to ~ tenere qcno in ostaggio (per il riscatto)

rant /rænt/ vi ~ [and rave] inveire;

what's he ~ing on about? cosa sta blaterando?

rap /ræp/ n colpo m [secco]; Mus rap m ● v (pt/pp rapped) ● vt dare colpetti a ● vi ~ at bussare a

rape /reɪp/ n (sexual) stupro m ● vt violentare, stuprare

rapid /ˈræpɪd/ a rapido. **~ity** /rəˈpɪdətɪ/ n rapidità f. **~ly** adv rapidamente

rapids /ˈræpɪdz/ npl rapida fsg

rapist /ˈreɪpɪst/ n violentatore m

rapport /ræˈpɔː(r)/ n rapporto m di intesa

raptur|e /ˈræptʃə(r)/ n estasi f. **~ous** /-rəs/ a entusiastico

rare¹ /reə(r)/ a raro. **~ly** adv raramente

rare² a Culin al sangue

rarefied /ˈreərɪfaɪd/ a rarefatto

rarity /ˈreərətɪ/ n rarità f inv

rascal /ˈrɑːskl/ n mascalzone m

rash¹ /ræʃ/ n Med eruzione f

rash² a avventato. **~ly** adv avventatamente

rasher /ˈræʃə(r)/ n fetta f di pancetta

rasp /rɑːsp/ n (noise) stridio m. **~ing** a stridente

raspberry /ˈrɑːzbərɪ/ n lampone m

rat /ræt/ n topo m; (fam: person) carogna f; smell a ~ fam sentire puzzo di bruciato

rate /reɪt/ n (speed) velocità f inv; (of payment) tariffa f; (of exchange) tasso m; ~s pl (taxes) imposte fpl comunali sui beni immobili; at any ~ in ogni caso; at this ~ di questo passo ● vt stimare; ~ among annoverare tra ● vi ~ as essere considerato

rather /ˈrɑːðə(r)/ adv piuttosto; ~! eccome!; ~ too... un po' troppo...

rati|fication /rætɪfɪˈkeɪʃn/ n ratifica f. **~fy** /ˈrætɪfaɪ/ vt (pt/pp -ied) ratificare

rating /ˈreɪtɪŋ/ n ~s pl Radio, TV indice m d'ascolto, audience f inv

ratio /ˈreɪʃɪəʊ/ n rapporto m

ration /ˈræʃn/ n razione f ● vt razionare

rational /ˈræʃənl/ a razionale. **~ize** vt/i razionalizzare

'rat race n fam corsa f al successo

rattle /ˈrætl/ n tintinnio m; (toy) sonaglio m ● vi tintinnare ● vt (shake) scuotere; fam innervosire. **rattle off** vt fam sciorinare

'rattlesnake n serpente m a sonagli

raucous /ˈrɔːkəs/ a rauco

rave /reɪv/ vi vaneggiare; ~ about andare in estasi per

raven /'reɪvn/ n corvo m imperiale

ravenous /'rævənəs/ a ⟨person⟩ affamato

ravine /rə'viːn/ n gola f

raving /'reɪvɪŋ/ a ~ **mad** fam matto da legare

ravishing /'rævɪʃɪŋ/ a incantevole

raw /rɔː/ a crudo; (not processed) grezzo; ⟨weather⟩ gelido; (inexperienced) inesperto; **get a ~ deal** fam farsi fregare. **~ materials** npl materie fpl prime

ray /reɪ/ n raggio m; **~ of hope** barlume m di speranza

raze /reɪz/ vt **~ to the ground** radere al suolo

razor /'reɪzə(r)/ n rasoio m. **~ blade** n lametta f da barba

re /riː/ prep con riferimento a

reach /riːtʃ/ n portata f; **within ~** a portata di mano; **out of ~ of** fuori dalla portata di; **within easy ~** facilmente raggiungibile ● vt arrivare a ⟨place, decision⟩; ⟨contact⟩ contattare; ⟨pass⟩ passare; **I can't ~ it** non ci arrivo ● vi arrivare (**to** a); **~ for** allungare la mano per prendere

re'act /rɪ-/ vi reagire

re'action /rɪ-/ n reazione f. **~ary** a & n reazionario, -a mf

reactor /rɪ'æktə(r)/ n reattore m

read /riːd/ vt (pt/pp **read** /red/) leggere; Univ studiare ● vi leggere; ⟨instrument:⟩ indicare. **read out** vt leggere ad alta voce

readable /'riːdəbl/ a piacevole a leggersi; (legible) leggibile

reader /'riːdə(r)/ n lettore, -trice mf; (book) antologia f

readi·ly /'redɪlɪ/ adv volentieri; (easily) facilmente. **~ness** n disponibilità f; **in ~ness** pronto

reading /'riːdɪŋ/ n lettura f

rea'djust /riː-/ vt regolare di nuovo ● vi riabituarsi (**to** a)

ready /'redɪ/ a (**-ier, -iest**) pronto; (quick) veloce; **get ~** prepararsi

ready· **~-'made** a confezionato. **~ 'money** n contanti mpl. **~-to-'wear** a prêt-à-porter

real /riːl/ a vero; ⟨increase⟩ reale ● adv Am fam veramente. **~ estate** n beni mpl immobili

realis·m /'rɪəlɪzm/ n realismo m. **~t** /-lɪst/ n realista mf. **~tic** /-'lɪstɪk/ a realistico

reality /rɪ'ælətɪ/ n realtà f inv

realization /rɪəlar'zeɪʃn/ n realizzazione f

realize /'rɪəlaɪz/ vt realizzare

really /'rɪəlɪ/ adv davvero

realm /relm/ n regno m

realtor /'rɪəltə(r)/ n Am agente mf immobiliare

reap /riːp/ vt mietere

reap'pear /riː-/ vi riapparire

rear¹ /rɪə(r)/ a posteriore; Auto di dietro; **~ end** fam didietro m ● n **the ~** (of building) il retro; (of bus, plane) la parte posteriore; **from the ~** da dietro

rear² vt allevare ● vi **~ [up]** ⟨horse:⟩ impennarsi

'rear-light n luce f posteriore

re'arm /riː-/ vt riarmare ● vi riarmarsi

rear'range /riː-/ vt cambiare la disposizione di

rear-view 'mirror n Auto specchietto m retrovisore

reason /'riːzn/ n ragione f; **within ~** nei limiti del ragionevole ● vi ragionare; **~ with** cercare di far ragionare. **~able** /-əbl/ a ragionevole. **~ably** /-əblɪ/ adv (in reasonable way, fairly) ragionevolmente

reas'sur·ance /riː-/ n rassicurazione f. **~e** vt rassicurare; **~e sb of sth** rassicurare qcno su qcsa. **~ing** a rassicurante

rebate /'riːbeɪt/ n rimborso m; (discount) deduzione f

rebel¹ /'rebl/ n ribelle mf

rebel² /rɪ'bel/ vi (pt/pp **rebelled**) ribellarsi. **~lion** /-ljən/ n ribellione f. **~lious** /-ljəs/ a ribelle

re'bound¹ /rɪ-/ vi rimbalzare; fig ricadere

'rebound² /riː-/ n rimbalzo m

rebuff /rɪ'bʌf/ n rifiuto m

re'build /riː-/ vt (pt/pp **-built**) ricostruire

rebuke /rɪ'bjuːk/ vt rimproverare

rebuttal /rɪ'bʌtl/ n rifiuto m

re'call /rɪ-/ n richiamo m; **beyond ~** irrevocabile ● vt richiamare; riconvocare ⟨diplomat, parliament⟩; (remember) rievocare

recap /'riːkæp/ vt/i fam = **recapitulate** ● n ricapitolazione f

recapitulate /riːkə'pɪtjʊleɪt/ vt/i ricapitolare

re'capture /riː-/ vt riconquistare; ricatturare ⟨person, animal⟩

reced·e /rɪ'siːd/ vi allontanarsi. **~ing** a ⟨forehead, chin⟩ sfuggente; **have ~ing hair** essere stempiato

receipt /rɪ'siːt/ n ricevuta f; (receiving) ricezione f; **~s** pl Comm entrate fpl

receive /rɪ'siːv/ vt ricevere. **~r** n Teleph ricevitore m; Radio, TV apparecchio m ricevente; (of stolen goods) ricettatore, -trice mf

recent /'riːsnt/ a recente. **~ly** adv recentemente

receptacle /rɪ'septəkl/ n recipiente m

reception /rɪ'sepʃn/ n ricevimento m; (welcome) accoglienza f; Radio ricezione f; **~ [desk]** (in hotel) reception f inv. **~ist** n persona f alla reception

receptive /rɪ'septɪv/ a ricettivo

recess /rɪ'ses/ n rientranza f; (holiday) vacanza f; Am Sch intervallo m

recession /rɪ'seʃn/ n recessione f

re'charge /riː-/ vt ricaricare

recipe /'resəpɪ/ n ricetta f

recipient /rɪ'sɪpɪənt/ n (of letter) destinatario, -a mf; (of money) beneficiario, -a mf

recipro|cal /rɪ'sɪprəkl/ a reciproco. **~cate** /-keɪt/ vt ricambiare

recital /rɪ'saɪtl/ n recital m inv

recite /rɪ'saɪt/ vt recitare; (list) elencare

reckless /'reklɪs/ a ⟨action, decision⟩ sconsiderato; **be a ~ driver** guidare in modo spericolato. **~ly** adv in modo sconsiderato. **~ness** n sconsideratezza f

reckon /'rekən/ vt calcolare; (consider) pensare. **reckon on/with** vt fare i conti con

re'claim /rɪ-/ vt reclamare; bonificare ⟨land⟩

reclin|e /rɪ'klaɪn/ vi sdraiarsi. **~ing** a ⟨seat⟩ reclinabile

recluse /rɪ'kluːs/ n recluso, -a mf

recognition /rekəg'nɪʃn/ n riconoscimento m; **beyond ~** irriconoscibile

recognize /'rekəgnaɪz/ vt riconoscere

re'coil /rɪ-/ vi (in fear) indietreggiare

recollect /rekə'lekt/ vt ricordare. **~ion** /-ekʃn/ n ricordo m

recommend /rekə'mend/ vt raccomandare. **~ation** /-'deɪʃn/ n raccomandazione f

recompense /'rekəmpens/ n ricompensa f

recon|cile /'rekənsaɪl/ vt riconciliare; conciliare ⟨facts⟩; **~cile oneself to** rassegnarsi a. **~ciliation** /-sɪlɪ'eɪʃn/ n riconciliazione f

recon'dition /riː-/ vt ripristinare. **~ed engine** n motore m che ha subito riparazioni

reconnaissance /rɪ'kɒnɪsns/ n Mil ricognizione f

reconnoitre /rekə'nɔɪtə(r)/ vi (pres p -tring) fare una ricognizione

recon'sider /riː-/ vt riconsiderare

recon'struct /riː-/ vt ricostruire. **~ion** n ricostruzione f

record[^1] /rɪ'kɔːd/ vt registrare; (make a note of) annotare

record[^2] /'rekɔːd/ n (file) documentazione f; Mus disco m; Sport record m inv; **~s** pl (files) schedario msg; **keep a ~ of** tener nota di; **off the ~** in via ufficiosa; **have a [criminal] ~** avere la fedina penale sporca

recorder /rɪ'kɔːdə(r)/ n Mus flauto m dolce

recording /rɪ'kɔːdɪŋ/ n registrazione f

'record-player n giradischi m inv

recount /rɪ'kaʊnt/ vt raccontare

re-'count[^1] /rɪ-/ vt ricontare ⟨votes etc⟩

're-count[^2] /'riː-/ n Pol nuovo conteggio m

recoup /rɪ'kuːp/ vt rifarsi di ⟨losses⟩

recourse /rɪ'kɔːs/ n **have ~ to** ricorrere a

re-'cover /riː-/ vt rifoderare

recover /rɪ'kʌvə(r)/ vt/i recuperare. **~y** n recupero m; (of health) guarigione f

recreation /rekrɪ'eɪʃn/ n ricreazione f. **~al** a ricreativo

recrimination /rɪkrɪmɪ'neɪʃn/ n recriminazione f

recruit /rɪ'kruːt/ n Mil recluta f; **new ~** (member) nuovo, -a adepto, -a mf; (worker) neoassunto, -a mf ● vt assumere ⟨staff⟩. **~ment** n assunzione f

rectang|le /'rektæŋgl/ n rettangolo m. **~ular** /-'tæŋgjʊlə(r)/ a rettangolare

rectify /'rektɪfaɪ/ vt (pt/pp -ied) rettificare

recuperate /rɪ'kuːpəreɪt/ vi ristabilirsi

recur /rɪ'kɜː(r)/ vi (pt/pp recurred) ricorrere; ⟨illness:⟩ ripresentarsi

recurren|ce /rɪ'kʌrəns/ n ricorrenza f; (of illness) ricomparsa f. **~t** a ricorrente

recycle /riː'saɪkl/ vt riciclare

red /red/ a (redder, reddest) rosso ● n rosso m; **in the ~** (account) scoperto. **R~ Cross** n Croce f rossa

redd|en /'redn/ vt arrossare ● vi arrossire. **~ish** a rossastro

re'decorate /riː-/ vt (paint) ridipingere; (wallpaper) ritappezzare

redeem /rɪ'diːm/ vt **~ing quality** unico aspetto m positivo

redemption /rɪ'dempʃn/ n riscatto m

rede'ploy /riː-/ vt ridistribuire

red: **~-haired** *a* con i capelli rossi. **~-'handed** *a* **catch sb ~-handed** cogliere qcno con le mani nel sacco. **'herring** *n* diversione *f.* **~-hot** a rovente. **~ 'light** *n Auto* semaforo *m* rosso

re'double /riː-/ *vt* raddoppiare

redress /rɪ'dres/ *n* riparazione *f* ● *vt* ristabilire ⟨*balance*⟩

red 'tape *n fam* burocrazia *f*

reduc|e /rɪ'djuːs/ *vt* ridurre; *Culin* far consumare. **~tion** /-'dʌkʃn/ *n* riduzione *f*

redundan|cy /rɪ'dʌndənsɪ/ *n* licenziamento *m*; ⟨*payment*⟩ cassa *f* integrazione. **~t** *a* superfluo; **make ~t** licenziare; **be made ~t** essere licenziato

reed /riːd/ *n Bot* canna *f*

reef /riːf/ *n* scogliera *f*

reek /riːk/ *vi* puzzare (**of** di)

reel /riːl/ *n* bobina *f* ● *vi* (*stagger*) vacillare. **reel off** *vt fig* snocciolare

refectory /rɪ'fektərɪ/ *n* refettorio *m*; *Univ* mensa *f* universitaria

refer /rɪ'fɜː(r)/ *v* (*pt/pp* **referred**) ● *vt* rinviare ⟨*matter*⟩ (**to** a); indirizzare ⟨*person*⟩ ● *vi* **~ to** fare allusione a; (*consult*) rivolgersi a ⟨*book*⟩

referee /refə'riː/ *n* arbitro *m*; (*for job*) garante *mf* ● *vt/i* (*pt/pp* **refereed**) arbitrare

reference /'refərəns/ *n* riferimento *m*; (*in book*) nota *f* bibliografica; (*for job*) referenza *f*, *Comm* **'your ~'** 'riferimento'; **with ~ to** con riferimento a; **make [a] ~ to** fare riferimento a. **~ book** *n* libro *m* di consultazione. **~ number** *n* numero *m* di riferimento

referendum /refə'rendəm/ *n* referendum *m inv*

re'fill¹ /riː-/ *vt* riempire di nuovo; ricaricare ⟨*pen, lighter*⟩

'refill² /'riː-/ *n* (*for pen*) ricambio *m*

refine /rɪ'faɪn/ *vt* raffinare. **~d** *a* raffinato. **~ment** *n* raffinatezza *f*; *Techn* raffinazione *f.* **~ry** /-ərɪ/ *n* raffineria *f*

reflect /rɪ'flekt/ *vt* riflettere; **be ~ed in** essere riflesso in ● *vi* (*think*) riflettere (**on** su); **~ badly on sb** *fig* mettere in cattiva luce qcno. **~ion** /-ekʃn/ *n* riflessione *f*; (*image*) riflesso *m*; **on ~ion** dopo riflessione. **~ive** /-ɪv/ *a* riflessivo. **~or** *n* riflettore *m*

reflex /'riːfleks/ *n* riflesso *m* ● *attrib* di riflesso

reflexive /rɪ'fleksɪv/ *a* riflessivo

reform /rɪ'fɔːm/ *n* riforma *f* ● *vt* riformare ● *vi* correggersi. **R~ation** /refə'meɪʃn/ *n Relig* Riforma *f.* **~er** *n* riformatore, -trice *mf*

refrain¹ /rɪ'freɪn/ *n* ritornello *m*

refrain² *vi* astenersi (**from** da)

refresh /rɪ'freʃ/ *vt* rinfrescare. **~ing** *a* rinfrescante. **~ments** *npl* rinfreschi *mpl*

refrigerat|e /rɪ'frɪdʒəreɪt/ *vt* conservare in frigo. **~or** *n* frigorifero *m*

re'fuel /riː-/ *v* (*pt/pp* -**fuelled**) ● *vt* rifornire (*di carburante*) ● *vi* fare rifornimento

refuge /'refjuːdʒ/ *n* rifugio *m*; **take ~** rifugiarsi

refugee /refjʊ'dʒiː/ *n* rifugiato, -a *mf*

'refund¹ /'riː-/ *n* rimborso *m*

re'fund² /rɪ-/ *vt* rimborsare

refurbish /riː'fɜːbɪʃ/ *vt* rimettere a nuovo

refusal /rɪ'fjuːzl/ *n* rifiuto *m*

refuse¹ /rɪ'fjuːz/ *vt/i* rifiutare; **~ to do sth** rifiutare di fare qcsa

refuse² /'refjuːs/ *n* rifiuti *mpl.* **~ collection** *n* raccolta *f* dei rifiuti

refute /rɪ'fjuːt/ *vt* confutare

re'gain /rɪ-/ *vt* riconquistare

regal /'riːgl/ *a* regale

regalia /rɪ'geɪlɪə/ *npl* insegne *fpl* reali

regard /rɪ'gɑːd/ *n* (*heed*) riguardo *m*; (*respect*) considerazione *f*; **~s** *pl* saluti *mpl*; **send/give my ~s to your brother** salutami tuo fratello ● *vt* (*consider*) considerare (**as** come); **as ~s** riguardo a. **~ing** *prep* riguardo a. **~less** *adv* lo stesso; **~ of** senza badare a

regatta /rɪ'gætə/ *n* regata *f*

regenerate /rɪ'dʒenəreɪt/ *vt* rigenerare ● *vi* rigenerarsi

regime /reɪ'ʒiːm/ *n* regime *m*

regiment /'redʒɪmənt/ *n* reggimento *m.* **~al** /-'mentl/ *a* reggimentale. **~ation** /-mən'teɪʃn/ *n* irreggimentazione *f*

region /'riːdʒən/ *n* regione *f*, **in the ~ of** *fig* approssimativamente. **~al** *a* regionale

register /'redʒɪstə(r)/ *n* registro *m* ● *vt* registrare; mandare per raccomandata ⟨*letter*⟩; assicurare ⟨*luggage*⟩; immatricolare ⟨*vehicle*⟩; mostrare ⟨*feeling*⟩ ● *vi* ⟨*instrument:*⟩ funzionare; ⟨*student:*⟩ iscriversi (**for** a); **~ with** iscriversi nella lista di ⟨*doctor*⟩

registrar /redʒɪ'strɑː(r)/ *n* ufficiale *m* di stato civile

registration /redʒɪ'streɪʃn/ *n* (*of vehicle*) immatricolazione *f*; (*of letter*) raccomandazione *f*; (*of luggage*) assicurazione *f*; (*for course*) iscrizione *f.* **~ number** *n Auto* [numero *m* di] targa *f*

registry office /'redʒɪstrɪ-/ n anagrafe f

regret /rɪ'gret/ n rammarico m ● vt (pt/pp **regretted**) rimpiangere; **I ~ that** mi rincresce che. **~fully** adv con rammarico

regrettab|le /rɪ'gretəbl/ a spiacevole. **~ly** adv spiacevolmente; (before adjective) deplorevolmente

regular /'regjʊlə(r)/ a regolare; (usual) abituale ● n cliente mf abituale. **~ity** /-'lærətɪ/ n regolarità f. **~ly** adv regolarmente

regulat|e /'regʊleɪt/ vt regolare. **~ion** /-'leɪʃn/ n (rule) regolamento m

rehabilitat|e /ri:hə'bɪlɪteɪt/ vt riabilitare. **~ion** /-'teɪʃn/ n riabilitazione f

rehears|al /rɪ'hɜːsl/ n Theat prova f. **~e** vt/i provare

reign /reɪn/ n regno m ● vi regnare

reimburse /ri:ɪm'bɜːs/ vt ~ **sb for sth** rimborsare qcsa a qcno

rein /reɪn/ n redine f

reincarnation /ri:ɪnkɑː'neɪʃn/ n reincarnazione f

reinforce /ri:ɪn'fɔːs/ vt rinforzare. **~d 'concrete** n cemento m armato. **~ment** n rinforzo m

reinstate /ri:ɪn'steɪt/ vt reintegrare

reiterate /ri:'ɪtəreɪt/ vt reiterare

reject /rɪ'dʒekt/ vt rifiutare. **~ion** /-ekʃn/ n rifiuto m; Med rigetto m

rejoic|e /rɪ'dʒɔɪs/ vi liter rallegrarsi. **~ing** n gioia f

rejuvenate /rɪ'dʒuːvəneɪt/ vt ringiovanire

relapse /rɪ'læps/ n ricaduta f ● vi ricadere

relate /rɪ'leɪt/ vt (tell) riportare; (connect) collegare ● vi ~ **to** riferirsi a; identificarsi con (person). **~d** a imparentato (**to** a); (ideas etc) affine

relation /rɪ'leɪʃn/ n rapporto m; (person) parente mf. **~ship** n rapporto m; (blood tie) parentela f; (affair) relazione f

relative /'relətɪv/ n parente mf ● a relativo. **~ly** adv relativamente

relax /rɪ'læks/ vt rilassare; allentare (pace, grip) ● vi rilassarsi. **~ation** /ri:læk'seɪʃn/ n rilassamento m, relax m; (recreation) svago m. **~ing** a rilassante

relay¹ /ri:'leɪ/ vt (pt/pp **-layed**) ritrasmettere; Radio, TV trasmettere

relay² /'ri:leɪ/ n Electr relais m inv; **work in ~s** fare i turni. ~ **[race]** n [corsa f a] staffetta f

release /rɪ'li:s/ n rilascio m; (of film) distribuzione f ● vt liberare; lasciare (hand); togliere (brake); distribuire (film); rilasciare (information etc)

relegate /'relɪgeɪt/ vt relegare; **be ~d** Sport essere retrocesso

relent /rɪ'lent/ vi cedere. **~less** a inflessibile; (unceasing) incessante. **~lessly** adv incessantemente

relevan|ce /'reləvəns/ n pertinenza f. **~t** a pertinente (**to** a)

reliab|ility /rɪlaɪə'bɪlətɪ/ n affidabilità f. **~le** /-'laɪəbl/ a affidabile. **~ly** adv in modo affidabile; **be ~ly informed** sapere da fonte certa

relian|ce /rɪ'laɪəns/ n fiducia f (**on** in). **~t** a fiducioso (**on** in)

relic /'relɪk/ n Relig reliquia f; **~s** pl resti mpl

relief /rɪ'li:f/ n sollievo m; (assistance) soccorso m; (distraction) diversivo m; (replacement) cambio m; (in art) rilievo m; **in ~** in rilievo. **~ map** n carta f in rilievo. ~ **train** n treno m supplementare

relieve /rɪ'li:v/ vt alleviare; (take over from) dare il cambio a; ~ **of** liberare da (burden)

religion /rɪ'lɪdʒən/ n religione f

religious /rɪ'lɪdʒəs/ a religioso. **~ly** adv (conscientiously) scrupolosamente

relinquish /rɪ'lɪŋkwɪʃ/ vt abbandonare; ~ **sth to sb** rinunciare a qcsa in favore di qcno

relish /'relɪʃ/ n gusto m; Culin salsa f ● vt fig apprezzare

relo'cate /ri:-/ vt trasferire

reluctan|ce /rɪ'lʌktəns/ n riluttanza f. **~t** a riluttante. **~tly** adv a malincuore

rely /rɪ'laɪ/ vi (pt/pp **-ied**) ~ **on** dipendere da; (trust) contare su

remain /rɪ'meɪn/ vi restare. **~der** n resto m. **~ing** a restante. **~s** npl resti mpl; (dead body) spoglie fpl

remand /rɪ'mɑːnd/ n **on ~** in custodia cautelare ● vt ~ **in custody** rinviare con detenzione provvisoria

remark /rɪ'mɑːk/ n osservazione f ● vt osservare. **~able** /-əbl/ a notevole. **~ably** adv notevolmente

remarry /ri:-/ vi (pt/pp **-ied**) risposarsi

remedial /rɪ'miːdɪəl/ a correttivo; Med curativo

remedy /'remədɪ/ n rimedio m (**for** contro) ● vt (pt/pp **-ied**) rimediare a

remember /rɪ'membə(r)/ vt ricordare,

ricordarsi; **~ to do sth** ricordarsi di fare qcsa; **~ me to him** salutamelo ● *vi* ricordarsi

remind /rɪˈmaɪnd/ *vt* **~ sb of sth** ricordare qcsa a qcno. **~er** *n* ricordo *m*; (*memo*) promemoria *m inv*; (*letter*) lettera *f* di sollecito

reminisce /remɪˈnɪs/ *vi* rievocare il passato. **~nces** /-ənsɪz/ *npl* reminiscenze *fpl*. **~nt** *a* **be ~nt of** richiamare alla memoria

remiss /rɪˈmɪs/ *a* negligente

remission /rɪˈmɪʃn/ *n* remissione *f*; (*of sentence*) condono *m*

remit /rɪˈmɪt/ *vt* (*pt/pp* **remitted**) rimettere ⟨*money*⟩. **~tance** *n* rimessa *f*

remnant /ˈremnənt/ *n* resto *m*; (*of material*) scampolo *m*; (*trace*) traccia *f*

remonstrate /ˈremənstreɪt/ *vi* fare rimostranze **(with sb** a qcno)

remorse /rɪˈmɔːs/ *n* rimorso *m*. **~ful** *a* pieno di rimorso. **~less** *a* spietato. **~lessly** *adv* senza pietà

remote /rɪˈməʊt/ *a* remoto; (*slight*) minimo. **~ access** *n* Comput accesso *m* remoto. **~ con'trol** *n* telecomando *m*. **~-con'trolled** *a* telecomandato. **~ly** *adv* lontanamente; **be not ~ly...** non essere lontanamente...

re'movable /rɪ-/ *a* rimovibile

removal /rɪˈmuːvl/ *n* rimozione *f*; (*from house*) trasloco *m*. **~ van** *n* camion *m inv* da trasloco

remove /rɪˈmuːv/ *vt* togliere; togliersi ⟨*clothes*⟩; eliminare ⟨*stain, doubts*⟩

remuneration /rɪmjuːnəˈreɪʃn/ *n* rimunerazione *f*. **~ive** /-ˈmjuːnərətɪv/ *a* rimunerativo

render /ˈrendə(r)/ *vt* rendere ⟨*service*⟩

rendering /ˈrend(ə)rɪŋ/ *n* Mus interpretazione *f*

renegade /ˈrenɪɡeɪd/ *n* rinnegato, -a *mf*

renew /rɪˈnjuː/ *vt* rinnovare ⟨*contract*⟩. **~al** *n* rinnovo *m*

renounce /rɪˈnaʊns/ *vt* rinunciare a

renovate /ˈrenəveɪt/ *vt* rinnovare. **~ion** /-ˈveɪʃn/ *n* rinnovo *m*

renown /rɪˈnaʊn/ *n* fama *f*. **~ed** *a* rinomato

rent /rent/ *n* affitto *m* ● *vt* affittare; **~ [out]** dare in affitto. **~al** *n* affitto *m*

renunciation /rɪnʌnsɪˈeɪʃn/ *n* rinuncia *f*

re'open /riː-/ *vt/i* riaprire

re'organize /riː-/ *vt* riorganizzare

rep /rep/ *n* Comm fam rappresentante *mf*; *Theat* ≈ teatro *m* stabile

repair /rɪˈpeə(r)/ *n* riparazione *f*; **in good/bad ~** in buone/cattive condizioni ● *vt* riparare

repatriate /riːˈpætrɪeɪt/ *vt* rimpatriare. **~ion** /-ˈeɪʃn/ *n* rimpatrio *m*

re'pay /riː-/ *vt* (*pt/pp* **-paid**) ripagare. **~ment** *n* rimborso *m*

repeal /rɪˈpiːl/ *n* abrogazione *f* ● *vt* abrogare

repeat /rɪˈpiːt/ *n* TV replica *f* ● *vt/i* ripetere; **~ oneself** ripetersi. **~ed** *a* ripetuto. **~edly** *adv* ripetutamente

repel /rɪˈpel/ *vt* (*pt/pp* **repelled**) respingere; *fig* ripugnare. **~lent** *a* ripulsivo

repent /rɪˈpent/ *vi* pentirsi. **~ance** *n* pentimento *m*. **~ant** *a* pentito

repercussions /riːpəˈkʌʃnz/ *npl* ripercussioni *fpl*

repertoire /ˈrepətwɑː(r)/ *n* repertorio *m*

repetition /repɪˈtɪʃn/ *n* ripetizione *f*. **~ive** /rɪˈpetɪtɪv/ *a* ripetitivo

re'place /rɪ-/ *vt* (*put back*) rimettere a posto; (*take the place of*) sostituire; **~ sth with sth** sostituire qcsa con qcsa. **~ment** *n* sostituzione *f*; (*person*) sostituto, -a *mf*. **~ment part** *n* pezzo *m* di ricambio

'replay /ˈriː-/ *n* Sport partita *f* ripetuta; **[action] ~** replay *m inv*

replenish /rɪˈplenɪʃ/ *vt* rifornire ⟨*stocks*⟩; (*refill*) riempire di nuovo

replica /ˈreplɪkə/ *n* copia *f*

reply /rɪˈplaɪ/ *n* risposta *f* **(to** a) ● *vt/i* (*pt/pp* **replied**) rispondere

report /rɪˈpɔːt/ *n* rapporto *m*; *TV, Radio* servizio *m*; *Journ* cronaca *f*; *Sch* pagella *f*; (*rumour*) diceria *f* ● *vt* riportare; **~ sb to the police** denunciare qcno alla polizia ● *vi* riportare; (*present oneself*) presentarsi **(to** a). **~edly** *adv* secondo quanto si dice. **~er** *n* cronista *mf*, reporter *mf inv*

repose /rɪˈpəʊz/ *n* riposo *m*

repos'sess /riː-/ *vt* riprendere possesso di

reprehensible /reprɪˈhensəbl/ *a* riprovevole

represent /reprɪˈzent/ *vt* rappresentare

representative /reprɪˈzentətɪv/ *a* rappresentativo ● *n* rappresentante *mf*

repress /rɪˈpres/ *vt* reprimere. **~ion** /-eʃn/ *n* repressione *f*. **~ive** /-ɪv/ *a* repressivo

reprieve /rɪˈpriːv/ *n* commutazione *f* della pena capitale; (*postponement*) sospensione *f* della pena capitale; *fig* tregua *f* ● *vt* sospendere la sentenza a; *fig* risparmiare

reprimand /'reprɪmɑ:nd/ *n* rimprovero *m* ● *vt* rimproverare

'reprint¹ /'ri:-/ *n* ristampa *f*

re'print² /ri:-/ *vt* ristampare

reprisal /rɪ'praɪzl/ *n* rappresaglia *f*; **in ~ for** per rappresaglia contro

reproach /rɪ'prəʊtʃ/ *n* ammonimento *m* ● *vt* ammonire. **~ful** *a* riprovevole. **~fully** *adv* con aria di rimprovero

repro'duc|e /ri:-/ *vt* riprodurre ● *vi* riprodursi. **~tion** /-'dʌkʃn/ *n* riproduzione *f*. **~tive** /-'dʌktɪv/ *a* riproduttivo

reprove /rɪ'pru:v/ *vt* rimproverare

reptile /'reptaɪl/ *n* rettile *m*

republic /rɪ'pʌblɪk/ *n* repubblica *f*. **~an** *a* repubblicano ● *n* repubblicano, -a *mf*

repudiate /rɪ'pju:dɪeɪt/ *vt* ripudiare; respingere ⟨view, suggestion⟩

repugnan|ce /rɪ'pʌgnəns/ *n* ripugnanza *f*. **~t** *a* ripugnante

repuls|ion /rɪ'pʌlʃn/ *n* repulsione *f*. **~ive** /-ɪv/ *a* ripugnante

reputable /'repjʊtəbl/ *a* affidabile

reputation /repjʊ'teɪʃn/ *n* reputazione *f*

repute /rɪ'pju:t/ *n* reputazione *f*. **~d** /-ɪd/ *a* presunto; **he is ~d to be** si presume che sia. **~dly** *adv* presumibilmente

request /rɪ'kwest/ *n* richiesta *f* ● *vt* richiedere. **~ stop** *n* fermata *f* a richiesta

require /rɪ'kwaɪə(r)/ *vt* ⟨need⟩ necessitare di; ⟨demand⟩ esigere. **~d** *a* richiesto; **I am ~d to do** si esige che io faccia. **~ment** *n* esigenza *f*; ⟨condition⟩ requisito *m*

requisite /'rekwɪzɪt/ *a* necessario ● *n* **toilet/travel ~s** *pl* articoli *mpl* da toilette/viaggio

re'sale /ri:-/ *n* rivendita *f*

rescue /'reskju:/ *n* salvataggio *m* ● *vt* salvare. **~r** *n* salvatore, -trice *mf*

research /rɪ'sɜ:tʃ/ *n* ricerca *f* ● *vt* fare ricerche su; *Journ* fare un'inchiesta su ● *vi* **~ into** fare ricerche su. **~er** *n* ricercatore, -trice *mf*

resem|blance /rɪ'zembləns/ *n* rassomiglianza *f*. **~ble** /-bl/ *vt* rassomigliare a

resent /rɪ'zent/ *vt* risentirsi per. **~ful** *a* pieno di risentimento. **~fully** *adv* con risentimento. **~ment** *n* risentimento *m*

reservation /rezə'veɪʃn/ *n* ⟨booking⟩ prenotazione *f*; ⟨doubt, enclosure⟩ riserva *f*

reserve /rɪ'zɜ:v/ *n* riserva *f*; ⟨shyness⟩ riserbo *m* ● *vt* riservare; riservarsi ⟨right⟩. **~d** *a* riservato

reservoir /'rezəvwɑ:(r)/ *n* bacino *m* idrico

re'shape /ri:-/ *vt* ristrutturare

re'shuffle /ri:-/ *n Pol* rimpasto *m* ● *vt Pol* rimpastare

reside /rɪ'zaɪd/ *vi* risiedere

residence /'rezɪdəns/ *n* residenza *f*; ⟨stay⟩ soggiorno *m*. **~ permit** *n* permesso *m* di soggiorno

resident /'rezɪdənt/ *a* residente ● *n* residente *mf*. **~ial** /-'denʃl/ *a* residenziale

residue /'rezɪdju:/ *n* residuo *m*

resign /rɪ'zaɪn/ *vt* dimettersi da; **~ oneself to** rassegnarsi a ● *vi* dare le dimissioni. **~ation** /rezɪg'neɪʃn/ *n* rassegnazione *f*; ⟨from job⟩ dimissioni *fpl*. **~ed** *a* rassegnato

resilient /rɪ'zɪlɪənt/ *a* elastico; *fig* con buone capacità di ripresa

resin /'rezɪn/ *n* resina *f*

resist /rɪ'zɪst/ *vt* resistere a ● *vi* resistere. **~ance** *n* resistenza *f*. **~ant** *a* resistente

resolut|e /'rezəlu:t/ *a* risoluto. **~ely** *adv* con risolutezza. **~ion** /-'lu:ʃn/ *n* risolutezza *f*

resolve /rɪ'zɒlv/ *vt* **~ to do** decidere di fare

resonan|ce /'rezənəns/ *n* risonanza *f*. **~t** *a* risonante

resort /rɪ'zɔ:t/ *n* ⟨place⟩ luogo *m* di villeggiatura; **as a last ~** come ultima risorsa ● *vi* **~ to** ricorrere a

resound /rɪ'zaʊnd/ *vi* risonare (**with** di). **~ing** *a* ⟨success⟩ risonante

resource /rɪ'sɔ:s/ *n* **~s** *pl* risorse *fpl*. **~ful** *a* pieno di risorse; ⟨solution⟩ ingegnoso. **~fulness** *n* ingegnosità *f*

respect /rɪ'spekt/ *n* rispetto *m*; ⟨aspect⟩ aspetto *m*; **with ~ to** per quanto riguarda ● *vt* rispettare

respectability /rɪspektə'bɪlətɪ/ *n* rispettabilità *f*

respect|able /rɪ'spektəbl/ *a* rispettabile. **~ably** *adv* rispettabilmente. **~ful** *a* rispettoso

respective /rɪ'spektɪv/ *a* rispettivo. **~ly** *adv* rispettivamente

respiration /respɪ'reɪʃn/ *n* respirazione *f*

respite /'respaɪt/ *n* respiro *m*

respond /rɪ'spɒnd/ *vi* rispondere; ⟨react⟩ reagire (**to** a); ⟨patient:⟩ rispondere (**to** a)

response /rɪ'spɒns/ n risposta f; (*reaction*) reazione f

responsibility /rɪspɒnsɪ'bɪlətɪ/ n responsabilità f inv

responsib|le /rɪ'spɒnsəbl/ a responsabile; ⟨*job*⟩ impegnativo

responsive /rɪ'spɒnsɪv/ a be ~ ⟨*audience etc.*⟩ reagire; ⟨*brakes*:⟩ essere sensibile

rest¹ /rest/ n riposo m; Mus pausa f; **have a ~** riposare ● vt riposare; (*lean*) appoggiare (**on** su); (*place*) appoggiare ● vi riposarsi; ⟨*elbows*:⟩ appoggiarsi; ⟨*hopes*:⟩ riposare; **it ~s with you** sta a te

rest² n **the ~** il resto; (*people*) gli altri

restaurant /'restərɒnt/ n ristorante m. **~ car** n vagone m ristorante

restful /'restfl/ a riposante

restive /'restɪv/ a irrequieto

restless /'restlɪs/ a nervoso

restoration /restə'reɪʃn/ n (*of building*) restauro m

restore /rɪ'stɔː(r)/ vt ristabilire; restaurare ⟨*building*⟩; (*give back*) restituire

restrain /rɪ'streɪn/ vt trattenere; **~ oneself** controllarsi. **~ed** a controllato. **~t** n restrizione f; (*moderation*) ritegno m

restrict /rɪ'strɪkt/ vt limitare; **~ oneself to** limitarsi a. **~ion** /-ɪkʃn/ n limite m; (*restraint*) restrizione f. **~ive** /-ɪv/ a limitativo

'rest room n Am toilette f inv

result /rɪ'zʌlt/ n risultato m; **as a ~** a causa (**of** di) ● vi **~ from** risultare da; **~ in** portare a

resume /rɪ'zjuːm/ vt/i riprendere

résumé /'rezjʊmeɪ/ n riassunto m; Am curriculum vitae m inv

resumption /rɪ'zʌmpʃn/ n ripresa f

resurgence /rɪ'sɜːdʒəns/ n rinascita f

resurrect /rezə'rekt/ vt fig risuscitare. **~ion** /-ekʃn/ n **the R~ion** Relig la Risurrezione

resuscitat|e /rɪ'sʌsɪteɪt/ vt rianimare. **~ion** /-'teɪʃn/ n rianimazione f

retail /'riːteɪl/ n vendita f al minuto o al dettaglio ● a & adv al minuto ● vt vendere al minuto ● vi **~ at** essere venduto al pubblico al prezzo di. **~er** n dettagliante mf

retain /rɪ'teɪn/ vt conservare; (*hold back*) trattenere

retaliat|e /rɪ'tælɪeɪt/ vi vendicarsi. **~ion** /-'eɪʃn/ n rappresaglia f; **in ~ion for** per rappresaglia contro

retarded /rɪ'tɑːdɪd/ a ritardato

retentive /rɪ'tentɪv/ a ⟨*memory*⟩ buono

rethink /riː'θɪŋk/ vt (*pt/pp* **rethought**) ripensare

reticen|ce /'retɪsəns/ n reticenza f. **~t** a reticente

retina /'retɪnə/ n retina f

retinue /'retɪnjuː/ n seguito m

retire /rɪ'taɪə(r)/ vi andare in pensione; (*withdraw*) ritirarsi ● vt mandare in pensione ⟨*employee*⟩. **~d** a in pensione. **~ment** n pensione f; **since my ~ment** da quando sono andato in pensione

retiring /rɪ'taɪərɪŋ/ a riservato

retort /rɪ'tɔːt/ n replica f ● vt ribattere

re'touch /riː-/ vt Phot ritoccare

re'trace /rɪ-/ vt ripercorrere; **~ one's steps** ritornare sui propri passi

retract /rɪ'trækt/ vt ritirare; ritrattare ⟨*statement, evidence*⟩ ● vi ritrarsi

re'train /riː-/ vt riqualificare ● vi riqualificarsi

retreat /rɪ'triːt/ n ritirata f; (*place*) ritiro m ● vi ritirarsi; Mil battere in ritirata

re'trial /riː-/ n nuovo processo m

retribution /retrɪ'bjuːʃn/ n castigo m

retrieval /rɪ'triːvəl/ n recupero m

retrieve /rɪ'triːv/ vt recuperare

retrograde /'retrəgreɪd/ a retrogrado

retrospect /'retrəspekt/ n **in ~** guardando indietro. **~ive** /-'spektɪv/ a retrospettivo; ⟨*legislation*⟩ retroattivo ● n retrospettiva f

return /rɪ'tɜːn/ n ritorno m; (*giving back*) restituzione f; Comm profitto m; (*ticket*) biglietto m di andata e ritorno; **by ~ [of post]** a stretto giro di posta; **in ~** in cambio (**for** di); **many happy ~s!** cento di questi giorni! ● vi ritornare ● vt (*give back*) restituire; ricambiare ⟨*affection, invitation*⟩; (*put back*) rimettere; (*send back*) mandare indietro; (*elect*) eleggere

return: ~ flight n volo m di andata e ritorno. **~ match** n rivincita f. **~ ticket** n biglietto m di andata e ritorno

reunion /riː'juːnjən/ n riunione f

reunite /riːjʊ'naɪt/ vt riunire

re'us|able /riː-/ a riutilizzabile. **~e** vt riutilizzare

rev /rev/ n Auto, fam giro m (*di motore*) ● v (*pt/pp* **revved**) ● vt **~ [up]** far andare su di giri ● vi andare su di giri

reveal /rɪ'viːl/ vt rivelare; ⟨*dress*:⟩ scoprire. **~ing** a rivelatore; ⟨*dress*⟩ osé inv

revel /'revl/ vi (*pt/pp* **revelled**) **~ in sth** godere di qcsa

revelation /revə'leɪʃn/ n rivelazione f
revelry /'revlrɪ/ n baldoria f
revenge /rɪ'vendʒ/ n vendetta f; Sport rivincita f; **take ~** vendicarsi ● vt vendicare
revenue /'revənju:/ n reddito m
reverberate /rɪ'vɜːbəreɪt/ vi riverberare
revere /rɪ'vɪə(r)/ vt riverire. **~nce** /'revərəns/ n riverenza f
Reverend /'revərənd/ a reverendo
reverent /'revərənt/ a riverente
reverse /rɪ'vɜːs/ a opposto; **in ~ order** in ordine inverso ● n contrario m; (back) rovescio m; Auto marcia m indietro ● vt invertire; **~ the car into the garage** entrare in garage a marcia indietro; **~ the charges** Teleph fare una telefonata a carico del destinatario ● vi Auto fare marcia indietro
revert /rɪ'vɜːt/ vi **~ to** tornare a
review /rɪ'vju:/ n (survey) rassegna f; (re-examination) riconsiderazione f; Mil rivista f; (of book, play) recensione f ● vt riesaminare (situation); Mil passare in rivista; recensire (book, play). **~er** n critico, -a m f
revile /rɪ'vaɪl/ vt ingiuriare
revis|e /rɪ'vaɪz/ vt rivedere; (for exam) ripassare. **~ion** /-'vɪʒn/ n revisione f; (for exam) ripasso m
revival /rɪ'vaɪvl/ n ritorno m; (of patient) recupero m; (from coma) risveglio m
revive /rɪ'vaɪv/ vt resuscitare; rianimare (person) ● vi riprendersi; (person:) rianimarsi
revoke /rɪ'vəʊk/ vt revocare
revolt /rɪ'vəʊlt/ n rivolta f ● vi ribellarsi ● vt rivoltare. **~ing** a rivoltante
revolution /revə'lu:ʃn/ n rivoluzione f; Auto **~s per minute** giri mpl al minuto. **~ary** /-ərɪ/ a & n rivoluzionario, -a m f. **~ize** vt rivoluzionare
revolve /rɪ'vɒlv/ vi ruotare; **~ around** girare intorno a
revolv|er /rɪ'vɒlvə(r)/ n rivoltella f, revolver m inv. **~ing** a ruotante
revue /rɪ'vju:/ n rivista f
revulsion /rɪ'vʌlʃn/ n ripulsione f
reward /rɪ'wɔːd/ n ricompensa f ● vt ricompensare. **~ing** a gratificante
re'write /ri:-/ vt (pt **rewrote**, pp **rewritten**) riscrivere
rhapsody /'ræpsədɪ/ n rapsodia f
rhetoric /'retərɪk/ n retorica f. **~al** /rɪ'tɒrɪkl/ a retorico

rheuma|tic /rʊ'mætɪk/ a reumatico. **~tism** /'ru:mətɪzm/ n reumatismo m
Rhine /raɪn/ n Reno m
rhinoceros /raɪ'nɒsərəs/ n rinoceronte m
rhubarb /'ru:bɑːb/ n rabarbaro m
rhyme /raɪm/ n rima f; (poem) filastrocca f ● vi rimare
rhythm /'rɪðm/ n ritmo m. **~ic[al]** a ritmico. **~ically** adv con ritmo
rib /rɪb/ n costola f
ribald /'rɪbld/ a spinto
ribbon /'rɪbən/ n nastro m; **in ~s** a brandelli
rice /raɪs/ n riso m
rich /rɪtʃ/ a ricco; (food) pesante ● n **the ~** pl i ricchi; **~es** pl ricchezze fpl. **~ly** adv riccamente; (deserve) largamente
rickety /'rɪkɪtɪ/ a malfermo
ricochet /'rɪkəʃeɪ/ vi rimbalzare ● n rimbalzo m
rid /rɪd/ vt (pt/pp **rid**, pres p **ridding**) sbarazzare (**of** di); **get ~ of** sbarazzarsi di
riddance /'rɪdns/ n **good ~!** che liberazione!
ridden /'rɪdn/ see **ride**
riddle /'rɪdl/ n enigma m
riddled /'rɪdld/ a **~ with** crivellato di
ride /raɪd/ n (on horse) cavalcata f; (in vehicle) giro m; (journey) viaggio m; **take sb for a ~** fam prendere qcno in giro ● v (pt **rode**, pp **ridden**) ● vt montare (horse); andare su (bicycle) ● vi andare a cavallo; (jockey, showjumper:) cavalcare; (cyclist:) andare in bicicletta; (in vehicle) viaggiare. **~r** n cavallerizzo, -a m f; (in race) fantino m; (on bicycle) ciclista m f; (in document) postilla f
ridge /rɪdʒ/ n spigolo m; (on roof) punta f; (of mountain) cresta f
ridicule /'rɪdɪkju:l/ n ridicolo m ● vt mettere in ridicolo
ridiculous /rɪ'dɪkjʊləs/ a ridicolo
riding /'raɪdɪŋ/ n equitazione f ● attrib d'equitazione
rife /raɪf/ a **be ~** essere diffuso; **~ with** pieno di
riff-raff /'rɪfræf/ n marmaglia f
rifle /'raɪfl/ n fucile m. **~-range** n tiro m al bersaglio ● vt **~ [through]** mettere a soqquadro
rift /rɪft/ n fessura f; fig frattura f
rig¹ /rɪg/ n equipaggiamento m; (at sea) piattaforma f [per trivellazioni subacquee] ● **rig out** vt (pt/pp **rigged**) equipaggiare. **rig up** vt allestire

rig² vt (pt/pp **rigged**) manovrare ⟨election⟩

right /raɪt/ a giusto; (not left) destro; **be ~** ⟨person:⟩ aver ragione; ⟨clock:⟩ essere giusto; **put ~** mettere all'ora ⟨clock⟩; correggere ⟨person⟩; rimediare a ⟨situation⟩; **that's ~!** proprio così! ● adv (correctly) bene; (not left) a destra; (directly) proprio; (completely) completamente; **~ away** immediatamente ● n giusto m; (not left) destra f; (what is due) diritto m; **on/to the ~** a destra; **be in the ~** essere nel giusto; **know ~ from wrong** distinguere il bene dal male; **by ~s** secondo giustizia; **the R~** Pol la destra ● vt raddrizzare; **~ a wrong** fig riparare a un torto. **~ angle** n angolo m retto

rightful /'raɪtfl/ a legittimo

right: ~-'handed a che usa la mano destra. **~-hand 'man** n fig braccio m destro

rightly /'raɪtlɪ/ adv giustamente

right: ~ of way n diritto m di transito; (path) passaggio m; Auto precedenza f. **~-'wing** a Pol di destra ● n Sport ala f destra

rigid /'rɪdʒɪd/ a rigido. **~ity** /-'dʒɪdətɪ/ n rigidità f

rigmarole /'rɪgmərəʊl/ n trafila f; (story) tiritera f

rigorous /'rɪgərəs/ a rigoroso

rile /raɪl/ vt fam irritare

rim /rɪm/ n bordo m; (of wheel) cerchione m

rind /raɪnd/ n (on fruit) scorza f; (on cheese) crosta f; (on bacon) cotenna f

ring¹ /rɪŋ/ n (circle) cerchio m; (on finger) anello m; (boxing) ring m inv; (for circus) pista f; **stand in a ~** essere in cerchio

ring² n suono m; **give sb a ~** Teleph dare un colpo di telefono a qcno ● v (pt **rang**, pp **rung**) ● vt suonare; **~ [up]** Teleph telefonare a ● vi suonare; Teleph **~ [up]** telefonare. **ring back** vt/i Teleph richiamare. **ring off** vi Teleph riattaccare

ring: ~leader n capobanda m. **~ road** n circonvallazione f

rink /rɪŋk/ n pista f di pattinaggio

rinse /rɪns/ n risciacquo m; (hair colour) cachet m inv ● vt sciacquare

riot /'raɪət/ n rissa f; (of colour) accozzaglia f; **~s** pl disordini mpl; **run ~** impazzare ● vi creare disordini. **~er** n dimostrante mf. **~ous** /-əs/ a sfrenato

rip /rɪp/ n strappo m ● vt (pt/pp **ripped**)

strappare; **~ open** aprire con uno strappo. **rip off** vt fam fregare

ripe /raɪp/ a maturo; ⟨cheese⟩ stagionato

ripen /'raɪpn/ vi maturare; ⟨cheese:⟩ stagionarsi ● vt far maturare; stagionare ⟨cheese⟩

ripeness /'raɪpnɪs/ n maturità f

'rip-off n fam frode f

ripple /'rɪpl/ n increspatura f; (sound) mormorio m ●

rise /raɪz/ n (of sun) levata f; (fig: to fame, power) ascesa f; (increase) aumento m; **give ~ to** dare adito a ● vi (pt **rose**, pp **risen**) alzarsi; ⟨sun:⟩ sorgere; ⟨dough:⟩ lievitare; ⟨prices, water level:⟩ aumentare; (to power, position) arrivare (**to** a). **~r** n **early ~r** persona f mattiniera

rising /'raɪzɪŋ/ a ⟨sun⟩ levante; **~ generation** nuova generazione f ● n (revolt) sollevazione f

risk /rɪsk/ n rischio m; **at one's own ~** a proprio rischio e pericolo ● vt rischiare

risky /'rɪskɪ/ a (**-ier, -iest**) rischioso

risqué /'rɪskeɪ/ a spinto

rite /raɪt/ n rito m; **last ~s** estrema unzione f

ritual /'rɪtjʊəl/ a rituale ● n rituale m

rival /'raɪvl/ a rivale ● n rivale mf; **~s** pl Comm concorrenti mpl ● vt (pt/pp **rivalled**) rivaleggiare con. **~ry** n rivalità f inv; Comm concorrenza f

river /'rɪvə(r)/ n fiume m. **~-bed** n letto m del fiume

rivet /'rɪvɪt/ n rivetto m ● vt rivettare; **~ed by** fig inchiodato da

Riviera /rɪvɪ'eərə/ n **the Italian ~** la riviera ligure

road /rəʊd/ n strada f, via f; **be on the ~** viaggiare

road: ~-block n blocco m stradale. **~-hog** n fam pirata m della strada. **~-map** n carta f stradale. **~ safety** n sicurezza f sulle strade. **~ sense** n prudenza f (per strada). **~side** n bordo m della strada. **~-sign** cartello m stradale. **~way** n carreggiata f, corsia f. **~-works** npl lavori mpl stradali. **~worthy** a sicuro

roam /rəʊm/ vi girovagare

roar /rɔː(r)/ n ruggito m; **~s of laughter** scroscio msg di risa ● vi ruggire; ⟨lorry, thunder:⟩ rombare; **~ with laughter** ridere fragorosamente. **~ing** a **do a ~ing trade** fam fare affari d'oro

roast /rəʊst/ a arrosto; **~ pork** arrosto

m di maiale ● *n* arrosto *m* ● *vt* arrostire ⟨*meat*⟩ ● *vi* arrostirsi

rob /rɒb/ *vt* (*pt/pp* **robbed**) derubare (**of** di); svaligiare ⟨*bank*⟩. **~ber** *n* rapinatore *m*. **~bery** *n* rapina *f*

robe /rəʊb/ *n* tunica *f*; (*Am: bathrobe*) accappatoio *m*

robin /'rɒbɪn/ *n* pettirosso *m*

robot /'rəʊbɒt/ *n* robot *m inv*

robust /rəʊ'bʌst/ *a* robusto

rock[1] /rɒk/ *n* roccia *f*; (*in sea*) scoglio *m*; (*sweet*) zucchero *m* candito. **on the ~s** ⟨*ship*⟩ incagliato; ⟨*marriage*⟩ finito; ⟨*drink*⟩ con ghiaccio

rock[2] *vt* cullare ⟨*baby*⟩; (*shake*) far traballare; (*shock*) scuotere ● *vi* dondolarsi

rock[3] *n Mus* rock *m*

rock-'bottom *a* bassissimo ● *n* livello *m* più basso

rockery /'rɒkərɪ/ *n* giardino *m* roccioso

rocket /'rɒkɪt/ *n* razzo *m* ● *vi* salire alle stelle

rocking /'rɒkɪŋ/: **~-chair** *n* sedia *f* a dondolo. **~-horse** *n* cavallo *m* a dondolo

rocky /'rɒkɪ/ *a* (**-ier, -iest**) roccioso; *fig* traballante

rod /rɒd/ *n* bacchetta *f*; (*for fishing*) canna *f*

rode /rəʊd/ *see* **ride**

rodent /'rəʊdnt/ *n* roditore *m*

roe /rəʊ/ *n* (*pl* **roe** *or* **roes**) **~[-deer]** capriolo *m*

rogue /rəʊg/ *n* farabutto *m*

role /rəʊl/ *n* ruolo *m*

roll /rəʊl/ *n* rotolo *m*; (*bread*) panino *m*; (*list*) lista *f*; (*of ship, drum*) rullio *m* ● *vi* rotolare; **be ~ing in money** *fam* nuotare nell'oro ● *vt* spianare ⟨*lawn, pastry*⟩. **roll over** *vi* rigirarsi. **roll up** *vt* arrotolare; rimboccarsi ⟨*sleeves*⟩ ● *vi fam* arrivare

'roll-call *n* appello *m*

roller /'rəʊlə(r)/ *n* rullo *m*; (*for hair*) bigodino *m*. **~ blind** *n* tapparella *f*. **~-coaster** *n* montagne *fpl* russe. **~-skate** *n* pattino *m* a rotelle

'rolling-pin *n* mattarello *m*

Roman /'rəʊmən/ *a* romano ● *n* romano, -a *mf*. **~ Catholic** *a* cattolico ● *n* cattolico, -a *mf*

romance /rəʊ'mæns/ *n* (*love-affair*) storia *f* d'amore; (*book*) romanzo *m* rosa

Romania /rəʊ'meɪnɪə/ *n* Romania *f*. **~n** *a* rumeno ● *n* rumeno, -a *mf*; (*language*) rumeno *m*

romantic /rəʊ'mæntɪk/ *a* romantico.

~ally *adv* romanticamente. **~ism** /-tɪsɪzm/ *n* romanticismo *m*

Rome /rəʊm/ *n* Roma *f*

romp /rɒmp/ *n* gioco *m* rumoroso ● *vi* giocare rumorosamente. **~ers** *npl* pagliaccetto *msg*

roof /ru:f/ *n* tetto *m*; (*of mouth*) palato *m* ● *vt* mettere un tetto su. **~-rack** *n* portabagagli *m inv*. **~-top** *n* tetto *m*

rook /rʊk/ *n* corvo *m*; (*in chess*) torre *f*

room /ru:m/ *n* stanza *f*; (*bedroom*) camera *f*; (*for functions*) sala *f*; (*space*) spazio *m*. **~y** *a* spazioso; ⟨*clothes*⟩ ampio

roost /ru:st/ *vi* appollaiarsi

root[1] /ru:t/ *n* radice *f*; **take ~** metter radici ● **root out** *vt fig* scovare

root[2] *vi* **~ about** grufolare; **~ for sb** *Am fam* fare il tifo per qcno

rope /rəʊp/ *n* corda *f*; **know the ~s** *fam* conoscere i trucchi del mestiere ● **rope in** *vt fam* coinvolgere

rosary /'rəʊzərɪ/ *n* rosario *m*

rose[1] /rəʊz/ *n* rosa *f*; (*of watering-can*) bocchetta *f*

rose[2] *see* **rise**

rosé /'rəʊzeɪ/ *n* [vino *m*] rosé *m inv*

rosemary /'rəʊzmərɪ/ *n* rosmarino *m*

rosette /rəʊ'zet/ *n* coccarda *f*

roster /'rɒstə(r)/ *n* tabella *f* dei turni

rostrum /'rɒstrəm/ *n* podio *m*

rosy /'rəʊzɪ/ *a* (**-ier, -iest**) roseo

rot /rɒt/ *n* marciume *m*; (*fam: nonsense*) sciocchezze *fpl* ● *vi* (*pt/pp* **rotted**) marcire

rota /'rəʊtə/ *n* tabella *f* dei turni

rotary /'rəʊtərɪ/ *a* rotante

rotat|e /rəʊ'teɪt/ *vt* far ruotare; avvicendare ⟨*crops*⟩ ● *vi* ruotare. **~ion** /-eɪʃn/ *n* rotazione *f*; **in ~ion** a turno

rote /rəʊt/ *n* **by ~** meccanicamente

rotten /'rɒtn/ *a* marcio; *fam* schifoso; ⟨*person*⟩ penoso

rotund /rəʊ'tʌnd/ *a* paffuto

rough /rʌf/ *a* (*not smooth*) ruvido; (*ground*) accidentato; (*behaviour*) rozzo; (*sport*) violento; (*area*) malfamato; ⟨*crossing, time*⟩ brutto; ⟨*estimate*⟩ approssimativo ● *adv* ⟨*play*⟩ grossolanamente; **sleep ~** dormire sotto i ponti ● *vt* **~ it** vivere senza confort. **rough out** *vt* abbozzare

roughage /'rʌfɪdʒ/ *n* fibre *fpl*

rough 'draft *n* abbozzo *m*

rough|ly /'rʌflɪ/ *adv* rozzamente; (*more or less*) pressappoco. **~ness** *n* ruvidità *f*; (*of behaviour*) rozzezza *f*

rough paper *n* carta *f* da brutta

roulette /ru:'let/ *n* roulette *f*

round /raʊnd/ *a* rotondo ● *n* tondo *m*; (*slice*) fetta *f*; (*of visits, drinks*) giro *m*; (*of competition*) partita *f*; (*boxing*) ripresa *f*, round *m inv*; **do one's ~s** (*doctor:*) fare il giro delle visite ● *prep* intorno a; **open ~ the clock** aperto ventiquattr'ore ● *adv* **all ~** tutt'intorno; **ask sb ~** invitare qcno; **go/come ~ to** (*a friend etc*) andare da; **turn/look ~** girarsi; **~ about** (*approximately*) intorno a ● *vt* arrotondare; girare (*corner*). **round down** *vt* arrotondare (*per difetto*). **round off** *vt* (*end*) terminare. **round on** *vt* aggredire. **round up** *vt* radunare; arrotondare (*prices*)

roundabout /'raʊndəbaʊt/ *a* indiretto ● *n* giostra *f*; (*for traffic*) rotonda *f*

round: **~ 'trip** *n* viaggio *m* di andata e ritorno

rous|e /raʊz/ *vt* svegliare; risvegliare (*suspicion, interest*). **~ing** *a* di incoraggiamento

route /ruːt/ *n* itinerario *m*; *Naut, Aeron* rotta *f*; (*of bus*) percorso *m*

routine /ruːˈtiːn/ *a* di routine ● *n* routine *f inv*; *Theat* numero *m*

rov|e /rəʊv/ *vi* girovagare. **~ing** *a* (*reporter, ambassador*) itinerante

row¹ /rəʊ/ *n* (*line*) fila *f*; **three years in a ~** tre anni di fila

row² *vi* (*in boat*) remare

row³ /raʊ/ *n fam* (*quarrel*) litigata *f*; (*noise*) baccano *m* ● *vi fam* litigare

rowdy /'raʊdɪ/ *a* (**-ier, -iest**) chiassoso

rowing boat /'rəʊɪŋ-/ *n* barca *f* a remi

royal /'rɔɪəl/ *a* reale

royalt|y /'rɔɪəltɪ/ *n* appartenenza *f* alla famiglia reale; (*persons*) i membri della famiglia reale. **~ies** *npl* (*payments*) diritti *mpl* d'autore

rpm *abbr* **revolutions per minute**

rub /rʌb/ *n* **give sth a ~** dare una sfregata a qcsa ● *vt* (*pt/pp* rubbed) sfregare. **rub in** *vt* **don't ~ it in** *fam* non rigirare il coltello nella piaga. **rub off** *vt* mandar via sfregando (*stain*); (*from blackboard*) cancellare ● *vi* andar via; **~ off on** essere trasmesso a. **rub out** *vt* cancellare

rubber /'rʌbə(r)/ *n* gomma *f*; (*eraser*) gomma *f* [da cancellare]. **~ band** *n* elastico *m*. **~y** *a* gommoso

rubbish /'rʌbɪʃ/ *n* immondizie *fpl*; (*fam: nonsense*) idiozie *fpl*; (*fam: junk*) robaccia *f* ● *vt fam* fare a pezzi. **~ bin** *n* pattumiera *f*. **~ dump** *n* discarica *f*; (*official*) discarica *f* comunale

rubble /'rʌbl/ *n* macerie *fpl*

ruby /'ruːbɪ/ *n* rubino *m* ● *attrib* di rubini; (*lips*) scarlatta

rucksack /'rʌksæk/ *n* zaino *m*

rudder /'rʌdə(r)/ *n* timone *m*

ruddy /'rʌdɪ/ *a* (**-ier, -iest**) rubicondo; *fam* maledetto

rude /ruːd/ *a* scortese; (*improper*) spinto. **~ly** *adv* scortesemente. **~ness** *n* scortesia *f*

rudiment /'ruːdɪmənt/ *n* **~s** *pl* rudimenti *mpl*. **~ary** /-'mentərɪ/ *a* rudimentale

rueful /'ruːfl/ *a* rassegnato

ruffian /'rʌfɪən/ *n* farabutto *m*

ruffle /'rʌfl/ *n* gala *f* ● *vt* scompigliare (*hair*)

rug /rʌg/ *n* tappeto *m*; (*blanket*) coperta *f*

rugby /'rʌgbɪ/ *n* **~ [football]** rugby *m*

rugged /'rʌgɪd/ *a* (*coastline*) roccioso

ruin /'ruːɪn/ *n* rovina *f*; **in ~s** in rovina ● *vt* rovinare. **~ous** /-əs/ *a* estremamente costoso

rule /ruːl/ *n* regola *f*; (*control*) ordinamento *m*; (*for measuring*) metro *m*; **~s** *pl* regolamento *msg*; **as a ~** generalmente ● *vt* governare; dominare (*colony, behaviour*); **~ that** stabilire (*che*) ● *vi* governare. **rule out** *vt* escludere

ruled /ruːld/ *a* (*paper*) a righe

ruler /'ruːlə(r)/ *n* capo *m* di Stato; (*sovereign*) sovrano, -a *mf*; (*measure*) righello *m*, regolo *m*

ruling /'ruːlɪŋ/ *a* (*class*) dirigente; (*party*) di governo ● *n* decisione *f*

rum /rʌm/ *n* rum *m inv*

rumble /'rʌmbl/ *n* rombo *m*; (*of stomach*) brontolio *m* ● *vi* rombare; (*stomach:*) brontolare

rummage /'rʌmɪdʒ/ *vi* rovistare (**in/through** in)

rummy /'rʌmɪ/ *n* ramino *m*

rumour /'ruːmə(r)/ *n* diceria *f* ● *vt* **it is ~ed that** si dice che

rump /rʌmp/ *n* natiche *fpl*. **~ steak** *n* bistecca *f* di girello

rumpus /'rʌmpəs/ *n fam* baccano *m*

run /rʌn/ *n* (*on foot*) corsa *f*; (*distance to be covered*) tragitto *m*; (*outing*) giro *m*; *Theat* rappresentazioni *fpl*; (*in skiing*) pista *f*; (*Am: ladder*) smagliatura *f* (*in calze*); **at a ~** di corsa; **~ of bad luck** periodo *m* sfortunato; **on the ~** in fuga; **have the ~ of** avere a disposizione; **in the long ~** a lungo termine ● *v* (*pt* **ran**, *pp* **run**, *pres p* **running**) ● *vi* correre; (*river:*) scorrere; (*nose, makeup:*) colare; (*bus:*) fare servizio; (*play:*) essere in cartellone; (*colours:*) sbiadire; (*in* *election*) presentarsi [come candidato] ● *vt* (*manage*) dirigere; tenere ⟨*house*⟩; (*drive*) dare un passaggio a; correre ⟨*risk*⟩; *Comput* lanciare; *Journ* pubblicare ⟨*article*⟩; (*pass*) far scorrere ⟨*eyes, hand*⟩; **~ a bath** far scorrere l'acqua per il bagno. **run across** *vt* (*meet, find*) imbattersi in. **run away** *vi* scappare [via]. **run down** *vi* scaricarsi; ⟨*clock:*⟩ scaricarsi; ⟨*stocks:*⟩ esaurirsi ● *vt Auto* investire; (*reduce*) esaurire; (*fam: criticize*) denigrare. **run in** *vi* entrare di corsa. **run into** *vi* (*meet*) imbattersi in; (*knock against*) urtare. **run off** *vi* andare via di corsa ● *vt* stampare ⟨*copies*⟩. **run out** *vi* uscire di corsa; ⟨*supplies, money:*⟩ esaurirsi; **~ out of** rimanere senza. **run over** *vi* correre; (*overflow*) traboccare ● *vt Auto* investire. **run through** *vi* scorrere. **run up** *vi* salire di corsa; (*towards*) arrivare di corsa ● *vt* accumulare ⟨*debts, bill*⟩; (*sew*) cucire

'**runaway** *n* fuggitivo, -a *mf*

run-'down *a* ⟨*area*⟩ in abbandono; ⟨*person*⟩ esaurito ● *n* analisi *f*

rung[1] /rʌŋ/ *n* (*of ladder*) piolo *m*

rung[2] *see* **ring**[2]

runner /'rʌnə(r)/ *n* podista *mf*; (*in race*) corridore, -trice *mf*; (*on sledge*) pattino *m*. **~ bean** *n* fagiolino *m*. **~-up** *n* secondo, -a *mf* classificato, -a

running /'rʌnɪŋ/ *a* in corsa; ⟨*water*⟩ corrente; **four times ~** quattro volte di

seguito ● *n* corsa *f*; (*management*) direzione *f*; **be in the ~** essere in lizza. **~ 'commentary** *n* cronaca *f*

runny /'rʌnɪ/ *a* semiliquido; **~ nose** naso che cola

run: ~-of-the-'mill *a* ordinario. **~-up** *n Sport* rincorsa *f*; **the ~-up to** il periodo precedente. **~way** *n* pista *f*

rupture /'rʌptʃə(r)/ *n* rottura *f*; *Med* ernia *f* ● *vt* rompere; **~ oneself** farsi venire l'ernia ● *vi* rompersi

rural /'rʊərəl/ *a* rurale

ruse /ru:z/ *n* astuzia *f*

rush[1] /rʌʃ/ *n Bot* giunco *m*

rush[2] *n* fretta *f*; **in a ~** di fretta ● *vi* precipitarsi ● *vt* far premura a; **~ sb to hospital** trasportare qcno di corsa all'ospedale. **~-hour** *n* ora *f* di punta

rusk /rʌsk/ *n* biscotto *m*

Russia /'rʌʃə/ *n* Russia *f*. **~n** *a* & *n* russo, -a *mf*; (*language*) russo *m*

rust /rʌst/ *n* ruggine *f* ● *vi* arrugginirsi

rustic /'rʌstɪk/ *a* rustico

rustle /'rʌsl/ *vi* frusciare ● *vt* far frusciare; *Am* rubare ⟨*cattle*⟩. **rustle up** *vt fam* rimediare

'**rustproof** *a* a prova di ruggine

rusty /'rʌstɪ/ *a* (**-ier, -iest**) arrugginito

rut /rʌt/ *n* solco *m*; **in a ~** *fam* nella routine

ruthless /'ru:θlɪs/ *a* spietato. **~ness** *n* spietatezza *f*

rye /raɪ/ *n* segale *f*

Ss

sabbath /'sæbəθ/ *n* domenica *f*; (*Jewish*) sabato *m*

sabbatical /sə'bætɪkl/ *n Univ* anno *m* sabbatico

sabot|age /'sæbətɑ:ʒ/ *n* sabotaggio *m* ● *vt* sabotare. **~eur** /-'tɜ:(r)/ *n* sabotatore, -trice *mf*

saccharin /'sæʃeɪ/ *n* saccarina *f*

sachet /'sæʃeɪ/ *n* bustina *f*; (*scented*) sacchetto *m* profumato

sack[1] /sæk/ *vt* (*plunder*) saccheggiare

sack[2] *n* sacco *m*; **get the ~** *fam* essere licenziato ● *vt fam* licenziare. **~ing** *n* tela *f* per sacchi; (*fam: dismissal*) licenziamento *m*

sacrament /'sækrəmənt/ *n* sacramento *m*

sacred /'seɪkrɪd/ *a* sacro

sacrifice /'sækrɪfaɪs/ *n* sacrificio *m* ● *vt* sacrificare

sacrilege /'sækrɪlɪdʒ/ *n* sacrilegio *m*

sad /sæd/ *a* (**sadder, saddest**) triste. **~den** *vt* rattristare

saddle /'sædl/ *n* sella *f* ● *vt* sellare; **I've been ~d with...** *fig* mi hanno affibbiato...

sadis|m /'seɪdɪzm/ *n* sadismo *m*. **~t** /-dɪst/ *n* sadico, -a *mf*. **~tic** /sə'dɪstɪk/ *a* sadico

sad|ly /'sædlɪ/ *adv* tristemente; (*unfor-*

tunately) sfortunatamente. **~ness** *n*
tristezza *f*

safe /seif/ *a* sicuro; (*out of danger*) salvo; (*object*) al sicuro; **~ and sound** sano e salvo ● *n* cassaforte *f*. **~guard** *n* protezione *f* ● *vt* proteggere. **~ly** *adv* in modo sicuro; (*arrive*) senza incidenti; (*assume*) con certezza

safety /'seifti/ *n* sicurezza *f*. **~-belt** *n* cintura *f* di sicurezza. **~-deposit box** *n* cassetta *f* di sicurezza. **~-pin** *n* spilla *f* di sicurezza *o* da balia. **~-valve** *n* valvola *f* di sicurezza

sag /sæg/ *vi* (*pt/pp* **sagged**) abbassarsi

saga /'sɑːgə/ *n* saga *f*

sage /seidʒ/ *n* (*herb*) salvia *f*

Sagittarius /sædʒɪ'teərɪəs/ *n* Sagittario *m*

said /sed/ *see* **say**

sail /seil/ *n* vela *f*; (*trip*) giro *m* in barca a vela ● *vi* navigare; *Sport* praticare la vela; (*leave*) salpare ● *vt* pilotare

'sailboard *n* tavola *f* del windsurf. **~ing** *n* windsurf *m inv*

sailing /'seilɪŋ/ *n* vela *f*. **~-boat** *n* barca *f* a vela. **~-ship** *n* veliero *m*

sailor /'seilə(r)/ *n* marinaio *m*

saint /seint/ *n* santo, -a *mf*. **~ly** *a* da santo

sake /seik/ *n* **for the ~ of** (*person*) per il bene di; (*peace*) per amor di; **for the ~ of it** per il gusto di farlo

salad /'sæləd/ *n* insalata *f*. **~ bowl** *n* insalatiera *f*. **~ cream** *n* salsa *f* per condire l'insalata. **~-dressing** *n* condimento *m* per insalata

salary /'sæləri/ *n* stipendio *m*

sale /seil/ *n* vendita *f*; (*at reduced prices*) svendita *f*; **for/on ~** in vendita. **'for ~'** 'vendesi'

sales|man /'seilzmən/ *n* venditore *m*; (*traveller*) rappresentante *m*. **~woman** *n* venditrice *f*

salient /'seilɪənt/ *a* saliente

saliva /sə'laivə/ *n* saliva *f*

sallow /'sæləʊ/ *a* giallastro

salmon /'sæmən/ *n* salmone *m*

saloon /sə'luːn/ *n* *Auto* berlina *f*; (*Am: bar*) bar *m*

salt /sɔːlt/ *n* sale *m* ● *a* salato; (*fish, meat*) sotto sale ● *vt* salare; (*cure*) mettere sotto sale. **~-cellar** *n* saliera *f*. **~ 'water** *n* acqua *f* di mare. **~y** *a* salato

salutary /'sæljʊtəri/ *a* salutare

salute /sə'luːt/ *Mil n* saluto *m* ● *vt* salutare ● *vi* fare il saluto

salvage /'sælvɪdʒ/ *n* *Naut* recupero *m* ● *vt* recuperare

salvation /sæl'veɪʃn/ *n* salvezza *f*. **S~ 'Army** *n* Esercito *m* della Salvezza

salvo /'sælvəʊ/ *n* salva *f*

same /seim/ *a* stesso (**as** di) ● *pron* **the ~** lo stesso; **be all the ~** essere tutti uguali ● *adv* **the ~** nello stesso modo; **all the ~** (*however*) lo stesso; **the ~ to you** altrettanto

sample /'sɑːmpl/ *n* campione *m* ● *vt* testare

sanatorium /sænə'tɔːrɪəm/ *n* casa *f* di cura

sanctimonious /sæŋktɪ'məʊnɪəs/ *a* moraleggiante

sanction /'sæŋkʃn/ *n* (*approval*) autorizzazione *f*; (*penalty*) sanzione *f* ● *vt* autorizzare

sanctity /'sæŋktəti/ *n* santità *f*

sanctuary /'sæŋktjʊəri/ *n* *Relig* santuario *m*; (*refuge*) asilo *m*; (*for wildlife*) riserva *f*

sand /sænd/ *n* sabbia *f* ● *vt* **~ [down]** carteggiare

sandal /'sændl/ *n* sandalo *m*

sand: ~bank *n* banco *m* di sabbia. **~paper** *n* carta *f* vetrata ● *vt* cartavetrare. **~-pit** *n* recinto *m* contenente sabbia dove giocano i bambini

sandwich /'sænwidʒ/ *n* tramezzino *m* ● *vt* **~ed between** schiacciato tra

sandy /'sændi/ *a* (**-ier, -iest**) (*beach, soil*) sabbioso; (*hair*) biondiccio

sane /sein/ *a* (*not mad*) sano di mente; (*sensible*) sensato

sang /sæŋ/ *see* **sing**

sanitary /'sænɪtəri/ *a* igienico; (*system*) sanitario. **~ napkin** *n Am*, **~ towel** *n* assorbente *m* igienico

sanitation /sænɪ'teɪʃn/ *n* impianti *mpl* igienici

sanity /'sænəti/ *n* sanità *f* di mente; (*common sense*) buon senso *m*

sank /sæŋk/ *see* **sink**

sapphire /'sæfaɪə(r)/ *n* zaffiro *m* ● *a* blu zaffiro *inv*

sarcas|m /'sɑːkæzm/ *n* sarcasmo *m*. **~tic** /-'kæstɪk/ *a* sarcastico

sardine /sɑː'diːn/ *n* sardina *f*

Sardinia /sɑː'dɪnɪə/ *n* Sardegna *f*. **~n** *a* & *n* sardo, -a *mf*

sardonic /sɑː'dɒnɪk/ *a* sardonico

sash /sæʃ/ *n* fascia *f*; (*for dress*) fusciacca *f*

sat /sæt/ *see* **sit**

satanic /sə'tænɪk/ *a* satanico

satchel /'sætʃl/ *n* cartella *f*

satellite /'sætəlait/ *n* satellite *m*. **~**

dish *n* antenna *f* parabolica. **~ television** *n* televisione *f* via satellite

satin /'sætɪn/ *n* raso *m* ● *attrib* di raso

satire /'sætaɪə(r)/ *n* satira *f*

satirical /sə'tɪrɪkl/ *a* satirico

satir|ist /'sætɪrɪst/ *n* scrittore, -trice *mf* satirico, -a; (*comedian*) comico, -a *mf* satirico, -a. **~ize** *vt* satireggiare

satisfaction /sætɪs'fækʃn/ *n* soddisfazione *f*; **be to sb's ~** soddisfare qcno

satisfactor|y /sætɪs'fæktərɪ/ *a* soddisfacente. **~ily** *adv* in modo soddisfacente

satisf|y /'sætɪsfaɪ/ *vt* (*pp/pp* **-ied**) soddisfare; (*convince*) convincere; **be ~ied** essere soddisfatto. **~ying** *a* soddisfacente

saturat|e /'sætʃəreɪt/ *vt* inzuppare (**with** di), *Chem*, *fig* saturare (**with** di). **~ed** *a* saturo

Saturday /'sætədeɪ/ *n* sabato *m*

sauce /sɔːs/ *n* salsa *f*; (*cheek*) impertinenza *f*. **~pan** *n* pentola *f*

saucer /'sɔːsə(r)/ *n* piattino *m*

saucy /'sɔːsɪ/ *a* (**-ier, -iest**) impertinente

Saudi Arabia /saʊdɪə'reɪbɪə/ *n* Arabia *f* Saudita

sauna /'sɔːnə/ *n* sauna *f*

saunter /'sɔːntə(r)/ *vi* andare a spasso

sausage /'sɒsɪdʒ/ *n* salsiccia *f*; (*dried*) salame *m*

savage /'sævɪdʒ/ *a* feroce; ⟨*tribe*, *custom*⟩ selvaggio ● *n* selvaggio, -a *mf* ● *vt* fare a pezzi. **~ry** *n* ferocia *f*

save /seɪv/ *n Sport* parata *f* ● *vt* salvare (**from** da); (*keep*, *collect*) tenere; risparmiare ⟨*time, money*⟩; (*avoid*) evitare; *Sport* parare ⟨*goal*⟩; *Comput* salvare, memorizzare ● *vi* **[up]** risparmiare ● *prep* salvo

saver /'seɪvə(r)/ *n* risparmiatore, -trice *mf*

savings /'seɪvɪŋz/ *npl* (*money*) risparmi *mpl*. **~ account** *n* libretto *m* di risparmio. **~ bank** *n* cassa *f* di risparmio

saviour /'seɪvjə(r)/ *n* salvatore *m*

savour /'seɪvə(r)/ *n* sapore *m* ● *vt* assaporare. **~y** *a* salato; *fig* rispettabile

saw¹ /sɔː/ *see* **see¹**

saw² /sɔː/ *n* sega *f* ● *vt/i* (*pt* **sawed**, *pp* **sawn** *or* **sawed**) segare. **~dust** *n* segatura *f*

saxophone /'sæksəfəʊn/ *n* sassofono *m*

say /seɪ/ *n* **have one's ~** dire la propria; **have a ~** avere voce in capitolo ● *vt/i* (*pt/pp* **said**) dire; **that is to ~** cioè; **that goes without ~ing** questo è ovvio; **when all is said and done** alla fine dei conti. **~ing** *n* proverbio *m*

scab /skæb/ *n* crosta *f*; *pej* crumiro *m*

scaffold /'skæfəld/ *n* patibolo *m*. **~ing** *n* impalcatura *f*

scald /skɔːld/ *vt* scottare; (*milk*) scaldare ● *n* scottatura *f*

scale¹ /skeɪl/ *n* (*of fish*) scaglia *f*

scale² *n* scala *f*; **on a grand ~** su vasta scale ● *vt* (*climb*) scalare. **scale down** *vt* diminuire

scales /skeɪlz/ *npl* (*for weighing*) bilancia *fsg*

scallop /'skɒləp/ *n* (*shellfish*) pettine *m*

scalp /skælp/ *n* cuoio *m* capelluto

scalpel /'skælpl/ *n* bisturi *m inv*

scam /skæm/ *n fam* fregatura *f*

scamper /'skæmpə(r)/ *vi* **~ away** sgattaiolare via

scampi /'skæmpɪ/ *npl* scampi *mpl*

scan /skæn/ *n Med* scanning *m inv*, scansioscintigrafia *f* ● *vt* (*pt/pp* **scanned**) scrutare; (*quickly*) dare una scorsa a; *Med* fare uno scanning di

scandal /'skændl/ *n* scandalo *m*; (*gossip*) pettegolezzi *mpl*. **~ize** /-d(ə)laɪz/ *vt* scandalizzare. **~ous** /-əs/ *a* scandaloso

Scandinavia /skændɪ'neɪvɪə/ *n* Scandinavia *f*. **~n** *a & n* scandinavo, -a *mf*

scanner /'skænə(r)/ *n Comput* scanner *m inv*

scant /skænt/ *a* scarso

scant|y /'skæntɪ/ *a* (**-ier, -iest**) scarso; (*clothing*) succinto. **~ily** *adv* scarsamente; ⟨*clothed*⟩ succintamente

scapegoat /'skeɪp-/ *n* capro *m* espiatorio

scar /skɑː(r)/ *n* cicatrice *f* ● *vt* (*pt/pp* **scarred**) lasciare una cicatrice a

scarc|e /skeəs/ *a* scarso; *fig* raro. **make oneself ~e** *fam* svignarsela. **~ely** *adv* appena; **~ely anything** quasi niente. **~ity** *n* scarsezza *f*

scare /skeə(r)/ *n* spavento *m*; (*panic*) panico *m* ● *vt* spaventare; **be ~d** aver paura (**of** di)

'scarecrow *n* spaventapasseri *m inv*

scarf /skɑːf/ *n* (*pl* **scarves**) sciarpa *f*; (*square*) foulard *m inv*

scarlet /'skɑːlət/ *a* scarlatto. **~ 'fever** *n* scarlattina *f*

scary /'skeərɪ/ *a* **be ~** far paura

scathing /'skeɪðɪŋ/ *a* mordace

scatter /'skætə(r)/ *vt* spargere; (*disperse*) disperdere ● *vi* disperdersi. **~-brained** *a fam* scervellato. **~ed** *a* sparso

scatty /'skætɪ/ a (**-ier, -iest**) *fam* svitato

scavenge /'skævɪndʒ/ vi frugare nella spazzatura. **~r** n persona f che fruga nella spazzatura

scenario /sɪ'nɑːrɪəʊ/ n scenario m

scene /siːn/ n scena f; (quarrel) scenata f; **behind the ~s** dietro le quinte

scenery /'siːnərɪ/ n scenario m

scenic /'siːnɪk/ a panoramico

scent /sent/ n odore m; (trail) scia f; (perfume) profumo m. **~ed** a profumato (**with** di)

sceptic|al /'skeptɪkl/ a scettico. **~ism** /-tɪsɪzm/ n scetticismo m

schedule /'ʃedjuːl/ n piano m, programma m; (of work) programma m; (timetable) orario m; **behind ~** indietro; **on ~** nei tempi previsti ● vt prevedere. **~d flight** n volo m di linea

scheme /skiːm/ n (plan) piano m; (plot) macchinazione f ● vi pej macchinare

schizophren|ia /skɪtsə'friːnɪə/ n schizofrenia f. **~ic** /-'frenɪk/ a schizofrenico

scholar /'skɒlə(r)/ n studioso, -a mf. **~ly** a erudito. **~ship** n erudizione f; (grant) borsa f di studio

school /skuːl/ n scuola f; (in university) facoltà f; (of fish) branco m

school: **~boy** n scolaro m. **~girl** n scolara f. **~ing** n istruzione f. **~-teacher** n insegnante mf

sciatica /saɪ'ætɪkə/ n sciatica f

scien|ce /'saɪəns/ n scienza f; **~ce fiction** fantascienza f. **~tific** /-'tɪfɪk/ a scientifico. **~tist** n scienziato, -a mf

scintillating /'sɪntɪleɪtɪŋ/ a brillante

scissors /'sɪzəz/ npl forbici fpl

scoff¹ /skɒf/ vi **~ at** schernire

scoff² vt fam divorare

scold /skəʊld/ vt sgridare. **~ing** n sgridata f

scone /skɒn/ n pasticcino m da tè

scoop /skuːp/ n paletta f; Journ scoop m inv ● **scoop out** vt svuotare. **scoop up** vt tirar su

scoot /skuːt/ vi fam filare. **~er** n motoretta f

scope /skəʊp/ n portata f; (opportunity) opportunità f inv

scorch /skɔːtʃ/ vt bruciare. **~er** n fam giornata f torrida. **~ing** a caldissimo

score /skɔː(r)/ n punteggio m; Mus partitura f; (for film, play) musica f; **a ~ [of]** (twenty) una ventina [di]; **keep [the] ~** tenere il punteggio; **on that ~** a questo proposito ● vt segnare ⟨goal⟩;

(cut) incidere ● vi far punti; (in football etc) segnare; (keep score) tenere il punteggio. **~r** n segnapunti m inv; (of goals) giocatore, -trice mf che segna

scorn /skɔːn/ n disprezzo m ● vt disprezzare. **~ful** a sprezzante

Scorpio /'skɔːpɪəʊ/ n Astr Scorpione m

scorpion /'skɔːpɪən/ n scorpione m

Scot /skɒt/ n scozzese mf

Scotch /skɒtʃ/ a scozzese ● n (whisky) whisky m [scozzese]

scotch vt far cessare

scot-'free a **get off ~** cavarsela impunemente

Scot|land /'skɒtlənd/ n Scozia f. **~s, ~tish** a scozzese

scoundrel /'skaʊndrəl/ n mascalzone m

scour¹ /'skaʊə(r)/ vt (search) perlustrare

scour² vt (clean) strofinare

scourge /skɜːdʒ/ n flagello m

scout /skaʊt/ n Mil esploratore m ● vi **~ for** andare in cerca di

Scout n [Boy] **~** [boy]scout m inv

scowl /skaʊl/ n sguardo m torvo ● vi guardare [di] storto

Scrabble® /'skræbl/ n Scarabeo® m

scraggy /'skrægɪ/ a (**-ier, -iest**) pej scarno

scram /skræm/ vi fam levarsi dai piedi

scramble /'skræmbl/ n (climb) arrampicata f ● vi (clamber) arrampicarsi; **~ for** azzuffarsi per ● vt Teleph creare delle interferenze in; (eggs) strapazzare

scrap¹ /skræp/ n (fam: fight) litigio m

scrap² n pezzetto m; (metal) ferraglia f; **~s** pl (of food) avanzi mpl ● vt (pt/pp **scrapped**) buttare via

'**scrap-book** n album m inv

scrape /skreɪp/ vt raschiare; (damage) graffiare. **scrape through** vi passare per un pelo. **scrape together** vt racimolare

scraper /'skreɪpə(r)/ n raschietto m

scrappy /'skræpɪ/ a frammentario

'**scrap-yard** n deposito m di ferraglia; (for cars) cimitero m delle macchine

scratch /skrætʃ/ n graffio m; (to relieve itch) grattata f; **start from ~** partire da zero; **up to ~** ⟨work⟩ all'altezza ● vt graffiare; (to relieve itch) grattare ● vi grattarsi. **~ card** n gratta e vinci m inv

scrawl /skrɔːl/ n scarabocchio m ● vt/i scarabocchiare

scrawny /'skrɔːnɪ/ a (**-ier, -iest**) pej magro

scream /skri:m/ *n* strillo *m* ● *vt/i* strillare

screech /skri:tʃ/ *n* stridore *m* ● *vi* stridere ● *vt* strillare

screen /skri:n/ *n* paravento *m*; *Cinema, TV* schermo *m* ● *vt* proteggere; (*conceal*) riparare; proiettare ⟨*film*⟩; (*candidates*) passare al setaccio; *Med* sottoporre a visita medica. **~ing** *n Med* visita *f* medica; (*of film*) proiezione *f*. **~play** *n* sceneggiatura *f*

screw /skru:/ *n* vite *f* ● *vt* avvitare. **screw up** *vt* (*crumple*) accartocciare; strizzare ⟨*eyes*⟩; storcere ⟨*face*⟩; (*sl: bungle*) mandare all'aria

'screwdriver *n* cacciavite *m inv*

screwy /'skru:ɪ/ *a* (**-ier, -iest**) *fam* svitato

scribble /'skrɪbl/ *n* scarabocchio *m* ● *vt/i* scarabocchiare

script /skrɪpt/ *n* scrittura *f* ⟨*a mano*⟩; (*of film*) sceneggiatura *f*

'script-writer *n* sceneggiatore, -trice *mf*

scroll /skrəʊl/ *n* rotolo *m* ⟨*di pergamena*⟩; (*decoration*) voluta *f*

scrounge /skraʊndʒ/ *vt/i* scroccare. **~r** *n* scroccone, -a *mf*

scrub[1] /skrʌb/ *n* ⟨*land*⟩ boscaglia *f*

scrub[2] *vt/i* (*pt/pp* **scrubbed**) strofinare; (*fam: cancel*) cancellare ⟨*plan*⟩

scruff /skrʌf/ *n* **by the ~ of the neck** per la collottola

scruffy /'skrʌfɪ/ *a* (**-ier, -iest**) trasandato

scrum /skrʌm/ *n* (*in rugby*) mischia *f*

scruple /'skru:pl/ *n* scrupolo *m*

scrupulous /'skru:pjʊləs/ *a* scrupoloso

scrutin|ize /'skru:tɪnaɪz/ *vt* scrutinare. **~y** *n* ⟨*look*⟩ esame *m* minuzioso

scuffle /'skʌfl/ *n* tafferuglio *m*

sculpt /skʌlpt/ *vt/i* scolpire. **~or** /'skʌlptə(r)/ *n* scultore *m*. **~ure** /-tʃə(r)/ *n* scultura *f*

scum /skʌm/ *n* schiuma *f*; (*people*) feccia *f*

scurrilous /'skʌrɪləs/ *a* scurrile

scurry /'skʌrɪ/ *vi* (*pt/pp* **-ied**) affrettare il passo

scuttle /'skʌtl/ *vi* (*hurry*) **~ away** correre via

sea /si:/ *n* mare *m*; **at ~** in mare; *fig* confuso; **by ~** via mare. **~board** *n* costiera *f*. **~food** *n* frutti *mpl* di mare. **~gull** *n* gabbiano *m*

seal[1] /si:l/ *n Zool* foca *f*

seal[2] *n* sigillo *m*; *Techn* chiusura *f* ermetica ● *vt* sigillare; *Techn* chiudere ermeticamente. **seal off** *vt* bloccare ⟨*area*⟩

'sea-level *n* livello *m* del mare

seam /si:m/ *n* cucitura *f*; (*of coal*) strato *m*

'seaman *n* marinaio *m*

seamless /'si:mlɪs/ *a* senza cucitura

seamy /'si:mɪ/ *a* sordido; ⟨*area*⟩ malfamato

seance /'seɪɑ:ns/ *n* seduta *f* spiritica

sea: ~plane *n* idrovolante *m*. **~port** *n* porto *m* di mare

search /sɜ:tʃ/ *n* ricerca *f*; (*official*) perquisizione *f*; **in ~ of** alla ricerca di ● *vt* frugare (**for** alla ricerca di); perlustrare ⟨*area*⟩; (*officially*) perquisire ● *vi* **~ for** cercare. **~ing** *a* penetrante

search: ~light *n* riflettore *m*. **~-party** *n* squadra *f* di ricerca

sea: ~sick *a* **be/get ~** avere il mal di mare. **~side** *n* **at/to the ~side** al mare. **~side resort** *n* stazione *f* balneare. **~side town** *n* città *f* di mare

season /'si:zn/ *n* stagione *f* ● *vt* (*flavour*) condire. **~able** /-əbl/ *a*, **~al** *a* stagionale. **~ing** *n* condimento *m*

'season ticket *n* abbonamento *m*

seat /si:t/ *n* (*chair*) sedia *f*; (*in car*) sedile *m*; (*place to sit*) posto *m* [a sedere]; (*bottom*) didietro *m*; (*of government*) sede *f*; **take a ~** sedersi ● *vt* mettere a sedere; (*have seats for*) aver posti [a sedere] per; **remain ~ed** mantenere il proprio posto. **~-belt** *n* cintura *f* di sicurezza

sea: ~weed *n* alga *f* marina. **~worthy** *a* in stato di navigare

secateurs /sekə'tɜ:z/ *npl* cesoie *fpl*

seclu|ded /sɪ'klu:dɪd/ *a* appartato. **~sion** /-ʒn/ *n* isolamento *m*

second[1] /sɪ'kɒnd/ *vt* (*transfer*) distaccare

second[2] /'sekənd/ *a* secondo; **on ~ thoughts** ripensandoci meglio ● *n* secondo *m*; **~s** *pl* (*goods*) merce *fsg* di seconda scelta; **have ~s** (*at meal*) fare il bis; **John the S~** Giovanni Secondo ● *adv* (*in race*) al secondo posto ● *vt* assistere; appoggiare ⟨*proposal*⟩

secondary /'sekəndrɪ/ *a* secondario. **~ school** *n* scuola *f* media (*inferiore e superiore*)

second: ~-best *a* secondo dopo il migliore; **be ~-best** *pej* essere un ripiego. **~ 'class** *adv* ⟨*travel, send*⟩ in seconda classe. **~-class** *a* di seconda classe

'second hand *n* (*on clock*) lancetta *f* dei secondi

second-'hand a & adv di seconda mano

secondly /'sekəndlɪ/ adv in secondo luogo

second-'rate a di second'ordine

secrecy /'si:krəsɪ/ n segretezza f; **in ~** in segreto

secret /'si:krɪt/ a segreto ● n segreto m

secretarial /sekrə'teərɪəl/ a ⟨work, staff⟩ di segreteria

secretary /'sekrətərɪ/ n segretario, -a mf

secret|e /sɪ'kri:t/ vt secernere ⟨poison⟩. **~ion** /-'i:ʃn/ n secrezione f

secretive /'si:krətɪv/ a riservato. **~ness** n riserbo m

secretly /'si:krɪtlɪ/ adv segretamente

sect /sekt/ n setta f. **~arian** a settario

section /'sekʃn/ n sezione f

sector /'sektə(r)/ n settore m

secular /'sekjʊlə(r)/ a secolare; ⟨education⟩ laico

secure /sɪ'kjʊə(r)/ a sicuro ● vt proteggere; chiudere bene ⟨door⟩; rendere stabile ⟨ladder⟩; ⟨obtain⟩ assicurarsi. **~ly** adv saldamente

securit|y /sɪ'kjʊərətɪ/ n sicurezza f; ⟨for loan⟩ garanzia f. **~ies** npl titoli mpl

sedate[1] /sɪ'deɪt/ a posato

sedate[2] vt somministrare sedativi a

sedation /sɪ'deɪʃn/ n somministrazione f di sedativi; **be under ~** essere sotto l'effetto di sedativi

sedative /'sedətɪv/ a sedativo ● n sedativo m

sedentary /'sedəntərɪ/ a sedentario

sediment /'sedɪmənt/ n sedimento m

seduce /sɪ'dju:s/ vt sedurre

seduct|ion /sɪ'dʌkʃn/ n seduzione f. **~ive** /-tɪv/ a seducente

see /si:/ v (pt saw, pp seen) ● vt vedere; ⟨understand⟩ capire; ⟨escort⟩ accompagnare; **go and ~** andare a vedere; ⟨visit⟩ andare a trovare; **~ you!** ci vediamo!; **~ you later!** a più tardi!; **~ing that** visto che ● vi vedere; ⟨understand⟩ capire; **~ that** ⟨make sure⟩ assicurarsi che; **~ about** occuparsi di. **see off** vt veder partire; ⟨chase away⟩ mandar via. **see through** vi vedere attraverso; fig non farsi ingannare da ● vt portare a buon fine. **see to** vi occuparsi di

seed /si:d/ n seme m; Tennis testa f di serie; **go to ~** fare seme; fig lasciarsi andare. **~ed player** n Tennis testa f di serie. **~ling** n pianticella f

seedy /'si:dɪ/ a (-ier, -iest) squallido

seek /si:k/ vt (pt/pp sought) cercare

seem /si:m/ vi sembrare. **~ingly** adv apparentemente

seen /si:n/ see see[1]

seep /si:p/ vi filtrare

see-saw /'si:sɔ:/ n altalena f

seethe /si:ð/ vi **~ with anger** ribollire di rabbia

'see-through a trasparente

segment /'segmənt/ n segmento m; ⟨of orange⟩ spicchio m

segregat|e /'segrɪgeɪt/ vt segregare. **~ion** /-'geɪʃn/ n segregazione f

seize /si:z/ vt afferrare; Jur confiscare. **seize up** vi Techn bloccarsi

seizure /'si:ʒə(r)/ n Jur confisca f; Med colpo m [apoplettico]

seldom /'seldəm/ adv raramente

select /sɪ'lekt/ a scelto; ⟨exclusive⟩ esclusivo ● vt scegliere; selezionare ⟨team⟩. **~ion** /-ekʃn/ n selezione f. **~ive** /-ɪv/ a selettivo. **~or** n Sport selezionatore, -trice mf

self /self/ n io m

self: **~-ad'dressed** a con il proprio indirizzo. **~-ad'hesive** a autoadesivo. **~-as'surance** n sicurezza f di sé. **~-as'sured** a sicuro di sé. **~-'catering** a in appartamento attrezzato di cucina. **~-'centred** a egocentrico. **~-'confidence** n fiducia f in se stesso. **~-'confident** a sicuro di sé. **~-'conscious** a impacciato. **~-con'tained** a ⟨flat⟩ con ingresso indipendente. **~-con'trol** n autocontrollo m. **~-de'fence** n autodifesa f; Jur legittima difesa f. **~-de'nial** n abnegazione f. **~-determi'nation** n autodeterminazione f. **~-em'ployed** a che lavora in proprio. **~-e'steem** n stima f di sé. **~-'evident** a ovvio. **~-'governing** a autonomo. **~-'help** n iniziativa f personale. **~-in'dulgent** a indulgente con se stesso. **~-'interest** n interesse m personale

self|ish /'selfɪʃ/ a egoista. **~ishness** n egoismo m. **~less** a disinteressato

self: **~-made** a che si è fatto da sé. **~-pity** n autocommiserazione f. **~-'portrait** n autoritratto m. **~-pos'sessed** a padrone di sé. **~-preser'vation** n istinto m di conservazione. **~-re'spect** n amor m proprio. **~-'righteous** a presuntuoso. **~-'sacrifice** n abnegazione f. **~-'satisfied** a compiaciuto di sé. **~-'service** n self-service m inv ● attrib

self-service. **~-suf'ficient** *a* autosuffi-
ciente. **~-'willed** *a* ostinato

sell /sel/ *v* (*pt/pp* **sold**) ● *vt* vendere; **be
sold out** essere esaurito ● *vi* vendersi.
sell off *vt* liquidare

seller /'selə(r)/ *n* venditore, -trice *mf*

Sellotape® /'seləʊ-/ *n* nastro *m* adesivo, scotch® *m*

'sell-out *n* (*fam: betrayal*) tradimento
m; **be a ~** ⟨*concert:*⟩ fare il tutto esaurito

selves /selvz/ *pl of* **self**

semen /'si:mən/ *n* Anat liquido *m* se-
minale

semester /sɪ'mestə(r)/ *n Am* semestre *m*

semi /'semɪ/: **~breve** /'semɪbri:v/ *n*
semibreve *f*. **~circle** /'semɪsɜ:k(ə)l/ *n*
semicerchio *m*. **~'circular** *a* semi-
circolare. **~'colon** *n* punto e virgola *m*.
~-de'tached *a* gemella ● *n* casa *f* gemella. **~-'final** *n* semifinale *f*

seminar /'semɪnɑ:(r)/ *n* seminario *m*.
~y /-nərɪ/ *n* seminario *m*

semolina /semə'li:nə/ *n* semolino *m*

senat|e /'senət/ *n* senato *m*. **~or** *n* se-
natore *m*

send /send/ *vt/i* (*pt/pp* **sent**) mandare;
~ for mandare a chiamare ⟨*person*⟩; far
venire ⟨*thing*⟩. **~er** *n* mittente *mf*. **~-off**
n commiato *m*

senil|e /'si:naɪl/ *a* arteriosclerotico; *Med*
senile. **~ity** /sɪ'nɪlətɪ/ *n* senilismo *m*

senior /'si:nɪə(r)/ *a* più vecchio; (*in
rank*) superiore ● *n* (*in rank*) superiore
mf; (*in sport*) senior *mf*; **she's two
years my ~** è più vecchia di me di due
anni. **~ 'citizen** *n* anziano, -a *mf*

seniority /si:nɪ'ɒrətɪ/ *n* anzianità *f* di
servizio

sensation /sen'seɪʃn/ *n* sensazione *f*.
~al *a* sensazionale. **~ally** *adv* in modo
sensazionale

sense /sens/ *n* senso *m*; (*common ~*)
buon senso *m*; **in a ~** in un certo senso;
make ~ aver senso ● *vt* sentire. **~less**
a insensato; (*unconscious*) privo di sensi

sensibl|e /'sensəbl/ *a* sensato;
(*suitable*) appropriato. **~y** *adv* in modo
appropriato

sensitiv|e /'sensətɪv/ *a* sensibile;
(*touchy*) suscettibile. **~ely** *adv* con sensibilità. **~ity** /-'tɪvɪtɪ/ *n* sensibilità *f inv*

sensory /'sensərɪ/ *a* sensoriale

sensual /'sensjʊəl/ *a* sensuale. **~ity**
/-'ælətɪ/ *n* sensualità *f inv*

sensuous /'sensjʊəs/ *a* voluttuoso

sent /sent/ *see* **send**

sentence /'sentəns/ *n* frase *f*; *Jur* sen-

tenza *f*; (*punishment*) condanna *f* ● *vt* **~
to** condannare a

sentiment /'sentɪmənt/ *n* sentimento
m; (*opinion*) opinione *f*; (*sentimentality*)
sentimentalismo *m*. **~al** /-'mentl/ *a* sen-
timentale; *pej* sentimentalista. **~ality**
/-'tælətɪ/ *n* sentimentalità *f inv*

sentry /'sentrɪ/ *n* sentinella *f*

separable /'sepərəbl/ *a* separabile

separate¹ /'sepərət/ *a* separato. **~ly**
adv separatamente

separat|e² /'sepəreɪt/ *vt* separare ● *vi*
separarsi. **~ion** /-'reɪʃn/ *n* separazione *f*

September /sep'tembə(r)/ *n* settem-
bre *m*

septic /'septɪk/ *a* settico; **go ~** infettarsi. **~ tank** *n* fossa *f* biologica

sequel /'si:kwəl/ *n* seguito *m*

sequence /'si:kwəns/ *n* sequenza *f*

sequin /'si:kwɪn/ *n* lustrino *m*,
paillette *f inv*

Serbia /'sɜ:bɪə/ *n* Serbia *f*

serenade /serə'neɪd/ *n* serenata *f* ● *vt*
fare una serenata a

seren|e /sɪ'ri:n/ *a* sereno. **~ity**
/-'renətɪ/ *n* serenità *f inv*

sergeant /'sɑ:dʒənt/ *n* sergente *m*

serial /'sɪərɪəl/ *n* racconto *m* a puntate;
TV sceneggiato *m* a puntate; *Radio* commedia *f* radiofonica a puntate. **~ize** *vt*
pubblicare a puntate; *Radio, TV* trasmettere a puntate. **~ killer** *n* serial killer *mf inv*. **~ number** *n* numero *m* di serie. **~ port** *n Comput* porta *f* seriale

series /'sɪəri:z/ *n* serie *f inv*

serious /'sɪərɪəs/ *a* serio; ⟨*illness,
error*⟩ grave. **~ly** *adv* seriamente; ⟨*ill*⟩
gravemente; **take ~ly** prendere sul serio. **~ness** *n* serietà *f*; (*of situation*) gravità *f*

sermon /'sɜ:mən/ *n* predica *f*

serpent /'sɜ:pənt/ *n* serpente *m*

serrated /se'reɪtɪd/ *a* dentellato

serum /'sɪərəm/ *n* siero *m*

servant /'sɜ:vənt/ *n* domestico, -a *mf*

serve /sɜ:v/ *n* Tennis servizio *m* ● *vt*
servire; scontare ⟨*sentence*⟩; **~ its
purpose** servire al proprio scopo; **it
~s you right!** ben ti sta!; **~s two** per
due persone ● *vi* prestare servizio; *Tennis* servire; **~ as** servire da

server /'sɜ:və(r)/ *n Comput* server *m
inv*

service /'sɜ:vɪs/ *n* servizio *m*; *Relig*
funzione *f*; (*maintenance*) revisione *f*;
~s *pl* forze *fpl* armate; (*on motorway*)
area *f* di servizio; **in the ~s** sotto le
armi; **of ~ to** utile a; **out of ~**

⟨*machine:*⟩ guasto ● *vt Techn* revisionare. **~able** /-əbl/ *a* utilizzabile; (*hard-
wearing*) resistente; (*practical*) pratico
service: ~ area *n* area *f* di servizio. **~
charge** *n* servizio *m*. **~man** *n* militare
m. **~ provider** *n Comput* fornitore *m* di
servizi. **~ station** *n* stazione *f* di servizio
serviette /sɜːvɪˈet/ *n* tovagliolo *m*
servile /ˈsɜːvaɪl/ *a* servile
session /ˈseʃn/ *n* seduta *f*; *Jur* sessione
f; *Univ* anno *m* accademico
set /set/ *n* serie *f inv*, set *m inv*; (*of
crockery, cutlery*) servizio *m*; *TV, Radio*
apparecchio *m*; *Math* insieme *m*; *Theat*
scenario *m*; *Cinema, Tennis* set *m inv*;
(*of people*) circolo *m*; (*of hair*) messa *f* in
piega ● *a* (*ready*) pronto; (*rigid*) fisso;
⟨*book*⟩ in programma; **be ~ on doing
sth** essere risoluto a fare qcsa; **be ~ in
one's ways** essere abitudinario ● *v*
(*pt/pp* set, *pres p* setting) ● *vt* mettere,
porre; mettere ⟨*alarm clock*⟩; assegnare
⟨*task, homework*⟩; fissare ⟨*date, limit*⟩;
chiedere ⟨*questions*⟩; montare ⟨*gem*⟩; as-
sestare ⟨*bone*⟩; apparecchiare ⟨*table*⟩; **~
fire to** dare fuoco a; **~ free** liberare
● *vi* ⟨*sun:*⟩ tramontare; ⟨*jelly, concrete:*⟩
solidificare; **~ about doing sth** mettersi a fare qcsa. **set back** *vt* mettere
indietro; (*hold up*) ritardare; (*fam: cost*)
costare a. **set off** *vi* partire ● *vt* avviare; mettere ⟨*alarm*⟩; fare esplodere
⟨*bomb*⟩. **set out** *vi* partire; **~ out to do
sth** proporsi di fare qcsa ● *vt* disporre;
(*state*) esporre. **set to** *vi* mettersi al-
l'opera. **set up** *vt* fondare ⟨*company*⟩;
istituire ⟨*committee*⟩
'set-back *n* passo *m* indietro
set 'meal *n* menù *m inv* fisso
settee /seˈtiː/ *n* divano *m*
setting /ˈsetɪŋ/ *n* scenario *m*; (*position*)
posizione *f*; (*of sun*) tramonto *m*; (*of
jewel*) montatura *f*
settle /ˈsetl/ *vt* (*decide*) definire; risolvere ⟨*argument*⟩; fissare ⟨*date*⟩; calmare
⟨*nerves*⟩; saldare ⟨*bill*⟩ ● *vi* (*to live*) sta-
bilirsi; ⟨*snow, dust, bird:*⟩ posarsi;
(*subside*) assestarsi; ⟨*sediment:*⟩ deposi-
tarsi. **settle down** *vi* sistemarsi; (*stop
making noise*) calmarsi. **settle for** *vt*
accontentarsi di. **settle up** *vi* regolare i
conti
settlement /ˈsetlmənt/ *n* (*agreement*)
accordo *m*; (*of bill*) saldo *m*; (*colony*) in-
sediamento *m*
settler /ˈsetlə(r)/ *n* colonizzatore, -trice
mf

'set-to *n fam* zuffa *f*; (*verbal*) battibecco *m*
'set-up *n* situazione *f*
seven /ˈsevn/ *a* & *n* sette *m*. **~'teen** *a*
& *n* diciassette *m*. **~'teenth** *a* & *n* di-
ciassettesimo, -a *mf*
seventh /ˈsevnθ/ *a* & *n* settimo, -a *mf*
seventieth /ˈsevntɪɪθ/ *a* & *n* settan-
tesimo, -a *mf*
seventy /ˈsevntɪ/ *a* & *n* settanta *m*
sever /ˈsevə(r)/ *vt* troncare ⟨*relations*⟩
several /ˈsevrəl/ *a* & *pron* parecchi
sever|e /sɪˈvɪə(r)/ *a* severo; (*pain*) vio-
lento; (*illness*) grave; (*winter*) rigido.
~ely *adv* severamente; (*ill*) gravemente. **~ity** /-ˈverətɪ/ *n* severità *f*; (*of pain*)
violenza *f*; (*of illness*) gravità *f*; (*of
winter*) rigore *m*
sew /səʊ/ *vt/i* (*pt* sewed, *pp* sewn or
sewed) cucire. **sew up** *vt* ricucire
sewage /ˈsuːɪdʒ/ *n* acque *fpl* di scolo
sewer /ˈsuːə(r)/ *n* fogna *f*
sewing /ˈsəʊɪŋ/ *n* cucito *m*; (*work*) lavoro *m* di cucito. **~ machine** *n* macchina
f da cucire
sewn /səʊn/ *see* sew
sex /seks/ *n* sesso *m*; **have ~** avere rapporti sessuali. **~ist** *a* sessista. **~
offence** *n* delitto *m* a sfondo sessuale
sexual /ˈseksjʊəl/ *a* sessuale. **~ 'intercourse** *n* rapporti *mpl* sessuali. **~ity**
/-ˈælətɪ/ *n* sessualità *f*. **~ly** *adv*
sessualmente
sexy /ˈseksɪ/ *a* (-ier, -iest) sexy *inv*
shabb|y /ˈʃæbɪ/ *a* (-ier, -iest) scialbo;
⟨*treatment*⟩ meschino. **~iness** *n* trasan-
datezza *f*; (*of treatment*) meschinità *f inv*
shack /ʃæk/ *n* catapecchia *f* ● **shack
up with** *vt fam* vivere con
shade /ʃeɪd/ *n* ombra *f*; (*of colour*) sfumatura *f*; (*for lamp*) paralume *m*; (*Am:
for window*) tapparella *f*; **a ~ better** un
tantino meglio ● *vt* riparare dalla luce;
(*draw lines on*) ombreggiare. **~s** *npl
fam* occhiali *mpl* da sole
shadow /ˈʃædəʊ/ *n* ombra *f*; **S~
Cabinet** governo *m* ombra ● *vt* (*follow*)
pedinare. **~y** *a* ombroso
shady /ˈʃeɪdɪ/ *a* (-ier, -iest) ombroso;
(*fam: disreputable*) losco
shaft /ʃɑːft/ *n Techn* albero *m*; (*of light*)
raggio *m*; (*of lift, mine*) pozzo *m*
shaggy /ˈʃægɪ/ *a* (-ier, -iest) irsuto;
⟨*animal*⟩ dal pelo arruffato
shake /ʃeɪk/ *n* scrollata *f* ● *v* (*pt*
shook, *pp* shaken) ● *vt* scuotere; agitare ⟨*bottle*⟩; far tremare ⟨*building*⟩; **~
hands with** stringere la mano a ● *vi*
tremare. **shake off** *vt* scrollarsi di dos-

so. **~-up** n Pol rimpasto m; Comm ristrutturazione f

shaky /'ʃeɪkɪ/ a (**-ier, -iest**) tremante; ‹table etc› traballante; (unreliable) vacillante

shall /ʃæl/ v aux **I ~ go** andrò; **we ~ see** vedremo; **what ~ I do?** cosa faccio?; **I'll come too, ~ I?** vengo anch'io, no?; **thou shalt not kill** liter non uccidere

shallow /'ʃæləʊ/ a basso, poco profondo; ‹dish› poco profondo; fig superficiale

sham /ʃæm/ a falso ● n finzione f; (person) spaccone, -a mf ● vt (pt/pp **shammed**) simulare

shambles /'ʃæmblz/ n baraonda fsg

shame /ʃeɪm/ n vergogna f; **it's a ~ that** è un peccato che; **what a ~!** che peccato! ● a vergognoso

shame|ful /'ʃeɪmfl/ a vergognoso. **~less** a spudorato

shampoo /ʃæm'puː/ n shampoo m inv ● vt fare uno shampoo a

shandy /'ʃændɪ/ n bevanda f a base di birra e gassosa

shan't /ʃɑːnt/ = **shall not**

shanty town /'ʃæntɪtaʊn/ n bidonville f inv, baraccopoli f inv

shape /ʃeɪp/ n forma f; (figure) ombra f; **take ~** prendere forma; **get back in ~** ritornare in forma ● vt dare forma a (**into** di) ● vi ~ [**up**] mettere la testa a posto; **~ up nicely** mettersi bene. **~less** a informe

shapely /'ʃeɪplɪ/ a (**-ier, -iest**) ben fatto

share /ʃeə(r)/ n porzione f; Comm azione f ● vt dividere; condividere ‹views› ● vi dividere. **~holder** n azionista mf

shark /ʃɑːk/ n squalo m, pescecane m; fig truffatore, -trice mf

sharp /ʃɑːp/ a ‹knife etc› tagliente; ‹pencil› appuntito; ‹drop› a picco; ‹reprimand› severo; ‹outline› marcato; ‹alert› acuto; ‹unscrupulous› senza scrupoli; **~ pain** fitta f ● adv in punto; Mus fuori tono; **look ~!** sbrigati! ● n Mus diesis m inv. **~en** vt affilare ‹knife›; appuntire ‹pencil›

shatter /'ʃætə(r)/ vt frantumare; fig mandare in frantumi; **~ed** (fam: exhausted) a pezzi ● vi frantumarsi

shav|e /ʃeɪv/ n rasatura f; **have a ~e** farsi la barba ● vt radere ● vi radersi. **~er** n rasoio m elettrico. **~ing-brush** n pennello m da barba; **~ing foam** n schiuma f da barba; **~ing soap** n sapone m da barba

shawl /ʃɔːl/ n scialle m

she /ʃiː/ pers pron lei

sheaf /ʃiːf/ n (pl **sheaves**) fascio m

shear /ʃɪə(r)/ vt (pt **sheared**, pp **shorn** or **sheared**) tosare

shears /ʃɪəz/ npl (for hedge) cesoie fpl

sheath /ʃiːθ/ n (pl ~s /ʃiːðz/) guaina f

shed[1] /ʃed/ n baracca f; (for cattle) stalla f

shed[2] vt (pt/pp **shed**, pres p **shedding**) perdere; versare ‹blood, tears›; **~ light on** far luce su

sheen /ʃiːn/ n lucentezza f

sheep /ʃiːp/ n inv pecora f. **~-dog** n cane m da pastore

sheepish /'ʃiːpɪʃ/ a imbarazzato. **~ly** adv con aria imbarazzata

'sheepskin n [pelle f di] montone m

sheer /ʃɪə(r)/ a puro; (steep) a picco; (transparent) trasparente ● adv a picco

sheet /ʃiːt/ n lenzuolo m; (of paper) foglio m; (of glass, metal) lastra f

shelf /ʃelf/ n (pl **shelves**) ripiano m; (set of shelves) scaffale m

shell /ʃel/ n conchiglia f; (of egg, snail, tortoise) guscio m; (of crab) corazza f; (of unfinished building) ossatura f; Mil granata f ● vt sgusciare ‹peas›; Mil bombardare. **shell out** vi fam sborsare

'shellfish n inv mollusco m; Culin frutti mpl di mare

shelter /'ʃeltə(r)/ n rifugio m; (air raid ~) rifugio m antiaereo ● vt riparare (**from** da); fig mettere al riparo; (give lodging to) dare asilo a ● vi rifugiarsi. **~ed** a ‹spot› riparato; ‹life› ritirato

shelve /ʃelv/ vt accantonare ‹project›

shelves /ʃelvz/ see **shelf**

shelving /'ʃelvɪŋ/ n (shelves) ripiani mpl

shepherd /'ʃepəd/ n pastore m ● vt guidare. **~'s pie** n pasticcio m di carne tritata e patate

sherry /'ʃerɪ/ n sherry m inv

shield /ʃiːld/ n scudo m; (for eyes) maschera f; Techn schermo m ● vt proteggere (**from** da)

shift /ʃɪft/ n cambiamento m; (in position) spostamento m; (at work) turno m ● vt spostare; (take away) togliere; riversare ‹blame› ● vi spostarsi; ‹wind:› cambiare; (fam: move quickly) darsi una mossa

'shift work n turni mpl

shifty /'ʃɪftɪ/ a (**-ier, -iest**) pej losco; ‹eyes› sfuggente

shilly-shally /'ʃɪlɪʃælɪ/ vi titubare

shimmer /'ʃɪmə(r)/ n luccichio m ● vi luccicare

shin /ʃɪn/ n stinco m

shine /ʃaɪn/ n lucentezza f; **give sth a ~** dare una lucidata a qcsa ● v (pt/pp **shone**) ● vi splendere; (reflect light) brillare; ⟨hair, shoes:⟩ essere lucido ● vt **~ a light on** puntare una luce su

shingle /'ʃɪŋgl/ n (pebbles) ghiaia f

shingles /'ʃɪŋglz/ n Med fuochi mpl di Sant'Antonio

shiny /'ʃaɪnɪ/ a (-ier, -iest) lucido

ship /ʃɪp/ n nave f ● vt (pt/pp **shipped**) spedire; (by sea) spedire via mare

ship: **~ment** n spedizione f; (consignment) carico m. **~per** n spedizioniere m. **~ping** n trasporto m; (traffic) imbarcazioni fpl. **~shape** a & adv in perfetto ordine. **~wreck** n naufragio m. **~wrecked** a naufragato. **~yard** n cantiere m navale

shirk /ʃɜːk/ vt scansare. **~er** n scansafatiche mf inv

shirt /ʃɜːt/ n camicia f; **in ~-sleeves** in maniche di camicia

shit /ʃɪt/ vulg n & int merda f ● vi (pt/pp **shit**) cagare

shiver /'ʃɪvə(r)/ n brivido m ● vi rabbrividire

shoal /ʃəʊl/ n (of fish) banco m

shock /ʃɒk/ n (impact) urto m; Electr scossa f [elettrica]; fig colpo m, shock m inv; Med shock m inv; **get a ~** Electr prendere la scossa ● vt scioccare. **~ing** a scioccante; ⟨fam: weather, handwriting etc⟩ tremendo

shod /ʃɒd/ see **shoe**

shoddy /'ʃɒdɪ/ a (-ier, -iest) scadente

shoe /ʃuː/ n scarpa f; (of horse) ferro m ● vt (pt/pp **shod**, pres p **shoeing**) ferrare ⟨horse⟩

shoe: **~horn** n calzante m. **~-lace** n laccio m da scarpa. **~maker** n calzolaio m. **~-shop** n calzoleria f. **~-string** n **on a ~-string** fam con una miseria

shone /ʃɒn/ see **shine**

shoo /ʃuː/ vt **~ away** cacciar via ● int sciò

shook /ʃʊk/ see **shake**

shoot /ʃuːt/ n Bot germoglio m; (hunt) battuta f di caccia ● v (pt/pp **shot**) ● vt sparare; girare ⟨film⟩ ● vi (hunt) andare a caccia. **shoot down** vt abbattere. **shoot out** vi (rush) precipitarsi fuori. **shoot up** vi (grow) crescere in fretta; ⟨prices:⟩ salire di colpo

'shooting-range n poligono m di tiro

shop /ʃɒp/ n negozio m; (workshop) officina f; **talk ~** fam parlare di lavoro ● vi (pt/pp **shopped**) far compere; **go ~ping** andare a fare compere. **shop around** vi confrontare i prezzi

shop: **~ assistant** n commesso, -a mf. **~keeper** n negoziante mf. **~-lifter** n taccheggiatore, -trice mf. **~-lifting** n taccheggio m; **~per** n compratore, -trice mf

shopping /'ʃɒpɪŋ/ n compere fpl; (articles) acquisti mpl; **do the ~** fare la spesa. **~ bag** n borsa f per la spesa. **~ centre** n centro m commerciale. **~ trolley** n carrello m

shop: **~-steward** n rappresentante mf sindacale. **~-'window** n vetrina f

shore /ʃɔː(r)/ n riva f

shorn /ʃɔːn/ see **shear**

short /ʃɔːt/ a corto; (not lasting) breve; ⟨person⟩ basso; (curt) brusco; **a ~ time ago** poco tempo fa; **be ~ of** essere a corto di; **be in ~ supply** essere scarso; fig essere raro; **Mick is ~ for Michael** Mick è il diminutivo di Michael ● adv bruscamente; **in ~** in breve; **~ of doing** a meno di fare; **go ~** essere privato ⟨of di⟩; **stop ~ of doing sth** non arrivare fino a fare qcsa; **cut ~** interrompere ⟨meeting, holiday⟩; **to cut a long story ~** per farla breve

shortage /'ʃɔːtɪdʒ/ n scarsità f inv

short: **~bread** n biscotto m di pasta frolla. **~ 'circuit** n corto m circuito. **~coming** n difetto m. **~ 'cut** n scorciatoia f

shorten /'ʃɔːtn/ vt abbreviare; accorciare ⟨garment⟩

short: **~hand** n stenografia f. **~-'handed** a a corto di personale. **~hand 'typist** n stenodattilografo, -a mf. **~ list** n lista f dei candidati selezionati per un lavoro. **~-lived** /-lɪvd/ a di breve durata

short|ly /'ʃɔːtlɪ/ adv presto; **~ly before/after** poco prima/dopo. **~ness** n brevità f inv; (of person) bassa statura f

short-range a di breve portata

shorts /ʃɔːts/ npl calzoncini mpl corti

short: **~-'sighted** a miope. **~-'sleeved** a a maniche corte. **~-'staffed** a a corto di personale. **~ 'story** n racconto m, novella f. **~-'tempered** a irascibile. **~-term** a a breve termine. **~ wave** n onde fpl corte

shot /ʃɒt/ see **shoot** ● n colpo m; (person) tiratore m; Phot foto f inv; (injection) puntura f; (fam: attempt) prova *f*; **like a ~** *fam* come un razzo. **~gun** *n* fucile *m* da caccia

should /ʃʊd/ *v aux* **I ~ go** dovrei andare; **I ~ have seen him** avrei dovuto vederlo; **I ~ like** mi piacerebbe; **this ~ be enough** questo dovrebbe bastare; **if he ~ come** se dovesse venire

shoulder /'ʃəʊldə(r)/ *n* spalla *f* ● *vt* mettersi in spalla; *fig* accollarsi. **~-bag** *n* borsa *f* a tracolla. **~-blade** *n* scapola *f*. **~-strap** *n* spallina *f*; (*of bag*) tracolla *f*

shout /ʃaʊt/ *n* grido *m* ● *vt/i* gridare. **shout at** *vi* alzar la voce con. **shout down** *vt* azzittire gridando

shouting /'ʃaʊtɪŋ/ *n* grida *fpl*

shove /ʃʌv/ *n* spintone *m* ● *vt* spingere; (*fam: put*) ficcare ● *vi* spingere. **shove off** *vi fam* togliersi di torno

shovel /'ʃʌvl/ *n* pala *f* ● *vt* (*pt/pp* **shovelled**) spalare

show /ʃəʊ/ *n* (*display*) manifestazione *f*; (*exhibition*) mostra *f*; (*ostentation*) ostentazione *f*; *Theat, TV* spettacolo *m*; (*programme*) programma *m*; **on ~** esposto ● *v* (*pt* **showed**, *pp* **shown**) ● *vt* mostrare; (*put on display*) esporre; proiettare ⟨film⟩ ● *vi* ⟨film:⟩ essere proiettato; **your slip is ~ing** ti si vede la sottoveste. **show in** *vt* fare accomodare. **show off** *vi fam* mettersi in mostra ● *vt* mettere in mostra. **show up** *vi* risaltare; (*fam: arrive*) farsi vedere ● *vt* (*fam: embarrass*) far fare una brutta figura a

'show-down *n* regolamento *m* dei conti

shower /'ʃaʊə(r)/ *n* doccia *f*; (*of rain*) acquazzone *m*; **have a ~** fare la doccia ● *vt* **~ with** coprire di ● *vi* fare la doccia. **~-proof** *a* impermeabile. **~y** *a* da acquazzoni

'show-jumping *n* concorso *m* ippico

shown /ʃəʊn/ *see* **show**

'show-off *n* esibizionista *mf*

showy /'ʃəʊɪ/ *a* appariscente

shrank /ʃræŋk/ *see* **shrink**

shred /ʃred/ *n* brandello *m*; *fig* briciolo *m* ● *vt* (*pt/pp* **shredded**) fare a brandelli; *Culin* tagliuzzare. **~der** *n* distruttore *m* di documenti

shrewd /ʃruːd/ *a* accorto. **~ness** *n* accortezza *f*

shriek /ʃriːk/ *n* strillo *m* ● *vt/i* strillare

shrift /ʃrɪft/ *n* **give sb short ~** liquidare qcno rapidamente

shrill /ʃrɪl/ *a* penetrante

shrimp /ʃrɪmp/ *n* gamberetto *m*

shrine /ʃraɪn/ *n* (*place*) santuario *m*

shrink /ʃrɪŋk/ *vi* (*pt* **shrank**, *pp* **shrunk**) restringersi; (*draw back*) ritrarsi (**from** da)

shrivel /'ʃrɪvl/ *vi* (*pt/pp* **shrivelled**) raggrinzare

shroud /ʃraʊd/ *n* sudario *m*; *fig* manto *m*

Shrove /ʃrəʊv/ *n* **~ 'Tuesday** martedì *m* grasso

shrub /ʃrʌb/ *n* arbusto *m*

shrug /ʃrʌg/ *n* scrollata *f* di spalle ● *vt/i* (*pt/pp* **shrugged**) **~** [**one's shoulders**] scrollare le spalle

shrunk /ʃrʌŋk/ *see* **shrink**. **~en** *a* rimpicciolito

shudder /'ʃʌdə(r)/ *n* fremito *m* ● *vi* fremere

shuffle /'ʃʌfl/ *vi* strascicare i piedi ● *vt* mescolare ⟨cards⟩

shun /ʃʌn/ *vt* (*pt/pp* **shunned**) rifuggire

shunt /ʃʌnt/ *vt* smistare

shush /ʃʊʃ/ *int* zitto!

shut /ʃʌt/ *v* (*pt/pp* **shut**, *pres p* **shutting**) ● *vt* chiudere ● *vi* chiudersi; ⟨shop:⟩ chiudere. **shut down** *vt/i* chiudere. **shut up** *vt* chiudere; *fam* far tacere ● *vi fam* stare zitto; **~ up!** stai zitto!

'shut-down *n* chiusura *f*

shutter /'ʃʌtə(r)/ *n* serranda *f*; *Phot* otturatore *m*

shuttle /'ʃʌtl/ *n* navetta *f* ● *vi* far la spola

shuttle: ~cock *n* volano *m*. **~ service** *n* servizio *m* pendolare

shy /ʃaɪ/ *a* (*timid*) timido. **~ness** *n* timidezza *f*

Siamese /saɪə'miːz/ *a* siamese

sibling /'sɪblɪŋz/ *n* (*brother*) fratello *m*; (*sister*) sorella *f*; **~s** *pl* fratelli *mpl*

Sicil|y /'sɪsɪlɪ/ *n* Sicilia *f*. **~ian** *a* & *n* siciliano, -a *mf*

sick /sɪk/ *a* ammalato; ⟨humour⟩ macabro; **be ~** (*vomit*) vomitare; **be ~ of sth** *fam* essere stufo di qcsa; **feel ~** aver la nausea

sicken /'sɪkn/ *vt* disgustare ● *vi* **be ~ing for something** covare qualche malanno. **~ing** *a* disgustoso

sick|ly /'sɪklɪ/ *a* (**-ier, -iest**) malaticcio. **~ness** *n* malattia *f*; (*vomiting*) nausea *f*. **~ness benefit** *n* indennità *f* di malattia

side /saɪd/ *n* lato *m*; (*of person, mountain*) fianco *m*; (*of road*) bordo *m*; **on the ~** (*as sideline*) come attività secondaria; **~ by ~** fianco a fianco; **take ~s** immischiarsi; **take sb's ~** prendere le parti di qcno; **be on the safe ~**

andare sul sicuro ● *attrib* laterale ● *vi*
~ **with** parteggiare per

side: **~board** *n* credenza *f*. **~burns** *npl*
basette *fpl*. **~-effect** *n* effetto *m*
collaterale. **~lights** *npl* luci *fpl* di posizione. **~line** *n* attività *f inv* complementare. **~-show** *n* attrazione *f*. **~-step** *vt*
schivare. **~-track** *vt* sviare. **~walk** *n*
Am marciapiede *m*. **~ways** *adv* obliquamente

siding /'saɪdɪŋ/ *n* binario *m* di raccordo

sidle /'saɪdl/ *vi* camminare furtivamente (**up to** verso)

siege /si:dʒ/ *n* assedio *m*

sieve /sɪv/ *n* setaccio *m* ● *vt* setacciare

sift /sɪft/ *vt* setacciare; ~ [**through**] *fig*
passare al setaccio

sigh /saɪ/ *n* sospiro *m* ● *vi* sospirare

sight /saɪt/ *n* vista *f*; (*on gun*) mirino *m*;
the ~s *pl* le cose da vedere; **at first** ~ a
prima vista; **be within/out of** ~
essere/non essere in vista; **lose** ~ **of**
perdere di vista; **know by** ~ conoscere
di vista. **have bad** ~ vederci male ● *vt*
avvistare

'sightseeing *n* **go** ~ andare a visitare
posti

sign /saɪn/ *n* segno *m*; (*notice*) insegna *f*
● *vt/i* firmare. **sign on** *vi* (*as
unemployed*) presentarsi all'ufficio di
collocamento; *Mil* arruolarsi

signal /'sɪgnl/ *n* segnale *m* ● *v* (*pt/pp*
signalled) ● *vt* segnalare ● *vi* fare segnali; ~ **to sb** far segno a qcno (**to** di).
~-box *n* cabina *f* di segnalazione

signature /'sɪgnətʃə(r)/ *n* firma *f*. ~
tune *n* sigla *f* [musicale]

signet-ring /'sɪgnɪt-/ *n* anello *m* con sigillo

significan|ce /sɪg'nɪfɪkəns/ *n* significato *m*. **~t** *a* significativo

signify /'sɪgnɪfaɪ/ *vt* (*pt/pp* **-ied**) indicare

sign-language *n* linguaggio *m* dei segni

signpost /'saɪn-/ *n* segnalazione *f* stradale

silence /'saɪləns/ *n* silenzio *m* ● *vt* far
tacere. **~r** *n* (*on gun*) silenziatore *m*;
Auto marmitta *f*

silent /'saɪlənt/ *a* silenzioso; (*film*)
muto; **remain** ~ rimanere in silenzio.
~ly *adv* silenziosamente

silhouette /sɪlʊ'et/ *n* sagoma *f*, silhouette *f inv* ● *vt* **be ~d** profilarsi

silicon /'sɪlɪkən/ *n* silicio *m*. ~ **chip**
piastrina *f* di silicio

silk /sɪlk/ *n* seta *f*. ● *attrib* di seta.
~worm *n* baco *m* da seta

silky /'sɪlkɪ/ *a* (**-ier, -iest**) come la seta

sill /sɪl/ *n* davanzale *m*

silly /'sɪlɪ/ *a* (**-ier, -iest**) sciocco

silo /'saɪləʊ/ *n* silo *m*

silt /sɪlt/ *n* melma *f*

silver /'sɪlvə(r)/ *a* d'argento; (*paper*)
argentato ● *n* argento *m*; (*silverware*)
argenteria *f*

silver: **~-plated** *a* placcato d'argento.
~ware *n* argenteria *f*. ~ **'wedding** *n*
nozze *fpl* d'argento

similar /'sɪmɪlə(r)/ *a* simile. **~ity**
/-'lærətɪ/ *n* somiglianza *f*. **~ly** *adv* in
modo simile

simile /'sɪmɪlɪ/ *n* similitudine *f*

simmer /'sɪmə(r)/ *vi* bollire lentamente ● *vt* far bollire lentamente. **simmer
down** *vi* calmarsi

simple /'sɪmpl/ *a* semplice; (*person*)
sempliciotto. **~-'minded** *a* sempliciotto

simplicity /sɪm'plɪsətɪ/ *n* semplicità *f*

simpli|fication /sɪmplɪfɪ'keɪʃn/ *n*
semplificazione *f*. **~fy** /'sɪmplɪfaɪ/ *vt*
(*pt/pp* **-ied**) semplificare

simply /'sɪmplɪ/ *adv* semplicemente

simulat|e /'sɪmjʊleɪt/ *vt* simulare.
~ion /-'leɪʃn/ *n* simulazione *f*

simultaneous /sɪml'teɪnɪəs/ *a* simultaneo

sin /sɪn/ *n* peccato *m* ● *vi* (*pt/pp*
sinned) peccare

since /sɪns/ *prep* da ● *adv* da allora
● *conj* da quando; (*because*) siccome

sincere /sɪn'sɪə(r)/ *a* sincero. **~ly** *adv*
sinceramente; **Yours ~ly** distinti saluti

sincerity /sɪn'serətɪ/ *n* sincerità *f*

sinful /'sɪnfl/ *a* peccaminoso

sing /sɪŋ/ *vt/i* (*pt* **sang**, *pp* **sung**) cantare

singe /sɪndʒ/ *vt* (*pres p* **singeing**) bruciacchiare

singer /'sɪŋə(r)/ *n* cantante *mf*

single /'sɪŋgl/ *a* solo; (*not double*) semplice; (*unmarried*) celibe; (*woman*) nubile; (*room*) singolo; (*bed*) a una piazza
● *n* (*ticket*) biglietto *m* di sola andata;
(*record*) singolo *m*; **~s** *pl Tennis* singolo
m ● **single out** *vt* scegliere; (*distinguish*) distinguere

single: **~-breasted** *a* a un petto.
~-handed *a & adv* da solo. **~-minded** *a*
risoluto. ~ **'parent** *n* genitore *m* che alleva il figlio da solo

singly /'sɪŋglɪ/ *adv* singolarmente

singular /'sɪŋgjʊlə(r)/ *a Gram* singolare ● *n* singolare *m*. **~ly** *adv* singolarmente

sinister /'sɪnɪstə(r)/ *a* sinistro

sink /sɪŋk/ *n* lavandino *m* ● *v* (*pt* **sank**, *pp* **sunk**) ● *vi* affondare ● *vt* affondare ⟨*ship*⟩; scavare ⟨*shaft*⟩; investire ⟨*money*⟩. **sink in** *vi* penetrare; **it took a while to ~ in** ⟨*fam: be understood*⟩ c'è voluto un po' a capirlo

sinner /'sɪnə(r)/ *n* peccatore, -trice *mf*

sinus /'saɪnəs/ *n* seno *m* paranasale. **~itis** *n* sinusite *f*

sip /sɪp/ *n* sorso *m* ● *vt* (*pt/pp* **sipped**) sorseggiare

siphon /'saɪfn/ *n* (*bottle*) sifone *m* ● **siphon off** *vt* travasare (*con sifone*)

sir /sɜ:(r)/ *n* signore *m*; **S~** ⟨*title*⟩ Sir *m*; **Dear S~s** Spettabile ditta

siren /'saɪrən/ *n* sirena *f*

sissy /'sɪsɪ/ *n* femminuccia *f*

sister /'sɪstə(r)/ *n* sorella *f*; (*nurse*) [infermiera *f*] caposala *f*. **~-in-law** *n* (*pl* **~s-in-law**) cognata *f*. **~ly** *a* da sorella

sit /sɪt/ *v* (*pt/pp* **sat**, *pres p* **sitting**) ● *vi* essere seduto; (*sit down*) sedersi; ⟨*committee:*⟩ riunirsi ● *vt* sostenere ⟨*exam*⟩. **sit back** *vi fig* starsene con le mani in mano. **sit down** *vi* mettersi a sedere. **sit up** *vi* mettersi seduto; (*not slouch*) star seduto diritto; (*stay up*) stare alzato

site /saɪt/ *n* posto *m*; *Archaeol* sito *m*; (*building ~*) cantiere *m* ● *vt* collocare

sit-in /'sɪtɪn/ *n* occupazione *f* (*di fabbrica ecc*)

sitting /'sɪtɪŋ/ *n* seduta *f*; (*for meals*) turno *m*. **~-room** *n* salotto *m*

situat|e /'sɪtjʊeɪt/ *vt* situare. **~ed** *a* situato. **~ion** /-'eɪʃn/ *n* situazione *f*; (*location*) posizione *f*; (*job*) posto *m*

six /sɪks/ *a & n* sei *m*. **~teen** *a & n* sedici *m*. **~teenth** *a & n* sedicesimo, -a *mf*

sixth /sɪksθ/ *a & n* sesto, -a *mf*

sixtieth /'sɪkstɪɪθ/ *a & n* sessantesimo, -a *mf*

sixty /'sɪkstɪ/ *a & n* sessanta *m*

size /saɪz/ *n* dimensioni *fpl*; (*of clothes*) taglia *f*, misura *f*; (*of shoes*) numero *m*; **what ~ is the room?** che dimensioni ha la stanza? ● **size up** *vt fam* valutare

sizeable /'saɪzəbl/ *a* piuttosto grande

sizzle /'sɪzl/ *vi* sfrigolare

skate[1] /skeɪt/ *n inv* (*fish*) razza *f*

skate[2] /skeɪt/ *n* pattino *m* ● *vi* pattinare

skateboard /'skeɪtbɔ:d/ *n* skate-board *m inv*

skater /'skeɪtə(r)/ *n* pattinatore, -trice *mf*

skating /'skeɪtɪŋ/ *n* pattinaggio *m*. **~-rink** *n* pista *f* di pattinaggio

skeleton /'skelɪtn/ *n* scheletro *m*. **~ 'key** *n* passe-partout *m inv*. **~ 'staff** *n* personale *m* ridotto

sketch /sketʃ/ *n* schizzo *m*; *Theat* sketch *m inv* ● *vt* fare uno schizzo di

sketch|y /'sketʃɪ/ *a* (**-ier**, **-iest**) abbozzato. **~ily** *adv* in modo abbozzato

skewer /'skjʊə(r)/ *n* spiedo *m*

ski /ski:/ *n* sci *m inv* ● *vi* (*pt/pp* **skied**, *pres p* **skiing**) sciare; **go ~ing** andare a sciare

skid /skɪd/ *n* slittata *f* ● *vi* (*pt/pp* **skidded**) slittare

skier /'ski:ə(r)/ *n* sciatore, -trice *mf*

skiing /'ski:ɪŋ/ *n* sci *m*

skilful /'skɪlfl/ *a* abile

'ski-lift *n* impianto *m* di risalita

skill /skɪl/ *n* abilità *f inv*. **~ed** *a* dotato; ⟨*worker*⟩ specializzato

skim /skɪm/ *vt* (*pt/pp* **skimmed**) schiumare; scremare ⟨*milk*⟩. **skim off** *vt* togliere. **skim through** *vt* scorrere

skimp /skɪmp/ *vi* **~ on** lesinare su

skimpy /'skɪmpɪ/ *a* (**-ier**, **-iest**) succinto

skin /skɪn/ *n* pelle *f*; (*on fruit*) buccia *f* ● *vt* (*pt/pp* **skinned**) spellare

skin: ~-deep *a* superficiale. **~-diving** *n* nuoto *m* subacqueo

skinflint /'skɪnflɪnt/ *n* miserabile *mf*

skinny /'skɪnɪ/ *a* (**-ier**, **-iest**) molto magro

skip[1] /skɪp/ *n* (*container*) benna *f*

skip[2] /skɪp/ *n* salto *m* ● *v* (*pt/pp* **skipped**) ● *vi* saltellare; (*with rope*) saltare la corda ● *vt* omettere

skipper /'skɪpə(r)/ *n* skipper *m inv*

skipping-rope /'skɪpɪŋrəʊp/ *n* corda *f* per saltare

skirmish /'skɜ:mɪʃ/ *n* scaramuccia *f*

skirt /skɜ:t/ *n* gonna *f* ● *vt* costeggiare

skit /skɪt/ *n* bozzetto *m* comico

skittle /'skɪtl/ *n* birillo *m*

skive /skaɪv/ *vi fam* fare lo scansafatiche

skulk /skʌlk/ *vi* aggirarsi furtivamente

skull /skʌl/ *n* cranio *m*

skunk /skʌŋk/ *n* moffetta *f*

sky /skaɪ/ *n* cielo *m*. **~light** *n* lucernario *m*. **~scraper** *n* grattacielo *m*

slab /slæb/ *n* lastra *f*; (*slice*) fetta *f*; (*of chocolate*) tavoletta *f*

slack /slæk/ *a* lento; ⟨*person*⟩ fiacco ● *vi* fare lo scansafatiche. **slack off** *vi* rilassarsi

slacken /'slækn/ *vi* allentare; **~ [off]**

⟨*trade:*⟩ rallentare; ⟨*speed, rain:*⟩ diminuire ● *vt* allentare; diminuire ⟨*speed*⟩

slacks /slæks/ *npl* pantaloni *mpl* sportivi

slag /slæg/ *n* scorie *fpl* ● **slag off** *vt* ⟨*pt/pp* **slagged**⟩ *Br fam* criticare

slain /slem/ *see* **slay**

slam /slæm/ *v* ⟨*pt/pp* **slammed**⟩ ● *vt* sbattere; ⟨*fam: criticize*⟩ stroncare ● *vi* sbattere

slander /'slɑːndə(r)/ *n* diffamazione *f* ● *vt* diffamare. **~ous** /-rəs/ *a* diffamatorio

slang /slæŋ/ *n* gergo m. **~y** *a* gergale

slant /slɑːnt/ *n* pendenza *f*; ⟨*point of view*⟩ angolatura *f*; **on the ~** in pendenza ● *vt* pendere; *fig* distorcere ⟨*report*⟩ ● *vi* pendere

slap /slæp/ *n* schiaffo m ● *vt* ⟨*pt/pp* **slapped**⟩ schiaffeggiare; ⟨*put*⟩ schiaffare ● *adv* in pieno

slap: **~-dash** *a fam* frettoloso. **~-up** *a fam* di prim'ordine

slash /slæʃ/ *n* taglio m ● *vt* tagliare; ridurre drasticamente ⟨*prices*⟩

slat /slæt/ *n* stecca *f*

slate /sleɪt/ *n* ardesia *f* ● *vt fam* fare a pezzi

slaughter /'slɔːtə(r)/ *n* macello m; ⟨*of people*⟩ massacro m ● *vt* macellare; massacrare ⟨*people*⟩. **~house** *n* macello m

Slav /slɑːv/ *a* slavo ● *n* slavo, -a *mf*

slave /sleɪv/ *n* schiavo, -a *mf* ● *vi* **~ [away]** lavorare come un negro. **~-driver** *n* schiavista *mf*

slav|ery /'sleɪvəri/ *n* schiavitù *f*. **~ish** *a* servile

Slavonic /slə'vɒnɪk/ *a* slavo

slay /sleɪ/ *vt* ⟨*pt* **slew**, *pp* **slain**⟩ ammazzare

sleazy /'sliːzɪ/ *a* (**-ier, -iest**) sordido

sledge /sledʒ/ *n* slitta *f*. **~-hammer** *n* martello m

sleek /sliːk/ *a* liscio, lucente; ⟨*well-fed*⟩ pasciuto

sleep /sliːp/ *n* sonno m; **go to ~** addormentarsi; **put to ~** far addormentare ● *v* ⟨*pt/pp* **slept**⟩ ● *vi* dormire ● *vt* **~s six** ha sei posti letto. **~er** *n Rail* treno m con vagoni letto; ⟨*compartment*⟩ vagone m letto; **be a light/heavy ~er** avere il sonno leggero/pesante

sleeping: **~-bag** *n* sacco m a pelo. **~-car** *n* vagone m letto. **~-pill** *n* sonnifero m

sleep: **~less** *a* insonne. **~lessness** *n* insonnia *f*. **~-walker** *n* sonnambulo, -a *mf*. **~-walking** *n* sonnambulismo m

sleepy /'sliːpɪ/ *a* (**-ier, -iest**) assonnato; **be ~** aver sonno

sleet /sliːt/ *n* nevischio m ● *vi* **it is ~ing** nevischia

sleeve /sliːv/ *n* manica *f*; ⟨*for record*⟩ copertina *f*. **~less** *a* senza maniche

sleigh /sleɪ/ *n* slitta *f*

sleight /slaɪt/ *n* **~ of hand** gioco m di prestigio

slender /'slendə(r)/ *a* snello; ⟨*fingers, stem*⟩ affusolato; *fig* scarso; ⟨*chance*⟩ magro

slept /slept/ *see* **sleep**

sleuth /sluːθ/ *n* investigatore m, detective m *inv*

slew[1] /sluː/ *vi* girare

slew[2] *see* **slay**

slice /slaɪs/ *n* fetta *f* ● *vt* affettare; **~d bread** pane m a cassetta

slick /slɪk/ *a* liscio; ⟨*cunning*⟩ astuto ● *n* ⟨*of oil*⟩ chiazza *f* di petrolio

slid|e /slaɪd/ *n* scivolata *f*; ⟨*in playground*⟩ scivolo m; ⟨*for hair*⟩ fermaglio m ⟨*per capelli*⟩; *Phot* diapositiva *f* ● *v* ⟨*pt/pp* **slid**⟩ ● *vi* scivolare ● *vt* far scivolare. **~-rule** *n* regolo m calcolatore. **~ing** *a* ⟨*door, seat*⟩ scorrevole. **~ing scale** *n* scala *f* mobile

slight /slaɪt/ *a* leggero; ⟨*importance*⟩ poco; ⟨*slender*⟩ esile. **~est** minimo; **not in the ~est** niente affatto ● *vt* offendere ● *n* offesa *f*. **~ly** *adv* leggermente

slim /slɪm/ *a* (**slimmer, slimmest**) snello; *fig* scarso; ⟨*chance*⟩ magro ● *vi* dimagrire

slim|e /slaɪm/ *n* melma *f*. **~y** *a* melmoso; *fig* viscido

sling /slɪŋ/ *n Med* benda *f* al collo ● *vt* ⟨*pt/pp* **slung**⟩ *fam* lanciare

slip /slɪp/ *n* scivolata *f*; ⟨*mistake*⟩ lieve errore m; ⟨*petticoat*⟩ sottoveste *f*; ⟨*for pillow*⟩ federa *f*; ⟨*paper*⟩ scontrino m; **give sb the ~** *fam* sbarazzarsi di qcno; **~ of the tongue** lapsus m *inv* ● *v* ⟨*pt/pp* **slipped**⟩ ● *vi* scivolare; ⟨*go quickly*⟩ sgattaiolare; ⟨*decline*⟩ retrocedere ● *vt* **he ~ped it into his pocket** se l'è infilato in tasca; **~ sb's mind** sfuggire di mente a qcno. **slip away** *vi* sgusciar via; ⟨*time:*⟩ sfuggire. **slip into** *vi* infilarsi ⟨*clothes*⟩. **slip up** *vi fam* sbagliare

slipped 'disc *n Med* ernia *f* del disco

slipper /'slɪpə(r)/ *n* pantofola *f*

slippery /'slɪpərɪ/ *a* scivoloso

slip-road *n* bretella *f*

slipshod /'slɪpʃɒd/ *a* trascurato

'slip-up *n fam* sbaglio m

slit /slɪt/ n spacco m; (*tear*) strappo m; (*hole*) fessura f ● vt (*pt/pp* **slit**) tagliare

slither /ˈslɪðə(r)/ vi scivolare

sliver /ˈslɪvə(r)/ n scheggia f

slobber /ˈslɒbə(r)/ vi sbavare

slog /slɒg/ n [hard] ~ sgobbata f ● vi (*pt/pp* **slogged**) (*work*) sgobbare

slogan /ˈsləʊgən/ n slogan m inv

slop /slɒp/ v (*pt/pp* **slopped**) ● vt versare. **slop over** vi versarsi

slop|e /sləʊp/ n pendenza f; (*ski* ~) pista f ● vi essere inclinato, inclinarsi. **~ing** a in pendenza

sloppy /ˈslɒpɪ/ a (**-ier, -iest**) (*work*) trascurato; (*worker*) negligente; (*in dress*) sciatto; (*sentimental*) sdolcinato

slosh /slɒʃ/ vi fam (*person, feet:*) sguazzare; (*water:*) scrosciare ● vt (*fam: hit*) colpire

sloshed /slɒʃt/ a fam sbronzo

slot /slɒt/ n fessura f; (*time-*~) spazio m ● v (*pt/pp* **slotted**) ● vt infilare. **slot in** vi incastrarsi

'slot-machine n distributore m automatico; (*in gambling*) slot-machine f inv

slouch /slaʊtʃ/ vi (*in chair*) stare scomposto

Slovakia /sləˈvækɪə/ n Slovacchia f

Slovenia /sləˈviːnɪə/ n Slovenia f

slovenl|y /ˈslʌvnlɪ/ a sciatto. **~iness** n sciatteria f

slow /sləʊ/ a lento; **be ~** (*clock:*) essere indietro; **in ~ motion** al rallentatore ● adv lentamente ● **slow down/up** vt/i rallentare

slow: **~coach** n fam tartaruga f. **~ly** adv lentamente. **~ness** n lentezza f

sludge /slʌdʒ/ n fanghiglia f

slug /slʌg/ n lumacone m; (*fam: bullet*) pallottola f

sluggish /ˈslʌgɪʃ/ a lento

sluice /sluːs/ n chiusa f

slum /slʌm/ n (*house*) tugurio m; **~s** pl bassifondi mpl

slumber /ˈslʌmbə(r)/ vi dormire

slump /slʌmp/ n crollo m; (*economic*) depressione f ● vi crollare

slung /slʌŋ/ see **sling**

slur /slɜː(r)/ n (*discredit*) calunnia f ● vt (*pt/pp* **slurred**) biascicare

slurp /slɜːp/ vt/i bere rumorosamente

slush /slʌʃ/ n pantano m nevoso; fig sdolcinatezza f. **~ fund** n fondi mpl neri

slushy /ˈslʌʃɪ/ a fangoso; (*sentimental*) sdolcinato

slut /slʌt/ n sgualdrina f

sly /slaɪ/ a (**-er, -est**) scaltro ● n on the ~ di nascosto

smack¹ /smæk/ n (*on face*) schiaffo m; (*on bottom*) sculaccione m ● vt (*on face*) schiaffeggiare; (*on bottom*) sculacciare; **~ one's lips** far schioccare le labbra ● adv fam in pieno

smack² vi ~ **of** fig sapere di

small /smɔːl/ a piccolo; **be out/work until the ~ hours** fare le ore piccole ● adv **chop up ~** fare a pezzettini ● n **the ~ of the back** le reni

small: **~ ads** npl annunci mpl [commerciali]. **~ change** n spiccioli mpl. **~-holding** n piccola tenuta f. **~pox** n vaiolo m. **~ talk** n chiacchiere fpl

smarmy /ˈsmɑːmɪ/ a (**-ier, -iest**) fam untuoso

smart /smɑːt/ a elegante; (*clever*) intelligente; (*brisk*) svelto; **be ~** (*fam: cheeky*) fare il furbo ● vi (*hurt*) bruciare

smarten /ˈsmɑːtn/ vt ~ **oneself up** farsi bello

smash /smæʃ/ n fragore m; (*collision*) scontro m; *Tennis* schiacciata f ● vt spaccare; *Tennis* schiacciare ● vi spaccarsi; (*crash*) schiantarsi (**into** contro). **~ [hit]** n successo m. **~ing** a fam fantastico

smattering /ˈsmætərɪŋ/ n infarinatura f

smear /smɪə(r)/ n macchia f; *Med* striscio m ● vt imbrattare; (*coat*) spalmare (**with** di); fig calunniare

smell /smel/ n odore m; (*sense*) odorato m ● v (*pt/pp* **smelt** or **smelled**) ● vt odorare; (*sniff*) annusare ● vi odorare (**of** di)

smelly /ˈsmelɪ/ a (**-ier, -iest**) puzzolente

smelt¹ /smelt/ see **smell**

smelt² vt fondere

smile /smaɪl/ n sorriso m ● vi sorridere; **~ at** sorridere a (*sb*); sorridere di (*sth*)

smirk /smɜːk/ n sorriso m compiaciuto

smithereens /smɪðəˈriːnz/ npl **to/in ~** in mille pezzi

smitten /ˈsmɪtn/ a ~ **with** tutto preso da

smock /smɒk/ n grembiule m

smoke /sməʊk/ n fumo m ● vt/i fumare. **~less** a senza fumo; (*fuel*) che non fa fumo

smoker /ˈsməʊkə(r)/ n fumatore, -trice mf; *Rail* vagone m fumatori

'smoke-screen n cortina f di fumo

smoking /ˈsməʊkɪŋ/ n fumo m; **'no ~'** 'vietato fumare'

smoky /'sməʊkɪ/ a (**-ier, -iest**) fumoso; ⟨taste⟩ di fumo

smooth /smu:ð/ a liscio; ⟨movement⟩ scorrevole; ⟨sea⟩ calmo; ⟨manners⟩ mellifluo ● vt lisciare. **smooth out** vt lisciare. **~ly** adv in modo scorrevole

smother /'smʌðə(r)/ vt soffocare

smoulder /'sməʊldə(r)/ vi fumare; (with rage) consumarsi

smudge /smʌdʒ/ n macchia f ● vt/i imbrattare

smug /smʌg/ a (**smugger, smuggest**) compiaciuto. **~ly** adv con aria compiaciuta

smuggl|e /'smʌgl/ vt contrabbandare. **~er** n contrabbandiere, -a mf. **~ing** n contrabbando m

smut /smʌt/ n macchia f di fuliggine; fig sconcezza f

smutty /'smʌtɪ/ a (**-ier, -iest**) fuligginoso; fig sconcio

snack /snæk/ n spuntino m. **~-bar** n snack bar m inv

snag /snæg/ n (problem) intoppo m

snail /sneɪl/ n lumaca f; **at a ~'s pace** a passo di lumaca

snake /sneɪk/ n serpente m

snap /snæp/ n colpo m secco; (photo) istantanea f ● attrib ⟨decision⟩ istantaneo ● v (pt/pp **snapped**) ● vi (break) spezzarsi; **~ at** ⟨dog:⟩ cercare di azzannare; ⟨person:⟩ parlare seccamente a ● vt (break) spezzare; (say) dire seccamente; Phot fare un'istantanea di. **snap up** vt afferrare

snappy /'snæpɪ/ a (**-ier, -iest**) scorbutico; (smart) elegante; **make it ~!** sbrigati!

'snapshot n istantanea f

snare /sneə(r)/ n trappola f

snarl /snɑ:l/ n ringhio m ● vi ringhiare

snatch /snætʃ/ n strappo m; (fragment) brano m; (theft) scippo m; **make a ~ at sth** cercare di afferrare qcsa ● vt strappare [di mano] (**from** a); (steal) scippare; rapire ⟨child⟩

sneak /sni:k/ n fam spia mf ● vi (fam: tell tales) fare la spia ● vt (take) rubare; **~ a look at** dare una sbirciata a. **sneak in/out** vi sgattaiolare dentro/fuori

sneakers /'sni:kəz/ npl Am scarpe fpl da ginnastica

sneaking /'sni:kɪŋ/ a furtivo; ⟨suspicion⟩ vago

sneaky /'sni:kɪ/ a sornione

sneer /snɪə(r)/ n ghigno m ● vi sogghignare; (mock) ridere di

sneeze /sni:z/ n starnuto m ● vi starnutire

snide /snaɪd/ a fam insinuante

sniff /snɪf/ n (of dog) annusata f ● vi tirare su col naso ● vt odorare ⟨flower⟩; sniffare ⟨glue, cocaine⟩; ⟨dog:⟩ annusare

snigger /'snɪgə(r)/ n risatina f soffocata ● vi ridacchiare

snip /snɪp/ n taglio m; (fam: bargain) affare m ● vt/i (pt/pp **snipped**) **~ [at]** tagliare

snipe /snaɪp/ vi **~ at** tirare su; fig sparare a zero su. **~r** n cecchino m

snippet /'snɪpɪt/ n **a ~ of information/news** una breve notizia/informazione

snivel /'snɪvl/ vi (pt/pp **snivelled**) piagnucolare. **~ling** a piagnucoloso

snob /snɒb/ n snob mf inv. **~bery** n snobismo m. **~bish** a da snob

snooker /'snu:kə(r)/ n snooker m

snoop /snu:p/ n spia f ● vi fam curiosare

snooty /'snu:tɪ/ a fam sdegnoso

snooze /snu:z/ n sonnellino m ● vi fare un sonnellino

snore /snɔ:(r)/ vi russare

snorkel /'snɔ:kl/ n respiratore m

snort /snɔ:t/ n sbuffo n ● vi sbuffare

snout /snaʊt/ n grugno m

snow /snəʊ/ n neve f ● vi nevicare; **~ed under with** fig sommerso di

snow: **~ball** n palla f di neve ● vi fare a palle di neve. **~-drift** n cumulo m di neve. **~drop** n bucaneve m inv. **~fall** n nevicata f. **~flake** n fiocco m di neve. **~man** n pupazzo m di neve. **~-plough** n spazzaneve m inv. **~storm** n tormenta f. **~y** a nevoso

snub /snʌb/ n sgarbo m ● vt (pt/pp **snubbed**) snobbare

'snub-nosed a dal naso all'insù

snuff /snʌf/ n tabacco m da fiuto

snug /snʌg/ a (**snugger, snuggest**) comodo; (tight) aderente

snuggle /'snʌgl/ vi rannicchiarsi (**up to** accanto a)

so /səʊ/ adv così; **so far** finora; **so am I** anch'io; **so I see** così pare; **that is so** è così; **so much** così tanto; **so much the better** tanto meglio; **so it is** proprio così; **if so** se è così; **so as to** in modo da; **so long!** fam a presto! ● pron **I hope/think/am afraid so** spero/penso/temo di sì; **I told you so** te l'ho detto; **because I say so** perché lo dico io; **I did so!** è vero!; **so saying/doing,...** così dicendo/facendo,...; **or so**

209

soak | somebody

circa; **very much so** sì, molto; **and so forth** or **on** e così via ● conj (therefore) perciò; (in order that) così; **so that** affinché; **so there!** ecco!; **so what?** e allora?; **so where have you been?** allora, dove sei stato?

soak /səʊk/ vt mettere a bagno● vi stare a bagno; ~ **into** ⟨liquid:⟩ penetrare. **soak up** vt assorbire

soaking /'səʊkɪŋ/ n ammollo m ● a & adv ~ **[wet]** fam inzuppato

so-and-so /'səʊənsəʊ/ n Tal dei Tali mf; (euphemism) specie f di imbecille

soap /səʊp/ n sapone m. ~ **opera** n telenovella f, soap opera f inv. ~ **powder** n detersivo m in polvere

soapy /'səʊpɪ/ a (-ier, -iest) insaponato

soar /sɔː(r)/ vi elevarsi; ⟨prices:⟩ salire alle stelle

sob /sɒb/ n singhiozzo m ● vi (pt/pp **sobbed**) singhiozzare

sober /'səʊbə(r)/ a sobrio; (serious) serio ● **sober up** vi ritornare sobrio

'so-called a cosiddetto

soccer /'sɒkə(r)/ n calcio m

sociable /'səʊʃəbl/ a socievole

social /'səʊʃl/ a sociale; (sociable) socievole

socialis|m /'səʊʃəlɪzm/ n socialismo m. ~**t** /-ɪst/ a socialista ● n socialista mf

socialize /'səʊʃəlaɪz/ vi socializzare

socially /'səʊʃəlɪ/ adv socialmente; **know sb** ~ frequentare qcno

social: ~ **se'curity** n previdenza f sociale. ~ **work** n assistenza f sociale. ~ **worker** n assistente mf sociale

society /sə'saɪətɪ/ n società f inv

sociolog|ist /səʊsɪ'ɒlədʒɪst/ n sociologo, -a mf. ~**y** n sociologia f

sock¹ /sɒk/ n calzino m; (kneelength) calza f

sock² fam n pugno m ● vt dare un pugno a

socket /'sɒkɪt/ n (wall plug) presa f [di corrente]; (for bulb) portalampada m inv

soda /'səʊdə/ n soda f; Am gazzosa f. ~ **water** n seltz m inv

sodden /'sɒdn/ a inzuppato

sodium /'səʊdɪəm/ n sodio m

sofa /'səʊfə/ n divano m. ~ **bed** n divano m letto

soft /sɒft/ a morbido, soffice; ⟨voice⟩ sommesso; ⟨light, colour⟩ tenue; (not strict) indulgente; (fam: silly) stupido; **have a** ~ **spot for sb** avere un debole per qcno. ~ **drink** n bibita f analcolica

soften /'sɒfn/ vt ammorbidire; fig attenuare ● vi ammorbidirsi

softly /'sɒftlɪ/ adv (say) sottovoce; (treat) con indulgenza; (play music) in sottofondo

soft: ~ **toy** n pupazzo m di peluche. ~**ware** n software m

soggy /'sɒgɪ/ a (-ier, -iest) zuppo

soil¹ /sɔɪl/ n suolo m

soil² vt sporcare

solar /'səʊlə(r)/ a solare

sold /səʊld/ see **sell**

solder /'səʊldə(r)/ n lega f da saldatura ● vt saldare

soldier /'səʊldʒə(r)/ n soldato m ● **soldier on** vi perseverare

sole¹ /səʊl/ n (of foot) pianta f; (of shoe) suola f

sole² n (fish) sogliola f

sole³ a unico, solo. ~**ly** adv unicamente

solemn /'sɒləm/ a solenne. ~**ity** /sə'lemnətɪ/ n solennità f inv

solicit /sə'lɪsɪt/ vt sollecitare ● vi ⟨prostitute:⟩ adescare

solicitor /sə'lɪsɪtə(r)/ n avvocato m

solid /'sɒlɪd/ a solido; ⟨oak, gold⟩ massiccio ● n (figure) solido m; ~**s** pl (food) cibi mpl solidi

solidarity /sɒlɪ'dærətɪ/ n solidarietà f inv

solidify /sə'lɪdɪfaɪ/ vi (pt/pp **-ied**) solidificarsi

soliloquy /sə'lɪləkwɪ/ n soliloquio m

solitaire /sɒlɪ'teə(r)/ n solitario m

solitary /'sɒlɪtərɪ/ a solitario; (sole) solo. ~ **con'finement** n cella f di isolamento

solitude /'sɒlɪtjuːd/ n solitudine f

solo /'səʊləʊ/ n Mus assolo m ● a ⟨flight⟩ in solitario ● adv in solitario. ~**ist** n solista mf

solstice /'sɒlstɪs/ n solstizio m

soluble /'sɒljʊbl/ a solubile

solution /sə'luːʃn/ n soluzione f

solve /sɒlv/ vt risolvere

solvent /'sɒlvənt/ a solvente ● n solvente m

sombre /'sɒmbə(r)/ a tetro; ⟨clothes⟩ scuro

some /sʌm/ a (a certain amount of) del; (a certain number of) qualche, alcuni; ~ **day** un giorno o l'altro; **I need** ~ **money/books** ho bisogno di soldi/libri; **do** ~ **shopping** fare qualche acquisto ● pron (a certain amount) un po'; (a certain number) alcuni; **I want** ~ ne voglio

some: ~**body** /-bədɪ/ pron & n qualcuno *m*. **~how** *adv* in qualche modo; **~how or other** in un modo o nell'altro. **~one** *pron & n* = **somebody**

somersault /'sʌməsɔːlt/ *n* capriola *f*; **turn a ~** fare una capriola

'something *pron* qualche cosa, qualcosa; **~ different** qualcosa di diverso; **~ like** un po' come; (*approximately*) qualcosa come; **see ~ of sb** vedere qcno un po'

some: **~time** *adv* un giorno o l'altro; **~time last summer** durante l'estate scorsa. **~times** *adv* qualche volta. **~what** *adv* piuttosto. **~where** *adv* da qualche parte ● *pron* **~where to eat** un posto in cui mangiare

son /sʌn/ *n* figlio *m*

sonata /sə'nɑːtə/ *n* sonata *f*

song /sɒŋ/ *n* canzone *f*

sonic /'sɒnɪk/ *a* sonico. **~ 'boom** *n* bang *m inv* sonico

'son-in-law *n* (*pl* **~s-in-law**) genero *m*

sonnet /'sɒnɪt/ *n* sonetto *m*

soon /suːn/ *adv* presto; (*in a short time*) tra poco; **as ~ as** [non] appena; **as ~ as possible** il più presto possibile; **~er or later** prima o poi; **the ~er the better** prima è, meglio è; **no ~er had I arrived than...** ero appena arrivato quando...; **I would ~er go** preferirei andare; **~ after** subito dopo

soot /sʊt/ *n* fuliggine *f*

sooth|e /suːð/ *vt* calmare

sooty /'sʊtɪ/ *a* fuligginoso

sophisticated /sə'fɪstɪkeɪtɪd/ *a* sofisticato

soporific /sɒpə'rɪfɪk/ *a* soporifero

sopping /'sɒpɪŋ/ *a & adv* **be ~ [wet]** essere bagnato fradicio

soppy /'sɒpɪ/ *a* (**-ier, -iest**) *fam* svenevole

soprano /sə'prɑːnəʊ/ *n* soprano *m*

sordid /'sɔːdɪd/ *a* sordido

sore /sɔː(r)/ *a* dolorante; (*Am: vexed*) arrabbiato; **it's ~** fa male; **have a ~ throat** avere mal di gola ● *n* piaga *f*. **~ly** *adv* (*tempted*) seriamente

sorrow /'sɒrəʊ/ *n* tristezza *f*. **~ful** *a* triste

sorry /'sɒrɪ/ *a* (**-ier, -iest**) (*sad*) spiacente; (*wretched*) pietoso; **you'll be ~!** te ne pentirai!; **I am ~** mi dispiace; **be or feel ~ for** provare compassione per; **~!** scusa!; (*more polite*) scusi!

sort /sɔːt/ *n* specie *f*; (*fam: person*) tipo *m*; **it's a ~ of fish** è un tipo di pesce; **be out of ~s** (*fam: unwell*) stare poco bene ● *vt* classificare. **sort out** *vt* sele-

zionare ⟨*papers*⟩; *fig* risolvere ⟨*problem*⟩; occuparsi di ⟨*person*⟩

'so-so *a & adv* così così

sought /sɔːt/ *see* **seek**

soul /səʊl/ *n* anima *f*

sound¹ /saʊnd/ *a* sano; (*sensible*) saggio; (*secure*) solido; (*thrashing*) clamoroso ● *adv* **~ asleep** profondamente addormentato

sound² *n* suono *m*; (*noise*) rumore *m*; **I don't like the ~ of it** *fam* non mi suona bene ● *vi* suonare; (*seem*) aver l'aria ● *vt* (*pronounce*) pronunciare; *Med* auscultare ⟨*chest*⟩. **~ barrier** *n* muro *m* del suono. **~ card** *n* *Comput* scheda *f* sonora. **~less** *a* silenzioso. **sound out** *vt fig* sondare

soundly /'saʊndlɪ/ *adv* ⟨*sleep*⟩ profondamente; ⟨*defeat*⟩ clamorosamente

'sound: **~proof** *a* impenetrabile al suono. **~-track** *n* colonna *f* sonora

soup /suːp/ *n* minestra *f*. **~ed-up** *a* *fam* ⟨*engine*⟩ truccato

soup: **~-plate** *n* piatto *m* fondo. **~-spoon** *n* cucchiaio *m* da minestra

sour /'saʊə(r)/ *a* agro; (*not fresh & fig*) acido

source /sɔːs/ *n* fonte *f*

south /saʊθ/ *n* sud *m*; **to the ~ of** a sud di ● *a* del sud, meridionale ● *adv* verso il sud

south: **S~ 'Africa** *n* Sudafrica *f*. **S~ A'merica** *n* America *f* del Sud. **S~ American** *a & n* sud-americano, -a *mf*. **~-'east** *n* sud-est *m*

southerly /'sʌðəlɪ/ *a* del sud

southern /'sʌðən/ *a* del sud, meridionale; **~ Italy** il Mezzogiorno. **~er** *n* meridionale *mf*

South 'Pole *n* polo *m* Sud

'southward[s] /-wəd[z]/ *adv* verso sud

souvenir /suːvə'nɪə(r)/ *n* ricordo *m*, souvenir *m inv*

sovereign /'sɒvrɪn/ *a* sovrano ● *n* sovrano, -a *mf*. **~ty** *n* sovranità *f inv*

Soviet /'səʊvɪət/ *a* sovietico; **~ Union** Unione *f* Sovietica

sow¹ /saʊ/ *n* scrofa *f*

sow² /səʊ/ *vt* (*pt* **sowed**, *pp* **sown** or **sowed**) seminare

soya /'sɔɪə/ *n* **~ bean** soia *f*

spa /spɑː/ *n* stazione *f* termale

space /speɪs/ *n* spazio *m* ● *a* ⟨*research etc*⟩ spaziale ● *vt* **~ [out]** distanziare

space: **~ship** *n* astronave *f*. **~ shuttle** *n* navetta *f* spaziale

spacious /'speɪʃəs/ *a* spazioso

spade /speɪd/ n vanga f; (for child) paletta f; **~s** pl (in cards) picche fpl. **~work** n lavoro m preparatorio

Spain /speɪn/ n Spagna f

span[1] /spæn/ n spanna f; (of arch) luce f; (of time) arco m; (of wings) apertura f ● vt (pt/pp **spanned**) estendersi su

span[2] see **spick**

Span|iard /'spænjəd/ n spagnolo, -a mf. **~ish** a spagnolo ● n (language) spagnolo m; **the ~ish** pl gli spagnoli

spank /spæŋk/ vt sculacciare. **~ing** n sculacciata f

spanner /'spænə(r)/ n chiave f inglese

spar /spɑː(r)/ vi (pt/pp **sparred**) (boxing) allenarsi; (argue) litigare

spare /speə(r)/ a (surplus) in più; (additional) di riserva ● n (part) ricambio m ● vt risparmiare; (do without) fare a meno di; **can you ~ five minutes?** avresti cinque minuti?; **to ~** (surplus) in eccedenza. **~ part** n pezzo m di ricambio. **~ time** n tempo m libero. **~ 'wheel** n ruota f di scorta

sparing /'speərɪŋ/ a parco (**with** di). **~ly** adv con parsimonia

spark /spɑːk/ n scintilla f. **~ing-plug** n Auto candela f

sparkl|e /'spɑːkl/ n scintillio m ● vi scintillare. **~ing** a frizzante; ⟨wine⟩ spumante

sparrow /'spærəʊ/ n passero m

sparse /spɑːs/ a rado. **~ly** adv scarsamente; **~ly populated** a bassa densità di popolazione

spartan /'spɑːtn/ a spartano

spasm /'spæzm/ n spasmo m. **~odic** /-'mɒdɪk/ a spasmodico

spastic /'spæstɪk/ a spastico ● n spastico, -a mf

spat /spæt/ see **spit**[1]

spate /speɪt/ n (series) successione f; **be in full ~** essere in piena

spatial /'speɪʃl/ a spaziale

spatter /'spætə(r)/ vt schizzare

spatula /'spætjʊlə/ n spatola f

spawn /spɔːn/ n uova fpl (di pesci, rane ecc) ● vi deporre le uova ● vt fig generare

spay /speɪ/ vt sterilizzare

speak /spiːk/ v (pt **spoke**, pp **spoken**) ● vi parlare (**to** a); **~ing!** Teleph sono io! ● vt dire; **~ one's mind** dire quello che si pensa. **speak for** vi parlare a nome di. **speak up** vi parlare più forte; **~ up for oneself** farsi valere

speaker /'spiːkə(r)/ n parlante mf; (in public) oratore, -trice mf; (of stereo) cassa f

spear /spɪə(r)/ n lancia f

spec /spek/ n **on ~** fam senza certezza

special /'speʃl/ a speciale. **~ist** n specialista mf. **~ity** /-ʃɪ'ælətɪ/ n specialità f inv

special|ize /'speʃəlaɪz/ vi specializzarsi. **~ly** adv specialmente; (particularly) particolarmente

species /'spiːʃiːz/ n specie f inv

specific /spə'sɪfɪk/ a specifico. **~ally** adv in modo specifico

specifications /spesɪfɪ'keɪʃnz/ npl descrizione f

specify /'spesɪfaɪ/ vt (pt/pp **-ied**) specificare

specimen /'spesɪmən/ n campione m

speck /spek/ n macchiolina f; (particle) granello m

speckled /'spekld/ a picchiettato

specs /speks/ npl fam occhiali mpl

spectacle /'spektəkl/ n (show) spettacolo m. **~s** npl occhiali mpl

spectacular /spek'tækjʊlə(r)/ a spettacolare

spectator /spek'teɪtə(r)/ n spettatore, -trice mf

spectre /'spektə(r)/ n spettro m

spectrum /'spektrəm/ n (pl **-tra**) spettro m; fig gamma f

speculat|e /'spekjʊleɪt/ vi speculare. **~ion** /-'leɪʃn/ n speculazione f. **~ive** /-ɪv/ a speculativo. **~or** n speculatore, -trice mf

sped /sped/ see **speed**

speech /spiːtʃ/ n linguaggio m; (address) discorso m. **~less** a senza parole

speed /spiːd/ n velocità f inv; (gear) marcia f; **at ~** a tutta velocità ● vi (pt/pp **sped**) andare veloce; (pt/pp **speeded**) (go too fast) andare a velocità eccessiva. **speed up** (pt/pp **speeded up**) vt/i accelerare

'speedboat n motoscafo m

speedily /'spiːdɪlɪ/ adv rapidamente

speeding /'spiːdɪŋ/ n eccesso m di velocità

'speed limit n limite m di velocità

speedometer /spiː'dɒmɪtə(r)/ n tachimetro m

speedy /'spiːdɪ/ a (**-ier, -iest**) rapido

spell[1] /spel/ n (turn) turno m; (of weather) periodo m

spell[2] v (pt/pp **spelled** or **spelt**) ● vt **how do you ~...?** come si scrive...?; **could you ~ that for me?** me lo può compitare?; **~ disaster** essere disastroso ● *vi* **he can't ~** fa molti errori d'ortografia

spell³ *n* (*magic*) incantesimo *m*. **~bound** *a* affascinato

spelling /'spelɪŋ/ *n* ortografia *f*

spelt /spelt/ *see* **spell²**

spend /spend/ *vt/i* (*pt/pp* **spent**) spendere; passare ⟨*time*⟩

spent /spent/ *see* **spend**

sperm /spɜːm/ *n* spermatozoo *m*; (*semen*) sperma *m*

spew /spjuː/ *vt/i* vomitare

spher|e /sfɪə(r)/ *n* sfera *f*. **~ical** /'sferɪkl/ *a* sferico

spice /spaɪs/ *n* spezia *f*; *fig* pepe *m*

spick /spɪk/ *a* **~ and span** lindo

spicy /'spaɪsɪ/ *a* piccante

spider /'spaɪdə(r)/ *n* ragno *m*

spik|e /spaɪk/ *n* punta *f*; *Bot, Zool* spina *f*; (*on shoe*) chiodo *m*. **~y** *a* ⟨*plant*⟩ pungente

spill /spɪl/ *v* (*pt/pp* **spilt** *or* **spilled**) ● *vt* versare ● *vi* rovesciarsi

spin /spɪn/ *v* (*pt/pp* **spun**, *pres p* **spinning**) ● *vt* far girare; filare ⟨*wool*⟩; centrifugare ⟨*washing*⟩ ● *vi* girare; ⟨*washing machine:*⟩ centrifugare ● *n* rotazione *f*; (*short drive*) giretto *m*. **spin out** *vt* far durare

spinach /'spɪnɪdʒ/ *n* spinaci *mpl*

spinal /'spaɪnl/ *a* spinale. **~ 'cord** *n* midollo *m* spinale

spindl|e /'spɪndl/ *n* fuso *m*. **~y** *a* affusolato

spin-'drier *n* centrifuga *f*

spine /spaɪn/ *n* spina *f* dorsale; (*of book*) dorso *m*; *Bot, Zool* spina *f*. **~less** *a* *fig* smidollato

spinning /'spɪnɪŋ/ *n* filatura *f*. **~-wheel** *n* filatoio *m*

'spin-off *n* ricaduta *f*

spiral /'spaɪrəl/ *a* a spirale ● *n* spirale *f* ● *vi* (*pt/pp* **spiralled**) formare una spirale. **~ 'staircase** *n* scala *f* a chiocciola

spire /'spaɪə(r)/ *n* guglia *f*

spirit /'spɪrɪt/ *n* spirito *m*; (*courage*) ardore *m*; **~s** *pl* (*alcohol*) liquori *mpl*; **in good ~s** di buon umore; **in low ~s** abbattuto

spirited /'spɪrɪtɪd/ *a* vivace; (*courageous*) pieno d'ardore

spirit: ~-level *n* livella *f* a bolla d'aria. **~ stove** *n* fornellino *m* [da campeggio]

spiritual /'spɪrɪtjʊəl/ *a* spirituale ● *n* spiritual *m*. **~ism** /-ɪzm/ *n* spiritismo *m*. **~ist** /-ɪst/ *n* spiritista *mf*

spit¹ /spɪt/ *n* (*for roasting*) spiedo *m*

spit² *n* sputo *m* ● *vt/i* (*pt/pp* **spat**, *pres*

p **spitting**) sputare; ⟨*cat:*⟩ soffiare; ⟨*fat:*⟩ sfrigolare; **it's ~ting [with rain]** pioviggina; **the ~ting image of** il ritratto spiccicato di

spite /spaɪt/ *n* dispetto *m*; **in ~ of** malgrado ● *vt* far dispetto a. **~ful** *a* indispettito

spittle /'spɪtl/ *n* saliva *f*

splash /splæʃ/ *n* schizzo *m*; (*of colour*) macchia *f*; (*fam: drop*) goccio *m* ● *vt* schizzare; **~ sb with sth** schizzare qcno di qcsa ● *vi* schizzare. **splash about** *vi* schizzarsi. **splash down** *vi* ⟨*spacecraft:*⟩ ammarare

spleen /spliːn/ *n* *Anat* milza *f*

splendid /'splendɪd/ *a* splendido

splendour /'splendə(r)/ *n* splendore *m*

splint /splɪnt/ *n* *Med* stecca *f*

splinter /'splɪntə(r)/ *n* scheggia *f* ● *vi* scheggiarsi

split /splɪt/ *n* fessura *f*; (*quarrel*) rottura *f*; (*division*) scissione *f*; (*tear*) strappo *m* ● *v* (*pt/pp* **split**, *pres p* **splitting**) ● *vt* spaccare; (*share, divide*) dividere; (*tear*) strappare ● *vi* spaccarsi; (*tear*) strapparsi; (*divide*) dividersi; **~ on sb** denunciare qcno ● *a* **a ~ second** una frazione di secondo. **split up** *vt* dividersi ● *vi* ⟨*couple:*⟩ separarsi

splutter /'splʌtə(r)/ *vi* farfugliare

spoil /spɔɪl/ *n* **~s** *pl* bottino *msg* ● *v* (*pt/pp* **spoilt** *or* **spoiled**) ● *vt* rovinare; viziare ⟨*person*⟩ ● *vi* andare a male. **~sport** *n* guastafeste *mf* *inv*

spoke¹ /spəʊk/ *n* raggio *m*

spoke², **spoken** /'spəʊkn/ *see* **speak**

'spokesman *n* portavoce *m* *inv*

sponge /spʌndʒ/ *n* spugna *f* ● *vt* pulire (*con la spugna*) ● *vi* **~ on** *fam* scroccare da. **~-cake** *n* pan *m* di Spagna

spong|er /'spʌndʒə(r)/ *n* scroccone, -a *mf*. **~y** *a* spugnoso

sponsor /'spɒnsə(r)/ *n* garante *mf*; *Radio, TV* sponsor *m* *inv*; (*god-parent*) padrino *m*, madrina *f*; (*for membership*) socio, -a *mf* garante ● *vt* sponsorizzare. **~ship** *n* sponsorizzazione *f*

spontaneous /spɒn'teɪnɪəs/ *a* spontaneo

spoof /spuːf/ *n* *fam* parodia *f*

spooky /'spuːkɪ/ *a* (**-ier, -iest**) *fam* sinistro

spool /spuːl/ *n* bobina *f*

spoon /spuːn/ *n* cucchiaio *m* ● *vt* mettere col cucchiaio. **~-feed** *vt* (*pt/pp* **-fed**) *fig* imboccare. **~ful** *n* cucchiaiata *f*

sporadic /spə'rædɪk/ *a* sporadico

sport /spɔːt/ *n* sport *m* *inv* ● *vt* sfoggia-

213 **sportscar | squash**

re. **~ing** *a* sportivo; **~ing chance** possibilità *f inv*

sports: ~car *n* automobile *f* sportiva. **~ coat** *n*, **~ jacket** *n* giacca *f* sportiva. **~man** *n* sportivo *m*. **~woman** *n* sportiva *f*

sporty /'spɔːtɪ/ *a* (**-ier, -iest**) sportivo

spot /spɒt/ *n* macchia *f*; (*pimple*) brufolo *m*; (*place*) posto *m*; (*in pattern*) pois *m inv*; (*of rain*) goccia *f*; (*of water*) goccio *m*; **~s** *pl* (*rash*) sfogo *msg*; **a ~ of** *fam* un po' di; **a ~ of bother** qualche problema; **on the ~** sul luogo; (*immediately*) immediatamente; **in a [tight] ~** *fam* in difficoltà ● *vt* (*pt/pp* **spotted**) macchiare; (*fam: notice*) individuare

spot: ~ 'check *n* (*without warning*) controllo *m* a sorpresa; **do a ~ check on sth** dare una controllata a qcsa. **~less** *a* immacolato. **~light** *n* riflettore *m*

spotted /'spɒtɪd/ *a* ⟨*material*⟩ a pois

spotty /'spɒtɪ/ *a* (**-ier, -iest**) (*pimply*) brufoloso

spouse /spaʊz/ *n* consorte *mf*

spout /spaʊt/ *n* becco *m* ● *vi* zampillare (**from** da)

sprain /spreɪn/ *n* slogatura *f* ● *vt* slogare

sprang /spræŋ/ *see* **spring²**

sprawl /sprɔːl/ *vi* (*in chair*) stravaccarsi; ⟨*city etc*⟩ estendersi; **go ~ing** (*fall*) cadere disteso

spray /spreɪ/ *n* spruzzo *m*; (*preparation*) spray *m inv*; (*container*) spruzzatore *m* ● *vt* spruzzare. **~-gun** *n* pistola *f* a spruzzo

spread /spred/ *n* estensione *f*; (*of disease*) diffusione *f*; (*paste*) crema *f*; (*fam: feast*) banchetto *m* ● *v* (*pt/pp* **spread**) ● *vt* spargere; spalmare ⟨*butter, jam*⟩; stendere ⟨*cloth, arms*⟩; diffondere ⟨*news, disease*⟩; dilazionare ⟨*payments*⟩; **~ sth with** spalmare qcsa di ● *vi* spargersi; ⟨*butter:*⟩ spalmarsi; ⟨*disease:*⟩ diffondersi. **~sheet** *n* Comput foglio *m* elettronico. **spread out** *vt* sparpagliare ● *vi* sparpagliarsi

spree /spriː/ *n fam* **go on a ~** far baldoria; **go on a shopping ~** fare spese folli

sprig /sprɪg/ *n* rametto *m*

sprightly /'spraɪtlɪ/ *a* (**-ier, -iest**) vivace

spring¹ /sprɪŋ/ *n* primavera *f* ● *attrib* primaverile

spring² *n* (*jump*) balzo *m*; (*water*) sor-gente *f*; (*device*) molla *f*; (*elasticity*) elasticità *f* ● *v* (*pt* **sprang**, *pp* **sprung**) ● *vi* balzare; (*arise*) provenire (**from** da) ● *vt* **he just sprang it on me** me l'ha detto a cose fatte compiuto. **spring up** balzare; *fig* spuntare

spring: ~board *n* trampolino *m*. **~-'cleaning** *n* pulizie *fpl* di Pasqua. **~time** *n* primavera *f*

sprinkl|e /'sprɪŋkl/ *vt* (*scatter*) spruzzare ⟨*liquid*⟩; spargere ⟨*flour, cocoa*⟩; **~ sth with** spruzzare qcsa di ⟨*liquid*⟩; cospargere qcsa di ⟨*flour, cocoa*⟩. **~er** *n* sprinkler *m inv*; (*for lawn*) irrigatore *m*. **~ing** *n* (*of liquid*) spruzzatina *f*; (*of pepper, salt*) pizzico *m*; (*of flour, sugar*) spolveratina *f*; (*of knowledge*) infarinatura *f*; (*of people*) pugno *m*

sprint /sprɪnt/ *n* sprint *m inv* ● *vi* fare uno sprint; *Sport* sprintare. **~er** *n* sprinter *mf inv*

sprout /spraʊt/ *n* germoglio *m*; [**Brussels**] **~s** *pl* cavolini *mpl* di Bruxelles ● *vi* germogliare

spruce /spruːs/ *a* elegante ● *n* abete *m*

sprung /sprʌŋ/ *see* **spring²** ● *a* molleggiato

spud /spʌd/ *n fam* patata *f*

spun /spʌn/ *see* **spin**

spur /spɜː(r)/ *n* sperone *m*; (*stimulus*) stimolo *m*; (*road*) svincolo *m*. **on the ~ of the moment** su due piedi ● *vt* (*pt/pp* **spurred**) **~ [on]** *fig* spronare [a]

spurious /'spjʊərɪəs/ *a* falso

spurn /spɜːn/ *vt* sdegnare

spurt /spɜːt/ *n* getto *m*; *Sport* scatto *m*; **put on a ~** fare uno scatto ● *vi* sprizzare; (*increase speed*) scattare

spy /spaɪ/ *n* spia *f* ● *v* (*pt/pp* **spied**) ● *vi* spiare ● *vt* (*fam: see*) spiare. **spy on** *vi* spiare

spying /'spaɪɪŋ/ *n* spionaggio *m*

squabble /'skwɒbl/ *n* bisticcio *m* ● *vi* bisticciare

squad /skwɒd/ *n* squadra *f*

squadron /'skwɒdrən/ *n Mil* squadrone *m*; *Aeron, Naut* squadriglia *f*

squalid /'skwɒlɪd/ *a* squallido

squalor /'skwɒlə(r)/ *n* squallore *m*

squander /'skwɒndə(r)/ *vt* sprecare

square /skweə(r)/ *a* quadrato; ⟨*meal*⟩ sostanzioso; (*fam: old-fashioned*) vecchio stampo; **all ~** *fam* pari ● *n* quadrato *m*; (*in city*) piazza *f*; (*on chessboard*) riquadro *m* ● *vt* (*settle*) far quadrare; *Math* elevare al quadrato ● *vi* (*agree*) armonizzare

squash /skwɒʃ/ *n* (*drink*) spremuta *f*;

(*sport*) squash *m*; (*vegetable*) zucca *f* ● *vt* schiacciare; soffocare ⟨*rebellion*⟩

squat /skwɒt/ *a* tarchiato ● *n fam* edificio *m* occupato abusivamente. ● *vi* (*pt/pp* **squatted**) accovacciarsi; **~ in** occupare abusivamente. **~ter** *n* occupante *mf* abusivo, -a

squawk /skwɔːk/ *n* gracchio *m* ● *vi* gracchiare

squeak /skwiːk/ *n* squittio *m*; (*of hinge, brakes*) scricchiolio *m* ● *vi* squittire; ⟨*hinge, brakes:*⟩ scricchiolare

squeal /skwiːl/ *n* strillo *m*; (*of brakes*) cigolio *m* ● *vi* strillare; *sl* spifferare

squeamish /ˈskwiːmɪʃ/ *a* dallo stomaco delicato

squeeze /skwiːz/ *n* stretta *f*; (*crush*) pigia pigia *m inv* ● *vt* premere; (*to get juice*) spremere; stringere ⟨*hand*⟩; (*force*) spingere a forza; (*fam: extort*) estorcere (**out of** da). **squeeze in/out** *vi* sgusciare dentro/fuori. **squeeze up** *vi* stringersi

squelch /skweltʃ/ *vi* sguazzare

squid /skwɪd/ *n* calamaro *m*

squiggle /ˈskwɪgl/ *n* scarabocchio *m*

squint /skwɪnt/ *n* strabismo *m* ● *vi* essere strabico

squire /ˈskwaɪə(r)/ *n* signorotto *m* di campagna

squirm /skwɜːm/ *vi* contorcersi; (*feel embarrassed*) sentirsi imbarazzato

squirrel /ˈskwɪrəl/ *n* scoiattolo *m*

squirt /skwɜːt/ *n* spruzzo *m*; (*fam: person*) presuntuoso *m* ● *vt/i* spruzzare

St *abbr* (**Saint**) S; *abbr* **Street**

stab /stæb/ *n* pugnalata *f*, coltellata *f*; (*sensation*) fitta *f*; (*fam: attempt*) tentativo *m* ● *vt* (*pt/pp* **stabbed**) pugnalare, accoltellare

stability /stəˈbɪlətɪ/ *n* stabilità *f inv*

stabilize /ˈsteɪbɪlaɪz/ *vt* stabilizzare ● *vi* stabilizzarsi

stable¹ /ˈsteɪbl/ *a* stabile

stable² *n* stalla *f*; (*establishment*) scuderia *f*

stack /stæk/ *n* catasta *f*; (*of chimney*) comignolo *m*; (*chimney*) ciminiera *f*; (*fam: large quantity*) montagna *f* ● *vt* accatastare

stadium /ˈsteɪdɪəm/ *n* stadio *m*

staff /stɑːf/ *n* (*stick*) bastone *m*; (*employees*) personale *m*; (*teachers*) corpo *m* insegnante; *Mil* Stato *m* Maggiore ● *vt* fornire di personale. **~-room** *n Sch* sala *f* insegnanti

stag /stæg/ *n* cervo *m*

stage /steɪdʒ/ *n* palcoscenico *m*;

(*profession*) teatro *m*; (*in journey*) tappa *f*; (*in process*) stadio *m*; **go on the ~** darsi al teatro; **by** or **in ~s** a tappe ● *vt* mettere in scena; (*arrange*) organizzare

stage: ~ door *n* ingresso *m* degli artisti. **~ fright** *n* panico *m* da scena. **~ manager** *n* direttore, -trice *mf* di scena

stagger /ˈstægə(r)/ *vi* barcollare ● *vt* sbalordire; scaglionare ⟨*holidays etc*⟩; **I was ~ed** sono rimasto sbalordito ● *n* vacillamento *m*. **~ing** *a* sbalorditivo

stagnant /ˈstægnənt/ *a* stagnante

stagnat|e /stægˈneɪt/ *vi fig* [ri]stagnare. **~ion** /-ˈneɪʃn/ *n fig* inattività *f*

'stag party *n* addio *m* al celibato

staid /steɪd/ *a* posato

stain /steɪn/ *n* macchia *f*; (*for wood*) mordente *m* ● *vt* macchiare; ⟨*wood*⟩ dare il mordente a; **~ed glass** vetro *m* colorato; **~ed-glass window** vetrata *f* colorata. **~less** *a* senza macchia; ⟨*steel*⟩ inossidabile. **~ remover** *n* smacchiatore *m*

stair /steə(r)/ *n* gradino *m*; **~s** *pl* scale *fpl*. **~case** *n* scale *fpl*

stake /steɪk/ *n* palo *m*; (*wager*) posta *f*; *Comm* partecipazione *f*; **at ~** in gioco ● *vt* puntellare; (*wager*) scommettere

stale /steɪl/ *a* stantio; (*air*) viziato; (*uninteresting*) trito [e ritrito]. **~mate** *n* (*in chess*) stallo *m*; (*deadlock*) situazione *f* di stallo

stalk¹ /stɔːk/ *n* gambo *m*

stalk² *vt* inseguire ● *vi* camminare impettito

stall /stɔːl/ *n* box *m inv*; (*in market*) bancarella *f*. **~s** *pl Theat* platea *f* ● *vi* ⟨*engine:*⟩ spegnersi; *fig* temporeggiare ● *vt* far spegnere ⟨*engine*⟩; tenere a bada ⟨*person*⟩

stallion /ˈstæljən/ *n* stallone *m*

stalwart /ˈstɔːlwət/ *a* fedele

stamina /ˈstæmɪnə/ *n* [capacità *f inv* di] resistenza *f*

stammer /ˈstæmə(r)/ *n* balbettio *m* ● *vt/i* balbettare

stamp /stæmp/ *n* (*postage ~*) francobollo *m*; (*instrument*) timbro *m*; *fig* impronta *f* ● *vt* affrancare ⟨*letter*⟩; timbrare ⟨*bill*⟩; battere ⟨*feet*⟩. **stamp out** *vt* spegnere; *fig* soffocare

stampede /stæmˈpiːd/ *n* fuga *f* precipitosa, fuggi-fuggi *m inv fam* ● *vi* fuggire precipitosamente

stance /stɑːns/ *n* posizione *f*

stand /stænd/ *n* (*for bikes*) rastrelliera *f*; (*at exhibition*) stand *m inv*; (*in market*) bancarella *f*; (*in stadium*) gradinata *f*; *fig* posizione *f* ● *v* (*pt/pp* **stood**) ● *vi* stare in piedi; (*rise*) alzarsi [in piedi]; (*be*) trovarsi; (*be candidate*) essere candidato (**for** a); (*stay valid*) rimanere valido; **~ still** non muoversi; **I don't know where I ~** non so qual'è la mia posizione; **~ firm** *fig* tener duro; **~ together** essere solidali; **~ to lose/ gain** rischiare di perdere/vincere; **~ to reason** essere logico ● *vt* (*withstand*) resistere a; (*endure*) sopportare; (*place*) mettere; **~ a chance** avere una possibilità; **~ one's ground** tener duro; **~ the test of time** superare la prova del tempo; **~ sb a beer** offrire una birra a qcno. **stand by** *vi* stare a guardare; (*be ready*) essere pronto ● *vt* (*support*) appoggiare. **stand down** *vi* (*retire*) ritirarsi. **stand for** *vt* (*mean*) significare; (*tolerate*) tollerare. **stand in for** *vt* sostituire. **stand out** *vi* spiccare. **stand up** *vi* alzarsi [in piedi]. **stand up for** *vt* prendere le difese di; **~ up for oneself** farsi valere. **stand up to** *vt* affrontare

standard /'stændəd/ *a* standard; **be ~ practice** essere pratica corrente ● *n* standard *m inv*; *Techn* norma *f*; (*level*) livello *m*; (*quality*) qualità *f inv*; (*flag*) stendardo *m*; **~s** *pl* (*morals*) valori *mpl*; **~ of living** tenore *m* di vita. **~ize** *vt* standardizzare

'**standard lamp** *n* lampada *f* a stelo
'**stand-by** *n* riserva *f*; **on ~** (*at airport*) in lista d'attesa
'**stand-in** *n* controfigura *f*
standing /'stændɪŋ/ *a* (*erect*) in piedi; (*permanent*) permanente ● *n* posizione *f*; (*duration*) durata *f*. ~ '**order** *n* addebitamento *m* diretto. **~-room** *n* posti *mpl* in piedi
stand: **~-offish** /stænd'ɒfɪʃ/ *a* scostante. **~point** *n* punto *m* di vista. **~still** *n* come to a **~still** fermarsi; **at a ~still** in un periodo di stasi
stank /stæŋk/ *see* **stink**
staple[1] /'steɪpl/ *n* (*product*) prodotto *m* principale
staple[2] *n* graffa *f* ● *vt* pinzare. **~r** *n* pinzatrice *f*, cucitrice *f*
star /stɑː(r)/ *n* stella *f*; (*asterisk*) asterisco *m*; *Theat, Cinema, Sport* divo, -a *mf*, stella *f* ● *vi* (*pt/pp* **starred**) essere l'interprete principale
starboard /'stɑːbəd/ *n* tribordo *m*
starch /stɑːtʃ/ *n* amido *m* ● *vt* inamidare. **~y** *a* ricco di amido; *fig* compito
stare /steə(r)/ *n* sguardo *m* fisso ● *vi*

it's rude to ~ è da maleducati fissare la gente; **~ at** fissare; **~ into space** guardare nel vuoto
'**starfish** *n* stella *f* di mare
stark /stɑːk/ *a* austero; (*contrast*) forte ● *adv* completamente; **~ naked** completamente nudo
starling /'stɑːlɪŋ/ *n* storno *m*
'**starlit** *a* stellato
starry /'stɑːrɪ/ *a* stellato
start /stɑːt/ *n* inizio *m*; (*departure*) partenza *f*; (*jump*) sobbalzo *m*; **from the ~** [fin] dall'inizio; **for a ~** tanto per cominciare; **give sb a ~** *Sport* dare un vantaggio a qcno ● *vi* [in]cominciare; (*set out*) avviarsi; (*engine, car:*) partire; (*jump*) trasalire; **to ~ with,...** tanto per cominciare,... ● *vt* [in]cominciare; (*cause*) dare inizio a; (*found*) mettere su; mettere in moto (*car*); mettere in giro (*rumour*). **~er** *n* *Culin* primo *m* [piatto *m*]; (*in race: giving signal*) starter *m inv*; (*participant*) concorrente *mf*; *Auto* motorino *m* d'avviamento. **~ing-point** *n* punto *m* di partenza
startle /'stɑːtl/ *vt* far trasalire; (*news:*) sconvolgere
starvation /stɑːˈveɪʃn/ *n* fame *f*
starve /stɑːv/ *vi* morire di fame ● *vt* far morire di fame
stash /stæʃ/ *vt fam* **~ [away]** nascondere
state /steɪt/ *n* stato *m*; (*grand style*) pompa *f*; **~ of play** punteggio *m*; **be in a ~** (*person:*) essere agitato; **lie in ~** essere esposto ● *attrib* di Stato; *Sch* pubblico; (*with ceremony*) di gala ● *vt* dichiarare; (*specify*) precisare. **~less** *a* apolide
stately /'steɪtlɪ/ *a* (**-ier, -iest**) maestoso. **~ 'home** *n* dimora *f* signorile
statement /'steɪtmənt/ *n* dichiarazione *f*; *Jur* deposizione *f*; (*in banking*) estratto *m* conto; (*account*) rapporto *m*
'**statesman** *n* statista *m*
static /'stætɪk/ *a* statico
station /'steɪʃn/ *n* stazione *f*; (*police*) commissariato *m* ● *vt* appostare (*guard*); **be ~ed in Germany** essere di stanza in Germania. **~ary** /-ərɪ/ *a* immobile
stationer /'steɪʃənə(r)/ *n* **~'s [shop]** cartoleria *f*. **~y** *n* cartoleria *f*
'**station-wagon** *n Am* familiare *f*
statistic|al /stəˈtɪstɪkl/ *a* statistico. **~s** *n & pl* statistica *f*
statue /'stætjuː/ *n* statua *f*
stature /'stætʃə(r)/ *n* statura *f*

status /'steɪtəs/ *n* condizione *f*; *(high rank)* alto rango *m*. **~ symbol** *n* status symbol *m inv*

statut|e /'stætjuːt/ *n* statuto *m*. **~ory** *a* statutario

staunch /stɔːntʃ/ *a* fedele. **~ly** *adv* fedelmente

stave /steɪv/ *vt* **~ off** tenere lontano

stay /steɪ/ *n* soggiorno *m* ● *vi* restare, rimanere; *(reside)* alloggiare; **~ the night** passare la notte; **~ put** non muoversi ● *vt* **~ the course** resistere fino alla fine. **stay away** *vi* stare lontano. **stay behind** *vi* non andare con gli altri. **stay in** *vi* *(at home)* stare in casa; *Sch* restare a scuola dopo le lezioni. **stay up** *vi* stare su; ⟨*person:*⟩ stare alzato

stead /sted/ *n* in his **~** in sua vece; **stand sb in good ~** tornare utile a qcno. **~fast** *a* fedele; ⟨*refusal*⟩ fermo

steadily /'stedɪlɪ/ *adv* *(continually)* continuamente

steady /'stedɪ/ *a* **(-ier, -iest)** saldo, fermo; ⟨*breathing*⟩ regolare; ⟨*job, boyfriend*⟩ fisso; *(dependable)* serio

steak /steɪk/ *n* *(for stew)* spezzatino *m*; *(for grilling, frying)* bistecca *f*

steal /stiːl/ *v* *(pt* **stole***, pp* **stolen***)* ● *vt* rubare **(from** da). **steal in/out** *vi* entrare/uscire furtivamente

stealth /stelθ/ *n* **by ~** di nascosto. **~y** *a* furtivo

steam /stiːm/ *n* vapore *m*; **under one's own ~** *fam* da solo ● *vt* Culin cucinare a vapore ● *vi* fumare. **steam up** *vi* appannarsi

'steam-engine *n* locomotiva *f*

steamer /'stiːmə(r)/ *n* piroscafo *m*; *(saucepan)* pentola *f* a vapore

'steamroller *n* rullo *m* compressore

steamy /'stiːmɪ/ *a* appannato

steel /stiːl/ *n* acciaio *m* ● *vt* **~ oneself** temprarsi

steep[1] /stiːp/ *vt* *(soak)* lasciare a bagno

steep[2] *a* ripido; ⟨*fam: price*⟩ esorbitante. **~ly** *adv* ripidamente

steeple /'stiːpl/ *n* campanile *m*. **~chase** *n* corsa *f* ippica a ostacoli

steer /stɪə(r)/ *vt/i* guidare; **~ clear of** stare alla larga da. **~ing** *n* Auto sterzo *m*. **~ing-wheel** *n* volante *m*

stem[1] /stem/ *n* stelo *m*; *(of glass)* gambo *m*; *(of word)* radice *f* ● *vi* *(pt/pp* **stemmed***)* **~ from** derivare da

stem[2] *vt* *(pt/pp* **stemmed***)* contenere

stench /stentʃ/ *n* fetore *m*

step /step/ *n* passo *m*; *(stair)* gradino *m*; **~s** *pl* *(ladder)* scala *f* portatile; **in ~** al passo; **be out of ~** non stare al passo; **~ by ~** un passo alla volta ● *vi* *(pt/pp* **stepped***)* **~ into** entrare in; **~ out of** uscire da; **~ out of line** sgarrare. **step down** *vi fig* dimettersi. **step forward** *vi* farsi avanti. **step in** *vi fig* intervenire. **step up** *vt* *(increase)* aumentare

step: ~brother *n* fratellastro *m*. **~child** *n* figliastro, -a *mf*. **~daughter** *n* figliastra *f*. **~father** *n* patrigno *m*. **~-ladder** *n* scala *f* portatile. **~mother** *n* matrigna *f*

'stepping-stone *n* pietra *f* per guadare; *fig* trampolino *m*

step: ~sister *n* sorellastra *f*. **~son** *n* figliastro *m*

stereo /'sterɪəʊ/ *n* stereo *m*; **in ~** in stereofonia. **~phonic** /-'fɒnɪk/ *a* stereofonico

stereotype /'sterɪətaɪp/ *n* stereotipo *m*. **~d** *a* stereotipato

steril|e /'steraɪl/ *a* sterile. **~ity** /stə'rɪlətɪ/ *n* sterilità *f*

steriliz|ation /steralaɪ'zeɪʃn/ *n* sterilizzazione *f*. **~e** /'ster-/ *vt* sterilizzare

sterling /'stɜːlɪŋ/ *a* fig apprezzabile; **~ silver** argento *m* pregiato ● *n* sterlina *f*

stern[1] /stɜːn/ *a* severo

stern[2] *n* *(of boat)* poppa *f*

stethoscope /'steθəskəʊp/ *n* stetoscopio *m*

stew /stjuː/ *n* stufato *m*; **in a ~** *fam* agitato ● *vt/i* cuocere in umido; **~ed fruit** frutta *f* cotta

steward /'stjuːəd/ *n* *(at meeting)* organizzatore, -trice *mf*; *(on ship, aircraft)* steward *m inv*. **~ess** *n* hostess *f inv*

stick[1] /stɪk/ *n* bastone *m*; *(of celery, rhubarb)* gambo *m*; Sport mazza *f*

stick[2] *v* *(pt/pp* **stuck***)* ● *vt* *(stab)* [con]ficcare; *(glue)* attaccare; *(fam: put)* mettere; *(fam: endure)* sopportare ● *vi* *(adhere)* attaccarsi **(to** a); *(jam)* bloccarsi; **~ to** attenersi a ⟨*facts*⟩; mantenere ⟨*story*⟩; perseverare in ⟨*task*⟩; **~ at it** *fam* tener duro; **~ at nothing** *fam* non fermarsi di fronte a niente; **be stuck** ⟨*vehicle, person:*⟩ essere bloccato; ⟨*drawer:*⟩ essere incastrato; **be stuck with sth** *fam* farsi incastrare con qcsa. **stick out** *vi* *(project)* sporgere; *(fam: catch the eye)* risaltare ● *vt fam* fare ⟨*tongue*⟩. **stick up for** *vt fam* difendere

sticker /'stɪkə(r)/ *n* autoadesivo *m*

'sticking plaster *n* cerotto *m*

stick-in-the-mud *n* retrogrado *m*

stickler /'stɪklə(r)/ *n* **be a ~ for** tenere molto a

sticky /'stɪkɪ/ a (**-ier, -iest**) appiccicoso; (*adhesive*) adesivo; (*fig: difficult*) difficile

stiff /stɪf/ a rigido; ⟨*brush, task*⟩ duro; ⟨*person*⟩ controllato; ⟨*drink*⟩ forte; ⟨*penalty*⟩ severo; ⟨*price*⟩ alto; **bored ~** *fam* annoiato a morte; **~ neck** torcicollo *m*. **~en** *vt* irrigidire ● *vi* irrigidirsi. **~ness** *n* rigidità *f*

stifl|e /'staɪfl/ *vt* soffocare. **~ing** a soffocante

stigma /'stɪgmə/ *n* marchio *m*

stiletto /stɪ'letəʊ/ *n* stiletto *m*; **~ heels** tacchi *mpl* a spillo; **~s** (*pl: shoes*) scarpe *fpl* coi tacchi a spillo

still[1] /stɪl/ *n* distilleria *f*

still[2] a fermo; ⟨*drink*⟩ non gasato; **keep/stand ~** stare fermo ● *n* quiete *f*; (*photo*) posa *f* ● *adv* ancora; (*nevertheless*) nondimeno, comunque; **I'm ~ not sure** non sono ancora sicuro

'stillborn a nato morto

still 'life *n* natura *f* morta

stilted /'stɪltɪd/ a artificioso

stilts /stɪlts/ *npl* trampoli *mpl*

stimulant /'stɪmjʊlənt/ *n* eccitante *m*

stimulat|e /'stɪmjʊleɪt/ *vt* stimolare. **~ion** /-'leɪʃn/ *n* stimolo *m*

stimulus /'stɪmjʊləs/ *n* (*pl* **-li** /-laɪ/) stimolo *m*

sting /stɪŋ/ *n* puntura *f*; (*organ*) pungiglione *m* ● *v* (*pt/pp* **stung**) ● *vt* pungere; ⟨*jellyfish:*⟩ pizzicare ● *vi* ⟨*insect:*⟩ pungere. **~ing nettle** *n* ortica *f*

stingy /'stɪndʒɪ/ a (**-ier, -iest**) tirchio

stink /stɪŋk/ *n* puzza *f* ● *vi* (*pt* **stank**, *pp* **stunk**) puzzare

stint /stɪnt/ *n* lavoro *m*; **do one's ~** fare la propria parte ● *vt* **~ on** lesinare su

stipulat|e /'stɪpjʊleɪt/ *vt* porre come condizione. **~ion** /-'leɪʃn/ *n* condizione *f*

stir /stɜː(r)/ *n* mescolata *f*; (*commotion*) trambusto *m* ● *v* (*pt/pp* **stirred**) ● *vt* muovere; (*mix*) mescolare ● *vi* muoversi

stirrup /'stɪrəp/ *n* staffa *f*

stitch /stɪtʃ/ *n* punto *m*; (*in knitting*) maglia *f*; (*pain*) fitta *f*; **have sb in ~es** *fam* far ridere qcno a crepapelle ● *vt* cucire

stock /stɒk/ *n* (*for use or selling*) scorta *f*, stock *m inv*; (*livestock*) bestiame *m*; (*lineage*) stirpe *f*; *Fin* titoli *mpl*; *Culin* brodo *m*; **in ~** disponibile; **out of ~** esaurito; **take ~** *fig* fare il punto ● a solito ● *vt* ⟨*shop:*⟩ vendere; approvvigio-

nare ⟨*shelves*⟩. **stock up** *vi* far scorta (**with** di)

stock: ~broker *n* agente *m* di cambio. **~ cube** *n* dado *m* [da brodo]. **S~ Exchange** *n* Borsa *f* Valori

stocking /'stɒkɪŋ/ *n* calza *f*

stockist /'stɒkɪst/ *n* rivenditore *m*

stock: ~market *n* mercato *m* azionario. **~pile** *vt* fare scorta di ● *n* riserva *f*. **~-'still** a immobile. **~-taking** *n* *Comm* inventario *m*

stocky /'stɒkɪ/ a (**-ier, -iest**) tarchiato

stodgy /'stɒdʒɪ/ a indigesto

stoic /'stəʊɪk/ *n* stoico, -a *mf*. **~al** a stoico. **~ism** /-sɪzm/ *n* stoicismo *m*

stoke /stəʊk/ *vt* alimentare

stole[1] /stəʊl/ *n* stola *f*

stole[2], **stolen** /'stəʊln/ *see* **steal**

stolid /'stɒlɪd/ a apatico

stomach /'stʌmək/ *n* pancia *f*; *Anat* stomaco *m* ● *vt fam* reggere. **~-ache** *n* mal *m* di pancia

stone /stəʊn/ *n* pietra *f*; (*in fruit*) nocciolo *m*; *Med* calcolo *m*; (*weight*) 6,348 *kg* ● a di pietra; ⟨*wall, Age*⟩ della pietra ● *vt* snocciolare ⟨*fruit*⟩. **~-cold** a gelido. **~-'deaf** a *fam* sordo come una campana

stony /'stəʊnɪ/ a pietroso; ⟨*glare*⟩ glaciale

stood /stʊd/ *see* **stand**

stool /stuːl/ *n* sgabello *m*

stoop /stuːp/ *n* curvatura *f* ● *vi* stare curvo; (*bend down*) chinarsi; *fig* abbassarsi

stop /stɒp/ *n* (*break*) sosta *f*; (*for bus, train*) fermata *f*; *Gram* punto *m*; **come to a ~** fermarsi; **put a ~ to sth** mettere fine a qcsa ● *v* (*pt/pp* **stopped**) ● *vt* fermare; arrestare ⟨*machine*⟩; (*prevent*) impedire; **~ sb doing sth** impedire a qcno di fare qcsa; **~ doing sth** smettere di fare qcsa; **~ that!** smettila! ● *vi* fermarsi; ⟨*rain:*⟩ smettere ● *int* fermo!. **stop off** *vi* fare una sosta. **stop up** *vt* otturare ⟨*sink*⟩; tappare ⟨*hole*⟩. **stop with** *vi* (*fam: stay with*) fermarsi da

stop: ~gap *n* palliativo *m*; (*person*) tappabuchi *m inv*. **~-over** *n* sosta *f*; *Aeron* scalo *m*

stoppage /'stɒpɪdʒ/ *n* ostruzione *f*; (*strike*) interruzione *f*; (*deduction*) trattenute *fpl*

stopper /'stɒpə(r)/ *n* tappo *m*

stop: ~-press *n* ultimissime *fpl*. **~-watch** *n* cronometro *m*

storage /'stɔːrɪdʒ/ *n* deposito *m*; (*in*

warehouse) immagazzinaggio *m*; Comput memoria *f*

store /stɔ:(r)/ *n* (*stock*) riserva *f*; (*shop*) grande magazzino *m*; (*depot*) deposito *m*; **in ~** in deposito; **what the future has in ~ for me** cosa mi riserva il futuro; **set great ~ by** tenere in gran conto ● *vt* tenere; (*in warehouse, Comput*) immagazzinare. **~-room** *n* magazzino *m*

storey /'stɔ:rɪ/ *n* piano *m*

stork /stɔ:k/ *n* cicogna *f*

storm /stɔ:m/ *n* temporale *m*; (*with thunder*) tempesta *f* ● *vt* prendere d'assalto. **~y** *a* tempestoso

story /'stɔ:rɪ/ *n* storia *f*; (*in newspaper*) articolo *m*

stout /staʊt/ *a* (*shoes*) resistente; (*fat*) robusto; (*defence*) strenuo

stove /stəʊv/ *n* stufa *f*; (*for cooking*) cucina *f* [economica]

stow /stəʊ/ *vt* metter via. **~away** *n* passeggero, -a *mf* clandestino, -a

straddle /'strædl/ *vt* stare a cavalcioni su; (*standing*) essere a cavallo su

straggl|e /'strægl/ *vi* crescere disordinatamente; (*dawdle*) rimanere indietro. **~er** *n* persona *f* che rimane indietro. **~y** *a* in disordine

straight /streɪt/ *a* diritto, dritto; (*answer, question, person*) diretto; (*tidy*) in ordine; (*drink, hair*) liscio ● *adv* diritto, dritto; (*directly*) direttamente; **~ away** immediatamente; **~ on** *or* **ahead** diritto; **~ out** *fig* apertamente; **go ~** *fam* rigare diritto; **put sth ~** mettere qcsa in ordine; **sit/stand up ~** stare diritto

straighten /'streɪtn/ *vt* raddrizzare ● *vi* raddrizzarsi; **~ [up]** (*person:*) mettersi diritto. **straighten out** *vt fig* chiarire (*situation*)

straight'forward *a* franco; (*simple*) semplice

strain¹ /streɪn/ *n* (*streak*) vena *f*; *Bot* varietà *f inv*; (*of virus*) forma *f*

strain² *n* tensione *f*; (*injury*) stiramento *m*; **~s** *pl* (*of music*) note *fpl* ● *vt* tirare; sforzare (*eyes, voice*); stirarsi (*muscle*); Culin scolare ● *vi* sforzarsi. **~ed** *a* (*relations*) teso. **~er** *n* colino *m*

strait /streɪt/ *n* stretto *m*; **in dire ~s** in serie difficoltà. **~-jacket** *n* camicia *f* di forza. **~-'laced** *a* puritano

strand¹ /strænd/ *n* (*of thread*) gugliata *f*; (*of beads*) filo *m*; (*of hair*) capello *m*

strand² *vt* **be ~ed** rimanere bloccato

strange /streɪndʒ/ *a* strano; (*not*

known) sconosciuto; (*unaccustomed*) estraneo. **~ly** *adv* stranamente; **~ly enough** curiosamente. **~r** *n* estraneo, -a *mf*

strangle /'stræŋgl/ *vt* strangolare; *fig* reprimere

strangulation /stræŋgjʊ'leɪʃn/ *n* strangolamento *m*

strap /stræp/ *n* cinghia *f*; (*to grasp in vehicle*) maniglia *f*; (*of watch*) cinturino *m*; (*shoulder ~*) bretella *f*, spallina *f* ● *vt* (*pt/pp* **strapped**) legare; **~ in** *or* **down** assicurare

strapping /'stræpɪŋ/ *a* robusto

strata /'strɑːtə/ *npl see* **stratum**

stratagem /'strætədʒəm/ *n* stratagemma *f*

strategic /strə'tiːdʒɪk/ *a* strategico

strategy /'strætɪdʒɪ/ *n* strategia *f*

stratum /'strɑːtəm/ *n* (*pl* **strata**) strato *m*

straw /strɔ:/ *n* paglia *f*; (*single piece*) fuscello *m*; (*for drinking*) cannuccia *f*; **the last ~** l'ultima goccia

strawberry /'strɔ:bərɪ/ *n* fragola *f*

stray /streɪ/ *a* (*animal*) randagio ● *n* randagio *m* ● *vi* andarsene per conto proprio; (*deviate*) deviare (**from** da)

streak /striːk/ *n* striatura *f*; (*fig: trait*) vena *f* ● *vi* sfrecciare. **~y** *a* striato; (*bacon*) grasso

stream /striːm/ *n* ruscello *m*; (*current*) corrente *f*; (*of blood, people*) flusso *m*; *Sch* classe *f* ● *vi* scorrere. **stream in/out** *vi* entrare/uscire a fiotti

streamer /'striːmə(r)/ *n* (*paper*) stella *f* filante; (*flag*) pennone *m*

'streamline *vt* rendere aerodinamico; (*simplify*) snellire. **~d** *a* aerodinamico

street /striːt/ *n* strada *f*. **~car** *n* Am tram *m inv*. **~lamp** *n* lampione *m*

strength /streŋθ/ *n* forza *f*; (*of wall, bridge etc*) solidità *f*; **~s** *pl* punti *mpl* forti; **on the ~ of** grazie a. **~en** *vt* rinforzare

strenuous /'strenjʊəs/ *a* faticoso; (*attempt, denial*) energico

stress /stres/ *n* (*emphasis*) insistenza *f*; *Gram* accento *m* tonico; (*mental*) stress *m inv*; *Mech* spinta *f* ● *vt* (*emphasize*) insistere su; *Gram* mettere l'accento [tonico] su. **~ed** *a* (*mentally*) stressato. **~ful** *a* stressante

stretch /stretʃ/ *n* stiramento *m*; (*period*) periodo *m* di tempo; (*of road*) tratto *m*; (*elasticity*) elasticità *f*; **at a ~** di fila; **have a ~** stirarsi ● *vt* tirare; allargare (*shoes, arms etc*); (*person:*) allungare ● *vi* (*become wider*) allargarsi; (*extend*) estendersi; ⟨*person:*⟩ stirarsi. **~er** *n* barella *f*

strew /stru:/ *vt* (*pp* **strewn** *or* **strewed**) sparpagliare

stricken /'strɪkn/ *a* prostrato; **~ with** affetto da ⟨*illness*⟩

strict /strɪkt/ *a* severo; (*precise*) preciso. **~ly** *adv* severamente; **~ly speaking** in senso stretto

stride /straɪd/ *n* [lungo] passo *m*; **take sth in one's ~** accettare qcsa con facilità ● *vi* (*pt* **strode**, *pp* **stridden**) andare a gran passi

strident /'straɪdənt/ *a* stridente; ⟨*colour*⟩ vistoso

strife /straɪf/ *n* conflitto *m*

strike /straɪk/ *n* sciopero *m*; *Mil* attacco *m*; **on ~** in sciopero ● *v* (*pt/pp* **struck**) ● *vt* colpire; accendere ⟨*match*⟩; trovare ⟨*oil, gold*⟩; (*delete*) depennare; (*occur to*) venire in mente a; *Mil* attaccare ● *vi* ⟨*lightning:*⟩ cadere; ⟨*clock:*⟩ suonare; *Mil* attaccare; ⟨*workers:*⟩ scioperare; **~ lucky** azzeccarla. **strike off**, **strike out** *vt* eliminare. **strike up** *vt* fare ⟨*friendship*⟩; attaccare ⟨*conversation*⟩. **~-breaker** *n* persona *f* che non aderisce a uno sciopero

striker /'straɪkə(r)/ *n* scioperante *mf*

striking /'straɪkɪŋ/ *a* impressionante; (*attractive*) affascinante

string /strɪŋ/ *n* spago *m*; (*of musical instrument, racket*) corda *f*; (*of pearls*) filo *m*; (*of lies*) serie *f*; **the ~s** *pl Mus* gli archi; **pull ~s** *fam* usare le proprie conoscenze ● *vt* (*pt/pp* **strung**) (*thread*) infilare ⟨*beads*⟩. **~ed** *a* ⟨*instrument*⟩ a corda

stringent /'strɪndʒənt/ *a* rigido

strip /strɪp/ *n* striscia *f* ● *v* (*pt/pp* **stripped**) ● *vt* spogliare; togliere le lenzuola da ⟨*bed*⟩; scrostare ⟨*wood, furniture*⟩; smontare ⟨*machine*⟩; (*deprive*) privare (**of** di) ● *vi* (*undress*) spogliarsi. **~ cartoon** *n* striscia *f*. **~ club** *n* locale *m* di strip-tease

stripe /straɪp/ *n* striscia *f*; *Mil* gallone *m*. **~d** *a* a strisce

'striplight *n* tubo *m* al neon

stripper /'strɪpə(r)/ *n* spogliarellista *mf*; (*solvent*) sverniciatore *m*

strip-'tease *n* spogliarello *m*, strip-tease *m inv*

strive /straɪv/ *vi* (*pt* **strove**, *pp* **striven**) sforzarsi (**to** di); **~ for** sforzarsi di ottenere

strode /strəʊd/ *see* **stride**

stroke[1] /strəʊk/ *n* colpo *m*; (*of pen*) tratto *m*; (*in swimming*) bracciata *f*; *Med* ictus *m inv*; **~ of luck** colpo *m* di fortuna; **put sb off his ~** far perdere il filo a qcno

stroke[2] *vt* accarezzare

stroll /strəʊl/ *n* passeggiata *f* ● *vi* passeggiare. **~er** *n* (*Am: push-chair*) passeggino *m*

strong /strɒŋ/ *a* (**-er** /-gə(r)/, **-est** /-gɪst/) forte; ⟨*argument*⟩ valido

strong: **~-box** *n* cassaforte *f*. **~hold** *n* roccaforte *f*. **~ly** *adv* fortemente. **~-'minded** *a* risoluto. **~-room** *n* camera *f* blindata

stroppy /'strɒpɪ/ *a* scorbutico

strove /strəʊv/ *see* **strive**

struck /strʌk/ *see* **strike**

structural /'strʌktʃərəl/ *a* strutturale. **~ly** *adv* strutturalmente

structure /'strʌktʃə(r)/ *n* struttura *f*

struggle /'strʌgl/ *n* lotta *f*; **with a ~** con difficoltà ● *vi* lottare; **~ for breath** respirare con fatica; **~ to do sth** fare fatica a fare qcsa; **~ to one's feet** alzarsi con fatica

strum /strʌm/ *vt/i* (*pt/pp* **strummed**) strimpellare

strung /strʌŋ/ *see* **string**

strut[1] /strʌt/ *n* (*component*) puntello *m*

strut[2] *vi* (*pt/pp* **strutted**) camminare impettito

stub /stʌb/ *n* mozzicone *m*; (*counterfoil*) matrice *f* ● *vt* (*pt/pp* **stubbed**) **~ one's toe** sbattere il dito del piede (**on** contro). **stub out** *vt* spegnere ⟨*cigarette*⟩

stubb|le /'stʌbl/ *n* barba *f* ispida. **~ly** *a* ispido

stubborn /'stʌbən/ *a* testardo; ⟨*refusal*⟩ ostinato

stubby /'stʌbɪ/ *a* (**-ier, -iest**) tozzo

stucco /'stʌkəʊ/ *n* stucco *m*

stuck /stʌk/ *see* **stick**[2]. **~-'up** *a fam* snob *inv*

stud[1] /stʌd/ *n* (*on boot*) tacchetto *m*; (*on jacket*) borchia *f*; (*for ear*) orecchino *m* [a bottone]

stud[2] *n* (*of horses*) scuderia *f*

student /'stju:dənt/ *n* studente *m*, studentessa *f*; (*school child*) scolaro, -a *mf*. **~ nurse** *n* studente, studentessa infermiere, -a

studied /'stʌdɪd/ *a* intenzionale; ⟨*politeness*⟩ studiato

studio /'stju:dɪəʊ/ *n* studio *m*

studious /'stju:dɪəs/ *a* studioso; ⟨*attention*⟩ studiato

study /'stʌdɪ/ n studio m ● vt/i (pt/pp **studied**) studiare

stuff /stʌf/ n materiale m; (fam: things) roba f ● vt riempire; (with padding) imbottire; Culin farcire; ~ **sth into a drawer/one's pocket** ficcare qcsa alla rinfusa in un cassetto/in tasca. ~**ing** n (padding) imbottitura f; Culin ripieno m

stuffy /'stʌfɪ/ a (-ier, -iest) che sa di chiuso; (old-fashioned) antiquato

stumbl|e /'stʌmbl/ vi inciampare; ~**e across** or **on** imbattersi in. ~**ing-block** n ostacolo m

stump /stʌmp/ n ceppo m; (of limb) moncone m. ~**ed** a fam perplesso ● **stump up** vt/i fam sganciare

stun /stʌn/ vt (pt/pp **stunned**) stordire; (astonish) sbalordire

stung /stʌŋ/ see **sting**

stunk /stʌŋk/ see **stink**

stunning /'stʌnɪŋ/ a fam favoloso; (blow, victory) sbalorditivo

stunt[1] /stʌnt/ n fam trovata f pubblicitaria

stunt[2] vt arrestare lo sviluppo di. ~**ed** a stentato

stupendous /stju:'pendəs/ a stupendo. ~**ly** adv stupendamente

stupid /'stju:pɪd/ a stupido. ~**ity** /-'pɪdətɪ/ n stupidità f. ~**ly** adv stupidamente

stupor /'stju:pə(r)/ n torpore m

sturdy /'stɜ:dɪ/ a (-ier, -iest) robusto; (furniture) solido

stutter /'stʌtə(r)/ n balbuzie f ● vt/i balbettare

sty, stye /staɪ/ n (pl **styes**) Med orzaiolo m

style /staɪl/ n stile m; (fashion) moda f; (sort) tipo m; (hair~) pettinatura f; **in ~** in grande stile

stylish /'staɪlɪʃ/ a elegante. ~**ly** adv con eleganza

stylist /'staɪlɪst/ n stilista mf; (hair-~) parrucchiere, -a mf. ~**ic** /-'lɪstɪk/ a stilistico

stylized /'staɪlaɪzd/ a stilizzato

stylus /'staɪləs/ n (on record player) puntina f

suave /swɑ:v/ a dai modi garbati

sub'conscious /sʌb-/ a subcosciente ● n subcosciente m. ~**ly** adv in modo inconscio

subcon'tract vt subappaltare (**to** a). ~**or** n subappaltatore m

'subdivi|de vt suddividere. ~**sion** n suddivisione f

subdue /səb'dju:/ vt sottomettere;

(make quieter) attenuare. ~**d** a (light) attenuato; (person, voice) pacato

subhuman /sʌb'hju:mən/ a disumano

subject[1] /'sʌbdʒɪkt/ a ~ **to** soggetto a; (depending on) subordinato a; ~ **to availability** nei limiti della disponibilità ● n soggetto m; (of ruler) suddito, -a mf; Sch materia f

subject[2] /səb'dʒekt/ vt (to attack, abuse) sottoporre; assoggettare (country)

subjective /səb'dʒektɪv/ a soggettivo. ~**ly** adv soggettivamente

subjugate /'sʌbdʒʊgeɪt/ vt soggiogare

subjunctive /səb'dʒʌŋktɪv/ a & n congiuntivo m

sub'let vt (pt/pp -**let**, pres p -**letting**) subaffittare

sublime /sə'blaɪm/ a sublime. ~**ly** adv sublimamente

subliminal /sə'blɪmɪnl/ a subliminale

sub-ma'chine-gun n mitraglietta f

subma'rine n sommergibile m

submerge /səb'mɜ:dʒ/ vt immergere; **be ~d** essere sommerso ● vi immergersi

submiss|ion /səb'mɪʃn/ n sottomissione f. ~**ive** /-sɪv/ a sottomesso

submit /səb'mɪt/ v (pt/pp -**mitted**, pres p -**mitting**) ● vt sottoporre ● vi sottomettersi

subordinate /sə'bɔ:dɪneɪt/ vt subordinare (**to** a)

subscribe /səb'skraɪb/ vi contribuire; ~ **to** abbonarsi a (newspaper); sottoscrivere (fund); fig aderire a. ~**r** n abbonato, -a mf

subscription /səb'skrɪpʃn/ n (to club) sottoscrizione f; (to newspaper) abbonamento m

subsequent /'sʌbsɪkwənt/ a susseguente. ~**ly** adv in seguito

subservient /səb'sɜ:vɪənt/ a subordinato; (servile) servile. ~**ly** adv servilmente

subside /səb'saɪd/ vi sprofondare; (ground:) avvallarsi; (storm:) placarsi

subsidiary /səb'sɪdɪərɪ/ a secondario ● n [**company**] filiale f

subsid|ize /'sʌbsɪdaɪz/ vt sovvenzionare. ~**y** n sovvenzione f

subsist /səb'sɪst/ vi vivere (**on** di). ~**ence** n sussistenza f

substance /'sʌbstəns/ n sostanza f

sub'standard a di qualità inferiore

substantial /səb'stænʃl/ a solido; (meal) sostanzioso; (considerable) notevole. **~ly** *adv* notevolmente; (*essentially*) sostanzialmente

substantiate /səb'stænʃɪeɪt/ *vt* comprovare

substitut|e /'sʌbstɪtjuːt/ *n* sostituto *m* ● *vt* **~e A for B** sostituire B con A ● *vi* **~e for sb** sostituire qcno. **~ion** /-'tjuːʃn/ *n* sostituzione *f*

subterranean /sʌbtə'reɪnɪən/ *a* sotterraneo

'**subtitle** *n* sottotitolo *m*

sub|tle /'sʌtl/ *a* sottile; (*taste, perfume*) delicato. **~tlety** *n* sottigliezza *f*. **~tly** *adv* sottilmente

subtract /səb'trækt/ *vt* sottrare. **~ion** /-ækʃn/ *n* sottrazione *f*

suburb /'sʌbɜːb/ *n* sobborgo *m*; **in the ~s** in periferia. **~an** /sə'bɜːbən/ *a* suburbano. **~ia** /sə'bɜːbɪə/ *n* sobborghi *mpl*

subversive /səb'vɜːsɪv/ *a* sovversivo

'**subway** *n* sottopassagio *m*; (*Am: railway*) metropolitana *f*

succeed /sək'siːd/ *vi* riuscire; (*follow*) succedere a; **~ in doing** riuscire a fare ● *vt* succedere a (*king*). **~ing** *a* successivo

success /sək'ses/ *n* successo *m*; **be a ~** (*in life*) aver successo. **~ful** *a* riuscito; (*businessman, artist etc*) di successo. **~fully** *adv* con successo

succession /sək'seʃn/ *n* successione *f*; **in ~** di seguito

successive /sək'sesɪv/ *a* successivo. **~ly** *adv* successivamente

successor /sək'sesə(r)/ *n* successore *m*

succinct /sək'sɪŋkt/ *a* succinto

succulent /'sʌkjʊlənt/ *a* succulento

succumb /sə'kʌm/ *vi* soccombere (**to** a)

such /sʌtʃ/ *a* tale; **~ a book** un libro di questo genere; **~ a thing** una cosa di questo genere; **~ a long time ago** talmente tanto tempo fa; **there is no ~ thing** non esiste una cosa così; **there is no ~ person** non esiste una persona così ● *pron* **as** ~ come tale; **~ as** chi; **and ~** e simili; **~ as it is** così com'è. **~like** *pron* fam di tal genere

suck /sʌk/ *vt* succhiare. **suck up** *vt* assorbire. **suck up to** *vt fam* fare il lecchino con

sucker /'sʌkə(r)/ *n Bot* pollone *m*; (*fam: person*) credulone, -a *mf*

suction /'sʌkʃn/ *n* aspirazione *f*

sudden /'sʌdn/ *a* improvviso ● *n* **all of a ~** all'improvviso. **~ly** *adv* improvvisamente

sue /suː/ ● *v* (*pres p* **suing**) ● *vt* fare causa a (**for** per) ● *vi* fare causa

suede /sweɪd/ *n* pelle *f* scamosciata

suet /'suːɪt/ *n* grasso *m* di rognone

suffer /'sʌfə(r)/ *vi* soffrire (**from** per) ● *vt* soffrire; subire (*loss etc*); (*tolerate*) subire. **~ing** *n* sofferenza *f*

suffice /sə'faɪs/ *vi* bastare

sufficient /sə'fɪʃənt/ *a* sufficiente. **~ly** *adv* sufficientemente

suffix /'sʌfɪks/ *n* suffisso *m*

suffocat|e /'sʌfəkeɪt/ *vt/i* soffocare. **~ion** /-'keɪʃn/ *n* soffocamento *m*

sugar /'ʃʊgə(r)/ *n* zucchero *m* ● *vt* zuccherare. **~ basin**, **~-bowl** *n* zuccheriera *f*. **~y** *a* zuccheroso; *fig* sdolcinato

suggest /sə'dʒest/ *vt* suggerire; (*indicate, insinuate*) fare pensare a. **~ion** /-estʃən/ *n* suggerimento *m*; (*trace*) traccia *f*. **~ive** /-ɪv/ *a* allusivo. **~ively** *adv* in modo allusivo

suicidal /suːɪ'saɪdl/ *a* suicida

suicide /'suːɪsaɪd/ *n* suicidio *m*; (*person*) suicida *mf*; **commit ~** suicidarsi

suit /suːt/ *n* vestito *m*; (*woman's*) tailleur *m inv*; (*in cards*) seme *m*; *Jur* causa *f*; **follow ~** *fig* fare lo stesso ● *vt* andar bene a; (*adapt*) adattare (**to** a); (*be convenient for*) andare bene per; **be ~ed to** *or* **for** essere adatto a; **~ yourself!** fa' come vuoi!

suitabl|e /'suːtəbl/ *a* adatto. **~y** *adv* convenientemente

'**suitcase** *n* valigia *f*

suite /swiːt/ *n* suite *f inv*; (*of furniture*) divano *m* e poltrone *fpl* assortiti

sulk /sʌlk/ *vi* fare il broncio. **~y** *a* imbronciato

sullen /'sʌlən/ *a* svogliato

sulphur /'sʌlfə(r)/ *n* zolfo *m*. **~ic** /-'fjuːrɪk/ **~ic acid** *n* acido *m* solforico

sultana /sʌl'tɑːnə/ *n* uva *f* sultanina

sultry /'sʌltrɪ/ *a* (**-ier, -iest**) (*weather*) afoso; *fig* sensuale

sum /sʌm/ *n* somma *f*; *Sch* addizione *f* ● **sum up** ● *v* (*pt/pp* **summed**) ● *vi* riassumere ● *vt* valutare

summar|ize /'sʌməraɪz/ *vt* riassumere. **~y** *n* sommario *m* ● *a* sommario; (*dismissal*) sbrigativo

summer /'sʌmə(r)/ *n* estate *f*. **~-house** *n* padiglione *m*. **~time** *n* (*season*) estate *f*

summery /'sʌmərɪ/ *a* estivo

summit /'sʌmɪt/ *n* cima *f*. **~ conference** *n* vertice *m*

summon /'sʌmən/ *vt* convocare; *Jur* citare. **summon up** vt raccogliere ⟨strength⟩; rievocare ⟨memory⟩

summons /'sʌmənz/ n Jur citazione f ● vt citare in giudizio

sump /sʌmp/ n Auto coppa f dell'olio

sumptuous /'sʌmptjʊəs/ a sontuoso. **~ly** adv sontuosamente

sun /sʌn/ n sole m ● vt (pt/pp sunned) **~ oneself** prendere il sole

sun: ~bathe vi prendere il sole. **~-bed** n lettino m solare. **~burn** n scottatura f (solare). **~burnt** a scottato (dal sole)

sundae /'sʌndeɪ/ n gelato m guarnito

Sunday /'sʌndeɪ/ n domenica f

'sundial n meridiana f

sundry /'sʌndrɪ/ a svariati; **all and ~** tutti quanti

'sunflower n girasole m

sung /sʌŋ/ see sing

'sun-glasses npl occhiali mpl da sole

sunk /sʌŋk/ see sink

sunken /'sʌŋkn/ a incavato

'sunlight n [luce f del] sole m

sunny /'sʌnɪ/ a (-ier, -iest) assolato

sun: ~rise n alba f. **~-roof** n Auto tettuccio m apribile. **~set** n tramonto m. **~shade** n parasole m. **~shine** n [luce f del] sole m. **~stroke** n insolazione f. **~-tan** n abbronzatura f. **~-tanned** a abbronzato. **~-tan oil** n olio m solare

super /'su:pə(r)/ a fam fantastico

superb /sʊ'pɜ:b/ a splendido

supercilious /su:pə'sɪlɪəs/ a altezzoso

superficial /su:pə'fɪʃl/ a superficiale. **~ly** adv superficialmente

superfluous /sʊ'pɜ:flʊəs/ a superfluo

super'human a sovrumano

superintendent /su:pərɪn'tendənt/ n (of police) commissario m di polizia

superior /su:'pɪərɪə(r)/ a superiore ● n superiore, -a mf. **~ity** /-'ɒrətɪ/ n superiorità f

superlative /su:'pɜ:lətɪv/ a eccellente ● n superlativo m

'superman n superuomo m

'supermarket n supermercato m

'supermodel n top model f inv

super'natural a soprannaturale

'superpower n superpotenza f

supersede /su:pə'si:d/ vt rimpiazzare

super'sonic a supersonico

superstiti|on /su:pə'stɪʃn/ n superstizione f. **~ous** /-'stɪʃəs/ a superstizioso

supervis|e /'su:pəvaɪz/ vt supervisionare. **~ion** /-'vɪʒn/ n supervisione f. **~or** n supervisore m

supper /'sʌpə(r)/ n cena f

supple /'sʌpl/ a slogato

supplement /'sʌplɪmənt/ n supplemento m ● vt integrare. **~ary** /-'mentərɪ/ a supplementare

supplier /sə'plaɪə(r)/ n fornitore, -trice mf

supply /sə'plaɪ/ n fornitura f; (in economics) offerta f; **supplies** pl Mil approvvigionamenti mpl ● vt (pt/pp -ied) fornire; **~ sb with sth** fornire qcsa a qcno

support /sə'pɔ:t/ n sostegno m; (base) supporto m; (keep) sostentamento m ● vt sostenere; mantenere ⟨family⟩; (give money to) mantenere finanziariamente; Sport fare il tifo per. **~er** n sostenitore, -trice mf; Sport tifoso, -a mf. **~ive** /-ɪv/ a incoraggiante

suppose /sə'pəʊz/ vt (presume) supporre; (imagine) pensare; **be ~d to do** dover fare; **not be ~d to** fam non avere il permesso di; **I ~ so** suppongo di sì. **~dly** /-ɪdlɪ/ adv presumibilmente

suppress /sə'pres/ vt sopprimere. **~ion** /-eʃn/ n soppressione f

supremacy /su:'preməsɪ/ n supremazia f

supreme /su:'pri:m/ a supremo

surcharge /'sɜ:tʃɑ:dʒ/ n supplemento m

sure /ʃʊə(r)/ a sicuro, certo; **make ~** accertarsi; **be ~ to do it** mi raccomando di farlo ● adv Am fam certamente; **~ enough** infatti. **~ly** adv certamente; (Am: gladly) volentieri

surety /'ʃʊərətɪ/ n garanzia f; **stand ~ for** garantire per

surf /sɜ:f/ n schiuma f ● vt Comput **~ the Net** surfare in Internet

surface /'sɜ:fɪs/ n superficie f; **on the ~** fig in apparenza ● vi (emerge) emergere. **~ mail** n **by ~ mail** per posta ordinaria

'surfboard n tavola f da surf

surfing /'sɜ:fɪŋ/ n surf m inv

surge /sɜ:dʒ/ n (of sea) ondata f; (of interest) aumento m; (in demand) impennata f; (of anger, pity) impeto m ● vi riversarsi; **~ forward** buttarsi in avanti

surgeon /'sɜ:dʒən/ n chirurgo m

surgery /'sɜ:dʒərɪ/ n chirurgia f; (place, consulting room) ambulatorio m; (hours) ore fpl di visita; **have ~** subire un'intervento [chirurgico]

surgical /'sɜ:dʒɪkl/ a chirurgico

surly /'sɜ:lɪ/ a (-ier, -iest) scontroso

surmise /sə'maɪz/ vt supporre

surmount /sə'maʊnt/ vt sormontare

surname /'sɜ:neɪm/ n cognome m

surpass /sə'pɑːs/ vt superare

surplus /'sɜːpləs/ a d'avanzo ● n sovrappiù m

surpris|e /sə'praɪz/ n sorpresa f ● vt sorprendere; **be ~ed** essere sorpreso (**at** da). **~ing** a sorprendente. **~ingly** adv sorprendentemente

surrender /sə'rendə(r)/ n resa f ● vi arrendersi ● vt cedere

surreptitious /sʌrəp'tɪʃəs/ a & adv di nascosto

surrogate /'sʌrəgət/ n surrogato m. **~ 'mother** n madre f surrogata

surround /sə'raʊnd/ vt circondare. **~ing** a circostante. **~ings** npl dintorni mpl

surveillance /sə'veɪləns/ n sorveglianza f

survey[1] /'sɜːveɪ/ n sguardo m; (poll) sondaggio m; (investigation) indagine f; (of land) rilevamento m; (of house) perizia f

survey[2] /sə'veɪ/ vt esaminare; fare un rilevamento di (land); fare una perizia di (building). **~or** n perito m; (of land) topografo, -a f

survival /sə'vaɪvl/ n sopravvivenza f; (relic) resto m

surviv|e /sə'vaɪv/ vt sopravvivere a ● vi sopravvivere. **~or** n superstite mf; **be a ~or** fam riuscire sempre a cavarsela

susceptible /sə'septəbl/ a influenzabile; **~ to** sensibile a

suspect[1] /sə'spekt/ vt sospettare; (assume) supporre

suspect[2] /'sʌspekt/ a & n sospetto, -a mf

suspend /sə'spend/ vt appendere; (stop, from duty) sospendere. **~er belt** n reggicalze m inv. **~ders** npl giarrettiere fpl; (Am: braces) bretelle fpl

suspense /sə'spens/ n tensione f; (in book etc) suspense f

suspension /sə'spenʃn/ n Auto sospensione f. **~ bridge** n ponte m sospeso

suspici|on /sə'spɪʃn/ n sospetto m; (trace) pizzico m; **under ~on** sospettato. **~ous** /-ʃəs/ a sospettoso; (arousing suspicion) sospetto. **~ously** adv sospettosamente; (arousing suspicion) in modo sospetto

sustain /sə'steɪn/ vt sostenere; mantenere (life); subire (injury)

sustenance /'sʌstɪnəns/ n nutrimento m

swab /swɒb/ n Med tampone m

swagger /'swægə(r)/ vi pavoneggiarsi

swallow[1] /'swɒləʊ/ vt/i inghiottire. **swallow up** vt divorare; (earth, crowd:) inghiottire

swallow[2] n (bird) rondine f

swam /swæm/ see **swim**

swamp /swɒmp/ n palude f ● vt fig sommergere. **~y** a paludoso

swan /swɒn/ n cigno m

swap /swɒp/ n fam scambio m ● vt (pt/pp **swapped**) fam scambiare (**for** con) ● vi fare cambio

swarm /swɔːm/ n sciame m ● vi sciamare; **be ~ing with** brulicare di

swarthy /'swɔːðɪ/ a (-ier, -iest) di carnagione scura

swastika /'swɒstɪkə/ n svastica f

swat /swɒt/ vt (pt/pp **swatted**) schiacciare

sway /sweɪ/ n fig influenza f ● vi oscillare; (person:) ondeggiare ● vt (influence) influenzare

swear /sweə(r)/ v (pt **swore**, pp **sworn**) ● vt giurare ● vi giurare; (curse) dire parolacce; **~ at sb** imprecare contro qcno; **~ by** fam credere ciecamente in. **~-word** n parolaccia f

sweat /swet/ n sudore m ● vi sudare

sweater /'swetə(r)/ n golf m inv

sweaty /'swetɪ/ a sudato

swede /swiːd/ n rapa f svedese

Swed|e n svedese mf. **~en** n Svezia f. **~ish** a svedese ● n (language) svedese m

sweep /swiːp/ n scopata f, spazzata f; (curve) curva f; (movement) movimento m ampio; **make a clean ~** fig fare piazza pulita ● v (pt/pp **swept**) ● vt scopare, spazzare; (wind:) spazzare ● vi (go swiftly) andare rapidamente; (wind:) soffiare. **sweep away** vt fig spazzare via. **sweep up** vt spazzare

sweeping /'swiːpɪŋ/ a (gesture) ampio; (statement) generico; (changes) radicale

sweet /swiːt/ a dolce; **have a ~ tooth** essere goloso ● n caramella f; (dessert) dolce m. **~ corn** n mais m

sweet: ~heart n innamorato, -a mf; **hi, ~heart** ciao, tesoro. **~ness** n dolcezza f. **~ 'pea** n pisello m odoroso. **~-shop** n negozio m di dolciumi

swell /swel/ ● v (pt **swelled**, pp **swollen** or **swelled**) ● vi gonfiarsi; (increase) aumentare ● vt gonfiare; (increase) far salire. **~ing** n gonfiore m

swelter /'sweltə(r)/ vi soffocare [dal caldo]

swept /swept/ see **sweep**

swerve /swɜ:v/ *vi* deviare bruscamente

swift /swɪft/ *a* rapido. **~ly** *adv* rapidamente

swig /swɪg/ *n fam* sorso *m* ● *vt* (*pt/pp* **swigged**) *fam* scolarsi

swill /swɪl/ *n* (*for pigs*) brodaglia *f* ● *vt* **~** [**out**] risciacquare

swim /swɪm/ *n* **have a ~** fare una nuotata ● *v* (*pt* **swam**, *pp* **swum**) ● *vi* nuotare; (*room:*) girare; **my head is ~ming** mi gira la testa ● *vt* percorrere a nuoto. **~mer** *n* nuotatore, -trice *mf*

swimming /'swɪmɪŋ/ *n* nuoto *m*. **~-baths** *npl* piscina *fsg*. **~ costume** *n* costume *m* da bagno. **~-pool** *n* piscina *f*. **~ trunks** *npl* calzoncini *mpl* da bagno

'swim-suit *n* costume *m* da bagno

swindle /'swɪndl/ *n* truffa *f* ● *vt* truffare. **~r** *n* truffatore, -trice *mf*

swine /swaɪn/ *n fam* porco *m*

swing /swɪŋ/ *n* oscillazione *f*; (*shift*) cambiamento *m*; (*seat*) altalena *f*; *Mus* swing *m*; **in full ~** in piena attività ● *v* (*pt/pp* **swung**) ● *vi* oscillare; (*on swing, sway*) dondolare; (*dangle*) penzolare; (*turn*) girare ● *vt* oscillare; far deviare (*vote*). **~-'door** *n* porta *f* a vento

swingeing /'swɪndʒɪŋ/ *a* (*increase*) drastico

swipe /swaɪp/ *n fam* botta *f* ● *vt fam* colpire; (*steal*) rubare; far passare nella macchinetta (*credit card*)

swirl /swɜ:l/ *n* (*of smoke, dust*) turbine *m* ● *vi* (*water:*) fare mulinello

swish /swɪʃ/ *a fam* chic ● *vi* schioccare

Swiss /swɪs/ *a & n* svizzero, -a *mf*; **the ~** *pl* gli svizzeri. **~ 'roll** *n* rotolo *m* di pan di Spagna ripieno di marmellata

switch /swɪtʃ/ *n* interruttore *m*; (*change*) mutamento *m* ● *vt* cambiare; (*exchange*) scambiare ● *vi* cambiare; **~ to** passare a. **switch off** *vt* spegnere. **switch on** *vt* accendere

switch: **~back** *n* montagne *fpl* russe. **~board** *n* centralino *m*

Switzerland /'swɪtsələnd/ *n* Svizzera *f*

swivel /'swɪvl/ *v* (*pt/pp* **swivelled**) ● *vt* girare ● *vi* girarsi

swollen /'swəʊlən/ *see* **swell** ● *a* gonfio. **~-'headed** *a* presuntuoso

swoop /swu:p/ *n* (*by police*) incursione *f* ● *vi* **~** [**down**] (*bird:*) piombare; *fig* fare un'incursione

sword /sɔ:d/ *n* spada *f*

swore /swɔ:(r)/ *see* **swear**

sworn /swɔ:n/ *see* **swear**

swot /swɒt/ *n fam* sgobbone, -a *mf* ● *vt* (*pt/pp* **swotted**) *fam* sgobbare

swum /swʌm/ *see* **swim**

swung /swʌŋ/ *see* **swing**

syllable /'sɪləbl/ *n* sillaba *f*

syllabus /'sɪləbəs/ *n* programma *m* [dei corsi]

symbol /'sɪmbl/ *n* simbolo *m* (**of** di). **~ic** /-'bɒlɪk/ *a* simbolico. **~ism** /-ɪzm/ *n* simbolismo *m*. **~ize** *vt* simboleggiare

symmetr|ical /sɪ'metrɪkl/ *a* simmetrico. **~y** /'sɪmətrɪ/ *n* simmetria *f*

sympathetic /sɪmpə'θetɪk/ *a* (*understanding*) comprensivo; (*showing pity*) compassionevole. **~ally** *adv* con comprensione/compassione

sympathize /'sɪmpəθaɪz/ *vi* capire; (*in grief*) solidarizzare; **~ with sb** capire qcno/solidarizzare con qcno. **~r** *n Pol* simpatizzante *mf*

sympathy /'sɪmpəθɪ/ *n* comprensione *f*; (*pity*) compassione *f*; (*condolences*) condoglianze *fpl*; **in ~ with** (*strike*) per solidarietà con

symphony /'sɪmfənɪ/ *n* sinfonia *f*

symptom /'sɪmptəm/ *n* sintomo *m*. **~atic** /-'mætɪk/ *a* sintomatico (**of** di)

synagogue /'sɪnəgɒg/ *n* sinagoga *f*

synchronize /'sɪŋkrənaɪz/ *vt* sincronizzare

syndicate /'sɪndɪkət/ *n* gruppo *m*

syndrome /'sɪndrəʊm/ *n* sindrome *f*

synonym /'sɪnənɪm/ *n* sinonimo *m*. **~ous** /-'nɒnɪməs/ *a* sinonimo

synopsis /sɪ'nɒpsɪs/ *n* (*pl* **-opses** /-si:z/) (*of opera, ballet*) trama *f*; (*of book*) riassunto *m*

syntax /'sɪntæks/ *n* sintassi *f inv*

synthesize /'sɪnθəsaɪz/ *vt* sintetizzare. **~r** *n Mus* sintetizzatore *m*

synthetic /sɪn'θetɪk/ *a* sintetico ● *n* fibra *f* sintetica

Syria /'sɪrɪə/ *n* Siria *f*. **~n** *a & n* siriano, -a *mf*

syringe /sɪ'rɪndʒ/ *n* siringa *f*

syrup /'sɪrəp/ *n* sciroppo *m*; *Br* tipo *m* di melassa

system /'sɪstəm/ *n* sistema *m*. **~atic** /-'mætɪk/ *a* sistematico

Tt

tab /tæb/ n linguetta f; (with name) etichetta f; **keep ~s on** fam sorvegliare; **pick up the ~** fam pagare il conto

tabby /'tæbɪ/ n gatto m tigrato

table /'teɪbl/ n tavolo m; (list) tavola f; **at [the] ~** a tavola; **~ of contents** tavola f delle materie ● vt proporre. **~-cloth** n tovaglia f. **~spoon** n cucchiaio m da tavola. **~spoon|ful** n cucchiaiata f

tablet /'tæblɪt/ n pastiglia f; (slab) lastra f; **~ of soap** saponetta f

'table tennis n tennis m da tavolo; (everyday level) ping pong m

tabloid /'tæblɔɪd/ n [giornale m formato] tabloid m inv; pej giornale m scandalistico

taboo /tə'buː/ a tabù inv ● n tabù m inv

tacit /'tæsɪt/ a tacito

taciturn /'tæsɪtɜːn/ a taciturno

tack /tæk/ n (nail) chiodino m; (stitch) imbastitura f; Naut virata f; fig linea f di condotta ● vt inchiodare; (sew) imbastire ● vi Naut virare

tackle /'tækl/ n (equipment) attrezzatura f; (football etc) contrasto m, tackle m inv ● vt affrontare

tacky /'tækɪ/ a (paint) non ancora asciutto; (glue) appiccicoso; fig pacchiano

tact /tækt/ n tatto m. **~ful** a pieno di tatto; (remark) delicato. **~fully** adv con tatto

tactic|al /'tæktɪkl/ a tattico. **~s** npl tattica fsg

tactless /'tæktlɪs/ a privo di tatto. **~ly** adv senza tatto. **~ness** n mancanza f di tatto; (of remark) indelicatezza f

tadpole /'tædpəʊl/ n girino m

tag¹ /tæg/ n (label) etichetta f ● vt (pt/pp **tagged**) attaccare l'etichetta a. **tag along** vi seguire passo passo

tag² n (game) acchiapparello m

tail /teɪl/ n coda f; **~s** pl (tailcoat) frac m inv ● vt (fam: follow) pedinare. **tail off** vi diminuire

tail: **~back** n coda f. **~-end** n parte f finale; (of train) coda f. **~ light** n fanalino m di coda

tailor /'teɪlə(r)/ n sarto m. **~-made** a fatto su misura

'tail wind n vento m di coda

taint /teɪnt/ vt contaminare

take /teɪk/ n Cinema ripresa f ● v (pt **took**, pp **taken**) ● vt prendere; (to a place) portare (person, object); (contain) contenere (passengers etc); (endure) sopportare; (require) occorrere; (teach) insegnare; (study) studiare (subject); fare (exam, holiday, photograph, walk, bath); sentire (pulse); misurare (sb's temperature); **~ sb prisoner** fare prigioniero qcno; **be ~n ill** ammalarsi; **~ sth calmly** prendere con calma qcsa ● vi (plant:) attecchire. **take after** vt assomigliare a. **take away** vt (with one) portare via; (remove) togliere; (subtract) sottrarre; **'to ~ away'** 'da asporto'. **take back** vt riprendere; ritirare (statement); (return) riportare [indietro]. **take down** vt portare giù; (remove) tirare giù; (write down) prendere nota di. **take in** vt (bring indoors) portare dentro; (to one's home) ospitare; (understand) capire; (deceive) ingannare; riprendere (garment); (include) includere. **take off** vt togliersi (clothes); (deduct) togliere; (mimic) imitare; **~ time off** prendere delle vacanze; **~ oneself off** andarsene ● vi Aeron decollare. **take on** vt farsi carico di; assumere (employee); (as opponent) prendersela con. **take out** vt portare fuori; togliere (word, stain); (withdraw) ritirare (money, books); **~ out a subscription to sth** abbonarsi a qcsa; **~ it out on sb** fam prendersela con qcno. **take over** vt assumere il controllo di (firm) ● vi **~ over from sb** sostituire qcno; (permanently) succedere a qcno. **take to** vt (as a habit) darsi a; **I took to her** (liked) mi è piaciuta. **take up** vt portare su; accettare (offer); intraprendere (profession); dedicarsi a (hobby); prendere (time); occupare (space); tirare su (floor-boards); accorciare (dress); **~ sth up with sb** discutere qcsa con qcno ● vi **~ up with sb** legarsi a qcno

take: **~-away** n (meal) piatto m da asporto; (restaurant) ristorante m che prepara piatti da asporto. **~-off** n Aeron decollo *m*. **~-over** *n* rilevamento *m*. **~-over bid** *n* offerta *f* di assorbimento

takings /'teɪkɪnz/ *npl* incassi *mpl*

talcum /'tælkəm/ *n* ~ [**powder**] talco *m*

tale /teɪl/ *n* storia *f*; *pej* fandonia *f*

talent /'tælənt/ *n* talento *m*. **~ed** *a* [ricco] di talento

talk /tɔːk/ *n* conversazione *f*; (*lecture*) conferenza *f*; (*gossip*) chiacchere *fpl*; **make small** ~ parlare del più e del meno ● *vi* parlare ● *vt* parlare di (*politics etc*); **~ sb into sth** convincere qcno di qcsa. **talk over** *vt* discutere

talkative /'tɔːkətɪv/ *a* loquace

'talking-to *n* sgridata *f*

talk show *n* talk show *m inv*

tall /tɔːl/ *a* alto. **~boy** *n* cassettone *m*. **~ order** *n* impresa *f* difficile. **~ 'story** *n* frottola *f*

tally /'tælɪ/ *n* conteggio *m*; **keep a ~ of** tenere il conto di ● *vi* coincidere

tambourine /tæmbə'riːn/ *n* tamburello *m*

tame /teɪm/ *a* (*animal*) domestico; (*dull*) insulso ● *vt* domare. **~ly** *adv* docilmente. **~r** *n* domatore, -trice *mf*

tamper /'tæmpə(r)/ *vi* ~ **with** manomettere

tampon /'tæmpɒn/ *n* tampone *m*

tan /tæn/ *a* marrone rossiccio ● *n* marrone *m* rossiccio; (*from sun*) abbronzatura *f* ● *v* (*pt/pp* **tanned**) ● *vt* conciare (*hide*) ● *vi* abbronzarsi

tang /tæŋ/ *n* sapore *m* forte; (*smell*) odore *m* penetrante

tangent /'tændʒənt/ *n* tangente *f*

tangible /'tændʒɪbl/ *a* tangibile

tangle /'tæŋgl/ *n* groviglio *m*; (*in hair*) nodo *m* ● *vt* ~ [**up**] aggrovigliare ● *vi* aggrovigliarsi

tango /'tæŋgəʊ/ *n* tango *m inv*

tank /tæŋk/ *n* contenitore *m*; (*for petrol*) serbatoio *m*; (*fish* ~) acquario *m*; *Mil* carro *m* armato

tankard /'tæŋkəd/ *n* boccale *m*

tanker /'tæŋkə(r)/ *n* nave *f* cisterna; (*lorry*) autobotte *f*

tanned /tænd/ *a* abbronzato

tantaliz|e /'tæntəlaɪz/ *vt* tormentare. **~ing** *a* allettante; (*smell*) stuzzicante

tantamount /'tæntəmaʊnt/ *a* ~ **to** equivalente a

tantrum /'tæntrəm/ *n* scoppio *m* d'ira

tap /tæp/ *n* rubinetto *m*; (*knock*) colpo *m*; **on** ~ *fig* a disposizione ● *v* (*pt/pp* **tapped**) ● *vt* dare un colpetto a; sfruttare (*resources*); mettere sotto controllo (*telephone*) ● *vi* picchiettare. **~-dance** *n* tip tap *m* ● *vi* ballare il tip tap

tape /teɪp/ *n* nastro *m*; (*recording*) cassetta *f* ● *vt* legare con nastro; (*record*) registrare

'tape: ~ **backup drive** *n* *Comput* unità *f* di backup a nastro. **~-deck** *n* piastra *f*. **~-measure** *n* metro *m* [a nastro]

taper /'teɪpə(r)/ *n* candela *f* sottile ● **taper off** *vi* assottigliarsi

'tape: ~ **recorder** *n* registratore *m*. ~ **recording** *n* registrazione *f*

tapestry /'tæpɪstrɪ/ *n* arazzo *m*

'tap water *n* acqua *f* del rubinetto

tar /tɑː(r)/ *n* catrame *m* ● *vt* (*pt/pp* **tarred**) incatramare

tardy /'tɑːdɪ/ *a* (**-ier, -iest**) tardivo

target /'tɑːgɪt/ *n* bersaglio *m*; *fig* obiettivo *m*

tariff /'tærɪf/ *n* (*price*) tariffa *f*; (*duty*) dazio *m*

Tarmac® /'tɑːmæk/ *n* macadam *m* al catrame. **tarmac** *n* *Aeron* pista *f* di decollo

tarnish /'tɑːnɪʃ/ *vi* ossidarsi ● *vt* ossidare; *fig* macchiare

tarpaulin /tɑː'pɔːlɪn/ *n* telone *m* impermeabile

tart¹ /tɑːt/ *a* aspro; *fig* acido

tart² *n* crostata *f*; (*individual*) crostatina *f*; (*sl: prostitute*) donnaccia *f* ● **tart up** *vt* *fam* ~ **oneself up** agghindarsi

tartan /'tɑːtn/ *n* tessuto *m* scozzese, tartan *m inv* ● *attrib* di tessuto scozzese

tartar /'tɑːtə(r)/ *n* (*on teeth*) tartaro *m*

tartar 'sauce /tɑːtə-/ *n* salsa *f* tartara

task /tɑːsk/ *n* compito *m*; **take sb to ~** riprendere qcno. ~ **force** *n* *Pol* commissione *f*; *Mil* task-force *f inv*

tassel /'tæsl/ *n* nappa *f*

taste /teɪst/ *n* gusto *m*; (*sample*) assaggio *m*; **get a ~ of sth** *fig* assaporare il gusto di qcsa ● *vt* sentire il sapore di; (*sample*) assaggiare ● *vi* sapere (**of** di); **it ~s lovely** è ottimo. **~ful** *a* di [buon] gusto. **~fully** *adv* con gusto. **~less** *a* senza gusto. **~lessly** *adv* con cattivo gusto

tasty /'teɪstɪ/ *a* (**-ier, -iest**) saporito

tat /tæt/ *see* **tit²**

tatter|ed /'tætəd/ *a* cencioso; (*pages*) stracciato. **~s** *npl* **in ~s** a brandelli

tattoo¹ /tæ'tuː/ *n* tatuaggio *m* ● *vt* tatuare

tattoo² *n* *Mil* parata *f* militare

tatty /'tætɪ/ *a* (**-ier, -iest**) (*clothes, person*) trasandato; (*book*) malandato

taught /tɔːt/ *see* **teach**

taunt /tɔːnt/ *n* scherno *m* ● *vt* schernire

Taurus /ˈtɔːrəs/ n Astr Toro m
taut /tɔːt/ a teso
tawdry /ˈtɔːdrɪ/ a (**-ier, -iest**) pacchiano
tax /tæks/ n tassa f; ⟨on income⟩ imposte
fpl; **before ~** ⟨price⟩ tasse escluse;
⟨salary⟩ lordo ● vt tassare; fig mettere
alla prova; **~ with** accusare di. **~able**
/-əbl/ a tassabile. **~ation** /-ˈseɪʃn/ n tasse fpl. **~ evasion** n evasione f fiscale.
~-free a esentasse. **~ haven** n paradiso m fiscale
taxi /ˈtæksɪ/ n taxi m inv ● vi (pt/pp
taxied, pres p **taxiing**) ⟨aircraft:⟩ rulla-
re. **~ driver** n tassista mf. **~ rank** n posteggio m per taxi
'**taxpayer** n contribuente mf
tea /tiː/ n tè m inv. **~-bag** n bustina f di
tè. **~-break** n intervallo m per il tè
teach /tiːtʃ/ vt/i (pt/pp **taught**) insegnare; **~ sb sth** insegnare qcsa a qcno.
~er n insegnante mf; ⟨primary⟩ maestro, -a mf. **~ing** n insegnamento m
tea: ~-cloth n ⟨for drying⟩
asciugapiatti m inv. **~cup** n tazza f da tè
teak /tiːk/ n tek m
'**tea-leaves** npl tè m inv sfuso; ⟨when
infused⟩ fondi mpl di tè
team /tiːm/ n squadra f, fig équipe f inv
● **team up** vi unirsi
'**team-work** n lavoro m di squadra; fig
lavoro m d'équipe
'**teapot** n teiera f
tear¹ /teə(r)/ n strappo m ● v (pt **tore**,
pp **torn**) ● vt strappare ● vi strappare;
⟨material:⟩ strapparsi; ⟨run⟩ precipitarsi. **tear apart** vt ⟨fig: criticize⟩ fare a
pezzi; ⟨separate⟩ dividere. **tear away** vt
~ oneself away andare via; **~
oneself away from** staccarsi da
⟨television⟩. **tear open** vt aprire strap-
pando. **tear up** vt strappare; rompere
⟨agreement⟩
tear² /tɪə(r)/ n lacrima f. **~ful** a
⟨person⟩ in lacrime; ⟨farewell⟩
lacrimevole. **~fully** adv in lacrime.
~gas n gas m lacrimogeno
tease /tiːz/ vt prendere in giro
⟨person⟩; tormentare ⟨animal⟩
tea: ~-set n servizio m da tè. **~ shop** n
sala f da tè. **~spoon** n cucchiaino m [da
tè]. **~spoon[ful]** n cucchiaino m
teat /tiːt/ n capezzolo m; ⟨on bottle⟩
tettarella f
'**tea-towel** n strofinaccio m [per i piatti]
technical /ˈteknɪkl/ a tecnico. **~ity**
/-ˈkælətɪ/ n tecnicismo m; Jur cavillo m
giuridico. **~ly** adv tecnicamente;
⟨strictly⟩ strettamente

technician /tekˈnɪʃn/ n tecnico, -a mf
technique /tekˈniːk/ n tecnica f
technological /teknəˈlɒdʒɪkl/ a tec-
nologico
technology /tekˈnɒlədʒɪ/ n tecnologia f
teddy /ˈtedɪ/ n ~ **[bear]** orsacchiotto m
tedious /ˈtiːdɪəs/ a noioso
tedium /ˈtiːdɪəm/ n tedio m
tee /tiː/ n ⟨in golf⟩ tee m inv
teem /tiːm/ vi ⟨rain⟩ piovere a dirotto;
be ~ing with ⟨full of⟩ pullulare di
teenage /ˈtiːneɪdʒ/ a per ragazzi; **~
boy/girl** adolescente mf. **~r** n adolescente mf
teens /tiːnz/ npl **the ~** l'adolescenza
fsg; **be in one's ~** essere adolescente
teeny /ˈtiːnɪ/ a (**-ier, -iest**) piccolissimo
teeter /ˈtiːtə(r)/ vi barcollare
teeth /tiːθ/ see **tooth**
teeth|e /tiːð/ vi mettere i [primi] denti.
~ing troubles npl fig difficoltà fpl ini-
ziali
teetotal /tiːˈtəʊtl/ a astemio. **~ler** n
astemio, -a mf
telecommunications /telɪkəm-
juːnɪˈkeɪʃnz/ npl telecomunicazioni fpl
telegram /ˈtelɪɡræm/ n telegramma m
telegraph /ˈtelɪɡrɑːf/ n telegrafo m.
~ic /-ˈɡræfɪk/ a telegrafico. **~ pole** n
palo m del telegrafo
telepathy /tɪˈlepəθɪ/ n telepatia f
telephone /ˈtelɪfəʊn/ n telefono m; **be
on the ~** avere il telefono; ⟨be
telephoning⟩ essere al telefono ● vt telefonare a ● vi telefonare
telephone: ~ book n elenco m telefonico. **~ booth** n, **~ box** n cabina f telefonica. **~ directory** n elenco m telefonico. **~ number** n numero m di telefono
'**telephoto** /telɪ-/ a ~ **lens** tele-obiet-
tivo m
telescop|e /ˈtelɪskəʊp/ n telescopio m.
~ic /-ˈskɒpɪk/ a telescopico
televise /ˈtelɪvaɪz/ vt trasmettere per
televisione
television /ˈtelɪvɪʒn/ n televisione f;
watch ~ guardare la televisione. **~
set** n televisore m
teleworking /ˈtelɪwɜːkɪŋ/ n tele-
lavoro m
telex /ˈteleks/ n telex m inv
tell /tel/ vt (pt/pp **told**) dire; raccontare
⟨story⟩; ⟨distinguish⟩ distinguere (**from**
da); **~ sb sth** dire qcsa a qcno; **~ the
time** dire l'ora; **I couldn't ~ why...**
non sapevo perché... ● vi ⟨produce an
effect⟩ avere effetto; **time will ~** il tempo ce lo dirà; **his age is beginning to**

~ l'età comincia a farsi sentire [per lui]; **you mustn't** ~ non devi dire niente. **tell off** *vt* sgridare

teller /'telə(r)/ *n* (*in bank*) cassiere, -a *mf*

telling /'telɪŋ/ *a* significativo; ⟨*argument*⟩ efficace

telly /'telɪ/ *n fam* tv *f inv*

temerity /tɪ'merətɪ/ *n* audacia *f*

temp /temp/ *n fam* impiegato, -a *mf* temporaneo, -a

temper /'tempə(r)/ *n* (*disposition*) carattere *m*; (*mood*) umore *m*; (*anger*) collera *f*; **lose one's** ~ arrabbiarsi; **be in a** ~ essere arrabbiato; **keep one's** ~ mantenere la calma

temperament /'temprəmənt/ *n* temperamento *m*. **~al** /-'mentl/ *a* (*moody*) capriccioso

temperate /'tempərət/ *a* ⟨*climate*⟩ temperato

temperature /'temprətʃə(r)/ *n* temperatura *f*; **have a** ~ avere la febbre

tempest /'tempɪst/ *n* tempesta *f*. **~uous** /-'pestjʊəs/ *a* tempestoso

temple[1] /'templ/ *n* tempio *m*

temple[2] *n Anat* tempia *f*

tempo /'tempəʊ/ *n* ritmo *m*; *Mus* tempo *m*

temporar|y /'tempərərɪ/ *a* temporaneo; ⟨*measure, building*⟩ provvisorio. **~ily** *adv* temporaneamente; ⟨*introduced, erected*⟩ provvisoriamente

tempt /tempt/ *vt* tentare; sfidare ⟨*fate*⟩; ~ **sb to** indurre qcno a; **be ~ed** essere tentato (**to** di); **I am ~ed by the offer** l'offerta mi tenta. **~ation** /-'teɪʃn/ *n* tentazione *f*. **~ing** *a* allettante; ⟨*food, drink*⟩ invitante

ten /ten/ *a* & *n* dieci *m*

tenable /'tenəbl/ *a fig* sostenibile

tenaci|ous /tɪ'neɪʃəs/ *a* tenace. **~ty** /-'næsətɪ/ *n* tenacia *f*

tenant /'tenənt/ *n* inquilino, -a *mf*; *Comm* locatario, -a *mf*

tend[1] /tend/ *vt* (*look after*) prendersi cura di

tend[2] *vi* ~ **to do sth** tendere a far qcsa

tendency /'tendənsɪ/ *n* tendenza *f*

tender[1] /'tendə(r)/ *n Comm* offerta *f*; **be legal** ~ avere corso legale ● *vt* offrire; presentare ⟨*resignation*⟩

tender[2] *a* tenero; (*painful*) dolorante. **~ly** *adv* teneramente. **~ness** *n* tenerezza *f*; (*painfulness*) dolore *m*

tendon /'tendən/ *n* tendine *m*

tenement /'tenəmənt/ *n* casamento *m*

tenner /'tenə(r)/ *n fam* biglietto *m* da dieci sterline

tennis /'tenɪs/ *n* tennis *m*. **~-court** *n* campo *m* da tennis. **~ player** *n* tennista *mf*

tenor /'tenə(r)/ *n* tenore *m*

tense[1] /tens/ *n Gram* tempo *m*

tense[2] *a* teso ● *vt* tendere ⟨*muscle*⟩. **tense up** *vi* tendersi

tension /'tenʃn/ *n* tensione *f*

tent /tent/ *n* tenda *f*

tentacle /'tentəkl/ *n* tentacolo *m*

tentative /'tentətɪv/ *a* provvisorio; ⟨*smile, gesture*⟩ esitante. **~ly** *adv* timidamente; ⟨*accept*⟩ provvisoriamente

tenterhooks /'tentəhʊks/ *npl* **be on** ~ essere sulle spine

tenth /tenθ/ *a* decimo ● *n* decimo, -a *mf*

tenuous /'tenjʊəs/ *a fig* debole

tepid /'tepɪd/ *a* tiepido

term /tɜːm/ *n* periodo *m*; *Sch Univ* trimestre *m*; (*expression*) termine *m*; **~s** *pl* (*conditions*) condizioni *fpl*; ~ **of office** carica *f*; **in the short/long** ~ a breve/lungo termine; **be on good/bad ~s** essere in buoni/cattivi rapporti; **come to ~s with** accettare ⟨*past, fact*⟩; **easy ~s** facilità *f* di pagamento

terminal /'tɜːmɪn(ə)l/ *a* finale; *Med* terminale ● *n Aeron* terminal *m inv*; *Rail* stazione *f* di testa; (*of bus*) capolinea *m*; (*on battery*) morsetto *m*; *Comput* terminale *m*. **~ly** *adv* **be ~ly ill** essere in fase terminale

terminat|e /'tɜːmɪneɪt/ *vt* terminare; rescindere ⟨*contract*⟩; interrompere ⟨*pregnancy*⟩ ● *vi* terminare; **~e in** finire in. **~ion** /-'neɪʃn/ *n* termine *m*; *Med* interruzione *f* di gravidanza

terminology /tɜːmɪ'nɒlədʒɪ/ *n* terminologia *f*

terminus /'tɜːmɪnəs/ *n* (*pl* -**ni** /-naɪ/) (*for bus*) capolinea *m*; (*for train*) stazione *f* di testa

terrace /'terəs/ *n* terrazza *f*; (*houses*) fila *f* di case a schiera; **the ~s** *pl Sport* le gradinate. **~d house** *n* casa *f* a schiera

terrain /te'reɪn/ *n* terreno *m*

terrib|le /'terəbl/ *a* terribile. **~y** *adv* terribilmente

terrier /'terɪə(r)/ *n* terrier *m inv*

terrific /tə'rɪfɪk/ *a fam* (*excellent*) fantastico; (*huge*) enorme. **~ally** *adv fam* terribilmente

terri|fy /'terɪfaɪ/ *vt* (*pt/pp* -**ied**) atterrire; **be ~fied** essere terrorizzato. **~fying** *a* terrificante

territorial /terɪ'tɔːrɪəl/ *a* territoriale

territory /'terɪtərɪ/ *n* territorio *m*

terror /'terə(r)/ *n* terrore *m*. **~ism**

/-ɪzm/ *n* terrorismo *m*. **~ist** /-ɪst/ *n* terrorista *mf*. **~ize** *vt* terrorizzare

terse /tɜːs/ *a* conciso

test /test/ *n* esame *m*; (*in laboratory*) esperimento *m*; (*of friendship, machine*) prova *f*; (*of intelligence, aptitude*) test *m* inv; **put to the ~** mettere alla prova ● *vt* esaminare; provare ⟨machine⟩

testament /'testəmənt/ *n* testamento *m*; **Old/New T~** Antico/Nuovo Testamento *m*

testicle /'testɪkl/ *n* testicolo *m*

testify /'testɪfaɪ/ *vt/i* (*pt/pp* **-ied**) testimoniare

testimonial /testɪ'məʊnɪəl/ *n* lettera *f* di referenze

testimony /'testɪmənɪ/ *n* testimonianza *f*

'test: ~ match *n* partita *f* internazionale. **~-tube** *n* provetta *f*. **~-tube 'baby** *n fam* bambino, -a *mf* in provetta

tetanus /'tetənəs/ *n* tetano *m*

tether /'teðə(r)/ *n* **be at the end of one's ~** non poterne più

text /tekst/ *n* testo *m*. **~book** *n* manuale *m*

textile /'tekstaɪl/ *a* tessile ● *n* stoffa *f*

texture /'tekstʃə(r)/ *n* (*of skin*) grana *f*; (*of food*) consistenza *f*; **of a smooth ~** (*to the touch*) soffice al tatto

Thai /taɪ/ *a* & *n* tailandese *mf*. **~land** *n* Tailandia *f*

Thames /temz/ *n* Tamigi *m*

than /ðən/, *accentato* /ðæn/ *conj* che; (*with numbers, names*) di; **older ~ me** più vecchio di me

thank /θæŋk/ *vt* ringraziare; **~ you [very much]** grazie [mille]. **~ful** *a* grato. **~fully** *adv* con gratitudine; (*happily*) fortunatamente. **~less** *a* ingrato

thanks /θæŋks/ *npl* ringraziamenti *mpl*; **~!** *fam* grazie!; **~ to** grazie a

that /ðæt/ *a* & *pron* (*pl* **those**) quel, quei *pl*; (*before s + consonant, gn, ps and z*) quello, quegli *pl*; (*before vowel*) quell' *mf*, quegli *mpl*, quelle *fpl*; **~ one** quello; **I don't like those** quelli non mi piacciono; **~** cioè; **is ~ you?** sei tu?; **who is ~?** chi è?; **what did you do after ~?** cosa hai fatto dopo?; **like ~** in questo modo, così; **a man like ~** un uomo così; **~ is why** ecco perché; **~'s it!** (*you've understood*) ecco!; (*I've finished*) ecco fatto!; (*I've had enough*) basta così!; (*there's nothing more*) tutto qui!; **~'s ~!** (*with job*) ecco fatto!; (*with relationship*) è tutto finito!; **and ~'s ~!** punto e basta! **all ~ I know** tutto quello che so ● *adv* così; **it wasn't ~ good** non era poi così buono ● *rel pron* che; **the man ~ I spoke to** l'uomo con cui ho parlato; **the day ~ I saw him** il giorno in cui l'ho visto; **all ~ I know** tutto quello che so ● *conj* che; **I think ~...** penso che...

thatch /θætʃ/ *n* tetto *m* di paglia. **~ed** *a* coperto di paglia

thaw /θɔː/ *n* disgelo *m* ● *vt* fare scongelare ⟨food⟩ ● *vi* ⟨food:⟩ scongelarsi; **it's ~ing** sta sgelando

the /ðə/, *di fronte a una vocale* /ðiː/ *def art* il, la *f*; i *mpl*, le *fpl*; (*before s + consonant, gn, ps and z*) lo, gli *mpl*; (*before vowel*) l' *mf*, gli *mpl*, le *fpl*; **at ~ cinema/station** al cinema/alla stazione; **from ~ cinema/station** dal cinema/dalla stazione ● *adv* **~ more ~ better** più ce n'è meglio è; (*with reference to pl*) più ce ne sono, meglio è; **all ~ better** tanto meglio

theatre /'θɪətə(r)/ *n* teatro *m*; *Med* sala *f* operatoria

theatrical /θɪ'ætrɪkl/ *a* teatrale; (*showy*) melodrammatico

theft /θeft/ *n* furto *m*

their /ðeə(r)/ *poss a* il loro *m*, la loro *f*, i loro *mpl*, le loro *fpl*; **~ mother/father** la loro madre/il loro padre

theirs /ðeəz/ *poss pron* il loro *m*, la loro *f*, i loro *mpl*, le loro *fpl*; **a friend of ~** un loro amico; **friends of ~** dei loro amici; **those are ~** quelli sono loro; (*as opposed to ours*) quelli sono i loro

them /ðem/ *pron* (*direct object*) li *m*, le *f*; (*indirect object*) gli, loro *fml*; (*after prep: with people*) loro; (*after preposition: with things*) essi; **we haven't seen ~** non li/le abbiamo visti/viste; **give ~ the money** dai loro *or* dagli i soldi; **give it to ~** daglielo; **I've spoken to ~** ho parlato con loro; **it's ~** sono loro

theme /θiːm/ *n* tema *m*. **~ song** *n* motivo *m* conduttore

them'selves *pers pron* (*reflexive*) si; (*emphatic*) se stessi; **they poured ~ a drink** si sono versati da bere; **they said so ~** lo hanno detto loro stessi; **they kept it to ~** se lo sono tenuti per sé; **by ~ da soli**

then /ðen/ *adv* allora; (*next*) poi; **by ~** (*in the past*) ormai; (*in the future*) per allora; **since ~** sin da allora; **before ~** prima di allora; **from ~ on** da allora in poi; **now and ~** ogni tanto; **there and ~** all'istante ● *a* di allora

theolog|ian /θɪə'ləʊdʒɪən/ *n* teologo, -a *mf*. **~y** /-'ɒlədʒɪ/ *n* teologia *f*

theorem /'θɪərəm/ *n* teorema *m*

theoretical /θɪə'retɪkl/ *a* teorico

theory /ˈθɪərɪ/ n teoria f; **in ~** in teoria

therapeutic /θerəˈpjuːtɪk/ a terapeutico

therap|ist /ˈθerəpɪst/ n terapista mf. **~y** n terapia f

there /ðeə(r)/ adv là, lì; **down/up ~** laggiù/lassù; **~ is/are** c'è/ci sono; **he/she is** eccolo/eccola ● int **~, ~!** dai, su!

there: ~abouts adv [or] **~abouts** (roughly) all'incirca. **~'after** adv dopo di che. **~by** adv in tal modo. **~fore** /-fɔː(r)/ adv perciò

thermal /ˈθɜːm(ə)l/ a termale; **~ 'underwear** n biancheria f che mantiene la temperatura corporea

thermometer /θəˈmɒmɪtə(r)/ n termometro m

Thermos® /ˈθɜːməs/ n **~ [flask]** termos m inv

thermostat /ˈθɜːməstæt/ n termostato m

thesaurus /θɪˈsɔːrəs/ n dizionario m dei sinonimi

these /ðiːz/ see **this**

thesis /ˈθiːsɪs/ n (pl **-ses** /-siːz/) tesi f inv

they /ðeɪ/ pron loro; **~ are tired** sono stanchi; **we're going, but ~ are not** noi andiamo, ma loro no; **~ say** (generalizing) si dice; **~ are building a new road** stanno costruendo una nuova strada

thick /θɪk/ a spesso; ⟨forest⟩ fitto; ⟨liquid⟩ denso; ⟨hair⟩ folto; ⟨fam: stupid⟩ ottuso; ⟨fam: close⟩ molto unito; **be 5 mm ~** essere 5 mm di spessore ● adv densamente ● n **in the ~ of** nel mezzo di. **~en** vt ispessire ⟨sauce⟩ ● vi ispessirsi; ⟨fog:⟩ infittirsi. **~ly** adv densamente; ⟨cut⟩ a fette spesse. **~ness** n spessore m

thick: ~set a tozzo. **~-'skinned** a fam insensibile

thief /θiːf/ n (pl **thieves**) ladro, -a mf

thieving /ˈθiːvɪŋ/ a ladro ● n furti mpl

thigh /θaɪ/ n coscia f

thimble /ˈθɪmbl/ n ditale m

thin /θɪn/ a (**thinner, thinnest**) sottile; ⟨shoes, sweater⟩ leggero; ⟨liquid⟩ liquido; ⟨person⟩ magro; ⟨fig: excuse, plot⟩ inconsistente ● adv = **thinly** ● v (pt/pp **thinned**) ● vt diluire ⟨liquid⟩ ● vi diradarsi. **thin out** vi diradarsi. **~ly** adv ⟨populated⟩ scarsamente; ⟨disguised⟩ leggermente; ⟨cut⟩ a fette sottili

thing /θɪŋ/ n cosa f; **~s** pl (belongings) roba fsg; **for one ~** in primo luogo; **the right ~** la cosa giusta; **just the ~!** pro-

prio quel che ci vuole!; **how are ~s?** come vanno le cose?; **the latest ~** fam l'ultima cosa; **the best ~ would be** la cosa migliore sarebbe; **poor ~!** poveretto!

think /θɪŋk/ vt/i (pt/pp **thought**) pensare; (believe) credere; **I ~ so** credo di sì; **what do you ~?** (what is your opinion?) cosa ne pensi?; **~ of/about** pensare a; **what do you ~ of it?** cosa ne pensi di questo?. **think over** vt riflettere su. **think up** vt escogitare

third /θɜːd/ a & n terzo, -a mf. **~ly** adv terzo. **~-rate** a scadente

thirst /θɜːst/ n sete f. **~ily** adv con sete. **~y** a assetato; **be ~y** aver sete

thirteen /θɜːˈtiːn/ a & n tredici m. **~th** a & n tredicesimo, -a mf

thirtieth /ˈθɜːtɪɪθ/ a & n trentesimo, -a mf

thirty /ˈθɜːtɪ/ a & n trenta m

this /ðɪs/ a (pl **these**) questo; **~ man/ woman** quest'uomo/questa donna; **these men/women** questi uomini/ queste donne; **~ one** questo; **~ morning/evening** stamattina/stasera ● pron (pl **these**) questo; **we talked about ~ and that** abbiamo parlato del più e del meno; **like ~** così; **~ is Peter** questo è Peter; Teleph sono Peter; **who is ~?** chi è?; Teleph chi parla? ● adv così; **~ big** così grande

thistle /ˈθɪsl/ n cardo m

thorn /θɔːn/ n spina f. **~y** a spinoso

thorough /ˈθʌrə/ a completo; ⟨knowledge⟩ profondo; ⟨clean, search, training⟩ a fondo; ⟨person⟩ scrupoloso

thorough: ~bred n purosangue m inv. **~fare** n via f principale; **'no ~fare'** 'strada non transitabile'

thorough|ly /ˈθʌrəlɪ/ adv ⟨clean, search, know sth⟩ a fondo; (extremely) estremamente. **~ness** n completezza f

those /ðəʊz/ see **that**

though /ðəʊ/ conj sebbene; **as ~** come se ● adv fam tuttavia

thought /θɔːt/ see **think** ● n pensiero m; (idea) idea f. **~ful** a pensieroso; (considerate) premuroso. **~fully** adv pensierosamente; (considerately) premurosamente. **~less** a (inconsiderate) sconsiderato. **~lessly** adv con noncuranza

thousand /ˈθaʊznd/ a **one/a ~** mille m inv ● n mille m inv; **~s of** migliaia fpl di. **~th** a millesimo ● n millesimo, -a mf

thrash /θræʃ/ vt picchiare; (defeat) sconfiggere. **thrash out** vt mettere a punto

thread /θred/ n filo m; (of screw) filetto

● *vt* infilare ⟨*beads*⟩; ~ **one's way through** farsi strada fra. **~bare** *a* logoro

threat /θret/ *n* minaccia *f*

threaten /ˈθretn/ *vt* minacciare (**to do** di fare) ● *vi fig* incalzare. **~ing** *a* minaccioso; ⟨*sky, atmosphere*⟩ sinistro

three /θriː/ *a & n* tre *m*. **~fold** *a & adv* triplo. **~some** /-səm/ *n* trio *m*

thresh /θreʃ/ *vt* trebbiare

threshold /ˈθreʃəʊld/ *n* soglia *f*

threw /θruː/ *see* **throw**

thrift /θrɪft/ *n* economia *f*. **~y** *a* parsimonioso

thrill /θrɪl/ *n* emozione *f*; ⟨*of fear*⟩ brivido *m* ● *vt* entusiasmare; **be ~ed with** essere entusiasta di. **~er** *n* ⟨*book*⟩ [romanzo *m*] giallo *m*; ⟨*film*⟩ [film *m*] giallo *m*. **~ing** *a* eccitante

thrive /θraɪv/ *vi* (*pt* thrived *or* throve, *pp* thrived *or* thriven /ˈθrɪvn/) ⟨*business:*⟩ prosperare; ⟨*child, plant:*⟩ crescere bene; **I ~ on pressure** mi piace essere sotto tensione

throat /θrəʊt/ *n* gola *f*; **sore ~** mal *m* di gola

throb /θrɒb/ *n* pulsazione *f*; ⟨*of heart*⟩ battito *m* ● *vi* (*pt/pp* throbbed) ⟨*vibrate*⟩ pulsare; ⟨*heart:*⟩ battere

throes /θrəʊz/ *npl* **in the ~ of** *fig* alle prese con

thrombosis /θrɒmˈbəʊsɪs/ *n* trombosi *f*

throne /θrəʊn/ *n* trono *m*

throng /θrɒŋ/ *n* calca *f*

throttle /ˈθrɒtl/ *n* (*on motorbike*) manopola *f* di accelerazione ● *vt* strozzare

through /θruː/ *prep* attraverso; ⟨*during*⟩ durante; ⟨*by means of*⟩ tramite; ⟨*thanks to*⟩ grazie a; **Saturday ~ Tuesday** *Am* da sabato a martedì incluso ● *adv* attraverso; **~ and ~** fino in fondo; **wet ~** completamente bagnato; **read sth ~** dare una lettura a qcsa; **let ~** lasciar passare ⟨*sb*⟩ ● *a* ⟨*train*⟩ diretto; **be ~** ⟨*finished*⟩ aver finito; *Teleph* avere la comunicazione

throughout /θruːˈaʊt/ *prep* per tutto ● *adv* completamente; ⟨*time*⟩ per tutto il tempo

throw /θrəʊ/ *n* tiro *m* ● *vt* (*pt* threw, *pp* thrown) lanciare; ⟨*throw away*⟩ gettare; azionare ⟨*switch*⟩; disarcionare ⟨*rider*⟩; ⟨*fam: disconcert*⟩ disorientare; *fam* dare ⟨*party*⟩. **throw away** *vt* gettare via. **throw out** *vt* gettare via; rigettare ⟨*plan*⟩; buttare fuori ⟨*person*⟩. **throw up** *vt* alzare ● *vi* ⟨*vomit*⟩ vomitare

ˈthrow-away *a* ⟨*remark*⟩ buttato lì; ⟨*paper cup*⟩ usa e getta *inv*

thrush /θrʌʃ/ *n* tordo *m*

thrust /θrʌst/ *n* spinta *f* ● *vt* (*pt/pp* thrust) ⟨*push*⟩ spingere; ⟨*insert*⟩ conficcare; ~ **[up]on** imporre a

thud /θʌd/ *n* tonfo *m*

thug /θʌg/ *n* delinquente *m*

thumb /θʌm/ *n* pollice *m*; **as a rule of ~** come regola generale; **under sb's ~** succube di qcno ● *vt* ~ **a lift** fare l'autostop. **~-index** *n* indice *m* a rubrica. **~tack** *n Am* puntina *f* da disegno

thump /θʌmp/ *n* colpo *m*; ⟨*noise*⟩ tonfo *m* ● *vt* battere su ⟨*table, door*⟩; battere ⟨*fist*⟩; colpire ⟨*person*⟩ ● *vi* battere (**on** su); ⟨*heart:*⟩ battere forte. **thump about** *vi* camminare pesantemente

thunder /ˈθʌndə(r)/ *n* tuono *m*; ⟨*loud noise*⟩ rimbombo *m* ● *vi* tuonare; ⟨*make loud noise*⟩ rimbombare. **~clap** *n* rombo *m* di tuono. **~storm** *n* temporale *m*. **~y** *a* temporalesco

Thursday /ˈθɜːzdeɪ/ *n* giovedì *m inv*

thus /ðʌs/ *adv* così

thwart /θwɔːt/ *vt* ostacolare

thyme /taɪm/ *n* timo *m*

Tiber /ˈtaɪbə(r)/ *n* Tevere *m*

tick /tɪk/ *n* ⟨*sound*⟩ ticchettio *m*; ⟨*mark*⟩ segno *m*; ⟨*fam: instant*⟩ attimo *m* ● *vi* ticchettare. **tick off** *vt* spuntare; *fam* sgridare. **tick over** *vi* ⟨*engine:*⟩ andare al minimo

ticket /ˈtɪkɪt/ *n* biglietto *m*; ⟨*for item deposited, library*⟩ tagliando *m*; ⟨*label*⟩ cartellino *m*; ⟨*fine*⟩ multa *f*. **~-collector** *n* controllore *m*. **~-office** *n* biglietteria *f*

tick|le /ˈtɪkl/ *n* solletico *m* ● *vt* fare il solletico a; ⟨*amuse*⟩ divertire ● *vi* fare prurito. **~lish** /ˈtɪklɪʃ/ *a* che soffre il solletico

tidal /ˈtaɪdl/ *a* ⟨*river, harbour*⟩ di marea. **~ wave** *n* onda *f* di marea

tiddly-winks /ˈtɪdlɪwɪŋks/ *n* gioco *m* delle pulci

tide /taɪd/ *n* marea *f*; ⟨*of events*⟩ corso *m*; **the ~ is in/out** c'è alta/bassa marea ● **tide over** *vt* ~ **sb over** aiutare qcno a andare avanti

tidily /ˈtaɪdɪlɪ/ *adv* in modo ordinato

tidiness /ˈtaɪdɪnɪs/ *n* ordine *m*

tidy /ˈtaɪdɪ/ *a* (**-ier, -iest**) ordinato; ⟨*fam: amount*⟩ bello ● *vt* (*pt/pp* -ied) ~ **[up]** ordinare; ~ **oneself up** mettersi in ordine

tie /taɪ/ *n* cravatta *f*; ⟨*cord*⟩ legaccio *m*; ⟨*fig: bond*⟩ legame *m*; ⟨*restriction*⟩ impedimento *m*; *Sport* pareggio *m* ● *v* (*pres p* tying) ● *vt* legare; fare ⟨*knot*⟩; **be ~d**

(*in competition*) essere in parità ● *vi* pareggiare. **tie in with** *vi* corrispondere a. **tie up** *vt* legare; vincolare ‹*capital*›; **be ~d up** (*busy*) essere occupato

tier /tɪə(r)/ *n* fila *f;* (*of cake*) piano *m;* (*in stadium*) gradinata *f*

tiff /tɪf/ *n* battibecco *m*

tiger /'taɪɡə(r)/ *n* tigre *f*

tight /taɪt/ *a* stretto; (*taut*) teso; (*fam: drunk*) sbronzo; (*fam: mean*) spilorcio; **~ corner** *fam* brutta situazione *f* ● *adv* strettamente; ‹*hold*› forte; ‹*closed*› bene

tighten /'taɪtn/ *vt* stringere; avvitare ‹*screw*›; intensificare ‹*control*› ● *vi* stringersi

tight: ~-'fisted *a* tirchio. **~-fitting** *a* aderente. **~ly** *adv* strettamente; ‹*hold*› forte; ‹*closed*› bene. **~rope** *n* fune *f* (*da funamboli*)

tights /taɪts/ *npl* collant *m inv*

tile /taɪl/ *n* mattonella *f;* (*on roof*) tegola *f* ● *vt* rivestire di mattonelle ‹*wall*›

till¹ /tɪl/ *prep & conj* = **until**

till² *n* cassa *f*

tiller /'tɪlə(r)/ *n* barra *f* del timone

tilt /tɪlt/ *n* inclinazione *f;* **at full ~** a tutta velocità ● *vt* inclinare ● *vi* inclinarsi

timber /'tɪmbə(r)/ *n* legname *m*

time /taɪm/ *n* tempo *m;* (*occasion*) volta *f;* (*by clock*) ora *f;* **two ~s four** due volte quattro; **at any ~** in qualsiasi momento; **this ~** questa volta; **at ~s, from ~ to ~** ogni tanto; **~ and again** cento volte; **two at a ~** due alla volta; **on ~** in orario; **in ~** in tempo; (*eventually*) col tempo; **in ~ at all** velocemente; **in a year's ~** fra un anno; **behind ~** in ritardo; **behind the ~s** antiquato; **for the ~ being** per il momento; **what is the ~?** che ora è?; **by the ~ we arrive** quando arriviamo; **did you have a nice ~?** ti sei divertito?; **have a good ~!** divertiti! ● *vt* scegliere il momento per; cronometrare ‹*race*›; **be well ~d** essere ben calcolato

time: ~ bomb *n* bomba *f* a orologeria. **~-lag** *n* intervallo *m* di tempo. **~less** *a* eterno. **~ly** *a* opportuno. **~-switch** *n* interruttore *m* a tempo. **~-table** *n* orario *m*

timid /'tɪmɪd/ *a* (*shy*) timido; (*fearful*) timoroso

timing /'taɪmɪŋ/ *n* Sport, Techn cronometraggio *m;* **the ~ of the election** il momento scelto per le elezioni

tin /tɪn/ *n* stagno *m;* (*container*) barattolo *m* ● *vt* (*pt/pp* **tinned**) inscatolare. **~ foil** *n* [carta *f*] stagnola *f*

tinge /tɪndʒ/ *n* sfumatura *f* ● *vt* **~d with** *fig* misto a

tingle /'tɪŋɡl/ *vi* pizzicare

tinker /'tɪŋkə(r)/ *vi* armeggiare

tinkle /'tɪŋkl/ *n* tintinnio *m;* (*fam: phone call*) colpo *m* di telefono ● *vi* tintinnare

tinned /tɪnd/ *a* in scatola

'tin opener *n* apriscatole *m inv*

tinsel /'tɪnsl/ *n* filo *m* d'argento

tint /tɪnt/ *n* tinta *f* ● *vt* tingersi ‹*hair*›

tiny /'taɪnɪ/ *a* (**-ier, -iest**) minuscolo

tip¹ /tɪp/ *n* punta *f*

tip² *n* (*money*) mancia *f;* (*advice*) consiglio *m;* (*for rubbish*) discarica *f* ● *v* (*pt/pp* **tipped**) ● *vt* (*tilt*) inclinare; (*overturn*) capovolgere; (*pour*) versare; (*reward*) dare una mancia a ● *vi* inclinarsi; (*overturn*) capovolgersi. **tip off** *vt* **~ sb off** (*inform*) fare una soffiata a qcno. **tip out** *vt* rovesciare. **tip over** *vt* capovolgere ● *vi* capovolgersi

'tip-off *n* soffiata *f*

tipped /tɪpt/ *a* ‹*cigarette*› col filtro

tipsy /'tɪpsɪ/ *a fam* brillo

tiptoe /'tɪptəʊ/ *n* **on ~** in punta di piedi

tiptop /tɪp'tɒp/ *a fam* in condizioni perfette

tire /'taɪə(r)/ *vt* stancare ● *vi* stancarsi. **~d** *a* stanco; **~d of** stanco di; **~d out** stanco morto. **~less** *a* instancabile. **~some** /-səm/ *a* fastidioso

tiring /'taɪərɪŋ/ *a* stancante

tissue /'tɪʃuː/ *n* tessuto *m;* (*handkerchief*) fazzolettino *m* di carta. **~-paper** *n* carta *f* velina

tit¹ /tɪt/ *n* (*bird*) cincia *f*

tit² *n* **~ for tat** pan per focaccia

title /'taɪtl/ *n* titolo *m.* **~-deed** *n* atto *m* di proprietà. **~-role** *n* ruolo *m* principale

tittle-tattle /'tɪtltætl/ *n* pettegolezzi *mpl*

to /tuː/, *atono* /tə/ *prep* a; (*to countries*) in; (*towards*) verso; (*up to, until*) fino a; **I'm going to John's/the butcher's** vado da John/dal macellaio; **come/go to sb** venire/andare da qcno; **to Italy/ Switzerland** in Italia/Svizzera; **I've never been to Rome** non sono mai stato a Roma; **go to the market** andare al mercato; **to the toilet/my room** in bagno/camera mia; **to an exhibition** a una mostra; **to university** all'università; **twenty/quarter to eight** le otto meno venti/un quarto; **5 to 6 kilos** da 5 a 6 chili; **to the end** alla fine; **to this day** fino a oggi; **to the best of my recollection** per quanto mi possa ricordare; **give/say sth to sb** dare/dire qcsa a qcno; **give it to me** dammelo; **there's nothing to it** è una cosa da niente ● *verbal constructions*

to go andare; **learn to swim** imparare a nuotare; **I want to/have to go** voglio/devo andare; **it's easy to forget** è facile da dimenticare; **too ill/tired to** troppo malato/stanco per andare; **you have to** devi; **I don't want to** non voglio; **live to be 90** vivere fino a 90 anni; **he was the last to arrive** è stato l'ultimo ad arrivare; **to be honest,...** per essere sincero,... ● *adv* **pull to** chiudere; **to and fro** avanti e indietro

toad /təʊd/ *n* rospo *m*. **~stool** *n* fungo *m* velenoso

toast /təʊst/ *n* pane *m* tostato; ⟨*drink*⟩ brindisi *m* *inv* ● *vt* tostare ⟨*bread*⟩; ⟨*drink a ~ to*⟩ brindare a. **~er** *n* tostapane *m* *inv*

tobacco /təˈbækəʊ/ *n* tabacco *m*. **~nist's** [**shop**] *n* tabaccheria *f*

toboggan /təˈbɒɡən/ *n* toboga *m* *inv* ● *vi* andare in toboga

today /təˈdeɪ/ *a* & *adv* oggi *m*; **a week ~** una settimana a oggi; **~'s paper** il giornale di oggi

toddler /ˈtɒdlə(r)/ *n* bambino, -a *mf* ai primi passi

to-do /təˈduː/ *n fam* baccano *m*

toe /təʊ/ *n* dito *m* del piede; ⟨*of footwear*⟩ punta *f*; **big ~** alluce *m* ● *vt* **~ the line** rigar diritto. **~nail** *n* unghia *f* del piede

toffee /ˈtɒfɪ/ *n* caramella *f* al mou

together /təˈɡeðə(r)/ *adv* insieme; ⟨*at the same time*⟩ allo stesso tempo; **~ with** insieme a

toilet /ˈtɔɪlɪt/ *n* ⟨*lavatory*⟩ gabinetto *m*. **~ paper** *n* carta *f* igienica

toiletries /ˈtɔɪlɪtrɪz/ *npl* articoli *mpl* da toilette

toilet: **~ roll** *n* rotolo *m* di carta igienica. **~ water** *n* acqua *f* di colonia

token /ˈtəʊkən/ *n* segno *m*; ⟨*counter*⟩ gettone *m*; ⟨*voucher*⟩ buono *m* ● *attrib* simbolico

told /təʊld/ *see* **tell** ● *a* **all ~** in tutto

tolerab|le /ˈtɒl(ə)rəbl/ *a* tollerabile; ⟨*not bad*⟩ discreto. **~y** *adv* discretamente

toleran|ce /ˈtɒl(ə)r(ə)ns/ *n* tolleranza *f*. **~t** *a* tollerante. **~tly** *adv* con tolleranza

tolerate /ˈtɒləreɪt/ *vt* tollerare

toll[1] /təʊl/ *n* pedaggio *m*; **death ~** numero *m* di morti

toll[2] *vi* suonare a morto

tom /tɒm/ *n* ⟨*cat*⟩ gatto *m* maschio

tomato /təˈmɑːtəʊ/ *n* (*pl* **-es**) pomodoro *m*. **~ ketchup** *n* ketchup *m*. **~ purée** *n* concentrato *m* di pomodoro

tomb /tuːm/ *n* tomba *f*

'tomboy *n* maschiaccio *m*

'tombstone *n* pietra *f* tombale

'tom-cat *n* gatto *m* maschio

tomfoolery /tɒmˈfuːlərɪ/ *n* stupidaggini *fpl*

tomorrow /təˈmɒrəʊ/ *a* & *adv* domani; **~ morning** domani mattina; **the day after ~** dopodomani; **see you ~!** a domani!

ton /tʌn/ *n* tonnellata *f* (= *1,016 kg.*); **~s of** *fam* un sacco di

tone /təʊn/ *n* tono *m*; ⟨*colour*⟩ tonalità *f* *inv* ● **tone down** *vt* attenuare. **tone up** *vt* tonificare ⟨*muscles*⟩

toner /ˈtəʊnə(r)/ *n* toner *m*

tongs /tɒŋz/ *npl* pinze *fpl*

tongue /tʌŋ/ *n* lingua *f*; **~ in cheek** ⟨*fam: say*⟩ ironicamente. **~-twister** *n* scioglilingua *m* *inv*

tonic /ˈtɒnɪk/ *n* tonico *m*; ⟨*for hair*⟩ lozione *f* per i capelli; *fig* toccasana *m* *inv*; **~ [water]** acqua *f* tonica

tonight /təˈnaɪt/ *adv* stanotte; ⟨*evening*⟩ stasera ● *n* questa notte *f*; ⟨*evening*⟩ questa sera *f*

tonne /tʌn/ *n* tonnellata *f* metrica

tonsil /ˈtɒnsl/ *n Anat* tonsilla *f*. **~litis** /-səˈlaɪtɪs/ *n* tonsillite *f*

too /tuː/ *adv* troppo; ⟨*also*⟩ anche; **~ many** troppi; **~ much** troppo; **~ little** troppo poco

took /tʊk/ *see* **take**

tool /tuːl/ *n* attrezzo *m*

toot /tuːt/ *n* suono *m* di clacson ● *vi* *Auto* clacsonare

tooth /tuːθ/ *n* (*pl* **teeth**) dente *m*

tooth: **~ache** *n* mal *m* di denti. **~brush** *n* spazzolino *m* da denti. **~less** *a* sdentato. **~paste** *n* dentifricio *m*. **~pick** *n* stuzzicadenti *m* *inv*

top[1] /tɒp/ *n* ⟨*toy*⟩ trottola *f*

top[2] *n* cima *f*; *Sch* primo, -a *mf*; ⟨*upper part or half*⟩ parte *f* superiore; ⟨*of page, list, street*⟩ inizio *m*; ⟨*upper surface*⟩ superficie *f*; ⟨*lid*⟩ coperchio *m*; ⟨*of bottle*⟩ tappo *m*; ⟨*garment*⟩ maglia *f*; ⟨*blouse*⟩ camicia *f*; *Auto* marcia *f* più alta; **at the ~** *fig* al vertice; **at the ~ of one's voice** a squarciagola; **on ~/on ~ of** sopra; **on ~ of that** ⟨*besides*⟩ per di più; **from ~ to bottom** da cima a fondo ● *a* in alto; ⟨*official, floor of building*⟩ migliore; ⟨*speed*⟩ massimo ● *vt* (*pt/pp* **topped**) essere in testa a ⟨*list*⟩; ⟨*exceed*⟩ sorpassare; **~ped with ice-cream** ricoperto di gelato. **top up** *vt* riempire

top: **~ 'floor** *n* ultimo piano *m*. **~ hat** *n*

cilindro m. **~-heavy** a con la parte superiore sovraccarica

topic /'tɒpɪk/ n soggetto m; (of conversation) argomento m. **~al** a d'attualità

top: **~less** a & adv topless. **~most** a più alto

topple /'tɒpl/ vt rovesciare ● vi rovesciarsi. **topple off** vi cadere

top-'secret a segretissimo, top secret inv

torch /tɔ:tʃ/ n torcia f [elettrica]; (flaming) fiaccola f

tore /tɔ:(r)/ see **tear¹**

torment¹ /'tɔ:ment/ n tormento m

torment² /tɔ:'ment/ vt tormentare

torn /tɔ:n/ see **tear¹** ● a bucato

tornado /tɔ:'neɪdəʊ/ n (pl **-es**) tornado m inv

torpedo /tɔ:'pi:dəʊ/ n (pl **-es**) siluro m ● vt silurare

torrent /'tɒrənt/ n torrente m. **~ial** /tə'renʃl/ a ⟨rain⟩ torrenziale

torso /'tɔ:səʊ/ n torso m; (in art) busto m

tortoise /'tɔ:təs/ n tartaruga f

tortuous /'tɔ:tʃʊəs/ a tortuoso

torture /'tɔ:tʃə(r)/ n tortura f ● vt torturare

Tory /'tɔ:rɪ/ a & n fam conservatore, -trice mf

toss /tɒs/ vt gettare; (into the air) lanciare in aria; (shake) scrollare; ⟨horse:⟩ disarcionare; mescolare ⟨salad⟩ rivoltare facendo saltare in aria ⟨pancake⟩; **~ a coin** fare testa o croce ● vi **~ and turn** (in bed) rigirarsi; **let's ~ for it** facciamo testa o croce

tot¹ /tɒt/ n bimbetto, -a mf; (fam: of liquor) goccio m

tot² vt (pt/pp **totted**) **~ up** fam fare la somma di

total /'təʊtl/ a totale ● n totale m ● vt (pt/pp **totalled**) ammontare a; (add up) sommare

totalitarian /təʊtælɪ'teərɪən/ a totalitario

totally /'təʊtəlɪ/ adv totalmente

totter /'tɒtə(r)/ vi barcollare; ⟨government:⟩ vacillare

touch /tʌtʃ/ n tocco m; (sense) tatto m; (contact) contatto m; (trace) traccia f; (of irony, humour) tocco m; **get/be in ~** mettersi/essere in contatto ● vt toccare; (lightly) sfiorare; (equal) eguagliare; (fig: move) commuovere ● vi toccarsi. **touch down** vi Aeron atterrare. **touch on** vt fig accennare a. **touch up** vt ritoccare ⟨painting⟩

touch|ing /'tʌtʃɪŋ/ a commovente. **~screen** n touchscreen m inv. **~-tone** a a tastiera. **~y** a permaloso; ⟨subject⟩ delicato

tough /tʌf/ a duro; (severe, harsh) severo; (durable) resistente; (resilient) forte

toughen /'tʌfn/ vt rinforzare. **toughen up** vt rendere più forte ⟨person⟩

tour /tʊə(r)/ n giro m; (of building, town) visita f; Theat, Sport tournée f inv; (of duty) servizio m ● vt visitare ● vi fare un giro turistico; Theat essere in tournée

touris|m /'tʊərɪzm/ n turismo m. **~t** /-rɪst/ n turista mf ● attrib turistico. **~t office** n ufficio m turistico

tournament /'tʊənəmənt/ n torneo m

'tour operator n tour operator mf inv, operatore, -trice mf turistico, -a

tousle /'taʊzl/ vt spettinare

tout /taʊt/ n (ticket ~) bagarino m; (horse-racing) informatore m ● vi **~ for** sollecitare

tow /təʊ/ n rimorchio m; **'on ~'** 'a rimorchio'; **in ~** fam al seguito ● vt rimorchiare. **tow away** vt portare via col carro attrezzi

toward[s] /tə'wɔ:d(z)/ prep verso; (with respect to) nei riguardi di

towel /'taʊəl/ n asciugamano m. **~ling** n spugna f

tower /'taʊə(r)/ n torre f ● vi **~ above** dominare. **~ block** n palazzone m. **~ing** a torreggiante; ⟨rage⟩ violento

town /taʊn/ n città f inv. **~ 'hall** n municipio m

tow: **~-path** n strada f alzaia. **~-rope** n cavo m da rimorchio

toxic /'tɒksɪk/ a tossico

toxin /'tɒksɪn/ n tossina f

toy /tɔɪ/ n giocattolo m. **~shop** n negozio m di giocattoli. **toy with** vt giocherellare con

trace /treɪs/ n traccia f ● vt seguire le tracce di; (find) rintracciare; (draw) tracciare; (with tracing-paper) ricalcare

track /træk/ n traccia f; (path, Sport) pista f; Rail binario m; **keep ~ of** tenere d'occhio ● vt seguire le tracce di. **track down** vt scovare

'track: **~ball** n Comput trackball f inv. **~suit** n tuta f da ginnastica

tractor /'træktə(r)/ n trattore m

trade /treɪd/ n commercio m; (line of business) settore m; (craft) mestiere m; **by ~** di mestiere ● vt commerciare; **~ sth for sth** scambiare qcsa per qcsa ● vi commerciare. **trade in** vt (give in

235   **trade mark | trauma**

part exchange) dare in pagamento parziale

'**trade mark** *n* marchio *m* di fabbrica

trader /'treɪdə(r)/ *n* commerciante *mf*

trade: ~**sman** *n* (*joiner etc*) operaio *m*.
~ '**union** *n* sindacato *m*. ~ '**unionist** *n* sindacalista *mf*

trading /'treɪdɪŋ/ *n* commercio *m*. ~ **estate** *n* zona *f* industriale

tradition /trə'dɪʃn/ *n* tradizione *f*. ~**al** *a* tradizionale. ~**ally** *adv* tradizionalmente

traffic /'træfɪk/ *n* traffico *m* ● *vi* (*pt/pp* **trafficked**) trafficare

traffic: ~ **circle** *n* *Am* isola *f* rotatoria. ~ **jam** *n* ingorgo *m*. ~ **lights** *npl* semaforo *msg*. ~ **warden** *n* vigile *m* [urbano]; (*woman*) vigilessa *f*

tragedy /'trædʒədɪ/ *n* tragedia *f*

tragic /'trædʒɪk/ *a* tragico. ~**ally** *adv* tragicamente

trail /treɪl/ *n* traccia *f*; (*path*) sentiero *m* ● *vi* strisciare; ⟨*plant:*⟩ arrampicarsi; ~ [**behind**] rimanere indietro; (*in competition*) essere in svantaggio ● *vt* trascinare

trailer /'treɪlə(r)/ *n* *Auto* rimorchio *m*; (*Am: caravan*) roulotte *f inv;* (*film*) presentazione *f* (*di un film*)

train /treɪn/ *n* treno *m*; ~ **of thought** filo *m* dei pensieri ● *vt* formare professionalmente; *Sport* allenare; (*aim*) puntare; educare ⟨*child*⟩; addestrare ⟨*animal, soldier*⟩ ● *vi* fare il tirocinio; *Sport* allenarsi. ~**ed** *a* ⟨*animal*⟩ addestrato (**to do** a fare)

trainee /treɪ'niː/ *n* apprendista *mf*

train|er /'treɪnə(r)/ *n* *Sport* allenatore, -trice *mf*; (*in circus*) domatore, -trice *mf*; (*of dog, race-horse*) addestratore, -trice *mf*; ~**ers** *pl* scarpe *fpl* da ginnastica. ~**ing** *n* tirocinio *m*; *Sport* allenamento *m*; (*of animal, soldier*) addestramento *m*

traipse /treɪps/ *vi* ~ **around** *fam* andare in giro

trait /treɪt/ *n* caratteristica *f*

traitor /'treɪtə(r)/ *n* traditore, -trice *mf*

tram /træm/ *n* tram *m inv*. ~-**lines** *npl* rotaie *fpl* del tram

tramp /træmp/ *n* (*hike*) camminata *f*; (*vagrant*) barbone, -a *mf*; (*of feet*) calpestio *m* ● *vi* camminare con passo pesante; (*hike*) percorrere a piedi

trample /'træmpl/ *vt/i* ~ [**on**] calpestare

trampoline /'træmpəliːn/ *n* trampolino *m*

trance /trɑːns/ *n* trance *f inv*

tranquil /'træŋkwɪl/ *a* tranquillo. ~**lity** /-'kwɪlətɪ/ *n* tranquillità *f*

tranquillizer /'træŋkwɪlaɪzə(r)/ *n* tranquillante *m*

transact /træn'zækt/ *vt* trattare. ~**ion** /-ækʃn/ *n* transazione *f*

transatlantic /trænzət'læntɪk/ *a* transatlantico

transcend /træn'send/ *vt* trascendere

transfer[1] /'trænsfɜː(r)/ *n* trasferimento *m*; *Sport* cessione *f*; (*design*) decalcomania *f*

transfer[2] /træns'fɜː(r)/ *v* (*pt/pp* **transferred**) ● *vt* trasferire; *Sport* cedere ● *vi* trasferirsi; (*when travelling*) cambiare. ~**able** /-əbl/ *a* trasferibile

transform /træns'fɔːm/ *vt* trasformare. ~**ation** /-fə'meɪʃn/ *n* trasformazione *f*. ~**er** *n* trasformatore *m*

transfusion /træns'fjuːʒn/ *n* trasfusione *f*

transient /'trænzɪənt/ *a* passeggero

transistor /træn'zɪstə(r)/ *n* transistor *m inv*; (*radio*) radiolina *f* a transistor

transit /'trænzɪt/ *n* transito *m*; **in** ~ ⟨*goods*⟩ in transito

transition /træn'zɪʃn/ *n* transizione *f*. ~**al** *a* di transizione

transitive /'trænzɪtɪv/ *a* transitivo

transitory /'trænzɪtərɪ/ *a* transitorio

translat|e /trænz'leɪt/ *vt* tradurre. ~**ion** /-'leɪʃn/ *n* traduzione *f*. ~**or** *n* traduttore, -trice *mf*

transmission /trænz'mɪʃn/ *n* trasmissione *f*

transmit /trænz'mɪt/ *vt* (*pt/pp* **transmitted**) trasmettere. ~**ter** *n* trasmettitore *m*

transparen|cy /træn'spærənsɪ/ *n* *Phot* diapositiva *f*. ~**t** *a* trasparente

transpire /træn'spaɪə(r)/ *vi* emergere; (*fam: happen*) accadere

transplant[1] /'trænsplɑːnt/ *n* trapianto *m*

transplant[2] /træns'plɑːnt/ *vt* trapiantare

transport[1] /'trænspɔːt/ *n* trasporto *m*

transport[2] /træn'spɔːt/ *vt* trasportare. ~**ation** /-teɪʃn/ *n* trasporto *m*

transvestite /trænz'vestaɪt/ *n* travestito, -a *mf*

trap /træp/ *n* trappola *f*; (*fam: mouth*) boccaccia *f* ● *vt* (*pt/pp* **trapped**) intrappolare; schiacciare ⟨*finger in door*⟩. ~'**door** *n* botola *f*

trapeze /trə'piːz/ *n* trapezio *m*

trash /træʃ/ *n* robaccia *f*; (*rubbish*) spazzatura *f*; (*nonsense*) schiocchezze *fpl*. ~**can** *n* *Am* secchio *m* della spazzatura. ~**y** *a* scadente

trauma /'trɔːmə/ *n* trauma *m*. ~**tic**

/-'mætɪk/ *a* traumatico. **~tize** /-taɪz/ traumatizzare

travel /'trævl/ *n* viaggi *mpl* ● *v* (*pt/pp* **travelled**) ● *vi* viaggiare; (*to work*) andare ● *vt* percorrere ‹*distance*›. **~ agency** *n* agenzia *f* di viaggi. **~ agent** *n* agente *mf* di viaggio

traveller /'trævələ(r)/ *n* viaggiatore, -trice *mf*; *Comm* commesso *m* viaggiatore; **~s** *pl* (*gypsies*) zingari *mpl*. **~'s cheque** *n* traveller's cheque *m inv*

trawler /'trɔːlə(r)/ *n* peschereccio *m*

tray /treɪ/ *n* vassoio *m*; (*for baking*) teglia *f*; (*for documents*) vaschetta *f* sparticarta; (*of printer, photocopier*) vassoio *m*

treacher|ous /'tretʃərəs/ *a* traditore; ‹*weather, currents*› pericoloso. **~y** *n* tradimento *m*

treacle /'triːkl/ *n* melassa *f*

tread /tred/ *n* andatura *f*; (*step*) gradino *m*; (*of tyre*) battistrada *m inv* ● *v* (*pt* **trod**, *pp* **trodden**) ● *vi* (*walk*) camminare. **tread on** *vt* calpestare ‹*grass*›; pestare ‹*foot*›

treason /'triːzn/ *n* tradimento *m*

treasure /'treʒə(r)/ *n* tesoro *m* ● *vt* tenere in gran conto. **~r** *n* tesoriere, -a *mf*

treasury /'treʒərɪ/ *n* **the T~** il Ministero del Tesoro

treat /triːt/ *n* piacere *m*; (*present*) regalo *m*; **give sb a ~** fare una sorpresa a qcno ● *vt* trattare; *Med* curare; **~ sb to sth** offrire qcsa a qcno

treatise /'triːtɪz/ *n* trattato *m*

treatment /'triːtmənt/ *n* trattamento *m*; *Med* cura *f*

treaty /'triːtɪ/ *n* trattato *m*

treble /'trebl/ *a* triplo ● *n* *Mus* (*voice*) voce *f* bianca ● *vt* triplicare ● *vi* triplicarsi. **~ clef** *n* chiave *f* di violino

tree /triː/ *n* albero *m*

trek /trek/ *n* scarpinata *f*; (*as holiday*) trekking *m inv* ● *vi* (*pt/pp* **trekked**) farsi una scarpinata; (*on holiday*) fare trekking

tremble /'trembl/ *vi* tremare

tremendous /trɪ'mendəs/ *a* (*huge*) enorme; (*fam: excellent*) formidabile. **~ly** *adv* (*very*) straordinariamente; (*a lot*) enormemente

tremor /'tremə(r)/ *n* tremito *m*; [**earth**] **~** scossa *f* [sismica]

trench /trentʃ/ *n* fosso *m*; *Mil* trincea *f*. **~ coat** *n* trench *m inv*

trend /trend/ *n* tendenza *f*; (*fashion*) moda *f*. **~y** *a* (*-ier, -iest*) *fam* di *or* alla moda

trepidation /trepɪ'deɪʃn/ *n* trepidazione *f*

trespass /'trespəs/ *vi* **~ on** introdursi abusivamente in; *fig* abusare di. **~er** *n* intruso, -a *mf*

trial /'traɪəl/ *n* *Jur* processo *m*; (*test, ordeal*) prova *f*; **on ~** in prova; *Jur* in giudizio; **by ~ and error** per tentativi

triang|le /'traɪæŋgl/ *n* triangolo *m*. **~ular** /-'æŋgjʊlə(r)/ *a* triangolare

tribe /traɪb/ *n* tribù *f inv*

tribulation /trɪbjʊ'leɪʃn/ *n* tribolazione *f*

tribunal /traɪ'bjuːnl/ *n* tribunale *m*

tributary /'trɪbjʊtərɪ/ *n* affluente *m*

tribute /'trɪbjuːt/ *n* tributo *m*; **pay ~** rendere omaggio

trice /traɪs/ *n* **in a ~** in un attimo

trick /trɪk/ *n* trucco *m*; (*joke*) scherzo *m*; (*in cards*) presa *f*; **do the ~** *fam* funzionare; **play a ~ on** fare uno scherzo a ● *vt* imbrogliare

trickle /'trɪkl/ *vi* colare

trick|ster /'trɪkstə(r)/ *n* imbroglione, -a *mf*. **~y** *a* (*-ier, -iest*) *a* ‹*operation*› complesso; ‹*situation*› delicato

tricycle /'traɪsɪkl/ *n* triciclo *m*

tried /traɪd/ *see* **try**

trifl|e /'traɪfl/ *n* inezia *f*; *Culin* zuppa *f* inglese. **~ing** *a* insignificante

trigger /'trɪgə(r)/ *n* grilletto *m* ● *vt* **~ [off]** scatenare

trigonometry /trɪgə'nɒmɪtrɪ/ *n* trigonometria *f*

trim /trɪm/ *a* (**trimmer, trimmest**) curato; ‹*figure*› snello ● *n* (*of hair, hedge*) spuntata *f*; (*decoration*) rifinitura *f*; **in good ~** in buono stato; ‹*person*› in forma ● *vt* (*pt/pp* **trimmed**) spuntare ‹*hair etc*›; (*decorate*) ornare; *Naut* orientare. **~ming** *n* bordo *m*; **~mings** *pl* (*decorations*) guarnizioni *fpl*; **with all the ~mings** *Culin* guarnito

trinket /'trɪŋkɪt/ *n* ninnolo *m*

trio /'triːəʊ/ *n* trio *m*

trip /trɪp/ *n* (*excursion*) gita *f*; (*journey*) viaggio *m*; (*stumble*) passo *m* falso ● *v* (*pt/pp* **tripped**) ● *vt* far inciampare ● *vi* inciampare (**on/over** in). **trip up** *vt* far inciampare

tripe /traɪp/ *n* trippa *f*; (*sl: nonsense*) fesserie *fpl*

triple /'trɪpl/ *a* triplo ● *vt* triplicare ● *vi* triplicarsi

triplets /'trɪplɪts/ *npl* tre gemelli *mpl*

triplicate /'trɪplɪkət/ *n* **in ~** in triplice copia

tripod /'traɪpɒd/ *n* treppiede *m inv*

tripper /'trɪpə(r)/ *n* gitante *mf*

trite /traɪt/ a banale

triumph /'traɪʌmf/ n trionfo m ●vi trionfare (**over** su). **~ant** /-'ʌmf(ə)nt/ a trionfante. **~antly** adv ⟨exclaim⟩ con tono trionfante

trivial /'trɪvɪəl/ a insignificante. **~ity** /-'ælətɪ/ n banalità f inv

trod, trodden /trɒd, 'trɒdn/ see **tread**

trolley /'trɒlɪ/ n carrello m; (Am: tram) tram m inv. **~ bus** n filobus m inv

trombone /trɒm'bəʊn/ n trombone m

troop /truːp/ n gruppo m; **~s** pl truppe fpl ●vi **~ in/out** entrare/uscire in gruppo

trophy /'trəʊfɪ/ n trofeo m

tropic /'trɒpɪk/ n tropico m; **~s** pl tropici mpl. **~al** a tropicale

trot /trɒt/ n trotto m ●vi (pt/pp **trotted**) trottare

trouble /'trʌbl/ n guaio m; (difficulties) problemi mpl; (inconvenience, Med) disturbo m; (conflict) conflitto m; **be in ~** essere nei guai; ⟨swimmer, climber:⟩ essere in difficoltà; **get into ~** finire nei guai; **get sb into ~** mettere qcno nei guai; **take the ~ to do sth** darsi la pena di far qcsa ●vt (worry) preoccupare; (inconvenience) disturbare; ⟨conscience, old wound:⟩ tormentare ●vi **don't ~!** non ti disturbare!. **~-maker** n **be a ~-maker** seminare zizzania. **~some** /-səm/ a fastidioso

trough /trɒf/ n trogolo m; (atmospheric) depressione f

trounce /traʊns/ vt (in competition) schiacciare

troupe /truːp/ n troupe f inv

trousers /'traʊzəz/ npl pantaloni mpl

trout /traʊt/ n inv trota f

trowel /'traʊəl/ n (for gardening) paletta f; (for builder) cazzuola f

truant /'truːənt/ n **play ~** marinare la scuola

truce /truːs/ n tregua f

truck /trʌk/ n (lorry) camion m inv

trudge /trʌdʒ/ n camminata f faticosa ●vi arrancare

true /truː/ a vero; **come ~** avverarsi

truffle /'trʌfl/ n tartufo m

truism /'truːɪzm/ n truismo m

truly /'truːlɪ/ adv veramente; **Yours ~** distinti saluti

trump /trʌmp/ n (in cards) atout m inv

trumpet /'trʌmpɪt/ n tromba f. **~er** n trombettista mf

truncheon /'trʌntʃn/ n manganello m

trunk /trʌŋk/ n (of tree, body) tronco m; (of elephant) proboscide f; (for travelling, storage) baule m; (Am: of car) bagagliaio m; **~s** pl calzoncini mpl da bagno

truss /trʌs/ n Med cinto m erniario

trust /trʌst/ n fiducia f; (group of companies) trust m inv; (organization) associazione f; **on ~** sulla parola ●vt fidarsi di; (hope) augurarsi ●vi **~ in** credere in; **~ to** affidarsi a. **~ed** a fidato

trustee /trʌs'tiː/ n amministratore, -trice mf fiduciario, -a

'trust|ful /'trʌstfl/ a fiducioso. **~ing** a fiducioso. **~worthy** a fidato

truth /truːθ/ n (pl -s /truːðz/) verità f inv. **~ful** a veritiero. **~fully** adv sinceramente

try /traɪ/ n tentativo m, prova f; (in rugby) meta f ●v (pt/pp **tried**) ●vt provare; (be a strain on) mettere a dura prova; Jur processare ⟨person⟩; discutere ⟨case⟩; **~ to do sth** provare a fare qcsa ●vi provare. **try on** vt provarsi ⟨garment⟩. **try out** vt provare

trying /'traɪɪŋ/ a duro; ⟨person⟩ irritante

T-shirt /'tiː-/ n maglietta f

tub /tʌb/ n tinozza f; (carton) vaschetta f; (bath) vasca f da bagno

tuba /'tjuːbə/ n Mus tuba f

tubby /'tʌbɪ/ a (-ier, -iest) tozzo

tube /tjuːb/ n tubo m; (of toothpaste) tubetto m; Rail metro f

tuber /'tjuːbə(r)/ n tubero m

tuberculosis /tjuːbɜːkjʊ'ləʊsɪs/ n tubercolosi f

tubular /'tjuːbjʊlə(r)/ a tubolare

tuck /tʌk/ n piega f ●vt (put) infilare. **tuck in** vt rimboccare; **~ sb in** rimboccare le coperte a qcno ●vi (fam: eat) mangiare con appetito. **tuck up** vt rimboccarsi ⟨sleeves⟩; (in bed) rimboccare le coperte a

Tuesday /'tjuːzdeɪ/ n martedì m inv

tuft /tʌft/ n ciuffo m

tug /tʌg/ n strattone m; Naut rimorchiatore m ●v (pt/pp **tugged**) ●vt tirare ●vi dare uno strattone. **~ of war** n tiro m alla fune

tuition /tjuː'ɪʃn/ n lezioni fpl

tulip /'tjuːlɪp/ n tulipano m

tumble /'tʌmbl/ n ruzzolone m ●vi ruzzolare. **~down** a cadente. **~-drier** n asciugabiancheria f

tumbler /'tʌmblə(r)/ n bicchiere m (senza stelo)

tummy /'tʌmɪ/ n fam pancia f

tumour /'tjuːmə(r)/ n tumore m

tumult /'tjuːmʌlt/ n tumulto m. **~uous** /-'mʌltjʊəs/ a tumultuoso

tuna /'tjuːnə/ n tonno m

tune /tjuːn/ *n* motivo *m*; **out of/in ~** ⟨*instrument*⟩ scordato/accordato; ⟨*person*⟩ stonato/intonato; **to the ~ of** *fam* per la modesta somma di ● *vt* accordare ⟨*instrument*⟩; sintonizzare ⟨*radio, TV*⟩; mettere a punto ⟨*engine*⟩. **tune in** *vt* sintonizzare ● *vi* sintonizzarsi (**to** su). **tune up** *vi Mus* accordare gli strumenti

tuneful /'tjuːnfl/ *a* melodioso

tuner /'tjuːnə(r)/ *n* accordatore, -trice *mf*; *Radio, TV* sintonizzatore *m*

tunic /'tjuːnɪk/ *n* tunica *f*; *Mil* giacca *f*; *Sch* grembiule *m*

Tunisia /tjuː'nɪzɪə/ *n* Tunisia *f*. **~n** *a* & *n* tunisino, -a *mf*

tunnel /'tʌnl/ *n* tunnel *m* inv ● *vi* (*pt/pp* **tunnelled**) scavare un tunnel

turban /'tɜːbən/ *n* turbante *m*

turbine /'tɜːbaɪn/ *n* turbina *f*

turbulen|ce /'tɜːbjʊləns/ *n* turbolenza *f*. **~t** *a* turbolento

turf /tɜːf/ *n* erba *f*; ⟨*segment*⟩ zolla *f* erbosa ● **turf out** *vt fam* buttar fuori

Turin /tjuˈrɪn/ *n* Torino *f*

Turk /tɜːk/ *n* turco, -a *mf*

turkey /'tɜːkɪ/ *n* tacchino *m*

Turk|ey *n* Turchia *f*. **~ish** *a* turco

turmoil /'tɜːmɔɪl/ *n* tumulto *m*

turn /tɜːn/ *n* (*rotation, short walk*) giro *m*; (*in road*) svolta *f*, curva *f*; (*development*) svolta *f*; *Theat* numero *m*; (*fam: attack*) crisi *f* inv; **a ~ for the better/worse** un miglioramento/peggioramento; **do sb a good ~** rendere un servizio a qcno; **take ~s** fare a turno; **in ~** a turno; **out of ~** ⟨*speak*⟩ a sproposito; **it's your ~** tocca a te ● *vt* girare; voltare ⟨*back, eyes*⟩; dirigere ⟨*gun, attention*⟩ ● *vi* girare; ⟨*person:*⟩ girarsi; ⟨*leaves:*⟩ ingiallire; (*become*) diventare; **~ right/left** girare a destra/sinistra; **~ sour** inacidirsi; **~ to sb** girarsi verso qcno; *fig* rivolgersi a qcno. **turn against** *vi* diventare ostile a ● *vt* mettere contro. **turn away** *vt* mandare via ⟨*people*⟩; girare dall'altra parte ⟨*head*⟩ ● *vi* girarsi dall'altra parte. **turn down** *vt* piegare ⟨*collar*⟩; abbassare ⟨*heat, gas, sound*⟩; respingere ⟨*person, proposal*⟩. **turn in** *vt* ripiegare in dentro ⟨*edges*⟩; consegnare ⟨*lost object*⟩ ● *vi* (*fam: go to bed*) andare a letto; **~ into the drive** entrare nel viale. **turn off** *vt* spegnere; chiudere ⟨*tap, water*⟩ ● *vi* ⟨*car:*⟩ girare. **turn on** *vt* accendere; aprire ⟨*tap, water*⟩; (*fam: attract*) eccitare ● *vi* (*attack*) attaccare. **turn out** *vt* (*expel*) mandar via; spegnere ⟨*light,*

gas⟩; (*produce*) produrre; (*empty*) svuotare ⟨*room, cupboard*⟩ ● *vi* (*transpire*) risultare; **~ out well/badly** ⟨*cake, dress:*⟩ riuscire bene/male; ⟨*situation:*⟩ andare bene/male. **turn over** *vt* girare ● *vi* girarsi; **please ~ over** vedi retro. **turn round** *vi* girarsi; ⟨*car:*⟩ girare. **turn up** *vt* tirare su ⟨*collar*⟩; alzare ⟨*heat, gas, sound, radio*⟩ ● *vi* farsi vedere

turning /'tɜːnɪŋ/ *n* svolta *f*. **~-point** *n* svolta *f* decisiva

turnip /'tɜːnɪp/ *n* rapa *f*

turn: ~-out *n* (*of people*) affluenza *f*. **~over** *n Comm* giro *m* d'affari; (*of staff*) ricambio *m*. **~pike** *n Am* autostrada *f*. **~stile** *n* cancelletto *m* girevole. **~table** *n* piattaforma *f* girevole; (*on record-player*) piatto *m* (*di giradischi*). **~-up** *n* (*of trousers*) risvolto *m*

turpentine /'tɜːpəntaɪn/ *n* trementina *f*

turquoise /'tɜːkwɔɪz/ *a* (*colour*) turchese ● *n* turchese *m*

turret /'tʌrɪt/ *n* torretta *f*

turtle /'tɜːtl/ *n* tartaruga *f* acquatica

tusk /tʌsk/ *n* zanna *f*

tussle /'tʌsl/ *n* zuffa *f* ● *vi* azzuffarsi

tutor /'tjuːtə(r)/ *n* insegnante *mf* privato, -a; *Univ* insegnante *mf* universitario, -a che segue individualmente un ristretto numero di studenti. **~ial** /-'tɔːrɪəl/ *n* discussione *f* col tutor

tuxedo /tʌk'siːdəʊ/ *n Am* smoking *m* inv

TV *n abbr* (**television**) tv *f* inv, tivù *f* inv

twaddle /'twɒdl/ *n* scemenze *fpl*

twang /twæŋ/ *n* (*in voice*) suono *m* nasale ● *vt* far vibrare

tweed /twiːd/ *n* tweed *m* inv

tweezers /'twiːzəz/ *npl* pinzette *fpl*

twelfth /twelfθ/ *a* & *n* dodicesimo, -a *mf*

twelve /twelv/ *a* & *n* dodici *m*

twentieth /'twentɪɪθ/ *a* & *n* ventesimo, -a *mf*

twenty /'twentɪ/ *a* & *n* venti *m*

twerp /twɜːp/ *n fam* stupido, -a *mf*

twice /twaɪs/ *adv* due volte

twiddle /'twɪdl/ *vt* giocherellare con; **~ one's thumbs** *fig* girarsi i pollici

twig[1] /twɪg/ *n* ramoscello *m*

twig[2] *vt/i* (*pt/pp* **twigged**) *fam* intuire

twilight /'twaɪ-/ *n* crepuscolo *m*

twin /twɪn/ *n* gemello, -a *mf* ● *attrib* gemello. **~ beds** *npl* letti *mpl* gemelli

twine /twaɪn/ *n* spago *m* ● *vi* intrecciarsi; ⟨*plant:*⟩ attorcigliarsi ● *vt* intrecciare

twinge /twɪndʒ/ *n* fitta *f*; **~ of conscience** rimorso *m* di coscienza

twinkle /'twɪŋkl/ n scintillio m ● vi scintillare

twin 'town n città f inv gemellata

twirl /twɜːl/ vt far roteare ● vi volteggiare ● n piroetta f

twist /twɪst/ n torsione f; (curve) curva f; (in rope) attorcigliata f; (in book, plot) colpo m di scena ● vt attorcigliare ⟨rope⟩; torcere ⟨metal⟩; girare ⟨knob, cap⟩; (distort) distorcere; **~ one's ankle** storcersi la caviglia ● vi attorcigliarsi; ⟨road:⟩ essere pieno di curve

twit /twɪt/ n fam cretino, -a mf

twitch /twɪtʃ/ n tic m inv; (jerk) strattone m ● vi contrarsi

twitter /'twɪtə(r)/ n cinguettio m ● vi cinguettare; ⟨person:⟩ cianciare

two /tuː/ a & n due m

two: **~-faced** a falso. **~-piece** a (swimsuit) due pezzi m inv; (suit) comple-

to m. **~some** /-səm/ n coppia f. **~-way** a ⟨traffic⟩ a doppio senso di marcia

tycoon /taɪ'kuːn/ n magnate m

tying /'taɪɪŋ/ see **tie**

type /taɪp/ n tipo m; (printing) carattere m [tipografico] ● vt/i scrivere a macchina. **~writer** n macchina f da scrivere. **~written** a dattiloscritto

typhoid /'taɪfɔɪd/ n febbre f tifoidea

typical /'tɪpɪkl/ a tipico. **~ly** adv tipicamente; (as usual) come al solito

typify /'tɪpɪfaɪ/ vt (pt/pp -ied) essere tipico di

typing /'taɪpɪŋ/ n dattilografia f

typist /'taɪpɪst/ n dattilografo, -a mf

typography /taɪ'pɒɡrəfɪ/ n tipografia f

tyrannical /tɪ'rænɪkl/ a tirannico

tyranny /'tɪrənɪ/ n tirannia f

tyrant /'taɪrənt/ n tiranno, -a mf

tyre /'taɪə(r)/ n gomma f, pneumatico m

Uu

ubiquitous /juː'bɪkwɪtəs/ a onnipresente

udder /'ʌdə(r)/ n mammella f (di vacca, capra etc)

ugl|iness /'ʌɡlɪnɪs/ n bruttezza f. **~y** a (-ier, -iest) brutto

UK n abbr **United Kingdom**

ulcer /'ʌlsə(r)/ n ulcera f

ulterior /ʌl'tɪərɪə(r)/ a **~ motive** secondo fine m

ultimate /'ʌltɪmət/ a definitivo; (final) finale; (fundamental) fondamentale. **~ly** adv alla fine

ultimatum /ʌltɪ'meɪtəm/ n ultimatum m inv

ultrasound /'ʌltrə-/ n Med ecografia f

ultra'violet a ultravioletto

umbilical /ʌm'bɪlɪkl/ a **~ cord** cordone m ombelicale

umbrella /ʌm'brelə/ n ombrello m

umpire /'ʌmpaɪə(r)/ n arbitro m ● vt/i arbitrare

umpteen /ʌmp'tiːn/ a fam innumerevole. **~th** a fam ennesimo; **for the ~th time** per l'ennesima volta

UN n abbr (**United Nations**) ONU f

un'able /ʌn-/ a **be ~ to do sth** non po-

tere fare qcsa; (not know how) non sapere fare qcsa

una'bridged a integrale

unac'companied a non accompagnato; ⟨luggage⟩ incustodito

unac'countabl|e a inspiegabile. **~y** adv inspiegabilmente

unac'customed a insolito; **be ~ to** non essere abituato a

una'dulterated a ⟨water⟩ puro; ⟨wine⟩ non sofisticato; fig assoluto

un'aided a senza aiuto

unanimity /juːnə'nɪmətɪ/ n unanimità f

unanimous /juː'nænɪməs/ a unanime. **~ly** adv all'unanimità

un'armed a disarmato. **~ combat** n lotta f senza armi

unas'suming a senza pretese

unat'tached a staccato; ⟨person⟩ senza legami

unat'tended a incustodito

un'authorized a non autorizzato

una'voidable a inevitabile

una'ware a **be ~ of sth** non rendersi conto di qcsa. **~s** /-eəz/ adv **catch sb ~s** prendere qcno alla sprovvista

un'balanced a non equilibrato; (mentally) squilibrato

un'bearabl|e *a* insopportabile. **~y** *adv* insopportabilmente

unbeat|able /ʌn'bi:təbl/ *a* imbattibile. **~en** *a* imbattuto

unbeknown /ʌnbɪ'nəʊn/ *a fam* **~ to me** a mia insaputa

unbe'lievable *a* incredibile

un'bend *vi* (*pt/pp* **-bent**) ⟨*relax*⟩ distendersi

un'biased *a* obiettivo

un'block *vt* sbloccare

un'bolt *vt* togliere il chiavistello di

un'breakable *a* infrangibile

unbridled /ʌn'braɪdld/ *a* sfrenato

un'burden *vt* **~ oneself** *fig* sfogarsi (**to** con)

un'button *vt* sbottonare

uncalled-for /ʌn'kɔ:ldfɔ:(r)/ *a* fuori luogo

un'canny *a* sorprendente; ⟨*silence, feeling*⟩ inquietante

un'ceasing *a* incessante

uncere'monious *a* ⟨*abrupt*⟩ brusco. **~ly** *adv* senza tante cerimonie

un'certain *a* incerto; ⟨*weather*⟩ instabile; **in no ~ terms** senza mezzi termini. **~ty** *n* incertezza *f*

un'changed *a* invariato

un'charitable *a* duro

uncle /'ʌŋkl/ *n* zio *m*

un'comfortabl|e *a* scomodo; imbarazzante ⟨*silence, situation*⟩; **feel ~e** *fig* sentirsi a disagio. **~y** *adv* ⟨*sit*⟩ scomodamente; (*causing alarm etc*) spaventosamente

un'common *a* insolito

un'compromising *a* intransigente

uncon'ditional *a* incondizionato. **~ly** *adv* incondizionatamente

un'conscious *a* privo di sensi; (*unaware*) inconsapevole; **be ~ of sth** non rendersi conto di qcsa. **~ly** *adv* inconsapevolmente

uncon'ventional *a* poco convenzionale

unco'operative *a* poco cooperativo

un'cork *vt* sturare

uncouth /ʌn'ku:θ/ *a* zotico

un'cover *vt* scoprire; portare alla luce ⟨*buried object*⟩

unde'cided *a* indeciso; (*not settled*) incerto

undeniabl|e /ʌndɪ'naɪəbl/ *a* innegabile. **~y** *adv* innegabilmente

under /'ʌndə(r)/ *prep* sotto; (*less than*) al di sotto di; **~ there** lì sotto; **~ repair/construction** in riparazione/ costruzione; **~ way** *fig* in corso ● *adv*

(**~ water**) sott'acqua; (*unconscious*) sotto anestesia

'undercarriage *n Aeron* carrello *m*

'underclothes *npl* biancheria *fsg* intima

under'cover *a* clandestino

'undercurrent *n* corrente *f* sottomarina; *fig* sottofondo *m*

under'cut *vt* (*pt/pp* **-cut**) *Comm* vendere a minor prezzo di

'underdog *n* perdente *m*

under'done *a* ⟨*meat*⟩ al sangue

under'estimate *vt* sottovalutare

under'fed *a* denutrito

under'foot *adv* sotto i piedi; **trample ~** calpestare

under'go *vt* (*pt* **-went**, *pp* **-gone**) subire ⟨*operation, treatment*⟩; **~ repair** essere in riparazione

under'graduate *n* studente, -tessa *mf* universitario, -a

under'ground¹ *adv* sottoterra

'underground² *a* sotterraneo; (*secret*) clandestino ● *n* (*railway*) metropolitana *f*. **~ car park** *n* parcheggio *m* sotterraneo

'undergrowth *n* sottobosco *m*

'underhand *a* subdolo

'underlay *n* strato *m* di gomma o feltro posto sotto la moquette

under'lie *vt* (*pt* **-lay**, *pp* **-lain**, *pres p* **-lying**) *fig* essere alla base di

under'line *vt* sottolineare

underling /'ʌndəlɪŋ/ *n pej* subalterno, -a *mf*

under'lying *a fig* fondamentale

under'mine *vt fig* minare

underneath /ʌndə'ni:θ/ *prep* sotto; **~ it** sotto ● *adv* sotto

under'paid *a* mal pagato

'underpants *npl* mutande *fpl*

'underpass *n* sottopassaggio *m*

under'privileged *a* non abbiente

under'rate *vt* sottovalutare

'underseal *n Auto* antiruggine *m inv*

'undershirt *n Am* maglia *f* della pelle

understaffed /-'stɑ:ft/ *a* a corto di personale

under'stand *vt* (*pt/pp* **-stood**) capire; **I ~ that...** (*have heard*) mi risulta che... ● *vi* capire. **~able** /-əbl/ *a* comprensibile. **~ably** /-əblɪ/ *adv* comprensibilmente

under'standing *a* comprensivo ● *n* comprensione *f*; (*agreement*) accordo *m*; **on the ~ that** a condizione che

'understatement *n* understatement *m inv*

'understudy *n Theat* sostituto, -a *mf*

under'take *vt* (*pt* **-took**, *pp* **-taken**)

intraprendere; **~ to do sth** impegnarsi a fare qcsa

'undertaker *n* impresario *m* di pompe funebri; [**firm of**] **~s** *n* impresa *f* di pompe funebri

under'taking *n* impresa *f*; ⟨*promise*⟩ promessa *f*

'undertone *n* *fig* sottofondo *m*; **in an ~** sottovoce

under'value *vt* sottovalutare

'underwater[1] *a* subacqueo

under'water[2] *adv* sott'acqua

'underwear *n* biancheria *f* intima

under'weight *a* sotto peso

'underworld *n* ⟨*criminals*⟩ malavita *f*

'underwriter *n* assicuratore *m*

unde'sirable *a* indesiderato; ⟨*person*⟩ poco raccomandabile

undies /'ʌndɪz/ *npl fam* biancheria *fsg* intima (*da donna*)

un'dignified *a* non dignitoso

un'do *vt* (*pt* **-did**, *pp* **-done**) disfare; slacciare ⟨*dress, shoes*⟩; sbottonare ⟨*shirt*⟩; *fig, Comput* annullare

un'done *a* ⟨*shirt, button*⟩ sbottonato; ⟨*shoes, dress*⟩ slacciato; (*not accomplished*) non fatto; **leave ~** ⟨*job*⟩ tralasciare

un'doubted *a* indubbio. **~ly** *adv* senza dubbio

un'dress *vt* spogliare; **get ~ed** spogliarsi ● *vi* spogliarsi

un'due *a* eccessivo

undulating /'ʌndjʊleɪtɪŋ/ *a* ondulato; ⟨*country*⟩ collinoso

un'duly *adv* eccessivamente

un'dying *a* eterno

un'earth *vt* dissotterrare; *fig* scovare; scoprire ⟨*secret*⟩. **~ly** *a* soprannaturale; **at an ~ly hour** *fam* a un'ora impossibile

un'eas|e *n* disagio *m*. **~y** *a* a disagio; ⟨*person*⟩ inquieto; ⟨*feeling*⟩ inquietante; (*truce*) precario

un'eatable *a* immangiabile

uneco'nomic *a* poco remunerativo

uneco'nomical *a* poco economico

unem'ployed *a* disoccupato ● *npl* the **~** i disoccupati

unem'ployment *n* disoccupazione *f*. **~ benefit** *n* sussidio *m* di disoccupazione

un'ending *a* senza fine

un'equal *a* disuguale; ⟨*struggle*⟩ impari; **be ~ to a task** non essere all'altezza di un compito

unequivocal /ʌnɪ'kwɪvəkl/ *a* inequivocabile; ⟨*person*⟩ esplicito

unerring /ʌn'ɜːrɪŋ/ *a* infallibile

un'ethical *a* immorale

un'even *a* irregolare; ⟨*distribution*⟩ ineguale; ⟨*number*⟩ dispari

unex'pected *a* inaspettato. **~ly** *adv* inaspettatamente

un'failing *a* infallibile

un'fair *a* ingiusto. **~ly** *adv* ingiustamente. **~ness** *n* ingiustizia *f*

un'faithful *a* infedele

unfa'miliar *a* sconosciuto; **be ~ with** non conoscere

un'fasten *vt* slacciare; (*detach*) staccare

un'favourable *a* sfavorevole; ⟨*impression*⟩ negativo

un'feeling *a* insensibile

un'finished *a* da finire; ⟨*business*⟩ in sospeso

un'fit *a* inadatto; (*morally*) indegno; *Sport* fuori forma; **~ for work** non in grado di lavorare

unflinching /ʌn'flɪntʃɪŋ/ *a* risoluto

un'fold *vt* spiegare; (*spread out*) aprire; *fig* rivelare ● *vi* ⟨*view:*⟩ spiegarsi

unfore'seen *a* imprevisto

unforgettable /ʌnfə'getəbl/ *a* indimenticabile

unforgivable /ʌnfə'gɪvəbl/ *a* imperdonabile

un'fortunate *a* sfortunato; (*regrettable*) spiacevole; ⟨*remark, choice*⟩ infelice. **~ly** *adv* purtroppo

un'founded *a* infondato

unfurl /ʌn'fɜːl/ *vt* spiegare

un'furnished *a* non ammobiliato

ungainly /ʌn'geɪnlɪ/ *a* sgraziato

ungodly /ʌn'gɒdlɪ/ *a* empio; **~ hour** *fam* ora *f* impossibile

un'grateful *a* ingrato. **~ly** *adv* senza riconoscenza

un'happi|ly *adv* infelicemente; (*unfortunately*) purtroppo. **~ness** *n* infelicità *f*

un'happy *a* infelice; (*not content*) insoddisfatto (**with** di)

un'harmed *a* incolume

un'healthy *a* poco sano; (*insanitary*) malsano

un'hook *vt* sganciare

un'hurt *a* illeso

unhy'gienic *a* non igienico

unification /juːnɪfɪ'keɪʃn/ *n* unificazione *f*

uniform /'juːnɪfɔːm/ *a* uniforme ● *n* uniforme *f*. **~ly** *adv* uniformemente

unify /'juːnɪfaɪ/ *vt* (*pt/pp* **-ied**) unificare

uni'lateral /juːnɪ-/ *a* unilaterale

uni'maginable *a* inimmaginabile

unim'portant *a* irrilevante

unin'habited *a* disabitato

unin'tentional *a* involontario. **~ly**
adv involontariamente

union /'ju:nɪən/ *n* unione *f*; (*trade ~*)
sindacato *m*. **U~** Jack *n* bandiera *f* del
Regno Unito

unique /ju:'ni:k/ *a* unico. **~ly** *adv* unicamente

unison /'ju:nɪsn/ *n* **in ~** all'unisono

unit /'ju:nɪt/ *n* unità *f inv*; (*department*)
reparto *m*; (*of furniture*) elemento *m*

unite /ju:'naɪt/ *vt* unire ● *vi* unirsi

united /ju:'naɪtɪd/ *a* unito. **U~**
'**Kingdom** *n* Regno *m* Unito. **U~**
'**Nations** *n* [Organizzazione *f* delle] Nazioni Unite *fpl*. **U~ States [of Ameri-
ca]** *n* Stati *mpl* Uniti [d'America]

unity /'ju:nətɪ/ *n* unità *f*; (*agreement*) accordo *m*

universal /ju:nɪ'vɜ:sl/ *a* universale.
~ly *adv* universalmente

universe /'ju:nɪvɜ:s/ *n* universo *m*

university /ju:nɪ'vɜ:sətɪ/ *n* università *f
inv* ● *attrib* universitario

un'just *a* ingiusto

unkempt /ʌn'kempt/ *a* trasandato;
(*hair*) arruffato

un'kind *a* scortese. **~ly** *adv* in modo
scortese. **~ness** *n* mancanza *f* di gentilezza

un'known *a* sconosciuto

un'lawful *a* illecito, illegale

unleaded /ʌn'ledɪd/ *a* senza piombo

un'leash *vt fig* scatenare

unless /ən'les/ *conj* a meno che; **~ I am
mistaken** se non mi sbaglio

un'like *a* (*not the same*) diversi ● *prep*
diverso da; **that's ~ him** non è da lui;
~ me, he... diversamente da me, lui...

un'likely *a* improbabile

un'limited *a* illimitato

un'load *vt* scaricare

un'lock *vt* aprire (*con chiave*)

un'lucky *a* sfortunato; **It's ~ to...** porta sfortuna...

un'manned *a* senza equipaggio

un'married *a* non sposato. **~ 'mother**
n ragazza *f* madre

un'mask *vt fig* smascherare

unmistak|e /ʌnmɪ'steɪkəbl/ *a*
inconfondibile. **~y** *adv* chiaramente

un'mitigated *a* assoluto

un'natural *a* innaturale; *pej* anormale. **~ly** *adv* in modo innaturale; *pej* in
modo anormale

unneces'sarily *adv* inutilmente

un'necessary *a* inutile

un'noticed *a* inosservato

unob'tainable *a* (*products etc*) intro-

vabile; (*telephone number*) non ottenibile

unob'trusive *a* discreto. **~ly** *adv* in
modo discreto

unof'ficial *a* non ufficiale. **~ly** *adv* uf-
ficiosamente

un'pack *vi* disfare le valigie ● *vt* svuotare (*parcel*); spacchettare (*books*); **~**
one's case disfare la valigia

un'paid *a* da pagare; (*work*) non retri-
buito

un'palatable *a* sgradevole

un'paralleled *a* senza pari

un'pick *vt* disfare

un'pleasant *a* sgradevole; (*person*)
maleducato. **~ly** *adv* sgradevolmente;
(*behave*) maleducatamente. **~ness** *n*
(*bad feeling*) tensioni *fpl*

un'plug *vt* (*pt/pp* -**plugged**) staccare

un'popular *a* impopolare

un'precedented *a* senza precedenti

unpre'dictable *a* imprevedibile

unpre'meditated *a* involontario

unpre'pared *a* impreparato

unpre'tentious *a* senza pretese

un'principled *a* senza principi;
(*behaviour*) scorretto

unpro'fessional *a* non professionale;
it's ~ è una mancanza di professionalità

un'profitable *a* non redditizio

un'qualified *a* non qualificato; (*fig:
absolute*) assoluto

un'questionable *a* incontestabile

un'quote *vi* chiudere le virgolette

unravel /ʌn'rævl/ *vt* (*pt/pp* -**ravelled**)
districare; (*in knitting*) disfare

un'real *a* irreale; *fam* inverosimile

un'reasonable *a* irragionevole

unre'lated *a* (*fact*) senza rapporto (**to**
con); (*person*) non imparentato (**to** con)

unre'liable *a* inattendibile; (*person*)
inaffidabile, che non dà affidamento

unrequited /ʌnrɪ'kwaɪtɪd/ *a* non cor-
risposto

unreservedly /ʌnrɪ'zɜ:vɪdlɪ/ *adv* senza riserve; (*frankly*) francamente

un'rest *n* fermenti *mpl*

un'rivalled *a* ineguagliato

un'roll *vt* srotolare ● *vi* srotolarsi

unruly /ʌn'ru:lɪ/ *a* indisciplinato

un'safe *a* pericoloso

un'said *a* inespresso

un'salted *a* non salato

unsatis'factory *a* poco soddisfacente

un'savoury *a* equivoco

unscathed /ʌn'skeɪðd/ *a* illeso

un'screw *vt* svitare

un'scrupulous *a* senza scrupoli

un'seemly *a* indecoroso
un'selfish *a* disinteressato
un'settled *a* in agitazione; ⟨weather⟩ variabile; ⟨bill⟩ non saldato
unshakeable /ʌnˈʃeɪkəbl/ *a* categorico
unshaven /ʌnˈʃeɪvn/ *a* non rasato
unsightly /ʌnˈsaɪtlɪ/ *a* brutto
un'skilled *a* non specializzato. **~ worker** *n* manovale *m*
un'sociable *a* scontroso
unso'phisticated *a* semplice
un'sound *a* ⟨building, reasoning⟩ poco solido; ⟨advice⟩ poco sensato; **of ~ mind** malato di mente
unspeakable /ʌnˈspiːkəbl/ *a* indicibile
un'stable *a* instabile; (mentally) squilibrato
un'steady *a* malsicuro
un'stuck *a* **come ~** staccarsi; (fam: project) andare a monte
unsuc'cessful *a* fallimentare; **be ~** (in attempt) non aver successo. **~ly** *adv* senza successo
un'suitable *a* (inappropriate) inadatto; (inconvenient) inopportuno
unsu'specting *a* fiducioso
unthinkable /ʌnˈθɪŋkəbl/ *a* impensabile
un'tidiness *n* disordine *m*
un'tidy *a* disordinato
un'tie *vt* slegare
until /ənˈtɪl/ *prep* fino a; **not ~** non prima di; **~ the evening** fino alla sera; **~ his arrival** fino al suo arrivo ● *conj* finché, fino a quando; **not ~ you've seen it** non prima che tu l'abbia visto
untimely /ʌnˈtaɪmlɪ/ *a* inopportuno; (premature) prematuro
un'tiring *a* instancabile
un'told *a* ⟨wealth⟩ incalcolabile; ⟨suffering⟩ indescrivibile; ⟨story⟩ inedito
unto'ward *a* **if nothing ~ happens** se non capita un imprevisto
un'true *a* falso; **that's ~** non è vero
unused¹ /ʌnˈjuːzd/ *a* non [ancora] usato
unused² /ʌnˈjuːst/ *a* **be ~ to** non essere abituato a
un'usual *a* insolito. **~ly** *adv* insolitamente
un'veil *vt* scoprire
un'wanted *a* indesiderato
un'warranted *a* ingiustificato
un'welcome *a* sgradito
un'well *a* indisposto
unwieldy /ʌnˈwiːldɪ/ *a* ingombrante
un'willing *a* riluttante. **~ly** *adv* malvolentieri
un'wind *v* (pt/pp **unwound**) ● *vt* svolgere, srotolare ● *vi* svolgersi, srotolarsi; (fam: relax) rilassarsi
un'wise *a* imprudente
unwitting /ʌnˈwɪtɪŋ/ *a* involontario; ⟨victim⟩ inconsapevole. **~ly** *adv* involontariamente
un'worthy *a* non degno
un'wrap *vt* (pt/pp **-wrapped**) scartare ⟨present, parcel⟩
un'written *a* tacito
up /ʌp/ *adv* su; (not in bed) alzato; ⟨road⟩ smantellato; ⟨theatre curtain, blinds⟩ alzato; ⟨shelves, tent⟩ montato; ⟨notice⟩ affisso; ⟨building⟩ costruito; **prices are up** i prezzi sono aumentati; **be up for sale** essere in vendita; **up here/there** quassù/lassù; **time's up** tempo scaduto; **what's up?** fam cosa è successo?; **up to** (as far as) fino a; **be up to** essere all'altezza di ⟨task⟩; **what's he up to?** fam cosa sta facendo?; (plotting) cosa sta combinando?; **I'm up to page 100** sono arrivato a pagina 100; **feel up to it** sentirsela; **be one up on sb** fam essere in vantaggio su qcno; **go up** salire; **lift up** alzare; **up against** fig alle prese con ● *prep* su; **the cat ran/is up the tree** il gatto è salito di corsa/è sull'albero; **further up this road** più avanti su questa strada; **row up the river** risalire il fiume; **go up the stairs** salire su per le scale; **be up the pub** fam essere al pub; **be up on** or **in sth** essere bene informato su qcsa ● *n* **ups and downs** npl alti mpl e bassi
'upbringing *n* educazione *f*
up'date¹ *vt* aggiornare
'update² *n* aggiornamento *m*
up'grade *vt* promuovere ⟨person⟩; modernizzare ⟨equipment⟩
upgradeable /ʌpˈgreɪdəbl/ *a* Comput upgradabile
upheaval /ʌpˈhiːvl/ *n* scompiglio *m*
up'hill *a* in salita; fig arduo ● *adv* in salita
up'hold *vt* (pt/pp **upheld**) sostenere ⟨principle⟩; confermare ⟨verdict⟩
upholster /ʌpˈhəʊlstə(r)/ *vt* tappezzare. **~er** *n* tappezziere, -a *mf*. **~y** *n* tappezzeria *f*
'upkeep *n* mantenimento *m*
up-'market *a* di qualità
upon /əˈpɒn/ *prep* su; **~ arriving home** una volta arrivato a casa
upper /ˈʌpə(r)/ *a* superiore ● *n* (of shoe) tomaia *f*
upper: ~ circle *n* seconda galleria *f*. **~ class** *n* alta borghesia *f*. **~ hand** *n* **have the ~ hand** avere il sopravvento.

~most *a* più alto; **that's ~most in my mind** è la mia preoccupazione principale

'upright *a* dritto; ⟨*piano*⟩ verticale; ⟨*honest*⟩ retto ● *n* montante *m*

'uprising *n* rivolta *f*

'uproar *n* tumulto *m*; **be in an ~** essere in trambusto

up'root *vt* sradicare

up'set[1] *vt* (*pt/pp* upset, *pres p* upsetting) rovesciare; sconvolgere ⟨*plan*⟩; ⟨*distress*⟩ turbare; **get ~ about sth** prendersela per qcsa; **be very ~** essere sconvolto; **have an ~ stomach** avere l'intestino disturbato

'upset[2] *n* scombussolamento *m*

'upshot *n* risultato *m*

upside 'down *adv* sottosopra; **turn ~ ~** capovolgere

up'stairs[1] *adv* [al piano] di sopra

'upstairs[2] *a* del piano superiore

'upstart *n* arrivato, -a *mf*

up'stream *adv* controcorrente

'upsurge *n* ⟨*in sales*⟩ aumento *m* improvviso; ⟨*of enthusiasm, crime*⟩ ondata *f*

'uptake *n* **be slow on the ~** essere lento nel capire; **be quick on the ~** capire le cose al volo

up'tight *a* teso

up-to-'date *a* moderno; ⟨*news*⟩ ultimo; ⟨*records*⟩ aggiornato

'upturn *n* ripresa *f*

upward /'ʌpwəd/ *a* verso l'alto, in su; **~ slope** salita *f* ● *adv* **~[s]** verso l'alto; **~s of** oltre

uranium /jʊˈreɪmɪəm/ *n* uranio *m*

urban /'ɜ:bən/ *a* urbano

urge /ɜ:dʒ/ *n* forte desiderio *m* ● *vt* esortare (**to** a). **urge on** *vt* spronare

urgen|cy /'ɜ:dʒənsɪ/ *n* urgenza *f*. **~t** *a* urgente

urinate /'jʊərmeɪt/ *vi* urinare

urine /'jʊərɪn/ *n* urina *f*

urn /ɜ:n/ *n* urna *f*; ⟨*for tea*⟩ contenitore *m* munito di cannella che si trova nei self-service, mense ecc

us /ʌs/ *pers pron* ci; ⟨*after prep*⟩ noi; **they know us** ci conoscono; **give us the money** dateci i soldi; **give it to us** datecelo; **they showed it to us** ce l'hanno fatto vedere; **they meant us, not you** intendevano noi, non voi; **it's us** siamo noi; **she hates us** ci odia

US[A] *n[pl] abbr* (**United States [of America]**) U.S.A. *mpl*

usable /'ju:zəbl/ *a* usabile

usage /'ju:sɪdʒ/ *n* uso *m*

use[1] /ju:s/ *n* uso *m*; **be of ~** essere utile; **be of no ~** essere inutile; **make ~ of** usare; ⟨*exploit*⟩ sfruttare; **it is no ~** è inutile; **what's the ~?** a che scopo?

use[2] /ju:z/ *vt* usare. **use up** *vt* consumare

used[1] /ju:zd/ *a* usato

used[2] /ju:st/ *pt* **be ~ to sth** essere abituato a qcsa; **get ~ to** abituarsi a; **he ~ to live here** viveva qui

useful /'ju:sfl/ *a* utile. **~ness** *n* utilità *f*

useless /'ju:slɪs/ *a* inutile; ⟨*fam: person*⟩ incapace

user /'ju:zə(r)/ *n* utente *mf*. **~-'friendly** *a* facile da usare

usher /'ʌʃə(r)/ *n Theat* maschera *f*; *Jur* usciere *m*; ⟨*at wedding*⟩ persona *f* che accompagna gli invitati a un matrimonio ai loro posti in chiesa ● **usher in** *vt* fare entrare

usherette /ʌʃəˈret/ *n* maschera *f*

usual /'ju:ʒʊəl/ *a* usuale; **as ~** come al solito. **~ly** *adv* di solito

usurp /jʊˈzɜ:p/ *vt* usurpare

utensil /jʊˈtensl/ *n* utensile *m*

uterus /'ju:tərəs/ *n* utero *m*

utilitarian /jʊtɪlɪˈteərɪən/ *a* funzionale

utility /jʊˈtɪlɪtɪ/ *n* servizio *m*. **~ room** *n* stanza *f* in casa privata per il lavaggio, la stiratura dei panni ecc

utilize /'ju:tɪlaɪz/ *vt* utilizzare

utmost /'ʌtməʊst/ *a* estremo ● *n* **one's ~** tutto il possibile

utter[1] /'ʌtə(r)/ *a* totale. **~ly** *adv* completamente

utter[2] *vt* emettere ⟨*sigh, sound*⟩; proferire ⟨*word*⟩. **~ance** /-əns/ *n* dichiarazione *f*

U-turn /'ju:-/ *n Auto* inversione *f* a U; *fig* marcia *f* in dietro

Vv

vacan|cy /'veɪk(ə)nsɪ/ n ⟨job⟩ posto m vacante; ⟨room⟩ stanza f disponibile. **~t** a libero; ⟨position⟩ vacante; ⟨look⟩ assente

vacate /vəˈkeɪt/ vt lasciare libero

vacation /vəˈkeɪʃn/ n Univ & Am vacanza f

vaccinat|e /'væksɪneɪt/ vt vaccinare. **~ion** /-ˈneɪʃn/ n vaccinazione f

vaccine /'væksi:n/ n vaccino m

vacuum /'vækjʊəm/ n vuoto m ● vt passare l'aspirapolvere in/su. **~ cleaner** n aspirapolvere m inv. **~ flask** n thermos® m inv. **~-packed** a confezionato sottovuoto

vagabond /'vægəbɒnd/ n vagabondo, -a mf

vagina /vəˈdʒaɪnə/ n Anat vagina f

vagrant /'veɪgrənt/ n vagabondo, -a mf

vague /veɪg/ a vago; ⟨outline⟩ impreciso; ⟨absent-minded⟩ distratto; **I'm still ~ about it** non ho ancora le idee chiare in proposito. **~ly** adv vagamente

vain /veɪn/ a vanitoso; ⟨hope, attempt⟩ vano; **in ~** invano. **~ly** adv vanamente

valentine /'væləntaɪn/ n ⟨card⟩ biglietto m di San Valentino

valiant /'væliənt/ a valoroso

valid /'vælɪd/ a valido. **~ate** vt ⟨confirm⟩ convalidare. **~ity** /vəˈlɪdətɪ/ n validità f

valley /'vælɪ/ n valle f

valour /'vælə(r)/ n valore m

valuable /'væljʊəbl/ a di valore; fig prezioso. **~s** npl oggetti mpl di valore

valuation /væljʊˈeɪʃn/ n valutazione f

value /'vælju:/ n valore m; ⟨usefulness⟩ utilità f ● vt valutare; ⟨cherish⟩ apprezzare. **~ 'added tax** n imposta f sul valore aggiunto

valve /vælv/ n valvola f

vampire /'væmpaɪə(r)/ n vampiro m

van /væn/ n furgone m

vandal /'vændl/ n vandalo, -a mf. **~ism** /-ɪzm/ n vandalismo m. **~ize** vt vandalizzare

vanilla /vəˈnɪlə/ n vaniglia f

vanish /'vænɪʃ/ vi svanire

vanity /'vænətɪ/ n vanità f. **~ bag** or **case** n beauty-case m inv

vantage-point /'vɑ:ntɪdʒ-/ n punto m d'osservazione; fig punto m di vista

vapour /'veɪpə(r)/ n vapore m

variable /'veərɪəbl/ a variabile; ⟨adjustable⟩ regolabile

variance /'veərɪəns/ n **be at ~** essere in disaccordo

variant /'veərɪənt/ n variante f

variation /veərɪˈeɪʃn/ n variazione f

varicose /'værɪkəʊs/ a **~ veins** vene fpl varicose

varied /'veərɪd/ a vario; ⟨diet⟩ diversificato; ⟨life⟩ movimentato

variety /vəˈraɪətɪ/ n varietà f inv

various /'veərɪəs/ a vario

varnish /'vɑ:nɪʃ/ n vernice f; ⟨for nails⟩ smalto m ● vt verniciare; **~ one's nails** mettersi lo smalto

vary /'veərɪ/ vt/i (pt/pp -ied) variare. **~ing** a variabile; ⟨different⟩ diverso

vase /vɑ:z/ n vaso m

vast /vɑ:st/ a vasto; ⟨difference, amusement⟩ enorme. **~ly** adv ⟨superior⟩ di gran lunga; ⟨different, amused⟩ enormemente

vat /væt/ n tino m

VAT /vi:eɪ'ti:, væt/ n abbr (**value added tax**) I.V.A. f

vault[1] /vɔ:lt/ n ⟨roof⟩ volta f; ⟨in bank⟩ caveau m inv; ⟨tomb⟩ cripta f

vault[2] n salto m ● vt/i **~ [over]** saltare

VDU n abbr (**visual display unit**) VDU m

veal /vi:l/ n carne f di vitello ● attrib di vitello

veer /vɪə(r)/ vi cambiare direzione; Naut, Auto virare

vegetable /'vedʒtəbl/ n ⟨food⟩ verdura f; ⟨when growing⟩ ortaggio m ● attrib ⟨oil, fat⟩ vegetale

vegetarian /vedʒɪˈteərɪən/ a & n vegetariano, -a mf

vegetat|e /'vedʒɪteɪt/ vi vegetare. **~ion** /-ˈteɪʃn/ n vegetazione f

vehemen|ce /'vi:əməns/ n veemenza f. **~t** a veemente. **~tly** adv con veemenza

vehicle /'vi:ɪkl/ n veicolo m; ⟨fig: medium⟩ mezzo m

veil /veɪl/ n velo m ● vt velare

vein /veɪn/ n vena f; (mood) umore m; (manner) tenore m. **~ed** a venato

Velcro® /'velkrəʊ/ n **~ fastening** chiusura f con velcro®

velocity /vɪ'lɒsətɪ/ n velocità f

velvet /'velvɪt/ n velluto m. **~y** a vellutato

vendetta /ven'detə/ n vendetta f

vending-machine /'vendɪŋ-/ n distributore m automatico

veneer /və'nɪə(r)/ n impiallacciatura f; fig vernice f. **~ed** a impiallacciato

venereal /vɪ'nɪərɪəl/ a **~ disease** malattia f venerea

Venetian /və'ni:ʃn/ a & n veneziano, -a mf. **v~ blind** n persiana f alla veneziana

vengeance /'vendʒəns/ n vendetta f; **with a ~** fam a più non posso

Venice /'venɪs/ n Venezia f

venison /'venɪsn/ n Culin carne f di cervo

venom /'venəm/ n veleno m. **~ous** /-əs/ a velenoso

vent¹ /vent/ n presa f d'aria; **give ~ to** fig dar libero sfogo a ● vt fig sfogare ⟨anger⟩

vent² n (in jacket) spacco m

ventilat|e /'ventɪleɪt/ vt ventilare. **~ion** /-'leɪʃn/ n ventilazione f; (installation) sistema m di ventilazione. **~or** n ventilatore m

ventriloquist /ven'trɪləkwɪst/ n ventriloquo, -a mf

venture /'ventʃə(r)/ n impresa f ● vt azzardare ● vi avventurarsi

venue /'venju:/ n luogo m (di convegno, concerto, ecc.)

veranda /və'rændə/ n veranda f

verb /vɜ:b/ n verbo m. **~al** a verbale

verbatim /vɜ:'beɪtɪm/ a letterale ● adv parola per parola

verbose /vɜ:'bəʊs/ a prolisso

verdict /'vɜ:dɪkt/ n verdetto m; (opinion) parere m

verge /vɜ:dʒ/ n orlo m; **be on the ~ of doing sth** essere sul punto di fare qcsa ● **verge on** vt fig rasentare

verger /'vɜ:dʒə(r)/ n sagrestano m

verify /'verɪfaɪ/ vt (pt/pp -ied) verificare; (confirm) confermare

vermin /'vɜ:mɪn/ n animali mpl nocivi

vermouth /'vɜ:məθ/ n vermut m inv

vernacular /və'nækjʊlə(r)/ n vernacolo m

versatil|e /'vɜ:sətaɪl/ a versatile. **~ity** /-'tɪlətɪ/ n versatilità f

verse /vɜ:s/ n verso m; (of Bible) versetto m; (poetry) versi mpl

versed /vɜ:st/ a **~ in** versato in

version /'vɜ:ʃn/ n versione f

versus /'vɜ:səs/ prep contro

vertebra /'vɜ:tɪbrə/ n (pl -brae /-bri:/) Anat vertebra f

vertical /'vɜ:tɪkl/ a & n verticale m

vertigo /'vɜ:tɪgəʊ/ n Med vertigine f

verve /vɜ:v/ n verve f

very /'verɪ/ adv molto; **~ much** molto; **~ little** pochissimo; **~ many** moltissimi; **~ few** pochissimi; **~ probably** molto probabilmente; **~ well** benissimo; **at the ~ most** tutt'al più; **at the ~ latest** al più tardi ● a **the ~ first** il primissimo; **the ~ thing** proprio ciò che ci vuole; **at the ~ end/beginning** proprio alla fine/all'inizio; **that ~ day** proprio quel giorno; **the ~ thought** la sola idea; **only a ~ little** solo un pochino

vessel /'vesl/ n nave f

vest /vest/ n maglia f della pelle; (Am: waistcoat) gilè m inv. **~ed interest** n interesse m personale

vestige /'vestɪdʒ/ n (of past) vestigio m

vestment /'vestmənt/ n Relig paramento m

vestry /'vestrɪ/ n sagrestia f

vet /vet/ n veterinario, -a mf ● vt (pt/pp vetted) controllare minuziosamente

veteran /'vetərən/ n veterano, -a mf

veterinary /'vetərɪnərɪ/ a veterinario. **~ surgeon** n medico m veterinario

veto /'vi:təʊ/ n (pl -es) veto m ● vt proibire

vex /veks/ vt irritare. **~ation** /-'seɪʃn/ n irritazione f. **~ed** a irritato; **~ed question** questione f controversa

VHF n abbr (very high frequency) VHF

via /'vaɪə/ prep via; (by means of) attraverso

viable /'vaɪəbl/ a ⟨life form, relationship, company⟩ in grado di sopravvivere; ⟨proposition⟩ attuabile

viaduct /'vaɪədʌkt/ n viadotto m

vibrat|e /vaɪ'breɪt/ vi vibrare. **~ion** /-'breɪʃn/ n vibrazione f

vicar /'vɪkə(r)/ n parroco m (protestante). **~age** /-rɪdʒ/ n casa f parrocchiale

vicarious /vɪ'keərɪəs/ a indiretto

vice¹ /vaɪs/ n vizio m

vice² n Techn morsa f

vice 'chairman n vicepresidente mf

vice 'president n vicepresidente mf

vice versa /vaɪsɪ'vɜ:sə/ adv viceversa

vicinity /vɪ'sɪnətɪ/ n vicinanza f; **in the ~ of** nelle vicinanze di

vicious /'vɪʃəs/ a cattivo; ⟨attack⟩ brutale; ⟨*animal*⟩ pericoloso. ~ **'circle** *n* circolo *m* vizioso. ~**ly** *adv* ⟨*attack*⟩ brutalmente

victim /'vɪktɪm/ *n* vittima *f*. ~**ize** *vt* fare delle rappresaglie contro

victor /'vɪktə(r)/ *n* vincitore *m*

victor|ious /vɪk'tɔːrɪəs/ *a* vittorioso. ~**y** /'vɪktərɪ/ *n* vittoria *f*

video /'vɪdɪəʊ/ *n* video *m*; ⟨*cassette*⟩ videocassetta *f*; ⟨*recorder*⟩ videoregistratore *m* ● *attrib* video ● *vt* registrare

video: ~ **card** *n* Comput scheda *f* video. ~ **cas'sette** *n* videocassetta *f*. ~**conference** *n* videoconferenza *f*. ~ **game** *n* videogioco *m*. ~ **recorder** *n* videoregistratore *m*. ~**-tape** *n* videocassetta *f*

vie /vaɪ/ *vi* (*pres p* **vying**) rivaleggiare

view /vjuː/ *n* vista *f*; (*photographed, painted*) veduta *f*; (*opinion*) visione *f*; **look at the** ~ guardare il panorama; **in my** ~ secondo me; **in** ~ **of** in considerazione di; **on** ~ esposto; **with a** ~ **to** con l'intenzione di ● *vt* visitare ⟨*house*⟩; (*consider*) considerare ● *vi* TV guardare. ~**er** *n* TV telespettatore, -trice *mf*; Phot visore *m*

view: ~**finder** *n* Phot mirino *m*. ~**point** *n* punto *m* di vista

vigil /'vɪdʒɪl/ *n* veglia *f*

vigilan|ce /'vɪdʒɪləns/ *n* vigilanza *f*. ~**t** *a* vigile

vigorous /'vɪgərəs/ *a* vigoroso

vigour /'vɪgə(r)/ *n* vigore *m*

vile /vaɪl/ *a* disgustoso; ⟨*weather*⟩ orribile; ⟨*temper, mood*⟩ pessimo

villa /'vɪlə/ *n* (*for holidays*) casa *f* di villeggiatura

village /'vɪlɪdʒ/ *n* paese *m*. ~**r** *n* paesano, -a *mf*

villain /'vɪlən/ *n* furfante *m*; (*in story*) cattivo *m*

vindicate /'vɪndɪkeɪt/ *vt* (*from guilt*) discolpare; **you are** ~**d** ti sei dimostrato nel giusto

vindictive /vɪn'dɪktɪv/ *a* vendicativo

vine /vaɪn/ *n* vite *f*

vinegar /'vɪnɪgə(r)/ *n* aceto *m*

vineyard /'vɪnjɑːd/ *n* vigneto *m*

vintage /'vɪntɪdʒ/ *a* ⟨*wine*⟩ d'annata ● *n* (*year*) annata *f*

viola /vɪ'əʊlə/ *n* Mus viola *f*

violat|e /'vaɪəleɪt/ *vt* violare. ~**ion** /-'leɪʃn/ *n* violazione *f*

violen|ce /'vaɪələns/ *n* violenza *f*. ~**t** *a* violento

violet /'vaɪələt/ *a* violetto ● *n* (*flower*) violetta *f*; (*colour*) violetto *m*

violin /vaɪə'lɪn/ *n* violino *m*. ~**ist** *n* violinista *mf*

VIP *n abbr* (**very important person**) vip *mf*

virgin /'vɜːdʒɪn/ *a* vergine ● *n* vergine *f*. ~**ity** /-'dʒɪnətɪ/ *n* verginità *f*

Virgo /'vɜːgəʊ/ *n* Astr Vergine *f*

viril|e /'vɪraɪl/ *a* virile. ~**ity** /-'rɪlətɪ/ *n* virilità *f*

virtual /'vɜːtjʊəl/ *a* effettivo. ~ **reality** *n* realtà *f* virtuale. ~**ly** *adv* praticamente

virtue /'vɜːtjuː/ *n* virtù *f inv*; (*advantage*) vantaggio *m*; **by** *or* **in** ~ **of** a causa di

virtuoso /vɜːtʊ'əʊzəʊ/ *n* (*pl* **-si** /-zɪ:/) virtuoso *m*

virtuous /'vɜːtjʊəs/ *a* virtuoso

virulent /'vɪrʊlənt/ *a* virulento

virus /'vaɪərəs/ *n* virus *m inv*

visa /'viːzə/ *n* visto *m*

vis-à-vis /viːzɑː'viː/ *prep* rispetto a

viscount /'vaɪkaʊnt/ *n* visconte *m*

viscous /'vɪskəs/ *a* vischioso

visibility /vɪzə'bɪlətɪ/ *n* visibilità *f*

visibl|e /'vɪzəbl/ *a* visibile. ~**y** *adv* visibilmente

vision /'vɪʒn/ *n* visione *f*; (*sight*) vista *f*

visit /'vɪzɪt/ *n* visita *f* ● *vt* andare a trovare ⟨*person*⟩; andare da ⟨*doctor etc*⟩; visitare ⟨*town, building*⟩. ~**ing hours** *npl* orario *m* delle visite. ~**or** *n* ospite *mf*; (*of town, museum*) visitatore, -trice *mf*; (*in hotel*) cliente *mf*

visor /'vaɪzə(r)/ *n* visiera *f*; Auto parasole *m*

vista /'vɪstə/ *n* (*view*) panorama *m*

visual /'vɪzjʊəl/ *a* visivo. ~ **aids** *npl* supporto *m* visivo. ~ **dis'play unit** *n* visualizzatore *m*. ~**ly** *adv* visualmente; ~**ly handicapped** non vedente

visualize /'vɪzjʊəlaɪz/ *vt* visualizzare

vital /'vaɪtl/ *a* vitale. ~**ity** /vaɪ'tælətɪ/ *n* vitalità *f*. ~**ly** /'vaɪtəlɪ/ *adv* estremamente

vitamin /'vɪtəmɪn/ *n* vitamina *f*

vivaci|ous /vɪ'veɪʃəs/ *a* vivace. ~**ty** /-'væsətɪ/ *n* vivacità *f*

vivid /'vɪvɪd/ *a* vivido. ~**ly** *adv* in modo vivido

vocabulary /və'kæbjʊlərɪ/ *n* vocabolario *m*; (*list*) glossario *m*

vocal /'vəʊkl/ *a* vocale; (*vociferous*) eloquente. ~ **cords** *npl* corde *fpl* vocali

vocalist /'vəʊkəlɪst/ *n* vocalista *mf*

vocation /və'keɪʃn/ *n* vocazione *f*. ~**al** *a* di orientamento professionale

vociferous /və'sɪfərəs/ *a* vociante

vodka /'vɒdkə/ *n* vodka *f inv*

vogue /vəʊg/ *n* moda *f*; **in** ~ in voga

voice /vɔɪs/ *n* voce *f* ● *vt* esprimere. **~mail** *n* posta *f* elettronica vocale

void /vɔɪd/ *a* (*not valid*) nullo; **~ of** privo di ● *n* vuoto *m*

volatile /ˈvɒlətaɪl/ *a* volatile; (*person*) volubile

volcanic /vɒlˈkænɪk/ *a* vulcanico

volcano /vɒlˈkeɪnəʊ/ *n* vulcano *m*

volition /vəˈlɪʃn/ *n* **of his own ~** di sua spontanea volontà

volley /ˈvɒlɪ/ *n* (*of gunfire*) raffica *f*; *Tennis* volée *f inv*

volt /vəʊlt/ *n* volt *m inv*. **~age** /-ɪdʒ/ *n Electr* voltaggio *m*

volubl|e /ˈvɒljʊbl/ *a* loquace

volume /ˈvɒljuːm/ *n* volume *m*; (*of work, traffic*) quantità *f inv*. **~ control** *n* volume *m*

voluntar|y /ˈvɒləntərɪ/ *a* volontario. **~y work** *n* volontariato *m*. **~ily** *adv* volontariamente

volunteer /vɒlənˈtɪə(r)/ *n* volontario, -a *mf* ● *vt* offrire volontariamente ⟨*information*⟩ ● *vi* offrirsi volontario; *Mil* arruolarsi come volontario

voluptuous /vəˈlʌptjʊəs/ *a* voluttuoso

vomit /ˈvɒmɪt/ *n* vomito *m* ● *vt/i* vomitare

voracious /vəˈreɪʃəs/ *a* vorace

vot|e /vəʊt/ *n* voto *m*; (*ballot*) votazione *f*; (*right*) diritto *m* di voto; **take a ~e on** votare su ● *vi* votare ● *vt* **~e** sb **president** eleggere qcno presidente. **~er** *n* elettore, -trice *mf*. **~ing** *n* votazione *f*

vouch /vaʊtʃ/ *vi* **~ for** garantire per. **~er** *n* buono *m*

vow /vaʊ/ *n* voto *m* ● *vt* giurare

vowel /ˈvaʊəl/ *n* vocale *f*

voyage /ˈvɔɪdʒ/ *n* viaggio *m* [marittimo]; (*in space*) viaggio *m* [nello spazio]

vulgar /ˈvʌlgə(r)/ *a* volgare. **~ity** /-ˈgærətɪ/ *n* volgarità *f inv*

vulnerable /ˈvʌlnərəbl/ *a* vulnerabile

vulture /ˈvʌltʃə(r)/ *n* avvoltoio *m*

vying /ˈvaɪɪŋ/ *see* **vie**

Ww

wad /wɒd/ *n* batuffolo *m*; (*bundle*) rotolo *m*. **~ding** *n* ovatta *f*

waddle /ˈwɒdl/ *vi* camminare ondeggiando

wade /weɪd/ *vi* guadare; **~ through** *fam* procedere faticosamente in ⟨*book*⟩

wafer /ˈweɪfə(r)/ *n* cialda *f*, wafer *m inv*; *Relig* ostia *f*

waffle[1] /ˈwɒfl/ *vi fam* blaterare

waffle[2] *n Culin* cialda *f*

waft /wɒft/ *vt* trasportare ● *vi* diffondersi

wag /wæg/ *v* (*pt/pp* **wagged**) ● *vt* agitare ● *vi* agitarsi

wage[1] /weɪdʒ/ *vt* dichiarare ⟨*war*⟩; lanciare ⟨*campaign*⟩

wage[2] *n*, & **~s** *pl* salario *msg*. **~ packet** *n* busta *f* paga

waggle /ˈwægl/ *vt* dimenare ● *vi* dimenarsi

wagon /ˈwægən/ *n* carro *m*; *Rail* vagone *m* merci

wail /weɪl/ *n* piagnucolio *m*; (*of wind*) lamento *m*; (*of baby*) vagito *m* ● *vi* piagnucolare; ⟨*wind:*⟩ lamentarsi; ⟨*baby:*⟩ vagire

waist /weɪst/ *n* vita *f*. **~coat** /ˈweɪskəʊt/ *n* gilè *m inv*; (*of man's suit*) panciotto *m*. **~line** *n* vita *f*

wait /weɪt/ *n* attesa *f*; **lie in ~ for** appostarsi per sorprendere ● *vi* aspettare; **~ for** aspettare ● *vt* **~ one's turn** aspettare il proprio turno. **wait on** *vt* servire

waiter /ˈweɪtə(r)/ *n* cameriere *m*

waiting: **~-list** *n* lista *f* d'attesa. **~-room** *n* sala *f* d'aspetto

waitress /ˈweɪtrɪs/ *n* cameriera *f*

waive /weɪv/ *vt* rinunciare a ⟨*claim*⟩; non tener conto di ⟨*rule*⟩

wake[1] /weɪk/ *n* veglia *f* funebre ● *v* (*pt* **woke**, *pp* **woken**) **~ [up]** ● *vt* svegliare ● *vi* svegliarsi

wake[2] *n Naut* scia *f*; **in the ~ of** *fig* nella scia di

waken /ˈweɪkn/ *vt* svegliare ● *vi* svegliarsi

Wales /weɪlz/ *n* Galles *m*

walk /wɔːk/ *n* passeggiata *f*; (*gait*) andatura *f*; (*path*) sentiero *m*; **go for a ~** andare a fare una passeggiata ● *vi* camminare; (*as opposed to drive etc*) andare a piedi; (*ramble*) passeggiare ● *vt* portare a spasso (*dog*); percorrere (*streets*). **walk out** *vi* (*husband, employee:*) andarsene; (*workers:*) scioperare. **walk out on** *vt* lasciare

walker /'wɔːkə(r)/ *n* camminatore, -trice *mf*; (*rambler*) escursionista *mf*

walking /'wɔːkɪŋ/ *n* camminare *m*; (*rambling*) fare *m* delle escursioni. **~-stick** *n* bastone *m* da passeggio

'Walkman® *n* Walkman *m inv*

walk: ~-out *n* sciopero *m*. **~-over** *n fig* vittoria *f* facile

wall /wɔːl/ *n* muro *m*; **go to the ~** *fam* andare a rotoli; **drive sb up the ~** *fam* far diventare matto qcno

wallet /'wɒlɪt/ *n* portafoglio *m*

wallop /'wɒləp/ *n fam* colpo *m*

wallow /'wɒləʊ/ *vi* sguazzare; (*in self-pity, grief*) crogiolarsi

'wallpaper *n* tappezzeria *f* ● *vt* tappezzare

walnut /'wɔːlnʌt/ *n* noce *f*

waltz /wɔːlts/ *n* valzer *m inv* ● *vi* ballare il valzer

wan /wɒn/ *a* esangue

wand /wɒnd/ *n* (*magic ~*) bacchetta *f* [magica]

wander /'wɒndə(r)/ *vi* girovagare; (*fig: digress*) divagare. **wander about** *vi* andare a spasso

wane /weɪn/ *n* **be on the ~** essere in fase calante ● *vi* calare

wangle /'wæŋgl/ *vt fam* rimediare (*invitation, holiday*)

want /wɒnt/ *n* (*hardship*) bisogno *m*; (*lack*) mancanza *f* ● *vt* volere; (*need*) aver bisogno di; **~ [to have] sth** volere qcsa; **~ to do sth** voler fare qcsa; **we ~ to stay** vogliamo rimanere; **I ~ you to go** voglio che tu vada; **it ~s painting** ha bisogno d'essere dipinto; **you ~ to learn to swim** bisogna che impari a nuotare ● *vi* **~ for** mancare di. **~ed** *a* ricercato. **~ing** *a* **be ~ing** mancare; **~ing in** mancare di

wanton /'wɒntən/ *a* (*cruelty, neglect*) gratuito; (*morally*) debosciato

WAP /wæp/ *n abbr* (**wireless application protocol**) WAP *m inv*

war /wɔː(r)/ *n* guerra *f*; *fig* lotta *f* (**on** contro); **at ~** in guerra

ward /wɔːd/ *n* (*in hospital*) reparto *m*; (*child*) minore *m* sotto tutela ● **ward off** *vt* evitare; parare (*blow*)

warden /'wɔːdn/ *n* guardiano, -a *mf*

warder /'wɔːdə(r)/ *n* guardia *f* carceraria

wardrobe /'wɔːdrəʊb/ *n* guardaroba *m*

warehouse /'weəhaʊs/ *n* magazzino *m*

war: ~fare *n* guerra *f*. **~head** *n* testata *f*

warily /'weərɪlɪ/ *adv* cautamente

'warlike *a* bellicoso

warm /wɔːm/ *a* caldo; (*welcome*) caloroso; **be ~** (*person:*) aver caldo; **it is ~** (*weather*) fa caldo ● *vt* scaldare. **warm up** *vt* scaldare ● *vi* scaldarsi; *fig* animarsi. **~-hearted** *a* espansivo. **~ly** *adv* (*greet*) calorosamente; (*dress*) in modo pesante

warmth /wɔːmθ/ *n* calore *m*

warn /wɔːn/ *vt* avvertire. **~ing** *n* avvertimento *m*; (*advance notice*) preavviso *m*

warp /wɔːp/ *vt* deformare; *fig* distorcere ● *vi* deformarsi

'war-path *n* **on the ~** sul sentiero di guerra

warped /wɔːpt/ *a fig* contorto; (*sexuality*) deviato; (*view*) distorto

warrant /'wɒrənt/ *n* (*for arrest, search*) mandato *m* ● *vt* (*justify*) giustificare; (*guarantee*) garantire

warranty /'wɒrəntɪ/ *n* garanzia *f*

warring /'wɔːrɪŋ/ *a* in guerra

warrior /'wɒrɪə(r)/ *n* guerriero, -a *mf*

'warship *n* nave *f* da guerra

wart /wɔːt/ *n* porro *m*

'wartime *n* tempo *m* di guerra

wary /'weərɪ/ *a* (**-ier, -iest**) (*careful*) cauto; (*suspicious*) diffidente

was /wɒz/ *see* **be**

wash /wɒʃ/ *n* lavata *f*; (*clothes*) bucato *m*; (*in washer*) lavaggio *m*; **have a ~** darsi una lavata ● *vt* lavare; (*sea:*) bagnare; **~ one's hands** lavarsi le mani ● *vi* lavarsi. **wash out** *vt* sciacquare (*soap*); sciacquarsi (*mouth*). **wash up** *vt* lavare ● *vi* lavare i piatti; *Am* lavarsi

washable /'wɒʃəbl/ *a* lavabile

wash: ~-basin *n* lavandino *m*. **~ cloth** *n Am* guanto *m* da bagno

washed 'out *a* (*faded*) scolorito; (*tired*) spossato

washer /'wɒʃə(r)/ *n Techn* guarnizione *f*; (*machine*) lavatrice *f*

washing /'wɒʃɪŋ/ *n* bucato *m*. **~-machine** *n* lavatrice *f*. **~-powder** *n* detersivo *m*. **~-'up** *n* do the ~-up lavare i piatti. **~-'up liquid** *n* detersivo *m* per i piatti

wash: ~-out *n* disastro *m*. **~-room** *n* bagno *m*

wasp /wɒsp/ *n* vespa *f*

wastage /'weɪstɪdʒ/ *n* perdita *f*

waste /weɪst/ *n* spreco *m*; (*rubbish*) ri-

fiuto *m*; **~ of time** perdita *f* di tempo
● *a* ⟨*product*⟩ di scarto; ⟨*land*⟩ desolato;
lay ~ devastare ● *vt* sprecare. **waste
away** *vi* deperire

waste: **~-di'sposal unit** *n* eliminatore
m di rifiuti. **~ful** *a* dispendioso. **~ 'paper**
n carta *f* straccia. **~-'paper basket** *n* cestino *m* per la carta [straccia]

watch /wɒtʃ/ *n* guardia *f*; (*period of
duty*) turno *m* di guardia; (*timepiece*)
orologio *m*; **be on the ~** stare all'erta
● *vt* guardare ⟨*film, match, television*⟩;
(*be careful of, look after*) stare attento a
● *vi* guardare. **watch out** *vi* (*be careful*)
stare attento (**for** a). **watch out for** *vt*
(*look for*) fare attenzione all'arrivo di
⟨*person*⟩

watch: **~-dog** *n* cane *m* da guardia.
~ful *a* attento. **~maker** *n* orologiaio, -a
mf. **~man** *n* guardiano *m*. **~-strap** *n*
cinturino *m* dell'orologio. **~word** *n*
motto *m*

water /'wɔːtə(r)/ *n* acqua *f* ● *vt* annaf-
fiare ⟨*garden, plant*⟩; (*dilute*) annacqua-
re ● *vi* ⟨*eyes:*⟩ lacrimare; **my mouth
was ~ing** avevo l'acquolina in bocca.
water down *vt* diluire; *fig* attenuare

water: **~-colour** *n* acquerello *m*.
~cress *n* crescione *m*. **~fall** *n* cascata *f*
'watering-can *n* annaffiatoio *m*

water: **~-lily** *n* ninfea *f*. **~logged** *a* inzuppato. **~-main** *n* conduttura *f* dell'acqua. **~ polo** *n* pallanuoto *f*. **~-power** *n*
energia *f* idraulica. **~proof** *a* impermeabile. **~shed** *n* spartiacque *m inv*; *fig*
svolta *f*. **~-skiing** *n* sci *m* nautico.
~tight *a* stagno; *fig* irrefutabile. **~way**
n canale *m* navigabile

watery /'wɔːtərɪ/ *a* acquoso; ⟨*eyes*⟩ la-
crimoso

watt /wɒt/ *n* watt *m inv*

wave /weɪv/ *n* onda *f*; (*gesture*) cenno
m; *fig* ondata *f* ● *vt* agitare; **~ one's
hand** agitare la mano ● *vi* far segno;
⟨*flag:*⟩ sventolare. **~length** *n* lunghezza
f d'onda

waver /'weɪvə(r)/ *vi* vacillare; (*hesitate*)
esitare

wavy /'weɪvɪ/ *a* ondulato

wax[1] /wæks/ *vi* ⟨*moon:*⟩ crescere; (*fig:
become*) diventare

wax[2] *n* cera *f*; (*in ear*) cerume *m* ● *vt*
dare la cera a. **~works** *n* museo *m* delle
cere

way /weɪ/ *n* percorso *m*; (*direction*) direzione *f*; (*manner, method*) modo *m*; **~s** *pl*
(*customs*) abitudini *fpl*; **be in the ~** essere in mezzo; **on the ~ to Rome** an-

dando a Roma; **I'll do it on the ~** lo
faccio mentre vado; **it's on my ~** è sul
mio percorso; **a long ~ off** lontano;
this ~ da questa parte; (*like this*) così;
by the ~ a proposito; **by ~ of** come;
(*via*) via; **either ~** (*whatever we do*) in
un modo o nell'altro; **in some ~s** sotto
certi aspetti; **in a ~** in un certo senso;
in a bad ~ ⟨*person*⟩ molto grave; **out of
the ~** fuori mano; **under ~** in corso;
lead the ~ far strada; *fig* aprire la strada; **make ~** far posto (**for** a); **give ~**
Auto dare la precedenza; **go out of
one's ~** *fig* scomodarsi (**to** per); **get
one's [own] ~** averla vinta ● *adv* **~
behind** molto indietro. **~ 'in** *n* entrata *f*

way'lay *vt* (*pt/pp* **-laid**) aspettare al
varco ⟨*person*⟩

way 'out *n* uscita *f*; *fig* via *f* d'uscita

way-'out *a fam* eccentrico

wayward /'weɪwəd/ *a* capriccioso

WC *n abbr* WC; **the WC** il gabinetto

we /wiː/ *pers pron* noi; **we're the last**
siamo gli ultimi; **they're going, but
we're not** loro vanno, ma noi no

weak /wiːk/ *a* debole; ⟨*liquid*⟩ leggero.
~en *vt* indebolire ● *vi* indebolirsi.
~ling *n* smidollato, -a *mf*. **~ness** *n* debolezza *f*; (*liking*) debole *m*

wealth /welθ/ *n* ricchezza *f*; *fig* gran
quantità *f*. **~y** *a* (**-ier, -iest**) ricco

wean /wiːn/ *vt* svezzare

weapon /'wepən/ *n* arma *f*

wear /weə(r)/ *n* (*clothing*) abbigliamento *m*; **for everyday ~** da portare tutti i
giorni; **~ [and tear]** usura *f* ● *v* (*pt*
wore, *pp* **worn**) ● *vt* portare; (*damage*)
consumare; **~ a hole in sth** logorare
qcsa fino a fare un buco; **what shall I
~?** cosa mi metto? ● *vi* consumarsi;
(*last*) durare. **wear off** *vi* scomparire;
⟨*effect:*⟩ finire. **wear out** *vt* consumare
[fino in fondo]; (*exhaust*) estenuare ● *vi*
estenuarsi

wearable /'weərəbl/ *a* portabile

wear|y /'wɪərɪ/ *a* (**-ier, -iest**) sfinito ● *v*
(*pt/pp* **wearied**) ● *vt* sfinire ● *vi* **~y of**
stancarsi di. **~ily** *adv* stancamente

weasel /'wiːzl/ *n* donnola *f*

weather /'weðə(r)/ *n* tempo *m*; **in this
~** con questo tempo; **under the ~** *fam*
giù di corda ● *vt* sopravvivere a ⟨*storm*⟩

weather: **~-beaten** *a* ⟨*face*⟩ segnato
dalle intemperie. **~cock** *n* gallo *m*
segnavento. **~ forecast** *n* previsioni
fpl del tempo

weave[1] /wiːv/ *vi* (*pt/pp* **weaved**)
(*move*) zigzagare

weave² n tessuto m ● vt (pt **wove**, pp **woven**) tessere; intrecciare ⟨flowers etc⟩; intrecciare le fila di ⟨story etc⟩. **~r** n tessitore, -trice mf

web /web/ n rete f; (of spider) ragnatela f; **W~** Comput Web m inv, Rete f. **~bed feet** npl piedi mpl palmati. **~cam** n webcam f inv. **~ page** n Comput pagina f web. **~ site** n Comput sito m web

wed /wed/ vt (pt/pp **wedded**) sposare ● vi sposarsi. **~ding** n matrimonio m

wedding: **~ cake** n torta f nuziale. **~ day** n giorno m del matrimonio. **~ dress** n vestito m da sposa. **~-ring** n fede f

wedge /wedʒ/ n zeppa f; (for splitting wood) cuneo m; (of cheese) fetta f ● vt (fix) fissare

wedlock /'wedlɒk/ n **born out of ~** nato fuori dal matrimonio

Wednesday /'wenzdeɪ/ n mercoledì m inv

wee¹ /wiː/ a fam piccolo

wee² vi fam fare la pipì

weed /wiːd/ n erbaccia f; (fam: person) mollusco m ● vt estirpare le erbacce da ● vi estirpare le erbacce. **weed out** vt fig eliminare

'weed-killer n erbicida m

week /wiːk/ n settimana f. **~day** n giorno m feriale. **~end** n fine m settimana

weekly /'wiːklɪ/ a settimanale ● n settimanale m ● adv settimanalmente

weep /wiːp/ vi (pt/pp **wept**) piangere

weigh /weɪ/ vt/i pesare; **~ anchor** levare l'ancora. **weigh down** vt fig piegare. **weigh up** vt fig soppesare; valutare ⟨person⟩

weight /weɪt/ n peso m; **put on/lose ~** ingrassare/dimagrire. **~ing** n (allowance) indennità f inv

weight: **~lessness** n assenza f di gravità. **~-lifting** n sollevamento m pesi

weighty /'weɪtɪ/ a (-ier, -iest) pesante; (important) di un certo peso

weir /wɪə(r)/ n chiusa f

weird /wɪəd/ a misterioso; (bizarre) bizzarro

welcome /'welkəm/ a benvenuto; **you're ~!** prego!; **you're ~ to have it/to come** prendilo/vieni pure ● n accoglienza f ● vt accogliere; (appreciate) gradire

weld /weld/ vt saldare. **~er** n saldatore m

welfare /'welfeə(r)/ n benessere m; (aid) assistenza f. **W~ State** n Stato m assistenziale

well¹ /wel/ n pozzo m; (of staircase) tromba f

well² adv (**better**, **best**) bene; **as ~** anche; **as ~ as** (in addition) oltre a; **~ done!** bravo!; **very ~** benissimo ● a **he is not ~** non sta bene; **get ~ soon!** guarisci presto! ● int beh!; **~ I never!** ma va!

well: **~-behaved** a educato. **~-being** n benessere m. **~-bred** a beneducato. **~-heeled** a fam danaroso

wellingtons /'welɪŋtənz/ npl stivali mpl di gomma

well: **~-known** a famoso. **~-meaning** a con buone intenzioni. **~-meant** a con le migliori intenzioni. **~-off** a benestante. **~-read** a colto. **~-to-do** a ricco

Welsh /welʃ/ a & n gallese; (language) gallese m; **the ~** pl i gallesi. **~man** n gallese m. **~ rabbit** n toast m inv al formaggio

went /went/ see **go**

wept /wept/ see **weep**

were /wɜː(r)/ see **be**

west /west/ n ovest m; **to the ~ of** a ovest di; **the W~** l'Occidente m ● a occidentale ● adv verso occidente; **go ~** fam andare in malora. **~erly** a verso ovest; occidentale ⟨wind⟩. **~ern** a occidentale ● n western m inv

West: **~ 'Germany** n Germania f Occidentale. **~ 'Indian** a & n antillese mf. **~ 'Indies** /'ɪndɪz/ npl Antille fpl

'westward[s] /-wəd[z]/ adv verso ovest

wet /wet/ a (**wetter**, **wettest**) bagnato; fresco ⟨paint⟩; (rainy) piovoso; ⟨fam: person⟩ smidollato; **get ~** bagnarsi ● vt (pt/pp **wet**, **wetted**) bagnare. **~ 'blanket** n guastafeste mf inv

whack /wæk/ n fam colpo m ● vt fam dare un colpo a. **~ed** a fam stanco morto. **~ing** a (fam: huge) enorme

whale /weɪl/ n balena f; **have a ~ of a time** fam divertirsi un sacco

wham /wæm/ int bum

wharf /wɔːf/ n banchina f

what /wɒt/ pron che, [che] cosa; **~ for?** perché?; **~ is that for?** a che cosa serve?; **~ is it?** (what do you want) cosa c'è?; **~ is it like?** com'è?; **~ is your name?** come ti chiami?; **~ is the weather like?** com'è il tempo?; **~ is the film about?** di cosa parla il film?; **~ is he talking about?** di cosa sta parlando?; **he asked me ~ she had said** mi ha chiesto cosa ha detto; **~ about going to the cinema?** e se andassimo al cinema?; ~ **about the children?** (*what will they do*) e i bambini?; ~ **if it rains?** e se piove? ● *a* quale, che; **take ~ books you want** prendi tutti i libri che vuoi; ~ **kind of a** che tipo di; **at ~ time?** a che ora? ● *adv* che; ~ **a lovely day!** che bella giornata! ● *int* ~! [che] cosa!; ~? [che] cosa?

what'ever *a* qualunque ● *pron* qualsiasi cosa; ~ **is it?** cos'è?; ~ **he does** qualsiasi cosa faccia; ~ **happens** qualunque cosa succeda; **nothing ~** proprio niente

whatso'ever *a & pron* = **whatever**

wheat /wi:t/ *n* grano *m*, frumento *m*

wheedle /'wi:d(ə)l/ *vt* ~ **sth out of sb** ottenere qcsa da qualcuno con le lusinghe

wheel /wi:l/ *n* ruota *f*; (*steering ~*) volante *m*; **at the ~** al volante ● *vt* (*push*) spingere ● *vi* (*circle*) ruotare; ~ **[round]** ruotare

wheel: ~**barrow** *n* carriola *f*. ~**chair** *n* sedia *f* a rotelle. ~**-clamp** *n* ceppo *m* bloccaruote

wheeze /wi:z/ *vi* ansimare

when /wen/ *adv & conj* quando; **the day ~** il giorno in cui; ~ **swimming/ reading** nuotando/leggendo

when'ever *adv & conj* in qualsiasi momento; (*every time that*) ogni volta che; ~ **did it happen?** quando è successo?

where /weə(r)/ *adv & conj* dove; **the street ~ I live** la via in cui abito; ~ **do you come from?** da dove vieni?

whereabouts[1] /weərə'baʊts/ *adv* dove

'whereabouts[2] *n* **nobody knows his ~** nessuno sa dove si trova

where'as *conj* dal momento che; (*in contrast*) mentre

where'by *adv* attraverso il quale

whereu'pon *adv* dopo di che

wher'ever *adv & conj* dovunque; ~ **is he?** dov'è mai?; ~ **possible** dovunque sia possibile

whet /wet/ *vt* (*pt/pp* **whetted**) aguzzare (*appetite*)

whether /'weðə(r)/ *conj* se; ~ **you like it or not** che ti piaccia o no

which /wɪtʃ/ *a & pron* quale; ~ **one?** quale?; ~ **one of you?** chi di voi?; ~ **way?** (*direction*) in che direzione? ● *rel pron* (*object*) che; ~ **he does frequently** cosa che fa spesso; **after ~** dopo di che; **on/in ~** su/in cui

which'ever *a & pron* qualunque; ~ **it is** qualunque sia; ~ **one of you** chiunque tra voi

whiff /wɪf/ *n* zaffata *f*; **have a ~ of sth** odorare qcsa

while /waɪl/ *n* un bel po'; **a little ~** un po' ● *conj* mentre; (*as long as*) finché; (*although*) sebbene ● **while away** *vt* passare (*time*)

whilst /waɪlst/ *conj see* **while**

whim /wɪm/ *n* capriccio *m*

whimper /'wɪmpə(r)/ *vi* piagnucolare; (*dog:*) mugolare

whimsical /'wɪmzɪkl/ *a* capriccioso; (*story*) fantasioso

whine /waɪn/ *n* lamento *m*; (*of dog*) guaito *m* ● *vi* lamentarsi; (*dog:*) guaire

whip /wɪp/ *n* frusta *f*; (*Pol: person*) parlamentare *mf* incaricato, -a di assicurarsi della presenza dei membri del suo partito alle votazioni ● *vt* (*pt/pp* **whipped**) frustare; *Culin* sbattere; (*snatch*) afferrare; (*fam: steal*) fregare. **whip up** *vt* (*incite*) stimolare; *fam* improvvisare (*meal*). ~**ped 'cream** *n* panna *f* montata

whirl /wɜ:l/ *n* (*movement*) rotazione *f*; **my mind's in a ~** ho le idee confuse ● *vi* girare rapidamente ● *vt* far girare rapidamente. ~ **pool** *n* vortice *m*. ~ **wind** *n* turbine *m*

whirr /wɜ:(r)/ *vi* ronzare

whisk /wɪsk/ *n Culin* frullino *m* ● *vt Culin* frullare. **whisk away** *vt* portare via

whisker /'wɪskə(r)/ *n* ~**s** baffi *mpl*; (*on man's face*) basette *fpl*; **by a ~** per un pelo

whisky /'wɪskɪ/ *n* whisky *m inv*

whisper /'wɪspə(r)/ *n* sussurro *m*; (*rumour*) diceria *f* ● *vt/i* sussurrare

whistle /'wɪsl/ *n* fischio *m*; (*instrument*) fischietto *m* ● *vt* fischiettare ● *vi* fischiettare; (*referee*) fischiare

white /waɪt/ *a* bianco; **go ~** (*pale*) sbiancare ● *n* bianco *m*; (*of egg*) albume *m*; (*person*) bianco, -a *mf*

white: ~ **'coffee** *n* caffè *m inv* macchiato. ~**-'collar worker** *n* colletto *m* bianco

'Whitehall *n* strada *f* di Londra, sede degli uffici del governo britannico; *fig* amministrazione *f* britannica

white 'lie *n* bugia *f* pietosa

whiten /'waɪtn/ *vt* imbiancare ● *vi* sbiancare

whiteness /'waɪtnɪs/ *n* bianchezza *f*

'whitewash *n* intonaco *m*; *fig* copertura *f* ● *vt* dare una mano d'intonaco a; *fig* coprire

Whitsun /'wɪtsn/ *n* Pentecoste *f*

whittle /'wɪtl/ *vt* ~ **down** ridurre

whiz[z] /wɪz/ *vi* (*pt/pp* **whizzed**) sibilare. **~-kid** *n fam* giovane *m* prodigio

who /huː/ *inter pron* chi ● *rel pron* che; **the children, ~ were all tired,...** i bambini, che erano tutti stanchi,...

who'ever *pron* chiunque; **~ he is** chiunque sia; **~ can that be?** chi può mai essere?

whole /həʊl/ *a* tutto; (*not broken*) intatto; **the ~ truth** tutta la verità; **the ~ world** il mondo intero; **the ~ lot** (*everything*) tutto; (*pl*) tutti; **the ~ lot of you** tutti voi ● *n* tutto *m*; **as a ~** nell'insieme; **on the ~** tutto considerato; **the ~ of Italy** tutta l'Italia

whole-: **~food** *n* cibo *m* macrobiotico. **~-'hearted** *a* di tutto cuore. **~meal** *a* integrale

'wholesale *a & adv* all'ingrosso; *fig* in massa. **~r** *n* grossista *mf*

wholesome /'həʊlsəm/ *a* sano

wholly /'həʊlɪ/ *adv* completamente

whom /huːm/ *rel pron* che; **the man ~ I saw** l'uomo che ho visto; **to/with ~** a/con cui ● *inter pron* chi; **to ~ did you speak?** con chi hai parlato?

whooping cough /'huːpɪŋ/ *n* pertosse *f*

whopping /'wɒpɪŋ/ *a fam* enorme

whore /hɔː(r)/ *n* puttana *f vulg*

whose /huːz/ *rel pron* il cui; **people ~ name begins with D** le persone i cui nomi cominciano con la D ● *inter pron* di chi; **~ is that?** di chi è quello? ● *a* **~ car did you use?** di chi è la macchina che hai usato?

why /waɪ/ *adv* (*inter*) perché; **the reason ~** la ragione per cui; **that's ~** per questo ● *int* diamine

wick /wɪk/ *n* stoppino *m*

wicked /'wɪkɪd/ *a* cattivo; (*mischievous*) malizioso

wicker /'wɪkə(r)/ *n* vimini *mpl* ● *attrib* di vimini

wide /waɪd/ *a* largo; (*experience, knowledge*) vasto; (*difference*) profondo; (*far from target*) lontano; **10 cm ~** largo 10 cm; **how ~ is it?** quanto è largo? ● *adv* (*off target*) lontano dal bersaglio; **~ awake** del tutto sveglio; **~ open** spalancato; **far and ~** in lungo e in largo. **~ly** *adv* largamente; (*known, accepted*) generalmente; (*different*) profondamente

widen /'waɪdn/ *vt* allargare ● *vi* allargarsi

'widespread *a* diffuso

widow /'wɪdəʊ/ *n* vedova *f*. **~ed** *a* vedovo. **~er** *n* vedovo *m*

width /wɪdθ/ *n* larghezza *f*; (*of material*) altezza *f*

wield /wiːld/ *vt* maneggiare; esercitare (*power*)

wife /waɪf/ *n* (*pl* **wives**) moglie *f*

wig /wɪg/ *n* parrucca *f*

wiggle /'wɪgl/ *vi* dimenarsi ● *vt* dimenare

wild /waɪld/ *a* selvaggio; (*animal, flower*) selvatico; (*furious*) furibondo; (*applause*) fragoroso; (*idea*) folle; (*with joy*) pazzo; (*guess*) azzardato; **be ~ about** (*keen on*) andare pazzo per ● *adv* **run ~** crescere senza controllo ● *n* **in the ~** allo stato naturale; **the ~s** *pl* le zone sperdute

wilderness /'wɪldənɪs/ *n* deserto *m*; (*fig: garden*) giungla *f*

'wildfire *n* **spread like ~** allargarsi a macchia d'olio

wild-: **~-'goose chase** *n* ricerca *f* inutile. **~life** *n* animali *mpl* selvatici

wilful /'wɪlfl/ *a* intenzionale; (*person, refusal*) ostinato. **~ly** *adv* intenzionalmente; (*refuse*) ostinatamente

will¹ /wɪl/ *v aux* **he ~ arrive tomorrow** arriverà domani; **I won't tell him** non glielo dirò; **you ~ be back soon, won't you?** tornerai presto, no?; **he ~ be there, won't he?** sarà là, no?; **she ~ be there by now** sarà là ormai; **~ you go?** (*do you intend to go*) pensi di andare?; **~ you go to the baker's and buy...?** puoi andare dal panettiere a comprare...?; **~ you be quiet!** vuoi stare calmo!; **~ you have some wine?** vuoi del vino?; **the engine won't start** la macchina non parte

will² *n* volontà *f inv*; (*document*) testamento *m*

willing /'wɪlɪŋ/ *a* disposto; (*eager*) volonteroso. **~ly** *adv* volentieri. **~ness** *n* buona volontà *f*

willow /'wɪləʊ/ *n* salice *m*

'will-power *n* forza *f* di volontà

willy-'nilly *adv* (*at random*) a casaccio; (*wanting to or not*) volente o nolente

wilt /wɪlt/ *vi* appassire

wily /'waɪlɪ/ *a* (**-ier, -iest**) astuto

wimp /wɪmp/ *n* rammollito, -a *mf*

win /wɪn/ *n* vittoria *f*; **have a ~** riportare una vittoria ● *v* (*pt/pp* **won**; *pres p* **winning**) ● *vt* vincere; conquistare (*fame*) ● *vi* vincere. **win over** *vt* convincere

wince /wɪns/ vi contrarre il viso

winch /wɪntʃ/ n argano m

wind¹ /wɪnd/ n vento m; (breath) fiato m; (fam: flatulence) aria f; **get/have the ~ up** fam aver fifa; **get ~ of** aver sentore di; **in the ~** nell'aria ● vt **~ sb** lasciare qcno senza fiato

wind² /waɪnd/ v (pt/pp **wound**) ● vt (wrap) avvolgere; (move by turning) far girare; caricare (clock) ● vi (road:) serpeggiare. **wind up** vt caricare (clock); concludere (proceedings); fam prendere in giro (sb)

wind /wɪnd/: **~fall** n fig fortuna f inaspettata

winding /'waɪndɪŋ/ a tortuoso

wind: **~ instrument** n strumento m a fiato. **~mill** n mulino m a vento

window /'wɪndəʊ/ n finestra f; (of car) finestrino m; (of shop) vetrina f

window: **~-box** n cassetta f per i fiori. **~-cleaner** n (person) lavavetri m inv. **~-dresser** n vetrinista mf. **~-dressing** n vetrinistica f; fig fumo m negli occhi. **~-pane** n vetro m. **~-shopping** n: **go ~-shopping** andare in giro a vedere le vetrine. **~-sill** n davanzale m

'windscreen n, Am **'windshield** n parabrezza m inv. **~ washer** n getto m d'acqua. **~-wiper** n tergicristallo m

wind: **~ surfing** n windsurf m inv. **~swept** a esposto al vento; (person) scompigliato

windy /'wɪndɪ/ a (-ier, -iest) ventoso

wine /waɪn/ n vino m

wine: **~-bar** n ≈ enoteca f. **~glass** n bicchiere m da vino. **~-list** n carta f dei vini

winery /'waɪnərɪ/ n Am vigneto m

'wine-tasting n degustazione f dei vini

wing /wɪŋ/ n ala f; Auto parafango m; **~s** pl Theat quinte fpl. **~er** n Sport ala f

wink /wɪŋk/ n strizzata f d'occhio; **not sleep a ~** non chiudere occhio ● vi strizzare l'occhio; (light:) lampeggiare

winner /'wɪnə(r)/ n vincitore, -trice mf

winning /'wɪnɪŋ/ a vincente; (smile) accattivante. **~-post** n linea f d'arrivo. **~s** npl vincite fpl

wint|er /'wɪntə(r)/ n inverno m. **~ry** a invernale

wipe /waɪp/ n passata f; (to dry) asciugata f ● vt strofinare; (dry) asciugare. **wipe off** vt asciugare; (erase) cancellare. **wipe out** vt annientare; eliminare (village); estinguere (debt). **wipe up** vt asciugare (dishes)

wire /'waɪə(r)/ n fil m di ferro; (electrical) filo m elettrico

wireless /'waɪəlɪs/ n radio f inv

wire 'netting n rete f metallica

wiring /'waɪərɪŋ/ n impianto m elettrico

wiry /'waɪərɪ/ a (-ier, -iest) (person) dal fisico asciutto; (hair) ispido

wisdom /'wɪzdəm/ n saggezza f; (of action) sensatezza f. **~ tooth** n dente m del giudizio

wise /waɪz/ a saggio; (prudent) sensato. **~ly** adv saggiamente; (act) sensatamente

wish /wɪʃ/ n desiderio m; **make a ~** esprimere un desiderio; **with best ~es** con i migliori auguri ● vt desiderare; **~ sb well** fare tanti auguri a qcno; **I ~ you every success** ti auguro buona fortuna; **I ~ you could stay** vorrei che tu potessi rimanere ● vi **~ for sth** desiderare qcsa. **~ful** a **~ful thinking** illusione f

wishy-washy /'wɪʃɪwɒʃɪ/ a (colour) spento; (personality) insignificante

wisp /wɪsp/ n (of hair) ciocca f; (of smoke) filo m; (of grass) ciuffo m

wistful /'wɪstfl/ a malinconico

wit /wɪt/ n spirito m; (person) persona f di spirito; **be at one's ~s' end** non saper che pesci pigliare

witch /wɪtʃ/ n strega f. **~craft** n magia f. **~-hunt** n caccia f alle streghe

with /wɪð/ prep con; (fear, cold, jealousy etc) di; **I'm not ~ you** fam non ti seguo; **can I leave it ~ you?** <task> puoi occupartene tu?; **~ no regrets/money** senza rimpianti/soldi; **be ~ it** fam essere al passo coi tempi; (alert) essere concentrato

with'draw v (pt **-drew**, pp **-drawn**) ● vt ritirare; prelevare (money) ● vi ritirarsi. **~al** n ritiro m; (of money) prelevamento m; (from drugs) crisi f inv di astinenza; Psych chiusura f in se stessi. **~al symptoms** npl sintomi mpl da crisi di astinenza

with'drawn see **withdraw** ● a (person) chiuso in se stesso

wither /'wɪðə(r)/ vi (flower:) appassire

with'hold vt (pt/pp **-held**) rifiutare (consent) (**from** a); nascondere (information) (**from** a); trattenere (smile)

with'in prep (inside) entro; (before the end of) entro; **~ the law** legale ● adv all'interno

with'out prep senza; **~ stopping** senza fermarsi

with'stand vt (pt/pp **-stood**) resistere a

witness /'wɪtnɪs/ n testimone mf ● vt autenticare (signature); essere testimone di (accident). **~-box**, Am **~-stand** n banco m dei testimoni

witticism /'wɪtɪsɪzm/ *n* spiritosaggine *f*

wittingly /'wɪtɪŋlɪ/ *adv* consapevolmente

witty /'wɪtɪ/ *a* (**-ier, -iest**) spiritoso

wives /waɪvz/ *see* **wife**

wizard /'wɪzəd/ *n* mago *m*. **~ry** *n* stregoneria *f*

wobb|le /'wɒbl/ *vi* traballare. **~ly** *a* traballante

wodge /wɒdʒ/ *n fam* mucchio *m*

woe /wəʊ/ *n* afflizione *f*

woke, woken /wəʊk, 'wəʊkn/ *see* **wake**[1]

wolf /wʊlf/ *n* (*pl* **wolves** /wʊlvz/) lupo *m*; (*fam: womanizer*) donnaiolo *m* ● *vt* **~** [**down**] divorare. **~ whistle** *n* fischio *m* ● *vi* **~-whistle at sb** fischiare dietro a qcno

woman /'wʊmən/ *n* (*pl* **women**) donna *f*. **~izer** *n* donnaiolo *m*. **~ly** *a* femmineo

womb /wu:m/ *n* utero *m*

women /'wɪmn/ *see* **woman**. **W~'s Libber** /'lɪbə(r)/ *n* femminista *f*. **W~'s Liberation** *n* movimento *m* femminista

won /wʌn/ *see* **win**

wonder /'wʌndə(r)/ *n* meraviglia *f*; (*surprise*) stupore *m*; **no ~!** non c'è da stupirsi!; **it's a ~ that...** è incredibile che... ● *vi* restare in ammirazione; (*be surprised*) essere sorpreso; **I ~** è quello che mi chiedo; **I ~ whether she is ill** mi chiedo se è malata?. **~ful** *a* meraviglioso. **~fully** *adv* meravigliosamente

won't /wəʊnt/ = **will not**

woo /wu:/ *vt* corteggiare; *fig* cercare di accattivarsi (*voters*)

wood /wʊd/ *n* legno *m*; (*for burning*) legna *f*; (*forest*) bosco *m*; **out of the ~** *fig* fuori pericolo; **touch ~!** tocca ferro!

wood: **~ed** /-ɪd/ *a* boscoso. **~en** *a* di legno; *fig* legnoso. **~ wind** *n* strumenti *mpl* a fiato. **~work** *n* (*wooden parts*) parti *fpl* in legno; (*craft*) falegnameria *f*. **~worm** *n* tarlo *m*. **~y** *a* legnoso; (*hill*) boscoso

wool /wʊl/ *n* lana *f* ● *attrib* di lana. **~len** *a* di lana. **~lens** *npl* capi *mpl* di lana

woolly /'wʊlɪ/ *a* (**-ier, -iest**) (*sweater*) di lana; *fig* confuso

word /wɜ:d/ *n* parola *f*; (*news*) notizia *f*; **by ~ of mouth** a viva voce; **have a ~ with** dire due parole a; **have ~s** bisticciare; **in other ~s** in altre parole. **~ing** *n* parole *fpl*. **~ processor** *n* programma *m* di videoscrittura, word processor *m inv*

wore /wɔ:(r)/ *see* **wear**

work /wɜ:k/ *n* lavoro *m*; (*of art*) opera *f*; **~s** *pl* (*factory*) fabbrica *fsg*; (*mechanism*) meccanismo *msg*; **at ~** al lavoro; **out of ~** disoccupato ● *vi* lavorare; (*machine, ruse:*) funzionare; (*study*) studiare ● *vt* far funzionare (*machine*); far lavorare (*employee*); far studiare (*student*). **work off** *vt* sfogare (*anger*); lavorare per estinguere (*debt*); fare sport per smaltire (*weight*). **work out** *vt* elaborare (*plan*); risolvere (*problem*); calcolare (*bill*); **I ~ed out how he did it** ho capito come l'ha fatto ● *vi* evolvere. **work up** *vt* **I've ~ed up an appetite** mi è venuto appetito; **don't get ~ed up** (*anxious*) non farti prendere dal panico; (*angry*) non arrabbiarti

workable /'wɜ:kəbl/ *a* (*feasible*) fattibile

workaholic /wɜ:kə'hɒlɪk/ *n* staccanovista *mf*

worker /'wɜ:kə(r)/ *n* lavoratore, -trice *mf*; (*manual*) operaio, -a *mf*

working /'wɜ:kɪŋ/ *a* (*clothes etc*) da lavoro; (*day*) feriale; **in ~ order** funzionante. **~ class** *n* classe *f* operaia. **~-class** *a* operaio

work: **~man** *n* operaio *m*. **~manship** *n* lavorazione *f*. **~-out** *n* allenamento *m*. **~shop** *n* officina *f*; (*discussion*) dibattito *m*

world /wɜ:ld/ *n* mondo *m*; **a ~ of difference** una differenza abissale; **out of this ~** favoloso; **think the ~ of sb** andare matto per qcno. **~ly** *a* materiale; (*person*) materialista. **~-'wide** *a* mondiale ● *adv* mondialmente

worm /wɜ:m/ *n* verme *m* ● *vt* **~ one's way into sb's confidence** conquistarsi la fiducia di qcno in modo subdolo. **~-eaten** *a* tarlato

worn /wɔ:n/ *see* **wear** ● *a* sciupato. **~-out** *a* consumato; (*person*) sfinito

worried /'wʌrɪd/ *a* preoccupato

worr|y /'wʌrɪ/ *n* preoccupazione *f* ● *v* (*pt/pp* **worried**) ● *vt* preoccupare; (*bother*) disturbare ● *vi* preoccuparsi. **~ing** *a* preoccupante

worse /wɜ:s/ *a* peggiore ● *adv* peggio ● *n* peggio *m*

worsen /'wɜ:sn/ *vt/i* peggiorare

worship /'wɜ:ʃɪp/ *n* culto *m*; (*service*) funzione *f*; **Your/His W~** (*to judge*) signor giudice/il giudice ● *v* (*pt/pp* **-shipped**) ● *vt* venerare ● *vi* andare a messa

worst /wɜ:st/ *a* peggiore ● *adv* peggio [di tutti] ● *n* **the ~** il peggio; **get the ~**

of it avere la peggio; **if the ~ comes to the ~** nella peggiore delle ipotesi

worth /wɜːθ/ n valore m; **£10 ~ of petrol** 10 sterline di benzina ● a **be ~** valere; **be ~ it** fig valerne la pena; **it's ~ trying** vale la pena di provare; **it's ~ my while** mi conviene. **~less** a senza valore. **~while** a che vale la pena; ⟨cause⟩ lodevole

worthy /ˈwɜːðɪ/ a degno; ⟨cause, motive⟩ lodevole

would /wʊd/ v aux **I ~ do it** lo farei; **~ you go?** andresti?; **~ you mind if I opened the window?** ti dispiace se apro la finestra?; **he ~ come if he could** verrebbe se potesse; **he said he ~n't** ha detto di no; **~ you like a drink?** vuoi qualcosa da bere?; **what ~ you like to drink?** cosa prendi da bere?; **you ~n't, ~ you?** non lo faresti, vero?

wound¹ /wuːnd/ n ferita f ● vt ferire

wound² /waʊnd/ see **wind²**

wove, woven /wəʊv, ˈwəʊvn/ see **weave²**

wrangle /ˈræŋgl/ n litigio m ● vi litigare

wrap /ræp/ n ⟨shawl⟩ scialle m ● vt (pt/pp **wrapped**) **~ [up]** avvolgere; incartare ⟨present⟩; **be ~ped up in** fig essere completamente preso da ● vi **~ up warmly** coprirsi bene. **~per** n (for sweet) carta f [di caramella]. **~ping** n materiale m da imballaggio. **~ping paper** n carta f da pacchi; (for gift) carta f da regalo

wrath /rɒθ/ n ira f

wreak /riːk/ vt **~ havoc with sth** scombussolare qcsa

wreath /riːθ/ n (pl **~s** /-ðz/) corona f

wreck /rek/ n (of ship) relitto m; (of car) carcassa f; (person) rottame m ● vt far naufragare; demolire ⟨car⟩. **~age** /-ɪdʒ/ n rottami mpl; fig brandelli mpl

wrench /rentʃ/ n (injury) slogatura f; (tool) chiave f inglese; (pull) strattone m ● vt strappare; slogarsi ⟨wrist, ankle etc⟩

wrest /rest/ vt strappare (**from** a)

wrestl|e /ˈresl/ vi lottare corpo a cor-

po; fig lottare. **~er** n lottatore, -trice mf. **~ing** n lotta f libera; (all-in) catch m

wretch /retʃ/ n disgraziato, -a mf. **~ed** /-ɪd/ a odioso; ⟨weather⟩ orribile; **feel ~ed** (unhappy) essere triste; (ill) sentirsi malissimo

wriggle /ˈrɪgl/ n contorsione f ● vi contorcersi; (move forward) strisciare; **~ out of sth** fam sottrarsi a qcsa

wring /rɪŋ/ vt (pt/pp **wrung**) torcere ⟨sb's neck⟩; strizzare ⟨clothes⟩; **~ one's hands** torcersi le mani; **~ing wet** inzuppato

wrinkle /ˈrɪŋkl/ n grinza f; (on skin) ruga f ● vt/i raggrinzire. **~d** a ⟨skin, face⟩ rugoso; ⟨clothes⟩ raggrinzito

wrist /rɪst/ n polso m. **~-watch** n orologio m da polso

writ /rɪt/ n Jur mandato m

write /raɪt/ vt/i (pt **wrote**, pp **written**, pres p **writing**) scrivere. **write down** vt annotare. **write off** vt cancellare ⟨debt⟩; distruggere ⟨car⟩

'write-off n (car) rottame m

writer /ˈraɪtə(r)/ n autore, -trice mf; **she's a ~** è una scrittrice

'write-up n (review) recensione f

writhe /raɪð/ vi contorcersi

writing /ˈraɪtɪŋ/ n (occupation) scrivere m; (words) scritte fpl; (handwriting) scrittura f; **in ~** per iscritto. **~-paper** n carta f da lettera

written /ˈrɪtn/ see **write**

wrong /rɒŋ/ a sbagliato; **be ~** ⟨person:⟩ sbagliare; **what's ~?** cosa c'è che non va? ● adv ⟨spelt⟩ in modo sbagliato; **go ~** ⟨person:⟩ sbagliare; ⟨machine:⟩ funzionare male; ⟨plan:⟩ andar male ● n ingiustizia f; **in the ~** dalla parte del torto; **know right from ~** distinguere il bene dal male ● vt fare torto a. **~ful** a ingiusto. **~ly** adv in modo sbagliato; ⟨accuse, imagine⟩ a torto; ⟨informed⟩ male

wrote /rəʊt/ see **write**

wrought'iron /rɔːt-/ n ferro m battuto ● attrib di ferro battuto

wrung /rʌŋ/ see **wring**

wry /raɪ/ a (**-er, -est**) ⟨humour, smile⟩ beffardo

Xmas /'krɪsməs/ *n fam* Natale *m*
'X-ray *n* (*picture*) radiografia *f*; **have**
an ~ farsi fare una radiografia ● *vt*
passare ai raggi X

yacht /jɒt/ *n* yacht *m inv*; (*for racing*)
bàrca *f* a vela. **~ing** *n* vela *f*
Yank /jæŋk/ *n fam* americano, -a *mf*
yank *vt fam* tirare
yap /jæp/ *vi* (*pt/pp* **yapped**) ⟨*dog:*⟩ guaire
yard¹ /jɑːd/ *n* cortile *m*; (*for storage*) deposito *m*
yard² *n* iarda *f* (= 91,44 *cm*). **~stick** *n fig*
pietra *f* di paragone
yarn /jɑːn/ *n* filo *m*; (*fam: tale*) storia *f*
yawn /jɔːn/ *n* sbadiglio *m* ● *vi* sbadigliare. **~ing** *a* **~ing gap** sbadiglio *m*
year /jɪə(r)/ *n* anno *m*; (*of wine*) annata *f*;
for ~s *fam* da secoli. **~-book** *n* annuario
m. **~ly** *a* annuale ● *adv* annualmente
yearn /jɜːn/ *vi* struggersi. **~ing** *n* desiderio *m* struggente
yeast /jiːst/ *n* lievito *m*
yell /jel/ *n* urlo *m* ● *vi* urlare
yellow /'jeləʊ/ *a & n* giallo *m*
yelp /jelp/ *n* (*of dog*) guaito *m* ● *vi* ⟨*dog:*⟩ guaire
yen /jen/ *n* forte desiderio *m* (**for** di)
yes /jes/ *adv* sì ● *n* sì *m inv*
yesterday /'jestədeɪ/ *n & adv* ieri *m inv*; **~'s paper** il giornale di ieri; **the day before ~** l'altroieri
yet /jet/ *adv* ancora; **as ~** fino ad ora;
not ~ non ancora; **the best ~** il migliore finora ● *conj* eppure
yew /juː/ *n* tasso *m* (*albero*)
yield /jiːld/ *n* produzione *f*; (*profit*) reddito *m* ● *vt* produrre; fruttare ⟨*profit*⟩
● *vi* cedere; *Am Auto* dare la precedenza
yodel /'jəʊdl/ *vi* (*pt/pp* **yodelled**) cantare jodel

yoga /'jəʊgə/ *n* yoga *m*
yoghurt /'jɒgət/ *n* yogurt *m inv*
yoke /jəʊk/ *n* giogo *m*; (*of garment*)
carré *m inv*
yokel /'jəʊkl/ *n* zotico, -a *mf*
yolk /jəʊk/ *n* tuorlo *m*
you /juː/ *pers pron* (*subject*) tu, voi *pl*;
(*formal*) lei, voi *pl*; (*direct/indirect object*)
ti, vi *pl*; (*formal: direct object*) la; (*formal:
indirect object*) le; (*after prep*) te, voi *pl*;
(*formal: after prep*) lei; **~ are very kind**
(*sg*) sei molto gentile; (*formal*) è molto
gentile; (*pl & formal pl*) siete molto gentili; **~ can stay, but he has to go** (*sg*) tu
puoi rimanere, ma lui deve andarsene;
(*pl*) voi potete rimanere, ma lui deve andarsene; **all of ~** tutti voi; **I'll give ~ the
money** (*sg*) ti darò i soldi; (*pl*) vi darò i
soldi; **I'll give it to ~** (*sg*) te/(*pl*) ve lo
darò; **it was ~!** (*sg*) eri tu!; (*pl*) eravate
voi!; **~ have to be careful** (*one*) si deve
fare attenzione
young /jʌŋ/ *a* giovane ● *npl* (*animals*)
piccoli *mpl*; **the ~** (*people*) i giovani. **~
lady** *n* signorina *f*. **~ man** *n* giovanotto
m. **~ster** *n* ragazzo, -a *mf*; (*child*) bambino, -a *mf*
your /jɔː(r)/ *poss a* il tuo *m*, la tua *f*, i
tuoi *mpl*, le tue *fpl*; (*formal*) il suo *m*, la
sua *f*, i suoi *mpl*, le sue *fpl*; (*pl & formal
pl*) il vostro *m*, la vostra *f*, i vostri *mpl*,
le vostre *fpl*; **~ mother/father** tua
madre/tuo padre; (*formal*) sua
madre/suo padre; (*pl & formal pl*) vostra madre/vostro padre
yours /jɔːz/ *poss pron* il tuo *m*, la tua *f*, i
tuoi *mpl*, le tue *fpl*; (*formal*) il suo *m*, la

sua *f*, i suoi *mpl*, le sue *fpl*; (*pl &
formal pl*) il vostro *m*, la vostra *f*,
i vostri *mpl*, le vostre *fpl*; **a friend of
~** un tuo/suo/vostro amico; **friends
of ~** dei tuoi/vostri/suoi amici; **that
is ~** quello è tuo/vostro/suo; (*as
opposed to mine*) quello è il tuo/il
vostro/il suo

your'self *pers pron* (*reflexive*) ti; (*formal*) si; (*emphatic*) te stesso; (*formal*)
sé, se stesso; **do pour ~ a drink** versati
da bere; (*formal*) si versi da bere; **you
said so ~** lo hai detto tu stesso;
(*formal*) lo ha detto lei stesso; **you can**

be proud of ~ puoi essere fiero di te/di
sé; **by ~** da solo

your'selves *pers pron* (*reflexive*) vi;
(*emphatic*) voi stessi; **do pour ~ a drink**
versatevi da bere; **you said so ~** lo avete
detto voi stessi; **you can be proud of ~**
potete essere fieri di voi; **by ~** da soli

youth /ju:θ/ *n* (*pl* **youths** /-ð:z/) gioventù *f inv*; (*boy*) giovanetto *m*; **the ~**
(*young people*) i giovani. **~ful** *a* giovanile. **~ hostel** *n* ostello *m* [della gioventù]

Yugoslav /'ju:gəslɑ:v/ *a & n* jugoslavo,
-a *mf*

Yugoslavia /-'slɑ:vɪə/ *n* Jugoslavia *f*

Zz

---

zany /'zeɪnɪ/ *a* (**-ier, -iest**) demenziale

zeal /zi:l/ *n* zelo *m*

zealous /'zeləs/ *a* zelante. **~ly** *adv* con
zelo

zebra /'zebrə/ *n* zebra *f*. **~-'crossing** *n*
passaggio *m* pedonale, zebre *fpl*

zero /'zɪərəʊ/ *n* zero *m*

zest /zest/ *n* gusto *m*

zigzag /'zɪgzæg/ *n* zigzag *m inv* ● *vi*
(*pt/pp* **-zagged**) zigzagare

zilch /zɪltʃ/ *n fam* zero *m* assoluto

zinc /zɪŋk/ *n* zinco *m*

zip /zɪp/ *n* **~** [**fastener**] cerniera *f* [lampo] ● *vt* (*pt/pp* **zipped**) **~** [**up**] chiudere
con la cerniera [lampo]

'Zip code *n Am* codice *m* postale

zipper /'zɪpə(r)/ *n Am* cerniera *f* [lampo]

zodiac /'zəʊdɪæk/ *n* zodiaco *m*

zombie /'zɒmbɪ/ *n fam* zombi *mf inv*

zone /zəʊn/ *n* zona *f*

zoo /zu:/ *n* zoo *m inv*

zoolog|ist /zəʊ'ɒlədʒɪst/ *n* zoologo, -a
mf. **~y** zoologia *f*

zoom /zu:m/ *vi* sfrecciare. **~ lens** *n*
zoom *m inv*

ITALIAN VERB TABLES

REGULAR VERBS:

1. in **-are** (*eg* **compr|are**)

   Present ~o, ~i, ~a, ~iamo, ~ate, ~ano
   Imperfect ~avo, ~avi, ~ava, ~avamo, ~avate, ~avano
   Past historic ~ai, ~asti, ~ò, ~ammo, ~aste, ~arono
   Future ~erò, ~erai, ~erà, ~eremo, ~erete, ~eranno
   Present subjunctive ~i, ~i, ~i, ~iamo, ~iate, ~ino
   Past subjunctive ~assi, ~assi, ~asse, ~assimo, ~aste, ~assero
   Present participle ~ando
   Past participle ~ato
   Imperative ~a (*fml* ~i), ~iamo, ~ate
   Conditional ~erei, ~eresti, ~erebbe, ~eremmo, ~ereste, ~erebbero

2. in **-ere** (*eg* **vend|ere**)

   Pres ~o, ~i, ~e, ~iamo, ~ete, ~ono
   Impf ~evo, ~evi, ~eva, ~evamo, ~evate, ~evano
   Past hist ~ei *or* ~etti, ~esti, ~è *or* ~ette, ~emmo, ~este, ~erono *or* ~ettero
   Fut ~erò, ~erai, ~erà, ~eremo, ~erete, ~eranno
   Pres sub ~a, ~a, ~a, ~iamo, ~iate, ~ano
   Past sub ~essi, ~essi, ~esse, ~essimo, ~este, ~essero
   Pres part ~endo
   Past part ~uto
   Imp ~i (*fml* ~a), ~iamo, ~ete
   Cond ~erei, ~eresti, ~erebbe, ~eremmo, ~ereste, ~erebbero

3. in **-ire** (*eg* **dorm|ire**)

   Pres ~o, ~i, ~e, ~iamo, ~ite, ~ono
   Impf ~ivo, ~ivi, ~iva, ~ivamo, ~ivate, ~ivano
   Past hist ~ii, ~isti, ~ì, ~immo, ~iste, ~irono
   Fut ~irò, ~irai, ~irà, ~iremo, ~irete, ~iranno
   Pres sub ~a, ~a, ~a, ~iamo, ~iate, ~ano
   Past sub ~issi, ~issi, ~isse, ~issimo, ~iste, ~issero
   Pres part ~endo
   Past part ~ito
   Imp ~i (*fml* ~a), ~iamo, ~ite
   Cond ~irei, ~iresti, ~irebbe, ~iremmo, ~ireste, ~irebbero

Notes

- Many verbs in the third conjugation take *isc* between the stem and the ending in the first, second, and third person singular and in the third person plural of the present, the present subjunctive, and the imperative: fin|ire **Pres** ~isco, ~isci, ~isce, ~iscono. **Pres sub** ~isca, ~iscano **Imp** ~isci.

- The three forms of the imperative are the same as the corresponding forms of the present for the second and third conjugation. In the first conjugation the forms are also the same except for the second person singular: present *compri*, imperative *compra*. The negative form of the second person singular is formed by putting *non* before the infinitive for all conjugations: *non comprare*. In polite forms the third person of the present subjunctive is used instead for all conjugations: *compri*.

IRREGULAR VERBS:

Certain forms of all irregular verbs are regular (except for *essere*). These are: the second person plural of the present, the past subjunctive, and the present participle. All forms not listed below are regular and can be derived from the parts given. Only those irregular verbs considered to be the most useful are shown in the tables.

accadere	*as* **cadere**
accendere	• **Past hist** accesi, accendesti • **Past part** acceso
affliggere	• **Past hist** afflissi, affliggesti • **Past part** afflitto
ammettere	*as* **mettere**
andare	• **Pres** vado, vai, va, andiamo, andate, vanno • **Fut** andrò *etc* • **Pres sub** vada, vadano • **Imp** va', vada, vadano
apparire	• **Pres** appaio *or* apparisco, appari *or* apparisci, appare *or* apparisce, appaiono *or* appariscono • **Past hist** apparvi *or* apparsi, apparisti, apparve *or* apparì *or* apparse, apparvero *or* apparirono *or* apparsero • **Pres sub** appaia *or* apparisca
aprire	• **Pres** apro • **Past hist** aprii, apristi • **Pres sub** apra • **Past part** aperto
avere	• **Pres** ho, hai, ha, abbiamo, hanno • **Past hist** ebbi, avesti, ebbe, avemmo, aveste, ebbero • **Fut** avrò *etc* • **Pres sub** abbia *etc* • **Imp** abbi, abbia, abbiate, abbiano
bere	• **Pres** bevo *etc* • **Impf** bevevo *etc* • **Past hist** bevvi *or* bevetti, bevesti • **Fut** berrò *etc* • **Pres sub** beva *etc* • **Past sub** bevessi *etc* • **Pres part** bevendo • **Cond** berrei *etc*
cadere	• **Past hist** caddi, cadesti • **Fut** cadrò *etc*
chiedere	• **Past hist** chiesi, chiedesti • **Pres sub** chieda *etc* • **Past part** chiesto *etc*
chiudere	• **Past hist** chiusi, chiudesti • **Past part** chiuso
cogliere	• **Pres** colgo, colgono • **Past hist** colsi, cogliesti • **Pres sub** colga • **Past part** colto
correre	• **Past hist** corsi, corresti • **Past part** corso
crescere	• **Past hist** crebbi • **Past part** cresciuto
cuocere	• **Pres** cuocio, cuociamo, cuociono • **Past hist** cossi, cocesti • **Past part** cotto
dare	• **Pres** do, dai, da, diamo, danno • **Past hist** diedi *or* detti, desti • **Fut** darò *etc* • **Pres sub** dia *etc* • **Past sub** dessi *etc* • **Imp** da' (*fml* dia)

dire
• **Pres** dico, dici, dice, diciamo, dicono • **Impf** dicevo *etc* • **Past hist** dissi, dicesti • **Fut** dirò *etc* • **Pres sub** dica, diciamo, diciate, dicano • **Past sub** dicessi *etc* • **Pres part** dicendo • **Past part** detto • **Imp** di' (*fml* dica)

dovere
• **Pres** devo *or* debbo, devi, deve, dobbiamo, devono *or* debbono • **Fut** dovrò *etc* • **Pres sub** deva *or* debba, dobbiamo, dobbiate, devano *or* debbano • **Cond** dovrei *etc*

essere
• **Pres** sono, sei, è, siamo, siete, sono • **Impf** ero, eri, era, eravamo, eravate, erano • **Past hist** fui, fosti, fu, fummo, foste, furono • **Fut** sarò *etc* • **Pres sub** sia *etc* • **Past sub** fossi, fossi, fosse, fossimo, foste, fossero • **Past part** stato • **Imp** sii (*fml* sia), siate • **Cond** sarei *etc*

fare
• **Pres** faccio, fai, fa, facciamo, fanno • **Impf** facevo *etc* • **Past hist** feci, facesti • **Fut** farò *etc* • **Pres sub** faccia *etc* • **Past sub** facessi *etc* • **Pres part** facendo • **Past part** fatto • **Imp** fa' (*fml* faccia) • **Cond** farei *etc*

fingere
• **Past hist** finsi, fingesti, finsero • **Past part** finto

giungere
• **Past hist** giunsi, giungesti, giunsero • **Past part** giunto

leggere
• **Past hist** lessi, leggesti • **Past part** letto

mettere
• **Past hist** misi, mettesti • **Past part** messo

morire
• **Pres** muoio, muori, muore, muoiono • **Fut** morirò *or* morrò *etc* • **Pres sub** muoia • **Past part** morto

muovere
• **Past hist** mossi, movesti • **Past part** mosso

nascere
• **Past hist** nacqui, nascesti • **Past part** nato

offrire
• **Past hist** offersi *or* offrii, offristi • **Pres sub** offra • **Past part** offerto

parere
• **Pres** paio, pari, pare, pariamo, paiono • **Past hist** parvi *or* parsi, paresti • **Fut** parrò *etc* • **Pres sub** paia, paiamo *or* pariamo, pariate, paiano • **Past part** parso

piacere
• **Pres** piaccio, piaci, piace, piacciamo, piacciono • **Past hist** piacqui, piacesti, piacque, piacemmo, piaceste, piacquero • **Pres sub** piaccia *etc* • **Past part** piaciuto

porre
• **Pres** pongo, poni, pone, poniamo, ponete, pongono • **Impf** ponevo *etc* • **Past hist** posi, ponesti • **Fut** porrò *etc* • **Pres sub** ponga, poniamo, poniate, pongano • **Past sub** ponessi *etc*

potere
• **Pres** posso, puoi, può, possiamo, possono • **Fut** potrò *etc* • **Pres sub** possa, possiamo, possiate, possano • **Cond** potrei *etc*

prendere
• **Past hist** presi, prendesti • **Past part** preso

ridere
• **Past hist** risi, ridesti • **Past part** riso

rimanere • **Pres** rimango, rimani, rimane, rimaniamo, rimangono • **Past hist** rimasi, rimanesti • **Fut** rimarrò *etc* • **Pres sub** rimanga • **Past part** rimasto • **Cond** rimarrei

salire • **Pres** salgo, sali, sale, saliamo, salgono • **Pres sub** salga, saliate, salgano

sapere • **Pres** so, sai, sa, sappiamo, sanno • **Past hist** seppi, sapesti • **Fut** saprò *etc* • **Pres sub** sappia *etc* • **Imp** sappi (*fml* sappia), sappiate • **Cond** saprei *etc*

scegliere • **Pres** scelgo, scegli, sceglie, scegliamo, scelgono • **Past hist** scelsi, scegliesti *etc* • **Past part** scelto

scrivere • **Past hist** scrissi, scrivesti *etc* • **Past part** scritto

sedere • **Pres** siedo *or* seggo, siedi, siede, siedono • **Pres sub** sieda *or* segga

spegnere • **Pres** spengo, spengono • **Past hist** spensi, spegnesti • **Past part** spento

stare • **Pres** sto, stai, sta, stiamo, stanno • **Past hist** stetti, stesti • **Fut** starò *etc* • **Pres sub** stia *etc* • **Past sub** stessi *etc* • **Past part** stato • **Imp** sta' (*fml* stia)

tacere • **Pres** taccio, tacciono • **Past hist** tacqui, tacque, tacquero • **Pres sub** taccia

tendere • **Past hist** tesi • **Past part** teso

tenere • **Pres** tengo, tieni, tiene, tengono • **Past hist** tenni, tenesti • **Fut** terrò *etc* • **Pres sub** tenga

togliere • **Pres** tolgo, tolgono • **Past hist** tolsi, tolse, tolsero • **Pres sub** tolga, tolgano • **Past part** tolto • *Imp fml* tolga

trarre • **Pres** traggo, trai, trae, traiamo, traete, traggono • **Past hist** trassi, traesti • **Fut** trarrò *etc* • **Pres sub** tragga • **Past sub** traessi *etc* • **Past part** tratto

uscire • **Pres** esco, esci, esce, escono • **Pres sub** esca • **Imp** esci (*fml* esca)

valere • **Pres** valgo, valgono • **Past hist** valsi, valesti • **Fut** varrò *etc* • **Pres sub** valga, valgano • **Past part** valso • **Cond** varrei *etc*

vedere • **Past hist** vidi, vedesti • **Fut** vedrò *etc* • **Past part** visto *or* veduto • **Cond** vedrei *etc*

venire • **Pres** vengo, vieni, viene, vengono • **Past hist** venni, venisti • **Fut** verrò *etc*

vivere • **Past hist** vissi, vivesti • **Fut** vivrò *etc* • **Past part** vissuto • **Cond** vivrei *etc*

volere • **Pres** voglio, vuoi, vuole, vogliamo, volete, vogliono • **Past hist** volli, volesti • **Fut** vorrò *etc* • **Pres sub** voglia *etc* • **Imp** vogliate • **Cond** vorrei *etc*

263

English irregular verbs

Infinitive / *Infinito*	Past Tense / *Passato*	Past Participle / *Participio passato*	Infinitive / *Infinito*	Past Tense / *Passato*	Past Participle / *Participio passato*
arise	arose	arisen	feed	fed	fed
awake	awoke	awoken	feel	felt	felt
be	was	been	fight	fought	fought
bear	bore	borne	find	found	found
beat	beat	beaten	flee	fled	fled
become	became	become	fling	flung	flung
begin	began	begun	fly	flew	flown
behold	beheld	beheld	forbid	forbade	forbidden
bend	bent	bent	forget	forgot	forgotten
beseech	beseeched	beseeched	forgive	forgave	forgiven
	besought	besought	forsake	forsook	forsaken
bet	bet,	bet,	freeze	froze	frozen
	betted	betted	get	got	got,
bid	bade,	bidden,			gotten *Am*
	bid	bid	give	gave	given
bind	bound	bound	go	went	gone
bite	bit	bitten	grind	ground	ground
bleed	bled	bled	grow	grew	grown
blow	blew	blown	hang	hung,	hung,
break	broke	broken		hanged (*vt*)	hanged
breed	bred	bred	have	had	had
bring	brought	brought	hear	heard	heard
build	built	built	hew	hewed	hewed,
burn	burnt,	burnt,			hewn
	burned	burned	hide	hid	hidden
burst	burst	burst	hit	hit	hit
bust	busted,	busted,	hold	held	held
	bust	bust	hurt	hurt	hurt
buy	bought	bought	keep	kept	kept
cast	cast	cast	kneel	knelt	knelt
catch	caught	caught	know	knew	known
choose	chose	chosen	lay	laid	laid
cling	clung	clung	lead	led	led
come	came	come	lean	leaned,	leaned,
cost	cost,	cost,		leant	leant
	costed (*vt*)	costed	leap	leapt,	leapt,
creep	crept	crept		leaped	leaped
cut	cut	cut	learn	learnt,	learnt,
deal	dealt	dealt		learned	learned
dig	dug	dug	leave	left	left
do	did	done	lend	lent	lent
draw	drew	drawn	let	let	let
dream	dreamt,	dreamt,	lie[2]	lay	lain
	dreamed	dreamed	light	lit,	lit,
drink	drank	drunk		lighted	lighted
drive	drove	driven	lose	lost	lost
dwell	dwelt	dwelt	make	made	made
eat	ate	eaten	mean	meant	meant
fall	fell	fallen	meet	met	met

Infinitive / *Infinito*	Past Tense / *Passato*	Past Participle / *Participio passato*	Infinitive / *Infinito*	Past Tense / *Passato*	Past Participle / *Participio passato*
mow	mowed	mown, mowed	spend	spent	spent
			spill	spilt, spilled	spilt, spilled
overhang	overhung	overhung			
pay	paid	paid	spin	spun	spun
put	put	put	spit	spat	spat
quit	quitted, quit	quitted, quit	split	split	split
			spoil	spoilt, spoiled	spoilt, spoiled
read	read /red/	read /red/			
rid	rid	rid	spread	spread	spread
ride	rode	ridden	spring	sprang	sprung
ring[2]	rang	rung	stand	stood	stood
rise	rose	risen	steal	stole	stolen
run	ran	run	stick	stuck	stuck
saw	sawed	sawn, sawed	sting	stung	stung
			stink	stank	stunk
say	said	said	strew	strewed	strewn, strewed
see	saw	seen			
seek	sought	sought	stride	strode	stridden
sell	sold	sold	strike	struck	struck
send	sent	sent	string	strung	strung
set	set	set	strive	strove	striven
sew	sewed	sewn, sewed	swear	swore	sworn
			sweep	swept	swept
shake	shook	shaken	swell	swelled	swollen, swelled
shear	sheared	shorn, sheared			
			swim	swam	swum
shed	shed	shed	swing	swung	swung
shine	shone	shone	take	took	taken
shit	shit	shit	teach	taught	taught
shoe	shod	shod	tear	tore	torn
shoot	shot	shot	tell	told	told
show	showed	shown	think	thought	thought
shrink	shrank	shrunk	thrive	thrived, throve	thrived, thriven
shut	shut	shut			
sing	sang	sung	throw	threw	thrown
sink	sank	sunk	thrust	thrust	thrust
sit	sat	sat	tread	trod	trodden
slay	slew	slain	understand	understood	understood
sleep	slept	slept	undo	undid	undone
slide	slid	slid	wake	woke	woken
sling	slung	slung	wear	wore	worn
slit	slit	slit	weave[2]	wove	woven
smell	smelt, smelled	smelt, smelled	weep	wept	wept
			wet	wet, wetted	wet, wetted
sow	sowed	sown, sowed			
			win	won	won
speak	spoke	spoken	wind[2]	wound	wound
speed	sped, speeded	sped, speeded	wring	wrung	wrung
			write	wrote	written
spell	spelled, spelt	spelled, spelt			